The Treasury of Precious Instructions: Essential Teachings of the Eight Practice Lineages of Tibet

Volume 18: Jonang

The Tsadra Foundation Series

published by Snow Lion, an imprint of Shambhala Publications

Tsadra Foundation is a U.S.-based nonprofit organization that contributes to the ongoing development of wisdom and compassion in Western minds by advancing the combined study and practice of Tibetan Buddhism.

Taking its inspiration from the nineteenth-century nonsectarian Tibetan Buddhist scholar and meditation master Jamgön Kongtrul Lodrö Taye, Tsadra Foundation is named after his hermitage in eastern Tibet, Tsadra Rinchen Drak. The Foundation's various program areas reflect his values of excellence in both scholarship and contemplative practice, and the recognition of their mutual complementarity.

Tsadra Foundation envisions a flourishing community of Western contemplatives and scholar-practitioners who are fully trained in the traditions of Tibetan Buddhism. It is our conviction that, grounded in wisdom and compassion, these individuals will actively enrich the world through their openness and excellence.

This publication is a part of Tsadra Foundation's Translation Program, which aims to make authentic and authoritative texts from the Tibetan traditions available in English. The Foundation is honored to present the work of its fellows and grantees, individuals of confirmed contemplative and intellectual integrity; however, their views do not necessarily reflect those of the Foundation.

Tsadra Foundation is delighted to collaborate with Shambhala Publications in making these important texts available in the English language.

Jonang

The One Hundred and Eight Teaching Manuals

The Treasury of Precious Instructions:
Essential Teachings of the Eight Practice
Lineages of Tibet
Volume 18

Compiled by Jamgön Kongtrul Lodrö Taye

TRANSLATED BY
Gyurme Dorje

Snow Lion

Snow Lion
An imprint of Shambhala Publications, Inc.
4720 Walnut Street
Boulder, Colorado 80301
www.shambhala.com

Cover art: Thangka "The Jonang Practice Lineage of Tibetan Buddhism." Collection Eric Colombel. Photo: Rafael Ortet, 2018. © Eric Colombel, New York.
Interior design: Gopa and Ted2, Inc.

9 8 7 6 5 4 3 2 1

First Edition
Printed in the United States of America

♾ This edition is printed on acid-free paper that meets the American National Standards Institute z39.48 Standard.
♻ Shambhala Publications makes every effort to print on recycled paper.
For more information please visit www.shambhala.com.

Snow Lion is distributed worldwide by Penguin Random House, Inc., and its subsidiaries.

LIBRARY OF CONGRESS CATALOGING-IN-PUBLICATION DATA
Names: Kong-sprul Blo-gros-mtha'-yas, 1813–1899, author. | Gyurme Dorje, translator.
Title: Jonang: the one hundred and eight teaching manuals / compiled by Jamgön Kongtrul Lodrö Taye; translated by Gyurme Dorje.
Description: First edition. | Boulder, Colorado: Snow Lion, an imprint of Shambhala Publications, Inc., 2021. | Series: The treasury of precious instructions: essential teachings of the eight practice lineages of Tibet; volume 18 | Includes bibliographical references and index.
Identifiers: LCCN 2019052967 | ISBN 9781559394956 (hardback)
Subjects: LCSH: Spiritual life—Tantric Buddhism. | Tantric Buddhism—Tibet Region—Doctrines.
Classification: LCC BQ8938 .K6513 2021 | DDC 294.3/923–dc23
LC record available at https://lccn.loc.gov/2019052967

Contents

Detailed Contents of Chapter 9: The One Hundred and Eight Guidebooks vii

Foreword by the Seventeenth Karmapa xi

Translator's Introduction xiii

Technical Note xxvii

Publisher's Note xxix

Part One: History

1. Lineage Prayers of the One Hundred and Eight Guidebooks 3
2. Supplementary Prayer to the Lineage *by Losal Tenkyong* 123
3. The Life-Sustaining Prayer of the One Hundred and Eight Guidebooks 125
4. An Autobiographical Record of the One Hundred and Eight Guidebooks Received 131
5. Historical Anecdotes of the Lineage Holders 155
6. Supplementary Historical Anecdotes *by Tāranātha* 189

Part Two: Practice

7. The Ordinary Preliminary Practices 209

8. The Extraordinary Preliminary Practices 213

9. The One Hundred and Eight Guidebooks 219

Part Three: Supports

10. Marvelous Key to the Contents of the One Hundred and Eight Guidebooks 499

11. A List of the One Hundred and Eight Guidebooks with Their Protectors and Empowerments 507

12. Methods for the Conferral of the Empowerments *by Losal Tenkyong* 521

Concordance of Technical Terms 527

Concordance of Personal Names 573

Concordance of Place Names 617

Abbreviations 621

Notes 623

Bibliography 719

Index 789

Detailed Contents of Chapter 9: The One Hundred and Eight Guidebooks

1. The Parting from the Four Attachments 220
2. The Seven-Point Mind Training of the Great Vehicle 221
3. The Heart of Dependent Origination 226
4. The Carrying of Happiness and Suffering on the Path 228
5. The Mind Training according to Sumpa Lotsāwa 230
6. The Severance of Machik Labdron 230
7. The Three Essential Points 233
8. The Resting in the Nature of Mind 235
9. The Three Sorts of Person 236
10. The Sequence of the Buddhist Teaching 238
11. The Sameness of Existence and Quiescence 240
12. The Great Middle Way 241
13. The Hidden Guidance of Kadam 243
14. The Four Deities of Kadam: Munīndra 244
15. The Four Deities of Kadam: Acala 245
16. The Four Deities of Kadam: Avalokita 247
17. The Four Deities of Kadam: Tārā 248
18. The Parables of Potowa 250
19. The Sixteen Spheres of the Heart 257
20. The Six Descents of the Transcendent Perfection of Wisdom 260
21. The Five Paths of Pacification 261
22. The Three Stages of Meditation—Beginning, Middle, and Conclusive 266
23. The Five Doctrines of Maitreya 268
24. The View of Intrinsic Emptiness 270

25. The View of Extraneous Emptiness 271
26. The Elucidation of the Concealed Meanings of Yogatantra 272
27. The Guidance of Amitāyus 283
28. The Guidance of White Tārā 285
29. The Guidance of White Amitāyus 287
30. The Direct Guidance of Avalokiteśvara according to the Lakṣmī Tradition 289
31. The Direct Guidance of Avalokiteśvara according to the Candradhvaja Tradition 290
32. The Direct Guidance of Avalokiteśvara according to the Tsembupa Tradition 291
33. The Direct Guidance of Avalokiteśvara according to the Kyergangpa Tradition 293
34. The Direct Guidance of Cakrasaṃvara 294
35. The Direct Guidance of Hevajra 295
36. Vajrapāṇi in the Form Mahācakra 296
37. Vajrapāṇi in the Form Caṇḍa 299
38. Vārāhī in the Form Kurmapādā 301
39. The Secret Guidance of Kurukullā 302
40. The Six-Branch Yoga of Kālacakra 303
41. The Aural Lineage of Kālacakra 312
42. The Ritual Service and Attainment of the Three Adamantine Realities according to Orgyanpa 317
43. The Path and Its Fruition 321
44. The Inconceivables 333
45. The Nine Profound Methods 335
46. The Attainment of Coemergence 339
47. The Perfection of the Path of Fierce Inner Heat 341
48. The Straightening of Crooked Posture 343
49. The Path of the Female Mudra 344
50. The Great Seal Devoid of Letters 346
51. The Attainment in Proximity to a Stupa/The Determination of Mind 348
52. The Mingling of Sutra and Tantra 349
53. The Dispelling of Obstacles due to External Demons 350
54. The Dispelling of Obstacles due to the Agitation of the Physical Body by the Elements 351

55. The Dispelling of the Obstacles of Meditative Stability and Mind 351
56. The Great Seal Dispelling the Three Sorts of Suffering 352
57. The Clear Recollection of the Innate State 354
58. The Three Purities 356
59. The Twenty-Nine Essential Visualizations of Self-Consecration 359
60. The Exegesis of the Concealed Path 364
61. The Elucidation of the Symbolic Meaning 366
62. The Five Stages of the Secret Assembly 368
63. The Vital Essence of Liberation 375
64. The Unelaborate Practice of Red Yamāri 379
65. The Four-Stage Yoga 384
66. The Mental Focus on the Horns of Bhairava 386
67. The Central Channel Dependent on the Male Deity Cakrasaṃvara 388
68. The Central Channel Dependent on the Female Deity Vajravārāhī 390
69. The Five Stages according to Ghaṇṭāpāda 392
70. The Four Stages according to Kṛṣṇacārin 395
71. The Guidance of White Cakrasaṃvara 396
72. The Four Adamantine Seats 398
73. The Great Magical Emanation 401
74. The Kharamukha Cakrasaṃvara 405
75. The Six Meditations of Vajravārāhī 409
76. The Six Doctrines of Nāropā 410
77. The Six Doctrines of Nigumā 414
78. The Amulet Tradition of the Great Seal 421
79. The Three Aspects Carried on the Path 422
80. The Deathlessness of One's Own Mind 423
81. The Six Doctrines of Sukhasiddhi 425
82. The Inner Guidance of Nairātmyā/The Emanational Navel Cakra 427
83. The Coemergent Union of the Great Seal 428
84. The Fivefold Great Seal 432
85. The Four Syllables of the Great Seal 433
86. The Introduction to the Three Buddha Bodies 434
87. The Indivisibility of Subtle Energy and Mind 436

88. The Six Doctrines according to the Sekharma Tradition 437
89. The Mingling and Transformation of the Three Poisons 439
90. The Four Scrolls of the Aural Instructions 440
91. The Six Doctrines of Liberation through the Upper Gate according to the Aural Lineage 442
92. The Nine Doctrinal Cycles of Nirdehaḍākinī 445
93. The Elaborate Guidance according to Zhang Tselpa 454
94. The Six-Branch Yoga according to Pelchen Ga Lotsāwa 456
95. The Cycle of Pagmodru Densatel 459
96. The Unique Enlightened Intention according to the Drigung 465
97. The Six Doctrines according to Taklungpa 470
98. The Means for Attainment of the Guru, Auspicious Circumstances, and Common Savor 472
99. The Fivefold Capacity of Lorepa 475
100. The Six Primary Essentials for the Mountain Retreat of Yangonpa 477
101. The Four-Armed Mahākāla in the Form Kurakma 481
102. The Inner Guidance of Glorious Pañjaranātha 483
103. The Trilogy of Spiritual Songs 485
104. The Six Doctrines of the Accomplished Masters 486
105. The Gradual Path of Padmasambhava 488
106. The Collected Injunctions of the King 490
107. The Liberation by Seeing according to Norbu Rinchen 492
108. The Nature of Mind: The Wish-Fulfilling Gem 493

Foreword

In his vast work *The Treasury of Precious Instructions* (*gDams ngag rin po che'i mdzod*), Jamgön Kongtrul Lodrö Taye, that most eminent of Tibetan Buddhist masters, collected together all the empowerments, instructions, and practices of the eight great chariots of the practice lineages. Not only that, but he himself received the complete transmissions for all the practices, accomplished them including the retreats, and preserved them in his own mindstream. He then passed on the transmissions to his own students and all who requested them.

The Treasury of Precious Instructions exemplifies how Jamgön Kongtrul Lodrö Taye's whole life was dedicated to teaching and spreading the dharma, whether it be sutra or mantra, *kama* or *terma*, Old or New Translation school, free of sectarian bias. Without his supreme efforts, many traditions of Tibetan Buddhism would have been lost.

The teachings of the Buddha have now spread throughout the Western world, and there is a growing need for major texts to be translated into English so that Western dharma students and scholars have access to these essential teachings. I was, therefore, delighted to hear that having successfully published a translation in ten volumes of Jamgön Kongtrul Lodrö Taye's *Treasury of Knowledge* (*Shes bya kun khyab mdzod*), the Tsadra Foundation has embarked on a second major project, the translation of *The Treasury of Precious Instructions*, and I would like to express my gratitude to them.

May their work be of benefit to countless sentient beings.

His Holiness the Seventeenth Karmapa, Ogyen Trinley Dorje
Bodhgaya
February 21, 2016

Translator's Introduction

The life of Jamgön Kongtrul (1813–1899), extraordinary compiler and author of *The Treasury of Precious Instructions*, is well known from various sources.[1] Revered as a spiritual emanation of the great eighth-century translator Vairocana, he was born into a Bon family at Rongyab Pema Lhatsé in Drida Zelmogang, within the principality of Dergé. From his eighteenth year onward, he was introduced to the formal study and practice of Buddhism—initially at Zhechen under the tutelage of Gyurmé Tutob Namgyal (b. 1787) and subsequently at Palpung, which had been founded by Situ Chokyi Jungné (1700–1774). In these institutions he twice received the vows of monastic ordination—according to the lower and upper Vinaya lineages respectively. During these formative years, Kongtrul accepted Situ Pema Nyinjé (1774–1853) as his main teacher, receiving the Kagyu and Jonangpa transmissions from him and some sixty other teachers in all.[2]

In 1842, Situ Pema Nyinjé granted Kongtrul permission to leave the monastery and enter into a three-year solitary retreat at Tsadra Rinchen Drak, revered as one of the twenty-five foremost power places in Kham, specifically associated with the "mind aspect of Padmasambhava's enlightened attributes" (*yon tan gyi thugs*). At Tsadra, on a concealed ridge, high above Palpung Monastery, Kongtrul founded the hermitage of Kunzang Dechen Oseling. It was here that he completed his prodigious writings, passed long periods in isolated meditation, and first liaised with his closest associates—Jamyang Khyentsé Wangpo of Dzongsar (1820–1892), Chogyur Dechen Lingpa of Nangchen (1829–1870), and others—to establish the dynamic and all-embracing nonsectarian (*ris med*) tradition of eastern Tibet. Together they sought to preserve and integrate the diverse lineages of Tibetan Buddhism, large and small, without fear of persecution, in an age of increasing strife. Receptive to Padmasambhava's spiritual revelations, they also mapped out the twenty-five ancient sacred sites of eastern Tibet, which had been imbued with his blessings.

While Kongtrul uniquely juxtaposed the realizations of Tibet's diverse spiritual traditions, Buddhist and Bon, he had a special affinity with the Jonangpa and Shangpa Kagyu teachings maintained in the lineage of Tāranātha (1575–1634). His writings display a particular penchant for the views and expositions of this multitalented renaissance figure and later scholars who empathized with his approach—Nyingma masters such as Rigdzin Tsewang Norbu (1698–1755) and Gyurmé Tsewang Chokdrub (1761–1829) of Katok, and Sarma masters including the aforementioned Situ Chokyi Jungné of Palpung.

The collected writings of Jamgön Kongtrul are known as the "five great treasuries" (*mDzod chen lnga*)—a title prophetically bestowed upon them by Kongtrul's closest associate, Jamyang Khyentsé Wangpo, in 1864, when only the first of the five had been composed. That was *The Treasury of Knowledge* (*Shes bya kun khyab mdzod*), which, in an encyclopedic manner, covers the entire corpus of the Sutra and Mantra traditions, from the ordinary fields of Indo-Tibetan classical learning, all the way up to the uncommon teachings of Atiyoga, which is the culmination of the nine vehicles of Buddhist practice.[3] The other four include *The Treasury of Kagyu Mantras* (*bKa' brgyud sngags kyi mdzod*), *The Treasury of Precious Spiritual Revelations* (*Rin chen gter mdzod*),[4] *The Treasury of Jamgön Kongtrul's Own Uncommon Revelations* (*Thun mong ma yin pa'i mdzod*),[5] and *The Treasury of Precious Instructions* (*gDams ngag rin po che'i mdzod*).[6]

Among these, *The Treasury of Precious Instructions* draws together teachings associated with the "eight great conveyances forming the lineages of spiritual attainment" (*sgrub brgyud shing rta chen po brgyad*). In general, this genre of instructions (*gdams ngag*), whether imparted verbally or in writing, is characterized by an emphasis on practical and pithy "hands-on" advice, in contrast to more formal theoretical teachings, for which reason such instructions are often considered to be esoteric, regardless of whether their content is concerned with medicine, astronomy, worldly matters, or Buddhist meditative practices.

Jamgön Kongtrul appears to have compiled and gradually expanded *The Treasury of Precious Instructions* between 1870 and 1887. Woodblocks, amounting to ten volumes, were originally carved at Palpung Monastery, but the collection has continued to expand—the Kundeling edition (1971–1972) in twelve volumes,[7] the edition of His Holiness Dilgo Khyentse

Rinpoche (1979–1981) in eighteen volumes, and the most recent Shechen Publications edition (1998), also in eighteen volumes. The last mentioned is the source text for the present volume of translations.

The content of *The Treasury of Precious Instructions* structures the oral teachings and their transmission according to the "eight great conveyances," or traditions that form the distinct lineages of spiritual attainment. These may be summarized as follows:[8]

(i) The Nyingma tradition derives from the transmissions of Padmasambhava and Vimalamitra during the eighth century, along with the former's illustrious twenty-five disciples (*rje dbangs nyer lnga*) headed by the sovereign Tri Songdetsen.

(ii) The Kadam tradition derives from Atiśa (982–1054) and his Tibetan disciples headed by Dromton Gyelwei Jungné (1004–1063).

(iii) The Sakya tradition, emphasizing the system known as "the Path and Its Fruition," derives from Virūpa and his Tibetan disciple Drokmi Lotsāwa Śākya Yeshé (992–1072).

(iv) The Marpa Kagyu tradition derives from the Indian masters Tilopā, Nāropā, and Maitrīpā, along with their preeminent Tibetan disciple Marpa Chokyi Lodro (1012–1097).

(v) The Shangpa Kagyu tradition derives from the ḍākinī Nigumā and her Tibetan disciple Khyungpo Neljor Tsultrim Gonpo of Shang. According to tradition, Khyungpo Neljor founded one hundred and eight sites over a three-year period, including the main monastery at Zhangzhong Dorjeden in Shang (ca. 1021), but following his death (ca. 1123), the cremated relics were mostly divided among his followers, and due to ongoing disputation, the opportunity to institutionalize the tradition was lost. For the most part, the Shangpa teachings have been maintained and transmitted within other schools and lineages, despite having asserted their distinctive presence through the sixteenth century with the construction of monasteries and hermitages. In recent years, a number of rebuilt Shangpa sites have been documented, including those at Zhangzhong Dorjeden, Dzongsho, Tsokha Gon, and Bokar Gon.

(vi) Pacification and Severance derive from Padampa Sangyé (d. 1117) and his female Tibetan disciple, Machik Labkyi Dronma (ca. 1055–1143). As with the Shangpa tradition, these instructions have also been transmitted within the main schools of Tibetan Buddhism.

(vii) The Six-Branch Yoga of the *Kālacakra Tantra* derives from Somanātha and his Tibetan disciple Gyijo Lotsāwa Dawa Ozer during the early eleventh century, and was maintained preeminently through the lineages associated with Zhalu and Jonang.

(viii) The Ritual Service and Attainment of the Three Adamantine Realities derives from the revelations of the female deity Vajrayoginī, compiled by the Tibetan master Orgyanpa Rinchen Pel (1230–1309) during his travels in Oḍḍiyāna.

The origin of this eclectic eightfold classification, with some variation in order, has been attributed to the versified composition of Trengwo Terton Sherab Ozer (1517–1584), the founder of Pelri Monastery in Chongyé.[9] The illustrious upholders of these eight lineages of spiritual attainment are sometimes contrasted with the great masters revered as the "ten great pillars who supported the exegetical lineages" (*bshad brgyud 'degs pa'i ka chen bcu*).[10]

In the context of Jamgön Kongtrul's *The Treasury of Precious Instructions*, the eight lineages are structured according to the following arrangement:

Volumes 1–2: the Nyingma tradition of the way of Secret Mantra (*gsang sngags rnying ma*)
Volumes 3–4: the Kadampa tradition (*bka' gdams*)
Volumes 5–6: the Sakya tradition: Path and Its Fruition (*sa skya lam 'bras*)
Volumes 7–10: the Marpa Kagyu tradition (*mar pa bka' brgyud*)
Volumes 11–12: the Shangpa Kagyu tradition (*shangs pa bka' brgyud*)
Volumes 13–14: Pacification and Severance (*zhi byed dang gcod*)
Volume 15: Kālacakra and the Ritual Service and Attainment of Orgyanpa (*dus 'khor dang o rgyan bsnyen sgrub*)
Volumes 16–17: miscellaneous teachings (*khrid skor sna tshogs*)[11]
Volume 18: the Jonang tradition and the Catalog (*jo nang khrid brgya dang dkar chag*)[12]

Volume 18: Part One

The first part of volume 18, translated here, comprises the one hundred and eight guidebooks of Jonang (*Jo nang khrid brgya*), which were compiled by the Venerable Kunga Drolchok (1507–1566). This anthology includes terse instructions representing all the eight lineages of spiritual attainment and was clearly regarded by Jamgön Kongtrul as an inspirational precursor for his own larger compilation, which additionally includes Indic source texts, Tibetan antecedents, and later interpretations. It is clear from the anthology itself that Kunga Drolchok identifies these one hundred and eight guidebooks within the Kadam, Sakya, and Kagyu lineages, and to a lesser extent with the Nyingma tradition. Although a few of the transmissions do have connections with earlier masters of Jonang, the author does not distinguish these from the majority that are of Sakya and Kagyu provenance. The appellation "Jonang" in this case points more toward the setting in which the anthology was eventually composed and its later transmission through Kunga Drolchok's illustrious reincarnation Tāranātha and the later Shangpa Kagyu succession.

Kunga Drolchok was born in 1507 in Lowo Matang (gLo bo sman thang), the capital of the Mustang enclave of northwestern Nepal, which lies due south of Drongpa Tradun in present-day Zhigatse Prefecture and functioned as an autonomous kingdom from its foundation in 1380 until its absorption by Nepal in 1795.[13] The rulers of Lowo Matang were for the most part patrons of the Sakya school, and it was this tradition in which the young Kunga Drolchok was raised. In his fifth year (1511), he began his studies at the local Pupak Monastery (Phu phag dgon pa), which was under the tutelage of his uncle, Kunga Chogdrub, a disciple of the Sakya master Dakchen Lodro Gyeltsen (1444–1495). In his tenth year (1516), he was ordained as a novice monk by Kunga Chogdrub, who over the next four years imparted the empowerments and instructions of the Sakya tradition, including the Path and Its Fruition.

In his thirteenth year (1519), Kunga Drolchok traveled north from Lowo Matang, accompanied by his elder brother, to study in the great monasteries of Utsang. At Sakya and the nearby retreat center of Khawu Drakdzong, they initially studied under Kunpang Doringpa and then continued on to Serdokchen, the seat of Paṇchen Śākya Chokden (1428–1507), where they began the study of Sakya epistemology and other fields of classical learning under the guidance of Śākya Chokden's disciple, Donyo Drubpa. A smallpox epidemic soon claimed the lives of nineteen of the twenty-two students there, including Kunga Drolchok's elder brother. To avoid the epidemic, as was the custom, Kunga Drolchok entered into retreat for the next eight months and memorized several treatises of epistemology. But he was admonished by Donyo Drubpa, who warned him that such scholarship would not result in enlightenment and instead taught him many meditative practices. After the epidemic had passed, he received further teachings of the Path and Its Fruition from Kunpang Doringpa, who had come to visit Serdokchen Monastery. Over a five-year period he studied all the major and minor fields of classical learning at Serdokchen and also at Ngor and Ngamring.

In his eighteenth year (1524), Kunga Drolchok returned to his native land, where he received the full monastic ordination from Kunga Chogdrub and Lhachok Sengé (1468–1535), the ninth preceptor of Ngor. After he was enthroned at Pupak Monastery, the deaths of both Kunga Chogdrub and his own father impelled him toward a life of meditative seclusion. Even so, he continued to teach Sakya Paṇḍita's *Treasury of Valid Cognition* at Pupak, and then in his twenty-third year (1529), the year after Paṇchen Jampa Lingpa had passed away, he occupied the latter's monastic seat where he taught intensively for the next three years, during that time visiting the famous pilgrimage site of Muktinath in Nepal.

In his twenty-seventh year (1533), Kunga Drolchok again traveled north from Lowo Matang to visit Lhasa and Tsurpu, where he received the Kagyu transmissions. On a return visit to his homeland, in his thirty-first year (1537), his mother passed away. Throughout his teaching career he frequently taught the Path and Its Fruition, but he also established close connections with the Shangpa Kagyu and Jonang traditions. Specifically, in the course of his peripatetic travels he received the Shangpa Kagyu teachings from Gyagom Lekpei Gyeltsen and others, and encountered the ḍākinī Nigumā in a vision, in consequence of which he widely taught the Six Doctrines of Nigumā. He then served as preceptor of the Jonang hermitage at Cholung Jangtsé, receiving the Six-Branch Yoga of Kālacakra from his relative Lochen Rinchen Zangpo (1489–1563). From his fortieth year (1546), Kunga Drolchok occupied the seat of Jonang Monastery, as the twenty-fourth lineage holder, and retained this position until his death in 1566, when he was succeeded on the throne of Jonang by his nephew, Kunga Pelzang (1513–1593).[14]

Kunga Drolchok's listed writings amount to seventy-nine distinct works, including eulogies, epistles, expositions, travelogues, biographies, mind training, exegeses of empowerments, means for attainment, lineage prayers, guidebooks of instruction, narratives, catalogs, and grammatical writings. There are extant compilations of his writings, including a two-volume collection from Dzamtang entitled *Miscellaneous Writings* (*gSung thor bu*),[15] and another one-volume collection printed at Gyantsé Dzong.[16] Apart from the One Hundred and Eight Guidebooks of Jonang, extensive autobiographical writings have survived.[17] These include the narratives of Kunga Drolchok's previous lives as Maitrīpā/Avadhūtipā, Kṛṣṇacārin (Nag po spyod pa), Ratanbhahula, Rongzom Chokyi Zangpo, Barompa Darma Wangchuk, Avadhūti Ozer Pel, Zhang Drukdra Gyeltsen, Nyo Gyelwa Lhanangpa, Kunkhyen Saṅghabhadra, Jamyang Tashi Palden, and Paṇḍita Chokyi Nyinmor Jepa. More significantly, they include eight distinct texts pertaining to Kunga Drolchok's outer, inner, and secret life, which offer ample resource materials for further research in this genre of Tibetan autobiographical literature, beyond the scope of the present work. These are respectively entitled: (i) *The Biography That Guides the Chariot of Faith for Those of Good Fortune* (*rNam thar skal bzang dad pa'i shing rta 'dren byed*), (ii) *The Continuation of the Biography That Guides the Chariot of Faith for Those of Good Fortune* (*rNam thar skal bzang dad pa'i shing rta 'dren byed kyi 'phros*), (iii) *The Supplement: A Beauteous Adornment* (*Zur 'debs mdzes rgyan*), (iv) *The Further Biography: The Inlaid Jewel Ornament* (*rNam thar yang rgyan nor bu'i phra bkod*), (v) *The Enhancing Biography: Necklace of Gemstone Ornaments* (*rNam thar spel rgyan nor bu'i do shal*), (vi) *The Biography Entitled Marvelous Ornament* (*rNam thar mtshar rgyan*), (vii) *The Biography of Ordinary Approach Entitled Ornamental Flower of Experience* (*Myong ba rgyan gyi me tog ces bya ba thun mong gi sgo'i rnam thar*), and (viii) *The Biography of Extraordinary Approach Entitled Ornamental Flower of Experience* (*Myong ba rgyan gyi me tog ces bya ba thun mong ma yin pa'i rnam thar*).

The Compilation of the One Hundred and Eight Guidebooks

In the fourth chapter of the present work, Kunga Drolchok describes how he was inspired by Sangyé Pel to seek out the respective lineage holders of the one hundred and eight guidebooks. Commencing in his seventh year (1514) and continuing through to his thirty-eighth year (1545) when he occupied the seat at Jonang, he traveled throughout Utsang, receiving these instructions from many diverse teachers, and sometimes on multiple occasions. The names of the foremost twenty-eight teachers are known from the lineage prayers in chapter 1. Among them, his uncle Kunga Chogdrub (fl. fifteenth–sixteenth centuries) was the most prolific, transmitting forty-one of the one hundred and eight guidebooks to Kunga Drolchok. These included the Sakya instructions of *Parting from the Four Attachments* (1),

The Path and Its Fruition (43), *The Inconceivables* (44), *The Nine Profound Methods* (45), *The Attainment of Coemergence* (46), *The Perfection of the Path of Fierce Inner Heat* (47), *The Straightening of Crooked Posture* (48), *The Path of the Female Mudra* (49), *The Great Seal Devoid of Letters* (50), *The Determination of Mind* (51), *The Mingling of Sutra and Tantra* (52), *The Dispelling of Obstacles due to External Demons* (53), *The Dispelling of Obstacles due to the Agitation of the Physical Body by the Elements* (54), *The Dispelling of the Obstacles of Meditative Stability and Mind* (55), *The Great Seal Dispelling the Three Sorts of Suffering* (56), *The Clear Recollection of the Innate State* (57), *The Twenty-Nine Essential Visualizations of Self-Consecration* (59), *The Exegesis of the Concealed Path* (60), and *The Elucidation of Symbolic Meaning* (61). Kunga Chogdrub was also responsible for transmitting Kadam instructions, including *The Seven-Point Mind Training of the Great Vehicle* (2), *The Heart of Dependent Origination* (3), *The Carrying of Happiness and Suffering on the Path* (4), *The Mind Training according to Sumpa Lotsāwa* (5), *The Three Essential Points* (7), *The Three Sorts of Person* (9), *The Sequence of the Buddhist Teaching* (10), *The Sameness of Existence and Quiescence* (11), *The Great Middle Way* (12), *The Hidden Guidance of Kadam* (13), *The Four Deities of Kadam: Munīndra, Acala, Avalokita, and Tārā* (14–17), and *The Parables of Potowa* (18). Furthermore, he transmitted *The Five Doctrines of Maitreya* (23), *The Direct Guidance of Avalokiteśvara according to the Lakṣmī, Candradhvaja, and Tsembupa Traditions* (30–32), as well as *The Unelaborate Practice of Red Yamāri* (64), *The Four-Stage Yoga* (65), and *The Gradual Path of Padmasambhava* (105).

Lowo Khenchen Sonam Lhundrub (1456–1532) was responsible for transmitting ten of the one hundred and eight guidebooks, including *The Six Descents of the Transcendent Perfection of Wisdom* (20), *The Three Stages of Meditation* (22), *The Three Purities* (58), *The Mental Focus on the Horns of Bhairava* (66), *The Central Channel Dependent on the Male Deity Cakrasaṃvara* (67), *The Central Channel Dependent on the Female Deity Vajravārāhī* (68), *The Five Stages according to Ghaṇṭāpāda* (69), *The Four Stages according to Kṛṣṇacārin* (70), *The Kharamukha Cakrasaṃvara* (74), and *The Six Meditations of Vajravārāhī* (75).

The remaining guidebooks were received from lineage holders outside his native Lowo Matang, among whom Changlungpa Zhonu Chodrub (fl. fifteenth–sixteenth centuries) transmitted ten instructions including *The Five Paths of Pacification* (21), *The Guidance of White Tārā* (28), *The Direct*

Guidance of Cakrasaṃvara and Hevajra (34–35), *Ritual Service and Attainment of the Three Adamantine Realities* (42), *The Six Doctrines of Sukhasiddhi* (81), *The Fivefold Great Seal* (84), *The Four Syllables of the Great Seal* (85), *The Cycle of Pagmodru Densatel* (95), and *The Nature of Mind: The Wish-Fulfilling Gem* (108).

The Shangpa Kagyu master Gyagom Lekpei Gyeltsen (fl. fifteenth–sixteenth centuries) transmitted six instructions including *The Direct Guidance of Avalokiteśvara according to the Kyergangpa Tradition* (33), *The Six Doctrines of Nigumā* (77), *The Amulet Tradition of the Great Seal* (78), *The Three Aspects Carried on the Path* (79), *The Deathlessness of One's Own Mind* (80), and *The Lineage of the Emanational Navel Cakra* (82), the last of which is sometimes substituted by *The Inner Guidance of Nairātmyā*.

As for the Marpa Kagyu traditions, Kunga Drolchok received five instructions from Ngok Lodro Pelzangpo (fl. fifteenth–sixteenth centuries), including *The Four Adamantine Seats* (72), *The Great Magical Emanation* (73), *The Six Doctrines according to the Sekharma Tradition* (88), *The Mingling and Transformation of the Three Poisons* (89), and *The Four Scrolls of the Aural Instruction* (90); and a further four from Trewo Chokyi Gyatso (d. 1547), including *Guidance on Amitāyus* (27), *The Six Doctrines of Nāropā* (76), *The Indivisibility of Subtle Energy and Mind* (87), and *The Six Doctrines of the Accomplished Masters* (104).

His relative Lotsāwa Rinchen Zangpo (1489–1563), who was affiliated to Jonang, transmitted a further four instructions including *The Six-Branch Yoga of Kālacakra* (40), *The Aural Lineage of Kālacakra* (41), *The Six Doctrines of Liberation through the Upper Gate, according to the Aural Lineage of Cakrasaṃvara* (91), and *The Doctrinal Cycle of Nirdehaḍākinī* (92).

Rabsel Dawa Gon (fl. fifteenth–sixteenth centuries) transmitted *Vajrapāṇi in the Form Caṇḍa* (37), *The Five Stages of the Secret Assembly* (62), and *The Vital Essence of Liberation* (63). Taklung Tulku Namgyel Tashi (1524–1563) transmitted *The Unique Enlightened Intention* (96), *The Six Doctrines according to Taklungpa* (97), and *Four-Armed Mahākāla in the Form Kurakma* (101). The latter's associate Ngawang Tulku of Taklung (fl. fifteenth–sixteenth centuries) transmitted *The Elaborate Guidance of Zhang Tselpa* (93) and *Lorepa's Fivefold Capacity* (99).

Kunpang Chokyi Nyima (1449–1524) transmitted *Resting in the Nature of Mind* (8) and *Vārāhī in the Form Kurmapādā* (38). Paṇchen Amogha Donyo Drubpa (fl. fifteenth–sixteenth centuries) transmitted *The View of*

Intrinsic Emptiness (24) and *The Trilogy of Spiritual Songs* (103). Yigdruk Sherab Peljor (b. fifteenth century) transmitted the instructions on Severance (6) and *The Collected Injunctions of the King* (106).

In addition, there were a further fourteen teachers responsible for transmitting a single guidebook. Among them, Avadhūtipā Namgyel Drakpa (1469–1530) transmitted *The Sixteen Spheres of the Heart* (19), Pelden Tsultrim (1333–1399) transmitted *The View of Extraneous Emptiness* (25), Zelmo Drakpa Drakpa Yeshé (fl. fifteenth–sixteenth centuries) of the Bodong lineage transmitted *The Elucidation of the Concealed Meanings of Yogatantra* (26), Trariwa Rinchen Gyelchok transmitted *The Guidance of White Amitāyus* (29), Tashi Namgyel (1490–1518) of Ngor transmitted *Vajrapāṇi in the Form Mahācakra* (36), Gugé Paṇchen Sonam Lhundrub (fl. fifteenth–sixteenth centuries) transmitted *Kurukullā* (39), Muchen Sangyé Rinchen (1450–1524) transmitted *White Cakrasaṃvara* (71), Drukchen Ngawang Chokyi Gyelpo (1465–1540) transmitted *The Coemergent Union of the Great Seal* (83), Karma Trinlepa (1456–1539) transmitted *The Introduction to the Three Buddha Bodies* (86), Paṇchen Donyo Sengé (fl. fifteenth–sixteenth centuries) transmitted *The Six-Branch Yoga according to Pelchen Ga Lotsāwa* (94), Ngawang Chogyel (1465–1540) transmitted *The Means for Attainment of the Teacher, Auspicious Circumstances, and Common Savor* (98), Sonam Gyelchok (fl. fifteenth–sixteenth centuries) transmitted *The Six Primary Essentials for Mountain Retreat* (100), Lhachok Sengé (fl. fifteenth–sixteenth centuries) transmitted *The Inner Guidance of Glorious Pañjaranātha* (102), and Norbu Rinchen (fl. sixteenth century) transmitted *Norbu Rinchen's Liberation by Seeing* (107).

After the death of Kunga Drolchok, the transmission of the complete collection was handed down within the Jonang and Shangpa Kagyu lineages through his own acknowledged reincarnation Drolmei Gonpo Tāranātha (1575–1634), as well as Rinchen Dorjéma Ratnavajriṇī (1585–1668), Katok Tsewang Norbu (1698–1755), Zhalu Lotsāwa Losal Tenkyong (b. 1804), and Jamyang Khyentsé Wangpo (1820–1892). Among these later lineage holders, Tāranātha authored chapter 6 of the present text, entitled "Supplementary Historical Anecdotes"; and Losal Tenkyong authored chapter 2, "Supplementary Prayer to the Lineage," and chapter 12, "Methods for the Conferral of the Empowerments." The other nine chapters are the work of Kunga Drolchok himself.

The Jonang Tradition

The Jonang tradition is not included among the eight lineages of spiritual attainment in that it was considered an affiliate of Sakya, probably on account of the background of its fourth incumbent, Dolpopa Sherab Gyeltsen. It is clear from Kunga Drolchok's own analysis of the structure and content of the One Hundred and Eight Guidebooks (chapter 10) that the Sarma texts within the collection are recognized to be of either Sakya, Kagyu, or Kadam provenance. On the other hand, it was after receiving all these instructions that Kunga Drolchok compiled them in textual form while occupying the seat of Jonang Monastery. So the importance of Jonang and the Shangpa Kagyu lineage for the subsequent transmission of the collection cannot be overestimated.

Jonang (Jomonang) is said to have been founded in 1294 by Kunpang Tukjé Tsondru (1243–1313), a lineage holder of Yumo Mikyo Dorjé who had received the instructions on the Six-Branch Yoga of Kālacakra from the Kashmiri paṇḍita Somanātha in the eleventh century. Previously the upper and lower meditation caves of Mount Jomo Nagyel (5,744 meters) had been frequented by Guru Padmasambhava and his disciples, such as Nub Namkei Nyingpo, during the eighth century, and later by the accomplished master Darchar Rinchen Zangpo. According to legend, Kungpangpa was invited to reside there by the local protector deity Jomo Ngak Gyelmo. He and his immediate successors, Jangsem Gyelwa Yeshé and Khetsun Yonten Gyatso, are collectively known as the three original teachers of the Jonangpa lineage. The fourth incumbent, the illustrious Dolpopa Sherab Gyeltsen (1292–1361), was a prolific commentator on the sutras and tantras, integrating the philosophical perspective known as "extraneous emptiness" (*gzhan stong*), which is based on the third-turning tathāgatagarbha sutras and their commentaries by Maitreya,[18] with the Six-Branch Yoga of Kālacakra. In 1354, near his own hermitage, he constructed the twenty-meter-high Kumbum-style stupa named Tongdrol Chenmo, which is octagonal in shape with seven stories. The extant murals are said to reflect the provincial Lato style, which represents an early synthesis of Newar and indigenous Tibetan elements, incorporating fewer Chinese-inspired features than the better-known paintings of Zhalu or Gyantsé.

When Kunga Drolchok occupied the monastic seat as the twenty-fifth incumbent in 1545, he resided at Cholung Jangtsé, where all but three of the texts forming the *One Hundred and Eight Guidebooks of Jonang* were composed. His incarnation, the twenty-seventh incumbent Drolmei Gonpo Tāranātha (1575–1634), founded the grand monastery of Takten Puntsoling in 1615[19] and refurbished the Tongdrol Chenmo under the patronage of the king of Tsang, Puntsok Namgyel, who at that time ruled Tibet from his fortress in Zhigatse. Tāranātha is respected as one of Tibet's greatest writers and polymaths, his *Collected Works* (2008 edition) amounting to forty-five volumes. His successors, the twenty-eighth incumbent Sangyé Gyatso and the twenty-ninth Kunga Rinchen Gyatso, ensured the continuity of his legacy, but in consequence of Jonang's support for the vanquished Tsangpa faction in the civil war of the seventeenth century, the monastery, along with its local branches, was taken over by the Gelukpa establishment during the lifetime or after the death of the thirtieth incumbent Lodro Namgyel (1618–1683) and renamed Geden Puntsoling. Although philosophical differences between the Jonangpa view of extraneous emptiness and the prevailing view of intrinsic emptiness are sometimes cited as a pretext for the closure of Takten Puntsolung, and the writings of Dolpopa on that subject were proscribed,[20] the Gelukpa in fact absorbed many of the Jonang teachings, particularly concerning the Six-Branch Yoga of Kālacakra. During this period of Gelukpa ascendancy, Ngawang Trinlé (1657–1723), a nephew and disciple of Lodro Namgyel who had also studied under the Fifth Dalai Lama, established Jonang teachings, particularly those concerning Kālacakra, within the curriculum of Drepung and Ganden. Having lived for years as a hermit, he became renowned throughout central Tibet for his nonsectarian approach, transmitting the Shangpa Kagyu and Jonang empowerments in Gelukpa circles, as well as to Mokchok Tulku.

The actual reasons for the Gelukpa suppression of the Jonangpa appear to have been political rather than doctrinal schism. Not only were they allied with the Kagyu traditions to the Tsangpa faction during the civil war, but also there were genuine fears the Jonangpa would have increasing influence in Mongolia, especially after Tāranātha's reincarnation was discovered to be Zanabazar, the son of Tushiyetu Khan, the prince of Central Khalkha. Tushiyetu Khan and his son were of Borjigin lineage (the imperial clan of Genghis Khan). When the young boy was declared spiritual leader of all of Mongolia, the Gelukpa acted to take control of the Jonangpa monasteries, along with others of Kagyu persuasion.[21]

Ngawang Trinlé also taught widely in the Jonang monasteries of the remote grasslands of northeastern Tibet, which were beyond the political jurisdiction of the Ganden Palace.[22] Peljam in his *Abridged History of the*

Abbatial Succession of the Jonangwa recounts the origins of the Jonang monasteries that survived and prospered in the Amdo grasslands. Their expansion in the region began in the mid-thirteenth century during the lifetime of Dolpopa and spread to Dzamtang in the fourteenth century. Three encampments or monastic communities were established there, including Chojé Dratsang, Tsechu Dratsang, and Tsangwa Dratsang.[23] The last of these has been maintained since the seventeenth century in a line extending from the aforementioned Lodro Namgyel and Ngawang Trinlé, through the latter's disciple Ngawang Tenzin Namgyel, and so on down to the fifty-third incumbent, Khentrul Jampel Lodro. The same source identifies a further eighteen Jonang monasteries and hermitages in Amdo, along with nine in Ngawa, seventeen further south in Gyarong, and fifteen in Golok. The final three chapters of Peljam's work pertain to Jonangpa activities in mainland China, Mongolia, and the United States.

The Content of the *One Hundred and Eight Guidebooks of Jonang*

The collection divides neatly into three components: History (chaps. 1–6), Practice (chaps. 7–9), and Supports (chaps. 10–12).[24]

The historical section includes prayers dedicated to the lineage of the One Hundred and Eight Guidebooks with a supplement composed by Losal Tenkyong (chaps. 1–2). The versified life-sustaining prayer (chap. 3) is followed by an autobiographical record of teachings received (chap. 4), and historical anecdotes written by Kunga Drolchok himself up to the end of the seventy-fourth guidebook, and thereafter by Tāranātha (chaps. 5–6).

The practice section includes two chapters concerning the discursive preliminaries and the extraordinary accumulations of the refuge, the enlightened mind, the purification of negativity, and the offering of the mandala (chaps. 7–8). Following these prerequisites, it then proceeds to the main content of the collection, the actual one hundred and eight guidebooks (chap. 9).

The final supporting section includes Kunga Drolchok's important analysis of the structure and content of the guidebooks (chap. 10), along with lists of their corresponding protector deities and empowerments (chap. 11) and a method for the conferral of blessing through the empowerment rite of the sacred book containing the One Hundred and Eight Guidebooks, the last of which was composed by Losal Tenkyong. Throughout this translation, the pagination of the Tibetan text (Shechen edition) has been retained in curly brackets for the benefit of Tibetan readers who may wish to access the original.

Each chapter is introduced by a short preamble, summarizing its content and drawing attention to certain technical issues. Readers should note that in chapter 9 the endnotes and corresponding bibliography entries frequently differentiate between the primary Tibetan sources that Kunga Drolchok accessed when writing his terse summaries and the corresponding original Indic sources or Tibetan antecedents. In some cases, later interpretations of Tāranātha and Jamyang Khyentsé Wangpo have also been referenced.

Acknowledgments

I would like to thank Eric Colombel of the Tsadra Foundation, who asked me to participate in this project and who provided generous funding as I translated and annotated the *One Hundred and Eight Guidebooks of Jonang*, working on a part-time basis from April 2016. I am also grateful to Ringu Tulku, who carefully reviewed my list of obscure points, and to Sarah Harding, Cyrus Stearns, and Stephen Gethin, with whom I discussed specific topics. My wife, Xiaohong, helped with the preparation of the bibliography. My old friend Martin Boord read through the entire manuscript with his customary and methodical attention to detail. Finally, heartfelt thanks are due to Nikko Odiseos of Shambhala Publications and to Michael Wakoff, our in-house editor.

Gyurme Dorje
Crieff, June 2019

Technical Note

THIS TRANSLATION is based on the version of the Tibetan text found in the first part of the eighteenth volume (*tsha*) of the Shechen edition of *The Treasury of Precious Instructions* (*gDams ngag rin po che'i mdzod*), pp. 1–380. The page numbers in curly brackets { } throughout this book indicate the arabic page numbers of that particular edition. The earlier Kundeling and Palpung editions of the same anthology were also occasionally consulted when specific passages or terms appeared to be unclear. In addition, there were instances where typographical errors and obscurities found in all these anthologies were resolved through consultation with the 1984 reproduction of a rare manuscript of the *One Hundred and Eight Guidebooks of Jonang* (*Jo nang khrid brgya*), from the library of His Holiness Sakya Trizin, published by Migmar Tseten in Dehradun, India.

Throughout this book, any text found in square brackets [ ] has been added to aid the reader's comprehension. The sources from which many of these inserts derive are mentioned in the corresponding endnotes. The preambles to each of the twelve chapters, written by the translator, are formatted differently than the main text.

With a few exceptions, Tibetan and Sanskrit technical terms have been rendered into English. To assist general readers and scholars alike, there are trilingual concordances of terminology and of personal and place names, all of which follow the last chapter of the translation. In these concordances and in the back matter as a whole, Tibetan words are transliterated according to a widely accepted variant of the extended Wylie system. In the main text, however, the Tibetan names of persons, deities, and places appear in a simplified phonetic system that makes use of the acute and umlaut accents above the vowels *e* and *o*, and that takes elision into account.

In the case of Sanskrit terms and names, the traditional system of transliteration using diacritics, universally accepted in academic circles, has been employed. Though this needs no introduction to scholars, for the benefit of the general reader the following guidelines will be useful: Among the short vowels, *a*, *i*, *u*, *e*, and *o* are pronounced as in Italian, while *ṛ* is pronounced like the *ri* sound of the English word *brick*, and the rarely found *ḷ* is pronounced as the *li* sound in *click*. Among the long vowels, most of which employ the superscript macron (-), *ā*, *ī*, and *ū* are respectively pronounced like the *a* in *father*, the *ea* in *seat*, and the *oo* in *boot*. Other long vowels include *ai*, which resembles the *y* sound in *by*; *au*, which resembles the *ow* sound in *now*; and the long versions of *ṛ* and *ḷ*, which respectively resemble the *rea* sound in *reach* and the *lea* sound in *leach*. Vowels may also be followed by *ṃ* and *ḥ*, which respectively indicate their nasalization and aspiration. As far as the Sanskrit consonants are concerned, *c* is pronounced as the *ch* sound in *church* but without strong aspiration. The consonants *th* and *ph* are respectively pronounced like *t* and *p* with strong aspiration, and **never** like the *th* in *that* and the *ph* in *phone*. Retroflex consonants with a subscript dot—*ṭ*, *ṭha*, *ḍ*, *ḍha*, and *ṇ*—indicate that they are pronounced with the tongue striking the roof of the mouth, while the corresponding dental set, without the subscript dot, indicates that they are pronounced with the tongue striking the upper incisors. The nasal consonants *ṅ* and *ñ* are respectively pronounced like the *ng* in *king*, and the *ny* in *canyon*. Finally, *ś* and *ṣ* are variants of the English *sh* sound, but with the tongue positioned forward in the former case and backward in the latter case. Throughout this text, mantra syllables are transliterated in small caps, their font size smaller than that of the surrounding text.

Most references to primary and secondary sources in the bibliography and endnotes are identified by abbreviations indicating the collections to which they belong or their catalog numbers in the indispensable digital library at the Buddhist Digital Resource Center (BDRC, formerly TBRC). For a complete listing, see the list of abbreviations, which precedes the notes.

Publisher's Note

THE TRANSLATOR of this volume, Gyurme Dorje, one of the giants of Tibetan translation and practice, passed away on February 5, 2020, the anniversary of the passing of his teacher Kangyur Rinpoche.

Gyurme spent many years in Asia, studying with many of the greatest masters of our day: Dudjom Rinpoche, Kangyur Rinpoche, Chatral Rinpoche, and Dilgo Khyentse Rinpoche. His translation work has been inestimably important to thousands of people. In the 1990s, there were far fewer books available for practitioners, and one of the essential volumes for many was *The History of the Nyingma School*, which he cotranslated with Matthew Kapstein. This is much more than a history, as it embodies the living tradition. He also is renowned for his three-volume dissertation on, and translation of, the *Guhyagarbha Tantra*, which runs over three thousand pages.

Gyurme's *Tibet Handbook* and *Bhutan Handbook* have been the companions of thousands as they trekked, made pilgrimage, and visited the sacred places of those blessed lands. And he published a dictionary and a wide variety of other works on Tibetan culture including books on divination, art, sacred architecture, and more. His translation of *The Tibetan Book of the Dead* is considered one of the very best.

Most recently he published several immensely important works, including (1) *Indo-Tibetan Classical Learning and Buddhist Phenomenology*, book 6, parts 1 and 2, in Jamgön Kongtrul's series *The Treasury of Knowledge*; (2) *Philosophical Systems and Lines of Transmission*, book 13, in Choying Tobden Dorje's series *The Complete Nyingma Tradition from Sutra to Tantra*; and (3) the two-volume set *The Essential Tantras of Mahayoga* (based on the *Guhyagarbha Tantra*), books 15–17, also in the series *The Complete Nyingma Tradition from Sutra to Tantra*.

All of us here at Shambhala Publications are extremely grateful to

Gyurme's immeasurable contribution to our understanding, experience, and appreciation of the Tibetan tradition.

I would also like to thank the translator and teacher Sarah Harding, Gyurme's longtime friend, who made a significant effort to complete the final edits and notes on this volume.

Nikko Odiseos
August 2020
Boulder, CO

PART ONE

History

1. Lineage Prayers of the One Hundred and Eight Guidebooks

The following prayers intone the names of the progenitors or inspirational sources of the One Hundred and Eight Guidebooks and their successive historical lineage holders in India and Tibet through to the time of their compiler, Kunga Drolchok (1507–1565). Jamgön Kongtrul Lodrö Taye (1813–1899) later extended the lineage of the first prayer, Parting from the Four Attachments, *by adding the names of subsequent lineage holders who followed Kunga Drolchok, including the latter's acknowledged reincarnation Drolmei Gonpo Tāranātha (1575–1634), as well as Rinchen Dorjéma Ratnavajriṇī (1585–1668), Katok Tsewang Norbu (1698–1755), Zhalu Lotsāwa Losal Tenkyong (b. 1804), and Jamyang Khyentsé Wangpo (1820–1892). Readers should understand that this extended lineage is to be appended to each of the one hundred and eight guidebooks in turn.*

Each prayer concludes with a pithy quatrain requesting the blessings of the lineage holders and alluding tersely to the doctrinal content of the lineage in question. In a few instances, explanatory notes have been added, but in general the reader should understand that these allusions and technicalities are explained in the corresponding guidebooks themselves (chap. 9).

In his concluding remarks at the end of this chapter, Kunga Drolchok comments on the difficulty he encountered in composing these versified prayers. In order to maintain the meter, he frequently resorted to a well-established poetic device—rendering the names of the successive lineage holders obliquely through epithets or contracted variant forms. For the aid of the reader, this translation presents these names not in metrical verse but in a simplified linear form, and each prayer is preceded by a short paragraph, which I have added, that dates the relevant chronology.

Formal Title

Supplication to the Lineage of the One Hundred and Eight Guidebooks, Easy to Recite and Clearly Listing to Some Extent the Names of the Lineage Holders[1] {2}

Introductory Verse

OṂ SVĀSTI SIDDHAṂ
Homage to the teachers and to Mañjughoṣa!

1. *Parting from the Four Attachments*

The progenitors of the first lineage are Śākyamuni Buddha and the bodhisattva Mañjughoṣa, whose revelation was transmitted to Sachen Kunga Nyingpo (1092–1158), the first of the five founders of Sakya Monastery. His successors, the hierarchs of Sakya, include Sonam Tsemo (1142–1182), Drakpa Gyeltsen (1147–1216), Sakya Paṇḍita Kunga Gyeltsen (1182–1251), Chogyel Pakpa Lodro Gyeltsen (1235–1280), Zhang Konchok Pel (1240–1317), Drakpukpa Sonam Pelwa (1277–1350), Lama Dampa Sonam Gyeltsen (1312–1375), Lama Dampa Pelden Tsultrim (1333–1399), Sharchen Yeshé Gyeltsen (1359–1406), Ngorchen Kunga Zangpo (1382–1456), Gyeltsab Kunga Wangchuk (1424–1478), and Kunga Chogdrub (fl. fifteenth–sixteenth centuries) who was an important teacher of Kunga Drolchok (1507–1565). The extended lineage (see above) includes: Choku Lhawang Drakpa (fl. sixteenth century), Tāranātha (1575–1634), Rinchen Dorjéma Ratnavajriṇī (1585–1668), Rinchen Gyatso (fl. seventeenth century), Nyingpo Tayepa (fl. seventeenth century), Kunzang Wangpo (fl. early eighteenth century), Katok Tsewang Norbu (1698–1755), Kunzang Choying Rangdrol, Kunzang Chojor, Lobzang Tutob (fl. late eighteenth–early nineteenth centuries), Nyima Chopelwa, Zhalu Lotsāwa Losal Tenkyong (b. 1804), and Jamyang Khyentsé Wangpo (1820–1892).

The lineage prayer of *Parting from the Four Attachments* is as follows:

- Śākyamuni
- Mañjughoṣa
- Sachen Kunga Nyingpo
- Sonam Tsemo

- Drakpa Gyeltsen
- Sakya Paṇḍita
- Chogyel Pakpa
- Zhang Konchok Pel
- Drakpukpa
- Sonam Gyeltsen
- Pelden Tsultrim
- Sharchen Yeshé Gyeltsen
- Ngorchen Kunga Zangpo
- Gyeltsab Kunga Wangchuk
- Kunga Chogdrub

Thereafter this guidebook was maintained by the lineage holders of the entire one hundred and eight guidebooks, as follows:

- Jetsun Kunga Drolchok
- Choku Lhawang Drakpa
- Drolmei Gonpo Tāranātha
- Ratnavajriṇī
- Rinchen Gyatso
- Nyingpo Tayepa
- Kunzang Wangpo
- Tsewang Norbu
- Choying Rangdrol
- Kunzang Chojor
- Lobzang Tutob
- Nyima Chopelwa
- Losal Tenkyong
- Khyentsé Wangpo . . .

I supplicate the teachers of the primary lineage.
Grant your blessing that the genuine coalescent middle way
Might arise in our minds,
Separated from all grasping,
Including attachment to this life,
Attachment to cyclic existence—the three world systems,
Attachment to self-interest, and attachment to prejudice.[2] {3}

2. *The Seven-Point Mind Training of the Great Vehicle*

The progenitors of this lineage are Śākyamuni Buddha and the bodhisattva Mahāmaitreya, whose revelations were received by Asaṅga (fl. late fourth–early fifth centuries). The latter's Indian successors included his brother Vasubandhu (fl. late fourth–early fifth centuries), as well as Ārya Vimuktisena (fl. fifth century), Bhaṭṭāraka Vimuktisena (fl. late fifth–early sixth centuries), Guṇamitra (fl. late sixth–early seventh centuries), Haribhadra (ca. 800), Pūrṇavardhana, the elder Kusulu Ratnabhadra, the younger Kusulu Mitrayogin, Dharmakīrti of Sumatra (b. tenth century), and Atiśa (982–1054). In Tibet, the lineage then descended through the Kadampa masters: Dromton Gyelwei Jungné (1004–1064), Potowa Rinchen Sel (1027–1105), Sharawa Yonten Drak (1070–1141), Chekhawa Yeshé Dorjé (1101–1175), Sechilbupa Chokyi Gyeltsen (1121–1189), Lhaton Ozer Lama (fl. twelfth century), Lhading Jangchub Bum (fl. twelfth century), Lhading Kunga Gyatso (fl. twelfth century), Umdzé Yonten Pel (fl. late twelfth– early thirteenth centuries), Dewa Pel (1231–1297), Drakpa Zhonu (1257–1315), Sonam Drakpa (1273–1345), Gyelsé Tokmé Zangpo (1295–1369), Drogon Pelden Yeshé (fl. fourteenth century), Hor Kabzhipa Sengé Gyeltsen (fl. late fourteenth–early fifteenth centuries), Pelden Zangpo, Neten Sampenpa Jangsem Jinpa, Raton Yonten Pelzang (fl. fifteenth century), and Kunga Chogdrub (fl. fifteenth–sixteenth centuries).

The lineage prayer of *The Seven-Point Mind Training of the Great Vehicle* is as follows:

- Śākyamuni
- Mahāmaitreya
- Asaṅga
- Vasubandhu
- Ārya Vimuktisena
- Bhaṭṭāraka Vimuktisena
- Guṇamitra
- Haribhadra
- Pūrṇavardhana
- Kusulu the Elder
- Kusulu the Younger
- Dharmakīrti of Sumatra
- Pelden Atiśa

- Dromton
- Potowa
- Shara Yonten Drak
- Chekhawa Yeshé Dorjé
- Sechilbupa Chokyi Gyeltsen
- Ozer Lama
- Lhading Jangchub Bum
- Kunga Gyatso
- Yonten Pel
- Dewa Pel
- Drakpa Zhonu
- Sonam Drakpa
- Gyelsé Tokmé Zangpo
- Pelden Yeshé
- Kabzhipa Sengé Gyeltsen
- Pelden Zangpo
- Sampenpa
- Raton Yonten Pelzang
- Kunga Chogdrub
- Jetsun Kunga Drolchok . . .

From this point on, the aforementioned extension of the lineage should be inserted.

Grant your blessing that those endowed with the preliminary supporting
teachings,
And refined in the twofold enlightened mind that constitutes the main
practice,
Having transformed [negative circumstances] into the path,
By the integration of experiential cultivation
Might esteem more than life itself
The reaching of the limits of mind training,
The precepts [of mind training], and the commitments [of mind
training]![3] {4}

3. *The Heart of Dependent Origination*

The progenitors of this lineage are Śākyamuni Buddha and the bodhisattva Mahāmaitreya, whose revelations were received by Dharmakīrti of Sumatra (b. tenth century). Atiśa (982–1054) then transmitted this instruction in Tibet through the Kadampa masters: Dromton Gyelwei Jungné (1004–1064), Potowa Rinchen Sel (1027–1105), Gyaton Chagriwa (fl. late eleventh–early twelfth centuries), Chokyi Yungdrung (fl. early twelfth century), Nyipuwa Gyergom Zhikpo (1090–1171), Gyagom Riwa Zhikpo, Drakrom, Nyenchenpa Sonam Tenpa (ca. 1222–1317), Sherab Bumpa (fl. thirteenth century), Gyelsé Tokmé Zangpo (1295–1369), Drogon Pelden Yeshé (fl. fourteenth century), Hor Kabzhipa Sengé Gyeltsen (fl. late fourteenth–early fifteenth centuries), Pelden Zangpo, Neten Sampenpa Jangsem Jinpa, Raton Yonten Pelzang (fl. fifteenth century), and Kunga Chogdrub (fl. fifteenth–sixteenth centuries) to Kunga Drolchok.

The lineage prayer of *The Heart of Dependent Origination* is as follows:

· Mahāmuni
· Maitreyanātha
· Dharmakīrti of Sumatra
· Pelden Atiśa
· Dromton
· Potowa
· Chagriwa
· Chokyi Yungdrung
· Nyipuwa Gyergom
· Gyagom Riwa
· Drakrom
· Nyenchenpa
· Sherab Bumpa
· Gyelsé Tokmé Zangpo
· Drogon Pelden Yeshé
· Kabzhipa
· Pelden Zangpo
· Sampenpa
· Yonten Pelzang
· Kunga Chogdrub . . .

Through the supplication and experiential cultivation of union with the teacher,
Grant your blessing that the mind endowed with loving-kindness, compassion,
And seven focuses[4] might arise uncontrived in the mental continuum,
And that all appearances whatsoever might arise as a magical net of auspicious circumstances!

4. *The Carrying of Happiness and Suffering on the Path*

The progenitor of this lineage is the female bodhisattva Bhaṭṭārikā Tārā, whose revelations were received by the great paṇḍita Śākyaśrī of Kashmir (1127–1225). He introduced this instruction in Tibet to Tropu Lotsāwa Jampapel (1173–1236), from whom it was transmitted through the Kadampa succession of Lhodrak Jangchub Pelzangpo (fl. early thirteenth century), Dewa Pel (1231–1297), Kabzhipa Drakpa Zhonu (1257–1315), Jangsem Sonam Drakpa (1273–1345), Gyelsépa Tokmé Zangpo (1295–1369), Remdawa Zhonu Lodro (1349–1412), Drakpa Gyeltsen, Konchok Gyeltsen, and Kunga Chogdrub (fl. fifteenth–sixteenth centuries), the teacher of Kunga Drolchok.

The lineage prayer of *The Carrying of Happiness and Suffering on the Path* is as follows:

- Bhaṭṭārikā Tārā
- Paṇchen Śākyaśrī
- Tropu Lotsāwa Jampapel
- Lhodrak Jangchub Pel
- Dewa Pel
- Drakpa Zhonu
- Sonam Drakpa
- Gyelsépa Tokmé Zangpo
- Zhonu Lodro
- Drakpa Gyeltsen
- Konchok Gyeltsen
- Kunga Chogdrub . . .

Grant your blessing that we may actualize the three buddha bodies:

The buddha body of reality in which happiness and suffering that arise are unfabricated,
The buddha body of perfect resource endowed with major and minor marks,
And the buddha body of emanation that nurtures all beings through spiritual and temporal well-being!

5. *The Mind Training according to Sumpa Lotsāwa*

The progenitors of this lineage are the female meditational deity Vajravārāhī and the female bodhisttva Bhaṭṭārikā Tārā, whose revelations were received by the Tibetan translator Sumpa Lotsāwa Darma Yonten (fl. twelfth century). He transmitted this instruction through a combined Sakya and Kadampa line that included Sakya Paṇḍita Kunga Gyeltsen (1182–1251), Chogyel Pakpa Lodro Gyeltsen (1235–1280), Zhangton Konchok Pel (1240–1317), Chojé Lama Dampa Sonam Gyeltsen (1312–1375), Gyelsé Tokmé Zangpo (1295–1369), Jangchub Tsemo (1303–1380), Hor Kabzhipa Sengé Gyeltsen (fl. late fourteenth–early fifteenth centuries), Pelden Zangpo, Neten Sampenpa Jangsem Jinpa, Raton Yonten Pelzang (fl. fifteenth century), and Kunga Chogdrub (fl. fifteenth–sixteenth centuries), the teacher of Kunga Drolchok.

The lineage prayer of *The Mind Training of Sumpa Lotsāwa* is as follows:

- Vajravārāhī
- Tārā
- Sumpa Lotsāwa
- Sakya Paṇḍita
- Pakpa
- Zhangton
- Drakpukpa
- Chojé Lama
- Tokmé Zangpo
- Jangchub Tsemo
- Kabzhipa
- Pelden Zangpo
- Sampenpa
- Raton Yonten Pel
- Kunga Chogdrub . . .

Grant your blessing that we may realize:
The state of mind that is satisfied with whatever arises,
The crucial experiential cultivation that is perfectly satisfied by resting
Where the nature of mind itself abides,
The lack of exhaustion of our own mind as it turns toward the sacred doctrine,
And the deathless abiding nature.

6. *The Severance of Machik Labdron*

The progenitors of this lineage are the female meditational deity Prajñāpāramitā—the Great Mother—and the bodhisattvas Mañjuśrī in the form Vādisiṃha and Bhaṭṭārikā Tārā, from whom the instruction was revealed in India to Sukhasiddhi, and thence to Aryadeva. The instruction of Severance was introduced to Tibet by Dampa Sangyé of South India (fl. eleventh–twelfth centuries), and then transmitted through the lineage holders: Kyoton Sonam Lama (fl. twelfth century), Machik Labkyi Dronma (1055–1149), Khugom Chokyi Sengé (fl. twelfth century), Dolpa Zangtalwa (fl. twelfth century), Gyanak Cherbu Sangyé Rabton, Sangyé Gelong, Rinchen Ozer, Tsetsa Repa Śāk Dor, Kyemé Dopa Chokyi Sherab Jodenpa, Chorin, Gangpa Rinchen Pelzangpo, Rinchen Zhonu, Samten Ozer, Namka Ozer, Śākya Ozer, Delek Gyeltsenpa, Onsé Cholek, and Yigdruk Sherab Peljor (b. fifteenth century), who transmitted it to Kunga Drolchok.

The lineage prayer of *Severance* is as follows:

- Prajñāpāramitā, the Great Mother
- Mañjuśrī Vādisiṃha, lord of the Buddhist teaching
- Bhaṭṭārikā Tārā
- Sukhasiddhi
- Aryadeva
- Dampa Sangyé
- Sonam Lama
- Machik Labkyi Dronma
- Khugom Chokyi Sengé
- Dolpa Zangtalwa
- Gyanak Cherbu {5}
- Sangyé Rabton
- Sangyé Gelong

- Rinchen Ozer
- Tsetsa Repa
- Kyeme Jodenpa
- Chorin
- Gangpa Rinchen Pelzangpo
- Rinchen Zhonu
- Samten Ozer
- Namka Ozer
- Śākya Ozer
- Delek Gyeltsenpa
- Onsé Cholek
- Yigdruk Sherab Pel . . .

Grant your blessing that, while purifying the mind by means of the preliminaries
And experientially cultivating the main practice,
We may sever the four malevolent forces[5] in the expanse of emptiness
And realize the unique determination of the unborn state,[6]
Free from pride and untainted by the corrosion of dualistic perception!

7. *The Three Essential Points*

The progenitors of this lineage are the bodhisattvas Avalokita and Matiratna, from whom the instruction was revealed in India to Tilopā (988–1069) and transmitted by him to Lalitavajra (fl. eleventh century) and Mitrayogin (fl. eleventh–twelfth centuries). The latter introduced it to Tropu Lotsāwa Jampa Pel of Tibet (1173–1236), and thereafter the instruction descended through the Tropu and Zhalu line of Sonam Wangchuk (b. thirteenth century), Sempa Ché Sonam Sengé (b. thirteenth century), Yangtsewa Rinchen Sengé (b. thirteenth century), Buton Rinchen Drub (1290–1364), Tukséwa Rinchen Namgyel (1318–1388), Jamyang Drakpa Gyeltsen (1365–1448), Trulzhik Tsultrim Gyeltsen (1399–1473), Khyenrab Chogdrub (1436–1497), and Kunga Chogdrub (fl. fifteenth–sixteenth centuries), who was the teacher of Kunga Drolchok.

The lineage prayer of *The Three Essential Points* is as follows:

- Avalokita
- Matiratna

- Tilopā
- unsullied and glorious [Lalitavajra]
- Mitrayogin
- Tropu Lotsāwa
- Sonam Wangchuk
- Sempa Ché
- Rinchen Sengé
- Buton
- Tuksėwa
- Jamyang Drakpa Gyeltsen
- Trulzhik Tsultrim Gyeltsen
- Khyenrab Chogdrub
- Kunga Chogdrub . . .

Grant your blessing that the three essential points might be manifested:
The yoga of continuous cultivation in this life,
The yoga of the transference [of consciousness] cultivated at the time of death,
And the yoga of mingling and transference cultivated in the intermediate state![7]

8. *Resting in the Nature of Mind*

The progenitors of this lineage are the bodhisattvas Avalokita in the form Khasarpaṇi and Matiratna, from whom the instruction was revealed in India to Tilopā (988–1069) and transmitted by him to Lalitavajra (fl. eleventh century) and Mitrayogin (fl. eleventh–twelfth centuries), and thence to Tropu Lotsāwa Jampa Pel (1173–1236) in Tibet. Thereafter the instruction descended through the same Tropu and Zhalu line as the aforementioned Three Essential Points, up to Khyenrab Chogdrub (1436–1497), who transmitted it to Kunpang Chokyi Nyima (1449–1524). The latter was a teacher of Kunga Drolchok.

The lineage prayer of *Resting in the Nature of Mind* is as follows:

- Khasarpaṇi
- Matiratna
- Tilopā
- Lalitavajra

- Mitrayogin
- Jampa Pel
- Lachen Sonam Wangchuk
- Sempa
- Yangtsewa
- Rinchen Drub
- Rinchen Namgyel
- Drakpa Gyeltsen
- Tsultrim Gyeltsen
- Khyenrab Chogdrub
- Kunpang Chokyi Nyima . . .

Grant your blessing that we may realize the innate abiding nature
By experientially cultivating the meditative stability of rest,
In which the continuum of awareness, not slowly but instantaneously,
Determines the tired mind without impediment as the power of luminosity!

9. *The Three Sorts of Person*

The progenitors of this lineage are Śākyamuni Buddha and the bodhisattva Maitreya, from whom the instruction was revealed to Asaṅga (fl. late fourth–early fifth centuries). The Indian transmission is through the latter's brother Vasubandhu (fl. late fourth–early fifth centuries), and thereafter: Ārya Vimuktisena (fl. fifth century), Bhaṭṭāraka Vimuktisena (fl. late fifth–early sixth centuries), Vairocanabhadra, Haribhadra (ca. 800), Ratnabhadra or Kusulu the Elder, Kusulu the Younger,[8] and Dharmakīrti of Sumatra (b. tenth century). The instruction was introduced to Tibet by Atiśa (982–1054) and thence transmitted through the Kadampa line of Ngok Lekpei Sherab (fl. tenth–eleventh centuries), Drolungpa Lodro Jungné (b. eleventh century), Khepa Tsangnak Repa (fl. eleventh–twelfth centuries), and Tumton Lodro Drak (1106–1166), the founder of Nartang Monastery. Thereafter the lineage descended through the abbatial succession of Nartang: Dutsi Drak (1153–1232), Zhangton Chokyi Lama (1184–1241), Sangyé Gompa Sengé Kyab (1179–1250), Chimchen Namka Drak (1210–1285), Monlam Tsultrim (1219–1299), Zewu Tsondru Drak (1253–1314), Drakpa Sherab (1259–1325), Chimton Lobzang Drak (1299–1375), Jangchub Tsemo (1303–1380), Sengé Gyeltsen (fl. fourteenth–fifteenth centuries), Pelden Zangpo (1402–1473),

Neten Sampenpa Jangsem Jinpa, Raton Yonten Pelzang (fl. fifteenth century), and Kunga Chogdrub (fl. fifteenth–sixteenth centuries), who was a teacher of Kunga Drolchok.

The lineage prayer of the gradual path entitled *The Three Sorts of Person* is as follows:

- Munīndra
- Maitreya
- Asaṅga
- Vasubandhu
- Ārya Vimuktisena
- Bhaṭṭāraka Vimuktisena
- Vairocanabhadra
- Haribhadra {6}
- Kusulu the Elder
- Kusulu the Younger
- Dharmakīrti of Sumatra
- Pelden Atiśa
- Lekpei Sherab
- Drolungpa Lodro Jungné
- Khepa Tsangnak
- Tumton Lodro Drak
- Dutsi Drak
- Zhangton Chokyi Lama
- Sangyé Gompa
- Chimchen Namka Drak
- Monlam Tsultrim
- Zewu Tsondru Drak
- Drakpa Sherab
- Chimton Lobzang Drak
- Jangchub Tsemo
- Sengé Gyeltsen
- Pelden Zangpo
- Neten Sampenpa
- Yonten Pelzang
- Kunga Chogdrub . . .

Grant your blessing that all beings may be established in bliss:

Persons of lesser capacity on the path that abandons negativity and practices virtue,
Persons of middling capacity on the path that combines loving-kindness and compassion,
And persons of greater capacity actualizing the twofold enlightened mind!

10. *The Sequence of the Buddhist Teaching*

The progenitors of this lineage are Śākyamuni Buddha and the bodhisattva Maitreyanātha, from whom the instruction was revealed to Asaṅga (fl. late fourth–early fifth centuries). The Indian transmission through to Atiśa (982–1054) is identical to that of the Three Sorts of Person. The instruction was introduced in Tibet to Dromton Gyelwei Jungné (1004–1064), and from him the lineage passed through the Kadampa line of Potowa Rinchen Sel (1027–1105), Sharawa Yonten Drak (1070–1141), and Tumton Lodro Drak (1106–1166), founder of Nartang Monastery. The abbatial succession of Nartang then maintained the lineage from Droton Dutsi Drak (1153–1232) through to Chimton Lobzang Drak (1299–1375). Thereafter it descended through Droton Kunga Gyeltsen (1338–1400/1401), Pangton Drubpa Sherab (1357–1423), Drakton Pelden Dondrub (b. fourteenth century), Raton Yonten Pelzang (fl. fourteenth–fifteenth centuries), and Kunga Chogdrub (fl. fifteenth–sixteenth centuries), who was a teacher of Kunga Drolchok.

The lineage prayer of *The Sequence of the Buddhist Teaching* is as follows:

- Mahāmuni
- Maitreyanātha
- Asaṅga
- Vasubandhu, the latter's brother
- Ārya Vimuktisena
- Bhaṭṭāraka Vimuktisena
- Vairocanabhadra
- Haribhadra
- Kusulu the Elder
- Kusulu the Younger
- Dharmakīrti of Sumatra
- Pelden Atiśa

- Dromton
- Potowa
- Sharawa
- Tumton
- Droton
- Zhangton
- Sangyé Gompa
- Chimchen Namka Drak
- Monlam Tsultrim
- Zewu
- Drakpa Sherab, the latter's brother
- Chimton Lobzang Drak
- Droton Kunga Gyeltsen
- Drubpa Sherab
- Pelden Dondrub
- Yonten Pelzang
- Kunga Chogdrub . . .

Grant your blessing that we may safeguard the seven renunciations[9]
That constitute the roots of the Buddhist teaching,
That we may maintain the Buddhist teaching without bewilderment,
Through compassion and emptiness,
Which constitute the conclusion of the Buddhist teaching—
Itself comprising the twofold enlightenment, aspirational and engaged,
That constitutes the nucleus of the Buddhist teaching!

11. *The Sameness of Existence and Quiescence*

The progenitors of this lineage are Śākyamuni Buddha and the bodhisattva Maitreya, from whom the instruction was revealed to Dharmakīrti of Sumatra (b. tenth century). Atiśa (982–1054) introduced it to Dromton Gyelwei Jungné (1004–1064) in Tibet, and thereafter it was transmitted through the Kadampa line of Chen Ngawa Tsultrim Bar (1038–1103), Jayulwa Zhonu O (1075–1138), Mumenpa Dutsi Charchen (fl. eleventh–twelfth centuries), Droton Dutsi Drak of Nartang (1153–1232), Zhangton Chokyi Lama (1184–1241), Sangyé Gompa Sengé Kyab (1179–1250), Chimchen Namka Drak (1210–1285), Kyoton Monlam Tsultrim (1219–1299), Chomden Rikpei Reldri (1227–1305), Droton Kunga Gyeltsen (1338–1400/1401),

Pangton Drubpa Sherab (1357–1423), Drakton Pelden Dondrub (b. fourteenth century), Raton Yonten Pelzang (fl. fourteenth–fifteenth centuries), and Kunga Chogdrub (fl. fifteenth–sixteenth centuries), who was a teacher of Kunga Drolchok.

The lineage prayer of *The Sameness of Existence and Quiescence* is as follows:

- Munīndra
- Maitreya
- Dharmakīrti of Sumatra
- Jowojé
- Dromton
- Tsultrim Bar
- Jayulwa
- Mumenpa
- Droton
- Zhangton
- Sangyé Gompa
- Chimchen
- Kyoton
- Chomden Rikpei Reldri
- Droton Kunga Gyeltsen
- Pangton Drubpa Sherab
- Drakton Pelden Dondrub
- Raton Yonten Pelzang
- Kunga Chogdrub . . . {7}

Grant your blessing that the two extremes of existence and quiescence might be abandoned
And that the expanse of reality might definitively emerge,
Along with the aspect of mind that simply maintains freedom from extremes
Having abandoned the abyss of eternalism and nihilism!

12. *The Great Middle Way*

The progenitors of this lineage are Śākyamuni Buddha and the bodhisattva Mañjughoṣa, who revealed the instruction to Nāgārjuna (fl. second century). The Indian inspirational transmission from him is through: Aryadeva (fl. second–third centuries), Candrakīrti (fl. seventh century), Vidyākokila (fl. tenth–eleventh centuries), and a Newar named Penyawa Ratnabhadra (fl. eleventh–twelfth centuries). It was the last mentioned who introduced this instruction to Jangsem Dawa Gyeltsen (fl. twelfth century) in Tibet, and from him the succession passed through Dzilungpa Ozer Drakpa (fl. twelfth century) to Droton Dutsi Drak of Nartang (1153–1232). Thereafter the lineage is identical to that of the Sequence of the Buddhist Teaching through to Kunga Drolchok.

The lineage prayer of *The Great Middle Way* is as follows:

- Mahāmuni
- Mañjughoṣa
- Nāgārjuna the father
- [Aryadeva] the son
- Candrakīrti
- Vidyākokila
- Penyawa, the Newar
- Dawa Gyeltsen
- Dzilungpa
- Droton Dutsi Drak
- Zhangton Chokyi Lama
- Gompa Sengé Kyab
- Chimchen
- Monlam Tsultrim
- Zewu
- [Zewu Drakpa Sherab,] the latter's brother
- Lobzang Drak
- Kunga Gyeltsen
- Drubpa Sherab
- Draktonpa
- Raton Yonten Pelzang
- Kunga Chogdrub . . .

Grant your blessing that we may realize the great middle way,
The expanse of the authentic view concerning subjective imagination,
Which does not perceive even minutely
The grasping for the perspectives

Of existence and nonexistence, eternalism and nihilism,
And that does not abide even in the middle between them!

13. *The Hidden Guidance of Kadam*

The progenitors of this lineage are Śākyamuni Buddha and the bodhisattva Maitreya, from whom the instruction was revealed to Dharmakīrti of Sumatra (b. tenth century). Atiśa (982–1054) introduced it in Tibet to Dromton Gyelwei Jungné (1004–1064), from whom it was then transmitted through the Kadampa line: Potowa Rinchen Sel (1027–1105), Sharawa Yonten Drak (1070–1141), Shawo Gangpa (fl. eleventh–twelfth centuries), and Mumenpa Dutsi Charchen (fl. eleventh–twelfth centuries) to Dromoché Dutsi Drak of Nartang (1153–1232). From this point on the lineage is identical to that of *The Great Middle Way*, through to Kunga Drolchok.

The lineage prayer of *The Hidden Guidance of Kadam* is as follows:

· Munīndra
· Maitreya
· Dharmakīrti of Sumatra
· Atiśa
· Dromton
· Potowa
· Sharawa
· Shawo Gangpa
· Mumenpa
· Dromoché
· Chokyi Lama
· Gompa Sengé Kyab
· Chimchen
· Monlam Tsultrim
· Tsondru Drak
· Drakpa Sherab
· Chimton
· Droton
· Pangton Drubpa Sherab
· Drakton Pelden
· Raton Yonten Pelzang
· Kunga Chogdrub . . .

Grant your blessing that we may perfect the hidden guidance,
Having trained our own minds, likened to a coracle on a dry river,
By determining the antidote of discipline
For the sake of this coarse mental continuum of ours
That is perpetually untamed!

14. *The Four Deities of Kadam: Munīndra*

The next four lineages (14–17) represent the descent of the Four Deities of Kadam, which were all introduced to Tibet directly by Atiśa (982–1054). The first of these concerns Śākyamuni Buddha and was revealed to Atiśa by Śākyamuni through revelatory means. In Tibet, the lineage descended through: Wangchuk Gyeltsen (1016–1082), Nezur Yeshé Bar (1042–1118), and Langri Tangpa Dorjé Sengé (1054–1123) to Zhangton Chokyi Lama (1184–1241). Thereafter the lineage is identical to that of *The Great Middle Way*, through to Kunga Drolchok.

The lineage prayer of *The Four Deities of Kadam: Munīndra* is as follows:

- Munīndra
- Glorious Atiśa
- Wangchuk Gyeltsen
- Nezur Yeshé Bar
- Dorjé Sengé
- Zhangton
- Gompa Sengé Kyab
- Chimchen
- Monlam Tsultrim
- Tsondru Drak
- Drakpa Sherab
- Chimton
- Droton
- Pangton Drubpa Sherab
- Draktonpa
- Raton Yonten Pelzang
- Kunga Chogdrub . . .

Grant your blessing that the golden-hued body of the Conqueror,
Blazing with major and minor marks,

Might arise, unfabricated, in our own minds,
And that, having pacified all grasping of subtle and coarse thoughts, {8}
We might realize the unmoving abiding nature of reality!

15. *The Four Deities of Kadam: Acala*

Here the lineage is identical to that of Munīndra, except that in this case, Atiśa received the instruction through revelatory means from the meditational deity Acala.

The lineage prayer of *The Four Deities of Kadam: Acala* is as follows:

- Acalanātha
- Glorious Atiśa . . .

And so forth, as above.

Grant your blessing that the one hundred thousand flames of pristine cognition,
Diffused from the actual body of fierce [Acala], combining all wrathful conquerors,
May banish to the distant ocean shores the enemies of the Buddhist teaching—
The hosts of evil spirits and obstructors who lead beings astray!

16. *The Four Deities of Kadam: Avalokita*

Here the lineage is identical to those of Munīndra and Acala, except that in this case, Atiśa received the instruction through revelatory means from Avalokiteśvara.

The lineage prayer of *The Four Deities of Kadam: Avalokita* is as follows:

- Avalokiteśvara
- Glorious Atiśa . . .

And so forth, as above.

Grant your blessing that the compassion that permeates space,
Diffusing in one hundred directions the white light of compassion

From all the pores of the Great Compassionate One
And from the heart of the Great Compassionate One,
Might be refined within our own bodies!

17. *The Four Deities of Kadam: Tārā*

Here the lineage is identical to those of Munīndra, Acala, and Avalokita, except that in this case, Atiśa received the instruction through revelatory means from Tārā.

The lineage prayer of *The Four Deities of Kadam: Tārā* is as follows:

- Venerable Tārā
- Glorious Atiśa . . .

And so forth, as above.

Grant your blessing that from the body of the Sublime Lady
Ten million light rays are diffused, and at their tips
The emanations of the Sublime Lady, who protects from fear, permeate space,
Protecting from the eight fears[10] all sentient beings who have been our mother
With the compassion of the Sublime Lady!

18. *The Parables of Potowa*

The progenitors of this lineage are Śākyamuni Buddha and the bodhisattva Mañjughoṣa, from whom the instruction was revealed in Tibet to Potowa Rinchen Sel (1027–1105). The transmission then continued through the Kadampa line: Drakarwa (1032–1111), Lopon Penyulwa Jangchub Nangwa (fl. eleventh–twelfth centuries), Chegom Dzogpaché Khakyong, Tanak Monlam Gom, Tanak Rinchen Yeshépa, Drogon Pelden Yeshé (fl. fourteenth century), Hor Kabzhipa Sengé Gyeltsen (fl. fourteenth–fifteenth centuries), Pelden Zangpo (1402–1473), Neten Sampenpa Jangsem Jinpa, Raton Yonten Pelzang (fl. fourteenth–fifteenth centuries), and Kunga Chogdrub (fl. fifteenth–sixteenth centuries), who was a teacher of Kunga Drolchok.

The lineage prayer of *The Parables of Potowa* is as follows:

- Munīndra
- Mañjughoṣa
- Potowa
- Drakarwa
- Lopon Penyulwa
- Chegom Dzogpaché
- Tanak Monlam Gom
- Rinchen Yeshépa
- Pelden Yeshé
- Kabzhipa
- Pelden Zangpo
- Neten Sampenpa
- Raton Yonten Pelzang
- Kunga Chogdrub . . .

Grant your blessing that we may plumb the depths of certainty
Concerning all sequences of the path for the three sorts of person,
Having purged the stains of the darkness of unknowing
By combining parables with meaningful exegesis!

19. *The Sixteen Spheres* [*of the Heart*]

The progenitors of this lineage are Śākyamuni Buddha and the female deity Tārā, from whom the instruction was revealed to Atiśa (982–1054). In Tibet, the lineage was transmitted through the following Kadampa line: Dromton Gyelwei Jungné (1004–1064), Ngok Lekpei Sherab (fl. tenth–eleventh centuries), Ngari Sherab Gyeltsen, Puchung Rinchen Gyeltsen (1031–1106), Zhangton Darma Gyeltsen (fl. eleventh–twelfth centuries), Rabkar Jangzangwa (fl. twelfth century), Drom Namka Rinchen (fl. twelfth century), Drom Zhonu Lodro (fl. twelfth–thirteenth centuries), Lhopa Kunkhyen Rinchen Pel (fl. twelfth–thirteenth centuries), Drapupa Chenpo, Galung Jangchub Pel, Sonam Ozer, Cholungpa Sonam Rinchen, Chodrak Zangpo, Khenchen Ratna Jamyang Rinchen Gyeltsen, Ngawang Drakpa (1418–1496), and Avadhūtipā Namgyel Drakpa (1469–1530), who taught Kunga Drolchok.

The lineage prayer of *The* [*Sixteen*] *Spheres of the Heart* is as follows:

- Munīndra
- Tārā
- Jowo
- Dromton
- Ngok
- Ngari Sherab Gyeltsen
- Puchung Rinchen Gyeltsen
- Darma Gyeltsen
- Rabkar Jangzangwa
- Namka Rinchen
- Zhonu Lodro
- Lhopa Kunkhyen
- Drapupa Chenpo
- Galung Jangchub Pel
- Sonam Ozer
- Sonam Rinchen
- Chodrak
- Khenchen Ratna {9}
- Ngawang Drakpa
- Avadhūtipā . . .

Grant your blessing that, upon a single seat, our experience and realization will be enhanced,
Through radiant and distinct meditative stability that permeates space
Within the [sixteen] spheres of the heart.
This is the essential elixir, experientially cultivating the four deities and three doctrines![11]

20. *The Six Descents of the Transcendent Perfection of Wisdom*

The progenitors of this lineage are Śākyamuni Buddha and the bodhisattva Mahāmaitreya, who is said to have revealed the instruction to Padampa Sangyé of South India (fl. eleventh–twelfth centuries). The latter introduced it to Jangsem Kunga (fl. eleventh–twelfth centuries) of Dingri in Tibet, and thereafter the lineage descended through Patsab Gompa Tsultrim Bar (1077–1156/58), Gyelwa Tené (ca. 1127–1217), Zhikpo Nyima Sengé (fl.

twelfth century), Nyemdo Sonam Pel (1217–1277), Gyelsé Kunga Zangpo (1258–1316), Kunga Dondrub, Ritro Wangchuk, Ngenlampa Tsul Pak, Sangyé On, Lodro Gyatso, Rongton Sheja Kunrik (1367–1449), Jamyang Sherab Gyatso (1396–1474), Raton Yonten Pelzang (fl. fourteenth–fifteenth centuries), and Lowo Khenchen Sonam Lhundrub (1456–1532). The last named was an influential teacher of Kunga Drolchok.

The lineage prayer of *The Six Descents of the Transcendent Perfection of Wisdom* is as follows:

- Munīndra
- Mahāmaitreya
- Dampa Gyakarwa
- Jangsem Kunga
- Patsab Tsultrim Bar
- Gyelwa Tené
- Zhikpo Nyima Sengé
- Nyemdo
- Gyelsé Kunga
- [Kunga Dondrub,] the latter's brother
- Ritro Wangchuk
- Tsul Pak
- Sangyé On
- Lodro Gyatso
- Rongton
- Sherab Gyatso
- Raton Yonten Pelzang
- Khenchen Sonam Lhundrub . . .

Grant your blessing that we may realize the abiding nature of reality,
By progressing at this time with the renunciations and realizations
That are associated with the levels and the paths
In the tradition of the *Sutra of the Transcendent Perfection of Wisdom*,
Endowed with six descents,[12]
The experiential cultivation of which is similar in its understanding to the way of mantra!

21. *The Five Paths of Pacification*

The progenitors of this lineage are Śākyamuni Buddha and the bodhisattva Mañjughoṣa in the form Vādīsiṃha, who revealed the instruction to Padampa Sangyé of South India (fl. eleventh–twelfth centuries). The latter introduced it to Jangsem Kunga (fl. eleventh–twelfth centuries) of Dingri in Tibet, and thereafter the lineage accorded with the transmission of the aforementioned *Six Descents of the Transcendent Perfection of Wisdom* through Patsab Gompa Tsultrim Bar, Gyelwa Tené, and Zhikpo Nyima Sengé. The succession that subsequently followed is through Trulzhik Darma Sengé, Nyemdo Sonam Pel (1217–1277), Kunga Zangpo, Pelchen Kunlhunpa, Chogyel Sherab Zangpo (1411–1475), Rongtö Gungru, Rinchen Khyenrab Chogdrub, and Changlungpa Zhonu Chodrub (fl. fifteenth–sixteenth centuries). The last mentioned was a teacher of Kunga Drolchok.

The lineage prayer of *The Five Paths of Pacification* is as follows:

- Munīndra
- Mañjughoṣa Vādīsiṃha
- Dampa Gyakarwa
- Jangsem Kunga
- Patsab Gompa
- Gyelwa Tené
- Zhikpo Nyima Sengé
- Trulzhik Darma Sengé
- Nyemdo
- [Kunga Zangpo,] the latter's son
- Pelchen Kunlhunpa
- Chogyel Sherab Zangpo
- Rongtö Gungru
- Khyenrab
- Changlungpa . . .

Grant your blessing that we may accomplish the supreme path of
Pacification,
Which actualizes all the renunciations and realizations
That are associated with the levels and the paths,
By definitively cultivating the sequences of the five paths,
Delivered through experiential cultivation of the three austerities![13]

22. *The Three Stages of Meditation*

The progenitors of this lineage are Śākyamuni Buddha and the bodhisattva Mañjughoṣa, who is said to have revealed the instruction to Śāntarakṣita (725–783) and Kamalaśīla (740–795). The latter introduced this treatise to Be Drum in Tibet, and thereafter the lineage descended through Gyelwa Yeshé, Dru Chok Yeshé, Setsun Wangchuk Zhonu, Gartsa Yonten Yungdrung, Khuton Tsondru Yungdrung (1011–1075), Ratri Zangbarwa, Loton Chodrak, Drangti Darma Nyingpo (b. eleventh century), Chim Tsondru Sengé, Gyangro Darma Gon, Chim Tsondru Gyeltsen, Shong Lotsāwa Dorjé Gyeltsen (b. thirteenth century), Mangkhar Lotsāwa Chokden Lekpei Lodro (fl. thirteenth century), Pang Lotsāwa Lodro Tenpa (1276–1342), Jangchub Tsemo (1303–1380), Nya-on Kunga Pel, Yagton Sangyé Pel (1348–1414), Rongton Sheja Kunrik (1367–1449), Jamyang Sherab Gyatso (1396–1474), Raton Yonten Pelzang (fl. fourteenth–fifteenth centuries), and Lowo Khenchen Sonam Lhundrub (1456–1532). The last mentioned taught Kunga Drolchok.

The lineage prayer of *The Three Stages of Meditation* is as follows:

- Munīndra
- Mañjughoṣa
- Śāntarakṣita
- Kamalaśīla
- Be Drum
- Gyelwa Yeshé
- Dru Chok Yeshé
- Setsun Wangchuk Zhonu
- Gartsa Yonten
- Khuton Tsondru
- Ratri Zangbarwa
- Loton Chodrak
- Drangti Darma Nyingpo
- Tsondru Sengé
- Gyangro Darma Gon
- Tsondru Gyeltsen
- Shong Lo
- Mangkhar Lotsāwa
- Pang Lo

- Jangchub Tsemo
- Nya-on Kunga Pel {10}
- Yag
- Rongton
- Sherab Gyatso
- Raton Yonten Pelzang
- Khenchen Sonam Lhundrub . . .

Grant your blessing that we may definitively realize the following triads:
The three sequences of the Buddhist teaching contained in the three promulgations,
And the three ways in which the three sorts of person traverse
The beginning, middle, and conclusion of the three stages of meditation![14]

23. *The Five Doctrines of Maitreya*

The progenitors of this lineage are Śākyamuni Buddha and the bodhisattva Maitreyanātha, who revealed the instruction to Asaṅga (fl. late fourth–early fifth centuries). The Indian transmission is through the latter's brother Vasubandhu (fl. late fourth–early fifth centuries), and thereafter: Sthiramati (ca. 470–550), Vidyākokila, Daṃṣṭrasena, Bhadrapāda, Atiśa (982–1054), Gaṅgabhadra, Puṇyaśrī, Gonpawa of Kashmir, Saṅgha the Brahmin, and Jñānaśrībhadra of Kashmir (fl. eleventh century). The last mentioned introduced the Five Doctrines of Maitreya to Tibet where the lineage passed through: Ngok Loden Sherab (1059–1109), Bareg Lotsāwa Sonam Gyeltsen, Bareg Tonkyab, Kyebu Yonten Ga, Tashi Dorjé, Dongtri Dulwadzin, Nyangton Konchok Dorjé, Jamyang Darma Ozer, Bagton Zhonu Tsultrim (fl. thirteenth century), Bagton Tsultrim Gyeltsen (fl. thirteenth–fourteenth centuries), Pangton Drubpa Sherab (fl. fourteenth century), Yagton Sangyé Pel (1348–1414), Rongton Sheja Kunrik (1367–1449), Donyo Pel, Raton Yonten Pelzang (fl. fourteenth–fifteenth centuries), and Kunga Chogdrub (fl. fifteenth–sixteenth centuries).

The lineage prayer of *The Five Doctrines of Maitreya* is as follows:

- Munīndra
- Maitreyanātha
- Asaṅga
- Vasubandhu

- Sthiramati
- Vidyākokila
- Daṃṣṭrasena
- Bhadrapāda
- Dīpaṃkara
- Gaṅgabhadra
- Puṇyaśrī
- Gonpawa of Kashmir
- Saṅgha the Brahmin
- Jñānaśrī of Kashmir
- Loden Sherab
- Bareg Lotsāwa
- Bareg Tonkyab
- Kyebu Yonten Ga
- Tashi Dorjé
- Dongtri Dulwadzin
- Nyangton Konchok Dorjé[15]
- Jamyang Darma Ozer
- Bagton Zhonu Tsultrim
- Tsultrim Gyeltsen
- Pangtonpa
- Yag
- Rongton
- Donyo Pel
- Raton Yonten Pelzang
- Kunga Chogdrub . . .

Grant your blessing that we may realize the sequence of the path
Comprising the Doctrines of Maitreya,
The tradition of the great bodhisattva of sublime enlightened mind,
Imparted from the mighty heart of Maitreya, embodiment of kindness and love,
In accordance with the words spoken by Maitreya in *The Five Doctrines of Maitreya*!

24. *The View of Intrinsic Emptiness*

The progenitors of this lineage are Śākyamuni Buddha and the bodhisattva Mañjughoṣa, who is said to have revealed the instruction to Nāgārjuna (fl. second century). The latter in turn inspired Candrakīrti (fl. seventh century), whose seminal commentaries were introduced to Tibet by Patsab Nyima Drak (b. 1055). Thereafter the lineage descended through Zhang Tangsagpa Yeshé Jungné (fl. eleventh century), Drom Wangchuk Drakpa (fl. eleventh–twelfth centuries), Sherab Dorjé, Lopon Tontsulwa, Sukhadeva, Jotsunpa, Urawa, Sherab Pel, Darma Sherab, Sherab Rinchen, Sonam Sengé, Pakton Samten Wang, Bagton Zhonu Tsultrim (fl. thirteenth century), Marton Samgyelwa, Bagton Zhonu Gyeltsen (fl. fourteenth century), Rongton Chenpo Sheja Kunrik (1367–1449), Śākya Chokden (1428–1507), and Paṇchen Amogha Donyo Drubpa (fl. fifteenth–sixteenth centuries). The last named was a teacher of Kunga Drolchok.

The lineage prayer of *The View of Intrinsic Emptiness* is as follows:

- Munīndra
- Mañjughoṣa
- Nāgārjuna
- Candrakīrti
- Patsab Nyima Drak
- Zhang Tangsagpa
- Wangchuk Drakpa
- Sherab Dorjé
- Lopon Tontsulwa
- Sukhadeva
- Jotsunpa
- Urawa
- Sherab Pel
- Darma Sherab
- Sherab Rinchen
- Sonam Sengé
- Pakton Samten Wang[16]
- Bagton Zhonu Tsultrim
- Marton Samgyelwa
- Zhonu Gyeltsen
- Rongton Chenpo

- Śākya Chokden
- Paṇchen Amogha . . .

Grant your blessing that, having abandoned the two extremes of eternalism and nihilism
Because all things have never existed from the beginning
And owing to interconnected dependent origination, {11}
We may realize the abiding nature of intrinsic emptiness!

25. *The View of Extraneous Emptiness*

The progenitors of this lineage are Śākyamuni Buddha and the bodhisattva Maitreyanātha, who revealed the instruction to Maitrīpā (ca. 986–1063 or 1007–1085). The latter's Indian successors were the great paṇḍita Ānandakīrti (fl. eleventh century) and Sajjana (fl. eleventh century), who introduced the instruction to the Tibetan translator Ngok Lotsāwa Loden Sherab (1059–1109). The succession then fell to Tsen Khawoché (b. 1021), Gya Marwa, Drolungpa Lodro Jungné (fl. eleventh–twelfth centuries), Chapa Chokyi Sengé (1109–1169), Dulkarwa, Tsangpa Dregurwa Dongtro Dulwadzin, Jamyang Darma Ozer, Drubpa Sengé, Bagton Tsultrim Gyeltsen (fl. thirteenth–fourteenth centuries), Pangton Drubpa Sherab (fl. fourteenth century), Yagton Sangyé Pel (1348–1414), Rongton Sheja Kunrik (1367–1449), Paṇchen Donyo Drubpa (fl. fifteenth–sixteenth centuries), and Pelden Tsultrim. The last mentioned taught Kunga Drolchok.

The lineage prayer of *The View of Extraneous Emptiness* is as follows:

- Munīndra
- Maitreyanātha
- Gyelsé Maitrīpā
- Paṇchen Ānandakīrti
- Sajjana
- Ngok Lotsāwa
- Khawoché
- Gya Marwa
- Drolungpa
- Chapa Chokyi Sengé
- Dulkarwa
- Dregurwa

- Dongtro
- Darma Ozer
- Drubpa Sengé
- Bagton Tsultrim Gyeltsen
- Pangton Drubpa Sherab
- Yag
- Rongton
- Paṇchen Donyo
- Pelden Tsultrimpa . . .

Grant your blessing that since the stains of dualistic appearance—the subject-object dichotomy—are primordially empty,
And the nature of reality is never empty,
We may realize the abiding nature of extraneous emptiness,
The perceptual range of the pristine cognition of particularizing intrinsic awareness!

26. *The Elucidation of the Concealed Meanings* [*of Yogatantra*]

The progenitors of this lineage are the meditational deities Vajrasattva and Vajrayoginī, the latter of whom revealed the instruction in Tibet to Bodong Paṇchen Jigdrel Sangwa Jin (1376–1451). The short lineage that ensued passed through Shangpa Rechen Sonam Chokgyur (fl. fifteenth century) and Zelmo Drakpa Drakpa Yeshé (fl. fifteenth–sixteenth centuries) to Kunga Drolchok.

The lineage prayer of *The Elucidation of the Concealed Meanings* [*of Yogatantra*] is as follows:

- Vajrasattva
- Vajrayoginī
- Jigdrel Sangwa Jin who gathered the elixir of scriptural transmission and realization of many learned and accomplished masters of India and Tibet
- Shangpa Rechen Sonam Chokgyur
- Zelmo Drakpa Drakpa Yeshé . . .

Grant your blessing that, having integrated all the experiential
cultivations of sutra and tantra
In unique meditative stability—the flow of the sacred doctrine—
We may realize the profoundly secret view,
The elixir of the most secret doctrine of the *Summation of the Real*![17]

27. *The Guidance of Amitāyus*

The progenitor of this lineage is the meditational deity Amitābha, who revealed the instruction in India to Siddhirājñi (fl. twelfth century). The latter's successor Tepuwa Pārvātapāda (fl. twelfth century) taught Rechungpa Dorjé Drak (1085–1161), who introduced it to Tibet. The lineage then descended through the following Drigung Kagyu succession: Milarepa (1052–1135), Gampopa Dakpo Lharjé (1079–1153), Pagmodrupa Dorjé Gyelpo (1110–1170), Drigungpa Jigten Sumgon (1143–1217), Chen Nga Drakpa Jungné (1175–1255), Yangonpa (1213–1258), Chen Ngawa Rinden (b. 1202), Zurpukpa Rinchen Pelzang (b. 1263), Barawa Choktrul Gyeltsen Pelzang (1310–1391), Nyen Repa Gendun Bum, Kyapchewa, and Trewo Chokyi Gyatso (d. 1547). The last mentioned taught Kunga Drolchok.

The lineage prayer of *The Guidance of Amitāyus* is as follows:

- Amitābha
- Siddhirājñi
- Tepuwa
- Rechung Dorjé Drak
- Milarepa
- Dakpo Lharjé
- Pagmodrupa
- Drigungpa
- Drakpa Jungné
- Yangonpa
- Chen Ngawa
- Zurpukpa
- Barawa Choktrul
- Nyen Repa
- Kyapchewa
- Trewo Chokyi Gyatso . . .

Grant your blessing that we may fill the vase of our own body
With the condensed elixirs of the four primary elements that enhance the life span,
In association with cyclic existence and nirvana,
And then find the path of the four delights through the sequence of the four empowerments
And attain the status of a deathless awareness holder![18]

28. *The Guidance of White Tārā*

The progenitors of this lineage are the meditational deities Amitāyus and Cintāmaṇicakra Tārā, who revealed the instruction in India to Vagīśvarakīrti. His lineage descended through Śraddhākara, Dharmakīrti of Sumatra (b. tenth century), and Atiśa (982–1054), who introduced the practice in Tibet to Dromton Gyelwei Jungné (1004–1064). Thereafter the lineage descended through the following, primarily Kadampa succession: Chen Ngawa Tsultrim Bar (1038–1103), Jayulwa Zhonu O (1075–1138), Chekhawa Yeshé Dorjé (1101–1175), Gyergom Zhikpo, Zhonu Drakpa, Sangyé Gompa Sengé Kyab (1179–1250), Chimchen Namka Drak (1210–1285), Gyangro Jangchub Bum (fl. thirteenth–fourteenth centuries), Chimton Lobzang Drak (1299–1375), Droton Kunga Gyeltsen (1338–1400/1401), Pangton Drubpa Sherab (fl. fourteenth century), Changlungpa Zhonu Lodro (1372–1475), Śākya Chokden (1428–1507), and Changlungpa Zhonu Chodrub (fl. fifteenth–sixteenth centuries). The last named taught the practice to Kunga Drolchok.

The lineage prayer of *The Guidance of White Tārā* is as follows: {12}

- Amitāyus
- Cintāmaṇicakra
- Vagīśvarakīrti
- Śraddhākara
- Dharmakīrti of Sumatra
- Jowo Atiśa
- Dromton
- Chen Ngawa
- Jayulwa
- Chekhawa

- Gyergom
- Zhonu Drakpa
- Gompa Sengé Kyab
- Chimchen Namka
- Gyangro Jangchub Bum
- Chimton Lobzang Drak
- Droton Kunga Gyeltsen
- Pangton Drubpa Sherab
- Changlungpa
- Śākya Chokden
- Zhonu Chodrub . . .

Grant your blessing that we may attain deathless spiritual accomplishment
Through the preliminary practice—essential union of winds enhancing life span and vitality—
The main practice—one-pointed meditative stability of long-life attainment—
And the subsequent practice—blissful triumph over the lord of death!

29. *The Guidance of White Amitāyus*

The progenitor of this lineage is the meditational deity Amitāyus, who revealed the instruction in India to Devaḍākinī. Thereafter the lineage descended through Mitrayogin, Ānandagupta, and Buddhaśrī (all fl. twelfth century), the last of whom introduced the practice in Tibet to Chak Lotsāwa Drachompa (1153–1216). His lineage then descended through Chak Lotsāwa Chojé Pel (1197–1263/4), Zhonu Gyeltsen, Jangchub Gyeltsen, Nyima Gyeltsen, Zangpo Pel, Yeshé Pelwa, Gyelsé Lobzang Peljor, Chak Lotsāwa Rinchen Chogyel (b. 1447), and Trariwa Rinchen Gyelchok, who was a teacher of Kunga Drolchok.

The lineage prayer of *The Guidance of White Amitāyus* is as follows:

- Amitāyus
- Devaḍākinī
- Mitrayogin
- Ānanda
- Buddhaśrī

- Chak Lotsāwa
- Chak Lotsāwa, the latter's nephew
- Zhonu
- Jangchub Gyeltsen
- Nyima Gyeltsen
- Zangpo Pel
- Yeshé Pelwa
- Lobzang Peljor
- Rinchen Chogyel
- Rinchen Gyelchok . . .

Grant your blessing that we may attain deathlessness through the three crucial points:
The crucial point of the preliminaries—extracting elixir that reduces the physical constituents—
The crucial point of the main practice—experientially cultivating the threefold descent, reversal, and diffusion [of vital essence]—
And the crucial point of the subsequent practice—relying on a female partner endowed with appropriate signs![19]

30. *The Direct Guidance of Avalokiteśvara according to the Lakṣmī Tradition*

The progenitor of this lineage is the bodhisattva Avalokiteśvara, who revealed the instruction to the nun Lakṣmī in India. Her successors were Śrībhadra, Samādhibhadra, and Atiśa (982–1054), the last of whom introduced this practice in Tibet to Yolton Chowang (fl. eleventh century). The transmission then follows this Kadampa lineage: Rogton, Tsi Tonpa, José Zhangton Chokyi Lama (1184–1241), Beton Zhikpo, Neljorpa Kyapsé, Sangyé Onpo, Duldzin Chewa Ratnapa, Jangsem Sonam Drakpa (1273–1345), Gyelsé Tokmé Zangpo (1295–1369), Gyamawa Yonten-o, Lotsāwa Drakpa Gyeltsen (ca. 1352–1405), Jangsem Konchok Gyeltsen (1388–1469), and Kunga Chogdrub (fl. fifteenth–sixteenth centuries).

The lineage prayer of *The Direct Guidance of Avalokiteśvara according to the Lakṣmī Tradition* is as follows:

- Avalokiteśvara
- Lakṣmī, the nun Dorjé

- Śrībhadra
- Samādhibhadra
- Jowojé
- Yolton Chowang
- Rogton
- Tsi Tonpa
- Zhangton
- Beton Zhikpo
- Neljorpa Kyapsé
- Sangyé Onpo
- Duldzin Chewa Ratnapa
- Jangsem Sonam Drakpa
- Tokmé Zangpo
- Gyamawa
- Lotsāwa Drakpa Gyeltsen
- Jangsem Konchok Gyeltsen
- Kunga Chogdrub . . .

Grant your blessing that we may attain the nature of Avalokiteśvara
Through preliminary practices integrating refuge and setting the mind on enlightenment;
The main practice, which is the vital experiential cultivation
Integrating generation and perfection stages;
And the subsequent practice—the yoga of continuous flow!

31. *The Direct Guidance of Avalokiteśvara according to the Candradhvaja Tradition*

The progenitor of this lineage is the bodhisattva Avalokiteśvara, who revealed the instruction directly to the bodhisattva Candradhvaja, also known as Jangsem Dawa Gyeltsen (fl. twelfth century). The practice was then transmitted through the following succession: Zhang Ring Kyitsa Ochen, Zhang Ukarwa, Zhang Lotsāwa Nyangenmé Pel, Zhang Rinchen Ozer, Zhangton Drukdra Gyeltsen, Nur Chopak Gyeltsen, Gyelsé Tokmé Zangpo (1295–1369), Gyamawa Yonten-o, Lotsāwa Drakpa Gyeltsen (ca. 1352–1405), Jangsem Konchok Gyeltsen (1388–1469), and Kunga Chogdrub (fl. fifteenth–sixteenth centuries).

The lineage prayer of *The Direct Guidance of Avalokiteśvara according to the Candradhvaja Tradition* is as follows: {13}

- Avalokiteśvara
- Jangsem Dawa Gyeltsen
- Zhang Ring Kyitsa Ochen
- Ukarwa
- Nyangenmé Pel
- Rinchen Ozer
- Zhangton Drukdra Gyeltsen
- Nur Chopak
- Gyelsé
- Gyamawa
- Drakpa Gyeltsen
- Konchok Gyeltsen
- Kunga Chogdrub . . .

The concluding quatrain should be repeated, as above.

32. *The Direct Guidance of Avalokiteśvara according to the Tsembupa Tradition*

The progenitor of this lineage is the primordial buddha Mahāvajradhara, along with the female deity Nairātmyā, who revealed this instruction directly to Drubchen Tsembupa (fl. twelfth century). Thereafter the lineage descended through Chiwo Lhepa (fl. thirteenth century), Drak Marwa, Lhatsun Gonserwa, Tukjé Tsondru Chojé (1243–1313), Gyelsé Sherab Bumpa (fl. fourteenth century), Gyelsé Tokmé Zangpo (1295–1369), Gyamawa Yonten-o, Lotsāwa Drakpa Gyeltsen (ca. 1352–1405), Jangsem Konchok Gyeltsen (1388–1469), and Kunga Chogdrub (fl. fifteenth–sixteenth centuries). The last mentioned was a teacher of Kunga Drolchok.

The lineage prayer of *The Direct Guidance of Avalokiteśvara according to the Tsembupa Tradition* is as follows:

- Mahāvajradhara
- Nairātmyā, the supreme mother
- Drubchen Tsembupa

- Chiwo Lhepa
- Drak Marwa
- Lhatsun Gonserwa
- Tukjé Tsondru Chojé
- Sherab Bum
- Gyelsé
- Gyamawa
- Drakpa Gyeltsen
- Konchok Gyeltsen
- Kunga Chogdrub . . .

The concluding quatrain should be repeated, as above.

33. *The Direct Guidance of Avalokiteśvara according to the Kyergangpa Tradition*

The progenitor of this lineage is the bodhisattva Avalokiteśvara, who revealed the instruction directly to the mahāsiddha Rāhula. His successor was Atiśa (982–1054), who introduced the practice in Tibet to Nagtso Lotsāwa Tsultrim Gyelwa (1011–1064). Thereafter the lineage descended through Rongpa Sherab Gyeltsen, Chegom Sherab Dorjé (fl. twelfth century), Kyergangpa Chokyi Sengé (1154–1217), Nyenton Rigongpa Chokyi Sherab (1175–1255), Sangyé Tonpa Tsondru Sengé (1207–1278), Tsangma Shangton (1234–1309), Khyungpo Tsultrim Gonpo (fl. thirteenth century), Jadrel Ritro Rechenpa (fl. fourteenth century), Shangkarwa Rinchen Gyeltsen (1353–1434), Sangyé Pelzangpo (1398–1465), Namka Gyeltsen (fl. fourteenth–fifteenth centuries), and Gyagom Lekpei Gyeltsen (fl. fifteenth–sixteenth centuries). The last mentioned was a teacher of Kunga Drolchok.

The lineage prayer of *The Direct Guidance of Avalokiteśvara according to the Kyergangpa Tradition* is as follows:

- Avalokiteśvara
- Rāhula, the great accomplished master
- Dīpaṃkara
- Nagtso Tsultrim Gyelwa
- Rongpa Sherab Gyeltsen
- Chegom Sherab Dorjé
- Kyergangpa

- Nyenton Rigongpa
- Sangyé Tonpa
- Tsangma Shangton
- Khyungpo Tsultrim Gonpo
- Ritro Rechenpa
- Shangkarwa Rinchen Gyeltsen
- Sangyé Pelzangpo
- Namka Gyeltsen
- Gyagom Lekpei Gyeltsen . . .

The concluding quatrain should be repeated, as above.

34. *The Direct Guidance of Cakrasaṃvara*

The progenitor of this lineage is the primordial buddha Mahāvajradhara, along with the female deity Vajravārāhī, who revealed this instruction directly to Ānandavajra. The succession was maintained in India by Vajrāsana the Elder and Vajrāsana the Younger, who was also known as Amoghavajra. The last mentioned introduced the practice to Bari Lotsāwa Rinchen Drak (1040–1112), after which it was transmitted, largely through the Sakya lineage in Tibet, as follows: Sachen Kunga Nyingpo (1092–1158), Sonam Tsemo (1142–1182), Drakpa Gyeltsen (1147–1216), Sakya Paṇḍita Kunga Gyeltsen (1182–1251), Chogyel Pakpa Lodro Gyeltsen (1235–1280), Zhangton Konchok Pel (1240–1317), Drakpukpa Sonam Pelwa (1277–1350), Pelden Lama Dampa Sonam Gyeltsen (1312–1375), Gyelsé Tokmé Zangpo (1295–1369), Jangsem Radengpa, Śākya Chokden (1428–1507), and Changlungpa Zhonu Chodrub (fl. fifteenth–sixteenth centuries).

The lineage prayer of *The Direct Guidance of Cakrasaṃvara* is as follows:

- Mahāvajradhara
- Vajravārāhī
- Ānandavajra
- Vajrāsana the Elder
- Vajrāsana the Younger
- Bari Lotsāwa
- Sachen Kunga Nyingpo
- Sonam Tsemo
- Drakpa Gyeltsen

- Sakya Paṇḍita Kunga Gyeltsen
- Chogyel Pakpa Lodro Gyeltsen
- Zhang
- Drakpuk
- Pelden Lama
- Gyelsé Tokmé Zangpo
- Jangsem Radengpa
- Śākya Chokden
- Zhonu Chodrub . . .

Grant your blessing that we may accomplish the power of Vajradhara,
Through the uncommon refuge and setting of the mind on enlightenment,
The generation stage of coemergence,
And the perfection stage of bliss and emptiness,
Comprising the six yogas of continuous flow![20]

35. *The Direct Guidance of Hevajra*

The lineage is identical to that of *The Direct Guidance of Cakrasaṃvara*.

The lineage prayer of *The Direct Guidance of Hevajra* is as follows:

- Mahāvajradhara
- Nairātmyā
- Ānandavajra, and so forth as above.

The concluding quatrain should be repeated, as above.

36. *Vajrapāṇi in the Form Mahācakra*

The progenitor of this lineage is the primordial buddha Mahāvajradhara, along with the female deity Ḍāki Siṃhavaktrā, who revealed this instruction directly to Śabaripā. The succession was maintained in India by Javaripā and Devapurṇamati, after whom it entered Tibet through Gar Lotsāwa Chokyi Zangpo. The succession there continued through the following Sakya line: Nyenton Rinchen Ngodrub, Marton Chokyi Gyeltsen, Mar Sherab Dorjé, Mar Tubpa Sherab, Mar Tsondru Sengé, Mar Chokyi Gyelpo (fl. twelfth century), Chagenpa, Dzinpa Rinchen Sherab, Mati Paṇchen

Lodro Gyeltsen (1294–1376), Sabzang Pakpa Zhonu Lodro (1358–1412), Ngorchen Kunga Zangpo (1382–1456), Drakar Sonam Rinchen (fl. fourteenth–fifteenth centuries), Sempa Sogyel, and Tashi Namgyel (1490–1518). The last named instructed Kunga Drolchok.

The lineage prayer of *Vajrapāṇi in the Form Mahācakra* is as follows:

- Vajradhara
- Ḍāki Siṃhavaktrā
- Śabaripā
- Javaripā {14}
- Devapurṇa
- Gar Lotsāwa Chokyi Zangpo
- Rinchen Ngodrub
- Marton Chokyi Gyeltsen
- Sherab Dorjé
- Mar Tubpa Sherab
- Mar Tsondru Sengé[21]
- Chokyi Gyelpo
- Chagenpa
- Dzinpa Rinchen Sherab
- Mati
- Sabzangwa
- Ngorchen
- Drakar Sonam Rinchen
- Sempa Sogyel
- Tashi Namgyel . . .

Grant your blessing that we may accomplish [the level of] Mahāvajradhara
Through the yoga of the two stages, generation and perfection, in coalescence:
The yoga of the generation stage endowed with four protections
And the yoga of the perfection stage endowed with four blessings!

37. *Vajrapāṇi in the Form Caṇḍa*

The progenitors of this lineage are the primordial buddha Mahāvajradhara and the bodhisattva Vajrapāṇi, who revealed this instruction to Karmavajra. The latter's immediate successors in India were Tang Lotsāwa, Shing

Lopa, Karṇaripā, and Valacaṇḍa. The lineage was introduced to Tibet by Rechungpa Dorjé Drak (1085–1161) and continued through the following, largely Drukpa Kagyu, transmission: Sumpa Repa Rinchen Gyeltsen (fl. twelfth century), Lingjé Repa Pema Dorjé (1128–1188), Dzongripa Konchok Zangpo, Riwo Gangpa, Uriwa, Sangdak Drubchen, Tulku Jodenpa (ca. 1292–1361), Gangtropa, Khenchen Jangchubsem, Sangyé Zangpo, Nesar Zhonu Drub, Lhundrub Dorjé, and Rabsel Dawa Gon (fl. fifteenth–sixteenth centuries). The last named was a teacher of Kunga Drolchok.

The lineage prayer of *Vajrapāṇi in the Form Caṇḍa* is as follows:

- Mahāvajradhara
- Vajrapāṇi
- Karmavajra
- Tang Lotsāwa
- Shing Lopa
- Karṇaripā
- Valacaṇḍa
- Rechung
- Sumpa Rinchen Gyeltsen
- Lingjé Repa
- Dzongripa
- Riwo Gangpa
- Uriwa
- Sangdak Drubchen
- Tulku Jodenpa
- Gangtropa
- Khenchen Jangchubsem[22]
- Sangyé Zangpo
- Nesar Zhonu Drub
- Lhundrub Dorjé
- Rabsel Dawa Gon . . .

Grant your blessing that we may attain the rank of Vajrapāṇi
Through the generation stage when the naturally arising body of the deity becomes radiant,
The perfection stage when divine appearances arise as a magical display,
And the natural unimpeded resonance of HŪṂ!

38. *Vārāhī in the Form Kurmapādā*

The progenitor of this lineage is the female meditational deity Vajravārāhī, who revealed the instruction directly to the mahāsiddha Śabaripā. The Indian transmission continued through Maitrīpā (ca. 986–1063 or 1007–1085), Nāyakapāda, Vikhyātadeva, the great paṇḍita Śākyaśrī of Kashmir (1127–1225), and Dānaśīla (fl. twelfth century), after whom it was introduced to Tibet by Chak Lotsāwa Chojé Pel (1197–1263/4). The lineage was then maintained by his successors: Zhonu Gyeltsen, Sherab Pel, Lekden Pelchen, Yeshé Pelwa, Gyelsé Lobzang Peljor, Chak Lotsāwa Rinchen Chogyel (b. 1447), and Kunpang Rinpoché Chokyi Nyima (1449–1524). The last named was a teacher of Kunga Drolchok.

The lineage prayer of *Vārāhī in the Form Kurmapādā* is as follows:

- Vajravārāhī
- Drubchen Śabaripā
- Maitrīpā
- Nāyakapāda, the glorious
- [Vikhyātadeva], receptive to the ten powers
- Paṇchen Śākyaśrī
- Dānaśīla
- Chak Lotsāwa
- Zhonu Gyel
- Sherab Pel
- Lekden Pelchen
- Yeshé Pelwa
- Lobzang Peljor
- Rinchen Chogyel
- Kunpang Rinpoche . . .

Grant your blessing that we may well realize the magical experiences
In which apparent forms are refined as deities
And all things are a magical display,
Just as magical emanations arise in space,
And may we then refine the meditative stability of the illusory body!

39. *Kurukullā*

The progenitor of this lineage is the female meditational deity Nairātmyā, who revealed the instruction directly to Virūpa. His Indian successors were the mahāsiddha Kṛṣṇapā, Vilāsa, Śīlacandra, and Dānaśīla (fl. twelfth century), the last of whom instructed Sakya Paṇḍita Kunga Gyeltsen (1182–1251) in Tibet. Thereafter the transmission was through the following Sakya lineage: Chogyel Pakpa Lodro Gyeltsen (1235–1280), Zhangton Konchok Pel (1240–1317), Drakpukpa Sonam Pelwa (1277–1350), Lama Dampa Sonam Gyeltsen (1312–1375), Pelden Tsultrim (1333–1399), Sharchen Yeshé Gyeltsen (ca. 1359–1406), Ngorchen Kunga Zangpo (1382–1456), and Gugé Paṇchen Sonam Lhundrub (fl. fifteenth–sixteenth centuries). The last named was a teacher of Kunga Drolchok.

The lineage prayer of *Kurukullā* is as follows:

- Bhagavatī Nairātmyā
- Virūpa
- Drubchen Kṛṣṇapā
- Vilāsa
- Śīlacandra {15}
- Dānaśīla
- Sakya Paṇḍita
- Pakpa
- Zhang
- Drakpuk
- Sonam Gyeltsen
- Pelden Tsultrim
- Sharchen Yeshé Gyeltsen
- Ngorchen Kunga Zangpo
- Gugé Paṇchen Sonam Lhundrub . . .

Grant your blessing that we may overpower all that appears and exists
By securing vitality within the long and short letters of the heart cakra
[That is supported upon] the triple channel intersection, resembling a wooden platform,
And by the hovering of the messenger bees of subtle energy and mind!

40. *The Six-Branch Yoga of Kālacakra*

The progenitors of this lineage are the three buddha bodies from whom the original transmission fell to the seven religious kings of Śambhala and the twenty-five Kulika kings of Śambhala. The succession of Indian masters then includes Caurayaśa (also known as Kālacakrapāda the Elder), Nālendrapā (also known as Kālacakrapāda the Younger, fl. eleventh century), and Somanātha of Kashmir (fl. eleventh century). Following the introduction of these practices to Tibet, the transmission was maintained in the Jonang succession: Drab Gompa Konchok Sungwa (fl. eleventh century), Droton Namlatsek (fl. eleventh century), Yumo Mikyo Dorjé (fl. eleventh century), Chokyi Wangchuk, Ḍāki Jobum-ma, Khangsarwa Namka Ozer, Semo Chewa Namka Gyeltsen (fl. twelfth century), Jamsarwa Sherab Ozer (fl. twelfth century), Gedingpa Choku Ozer (fl. twelfth–thirteenth centuries), Kunpang Tukjé Tsondru (1243–1313), Jangsem Gyelwa Yeshé (1247–1320), Yonten Gyatso (1260–1327), Dolpopa Sherab Gyeltsen (1292–1361), Choklé Namgyel (1306–1386), Nya-on Kunga Pel (1285–1379), Drubchen Kunlowa (fl. fourteenth century), Jamyang Konchok Zangpo (1398–1475), Namka Chokyong (1436–1507), Namka Pelzang (ca. 1464–1529), and Lochen Rinchen Zangpo (1489–1563). The last named taught Kunga Drolchok.

The lineage prayer of *The Six-Branch Yoga of Kālacakra* is as follows:

- Buddha body of reality
- Buddha body of perfect resource
- Buddha body of emanation
- The seven religious kings of Śambhala[23]
- The twenty-five Kulika kings of Śambhala[24]
- Kālacakrapāda the Elder
- Kālacakrapāda the Younger
- Somanātha of Kashmir
- Gompa Konchok
- Droton
- Yumo
- Chokyi Wangchuk
- Ḍāki Jobum-ma
- Namka Ozer
- Semo Chewa
- Jamsarwa

- Choku Ozer
- Tukjé Tsondru
- Gyelwa Yeshé
- Yonten Gyatso
- Kunkhyen Dolpopa
- Choklé Namgyel
- Nya-on Kunga
- Drubchen Kunlowa
- Jamyang Konchok Zangpo
- Namka Chokyong
- Namka Pelzang
- Lochen Ratnabhadra . . .

Grant your blessing that we may experientially cultivate the six-branch yoga—
Composure and meditative concentration that are virtuous in the beginning,
Breath control and retention that are virtuous in the middle,
And recollection and meditative stability that are virtuous in the end![25]

41. *The Aural Lineage of Kālacakra*

The progenitor of this lineage is the primordial buddha in the form Kālacakra, who revealed the transmission to the religious kings of Śambhala and to the three bodhisattvas known as the "lords of the three enlightened families." This lineage, distinct from the transmission of Somanātha, which is outlined in guidebook 40, appears to have entered Tibet somewhat later, through Menlung Guru Sonam Pel (b. 1239), who is known to have traveled to both Śambhala and Oḍḍiyāna. It was subsequently maintained in succession by Yarlungpa Lotsāwa Drakpa Gyeltsen, Nyemdo Kunga Dondrub (b. 1268), Kachupa Zhonu Sengé, Hūṃchen Namka Neljor, Hūṃ Gyel Lhundrub Rinchen, Rikgom Bepei Neljor, Chimé Drub, Drogon Chogyel Namka Pelzang (1462–1529), and Khewang Lotsāwa Rinchen Zangpo (1489–1563), the last of whom taught Kunga Drolchok.

The lineage prayer of *The Aural Lineage of Kālacakra* is as follows:

- Adibuddha
- The religious kings

- The lords of the three enlightened families
- Menlung Guru
- Lotsāwa Drakpa Gyeltsen
- Kunga Dondrub
- Kachupa Zhonu Sengé
- Hūṃchen Namka
- Hūṃ Gyel Lhundrub Rinchen
- Rikgom Bepei Neljor
- Chimé Drub
- Chogyel Pelzang
- Khewang Lotsāwa . . .

Grant your blessing that we may attain the ease of singular resolution—
The disposition of the Great Seal in which all things are liberated through singular knowledge,
The deep resonance of the uncreated syllable A, permeating all things in a singular utterance,
And the crucial five sibling frailties through which the knots are unraveled in a singular meditation![26]

42. *The Ritual Service and Attainment of the Three Adamantine Realities according to Orgyanpa*

The progenitor of this lineage is the primordial buddha Mahāvajradhara, along with the female deity Vajravārāhī, who revealed this instruction directly to Orgyanpa Rinchen Pel (1229–1309). From him the transmission continued in Tibet through Sonam Ozer (fl. thirteenth century), Barawa Gyeltsen Pelzang (1310–1391), Namka Sengé (fl. fourteenth century), Trulzhik Kunga Chogyel (1413–1509), Mondzong Rechen Dawa Gyeltsen (1418–1506), Rinchen Khyenrab Chogdrub (1436–1497), and Changlungpa Zhonu Chodrub (fl. fifteenth–sixteenth centuries). The last mentioned taught this practice to Kunga Drolchok.

The lineage prayer of *Ritual Service and Attainment of the Three Adamantine Realities according to Orgyanpa* is as follows: {16}

- Mahāvajradhara
- Vajravārāhī
- Khedrub Orgyanpa

- Sonam Ozer
- Gyeltsen Pelzang
- Namka Sengé
- Trulzhik Chogyel
- Monré Dawa Gyeltsen
- Khyenrab
- Changlungpa . . .

Grant your blessing that we may realize the perfection of ritual service and attainment—
The ritual service of buddha body that secures the essential posture of the physical body,
The attainment of buddha speech that entails recitation of adamantine syllables and breath control,
And the great attainment of buddha mind that secures the pure essences without leakage!

43. *The Path and Its Fruition*

The progenitor of this lineage is the primordial buddha Mahāvajradhara, along with the female deity Nairātmyā, who revealed this instruction directly to Virūpa. His Indian successors included Kṛṣṇacārin, Ḍamarupā, Avadhūtipā, and Gayādhara (fl. tenth–eleventh centuries), who introduced this cycle of practices to Tibet through the agency of Drokmi Lotsāwa Śākya Yeshé (992–1043). The lineage subsequently descended through the Sakya tradition as follows: Seton Kunrik (1029–1116), Zhangton Chobar (1053–1135), Sachen Kunga Nyingpo (1092–1158), Sonam Tsemo (1142–1182), Drakpa Gyeltsen (1147–1216), Sakya Paṇḍita Kunga Gyeltsen (1182–1251), Chogyel Pakpa Lodro Gyeltsen (1235–1280), Zhangton Konchok Pel (1240–1317), Namza Drakpuk Sonam Pelwa (1277–1350), Chojé Lama Dampa Sonam Gyeltsen (1312–1375), Pelden Tsultrim (1333–1399), Buddhaśrī Sangyé Pel (1339–1420), Ngorchen Kunga Zangpo (1382–1456), Pelden Dorjé (1411–1482), and Kunga Chogdrub (fl. fifteenth–sixteenth centuries). The last mentioned was a teacher of Kunga Drolchok.

The lineage prayer of *The Path and Its Fruition* is as follows:

- Vajradhara
- Nairātmyā

- Virūpa
- Kṛṣṇacārin
- Ḍamarupā
- Avadhūtipā
- Gayādhara
- Drokmi Lotsāwa
- Seton Kunrik
- Zhangton Chobar
- Sachen Kunga Nyingpo
- Sonam Tsemo
- Drakpa Gyeltsen
- Sakya Paṇḍita Kunga Gyeltsen
- Chogyel Pakpa Lodro Gyeltsen
- Konchok Pel
- Namza Drakpuk
- Chojé Lama
- Pelden Tsultrim
- Buddhaśrī
- Ngorchen Kunga Zangpo
- Pelden Dorjé
- Kunga Chogdrub . . .

Grant your blessing that, having trained our minds through the sequence of the path of sutra and mantra,
We may attain the rank of the four buddha bodies,
Through the short path of the meditative stabilities of ground, path, and fruition,
Experientially cultivating the four empowerments and meditating in four sessions!

44. *The Inconceivables*

The progenitor of this lineage is the primordial buddha Mahāvajradhara, along with the female deity Jñānaḍākinī, who revealed this instruction directly to Aśvottama. The Indian lineage is as follows: Vīṇapa, Indrabhūti, Lakṣmīkarā, Lalitavajra, Gundharipā, Padmavajra, Dhārmika, Bhadrapāda, Khanitra, Bhuṣaṇa, Dhamapa, Karṇa, and Vīravajra (fl. eleventh century), the last of whom instructed Drokmi Lotsāwa Śākya Yeshé (992–

1043). Thereafter the succession continued in Tibet through the mainstream Sakya lineage, similar to that of *The Path and Its Fruition*.

The lineage prayer of *The Inconceivables* is as follows:

- Mahāvajradhara
- Jñānaḍākinī
- Aśvottama
- Vīṇapa
- Indrabhūti
- Lakṣmīkarā
- Lalitavajra
- Gundharipā
- Padmavajra
- Dhārmika
- Bhadrapāda
- Khanitra
- Bhuṣaṇa
- Dhamapa
- Karṇa
- Vīravajra
- Drokmi Lotsāwa, and so forth, as above.

Grant your blessing that by experientially cultivating the five inconceivables,
We may dispel the obscurations of the expanse of space—
The nature of mind originally free from conceptual elaboration
Caused by thought clouds of dualistic perception,
And that the rain of nondual pristine cognition may fall!

45. *The Nine Profound Methods*

The progenitor of this lineage is the primordial buddha Mahāvajradhara, who revealed the instruction to Cintivilavavajra. The Indian succession includes Anaṅgavajra, Saroruha, Indrabhūti, Lakṣmīkarā, Kṛṣṇacārin, Śrīdhara, and Gayādhara (fl. tenth–eleventh centuries), the last of whom introduced the practice to Drokmi Lotsāwa Śākya Yeshé (992–1043). Thereafter the succession continued in Tibet through the mainstream Sakya lineage, similar to that of *The Path and Its Fruition*.

The lineage prayer of *The Nine Profound Methods of Padmavajra Saroruha* is as follows:

- Vajradhara
- Cintivilavavajra
- Anaṅgavajra
- Saroruha
- Indrabhūti
- Lakṣmīkarā
- Kṛṣṇacārin
- Śrīdhara
- Gayādhara
- Drokmi, and so forth, as above.

Grant your blessing that we may refine thoughts fixated on the inhabited world and its inhabitants through the nine profound methods, {17}
And then realize the coemergent pristine cognition,
Holding whatever appears within the maṇḍala of the deity
And experientially focusing on it in the manner of a flame tip!

46. *The Attainment of Coemergence*

The progenitor of this lineage is the primordial buddha Mahāvajradhara, along with the female deity Nairātmyā, who revealed this instruction directly to Ḍombipā. The Indian lineage is as follows: Alalavajra, Vanaprastha, Garbharipā, Jayaśrījñāna, Durjayacandra, and Vīravajra (fl. eleventh century), the last of whom instructed Drokmi Lotsāwa Śākya Yeshé (992–1043). Thereafter the succession continued in Tibet through the mainstream Sakya lineage, similar to that of *The Path and Its Fruition*.

The lineage prayer of *The Attainment of Coemergence* is as follows:

- Vajradhara
- Nairātmyā
- Ḍombipā
- Alalavajra
- Vanaprastha
- Garbharipā
- Jayaśrījñāna

- Durjayacandra
- Vīravajra
- Drokmi Lotsāwa, and so forth as above.

Grant your blessing that we may actualize the three buddha bodies—
The nature of mind without beginning or end that is the coemergence of the causal basis,
The inherent purity of the three poisons that is the coemergence of the path,
And the three gateways of liberation that are the coemergence of the fruition!

47. *The Perfection of the Path of Fierce Inner Heat*[27]

The progenitor of this lineage is the primordial buddha Mahāvajradhara, along with the female deity Vajravārāhī, who revealed this instruction directly to Ghaṇṭāpāda. The Indian lineage is as follows: Kūrmapādā, Jālandharapāda, Kṛṣṇacārin, Śrīdhara, and Gayādhara (fl. tenth–eleventh centuries), the last of whom instructed Drokmi Lotsāwa Śākya Yeshé (992–1043). Thereafter the succession continued in Tibet through the mainstream Sakya lineage, similar to that of *The Path and Its Fruition*.

The lineage prayer of *The Perfection of the Path of Fierce Inner Heat* is as follows:

- Vajradhara
- Vajravārāhī
- Ghaṇṭāpāda
- Kūrmapādā
- Jālandharapāda
- Kṛṣṇacārin
- Śrīdhara the Brahmin
- Gayādhara
- Drokmi, and so forth, as above.

Grant your blessing that we may actualize the four buddha bodies
Through the sequential experiential cultivation of the four phases—
Those of the continuum, mantra, pristine cognition, and secrecy,
And through the meditative stability that beholds liberation from the four limits![28]

48. *The Straightening of Crooked Posture*

The progenitor of this lineage is the primordial buddha Mahāvajradhara, who revealed this instruction directly to Īśvara. The Indian lineage is as follows: Kṛṣṇocita, Kṛṣṇacārin, Śrīdhara, and Gayādhara (fl. tenth–eleventh centuries), the last of whom instructed Drokmi Lotsāwa Śākya Yeshé (992–1043). Thereafter the succession continued in Tibet through the mainstream Sakya lineage, similar to that of *The Path and Its Fruition*.

The lineage prayer of *The Straightening of Crooked Posture* is as follows:

- Vajradhara
- Īśvara
- Ucita
- Kṛṣṇacārin
- Śrīdhara
- Gayādhara
- Drokmi, and so forth, as above and below.

Grant your blessing that we may definitively realize the abiding nature
Untainted by the stains of conceptual thought of dualizing perception,
By immutably inducting within the central channel the winds
That enter and move through the left and right channels,
Where semen and blood respectively arise![29]

49. *The Path of the Female Mudra*[30]

The progenitor of this lineage is the primordial buddha Mahāvajradhara, who revealed this instruction directly to Indrabhūti. Thereafter the succession is through: Śrībrahmā, Brahmāṇī, Siddhivajra, Middle Indrabhūti, Upama, Niḥsaṅgapāda, Jñānaśrībodhi, Padmavajra, Ḍombipā, Anaṅgavajra, Bhṛṅgapadminī, Lakṣmīkarā, Younger Indrabhūti, Ratnavajra, and Prajñāguhya (fl. eleventh century), the last of whom instructed Drokmi Lotsāwa Śākya Yeshé (992–1043). Thereafter the succession continued in Tibet through the mainstream Sakya lineage, similar to that of *The Path and Its Fruition*.

The lineage prayer of *The Path of the Female Mudra* is as follows:

- Vajradhara
- Indrabhūti

- Śrībrahmā
- Brahmāṇī
- Siddhivajra
- Middle Indrabhūti
- Upama
- Niḥsaṅgapāda
- Jñānaśrī
- Padmavajra
- Ḍombipā {18}
- Anaṅgavajra
- Bhṛṅgapadminī
- Lakṣmīkarā
- Younger Indrabhūti
- Ratnavajra
- Prajñāguhya
- Drokmi Lotsāwa, and so forth, as above.

Grant your blessing that we may realize through the essential female mudra
The unchanging supreme bliss with mastery over all entities,
The adamantine body that is not decayed by composite conditions,
The supremely short path of the messenger, experientially cultivating the four delights!

50. *The Great Seal Devoid of Letters*

The progenitor of this lineage is the female bodhisattva Tārā, who revealed this instruction directly to Vagīśvarakīrti. His successors were Devākaracandra and Amoghavajra, the last of whom instructed Drokmi Lotsāwa Śākya Yeshé (992–1043). Thereafter the succession continued in Tibet through the mainstream Sakya lineage, similar to that of *The Path and Its Fruition*.

The lineage prayer of *The Great Seal Devoid of Letters* is as follows:

- Tārā
- Vagīśvarakīrti
- Devākaracandra
- Amoghavajra
- Drokmi Lotsāwa, and so forth, as above.

Grant your blessing that we may realize the innate nature of mind,
Which has a relaxed and uncontrived disposition,
Resembling a trained elephant
Repeatedly goaded by the hook of its attendant
Toward the nature of mind, without falling into the two extremes!

51. *The Determination of Mind*[31]

The progenitor of this lineage is the primordial buddha Mahāvajradhara, who revealed this instruction directly to Nāgārjuna (fl. second century). The latter's succession included Āryadeva (fl. second–third centuries), Kṛṣṇacārin, Candrakīrti (fl. seventh century), Śrīdhara, and Vīravajra (fl. eleventh century), the last of whom instructed Drokmi Lotsāwa Śākya Yeshé (992–1043). Thereafter the succession continued in Tibet through the mainstream Sakya lineage, similar to that of *The Path and Its Fruition.*

The lineage prayer of *The Determination of Mind* is as follows:

- Mahāvajradhara
- Nāgārjuna
- Āryadeva
- Kṛṣṇacārin
- Candrakīrti
- Śrīdhara
- Vīravajra
- Drokmi Lotsāwa, and so forth, as above.

Grant your blessing that we may realize the profound emptiness
Uncontaminated by clinging to stains of conceptual thought,
The compassion and enlightened mind of all the buddhas,
And the apperception of self and the aggregates, and so forth!

52. *The Mingling of Sutra and Tantra*

The progenitor of this lineage is the bodhisattva Mañjughoṣa, who revealed this instruction directly to Śāntipa. He in turn taught Drokmi Lotsāwa Śākya Yeshé (992–1043), who introduced the practice to Tibet. The succession that follows included: Ngaripa Selnying (fl. eleventh century), Khon Kyichuwa Dralha Bar (fl. eleventh century), Sachen Kunga Nyingpo

(1092–1158), Sonam Tsemo (1142–1182), Drakpa Gyeltsen (1147–1216), Sakya Paṇḍita Kunga Gyeltsen (1182–1251), Lungpuwa (fl. thirteenth century), Zhonu Drubpa (fl. thirteenth century), Jangchub Yeshé, Lama Dampa Sonam Gyeltsen (1312–1375), Pelden Tsultrim (1333–1399), Buddhaśrī Sangyé Pel (1339–1420), Ngorchen Kunga Zangpo (1382–1456), Pelden Dorjé (1411–1482), and Kunga Chogdrub (fl. fifteenth–sixteenth centuries). The last named was a teacher of Kunga Drolchok.

The lineage prayer of *The Mingling of Sutra and Tantra* is as follows:

- Mañjughoṣa
- Śāntipa
- Lachen Drokmi
- Ngaripa Selnying
- Kyichuwa
- Sachen Kunga Nyingpo
- Sonam Tsemo
- Drakpa Gyeltsen
- Sakya Paṇḍita Kunga Gyeltsen
- Lungpuwa
- Zhonu Drubpa
- Jangchub Yeshé
- Pelden Lama
- Pelden Tsultrim
- Buddhaśrī
- Ngorchen
- Pelden Dorjé
- Kunga Chogdrub . . .

Grant your blessing that we may realize the natural momentum of the essential [paths]
Through spontaneous experiential cultivation of the disposition of magical display—
The pristine cognition of particularizing intrinsic awareness,
Extracted from the profound key points of sutra and mantra!

53. *The Dispelling of Obstacles due to External Demons*

The progenitor of this lineage is the bodhisattva Vajrapāṇi in the form Guhyapati, who revealed the instruction directly to Prajñākaramati. He in turn taught Drokmi Lotsāwa Śākya Yeshé (992–1043), who introduced the practice to Tibet. His successors within the Sakya lineage included Seton Kunrik (ca. 1026–ca. 1112), Shengom Rokpo, Nyo, Yerpa Gomseng, Drubtob Lhabar, Kharak Gompa, Lungpuwa (fl. thirteenth century), Zhonu Drubpa (fl. thirteenth century), Jangchub Yeshé, Lama Dampa Sonam Gyeltsen (1312–1375), Pelden Tsultrim (1333–1399), Buddhaśrī Sangyé Pel (1339–1420), Ngorchen Kunga Zangpo (1382–1456), Pelden Dorjé (1411–1482), and Kunga Chogdrub (fl. fifteenth–sixteenth centuries). The last mentioned taught Kunga Drolchok.

The lineage prayer of *The Dispelling of Obstacles due to External Demons*—among the *Dispelling of Three Sorts of Obstacles*—is as follows:

- Guhyapati
- Prajñākaramati
- Lachen Drokmi
- Sé
- Rok
- Nyo
- Yerpa Gomseng
- Drubtob Lhabar
- Kharak Gompa
- Lungpuwa
- Zhonu Drubpa
- Jangchub Yeshé
- Sonam Gyeltsen
- Pelden Tsultrim
- Buddhaśrī
- Ngorchen
- Pelden Dorjé
- Kunga Chogdrub . . .

Grant your blessing that we may subdue non-Buddhist forces, evil spirits,
and obstructors
By the fierce resonance of the syllable HŪṂ, blazing forth the light of splendor

Within the firelight of the adamantine tent that diffuses clarity
From the seed within the heart cakra of our own body, naturally arisen as the deity!

54. *The Dispelling of Obstacles due to the Agitation of the Physical Body by the Elements*

The progenitor of this lineage is the bodhisattva Vajrapāṇi in the form Guhyapati, who revealed the instruction directly to Ratnavajra. He in turn taught Drokmi Lotsāwa Śākya Yeshé (992–1043), who introduced the practice to Tibet. His successors within the Sakya lineage included Seton Kunrik (ca. 1026–ca. 1112), Shengom Rokpo, and so forth, as above.

The lineage prayer of *The Dispelling of Obstacles That Agitate the Physical Body*—among the *Dispelling of Three Sorts of Obstacles*—is as follows:

- Guhyapati
- Ratnavajra
- Lachen Drokmi {19}
- Se
- Rok, and so forth, as above.

Grant your blessing that we may eradicate entirely
All pathological roots of fever and cold in the upper and lower body,
Through the rosaries of the sunlight and moonlight vital essences
At its upper and lower gates,
Which are in association with the adamantine axis of vitality—
The central channel within the body!

55. *The Dispelling of the Obstacles of Meditative Stability and Mind*

The progenitor of this lineage is the bodhisattva Vajrapāṇi in the form Guhyapati, who revealed the instruction directly to Jñānaśrībodhi. He in turn taught Drokmi Lotsāwa Śākya Yeshé (992–1043), who introduced the practice to Tibet. His successors within the Sakya lineage included Seton Kunrik (ca. 1026–ca. 1112), Shengom Rokpo, and so forth, as above.

The lineage prayer of *The Dispelling of the Obstacles of Meditative Stability and Mind*—among the *Dispelling of Three Sorts of Obstacles*—is as follows:

- Guhyapati
- Jñānaśrī
- Lachen Drokmi
- Se
- Rok, and so forth, as above.

Grant your blessing that we may forsake the mind that grasps
The extremes of beginning, middle, and end—
That grasps a beginning and an end—
And that we may then reach the path of meditative stability
Through experiential cultivation, without intervening obstacles!

56. *The Great Seal Dispelling the Three Sorts of Suffering*

The progenitor of this lineage is the bodhisattva Avalokiteśvara, who revealed the instruction directly to Nāropā Jñānasiddhi (1016–1100). The latter passed the instruction to Drokmi Lotsāwa Śākya Yeshé (992–1043), who taught Ngaripa Selnying (fl. eleventh century). Thereafter the practice was handed down through the Sakya line—Khon Kyichuwa Dralha Bar, Sachen Kunga Nyingpo, and so forth—as in the aforementioned lineage of *The Mingling of Sutra and Tantra*.

The lineage prayer of *The Great Seal Dispelling the Three Sorts of Suffering* is as follows:

- Avalokiteśvara
- Nāropā
- Lachen Drokmi
- Ngaripa Selnying, and so forth, as in the aforementioned lineage of the guidebook *The Mingling of Sutra and Tantra*.

Grant your blessing that the minds of all beings,
Tormented by the three sorts of suffering,
Might be transformed in the presence of the three buddha bodies,
And may all suffering, without exception, be dispelled
Through the natural descent of physical, mental, and cognitive well-being!

57. *The Clear Recollection of the Innate State*

The progenitor of this lineage is the female bodhisattva Tārā, who revealed this instruction directly to Vagīśvarakīrti. The latter's successors, within the Sakya lineage, were Drokmi Lotsāwa Śākya Yeshé (992–1043), Khon Konchok Gyelpo (1034–1102), Lama Shang Khyungpo Neljor (978–1127), Sachen Kunga Nyingpo (1092–1158), Sonam Tsemo (1142–1182), Drakpa Gyeltsen (1147–1216), Sakya Paṇḍita Kunga Gyeltsen (1182–1251), Lungpuwa (fl. thirteenth century), Zhonu Drubpa (fl. thirteenth century), Zhang Jangchub Sherab, Lama Dampa Sonam Gyeltsen (1312–1375), Pelden Tsultrim (1333–1399), Buddhaśrī Sangyé Pel (1339–1420) Ngorchen Kunga Zangpo (1382–1456), Pelden Dorjé (1411–1482), and Kunga Chogdrub (fl. fifteenth–sixteenth centuries). The last named taught Kunga Drolchok.

The lineage prayer of *The Clear Recollection of the Innate State* is as follows:

- Tārā
- Vāgīśvara
- Drokmi
- Konchok Gyelpo
- Lama Shang
- Sachen Kunga Nyingpo
- Sonam Tsemo
- Drakpa Gyeltsen
- Sakya Paṇḍita Kunga Gyeltsen
- Lungpuwa
- Zhonu Drubpa
- Jangchub Sherab
- Sonam Gyeltsen
- Pelden Tsultrim
- Buddhaśrī
- Ngorchen
- Pelden Dorjé
- Kunga Chogdrub . . .

Grant your blessing that we may realize the supreme essentials of the four empowerments,
Through the short path that engages the host of deities within the six cakras—

The celestial palaces innately present from the beginning within our own body,
And that cultivates the four delights associated with blazing, secretion, bliss, and warmth [of vital essences]!

58. *The Three Purities*

The progenitor of this lineage is the primordial buddha Mahāvajradhara, along with the female deity Nairātmyā, who revealed this instruction directly to Ḍombipā. His Indian successors included Alalavajra, Vanaprastha, Garbharipā, Jayaśrījñāna, Durjayacandra, and Vīravajra (fl. eleventh century). Thereafter the transmission was introduced to Tibet by Drokmi Lotsāwa Śākya Yeshé (992–1043). The Tibetan lineage holders who followed him included Seton Kunrik (ca. 1026–ca. 1112), Zhangton Chobar (1053–1135), Sachen Kunga Nyingpo (1092–1158), Sonam Tsemo (1142–1182), Drakpa Gyeltsen (1147–1216), Sakya Paṇḍita Kunga Gyeltsen (1182–1251), Zhangton Gadenpa Kunga Sonam (fl. thirteenth century), Namza Drakpuk Sonam Pelwa (1277–1350), Pang Lotsāwa Lodro Tenpa (1276–1342), Pelden Tsultrim (1333–1399), Sharwa Yeshé Gyeltsen (ca. 1359–1406), Ngorchen Kunga Zangpo (1382–1456), Gugé Paṇchen Drakpa Gyeltsen (d. 1486), and Lowo Khenchen Sonam Lhundrub (fl. fifteenth–sixteenth centuries). The last mentioned was a teacher of Kunga Drolchok.

The lineage prayer of the guidance on *The Three Purities* is as follows:

- Vajradhara
- Nairātmyā
- Ḍombipā
- Alalavajra
- Vanaprastha
- Garbharipā
- Jayaśrījñāna
- Durjayacandra
- Vīravajra
- Drokmi
- Se
- Zhang
- Sachen Kunga Nyingpo
- Sonam Tsemo

- Drakpa Gyeltsen
- Sakya Paṇḍita Kunga Gyeltsen
- Gadenpa
- Drakpuk
- Lodro Tenpa
- Pelden Tsultrim
- Sharwa
- Ngorchen
- Paṇchen Drakpa Gyeltsen
- Khenchen Sonam Lhundrub . . .

Grant your blessing that we may perfect the three purities:
Refinement through the purity of the true nature, {20}
The arising of appearances as the purity of the deities,
And the realization of reality as the purity of intrinsic awareness!

59. *The Twenty-Nine Essential Visualizations of Self-Consecration*

The progenitor of this lineage is the primordial buddha Mahāvajradhara, along with the female deity Nairātmyā, who revealed this instruction directly to Ḍombipā. The latter's Indian and Tibetan successors from Alalavajra through to Sakya Paṇḍita Kunga Gyeltsen (1182–1251) are identical to those in the transmission of the Three Purities. Thereafter the lineage descended to Tsokgom Kunga Pel (1210–1307), Nyagton Nyingpo Gyeltsen (fl. thirteenth century), Gyelwa Bum (fl. thirteenth–fourteenth centuries), Lama Dampa Sonam Gyeltsen (1312–1375), Pelden Tsultrim (1333–1399), Buddhaśrī Sangyé Pel (1339–1420), Ngorchen Kunga Zangpo (1382–1456), Pelden Dorjé (1411–1482), and Kunga Chogdrub (fl. fifteenth–sixteenth centuries). The last named instructed Kunga Drolchok.

The lineage prayer of *The Twenty-Nine Essential Visualizations of Self-Consecration* is as follows:

- Vajradhara
- Nairātmyā
- Ḍombipā
- Alalavajra

- Vanaprastha
- Garbharipā
- Jayaśrījñāna
- Durjayacandra
- Vīravajra
- Drokmi
- Se
- Zhang
- Sachen Kunga Nyingpo
- Sonam Tsemo
- Drakpa Gyeltsen
- Sakya Paṇḍita Kunga Gyeltsen
- Tsokgom
- Nyagton Nyingpo
- Gyelwa Bum
- Sonam Gyeltsen
- Pelden Tsultrim
- Buddhaśrī
- Ngorchen Kunga Zangpo
- Pelden Dorjé
- Kunga Chogdrub[32]

Grant your blessing that the illustrative and genuine pristine cognitions may arise
Through the yogas attained, engaged, and cultivated individually,
In each of the twenty-nine essential visualizations,
Experientially cultivated through self-consecration!

60. *The Exegesis of the Concealed Path*

The progenitor of this lineage is the primordial buddha Mahāvajradhara, along with the female deity Nairātmyā, who revealed this instruction directly to Virūpa. His successors in Tibet included Sachen Kunga Nyingpo (1092–1158), Sonam Tsemo (1142–1182), Drakpa Gyeltsen (1147–1216), Sakya Paṇḍita Kunga Gyeltsen (1182–1251), Chogyel Pakpa Lodro Gyeltsen (1235–1280), Zhangton Gadenpa Kunga Sonam (fl. thirteenth century), Namza Drakpuk Sonam Pelwa (1277–1350), Chojé Lama Dampa Sonam Gyeltsen

(1312–1375), Pelden Tsultrim (1333–1399), Buddhaśrī Sangyé Pel (1339–1420), Ngorchen Kunga Zangpo (1382–1456), Pelden Dorjé (1411–1482), and Kunga Chogdrub (fl. fifteenth–sixteenth centuries).

The lineage prayer of *The Exegesis of the Concealed Path* is as follows:

- Vajradhara
- Nairātmyā
- Virūpa
- Sachen Kunga Nyingpo
- Sonam Tsemo
- Drakpa Gyeltsen
- Sakya Paṇḍita Kunga
- Pakpa Lodro Gyeltsen
- Zhang
- Drakpuk
- Chojé Lama
- Pelden Tsultrim
- Buddhaśrī
- Ngorchen
- Pelden Dorjé
- Kunga Chogdrub . . .

Grant your blessing that we may experientially cultivate the concealed exegesis
By revealing the five-aspected palace of adamantine buddha mind
And key points concerning the union of winds, yogic exercises, and vital essences,
Which are all present within the tent [of the subtle body],
In which the lungs, liver, and heart are inherently transformed!

61. *The Elucidation of the Symbolic Meaning*

The progenitor of this lineage is the primordial buddha Mahāvajradhara, who revealed this instruction directly to Virūpa. His successors in Tibet included Sachen Kunga Nyingpo (1092–1158), Drakpa Gyeltsen (1147–1216), Sakya Paṇḍita Kunga Gyeltsen (1182–1251), Lungpuwa (fl. thirteenth century), Zhonu Drubpa (fl. thirteenth century), Zhang Jangchub Sherab, Lama Dampa Sonam Gyeltsen (1312–1375), Pelden Tsultrim (1333–1399),

Buddhaśrī Sangyé Pel (1339–1420), Ngorchen Kunga Zangpo (1382–1456), Pelden Dorjé (1411–1482), and Kunga Chogdrub (fl. fifteenth–sixteenth centuries).

The lineage prayer of *The Elucidation of the Symbolic Meaning* is as follows:

- Vajradhara
- Virūpa
- Sakyapa
- Drakpa Gyeltsen
- Sakya Paṇḍita
- Lungpuwa
- Zhonu Drubpa
- Jangchub Sherab
- Sonam Gyeltsen
- Pelden Tsultrim
- Buddhaśrī
- Ngorchen
- Pelden Dorjé
- Kunga Chogdrub . . .

Grant your blessing that we may realize the supreme essentials of the Path and Its Fruition,
Through blessings that confer definitive wisdom by means of symbols,
And through the transformations of the *Instruction Entitled Three Emerging from Two*,
Concerning the essential visualizations of the three inaugural approaches—extensive, middling, and abridged![33]

62. *The Five Stages of the Secret Assembly*

The progenitors of this lineage are the primordial buddha Mahāvajradhara and the bodhisattva Vajrapāṇi, who revealed this instruction directly to Indrabhūti. The latter's Indian successors included Nāgayoginī, King Visukalpa, Saraha, Nāgārjuna, Āryadeva, Śākyamitra, Nāgabodhi, Candrakīrti, Śiṣyavajra, Kṛṣṇacārin in the form Caryāvajra, and Gomiśra, who introduced it to Tsondru Zangpo in Tibet. Thereafter the lineage is through Go Lotsāwa Khukpa Lhetsé (fl. eleventh century), Mangrawa Sengé Gyeltsen (fl. twelfth century), Ngok Yeshé Sengé (fl. twelfth century), Ngok Nyima Sengé, Lentsangtsa Nyima Cham, Ngok Pakpa Lha (fl. twelfth century), Gyakar Tangbewa Pakpa Kyab (fl. twelfth century), Serdingpa Zhonu O (fl. twelfth century), Choku Ozer (fl. twelfth–thirteenth centuries), Jotsowa Pakpa Ozer (fl. thirteenth century), Buton Rinchen Drub (1290–1364), Khyung Lhepa Zhonu Sonam (fl. fourteenth century), Sharchen Yeshé Gyeltsen (1359–1406), Ngorchen Kunga Zangpo (1382–1456), Śākya Chokden (1428–1507), and Rabsel Dawa Gon (fl. fifteenth–sixteenth centuries). The last named was a teacher of Kunga Drolchok.

The lineage prayer of *The Five Stages of the Secret Assembly* according to the tradition of Sublime Nāgārjuna is as follows: {21}

- Mahāvajradhara
- Vajrapāṇi
- Indrabhūti
- Nāgayoginī
- Visukalpa
- Saraha
- Sublime Nāgārjuna
- Āryadeva
- Śākyamitra
- Nāgabodhi
- Candrakīrti
- Śiṣyavajra
- Caryāvajra
- Gomiśra
- Tsondru Zangpo
- Go Lotsāwa Khugpa
- Mangrawa Sengé Gyeltsen
- Yeshé Sengé
- Nyima Sengé
- Nyima Cham
- Pakpa Lha
- Pakpa Kyab
- Zhonu O
- Choku Ozer
- Pakpa Ozer

- Rinchen Drub
- Khyung Lhepa
- Sharchen Yeshé Gyeltsen
- Ngorchen Kunga Zangpo
- Śākya Chokden
- Rabsel Dawa Gon . . .

Grant your blessing that we may accomplish the supreme path of the five stages:
The adamantine buddha body in which the rainbow body is perfected through isolation of the physical body,
The adamantine buddha speech in which the three seed syllables are perfected through isolation of speech,
And the coalescent buddha mind in which luminosity is perfected through isolation of the mind!

63. *The Vital Essence of Liberation*

The progenitor of this lineage is the bodhisattva Mañjughoṣa, who revealed this instruction directly to Buddhajñānapāda. His Indian successors were Dīpaṃkarabhadra, Śrīsukha, Vimalagupta, Ratnavajra, Ratnakīrti, Kandarayoginī, and Pandeva. The practice was introduced into Tibet by Nyan Lotsāwa Darma Drak (fl. eleventh century) and continued through the following Sakya line of transmission: Nam Khawupa Chokyi Gyeltsen, Jetsun Tsewa Chenpo Sachen Kunga Nyingpo (1092–1158), Sonam Tsemo (1142–1182), Drakpa Gyeltsen (1147–1216), Sakya Paṇḍita Kunga Gyeltsen (1182–1251), Chogyel Pakpa Lodro Gyeltsen (1235–1280), Anyen Dampa Kunga Drak (1230–1303), Gadenpa Kunga Sonam (fl. thirteenth century), Gadenpa Tashi Pel (fl. thirteenth century), Khampa Dorjé Pel (fl. thirteenth century), Drakchen Donmoripa (fl. thirteenth century), Gangtropa Drakpa Gyeltsen (fl. fourteenth century), Sabzang Mati Paṇchen Lodro Gyeltsen (1294–1376), Sabzang Pakpa Zhonu Lodro (1358–1412/24), Ngorchen Kunga Zangpo (1382–1456), Gyeltsab Kunga Wangchuk (1424–1478), Paṇchen Drakmar Kunga Tsepel (fl. fifteenth century), and Rabsel Dawa Gon (fl. fifteenth–sixteenth centuries). The last mentioned taught Kunga Drolchok.

The lineage prayer of *The Vital Essence of Liberation* according to the tradition of Buddhajñānapāda is as follows:

- Mañjughoṣa
- Buddhajñānapāda
- Dīpaṃkarabhadra
- Śrīsukha
- Vimalagupta
- Ratna
- Kandarayoginī
- Pandeva
- Nyan Lotsāwa Darma Drak
- Chokyi Gyeltsen
- Jetsun Sachen Kunga Nyingpo
- Sonam Tsemo
- Drakpa Gyeltsen
- Sakya Paṇḍita Kunga Gyeltsen
- Pakpa Lodro Gyeltsen
- Anyen Dampa
- Kunga Sonam
- Tashipel
- Dorjépel
- Drakchen
- Gangtropa
- Sabzang
- Pakpa
- Ngorchen Kunga Zangpo
- Gyeltsab
- Paṇchen Drakmar
- Rabsel Dawa Gon . . .

Grant your blessing that, having abandoned the propensities of dark ignorance
By means of the garland of light of the imperishable vital essence within the heart,
We may radiantly discern the mind as Mañjuvajra
And realize the nonduality of the expanse and awareness!

64. *The Unelaborate Practice of Red Yamāri*

The progenitors of this lineage are the bodhisattva Mañjughoṣa and the meditational deity Yamāntaka, who revealed this instruction directly to Ḍombipā. The latter's Indian successors included Virūpa, Śrīdhara, Sumati, and Darpaṇa Acārya (fl. twelfth century). The practice was introduced into Tibet by Lowo Lotsāwa Sherab Rinchen (fl. twelfth–thirteenth centuries) and transmitted by his successors: Lodro Gyeltsen (1235–1280), Mangkhar Lotsāwa Chokden Lekpei Lodro, Lowo Lotsāwa [Sangyé Sé], Bagton Zhonu Tsultrim (fl. thirteenth century), Tsultrim Gyeltsen (fl. thirteenth–fourteenth centuries), Pangton Drubpa Sherab (1357–1423), Jamyang Sherab Gyatso (1396–1474), Raton Yonten Pelzang (fl. fourteenth–fifteenth centuries), and Kunga Chogdrub (fl. fifteenth–sixteenth centuries).

The lineage prayer of *The Unelaborate Practice of Red Yamāri* is as follows:

- Mañjuśrī
- Yamāntaka
- Ḍombipā
- Virūpa
- Śrīdhara
- Sumati
- Darpaṇa
- Sherab Rinchen
- [Lodro Gyeltsen,] the latter's disciple
- Lotsāwa Chokden
- Lowo Lotsāwa {22}
- Bagton
- Tsultrim Gyeltsen
- Drubpa Sherab
- Sherab Gyatso
- Raton
- Kunga Chogdrub . . .

Grant your blessing that we may accomplish the utterly unelaborate
expanse of space,
[Union of] emptiness and radiance, free from all grasping,
Through devout application, devotion to the guru, and luminosity,
As well as the six methods of setting the mind on enlightenment,

And having eliminated all obstacles!

65. *The Four-Stage Yoga*

This transmission is identical to the foregoing *Unelaborate Practice of Red Yamāri.*

The lineage prayer of *The Four-Stage Yoga* is as follows:

- Mañjuśrī,
- Yamāntaka, and so forth, as above.

Grant your blessing that we may accomplish the four-stage yoga, including:
Self-consecration through which our own physical body becomes the body of the deity,
Adamantine sound through which our own speech naturally arises in an indestructible manner,
And the Great Seal in which our own mind is naturally unfabricated!

66. *The Mental Focus on the Horns of Bhairava*

The progenitors of this lineage are the meditational deities Vajrabhairava and Jñānaḍākinī, who revealed this instruction directly to Lalitavajra. The latter's Indian successors included Mañjuśrīmitra, Amoghavajra the Elder, and Amoghavajra the Younger. The practice was introduced to Tibet by Kyoton Ojung, and maintained thereafter in the following succession: Kyoton's brother, José Khampa, Nyenton Rinchen Tenpa, Nyenton Osung, Nyenton Chogyel, Dzinpa Rinchen Sherab, Khonton Tukjé Rinchen, Dung-gyu Rinchen Gyeltsen, Chagenpa, Drakchen Donmoripa (fl. thirteenth century), Gangtropa Drakpa Gyeltsen (fl. fourteenth century), Sabzang Mati Paṇchen Lodro Gyeltsen (1294–1376), Sabzang Pakpa Zhonu Lodro (1358–1412/24), Ngorchen Kunga Zangpo (1382–1456), Gugé Paṇchen Drakpa Gyeltsen (d. 1486), and Lowo Khenchen Sonam Lhundrub (fl. fifteenth–sixteenth centuries). The last mentioned taught Kunga Drolchok.

The lineage prayer of *The Mental Focus on the Horns of Bhairava* is as follows:

- Vajrabhairava
- Jñānaḍākinī

- Lalita
- Mañjuśrīmitra
- Amoghavajra the Elder
- Amoghavajra the Younger
- Kyo Ojung
- The brother of Kyoton[34]
- Khampa
- Rinchen Tenpa
- Nyenton Osung
- Chogyel
- Rinchen Sherab
- Tukjé Rinchen
- Rinchen Gyeltsen
- Chagenpa
- Drakchen
- Gangtropa
- Mati
- Sabzang
- Ngorchen Kunga Zangpo
- Drakpa Gyeltsen
- Sonam Lhundrub . . .

Grant your blessing that we may fearlessly cultivate the Nocturnal Motion,
With divine pride that naturally arises
Through *The Mental Focus on the Horns of Bhairava*,
And that we may then actualize the perfection stage
Of the Erect Penis [of Bhairava], relying on the flow of bliss!

67. *The Central Channel Dependent on the Male Deity Cakrasaṃvara*

The progenitors of this lineage are the primordial buddha Mahāvajradhara and the bodhisattva Vajrapāṇi, who revealed this instruction directly to Saraha. The Indian succession includes Nāgārjuna, Śabaripā, Luipā, Dhārikpa, Andharapa, Tilopā (988–1069), Nāropā Jñānasiddhi (1016–1100), and the Newar Phamtingwa Abhayakīrti (fl. eleventh century). The practice was introduced to Tibet by Mal Lotsāwa Lodro Drak (fl. eleventh century), and thereafter transmitted through the following Sakya line: Sachen Kunga Nyingpo (1092–1158), Sonam Tsemo (1142–1182), Drakpa Gyeltsen (1147–1216), Sakya Paṇḍita Kunga Gyeltsen (1182–1251), Zhangton Gadenpa Kunga Sonam (fl. thirteenth century), Namza Drakpuk Sonam Pelwa (1277–1350), Lama Dampa Sonam Gyeltsen (1312–1375), Pelden Tsultrim (1333–1399), Sharwa Yeshé Gyeltsen (ca. 1359–1406), Ngorchen Kunga Zangpo (1382–1456), Gugé Paṇchen Drakpa Gyeltsen (d. 1486), and Lowo Khenchen Sonam Lhundrub (fl. fifteenth–sixteenth centuries).

The lineage prayer of *The Central Channel Dependent on the Male Deity Cakrasaṃvara* is as follows:

- Mahāvajradhara
- Vajrapāṇi
- Saraha
- Nāgārjuna
- Śabaripā
- Luipā
- Dhārikpa
- Andharapa
- Tilopā
- Nāropā
- Phamtingwa
- Mal Lotsāwa Lodro Drak
- Sachen Kunga Nyingpo
- Sonam Tsemo
- Drakpa Gyeltsen
- Sakya Paṇḍita Kunga Gyeltsen
- Zhangton
- Drakpuk
- Chojé Lama
- Pelden Tsultrim
- Sharwa Yeshé Gyeltsen
- Ngorchen Kunga Zangpo
- Gugé Paṇchen
- Sonam Lhundrub . . .

Grant your blessing that we may apply the symbolic method
In accordance with the common and extraordinary examples,

And then, with all the winds of past actions in their entirety absorbed
In the great pathway of the central channel,
And relying on the short path of the messenger of the Great Seal, {23}
May we manifestly accomplish the rainbow body!

68. *The Central Channel Dependent on the Female Deity Vajravārāhī*

The progenitors of this lineage are the primordial buddha Mahāvajradhara and the female deity Vajravārāhī, who revealed this instruction directly to Nāropā Jñānasiddhi (1016–1100). His successors included the Newar Phamtingwa brothers Abhayakīrti and Vāgīśvara (fl. eleventh century). The practice was introduced to Tibet by Lokya Lotsāwa Sherab Tsekpa (fl. eleventh century) and thereafter transmitted through Mal Lotsāwa Lodro Drak (fl. eleventh century), Sachen Kunga Nyingpo (1092–1158), Sonam Tsemo (1142–1182), Drakpa Gyeltsen (1147–1216), and Sakya Paṇḍita Kunga Gyeltsen (1182–1251), after whom the line of transmission is identical to that of the foregoing lineage prayer of *The Central Channel Dependent on the Male Deity Cakrasaṃvara*.

The lineage prayer of *The Central Channel Dependent on the Female Deity Vajravārāhī* is as follows:

- Mahāvajradhara
- Vajravārāhī
- Nāropā
- Phamtingwa brothers
- Lokya Sherab Tsekpa
- Mal Lotsāwa Lodro Drak
- Sachen Kunga Nyingpo
- Sonam Tsemo
- Drakpa Gyeltsen
- Sakya Paṇḍita Kunga Gyeltsen, and so forth, as above.

Grant your blessing that, consequent on the generation stage
In which the blissful body is arrayed with the four empowerments [of Khecarī],
On the path of the messenger who reveals without attachment the path of the four delights,

We may accomplish the coalescence of the syllables E and VAṂ,
Which comprise within them the five syllables of great emptiness and the six syllables of the vital essence![35]

69. *The Five Stages according to Ghaṇṭāpāda*

The progenitors of this lineage are the primordial buddha Mahāvajradhara and the female deity Vajravārāhī, who revealed this instruction directly to Ghaṇṭāpāda. In India his successors included Kūrmapādā, Jālandharipā, Kṛṣṇacārin, Guhyavijaya, Tilopā (988–1069), and the Newar Phamtingwa Abhayakīrti (fl. eleventh century). The practice was introduced to Tibet by Mal Lotsāwa Lodro Drak (fl. eleventh century), and transmitted thereafter through the following Sakya and Bodongpa line: Sachen Kunga Nyingpo (1092–1158), Sonam Tsemo (1142–1182), Drakpa Gyeltsen (1147–1216), Sakya Paṇḍita Kunga Gyeltsen (1182–1251), Bodong Tsondru Dorjé (fl. twelfth–thirteenth centuries), Yangtsewa Rinchen Sengé (fl. thirteenth century), Tashi Zangpo, Khyung Lhepa Zhonu Sonam (fl. fourteenth century), Sharwa Yeshé Gyeltsen (ca. 1359–1406), Ngorchen Kunga Zangpo (1382–1456), Gugé Paṇchen Drakpa Gyeltsen (d. 1486), and Lowo Khenchen Sonam Lhundrub (fl. fifteenth–sixteenth centuries).

The lineage prayer of *The Five Stages according to Ghaṇṭāpāda* is as follows:

- Mahāvajradhara
- Vajravārāhī
- Ghaṇṭāpāda
- Kūrmapādā
- Jālandharipā
- Kṛṣṇacārin
- Guhyavijaya
- Tilopā
- Phamtingwa
- Mal Lotsāwa
- Sachen Kunga Nyingpo
- Sonam Tsemo
- Drakpa Gyeltsen
- Sakya Paṇḍita
- Tsondru Dorjé

- Yangtsewa Rinchen Sengé
- Tashi Zangpo
- Khyung Lhepa
- Sharwa
- Ngorchen
- Gugé Paṇchen
- Sonam Lhundrub . . .

Grant your blessing that we may accomplish the inconceivable realm,
Having excellently purified sense objects and mind in supreme bliss
Through the guidance on the path of the five stages that disclose blessings
And the refinement of the subtle vital essence, starting with
self-consecration!

70. *The Four Stages according to Kṛṣṇacārin*

The progenitors of this lineage are identical to those of the foregoing Five Stages according to Ghaṇṭāpāda. The Indian and Tibetan transmissions through to Sakya Paṇḍita Kunga Gyeltsen (1182–1251) are also identical. Thereafter the succession is through Chogyel Pakpa Lodro Gyeltsen (1235–1280), Zhangton Konchok Pel (fl. thirteenth century), Namza Drakpuk Sonam Pelwa (1277–1350), Pang Lotsāwa Lodro Tenpa (1276–1342), Pelden Tsultrim (1333–1399), Sharwa Yeshé Gyeltsen (ca. 1359–1406), Ngorchen Kunga Zangpo (1382–1456), Gugé Paṇchen Drakpa Gyeltsen (d. 1486), and Lowo Khenchen Sonam Lhundrub (fl. fifteenth–sixteenth centuries).

The lineage prayer of *The Four Stages according to Kṛṣṇacārin* is as above, from Mahāvajradhara up to Sakya Paṇḍita, and then:

- Chogyel Pakpa
- Zhangton
- Drakpuk
- Lodro Tenpa
- Pelden Tsultrim
- Sharwa
- Ngorchen
- Gugé Paṇchen
- Lowo Khenchen . . .

Grant your blessing that we may accomplish the fruitional stages of the path,
Through having refined the stage of the continuum
And cultivated the stage of mantra,
And through the arising of the stage of realized pristine cognition
And the completion of the crucial secret stage concerning subtle energy!

71. *The Guidance of White Cakrasaṃvara*

The progenitors of this lineage are the meditational deities Cakrasaṃvara and Vajrayoginī, who revealed this instruction directly to Śākyaśrī of Kashmir (1127–1225). He in turn introduced the practice to Tibet where it was maintained in the following line of transmission: Sakya Paṇḍita Kunga Gyeltsen (1182–1251), Yagdé Lotsāwa Sonam Sengé (fl. thirteenth century), Dremarwa Sangyé Yeshé (fl. thirteenth century), Gyawo Khenchen Sonam Drak (1280–1358), Drakpa Tsultrim (fl. thirteenth century), Jangsem Jadeng, Sabzang Mati Paṇchen Lodro Gyeltsen (1294–1376), Sabzang Pakpa Chok Zhonu Lodro (1358–1412/24), Ngorchen Kunga Zangpo (1382–1456), Sonam Wangchuk, Drungtsun Pelden Gyelpo, and Muchen Sangyé Rinchen (1450–1524). The last named taught Kunga Drolchok.

The lineage prayer of *White Cakrasaṃvara* is as follows:

- Cakrasaṃvara
- Vajrayoginī
- Śākyaśrī
- Sakya Paṇḍita
- Yagdé Lotsāwa
- Sangyé Yeshé
- Khenchen Sonam Drak
- Drakpa Tsultrim
- Jangsem Jadeng
- Sabzang
- Pakpa Chok {24}
- Kunga Zangpo
- Sonam Wangchuk
- Drungtsun Pelden Gyelpo
- Sangyé Rinchen . . .

Grant your blessing that we may realize the coemergent coalescence:
Through the yoga of the generation stage without grasping radiance and emptiness,
The yoga of the vital essence without grasping bliss and emptiness,
And the yoga of ultimate reality without grasping awareness and emptiness!

72. *The Four Adamantine Seats*

The progenitors of this lineage are the primordial buddha Mahāvajradhara and the female deity Kadalīmañjarī, who revealed the instruction directly to Marpa Lotsāwa Chokyi Lodro (1012–1097). Thereafter it was maintained in the following Ngok familial line of transmission: Ngokton Choku Dorjé (1036–1097), Ngok Zhedang Dorjé (fl. eleventh century), Gyeltsa Ramo, Ngok Tsa Choku Dorjé (b. 1246), Ngok Konchok Pel, Drenton Tadrel, Drenton Sherab Zangpo, Menlung Guru Sonam Pel (b. 1239), Menlung Kunkhyen, Tsultrim Gonpo, Ngokton Jangchub Pel, Ngok Tashi Peldrub, Bodhiśrī Ngok Jangchub Peldrub (1360–1446), Ngok Jangchub Drakpa (fl. fifteenth century), and Ngok Lodro Pelzangpo (fl. fifteenth–sixteenth centuries). The last named was a teacher of Kunga Drolchok.

The lineage prayer of *The Four Adamantine Seats* is as follows:

- Vajradhara
- Kadalīmañjarī
- Marpa Chokyi Lodro
- Ngokton Choku Dorjé
- Zhedang Dorjé
- Gyeltsa Ramo
- Ngok Tsa Choku
- Konchok Pel
- Drenton Tadrel
- Sherab Zangpo
- Menlung Guru
- Menlung Kunkhyen
- Tsultrim Gonpo
- Ngokton Jangchub Pel
- Tashi Peldrub

- Ngok Jangchub Peldrub
- Jangchub Drakpa
- Lodro Pelzangpo . . .

Grant your blessing that we may cultivate the thirteen syllables,
Starting with the application at the spleen and kidney cavities,
The meditative concentration of the "cow udder" [at the navel cakra]
The "awns of the plantain" [at the central channel],
And the "hoofprint of a bull" [at the heart cakra],
And that we may accomplish the space of yoga through meditative stability![36]

73. *The Great Magical Emanation*

The progenitors of this lineage are the primordial buddha Mahāvajradhara and the female deity Jñānaḍākinī, who revealed the instruction directly to Kukkurāja. His disciples included Marpa Lotsāwa Chokyi Lodro (1012–1097), who introduced the practice to Tibet. The latter's successors were Ngokton Choku Dorjé (1036–1097), Ngok Dodé (fl. eleventh–twelfth centuries), Ngok Kunga Dorjé (d. 1234), Ziji Drakpa, Rinchen Zangpo, Cho Gyelwa, Dondrub Pel, Ngokton Jangchub Pel, and Ngok Tashi Peldrub, Bodhiśrī Ngok Jangchub Peldrub (1360–1446), Ngok Jangchub Drakpa (fl. fifteenth century), and Ngok Lodro Pelzangpo (fl. fifteenth–sixteenth centuries). The last named taught Kunga Drolchok.

The lineage prayer of *The Great Magical Emanation* is as follows:

- Mahāvajradhara
- Jñānaḍākinī
- Kukkurāja
- Marpa Lotsāwa
- Choku Dorjé
- Dodé
- Kunga
- Ziji
- Rinchen Zangpo
- Cho Gyelwa
- Dondrub Pel
- Ngokton Jangchub Pel
- Tashi Peldrub, and so forth, as above.

Grant your blessing that we may accomplish the skillful means
Of the generation stage, liberated from delusion,
And the three phases of yoga that comprise
The paths of lower forms and of profound mantras,
Along with the Great Seal of conclusive attributes!

74. *The Kharamukha Cakrasaṃvara*

The progenitors of this lineage are the meditational deities Cakrasaṃvara and the female deity Vajravārāhī, who revealed the instruction directly to the paṇḍita Bhavyabodhi of Kathmandu. His successors were the Newars Jīvabodhi and Mahābodhi (fl. fifteenth century), the latter of whom introduced the practice in Tibet to Samten Ozer (fl. fifteenth century). Thereafter the short transmission is through Gugé Paṇchen Drakpa Gyeltsen (d. 1486) and Lowo Khenchen Sonam Lhundrub (fl. fifteenth–sixteenth centuries). The last named instructed Kunga Drolchok.

The lineage prayer of *The Kharamukha Cakrasaṃvara* is as follows:

- Cakrasaṃvara
- Vajravārāhī
- Bhavyabodhi
- Jīvabodhi
- Mahābodhi
- Samten Ozer
- Gugé Drakpa Gyeltsen
- Khenchen Sonam Lhundrub . . .

Grant your blessing that the buddha body of reality might arise, in the manner of space,
From the mirror in which the vital essence within the heart cakra appears,
Through the yoga of subtle vital essence that is without grasping
In respect of all the objects of the five sensory consciousnesses that appear! {25}

75. *The Six Meditations of Vajravārāhī*

The progenitor of this lineage is the female deity Vajrayoginī, who revealed the instruction directly to Lakṣmīkarā. Her successors in India included

Virūpa, Avadhūtipā (also known as Maitrīpā, ca. 986–1063 or 1007–1085), Samādhivajra (also known as Dondarwa), Jinadatta (also known as Sonyompa), Buddhadatta (also known as Sonyompa), and the Newar Hadu Karpo. The practice was introduced to Tibet by Chel Lotsāwa Kunga Dorjé, and thereafter transmitted in the following succession: Chel Lotsāwa Kunga Drakpa, Chel Lotsāwa Chokyi Zangpo (fl. twelfth century), Rongpa Ga Lotsāwa Namgyel Dorjé (1203–1282), Rongpa Sherab Sengé (1231–1315), Bagton Zhonu Tsultrim (fl. thirteenth century), Tsultrim Gyeltsen (fl. thirteenth–fourteenth centuries), Pelden Tsultrim (1333–1399), Sangyé Pel Buddhaśrī (1339–1420), Ngorchen Kunga Zangpo (1382–1456), Gugé Paṇchen Drakpa Gyeltsen (d. 1486), and Lowo Khenchen Sonam Lhundrub (fl. fifteenth–sixteenth centuries).

The lineage prayer of *The Six Meditations of Vajravārāhī* is as follows:

· Vajrayoginī
· Lakṣmīkarā
· Virūpa
· Avadhūtipā
· Dondarwa
· Jinadatta
· Buddhadatta
· Hadu Karpo
· Chel Lotsāwa Kunga Dorjé
· Kunga Drakpa
· Chokyi Zangpo
· Rongpa Ga Lotsāwa
· Sherab Sengé
· Bagton
· Tsultrim Gyeltsen
· Pelden Tsultrim
· Sangyé Pel
· Ngorchen Kunga
· Gugé Paṇchen
· Lowo Khenchen . . .

Grant your blessing that we may perfectly accomplish the six meditations—
The generation stage of meditation, the radiant appearance of the deity,

The mantra recitations, the essential application of the visualization of mantra letters,
The luminosity of the nature of mind, and the disposition of the Great Seal!

76. *The Six Doctrines of Nāropā*

The progenitor of this lineage is the primordial buddha Mahāvajradhara, who revealed the instruction directly to Tilopā (988–1069). The latter instructed Nāropā Jñānasiddhi (1016–1100), whose disciple Marpa Lotsāwa Chokyi Lodro (1012–1097) introduced the practice to Tibet. Thereafter the transmission passed through the Karma Kagyu lineage, as follows: Milarepa (1040–1112), Dakpo Lharjé Gampopa (1079–1153), Karmapa I Dusum Khyenpa (1110–1193), Sangyé Rechen Peldrak (1148–1218), Pomdrakpa Sonam Dorjé (1170–1249), Drubchen Karma Pakshi (1204–1283), Nyen Repa Gendun Bum (fl. thirteenth–fourteenth centuries), Karmapa III Rangjung Dorjé (1284–1339), Tokden Gonpo Gyeltsen, Karmapa IV Rolpei Dorjé (1340–1383), Zhamar II Khacho Wangpo (1350–1405), Karmapa V Dezhin Shekpa (1384–1415), Sok-on Kabzhipa Rikpei Reldri, Karmapa VI Tongwa Donden (1416–1453), Bengarwa Jampel Zangpo (fl. fifteenth century), Karmapa VII Chodrak Gyatso (1454–1506), and Kyapjé Tokden Trewo Chokyi Gyatso (d. 1547). The last named was a teacher of Kunga Drolchok.

The lineage prayer of *The Six Doctrines of Nāropā* is as follows:

- Mahāvajradhara
- Tilopā
- Nāropā
- Marpa
- Mila
- Dakpo
- Dusum Khyenpa
- Rechen
- Pomdrakpa
- Drubchen Karma
- Nyen Repa
- Rangjung
- Gonpo Gyeltsen

- Rolpei Dorjé
- Khacho Wangpo
- Dezhin Shekpa
- Sok-on Rikpei Reldri
- Tongwa Donden
- Jampel Zangpo
- Chodrak Gyatso
- Kyapjé Tokden Trewo Chokyi Gyatso . . .

Grant your blessing that we may perfectly realize the path of the six doctrines—
The blissful warmth of the fierce inner heat, the definitive realization of illusory body,
And the refinement of dreams, luminosity,
consciousness transference, and the intermediate state;
And may we then attain the accomplishment of Vajradhara!

77. *The Six Doctrines of Nigumā*

The progenitor of this lineage is the primordial buddha Mahāvajradhara, who revealed the instruction directly to the ḍākinī Nigumā. The subsequent line of transmission through the Shangpa Kagyu tradition in Tibet is as follows: Khyungpo Neljor (990–1127), Mokchokpa Rinchen Tsondru (1110–1170), Kyergangpa Chokyi Sengé (1154–1217), Nyenton Chokyi Sherab (1175–1255), Sangyé Tonpa Tsondru Sengé (1207–1278), Tsangma Shangton (1234–1309), Khyungpo Tsultrim Gonpo (fl. thirteenth century), Jadrel Ritro Rechen (fl. fourteenth century), Shangkarwa Rinchen Gyeltsen (1353–1434), Kunglung Sangyé Pelzangpo (1398–1465), Drubchen Namka Gyeltsen (fl. fourteenth–fifteenth centuries), and Gyagom Lekpei Gyeltsen (fl. fifteenth–sixteenth centuries). The last mentioned taught Kunga Drolchok.

The lineage prayer of *The Six Doctrines of Nigumā* is as follows:

- Mahāvajradhara
- Ḍākinī Nigumā
- Khyungpo Neljor
- Mokchokpa
- Kyergangpa

- Nyenton
- Sangyé Tonpa
- Shangton
- Khyungpo Tsultrim Gonpo
- Ritro Rechen
- Shangkarwa Rinchen Gyeltsen
- Kunglung Sangyé Pel {26}
- Namka Gyeltsen
- Gyagom Lekpei Gyeltsen . . .

Grant your blessing that we may excellently complete the blissful warmth of the fierce inner heat,
The natural experiences of the illusory body, and dream yoga,
And that luminosity might effortlessly arise,
That excellent realization will come without consciousness transference,
And that in the first phase of the intermediate state
Our own mind might arise as the buddha body of reality!

78. *The Amulet Tradition of the Great Seal*

This lineage is identical to that of *The Six Doctrines of Nigumā*.

The lineage prayer of *The Amulet Tradition of the Great Seal* is as follows:

- Mahāvajradhara
- Ḍākinī Nigumā
- Khyungpo Neljor
- Mokchokpa
- Kyergangpa
- Nyenton
- Sangyé Tonpa
- Shangton
- Khyungpo Tsultrim Gonpo
- Ritro Rechen
- Shangkarwa Rinchen Gyeltsen
- Kunglung Sangyé Pel
- Namka Gyeltsen
- Gyagom Lekpei Gyeltsen . . .

Grant your blessing that by refining the three natural states according to the preliminary practices
And experientially cultivating freedom from the four defects according to the main practice,
We may realize the abiding nature of the Great Seal,
Naturally arising and spontaneously present as the four perfected buddha bodies!

79. *The Three Aspects Carried on the Path*

This lineage is identical to that of *The Six Doctrines of Nigumā*.

The lineage prayer of *The Three Aspects Carried on the Path* is as follows:

- Mahāvajradhara
- Ḍākinī Nigumā
- Khyungpo Neljor
- Mokchokpa
- Kyergangpa
- Nyenton
- Sangyé Tonpa
- Shangton
- Khyungpo Tsultrim Gonpo
- Ritro Rechen
- Shangkarwa Rinchen Gyeltsen
- Kunglung Sangyé Pel
- Namka Gyeltsen
- Gyagom Lekpei Gyeltsen . . .

Grant your blessing that we may carry all diverse appearances in all modes of conduct
On the path of the guru, meditational deity, and magical display,
And that signs and concepts may then be liberated right where they are,
Through the crucial nongrasping of the nature of mind and luminosity!

80. *The Deathlessness of One's Own Mind*

This lineage is identical to that of *The Six Doctrines of Nigumā*.

The lineage prayer of *The Deathlessness of One's Own Mind* is as follows:

- Mahāvajradhara
- Ḍākinī Nigumā
- Khyungpo Neljor
- Mokchokpa
- Kyergangpa
- Nyenton
- Sangyé Tonpa
- Shangton
- Khyungpo Tsultrim Gonpo
- Ritro Rechen
- Shangkarwa Rinchen Gyeltsen
- Kunglung Sangyé Pel
- Namka Gyeltsen
- Gyagom Lekpei Gyeltsen . . .

Grant your blessing that we may abandon all stains of mentally fabricated effort
And that our own minds may realize deathlessness—
The body of the deity that appears though lacking inherent existence,
Where the attachment that apprehends ordinary appearances is naturally pure!

81. *The Six Doctrines of Sukhasiddhi*

The progenitors of this lineage are the primordial buddha Mahāvajradhara and the female deity Nairātmyā, who revealed the instruction directly to Virūpa. The latter's disciple Sukhasiddhi instructed Khyungpo Neljor (990–1127), after whom the line of transmission primarily follows the Shangpa tradition through Mokchokpa Rinchen Tsondru (1110–1170), Kyergangpa Chokyi Sengé (1154–1217), Nyenton Chokyi Sherab (1175–1255), Sangyé Tonpa Tsondru Sengé (1207–1278), Tsangma Shangton (1234–1309), Shangpa Rikpei Dorjé (fl. thirteenth century), Zhuton Tsultrim Gon (fl. thirteenth–fourteenth centuries), Chopel Zangpo (fl. fourteenth century), Tsultrim Gyeltsen (fl. fourteenth–fifteenth centuries), Khyenrab Chojé Rinchen Chokdrub Pelzang (1436–1497), and Changlungpa Zhonu Chodrub (fl. fifteenth–sixteenth centuries). The last named taught Kunga Drolchok.

The lineage prayer of *The Six Doctrines of Sukhasiddhi* is as follows:

- Vajradhara
- Nairātmyā
- Virūpa
- Sukhasiddhi
- Khyungpo Neljor
- Mokchokpa
- Kyergangpa
- Chokyi Sherab
- Tsondru Sengé
- Shangton
- Rikpei Dorjé
- Zhuton Tsultrim Gon
- Chopel Zangpo
- Tsultrim Gyeltsen
- Khyenrab Chojé
- Zhonu Chodrub . . .

Grant your blessing that by experientially cultivating the six doctrines,
Retaining the four [syllables] of the fierce inner heat,[37]
Excellently refining the illusory body, mastering dream yoga,
And actualizing luminosity, along with consciousness transference and the intermediate state,
We may then accomplish conclusive buddhahood!

82. *The Lineage of the Emanational Navel Cakra*[38]

The progenitors of this lineage are the primordial buddha Mahāvajradhara and the female deity Nairātmyā, who revealed the instruction directly to Sukhasiddhi. The latter taught Āryadeva, after whom the line of transmission in Tibet primarily passed through the Shangpa tradition, as follows: Khyungpo Neljor (990–1127), Mokchokpa Rinchen Tsondru (1110–1170), Kyergangpa Chokyi Sengé (1154–1217), Nyenton Chokyi Sherab (1175–1255), Sangyé Tonpa Tsondru Sengé (1207–1278), Tsangma Shangton (1234–1309), Shangpa Rikpei Dorjé (fl. thirteenth century), Khyungpo Tsultrim Gonpo (fl. thirteenth century), Jadrel Ritro Rechen (fl. fourteenth century), Shangkarwa Rinchen Gyeltsen (1353–1434), Kunglung Sangyé Pelzangpo (1398–1465), Drubchen Namka Gyeltsen, and Gyagom Lekpei Gyeltsen (fl. fifteenth–sixteenth centuries). The last named taught Kunga Drolchok.

The lineage prayer of *The Lineage of the Emanational Navel Cakra* is as follows:

- Vajradhara
- Nairātmyā
- Sukhasiddhi
- Āryadeva
- Khyungpo Neljor
- Mokchokpa
- Kyergangpa
- Nyenton {27}
- Sangyé Tonpa
- Tsangma Shangton
- Tsultrim Gonpo
- Ritro Rechen
- Shangkarwa Rinchen Gyeltsen
- Sangyé Pelzangpo
- Namka Gyeltsen
- Gyagom Lekpei Gyeltsen . . .

Grant your blessing that the springtime rains of experiential cultivation
Of the channels, winds, and vital essences,
In the field of the yogic exercises of the navel cakra within one's own body,
Might ripen the fruits of inexhaustible supreme bliss
And that we may attain the threefold accomplishment!

83. *The Coemergent Union of the Great Seal*

The progenitor of this lineage is the primordial buddha Mahāvajradhara, who revealed the instruction directly to Tilopā (988–1069). The latter instructed Nāropā Jñānasiddhi (1016–1100), whose disciple Marpa Lotsāwa Chokyi Lodro (1012–1097) introduced the practice to Tibet. Thereafter the transmission passed through the Drukpa Kagyu lineage, as follows: Milarepa (1040–1112), Dakpo Lharjé Gampopa (1079–1153), Pagmodrupa Dorjé Gyelpo (1110–1170), Ling Repa Pema Dorjé (1128–1188), Tsangpa Gyaré Yeshé Dorjé (1161–1211), Gotsangpa Gonpo Dorjé (1189–1258), Yangonpa Gyeltsen Pel (1213–1258), Chen Ngawa Rinchen Den (b. 1202), Zurpukpa

Rinchen Pelzang (b. 1263), Sherab Bumpa (fl. thirteenth–fourteenth centuries), Gyelsé Tokmé Zangpo (1295–1369), Nyen Repa Gendun Bum (fl. fourteenth–fifteenth centuries), Drukchen II Gyelwang Kunga Peljor (1428–1476), and Drukchen Ngawang Chokyi Gyelpo (1465–1540). The last named was a teacher of Kunga Drolchok.

The lineage prayer of *The Coemergent Union of the Great Seal* is as follows:

- Vajradhara
- Tilopā
- Nāropā
- Marpa
- Mila
- Dakpo
- Pagmodrupa
- Ling Repa
- Gyaré
- Gotsangpa
- Yangonpa
- Chen Nga
- Zurpukpa
- Sherab Bum
- Gyelsé Tokmé Zangpo
- Nyen Repa
- Gyelwang
- Ngawang Chokyi Gyelpo . . .

Grant your blessing that we may ourselves recognize coemergence—
The buddha body of reality coemergent with the nature of mind,
The light of phenomena coemergent with appearances,
And [coalescent] bliss and emptiness coemergent with indivisible
appearances and mind!

84. *The Fivefold Great Seal*

The progenitor of this lineage is the primordial buddha Mahāvajradhara, who revealed the instruction directly to Tilopā (988–1069). The latter taught Nāropā Jñānasiddhi (1016–1100), whose disciple Marpa Lotsāwa Chokyi Lodro (1012–1097) introduced the practice to Tibet. Thereafter the transmission passed primarily through the Drigung Kagyu lineage, as follows: Milarepa (1040–1112), Dakpo Lharjé Gampopa (1079–1153), Pagmodrupa Dorjé Gyelpo (1110–1170), Drigungpa I Jigten Sumgon (1143–1217), Drigungpa III Sonam Drakpa (1187–1234), Drigungpa V Telo Dorjé Drak (1210–1278), Drigungpa VI Tok Khawa Rinchen Sengé (1226–1284), Drigungpa VII Tsamché Drakpa Sonam (1238–1286), Drigungpa IX Chunyipa Dorjé Rinchen (1278–1314), Drigungpa X Nyergyepa Dorjé Gyelpo (1283–1350), Menpa Gomchen (fl. fourteenth century), Lapchiwa Dokton Namka Gyeltsen (fl. fourteenth–fifteenth centuries), Dulwadzinpa Ngagi Wangpo (fl. fourteenth–fifteenth centuries), Taklung Ngawang Drakpa (1418–1496), Śākya Chokden (1428–1507), and Changlungpa Zhonu Chodrub (fl. fifteenth–sixteenth centuries).

The lineage prayer of *The Fivefold Great Seal* is as follows:

· Vajradhara
· Tilopā
· Nāropā
· Marpa
· Mila
· Dakpo
· Pagmodrupa
· Jigten Sumgon
· Sonam Drakpa
· Dorjé Drak
· Tok
· Tsamché
· Chunyipa
· Nyergyepa
· Menpa Gomchen
· Lapchiwa
· Dulwadzinpa
· Ngawang Drakpa
· Śākya Chokden
· Changlungpa . . .

Grant your blessing that we may definitively realize the unique enlightened intention—
The experiential cultivations combining five aspects:

The ultimate enlightened mind, [visualizing] the deity's body with one's own face,[39]
Devotion to the teacher, the Great Seal,
And the inherent dedication of merit!

85. *The Four Syllables of the Great Seal*

The progenitors of this lineage are the primordial buddha Mahāvajradhara and the bodhisattva Vajragarbha, who revealed the instruction directly to Tilopā (988–1069). The latter taught Nāropā Jñānasiddhi (1016–1100), whose disciple Marpa Lotsāwa Chokyi Lodro (1012–1100) introduced the practice to Tibet. Thereafter the transmission passed primarily through the Pagdru Kagyu lineage, as follows: Milarepa (1040–1112), Dakpo Lharjé Gampopa (1079–1153), Pagmodrupa Dorjé Gyelpo (1110–1170), Kyergom Zhikpo Tsultrim Sengé (ca. 1144–1204), Serdingpa Zhonu O (fl. twelfth–thirteenth centuries), Gedingpa Choku Ozer (fl. twelfth–thirteenth centuries), Kunpang Tukjé Tsondru (1243–1313), Jangsem Gyelwa Yeshé (1247–1320), Lodro Zangpo (fl. thirteenth–fourteenth centuries), Menpa Gomchen Tsultrim Zangpo (fl. fourteenth century), Lapchiwa Dokton Namka Gyeltsen (fl. fourteenth–fifteenth centuries), Dulwadzinpa Ngawang Gyeltsen (fl. fourteenth–fifteenth centuries), Taklung Ngawang Drakpa (1418–1496), Zilung Paṇchen Śākya Chokden (1428–1507), and Changlungpa Zhonu Chodrub (fl. fifteenth–sixteenth centuries).

The lineage prayer of *The Four Syllables of the Great Seal* is as follows:

- Vajradhara
- Vajragarbha
- Tilopā
- Nāropā
- Marpa
- Mila
- Dakpo
- Pagmodrupa
- Kyergom Zhikpo
- Zhonu O
- Choku Ozer
- Tukjé Tsondru
- Gyelwa Yeshé

- Lodro Zangpo
- Menpa Gomchen
- Lapchiwa
- Dulwadzinpa
- Ngawang Drakpa
- Zilung Paṇchen
- Zhonu Chodrub, and so forth.[40] {28}

Grant your blessing that we may realize the Great Seal of the abiding nature,
Firstly, by determining the fundamental basis of the mind,
Then by the methods that establish [the view]
And protecting it from the abyss of deviation,
And, finally, by the crucial practice of carrying the nature of mind on the path!

86. *The Introduction to the Three Buddha Bodies*

The progenitors of this lineage are the primordial buddha Mahāvajradhara and the bodhisattva Matiratna, who revealed the instruction directly to Śabaripā. The latter's disciple Maitrīpā (ca. 986–1063 or 1007–1085) taught Tepuwa Pārvātapāda, and thereafter the transmission follows the Karma Kagyu line through Karma Pakshi (1204–1283), Orgyanpa Rinchen Pel (1229–1309), Karmapa III Rangjung Dorjé (1284–1339), Yungtonpa Dorjé Pel (1284–1365), Karmapa IV Rolpei Dorjé (1340–1383), Zhamar II Khacho Wangpo (1350–1405), Karmapa V Dezhin Shekpa (1384–1415), Sok-on Kabzhipa Rikpei Reldri, Karmapa VI Tongwa Donden (1416–1453), Bengarwa Jampel Zangpo (fl. fifteenth century), Karmapa VII Chodrak Gyatso (1454–1506), and Karma Trinlepa (1456–1539). The last mentioned taught Kunga Drolchok.

The lineage prayer of *The Introduction to the Three Buddha Bodies* is as follows:

- Vajradhara
- Matiratna
- Śabaripā
- Maitrīpā
- Tepuwa

- Karma Pakshi
- Orgyan
- Rangjung
- Yungtonpa
- Rolpei Dorjé
- Khacho Wangpo
- Dezhin Shekpa
- Sok-on Rikpei Reldri
- Tongwa Donden
- Jampel Zangpo
- Chodrak Gyatso
- Karma Trinlepa . . .

Grant your blessing that we may establish ourselves and others in bliss,
Having reached the depths of definitive realization of the essential points
Of the introduction to the nature of the three buddha bodies,
Just as they appeared [to Tilopā] in the upper, lower, and middle reaches of Pullahari!

87. *The Indivisibility of Subtle Energy and Mind*

The progenitors of this lineage are the primordial buddha Mahāvajradhara and the female deity Vajravārāhī, who revealed the instruction directly to Nāropā Jñānasiddhi (1016–1100). The practice was introduced to Tibet by his disciple Marpa Lotsāwa Chokyi Lodro (1012–1097), and thereafter it was transmitted through the following Karma Kagyu line: Milarepa (1040–1112), Dakpo Lharjé Gampopa (1079–1153), Karmapa I Dusum Khyenpa (1110–1193), Drogon Pagmodrupa Dorjé Gyelpo (1110–1170), Sangyé Rechen Peldrak (1148–1218), Gyelsé Pomdrakpa Sonam Dorjé (1170–1249), Karmapa II Karma Pakshi (1204–1283), Nyen Repa Gendun Bum (fl. thirteenth–fourteenth centuries), Karmapa III Rangjung Dorjé (1284–1339), Tokden Gonpo Gyeltsen, Karmapa IV Rolpei Dorjé (1340–1383), Yorpa Yeshé Pelwa (fl. fourteenth–fifteenth centuries), Tsurpu Jamyang Dondrub Ozer (fl. fifteenth century), and Tokden Trewo Chokyi Gyatso (d. 1547). The last named taught Kunga Drolchok.

The lineage prayer of *The Indivisibility of Subtle Energy and Mind* is as follows:

- Mahāvajradhara
- Vajravārāhī
- Nāropā
- Marpa
- Mila
- Dakpo
- Dusum Khyenpa
- Drogon
- Rechen
- Gyelsé Pomdrakpa
- Karma Pakshi
- Nyen Repa
- Rangjung Dorjé
- Gonpo Gyeltsen
- Rolpei Dorjé
- Yeshé Pelwa
- Tsurpu Jamyang
- Kyapjé Tokden Trewo Chokyi Gyatso . . .

Grant your blessing that we may accomplish the particular profundities of the instructions:
Through coemergence, which is the particular profundity of the generation stage;
Through the essential indivisibility of subtle energy and mind,
Which is the particular profundity of the perfection stage;
And through the swift ease of the generation and perfection stages,
Which is the particular profundity of experiential cultivation!

88. *The Six Doctrines according to the Sekharma Tradition*

The progenitor of this lineage is the primordial buddha Mahāvajradhara, who revealed the instruction directly to Tilopā (988–1069). The latter taught Nāropā Jñānasiddhi (1016–1100), whose disciple Marpa Lotsāwa Chokyi Lodro (1012–1100) introduced the practice to Tibet, handing it down to his own son, Dodé Bum (fl. twelfth century), who concealed it as treasure. The text was later discovered as a spiritual revelation at Sekhar

Gutok by Guru Chokyi Wangchuk (1212–1270) and transmitted in the following succession within the Lhodrak area: Lha Rinchen Wangyal (fl. thirteenth century), Rutsam Gomchen, Kyipukpa Tsultrim Dargyé, Olgom Janglingpa, Sangyé On Drakpa Pel (1251–1296), Rinchen Chung, Kabzhipa Drakpa Zhonu (1257–1315), Rinchen Gyeltsen, Khenchen Sengé Pel, Ngokton Jangchub Pel, Ngok Tashi Peldrub, Ngok Jangchub Peldrub (1360–1446), Ngok Jangchub Drakpa (fl. fifteenth century), and Ngok Lodro Pelzangpo (fl. fifteenth–sixteenth centuries). The last named was a teacher of Kunga Drolchok.

The lineage prayer of *The Six Doctrines according to the Sekharma Tradition* is as follows:

- Mahāvajradhara
- Tilopā
- Nāropā
- Marpa
- Dodé Bum
- Guru Chokyi Wangchuk
- Rinchen Wangyal
- Rutsam Gomchen
- Kyipukpa
- Olgom Janglingpa
- Sangyé On
- Rinchen Chung
- Kabzhipa
- Rinchen Gyeltsen
- Khenchen Sengé Pel
- Ngokton Jangchub Pel
- Tashi Peldrub
- Jangchub Peldrub
- Jangchub Drakpa
- Lodro Pelzangpo . . .

Grant your blessing that we may definitively perfect unimpeded
experiential cultivation
Through this nectar of supreme buddha speech,
The aspiration of the entrustment seal [of Guru Chowang],[41] {29}

And then acquire certainty in the marvelous and auspicious
Enlightened intention of Marpa—father and son!

89. *The Mingling and Transformation of the Three Poisons*

The progenitor of this lineage is the primordial buddha Mahāvajradhara, who revealed the instruction directly to Nāgārjuna. The Indian succession is through Āryadeva, Tilopā (988–1069), and Nāropā Jñānasiddhi (1016–1100). The practice was introduced to Tibet by Ngok Choku Dorjé (1036–1097) and transmitted through the Ngok familial line as follows: Ngok Zhedang Dorjé (fl. eleventh century), Ngok Kunga Dorjé (d. 1234), Ziji Drakpa, Rinchen Zangpo, Chokyi Gyeltsen, Dondrub Pel, Ngokton Jangchub Pel, Ngok Tashi Peldrub, Ngok Jangchub Peldrub (1360–1446), Ngok Jangchub Drakpa (fl. fifteenth century), and Ngok Lodro Pelzangpo (fl. fifteenth–sixteenth centuries). The last mentioned taught Kunga Drolchok.

The lineage prayer of *The Mingling and Transformation of the Three Poisons* is as follows:

- Mahāvajradhara
- Nāgārjuna
- Āryadeva
- Tilopā
- Nāropā
- Ngok Choku Dorjé
- Zhedang Dorjé
- Kunga
- Ziji Drakpa
- Rinchen Zangpo
- Chokyi Gyeltsen
- Dondrub Pel
- Jangchub Pel
- Tashi Peldrub
- Jangchub Peldrub
- Jangchub Drakpa
- Lodro Pelzangpo . . .

Grant your blessing that we may accomplish medicinal nectar,
Transforming base metal into gold through experiential cultivation of
Secret Mantra
That mingles and transforms the three poisons,
Connecting the following poisons with the path:
Attachment with the practice of the fierce inner heat,
Hatred with the practice of the illusory body,
And delusion with the practice of luminosity!

90. *The Four Scrolls of the Aural Instructions*

The progenitors of this lineage are the primordial buddha Mahāvajradhara and the female deity Asthikhaṇḍaḍākinī, who revealed the instruction directly to Pendhapā. The practice was introduced to Tibet by Marpa Lotsāwa Chokyi Lodro (1012–1100) and thereafter transmitted through the following succession: Tsurton Wang-gi Dorjé (fl. eleventh century), Nyag-gom Marpo, Dungtsé Nyimalung, Gar Repa, Rok Tselha Gangpa, Nyemdo Kunga Dondrub (b. 1268), Yungtonpa Dorjé Pel (1284–1365), Lachen Sonam Zangpo, Tsultrim Gonpo, Sonam Gyeltsen, Nyakpu Sengé Pelwa, Ngokton Jangchub Pel, Ngok Tashi Peldrub, Ngok Jangchub Peldrub (1360–1446), Ngok Jangchub Drakpa (fl. fifteenth century), and Ngok Lodro Pelzangpo (fl. fifteenth–sixteenth centuries).

The lineage prayer of *The Four Scrolls of the Aural Instructions* is as follows:

- Mahāvajradhara
- Asthikhaṇḍaḍākinī
- Pendhapā
- Marpa
- Tsurton Wang-gi Dorjé
- Nyag-gom Marpo
- Dungtsé Nyimalung
- Gar Repa
- Tse Gangpa
- Nyemdo
- Yungtonpa
- Lachen Sonam Zangpo
- Tsultrim Gonpo
- Sonam Gyeltsen

- Nyakpu Sengé Pelwa
- Jangchub Pel
- Tashi Peldrub
- Jangchub Peldrub
- Jangchub Drakpa
- Lodro Pelzangpo . . .

Grant your blessing that we may attain buddhahood in a single lifetime,
Through diligent cultivation, maintaining commitments
In accordance with the scrolls of aural instruction,
Which are extracts of four tantras—
Four Adamantine Seats, *Great Magical Emanation*, *Secret Assembly*, and *Hevajra*!

91. *The Six Doctrines of Liberation through the Upper Gate according to the Aural Lineage*

The progenitors of this lineage are the primordial buddha Mahāvajradhara and the female deity Vajrayoginī, who revealed the instruction directly to Tilopā (988–1069). The latter instructed Nāropā Jñānasiddhi (1016–1100), whose disciple Marpa Lotsāwa Chokyi Lodro (1012–1097) introduced the practice to Tibet. Thereafter the transmission was as follows: Milarepa (1040–1112), Rechungpa Dorjé Drak (1085–1161), Khyungtsang Yeshé Lama (1115–1176), Machik Angjo (fl. twelfth–thirteenth centuries), Zhang Lotsāwa Jangchub-o (b. 1237), Drogon Dharaśrī (fl. thirteenth century), Jangsem Sonam Gyeltsen (fl. fourteenth century), Kunden Repa (fl. fourteenth century), Khetsun Ziji Gyeltsen (fl. fourteenth century), Rinchen Gyatso, Lopon Chodrak, Jangchub Zangpo, Rabjor Sengé, Chodrub Sengé, and Lotsāwa Rinchen Zangpo (1489–1563).

The lineage prayer of *The Six Doctrines of Liberation through the Upper Gate according to the Aural Lineage* is as follows:

- Mahāvajradhara
- Vajrayoginī
- Tilopā
- Nāropā
- Marpa
- Mila

- Rechung Dorjé Drak
- Khyungtsang Yeshé Lama
- Machik Angjo
- Zhang Lotsāwa Jangchub-o
- Drogon Dhara
- Jangsem Sonam Gyeltsen
- Kunden Repa
- Ziji Gyeltsen
- Rinchen Gyatso
- Lopon Chodrakpa
- Jangchub Zangpo {30}
- Rabjor Sengé
- Chodrub Sengé
- Lotsāwa Rinchen Zangpo . . .

Grant your blessing that the teaching of Secret Mantra may flourish
Through the tradition of the auspicious and marvelous path—
Comprising the six doctrines that confer liberation according to the upper gate
And the secret pathway of the ḍākinī of supreme bliss according to the lower gate!

92. *The Doctrinal Cycle of Nirdehaḍākinī*

The progenitors of this lineage are the primordial buddha Mahāvajradhara and the female deity Nirdehaḍākinī, who revealed the instruction directly to Tilopā (988–1069). The latter instructed Nāropā Jñānasiddhi (1016–1100), whose disciple Vimalamitra introduced the practice to Rechungpa Dorjé Drak (1085–1161). Thereafter the lineage is identical to that of the foregoing *Six Doctrines of the Upper Gate.*

The lineage prayer of *The Nine Doctrinal Cycles of Nirdehaḍākinī* is as follows:

- Mahāvajradhara
- Nirdehaḍākinī
- Tilopā
- Nāropā

- Vimalamitra
- Rechung Dorjé Drak
- Khyungtsang Yeshé Lama
- Machik Angjo
- Zhang Lotsāwa Jangchub-o
- Drogon Dhara
- Jangsem Sonam Gyeltsen
- Kunden Repa
- Ziji Gyeltsen
- Rinchen Gyatso
- Lopon Chodrakpa
- Jangchub Zangpo
- Rabjor Sengé
- Chodrub Sengé
- Lotsāwa Rinchen Zangpo . . .

Grant your blessing that the treasury of instructions of Secret Mantra,
Integrating mother and child, may never decline,
In the manner of the austerities adopted by the unique disciple Rechungpa
That satisfied the enlightened intention of his teacher
With the five additional instructions of Nirdehaḍākinī!

93. *The Elaborate Guidance according to Zhang Tselpa*

The progenitors of this lineage are the primordial buddha Mahāvajradhara and the four definitive presences of Cakrasaṃvara, Vārāhī, Tārā, and Śākyamuni. The transmission was received directly by Dakpo Gomtsul Nyingpo (1116–1169), and thereafter handed down through the Tselpa succession as follows: Pelchen Ga Lotsāwa Zhonu Pel (fl. twelfth century), Malton Yerpawa (fl. twelfth century), Vairocanabhadra (also known as Ngulchu Bairo, fl. twelfth century), Lama Zhang Tselpa Tsondru Drak (1123–1193), Śākya Yeshé, Sangyé Nyingpo (d. 1237), Sangyé Zhonu (d. 1260), Serkhang Tengpa Kunga Gyeltsen (1223–1292), Sangyé Rinchen (1247–1301), Śākya Bumpa (1263–1310), Śākya Sonam, Onpo Chozang, Drakton Donchok, Sonam Drubpa, Drakpa, Lama Tokdenpa, Lhundrub Dechen Rabjampa, and Ngawang Tulku of Taklung (fl. fifteenth–sixteenth centuries). The last named was a teacher of Kunga Drolchok.

The lineage prayer of *The Elaborate Guidance according to Zhang Tselpa* is as follows:

- Vajradhara—from whose distinctive lineage traditions there are:
- Four Definitive Presences [of Cakrasaṃvara, Vārāhī, Tārā, and Śākyamuni]
- Dakpo Gomtsul
- Pelchen Ga Lotsāwa
- Malton Yerpawa
- Ngulchu Bairo
- Tselpa Tsondru Drak
- Śākya Yeshé
- Sangyé Nyingpo
- Sangyé Zhonu
- Ser Tengpa
- Sangyé Rinchen
- Śākya Bumpa
- Śākya Sonam
- Chozang
- Drakton
- Sonam Drubpa
- Drakpa
- Tokdenpa
- Lhundrub Dechen
- Ngawang Tulku . . .

Grant your blessing that we may be free of hesitation, anger, or lust
In respect of the most secret wondrous approaches of the sacred doctrine
That cause the host of unfortunate, fox-like cowards to tremble
At the lion's roar of the elaborate realization of Zhang Tselpa!

94. *The Six-Branch Yoga according to Pelchen Ga Lotsāwa*

The progenitor of this lineage is the meditational deity Kālacakra, who revealed the instruction directly to Tsami Sangyé Drak (fl. eleventh century). The line of transmission that followed included Abhayākaragupta (fl. eleventh–twelfth centuries), Pelchen Ga Lotsāwa Namgyel Dorjé (fl.

twelfth century), Zhang Tselpa Tsondru Drak (1123–1193), Rechen Ronyompa, Rechen Lhundrubpa, Yangonpa Gyeltsen Pel (1213–1258), Chen Ngawa Rinchen Den (b. 1202), Zurpukpa Rinchen Pelzang (b. 1263), Barawa Gyeltsen Pelzang (1310–1391), Pago Jamyang Chojé, Kundar Rema, Ngok Drakpa Peljor, Rinchen Chodar, and Paṇchen Donyo Sengé (fl. fifteenth–sixteenth centuries). The last named was a teacher of Kunga Drolchok.

The lineage prayer of *The Six-Branch Yoga according to Pelchen Ga Lotsāwa* is as follows:

- Kālacakra
- Tsami Sangyé Drak
- Abhaya
- Pelchen Ga Lotsāwa
- Lama Zhang
- Ronyompa[42]
- Lhundrubpa
- Yangonpa
- Chen Ngawa
- Zurpukpa
- Gyeltsen Pelzang
- Jamyang Chojé
- Kundar Rema
- Drakpa Peljor
- Rinchen Chodar
- Amoghasiṃha {31}

Grant your blessing concerning the precious forceful method of the six-branch yoga,
That those of subtle vision might rely on the main path
Among the paths of supreme accomplishment
And, over seven days, refine the channels and winds of "melting bliss"
Through the fire and light of the fierce inner heat within the body!

95. *The Cycle of Pagmodru Densatel*

The progenitor of this lineage is the primordial buddha Mahāvajradhara, who revealed the instruction directly to Tilopā (988–1069). The latter taught Nāropā Jñānasiddhi (1016–1100), whose disciple Marpa Lotsāwa

Chokyi Lodro (1012–1100) introduced the practice to Tibet. Thereafter the transmission passed primarily through the Drigung Kagyu lineage, as follows: Milarepa (1040–1112), Dakpo Lharjé Gampopa (1079–1153), Pagmodrupa Dorjé Gyelpo (1110–1170), Drigungpa I Jigten Sumgon (1143–1217), Drigungpa IV Chen Nga Drakpa Jungné (1175–1255), Rinchen Dorjé, Drakpa Gyeltsen, Rinchen Gyeltsen, Drakpa Zhonu, Sonam Gyeltsenpa, and Changlungpa Zhonu Chodrub (fl. fifteenth–sixteenth centuries). The lineage prayer of *The Cycle of Pagmodru Densatel* is as follows:

- Mahāvajradhara
- Tilopā
- Nāropā
- Marpa
- Mila
- Dakpo
- Dorjé Gyelpo
- Jigten Sumgon
- Chen Nga Drakpa Jungné
- Rinchen Dorjé
- Drakpa Gyeltsen
- Rinchen Gyeltsen
- Drakpa Zhonu
- Sonam Gyeltsenpa
- Zhonu Chodrub . . .

Grant your blessing that we may open the storeroom of most secret instruction
With the miraculous key of Pagmodrupa's symbolic empowerment
And uphold the victory banner of attainment—
The gemstone crest of experiential cultivation of the six doctrines and the Great Seal!

96. *The Unique Enlightened Intention according to the Cycle of Drigung*

The progenitor of this lineage is the primordial buddha Mahāvajradhara, who revealed the instruction directly to Tilopā (988–1069). The latter taught Nāropā Jñānasiddhi (1016–1100), whose disciple Marpa Lotsāwa Chokyi Lodro (1012–1100) introduced the practice to Tibet. Thereafter the transmission passed primarily through the Drigung Kagyu lineage, as follows: Milarepa (1040–1112), Dakpo Lharjé Gampopa (1079–1153), Pagmodrupa Dorjé Gyelpo (1110–1170), Drigungpa I Jigten Sumgon (1143–1217), Drigungpa III Sonam Drakpa (1187–1234), Drigungpa V Telo Dorjé Drak (1210–1278), Drigungpa VI Tok Khawa Rinchen Sengé (1226–1284), Drigungpa VII Tsamché Drakpa Sonam (1238–1286), Drigungpa IX Chunyipa Dorjé Rinchen (1278–1314), Drigungpa X Nyergyepa Dorjé Gyelpo (1283–1350), Chen Nga Chokyi Gyelpo (1335–1407), Menpa Gomchen (fl. fourteenth century), Lapchiwa Dokton Namka Gyeltsen (fl. fourteenth–fifteenth centuries), Dulwadzinpa Ngagi Wangpo (fl. fourteenth–fifteenth centuries), Drukpa Ngawang Chogyel (1465–1540), Taklung Tulku Namgyel Tashi (1524–1563). The last named was a teacher of Kunga Drolchok.

The lineage prayer of *The Unique Enlightened Intention according to the Cycle of Drigung* is as follows:

- Mahāvajradhara
- Tilopā
- Nāropā
- Marpa
- Mila
- Dakpo
- Pagmodrupa
- Jigten Gonpo
- Onpo Sonam Drakpa
- Dorjé Drakpa
- Tok Khawa
- Tsamchépa
- Chunyipa
- Nyergyepa
- Chokyi Gyelpo
- Mengompa
- Lapchiwa
- Duldzinpa
- Ngawang Chogyel
- Taklung Tulku . . .

Grant your blessing that we may hammer the nails of the *Tenfold Doctrinal Instruction*,[43]
Resorting to the unique enlightened intention of all the buddhas,
Provisional and definitive, undistracted by winds of conceptual thought,
And may we realize the "liberation of all through singular knowledge"!

97. *The Six Doctrines according to Taklungpa*

The progenitor of this lineage is the primordial buddha Mahāvajradhara, who revealed the instruction directly to Tilopā (988–1069). The latter taught Nāropā Jñānasiddhi (1016–1100), whose disciple Marpa Lotsāwa Chokyi Lodro (1012–1100) introduced the practice to Tibet. Thereafter the transmission passed through the Taklung Kagyu lineage, as follows: Milarepa (1040–1112), Dakpo Lharjé Gampopa (1079–1153), Pagmodrupa Dorjé Gyelpo (1110–1170), Tangpa Tashi Pel (1142–1236), Kuyalwa Rinchen Gonpo (1190–1236), Sangyé Yarjon (1203–1272), Tashi Lama (1231–1297), Sangyé Pelzangpo (1257–1310), Ratnaguru (1288–1339), Ratnākara (1300–1361), Kunpang Namka Pelyang (1333–1379), Tashi Peltsek (1359–1424), Jangchub Gyatso (1403–1448), Ngawang Drakpa Pelzangpo (1418–1496), Namgyel Drakpa (1469–1530), and Taklung Tulku Namgyel Tashi (1524–1563). The last named was a teacher of Kunga Drolchok.

The lineage prayer of *The Six Doctrines according to Taklungpa* is as follows:

- Mahāvajradhara
- Tilopā
- Nāropā
- Marpa
- Mila
- Dakpo
- Pagmodrupa
- Tangpa Tashi Pel
- Kuyalwa
- Sangyé Yarjon
- Tashi Lama
- Sangyé Pelzangpo
- Ratnaguru

- Ratnākara
- Kunpang
- Tashi Peltsek
- Jangchub Gyatso
- Ngawang Drakpa Pelzangpo
- Namgyel Drakpa
- Taklung Tulku . . . {32}

Grant your blessing that we may enter again
Upon the unerring path resembling the supreme wish-fulfilling gem,
Which is the tradition disclosed by the founder of Taklung, that wish-fulfilling gem,
Forming a garland of white light, an auspicious mound of glory![44]

98. *The Means for Attainment of the Guru, Auspicious Circumstances, and Common Savor*

The progenitor of this lineage is the primordial buddha Mahāvajradhara, who revealed the instruction directly to Tilopā (988–1069). The latter taught Nāropā Jñānasiddhi (1016–1100), whose disciple Marpa Lotsāwa Chokyi Lodro (1012–1100) introduced the practice to Tibet. Thereafter the transmission passed through the Taklung Kagyu lineage, as follows: Milarepa (1040–1112), Dakpo Lharjé Gampopa (1079–1153), Pagmodrupa Dorjé Gyelpo (1110–1170), Tepuwa Pārvātapāda (fl. twelfth century), Rechungpa Dorjé Drak (1085–1161), Gyelwa Lorepa Darma Wangchuk Tsondru (1187–1250),[45] Sumpa Repa (fl. twelfth century), Ling Repa Pema Dorjé (1128–1188), Tsangpa Gyaré Yeshé Dorjé (also known as Sangyé Rabdun, 1161–1211), On Repa Darma Sengé (1177–1238), Zhonu Sengé (1200–1266), Nyima Sengé (1251–1287), Sengé Sherab (1236–1280), Pokya Rinchen Sengéwa (1258–1313), Sengé Gyelpo (1289–1325), Jamyang Kunga Sengé (1314–1347), Dorjé Rinchen (fl. fourteenth century), Jamyang Lodro Sengé (1345–1390), Khyentsé Tokden (fl. fourteenth–fifteenth centuries), Trulzhik Namkei Neljorpa (fl. fifteenth century), Gyelwang Kunga Peljor (1428–1476), Śākya Yarpel (b. fifteenth century), and Ngawang Chogyel (1465–1540). The last named was a teacher of Kunga Drolchok.

The lineage prayer of *The Means for Attainment of the Guru, Auspicious Circumstances, and Common Savor*, which are instructions of the Middle Drukpa, is as follows:

- Mahāvajradhara
- Tilopā
- Nāropā
- Marpa
- Mila
- Dakpo
- Pagmodrupa
- Tepuwa
- Rechung Dorjé
- Gyelwa Lo
- Sumpa
- Ling Repa
- Sangyé Rabdun
- On Repa Darma Sengé
- Zhonu Sengé
- Nyima Sengé
- Sengé Sherab
- Pokya Rinchen Sengéwa
- Sengé Gyelpo
- Jamyang Kunga Sengé
- Dorjé Rinchen
- Jamyang Lodro Sengé
- Khyentsé Tokden
- Namkei Neljorpa
- Gyelwang
- Śākya Yarpel
- Ngawang Chogyel . . .

Grant your blessing that we may bring forth the treasure of all desired auspicious circumstances, major and minor,
From the storeroom of devotion to the attainment of the teacher as the three buddha bodies,
And alleviate poverty in respect of the lineage of attainment
Through the gift that yields the common savor of contentment!

99. *The Fivefold Capacity of Lorepa*

The progenitor of this lineage is the primordial buddha Mahāvajradhara, who revealed the instruction directly to Tilopā (988–1069). The latter taught Nāropā Jñānasiddhi (1016–1100), whose disciple Marpa Lotsāwa Chokyi Lodro (1012–1097) introduced the practice to Tibet. Thereafter the transmission passed through the Taklung Kagyu lineage, as follows: Milarepa (1040–1112), Dakpo Lharjé Gampopa (1079–1153), Pagmodrupa Dorjé Gyelpo (1110–1170), Ling Repa Pema Dorjé (1128–1188), Tsangpa Gyaré Yeshé Dorjé (1161–1211), Lorepa Darma Wangchuk Tsondru (1187–1250), Dra Gandenpa, Onpo Sonam Dar, Girpuwa Ngejung Dar, Ozer Gyatso, Sangyé Repa, Kyechok Monlampa (b. fifteenth century), Yamkyilwa Lodro Chogyel (b. fifteenth century), and Ngawang Tulku (fl. fifteenth–sixteenth centuries). The last named taught Kunga Drolchok.

The lineage prayer of *The Fivefold Capacity of Lorepa*, which are the instructions of the Lower Drukpa, is as follows:

- Mahāvajradhara
- Tilopā
- Nāropā
- Ling Repa
- Gyaré
- Lorepa Darma Wang
- Gandenpa
- Sonam Dar
- Girpuwa Ngejung Dar
- Ozer Gyatso
- Sangyé Repa
- Kyechok Monlampa
- Yamkyilwa Lodro Chogyel
- Ngawang Tulku . . .

Grant your blessing that we may uphold the tradition of instruction of the Fivefold Capacity,
The yoga that, without attachment, abandons thoughts of this life,
And may we arrive at the doctrinal path of death
In haunted mountain ranges, uninhabited empty places!

100. *The Six Primary Essentials for the Mountain Retreat of Yangonpa*

The progenitor of this lineage is the primordial buddha Mahāvajradhara, who revealed the instruction directly to Tilopā (988–1069). The latter taught Nāropā Jñānasiddhi (1016–1100), whose disciple Marpa Lotsāwa Chokyi Lodro (1012–1097) introduced the practice to Tibet. Thereafter the transmission passed through the Taklung Kagyu lineage, as follows: Milarepa (1040–1112), Dakpo Lharjé Gampopa (1079–1153), Pagmodrupa Dorjé Gyelpo (1110–1170), Ling Repa Pema Dorjé (1128–1188), Tsangpa Gyaré Yeshé Dorjé (1161–1211), Kodrakpa Sonam Gyeltsen (1182–1261), Gotsangpa Gonpo Dorjé (1189–1258), Sakya Paṇḍita Kunga Gyeltsen (1182–1251), Drigung On Sonam Drakpa (1187–1234), Yangonpa Gyeltsen Pel (1213–1258), Chen Ngawa Rinchen Den (b. 1202), Zurpukpa Rinchen Pelzang (b. 1263), Barawa Gyeltsen Pelzang (1310–1391), Monlampa, Lechungwa Sonam Pelzang, Yargyab Kunpang Chokor Gangpa, and Sonam Gyelchok (fl. fifteenth–sixteenth centuries). The last named taught Kunga Drolchok.

The lineage prayer of *The Six Primary Essentials for the Mountain Retreat*, which is the instruction of the Upper Drukpa, is as follows:

- Mahāvajradhara
- Tilopā, gatherer of the lineage elixir of four transmitted teachings
- Nāropā
- Marpa
- Milarepa
- Dakpo
- Pagmodrupa
- Ling Repa
- Gyaré
- Kodrakpa
- Gotsangpa
- Sakya Paṇḍita
- Drigung On
- Yangonpa, the spiritual son of these four precious masters[46]
- Chen Ngawa
- Zurpukpa
- Barawa
- Monlampa {33}

- Lechungwa Sonam Pelzang
- Yargyab Kunpang
- Sonam Gyelchok . . .

Grant your blessing that we may open the treasure of instruction
By disclosing once or many times
The *Trilogy on Mountain Retreat*—
Comprising the *Source of All That Is Desired*,
The *Liberation from the Dangerous Passageway of the Intermediate State*,
And the [*Concealed Exegesis of the*] *Adamantine Body*.

101. *The Four-Armed Mahākāla in the Form Kurakma*

The progenitor of this lineage is the primordial buddha Mahāvajradhara, who revealed the instruction directly to Nāgārjuna (fl. second century). The latter's Indian successors included Āryadeva (fl. second–third centuries), Aśvaghoṣa (ca. 80–150), and Vajrāsana (fl. tenth–eleventh centuries), who imparted the instruction to Tsami Sangyé Drak (fl. eleventh century). Introduced in this manner to Tibet, the practice was thereafter transmitted in the following Kagyu line: Pelchen Ga Lotsāwa (fl. twelfth century), Khampa Aseng (fl. eleventh–twelfth centuries), Pagmodrupa Dorjé Gyelpo (1110–1170), Gyelwa Rinchen Gon (1118–1195), Olkha Lama, Rinchen Gyeltsen, Dorjé Rinchen, Gonpo Zhonu, Yarlungpa Sengé Gyeltsen (1345–1413), On Sonam Gyelwa Choyang (fl. fourteenth–fifteenth centuries), Dakchen Drakpa Lodro (1367–1446), Ngawang Drakpa Pelzangpo (1418–1496), Tsultrim Chogdrub (fl. fifteenth–sixteenth centuries), and Taklung Tulku Namgyel Tashi (1524–1563). The last named was a teacher of Kunga Drolchok.

The lineage prayer of the cycle of *The Four-Armed Mahākāla in the Form Kurakma* is as follows:

- Mahāvajradhara
- Nāgārjuna
- Āryadeva
- Aśvaghoṣa
- Vajrāsana
- Tsami Sangyé Drak
- Pelchen Ga Lotsāwa

- Aseng
- Pagmodrupa
- Gyelwa Rinchen
- Olkha Lama
- Gelong Rin Gyel
- Lopon Dor Rinpa
- Gonpo Zhonu
- Sengé Gyeltsen
- On Gyelwa Choyang
- Drakpa Lodro
- Ngawang Drakpa
- Tsultrim Chogdrub
- Taklung Tulku . . .

Grant your blessing that in the palace of the five cakras of our own body
Through the attainment of the five aspects of Mahākāla,
By means of buddha body, speech, mind, attributes, and activities,
And combined with some meditation and mantra recitation,
We may easily accomplish the four rites![47]

102. *The Inner Guidance of Glorious Pañjaranātha*

The progenitor of this lineage is the primordial buddha Mahāvajradhara, who revealed the instruction directly to Vararuci. In his Indian succession were Maṇidvīpa Sukhavajra and Śraddhākaravarman (fl. tenth–eleventh centuries). The practice was introduced to Tibet by Lochen Rinchen Zangpo (958–1055) and thereafter transmitted in the following Sakya line: Drakteng Yonten Tsultrim (fl. eleventh century), Mal Lotsāwa Lodro Drak (fl. eleventh century), Sachen Kunga Nyingpo (1092–1158), Yargom Sewo (fl. twelfth century), Gyeltsa Lungmang Chokyi Wangchuk, Khepa Yonten Tri (fl. thirteenth century), Drinchen Sengé Zangpo (fl. fourteenth century), Yarlungpa Sengé Gyeltsen (1345–1413), Sonam Gyelwa Choyang (fl. fourteenth–fifteenth centuries), Dakchen Jamyang Namka Gyeltsen (1398–1472), Dakchen Dorjé Chang Lodro Gyeltsen (fl. fifteenth century), Lama Dampa Pelden Gyelwa (fl. fifteenth century), Ngor Khenchen Sangyé Rinchen (1450–1524), and Lhachok Sengé (fl. fifteenth–sixteenth centuries). The last named taught Kunga Drolchok.

The lineage prayer of *The Inner Guidance of Glorious Pañjaranātha* is as follows:

- Mahāvajradhara
- Brahmin Vararuci
- Maṇidvīpa
- Śraddhākara
- Lochen Rinchen Zangpo
- Drakteng
- Mel Lotsāwa
- Sachen Kunga Nyingpo
- Yargom Sewo
- Gyeltsa Lungmang
- Khepa Yonten Tri
- Sengé Zangpo
- Sengé Gyeltsen
- Sonam Gyelwa Choyang
- Dakchen Namka Gyeltsen
- Lodro Gyeltsen
- Pelden Gyelwa
- Sangyé Rinchen
- Lhachok Sengé . . .

Grant your blessing that we may make malleable the channels and winds
of inner experiential cultivation
Whereby the subtle melting essences of the light of Ekajaṭī
That derive from the uncreated syllable A in the cakra of emanation
Are transformed into Śrīdevī, Mahākāla, and so forth!

103. *The Trilogy of Spiritual Songs*

The progenitor of this lineage is the primordial buddha Mahāvajradhara, who revealed the instruction directly to Sukhanātha. The latter's Indian successors included Saraha, Nāgārjuna, Śabaripā, Maitrīpā (ca. 986–1063 or 1007–1085), and Vajrapāṇi (fl. eleventh century). Introduced into Tibet by Joden Lama Ngaripa Zhang Joton, this practice was thereafter transmitted in the following Jonangpa line: Drushulwa Chorab Drakpa, Parpuwa

Lodro Sengé (b. twelfth century), Gyergom Zhikpo (1090–1171), Sangyé On, Drak Burwa, Ripa Zhonu Rinchen, Konchok Dorjé, Chogowa Chopel Sherab (b. fourteenth century), Joton Dzakhol Drubchen, Kyechok Monlampa (b. fifteenth century), Ngawang Drakpa Pelzangpo (1418–1496), and the great paṇḍita Donyo Drubpa (fl. fifteenth–sixteenth centuries). The last named was a teacher of Kunga Drolchok.

The lineage prayer of *The Trilogy of Spiritual Songs* is as follows:

· Mahāvajradhara
· Sukhanātha
· Saraha
· Nāgārjuna
· Śabaripā
· Maitrīpā
· Vajrapāṇi of India
· Joden Ngaripa {34}
· Drushulwa[48]
· Parpuwa
· Gyergom Zhikpo
· Sangyé On
· Drak Burwa
· Zhonu Rinchen
· Konchok Dorjé
· Chogowa Pel Sherab
· Dzakhol Drubchen
· Kyechok Monlampa
· Ngawang Drakpa
· Amoghasiddhi . . .

Grant your blessing that we may realize in a single savor
The manifold objects of knowledge and philosophical systems
And the many distinct inferences of different perspectives of realization
Contained within *The Trilogy* [*of Spiritual Songs*]:
The Spiritual Songs of the King, *The Spiritual Songs of the Queen*,
And *The Spiritual Songs of the Populace*!

104. *The Six Doctrines of the Accomplished Masters*

The progenitor of this lineage is the primordial buddha Mahāvajradhara, who revealed the instruction directly to the eighty-four mahāsiddhas.[49] Their Indian successors included the ḍākinī Kokalī, the ḍākinī Dharmavaṃ, Vīraraśmi, the great paṇḍita Kamala, Tsawaripa, and Abhayadattaśrī, author of the biographies of the mahāsiddhas. The practice was introduced to Tibet by Tsami Lotsāwa Mondrub Sherab, who taught his own son Rinchen. The transmission thereafter descended in the following line: Ratnaguru (1288–1327), Drubtob Hūṃ Barwa, Genmo Lhepa Jangchub Pel, Tagton Zhonu Dar, Bagton Zhonu Tsultrim (fl. thirteenth century), Densatel Khenchen Sherab Dorjé (fl. thirteenth–fourteenth centuries), Nyelwa Delekpa (fl. fourteenth–fifteenth centuries), Pak Chok Sonam Dar (fl. fifteenth century), Marton Gyeltsen Ozer (fl. fifteenth century), Kangyurwa Śākya Gyeltsen (fl. fifteenth century), Nyukla Paṇchen Ngawang Drakpa (1458–1515), and Trewo Chokyi Gyatso (d. 1547).

The lineage prayer of *The Six Doctrines of the Accomplished Masters* is as follows:

- Mahāvajradhara
- Eighty-four mahāsiddhas
- Ḍākinī Kokalī
- Ḍākinī Dharmavaṃ
- Mondrub Sherab
- Vīraraśmi
- Paṇchen Kamala
- Tsawaripa[50]
- Abhayadattaśrī
- Rinchen, the latter's son
- Ratnaguru
- Drubtob Hūṃ Barwa
- Genmo Lhepa Jangchub Pel
- Tagton Zhonu Dar
- Bagton Zhonu Tsultrim
- Sherab Dorjé
- Nyelwa Delekpa
- Pak Chok Sonam Dar

- Gyeltsen Ozer
- Kangyurwa Śākya Gyeltsen[51]
- Nyukla Paṇchen
- Trewo Chokyi Gyatso . . .

Grant your blessing that we may drink the nectar elixir
Vomited from the experiences of the eighty male accomplished masters,
Who number eighty-four with the addition of their four sisters,
Endowed with realization and liberation,
And may we then attain the rank of an accomplished master!

105. *The Gradual Path of Padmasambhava*

The progenitor of this lineage is the primordial buddha Samantabhadra and the buddha body of perfect resource Vajrasattva, who revealed the instruction directly to Padmākara, the buddha body of emanation. In Tibet the latter imparted the instruction through the long oral lineage (*ring brgyud bka' ma*) to Nyak Lotsāwa Yeshé Zhonu (fl. eighth–ninth centuries), and thereafter it was transmitted in the following Nyingma line of succession: Nubchen Sangyé Yeshé (fl. ninth century), Nub Khulungpa Yonten Gyatso (fl. ninth–tenth centuries), Nyangton Yeshé Jungné (b. tenth century), Zurchen Śākya Jungné (1002–1062), Zurchung Sherab Drak (1014–1074), Śākya Zangpo (fl. eleventh century), Zur Dropukpa Śākya Sengé (1074–1135), Tsaktsa Śākya Dorjé (fl. twelfth century), Nyonak Gyeltsen, Banrik Gyelkhampa, Zur Śākya Pelwa, Śākya Sengé, Kunga Rinchen, Rinchen Gyeltsen, Konchok Zangpo, Zurhaṃ Śākya Jungné (fl. thirteenth–fourteenth centuries), Śākya Pelzang, Zurhaṃ Shenyen, Khampa Drakpa Gyeltsen, Seton Chenpo, Rechen Namka Gyeltsen, Nyelwa Delekpa (fl. fourteenth–fifteenth centuries), and Kunga Chogdrub (fl. fifteenth–sixteenth centuries).

The lineage prayer of *The Gradual Path of Padmasambhava* is as follows:

- Samantabhadra, the buddha body of reality
- Vajrasattva, the buddha body of perfect resource
- Padmākara, the buddha body of emanation
- Nyak Lotsāwa Yeshé Zhonu
- Nubchen Sangyé Yeshé
- Yonten Gyatso
- Nyangton Yeshé Jungné

- Zurchen Śākya Jungné
- Zurchung Sherab Drak
- Śākya Zangpo
- Śākya Sengé
- Tsaktsa Śākya Dorjé
- Nyonak Gyeltsen
- Banrik Gyelkhampa
- Śākya Pelwa
- Śākya Sengé
- Kunga Rinchen
- Rinchen Gyeltsen
- Konchok Zangpo
- Zurhaṃ Śākya Jungné {35}
- Śākya Pelzang
- Shenyen
- Khampa Drakpa Gyeltsen
- Seton Chenpo
- Rechen Namka Gyeltsen
- Delekpa
- Kunga Chogdrub . . .

Grant your blessing that we may complete the fortunate path of liberation,
The essential of the path that nakedly reveals the nature of mind,
Well maintained through the practical guidance and adamantine verses
  spoken by Padmākara,
Exemplified by him pointing it out to an old man with a walking stick
And pointing it out to an old lady with his finger!

106. *The Collected Injunctions of the King*

The progenitor of this lineage is the buddha body of reality in the form of Amitābha and the buddha body of perfect resource in the form of Avalokiteśvara, who revealed the instruction directly to Songtsen Gampo, the buddha body of emanation (617–650). Later Padmākara (fl. eighth–ninth centuries) also instructed Tri Songdetsen (742–797), but the revelations of the king are said to have been rediscovered and redacted in their present form by the accomplished master Ngodrub (fl. eleventh–twelfth centuries) and Ngadak Nyangrel Nyima Ozer (ca. 1124–1192). Thereafter, the transmission was maintained through the latter's disciple Menlungpa Mikyo Dorjé (fl. twelfth century), Śākya Zangpo, Lharjé Gewa Bum (b. twelfth century) to whom authorship of the present guidebook is attributed, Chammo Yeshé Chok, Chugompa, Tazhi Jadrel, Tsulchen Sonam Sengé, Tashi Gyeltsen, Churak Lodro Gyeltsen, Pak Chok Norzang, Hor Kabzhipa Sengé Gyeltsen (fl. fourteenth–fifteenth centuries), Pelden Lekpa, Kachu Jangchub Pel, Pakpa Lodro Rinchen, and Yigdruk Sherab Peljor (fl. fifteenth–sixteenth centuries). The last named was a teacher of Kunga Drolchok.

The lineage prayer of *The Collected Injunctions of the King* is as follows:

- Amitābha, the buddha body of reality
- Avalokiteśvara, the buddha body of perfect resource
- Songtsen Gampo, the buddha body of emanation
- Padmākara
- Tri Songdetsen
- Ngodrub, accomplished master
- Ngadak Nyangrel Nyima Ozer
- Mikyo Dorjé
- Śākya Zangpo
- Lharjé Gewa Bum
- Chammo Yeshé Chok
- Chugompa
- Tazhi Jadrel
- Tsulchen Sonam Sengé
- Tashi Gyeltsen
- Churak Lodro Gyeltsen
- Pak Chok Norzang
- Hor Kabzhipa
- Pelden Lekpa
- Kachu Jangchub Pel
- Lodro Rinchen
- Yigdruk Sherab Peljor . . .

Grant your blessing that we may be led from abodes of great negativity
Through the guidance of buddha body concerning the generation stage
And its consciousness transference in the manner of a mustard seed,
Through the guidance of buddha speech concerning mantra recitation

And its consciousness transference in the manner of a seed syllable,
And through the guidance of buddha mind concerning luminosity
And its consciousness transference in the manner of a butter lamp!

107. *The Liberation by Seeing according to Norbu Rinchen*

The progenitor of this lineage is the buddha body of reality in the form of Samantabhadra, and Vajradhara, who revealed the instruction directly to four male accomplished masters: Saraha, Śabaripā, Mitrayogin, and Padmākara (fl. eighth–ninth centuries), along with their four female consorts, the ḍākinīs of pristine cognition. The practice was revealed in Tibet as treasure by Drampa Kunga Zangpo and then transmitted in the following line: Trulzhik Kundarma, Ngokton the Great, Drakpa Peljor, and Norbu Rinchen, the last of whom instructed Kunga Drolchok.

The lineage prayer of *Norbu Rinchen's Liberation by Seeing* is as follows:

- Samantabhadra
- Vajradhara
- Eight great accomplished masters—namely, the four male ones:
- Saraha
- Śabaripā
- Mitrayogin
- And Padmākara
- Along with their four female consorts
- Drampa Kunga Zangpo, revealer of treasure
- Trulzhik Kundarma
- Ngokton the Great
- Drakpa Peljor
- Norbu Rinchen . . .

Grant your blessing that we may realize the primordially pure buddha
body of reality
In the gorge of instruction where the two rivers of Great Seal and Great
Perfection converge,
Through multiplication of the four mothers and seventeen offspring,
And may our minds not grasp the ten signs [of realization]
That would be indicative of the abyss of eternalism and nihilism![52]

108. *The Nature of Mind: The Wish-Fulfilling Gem*

The progenitor of this lineage is the primordial buddha Mahāvajradhara, who revealed the instruction directly to Tilopā (988–1069). The latter taught Nāropā Jñānasiddhi (1016–1100), and his disciple Marpa Lotsāwa Chokyi Lodro (1012–1100) introduced the practice to Tibet, where the transmission passed through Milarepa (1040–1112), Dakpo Lharjé Gampopa (1079–1153), Kyebu Yeshé Dorjé, and the treasure revealer Drogon Dungtso Repa (fl. thirteenth–fourteenth centuries). Thereafter the instruction was handed down through Newu Repa, Choying Wangchuk, Garjong Gonpo Gyeltsen, Trulzhik Tsultrim Gyeltsen (fl. fourteenth–fifteenth centuries), Śākya Chokden (1428–1507), and Changlungpa Zhonu Chodrub (fl. fifteenth–sixteenth centuries). The last named was a teacher of Kunga Drolchok.

The lineage prayer of *The Nature of Mind: The Wish-Fulfilling Gem* is as follows:

- Mahāvajradhara
- Tilopā
- Nāropā {36}
- Marpa
- Mila
- Gampopa
- Kyebu Yeshé Dorjé
- Drogon Dungtso Repa
- Newu Repa
- Choying Wangchuk
- Garjong
- Trulzhik Tsultrim Gyeltsen
- Khyenrab Chojé
- Zhonu Chodrub Chok . . .

Grant your blessing that we may be guided from this uncertainty
As to where the nature of mind impartially goes,
On the main path of experiential cultivation and oral instruction,
And may we then see the natural face of original reality,
The unfabricated, ever-present isle of the wish-fulfilling gem!

Author's Comment

This supplication to the lineage of teachers who transmitted the One Hundred and Eight Guidebooks is easy to recite, listing the names of the lineage holders, and it should be chanted many times. Each time it is recited, we should consider the great difficulty that was incurred while composing, expressing, collating, and refining the prayer. I composed these verses, having thoroughly grasped the gist of their essential points, which are extensive in the manner of a string of auspicious gems. When there are doubts based on misunderstanding of the oblique references to the names of the teachers, these have been elucidated and clarified by annotations. As for the usefulness of reciting this prayer from beginning to end, I have always kept in mind the simple thought and meditation that I should painstakingly commit this supplication to writing, but, owing to my physical distractions and idleness, I was in a state of apathy that deterred me from taking it in hand. At that time, my committed disciple Namdrol Sengé Pelzangpo[53] would encourage me repeatedly, each day. It was in this context that these verses have emerged from the ornaments of the mind of Kunga Drolchok.

Concluding Verses

It is said we should look to teachers for sacred doctrines and their transmissions.
This mode of activity is absent from our own mind with its conceited conduct,
But present in the essential buddha speech of Munīndra.
By persevering in conformity with it,
May we successfully acquire the freedoms and opportunities![54]

The supplicatory verses to the names of the lineages holders,
Embodiments of the sacred doctrine,
Are enhanced by [honorific terminations such as] *-zhabs.*
The armor [of bodhisattvas] that can withstand hardships
Arises from such subtle modes of expression.

Each one of these profound guidebooks
Constitutes a path that is naturally beneficial.
May the words spoken by these teachers,
Unerring, unadulterated, and without contradiction,

Untainted by mental analysis and conceptual thought,
Exactly come to pass, and flourish within our hearts!

By virtue of such merits of body and speech, well conducted {37}
And in association with the mind, wherever I have gathered them,
I dedicate these so that all beings, relying on the sacred doctrine,
Might abandon all the obscurations of past actions
And come to attain buddhahood.

Through the melodious voice of Mañjughoṣa—
Mighty lord of speech who is skilled in speech—
May our speech, skilled in verbalizing beautiful verses,
Melodious words free from negativity,
Auspiciously acquire the eloquent level of Vagīśvara!

The writer of this benediction is Kunga Lekgyel.[55]

Colophon

This basic supplication to the lineage, which was composed by Venerable Kunga Drolchok, employs very concise words that, as it were, refresh the memory. For this reason, it is not easy to retain or recite, and it has become customary to embellish it for the most part with annotations.[56] Yet the original text itself is entirely flawless, and, besides that, it becomes extremely difficult to chant when these annotations are inscribed. But when the supplication lists the names alone, the text is not too verbose. I have, therefore, left the primary text unchanged, with all sorts of inconsistent variant forms of the names for the lineage holders, and I have discarded all the annotations. Having deleted the series of annotated names that were needlessly inserted, with the exception of those found in the supplement to the lineage that follows, the yogācārin Lodrö Tayé[57] then arranged the root verses as a ritual for reading aloud. I apologize for and confess any errors, mistakes, or faults that there may be to the teachers, the conquerors, and their heirs.

May this merit become the causal basis for the noble tradition of the profound One Hundred and Eight Guidebooks to flourish and expand, without decline, until the end of the rebirth process!

Let virtue prevail!

2. Supplementary Prayer to the Lineage

Losal Tenkyong

The supplementary lineage prayer that forms the content of the short second chapter was composed by Losal Tenkyong of Zhalu at the behest of Jamyang Khyentsé Wangpo. It commences with Kunga Drolchok (1507–1565), the compiler of the One Hundred and Eight Guidebooks, and continues through the Jonang line of transmission as follows: the latter's disciple Draktopa Choku Lhawang Drakpa (fl. sixteenth century), and reincarnation Tāranātha (also known as Drolwei Gonpo Kunga Nyingpo, 1575–1634), the ḍākinī Ratnavajriṇī (also known as Jonang Jetsunma Kunga Trinle Pelwangmo, 1585–1668), Khenchen Rinchen Gyatso Neten Dorjedzin (fl. seventeenth century), Nyingpo Lodro Tayé (fl. seventeenth century), Dzalongkar Lama Drubwang Kunzang Wangpo (fl. early eighteenth century), Katok Rigdzin Tsewang Norbu (1698–1755), Ngawang Nampar Gyelwa, On Dzalongkar Lama Kunzang Chojor, Drinchen Lobzang Tutob (fl. late eighteenth–early nineteenth centuries), Chakzampa Tulku Nyima Chopel, and the hermit Zhalu Lotsāwa Losal Tenkyong (b. 1804). Thereafter the lineage passed to Jamyang Khyentsé Wangpo (1820–1892) and Jamgön Kongtrul Lodrö Tayé (1813–1899), compiler of The Treasury of Precious Instructions.

Formal Title

Supplement to the Supplication of the Lineage of the One Hundred and Eight Guidebooks[1] {39}

We pray to the teachers of the root lineage:

- Kunga Drolchok, in whom all the streams of the lineage converged
- Draktopa Choku Lhawang Drakpa,[2] seer of the innate truth of reality

- Drolwei Gonpo Kunga Nyingpo, great promulgator of sutra and tantra
- Jonang Jetsunma Trinle Pelwangmo,[3] foremost of sky-farers
- Rinchen Gyatso Neten Dorjédzin
- Nyingpo Tayé, foremost of hidden accomplished masters
- Kunzang Wangpo, great emanation of Vajradhara, lord of the doctrinal wheel
- Tsewang Norbu[4]
- Ngawang Nampar Gyelwa[5]
- On Dzalongkar Lama Kunzang Chojor, who gained maturation in the essentials of experiential cultivation
- Drinchen Lobzang Tutob[6]
- Chakzampa Tulku Nyima Chopel[7]
- The hermit Losal Tenkyong . . .

Colophon

Giving continuity to the words of Rigdzin Tsewang Norbu,[8] this *Supplement to the Supplication to the Lineage of the One Hundred and Eight Guidebooks* was written by the venerable monk Losal Tenkyong at the behest of Jetsun Dampa Jamyang Khyentsé Wangpo.

SARVA MAṄGALAṂ {41}

3. The Life-Sustaining Prayer of the One Hundred and Eight Guidebooks

Having requested the blessings of the lineage holders of the past, Kunga Drolchok now offers a prayer to sustain the lives and enhance the enlightened activities of those, such as himself, who recount the history of the One Hundred and Eight Guidebooks, over successive lifetimes. The prayer contrasts the rarity of the sacred doctrine with counterfeit forms that would lead beings astray through sophistry, and dedicates the merit accrued by his documenting the One Hundred and Eight Guidebooks for the sake of buddhahood on behalf of all sentient beings.

Formal Title

The Life-Sustaining Verses for Those Introducing the Sources of the One Hundred and Eight Profound Guidebooks[1] {42}

Preamble

The following verses will excellently enhance even those who partially recount the historical narratives of the past that introduce the sources of the one hundred and eight guidebooks.

The Life-Sustaining Verses

Supreme gems of buddha mind,
Gathering the elixir of the enlightened intention
Of all the conquerors, their heirs, and emanations,
May we realize at this time the profound ocean depths

Of your respective manifestations,
Unadulterated and untainted in many ways!

Through my good fortune as the boatman of liberation,
May hosts of beings, ten million in number, find the wish-fulfilling gems—
The repository of gems forming the instructions of the ocean of sacred doctrine
Handed down through the lineage of learned and accomplished mighty nāgas!

Like gems with their attributes, colors, and functions,
The sacred doctrine guides mental capacities by superior and inferior means.
This is a wondrous and marvelous drama of multiplicity—not singularity—
Resembling the efficacy of medications that alleviate disease.

This sacred doctrine may also be exemplified by the light
That radiates the diversity of sparkling gems.
Although it is no different from the light that is the color of quartz,
Ignorant fools abandon the supremely precious light
And accept one that is inferior. {43}

A gem such as this in which the wise rejoice
Is not an inferior object but renowned
As the crest of an empowered nāga king
Within lakes of glacial origin.

This resembles a fisherman, unable to expose by burning, cutting, or grasping
A wish-fulfilling gem found within a fish,
Who then, with pointless frustration, as if pearl were stone,
Casts the large fish back into the lake whence it came.

Those endowed with good fortune at the present day
In respect of the essential words and meanings
Contained within the great ocean of scripture of the present day

Adhere at the present day to topics appraised through pride in learning,
And, finally, at the present day they laboriously reject authentic words.

"How amazing are the words of our predecessors
That any unfortunate person who accepts the secret doctrine
Will, through the power of merit, excellently realize its words and meanings!"
So they say with the purposeful words of an old worldly person,
But the thoughts and deeds of demonic forces
Lead oneself and others astray through the common desire for knowledge,
Causing dissension within the sacred doctrine.

How pitiful are those in whose minds arise
Convictions opposed to the discussions of their teachers!
The lowest of the low are those possessed by all the well-known obstacles
That distort the view and practice. {44}

Under the sway of the most degenerate of all degenerations,
Those who shrink from acting to complete the accumulation of merit,
But who right here, starkly and with wide-eyed clarity
Resembling the magic of a Chinese weaving,[2]
Disclose the different patterns of the sacred doctrine
And the different nuances of exegesis
As objects to be manifoldly refined by their manifold erudition,
Have led beings according to the path of reason
That glibly employs words of sophistry,
Guiding them [ostensibly] toward intrinsic knowledge.
For them, the ordinary scriptures
And the infinite profound secrets of the way of Secret Mantra
Resemble poisoned foods of one hundred flavors.

Therefore, the omniscient ones who bear witness to authentic cognition
Should persevere to acquire the true meaning of study,
Without doubting the transmitted teachings of the Conqueror
And the lineage traditions that comment on their enlightened intention,
Exactly as they have been explained!

May I, too, have faith in the impartial Buddhist teaching
And take responsibility without degeneration

For the experiential cultivation of the Sakya tradition
Upheld by Mañjughoṣa in human form,
And apart from that may I not mistakenly impose hatred or attachment
upon anyone!

May I liberate the minds of those who question and discuss
The philosophical systems of the elders of the past,
And any of their experiential cultivations, exegeses, or doctrinal
discourses.
Oh! When I return to this world in the future,
May I persevere each day, again and again,
So that, with regard to the essentials of the sacred doctrine,
I may not inspect even a mere letter
Of books that have been fabricated;
And with my mind not exhibiting this excessively delusional approach,
Whether for a short time or when death is certain,
May my mind never waver for a mere instant
Toward unfinished study, reflection, and meditation
That resemble a pointless millstone in a terrifying gorge!

In order to achieve life-sustaining leisure
I will simply fulfill each latent impulse
That generates an advantageous foundation
Exclusively for the benefit of the sacred tradition in which I persevere {45}
And [in general] for the Buddhist teaching and living beings.

In sadness due to terrifying fear of the aeon of darkness,
Afraid of fabrications that resemble the sacred doctrine,
I weep excessively, thinking how things will turn out in other lives
If I have no independence.

With a mind that inspects the one hundred and eight guidebooks
And ponders their meaning,
Listens to the one hundred and eight guidebooks
And cultivates their meaning,
And confers their one hundred and eight empowerments,
As my own ordinary life manifestly passes away,
And the chariot of my mental faculty is driven

By the messenger of aging, the mighty lord of death,
While I can still write and see,
I have penned this as the legacy of my studies,
So that unfinished tasks may be swiftly carried out.

These purposeful life-sustaining verses that resemble a [rare] daytime star
Should be offered whenever they may possibly be of benefit,
But, in addition, they will exclusively sustain the propensities for study
In your own future lives.

I dedicate the stock of merit that originates from having composed this prayer,
That through its purity, resembling a conch or a snow mountain peak,
All obscurations of past actions might be renounced, dependent on the sacred doctrine,
And that omniscient buddhahood might be attained.

By the force of my faith of conviction in genuine buddha speech,
By the power of the truth of having accumulated virtue devoid of negativity,
By however many means and at all times,
May the good auspices of practicing in accord with the sacred doctrine be granted!

Colophon

In the service of those who concisely document the narrative of the sources of the profound One Hundred and Eight Guidebooks, these life-sustaining verses originated from the oceanic mind of glorious Kunga Drolchok Losel Gyatsodé.

Concluding Verses

How could this be written in more detail!
It virtuously abides in its entirety in the mind.
If there are any wise persons,
It is right for them to ponder this partial illustration. {46}

Practice the sacred doctrine diligently in this manner!
This is a veritable treasure store of study, a supreme treasure store.
As for your material wealth,
If any of you are zealous in the correct manner,
It will be inexhaustible, never stolen by thieves.
Therefore, this meaningful study
Is the most essential possession in hand.
It is the pathway to great merit.

Benediction

May you reach this authenticity in the wake of the authentic ones who have departed!

MAṄGALAṂ

Let virtue prevail! {47}

4. An Autobiographical Record of the One Hundred and Eight Guidebooks Received

In this personal statement Kunga Drolchok describes how he was inspired by Sangyé Pel to seek out the respective lineage holders of the one hundred and eight guidebooks. Over thirty-one years, starting from the young age of seven through to his thirty-eighth year, he assiduously acquired these diverse teachings and here he presents his achievement in the well-established format of a "record of teachings received" (thob yig, bsan yig)*. The names of the teachers from whom he obtained each lineage are documented here, including his own root guru, Kunga Chogdrub, to whom he respectfully refers not by name, but by the epithet "venerable hidden buddha"* (rje sbas pa'i sangs rgyas)*.*

Kunga Drolchok also provides a wealth of information concerning the names of the Tibetan authors and redactors of these guidebooks, where they are known, and in cases where the authorship is unclear, he remarks that they derive from unspecified ancient writings. There is evidence of an incisive critical faculty in the way in which he occasionally differentiates between multiple strands of a given lineage, indicating which are to be included in the anthology and which are not. Further information on these primary sources, their antecedents, and so forth can be found in the bibliography and also in the initial note to each of the one hundred and eight actual guidebooks in chapter 9.

The chapter begins with a "signature" quatrain, in which the four syllables of Kunga Drolchok's own name are embedded within the lines of verse, and it ends with a poetic dedication of merit and a colophon.

Formal Title

Multiple Approaches of the Wondrous Doctrine, Enhancing the Summary of the One Hundred and Eight Guidebooks[1] {48}

Introductory Verses

OṂ Let there be good auspices!
Homage to the supreme primordial buddha, original lord-protector![2]

Though manifestly perfect **in totality** (*kun*) from the beginning,
With **delight** (*dga'*) for the sake of living beings in this basket of cyclic existence,
Devoid of craving through expressions that are neither singular nor multiple,
May this **supreme liberation** (*grol mchog*) from fear of the abyss
Of eternalism and nihilism be victorious![3]

May good auspices be bestowed by the Great Seal
Unguarded by attachment to the action seal,
Unfixated on the magical display of the seal of pristine cognition,
And unfettered by the symbols of the commitment seal![4]

May "she who is endowed with all the finest aspects"[5] protect us
Without scrutiny, in the manner of the reflection on an oracular mirror,
Having abandoned analytical emptiness,
Our meditative experience devoid of the poisonous savor of emptiness.[6]

How wonderful! The rain of the sacred doctrine
Is not determined as singular,
But satisfies each according to need,
So that the aspirations of each bear fruit
In the fertile field of disciples to be trained.

May the unforgettable retention of this book within my own mind
Be verbally expressed by all sentient beings
And penned by scribes for one hundred aeons
On surfaces of dry land,

With ink of the four great lakes[7]
And pen lines of plants and forests! {49}

To that end I will proudly present in just a few words
That which is called "inexhaustible intelligence."[8]
Delighting intelligent persons,
This is the portal through which the chariot of confidence is steered,
Intimating in words the framing narratives
That describe authentic sources, without fictitious lies.

Through the power of the residual inheritance of past actions
I have listened to profound guidance since childhood.
By listening each time in the correct manner
To the words and syllables of the sacred doctrine,
My memory has been refreshed.

While diverse and dissimilar exegetical methods
Remain individually and distinctly in my own mind,
I persevere to distinguish their exegetical sources,
Untainted and not conflated with one another.

May the doctrinal traditions, eloquently expressed,
Be enhanced in accordance with the respective sutras and tantras
Established as sources of their respective textual traditions.

Though learned and accomplished masters
May repeat insinuations regarding one another,[9]
We accept all traditions entirely on the basis of our faith,
Holding all of them to be interdependent, and without error,
Just as the eighteen schools [of monastic discipline][10]
Had points that were permissible and impermissible,
And yet we regard them all with devotion and confidence.

May any who have not savored
The conquerors' authentic teachings and transmissions
And are themselves endowed with a share of merit {50}
Drink of this nectar elixir!

O heart sons, endowed with pristine cognition,
Holding me with faith in your minds,
If you wish to establish the real nature, just as it is,
You should secure the nail of speech inherent in my explanations.
And when the actual sources are revealed without fabrication,
Devoid of my own creations,
Such that this point does not transgress that one,
Low-level secrets will emerge through these written exegeses,
And then the real nature will become clear,
When my own unwritten explanations
And those that are most subtle—not low-level matters for discussion—
Flourish in beings whose minds have been refined.

In the face of those who nowadays do as they wish,
Who stammer with childish expression,
And with the negative perspective of fools and nursemaids,
The mighty lord of speech yet prevails on earth.
Avoiding fame, meager in wisdom but great in perseverance,
May I find an opportunity to protect the traditions of my predecessors
In the correct manner, unfabricated by my own mind!

Owing to manifold efforts in this life,
The doctrines that I have heard
From the words of my teachers
Resemble the honey on an anthill.
Such are the definitive essentials of the One Hundred and Eight
Guidebooks.

Preamble

When I was young, according to the words of one of my disciples who journeyed from the land of Utsang, my mind was greatly moved upon hearing the introductory narrative of the One Hundred and Eight Guidebooks given by the teacher named Sangyé Pel. He himself emphasized the approach that nurtures guidance rather than empowerments and transmissions. So as the first of the guidebooks on the transmitted teachings that I heard—that which first penetrated my ears, I received excellent instruction on the *Oral Transmission of Venerable Mañjughoṣa: Parting from the Four Attachments.*

Thereby at the age of seven, my resolve with respect to the three kinds of faith[11] became much stronger, inspired by an intense disillusionment that was without attachment to the comforts of worldly existence, and that was not impoverished—owing to the nectar of meditative concentration. Starting from then, as I developed as a youth, I obtained other memorable and profound instructions, {51} but because I obtained so many, for the while it was simply that original guidance to which I adhered as the acceptable standard when enumerating the one hundred and eight guidebooks, up to and including the last of them, which is entitled *The Nature of Mind: The Wish-Fulfilling Gem*.

Thereafter, too, while my own mind was enriched by the responsibilities associated with the many acquisitions of the sacred doctrine that I had, there was no guidebook that I newly obtained through the acceptance or rejection of the earlier ones. Contrary to those who, having attended upon many unsuitable teachers, simply conduct funeral ceremonies in pursuit of fame, I do not reject those who arrive at true convictions by analyzing authentic words and meanings. But thinking that I should be of benefit to small-minded persons who have not acquired extensive experience and who lack understanding, I propagate writings that bring forth the essence of the words and meanings of the old texts that do not reiterate one another's methods of guidance.

If, at the outset, I may briefly comment in general on these anthologized teachings, from our perspective as beings of lesser aspiration, these approaches are all indicative of the pure sacred doctrine, unadulterated and untainted by the absence of the doctrine, and extracted from the great pathway of the sutras, tantras, and treatises in accordance with the singular true utterance, devoid of falsehood, of all the saintly beings of India and Tibet who grasped the essential mind of the buddhas and bodhisattvas. Since each individual may attain perfection by means of each of these guidebooks, the essential points firmly conveying beings to the state of buddhahood are unmistaken.

On that basis, the anthology is exemplified by these guidebooks that summarize the extensive sutras and are derived from the Kadampa tradition of Jowo Atiśa, commencing from the acceptance and rejection of past actions and their fruits in the context of mind training that delineates persons of superior, middling, and inferior capacity, and continuing through to the perfection of loving-kindness, compassion, and the two precious aspects of enlightened mind.[12] But the anthology is also exemplified by the oral transmission of the great, supremely accomplished masters of the Sakya and Kagyu traditions, who have extracted the definitive secrets of the profound tantras.[13] {52} Entering through the supreme way of the two stages of the path,[14] these two modes of guidance [of the Sakya and Kagyu traditions] that reach the level of an adamantine holder[15] are the essence that is to be explained in this anthology. Derived from these traditions are quintessential instructions through which one correctly achieves supreme confidence based on the subtleties of the direct teachings of the conquerors and their heirs, and which are disclosed directly, indirectly, or covertly based on the testimony of the sutras and tantras in the joyous tradition of the buddhas. Through them, without straying from the acquisition of the conclusive four reliances,[16] the introduction to the nature of reality that secures the nail [of firm realization] then takes effect. This is because there are no valid expositors surpassing the conquerors in the ways of the sacred doctrine.

The definitive topics in all the profound guidebooks that I obtained in accordance with my good fortune are without even a single adulteration that would come about by juxtaposing with them biased writings indicative of mere discussions I had with teachers that are but the excellent imaginings, analyses, or inclinations of my own appraisal. Those who see with the eye of the sacred doctrine, by investigating exemplary topics, do not harbor doubt owing to their enlightened intention and their faculty of discriminative awareness. Therefore this preamble to the One Hundred and Eight Guidebooks sets forth in writing the concise points that I have obtained through the kindness of my root teachers, and that have been embraced, as it were, by one who has the name of a writer.

You should know and understand that the gradual propagation of the names of all these lineages without exception will be contingent on the increase in the number of good auspices that flow from attending to the supplication prayers of their lineages and their presentation of the content of the [two] stages of the path.

The First Guidebook

The first of the eloquent instructions of profound guidance that I heard in my lifetime was the guidebook entitled *Parting from the Four Attachments*, which I received from my teacher, the venerable hidden buddha Kunga Chogdrub {53}, and which is itself the nectar elixir of Mañjughoṣa's oral transmission. This includes the *Root Verses of the Account of Sachen Kunga*

Nyingpo's Encounter with Mañjughoṣa, the *Versified Instruction on Parting from the Four Attachments* by Jetsun Rinpoché Drakpa Gyeltsen, and the *Songs of Meditative Experience* by Jetsun Drakpa Gyeltsen, which were imparted in support of this doctrine. It further includes the *List of Instructions in the Form of a Memorandum* that Nubpa Rigdzin Drak composed on the teachings of Jetsun Rinpoché,[17] and then, based on the notes of the great teacher [Sakya Paṇḍita] and Chogyel Pakpa,[18] it includes the *Essence of the Focus on Guidance* that was composed by Zarjang Pukpa Kunga Lekpa Rinchen.[19]

You should keep this instruction in your heart as the strength of your conviction. Since the pure seed of virtuous action is found in this initial guidebook through devotion, including faith, I esteem it emphatically. If any faithful disciple of mine should appear, placing their hopes in me, I think I would instruct them through this, opening the portal of the first guidebook.

Furthermore, with regard to this guidebook, I later requested Ngorchen Lhachok Sengé for the instruction composed by the omniscient Gorampa Sonam Sengé,[20] and I also heard instruction from Changlung Rinpoché [Zhonu Chodrub] based on the guidance of [Kunga Tashi], doctrinal lord of the Great Vehicle.[21]

Since I myself have relied on the very first and earliest transmission that I excellently received, I have transcribed the lineage accordingly in the *Supplication to the Lineage of the One Hundred and Eight Guidebooks*. Acting with faith and devotion, each of us should assiduously accept responsibility in this manner for the respective lineages to which we are devoted. This instruction was also the one that I had a need to request and receive repeatedly from different teachers. So, after initially receiving this guidance on virtuous action, it indeed became the foundation of my experiential cultivation of the Great Vehicle.

The Second Guidebook

With regard to the second guidebook that I heard, entitled *The Seven-Point Mind Training of the Great Vehicle*,[22] there are approximately sixty texts of Indian and Tibetan origin. {54} As an exegetical transmission, I received their synopsis in the form of the *Compendium of Eloquence*, compiled by Gangtropa Gyelsé Konchok Bang of Bulé, who was also called Sempa Zhonu Gyelchok.[23] The quintessential points were composed by Drogon

Pelden Yeshé according to the sayings of Gyelsé Sempa Chenpo Ngulchu Chodzongpa,[24] and the pith instructions derived from his teachings that emerged as an aural transmission were compiled as a supplement in five notebooks by Hor Kabzhipa Sengé Gyeltsen.[25] After completing the preliminary practice entitled the *Supporting Doctrine*, I directly obtained a text entitled *Cycle That Adopts the Calmness of Visualization* for the main practice, while setting my mind on altruistic engagement.[26]

The Third to Fifth Guidebooks

Thereafter [the following were bestowed upon me]: the third guidebook, the pith instruction entitled *The Heart of Dependent Origination*, which was based on the extensive introductory narrative composed by Muchen Gyeltsen Pelzangpo;[27] the fourth guidebook, entitled *The Carrying of Happiness and Suffering on the Path*,[28] according to Remdawa Zhonu Lodro's *Memorandum on the Teaching of Gyelsépa*;[29] and the fifth guidebook, entitled *The Mind Training according to Sumpa Lotsāwa*, according to the composition by Chojé Pelden Lama.[30]

I then received *The Direct Guidance of Avalokiteśvara* according to the tradition of Drubchen Tsembupa,[31] and in addition I searched in Utsang and definitively obtained the memorandum that Gyamawa Lodro Gyeltsen had written on the teachings of Gyelsépa entitled *The Coemergent Union of the Great Seal*.[32] These are both found below. My teacher, the venerable hidden buddha Kunga Chogdrub, said that these completed the six instructions of Gyelsé Tokmé Zangpo.[33]

The Sixth Guidebook

On one occasion when I was inclined toward the instructions of Machik Labkyi Dronma on Severance,[34] I received so many instructions, including *The Six Approaches of the Profound Meaning* according to the tradition of Kyemé Dopa [Chokyi Sherab Jodenpa][35] and *The Striking* by Tokden [Gangpa Rinchen] Pelzangpo, and subsequently I acquired confidence in *The New Pronouncement and Eight Appendices* of Nyakton Samten Ozer. {55} It contains within it *The Wish-Fulfilling Gem: An Instruction on the Inner Meaning*, which is indeed to be counted as this sixth guidebook. That I acquired from Yidruk Sherab Peljor.

The Seventh Guidebook

Again, under my teacher, the venerable hidden buddha Kunga Chogdrub, I studied to the point of maturation the seventh guidebook, entitled *The Three Essential Points*, which is based on the writings of Tropu Lotsāwa. Subsequently I also heard it from Changlungpa Zhonu Chodrub in accordance with the inner examples that Paṇchen Rinpoché [Śākya Chokden] had composed on behalf of that venerable lord of the sacred doctrine.[36]

The Eighth Guidebook

Again, as far as the eighth guidebook, entitled *Resting in the Nature of Mind*, is concerned, I received it based on the writings of Tropu [Lotsāwa Jampa Pel] and the instruction of Yangtsewa [Rinchen Sengé] from Kunpang Rinpoché Chokyi Nyima, who named it the "Great Guidance of Zhalupa."[37]

The Ninth to Seventeenth Guidebooks

Then I received the ninth guidebook, entitled *The Three Sorts of Person*, according to Kadam; the tenth guidebook, entitled *The Sequence of the Buddhist Teaching*; the eleventh guidebook, entitled *The Sameness of Existence and Quiescence*; the twelfth guidebook, entitled *The Great Middle Way*; the thirteenth guidebook, entitled *The Hidden Guidance of Kadam* by Shawo Gangpa, which is also known as the *Trilogy of Pulverizing*; the fourteenth guidebook, entitled *Munīndra*, on which the mental focus of calm abiding depends; the fifteenth guidebook, entitled *Acala*, on which the pervasion of space with compassion depends; the sixteenth guidebook, entitled *Avalokita*, on which the protection from fierce impediments depends; and the seventeenth guidebook, entitled *Tārā*, on which the foreordaining of extrasensory powers depends—the last four being the guidebooks associated with the four deities of Kadam.

These instructions on the three sorts of person and so forth were based exclusively on the adaptations of Chimchen Namka Drak.[38] My teacher, the venerable hidden buddha Kunga Chogdrub, joyfully conferred upon me the transmissions that Raton Yonten Pelzangpo had received in the presence of Drakpa Pelden Dondrub, the monastic preceptor of Nartang, in that very seminary where he had resided for three years.

The Eighteenth and Nineteenth Guidebooks

Then, continuing as before, I received the eighteenth guidebook, {56} the guidance that introduces *The Parables of Potowa* based on the writings of Hor Kabzhipa Sengé Gyeltsen; and the nineteenth guidebook, the guidance entitled *The Sixteen Spheres of the Heart* according to *The Book of Kadam*, which I requested from Kunpang Rinpoché [Chokyi Nyima], based on the writings of Nyukla Paṇchen. Having also studied that in the context of the aforementioned guidebooks on the four deities of Kadam, I was convinced that this was contrived and inauthentic, quite dissimilar to the former.

The Twentieth to Twenty-Third Guidebooks

I then received the twentieth guidebook, entitled *The Six Descents of the Transcendent Perfection of Wisdom*, from the mouth of the masterly scholar [Lowo Khenchen Sonam Lhundrub], based on the composition of Rongton Sheja Kunrik, and in conjunction with the latter's *Commentary on the Transcendent Perfection of Wisdom in One Hundred Thousand Lines*.[39]

In the presence of Changlungpa [Zhonu Chodrub] I also received the twenty-first guidebook, entitled *The Five Paths of Pacification*, according to the writings of Rongton. I have listed this only once, although I also obtained some sixteen methods of instruction that are preserved within the later lineages of the trio Ma [Chokyi Sherab], So [Chung Gedunbar], and Kam [Yeshé Gyeltsen], and so forth, but I did not list them.[40] This guidebook discloses the essentials of the *Three Stages of Meditation* by Kamalaśīla, who was identical in nature with Dampa Sangyé.

Then I excellently obtained the twenty-second guidebook, entitled *The Three Stages of Meditation*, which is established as an exemplar of the Svāntantrika Mādhyamika, in the presence of the masterly scholar [Lowo Khenchen Sonam Lhundrub], on the basis of the writings of Rongton.

I also received in ripening manner the twenty-third guidebook, entitled *The Five Doctrines of Maitreya*, from my teacher, the venerable hidden buddha Kunga Chogdrub—a transmission that Raton Yonten Pelzang had obtained from Kunkhyen Donyo Pelwa, through the lineage of Tsen Khawoché and based on the writings of Chomden Rikpei Reldri. While he pointed out the Five Doctrines of Maitreya to me on a hundred occasions, the learned master Zangpo Tenpa also entrusted this instruction to me by pointing it out.

The Twenty-Fourth and Twenty-Fifth Guidebooks

I perfected the definitive topics of the Prāsaṅgika Mādhyamika—the oral transmission of glorious Candrakīrti, which descended through the lineage from Patsab Lotsāwa, {57} in accordance with the writings of Remdawa. This is to be counted as the twenty-fourth guidebook [entitled *The View of Intrinsic Emptiness*].

Then I requested the twenty-fifth guidebook based on the text entitled *Hook of the Lotus*, which derives from the lineage of the aforementioned Tsen Khawoché. Two of its extracts forming the guidance on *The View of Extraneous Emptiness* were adorned with the words of my learned master [Pelden Tsultrim].

The Twenty-Sixth Guidebook

I received the twenty-sixth guidebook, *The Elucidation of the Concealed Meanings* [*of Yogatantra*], from Zelmo Drakpa Drakpa Yeshé, who pointed it out in two hundred and thirty instructions.

The Twenty-Seventh to Twenty-Ninth Guidebooks

I then earnestly requested the twenty-seventh guidebook, entitled *Guidance of Amitāyus*, according to the tradition of Siddhirājñi, based on the instructions of the supreme incarnation Barawa [Gyeltsen Pelzang], which I received in succession—initially from Kunpang Rinpoché [Chokyi Nyima], next from Gyagom and Trewo Chokyi Gyatso, and finally from Changlungpa [Zhonu Chodrub].

As for the twenty-eighth guidebook, the instruction on long life entitled *The Guidance of White Tārā*, I received in succession two traditions—the lineage derived from Jowo Atiśa and the lineage derived from Karmapa Rolpei Dorjé. But on this occasion I am counting the special tradition of Jowo Atiśa, perceiving that it is worthy of confidence.

I obtained the twenty-ninth guidebook, entitled *The Guidance of White Amitāyus*, according to the lineage that Mitrayogin received from Devaḍākinī, and also according to the two aforementioned lineages, from my precious teacher, Trariwa [Rinchen Gyelchok].

The Thirtieth to Thirty-Third Guidebooks

The thirtieth guidebook, entitled *The Direct Guidance of Avalokiteśvara according to the Lakṣmī Tradition*,[41] is an ancient instruction documented by Yolgom Chowang, based on the teachings of Jowo Atiśa.

The thirty-first guidebook, concerning *The Direct Guidance of Avalokiteśvara according to the Candradhvaja Tradition*, is based on three works—the brief notes of Zhang [Ring] Kyitsa Ochen, the extensive analysis by Dzimchen Gyeltsen Pelzang, and the actual guidebook of Rongton.

As for the thirty-second guidebook, concerning *The Direct Guidance of Avalokiteśvara according to the Tsembupa Tradition*, I obtained higher maturation [of empowerment] through experiential guidance based on the instruction manual of Rinpoche Sherab Bumpa, and as the supporting transmission I received from my teacher, the venerable hidden buddha Kunga Chogdrub, the transmission of the *Great Guidebook* composed by Chojé Lama Dampa [Sonam Gyeltsen].[42] {58}

Jangchub Zangpo had also requested it from Avalokiteśvara in person, and he had transmitted it to the supreme incarnation Barawa Gyeltsen Pelzang; he [then transmitted it] to Namka Sengé, Maṇiwa Lekpei Gyeltsen, and Maṇiwa Drakpa Sonam; and from them it was maintained by the venerable hidden buddha Kunga Chogdrub. Though I indeed obtained that transmission, I have not counted it.[43]

Later on, from Changlungpa [Zhonu Chodrub] I further obtained the transmission of the instruction composed by the bodhisattva Gyelwa Yeshé, and from Trewo Chokyi Gyatso the transmission of the instruction composed by Tokden Khacho Wangpo, both of which pertain to the tradition of Tsembu.

The Direct Guidance of Avalokiteśvara according to the Kyergangpa Tradition is to be counted here as the thirty-third guidebook. I obtained from Gyagom the instruction manual on this composed by Choku Śākya Rinchen.

The Thirty-Fourth and Thirty-Fifth Guidebooks

I obtained both the thirty-fourth guidebook, *The Direct Guidance of Cakrasaṃvara*, and the thirty-fifth guidebook, *The Direct Guidance of Hevajra*, which were both established by Ānandavajra according to the respective Sanskrit texts that concern Cakrasaṃvara and Hevajra in the form of a solitary hero.[44] These were later elucidated in [Tokmé Zangpo's] *Direct Guidance on All the Meditational Deities in General.* I obtained this elixir of the mind of Gyelsé Tokmé Zangpo from Changlungpa [Zhonu Chodrub] through the lineage descended from Radengpa [Śākya Sonam].

The Thirty-Sixth and Thirty-Seventh Guidebooks

I obtained the thirty-sixth guidebook, entitled *Vajrapāṇi in the Form Mahācakra*, which is based on the direct writings on the perfection stage endowed with four blessings from Khenchen Rinpoché [Tashi Namgyel], through the lineage descended from Drakar Sempa Chenpo [Sonam Rinchen]. Then, as for the thirty-seventh guidebook, I received the inconceivably secret guidance of *Vajrapāṇi in the Form Caṇḍa*[45] from Mangkharwa [Rabsel] Dawa Gonpo, based on the writings composed by Sangdak Drubchen.

The Thirty-Eighth and Thirty-Ninth Guidebooks

As for the thirty-eighth guidebook, concerning yellow *Vārāhī in the Form Kurmapādā*, according to the tradition of Chak Lotsāwa, this was especially conferred upon me along with a painting by Kunpang Rinpoché [Chokyi Nyima]. {59}

As for the thirty-ninth guidebook, entitled *The Secret Guidance of Kurukullā*,[46] I requested this, paying homage to the wondrous and marvelous crown ornament of learning [Gugé Paṇchen Sonam Lhundrub].

The Fortieth and Forty-First Guidebooks

As for the fortieth guidebook, entitled *The Six-Branch Yoga of the Kālacakra*, although I received this many times according to all the Sanskrit and Tibetan recensions of the Six-Branch Yoga elucidated in the writings of Pelden Lama [Dampa Sonam Gyeltsen], as well as the different exegetical traditions of Jonang and Zhalu, and the tradition of Paṇchen Vanaratna that subsequently appeared, and so forth, here I have counted the actual *Commentary on the Tantra* [*of the Kālacakra*] revealed according to [the translation of] Somanātha and the questions addressed to Somanātha. This I earnestly requested, initially from the Venerable Lochen Rinchen Zangpo (1489–1563), next from Trariwa, and finally from Changlungpa [Zhonu Chodrub].

As for the forty-first guidebook, entitled the unwritten *Aural Lineage of Kālacakra*,[47] this was initially conferred upon me when I requested guidance from the Venerable Lochen Rinchen Zangpo.

The Forty-Second Guidebook

I obtained, initially from Trewo Chokyi Gyatso, the forty-second guidebook, entitled *The Ritual Service and Attainment of the Three Adamantine Realities according to Orgyanpa*, based on the instruction manual of Venerable Karmapa III Rangjung Dorjé. Next, from Venerable Lochen Rinchen Zangpo I obtained the transmission and guidance based on the instruction manual of Dawa Sengé; and finally, from Changlungpa Zhonu Chodrub, I requested authentic guidance on practices undertaken in dark retreat, based on the instruction manual of Sonam Ozer. These are the ones I have counted.

The Forty-Third Guidebook

As for the forty-third guidebook, entitled *The Path and Its Fruition*,[48] this is based on the eighteen traditions of common descent[49] and comprises twenty-four extensive subdivisions, or twelve when these are condensed.[50] When further condensed, these may be subsumed in four primary divisions, or again in the two traditions of Drokmi and Gyijo.[51]

Among the twenty-five authentic transmissions, leaving aside the tradition of Zhama, there are twenty-four lineage traditions in the Sakya tradition alone. Their subdivisions include both the tradition of the Great Vehicle and the tradition of Ngor.[52] Changlungpa received the Path and Its Fruition according to the former lineage, descended from the tradition of the Great Vehicle, with all its components intact when he had reached the age of one hundred. As for the second lineage that descended from Ngorchen Kunga Zangpo, I received this three times, in turn, from my teacher, the venerable hidden buddha Kunga Chogdrub, {60} based exclusively on the *Instruction Manual Elucidating the Concealed Meaning*.[53] I also received it respectfully three times at the feet of Lowo Khenchen Rinpoché [Sonam Lhundrub], based on that same instruction manual.

In the presence of Ngorchen Lhachok Sengé, I then received the *Religious History of the Path and Its Fruition*, which had been composed by the omniscient [Ngorchen Kunga Zangpo], and *The Treasure That Brings Forth Accomplishment*—an extremely ripening exegetical method that resembled a baby placed in its mother's lap[54]—which was the work of Venerable [Jamyang] Sangyé Rinchen. These are to be counted here.

Since in the two lineage prayers [of the traditions of the Great Vehicle and Ngor] Tsangpa Gyaré is missing, my teacher, the venerable hidden buddha Kunga Chogdrub, cited this as an example of the succession of Ling Repa being interrupted.

The Forty-Fourth to Fifty-First Guidebooks

The following [guidebooks] are the eight subsidiary cycles of the path that derive from this same lineage [of Drokmi]:[55] The forty-fourth guidebook, entitled *The Inconceivables*; the forty-fifth guidebook, entitled *The Nine Profound Methods*; the forty-sixth guidebook, entitled *The Attainment of Coemergence*; the forty-seventh guidebook, entitled *The Perfection of the Path of Fierce Inner Heat*; the forty-eighth guidebook, entitled *The Straightening of Crooked Posture*; the forty-ninth guidebook, entitled *The Path of the Female Mudra*; the fiftieth guidebook, entitled *The Great Seal Devoid of Letters*; and the fifty-first guidebook, entitled *The Determination of Mind.*

The Fifty-Second to Fifty-Eighth Guidebooks

The fifty-second guidebook is entitled *The Mingling of Sutra and Tantra*, the fifty-third guidebook is entitled *The Dispelling of Obstacles due to External Demons*, the fifty-fourth guidebook is entitled *The Dispelling of Obstacles due to the Agitation of the Physical Body by the Elements*, the fifty-fifth guidebook is entitled *The Dispelling of the Obstacles of Meditative Stability and Mind*, the fifty-sixth guidebook is entitled *The Great Seal Dispelling the Three Sorts of Suffering*, and the fifty-seventh guidebook is entitled *The Clear Recollection of the Innate State*. These are known as *The Spiritual Connections with the Six Gatekeepers.*[56]

All these I received through the kindness of Lowo Khenchen Rinpoché [Sonam Lhundrub], along with the fifty-eighth guidebook, entitled *The Three Purities*, which accords with the instruction manual of Pakpa Rinpoché.

The Fifty-Ninth to Sixty-First Guidebooks

Then I received the fifty-ninth guidebook, entitled *Twenty-Nine Essential Visualizations of Self-Consecration*, from Pelden Tsultrim, a venerable lord of learning; and in accordance with the lineage of the Path and Its Fruition, I also received the sixtieth guidebook, entitled *The Exegesis of the Concealed Path*, and the sixty-first guidebook, entitled *The Elucidation of the Symbolic Meaning*.

The Sixty-Second and Sixty-Third Guidebooks

I received the sixty-second guidebook, entitled *The Five Stages of the Secret Assembly*, {61} from Venerable Rabsel Dawa Gonpo. This had been composed by Mangkharwa Lodro Gyeltsen as a memorandum on the teachings of Muchen within the tradition of Go Khukpa Lhetsé. I counted this as the sixty-second guidebook, even though I had also obtained detailed and extensive exegetical transmissions on the direct guidance of the Mar tradition based on the writings of Venerable Lochen [Marpa Chokyi Lodro] himself.

Then, in the above manner[—that is, from Rabsel Dawa Gon—]I received the sixty-third guidebook, concerning *The Vital Essence of Liberation*, which constitutes the perfection stage of the guidance on the Secret Assembly in the form of Mañjuvajra, based on the memorandum of Drakmar Kunga Tsepel.

The Sixty-Fourth to Sixty-Sixth Guidebooks

I count as the sixty-fourth guidebook *The Unelaborate Practice of Red Yamāri*, which I obtained from my teacher, the venerable hidden buddha Kunga Chogdrub, through the lineage descended from Drubpa Sherab, the monastic preceptor of Nartang. The empowerments and guidance that I had received according to the instruction of Lowo Lotsāwa [Sherab Rinchen] are also to be taken into account. In addition, I had previously obtained from three masters—Lowo Khenchen Rinpoché [Sonam Lhundrub], Ngorchen Lhachok Sengé, and Tsok Khenchen Rinpoché—the foundation of the *Beauteous Unelaborate Ornament* [of Kunga Zangpo], which constitutes the empowerment [of Red Yamāri] according to the Chak tradition.

From my teacher, the venerable hidden buddha Kunga Chogdrub, I requested the sixty-fifth guidebook, concerning the Four-Stage Yoga, based on the guidance of Lowo Lotsāwa [Sherab Rinchen].

I obtained the cycle of *The Mental Focus on the Horns of Bhairava* from Lowo Khenchen Rinpoché [Sonam Lhundrub], based on the memorandum of Tsawarongpa Śākya Gyeltsen, and also from the lord of learning Pelden Tsultrim, based on the guidance of Chojé Gewa Gyeltsen. But I count the former as the sixty-sixth guidebook.

The Sixty-Seventh to Seventy-First Guidebooks

I obtained and count as the sixty-seventh guidebook *The Central Channel Dependent on the Male Deity Cakrasaṃvara* according to the *Array of the Seats of the Syllables* by Jetsun Drakpa Gyeltsen; and, as the sixty-eighth guidebook, *The Central Channel Dependent on the Female Deity Vajravārāhī*, in which the "referential basis" is established as the male deity and the "referential object" is artfully adopted as the female deity.[57] As the sixty-ninth guidebook I count the maturational empowerment that I received in the presence of Lowo Khenchen Rinpoché [Sonam Lhundrub], based on the writings of Jetsun Drakpa Gyeltsen concerning *The Five Stages according to Ghaṇṭāpāda*. I also obtained [the last of these] from the lord of scholars Pelden Tsultrim, based on the guidance of Pakpa [entitled *Pith Instructions of the Five Stages*], and from Je Dawa Gonpo based on the guidance of Tsok Gompa [Kunga Pel]. {62}

I obtained to the point of maturation the seventieth guidebook, concerning *The Four Stages according to Kṛṣṇacārin*, at the feet of Lowo Khenchen Rinpoché [Sonam Lhundrub], based on the venerable one's own memorandum. I had also requested it from Ngorchen Lhachok Sengé, based on the guidance of Kunkhyen Rinpoché [Kunga Zangpo], and from Mangkharwa Dawa Gonpo, based on the memorandum of Langtangpa Chen Nga Kunga Dorjé.

I excellently obtained the seventy-first guidebook, concerning *The Guidance of White Cakrasaṃvara* from Venerable [Muchen] Sangyé Rinchen, based on the instruction manual of Chel Amogha. Later I also received it from Mangkharwa Dawa Gonpo, based on that same instruction manual.

The Seventy-Second to Seventy-Fifth Guidebooks

I requested the seventy-second guidebook, including the annotations on *The Four Adamantine Seats*, from Lodro Pelzangpo, a familial descendant of Ngok, in accordance with the ancient writings of Lord Marpa.

Then I also requested the seventy-third guidebook, the guidance concerning *The Great Magical Emanation*, from that same familial descendant of Ngok, in accordance with the ancient writings of Lord Marpa.

I excellently studied the seventy-fourth guidebook, concerning the subtle vital essence of the perfection stage in respect of *The Kharamukha Cakrasaṃvara*, in the presence of Lowo Khenchen Rinpoché [Sonam Lhundrub]. This was a distinctive teaching of the Newar lama Mahābodhi, transmitted from mouth to ear. He himself had also composed a memorandum concerning the advice that he had kept in mind.

I heard the seventy-fifth guidebook, concerning *The Six Meditations of Vajravārāhī*, from Lowo Khenchen Rinpoché [Sonam Lhundrub], in accordance with the writings of Chel Kunga Dorjé.

The Seventy-Sixth and Seventy-Seventh Guidebooks

Although I many times obtained the tradition of *The Six Doctrines of Nāropā*, the instructions that are to be counted as the seventy-sixth guidebook comprise the *Molten Gold of the Six Doctrines*, composed by Lord Rangjung Dorjé, which I obtained from Trewo Chokyi Gyatso.

As for the cycle of *The Six Doctrines of Nigumā*, which is the seventy-seventh guidebook, in general there are twenty-five lineages, among which the long lineage that the accomplished master Tangtong Gyelpo had received from Jangsem Jinpa Zangpo, {63} otherwise known as the Chakzam tradition, exclusively refers to the tradition of Mu. This also separately evolved in an unwritten symbolic method that Nigumā imparted directly to the accomplished master Tangtong Gyelpo. The other twenty-four lineages were consolidated by Jakchen Jampa Pel and Samdingpa Zhonu Drub, so that they all came to be subsumed in these two transmissions. Subsequently, the lineages that derived respectively from each of these two also evolved distinctly and were no longer considered to be subbranches. I actually obtained from Gyagom [Lek Gyeltsen] the instruction that is to be counted, which derives from the lineages of Aseng of Nenying and Rechen Peljor Zangpo.

The Seventy-Eighth to Eighty-First Guidebooks

The seventy-eighth guidebook is entitled *The Amulet Tradition of the Great Seal* and it comprises the instruction manuals of both Jakchen Jampa Pel and Samdingpa Zhonu Drub. Similarly, the seventy-ninth guidebook is entitled *The Three Aspects Carried on the Path*. The eightieth guidebook is the instruction on *The Deathlessness of One's Own Mind* and the eighty-first guidebook is *The Six Doctrines of Sukhasiddhi*. All these are not differentiated in the ancient writings of the Shangpa tradition, and I obtained them from Kunpang Rinpoché [Chokyi Nyima], in accordance with the instruction manual subsequently composed by Lord Khyenrab of Zhalu.[58]

The Eighty-Second to Eighty-Seventh Guidebooks

I received the eighty-second guidebook, concerning *The Emanational Navel Cakra*, from Gyagom Chenpo [Lekpei Gyeltsen], in accordance with the ancient writings of Khyungpo Neljor, which constitute *The Inner Guidance of Nairātmyā*;[59] and although I obtained *The Coemergent Union of the Great Seal* an inestimable number of times, I count as the eighty-third guidebook the lineage descended from Gyelsé Chodzong [Tokmé Zangpo].

From Changlungpa [Zhonu Chodrub] I obtained the eighty-fourth guidebook, concerning *The Fivefold Great Seal*, based on the instruction manual of Chen Nga Nyernyipa Chokyi Gyelpo; and the eighty-fifth guidebook, entitled *The Four Syllables of the Great Seal*, based on the instruction manual of Yagdé Paṇchen.

I requested the eighty-sixth guidebook, entitled *The Introduction to the Three Buddha Bodies*, based on the instruction manual of Lord Rangjung Dorjé from Karma Trinlepa, who was entrusted with this charge by Trewo Chokyi Gyatso.

I obtained the eighty-seventh guidebook, entitled *The Indivisibility of Subtle Energy and Mind*, from Trewo Chokyi Gyatso, based on the memorandum of Lhazik Repa, in the teaching transmission of Zhamar II Khacho Wangpo.

The Eighty-Eighth to Ninety-Second Guidebooks

Under the familial descendant of Ngok I studied the eighty-eighth guidebook, entitled *The Six Doctrines according to the Sekharma Tradition* of Lord

Marpa, which had been revealed as spiritual treasure by the treasure finder Chowang and subsequently maintained intact, without adulteration; {64} the eighty-ninth guidebook, entitled *The Mingling and Transformation of the Three Poisons*, which represents the perfection stage of Hevajra according to the Ngok tradition; and the ninetieth guidebook, entitled *The Four Scrolls of the Aural Instructions.*

From Lochen I obtained the ninety-first guidebook according to Rechungpa's ancient Aural Lineage [of Cakrasaṃvara] [entitled *The Six Doctrines of Liberation through the Upper Gate*], which constitutes the oral teachings of Milarepa; and the ninety-second guidebook, entitled *The Nine Doctrinal Cycles of Nirdehaḍākinī*, which Rechungpa had introduced from India.

The Ninety-Third Guidebook

I received the ninety-third guidebook, entitled *The Elaborate Guidance according to Zhang Tselpa*, from Taklung Rinpoché [Ngawang Tulku].

The Ninety-Fourth and Ninety-Fifth Guidebooks

From Changlung Rinpoché I obtained the ninety-fourth guidebook [entitled *The Six-Branch Yoga of Pelchen Ga Lotsāwa*], which includes [Yangonpa's] *Seven Days of Fierce Inner Heat according to Pelchen Ga Lotsāwa*; and the ninety-fifth guidebook, concerning the traditions associated with *The Cycle of Pagmodru Densatel.* The latter includes the *Verses on the Great Seal* and the *Verses on the Path of Skillful Means*, which had been the practical application of Pagmodrupa.[60]

The Ninety-Sixth to One Hundredth Guidebooks

From Taklung Rinpoché I received the ninety-sixth guidebook, entitled [*The Unique Enlightened Intention according to Drigung*, along with] the *Revered Wheel of Vitality* of Drigungpa Jigten Gonpo; the ninety-seventh guidebook, entitled *The Six Doctrines according to Taklungpa [Tashipel]: The Wish-Fulfilling Gem*; the ninety-eighth guidebook, entitled *The Means for Attainment of the Guru, Auspicious Circumstances, and Common Savor*, which represents the Middle Drukpa; and the ninety-ninth guidebook, entitled *The Fivefold Capacity of Lorepa*, which represents Lower Drukpa.

I then decisively requested from the doctrinal cycle of Yangongpa the one hundredth guidebook [entitled *The Six Primary Essentials for Mountain Retreat*, which represents the Upper Drukpa], from the master Chokhor Gangpa, a lama who had studied under Lochen.

The One Hundred and First and One Hundred and Second Guidebooks

I also requested from Taklung Rinpoché the one hundred and first guidebook, comprising the cycles of *The Four-Armed Mahākāla in the Form Kurakma*.

I count here as the one hundred and second guidebook, entitled *The Inner Guidance of Glorious Pañjaranātha*, the transmission I received from Ngorchen Lhachok Sengé, based on the writings of Venerable Sangyé Rinchen,[61] but I also heard, following that, a somewhat incomplete instruction from Venerable Kunpang [Chokyi Nyima].

The One Hundred and Third and One Hundred and Fourth Guidebooks

I extensively studied the one hundred and third guidebook, entitled *The Trilogy of Spiritual Songs*, under the learned scholar [Paṇchen Donyo Drubpa]. I requested the one hundred and fourth guidebook, {65} entitled *The Six Doctrines of the Accomplished Masters*, from Trewo Chokyi Gyatso.

The One Hundred and Fifth to One Hundred and Eighth Guidebooks

The one hundred and fifth guidebook, which is the cycle of *The Gradual Path of Padmasambhava*, was bestowed upon me by my teacher, the venerable hidden buddha Kunga Chogdrub. The one hundred and sixth guidebook, concerning the six-syllable mantra, which is the authentic guidance entitled *The Collected Injunctions of the King*, was granted me by Yigdruk Sherab Peljor.

I purposefully requested the one hundred and seventh guidebook, entitled *The Liberation by Seeing according to Norbu Rinchen*, from Changlungpa [Zhonu Chodrub].

Then I requested from Changlungpa [Zhonu Chodrub] the guidance of the final one hundred and eighth guidebook, entitled *The Nature of Mind: The Wish-Fulfilling Gem*, based on the great instruction manual of Tokden Chonyi Rangdrol. Previously I had also received to some extent this transmission and guidance from Lord Lochen, based on the brief instructional notes of Zhalu Khyenrab Chojé.

Author's Statement

In this manner I have provisionally disclosed, without addition or omission, the extent of these one hundred and eight guidebooks that I painstakingly sought over thirty-one years, along with their manifold subdivisions, embellished by a clear summary of the teachers from whom I obtained them and the writings on the basis of which I obtained them.

May those who strive to study and receive such instructions
Consume this supreme drink, quenching the thirst of the rebirth process,
Its pure streams forming the syllables of sutra and tantra
Emerging from snow mountain ridges, bastions of the lineage!

As the taste and potency of rivers that freely flow
From this land become diluted,
The nectar of these instructions may seem to lack potency,
According to the analysis of unrefined and foolish persons;
But their respective modes of experiential cultivation,
Like medications that remedy diseases,
Serve as an antidote to eliminate corresponding afflictions,
In accord with our share of good fortune.

The approaches of the sacred doctrine are such
That they accord with the constitutions of infinite disciples.
Like serving clothes to those who are hungry,
How could mere beneficial thoughts offer this protection! {66}

Like the diverse and distinct colors of fine brocade,
Like the clouds of the heavens that diverge from one another,
Like rainbows in the sky, ever insatiably beheld,
The vitality of the sacred doctrine that appears to be one
Has manifold attributes that are all of a single savor.

We should indeed realize that,
Like rivers flowing into a great ocean,
These are not different!

And yet whatever words of fools out for reputation and praise
May, in the perception of the unrealized,
Roar like noisy tributaries,
Or slowly flow like wide rivers,
These are absent in the Buddhist teachings.

When pure vision is total and impartial,
Where could you find anything impure!
Wonderful is this simultaneous blessing
Of the all-pervasive objects of refuge, none excepted!

When the anthologies that collect these deep profundities
Are examined again and again, their reiteration
Is a treasure store of distinct teachings.
If we inspect them thoroughly, they cannot be exhausted!

Likened to rice paddies arduously cultivated,
With their excellent ripening harvest forming awns of grain,
They have the character of a contented, peaceful friend.

Although their felicity extends outwardly to all,
May the clear crystal of my own rejoicing mind,
Aspiring to and practicing the sacred doctrine over successive lives,
Confer liberation through the merit of this dedication
Upon virtuous minds, excellently free from negativity![62]

Colophon

After writing the first part of this text entitled *Multiple Approaches of the Wondrous Doctrine, Enhancing the Summary of the One Hundred and Eight Guidebooks*, I abandoned my somewhat lethargic endeavors at the behest of Namdrol Sengé Pelzangpo, a committed disciple who has long relinquished idleness in its entirety.

The transcription was undertaken by one Kunga Lekgyel, who excellently emerged from the ocean of the mind of Kunga Drolchok.

Thereby may all the multiple approaches of the Buddhist teaching endure for a long time, spreading and extending throughout all directions!

MAṄGALAṂ!

Let virtue prevail! {67}

5. Historical Anecdotes of the Lineage Holders

Chapters 5 and 6 contain diverse anecdotal accounts of the transmission of the One Hundred and Eight Guidebooks by earlier generations of lineage holders. Many peripheral texts associated with these cycles are also incidentally mentioned. References are generally found in the bibliography and in the notes to chapter 9.

Chapter 5, written by Kunga Drolchok, covers the anecdotal accounts of the first seventy-four guidebooks, commencing with Parting from the Four Attachments *and concluding with* The Kharamukha Cakrasaṃvara. *The supplement by Tāranātha, which is contained in chapter 6, completes the remainder, from the seventy-fifth to the one hundred and eighth.*

The introductory verses of chapter 5 are not balanced by any corresponding concluding verses, which may perhaps suggest that it was originally Kunga Drolchok's intention to complete these anecdotes himself. Tāranātha, the acknowledged reincarnation, may have considered this task as a personal responsibility.

Formal Title

Historical Anecdotes of the Lineage Holders of the One Hundred and Eight Guidebooks[1] {68}

Introductory Verses

OṂ SVĀSTI SIDDHAṂ

Respectful homage to the teachers and to the lord-protector Mañjughoṣa!

May the three precious jewels who have become a refuge
For living beings including the gods,
Along with Yongdzin Lama[2] and his teachers
Endowed with the great compassion of the perfect conquerors, unsurpassed by others,
Grant protection to the beings of this world including myself!

Now I will briefly introduce the lineage holders who initiated the tradition—
The tradition concerning all essentials of instruction, most secret—
The secret disclosed in one hundred and eight modes of guidance—
The guidance profound that is embraced by numerous good auspices.[3]

Inspired by faithful, devout, and respectful requests,
Here I will write a partial historical account
Of the most saintly individuals of the past,
Who maintained the ways of learning and accomplishment
In order to benefit others of equal fortune.

I do not dare to write verbosely the detailed biographies of the lineage holders. Instead, I will introduce to some extent the authentic sources of these respective instructions.

The First Guidebook

With regard to the historical account of the guidebook entitled *Parting from the Four Attachments*: At the time when the teacher Sakyapa the Great, Kunga Nyingpo, was in his twelfth year, estimated from the death of his father [Khon Konchok Gyelpo],[4] {69} the offerings presented on behalf of his deceased father were laid out near the main temple [of Zimkhang].[5] Those entering the monastic seat in a single day were such that the things they left behind were said to be meritorious and bountiful, whereupon his mother said, "Since your father indeed had conviction in the teachings associated with the teacher Bari Lotsāwa that are not counterfeit, you should invite Bariwa!"

After he did so, Bari said, "You, the son of that venerable father, should study! For that you need discriminative awareness. This is why you should propitiate Mañjughoṣa!" Bari then bestowed upon him the doctrinal cycle of Mañjuśrī in the form Arapacana, and he engaged in that practice. When slight indications of an obstacle arose, Bari conferred the initiation of blue Acala, along with the water protection rite, so that Sachen was set free from these obstacles. When six months had passed, he had a vision of sublime Mañjuśrī, seated in an elegant posture upon the precious teaching throne—the central figure along with a retinue of two bodhisattvas. Mañjuśrī intoned the root verses [of *Parting from the Four Attachments*], and Sachen acquired the meditative stability of continuous flow and unforgettable retention. In consideration of that, {70} the *Eulogy* [*to Sachen*] speaks of him in the following words:[6]

> Manifestly instructed by the speech of Lord Mañjuśrī,
> Vast in knowledge perceiving all that is knowable,
> Acting in accord with prophetic declaration and inspiration—
> Homage to him of perfect reasoning and liberation!

Jetsun Rinpoché [Drakpa Gyeltsen] also said, "Speech that is favored by Mañjughoṣa is renowned among all living creatures" and "You should know that all convincing rational axioms and all doctrines without exception are said to be within the buddha mind."[7]

All the lineage holders [in the familial descent from Sachen Kunga Nyingpo]—including Lopon Rinpoché [Sonam Tsemo], Jetsun Rinpoché [Drakpa Gyeltsen], Chojé Sakya Paṇḍita, Drogon Pakpa, and Chojé Lama Dampa [Sonam Gyeltsen]—were emanations and embodiments of Mañjughoṣa, as if the two retainers of Mañjughoṣa—Akṣayamati and Pratibhākuṭa—had emerged from an ancient painted scroll, and they were absolutely favored by him.

Arising from the basis of that conviction, this original instruction constituted the first guidebook to the sacred doctrine that I acquired in this lifetime.

The Second Guidebook

Immediately after that, with regard to the guidebook entitled *The Seven-Point Mind Training of the Great Vehicle*: Over the period of one year and in the context of sessions of practice that were not interrupted for a single day during that twelve-month period, my elder brother Drungtsun Zangpo Tenpa pointed out its interconnections based on the memorandum of

Drogon Pelden Yeshé, the senior disciple of Gyalse Chodzongpa [Tokmé Zangpo], and the five notebooks composed as a memorandum by Hor Kabzhipa [Sengé Gyeltsen] on this very teaching.[8] He began by citing the following verses:[9]

When sixty aeons have passed after the conqueror Maitreya
Has set his mind on enlightenment,
The Sugata himself, setting his mind on enlightenment,
Will cherish others above self
And attain buddhahood in the age of degeneration.
Emphasizing the teaching of loving-kindness, {71}
His former lives as the daughter of a friend and so forth
Set the framing narrative for this pith instruction.

Jowojé Atiśa called out the names of his teacher Dharmarakṣita, who was actually capable of granting his own flesh to others, and in addition of [Mitrayogin], the yogin of loving-kindness. Consequently, he had two actual visions of Ajita Maitreya, the heir of the conquerors. In the first of these he received *The Wheel of Sharp Weapons* and *The Peacock's Neutralizing of Poison*;[10] and in the second he received *The Adamantine Song of Chanting Meditation*.[11] Then crossing the Andaman Sea, he voyaged to the supreme sacred land of Sumatra, where he bowed at the lotus feet of a teacher known by the name of that very land[—that is, Serlingpa Dharmakīrti].[12] Atiśa excellently requested the essence of the teaching of enlightened mind, exchanging self with others in the context of the preliminary practice of setting the mind on enlightenment, and his mind was perfectly satisfied.

There are eighteen factors that are to be carried on the path, in association with [Serlingpa's] *Stages of the Heroic Mind*.[13] In that regard, the most secret counsel is contained in the following verses:[14]

Adverse conditions are your spiritual mentor,
Spirits and demons are emanations of the conquerors,
Sickness is a broom for negative obscuration,
And suffering is the display of reality.

Having realized the essential instructions concerning the tarnish of the mind according to the Lesser Vehicle, it is said that whenever Atiśa recalled leaving the silver reliquary of his peerless teacher [Serlingpa Dharmakīrti], he would burst into tears; and whenever he said or heard that name, he would place the palms of his hands together on the crown of his head.

Without interrupting the power of his resolve and the continuity of his fervent devotion, Atiśa transmitted this instruction [in Tibet], commencing from Dromton, the three dharma siblings [Putowa, Chen Ngawa, and Puchungwa], as well as Sharawa and Chekhawa; and it was finally epitomized by the practical application and pointing-out instructions in accord with reality that Gyelsé Rinpoché [Tokmé Zangpo] received from Jangsem Sonam Drakpa.

Nowadays in the heartlands of Utsang, not even a trace of the conferral of this experiential guidance is extant; {72} and in the northern direction the major, mediocre, and minor teachers feign contentment simply when the transmission of the *Compendium of Eloquence on Mind Training* of the great bodhisattva Venerable Zhonu Gyelchok is conferred.[15] But this may be refuted on the basis of the following words of Gyelsépa [Tokmé Zangpo], which are found in the latter work:

> The fundamental nature of nonarising awareness is examined in the memorandum of Drogon Pelden Yeshé.[16]

There were also points that reflected my own ideas and accorded with *Guidance on the View [of the Middle Way]* by Tsongkhapa the Great that were not within the perceptual range of any proud scholars, or points in which I had conviction but did not understand, wondering whether they were false examples or not. By rectifying these, I brought this train of thought to its conclusion. I saw and heard my monastic preceptor, the [veritable emanation of] the transcendent Lord Mañjughoṣa, confer praises extensively and continuously on this guidebook that is the quintessence of Hor Kabzhipa; and it is certain that Khen Rinpoché himself was indeed distraught because he had not received it. It was in these circumstances that I acquired conviction from the depths of my heart that there is no means higher than this guidance on the path for attaining buddhahood.

The Third Guidebook

Distinct from that, the guidebook entitled *The Heart of Dependent Origination* derives from that same lineage. The transmission of this teaching, through which Bodong Rinchen Tsemo averted leprosy, descended from the yogin Chokyi Yungdrung and Nyemo Gyagom [also known as Nyipuwa Gyergom Zhikpo] to Nyenchen Sonam Tenpa. Immediately after receiving this instruction, Sonam Tenpa planted the victory banner of attainment, abandoning the concerns of this life, and after he passed away, the anthology of his teachings that contained the following root verses of pith instruction resounded:[17]

> First you should cultivate loving-kindness,
> And inquire whether it has arisen or not.
> If it has arisen, you should cultivate compassion,
> Avert [the distinction between] self and others,
> And generate the mind of enlightenment.
> Then from within this mountainous disposition of wisdom {73}
> You should calm the diffusion and absorption of these cultivations!

The Fourth Guidebook

With regard to the guidebook entitled *The Carrying of Happiness and Suffering on the Path*: Paṇchen Śākyaśrī of Kashmir imparted this many times to the official attendants of his nine lesser paṇḍitas,[18] as well as to Indian nuns, invalids, and so forth. But, at the time when he was invited from Baiḍūr Tsongdu to Nezin in Pari, traveling uphill in a palanquin for almost half a month, Tropu Lotsāwa [Jampa Pel] and his disciples carried him with utmost care and responsibility, so that they were worn out. On that occasion, the following words of Paṇḍita Śākyaśrī imparted the guidance that introduces happiness and suffering as the three buddha bodies:[19]

> When there is happiness,
> I shall dedicate this happiness as the provision [of merit].
> May the sky be filled with spiritual and temporal well-being!
> When there is suffering,
> I shall carry the suffering of all [beings].
> May the ocean of suffering become dry!

This sacred doctrine was held, maintained, and mastered by the learned and accomplished masters of the Land of Snows in general and in particular by all those who became preceptors at the four monastic communities [of

Śākyaśrī].[20] It gained importance, was formulated as a guidebook, and was then conferred upon these communities as a group teaching, as a public teaching, and so forth. The transmission of this discursive discourse is undiminished at the present time.

The Fifth Guidebook

With regard to the guidebook [entitled *The Mind Training according to Sumpa Lotsāwa*], which is established in the distinctive teachings of Sumpa Lotsāwa Dharma Yonten: When Sumpa Lotsāwa was traveling back from India to Tibet, he refined the state of mind in which the physical elements are absorbed. He passed days and nights in a state of exhaustion, wondering if this were some premonition of impending death, or what he should do. Although the blessings of empowerment that he had received from his own teacher Paṇḍita Sergyi Bumpa and others were useful for focusing on the alleviation of disease, there was no benefit. At that time, he had a small amount of residual gold [for his travels], with which he sought out offering sacraments, including flowers, and then he went to make offerings to the Mahābodhi at Vajrāsana. In the sky above the inner sanctum {74} there were two women—one blue and one red. The blue one prostrated three times before the red one, saying, "Last night my mind was unhappy. It did not rest in the place where the mind should abide. I hope this is not some premonition about my death, for I am afraid of dying." She asked this question four times, and then the red woman, looking directly toward Sumpa Lotsāwa, replied, "Madam! If you are content with whatever thoughts arise, whatever you do will bring happiness. Your mind suffers because you are not content with whatever arises. Madam! If your mind rests where it is placed, it will be content even though you travel. Your mind suffers because it does not rest where it is placed. Madam! If your mind turns toward the sacred doctrine, it will be easy even when you die. Your mind suffers because it is not turned toward the sacred doctrine. Madam! If you realize that your own mind is immortal, there will be no death. Your mind suffers because you have not realized that your mind is immortal." As soon as Sumpa Lotsāwa heard these four replies, an extraordinary realization arose in his mind, and he said that these two women, blue and red, were none other than Vajravārāhī and Venerable Tārā.

All later spiritual mentors have esteemed this mode of guidance. Chojé Pelden Lama Dampa [Sonam Gyeltsen] is known to have conferred it when

Gyelsé Chodzongpa [Tokmé Zangpo] requested of him an instruction that had been the quintessence of his contemplation and that would benefit his mind. The actual guidebook is also said to have been composed at that time. Then, during the time when Lachen Lodro Gyeltsen became the familial lineage holder of the Sakyapa, Gyelsé Rinpoché went to escort him as far as Lhasa, and there, while acting as chant master, he also imparted this instruction as a public teaching in the courtyard [of the Great Temple] of Lhasa. This incident is illustrative, since it is mentioned in the biography of Gyelsépa.

The Sixth Guidebook

With regard to the guidebook entitled *The Severance of Machik Labdron*: There is a memorandum originating from India, composed by Āryadeva the Brahmin, of which greater and lesser verses are extant, {75} but it is not contained within the Tengyur [manuscripts] of Utsang.[21] In Tibet this system was propagated extensively by the mother, Jomo [Machik Labkyi Dronma] herself.[22]

When a *geshé* went to meet Rinchen Gangpa Śākya Shenyen, the latter was staying in a room with four pillars. All around them it was filled to the brim with labeled books. When the geshé asked what these books were, he replied, "They are exclusively Machik's cycle on Severance." The geshé was astonished and asked whether all these books naturally belonged to [the cycle on] Severance, to which he replied, "If the books of Severance were gathered together, they would not fit within a single valley!" So that is illustrative.

Among the manifold recensions of such [teachings on Severance], I had supreme confidence in the new pronouncement composed by Lama Gyeltangpa Samten Ozer, which is a commentary on *The Eight Appendices*.[23] From start to finish this work is excellently adorned with new revelations that were actually given to him by the mother Labdron, the secret ḍākinī of pristine cognition, and that are unknown in the earlier recensions on Severance. In addition, there is no higher teaching among those that sever the expanse of the four demonic forces than [the third of these appendices], the aptly titled *Wish-Fulfilling Gem: An Instruction on the Inner Meaning*. Manifestly disclosing the key points that directly reveal the nature of reality, this is indeed an expression of my inherited ancestral teachings.

The Seventh Guidebook

With regard to the guidebook entitled *The Three Essential Points*: Once upon a time there was a devout person in Tropu who heard someone say in a dream, "You should sweep your house clean each day! On this very day next year, Avalokiteśvara will come to rent a room." {76} He swept and cleaned it each day, and others would ask him, "Why are you doing this?" to which he replied, "I am doing this in accordance with a prophecy I received in a dream." And they would laugh because they did not believe this to be true. Then, when the great accomplished master Mitrayogin was invited by Tropu Lotsāwa, he arrived in Tropu and there was a commotion due to his fame. Thousands of geshés with parasols gathered there from all directions of upper and lower [Tibet], and they were so many that they could not be accommodated. Some were properly housed, but some had to stay in the open plain. Seeing this, the great accomplished master Mitrayogin offered the lodgings where he was staying to them. Then he directly knocked on the door of that devout householder and said, "Do lend a room to this Indian!" Since this accorded with the circumstances of his earlier dream, the certainty arose within the devotee that this Mitrayogin was actually Avalokiteśvara. He at once offered the fields, house, and all possessions that he owned, and requested an essential instruction, saying, "Because I am old, I do not understand the extensive and manifold nuances of the sacred doctrine." Thinking him to be worthy, with Tropu Lotsāwa translating, the great master taught him the root verses of the pith instructions, entitled *The Fourteen Quatrains on Resting in the Nature of Mind*,[24] which are carried through this life, at the time of death, and in the intermediate state, which he had himself received from Jowo Khasarpaṇi [Avalokiteśvara]. It includes the following verse:[25]

> Placing great compassion in front,
> Always looking at it, without distraction,
> Through the union of male and female deities,
> The practitioner should come to rest.

I heard that the scholars Yagdé Paṇchen and Rongton Sheja Kunrik, who possessed the eye of the sacred doctrine, also experientially cultivated this guidebook themselves and subsequently inaugurated the enlightened activity of teaching it to others. {77}

The Eighth Guidebook

With regard to the guidebook entitled *Resting in the Nature of Mind*: Immediately after explaining [*The Three Essential Points*], the great accomplished master Mitrayogin actually displayed a cubit-sized image of Jowo Khasarpaṇi upon the maṇḍala in front, and he then taught the twenty-five verses of *Resting in the Nature of Mind* in tandem with twenty-five meditative stabilities that are mentioned in the sublime *Sutra of the Transcendent Perfection of Wisdom in Eight Thousand Lines*. He established three metaphors indicative of nondistraction from the essential points of experiential cultivation—namely, an expert swordsman in battle, a wise person finding a bull without looking for it, and a bird flying aimlessly over a boat. The omniscient Buton Rinchen Drub, a percipient lineage holder who experientially applied these metaphors, also esteemed this guidebook, and it is said that he imparted his innermost thoughts on it to all his senior disciples.

The Ninth Guidebook

With regard to the profound teachings of Kadam, Ra Yonten Pelzangpo (fl. fifteenth century) stayed for three years at the great seminary of Nartang where these were all conferred upon him in the presence of Pelden Dondrub, who was renowned as an emperor among the accomplished monastic preceptors of Nartang. In this regard, he firstly received the guidebook entitled *The Three Sorts of Person*. Jowo Atiśa had transmitted this to Ngok Lekpei Sherab, he to Drolungpa Lodro Jungné, and the spiritual mentor Tsangnak Tsondru Sengé received it, in turn, from him. In his presence, Tumton Lodro Drakpa, the founder of the seminary of Nartang, received it.

Geshé Sharawa had offered alms three times to Tumton's community, and on the last of these occasions he said to Tumton, "You should acquire a monastery in the direction of Tsang. It will bring great benefit to living beings. These donations offered by my patron, the nāga king who provides all my necessities, will be dispatched henceforth to you." On the way up [to Nartang], directly above the road on which Tumton was traveling, there appeared a bee with tiger stripes and a large, coarse body, {78} making a loud buzzing sound. During the night it circled within his alms bowl. Then on reaching exactly the place where the courtyard of Nartang is now located, the bee vanished into a tree that still stands there today.

Thinking this to be the place prophesied by the lama Sharawa, he founded a monastery there.

There are six renowned texts of the Kadam tradition—namely, *Garland of Birth Stories* and *Collection of Aphorisms*, which are texts concerning faith; *Level of the Bodhisattvas* and *Ornament of the Sutras of the Great Vehicle*, which are texts concerning conduct; and *Compendium of Lessons* and *Introduction to the Conduct of a Bodhisattva*, which are texts concerning the view. Later, Chimchen Namka Drakpa composed his annotations and tables of contents to these texts, so that the ancient oral transmissions might not degenerate. Chomden Rikpei Reldri composed a supplement to the *Tales of Past Lives*, entitled *Flower Ornament of the Tales of Past Lives*. In this way the transmission was definitively conferred from the mouths [of the masters] upon the ears of the disciples.

The Tenth Guidebook

In addition, the guidebook entitled *The Sequence of the Buddhist Teaching*, which Tumton received from his spiritual mentor Sharawa in person, was also extensively propagated. Its oral transmission, later established by Chimton Lobzang Drak, is itself maintained by all those endowed with the clear eye of the sacred doctrine. Hor Kabzhipa said that the basis of the composition of his two doctrinal collections, large and small, was modeled on this alone.[26] It is said that at the end of his life, Tumtonpa returned to his native place in the northern direction, where he nurtured enlightened activity at the place known as Cholung Kunra, and then passed away.

The Eleventh Guidebook

With regard to the guidebook entitled *The Sameness of Existence and Quiescence*: Droton Dutsi Drakpa from the monastic seat of Tumton[—that is, Nartang—]received this from Mumenpa [Dutsi Charchen], a disciple of Geshe Jayulwa Zhonu O.

The Twelfth Guidebook

With regard to the guidebook entitled *The Great Middle Way*: Jangsem Dawa Gyeltsen received this from the Newar Penyawa [Ratnabhadra], a lineage holder of the teachings that had descended from Nāgārjuna the father and Aryadeva the son. He transmitted the instruction to Dzilungpa Ozer Drakpa, and Droton Dutsi Drak (1153–1232) requested it from him and then propagated it.

Though there are some who hold that this guidebook also accords with the lineage of the *Guidance on the View of the Middle Way*, which Venerable Remdawa [Zhonu Lodro] propagated from the highland region of Ngari, that is not certain, because it represents the original Mādhyamika texts—the old tradition where Prāsaṅgika and Svātantrika are not differentiated. {79} It is simply the case that the distinctions introduced by Remdawa accord with the adherents of the texts of Candrakīrti that uphold consequential reasoning.

The Thirteenth Guidebook

With regard to the guidebook entitled *The Hidden Guidance of Kadam*: Mumenpa Dutsi Charchen received this from Geshé Shawo Gangpa in person, and he conferred it upon Drotonpa Dutsi Drak.

These aforementioned four guidebooks entitled *The Three Sorts of Persons*, *The Sameness of Existence and Quiescence*, *The Great Middle Way*, and *The Hidden Guidance of Kadam* are known as the "four great guidebooks of the Kadampa."

The Fourteenth to Seventeenth Guidebooks

With regard to the guidebooks concerning the four deities of Kadam: At the time when Sangyé Gompa Chenpo [Sengé Kyab] came to Utsang in the entourage of Jowo Atiśa, he went directly to Langtang and received these teachings from Geshé Zhangpa [Chokyi Lama] at the monastic seat of Geshé Langri Tangpa.

As far as these guidebooks concerning the four deities [of Kadam] are concerned, there have been some later individuals with the title "master of the Kadampa teaching" who failed to understand that the *Cornucopia of Avalokiteśvara's Attributes* is associated [not with this guidebook on Avalokiteśvara but] with *The Direct Guidance of Avalokiteśvara according to the Tradition of Candradvaja*. They also seem to have juxtaposed and conflated the guidebook on Acala with the higher tantras that concern fierce inner heat, illusory body, dream yoga, luminosity, and so forth. In this context, however, the guidebook on Acala is the foremost instruction on the attainment of the yogic gaze of Acala, whose right and left eyes exclusively focus upward and downward. It is known as such because it originated from the ancient account of Geshé Neuzurpa Yeshé Bar who, after meditating in that manner, by gazing upward is said to have seen what a shepherd was doing on the cliff above, and by gazing downward saw a buddha field below. Similarly, with regard to the guidebooks on Munīndra and Tārā, the method of cultivating calm abiding and the establishment of protection from the eight fears are never secured apart from these instructions concerning the corresponding deities.

The Eighteenth Guidebook

With regard to the guidebook entitled *The Parables of Potowa*: this is an unsurpassed and supreme method of transforming the minds of beginners, based on worldly tales and orally transmitted stories concerning the three sorts of persons. {80}

The Nineteenth Guidebook

With regard to the guidebook entitled *The Sixteen Spheres of the Heart* according to Kadam: All the sutras and mantras that are the legacy of the lineage of experiential cultivation and blessing include the peerless profound sacred doctrine whereby, in a single seated posture, one concentrates intently and focuses on the sphere of the heart cakra. Yet there are proud geshés, responsible for abandoning the sacred doctrine, who insistently exclude this from the perspective of the Riwo Geden tradition, [saying] that there is no such lineage of this doctrine that derives from Venerable Tsongkhapa and his heirs. Indeed, they seek to make revisions, saying that it contains terms that are outside their view, such as *pure in the expanse* (*dbyings su dag pa*) and *absence of pointed focus* (*'dzug gu gtad sa mi gda' ba*).

The Twentieth Guidebook

With regard to the guidebook entitled *The Six Descents of the Transcendent Perfection of Wisdom*: As mentioned in the guidance on the transcendent perfection of wisdom by Venerable Rongton Sheja Kunrik, the transcendent lord Buddha appointed the noble Kāśyapa to preside over his actual monastic succession, and he was followed, in turn, by Ānanda, Śāṇavāsika, Upagupta, Dhītika, and so on, up to and including the arhat Siṃha[bodhi]. In this way the transmission was successively maintained at Vajrāsana through twenty-four successive hierarchs of the teaching.[27] Afterward, following subjugation by the Turuṣka army, the transmission of study and exegesis was interrupted. A heretical beggar propitiated the sun god utilizing the means for attainment of Sūrya, and consequently the great Buddhist temples were mostly incinerated.[28] Collections of scriptures comprising words, phrases, and letters were even turned into heaps of ashes.

At that time, for the sake of the Buddhist teaching, there was a brahmin nun named Prakāśaśīlā who, through union with a *kṣatriya*, gave birth to the sublime Asaṅga, and on consorting with a brahmin youth, gave birth to the master Vasubandhu. Asaṅga instantaneously arrived in Tuṣita, where he sojourned for fifty human years and received twenty doctrinal collections as a follower of Maitreya. {81} Thereafter he propagated those teachings extensively. The younger brother Vasubandhu committed to memory the entire meaning of the *Transcendent Perfection of Wisdom in One Hundred Thousand Lines*, and he would recite it aloud while submerged in a pool of sesame oil from the neck downward. Throughout the early and later parts of his life, he extensively propagated the approaches of the sacred doctrine, according to both the Great and Lesser Vehicles.[29]

[In Tibet,] it was Rongton the Great (1367–1449) who synthesized the essentials of experiential cultivation on these teachings concerning the Transcendent Perfection of Wisdom.

In earlier times, at a place known as Yumta Yulma in the uplands of Gyel in Penyul, someone requested Dampa Sangyé to consecrate a manuscript of *Extensive Mother* [which is the *Transcendent Perfection of Wisdom in One Hundred Thousand Lines*]. Dampa then sat upon the pile of books, and the supplicant took a negative view of that. Immediately the pages were all carried away into the sky by a strong wind that naturally arose, and they surged high into space. Dampa scattered consecrated barley upon them and recited the following offering verse from *Refutation of Disputed Topics*:[30]

Homage to Munīndra
Whose speech is peerless and supreme,
Through whom auspicious circumstances
Are of identical meaning in the Middle Way!

Thereupon, the pages descended onto their books in the correct order. Later, when Rongton saw that manuscript of *Extensive Mother*, the following words resounded from the formless dawn sky:[31]

> In the essential meaning there is no essence.
> Without essence is the essence.
> If you seek the essence, at Dingri
> The pacification of suffering will ensue.

In accordance with this prophetic declaration, the master [Rongton] and his disciples set out for the sake of the doctrine and arrived without impediment at Dingri Langkor in Lato. There Rongton received the cycle of the Six Descents from Venerable Lodro Gyatso and wrote down a memorandum, which is this guidebook, extant at the present day.

The Twenty-First and Twenty-Second Guidebooks

With regard to the guidebook concerning the direct guidance on *The Five Paths of Pacification*: {82} it is said that Dramen Chikpa[32] Sherab Zangpo (1411–1475) received this instruction [from Pelchen Kunlhunpa] and experientially cultivated it.

With regard to the guidebook entitled *The Three Stages of Meditation—Beginning, Middle, and Conclusive*, which is the work of Kamalaśīla: this is the essence of the teachings of Rongton, the marvelous tradition of the path that is the illustrative basis of the Svātantrika Mādhyamika.

The Twenty-Third Guidebook

[With regard to this guidebook:] Among *The Five Doctrines of Maitreya*, it is clear that the *Distinction between Phenomena and Actual Reality* and the *Supreme Continuum of the Great Vehicle* were not extant at the time when the master Haribhadra (late eighth century) was alive. This is understood because in his *Great Commentary on the Transcendent Perfection of Wisdom in Eight Thousand Lines*, he repeatedly cites *Ornament of Clear Realization*, *Ornament of the Sutras of the Great Vehicle*, and the *Distinction between the Middle and Extremes*, but he does not even mention the titles of the *Distinction between Phenomena and Actual Reality* and the *Supreme Continuum of the Great Vehicle.*

On an auspicious occasion, Lord Maitrīpā the Great restored a dilapidated stupa on which a ray of light shone. He saw a rainbow emerge from the gap formed by a crack, and inside found an old manuscript inscribed on bark. He then prayed one-pointedly to Maitreya to request its transmission, without focusing on any other object. Consequently, Maitreya revealed his visage from within the clouds of the sky and bestowed upon him its transmission, instruction, and further instruction. These texts became well known to all the paṇḍitas of India, and among them there is an unbroken lineage that was propagated in Tibet by Tsen Khawoché.[33]

The Twenty-Fourth Guidebook

[With regard to the guidebook entitled *The View of Intrinsic Emptiness*:] At the time when Patsab (b. 1055) roared the lion's roar that was the enlightened intention of glorious Candrakīrti, this was comprehended by all his contemporary scholars [in Tibet]. Above all, Geshé Sharawa sent a letter to Patsab Lotsāwa, asking certain questions. Patsab offered in reply his own explanation—*Abridgement of the Essentials of the Root and Commentary of the Introduction to the Middle Way*—under the headings view, meditation, and conduct. When it reached Sharawa, who was presiding over a molasses feast, {83} as soon as he saw Patsab's writings, tears flowed uncontrollably, and with his hand he scattered the molasses in front of him into the ten directions, saying, "This is an offering to Nāgārjuna, father and son! This is an offering to Candrakīrti! This is an offering to Patsab Nyima Drakpa! He understands the enlightened intention of Lord Nāgārjuna." In that very row of monks he proclaimed, "I will send a hundred young intelligent monks to study under Patsab." Patsab had studied in India under the paṇḍita Tīlakakalāśa and others.

Afterward, when Patsab went out one day for recreation in the midst of a forest, he met a paṇḍita wearing a black robe, with a light-bluish complexion, exuding the fragrance of supreme sandalwood, and walking with two monastic boots on his hands.[34] He paid homage and requested a blessing, whereupon the paṇḍita placed his two hands on his head and said, "You need not stay long in cyclic existence." When Patsab related this incident to other scholars, they encouraged him in one voice, saying, "You have great fortune. That paṇḍita is Candrakīrti. You met him while he was engaged in the conduct of the ascetic discipline of awareness." Henceforth it is said that Patsab could convey an extraordinary certainty concerning the essential points of the view.

Jowojé Atiśa also remarked that their views were identical, and indeed on that account praised Patsab greatly, saying, "For every hundred persons who have not set out on the path, there is one who has set out on the path. . . . For every hundred who propound the middle way between extremes, there is only one who propounds consequential reasoning." [Elsewhere] it is said in his biography that Patsab himself was also the reincarnation of Jowo Atiśa.

The Twenty-Fifth Guidebook

With regard to the guidebook entitled *The View of Extraneous Emptiness*: It says in the words of Tsen Khawoché, "The paṇḍita Sajjana of Kashmir has made the following most significant remark, 'The Conqueror turned the wheel of the sacred doctrine three times—teaching the four noble truths in the first turning, the absence of defining characteristics in the second, and the excellent analysis [of all buddha attributes] in the final promulgation. Among these, the first two did not differentiate between the real and the imputed, whereas the final turning did determine the ultimate truth. On that occasion, therefore, the Buddha taught the distinction between the middle way and extremes, and between phenomena and reality. {84} The original manuscripts of the *Distinction between Phenomena and Actual Reality* and the *Supreme Continuum of the Great Vehicle* were simply lent out [to Maitreya].[35] Indeed, if these two texts had vanished, it would have denoted Maitreya's passing away into bliss.'"

In this regard, there is an ancient memorandum entitled *Hook of the Lotus*, composed by Tsen Khawoché, forewarning against the later allegation that the term *extraneous emptiness* was unknown in India but appeared in Tibet through the omniscient Dolpopa. You may also investigate that in a response to questions composed by the all-knowing Buton Rinchen Drub, it says that there was an earlier philosophical tenet of Tanakpa Rinchen Yeshépa that was later enhanced and maintained by Dolpopa.[36]

The Twenty-Sixth Guidebook

With regard to the guidebook entitled *The Elucidation of the Concealed Meanings* [*of Yogatantra*]: The essentials of this teaching were bestowed by

Lord Vajrasattva at the entreaty of the transcendent lady Vajravārāhī. The essence [of this guidebook]—an enumeration [of two hundred and thirty instructions] associated with the original text of *Summation of the Real*—was brought forth [by Bodongpa].

The Twenty-Seventh Guidebook

With regard to the guidebook entitled *The Guidance of Amitāyus*, which was imparted to Siddhirājñi: It is certain that, starting from Rechungpa Dorjé Drak (1085–1161), who offered this to Milarepa, and continuing down to the supreme emanation Barawa Gyeltsen Pelzang (1310–1391), the line of transmission was from mouth to ear, maintained in a single succession as a sealed precept. Although there were also different teachers who extensively propagated the discourses of Siddhirājñi, even the names of their "single-deity single-vase" transmissions are unknown.[37]

The original source of the guidebook of Barawa Gyeltsen Pelzang, this supreme incarnation, was also previously unknown in the Land of Snows. In the latter's secret biography, it mentions that while he was focusing on this very practice at a hermitage in Paro Drang-gyé, he wrote down the instruction of the aural lineage, based on a prophecy he received from the glorious ḍākinī Guhyajñānā, and afterward he conferred the empowerment in a large public gathering.

Nowadays, whatever philosophical systems of the Sakya, Kagyu, and Geluk {85} are espoused, there is no one at all who performs this ritual that is beneficial to others. The long-life empowerment that is the foundation of this guidebook is, however, still conferred in the context of an empowerment rite. I have recited with my tongue many tens of thousands of times the liturgy of this empowerment rite, so I am convinced that if any empowerment is to be conferred, there will be no greater blessing that there is in this.

The Twenty-Eighth and Twenty-Ninth Guidebooks

With regard to the guidebook entitled *The Guidance of White Tārā*: this denotes the tradition of Jowojé Atiśa, with which all the renowned Kadampa geshés previously had a connection.

With regard to the guidebook concerning the secret *Guidance of White Amitāyus* that was conferred on Mitrayogin by Devaḍākinī: This in later times became known as the "secret path of Maitrīpā." It directly emphasizes the practical application [of the perfection stage], having abandoned the empowerments, deity meditation, and so forth.

THE THIRTIETH TO THIRTY-THIRD GUIDEBOOKS

All of these guidebooks entitled *The Direct Guidance of Avalokiteśvara* respectively accord with the tradition of the nun Lakṣmī, which Jowojé Atiśa conferred upon Tonpa Yolgom Chowang; [the tradition of the bodhisattva Candradhvaja,] which Zhang [Ring] Kyitsa Ochen requested from the bodhisattva Candradhvaja; [the tradition of Drubchen Tsembupa,] which the accomplished master Tsembupa actually received from Nairātmyā; and [the tradition of Kyergangpa,] which Lama Kyergangpa received from Chegompa [Sherab Dorpa] at Lupuk Karchung in Lhasa. These are four distinct lineages but, other than that, they constitute a single path.

THE THIRTY-FOURTH AND THIRTY-FIFTH GUIDEBOOKS

Later, when Gyelsé Chodzongpa [Tokmé Zangpo] stayed for some three years in central Tibet, he guided his disciples at Jang Radeng and so forth through his definitive work, *Direct Guidance on All the Meditational Deities in General*. Then he gave teaching, commenting separately on each of the following methods of direct guidance: [The thirty-fourth guidebook, entitled *The Direct Guidance of Cakrasaṃvara*,] which is based on the master Ghaṇṭāpāda's short treatise entitled *Innate Cakrasaṃvara*; and [the thirty-fifth guidebook, entitled *The Direct Guidance of Hevajra*,] which is based on Ānandavajra's Sanskrit text concerning Innate Cakrasaṃvara and Hevajra. On that occasion, all the meditational deities were transformed into their unsurpassed forms. The glorious Lama Dampa [Sonam Gyeltsen] is also said to have approved of this, and actually it puts to rest the notion that Gyelsépa [Tokmé Zangpo] never taught the way of Secret Mantra. {86}

THE THIRTY-SIXTH AND THIRTY-SEVENTH GUIDEBOOKS

With regard to the guidebook concerning the perfection stage of *Vajrapāṇi in the Form Mahācakra*: The lineage descended gradually from Lama Mar[ton Chokyi Gyeltsen]. There is also [a line of transmission] from Buton the Great, who purposefully propagated it.

With regard to the guidebook entitled *Vajrapāṇi in the Form Caṇḍa*: This denotes the perfected experiential cultivation of Sangak Drubchen [Jodenpa]. Later, however, in this northern direction, the application of this fierce guidance of Guhyapati Vajrapāṇi, which is inconceivably secret, appears to have been superficial.

The Thirty-Eighth and Thirty-Ninth Guidebooks

With regard to the guidebook concerning yellow *Vārāhī in the Form Kurmapādā*: this denotes the profound and uncommon sacred doctrine associated with the lineage of Chak Lotsāwa [Rinchen Chogyel].

With regard to the guidebook concerning the outer and inner *Secret Guidance of Kurukullā*: this denotes the wondrous and marvelous [Sakya and Ngorpa transmission], but there are some people who, without paying attention to that, boast deceitfully and spuriously of engaging in the practice of the fierce inner heat and the four cakras with reference to Hevajra.

The Fortieth, Forty-First, and Forty-Second Guidebooks

With regard to the guidebook entitled *The Six-Branch Yoga of Kālacakra*: Although there are many independently written commentaries extant throughout India and Tibet, here I have counted the *Commentary* [*Entitled Taintless Light*], which accords with Somanātha and the questions addressed to Somanātha, and in which word and meaning are indivisible. Having investigated the commentary on the tantra itself, I acquired conviction in it.

With regard to the guidebook entitled *The Aural Lineage of Kālacakra* according to Menlung Guru [Sonam Pel]: This later merged with the Great Perfection, so that it is hard to differentiate them. This method is incomplete when one is engaging in the path that explores the structure of the subtle body, and it employs the terms *disposition* (*ngang*) and *self* (*rang*) instead of the term *this* (*'di*). For these reasons it resembles the threshing stick of a blind man.

For a long time I was left without finding any method based on the practice of its ritual service and attainment or its guidance. Later on, however, my paternal uncle, who had previously received this along with my father, the great translator,[38] from Chojé Khewang Rinchen Chowang at Tsetang and had become a great master of this doctrine, came to Drakhar in U to confer a connection with this teaching on me. When I questioned him about it, he said Hūṃchen Namka Neljor and Hūṃchen Lhundrub Rinchen had modified [the terminology] because they had formerly doubted the additions and deletions made by Menlungpa himself, who distinctively added certain unrelated terms from *Tantra of Heruka Galpo* here.[39] He, however, was satisfied [with the original] because he had acquired certainty in the term *disposition* (*ngang*) and also in the term *mine* (*nga'i nga*), {87} understanding these to denote the purification of the seven aspects of consciousness, including the afflicted mental consciousness.[40] He also said that his name had originally been Rinchen Zangpo. Since he and my father had the same name, I was contented, thinking of him with gratitude. This illustrates that when one has never tested a guidebook at all, one should persist in examining precisely the actual source of the lineage from which it originated.

[With regard to the forty-second guidebook, entitled *Ritual Service and Attainment of the Three Adamantine Realities according to Orgyanpa*: there is no mention of this here in these historical anecdotes].

The Forty-Third Guidebook

With regard to the guidebook entitled *The Path and Its Fruition*: Firstly, Drokmi [Lotsāwa] and later Gyijo Dawa Ozer received this from the paṇḍita Gayādhara.[41] Fifteen major traditions evolved from Drokmi, along with their twenty-three offshoots, but they number only twelve when arranged according to those that are still extant.[42] Sachen Kunga Nyingpo received the long lineage from Seton Kunrik and Zhangton Chobar; and, in addition to the lineage of Drokmi, he also received it from Virūpa in person, forming a close lineage that is virtually unbroken at the present time.[43]

As far as the [distinct] tradition of Zhama is concerned, only the transmissions of the *Instruction Manual* and *Dispelling of Obstacles Entitled Ocean-Like Visualizations of Ha*, which were composed by Kodrakpa, are extant. I understand that Mar[ton] made an accurate investigation [of this transmission], although Gyijo had told him not to propagate it. But Gyijo did teach it to Khorewa Okyi Gyeltsen, and thereafter his transmission naturally continued down to Bardingpa Namka Gyeltsen.

The Forty-Fourth to Fifty-First Guidebooks

With regard to these guidebooks, which are collectively entitled *Eight Further Cycles of the Path*: There are six that engage with the perfection stage of the three meditational deities—Cakrasaṃvara, Hevajra, and Guhyasamāja—and two that comment on the tantras in general.[44] Among them, Ḍombipā's *The Attainment of Coemergence* and Saroruha's *The Nine Profound Methods* pertain to the commentarial tradition of Hevajra and the actual perfection stage of the Saroruha tradition. *The Perfection of the Path of Fierce Inner Heat* and *The Straightening of Crooked Posture* pertain to Cakrasaṃvara. *The Attainment in Proximity to a Stupa* [or *The Determination of Mind*] pertains to Guhyasamāja in the form Akṣobhya, and *The Great Seal Devoid of Letters* pertains to Guhyasamāja according to the Buddhajñānapāda tradition. *The Inconceivables* and the cycle of the path of Indrabhūti [entitled *The Path of the Female Mudra*] are both unquestionably practiced in the perfection stage of all the unsurpassed tantras without exception. {88}

Here, in the practical transmission that is perfectly implemented, *The Attainment of Coemergence* and *The Nine Profound Methods* are not conferred through their own individual maturational empowerments, which would respectively be the maṇḍala rite of Ḍombipā and the inaugural maṇḍala rite of Nelingma. Rather, the maturation of each of the *Eight Further Cycles of the Path* is exclusively rendered efficacious through the empowerments associated with the instructional tradition of Hevajra. Following this line of reasoning, it is unquestionable that the maturational empowerments of all the mantra-related sections of all the one hundred and eight could be performed according to the instructional tradition of Hevajra alone! The essential point here, however, is that although the lineages of maturational empowerment and liberating path coincide in both the aforementioned traditions of Ḍombipā and Saroruha, they have diverged in the other six. For example, in *The Perfection of the Path of Fierce Inner Heat* and *The Straightening of Crooked Posture*, the empowerment accords with the Kāṇha tradition of Cakrasaṃvara, whereas *The Attainment in Proximity to a Stupa* adopts the empowerment of Guhyasamāja in the form Akṣobhya, and *The Great Seal Devoid of Letters* adopts [the empowerment of Guhyasamāja in the form] Mañjuvajra. *The Inconceivables* and the cycle of the path of Indrabhūti [entitled *The Path of the Female Mudra*] adopt the maturational empowerment of the *Tantra of the Vital Essence of Union*. And yet, although the empowerments [of these six guidebooks] manifestly correspond to their respective tantras, since the lineages of their maturational empowerment and their liberating path have diverged, the maturational empowerment is best performed according to the instructional tradition [of Hevajra] alone, with that empowerment functioning as their inaugural rite. For the lineages of instruction in addition to that empowerment, however, one cannot find any method apart from their individual applications.

The Fifty-Second to Fifty-Seventh Guidebooks

With regard to these guidebooks, which are collectively known as *The Spiritual Connections with the Six Gatekeepers*: there are many instructions that stem from the *Nine Cycles of the Path*, including the Path and Its Fruition, but these six are illustrative.

The Fifty-Eighth and Fifty-Ninth Guidebooks

With regard to the guidebook entitled *The Three Purities*: This is said to be a term that is not at all found in *The Path and Its Fruition*. Formerly, at Mutso, the glorious lord of the sacred doctrine Gyelwa Bum first delivered an essential teaching on *Parting from the Four Attachments*. Afterward, when he taught at Jonshing, he gave teachings on the [absolute] setting of the mind on enlightenment, which is nonarising and indeterminate; and then he conferred empowerment in the commentarial tradition that accords with the maṇḍala rite of Ḍombipā. He began with the guidebook entitled *The Three Purities*, next he bestowed the related instruction entitled *The Inconceivables*, and finally he bestowed *The Twenty-Nine [Essential] Visualizations of Self-Consecration*. There is an actual detailed account of Ngari Ulekpa, the monk Aba Drakpa, and the others who were his disciples at the time when they acquired the title of "one who had reached the Path and Its Fruition of the Hevajra commentarial tradition." {89}

The Sixtieth Guidebook

With regard to the guidebook entitled *The Exegesis of the Concealed Path*: The portal of this teaching was opened through the transformative empowerments of the profound path, exclusively in the palace of Akṣobhya—the adamantine reality of buddha mind. Jetsun Drakpa Gyeltsen alludes to this in his *Analysis of Empowerment*.[45] This guidebook concerns the application and symbolism of yogic exercises that constitute the guidance of the five celestial palaces [of the body], according to the concealed exegesis.

The root verses of the concealed exegesis were originally in hybrid Sanskrit and Prakrit, as follows: AIKE JARAHUMARAHAMARAHU| AṂKE MUDRATUTRA AṂ BINTUDARBA| IKE APARAŚŪNYATĀSAGATI| AṂGE PARAŚUKRADHANU IBATĪṢṬA|. When translated into Tibetan, the word AṂKE [and its variants] indicate the vocative. The other expressions respectively mean "blazing, dynamic, and steadfast," "propitiate the mudra and retain the vital essence!," "realize that the self is empty!," and "manifest like an overpowering bow!"

With these words, Virūpa symbolically taught seventy-two tantras to Sachen Kunga Nyingpo, and in the same manner he also taught him the four profound doctrines [in secret], without going beyond the boundary wall [of his hermitage].[46] Sachen wrote down the elucidation of their meaning in a concordance of bilingual examples.[47]

The Sixty-First Guidebook

With regard to the guidebook entitled *The Elucidation of the Symbolic Meaning*: Sachen Kunga Nyingpo revealed this in a pure vision to Jetsun Drakpa Gyeltsen. He explained the essentials of the Path and Its Fruition by means of making symbolic signs on the white rock upon which he sat. It brings together extensive, middling, and concise visualizations. Later on, certain proud scholars said of this that its root verses had been deliberately distorted following the interpretation of the six-branch yoga of Hevajra according to the class of mother tantra, which Ga Lotsāwa had given to Sachen Kunga Nyingpo.

The Sixty-Second and Sixty-Third Guidebooks

With regard to the guidebook entitled *The Five Stages of the Secret Assembly*: The commentarial writings of Serdingpa Zhonu O on [Nāgārjuna's] *Five Stages* were extensive.[48] When [the exposition of this instruction] had become corrupted, {90} he composed his own exegesis that reestablished the [meaning of] the *Guhyasamāja*, according to his view, based on three scrolls of Go Khukpa Lhetsé that came into his possession.

With regard to the guidebook entitled *The Vital Essence of Liberation*: this comprises the six-branch yoga of the *Guhyasamāja*, as enunciated in the *Subsequent Tantra of the Secret Assembly*.

The Sixty-Fourth to Sixty-Sixth Guidebooks

As for the guidebook entitled *The Unelaborate Practice of Red Yamāri*: I acquired conviction in the tradition of Lowo Lotsāwa.

The guidebook entitled *The Four-Stage Yoga* is also based on the writings of Lowo Lotsāwa. Later, Ārya [Kanaśrī] from Upper Nyang and others made a false claim concerning a yogin named Karṇaripā, dissimulating that he had stayed for twelve years standing on one foot alongside [an image of] Khasarpaṇi, and in consequence of that actually obtained this instruction from Virūpa. This needs to be investigated since it is indeed a false assertion.

With regard to the guidebook entitled *The Mental Focus on the Horns of Bhairava* that accords with the Kyo tradition, and the associated *Nocturnal Motion* and *The Erect Penis* [*of Bhairava*]: These are authentic, and there are extant Sanskrit memoranda attributed to the Indian masters Amoghavajra, Lalitavajra, and Mañjuśrīmitra. [In addition], the Riwo Gedenpa composed a supporting text on the *Guhyasamāja*, which was arranged according to the great accomplished master Śrīdhara's *Four-Stage Yoga of Red Yamāri* and Śāntipa's *The Inner Yoga of the Communal Offering*.

The Sixty-Seventh and Sixty-Eighth Guidebooks

With regard to the guidebook entitled *The Central Channel Dependent on the Male Deity Cakrasaṃvara*: This denotes the teaching of Jetsun Drakpa Gyeltsen entitled *Elixir of the Buddha Mind of Nāropā*. The guidebook entitled *The Central Channel Dependent on the Female Deity Vajravārāhī*—in which the "referential basis" is established as the male deity who enters into union with the female deity, or "referential object"—is contextualized by Mu Konchok Gyeltsen as follows:[49] "*Vārāhī Khecarī of the Generation Stage* and *The Central Channel of the Perfection Stage* had been taught sequentially, but the two had not been taught together. It was the glorious Lama Dampa Sonam Gyeltsen who conferred instruction on Chojé Zung[50] that combined *The Central Channel* with Nāropā's *Khecarī* and this is said to have been his own formulation. It represents our own tradition—the guidance of the concise and cherished pith instructions of inner Pullahari." And, "Though Jetsun [Drakpa Gyeltsen] did explain them, integrating the three channels with the two structures of the body, in his *Catalog* he still refers to them [separately] as '*Khecarī*, *The Central Channel*, and so forth.'"[51] {91} In addition, the Venerable Dorjé Chang [Kunga Zangpo] speaks of "the yoga of Khecarī, the profound generation stage, and the yoga of the central channel of the perfection stage."[52] There is therefore no authentic basis for conflating them. On the other hand, when glorious Lama Dampa Sonam Gyeltsen received guidance on the central channel from Drakpukpa Sonam Pelwa, over seven days he did perfect the power of the fierce inner heat. Since this is mentioned in the *Biography* [*of Lama Dampa Sonam Gyeltsen*] composed by the great translator Jangchub Tsemo, [his differing opinion] should be properly considered.

The Sixty-Ninth Guidebook

With regard to the guidebook entitled *The Five Stages according to Ghaṇṭāpāda*: There is an extensive exegesis on this composed by Tsongkhapa in respect of which I never obtained the blessing of the preliminary practice.[53] There is also the insightful commentary by [Taktsang Lotsāwa] Drapa Sherab Rinchen for which I acquired the blessing and empowerment.[54] As far as my own tradition is concerned, I have confidence in the teaching of Jetsun Drakpa Gyeltsen, which is an injunction of Vajradhara, so how could I follow naive chatter?[55] Although there is also an instruction composed by Pakpa,[56] in this context I count the text of Tsokgompa [Kunga Pel], which was definitively written. It is the experiential guidance through which Tsokgompa acquired a precisely flowing and clear meditative stability while cultivating this instruction under Sakya Paṇḍita. There are also definitive notes on that by Zhang Dodé Pel.[57]

The Seventieth Guidebook

With regard to the guidebook entitled *The Four Stages according to Kṛṣṇacārin*: Mal Lotsāwa, Purang Lochung [of Kashmir], and Mardo [Chokyi Wangchuk]—those three—were generally similar in that they composed instructions that were later comparable to *The Perfection of the Path of Fierce Inner Heat*.[58]

Gungru Sherab Zangpo and others also composed tables of contents entitled *A General Description of the Four Stages* and *A Particular Exegesis of the Vital Essence of Spring*.[59] Then he came to know that the *Instruction Manual Entitled Oral Discussion* is mistaken in teaching that the *Vital Essence of Spring* illustrates only two cakras because the Sanskrit text of the *Vital Essence of Spring* absolutely does have an extensive exegesis of four cakras.[60]

Also, with regard to *Inciting the Path of the Four Stages*, it is said that the teaching transmission of Purang Lochung was committed to writing by Mar Chokyi Gyeltsen, and a definitive memorandum on Marpa Dopa's *Oral Discussion* was definitively recorded by Chokro Chokyi Gyeltsen. {92} Then there was Venerable Sachen Kunga Nyingpo's [*Commentary on*] *Inciting the Path of the Four Stages*. All three could withstand revisions and are reliable because they are in harmony with the pith instructions of Nāropā.

Nowadays all the most dignified geshés of the Sakyapa school proclaim with trepidation that the four stages of the path are extremely dangerous, but there is no basis for Kṛṣṇacārin's *Four Stages of the Path* being dangerous for the Sakyapas. The reason why it is widely reported that this instruction is very dangerous is that formerly when Chokro Chokyi Gyeltsen set out from Kham, all his relatives sent much gold. In particular, his mother sent a golden spoon inlaid with turquoise in order to sustain his acquisition of the sacred doctrine. On reaching Utsang, he stayed a long time at Yamdrok, where for twelve years he sat pillow to pillow with Mardo Chokyi Wangchuk. He received all the tantras and pith instructions pertaining to Cakrasaṃvara, and also wrote an exegetical commentary on the tantra according to the teachings of Mardo. Buton later praised that treatise immensely, saying among the indigenous Tibetan commentaries on Cakrasaṃvara, that one was excellent. Venerable Tsongkhapa was also attracted to that commentary.

At that time when Chokro Chokyi Gyeltsen was contented with the teachings he had received, Mardo's son José Namka-o saw that golden spoon in the hand of Chokro and said to him, "You are contented with those oral instructions, but you have not received the direct guidance on implementing the *Four Stages* [*of the Path*], which is the essence of the instructions. You should offer this golden spoon to the lama and request that!" So Chokro prepared an excellent communal offering, on top of which he offered the golden spoon inlaid with turquoise and requested *Inciting the Path of the Four Stages*. Marpa Dopa rose on his teaching throne {93} and said, "No one at all knows the name of this doctrine. Who told you about it?" Chokro replied that José had told him, whereupon he looked at José and said, "Greedy! Is your vital channel of life made of diamond! Now, even if your life is cut off, there is an auspicious circumstance indicating that the continuity of this instruction will not be interrupted in the future." Mardo Lotsāwa conferred the instruction, and as soon as he had done so, he passed away. And as his son got dressed in order to make the funerary offerings, thieves launched a nighttime raid and pierced his body with weapons, so that he also died after eleven days. Throughout the country this was taken as an indication that the instruction was dangerous. Nowadays, the transmission that Mardo imparted to Chokro is no longer extant, but the text that Chokro composed survives.

The Seventy-First Guidebook

With regard to the guidebook entitled *The Guidance of White Cakrasaṃvara*: This was supreme among the four extraordinary and special instructions through which Śākyaśrī, the paṇḍita of Kashmir, attained enlightenment. Although dissimilar to the exegetical methods of the Indian masters Abhayākaragupta, Atiśa, and paṇḍita Vibhūticandra, Śākyaśrī said that Vajravārāhī actually conferred this upon him.

Formerly white Cakrasaṃvara was the principal meditational deity of all the monastic preceptors of the four communities [established in Tibet by Śākyaśrī]. Considering that, Rongton Sheja Kunrik later traveled to Ngor to request Dorjé Chang Kunga Zangpo for instruction on white Cakrasaṃvara. The letter of request that he made at that time is even now kept in a relic box at Ngor. But he did not have an opportunity to receive it.

The Seventy-Second Guidebook

With regard to the guidebook entitled *The Four Adamantine Seats*: The profound gradation of guidance on *The Four Adamantine Seats* is extremely rare. When Buton Rinpoché was teaching this instruction, he would confer it in the same way as his teacher, facing in the same direction, and exactly at the same time of day, neither earlier nor later.

The Seventy-Third Guidebook

With regard to the guidebook entitled *The Great Magical Emanation*: Here I refer exclusively to the tradition that maintains the texts and lineage of Ngok Choku Dorjé. {94} It is said that Buton also requested this and never acquired it, but that later he eventually did receive it from Jamkya Namka Pelden. Khyungpo Lhepa [Zhonu Sonam] received it from Buton, the lama Tashi Rinchen received it from him, and Dorjé Chang [Kunga Zangpo] received it from the latter.

Later on, some years after Dorjé Chang had founded Ngor Monastery, a great monastic preceptor known as Rongchung Sherab Pelden came to attend upon him. He and Chojé Rongpo both had the same birthplace, and there was not the slightest difference between them in their erudition or learning. Even so, Rongchung said, "Taking our physical stature into account, you are known as Rongchen and I am Rongchung. Previously, apart from following the causal vehicle of defining characteristics alone, I have never heard a single teaching on the way of mantra. Confronted by death in my old age, I feel sad even though I have listened to exegeses. In this last part of my life, I think I should engage in some experiential cultivation. So, O Lama, since you are a master of the tantras, I request you to confer upon me a maturational empowerment, liberating path, or supporting tantric exegesis of the way of Secret Mantra that is brief and concise, easy to understand, and absolutely easy to carry [on the path]—for I have not trained in the way of Secret Mantra."

Dorjé Chang replied, "In that case, I will offer you this sacred doctrine through which our predecessor the lord-protector Chogyel Pakpa dispatched the Kadampa Namka Bum to the realm of the sky-farers." In the southern castle [at Ngor], in a public exegesis, he conferred upon Rongchung the empowerments and guidance of *Cakrasaṃvara* and the *Great Magical Emanation*, based on the Vajragarbha Ḍākinī. Rongchung stayed there for about eleven months and a supreme joy was born within him. He then returned home and took up residence within a grass hermitage at the foot of the palace known as Nub Cholung's Cakrasaṃvara Chapel.[61] There he nurtured his liberating career, planting the victory banner of attainment without distractions. {95}

When some three years had passed, a vulture fell down upon the residence of the Governor Norzang of the Rinpung Estate.[62] Astrologers and others predicted that "this hare year there will be a great disaster that cannot be averted by any longevity rites and so forth. It is certain that the Drungchen will die." Many random teachers of the Rong area and the Shong area also said that such signs had occurred in their dreams. So Drungchen Norzang was despondent. They said, "Since death is certainly approaching at this time, having in the past accumulated most severe negativity through your governorship, there will be nowhere at all for you to go but the hells. So, before the movement of your life-breath expires, you have no choice but to receive empowerments of Sarvavid Vairocana from a lama who knows the way of Secret Mantra. Nowadays there is no one in the Tsang area other than Ngorpa Dorjé Chang Kunga Zangpo who is adorned with the practical applications of Secret Mantra. You should invite him!"

An invitation duly arrived at Ngor Evaṃ Choden, outlining the reason for this request. At that time, Dorjé Chang had finished teaching the three appearances according to the Path and Its Fruition,[63] and it was the day on which he was conferring the vows of setting the mind on enlightenment. Learned persons from each of the residential houses within the monastery assembled, and they said, "If you go at this time, it will not be auspicious. Since this is the high point of the teaching that you are conferring, it will indeed be difficult to achieve anything." On the other hand, since he would be censured [if he did not go there] before the governor passed away, Dorjé Chang said, "The master Konchok Gyeltsen who has not actually come [to this meeting] should confer upon the community of practitioners the empowerment of Nairātmyā in a maṇḍala of colored sand, and after that, seated upon a cushion in front of the teaching throne, he should deliver an extensive exegesis on the indivisibility of cyclic existence and nirvana." Then Dorjé Chang directly set out on horseback.

At Rinpung he conferred upon the governor an elaborate ritual on cheating death according to the Sanskrit text of Jetāri,[64] and in association with a hundred long-life empowerments. {96} In that manner, the obstacles of that year were dispelled, and thereafter it is said that he would virtually make an annual visit [to Rinpung].

On the way back up [to Ngor], just above Soldro Jetang in Nub Cholung, they set up their fireplace, and Chojé Rongchung went there from his retreat hermitage to meet him. After the others had set out from Soldro, Rongchung stayed alone for a while in the presence of the Venerable Dorjé Chang, offering many prostrations and suggesting some reasons [for leaving his hermitage], but the lama was displeased.

The lama and his disciples were then invited to the palace, where they had excellent sweet tea. At the break of dawn when the horizon was still pale, Gugé Paṇḍita, who was the attendant at that time, went to disturb Venerable Dorjé Chang with an offering of some black tea. At that time the sky was entirely filled with light. Inspecting this in detail, he saw that the grass hermitage of Rongchungpa was shrouded by a seven-layered umbrella of rainbow light, its upturned staff in the form of a tube fashioned of five-colored rainbow light. In astonishment he went inside and reported this, but the lama did not say anything at all. At sunrise, the attendant of Rongchung arrived there and said that although Rongchung's complexion had not shown any signs of illness and the like, when he went to bring him morning soup he had already passed away. The lama then said, "Over the last three years he has increased his meditative commitments. Reaching the essential point, he has departed without impediment for the realm of the sky-farers. Since we are responsible for the funeral ceremony, we will stay for three days, after which you may cremate the body." Since Rongchung's mortal remains had dissolved into light owing to the rites of the *Great Magical Emanation* that the Venerable Dorjé Chang the Great had himself bestowed, the valley was permeated with a shower of flowers, a symphony of music, and an exquisite fragrance. He presented gifts at the crematorium and said they should not open it for seven days. Then he set out on the way back to Ngor. {97} When the crematorium was opened on the eighth day, they found that he had been invited by the ḍākinīs, leaving behind not even a single bone relic the size of a fingernail or a spoonful of funerary ash. When they asked if they should build a small brick reliquary stupa at the place where he had departed, no one said anything in reply. When they looked for a quantity of earth to make one, they did not find even the slightest trace.

The Seventy-Fourth Guidebook

With regard to the guidebook entitled *The Kharamukha Cakrasaṃvara*: This is a wondrous and marvelous profound teaching that had never previously been translated in Tibet. Dorjé Chang Kunga Zangpo visited Ngari Lowo [Khenchen Sonam Lhundrub] on three occasions. On the last occasion, at a place called Netsedrum in the connecting lower valley (*bar tshigs lung thur*) of Lowo, there was a lama named Samten Ozer who had received the empowerments and oral instructions of Kharamukha Cakrasaṃvara from the Newar Mahābodhi. He had practiced the generation and perfection stages of meditation without interruption and had completed seven hundred million recitations of the seven-syllable mantra and eighty thousand recitations of the *Litany of the Names of Mañjuśrī* in Sanskrit. Immediately after that he had lived as a hidden yogin, selling yeast for brewing ale.

Venerable Dorjé Chang summoned Samten Ozer to Drakar and also gave him precise training in the tradition for the conferral of empowerment, after which Samten Ozer was due to offer the empowerment the next morning. That evening, however, Samten Ozer ran away and entered the temple of Lower Rongting. Venerable Dorjé Chang then said, "If he cannot confer the empowerment on me, since otherwise the transmission of this teaching will be interrupted and ruined, let him confer it on these three disciples of mine!" The three—Chojé Peldenpa of Jampeling, Gugé Paṇḍita [Drakpa Gyeltsen], and Lama Gyelsé—then requested it, and Samten Ozer bestowed it upon them, after which he was sent on his way with inconceivably fine donations. As commanded, Samten Ozer took care when conferring the empowerment. He conferred the preparatory rite, and the following day, during the exegesis on the empowerment, he detailed the hierarchy of the five [downfalls], from the killing of life to sexual misconduct, and of the ten nonvirtuous actions; and then he continued with a teaching on the eight freedoms and ten advantages.[65] {98}

When those three returned into the presence of Venerable Dorjé Chang, he examined them in detail, asking about the practical application at the time when these empowerments were conferred. Drung Peldenpa reported it naturally, just as it had happened, so that the lama was pleased. Gugé Paṇḍita said, "I have offered a quatrain in praise of it." "That's right!" he replied. The glorious and precious root guru Lama Gyelsé then said, "He excellently taught the definitive order of the ten nonvirtuous actions, and then continued with the eighteen aspects of freedom and endowment. Let's pray to you, Transcendent Perfection of Wisdom!" It is said that the master and his disciples all laughed.

The transmission was not propagated by two of these teachers, but Gugé Paṇḍita did confer it upon Lowo Khen Rinpoché [Sonam Lhundrub] and Chojé Namka Tenpa. These two propagated it extensively, so that its transmission is indeed unbroken at the present time. Gugé Paṇḍita also composed an arrangement for the visualization maṇḍala, concluding with the words, "The perfection stage of that which is called the oral transmission of the hidden and great accomplished yogin Samten Ozer, disciple of the cakravartin Mahābodhi who belonged to the class of accomplished masters blessed by Vajravārāhī, concerns the yoga of subtle vital essence, and is also reckoned to include his memorandum on the words of the *Tantra of Clear Expression*, and an exegesis on the fierce inner heat of the blazing fire of *kuṇḍalinī* according to *The Kharamukha Cakrasaṃvara*,[66] which pertains to *The Four [Adamantine] Seats*. Since these are without error, it is said that in these sacred texts it appears that we encounter the Indian and Newar paṇḍitas themselves."

MAṄGALAṂ

Let virtue prevail! {99}

6. Supplementary Historical Anecdotes

Tāranātha

In 1607, Tāranātha completed this supplement to the historical anecdotes contained in the previous chapter. These cover the thirty-three remaining guidebooks, commencing from The Six Meditations of Vajravārāhī *and concluding with* The Nature of Mind: The Wish-Fulfilling Gem. *At the end of the chapter Tāranātha explains that he was encouraged to do so by his teacher Lhawang Drakpa, who himself had been a disciple of Kunga Drolchok.*

Formal Title

Supplement to the Historical Anecdotes of the Lineage of the One Hundred and Eight Guidebooks[1]

Introduction

SARVA MAṄGALAṂ {100}
NAMO GURU
Homage to the teacher!

Among the one hundred and eight profound guidebooks, the foregoing historical anecdotes up to and including the seventy-fourth, which concerns the perfection stage of *Kharamukha Cakrasaṃvara*, were composed by Jetsun Kunga Drolchok, but the remainder were left unfinished in that chapter. I [Tāranātha] have therefore presented them here in the form of a supplement.

The Seventy-Fifth Guidebook

With regard to the guidebook entitled *The Six Meditations of Vajravārāhī*: This is based on the longer and shorter texts concerning Vajravārāhī in the form Dvimukhā,[2] the longer and shorter texts on Vajravārāhī in the form Chinnamuṇḍā,[3] and the longer and shorter texts concerning Vajravārāhī in the form Sarvārthasiddhā,[4] which are collectively known as the *Six Texts concerning Vajravārāhī*; along with the supplementary text entitled *Rite of Burnt Offerings*.[5]

Concerning Vajravārāhī in the form Dvimukhā ("with two faces"), prior to the Indian and Newar lineage holders, this was known and highly esteemed as Vārāhī according to the pith instructions of Oḍḍiyāna.[6] The shorter text on Vajravārāhī in the form Dvimukhā composed by Śabaripā, who was also known by the name of the master Śūnyatāsamādhivajra, has an extremely great blessing. Although elsewhere this is reputed to have been composed by Indrabhūti the Younger, that is simply because Śūnyatāsamādhivajra had been accepted as a disciple by Indrabhūti the Younger. {101} Later, the master Śūnyatāsamādhivajra composed a most excellent poetic work entitled the *Means for Attainment of Jowo Bhugama*, and he revealed it to all the Indian and Newar paṇḍitas, who could not discern any flaws. He became renowned for his learning and was revered as a teacher by the chief minister of Nepal, who offered him Meñja Lingpa and its estate. His resources and merits were extremely great. At that time, with pride in his mastery of poetics, he composed the *Attainment of the Pristine Cognition of the Real*, which is also known as the "longer text on Vajravārāhī in the form Dvimukhā," and he also wrote the longer text on Vajravārāhī in the form Sarvārthasiddhā,[7] but these were not approved by the Ḍākinī. As a negative consequence of having interpreted the profound Secret Mantra in a poetic form, the infant child of the minister did not recover her health, a downpour of rain could not be stopped, and there was great damage inflicted on the harvest. The master's resources faded like a stream that had been cut off. After passing three further years engaged in a confession rite, the Venerable Vajravārāhī actually revealed her visage and delivered the following prophetic declaration: "If you had meditated instead of writing these treatises and had been transfigured into the rainbow light body, those obstacles could have been prevented. Henceforth, however, I will consecrate these two means for attainment, {102} so that they will be of benefit to many sentient beings, and all your activities will be accomplished unimpededly." Thereafter Śūnyatāsamādhivajra's merits increased a hundredfold more than before. He became the teacher of the kings of both Nepal and Magadha, and those texts of his were indeed propagated throughout India and Nepal. Later, Chel Lotsāwa Kunga Dorjé, the son of Chel Lotsāwa Sonam Gyeltsen, received them from Hadu Karpo, the master of this sacred doctrine, pleasing him with his conduct and offerings. In order to request this doctrinal cycle completely, he traveled three times to Nepal.

Under these circumstances the exegesis of all six texts spread extremely far and wide. Ngok Lotsāwa the Great also made a translation. Although there were many who were extremely adept in this entire oral instruction—including the translator Khu Netso, Maben Chobar, and Nubton Gyelyé—Chel [Lotsāwa Kunga Dorjé] was absolutely greater in his blessings and enlightened activities, owing to the power of his inestimable ascetic discipline and persistent endeavors. So it was said that "Vārāhī had encountered Chel."[8]

The Seventy-Sixth Guidebook

With regard to the guidebook entitled *The Six Doctrines of Nāropā*: This is the quintessence of the oral instructions of the lineage holders of the four transmitted teachings.[9] Essentially these comprise the oral instructions of the lineage blessed with experiential cultivation, revealing (i) the fierce inner heat and action seal extrapolated from the *Tantra of Hevajra*; (ii–iv) the illusory body, luminosity, and dream yoga extrapolated from the *Tantra of Guhyasamāja*; and (v–vi) the consciousness transference and resurrection extrapolated from the *Tantra of the Adamantine Four Seats*—the last two being ancillary aspects of the path. Although there are many dissimilar interpretations of the *Six Doctrines* that are extant, here the *Molten Gold of the Six Doctrines*[10] is to be counted as the seventy-sixth guidebook.

The Seventy-Seventh Guidebook

With regard to the guidebook entitled *The Six Doctrines of Nigumā*, and so forth: There are widespread accounts that Nigumā, the ḍākinī of pristine cognition, had been the wife of Nāropā,[11] and so forth. In particular, when she received some oral instruction from Lavapa in the eastern direction, {103} she meditated alongside the master himself for seven days, so that she was transformed into the rainbow light body of a ḍākinī of pristine cognition and actualized the realization of the eighth level. It is said that she left a claw-sized mark protruding from the crown of the easterner Lavapa's head. That was Lavapa the Younger.

As for the name Nigumā, the corresponding Sanskrit is *nigupta*, which is also known to mean "definitively secret" (*nges gsang*) or "definitively concealed" (*nges sbas*). Actually, it is a symbolic term for the "ḍākinīs of pristine cognition."

The great accomplished master Khyungpo Neljor, who was endowed with five culminations,[12] received many Sanskrit texts that were well known throughout the sublime land of India. In particular, in the evening of the fifteenth day of the month of Vaiśākha, as the pale moon rose, Nigumā conferred the great empowerment of the illusory body upon him in an emanational maṇḍala; and at dawn in a dream he received the *Six Doctrines* all at once. Later he received them from her twice in person, so that he actually received them on three occasions.

From Khyungpo Neljor through to Drogon Sangyé Tonpa, the teachings remained sealed, transmitted to a single lineage holder in each generation. Drogon Tonpa had an inestimable number of disciples whom he favored with the oral instructions of Pacification, Severance, and those of Jowojé Atiśa, Nāropā, and so forth; and with the oral instructions of Maitrīpā, Rāhula, Vajrāsanapāda, and the others that constitute the sacred doctrines of the Shangpa. Although there were an infinite number who obtained from him a portion of the oral instructions of Nigumā and Sukhasiddhi, there were three on whom he bestowed the maturational empowerments and liberating path along with ancillaries in their entirety—namely, the master Ayi Sengé, Khedrub Shangton, and Khedrub Zhonu Drub. Although there are an inestimable number of different lineage transmissions that derived from the last two, the symbolic meanings were never differentiated because they are contained in the Ḍākinī [Nigumā's] *Inventory* [*Clarifying the Six Doctrines*].[13] {104} Since they were without contrived views, they arrived at the summit of all the lineages of attainment.

The entire instructional cycle of Nigumā contains the enlightened intention of all the tantras in general, and in particular it is the essence of the five tantras that reveal the culmination. The most uncommon of them are said to be contained in essential extracts from the *Tantra of the Ocean of Vows* and the *Tantra of the Precious Ocean*.[14]

The Seventy-Eighth Guidebook

With regard to the guidebook entitled *The Amulet Tradition of the Great Seal*: Khyungpo Neljor inscribed the root verses of this instruction on palm leaves and inserted them into an amulet made of sandalwood. On his journey he carried it with great care. That is how the name "amulet" (*ga'u ma*) came about. An alternative interpretation suggesting that the "gemstone of awareness or mind was inserted within an amulet of skillful means and discriminative awareness" is pointless, nonsensical talk.

The oral instructions of this guidebook contain a preliminary, main practice, and conclusion, and they never transgress the speech of the ḍākinī Nigumā. The lineage holders of its authentic realization are distilled in the unique perspective that is the enlightened intention of the ḍākinī Nigumā, Sukhasiddhi, and Maitrīpā—these three. When it was first introduced [to Tibet], the great accomplished master Khyungpo Neljor coined the terminology of the three sealings in the following verse:

> External appearances are sealed with appearance and emptiness.
> Awareness or mind is sealed with radiance and emptiness.
> One's own body in which the deity is present is sealed with bliss and emptiness.[15]

When an inconceivable realization of the *Six Doctrines* was born in Venerable Mokchokpa, the accomplished master Khyungpo Neljor was not present, so in order to cut off his misconceptions, Venerable Mokchokpa studied the Great Seal under Venerable Gampopa and perfected the successful outcome of realizing the abiding nature. Then, in accordance with the explanation of Venerable Dakpo Gampopa, he coined terminology that excluded the term *sealing*.

The Seventy-Ninth Guidebook

With regard to the guidebook entitled *The Three Aspects Carried on the Path*: this is known as the "branches" [of the Five Golden Dharmas of Glorious Shangpa] because it derives from the three capacities—best, average, and inferior—that are outlined in the instruction on the illusory body, among the *Six Doctrines*.[16] {105}

The Eightieth Guidebook

With regard to the guidebook entitled *The Deathlessness of One's Own Mind*, which is devoid of error: this is known as the "fruit of deathlessness" because it essentializes the practices of luminosity, illusory body, and Great Seal.

The Eighty-First and Eighty-Second Guidebooks

With regard to the guidebook entitled *The Six Doctrines of Sukhasiddhi*: Although the great accomplished master Khyungpo Neljor did not receive the great word transmission in connection with the Sanskrit texts derived from the ḍākinī of pristine cognition Sukhasiddhi, her kindness was unsurpassed for the following three reasons: (i) she imparted the oral instruction of essential meaning; (ii) she conferred upon him the empowerment of profundity; and (iii) she blessed the mind of the great accomplished master himself, along with all of his lineage holders.

This instruction contains extremely profound doctrinal cycles, including *The Three Nails of the Pith Instructions of Secret Attainment*.[17] Derived from that, and also renowned within the Six Doctrines of Sukhasiddhi, is the instruction based on *The Emanational Cakra of the Navel*. Although there is a clear ancient document concerning this instruction that is extant, it was not widely propagated in the past. But later it was disseminated widely by the Venerable Kuzhang Khyenrab[—that is, Rinchen Khyenrab Chogdrub].[18]

With regard to the guidebook entitled *The Inner Guidance of Nairātmyā*: this is the doctrine of the accomplished master—Āryadeva the Brahmin, who was the maternal uncle of Dampa Sangyé.

For each of these doctrinal cycles of Sukhasiddhi, there is an oral instruction dating from the time of Khyungpo Neljor. In addition, all of them also contain the particularly profound points to be extrapolated concerning the instructions that the ḍākinī Sukhasiddhi actually conferred in person on Nyenton the Great Chokyi Sherab (1175–1255) over seven days at Yang Gon in Rigongpel.

The Eighty-Third Guidebook

With regard to the guidebook entitled *The Coemergent Union of the Great Seal:* Only the kernel of this instruction was transmitted from Nāropā and

Maitrīpā to Marpa and Milarepa, and apart from that there was no detailed guidance. The peerless Dakpo Lharjé Gampopa then directly received a prophetic declaration from Venerable Milarepa. After passing six years enhancing his realization at Sewalung in Nyel, where he meditated skillfully on the fierce inner heat, he then stayed for three years at Gelung in Olka, perfecting the realization of the abiding nature. {106} Thinking it would be of no benefit even if he were to explain this to others, with the exception of certain industrious persons, he did not teach others for some years, but thereafter he did teach it somewhat to certain persons, including Neljor Choyung. Consequently, in the manner of a flame that spreads from one butter lamp to the next, without hardship, the realization [of the abiding nature] was absolutely perfected and widely enhanced. This master of the Great Seal was universally of benefit to others. Henceforth most of the instructions on the nature of mind that were known among the new and old traditions of Secret Mantra practiced in Tibet could probably not stand comparison with this guidebook.

The Eighty-Fourth Guidebook

With regard to the guidebook entitled *The Fivefold Great Seal*: The five aspects[19] are devoid of essential nature. These five aspects are known as a distinctive feature of the Drigungpa because it was Venerable Drigungpa Jigten Sumgon who skillfully extracted certain crucial points from the public teachings of Pagmodrupa.

The Eighty-Fifth Guidebook

With regard to the guidebook entitled *The Four Syllables of the Great Seal*: These are the steps [of instruction] that Drogon Pagmodrupa definitively imparted to Kyergom Zhikpo, and which were later propagated extensively by Gyangro Serdingpa Zhonu O, father and son.

The Eighty-Sixth to Eighty-Eighth Guidebooks

With regard to the guidebook entitled *The Introduction to the Three Buddha Bodies*: This is the sacred doctrine that arose from the mind of Karma Pakshi, simply by following his predecessors; a teaching endowed with the authentic lineage of blessings. At the time when he entrusted the authentic lineage of all his doctrines to the accomplished master Orgyanpa Rinchen Pel, it is said that he bestowed this instruction alone.

With regard to the guidebook entitled *The Indivisibility of Subtle Energy and Mind*: this is a profound doctrine that is known within the Karma Kamtsang tradition.

With regard to the guidebook entitled *The Six Doctrines according to the Sekharma Tradition*: The Venerable Marpa imparted this instruction to his son Dodé Bum. The scrolls were concealed as treasure at Sekhar, and later brought forth from their treasure trove by the treasure finder Chowang Rinpoché. After transcribing them, he reinserted the originals in their proper resting place. Knowing this instruction to be the doctrinal fortune of Lha Rinchen Wangyel, he bestowed them upon him, and consequently it was extensively propagated by Lhapa. {107} Although this was preserved among the upholders of the Kagyu teaching until the time of Nyopa and his followers, the transmission became denigrated due to disputes and repeated insinuations within the Kagyu school.

The Eighty-Ninth Guidebook

With regard to the guidebook entitled *The Mingling and Transformation of the Three Poisons* according to Ngok: this is the unsurpassed profound pith instruction in conformity with the enlightened intention of the *Root Tantra of Hevajra* and its exegesis.

Lord Marpa, during his final pilgrimage, received a prophetic declaration from his teacher Sendhepa. He prayed for seven days in the service of glorious Nāropā, and actually beheld his visage. But when he ran toward him, thinking to request some blessing, there was no trace of Nāropā—only a skull cup filled with Vairocana (that is, excrement) and consecrated as nectar. Just by drinking it, an inestimable meditative stability arose. After praying again for seven days, he met glorious Nāropā, who said, "What do you want?" He requested an exegesis on Hevajra, whereupon Nāropā emanated the nine-deity maṇḍala and conferred the empowerment. He then gave a single teaching on the tantra and its instruction, introducing it in accordance with the meaning of the empowerment and cutting of all doubts. Marpa then thought, "Now I should request Cakrasaṃvara and Guhyasamāja," but Nāropā said, "Do you understand Hevajra?" "I do understand it," he replied. "Well then, that's enough!" Nāropā replied, and he vanished.

Earlier and later Marpa also attended upon Lord Maitrīpā for a long period of time and received an infinite number of oral instructions on the tantras, but he held the tradition of Nāropā to be foremost, crucially because the empowerment had been conferred in an emanational maṇḍala. At that time Marpa requested the empowerment following the example of Buddhajñānapāda. But what is the point of recounting his wrong choice and so forth.[20] {108}

The Ninetieth Guidebook

With regard to the guidebook entitled *The Four Scrolls of the Aural Instructions*:[21] This concerns each of the extraordinary profound points pertaining to *Hevajra*, *Secret Assembly*, *Great Magical Emanation*, and *Four Adamantine Seats*. At the time when Tsurton Wang-gi Dorjé presented four great offerings to Venerable Marpa, he received each of these oral instructions individually. There are many extant old writings concerning this guidebook, but nowadays there is a newly composed text with the title *Four Scrolls* that has become widespread.

The Ninety-First and Ninety-Second Guidebooks

With regard to the guidebook of Rechungpa's aural lineage [entitled *The Six Doctrines of Liberation through the Upper Gate according to the Aural Lineage (of Cakrasaṃvara)*]: this is known to have been transmitted to a single lineage holder for thirteen successive generations, and then extensively propagated from the time of Zhang Lotsāwa Drubpa Pel.[22]

With regard to the guidebook entitled *The Nine Doctrinal Cycles of Nirdehaḍākinī*: Once upon a time when the accomplished master Tilopā journeyed here [to India] from Oḍḍiyāna, each evening the ḍākinīs would invisibly recite root verses from the sky, so these became known as the "doctrinal cycles of Nirdehaḍākinī," the "disembodied ḍākinī." It is also said that this ḍākinī was actually Vārāhī in the form Sarvārthasiddhā. Of the nine cycles, the first four descended to Marpa and the last five were painstakingly sought from India by Rechungpa.

The Ninety-Third and Ninety-Fourth Guidebooks

With regard to the guidebook entitled *The Elaborate Guidance of Zhang Tselpa*: This comprises the common traditions of Drigom and Dakpo Gomtsul Nyingpo, and the uncommon traditions of Ga Lotsāwa and Vairocanabhadra. Known as the "four definitive presences," their instructions include (i) the definitive presence of Cakrasaṃvara according to Ga Lotsāwa, (ii) the definitive presence of Vārāhī according to [Drigom] Melton Yerpawa, (iii) the definitive presence of Tārā according to the Indian Vairocanabhadra, and (iv) the definitive presence of Buddha Śākyamuni according to Dakpo Gomtsul Nyingpo.

The nucleus of these oral instructions comprises the cycle of the one hundred teachings of the path of skillful means and the single scroll of instruction pertaining to the path of liberation, which are introduced to fortunate individuals in an immediate manner.

With regard to the guidebook entitled the cycle of *The Six-Branch Yoga according to Pelchen Ga Lotsāwa*: Ga Lotsāwa requested from Tsami Chenpo Sangyé Drak (fl. eleventh century) the oral instruction through which there would be no need to change focus from the time when one is a beginner until the attainment of buddhahood. He was therefore granted the teaching entitled *On a Single Seat*, which integrates Cakrasaṃvara of the generation stage with the six-branch yoga of the perfection stage.[23] {109} By meditating for seven years he obtained the indications of great warmth. He then practiced for eleven months at the Śītavana charnel ground, during which time the ḍākinīs also presented him with the *Seven Days of Fierce Inner Heat*. Then he effortlessly became an accomplished master, known throughout India and Tibet, and possessing infinite signs of spiritual accomplishment.

The Ninety-Fifth Guidebook

With regard to the guidebook entitled *The Cycle of Pagmodru Densatel*: This commenced with the Venerable Drigung IV Chen Nga Drakpa Jungné (1175–1255). Some also refer to this as the teaching tradition of the followers of Densatel. The guidebook was primarily based on *Verses on the Path of Skillful Means*, which Drogon Pagmodrupa bestowed upon Goton Cholo, and later on it accorded with the writings of Chen Nga Sonam Gyeltsenpa.

The Ninety-Sixth Guidebook

With regard to the guidebook concerning the uncommon tenets of the Drigungpa entitled *The Unique Enlightened Intention*: While Jigten Gonpo was residing at Wangmopuk Monastery in Yechung Pulung, the *Tenfold Doctrinal Instruction*[24] and *The Threefold Doctrine*[25] arose in his mind. Since he understood all the crucial points of auspicious circumstance, these tenets also arose in his mind. Later at the time when he met Dodé Rabjam, he is said to have presented these in accordance with the real enlightened intention of the teachings. Although these tenets are for the most part extremely noble in meaning, they have generally been subjected to refutation, owing to their incompatibility with other terminologies. Their adherents also say that *The Unique Enlightened Intention* represents a promulgation of the doctrinal wheel that was never turned by anyone else after the Buddha attained nirvana. It is prone to criticism on account of being incompatible with all other traditions, but that seems not to be the main point that is intended.

The Ninety-Seventh Guidebook

With regard to the guidebook entitled *The Six Doctrines according to Taklungpa*: this instruction contains some points that are more especially profound than the other recensions of *The Six Doctrines of Nāropā*, but fundamentally it is an instruction that does not diverge from the enlightened intention of Drogon Pagmodrupa. {110}

The Ninety-Eighth to One Hundredth Guidebooks

With regard to the guidebook of the cycle of the Middle Drukpa [entitled *The Means for Attainment of the Guru, Auspicious Circumstances, and Common Savor*]: The oral instructions that were transmitted to Drogon Tsangpa Gyaré, renowned as the glorious Drukpa, are said to be subsumed in three stems. These three stems comprise (i) the view that accords with the tradition of Gampopa, (ii) the oral instructions that accord with the tradition of Rechungpa, and (iii) the auspicious circumstances that accord with his own tradition.[26]

The first of these denotes *The Coemergent Union of the Great Seal*, which was transmitted from Gampopa to Pagmodrupa. The second denotes most of the empowerments and oral instructions associated with this Drukpa tradition that were transmitted from Lorepa Darma Wangchuk (1187–1250), Tsangpa Gyaré, and Sumpa Repa (fl. twelfth century). However, the main disseminator of these two stems was Ling Repa (1128–1188). The third is the instruction that Tsangpa Gyaré himself received in a vision of the seven generations of past buddhas.

Among these, the lineage of blessings contained in *The Means for Attainment of the Guru as the Three Buddha Bodies*, which is of useful practical application, is compatible with [the aforementioned lineage of] the *Six Doctrines*, whereas the essential points of its oral instructions follow the texts of Vibhūticandra.

The kernel of the *Six Cycles of Common Savor* appears to be contained completely in the [aforementioned] *Doctrinal Cycles of Nirdehaḍākinī*. On the other hand, the instructions concerning supreme common savor that are prevalent today[—that is, in the time of Tāranātha—]integrate together both the transmitted teachings that were preserved as an aural lineage and the revelations that were concealed as treasure at Kharchu by Venerable Rechungpa and later brought forth by Tsangpa Gyaré.

Although all the lineages of the disciples of Tsangpa Gyaré are compatible as far as his oral teachings and eight great instructions[27] are concerned, here I adhere to the Middle Drukpa tradition, which was transmitted through the nine who had the name Sengé,[28] and so forth.

With regard to the guidebook [entitled *The Fivefold Capacity of Lorepa*], which represents the cycle of the Lower Drukpa: The Venerable Lorepa (1187–1250) founded monasteries in the lower eastern parts of Tibet at Jang Uri and so forth, and he acted for the great benefit of living beings. His distinctive composition was entitled *The Fivefold Capacity*.

With regard to the guidebook [entitled *The Six Primary Essentials for Mountain Retreat*], which represents the cycle of the Upper Drukpa: This is the tradition of Gyelwa Gotsangpa Gonpo Dorjé (1189–1258) and his followers. {111} Foremost among the stalwarts of this tradition was Gyelwa Yangonpa Gyeltsen Pel (1213–1258), who composed many profound instructions concerning the new and old traditions of Secret Mantra in Tibet. Among them is *Trilogy on Mountain Retreat*, along with its ancillary texts that bring together all useful necessities for practitioners. The *Trilogy* includes (i) *Source of All Attributes*, (ii) *Liberation from the Dangerous Passageway of the Intermediate State*, and (iii) *Concealed Exegesis of the Adamantine Body*.

The One Hundred and First Guidebook

With regard to the guidebook entitled *The Four-Armed Mahākāla in the Form Kurakma*: This instruction is known as the "vitality essence" (*srog thig*).[29] In general, throughout India and Nepal, four-armed Mahākāla is the most renowned among all the classes of Mahākāla. Although there are many lineages that derive from different Tibetan translators, the tradition of Pelchen Ga Lotsāwa is unrivaled because he was appointed as an attendant of Mahākāla. He acquired three distinct instructions—namely, the cycle that he received from Tsami Sangyé Drak and Abhaya, the revelation that he brought forth from Śītavana, and the exegesis that he actually received from Mahākāla and his acolytes. In addition, the pith instructions that arose from his buddha mind were also innumerable.

Here [in Tibet], Pagmodrupa received these cycles of the supreme attainment from Khampa Aseng, the great disciple of Pelchen Ga Lotsāwa. Since he esteemed the *Instruction on the Book with a Sash* and so forth, [this form of raven-faced four-armed Mahākāla] became known as Kurakma (the one with a sash).[30] With regard to this form of the deity, there are traditions without profundity in which the deity has four or five cakras, as well as profoundly crucial teachings in which the deity is conclusively established to have two cakras or one cakra; but here, however, these are all integrated together.[31]

In olden times, the liturgical feast offerings associated with this deity were widely propagated, but its supreme rite of spiritual attainment was rare.[32] Consequently it was said:

Raven-faced Mahākāla (Bya rog ma) is extremely rare,
Although birdlike figures are widespread.

The One Hundred and Second Guidebook

With regard to the guidebook entitled *The Inner Guidance of Glorious Pañjaranātha*: Apart from just a few lines from an ancient manuscript that had been released in this direction [of Tibet], no such category was recognized until the time of glorious Lama Dampa Sonam Gyeltsen. {112} It is held that the first of the transcribed liturgical arrangements of the aural lineage was the extant guidebook of Yarlungpa Sengé Gyeltsen, a disciple renowned for his highest learning in the pith instructions of ritual feast offerings.

The One Hundred and Third Guidebook

With regard to the guidebook entitled *The Trilogy of Spiritual Songs*: The [first cycle] is known as *The Spiritual Songs of the Populace* and also as *The Treasury of Spiritual Songs*, including the [renowned] songs that concern the fettering [of cyclic existence]. In olden times, this cycle was not widely propagated in India. The books were simply kept in the two great temples of Ratnagiri and Devagiri.[33] However, when the transmission of *The Spiritual Songs of the Populace* had virtually come to an end, Maitrīpā (ca. 1007–1085) received them from Śabaripā and propagated them more strongly. Later, when Maitrīpā, in turn, was about to die, he foreordained that Vajrapāṇi, one of his four Indian disciples, would act for the welfare of living beings in the northern direction. The latter, accordingly, performed acts of great benefit for the sake of living beings throughout Nepal and Tibet, extensively propagating the exegesis and attainment of *The Seven Sections of Spiritual Attainment*, *The Six Essential Cycles*, *The Twenty-Two (or Twenty-Four) Doctrinal Cycles of Nonmentation*, and *The Four Doctrines Exhorted by Injunction*.[34]

This *Treasury of Spiritual Songs* had previously been established by Jowojé Atiśa, who delivered a lengthy exegesis on the extent of its pitfalls. When Nagtso Lotsāwa translated part of it, Dromton Gyelwei Jungné said, "What need is there for butter lamps! It seems that such words will not be of a single benefit to Tibet." Later, Nagtso Lotsāwa went off to Chimphu and continued with the translation. On reaching the words "Just as one possessing an antipoison mantra is unharmed by poison . . ."[35] he ceased to translate the remainder, saying, "This will bring nothing but harm to Tibet." It is said that he inserted the earlier part that he had translated into a stupa. {113}

This same text is also known to have been translated once in Ngari dependent on another translator, but that version was not propagated in Utsang. Later on, although it was also maintained through other lines of transmissions, principally it was bestowed upon one named Joden Ngaripa [Zhang Joton] by Vajrapāṇi from India, who prophesied, "Since you are learned in the middle way and the perspective of mind, you should master this essential cycle." Accordingly, it was widely propagated through him.

The other two cycles from *The Trilogy of Spiritual Songs* [entitled *The Spiritual Songs of the King* and *The Spiritual Songs of the Queen*] were not well known in India and Nepal but propagated extensively in Tibet. It must be the case that their lineage descended from the Newar Asu alone.

The One Hundred and Fourth Guidebook

With regard to the guidebook entitled *The Six Doctrines of the Accomplished Masters*: The eighty-four accomplished masters who had attained buddhahood instructed the two ḍākinīs named Kokolilā and Dharmaviṣā in *Pith Instruction Entitled Precious Garland* in order that they might assist a yakṣinī of Śītavana who was exhausted by suffering. Those two instructed the yakṣinī who, by cultivating this, became a great ḍākinī of pristine cognition, capable of seeing the truth.

In general, each of those known [collectively] as the eighty-four accomplished masters, from the "holder of the sword, bull, and fish" to the "holder of the peacock and treasure vase," attained spiritual accomplishment.[36] Having become masters of the very spiritual accomplishments that they had obtained, they were recognized as the originally present accomplished masters, eighty-four in number, endowed with occult power that was swifter than others.

As far as the eighty-four accomplished masters who are revealed in this specific guidebook are concerned, they are exclusively great masters of mantra who appeared in earlier and later times. Later, during the time of a king named Kunīka, in Kantamara, which belonged to the land of Saurāṣṭra in the west, the [aforementioned] two ḍākinīs, acting as intermediaries, actually invited the eighty-four accomplished masters. {114} They held a communal offering and sang songs of adamantine reality. The king also commissioned an image of each of them. It was in their presence that the spiritual songs they had sung were committed to writing. It is also said that later they would return there on a single occasion, until the fifth generation of kings.[37] On that last occasion, the paṇḍita Vīraraśmi is said to have encountered the accomplished masters, but he could not catch their footprints (*zhabs rjes ma zin*). Instead, the two ḍākinīs revealed all the oral instructions to him, so that he became accomplished, and compiled an anthology containing all the short spiritual songs together. The root verses of both the *Spiritual Songs* and the *Precious Garland*, translated by Minyak Lotsāwa Mondrub Sherab, were considered reliable by all undisputed scholars of Sanskrit texts. This lotsāwa is said to have also prepared a memorandum on the teachings of Paṇḍita Abhayadattaśrī, including the narratives and commentaries [concerning the eighty-four].[38]

The One Hundred and Fifth Guidebook

With regard to the guidebook entitled *The Gradual Path of Padmasambhava*: This denotes the actual source of the pith instructions of the Great Perfection—the enlightened intention of Master Padmasambhava, which were transmitted from Nubchen Sangyé Yeshé (fl. ninth century),[39] their descent eventually falling to Zur Śākya Jungné (1002–1062).[40]

Leaving aside the treasure revelations of Guru Padmasambhava, within the individual ancient translations collectively known as the "[distant lineage of] transmitted teachings," the doctrinal cycles of the Great Perfection mostly descended from Vimalamitra and Vairotsana;[41] but there are many other lines of transmission including those of Buddhaguhya, [the teachings of Anuyoga] that Nubchen adopted from Burushaski, the seven lineage holders of the Chinese Hoshang, the seven lineages of the Indian masters, and so forth.[42] It is clear, however, that this present guidebook exclusively represents the Great Perfection that descended from Master Padmasambhava.

The One Hundred and Sixth Guidebook

With regard to the guidebook entitled *The Collected Injunctions of the King*: The means for attainment of the deity [Avalokiteśvara] and the root verses of the oral instruction were certainly composed by the religious king Songtsen Gampo. These actual transmitted teachings of sublime Avalokiteśvara and the ancestral doctrines of Tibet that are extant in the Nyingma teachings themselves were known to have been concealed as treasure by Master Padmasambhava. {115} The chronicles and most of the ancillary texts were later compiled by the treasure finders Drubtob Ngodrub, Nyangrel Nyima Ozer, and so forth.[43]

The One Hundred and Seventh Guidebook

With regard to the guidebook entitled *The Liberation by Seeing according to Norbu Rinchen*: This comprises the complete meaning of both the Great Seal and the Great Perfection; and it was brought forth from its treasure trove by Drampa Kunga Zangpo. It is said to subsume the enlightened intention of eight individual accomplished masters—namely, Saraha, Śabaripā,

Mitrayogin, and Master Padmasambhava, along with their consorts, the four ḍākinīs of pristine cognition.

The One Hundred and Eighth Guidebook

With regard to the guidebook entitled *The Nature of Mind: The Wish-Fulfilling Gem*: This was bestowed by Venerable Dakpo Gampopa on Kyebu Sherab, in a single transmission. The latter opened the gateway to [the hidden land of] Tsāri, and he concealed the instructions in the form of treasure. Later, his own reincarnation Dungtso Repa brought them forth from the treasure trove and propagated them.[44]

Concluding Verses

Here it may be said:

I have presented here the most astonishing anecdotes
Concerning the sources of the unstructurable one hundred and eight
guidebooks—
The most profound instructions—experiences regurgitated by
accomplished masters,
Extracted from the enlightened intention of the profound sutras and tantras,
Supreme path in which the conquerors rejoice.
This account includes authentic sources,
Without pursuing false reports and mundane tittletattle
That resonate simply owing to bias and fixation.

Completing these unfinished anecdotes concerning the sources of the
lineage
That elucidate the actual circumstances of the one hundred and eight
guidebooks
Is certainly a deed endowed with meaningful intent,
So that our positive actions might be enhanced.

In order to fulfill the enlightened intention of the supreme masters of the
past,
And also benefit others who are of equal fortune,

Though it has been somewhat laborious to pen these anecdotes,
I rejoice in the thought that they are beneficial.

In particular, may those fellow travelers
On whom the definitively secret teachings of my supreme teachers are bestowed {116}
Never squander the enlightened activity of all the conquerors and their heirs!

So it was that in the presence of my venerable root guru Dorjé Chang Lhawang Drakpa, in whom all the teachers of the fundamental lineages are subsumed, I was urged to prepare this supplement to the historical anecdotes of the lineage holders of the One Hundred and Eight Guidebooks.

Colophon

Completed by the vagabond Tāranātha at the Doctrinal Palace of Dragto, on the first day of his thirty-third year.[45]

ŚUBHAMASTU SARVAJAGATĀṂ
May there be good auspices for all beings! {117}

PART TWO

PRACTICE

7. The Ordinary Preliminary Practices

Having presented the historical background in the foregoing chapters, in the second part of this book, Kunga Drolchok focuses on the actual experiential cultivation of the One Hundred and Eight Guidebooks. The ordinary and extraordinary preliminary practices, briefly presented in chapter 7 and chapter 8, respectively, are the prerequisites for those wishing to pursue any of the main practices that are compiled in the long chapter 9. Among them, chapter 7 outlines the preliminary approaches suitable for individuals of lowest, average, and superior capacity. The endnotes here refer to the detailed and succinct explanation of these topics found in Patrul Rinpoche's The Words of My Perfect Teacher. *As before, the chapter is introduced by auspicious verses and concludes with a signature quatrain.*

Formal Title

The Ordinary Preliminary Practices of the One Hundred and Eight Guidebooks[1] {118}

Introductory Verse

OṂ SVĀSTI SIDDHAṂ
Respectful homage to my teacher and to Lord Mañjughoṣa!

Limitless in quantity, though numbering one hundred and eight,
These guidebooks are excellently threaded together in numerical order.
Here I have composed the ordinary preliminary practices that subsume them in part—
The part that clarifies the abiding nature of the transcendent perfections.[2]

The Text

The essential points of the ordinary preliminary practices, which are applicable to all the one hundred and eight guidebooks without exception, are as follows:

You should gather all the objects of refuge in your teacher and resolve that they are indeed identical in essence to your root teacher. You should reflect that you have genuinely acquired the freedoms and advantages that are hard to obtain,[3] and then analyze the circumstances of death and impermanence through which you will not live long,[4] so that overwhelming sadness will arise due to disillusionment with the nature of conditioned and perishable phenomena, and fascination with the ways of this life, including the eight worldly concerns, will not arise, even in your dreams.[5] Mindful of this, you should distill your experiential cultivation, emphasizing the discipline of the self that, from the perspective of bewilderment, innately conflates the actor of past actions with the experiencer of their ripening effect. With steadfast certainty in the unfailing results of positive and negative actions, and without scorning even minutely the acceptance of virtuous actions and the rejection of negative actions, you should strive for this experiential cultivation that may be followed by persons of lowest capacity.[6] {119}

Then, after determining that all the tainted bliss and excellence of cyclic existence are imbued with suffering—mere reflections of an externally contrived happiness—you should resolve to be emancipated from all cyclic existence. Through study, reflection, and meditation, founded on the ethical discipline that you have adopted in your own mind, you should earnestly follow all the scriptures of the conquerors without exception, without partiality or bias, and practice them as they should be experientially cultivated by persons of average capacity.

Finally, you should cultivate love, understanding that all the living beings who fill space have been your gracious parents. Thereby you will acquire the higher aspiration that cherishes others more than yourself. Whatever you do, you should maintain the relative enlightened mind that is intent exclusively on the benefit of others.[7] You should abide in sky-like meditative equipoise, realizing that all phenomena of cyclic existence and nirvana, from an analytical perspective, are without any reliable inherent existence whatsoever, and also in postmeditation, realizing that all that appears manifests as a magical reflection, without inherent existence. Within that disposition resembling a magical illusion, you should earnestly and responsibly follow this experiential cultivation in all your recitations, meditations, movements, sitting, lying down, and standing, until the path of persons of superior capacity has been perfected.[8] {120}

Concluding Verse

Exemplifying the mind that is sky-like,
This precept—a book of few pages—
Controls **supreme** and lesser modes of **liberation**
From the bondage that **delights**
In aversion and attachment to certain **imaginations.**[9]

MAṄGALAṂ

Let virtue prevail! {121}

8. The Extraordinary Preliminary Practices

The more advanced visualizations of the extraordinary preliminaries outlined here are practiced in the contexts of taking refuge, setting the mind on enlightenment, ritual purification, and offering the body maṇḍala. These finally enable the practitioner to settle into the physical posture appropriate for calm abiding, and thence to undertake the main practices of the One Hundred and Eight Guidebooks that follow in the next chapter.

Formal Title

The Extraordinary Preliminary Practices of the One Hundred and Eight Guidebooks[1] {122}

Introductory Verses

OṂ SVĀSTI SIDDHI
Respectful homage to my teacher and to Lord Mañjughoṣa!

Of the two approaches leading toward the practice of the consecutively arranged one hundred and eight guidebooks, distinct and profound, the ordinary preliminaries have already been explained. There now follows an elucidation of the practical guidance that constitutes the extraordinary preliminaries.

Once the mindstream has been refined by means of the general preliminary practices in the above manner, you should imagine your residence as a pure land, with the words:

May the terrain in every way be pure,
Transformed into the exquisite nature of aquamarine,
Smooth like the palm of the hand,
Without gravel and so forth![2]

In the midst of this pure land, upon a wish-granting tree with extensive fruits and foliage that brings forth all that is desired, you should visualize in the manner of a dense cloud an assembly that includes the teachers of the fundamental lineage, an apparition that is essentially the source of all spiritual accomplishments; the meditational deities associated with the four classes of tantra, an apparition that essentially comprises the deities amassing your own past actions; the buddha bodies of perfect resource, an apparition that is essentially the nonarising buddha body of reality; the volumes of sutra and tantra, an apparition that is essentially the truth of cessation; {123} the bodhisattva heirs of the conquerors, an apparition that essentially comprises sublime beings abiding on the levels; and the doctrinal protectors and guardians, an apparition that is essentially the truth of the ten powers.[3]

You should visualize that, just like you, all sentient beings—an apparition that essentially comprises your gracious parents—respectfully seek refuge with body, speech, and mind; and then you should repeat one hundred thousand times the following words:[4]

I go for refuge to the teachers.
I go for refuge to the buddhas.
I go for refuge to the sacred doctrine.
I go for refuge to the monastic community.
I go for refuge to the deities of the maṇḍala.
I go for refuge to the doctrinal protectors.

Then, as before, you should cultivate love for the realms of sentient beings. You should repeat many times "SARVASATTVA KĀRUṆIKA—O you who are imbued with compassion for all beings!" And then,

Oh! Sentient beings are a field of suffering,
Fixated on conceptual thoughts.
To subdue their conceptual thoughts
I should attain perfect buddhahood![5]

Upon the crown of your head and those of all other sentient beings, arising from a sword marked with the letter KHAṂ that rests on a lotus and moon disk, you should visualize the transcendent lord Samayavajra, his body green in color, with one face, his two hands holding a sword and a bell, {124} embracing the female consort Samayatārā, who resembles him. Seated respectively in the adamantine posture and the lotus posture, they are united in equipoise. They each have three eyes and a tuft of matted hair, and they are each adorned with silks and precious gems, slightly wrathful in demeanor, and wearing a crown indicative of successful accomplishment. Their foreheads, throats, and hearts are marked respectively with the letters OṂ, ĀḤ, and HŪṂ, and within their hearts, light rays are diffused from the sword that is marked with the letter KHAṂ.

All the buddhas of the ten directions then appear in the form of Samayavajra:

OṂ VAJRA SAMĀJA JAḤ HŪṂ VAṂ HOḤ

I pray that the transcendent lord Samayavajra might refine and purify
All the mass of negative deeds, obscurations, downfalls, and stains
That I and all sentient beings have accumulated in cyclic existence, without beginning![6]

Visualize that from the letter KHAṂ within the heart a stream of nectar is exuded, filling the bodies of the male and female deities, and that from their point of union the downpour of nectar enters through the crown of your own head. Your entire body is cleared and purified, and negative obscurations and their propensities emerge in the form of smoke from the soles of the feet, the rectum, and the urethra.

Then, after reciting one hundred thousand times OṂ ĀḤ KHAṂ HŪṂ PHAṬ SVĀHĀ, you should confess all violations of the primary and ancillary commitments of buddha body, speech, and mind with the words:

May the transcendent lord Samayavajra
Purify all my downfalls in respect of the commitments!
May he purify my violations of the commitments,
And may he cleanse my commitments![7]
I pray that all the mass of my downfalls and stains might be purified and purged!

You should then visualize that the deities on the crown of your head dissolve into you, and that your body becomes translucent, like crystal.[8]

Then you should mentally tally the outer, inner, and secret [offerings].[9] That is to say, the mighty terrain of gold should be conflated with your physical frame covered with skin and blood, the substratum should be conflated with the moisture of your generative fluid, Mount Meru with the spinal bone, the root of the sacred doctrine with the mind, the four continents with the four arms, {125} the four immeasurable aspirations with the solar and lunar channels and the red and white vital essences, and the seven insignia of royal dominion with the five solid viscera and the six hollow viscera—seven along with the genitalia.[10] The seven aspects of sublime spiritual wealth are conflated with an uncultivated harvest,[11] the three naturally arising buddha bodies with the uninterrupted flow of enlightened activities, and the wish-granting cow with the uvula. The altruistic mind should be conflated with the wish-granting tree; the treasure vase with sacraments, clothing, and all resources without exception; and the channels, winds, and vital essences with the buddha bodies, pristine cognitions, and enlightened activities. Then you should make this maṇḍala offering with the words:

> In this pure land, I offer to the teachers and buddhas
> Mount Meru at the center and the four continents,
> Adorned with the five desirable attributes of the senses,
> And encircled by sun and moon,
> Along with the resources and excellences of gods and humans,
> The seven insignia of royal dominion and seven precious things,
> The wish-granting cow, the wish-fulfilling tree,
> Uncultivated harvests, gold, silver,
> Excellent grain, inconceivable resources,
> And exquisite, abundant material things.
> May I attain perfect buddhahood!

> OṂ GURU BUDDHA BODHISATTVA MAṆḌALA PŪJĀ
> MEGHA SAMUDRA SPHARAṆA SAMAYE HŪṂ[12]

You should make this offering as many times as possible.

After that, your mind should visualize your root teacher in the guise of Vajradhara, seated at the center of the objects of refuge; and then say:

I confidently offer to you, my teacher,
My enemies, relatives, and resources,
And indeed all the virtuous acts that I have accumulated through the three times.
Please receive them with your loving heart!

To the teacher who grants precious accomplishments,
Embodiment of all the buddhas of the three times,
I respectfully grant this sacred offering—
The nectar of pristine cognition.
Please receive this with love!

From the three seed syllables in the teacher's body, speech, and mind,
Three light rays of nectar are excellently diffused {126}
And the obfuscations of my body, speech, and mind are purified.
Please bestow the buddha level, manifesting the three buddha bodies!

After reciting this, let the objects of refuge dissolve into yourself, and then with legs crossed in the adamantine posture, place your hands four finger widths below the navel in the gesture of meditative equipoise, with the two thumbs properly positioned. Straighten your spine like a stack of disks, bend your head like a swan, let your tongue rest against the palate, and fix your eyes directly in front without contrivance. Having made the body into a worthy vessel for meditative concentration, you should then practice in accordance with each of the one hundred and eight guidebooks in succession, or else you may excellently guide your mind in whichever of them you prefer, and finally that itself will lead you to the supreme path.

Concluding Verse

By virtue of propagating in a **supreme** written form
This extraordinary preliminary practice for **all** the guidebooks,
Giving rise to **delight** and causing [beings]
To enter the path of **liberation**,
May experiential cultivation be rendered free from obstacles!

MAṄGALAṂ

Let virtue prevail! {127}

9. The One Hundred and Eight Guidebooks

*After completing the ordinary and extraordinary preliminaries outlined in the previous two chapters, practitioners may then undertake the main practices contained in the one hundred and eight guidebooks, which constitute by far the longest chapter of the book. These practices, collated by Kunga Drolchok, represent all eight authoritative lineages promulgated in Tibet—Nyingma, Kadam, Sakya, Kagyu, Severance and Pacification, Six-Branch Yoga, Shangpa Kagyu, and the Ritual Service and Attainment of Orgyanpa; and they derive from both the Sutra and Tantra traditions, the latter emphasizing the generation stage (*bskyed rim*) and perfection stage (*rdzogs rim*) of meditation, along with instruction on the Great Seal (*phyag rgya chen po*) and the Great Perfection (*rdzogs pa chen po*). The compiler advises, in his concluding verses, that these main practices are to be undertaken distinctly and individually in their own terms, without being intermingled. The intricate relationships between the guidebooks are set aside for discussion in a later chapter.*

*These one hundred and eight guidebooks are for the most part written in the terse, shorthand style of a memorandum (*zin bris*), for which reason, in this translation, it has often been necessary to add phrases or entire sentences in square brackets to elucidate the meaning. Such insertions derive from primary sources and related texts, found elsewhere in Jamgön Kongtrul's* Treasury of Precious Instructions, *or in the collected works of their original authors. In the introductory note to each guidebook I have indicated, wherever possible, its primary source and antecedents in Sanskrit or Tibetan literature. There are also some cases where the primary sources are no longer extant outside this anthology, and others where references are made to later commentaries by Tāranātha or Jamyang Khyentsé Wangpo. Readers will note that the order in which these guidebooks are presented corresponds for the most part to chapter*

9 of the Tibetan text, but there are a small number of exceptions where this sequence is at variance with that of the earlier historical chapters. Most notably, The Six-Branch Yoga of Kālacakra *(40) has been moved in the Tibetan text to be guidebook number 90, perhaps in consideration of its content. But for the sake of consistency, I have followed the ordering clearly stated in the earlier chapters.*

Formal Title

The Profound One Hundred and Eightfold Guidebooks[1] {128}

1. Guidebook Entitled *Parting from the Four Attachments*[2]

After taking refuge and setting the mind on enlightenment: (i) You should cultivate from the heart a desire to practice the sacred doctrine by means of three considerations: the consideration that the time of death is unknown since attachment to this life resembles a bubble of water and there is no value in being attached; the consideration that there are many circumstances giving rise to death; and the consideration that nothing at all is of benefit at the time of death. This is the principal instruction that leads the mind toward the sacred doctrine.

(ii) Next, you should consider the circumstances of cyclic existence, since this cyclic existence with its three world systems entirely resembles a poisonous fruit. Although it may be delicious in the moment, ultimately it causes pain and death. Anyone who has attachment to that is self-deluded. You should proceed on the path of the sacred doctrine, considering that even those who have acquired the kingship of an emperor will eventually die and perish, and they will not transcend suffering.

(iii) Then you should consider that attachment to self-interest resembles the raising of an enemy's son. Though this may ostensibly bring short-term happiness, in the long term it will be harmful. According to this example, even though there may be short-term happiness when you are attached to self-interest, in the long term it will impede the attainment of enlightenment. For there is no benefit in yourself alone attaining liberation from these three world systems, imbued with the nature of suffering. {129} Instead, you should eliminate the bewilderment of the path by intensely cultivating the following thought that easily arises again and again in the mind: "Until each of these sentient beings, all of whom have been my parents, attains buddhahood, supreme bliss, I will take birth from one aeon to the next, even in the hells!"

(iv) Finally, you should consider that when you are attached to entities and symbols, this resembles grasping the mirage of water. Even though a mirage may immediately appear as water, thirst will not be alleviated because there is nothing for the mouth to drink. Even though this cyclic existence appears to the bewildered mind, when genuinely investigated, it is without inherent existence in any respect whatsoever. Therefore, when all things are ascertained to be free from conceptual elaboration, without the mind dwelling on the past, without the mind dwelling on the future, and without consciousness dwelling on the present, it is said that bewildering appearances will arise as pristine cognition and buddhahood will be attained.

This sacred doctrine, the first of **all** that I received,
Guiding my own mental faculty to **delight** and joy,
The path revealing the **liberation** of the knots of the mind,
Was penned according to the words of my **supreme** teacher.

This guidebook entitled *Parting from the Four Attachments* was compiled by Nub Rigdzin Drak and embellished by Sakya Paṇḍita, glorious lord of the sacred doctrine.[3] {130}

2. Guidebook Entitled *The Seven-Point Mind Training of the Great Vehicle*[4]

After taking refuge and setting the mind on enlightenment: (i) you should accrue the supporting preliminary teachings,[5] and (ii) then cultivate the main practice that constitutes the two aspects of enlightened mind.[6]

Seated in an upright posture, you should count the exhalation and inhalation of breath, up to twenty-one times, without error. Phenomena appearing as perceived objects in the manner of a dream become manifest when the nature of mind has been bewildered, but there is nothing existing at all apart from the mind. After reflecting upon this, you should next inspect the fundamental state of nonarising awareness, and rest in the disposition of that fundamental state that is absolutely without inherent existence. After reflecting that objects and mind are both empty, you should then observe the essential nature and rest in the radiant clarity of the substratum, without grasping anything at all, your mind free from the diffusion and absorption of the seven aspects of consciousness.[7] Then, during postmeditation, you should regard the inhabited world and its inhabitants as a magical display.

At the outset you should meditate on the visualization of your dear mother. All the sufferings that arise in your mother's mind will manifest within your own heart. When they have manifested, you should cultivate an intense volition toward empathetic joy. You should send forth your own happiness and merit to your mother, and immediately after that bliss and harmonious circumstances will converge, and buddhahood will simply be obtained.

Then, in the same way, you should meditate upon all sentient beings, headed by your father. When the wind is exhaled, in association with that, you should meditate that all your happiness and joy is sent forth to others, and on breathing in, that all the negativity and sufferings of others manifest within yourself.

"May sentient beings in whom attachment, aversion, and delusion arise dependent on pleasant, unpleasant, or neutral sense objects possess the three virtuous actions [of body, speech, and mind]!"[8] These words should be repeated in the course of all your daily activities.[9]

As for the sequence in which this volition is to be adopted, you should accept right now the sufferings that would otherwise be purified in the future. You should take upon yourself the sufferings of sentient beings lest they might have the effects of negative actions: harm or degeneration. {131}

In particular, if harmful human or nonhuman beings arise, you should summon them through your own negative past actions and meditate intensely on the exchanging of compassion for the suffering of others,[10] reflecting that since these beings have a negative, harming influence on you, later, after experiencing their ripening suffering, you will have compassion for them. In the case of humans and dogs, for example, you should persevere with whatever actually brings them benefit. When evil spirits are present, you should turn your mind firmly toward the thought "Let my flesh and blood be consumed!"

(iii) [As for the transforming of negative circumstances into the path:][11] When you regard the bewildering appearances of suffering that afflict the inhabited world and its sentient inhabitants due to adverse circumstances as having the essential nature of unreality, like calamities that arise in a dream due to fire and flooding, at that time you will be introduced to the four buddha bodies—the nonarising buddha body of reality, the unimpeded buddha body of perfect resource, the nonabiding buddha body of emanation, and the indivisible buddha body of essentiality.

If you catch leprosy or other such illnesses, you should think, "If this disease were not present, I would be embroiled in the grandiose activities of this life. If I neglect to remember the sacred doctrine, this will induce me to do so! This very disease is the enlightened activity of the precious jewels!"

In brief, if you do not wish for suffering [and instead wish for happiness], you should reflect that this [suffering] is an indication that is indispensable [for happiness] and the like,[12] and you should say, "Grant your blessing that when I am ill, I may make offerings to the precious jewels, venerate the monastic community, present the torma offerings of the elemental spirts, and make a maṇḍala offering to my teacher! Also, when I recover, grant your blessing at the time of my recovery. When I am to die, grant your blessing at the time of death!" You should pray fervently in this manner, so that hope and doubt come to cease. When offering tormas to malign spirits, you should sincerely cut off hope and doubt, saying, "Thank you! May the sufferings of sentient beings ripen within me!"

(iv) [As for the integration of a lifetime's experiential cultivation:][13] With regard to this essential pith instruction, starting now and continuing through the months and years until you die, you should strongly propel your thoughts with the power of the seed of virtuous action and the power of propulsion that increases necessities and merits! {132} You should repeatedly refine the power of familiarity! You should reject the cherishing of self through the power of eradication. And as far as the power of aspirational prayer is concerned, at the conclusion of any virtuous activity you should say, "May I not be separated from the two aspects of enlightened mind!" Through these five powers all things are integrated within the syllable HŪṂ.[14]

At times when consciousness transference is applied, when death is certain or you are afflicted by illness, you should pray, saying, "Through [the power of] the seed of virtuous activity, [the power of propulsion] that enhances necessities and merits, and [the power of] aspirational prayer, grant your blessing that during the intermediate state and in all my subsequent lives, I may refine the two aspects of enlightened mind and encounter teachers who reveal this sacred doctrine!"

You should make this aspiration, reflecting that through the power of eradication the cherishing of the physical body is rejected, and that through the power of propulsion the enlightened mind is refined during the intermediate state.

Through the power of familiarity, your former memories and deeds will, at the time of death, cause you to lie down on your right side, and you will refine the two aspects of exchanging compassion with the suffering of others, regulated according to the exhalation and inhalation of breath. Your mind should not at all grasp the state where thoughts of birth and death arise. You should die while continuing to enhance and cultivate this practice.

(v) [As for the measure of mind training:][15] All the doctrines of the Great and Lesser Vehicles are subsumed in the overcoming of self-grasping. Since mind training is an antidote, you should endeavor not to deride yourself. By training the mind well, you will delight in whatever adverse circumstances arise. In addition, with regard to the adverse circumstances of others, just as a skilled horseman does not fall from his horse even though he sways, these very adverse circumstances will gradually come to assist in mind training.

(vi) [As for the commitments of mind training:][16] You should be most effective if you do not err in the commitments, do not lapse into nonsensical talk, do not fall into one-sided bias, and remain inconspicuous.

Do not speak of the faults of others. However great afflicted mental states may be, amass all things as an antidote. Abandon self-interest. Abandon grasping things as true. Abandon enmity. Abandon bad language, without resorting to it. Abandon recrimination. Do not dig up human frailties. {133} Do not target the recitation of life-extracting mantras and so forth toward nonhumans. Abandon the transferring of your own burdensome liabilities to others by devious means. Abandon the desire for good outcomes.

If, after cultivating mind training, your mind remains obdurate, this will have the opposite effect, like carrying a scapegoat effigy to the west gate when a demon is causing harm at the east gate. Therefore, you should dispense medications directly relevant for [the treatment of] diseases. You should abandon thoughts [of schadenfreude], such as thinking that if relatives should die, you will acquire food and property; if patrons should incur a fatal disease, you will acquire an accumulation of merit; if someone of a status equal to yourself should die, you alone will acquire merit; or if an enemy should die, you will be satisfied.

(vii) [As for the precepts of mind training:][17] The precepts concerning food and clothing are observed by all yogins who are absolutely of a mind to benefit others. You should practice the exchanging of compassion with the suffering of others to overcome all deviations.

There are two tasks, one at the start and one at the end. In the mornings, you should mindfully retain this thought: "May I not be separated from enlightened mind for the duration of this day!" And in the evenings, you should make a reckoning, saying, "If I have deviated from the enlightened mind, I am contemptible."

You should practice patience in both circumstances [of good and bad fortune]. That is to say, you should not be proud of your entourage, resources, and the like; and you should act without discouragement even in a state of extreme frailty.

You should guard dearer than life itself the commitments of the sacred doctrine in general and those pertaining to mind training. You should strive so that the three difficulties do not arise—namely, the difficulty of recollecting afflictive mental states, the difficulty of averting them, and the difficulty of eradicating them.

You should cultivate joy with respect to the three principal conditions—namely, meeting an excellent teacher, making your own mind malleable to mind training, and engaging in experiential cultivation in accordance with the ways of the sacred doctrine—and you should aspire that others also may completely possess these three principal conditions.

Then there are three nondegenerations—namely, nondegeneration of devotion to your teacher, nondegeneration of enthusiasm for cultivating mind training, and nondegeneration with regard to the slightest infringements of the precepts. There are three nonseparations—namely, the nonseparation of body, speech, and mind from virtuous action.

You should be unbiased in all respects and profoundly refine mind training with respect to all things, without merely paying lip service. As for the unpleasant tasks with which you are charged, you should carry these, above all, onto the path of enlightened mind.

With regard to foremost experiential cultivation, in this present life {134} the sacred doctrine is foremost, more important than this life. Even with regard to the sacred doctrine, practice is foremost; and with regard to practice, mind training is foremost. Furthermore, for those who would engage in this training by means of scriptural authority and logical reasoning, training in a concentrated manner dependent on the pith instructions is foremost.

There are six misplaced understandings: (i) Misplaced tolerance denotes the tolerance of suffering that comes from disciplining enemies and nurturing allies while lacking the tolerance of suffering associated with the practice of the sacred doctrine. (ii) Misplaced volition denotes acting according to the volitions of this life, without engaging in the volition to practice the sacred doctrine. (iii) Misplaced savoring denotes the savoring of mundane things without savoring the sacred doctrine. (iv) Misplaced compassion denotes the cultivation of compassion for those who practice austerities for the sake of the sacred doctrine, without having cultivated compassion for those who engage in negative actions. (v) Misplaced striving denotes the engagement in the affectations of this life, paying attention to oneself and not practicing the sacred doctrine. (vi) Misplaced rejoicing denotes the cultivation of empathetic joy when enemies experience suffering and the noncultivation of joy with respect to virtuous actions.

Refinement ensues once the mind is entirely transformed in mind training itself. Ideation and scrutiny abandon afflicted mental states through antidotes, dependent on whichever afflicted mental state is most dominant. You should practice the sacred doctrine without boasting and reminding others of your own kindness.

You should not retaliate, getting upset over small matters such as when you are humiliated by others. You should not have a fickle demeanor that likes or dislikes anything for even the slightest moment. You should not hope for gratitude or verbal rewards from those you have benefited. By acting in this manner throughout your entire life, you should plumb the depths of the training in the two aspects of enlightened mind, through both meditative equipoise and postmeditation.

The **supreme** path that **liberates** from bondage
Thoughts that are disturbed in **all** respects
And the mental faculty swayed by **delightful** and pleasant appearances
Arises as the path of this succinct guidebook.

This was compiled from the guidebook of Gyelsé Rinpoché [Tokmé Zangpo].

3. Guidebook Entitled *The Heart of Dependent Origination*[18]

After you have taken refuge and set the mind on enlightenment, there ensues the particular preliminary practice:[19] You should meditate that on the crown of your own head, {135} on a seat comprising a lotus and a moon disk, your teacher is present in the form of Avalokiteśvara, and in front you should visualize your actual mother.

[In the main practice] (i) the meditation on loving-kindness is as follows:[20] You should reflect on her, starting from your conception within her womb, through to your birth, and finally to her nurturing you into adulthood. Cultivate an intense power of love and repeat the words "My mother!" again and again. You should meditate in this manner until your body hairs are moved and you are brought to tears.

(ii) If that does not happen, the meditation on compassion should follow:[21] You should sit cross-legged with your knees touching your chest, your face lowered, your facial expression sad, your hands supporting your cheeks, and your ring finger inside your mouth. With the vital points of your body in this state of distress, you should meditate strongly on compassion, and pray with a loud voice, calling out for help: "Father, Teacher! Lead this kind mother of mine now on the path of liberation!"

(iii) After reaching the limits of this meditation, you should change focus and meditate, turning toward all six classes of living beings who have been your parents. Be mindful that the gods are subject to change at death; the antigods are quarrelsome; human beings experience sorrow and endure birth, aging, and death; animals are slaughtered and coerced to work; anguished spirits are prone to hunger and thirst; and denizens of the hells are tormented by heat, cold, roasting, and burning. You should generate compassion for them. (iv) Then, in gratitude, you should pray fervently, with focused attention, saying, "My outstanding father and mother!"

(v) After that, you should practice the exchanging [of self with others][22]—namely, the six classes of living beings who have been your mother. (vi) Then you should practice the giving [of compassion] to them and the taking of their sufferings,[23] and (vii) cultivate the power of tolerance.

(viii) Finally, you should rest in the disposition of space, free from conceptual elaboration, the sameness of self and others. Imbued with that essential disposition, [when adversities arise, in order to carry them onto the path], you should then resort to the [three ancillary] focuses that directly concern ill health, malign spirits, and enemies.[24]

In order to benefit the mind, I wrote down
This instruction that combines the profound essentials,
Resembling the **delight** of **omni**present dependent origination,
Revealing the **supreme** natural **liberation** of concepts.

This guidebook entitled *The Heart of Dependent Origination* was compiled and redacted from the guidance of Muchen Gyeltsen Pelzangpo. {136}

4. Guidebook Entitled *The Carrying of Happiness and Suffering on the Path*[25]

After you have taken refuge and set the mind on enlightenment, there ensues the carrying of happiness on the path and the carrying of suffering on the path, each of which is undertaken by means of relative enlightened mind and ultimate enlightened mind. Once you have acquired certainty in the former method [by means of relative enlightened mind], you can also acquire certainty in the latter method [by means of ultimate enlightened mind].

Carrying Happiness on the Path

The first method: When all the circumstances that converge are favorable—your physical body without ill health and your mind without suffering—you should reflect, "Who apart from me has happiness at the present?" At that time, you should think with a pure heart and also say aloud, "Just as I wish for happiness, so do all sentient beings also wish for that. Since each and every sentient being has been my parent, there is no one who has not helped me. Therefore, just as I have happiness, may all sentient beings who have been my mother also experience happiness!" You should determine that since this acquisition of happiness has indeed arisen through the power of past merits, if you wish henceforth also to experience happiness, you should persevere in virtuous actions; and then you should persevere in virtuous actions of body, speech, and mind.[26]

The second method, the carrying of happiness on the path by means of ultimate enlightened mind, has three parts:

(i) The first is the introduction to happiness in the buddha body of reality:[27] When you think, "I am happy now," is it the body or the mind that is happy? Apart from these two, nothing else could be the subject of happiness. If there were no mind, the body would be inert, like a corpse in a charnel ground, and so there would be no cause of felicity and no cause of happiness. Therefore, this perception of happiness did not arise from anywhere in the beginning, nor will it cease anywhere in the end. And if it appears to abide in the interim, it does not abide anywhere within the body, from the crown of the head to the soles of the feet. This fundamental nature in which entities such as colors, forms, and so forth are without inherent existence in all respects is termed the buddha body of reality.

(ii) Next, there is the introduction to happiness in the buddha body of perfect resource:[28] You should meditate that this nature of mind that is perceived as happiness {137} assumes the form of a white HRĪḤ, and that from its *visarga* the path manifests as Avalokiteśvara. Count the mantra OṂ MAṆI PADME HŪṂ as much as possible.

(iii) The third part is the introduction to happiness in the buddha body of emanation:[29] Here you should meditate that this nature of mind that perceives happiness and is diversely perceived in unceasing hues of blue, yellow, white, red, and so forth is the buddha body of emanation. After that you should say:

When happy, I dedicate this happiness as a provision of merit.
May space be filled with spiritual and temporal well-being![30]

Carrying Suffering on the Path

Secondly, with regard to the carrying of suffering on the path, the same meditations should be applied with appropriate modulations in the case of the methods of relative enlightened mind, ultimate enlightened mind, and the three buddha bodies.[31] Then in conclusion you should make the following aspiration prayers as before:

When suffering, I shall carry the suffering of all;
May the ocean of suffering become dry![32]

The notes of this **supremely** profound guidance—
Crucially illustrating the natural **liberation**
Of the perceptions of **delight** and sorrow
In **all** modes of happiness and suffering—
Have been penned just as I received them.

This guidebook entitled *The Carrying of Happiness and Suffering on the Path* was compiled and redacted from Venerable Lama Remdawa's memorandum, based on the teachings of Gyelsé Chodzongpa.

5. Guidebook Entitled *The Mind Training according to Sumpa Lotsāwa*[33]

After first taking refuge and setting the mind on enlightenment: (i) You should cultivate a sense of contentment, without reproach, concerning those appearances that now arise commensurate with the past actions that you have previously accumulated. You should relax your mind. Without mistaking the impact of past actions, you should determine in your mind the source from which body and mind acquire modes of happiness. When this is settled, happiness arises from within.

(ii) You should not cut off thoughts that have passed. Do not welcome those that have not yet come. You should rest in the disposition of the lucid consciousness of the present, without appraising anything. Even when thoughts are diffused from the disposition of this present consciousness, you will be perfectly contented, having bound them conveniently with the rope of mindfulness.

(iii) Whatever situation confronts you, when the mind turns toward the sacred doctrine without any ulterior purpose, even dying will be easy. {138} It will not be possible to be swayed from the path of liberation.

(iv) Your own mind is actually deathless, but it appears to arise. When you realize that it is merely imagined to die, the flaws of birth and death are eclipsed. You should completely determine in the dangerous passageway of the mental body[34] that, having seen the very face of innate deathlessness, how could you possibly die!

This presents the essential and crucial synopsis
Of the short path to **supreme** natural **liberation**,
A topic that, when pondered, enhances the **delight** of learned minds
With the most profound doctrine of **all**.

This was compiled from the guidebook of Chojé Pelden Lama Dampa [Sonam Gyeltsen].

6. Guidebook Entitled *The Severance of Machik Labdron*[35]

After you have taken refuge and set the mind on enlightenment, (i) there ensues the preliminary practice in which the view, the meaning of the "mother"—the transcendent perfection of wisdom (*prajñāpāramitā*)—is introduced:[36] You should rest on the basis of the abiding aspect of the uncontrived nature of mind, and your mental faculty should not engage in any activity at all. Your mind should not ponder anything at all. There is nothing it should pursue. You should bring forth the clarity aspect of awareness. Your eyeballs should not flicker, and your gaze should be instinctively focused.[37]

It will be excellent if you can establish this and, if you can meditate, you should meditate simply on that. Meditate on that state alone! But if you are not at all inclined to meditate, you should visualize in this space in front a miniature icon, one inch in size, in which your teacher and Machik are inseparable. From that icon an [immeasurable] fiery light is diffused, unimpeded in respect of any corporeal form, and imbued with the power to pierce [earth, stone, mountain, and rock], penetrating them outward and penetrating them inward. You should meditate that it pierces your own body, from the crown of your head to the soles of your feet, penetrating it outwardly and penetrating it inwardly with the unique resonance of PHAṬ—the wrathful syllable indicative of buddha speech.[38] Having done so, you should be introduced to the abiding aspect [of the nature of mind] that is free from the dynamic of conceptual thought, resembling the centerpoint of space. [At first] this should be induced to some extent by your teacher, and then your teacher should repeatedly reinforce the view associated with this guidance.[39]

The ultimate reality associated with this practice is the intrinsic face of the mother—the transcendent perfection of wisdom[40] that is the mind of the present moment, unrecognized, free from focus, devoid of positive gods, devoid of negative demons, free from the extreme of external inspection, {139} and free from the extreme of internal inspection.[41] It is dependent on this ultimate reality that all buddhas have attained buddhahood; and it is through realizing the meaning of this ultimate reality that buddhas of the future will come forth.[42] You should experientially cultivate this!

(ii) Next, you should engage in the main practice, where the four devils are severed in the expanse of reality.[43] After making that preliminary visualization your support and having been first introduced in that manner to ultimate reality, then you should settle in the disposition of the mother—the transcendent perfection of wisdom. You should summon the consciousness that is devoid of focus, since fundamentally it is without fixed conditions, and [sever the four devils as follows]:[44]

1. The Devil of Impeded Senses

You should sever within the disposition of the mother—the transcendent perfection of wisdom—the five sense organs and five sense objects, namely, the sights that appear to the eyes, the sounds that appear to the ears, the odors that appear to the nose, the tastes that appear to the tongue, and the tangibles that appear to the body. That is to say, as these arise on the path in your own mind, you should shout out PHAṬ and let your mind rest in a relaxed state. Thereby the continuity of attachment and aversion will be absolutely severed. You should abide with clarity in your own intrinsic nature, and starkly determine that natural state. Should attachment and aversion again arise on the path, sever them with PHAṬ, and settle into that disposition. Stark freedom from thought is the evidence of the successful outcome of this severance. You should experientially cultivate that![45]

2. The Devil of Unimpeded Thoughts

Then, since they constitute the devil [of unimpeded thoughts], the plethora of fleeting conceptual thoughts of the past, future, and present will then arise on the path—including joy, fear, terror, irritation, sadness, trepidation, desire, and nondesire. When you shout out PHAṬ and relax the mental faculty, the continuity of its mentation will be absolutely severed and the stark intrinsic nature of mind will be determined. The conceptual thoughts that arise on the path are established and severed in emptiness, without training and without grasping. The awareness of this intrinsic nature is the evidence of the successful outcome of this severance.[46]

3. The Devil That Induces Exaltation

Similarly, when exaltation manifests out of attachment to the sacred doctrine, there will arise on the path attachment to the notion that a teacher such as this is excellent, or a doctrine such as this is profound. You should shout out PHAṬ and rest the mental faculty in a relaxed state, and that exaltation will be absolutely severed. You should recognize with clarity the nature of mind without attachment. Should exaltation arise on the path, sever it with PHAṬ, settling into that disposition. The awareness of this intrinsic nature is the evidence of the successful outcome of this severance.[47]

4. The Devil That Induces Egotistical Pride

All [the other devils] may be subsumed in egotistical pride, for [the devil of] impeded senses is present in greater and lesser thoughts, {140} [the devil of] unimpeded thoughts is present in agreeable and disagreeable thoughts, and [the devil of] exaltation is present in the warmth of bliss, and so forth. You should let this egotistical pride rest radiantly in the disposition [of ultimate reality]. Shouting out PHAṬ, you should directly place your mental faculty in a state of clarity and be aware of its intrinsic nature.[48]

(iii) Finally, there is conduct during postmeditation:[49] After liberating these four devils in the disposition of the mother—the transcendent perfection of wisdom—during postmeditation, the common savor will arise on the path. Without being separated from that disposition [of ultimate reality], you should continue the practice of severance, in mountain retreats and all sorts of rugged places. Thereby meditative equipoise and postmeditation should be indivisibly mingled.[50]

How wonderful that the profound essentials of **all** the cycles of Severance
Have been released in written form—
Enhancing **delight** when pondered,
They are the **supreme** guidance and natural **liberation** of bondage!

This guidebook was compiled from the authentic guidance [of Nyakton Samten Ozer].

7. Guidebook Entitled *The Three Essential Points*[51]

After you have taken refuge and set the mind on enlightenment, (i) there then ensues the yoga of continuous cultivation in this life: Here, you should visualize that on a lotus and moon seat on the crown of your head, there is a stupa embodying the essential nature of your teacher's awareness with one thousand niches, within each of which one of the one thousand buddhas is present. Then recite aloud:

> I pray to the precious teacher—essential nature of the nonarising buddha body of reality.
> I pray to the precious teacher—essential nature of the unimpeded buddha body of perfect resource.

I pray to the precious teacher—essential nature of the nonabiding buddha body of emanation.
I pray to the precious teacher—essential nature of the supreme bliss of the three buddha bodies.

After that you should visualize that within your heart at the center of a one-thousand-petal red lotus flower there is the letter HRĪḤ, from which an inch-sized miniature image of Jowo Khasarpaṇi emerges, and on the petals are one thousand ĀḤ letters, resembling dew on blades of grass. Visualize that through the recitation of OṂ ĀḤ HŪṂ, the ĀḤ letters dissolve into nectar, filling your body and refining your negative obscurations. Finally, you should rest in the disposition of your own mind, which is nonarising.

(ii) After you arise from that state, there next ensues the yoga of the transference of consciousness at the time of death: Here you should visualize that your meditational deity plucks the skull from your gross material body and places it on the surface of a cooking tripod fashioned of skulls. This is then filled with the remnants of your body, and through recitation of OṂ ĀḤ HŪṂ, your impure propensities are refined. Transformed into uncontaminated nectar, this is then offered to the guests—mundane beings associated with cyclic existence and supramundane beings associated with nirvana, headed by Maitreya. {141} Finally, a tube of light with a hook emerges from the heart of Maitreya, and within it you yourself in the form of Khasarpaṇi shoot upward like a comet and are transferred to Tuṣita, where you listen to the sacred doctrine in the presence of Maitreya.

(iii) Finally, there ensues the yoga of mingling and transference in the intermediate state: in order to cultivate certainty with respect to your immediate perceptions [during the intermediate state],[52] you should meditate with absolute determination that all sights are deities, sounds are mantra, and recollected thoughts are the innate state of awareness.

Excellently demonstrating **all** essential points,
This unsurpassed meaning—the enlightened intent of Mitrayogin—
Was established here in written form by my mind,
Endowed with **delightful** and **supreme** natural **liberation**.

This guidance entitled *The Three Essential Points* was compiled from the writings of Tropu Lotsāwa [Jampapel].[53]

8. Guidebook Entitled *Resting in the Nature of Mind*[54]

After first taking refuge and setting the mind on enlightenment: (i) You should assume the seal of body that is to be secured with the sevenfold posture of Vairocana.[55] Also, the seal of speech that is to be recited is lucid in its disposition, without the movement of wind—that is to say, without purposeful exhalation or purposeful inhalation of breath. You should let it rest lucidly in the disposition of unwavering mind.

(ii) Next, the seal of mind that is to be cultivated does not pursue thoughts of the past. You should forsake notions of the past. You should not welcome those of the future, and you should cut off their association with the mental faculty.

Right now, you should apprehend the natural state of awareness, without pondering likes and dislikes, and then directly and without wavering, just like an expert swordsman engaging in battle, you should watch with mindfulness from a distance, without wavering anywhere from the disposition in which the mind is perfectly tensioned; and after that you should settle your mind fixedly in this unbewildered essence.

At intervals you may then let your mind relax wherever it alights, without purposefully holding it and without purposefully letting it go, and without turning away from its disposition of bliss, just as a skilled person can nurture a bull without seeking to do so.[56] You should not be confused by any thoughts, nor should you strive toward them. You should dispatch them, vanquished, into the expanse {142} without grasping.

(iii) Finally, just as a bird flying directly from a boat, without finding a perch to alight or any support apart from merely seeing the sky above and the sky below, will land naturally upon that very boat, in the same way, wherever the mind becomes diffused, you should cut off its diffusion, since it has been nurtured without contrivance. When this has been determined, you will establish with the conviction of recognition that the diffusion [of mind] implicitly abides, timeless in an unfabricated state, naturally alighting right where it is, through its modality of rest.[57]

The grove of **delight** where mind, beginningless and tired,
Comes **totally** to rest is the **supreme** essential,

The natural **liberation** from bondage,
Exemplified by an authentic fixed abode.

This was compiled from the guidebook of Yangtsewa [Rinchen Sengé].

9. Guidebook Entitled *The Three Sorts of Person*[58]

After first taking refuge and setting the mind on enlightenment: [You should distinguish between] (i) persons of lesser capacity, (ii) persons of middling capacity, and (iii) persons of greater capacity, each of which includes a particular meditation and a positive attainment.

Persons of Lesser Capacity

First, the meditation is as follows: You should meditate on that which you have achieved, because you have at least acquired a human body as a physical support. You should meditate on preparing for death, because you will assuredly die.

You should meditate on the unfailing nature of past actions and their results. You should be certain about the impact of past actions on account of their benefit, their swiftness of time, their inalienable nature, their frequency, their causal basis, and their examples.

You should meditate that you will soon die, that internal phenomena are impermanent, that external phenomena are impermanent, that they are certain to die, that the actual time of death is uncertain, that death cannot be averted by any means whatsoever, that there is an impermanence of temporal instants, that there is an impermanence of the serial continuity [of thought], that there is no one to increase the life span, and that death will come due to its decay.

There is no one who will not die. Death is the reality for sentient beings. You should examine the impermanence of outer phenomena—whether in the corpses of a charnel ground, the shade of a tree, or the constellations of the sky—and be certain that the results of past actions are unfailing. For this reason you should forsake negative actions and adopt positive actions. You should meditate that you are saddened by negative actions {143} and that you have confidence in virtuous actions. You should be saddened by nonvirtuous causes with results that bring forth suffering.

You should consider that there are four types of result: (i) the ripening results of past actions, (ii) results corresponding to their causes on the basis of past experience, (iii) results corresponding to their causes on the basis of past activity, and (iv) predominant results.[59] You should consider whether or not you can tolerate the results of negative ripening at the time when it is actually experienced—the strongest sort of negative ripening being rebirth among denizens of the hells, the middling sort being rebirth among anguished spirits, and the weakest sort being rebirth among animals.

Next, the positive attainment for persons of lesser capacity is as follows: you should attain your objective on the basis of going for refuge and with the support of ethical discipline, and with virtuous actions as your path.

Persons of Middling Capacity

First, the meditation is as follows: You should meditate on the defects of cyclic existence, the defects that the five acquisitive aggregates generate,[60] and the sufferings of human beings, the sufferings of the antigods, and the sufferings of the gods. Sentient beings encounter unpleasant circumstances—birth, aging, sickness, and death. They are without pleasant circumstances, and although they seek their desired outcomes, they do not find them. You should meditate that the five acquisitive aggregates are imbued with suffering—they are conceived in the womb; they are born; they experience the sufferings of childhood, the degeneration of aging, and the unpleasantness of ill health, death, and separation from places, wealth, friends, and the physical body.

The gods experience the signs of death and the signs of impending death. You should meditate on the defects of meditative stability in the higher world realms of form and formlessness, the degeneration of meditative stability, the necessity of lapsing into the lower world realm of desire, the nature of bewilderment, the bewilderment of thoughts, the bewilderment of sexual union, the uncertainty of birth, the uncertainty of friendships, the uncertainty of past actions, and the defects associated with the past actions of each of the six classes of sentient beings.

Next, the positive attainment for persons of middling capacity is as follows: you should attain your desired result on the same basis, support, and path as before.

Persons of Greater Capacity

First, the meditation is as follows: You should meditate on the compassion that is skillful means, the emptiness that is discriminative awareness, their basis that is immeasurable, their essential nature that is enlightened mind, the compassion that is the natural condition of this birth and the natural condition of other births, and finally the need to repay kindness owing to gratitude for all sentient beings and the loving-kindness that seeks happiness through the repayment of gratitude. You should repay the kindness of those who have benefited you, those who have afflicted you with suffering, and those who have given ineffectual assistance. You should wish that human beings should not have to bear their sufferings and that they should be separated from their sufferings. {144} You should cultivate the enlightened mind, exchanging self with others. You should pray that they will wish to attain buddhahood. You should cultivate the certainty that discriminative awareness is emptiness, that both the external inhabited world and the mind are without inherent existence, and that subtle and gross particles are each imbued with conscious awareness.

Next, the positive attainment for persons of greater capacity is as follows: starting with the basis, you should set your mind on engaged enlightenment, maintain the view that is the coalescence of the two truths, and attain the coalescence of practice and ethical discipline.

Here I have established the essence of the sacred doctrine in written form—
This tradition leading to the **supreme** field of **liberation**,
The **delightful** minds of those on the great pathway
Suitable for persons of **all** capacities—greater, middling, and lesser.

This was compiled from the guidebook of Chim[chen Namka Drak].

10. Guidebook Entitled *The Sequence of the Buddhist Teaching*[61]

After you have taken refuge and set the mind on enlightenment, (i) there then ensues the base of ethical discipline:[62] Just as in the past the teaching of the Buddha and his entourage emphasized the mendicant ordination, the full monastic ordination, and the precepts of individual liberation,[63] you should also aim to act accordingly. You should pledge the vows in that manner and carefully keep in mind the precepts of individual liberation, just as they have been upheld by the monastic preceptors and masters of the past.

Each day should comprise six sessions of practice, and during each of these sessions you should recollect in your mind the gross precepts according to the *Ground Rules of Monastic Discipline* and its synopses, and the downfalls that are mentioned in the *Analyses* [of monastic discipline for monks and nuns]. Thereby you should examine whether or not your own mind has been tainted by the generic downfalls and the specific subsidiary downfalls.[64] If it is untainted, you should cultivate empathetic rejoicing. But if it is tainted, you should confess those transgressions that are to be confessed, secure those vows that are to be secured, and reconsecrate those items that are to be consecrated. This confession should be undertaken in a timely manner. You should purify your own mind during each session with the fervent thought that your transgressions will not recur in the future.

Just as the elder sages of the past depended on the precious Buddhist teaching that is the source of spiritual and temporal well-being, and on the monastic community endowed with ethical discipline; and just as they trained in the precepts, including the monastic discipline that is the root of the Buddhist teaching; {145} so you yourself should emulate them and train in that manner.

(ii) Subsequently, with regard to study, reflection, and meditation:[65] You should recognize that this ethical discipline was experientially cultivated by all mendicants of the past and is itself the foremost of experiential cultivations. Through this, fortunate beings have attained liberation. You should adopt this monastic support that is revered by all. Anyone desirous of liberation who engages in this ethical discipline and also encourages others to engage in it should take as their witnesses those who are skilled in the ethical discipline of individual liberation. For those maintaining the pure unbewildered precepts of monastic discipline and all the bodhisattva heirs of the past have, without destitution, considered their own body and life, which are hard to dispense on behalf of sentient beings, as a means of generosity.

You should cultivate from the heart the unbiased, impartial love that understands the six classes of living beings to have been your parents. You should practice tolerance toward anyone whomsoever, without enmity. You should be mindfully aware that all sorts of criticism are incurred absolutely due to your self-grasping, and you should cultivate the particular antidotes. You should insistently refine in succession whatever directly and indirectly benefits others, along with forsaking negative deeds and adopting positive deeds according to past actions and their results, as well as loving-kindness and compassion, the integration of calm abiding with higher insight, and so forth.

Here I have presented in writing this sequence of the teaching—
Purest of **all** ethical disciplines,
The **supreme liberation** imbued with extensive **delight**,
Averting the thoughts and deeds of the pious attendants.

This was compiled from the ancient writings of Chimchen.

11. Guidebook Entitled *The Sameness of Existence and Quiescence*[66]

After you have taken refuge and set the mind on enlightenment, then (i) with regard to relative appearances:[67] The abiding modality of cyclic existence is imbued with suffering, like the revolving buckets of a waterwheel, and its apparent modality is imbued with the negative actions of your own suffering that you have incurred, like a blind person roaming in a rugged wilderness. By employing the watchman of acute mindfulness during six sessions of practice, day and night, you should, in the aforementioned manner, also confidently inspect the steadfast realm of quiescent nirvana, {146} the citadel of all blissful appearances, the excellent fields of the mature roots of virtuous action, and the array of the groves encompassing spiritual and temporal well-being. In this way, clear mindfulness of happiness and suffering, the rejecting of negative deeds and accepting of positive deeds, will surge within you.

At this juncture, if your mind is afraid and saddened at the modality of cyclic existence and becomes insistent on and attached to the abiding modality of nirvana, you may deviate toward the perspective of the pious attendants and hermit buddhas who maintain the Lesser Vehicle. But in this fearful dangerous pathway, there is no one among all the sentient beings of the three planes of existence who has not been your parent. How, then, is it permissible to cling shamelessly to your own happiness, as if setting aside the kindness of your actual parents, including all those who have acted in turn as your parents? Rather, you should strongly cultivate the following notion: "I should assign my own body, speech, and mind to engage in positive and virtuous actions, without interruption, day and night, to quell the sufferings of all sentient beings of the six classes who wander in this existence, along with the causes of their sufferings!" You should cultivate compassion for all unprotected sentient beings. You should practice loving-kindness, undertake acts of benefit, reverse negative actions, and train in the manner in which loving parents act toward their child. You should apply yourself to the teaching in a timely and inconspicuous manner, and obstruct the dangerous pathways of sheer doubt whereby this practice might itself become a causal basis for lackluster, narcissistic praise.

(ii) Finally, with regard to ultimate truth:[68] You should place your mind without hesitation in the natural state where the nature of existence and quiescence abides intrinsically and timelessly in sameness. You should dispel obstacles at will, without even the slightest trace of hope or doubt, and beneficially reflect upon and recite the following prayer: "By the power of whatever roots of virtuous action of body, speech, and mind that I possess, may all sentient beings, equal to space, who have been my mother, come to acquire provisional happiness and conclusive buddhahood!" It is said that an exemplary instance of this meditation reaching the crucial point will occur if you are without repulsion or attraction,[69] even when sandalwood paste is smeared to the right {147} and dog's dung to the left.

Here I have penned the guidance that excellently reveals
The intelligence in which existence and quiescence are **totally** the same,
The **supreme** mind, **liberation** from happiness and suffering,
That derives from diligent and **delightful** cultivation.

This was compiled from the instruction manual of Chimchen.

12. Guidebook Entitled *The Great Middle Way*[70]

After first taking refuge and setting the mind on enlightenment in the context of the preliminaries, then:[71]

1. As Far as Discriminative Awareness Is Concerned[72]

You should examine the abiding nature of appearances and emptiness. Here, *appearances* denotes this phenomenal world that arises diversely without impediment. *Emptiness* does not denote the emptiness that ensues when a vase has been broken, nor the emptiness that ensues when a vase is empty of being a blanket, nor the emptiness of sheer nothingness, like the horns of a hare, but rather intrinsic awareness, empty of inherent existence, at the very moment when things appear. Relative truth is empty, in the manner of a magical display. Ultimate truth is empty of essential nature, in the manner of space. In brief, however things appear, they are without true existence even to the extent of a hair tip. This is not the emptiness of the cessation [of appearances], and it is not the emptiness of things that have been fabricated. Rather, it is exactly the emptiness that refers to appearances themselves.

2. As Far as Skillful Means Is Concerned[73]

During experiential cultivation, you should adopt the physical posture for meditative concentration, and in this disposition you should start by slightly focusing your awareness and end by relaxing it. Beginners should do this in many short sessions.

3. As Far as the Outcome of This Skillful Means Is Concerned[74]

When you have meditated in that manner, the three experiences of clarity, bliss, and nonconceptuality will arise; and then the mind will come to a state of ease, without being diffused anywhere, like your hand resting where it is placed. Your awareness, too, will settle without conceptual elaboration in this disposition of nonconceptual reality.

(i) The inception of one-pointedness when the mind is not diffused toward unobscured radiance or circumstantial objects is termed *calm abiding*, {148} and (ii) its nonconceptual nature, devoid of [dualistic] recognition, like the circle of the sky, is termed *higher insight*. (iii) Composure then ensues, untouched by the intellect that adheres to objective referents. And then, during postmeditation, experiential cultivation entails the four sorts of physical activity,[75] with an awareness that has the modality of a dream or a magical display.

When hairline distinctions concerning existence and nonexistence forcefully arise, you should gradually refine your skill, and it is said that thereby you will come to encounter the face of the abiding nature that is untainted by stains of conceptual elaboration due to the eight extremes.[76]

This great middle way, essence of **all** doctrines,
Which is **delightful** to the learned,
Is the great **supreme** path free from extremes,
Liberation from unscrutinized and foolish objects of meditation.

This was compiled from the guidance of Jangsem Dawa Gyeltsen.[77]

13. Guidebook Entitled *The Hidden Guidance of Kadam*[78]

(i) After first taking refuge and setting the mind on enlightenment, (ii) you should visualize a flat stone and position your body upon it. Thereupon king spirits, attachment spirits, spirit lords of the soil, and cannibal spirits will assault you from the four directions, each carrying a hammer with which they beat your body, covering some two-thirds of its surface with drops of your flesh and blood. Then these king spirits, attachment spirits, spirit lords of the soil, and cannibal spirits will cut your body with knives.

Attachment, hatred, and delusion are then generated by a king spirit, an attachment spirit, and a nāga. You should visualize that by eating your own flesh, you summon the attachment spirit before you and cultivate compassion. The attachment spirit eats the putrefying flesh of your body, and she is satisfied with that. The mind of that attachment spirit then emerges from her heart in the form of a vital essence. Exiting from her right nostril, it settles in the sky in front. Then visualize that your own mind extends upward, also in the form of a vital essence. As the mind of the attachment spirit vanishes farther and farther into the sky, your own mind in the form of its own vital essence is absorbed into the left nostril of the attachment spirit, causing her body to vanish clearly into space. Then you should rest in that disposition.

After that you should offer your body to the king spirit in the same manner as before, and then summon the harmful nāga spirit in front. Visualize your torso as its palace, and visualize your stomach, blood, and serum as a lake, {149} with writhing snakes and also worms, spirit lords, tadpoles, and so forth moving around the small and large intestines, and the five solid viscera headed by the heart as five precious gems, their impurities and filth as perfume and incense.

(iii) You should then visualize that all the negativity and obscurations of all sentient beings headed by that nāga emerge, like a hide of leather being scraped with a knife, and that these are ripened within yourself. In exchange, imagine that all your own virtuous actions and happiness are ripened in them.

In this practice you should make the visualizations instantaneously, determine that this is the unique path, concentrate your volition, and suppress conceptual thoughts. You should not esteem any path other than this violent antidote. Today if the self perishes, today buddhahood may be attained. Tomorrow if the self is rendered nonexistent, tomorrow buddhahood may be attained. Once the self has been rendered nonexistent, buddhahood will be attained.

Here I have committed to writing this list of visualizations—
The means whereby the coarsest untamed minds of **all**
Delightfully and **supremely** abandon self-grasping
In the **liberating** manner of an uncoiling snake.

This was compiled from the old writings of Chimchen.

14. Guidebook Entitled *The Four Deities of Kadam: Munīndra*[79]

Among the four deities of Kadam, the guidebook concerning Munīndra is as follows: After first taking refuge and setting the mind on enlightenment, in front you should visualize the transcendent lord Munīndra, the master of the Buddhist teaching in this field, upon a lion throne with lotus and moon cushions. His body resembles a polished golden door bolt, blazing with light, wearing the three religious robes.[80] His hands are in the gestures of earth-touching and meditative equipoise, his legs in the adamantine posture, and he is adorned with the major and minor marks, diffusing rays of light throughout the ten directions.

You should compose your body, and then, as for the methods of settling the mind, you should engage in calm abiding with a support, calm abiding without a support, calm abiding with a partial support, or calm abiding with a perfect support.[81] Then you should apply the nine phases of calm abiding—namely, (i) mental placement, (ii) total or perpetual placement, (iii) definitive or integrated placement, (iv) intensified placement, (v) controlling, (vi) calming, (vii) intensified calming, (viii) perpetual or one-pointed placement, and (ix) placement in meditative equipoise.[82]

After that, you should meditate on higher insight, and make the following into the path by means of meditative equipoise: (i) the nonself of individual persons, (ii) the nonself of phenomena, {150} (iii) the nonself of the causal basis, and (iv) the nonself of the essential nature.[83]

Through postmeditation you should then cut off superimpositions: the nature of the causal basis is nonexistent, the nature of fruition is nonexistent, the nature of dependent origination is nonexistent, the nature of sense objects is nonexistent, the nature of subjective consciousness is nonexistent, the nature of all things is nonexistent, the nature of entities is nonexistent, the nature of nonentities is nonexistent, the nature of the inhabited world is nonexistent, and the nature of sentient beings is nonexistent.

Here I have elucidated in writing the list of visualizations
Concerning guidance on Munīndra, in whom **all** buddhas are gathered.
This is the instruction whereby the **supreme liberation**
Integrating **delight** and joy is swiftly traversed.

This has been compiled from ancient writings.

15. Guidebook Entitled *The Four Deities of Kadam: Acala*[84]

Among the four deities of Kadam, the guidebook concerning Acala is as follows: After first taking refuge and setting the mind on enlightenment, you should then be seated with the vital points of your body composed, and vibrantly visualize the body of the deity Acala, emerging instantaneously from the syllable HŪṂ. In this context, his body is blue, with one face and two arms, the right one brandishing the sword of pristine cognition and the left one holding an adamantine lasso while forming the gesture of menace at the heart. The hair of his head, beard, and eyebrows is reddish-yellow, blazing upward; and he has three flashing eyes, red and round. His teeth bite down on the lower lip. He is adorned with precious gems and the eight great nāgas,[85] and wears a skirt of tiger skin. His right leg is drawn in and the left leg extended, trampling upon Vināyaka, the king of impediments, who has an elephant's nose, diffusing and absorbing many lesser wrathful emanations, and present within the blazing fire of pristine cognition.

In his heart, upon a lotus and sun cushion, there is the syllable HŪṂ surrounded at its extremities by the ten-syllable mantra.[86] Fierce flames emerge from it, like the conflagration at the end of an aeon of destruction, blazing with seven defining characteristics—namely, (i) heat, (ii) harshness, (iii) wrath, (iv) sharpness, (v) power, (vi) strength, and (vii) swiftness.

At first, the HŪṂ and its mantra garland {151} burn noisily within the fire. Then more intensely, the curving flames fill the butter lamp inside your body and red flames dart from the nine orifices of your body, like the tongue of a snake. Finally, the reddish glow permeates all the pores of your body. It mingles with the tented aureole of fire on the outside, and from that it blazes, flickering as far as a double arm span or bow span, an earshot, and a yoking distance.[87] You should visualize that this fire expels and scatters the venomous enemies of the Buddhist teaching and the most powerful mistresses of disease and plague to the extremities of the ocean. Then you should recite the [aforementioned ten-syllable] mantra.

After that, you should visualize a solar disk arising from the syllable MAṂ within the right eye. It beholds the buddha fields and all phenomena of cyclic existence and nirvana that arise dependently through causes and results. You should visualize a lunar disk arising from the syllable A within the left eye. It beholds all phenomena as emptiness, nonapprehensible in all respects. Then within the space between those two eyes, another sparkling eye emerges. Visualize that it lucidly beholds the inseparability of skillful means and discriminative awareness, the coalescence of calm abiding and higher insight, the inseparability of eternalism and nihilism and of being and nonbeing, and so forth. Then remain in one-pointed meditative equipoise.

If you then practice consciousness transference, you should unite the upper and lower winds within the vital points of your body, and then meditate on the vibrant meditational deity Acala. With the mantra OṂ CAṆḌA MAHĀROṢANA HŪṂ, visualize that all phenomena are merely echoes. With the syllable PHAṬ, visualize that the nature of your mind resembles a fading echo, reverberating off a cliff.

At the time when the spiritual mentor Nezur Yeshé Bar passed away,[88] he recited the mantra OṂ CAṆḌA MAHĀROṢANA HŪṂ, and after sitting a while, he uttered PHAṬ, and departed with his eyes staring upward and wide open. The crown of his head exuded steam like that of an open teapot.

Here I have elucidated in writing the list of visualizations
Concerning guidance on Acala, in whom all wrathful conquerors are
gathered.

This is the instruction whereby the **supreme liberation**
Integrating **delight** and joy is swiftly traversed. {152}

This has been compiled from the ancient writings of the past.

16. Guidebook Entitled *The Four Deities of Kadam: Avalokita*[89]

Among the four deities of Kadam, the guidebook concerning Avalokita is as follows: After first taking refuge and setting the mind on enlightenment, you should visualize yourself instantly as sublime Avalokita, with one face and four arms, seated upon a lotus and moon cushion. At the aperture formed by the pore of his body that is named "sunlight"[90] there are many million trillion bodhisattvas and ten thousand golden mountains, each of which has twelve thousand peaks, adorned with many arrays of gemstone mansions, groves, and ornaments, resonant with the sound of the sacred doctrine—the six-syllable mantra OṂ MAṆI PADME HŪṂ.

Also within that pore, inside the cavity of an inner pore named "power of the conqueror,"[91] there are eighty thousand divine golden mountains with cliffs of gemstone, trees, food, and clothing—all materialized from the nature of the gods; and there are practicing bodhisattvas chanting the sacred doctrine of the six-syllable mantra.

After the visualization of that pore has passed, you should then imagine that inside the cavity of another pore named "great medication"[92] there are eighty thousand million trillion bodhisattvas who have just set their minds on enlightenment; and eighty thousand mountain peaks of diamond, silver, gold, sapphire, ruby, emerald, and crystal. The melody of the sacred doctrine of the six-syllable mantra emerges from the symphony of *gandharva* music; and those bodhisattvas who have initially set their minds on enlightenment are imbued with emptiness and signlessness. You should say, "Alas, what suffering there is! Protect us from birth, aging, sickness, death, and so forth!" Then take your place alongside them, with your legs crossed in the adamantine posture, your body straightened, and mindfulness clearly established.

When the visualization of that pore has also passed, you should imagine that inside the cavity of another pore named "king of diversity"[93] there are many hundred thousand million trillions of hermit buddhas, revealing diverse miracles, blazing with fire, and causing downpours of rain; and there are one hundred thousand kingly mountains fashioned of the seven kinds of precious gems, {153} from which grow wish-granting trees—with trunks and roots of pearl, leaves of silver and gold, and flowers of crystal—that bring forth all that is desired. Many ornaments and garments of *kāshikā* linen spill forth from them. On mountains such as these the hermit buddhas are seated, and the twelve branches of scripture are also revealed in the resonance of the six-syllable mantra.[94]

Last of all, inside the cavity of another pore named "king of victory banners"[95] there are eighty-four thousand gemstone mountains, with wish-granting trees and as many sandalwood and coral trees; and in a mansion of blazing gemstones, the body of the Tathāgata is seated, facing toward Jambudvīpa, teaching the sacred doctrine, and expounding the six transcendent perfections in the resonance of the six-syllable mantra.

In brief, within a mere pore, there are present as many buddhas and bodhisattvas as there are within the extent of the three times, and the melodic symphony of the six-syllable mantra resonates. The million trillion rays of light that they emanate then emerge from the billion apertures formed of their pores. In order to purify the propensities of the six classes of beings, without being separated from the disposition of your one-pointed focus, you should then recite OṂ MAṆI PADME HŪṂ as often as you can.

Here I have elucidated in writing the list of visualizations
Concerning guidance on Avalokita, in whom **all** peaceful deities are gathered.
This is the instruction whereby the **supreme liberation**
Integrating **delight** and joy is swiftly traversed.

This has been compiled from the instruction manual of Chimchen.

17. Guidebook Entitled *The Four Deities of Kadam: Tārā*[96]

Among the four deities of Kadam, the guidebook concerning Tārā is as follows: After first taking refuge and setting the mind on enlightenment, you should visualize the form of the sublime lady Tārā, seated on a lotus and moon cushion in the midst of a sandalwood forest, dense with many trees adorned with flowers and fruits. She is green in color, with a golden face and two arms, holding a lily stem, her legs in the bodhisattva posture; {154} she is adorned with gemstones and silk, her aureole formed of the moon, her hair in curls, and she has a smiling facial expression. You should visualize that from the pores of her body emanations of Tārā resembling herself are diffused, permeating space and dispelling the sufferings of the six classes of beings along with their causes, establishing them in states of bliss. You should then recite OṂ TĀRE TUTTĀRE TURE SVĀHĀ as often as you can.

You should meditate that Tārā offers protection from each of the eight fears: (i) To protect from fear of lions, meditate that she appears in a lion-faced form, with her fangs bared, her tongue flashing like lightning, her eyes reddish-yellow, her hair yellow, her hands forming the gesture of fearless generosity at her heart, and adorned with ornaments, liberating sentient beings from the fear of lions. (ii) To protect from fear of elephants, meditate that Tārā has an elephant face, with a high nose, her fangs bared and her belly the color of smoke, clearly extending her thumbs with both hands forming the gesture of menace, liberating sentient beings from the fear of elephants. (iii) To protect from fear of fire, meditate that Tārā is red in color, with a burning face and seven mouths and seven tongues, her hair blazing upward, her two hands forming the lotus gesture, adorned with many ornaments, and liberating sentient beings from the fear of fire. (iv) To protect from fear of snakes, meditate that Tārā is black in color, with ten snake hoods, her hair loose, adorned with ornaments, her two hands forming the gesture of fearless generosity, and liberating sentient beings from the fear of snakes. (v) To protect from fear of brigands, meditate that Tārā is green in color, her face wrinkled with frowns, the hair of her head billowing upward, her right hand holding a sword, her left hand forming the gesture of menace, adorned with ornaments, standing, and liberating sentient beings from the fear of brigands. {155} (vi) To protect from fear of imprisonment, meditate that Tārā is red in color, her right hand holding a hook and her left hand holding a noose, adorned with ornaments, standing and liberating sentient beings from the fear of imprisonment. (vii) To protect from fear of water, meditate that Tārā is white in color, her right hand holding a chain, her left hand forming the gesture of menace, standing upright in a peaceful form, and liberating sentient beings from the fear of water. (viii) To protect from fear of carnivorous beasts, meditate that Tārā is seated in the bodhisattva posture, her body the color of jasmine flowers and the moon, adorned with ornaments, her right hand in the gesture of offering and her left hand forming the gesture of fearlessness, liberating sentient beings from the fear of carnivorous beasts.[97]

Along with each of these visualizations, you should recite the [aforementioned] ten-syllable mantra with fervent devotion and conclude this mantra with two utterances, "Tārā, Tārā!" Finally, you should say, "Omniscient Tārā!"[98]

Here I have elucidated in writing the list of visualizations
Concerning guidance on Tārā, in whom **all** peaceful and wrathful deities are gathered.
This is the instruction whereby the **supreme liberation**
Integrating **delight** and joy is swiftly traversed.

This has been compiled from the instruction manual of Chimchen.

18. Guidebook Entitled *The Parables of Potowa*[99]

After taking refuge and setting the mind on enlightenment, it behooves worthy recipients of the teachings to be untainted by three flaws that resemble (i) an upturned vase, (ii) with a leaking base, and (iii) a bad odor.[100] [Those listening to the teachings] should be without the five stains of pride, disinterest, distraction, mental inertia,[101] and sadness.[102] They should turn away from misunderstandings concerning meanings, words, and symbols, and from objects of misapprehension.[103] They should cultivate the power of the four modes of faith—conviction, longing, confidence, and incontrovertibility.[104]

It is said [in the root verses]:

> The teachings revealed by means of the parables of pith instruction
> Resemble [a child] speaking in its father's voice,
> Or a testament addressed to the wind.[105] {156}

After that interlude, in the chapter on taking refuge, there are twenty-four parables of compatibility with refuge, starting with the parable of the universal emperor and continuing through to the parable of the wedding invitation.[106] There are sixteen applicable parables for incompatibility with refuge, starting with the parable of the north-facing cave and continuing through to the parable of the killing of a field mouse.[107]

In the chapter on the difficulty of obtaining the freedoms and advantages, there are twelve parables of compatibility with that reflection, starting from the parable of grass on a castle roof and continuing through to the parable of a castle watchtower.[108] There are sixteen parables of incompatibility with that reflection, starting from the parable of a child losing its last morsel of food [in a time of famine] and continuing through to the parable of cold sealing wax.[109]

In the chapter on the meaning of impermanence, there are thirty-nine parables of compatibility with that reflection, starting from the parable of dislike for this transient state and continuing through to the parable of the *sthavira* named Vṛddhaja ("born old") [who remained in his mother's womb for sixty years].[110] There are sixteen parables of incompatibility with that reflection, starting from the parable of clutching at death and continuing through to the parable of [procrastination in practice that resembles] grassland [unwarmed by the evening sun].[111]

In the chapter on the causes and results of past actions, there are twenty-nine parables of compatibility with that reflection, starting from the parable of [positive actions] with positive returns, and continuing through to the parables of [nonwithdrawal from the sacred doctrine] despite the trichiliocosm having been enslaved and of [not being swayed by hatred] even though one might be killed.[112] There are twenty-four parables of incompatibility with that reflection, starting from the parable of loss of good fortune and continuing through to the parable of being stuffed with tea and cheesecake [but lacking faith].[113] All the foregoing parables refer to and complete the path associated with persons of lesser capacity.

In the chapter on the defects of cyclic existence, there are thirteen parables of compatibility with that reflection, starting from the parable of Nanda [who was shown these defects by the Buddha], and continuing through to the parable of seeing the [irreversible] goal.[114] There are sixteen parables of incompatibility with that reflection, starting from the parable of a monkey in a trap and continuing through to the parable of [reversing] a falling boulder of copper ore.[115]

Having been emancipated from cyclic existence in that manner, in the chapter on the vows of individual liberation, there are fourteen parables of compatibility with the ethical discipline that engages with those vows, starting from the parable of bridling a horse and continuing through to the parable of the two divine princes [who swiftly attained liberation following their ordination by the Buddha].[116] There are twelve parables of incompatibility with that ethical discipline, starting from the parable of crossing a river without being able to ford a ditch [and continuing through to the parable of the eagle and the monkeys].[117]

[In the chapter on living in a conducive place, which is one of the four great factors for spiritual progress, there are ten parables of compatibility with that objective, starting from the parable of begging for alms] and continuing through to the parable of the two sibling monks of Gyel.[118] [There are eleven parables of incompatibility with that objective], starting from the parable of feeding off an invalid when hungry, in the manner of Bonpos and wild horses, and continuing through to the parable of finding a small shack [in a blizzard].[119] All the foregoing parables refer to and complete the path associated with persons of middling capacity.

In the chapter on [the characteristics of] the most saintly beings [who are to be venerated], there are eleven parables of compatibility with those characteristics, starting from the parable of a well of gold bursting forth and continuing through to the parable of a goat herder.[120] There are twelve parables of incompatibility with those characteristics, starting from the parable of a [functionless] water mill made of wood and continuing through to the parables of an [impotent] castrated bull and an ordinary agate stone [instead of a wish-fulfilling gem].[121]

In the chapter on [the characteristics of] disciples, there are ten parables of compatibility with those characteristics, starting from the parable of two [breastfed] babies—one with a mouth and one without a mouth—and continuing through to the parable of [Potowa's exemplary disciple] Sherab Yonten [who on falling ill, opted to die and be reborn in Tuṣita, rather than to recover].[122] There are fifteen parables of incompatibility with those characteristics, starting from the parable of [Potowa's failed disciple] Ngapa Gyagar and continuing through to the parable of the child named Analé [who misapplied certain rites and was an unworthy recipient].[123]

In the chapter on the way of attending upon a teacher, there are ten parables of compatibility, starting from the parable of a baby and a chick who are both dependent on their mothers and continuing through to the parable of [Nāgabodhi] swallowing [Nāgārjuna's] spittle [and attaining the first bodhisattva level].[124] There are eight parables of incompatibility, starting from the parable of [Atiśa's disciple] Shik Chawa [who failed to regard his teacher's bizarre conduct as pure] and continuing through to the parable of the monkey's [stash of stolen] food.[125] {157}

In the chapter on our own excellent aspirations, there are six parables of compatibility with them, starting from the parable of a sweet ball of molasses and continuing through to the parable of our past history [which has brought about our present excellent condition].[126] There are five parables of incompatibility with our excellent aspirations, starting with the parable of a [disconsolate bride] saying to her mother, "I have been [harmed]!" and continuing through to the parable of [accepting] an [inferior] goat or bird [as compensation] rather than a [superior] horse or a yak.[127]

In the chapter on accumulating merit, there are twelve parables of compatibility with that accumulation, starting from the parable of Atiśa [who accumulated merits in former lives] and continuing through to the parable of [meritoriously responding to Mangyul] while sitting on one's seat.[128] There are twelve parables of incompatibility with that accumulation, starting from the parable of having acquired a body with unfavorable conditions and continuing through to the parable of having sold a [wish-fulfilling] gem [for a pittance].[129] The [foregoing four chapters], in brief, concern monks who keep their precepts while endowed with the four progressive factors.[130]

In the chapter on entering upon the path of the Great Vehicle, there are five parables of compatibility with that objective, starting from the parable of the pathway [to enlightenment] and continuing through to the parable of the resemblance of [the remedial enlightened mind] to nectar.[131] There are five parables of incompatibility with that objective, starting from the parable of an [essenceless] plantain and continuing through to the parable of a [hibernating] marmot.[132]

In the chapter on cultivating awareness of and gratitude for the past actions [that all sentient beings as your mother] have done on your behalf, there are four parables of compatibility with that objective, starting from the parable of [a mother's nurturing of an infant from the size of] a worm [to the size of a yak] and continuing through to the parable of [the stabbing of] an enemy with a sword.[133] There are three parables of incompatibility with that objective—namely, [the story concerning the betrayal of the great ape by one in search of] a lost cow,[134] [the story concerning the betrayal of the ruru deer by one it had saved from being] carried off by water,[135] and [the betrayal of Bimbisāra by] Ajātaśatru.[136]

In the chapter on the cultivation of loving-kindness, there are six parables of compatibility with that objective, starting from the parable of a mother's [love] for her child and continuing through to the parable of [the kind sthavira] Gyelshé.[137] There are six parables of incompatibility with that objective, starting from the parable of the burning fire [of hatred] of his mother's suffering and continuing through to the parable of [the limited loving-kindness of Jangpa Sherab Bar].[138]

In the chapter on the cultivation of compassion, there are five parables of compatibility with that objective, starting from the parable of [compassion] for the blind roaming in a wilderness and continuing through to the parable of [the incident] at Nadong [where Khampa Jampel's mother suffered a dog bite].[139] There are four parables of incompatibility with that objective, starting from the parable of the [uncompassionate] mantrin who slew a goat and continuing through to the parable of the falcon and the wolf [who display utilitarian compassion toward their kin].[140]

In the chapter on setting the mind on aspirational enlightenment, there are twenty-two parables of compatibility, starting from the parable of the desire [of a thirsty man] for water and continuing through to the parable of training in seven attributes [of a bodhisattva].[141] There are twenty-one parables of incompatibility, starting from the parable of [inadequate aspiration] like a foe banished from the land and continuing through to the parable of a mantrin [deceitfully] selling butter.[142]

Among the six transcendent perfections [of the engaged enlightened mind] that extends from the setting of the mind on aspirational enlightenment until its maturation is reached, in the chapter on generosity, there are five parables of compatibility with material generosity, starting from the parable of the snake slithering from its hole [without attachment] and continuing through to the parable of [Jowo Rinpoché saying,] "I am skilled [in acts of liberality]." There are also two parables of doctrinal generosity, including the hermit monk [of India] and the reading aloud [of the sutras]; and there are two parables of fearless generosity, including the royal class [protecting the lowly] and the mendicant dwelling in a fearsome place.[143] There are four parables of incompatibility with material generosity, starting from the parable of an [oblivious] skunk attracted to butter and continuing through to the parable of an [unclean] feast offered by northern [brigands]. There is also one parable of incompatibility with doctrinal generosity—the wild [brigand] burned by fire—and there are two parables incompatible with fearless generosity, including the [deceitful] lion [in mendicant's garb] and the [hypocrite] licking a butter lamp.[144]

In the chapter on ethical discipline, there are nineteen parables of compatibility with the discipline of observing vows, starting from the parable of [nonattachment to] grass or impurities {158} and continuing through to the parable of one [hundred meritorious] gilded manuscripts of the *Transcendent Perfection of Wisdom*. There are also two parables compatible with the discipline of gathering virtuous attributes—namely, the absorbing [of all things] with moisture, and an [able-bodied] person with legs and eyes; and there are also four parables compatible with the discipline of acting for the benefit of sentient beings, starting from the parable of parents acting without sadness [on behalf of their child] and continuing through to the parable of [acting on behalf of others as you would in the case of] your own body.[145] There are thirteen parables of incompatibility with the discipline of observing vows, starting from the parable of the [greedy] dog and continuing through to the parable of raising oneself up and then crashing down. There are also two parables of incompatibility with the discipline of gathering virtuous attributes—namely, the incineration by the fire [of afflicted mental states], and the wingless bird [who cannot fly]; and there are also five parables of incompatibility with the discipline of acting for the benefit of sentient beings, starting from the parable of selling a blanket at a loss [as a ruse] and continuing through to the parable of [the northern brigands] inflicting harm instead of benefit.[146]

In the chapter on tolerance, there are twelve parables of compatibility with that transcendent perfection, starting from the parable of the earth [that supports all things] and continuing through to the parable of [the travails of] Sadāprarudita.[147] There are sixteen parables of incompatibility with that transcendent perfection, starting from the parable of the dog that cannot bear a load and continuing through to the parable of the glib [and false promise] of pleasant [outcomes without prior effort].[148]

In the chapter on perseverance, there are eighteen parables of compatibility with that transcendent perfection, starting from the parable of [Ma of Penyul] acquiring the fortress [of Dro] and continuing through to the parable of drinking [completely] whatever little one has.[149] There are twelve parables of incompatibility with that transcendent perfection, starting from the parable of [old] tripe [shriveling in] fire and continuing through to the parable of the [misplaced efforts of] Semodru [of U].[150]

In the chapter on meditative concentration, there are eleven parables of compatibility with that transcendent perfection, starting from the parable of pure water in a clean container and continuing through to the parable of seeing [one's past life] on the basis of an icon.[151] There are thirteen parables of incompatibility with that transcendent perfection, starting from the parable of an impure vessel and continuing through to the parable of the lady of the North [inexperienced in farming but proud of her harvest] and the parable of [a meditator] without signs [of realization].[152] The foregoing [five chapters] all pertain to the distinctive attributes of skillful means.

Now, in the chapter on wisdom, there are thirty-five parables of compatibility with that transcendent perfection, starting from the parable of a sighted person [leading the blind] and continuing through to the parable of an excellent vase [that is never diminished].[153] There are twenty-five parables of incompatibility with that transcendent perfection, starting from the parable of hundreds [of blind people without a guide] and continuing through to the parable of [a deer] chasing a mirage.[154]

In the chapter on the attributes of the way of mantras that concludes the vehicle, there are six parables of compatibility, starting from the parable of handcrafted [buddhahood] and continuing through to the parable of [a disciple who became accomplished despite misinterpreting] the mantra MARAṆA JAḤ. There are thirteen parables of incompatibility, starting from the parable of [Atiśa finding] no [suitable teacher of mantras] in Tibet and continuing through to the parable of Apo [passing the buck and] saying he did not know.[155]

In the chapter on the need to please the root teacher of the path, there are seven parables of compatibility, starting from the parable of [an irrigation pool] fed by a mountain spring and continuing through to the parable of Atiśa [encountering Ḍombipā who was] of an inferior social class.[156] There are six parables of incompatibility, starting from the parable of [a child who claimed not to be inferior to his] paternal ancestors and continuing through to the parable of [a brahmin who obtained the accomplishment of] swift-footedness [but trivialized it out of faithlessness].[157]

In the final chapter on the dedication of merit, there are nine parables of compatibility, starting from the parable of the [perfected workmanship] of a goldsmith or silversmith and continuing through to the parable of [a boatman crossing a river] with a safety towrope.[158] There are ten parables of incompatibility, starting from the parable of [a passing] comet [that self-destructs] and continuing through to the parable of offering someone a pull rope [after weighing him down with an anchor].[159] {159}

In the synopsis of all [these topics], there are [five] parables, including (i) the conclusive investigation of enemies [such as the aforementioned incompatible factors], (ii) [the balanced raising of a grain container from] its four corners, (iii) [the accurate counting of Bon ritual ingredients required] for a single doughball, (iv) [the persistent effort required when] rubbing sticks to make fire, and (v) [the exemplary pursuits of] Sadāprarudita and Subhadra.[160]

Having cultivated an understanding of these parables, this guidebook is a form of mind training for the sake of persons of the three capacities.

Here I have presented in writing the crucial teachings
Of Potowa's instruction manual entitled *Heap of Gems*
That trains the mind in **supreme liberation,**
Seeing **all** aspects of the sacred doctrine as parables—**delightful** topics.

This was compiled from the guidebook of Hor Kabzhipa.

19. Guidebook Entitled *The Sixteen Spheres of the Heart*[161]

After you have taken refuge and set the mind on enlightenment, there ensues the cultivation of the four spheres of the supporting maṇḍala, the six spheres of the supported deities, and the six spheres of the teachers of the root lineage. The coalescence of these sixteen is the sphere of enlightened mind.[162]

The Four Spheres of the Supporting Maṇḍala

As to the first group of four, these are respectively the spheres of (i) the inconceivable external array of the universe in general; (ii) the world of Patient Endurance within the trichiliocosm in particular; (iii) Tibet, the Land of Snows, more particularly; and (iv) the northern direction of Uru, most particularly.

As to the first of these spheres, this denotes the complete defining characteristics of the celestial palace, which is square with four gates and so forth. When this is respectfully observed, the white syllable OṂ appears at its zenith, white MA appears at the eastern gate, yellow ṆI appears at the southern gate, red PAD appears at the western gate, green ME appears at the northern gate, and blue HŪṂ appears at the nadir. At the center, within [the palace], there is a seat comprising a one-thousand-petal white lotus and a crystalized moon disk.[163]

As to the second sphere [the world of Patient Endurance within the trichiliocosm], this denotes the great sage Vairocana in the form Himamahāsāgara, yellow in color, who has the appearance of the buddha body of emanation, teaching the sacred doctrine.[164]

As to the third sphere [in the case of Tibet], this denotes Avalokiteśvara in the form Jinasāgara, with one thousand arms and one thousand eyes, seated in the [adamantine] posture.[165]

As to the fourth sphere [the northern direction of Uru], this denotes standing Padmapāṇi in the form of a crystal youth, according to Dromton. His right hand counts the beads of a crystal rosary and his left hand holds a crystal staff surmounted by a one-thousand-petal white lotus, at the center of which the Great Mother Prajñāpāramitā appears with Śākyamuni on her right, Jowo Atiśa in a not dissimilar form on her left, and on the one thousand petals are seated the one thousand buddhas of the Auspicious Aeon.[166] {160}

The Six Spheres of the Supported Deities

As to the second group of six spheres, these comprise the six meditational deities: (v) The Great Mother Prajñāpāramitā is yellow in color, with four arms, her first right hand holding a nine-pronged vajra, her first left hand in the gesture of meditative equipoise, her second right hand holding a rosary, and her second left hand holding a scripture. Her legs are in the adamantine posture, and she has gemstone ornaments. (vi) Śākyamuni appears in the Māra-subduing form, with his right hand in the earth-touching gesture and his left in the gesture of meditative equipoise. (vii) Avalokiteśvara has one face and four arms. (viii) Tārā is peaceful and greenish-yellow in color, and she liberates from [the fear of] sandalwood forests. (ix) The dark green and wrathful form of Tārā, with four arms, holds a knife and skull, *ḍamaru* and *khaṭvāṅga*, and has bone ornaments; the hair of her head is yellowish-red; her left leg is extended and upright, in a dancing posture. (x) Acala has one leg extended, the other drawn in, trampling upon Gaṇapati; he is wearing an elephant hide, holding a sword and a noose, the hair of his head yellowish-brown; and he is adorned with snakes.[167]

The Six Spheres of the Teachers of the Root Lineage

The five spheres of the teachers are those of (xi) the father Jowo Atiśa; (xii) the son Dromton; and (xiii–xv) the three deities Maitreya, Mañjughoṣa, and Vajradhara, who are respectively surrounded by the lineages of extensive conduct, profound view, and blessed experiential cultivation.[168]

(xvi) As for the sixteenth, this sphere denotes [Samantabhadra], the buddha body of reality, blue in color, with one face and two arms, forming the gesture of meditative stability, radiant and perfect in enlightened attributes and divine form. All the fifteen other spheres have an external divine form and an inner celestial palace. Within the heart of the sixteenth you should meditate and visualize with one-pointed focus that there appears a yellowish-white extremely minute sphere combining both subtle energy and mind, along with the modalities of the supporting palaces and supported deities. When this is diffused, it encompasses space. When it is absorbed, it assumes a form the size of a split pea; and around it, about the thickness of a white mustard seed, is the self-manifesting sphere of enlightened mind, diffusing five rays of light.[169]

Next, you should associate the [visualizations of the six deities] with the five recollections,[170] and at the time of making the recitations, you should say TADYATHĀ and so forth in the case of the Great Mother [Prajñāpāramitā], OṂ MUṆE MUṆE and so forth in the case of Śākyamuni, the six-syllable mantra [OṂ MAṆI PADME HŪṂ] in the case of Avalokiteśvara, TĀRE TUTTĀRE and so forth in the case of Tārā, {161} OṂ TĀRE TUTTĀRE TURE HŪṂ PHAṬ in the case of wrathful Tārā, and OṂ CANDA MAHĀROṢANA in the case of Acala. At that time, you should firmly close all the gateways of the senses and meditate one-pointedly.

Here, extracted from *The Book of Kadam*, I have penned

This quintessence of **all** Kadam instructions,
The release—**delightful** and exalted—
That swiftly confers **supreme liberation**.

Although I obtained this instruction entitled *The Sixteen Spheres of the Heart* based on the memorandum of Nyukla Paṇchen, I wrote down this specific guidebook, summarizing the inspection I myself made of *The Book of Kadam*.

20. Guidebook Entitled *The Six Descents of the Transcendent Perfection of Wisdom*[171]

After first taking refuge and setting the mind on enlightenment: (i) You should then meditate in a single sitting upon the eight phases [of clear realization] that derive from the regent Maitreya in the paradise of Tuṣita, source of happiness. These phases comprise the three understandings; the four applications; and the fruition, which is the buddha body of reality.[172] Having established this methodology to constitute the vitality of the path, you will have confidence in it.

(ii) In addition, the sixteen volumes of *Extensive Mother: The Transcendent Perfection of Wisdom in One Hundred Thousand Lines* were brought forth from the underworld of the nāgas, source of resources.[173]

(iii) When its content is analyzed in detail, it comprises the aforementioned eight phases as well as the [subsequent] division into six summations and the division into three summations,[174] along with the distinctions between analysis and meditative cultivation, and the distinctions between scriptural authority and logical reasoning established by the learned paṇḍitas of Bengal, source of awareness.

(iv) The sequence in which the path is cultivated—the sequential phases of application, including the four grades of ascertainment[175] and so forth—originated from the southern land of Beta, source of enlightened attributes.

(v) The sequence of the teaching and the compilation of the transmitted teachings, in which each of the six transcendent perfections is revealed to subsume within it all six, is the lineage originating from the speech of the ḍākinīs of the western land of Oḍḍiyāna, source of blessings.

(vi) In addition, with regard to the latter, the [related instructions on] pacification of all sufferings of mental anguish without exception originated from the isle of Viśvakoṭacandana, source of wonder.[176]

In sum, {162} from the perspective of analysis, the transcendent perfection of wisdom is ineffable, unthinkable, and indescribable. It is of the essential nature of space, without arising and without ceasing. And from the perspective of meditative equipoise, you should comprehend the perceptual range of pristine cognition—particularizing intrinsic awareness—that is termed the "mother of the conquerors of the three times."

Here I have elucidated in writing the meaning of the Mother—
This most essential of **all** descents of the transmitted teachings,

The expanse of great **delight** of intrinsic awareness,
The grand palace of **supreme liberation**.

This was compiled from the instruction manual of Rongton.

21. Guidebook Entitled *The Five Paths of Pacification*[177]

After first taking refuge and setting the mind on enlightenment, you should assess the five paths and three austerities.

The Five Paths

Among the five paths, the path of provisions entails mind training. The path of connection entails austerities. The path of insight entails subsequent applications. The path of meditation entails common savor. The path of conclusion entails freedom from activity.

1. The Path of Provisions That Entails Mind Training

On the crown of the head, you should visualize your actual teacher, imbued with radiance, upon a lotus, sun, and moon cushion that rests on the stem of a lotus. Stacked above and below are the four tiers of the teachers of the lineage. Dampa Gyagar's body is reddish-brown in color, the hair of his head bristling like [the leaves of] an elm tree,[178] overwhelming phenomenal existence. In all, there are fifty-four male and female accomplished masters. [To their rear] are the eleven teachers of dialectics and Sanskrit grammar, [headed by Nāgārjunagarbha]. [To their right] are the eleven teachers of the dynamic subtle energy [of the father tantras, headed by Buddhaguhya]. [To their left] are the eleven teachers of the blissful experience [of the mother tantras, headed Saroruhavajra]. [In front] are the eleven teachers of the symbolic [Great] Seal [headed by Saraha]. [In the intermediate directions] are the ten teachers who confer the introduction to awareness [headed by Sukhamahāsiddha]. [Above their heads] are the thirty-six teachers endowed with wondrous sky-faring ability, and [above their heads in turn] are the twelve teachers who are sugatas in steadfast meditation.[179] All of them are naked, clad in space, without the elaboration of costumes.

You should visualize that rays of light emerge from your own heart and are presented as offerings. You should pay homage to those teachers and go for refuge to them. Pray for their blessing, and then [dedicate your merits of the past, present, and] future in all respects.[180]

[To consecrate sights, sounds, thoughts, and all of these combined],[181] you should then recite four times: A Ā I Ī U Ū Ṛ Ṝ Ḷ Ḹ E AI O AU {163} AṂ AḤ KA KHA GA GHA ṄA CA CHA JA JHA ÑA ṬA ṬHA ḌA ḌHA ṆA TA THA DA DHA NA PA PHA BA BHA MA YA RA LA VA ŚA ṢA SA HA KṢA. After you complete the recitation of these Secret Mantra letters, they all vanish.

Then [as for the consecrations of the four cakras]: You should visualize that from OṂ [in the crown cakra], the seed syllable indicative of buddha body, a white [stream of] generative fluid flows down and fills the body. From ĀḤ [in the throat cakra], the seed syllable indicative of buddha speech, a red stream of generative fluid freely flows down and fills the body. From HŪṂ [in the heart cakra], the seed syllable indicative of buddha mind, a blue stream of generative fluid spreads forth and fills the body with bliss. From HRĪḤ [in the navel cakra], the seed syllable of buddha attributes, a stream of generative fluid emerges in diverse colors, transforming your body and mind into stark emptiness.[182]

Then, in order to carry the introduction [to awareness] on the path, you should cross your legs in the adamantine posture, with your hands in meditative equipoise, your spine straight, your neck [slightly] bent, your shoulders stretched out [like the wings of a *garuḍa*], your lips and teeth in their natural positions, and your eyes focusing on the tip of your nose.[183] Concentrate your eyes, nose, and mind together, and rest in their natural state, without conceptualizing. [Thereby nonconceptual pristine cognition will abide in its own intrinsic nature.] During postmeditation, all that appears is fictitious. You should make this determination [counterintuitively], having dried things in water![184]

Then you should count the eight-syllable mantra with intense longing: OṂ ĀḤ HŪṂ GURU SIDDHI HŪṂ. You should visualize that your actual teacher does not vanish [from the crown of your head] and that the blessings [of nondual bliss and emptiness] enter into you. At the session's end you should say, "May I become accomplished!"[185]

2. The Path of Connection That Entails Austerities

Here in particular you should visualize your teacher as the buddha body of perfect resource, adorned with the major and minor marks. The other steps are the same as above. You should recite the vowels and consonants four times. Then, as before, sights become deities, sounds become mantra, and thoughts become the four pristine cognitions.[186]

[With regard to the four empowerments that are associated with the four cakras:] At the crown of your head, the seed syllable indicative of your teacher's buddha body manifests as white Vairocana, in union with female consort. At the throat, the seed syllable indicative of his buddha speech manifests as red Amitābha, in union with female consort. At the heart, the seed syllable indicative of his buddha mind manifests as blue Akṣobhya, in union with female consort. At the navel, the seed syllable indicative of his buddha attributes manifests as yellow Ratnasambhava, in union with female consort. These are seated in the adamantine posture upon a lotus and moon cushion. The four empowerments should then be similarly received.[187]

You should regard subtle and gross conceptual thoughts with the five eyes. That is to say, you should regard such thoughts with the closed eyes of a turtle; you should regard them with eyes like cowrie shells, slightly open and squinting; you should regard them with eyes like a crescent moon, somewhat open; {164} you should regard them with eyes like kidneys, slightly open with admiration; and you should regard them with eyes like the full moon, open wide. You should bunch these conceptual thoughts together and smash them, and thereafter you will be entirely without thoughts.[188] Then you should pray as before, reciting OṂ ĀḤ HŪṂ GURU SIDDHI HŪṂ.[189]

3. The Path of Insight That Entails Subsequent Applications

The particular distinction here is that you should visualize your teacher naked with bone ornaments, and then recite the vowels and consonants four times. Then visualize the essential nature of sense objects—sights, sounds, [and thoughts]—as your teacher; and senses as the meditational deities—nonarising, nonabiding, nonceasing, nonexistent, empty of sights, empty of sounds, and empty of thoughts, without duality.[190]

With regard to the visualizations associated with the four empowerments, in order that beings might attain liberation in that state devoid of inherent existence, there are five gazes: the eyes should be turned downward in the gaze of pious attendants, upward in the gaze of hermit buddhas, to the zenith in the gaze of male bodhisattvas, to the left in the gaze of female bodhisattvas, and straight ahead in the gaze of sugatas. At those times, the relaxation of your mind should be maintained just the same as in the aforementioned austerity practices [and mind training]. Then recite OṂ ĀḤ HŪṂ GURU SIDDHI HŪṂ.[191]

4. The Path of Meditation That Entails Common Savor

The particular distinction here is that you should meditate on the teacher wearing indeterminate costumes. You should then recite the vowels and consonants as before, and as a result, sights, sounds, and thoughts will manifest as the teacher's buddha body, speech, and mind, without duality of bliss and emptiness.[192]

As for the particular visualization of the four empowerments, within the four cakras you should visualize the sugatas, and receive the empowerments from them in no particular order.

[As far as the practical application of meditative equipoise and postmeditation is concerned, Kamalaśrīvajra has said, "One who relies on beneficial things that facilitate the path] should fear the persistent grasping of entities. This is the crucial point that topples the established order in a carefree manner."[193]

[As far as the modes of conduct are concerned,] there are five sitting postures—namely, the cross-legged adamantine posture, the semi-cross-legged posture, the crouching posture, the leaning posture,[194] and the posture of royal ease. There are five sorts of movement: walking, dancing, running, jumping, and resting. There are five standing postures—namely, rising, half standing, standing, getting dressed, and stepping forward. There are five ways of reclining—namely, lying down on the right side, lying down on the left side, lying down on the back, lying down on the front, and covering the head. {165} You should bunch all of these modes of conduct together, destroy and smash them. After crushing them, you should rest in a relaxed and naked state.[195]

5. The Path of Conclusion That Entails Freedom from Activity

The particular distinction here is that you should visualize your teacher as the supreme buddha body of emanation, wearing the costume of a monk, and then recite the vowels and consonants four times. Thereupon, though sights, sounds, and thoughts may appear, they will be without inherent existence, like the vanishing of clouds in the sky or the melting of ice on an ocean.[196]

As for the four empowerments, the particular visualization of the four cakras is as follows: In the crown cakra, Vairocana dissolves and vanishes into his female consort. This ḍākinī of the buddha family is white in color, holding a wheel and a skull of blood, and she overwhelms extraneous appearances with her charisma. In the cakra of resources [in the throat], Amitābha dissolves in the same manner as before into his female consort. This ḍākinī of the lotus family is red in color, holding a lotus and a skull of blood, and she brings extraneous appearances under control. In the cakra of the phenomenal wheel [in the heart], Akṣobhya dissolves in the same manner as before into his female consort. This ḍākinī of the vajra family is blue in color, holding a vajra and a skull of blood, and she longs for disciples who have been gathered within her power. In the cakra of emanation in the navel, Ratnasambhava also dissolves in the same manner as before into his female consort. This ḍākinī of the ratna family is yellow in color, holding a gemstone and a skull of blood, and she is satisfied by the mental faculties and mental phenomena of others who are faithful.[197]

You should then reflect, "Henceforth I am not to view my own self-interest rather than the interests of other sentient beings. I should not have that view! Perish the hope of having that view! If I were to have that view, I would incur negativity. Henceforth I am not to meditate on my own self-interest rather than the interests of other sentient beings! I should not meditate on that! Perish the hope of meditating on that! If I were to meditate on that, I would incur negativity. Henceforth I am not to act out of my own self-interest rather than the interests of other sentient beings! I should not act in that manner! Perish the hope of acting in that manner! If I were to act in that manner, I would incur negativity. Henceforth I am not to accomplish my own self-interest rather than the interests of other sentient beings! I should not accomplish that! Perish the hope of accomplishing that! If I were to accomplish that, I would incur negativity." In this way, you should crush the grasping and clinging that ensnares you! OṂ ĀḤ HŪṂ GURU SIDDHI HŪṂ.[198]

The Three Austerities

Next, with regard to the assessment of the three sorts of austerity, this comprises the three examples, the three sorts of person, the three times for austerity, and the three methods for the conferral [of empowerment].[199]

The three examples are as follows: You should cut off exaggeration and deprecation in the manner of a pious attendant. You should practice alone in the manner of a hermit buddha. {166} And you should experientially cultivate the interest of others, in the manner of a bodhisattva.[200]

There are three sorts of persons—namely, [mendicants], who abandon worldly activities; [householders], who give no space for worldly activities; and [ascetics], who do not stockpile necessities.[201]

With regard to the three times for practicing austerities, the optimum period for maintaining them is three days, the mediocre is two days, and the worst is one day.[202]

As for the methods of conferring empowerment, you should not enter into experiential cultivation of the higher paths [of empowerment] without having completed the lower paths.

As for the fruition that is free from activity, the best achieve this goal within this very lifetime, the mediocre do so at the time of death, and the worst are reborn in accordance with their former talents through the intermediate state.[203]

Here I have extracted all the essentials of pacification in their **totality**,
This verbal support of the **delightful** mind,
Supreme nucleus of natural **liberation**,
Among the methods of obtaining release.

This was compiled from the instruction manual of Rongton Sheja Kunrik.

22. Guidebook Entitled *The Three Stages of Meditation—Beginning, Middle, and Conclusive*[204]

After first taking refuge and setting the mind on enlightenment: By understanding that conditioned phenomena are impermanent and that contaminated phenomena are imbued with suffering, which is the guidance of the path enunciated in the first turning of the doctrinal wheel, you should have confidence in the unfolding of actions and their results, the virtuous actions to be adopted, and the negative actions to be rejected. And then with absolute certainty that [specific] results will emerge in respect of the causes you have investigated, you should insistently pursue abandoning negativity and practicing virtue for the sake of yourself and others. You should abandon bad associates who confuse actions and their results, and you should attend upon spiritual mentors who reveal the unfailing relation between actions and results. You should strive on the path of study, reflection, and meditation. You should cultivate empathetic joy for those who have acquired a place for spiritual attainment in a land that supports the adopting [of virtuous actions] of body, speech, and mind. You should engage in acts of renunciation and remedial acceptance with respect to minor offenses. It is important to purify your own mind through discipline.

Then, in a grass hermitage free from distractions, as in the mountains of Prānta that were praised by the Conqueror, with a mind disillusioned with cyclic existence, you should focus your mind inwardly, with inspiration that is unattached and does not cling to anything at all. Place in front whatever you can find as a support for mental focus—a stick, a pebble, or a flower, for example—as enunciated in the second turning [of the doctrinal wheel]. {167} To impede the flow of thoughts that are diffused toward objects, your mind should be one-pointed, your body should settle into the adamantine posture, your hands should be placed in the gesture of meditative equipoise, your spine should be straightened, your eyes focused on the visualization support, your neck bent, and your teeth and lips not quite touching. You should not pursue any circumstantial object whatsoever. You should remain clear and vivid and be absolutely determined to sever the tree of subjective conceptual thoughts with the sword of discerning discriminative awareness.

Then you should rest in the disposition where all things are empty and without self. Never submit to sluggish inertia but let your awareness flourish. Do not relish the taste of quiescent and blissful nirvana. You should absolutely and completely banish self-grasping, the primary downfall. Do not objectify any determinations concerning the pretentious abyss of eternalism and nihilism, and dispel the darkness of deepest inertia that resembles entering a marmot's burrow. You should remain confident and undisturbed, subsuming naturally radiant intrinsic awareness within your own mind. Do not adopt an intellectually fabricated understanding that would establish from the perspective of logic that things are empty. Without determining any distinction between object and subject or between enemy and friend, you should absolutely resolve that whatever arises is the natural form of emptiness.

Next, you should analyze the testimony of your own experience and, without perpetuating that, train in natural liberation, just as the knots of a snake are naturally uncoiled. As far as conduct during postmeditation is concerned, without distinguishing between meditative equipoise and postmeditation, you should guard the prescribed boundaries according to the teachings of the Conqueror, as if they were your own eyes. You should insistently pursue an expansive view and precision of conduct.

You should hold dear this very text
That subsumes **all** stages of meditation from beginning to end
And demonstrates the essential integration of view and conduct—
The **supreme liberation** of **delightful** inspired speech.

This was compiled from the guidebook of Rongton Sheja Kunrik.

23. Guidebook Entitled *The Five Doctrines of Maitreya*[205]

After first taking refuge and setting the mind on enlightenment: At the outset [of this practice], you should recite the offering prayers. In that connection, the quintessential point of the *Ornament of Clear Realization* is that you should practice with reference to the three aspects of objective understanding on the path of provisions.[206] Through the four essential applications[—namely, warmth, peak experience, acceptance, and supremacy[207]—]you should then practice the six transcendent perfections that constitute the path.[208]

As far as the attainment of the armor of aspiration is concerned, there are six transcendent perfections, preceded by the taking of refuge. They comprise (i) the three aspects of generosity,[209] (ii) ethical discipline that has abandoned the attentiveness of the pious attendants and hermit buddhas, (iii) tolerance of unpleasant phenomena, (iv) perseverance that longs for the assembly of the Great Vehicle, (v) meditative concentration that is unadulterated with other vehicles, and (vi) wisdom that dedicates merit toward enlightenment. You should retain these without conceiving them in terms of the threefold interaction of subject and object. In addition, the provisions associated with the [ten bodhisattva] levels entail ten corresponding transcendent perfections through which the levels are chiefly refined.[210]

The quintessential point of the *Ornament of the Sutras of the Great Vehicle* is the experiential cultivation of the conduct of a bodhisattva. To that end: (i) You should act with resolve on the impure levels (*ma dag sa'i mos spyod*). (ii) You should have higher aspirations for the pure levels (*dag pa sa'i lhag bsam*). (iii) You should experientially cultivate the conduct of a bodhisattva. (iv) You should cultivate devotion for the attributes of the Great Vehicle with the thought of engaging in acts of benefit. (v) You should teach the sacred doctrine acquired for the sake of others with a disposition that does not mistakenly long to find it for your own sake. (vi) You should realize the actual nature of phenomena for your own sake during the main practice. (vii) You should teach the oral instructions and further instructions for the sake of others. (viii) You should skillfully maintain conduct for your own and others' benefit during postmeditation. (ix) You should frequent the pure levels, and (x) you should engage in conduct that is extensive and profound.[211]

The advantages are that by having experientially cultivated the attributes of the Great Vehicle, the ailments of afflicted mental states will be calmed. If you practice this, you will acquire power over enlightened attributes. If you hold it in mind, all sorts of external benefits will emerge, resembling the wish-fulfilling gem.

The quintessential point of the *Distinction between Phenomena and Actual Reality* is that the appearances of your own mind as conceptual thoughts associated with the eight aspects of consciousness arise when reality is not recognized, {169} but these are without true existence.[212] In order that these thoughts might not manifest, you are introduced to the appearance of genuine reality. Afflicted mental states develop due to fixation on bewildered thoughts that appear as both the internal mind and the external inhabited world with its inhabitants. But when the awareness that impedes conceptual thoughts and dualistic perceptions abides in reality, the nonconceptual pristine cognition then ensues. During postmeditation there is an absence of fixation and appearances arise like a magical display.[213]

The quintessential point of the *Distinction between the Middle and Extremes* is that once the mind has renounced mundane concerns, you should dedicate enlightenment for the sake of sentient beings. Commencing with the path of provisions and the path of preparation, on the first bodhisattva level magical display is attained. On the eighth bodhisattva level causally concordant conduct is attained,[214] while on the tenth bodhisattva level and on the buddha level the transcendent perfections are attained.[215] In terms of skillful means, you should resolve that self and others are the same. And then, in order to actualize nonconceptual pristine cognition, you should attain mastery in the meditative stability of the other transcendent perfections [in addition to skillful means],[216] and then practice the ten facilitating modes of doctrinal conduct,[217] along with unwavering calm abiding and unerring higher insight.[218]

The *Supreme Continuum of the Great Vehicle* establishes the entrance and support [for the path] since that is mentioned in its concluding verses of dedication.[219] The quintessential point is that this text is the essence of the four preceding doctrines of Maitreya that have already been explained.

This treatise explains the presence of natural luminosity in detail, and by means of seven adamantine topics[220] and nine examples.[221] After determining that innate pristine cognition, tarnished by the dualistic perceptions of the subject-object dichotomy, is the naturally radiant intrinsic awareness, free from grasping, your awareness should then obstruct the dangerous passageway of eternalist views by eliminating nihilistic views. Since the nature of mind is unchanging like space, the seed of buddha nature is uncovered by the afflicted mental states that emerge from inauthentic conceptual thoughts. To fortunate persons who receive this introduction, this actual book of Maitreya refines the instructions by pointing out the path.

Here I have presented the gist of this instruction
On **all** the *Five Doctrines of Maitreya*,
Which, like an occasional udumbara flower,
Delightful minds of natural **liberation**
Imbue with **supreme** confidence. {170}

This somewhat brief guidebook was compiled from the instruction manuals of Chomden Rikpei Reldri.

24. Guidebook Entitled *The View of Intrinsic Emptiness*[222]

After first taking refuge and setting the mind on enlightenment: You should engage with precision in experiential cultivation of the ground that is the middle way, adopting virtuous actions and rejecting nonvirtuous actions with respect to mere conventional appearances. You should engage in meditative equipoise that is free from the eight extremes, since there is no ceasing, no arising, no nihilism, no eternalism, no coming, no going, no diversity, and no unity. In postmeditation you should cultivate for a long period of time the view that appearances are like a magical display. When you are familiar with this practice, your mind may experience great bliss and your body hairs may stand on end, just when you hear the word *emptiness*. Your eyes will be disturbed by tears, and you will awaken to the enlightened heritage of the Great Vehicle. Manifestly realizing the crucial points, you will be liberated from the afflicted mental states that are to be abandoned. You will refine the experiential cultivation that is devoid of conceptual elaboration, without grasping and without clinging, and in that case, you need not emphasize engagement in virtuous actions of body and speech. If, however, you have not yet attained stability in the truth devoid of conceptual elaboration, you should continue to emphasize engagement in virtuous actions of body and speech.

Here I have presented in writing this guidebook on the **supreme** view
Of natural **liberation**, devoid of grasping—
The state of **delight** and exaltation like space, free from clouds
Of **all** elaborate accumulations that grasp extremes.

This was compiled from the instruction manual of Patsab Nyima Drak.

25. Guidebook Entitled *The View of Extraneous Emptiness*[223]

After first taking refuge and setting the mind on enlightenment, [you should understand that] clinging to bewilderment as true is imaginary. The inauthentic imaginary nature includes all aspects of clinging to the subject-object dichotomy as entities, in the manner in which a multicolored rope resembles a snake.

All things from physical forms to omniscience in respect of which the imaginary nature engages in grasping constitute the dependent nature that is contingent on causes and conditions. Although these phenomena diversely appear, they are simply realized to be inauthentic. Like that multicolored rope, all dependent phenomena from physical forms to omniscience are conceptualized in accordance with past actions and afflicted mental states.

The naturally present original reality {171} that permeates all these [dependent phenomena], in the manner of the space that permeates the multicolored rope, constitutes the incontrovertible consummate nature and the unchanging consummate nature, which respectively denote the two buddha bodies of form.[224]

The factors conducive to enlightenment, the truth of the path, and all things from physical forms to omniscience that are conventionally imagined are empty of defining characteristics. Although they are indeed established in terms of the three essenceless natures, when investigated, there is no dualizing perception apart from the mind, and so apparent phenomena are assigned to the dependent nature, and reality itself to the consummate nature. The latter alone denotes the immaculate and spontaneously present, unique reality.

So it is that imaginary things resemble the horns of a hare because they are empty of their own inherent existence. Dependent things resemble a magical display because they are empty of the imaginary. Consummate things resemble space because they are empty of both the imaginary and the dependent. All conventional appearances associated with the imaginary and dependent natures exist relatively but not ultimately. The consummate reality exists ultimately but is neither identical in nature with nor different from relative appearances. It denotes the great middle way that is devoid of all extremes.

Here I have elucidated in writing
The guidebook of **delightful** and **supreme** natural **liberation**
That subsumes **all** things within the three natures
And is untarnished by dualistic appearances.

This was compiled from the instruction manual of Tsen Khawoché.

26. Guidebook Entitled *The Elucidation of the Concealed Meanings* [*of Yogatantra*][225]

After you have taken refuge and set the mind on enlightenment: For those of highest capacity, their own intrinsic awareness in an instant innately and directly perceives the generation and perfection stages of meditation as primordially perfect. For those of average capacity, the glow of the nonarising fundamental nature unimpededly manifests, fresh and without effort, as the deities. For those of inferior capacity, the uncontrived essential nature of meditation forcefully emerges. For those of the worst capacity, the graduated path [of mind training and so forth] is established as mainstream, and the buddha body, speech, mind, and pristine cognition are established as the four adamantine realities. In this last context, [there are four sessions of practice of which] the first two respectively concern (i) the eradication of hostile and obstructing forces and (ii) the acceptance of fortunate disciples.[226] {172}

1. The Eradication of Hostile and Obstructing Forces: Vajrabhairava and So Forth

This denotes the Unelaborate Practice and the Four-Stage Yoga, which are meditations of the perfection stage pertaining to the generation stage of three deities: Red Yamāri, Black Yamāri, and Vajrabhairava.[227]

With regard to the deity Red Yamāri, the Unelaborate Practice has six lines of transmission—namely, (i) the tradition of Chel Lotsāwa that makes [the realization of] freedom from extremes into the path; (ii) the tradition of Chak Lotsāwa entitled the unique visualization that enters into the path of luminosity; (iii) the tradition of Lowo Lotsāwa that details the Unelaborate Practice dependent on the adamantine verses of Virūpa; (iv) the tradition of Dānaśīla that applies the path of the Great Seal; (v) the tradition of Tarpa Lotsāwa that constitutes a close lineage in respect of the Unelaborate Practice; and (vi) the oral tradition of upper Nyang that derives from Kanaśrī.[228]

In the case of the Four-Stage Yoga, there are also six approaches—namely, those of Chel Lotsāwa, Chak Lotsāwa, Lowo Lotsāwa, Dānaśīla, Tarpa Lotsāwa, and Ārya [Kanaśrī]. So, altogether there are twelve traditions [pertaining to the deity Red Yamāri].

Similarly, with regard to Black Yamāri, there are the four lineages of Ra Lotsāwa, Kyo Lotsāwa, Zhang Lotsāwa, and Sakya, each of which has both an exegetical tradition based on the translation of the *Tantra of the Black Slayer of Death* alone and a tradition of pith instruction.[229] On Black Yamāri there is also the text of Devākaracandra concerning the four seals.[230]

On Ṣaḍānana (the "six-faced form"of Black Yamāri), there are the two traditions of Vajrahāsya's *Array of the Staircase Differentiating the Stages* and the [extant] Indian manuscript. Also on Ṣaḍānana,[231] there are four summations of the visualization, and by way of commentary, four supplements and four steps of guidance, making eight [commentarial traditions] altogether.

As for Vajrabhairava, there are four distinct traditions—namely, *The Profound and Extensive Training* by Ra Lotsāwa; *The Mental Focus on the Horns of Bhairava* by Kyoton Lotsāwa; *The Inner Yoga of the Communal Offering: A Vase of Nectar* by Zhang Śāntipa; and Nāropā's pith instruction entitled *The Erect Penis [of Bhairava]*, which represents the Sakyapa school.[232] In brief, the methods of guidance on all those aspects of Yamāntaka [including Black Yamāri, Ṣaḍānana, and Vajrabhairava] number twenty-four.

[The guidance concerning] the four seals of Vajrārali, which are similar in approach, are also subdivided into twenty-four, according to [distinctions in] the bliss of the deities. When these are added together with the previous [twenty-four], the traditions of guidance number forty-eight. With the further addition of the related guidance on Vajrapāṇi in the form Mahācakra, they number forty-nine, and fifty with the further addition of *The Coemergent Union [of the Great Seal]* that represents the corresponding tradition of experiential cultivation.[233]

When all these are summarized, the visualization of Vajrabhairava should be clear, lucid, and unsullied. The deity arises without obscuration and is endowed with the three pure essences [of channels, winds, and generative fluids]. He has an extremely wrathful dark blue buffalo head, with three eyes that are wrathful, mottled, and round, and light-blue horns—wrinkled at the base, bent in the middle, and pointing sideways at the tip. His uppermost [central] face is bright red, shining red, like one hundred thousand rising suns, and it loudly bellows the laughter of HA HA! Above that is the yellowish-red face of Mañjuśrī. The eyebrows [of Vajrabhairava] are black and darting. His eyes are long and bright. His nose is tall and high, and his lips are slightly snarling. His right and left faces, along with his arms and legs and his mighty wrathful body, are variegated as a rainbow body, shimmering as a mass of light.

This visualization should be established and then examined. At that time, by the cultivated power of meditative concentration, the mind delights and there arises a state of joy and happiness, similar to the cheerful perceptions of human beings. You should remain in the coemergent union of this generation stage, which is associated with one-pointed unbewildered meditative concentration, and also indeed with emptiness, sameness, ineffability, and nonconceptualization.

Then, from within that disposition where the appearances of the three world systems arise as deities, you should engage in the perfection stage of meditation. On the two horns' tips there are generative essences, bright and shining. Like threaded webs, these converge at the throat, after which they dissolve into Mañjughoṣa within the heart. You should meditate that the body is filled with bliss and that there is no grasping. If this is further explored, you should engage in the coemergent union of the perfection stage, which concerns the luminous mind, the lucid winds, and the unsullied state transcending common objects. This completes the guidance of the first session.

2. The Acceptance of Fortunate Disciples: Akṣobhyavajra and So Forth

The second session concerns the pathway of Guhyasamāja, through which fortunate disciples are accepted. The relevant texts comprise the *Root Tantra of the Secret Assembly* itself and its six exegetical tantras—namely, the *Subsequent Tantra of the Secret Assembly*, the *Compendium of the Adamantine Reality of Pristine Cognition*, the *Tantra Requested by Four Goddesses*, the *Adamantine Garland*, the *Tantra of the Ornament of the Nucleus of Adamantine Reality*, and the *Tantra Requested by Devendra*.[234] These are further supplemented by the *Tantra of the Victory of Nondual Sameness*.

The practice of the four-session yoga is based on the distinction of the introductory narrative of the root tantra, which describes the thirty-two-deity assemblage of Akṣobhya. In addition, the body maṇḍala also may be presented based on the distinction between the twenty-five-deity assemblage of Akṣobhya according to Śāntipā; or the nineteen-, thirteen-, {174} or nine-deity assemblages; or else on the basis of the five enlightened families or the single enlightened family.

The tradition of Buddhajñānapāda then changes the principal deities based on the *Subsequent Tantra of the Secret Assembly*, extrapolating that there are nineteen deities in the assemblage of Mañjuvajra,[235] and identifying them with the nineteen deities in the assemblage of Avalokiteśvara.

Although there are no more than five transmissions actually revealed on the basis of the *Root Tantra of the Secret Assembly*, there are six ancillary traditions revealed on the basis of the *Subsequent Tantra of the Secret Assembly*. Among the latter, Yangonpa's *Three Crucial Points of the All-Pervasive Coemergent Union That Brings Forth the Miraculous Ability of the Esoteric*

Instructions has primacy, and there are eighteen further traditions stemming from that.

Above all, with regard to *The Five Stages of the Secret Assembly*,[236] you should examine and cultivate the exegetical tradition of Nāgārjuna, and the tradition of the paṇḍitas that establishes conviction in the words of the *Tantra of the Secret Assembly*, stemming from Āryadeva and Candrakīrti, as well as the experiential cultivation that accords with the tradition of the yogin Kusāli, and the two traditions of direct guidance that were imparted by Mataṅgi to Tilopā and Nāropā. This should be combined with Lochen Rinchen Zangpo's [translation of Candrakīrti's] *Clarifying Lamp* commentary.

In general, there have been ten [important transmissions of *The Five Stages* in Tibet], starting with the three scrolls that were separately presented by Samayavajra, Vajrāsana, and Devākaracandra. The fourth was Patsab Lotsāwa's *Eight Sacral Aspects*, and the fifth was his *Analytic Meditation*. The sixth was the guidance on the Five Stages that Jowo Atiśa received from Śāntipā; the seventh was Nāgabodhi's tradition of the Five Stages, which Dampa Gyagar imparted to Ma Lotsāwa; the eighth was the instruction through which Paṇchen Śākyaśrī of Kashmir guided Chel Lotsāwa; the ninth was Tarpa Lotsāwa's close lineage of the Five Stages; and the tenth was Chak Lotsāwa's annual cycle of the Five Stages.

In *The Five Stages Perfected on One Seat*, which is a distinctive doctrine of Marpa[237] based exclusively on the Indian texts, headed by those of Nāgārjuna and his disciple, there are two aspects—the direct guidance that is pointed out, and the black guidance that is discussed—or four with the additional explanation of the two gates—the upper gate and the lower gate. The practices pertaining to the upper gate include modes of guidance that are gradual and all-surpassing. The practices pertaining to the lower gate are sixfold, including both the traditions of Nāropā and Nigumā. The implementation of the forceful method is revealed separately as a sealed injunction, and it is not enunciated in this common presentation.

With regard to the deity Mañjuvajra, it is by means of Buddhajñānapāda's *Vital Essence of Liberation* that the *Subsequent Tantra of the Secret Assembly* is fully understood. {175} This work integrates the luminosity of The Five Stages, condensing the final dissolution [of luminosity during the generation stage] in the yoga of higher absorption [during the perfection stage]. Because this work is connected as the vital lifeline of [Yangonpa's aforementioned *Three Crucial Points of*] *the All-Pervasive Coemergent Union*, the eighteen derivative instructions are similar in their experiential cultivation of composure and similar in their meditative concentration, and so forth.[238]

When the visualization is established, the deity [Akṣobhya or Mañjuvajra] has three faces and six arms. His legs are in the adamantine posture, and he is embraced by a female consort resembling himself. On examination, you should visualize that his primary face is bright blue, shining blue, with black darting eyebrows and sparkling eyes that stare. His nose is blue and pointed. His mouth is partly blue, partly red. His teeth are slightly snarling. Visualize that his demeanor is partly wrathful, partly alluring. The face to the right is bright white, shining white; and the face to the left is bright red, shining red. He is irresistible to behold, with an alluring demeanor, radiant with the major and minor marks. That completes the second session.

3. The Third Session Concerns Cakrasaṃvara

There are three primary traditions—one revealed from the tantras, one extrapolated through commentarial writings, and one that appeared to the ḍākinīs.

According to the *Root Tantra of Cakrasaṃvara*, the veritable offering of Kulikā comprises the hexahedron of the letter E, which embodies the five syllables of great emptiness, and the letter VAṂ, which embodies the six syllables of the vital essence.[239]

This text also alludes to the blossoming of the lotus of the profound abodes—outer, inner, and extraneous—and the experiential guidance of the view that regards the stroke of the letter *a*, the *ashé* (Tib. *a shad*), as the naked intrinsic face of Vajravārāhī.[240]

It then describes Cakrasaṃvara in coemergent union, in whom the profound coemergent union previously mentioned in the context of the father tantras and the channels, winds, and vital essences elucidated in the context of the mother tantras are combined. Through this profound essential that relates to both the father tantras and the mother tantras, the coemergent union that directly sees the buddha body of reality is disclosed.[241]

Also, the text explains that just as the one hundred sacral aspects are mentioned in the father tantras, the empty vital essence is also said to comprise one hundred syllables.[242]

Contrary to that presentation [of the *Root Tantra*], in the *Supreme Tantra of Clear Expression*, the syllable VAṂ embodies the five syllables of great emptiness, and the syllable E embodies the six syllables of the vital essence. When these letters are subsumed in the imperishable [vital essence] of the heart cakra, there also emerges the union of Heruka {176} and Vajravārāhī that derives from the *Tantra of the Emancipation of Śrīheruka*, the face-to-face union of Vasantatilaka mentioned in the *Tantra of the Adamantine Sky-Farers*, the innate state of rest that derives from the *Tantra of the Habitual Practice of the Yoginīs*, the perfect elucidation of the five stages mentioned in the *Tantra of the Emergence of Cakrasaṃvara*, the acquisition of the three yogas mentioned in the *Tantra of Great Magical Emanation*,[243] the perfection of the four pristine cognitions mentioned in the *Buddhakapāla*, the acquisition of the four yogas mentioned in *The Four Adamantine Seats*,[244] the acquisition of the six branches mentioned in the *Ocean of Sky-Farers*, the guidance on the path of the Great Seal mentioned in the *Coalescent Union of the Four Yoginīs*, and the profound path of guidance mentioned in the *Adamantine Garland*.

Next, there are the [commentarial writings] on these tantras, which include Luipā's *Perfection Stage of Great Yoga*, Kṛṣṇacārin's *Vital Essence of Spring*,[245] Ghaṇṭāpāda's *Five Stages*,[246] Kukuripā's *Extremely Unelaborate* [*Perfection Stage*], Saraha's *Introduction to the Innate*, Āryadeva's *Guidance on the Four Yogas*, Śabaripā's *Six-Branch Yoga*, and Ratnarakṣita's *Practical Guidance on the Five Stages*.

The female consort Vajravārāhī may have an assemblage of thirty-seven female deities; or fifteen, thirteen, nine, seven, or five female deities; or else she may take the form Sahajā.[247]

For each of these deities there are different perfection-stage practices. For example, there are three perfection-stage practices dependent on the Innate White Cakrasaṃvara, according to Jowo Atiśa, Abhaya, and Paṇchen Śākyaśrī of Kashmir;[248] and there are other perfection-stage practices dependent on Innate Blue Cakrasaṃvara, according to Ghaṇṭāpāda, Prahevajra, and Abhaya.[249]

Lastly, as for the aural lineage of the ḍākinīs, there are modes of experiential cultivation that arise from thirty-seven distinct methods of guidance in the context of the mother tantras, including the texts retained by Tilopā and those of Nāropā, Nigumā, and Sukhasiddhi.[250]

As above, there now follows the standard description of Cakrasaṃvara: When the visualization is established, Cakrasaṃvara has four faces and his right leg is extended. He is embraced by the female consort Vajravārāhī. On examination, the face to the rear is bright yellow, shining yellow, diffusing a yellow light. His eyes are wide and slightly quivering, and he has an extremely sensuous demeanor. This completes the third session.

4. The Fourth Session Concerns Hevajra

The primary texts are the *Root Tantra of Hevajra*, the *Two-Chapter Tantra of Hevajra*, the *Tantra of the Adamantine Tent*, the *Tantra of the Vital Essence of Union*, and the *Ārali Trilogy* that Gayādhara received from the yoginī of Siṅghala. {177} The last mentioned are also called the "three lesser tantras," and they are arranged as a supplement to the experiential cultivation of the higher empowerments.

In general, the practices of the perfection stage derive from all these tantras, but [more specifically] there are sixteen methods of guidance that derive from the *Two-Chapter Tantra*—namely, (i) the guidance of the three purities;[251] (ii) the guidance of the three coemergent states; (iii) the continuous guidance of the profound and illuminating river; (iv) the guidance on the view that equipoises existence and quiescence;[252] (v) the guidance that introduces the meaning of the four innate states; (vi) the guidance on secret conduct with respect to the central channel by means of coercion; (vii) the guidance combining three concealed exegeses of the introductory narrative; (viii) the guidance on the six-branch yoga—composure, concentration, breath control, apprehension [of the complete deity], subsequent recollection, and meditative stability; (ix) the guidance on the three aspects of mingling, transformation, and discriminative awareness; (x) the guidance on the means of separation from attachment;[253] (xi) the guidance of the alluring messenger; (xii) the guidance on the balancing of the generation and perfection stages; (xiii) the guidance on the perfection stage in which the body appears as a deity; (xiv) the guidance on the final thoughts of clinging to the generation stage; (xv) the attainment of the three roots combined; and (xvi) the guidance on devotion and the vitality of the teacher.[254]

Once the perfection stage has been entirely comprehended, all the profound crucial points of the entire generation and perfection stages revealed in the *Tantra of Hevajra* are arranged as the path of the four empowerments; and the [related instruction on the] ground, path, and fruition greatly surpasses the sixteen just-mentioned modes of guidance. These are said to include the path and fruition that are the nondual enlightened intention of the *Tantra of the Vital Essence of Union,*[255] the infinite yoga of the vital essences derived from the *Tantra of the Adamantine Tent,* the twenty-nine visualizations of self-consecration according to the *Tantra of the Vital Essence of Union,*[256] and the inestimable yoga of the subtle vital essences that derives from the three subsequent lesser tantras.

Although there have been an inconceivable number of masters in India and Tibet who commented on the meaning of the *Tantra of Hevajra,* their subcategories may be condensed in a single tradition; and when they are examined in detail from the perspective of the pith instructions, all these modes of guidance are combined together. Here the experiential cultivation refers to the experiential cultivation of glorious Hevajra himself, the lord of all the tantras.

According to the essence of this text, {178} it is taught that on the basis of the guidance on Hevajra, the gist of the three other foregoing sessions of practice [on Vajrabhairava, Akṣobhya, and Cakrasaṃvara] may be subsumed herein. In that case, it entails four aspects—namely, (i) the view that concerns the three essential natures, (ii) the philosophical tenet that cyclic existence and nirvana are indivisible, (iii) the practice that resurrects at the time of death, and (iv) the fruition that is the innate deity.

Among these aspects, the three essential natures—the imaginary, the dependent, and the consummate—are to be known respectively in terms of (i) the objects of meditation, all the apparent aspects of consciousness that are coarsely visualized; (ii) the act of meditating, the skillful means of the symbolic generation stage concerning the deities, their faces, arms, [and so forth]; and (iii) the [fruitional] entry into the state of pristine cognition. That is to say, once the path of provisions according to the [tantras of] unsurpassed yoga have been perfected through this spacious, uncontrived path, you will acquire the fruition that is free from the ordinary body, speech, and mind.

It is taught that the very perception that nakedly realizes the intrinsic face of the inseparable generation and perfection stages is also a magical vision of skillful means, applied on the basis of the three essential natures. For when the form of Hevajra with eight faces and sixteen arms is visualized, that denotes the dependent nature. The consideration of oneself as ordinary, with one body and two arms, denotes the imaginary nature. The natural expression untainted by the stains of positive and negative attributes denotes the consummate nature.

When this same analysis is applied to the fundamental state of the abiding nature, the consideration of bewilderment in respect of the innate nature of mind denotes the imaginary nature. The freedom from extraneous conditions that characterizes the innate state denotes the dependent nature. The innate state that has never been tainted by bewilderment denotes the consummate nature.

Having definitively understood this, you should visualize the attributes of innate pristine cognition where the generation and perfection stages are indivisible as the deity and meditate on this coalescent essential nature that is empty of the imaginary.

When this visualization is established, you should visualize yourself as blue, resembling the color of Hevajra's body and primary face. The right face is white, and the left one is red. The two remaining faces are black, and the upper face is smoke colored. He has twenty-four eyes, and the crown of his head is marked with the crossed vajra. He has sixty arms, four legs, and is in union with his female consort. His essential nature, endowed with three imperishable pure essences [of channels, winds, and generative fluids], resembles the reflection in a mirror. {179}

On examining each of these features in turn, you should consider and meditate that the primary face is the color of turquoise, the right face is the color of the moon, the left face is the color of coral, the upper face is the color of smoky clouds, and the remaining faces are smoky colored. His body is adorned with the skulls of an elephant, horse, donkey, ox, camel, human being, śarabha deer, cat, earth deity, water deity, fire deity, wind deity, moon deity, sun deity, Yama, and Vasudhara. Beneath his two extended right legs, he stands upon a mat formed of Brahmā and Rudra, and his two left legs, which are drawn in, stand upon a mat formed of Indra and Upendra. In his lap there is the female deity Nairātmyā, holding a knife and skull. Her calves entwine the male consort, and she is of youthful appearance. Both the male and female have a crown of five dry skulls. They have a necklace of fifty skulls—dry in the case of the female and moist in the case of the male. Their hands are adorned respectively with six and five hand emblems, and they wear skirts of tiger hide.

At this time, guided by the appearance and emptiness of the deity's body, the mind is at ease, as if meeting an old acquaintance—it is joyous and happy; and when you settle in that state, like the moon's reflection in water, this is meditative concentration. By experientially cultivating that without dichotomy between equipoise and postmeditation, all appearances are then known to be the natural glow of the mind—devoid of appearance as a divine form, emptiness, sameness, or nonconceptuality.

When this examination has been perfected, you should not consider anything at all. You should not think, examine, or conceive of anything at all, but relax in that effortless disposition. After establishing mind training in the view that is beyond the intellect and free from extremes, you should experientially cultivate this in an integrated manner: OṂ ĀḤ HŪṂ KĀYA VĀG CITTA VAJRA SVABHĀVĀTMAKO'HAM. The entire environment becomes the celestial palace. All its sentient inhabitants become male and female deities. This intrinsic nature is spontaneously actualized.

With regard to the guidance on buddha body and the guidance on buddha speech, this entails the yoga of breath control, including gentle breathing, moderate breathing, and strong breathing. {180} This practice should precede the branch of meditative concentration.

As breath is inhaled, you should recite OṂ. As it is held within, you should recite ĀḤ. And as it is exhaled, you should recite HŪṂ. In the practice of moderate breathing, after inhaling as long a breath as you can, you should push out the abdomen as far as possible and settle both the upper wind and the lower wind directly there. After that, you should inhale, fill the channels, and disperse or breathe out, emitting the breath like an arrow.

Next there is the yoga of the vital essence, whether independent of the cakras or dependent on the cakras. Here you should rely on the crucial points of the pith instructions. According to this Hevajra tradition, the conclusive path of the secret empowerment entails experiential cultivation of the eighteen yogic exercises focusing on the fire within the channel of fierce inner heat.[257] You should also be encouraged [by restrictions on] diet and regimen, and combine all the crucial points for achieving success, dispelling obstacles, and so forth.

In addition, you should experientially cultivate the *Yogic Exercises of the Thirty-Two Activities*[258] and the ninety-six that may be practically applied either sequentially, in reverse order, or randomly.

The Four-Stage Adamantine Reality of the Wheel of Time

Then, in the context of the path of the third empowerment, there is also the four-stage adamantine reality of the Wheel of Time. There are twelve [distinct] traditions of guidance that have contributed to the vitality of this path, namely, those of the four earlier translators—Gyijo, Dro, Ra, and Chodrak of Dingri; those of the four who appeared in the intervening period—Menlung Guru,[259] Tarpa Lotsāwa, Orgyanpa Rinchen Pel, and Vibhūticandra; the first, second, and final transmissions of Śabaripā; and the short lineage of Vanaratna, which was the last to reach Tibet.[260]

This [instruction] is a condensation of the profound crucial points contained in six different cycles of the six-branch yoga according to Buton Rinchen Drub and twenty-six different cycles of the six-branch yoga maintained among the Sakyapa and so forth, which, according to Lama Dampa Sonam Gyeltsen, were previously nonexistent modes of experiential guidance.[261]

The teaching traditions that expound the two branches entitled apprehension [of the entire deity] and subsequent recollection should be discerned separately in their [appropriate] instructions of direct guidance.

Directly combining all these crucial points, this practice should be properly completed in a single sitting of meditation.

Here I have presented a synopsis of the *Guidance of Concealed Meaning*
That imbues with **delight all** the streams
Of [Bodongpa's] *Summation of the Real*—
A detailed commentary on **supreme liberation.**

This was compiled from my own extensive commentary. {181}

27. Guidebook Entitled *The Guidance of Amitāyus*[262]

After first taking refuge and setting the mind on enlightenment: You should visualize yourself as Amitāyus, with fervent devotion to the emanation [Barawa Gyeltsen Pelzang], lord of your enlightened heritage, who is seated before your piled hair. Visualize that from the syllable HRĪḤ in the teacher's heart, rays of light are diffused, summoning your vitality, and that the alms bowl in your hands is consecrated with a flow of nectar.

The same consecration should be enacted in respect of all the condensed elixirs of the four lower elements:[263] You should recite the mantra OṂ AMARAṆI JĪVANTI YE SVĀHĀ as the light rays of HRĪḤ are again diffused, accepting the consecration of the condensed elixir of the earth element. You should recite it as the light rays of HRĪḤ are again diffused, accepting the consecration of the condensed elixir of the water element. You should recite it as the light rays from HRĪḤ are again diffused, accepting the consecration of the condensed elixir of the burning fire element. You should recite it as the light rays from HRĪḤ are again diffused, accepting the consecration of the condensed elixir of the wind element. You should recite it as the light rays from HRĪḤ are again diffused, accepting the consecration of the condensed vitality of the entire world. And you should also recite it as the light rays from HRĪḤ are again diffused, accepting the consecration of the condensed blessings of the conquerors and their heirs. You should make these recitations, absolutely determining that your own body is the adamantine reality endowed with five pure essences,[264] without birth or death.

Then, in the center of your heart, upon a moon disk the size of a split pea, you should visualize an ashé (the stroke of the letter *a*), indicative of life breath, clear and bright, diffusing a pale-red light. The rays of light diffused from it form a garland of OṂ syllables, indicative of the elixir of immortal life, which enters through your left nostril and dissolves into the ashé within your heart.

Gentle breathing causes the short syllable A to emit light in the form of a garland of HŪṂ syllables, which thoroughly cleanses and expels the impure obscurations of enmity associated with the aspect of degenerate wind, including all the winds within the body, as if sweeping them clean with a brush.

You should then count the OṂ syllables during inhalation, ĀḤ during the retention of breath, and HŪṂ during exhalation.

In the navel cakra, the ashé then assumes the form of red Amitāyus, {182} and in the crown cakra HAṂ assumes the form of white Amitāyus. The anal wind in the form of YAṂ then causes fire to blaze at the triple intersection [below the navel]. It causes the contents of the vase in the hands of Amitāyus at the navel cakra to boil, and the vapor then rises upward within the central channel, to touch the body of Amitāyus within the crown cakra. It transforms into the red female consort Pāṇḍaravāsinī, who draws the lower winds upward and breathes in the upper winds. The place where these winds make contact is naturally warm, causing the contents of the vase in the hands of Amitāyus at the crown cakra to boil and the stream of nectar to flow downward within the central channel. It touches the body of red Amitāyus within the navel cakra, it transforms into the female consort red Pāṇḍaravāsinī, and they embrace. The upper winds should then be forced downward, and again, from that male-female union, the white and red vital essences distinctly fill the navel cakra of emanation and the crown cakra of supreme bliss; and similarly they fill to the brim the heart cakra of the phenomenal wheel and the throat cakra of perfect resource. You should then visualize that your own body is transformed into the natural expression of light, with the [upper and lower] winds united. From the vase in the hands of [Amitāyus within] the navel cakra nectar rises upward to be transformed into the sun at the heart cakra, and from within the vase in the hands of [Amitāyus in] the crown cakra nectar flows downward to be transformed into the moon [at the heart cakra]. At the union of sun and moon, within the central channel, intrinsic awareness appears in the form of a pale-red HRĪḤ, secured within a cross formed by the vowels and consonants.

Then you should visualize that within each of the two ring fingers, there is a red HŪṂ, diffusing fiery light.

When you have meditated on this sequence of visualization for twelve months, it is said that the life span will definitely be prolonged for ten years. You should therefore prolong the life span of this innate luminosity and rest in a state of natural energy that is fresh, naturally glowing, relaxed, and without hope or doubt.

Extracting Nutritious Elixir

There then follows the prolonging of the life span by means of extracting nutritious elixir. You should place in a skull container pills made of calcite, Solomon's seal, orchid, and golden myrobalan, along with some deer droppings, and train in visualizing the male and female Amitāyus within it for seven days. It is said that you may then rely on that concoction.

Here I have set forth in writing this **supreme** and clear instruction,
Renowned among **all** the kingly means for attainment of long life,
Maintaining the four **delights** that control the four elements,
The experiential cultivation combining maturation and **liberation.** {183}

This was compiled from my own instruction manual.

28. Guidebook Entitled *The Guidance of White Tārā*[265]

After first taking refuge and setting the mind on enlightenment: You should rest timelessly in the disposition of ultimate enlightened mind and reverse impure perceptions through the blessing of the intrinsic nature that comes about simply through the transformation of the mental faculty. In this way, the uncontrived mind becomes manifest.

You should then visualize that from the syllable BHRŪṂ, the inhabited world becomes a celestial palace of pure crystal, at the center of which light rays are diffused from the syllable TĀṂ, upon a lotus seat. These absorb all the accomplishments of long life in their entirety, transforming them within an imperishable, permanent, and steadfast *svāstika* motif that embraces all cyclic existence and nirvana. Instantly there then arises the body of immortal Tārā in the form Cintāmaṇicakra, white as the moon, clear as a crystal gem, diffusing taintless light rays of five colors. She has a most peaceful and smiling face, and seven eyes that are wide open like the petals of an udumbara lotus. Her right hand is in the gesture of supreme boon, and her left hand holds the stem of a white lotus between her thumb and fingers. She has a sensuous and attractive demeanor, has beautiful full breasts, and wears ornaments, the foremost of which are white pearls, an upper robe of white silk, and a skirt of multicolored silk. The topknot of her tresses that are tied back is swaying, her youthful body is seated in a dignified manner in the adamantine posture, and she has the moon disk as her aureole. Within her heart there is a wheel marked with the seed syllable TĀṂ, and on the crown of her head, upon a lotus and moon cushion, there is the lord of her enlightened heritage, Amitābha. On her left side she is adorned with a crescent moon of the first day of the lunar month.

Aroused by the light of her heart cakra, light is then diffused from the alms bowl of Amitābha, the lord of her enlightened heritage. It absorbs {184} the phenomena of the inhabited world and its sentient inhabitants together in the form of nectar, and reenters her body from the crown of the head.

You should remain as long as you can in the intrinsic face of that effortless, naked state, beyond the intellect, the immortal and innate expanse that, owing to its auspicious circumstances, is imperishable for an aeon by any conditions whatsoever. The crucial point is that while you repeatedly recall this appearance of White Tārā, you should practice the yoga of the associated mantra recitation.[266]

Here I have set forth in writing an aspect,
An aspect of confidence supreme,
Supreme in **liberation**, and bliss of the mental faculty,
The mental faculty of **delight**
Endowed with **all** the attainments of long life.[267]

This instruction has originated from the stream of the oral teachings.

[In the context of the inner attainment, there are fourteen attributes of the inhabited world and its sentient inhabitants that constitute cyclic existence and nirvana]:[268] (i) youth that is unaging, (ii) brilliant luminosity that is without conditioning, (iii) power that is without effort, (iv) energy that is endowed with strength, (v) accomplishment that is uncontaminated, (vi) merit that is balanced, (vii) glory that is extensive, (viii) majesty that is uncovered, (ix) vitality that is unagitated, (x) life breath that is immortal, (xi) life span that is unchanging, (xii) mind that is unimpeded, (xiii) inspired speech that is transformative, and (xiv) virtuous signs triumphant over all directions.

29. Guidebook Entitled *The Guidance of White Amitāyus*[269]

After first taking refuge and setting the mind on enlightenment: You should rest your mind in the unfabricated and uncontrived state. From that disposition, there arises the syllable HŪṂ, its protective circle forming a canopy of vajra prongs, dense with the flames of pristine cognition.

Within that expanse you should then visualize a syllable HRĪḤ, from which there arises a celestial palace of blazing lotuses, encompassing the inhabited world. And in its midst upon a seat comprising lotus, sun, and moon cushions, Amitāyus instantly arises. His body is white in color, and upon his two hands in the gesture of meditative equipoise he holds a vase filled with nectar. He is adorned with silks and ornaments of precious gems, embellished with the major and minor marks, and seated in the adamantine posture, within an aureole of blazing light.

Above the protuberance of his head upon lotus, sun, and moon cushions, there is your teacher {185} with the syllable BHRŪṂ in his heart. Through its rays of light, the glow of the four elements that form the inhabited world of both cyclic existence and nirvana, along with its sentient inhabitants, and all the general and particular accomplishments of their long life, merit, and pristine cognition are completely absorbed in the form of white and red rays of light. This constitutes the attainment of the [visualized] being of commitment.

The flow of nectar present within the vase [of Amitāyus] then manifests within your mouth. As it mingles in a single savor at your throat, your mind is imbued with bliss. Let your uvula suck it. Nurture its essence in your individual intrinsic awareness. From the throat it then fills [the central channel] as far as the heart and the navel cakras.

Next, in conjunction with an exhalation of breath, its rays of light strike the inhabited world, comprising both cyclic existence and nirvana. The actual nature of the material elements should then be absorbed completely in conjunction with an inhalation of breath, and you should firmly maintain this with the vase-shaped breath, hammering in the spike that secures a life span that will not perish for an aeon, due to any condition whatsoever.

Again you should engage in the exercises that cause the luster of the secret wind to arise as HŪṂ. All the generative fluid is inducted from the secret cakra, through the navel, heart, and throat, as far as the crown cakra, and the body of adamantine reality is thereby attained. At the upper extremity of the central channel, this movement is blocked by a white vital essence in the form of BHRŪṂ. Then you should exhale and inhale as before, completely absorb all the life spans [of all beings] of cyclic existence and nirvana, coarse and subtle, and hammer in the spike that secures an imperishable life span. Finally, you should cross both your arms and compress your shoulders. Let your uvula suck the nectar. Your body of adamantine reality will then merge with the essential nature of this melting and pouring [nectar]. Remain in meditative equipoise in this innate, deathless natural state, without effort and beyond the intellect. Without pursuing thoughts of conditioned perception, relax and rest in this disposition. By nurturing the practice in this manner, you will train in higher and higher extraordinary levels that are the essential nature of buddha body, speech, and mind, endowed with adamantine life span and immeasurable pristine cognition. {186}

At the conclusion of this session, you should learn by word of mouth in the context of this actual guidance on Amitāyus the secret procedures through which those whose physical constituents are fully developed may enter into union with a female mudra who has the appropriate signs.

Here I have set forth in writing merely a verbal instruction
Representing the concealed meaning and further concealed meaning of
Mitrayogin,
With **total delight** in the accomplishments of Amitāyus,
And **supreme** aspirational **liberation**.

This was compiled from the instruction manual of Chak Lotsāwa.

30. Guidebook Entitled *The Direct Guidance of Avalokiteśvara according to the Lakṣmī Tradition*[270]

After first taking refuge and setting the mind on enlightenment: You should visualize a white syllable A in your own heart, the light rays of which absorb the inhabited three world systems and their sentient inhabitants; and these then dissolve into yourself. Consequently, intrinsic awareness, devoid of objects to be grasped, manifests in the form of a lotus and moon cushion, from which the seed syllable HRĪḤ appears, and therefrom there arises a lotus, marked with that same seed syllable. Visualize that therefrom you yourself appear, standing upright, in the form of Jowo Mahākāruṇika. The three syllables [OṂ, ĀḤ, HŪṂ] are arrayed at their three respective places [forehead, throat, and heart], with the syllable HRĪḤ inside the heart. You should then invite the sublime [being of pristine cognition] resembling yourself and let it dissolve into that visualized form. Meditate that the teacher [is present above the crown of your head] as the lord of enlightened heritage, in the form of Amitābha, and recite MAṆI as often as possible.

Afterward, you should visualize the world systems of the six classes of living beings and generate strong and immeasurable compassion for their sufferings, repeating the words "My Mother!" After that, rest in a disposition free from conceptual elaboration.

Then in postmeditation you should make the dedication of merit and recite aspiration prayers. While eating, getting dressed, sitting, and sleeping, you should act within the disposition of enlightened mind that entails altruistic thoughts.

When practicing consciousness transference, you should absorb all phenomenal existence into yourself and your intrinsic awareness into the syllable A. Repeating "A A," visualize that the syllable A vanishes, as it were, into a rainbow in the sky.

When practicing the yoga of the intermediate state, you should carry sights onto the path as the meditational deity Avalokiteśvara, sounds as the MAṆI PADME mantra, and thoughts of recollection as emptiness and compassion.

Here this illustrates in writing the method through which
Lakṣmī subsumes in the intrinsic essence of the syllable A

All the pith instructions—the crucial points
Of **delightful** affection and natural **supreme liberation.** {189}

This was compiled from the ancient writings of Yolton Chowang.

31. Guidebook Entitled *The Direct Guidance of Avalokiteśvara according to the Candradhvaja Tradition*[271]

After first taking refuge and setting the mind on enlightenment: You should visualize that from the disposition of emptiness, in which all things are without inherent existence, there appears the syllable HRĪḤ upon a lotus and moon cushion, and from that there arises an eight-petal lotus, shining like pure gold and marked with HRĪḤ. Therefrom you yourself manifest in the form of Mahākāruṇika, with one face and four arms; the syllables OṂ, ĀḤ, HŪṂ are arrayed respectively at the brow, the throat, and the heart. Through their rays of light the being of pristine cognition is invited from Potālaka and dissolves therein. You should think that you are empowered by the five enlightened families and that, as a sign of this empowerment, you are crowned by the teacher in the form of Amitābha. At the heart on a lotus and moon cushion there appears HRĪḤ, surrounded by the MAṆI syllables. Reciting this as many times as possible, you should ascertain that the abiding nature of reality is originally present in the expanse of quiescence, and so you should let things be consumed without grasping them. Maintain the natural state of the luster of compassion.

During postmeditation, while eating, getting dressed, and sitting, you should be mindful and act with divine pride. When sleeping, you should focus awareness on HRĪḤ at the heart.

When practicing consciousness transference, you should eject the HRĪḤ like an arrow through the passageway of the central channel into the heart of the teacher [above your head].

For practicing the yoga of the intermediate state, it is said that you should train right now through the three deportments [of buddha body, speech, and mind],[272] in order to change your resolve.

Here I have subsumed the teachings of direct guidance of the bodhisattva
Candradhvaja
And **all** the instructions of Dzimchen [Gyeltsen Pelzang],

And here I have **delightfully** illustrated **supreme liberation**
By means of the eloquence of Rongton.

This subsumes the essence of the two instruction manuals [of Dzimchen and Rongton].

32. Guidebook Entitled *The Direct Guidance of Avalokiteśvara according to the Tsembupa Tradition*[273]

After first taking refuge and setting the mind on enlightenment: You should visualize that from the awakening of emptiness among the five awakenings,[274] the seed syllable HRĪḤ indicative of buddha speech arises within your own heart, which resembles an upright eggshell, upon a seat comprising lotus and moon cushions. From that seed syllable there then arises a white lotus, the hand emblem of buddha mind, marked with HRĪḤ; and from that you yourself appear as sublime Avalokita, completely perfect in body, white in color, with one face and four arms. The first pair of hands is placed together at the heart, a rosary of one hundred and eight beads dangles from the second right hand, and he holds a white lotus in the second left hand. His legs assume the adamantine posture. He has an upper robe of white silk, an antelope hide tied across his chest, and a lower robe of multicolored silk. His crown of braided hair is embellished with all sorts of precious ornaments, and white rays of light are diffused in the ten directions from the pores of his skin. He has a moon disk aureole, with the syllable OṂ at his brow, ĀḤ at his throat, HŪṂ above his heart, and HRĪḤ upon a lotus and moon cushion at his heart.

Light rays are then diffused from these syllables, inviting all the meditational deities without exception, who are then dissolved [within your body, assuming the form known as the] "Gathering of All Meditational Deities." Also, empowered by your own root teacher, Avalokita is present in the form of Amitābha, above the crown of your head, and all the gurus [of the lineage] dissolve therein, [assuming the form known as the] "Gathering of All Gurus."

At the periphery of the HRĪḤ within the heart, the HRĪḤ is encircled by the six-syllable mantra, {187} from which rays of light are diffused. You should visualize that all expressed meanings of the eighty-four thousand sections of the sacred doctrine are absorbed therein, and that there is an Avalokita present within each of the eighty-four thousand animalcules in your own body, within its twenty-one thousand hairs and its thirty-five million pores. Then visualize that these all simultaneously chant MAṆI.

After reciting this mantra as much as you can, in terms of the ground, you should maintain the view that is uncontrived and innate. In terms of the path, you should maintain the integrated cultivation of calm abiding and higher insight, refining meditative concentration that is relaxed and naturally liberated, and meditative stability that is undistracted.

After sealing this practice with the dedication of merit, during post-meditation you should then visualize that at mealtimes the inhabited world and its inhabitants are blessed by the three syllables, that you make offerings to the Gathering of All Gurus on the crown of the head and to the Gathering of All Meditational Deities within your own body, and then you may partake of food. The same is applicable in the case of clothing. Meditate that your residence is a pure land and that the six classes of living beings are Avalokita.

As for [the practice of] yoga during sleep, at the center of the being of pristine cognition within the heart, you should focus on the teacher, lord of your enlightened heritage who is present.

When practicing consciousness transference, you should meditate that within a light azure hexahedron at the navel, the mind is present in the central channel as a bluish-red vital essence, the thickness of a cane, with five rays of light; that the meditational deity is present within the heart, an inch in size; that at the upper extremity of the central channel the fontanel is blocked by a blue HAṂ, indicative of the hook of compassion; and that the teacher is present on the crown of your head in the form of Amitābha, with his right and left legs in the posture of Maitreya, placed upon the fontanel, and his back resting against your crown of braided hair. From that vital essence within your navel, you should then visualize that a bluish-red vital essence of intermingled wind and mind, the thickness of a pea, breaks upward, swiftly encircles the meditational deity within the heart three times, and dispels the HAṂ at the crown of the head. Rising to the tip of the hook of compassion, it just touches the heart of the teacher, before reversing. After repeating this four times, {188} finally the vital essence vanishes into the heart of the teacher, and the teacher suddenly departs.

When practicing the yoga of the intermediate state, you should resolve that sights are the deities, sounds are the mantras, and recollected thoughts are emptiness.

Here I have put into writing the tradition of Tsembu,
Perfect among **all** the essentials of direct guidance,
Excellently teaching with **delight**
The refinement of **supreme** natural **liberation**.

This was compiled from the instruction manual of Chojé Shebum.

33. Guidebook Entitled *The Direct Guidance of Avalokiteśvara according to the Kyergangpa Tradition*[275]

After first taking refuge and setting the mind on enlightenment: Your own mind should simply be aware of the present, without falling into extremes of past and future. Visualize that from the HRĪḤ upon a lotus and moon cushion there appears the lily hand emblem, marked with HRĪḤ, {190} and that therefrom you yourself manifest as the body of the sublime Avalokiteśvara with one face and four arms. The face has a rosy complexion, the first pair of hands assuming the gesture of equipoise, the [second] right hand holding a rosary of pearl, and the [second] left hand holding a white lily. His legs assume the adamantine posture, and he has a crown of piled hair. Covered in scarlet silk, he is adorned with silks and precious gems. His eyes gaze no farther than a double arm span, and he maintains a smiling, decorous demeanor. The head is crowned by the teacher in the form of Amitābha.

You should recite the six-syllable mantra, and then finally rest in the view of genuine reality, the nonarising fundamental nature that is the intrinsic face of Mahākāruṇika, the disposition that is resplendent in lustrous compassion. This same disposition should arise in all the phases of yoga—eating, getting dressed, sitting, and sleeping. When practicing the yoga of the intermediate state, you should be aware that sights are deities and sounds are mantras. Emptiness is the essential for experientially cultivating confidence through which you will understand that the mind is groundless and without foundation.

This definitively presents in writing
All the assertions of direct guidance according to Kyergangpa,
Combining with a **delightful** mind the essential
Experiential cultivation of **supreme liberation**.

This was compiled from the instruction manual of Choku Śākya Rinchen.

34. GUIDEBOOK ENTITLED *THE DIRECT GUIDANCE OF CAKRASAṂVARA*[276]

After first taking refuge and setting the mind on enlightenment: You should visualize that from the awakening of emptiness among the five awakenings, within your own heart that resembles an upright eggshell, and upon a seat comprising lotus and sun cushions, there arises a blue seed syllable HŪṂ and a five-pronged vajra hand emblem, marked at the center with HŪṂ. From these there then appears the completely perfect body of Cakrasaṃvara, blue in color, with one face, two arms, and three eyes. His two hands, holding the vajra and the bell, embrace the female consort Vārāhī. Surmounting his dreadlocks is the wish-fulfilling gem, on the left side of which there is the crescent moon of the first lunar day, and above his fontanel there is a crossed vajra. Standing within a blazing fire of pristine cognition, he wears a skirt of tiger hide and is adorned with a garland of bones and human heads. {191}

From the syllables OṂ, ĀḤ, HŪṂ, which are respectively at his brow, throat, and heart, light is diffused, and with [the resonance of] the syllables JAḤ HŪṂ VAṂ HOḤ, all the hosts of deities associated with the four classes of tantra are transformed into the Gathering of All Meditational Deities. [This deity] is empowered by your teacher, who then manifests [above the crown of the head] as the lord of enlightened heritage. All teachers without exception dissolve therein, and the Gathering of All Gurus becomes manifest.

You should clearly visualize your own twenty-one thousand hairs and three and a half million pores, and all sentient beings of the three world systems as the deity, and simultaneously you should recite the mantra OṂ HRĪḤ HA HA HŪṂ HŪṂ PHAṬ as much as possible, chanting it with conviction.

When eating, you should visualize the container as a skull and its contents as the five meats and five nectars.[277] Visualize your dress as bone ornaments and tiger hides, your residence as a charnel ground, and the protective circle as a celestial palace. When sleeping, let the appearance of the deity be absorbed in luminosity.

When practicing consciousness transference, visualize that the meditational deity is present within your heart, resembling yourself, one inch in height, and that at the lower end of the central channel within a hexahedron there is a bluish-red vital essence, imbued with five-colored light rays, from which a pale-blue vital essence, the size of a pea, breaks off, swiftly encircles the meditational deity at the heart three times, and then dispels the syllable HAṂ at the crown. Extracted by the hook of compassion, it is absorbed into the heart of the teacher [above your head], who then departs in the way of the sky-farers.

When practicing the yoga of the intermediate state, right now you should train that sights innately arise as deities, sounds as mantras, and thoughts of recollection as the nature of mind itself.

Here I of **supreme liberation** have set forth in writing
The distinctive mode of the speech of the Conqueror's heirs
That is **delightfully** esteemed and inferred to be
The "direct guidance of **all** meditational deities."

This was written based on an oral transmission.

35. Guidebook Entitled *The Direct Guidance of Hevajra*[278]

After first taking refuge and setting the mind on enlightenment: You should visualize that from the awakening of emptiness among the five awakenings, within your own heart, which resembles an upright eggshell, and upon a seat comprising lotus and sun cushions, there arises a blue seed syllable HŪṂ and a five-pronged vajra hand emblem marked at the center with HŪṂ. {192} From these there then appears the completely perfect body of Hevajra, blue in color, with one face, two arms, and three eyes. His right hand brandishes a vajra, and the left holds a skull of blood at the heart. There is a khaṭvāṅga in the crook of his arm, the hidden female consort. Standing within the blazing fire of pristine cognition, he wears a skirt of tiger hide and is adorned with a garland of bones and human heads. From the syllables OṂ, ĀḤ, HŪṂ—respectively at his brow, throat, and heart—light rays are diffused, and [with the resonance of] the syllables JAḤ HŪṂ VAṂ HOḤ, all the hosts of deities associated with the four classes of tantra are transformed into the Gathering of All Meditational Deities. [This deity] is empowered by your teacher, who then manifests [above the crown of the head] as the lord of enlightened heritage. All teachers without exception dissolve therein, and the Gathering of All Gurus becomes manifest.

You should clearly visualize your own twenty-one thousand hairs and three and a half million pores, and all sentient beings of the three world systems as the deity, and simultaneously you should recite the mantra OṂ DEVA PICU VAJRA HŪṂ HŪṂ HŪṂ PHAṬ SVĀHĀ as much as possible, chanting it with conviction.

When eating, you should visualize the container as a skull and its contents as the five meats and five nectars. You should visualize your dress as bone ornaments and tiger hides, your residence as a charnel ground, and the protective circle as a celestial palace. When sleeping, let the appearance of the deity be absorbed in luminosity.

When practicing consciousness transference, visualize that the meditational deity is present within your heart, resembling yourself, one inch in height, and that at the lower end of the central channel within a hexahedron there is a bluish-red vital essence, imbued with five-colored light rays, from which a pale-blue vital essence, the size of a pea, breaks off, swiftly encircles the meditational deity at the heart three times, and then dispels the HAṂ at the crown. Extracted by the hook of compassion, it is absorbed into the heart of the teacher [above your head], who then departs in the way of the sky-farers.

When practicing the yoga of the intermediate state, right now you should train that sights innately arise as deities, sounds as mantras, and thoughts of recollection as the nature of mind itself.

Here I of **supreme liberation** have set forth in writing
The distinctive mode of the speech of the Conqueror's heirs
That is **delightfully** esteemed and inferred to be
The "direct guidance of **all** meditational deities." {193}

This was written based on an oral transmission.

36. Guidebook Entitled *Vajrapāṇi in the Form Mahācakra*[279]

After you have taken refuge and set the mind on enlightenment, there ensues the generation stage endowed with four protections and the perfection stage endowed with four blessings.

The Generation Stage Endowed with Four Protections

The four protections comprise the protection of engagement, the protection of self, the protection of environment, and the protection of life breath. The three purifications comprise the purifications of death, the intermediate state, and rebirth.

(i) The protection of engagement denotes the setting of the mind on aspirational enlightenment for the sake of sentient beings.

(ii) As for the protection of self, light is diffused from the syllable HŪṂ on a sun cushion at your heart. It invites the meditational deities and buddhas who enter through the point between your eyebrows. The light from the HŪṂ then penetrates sentient beings, causing them to melt into light; and it penetrates the buddhas, causing them to melt into light; and these are then absorbed into yourself so that extraneous thoughts are abandoned. The light diffused from the HŪṂ then causes your body to disintegrate, and your awareness is visualized as HŪṂ so that thoughts of self are abandoned. Next, you yourself become manifest from the HŪṂ in a wrathful form, upon a lotus cushion, with a tent pitched above in the form of a lotus. At your heart, throat, and crown, respectively, are the three syllables HŪṂ, ĀḤ, and OṂ, so that thoughts of ordinary names and clans are abandoned. This denotes the protection of self.

(iii) As for the protection of environment, you should visualize that fire issues from the HŪṂ, and encircling flames blaze within range of your [upraised] hand, in the standing posture of Vajrapāṇi Mahācakra.

(iv) As for the protection of life breath, during inhalation of breath, consciousness is absorbed in the form of a blazing HŪṂ, and the three purifications ensue—the light from HŪṂ purifying death, the mere letter HŪṂ purifying the intermediate state, and the wrath of HŪṂ purifying rebirth.

You should then focus on the body [of the deity] as a magical display, reciting OṂ VAJRA PĀṆI HŪṂ and acting with divine pride.

The Perfection Stage Endowed with Four Blessings

The perfection stage is endowed with four blessings, pertaining respectively to body, speech, mind, and real nature.

(i) The blessing of body concerns the essential attributes within [the subtle body of] Vairocana. That is to say, the cakra of emanation at the navel, from which phenomenal existence has been created in [the dichotomy] of soul and egocentricity of primal matter,[280] has sixty-four branches, the cakra of the heart has eight, the cakra of the throat has sixteen, {194} and the cakra of the head has thirty-two.[281] The syllable HAṂ is at the upper end of the central channel, and the syllable OṂ at the lower end. Their thickness is that of a straw of wheat. The head of the OṂ at the navel slightly protrudes into the central channel. HŪṂ is at the heart, ĀḤ at the throat, and HAṂ at the crown.

(ii) The blessing of speech concerns subtle energy, where OṂ represents the aspiration of sound, HAṂ represents its articulation, and AṂ represents the wind of past actions. You should visualize that, in conjunction with the sound of OṂ, a warm sensation rises upward inside the central channel. Penetrating HAṂ at the crown, it exudes warmth. Then, from HAṂ, in conjunction with the sound of HIK, a cooling sensation occurs, flowing down inside the central channel where it penetrates the AṂ at the navel, exuding coolness. The syllables AṂHAṂ should then be recited one hundred times.

(iii) The blessing of mind concerns the essential nature in the form of a vital essence. Visualize that the letters AṂ and HAṂ melt and become the size of a mustard seed. The bliss that is thereby experienced is the exemplary pristine cognition, which descends successively through the crown, throat, heart, and navel, where it generates respectively delight, supreme delight, absence of delight, and coemergent delight. The practice is then applied in reverse sequence, from the bottom upward, in respect of the pea-sized vital essence below the navel. The focusing of the mind on the vital essences in that manner is termed the *blessing of the mind*.

(iv) The blessing of real nature concerns the lustrous, clear, nonconceptual, and taintless space, which manifests through the power of cultivating emptiness. Here appearances are unimpeded and clearly experienced.

The crucial points of this meditation are that wind is mostly located in the navel, and in the morning, bile is mostly located at the crown. In the afternoon, if your consciousness is restless, you should cultivate nonconceptualization, but if it is torpid, you should focus on bliss. When you have meditated accordingly, [experiences resembling] smoke, mirage, fireflies, burning lamps, and cloudless sky will occur. These are indications that you will attain supreme spiritual accomplishment.

Here I have clearly set forth the **supreme** instruction manual,
The experiential cultivation of Mahācakra,
Comprising **all** the generation- and perfection-stage practices,
Which integrates the four **delights** with the path of maturation and **liberation**.

This was compiled from an ancient instruction manual of direct guidance.

37. Guidebook Entitled *Vajrapāṇi in the Form Caṇḍa*[282]

After first taking refuge and setting the mind on enlightenment: {195} (i) With the pride of Vajrapāṇi who appears to the minds of living beings as a sentient being,[283] you should yourself resolve to eliminate the film of ripening propensities that obscure the intrinsic essence, so that you do not recognize it.

Reciting the mantra OṂ SVABHĀVA ŚUDDHĀḤ SARVADHARMĀḤ SVABHĀVA ŚUDDHO'HAṂ, when your own perception, free from the dualistic perception of the subject-object dichotomy, becomes like a cloudless sky—that is the Vajrapāṇi of genuine reality.

When you meditate that from this disposition, upon a lotus and sun cushion, awareness suddenly appears in the form of HŪṂ, burning with fire—that is the Vajrapāṇi of symbolic letter.

When light is diffused from that HŪṂ, scattering in the ten directions the celestial demonic forces and planetary divinities, the subterranean demonic forces and nāgas, and the terrestrial demonic forces and elementals who may all lead you astray, and pursuing them in the manner of windblown feathers, and when the HŪṂ is then transformed and from it a nine-pronged vajra of meteorite manifests, its base planted firmly on a solid seat, its tip spontaneously facing upward to the sky, and its center marked with the progenitor syllable HŪṂ, burning with fire—that is the Vajrapāṇi of emblematic material form.

(ii) Next, you should visualize with great clarity that through these rays of light glorious Vajrapāṇi who appears to fruitional minds as a buddha,[284] the lord of all the secret mantras and gnostic mantras, is invited from the supreme abode of Alakāvatī, surrounded by an entourage of ninety million vajra-holding bodhisattvas, and that these all dissolve [into the aforementioned symbolic form].

(iii) Instantaneously you then become glorious Vajrapāṇi who appears to the minds of those on the path as a sublime being.[285] His essential nature is that of the buddha body of reality, his demeanor is that of the buddha body of perfect resource, and his embodiment is that of the buddha body of emanation. With the appearance of a sixteen-year-old, his body is azure blue in color, like a clear and lustrous sky, untainted by particles, the hair of his head, eyebrows, and beard bristling upward like the spreading red clouds of daybreak or dusk and emitting sparks of fire. He has three eyes, red and round; the shoots of his teeth are snarling, grinning, haughty, and jovial. His right hand brandishes a vajra; {196} his left hand holds a bell while embracing his female consort. He is adorned with snakes and a skirt of tiger hide, tied at the back, and he is in a standing posture, with his right leg contracted and left leg extended.

In union with him[286] is the female consort Vajracaṇḍālī, bluish-green in color, youthful, holding a knife and skull, and embracing the male by the neck. Her left leg is contracted and the right leg extended, entwined around the male. She has three eyes, reddish-yellow hair that hangs downward, a crown of skulls, and bone ornaments. The vajra and lotus are in union, and both deities are present in the midst of the blazing fiery mass of pristine cognition.

You should focus one-pointedly on the aspects of the deity, without impediment: In your own heart, upon a sun disk visualize a resplendent HŪṂ, the color of aquamarine, from which one hundred HŪṂ syllables, one thousand HŪṂ syllables, ten thousand HŪṂ syllables, one hundred thousand HŪṂ syllables, and immeasurable HŪṂ syllables extend outward, increasingly wearing away your own body so that it resembles gristle filled with air, its inside distended by HŪṂ and consecrated by the entire power and might of glorious Vajrapāṇi. Cracked by the force of HŪṂ, it disintegrates exclusively into the form of HŪṂ. You should then visualize that the world systems in their entirety are filled with the sound of HŪṂ, and that all the buddha fields of the ten directions are pervaded by its thunderous resonance, so that beings are aroused to contemplation. Think that it reaches the ears of demonic forces and all those who may lead you astray, filling them with fear and terror. Thereupon your awareness will be invigorated and the optic nerve will be heightened. As consciousness is intensified, the louder the intonation of HŪṂ, the more you will develop the power to resonate it from the throat, without moving the base of the tongue. At first, this should be done gently, but having acquired experience, it should be recited more loudly.

When settling into a session of meditation, the fruitional form of that mantra recitation should be absorbed into the HŪṂ within your heart. Next, you should visualize repeatedly the billion pores and the twenty-one thousand hairs {197} of your body as HŪṂ. Without wavering from the lustrous and clear body of the deity, resembling the stars reflected on a lake, there then ensues the transformation into the nasal chanting of a single seed syllable HŪṂ.

This elucidates in writing the quintessential [instruction of] HŪṂ
According to the perfection stage of Mahācaṇḍa,
The mode of **supreme** understanding in the mind of natural **liberation**,
Seen to resemble the blissful **delight** that carries **all**.

This was compiled from the instruction manual of Sangdak Drubchen.

38. Guidebook Entitled *Vārāhī in the Form Kurmapādā*[287]

After first taking refuge and setting the mind on enlightenment: Initially you should display a painted icon nearby and make an incense offering of consecrated flesh to it. You should then meditate, focusing without distraction on the exemplary painted icon. If your eyes feel uncomfortable, close your eyes and meditate on a mental object similar to the painted icon.

With regard to the posture of this deity, *kurmapādā* (*rus sbal zhabs*) means "turtle feet." She is so named because she assumes a posture resembling that of a turtle.

The visualization should be maintained since, by meditating in that manner, there is no difference between a painted icon and a mentally present image.

Next, you should meditate that within your navel cakra, at the center of a white lotus with four petals or a multicolored lotus with eight petals, black Bhairava with one face and two arms is lying face downward, holding a curved knife and a skull and wearing a skirt of tiger hide and a moist human hide with bone ornaments. Upon him stands the Venerable Vārāhī, her body yellow in color, with one face and two arms, her right hand stretching downward and holding a curved knife, and her left hand holding a skull at the heart. The disheveled hair of her head hangs down, and she wears a garland of moist human heads. Her legs assume the dancing posture, and she wears the five symbolic regalia,[288] blazing with light rays like the fire at the end of an aeon. Her consciousness is wild, {198} her body trembling, and her body hairs standing on end. Having impeded external thoughts, it is as if she cannot move. If you meditate in that manner, you will obtain the supreme accomplishment of the Great Seal in this very lifetime.

This renowned and **supreme** instruction of [Kurma]pādā,
Excellently revealed in the yellow form

Among **all** the aspects of Vārāhī,
Is a distinctive doctrine of Chak Lotsāwa,
Conferring **liberation** through its swirl of **delight**.

This was compiled from the instruction manual of [Chak Lotsāwa] Rinchen Chogyel.

39. Guidebook Entitled *The Secret Guidance of Kurukullā*[289]

After first taking refuge and setting the mind on enlightenment: You should visualize yourself as the deity Kurukullā. At her navel cakra, the channel branches of enlightened attributes resemble a reclining dog [on all fours].[290] Supported upon that, the channel of enlightened attributes faces upward, and growing from it, in the manner of an open peppercorn, is the heart cakra, where the channel branches associated with the eight modes of consciousness resemble an open lily with eight petals.[291] At its center you should visualize the syllable HRĪḤ, the color of the rising sun, in which the channels, winds, and vital essences are combined, and recite the garland of mantra syllables just as they encircle it.

Next, you should visualize that the deity who is your object of attainment is in front. The three vertical channels are also present within her body, with the syllable HRĪḤ in her heart cakra and its eight channel branches marked with the eight short vowels. You should meditate that these are similarly present within your own heart. Then the essential nature of all the long life and glory embodied in [the heart of] the deity who is the object of your attainment arises as the corresponding long vowels, in which similar letters are exemplified as before, but in long form.

With divine pride, you should strongly recite OṂ KURU KULLE HRĪḤ SVĀHĀ. Consequently, summoned from the HRĪḤ within your heart, eight ḍākinīs with the power of proud spirits, in the form of red bees, emerge from your right ear, and via the notch on the lily-covered arrow in your hand, they enter through the ear of the deity who is your object of attainment. You should visualize that not long after, the vitality and sap of the vowels [of your own heart] are isolated and extracted, and the lily withers, but that vitality is then restored to the short vowels within your own heart via the previous pathway, enabling the corresponding long syllables to be recited. {199} After completing this mantra recitation, you should equipoise the mind in the meaning of the following verses:[292]

That in which there is neither beginning, middle, nor end,
Neither rebirth process nor nirvana,
Neither self nor others,
Is itself supreme great bliss.

Having engaged in the perfection stage of this deity—
The fierce lady with the **all**-pervasive four cakras,
To restore **delight** in accordance with the sacred doctrine,
Supreme liberation deeply laughs.

This was compiled from a selection [of instructions].

40. Guidebook Entitled *The Six-Branch Yoga of Kālacakra*[293]

After you have taken refuge and set the mind on enlightenment [there ensue the preliminaries and the main practice of the six-branch yoga].

The Preliminaries

You should make the proper arrangements, including a darkened room and a platform, and then you should adopt the standard posture, with the two hands in the earth-subduing gesture,[294] and successfully expel all sorts of poisons associated with subtle energy.

After that, as far as the essentials of the physical body are concerned, you should assume the adamantine cross-legged posture and position the supine or downward-facing fists of the hands upon the channels of the thighs, with both arms straight and aligned with the sides of the rib cage, and the spine erect. Alternatively, if that is impossible, you should adopt the bodhisattva posture, with the hands forming the gesture of meditative equipoise, the upper body stretching backward and the neck slightly bent, the chin almost touching the Adam's apple, the tongue touching the palate, and the lips resting in their natural position. You should maintain these essentials of the physical body, without swaying forward or backward, right or left.

As far as your gaze is concerned, you should focus one-pointedly and unwaveringly on the space sixteen finger widths from the tip of the nose, and then settle your mind in a nonconceptual disposition, eradicating and not welcoming thoughts of the past or future, and without even allowing your present awareness to diffuse or disintegrate. Maintaining the three isolations of body, speech, and mind in that manner, there are four things to disregard, among which [in this preliminary context] you should disregard physical, verbal, and mental resources.[295]

There Then Follows the Main Practice of the Six-Branch Yoga

1. The Branch of Composure {307}

Nonconceptualization arises [naturally], either after ascertaining the time when the wind of the earth element is in motion,[296] or even through the [extraordinary] circumstance when the movement of the wind of the right nostril accords with the phase of the dissolution [of the elements, thereby absorbing impure perceptions into the expanse].[297] You should therefore meditate at such times. You should also meditate at twilight and at dawn, and in the morning and in the afternoon. You should, however, rest at noon, at midnight, and at the monkey hour,[298] because these are the times of mental dullness and agitation.

You should adopt the essential posture of the body, as previously indicated, in conjunction with the expulsion of the poisons associated with subtle energy and, as far as your gaze is concerned, focus without distraction and directly in front, sixteen finger widths from the space between the eyebrows. Then let the wind of speech settle in its own natural position, and, above all, let the mind settle into a nonconceptual state. If at that time conceptual thoughts are slightly diffused, you should train your awareness by means of gazing. It is important to let your awareness settle one-pointedly, concentrating the mental faculty, the eyes, and the wind in a one-pointed manner. If even at that time conceptual thoughts should continue to circulate upon the basis of the sense objects, you should cut off those of both the past and the future and settle in the uncontrived awareness of the present. If awareness is aroused through the tension of these methods of mental settling, you should let go of that tense effort and let your awareness relax. Even so, you should still be somewhat watchful, with unwavering mindfulness.

When practicing daytime yoga [in contrast to the foregoing yoga of darkness or nighttime], in a place where the sky appears expansive in the east and the west, and there is no dazzling white [phenomenon] such as snow, and when there are no clouds or breezes, you should direct your gaze toward the west in the morning and toward the east in the afternoon. The essential posture of the body and the settling of the mind should be maintained in the aforementioned manner. At noon you should interrupt the session.

If there is a predominance of mental dullness at the time when those two yogas of the pith instructions [of the daytime and the nighttime or darkness] are practiced, you should adopt a cross-legged posture, covering your knees with your hands, and control the wind slightly while maintaining that essential posture. Then strongly exhale the wind from both your mouth and nostrils. If, however, there is a preponderance of diffusion and mental agitation, you should visualize the body transformed into a ball of light, {308} and then, as it becomes gradually smaller and subtler, it becomes imperceptible. In this way mental agitation will be dispelled.

By the power of having one-pointedly persevered in those [daytime and nighttime] yogas, the subtle energy and mind should then enter into the central channel from the pathway of the vajra (penis), and then you will extensively perceive the appearances of luminosity. Indeed, there are four signs indicative of that luminosity that will manifest during the night—namely, smoke, mirage, the appearance of fireflies in the sky, and [a phenomenon] resembling a burning lamp. And there are also six signs indicative of that luminosity that will arise during the day—namely, (i) the burning yellow appearance of blazing fire, (ii) the moon, (iii) the sun, (iv) the multifarious black shapes of an adamantine eclipse, (v) the supreme phenomenon resembling a flash of lightning, and (vi) the appearances of a blue sphere and so forth. Although these are established to be the principal signs associated with [the yoga of] the daytime and [the yoga of] the nighttime, [their actual manifestations] will be uncertain.[299] Through cultivation of [these yogas] in that manner over a long period of time, in the middle of that [just-mentioned] sphere, emptiness in all its finest aspects will manifest as form; and it will be experienced as [anything] from the unconquerable echo of sound to the vibration of touch.[300]

With regard to the reason for the appearance of such signs: Since these signs are also said to derive from the dynamic winds entering the central channel during the phase of dissolution [of the elements at death] and during the generation stage, one might think that the manifestations of these signs will definitively arise as and when the winds of the coarse respiration cycle gradually dissolve and become invisible. But, on the contrary, you should reflect that right now, by the power of nonconceptual mind, the subtle wind, riding on consciousness, reverses the movement of speech, and as it blocks any conceptual thoughts of dualistic grasping, the movements of the winds of the five elements dissolve sequentially and enter [into the central channel].

Those forms of emptiness are perceived by the eye of flesh, although the eye that perceives them is not itself ordinary. Moreover, it is exclusively explained that the manifestation of that faculty is a defining characteristic that approximates the actual manifestation of a yogin's unbewildered nonconceptual pristine cognition. {309} It is said that these signs and [the yogins] who possess them are known to be certain or definitive; and one should also understand that these signs are finely differentiated from the many diverse and uncertain signs that may appear in [ordinary] dream experiences, such as vases, woolen cloth, and yak woolen fabric.

2. The Branch of Meditative Concentration

Here, the mind one-pointedly abides in the forms of emptiness that were perceived during the previous branch of composure. This entails five ancillary aspects: (i) Discriminative awareness is the knowledge that, though the forms of emptiness at first arise diversely, their intrinsic nature is emptiness. You should be certain that if there is movement of conceptual thought, the forms of emptiness also move, and that when the mind is not diffused, they do not move. (ii) Ideation is that which simply apprehends the appearance of entities while they are empty. (iii) Scrutiny is that which definitively arises, along with certainty, with reference to all appearances—not solely the forms of emptiness. By these methods, you should avoid being tainted by attachment due to the mind totally abiding in those forms of emptiness or even by attachment that would grasp those objects as mental concepts. (iv) An extraordinary joy will then arise in the mind by experientially cultivating these [forms of emptiness] without error, and through the repeated experience of previous [states of joy], the mind and the forms of emptiness will merge, as it were, in a common savor. (v) The bliss of extreme physical refinement will then arise. This is called the unmoving bliss or the immovable bliss. If you persevere with these five ancillary aspects of meditative concentration,[301] the forms of emptiness will become stable.

If, on the one hand, the forms of emptiness are unclear when the eyes are closed, you should gradually establish during daytime yoga that the appearances of the aforementioned signs do arise in the sky. That is to say, you should focus your gaze one-pointedly upon any entities that appear on the basis of past actions, and by controlling the mind, block those things that appear in whatever form on the basis of past actions {310} so that the [appropriate] signs will then arise, merging with those appearances. If, on the other hand, the forms of emptiness are clear when the eyes are closed, the abiding aspect of mind will become stable, particularly if you control the mind in the central channel, at the triple intersection of the channels [below the navel].

Also, you should visualize the movement of the winds and the forms of emptiness in tandem directly in front, sixteen finger widths from the nostrils, and consequently you will perceive the colors of the winds and also accomplish the rites of pacification and enrichment. Then you should prepare a comfortable bed with a high pillow and adopt the essential physical posture of the reclining lion. Leaving the movement of the winds unchanged, and settling the mind in a nonconceptual disposition, you should fall asleep, such that no sorts of dream phenomena are present, and after waking up, your mind will abide in the coalescence of radiance and emptiness. This will put an end to dense confusion and your sleep will become extremely refined. That is to say, the forms of emptiness will indeed clearly arise, resembling phenomena that appear as white within darkness.

You should persevere in these practices by gradually merging meditative equipoise and postmeditation. The appearances of the signs associated with the previous branch of composure will become clear and extensively arise, perceptions of sound and smell and so forth will also arise, and a vital essence with five properties—diffused in diverse colors, subtle, shining, trembling, and hard to disintegrate—will also become manifest. In its midst the body of the buddha will appear, endowed with three certainties,[302] along with its [black] outline. You will obtain the five extrasensory powers of divine clairvoyance, clairaudience, miraculous abilities, knowledge of the minds of others, and the recollection of past lives; your channels will be purified; and you will accomplish the body of adamantine reality.[303]

3. The Branch of Breath Control

The descent of vital breath moving from above into the right and left channels should be blocked, and then exertion—the procedure through which it is inducted into the central channel—should be applied when there is movement of wind from the left side. {311} Mainly you should stay in a darkened room and adopt the essential physical posture—blocking the channel of the vajra (penis) and the rectum with the heel of the right foot while extending the left leg comfortably in front. You should position the crossed palms of the hands just upon the thighs and secure the posture of the [six] opposing stoves [of the hands, feet, and elbows][304] or else execute the gesture of the fist[305] in an embracing manner. As far as your gaze is concerned, you should look directly in front, sixteen finger widths from the place between the eyebrows, and then while contracting the abdomen, you should exhale about twenty-one times. At that time the wind will be expelled from all the channels of the body, the channels also will be perceived to straighten out kinks, the right and left channels will be balanced, and you will attain accomplishments, as appropriate, in accordance with the practical application.

Thereafter the pith instructions that are to be experientially cultivated are entitled the *Six Adamantine Verses* and descended through the lineage from Paṇchen Śākyaśrī of Kashmir.[306] According to this text, once the pathways of the channels have been refined by the adamantine recitation [of the preliminary practices],[307] (i) the wind is inducted into the central channel through the filling and release of gentle wind.[308] (ii) The wind that has been inducted into the central channel is then secured through the rough vase breathing.[309] (iii) If the induction and securing of wind by these means is not effected, there is said to be the "forceful method of rough breathing."[310]

The practice begins as follows: In the morning when the stomach is empty and so forth, you should assume either the bodhisattva posture or the adamantine posture. [You should examine the place from where the wind is moving].[311] When the wind is flowing from the left nostril, you should place your right fist upon the kidney channel and the breast of the left side and press it with the left elbow. You should then turn your face toward the right, slightly draw in the lower wind, and block the right nostril with the extended index finger of the left fist. Inhale strongly from the left nostril and compress the abdomen. After completing that, you should turn your face toward the left side, release the blockage of your index finger on the right nostril, and then block the left one, forcefully exhaling wind from the right nostril.

Similarly, when wind is flowing from the right nostril, you should press the left fist against the kidney channel and the breast of the right side. {312} You should turn your face toward the left, draw in the lower wind, and block the left nostril with the [extended] index finger of the right fist. Then after inhaling from the right nostril, you should turn your face toward the right side, block the right nostril with the [extended] index finger, and exhale from the left one. After alternating in this manner seven times and so forth, you should be able to practice this in a flow of equilibrium, and at that time you may rest.[312]

During these exercises of breath control, you may have a headache, feel the heart being compressed, and see hallucinations such as a wheel of light. If, thereafter, you see that same hallucination becoming more prominent at its zenith, you should interrupt the session for a while and revert to meditation on [the aforementioned yogas] of composure and meditative concentration.[313] The techniques of mingling the vital breath with the downward purgative wind and savoring the nectar of the uvula are both explained in addition.[314]

4. The Branch of Retention

Having mingled the vital breath with the downward purgative wind, you should next meditate on the branch of retention by dissolving the elements—earth into water, and so on, up to space into pristine cognition—in the middle of each respective cakra. The essential physical posture is as in the [aforementioned] vase breathing, or, alternatively, if the wind moves mainly through the left channel, you should compress the lower gate with the heel of the right foot, with the left leg extended slightly in front, in the posture of left-sided royal ease. If, however, the wind moves [mainly] through the right channel, you should do the reverse. The two hands should cover the knees, and the gaze should be as before.[315]

First, you should draw the lower wind upward and conduct the upper wind with the resonance of the long syllable HŪṂ, so that it is exhaled from both nostrils. Then inhale again and let the breath enter the abdomen with the short syllable HŪṂ, so that you can visualize the mingling of the vital breath with the downward purgative wind. Next, you should push out the abdomen several times and strongly conduct the secret wind upward with the short syllable HŪṂ. The eyes should be turned toward the space between the eyebrows, the tip of the tongue raised to the palate, and the lower wind drawn upward through mindfulness of the syllable PHAṬ.[316]

Then visualize the central channel in the middle of the body and meditate that the navel cakra has four, eight, twelve, and so forth channel branches,

{313} all of which have both inner and outer edges, and outside these are sixty-four channel branches, yellow in color.[317] Within the central channel you should visualize upon a moon disk a white OṂ with its crescent, *biṇḍu*, and vibration. You should draw the downward purgative wind upward and conduct the upper wind, as in the [aforementioned] phase of the harsh wind, and then do the vase breathing. Imagine that your mental faculty dissolves into a vital essence and focus upon it one-pointedly. Experiencing that, you should meditate that the forms of emptiness and your mental faculty merge together in a single savor. If you think that the wind is insufficient, you should release it slowly and then earnestly apply this exercise. You should then dissolve the channels, winds, and vital essence of the navel cakra into a single savor, draw in the downward purgative wind, and unite it with the upper wind. Then, focusing one-pointedly on the heart cakra, you should slowly release the upper wind.[318]

The three applications of [gentle, harsh, and forceful] wind are similar in the case of the remaining cakras.[319] In this regard, the visualization at the throat cakra is of four, eight, sixteen, and thirty-two channel branches, the outer layer of which is red in color and dissolves and so forth, as before, in a single savor with the channels, vital essence, and winds of the heart cakra.[320]

At the forehead there are four, eight, and sixteen channel branches, the outer layer of which [dissolves] in a single savor with the channels, vital essence, and winds of the throat cakra.[321] At the crown cakra there are four blue channel branches that [dissolve] in a single savor with the channels, vital essence, and winds of the forehead.[322]

At the secret cakra you should visualize that there are six, ten, and sixteen channel branches, the outer layer of which, green in color, dissolves inseparably with the channels, vital essence, and winds of the crown cakra.[323]

With respect to all these cakras, you should also apply the one-pointed meditative concentration that merges [your mental faculty] with the forms of emptiness.

Since the order of the first two branches and the middle two branches [of the six-branch yoga] is fixed, the sequence of meditation on these six cakras, commencing with the navel cakra, accords with that order. However, in the case of yogins [of lower, average, and superior capacity] whose generative fluid is respectively thin, slightly thick, or extremely thick, it is also explained that as a method of retaining it and so forth, they should engage respectively [with the three seals], starting from [those of lower capacity] who engage with the action seal.[324] {314}

5. The Branch of Recollection

Here, by contrast, supreme yogins should make the forms of emptiness into the path of the Great Seal. By realizing the unchanging great bliss of inner awareness, they will become accomplished without [the need for] consciousness transference, whereas those of average and lower capacity should experience the melting innate bliss dependent on two [other] seals.[325] In this way, the seminal fluid is transformed as if into a bond of mercury and the unchanging great bliss is actualized. So yogins should practice in accordance with this sequence.

You should visualize, as before, the central channel in the middle of the body, reaching the place between the eyebrows at its upper extremity, and with the six cakras. The two right and left channels that are located in the navel cakra commence from the crown of the head. That is to say, they connect with the central channel directly at each of the respective cakras and diverge to the right and left between the six cakras. From the secret cakra [downward], the central channel proceeds to the right, the *rasanā* (right channel) to the left and the *lalanā* (left channel) is in the middle; and it is therefrom that the feces, urine, and seminal fluid are respectively excreted. Therefore you should meditate in conformity with this framework of the channels.

You should then visualize that in the middle of the navel cakra there is the syllable HOḤ, from the transformation of which the fire of the fierce inner heat blazes upward—red, subtle, and sharp, four finger widths in size, its light rays permeating entirely the upper and lower extremities of the central channel. Then you should hold the mind steadily for a long time, either in conjunction with the gentle vase breathing or focusing on the fire alone. The generative fluid of the crown cakra or forehead cakra then moves in the form of the syllable HAṂ or else in the form of a vital essence. You should meditate that it sequentially permeates the minor channels also and that it reaches the central channel, from where it generates delight in the forehead and throat cakras, supreme delight in the heart cakra, extraordinary delight in the navel cakra, and the experience of coemergent delight in the secret cakra and the vajra (penis). Alternatively, it generates delight when passing from the crown to the forehead, supreme delight when passing from the throat to the heart, {315} absence of delight or diverse delight when passing from the navel cakra to the secret cakra, and the conclusive coemergent delight when passing from the secret cakra to the vajra. You should experientially cultivate these aspects that are the means to accomplish the body of pristine cognition—the deathless, supreme bliss.[326]

6. The Branch of Meditative Stability

Depending on that sequence [of meditation] in which the generative fluid is not ejaculated, you will obtain twenty-one thousand six hundred instances of bliss, and you will also commensurately block the [twenty-one thousand six hundred] winds of temporal conjunction.[327] On that basis you will become a mighty lord of the twelfth level. That is to say, dependent on the vital essence being stable at the tip of the vajra (penis), you will obtain the first instance of unchanging bliss. This is the start of meditative stability, and you will block a single cycle of respiration.[328] That will commensurately increase to 1,800 instances [of bliss], and you will block an equivalent number of respiration cycles. In succession you will then obtain the first and second levels in the secret cakra. It is demonstrably established that you will also attain the [corresponding] instances of bliss in the navel, heart, throat, forehead, and crown cakras, and that by this same method of blocking the winds of temporal conjunction, two levels will be obtained [in each of these five cakras]. The conclusive fruit, the body of pristine cognition, is unsurpassed buddhahood.[329]

This **supreme** path of pure **liberation**,
The doctrine that actually induces the four **delights**,
Particularly sublime among **all** the six branches,
Was brought forth from the tantras and their actual commentaries.

This was compiled from the tantras and their commentaries that resemble sandalwood and its fragrance.

41. Guidebook Entitled *The Aural Lineage of Kālacakra*[330]

After you have taken refuge and set the mind on enlightenment, then, in accordance with the following stanzas concerning the Great Seal:[331]

> At first since one is devoid of effort and attainment, [the body and mind] are inwardly relaxed.[332] Next, since one is devoid of

> hesitation, the mind rests in its uncontrived [and fresh] state. Finally, one should know that all occurrences and sensations are nonarising.

And in accordance with the stanzas of the *Total Liberation through Singular Knowledge*:[333]

> You should rest in the profound reality. You should analyze the mind. With regard to the expansive nature of mind, you should nurture the natural glow of reality.

In any sutra, tantra, pith instruction, or treatise that is experientially cultivated, where realizations are offered and introductions to reality are made, there may be verbal instructions on both mind and the nature of mind, and on both phenomena and reality; and verbal instructions that differentiate words and thoughts.

Here [in the generation stage] there are five things to be cultivated, four things to be explained, four determinations to be made, and three aspects of prayer.

Among these, the five things to be cultivated comprise (i) the lion throne, (ii) the lotus cushion, (iii) the moon cushion, (iv) the sun cushion, and (v) the teacher. The four things to be explained comprise (i) self, (ii) sentient beings, (iii) teacher, and (iv) refuge. The four determinations to be made are that (i) this present [state of mind] is buddha, (ii) buddha mind is nonconceptual pristine cognition, (iii) buddha speech is the sacred doctrine, and (iv) buddha body is the monastic community.

The three aspects of prayer constitute the threefold request that the teacher might confer on oneself the blessing of realizing the abiding nature of the Great Seal. The first aspect is the object of the meditation, the second is the ritual, and the third is the actual prayer. That is to say, the first is expressed in the words "my teacher," the second in the words "Great Seal," {200} and the third in the words of the prayer "May the guru confer on me the blessing so that the emptiness and compassion of the Great Seal may arise in my mind!" This should be brought about through the auspicious connection of the four empowerments.

Then you should aspire that the mind [of the teacher] and [your ordinary] mind intermingle and become unchanging. Afterward, you should recite the wrathful mantra [of Kālacakra] and pray as follows:[334]

Oh, this unique buddha body of reality
Is the realization that henceforth connects dualities,
The sole essential nature of the bewildered and unbewildered,
Not holding that living beings have two natures of mind.

Listen now, Vajrasattva!
Given that Samantabhadra, naturally originated awareness,
Is without words and letters, he has no master.
Given that he teaches himself, he is a master.
Given that he is intrinsically aware of himself, he is the buddha body of reality.
There is nothing to be observed
Apart from things expressed by the mind.
There is no need to search for or flee from external signs.
The enlightened intention of the buddhas is present in the mind.
The inspection of this by yourself in your own nature
Is like finding the proverbial wish-granting gem.

When analyzed according to skillful means,
There are one hundred and fifty writings.
When these are subsumed, they are gathered in thirty writings.
When these are again subsumed, they comprise five writings on great emptiness,
And when these are further subsumed,
They comprise two writings of skillful means and discriminative awareness.
When these are further subsumed,
They comprise the single writing that is most secret.

On the throne endowed with the pure ten signs,[335]
There is a sun cushion with the pure vowels,
A moon cushion with the pure consonants,
And a vital essence with the pure [form of] Rāhu.
In the letter [A] representing pure reality,
The pristine cognition that permeates all knowledge is present.
Aroused by this adamantine sound,
In a celestial palace of five pure lights,

Pristine cognition, intrinsic awareness, becomes radiant,
Arising as the spontaneously present body of supreme bliss.

Homage to the precious nature of mind!
The vital heart mantra of adamantine reality takes form
When recited for twenty-one thousand six hundred [breaths].[336]
Those who know the melody of the bees that is nonarising
Do not interrupt the spontaneous presence of the three buddha bodies. {201}

Homage to the precious nature of mind!
In the tent of the precious heart,
Extremely translucent, one-hundredth of a horse's tail hair,
The long syllable A, endowed with five colors, resounds,
And all knowable things are clear, as on a mirror.

Homage to the precious nature of mind!
According to those outside the path of liberation
This is a radiant great pervasion, mingling outer and inner aspects;
But it is the supremely unchanging great bliss
Purposefully conferred on yogins.

Homage to the precious nature of mind!
The syllable A transcends emptiness and nonemptiness.
As for its abode, it abides in nonarising.
As for its expression, it is expressed without interruption.
As for its pervasion, it permeates all living beings.
As for its sight, it is not seen by anyone at all.
As for its teacher, it is revealed by the genuine teacher.

Homage to the precious nature of mind!
Within the translucent vital essence of conclusive great emptiness,
There is a black outline, one-hundredth of a horse's tail hair,
And within it radiate the indefinite phenomena that fill the three world systems,
Including matter and the forms of the six classes of beings.

Diffusing taintless light, the form endowed with all finest aspects
Becomes Vajrasattva, the body of the conquerors of the three times.

Homage to the precious nature of mind!
Without [notions of] mine, me, myself, by me, for me,
I have, I lack, and I am not,
Lay down a mat of uncontrived freshness
And suddenly make freshness your pillow.
Clad inseparably in a natural translucence,
Lie down naked and complete twenty-one thousand six hundred [breaths],
Whereupon you yourself will become Vajrasattva.

Afterward there are nine paths on which things may be carried:
Great obfuscation is carried on the path of delusion.
Great acquisition is carried on the path of hatred.
Great loving-kindness is carried on the path of desire.
Invincible enemies are carried on the path of generosity.
Thieves are carried on the path of identification. {202}
Encounters are carried on the path of heroic determination.
Fearsome passageways are carried on the path of vigilance.
The deceived are carried on the path of deception.
Negativity is carried on the path of poisonous compounds.

In addition to the first three poisons, pride is added for those of great arrogance and jealousy for those of great rivalry, and these are said to be called the "five sibling frailties."[337]

All that the teacher sees in terms of all the three poisons is the mingling of buddha mind and ordinary mind. All that the teacher sees of the sacred representations [of buddha body, speech, and mind] is consecration. All that the teacher sees of sentient beings is compassion. All that the teacher hears of the deceased is the forty-nine-day ceremony. All that the teacher sees of appearances is the mingling of the expanse and awareness.

Then finally, for the practice of consciousness transference, the instruction on the unique syllable A is revealed.

Here, I, of **supreme liberation**, in a few words,
Have with **delight** excellently condensed and committed to writing

The aural transmission of Kālacakra,
Which comprises **all** the instructions of Menlungpa [Sonam Pel].

This partially presents the reliable [points of instruction] that I gleaned from the words of a disciple of Chojé Khewang [Rinchen Zangpo], from which the unoriginal vestiges of the Nyingma scriptural transmission of the *Tantra of* [*Heruka*] *Galpo* and so forth had been removed.

42. Guidebook Entitled *The Ritual Service and Attainment of the Three Adamantine Realities according to Orgyanpa*[338]

After you have taken refuge and set the mind on enlightenment [there then ensue the three adamantine realities]:

1. The Adamantine Reality of Buddha Body

You should meditate in a darkened hermitage on the channels as the adamantine reality of buddha body, practicing the three postures.[339] Meditate with the shoulders stretched out, the back straight, the neck bent, the tongue rolled back, the mouth and nose slightly taut, the ears closed, and the eyes gazing upward without focusing on any object of reference.[340] Thoughts of desire should be expelled. You should rest simply, without distraction. Rejecting the nutrients of the five sensory gates, you should be filled internally with the primary and ancillary winds. Then [the nonconceptual state will arise and] signs such as smoke will be seen.[341]

When forcing the winds upward,[342] [you should purify defects of the posture of the upper body and let the individual winds rest in their natural place. To that end,] you should adopt the posture of the lower body, which requires you to block both the lower orifices below the abdomen with your two feet and tighten [the abdomen] all over. Then you should focus the gaze [of Vairocana] downward.[343] Next, you should adopt the posture of the upper body, which will dispel the defects of the lower posture.[344] {203} [After you invigorate the postures of the upper and lower body, the winds will not remain constant there without your mastering] the posture of the middle body. To that end, you should bend the knees slightly, push out the abdomen, and eliminate all obstacles associated with the postures of the upper and lower body.[345]

You should meditate in the morning and afternoon with the sun and the breeze to the rear, but not at midday. You should meditate in a place where a clear cloudless sky can be seen under a veranda. During the daytime, six signs may be observed, and there are four signs that may be observed during the nighttime, as the winds of the [four] elements are retained [within the central channel]. The latter include: smoke, which is the sign that the wind of the earth element has been retained; mirage, which is the sign that the wind of the water element has been retained; fireflies, which are the sign that the wind of the fire element has been retained; and lamplight, which is the sign that the wind of the wind element has been retained. In addition, a [cloudless space] like the sky is the sign that the wind of the space element [has been impeded]. The aforementioned daytime signs include blazing firelight, moonlight, sunlight, dense eclipsing darkness, lightning, and an extremely subtle vital essence in the middle of which the buddha body of perfect resource is seen.[346] However, the six signs that occur during daytime are uncertain, for there are an inconceivably vast number [of others], including vases, blankets, ropes, and so forth. In addition, you should make this examination in accordance with the threefold experience, that is to say, with the experience of the body, the experience of the mind, and the experience of dreams.[347] Such are the ten signs.

The five ancillary aspects of meditative concentration—namely, discriminative awareness, ideation, scrutiny, delight, and unmoving bliss—will also be observed, and the five extrasensory powers will arise.[348]

2. The Adamantine Reality of Buddha Speech

This concerns the framework of channels, the resource of vital essences, the mastery of the winds, and the abiding of awareness on the supports [of the generative essences, the presence of which is prerequisite for life].[349]

You should expel the residual wind. Then the inhalation of breath is accompanied by OṂ, retention by ĀḤ, and exhalation by HŪṂ.[350] This recitation is undertaken after you have abandoned bead counting.[351]

Afterward, without confusing the winds, you should meditate on the five applications of the winds [of the elements]: The wind of space that arises is without sensation; it is gentle and evenly retained. The wind of fire is strong, short, and retained with gasping. The wind of water whistles through the closed teeth and is retained with sound. The wind of earth is slightly stronger than the wind of space and is retained with or without sensation.[352]

You should then meditate on the seat of the lower purgative wind and [above it] the stacked letters of the elements. At the navel there is the syllable E, triangular, blue, and clear like the sky. Upon it [stacked one above the other] are the bow-shaped black syllable YAṂ from which the maṇḍala of wind emerges, {204} the triangular red syllable RAṂ from which the maṇḍala of fire emerges, the circular white syllable VAṂ from which the maṇḍala of water emerges, and the square yellow syllable LAṂ from which the maṇḍala of earth emerges. And upon that is the seat of pristine cognition, green and circular. Rāhu, the sun, the moon, and Ketu (comet Enke) are circular, corresponding to the element of tangibles.[353]

Then, through the application of the upper wind, the garlands of vowels and consonants on the seats of these elements emerge as follows: You should visualize that the vowels and consonants [in association with the wind of the earth element] emerge yellow in color and in a string. As they alight on [the seat formed of] Ketu, all becomes yellow. When releasing that breath, you should meditate that the seed syllables rise upward [in association with the exhalation of breath]. Next, you should visualize that the vowels and consonants in association with the wind of the water element emerge pale gray and in a string. As they alight on the seat formed of the moon, all becomes white. Next, the vowels and consonants in association with the wind of the fire element emerge red in color and in a string. As they alight on the seat formed of the sun, all becomes red. Next, the vowels and consonants in association with the wind of the wind element emerge black in color and in a string. [As they alight on the seat formed of Rāhu, all becomes black. Next, the vowels and consonants in association with the wind of the space element[354] emerge aquamarine in color and in a string]. As they alight on the seat of pristine cognition, you should visualize that all becomes blue.[355]

At the start of every session of meditation, you should adopt this perspective, and by focusing on these [winds of the elements] respectively, you should retain the middle wind while relaxing the upper and lower winds.[356]

The seed syllables then suddenly rise up in the forms of their respective hand emblems—the blue vajra, the black sword, the red gemstone, the white lotus, and the yellow wheel. Visualize that these in turn rise up in the form of their respective deities, as Kālacakra [or Cakrasaṃvara] in male-female union.[357]

As for the observations associated with this subtle energy, the lower wind pertains to [the clear visualization of] the lower part of the deity's body, the middle wind pertains to [the clear visualization of] the deity's waist, and the upper wind pertains to [the clear visualization of] the deity's face and eyes.[358] The precious wind also generates the physical constitutions of fire, water, and earth. Thus, when wind arises in the pathways, a sensation of heat is felt at the navel of the deity that has the constitution of fire, and this fire causes [the generative fluids in the form of] the vowels and consonants to descend from above, from the seed syllable HAṂ [in the cakra of] supreme bliss, and permeate the body.[359]

If at that time the great rites are practiced, the fourfold union[360] of the wind of the water element denotes the rite of pacification. Here the deity is visualized as having the constitution of the water element, and the subtle energy of water is inducted into the central channel. Then the following mantra is recited: OṂ MĀMA KĪRIKĪRI so and so (*che ge mo*) ŚĀNTI KURU NAMAḤ.[361]

The fourfold union of the wind of the earth element denotes the rite of enrichment. Here the deity is visualized as having the constitution of the earth element, and the wind of the earth element is inducted into the central channel. Then the following mantra is recited: OṂ LOCANĀVAŚUDHE[362] so and so (*che ge mo*) PUṢṬIṂ KURU SVĀHĀ.[363]

The fourfold union of the wind of the fire element denotes the rite of subjugation. Here the deity is visualized as having the constitution of the fire element, and the wind of the fire element is inducted into the central channel. Then the following mantra is recited: OṂ PAṆḌARAVĀSINĪ SARATA so and so (*che ge mo*) VAIṢAṬA.[364]

The fourfold union of the wind of the wind element denotes the rite of wrath. Here the deity is visualized as having the constitution of the wind element, and the wind of the wind element {205} is inducted into the central channel. Then the following mantra is recited: OṂ TĀRE TUTTĀRE TURE so and so (*che ge mo*) MĀRAYA HŪṂ.[365]

Moreover, in the case of those practicing the twelve great rites[366]—which include ritual separation, paralysis, obfuscation, alleviation of poison, expulsion, affliction through fever, and the thrusting of the ritual spike—the deity is visualized as having the constitution of the space element, and the wind of the space element is inducted into the central channel. Through your meditating that the object of the attainment disappears, it does disappear. Through such experiential cultivation, the subtle energy of life breath is inducted into the vital essence and then retained.[367]

3. The Adamantine Reality of Buddha Mind

You should adopt the essential physical posture [as above]. Within the empty space of your own body, the central channel, with the thickness of an average reed, is the life-giving axis of the six cakras. At its upper extremity there is a white vital essence in the form of HAṂ, and at its lower extremity there is a red vital essence in the form of HOḤ, which resembles lightning. OṂ is at the brow, ĀḤ at the throat, HŪṂ at the heart, and KṢA at the secret cakra. A gentle, long breath should be refined, igniting the KṢA and burning propensities within the channels at the secret cakra and thereafter at the navel, at the heart, at the throat, and at the brow. From the HAṂ, generative fluid then arises, filling the channel branches [of the crown cakra] with fire. Then gradually it fills the throat, the heart, the navel, and the secret cakra. Recognizing this uncontaminated state, you should focus one-pointedly on the absence of thought, expelling the ocean [of thoughts], and do not block the wind but leave it in its natural place. Then you should push the upper and lower winds below the navel. Do not inhale the life breath. Mingle the three winds—upper, middle, and lower—and prolong them repeatedly. The lower wind should then be pushed out, and the subtle energy of life breath should be pushed into its natural location.

Behold the instruction on visualization
In the ritual service and attainment of the three adamantine
  realities
Which is here excellently set forth in writing!
This is the essential of **supreme liberation**
That gives **delight** to **all**.

This was compiled from the instruction manual of Daseng.

43. Guidebook Entitled *The Path and Its Fruition*[368]

After you have taken refuge and set the mind on enlightenment, there ensues the teaching on impure appearances.[369]

Impure Appearances

Although the sufferings of cyclic existence are inconceivable, when subsumed they comprise the suffering of suffering, the suffering of change, and the suffering of conditioned existence.[370]

As to the first of these, the suffering of suffering,[371] the hot hells comprise {206} (i) the reviving hell, (ii) the black line hell, (iii) the crushing hell, (iv) the howling hell, (v) the great howling hell, (vi) the heating hell, (vii) the intense heating hell, and (viii) the hell of ultimate torment.[372] The cold hells comprise (i) the blistering hell, (ii) the blister-bursting hell, (iii) the hell of groans, (iv) the hell of lamentations, (v) the hell of chattering teeth, (vi) the hell of lily-like cracks, (vii) the hell of lotus-like cracks, and (viii) the hell of large lotus-like cracks.[373] In addition, there are the ephemeral hells and the neighboring hells, the last of which are located in each of the four directions of the eight hot hells. They comprise (i) the pit of burning embers, (ii) the swamp of putrefied corpses, (iii) the plain of razors, (iv) the forest of sword-like leaves, and (v) the hill of iron shamali trees.[374]

The anguished spirits comprise (i) those who suffer from external obscurations, (ii) those who suffer from internal obscurations, and (iii) those who suffer from obscurations about food and drink.[375]

The animal realm comprises (i) those living in the ocean depths and (ii) those who are scattered elsewhere.[376]

You should reflect that you have no choice but to avoid being born in these lower realms.

As for the suffering of change:[377] Cyclic existence is impermanent and pointless. Having been born as Śakra, one will again fall to earth. Having been born as a universal emperor, one will be reborn as the lowest of servants. Having attained the realms of the gods, one will be reborn in the hells. The sun and moon will enter into darkness. The wealthy will become impoverished. The strong will become weak. Enemies will become friends. Friends will become foes. If one considers people who are natives and migrants, they were not so in the past, but gradually their circumstances came about through change.

As for the suffering of conditioned existence:[378] Even after the aged have died, they will have no satisfaction, and even after acting through a succession of lives, their karma will not be ended. By reflecting in this manner, if you think decisively that wherever you may be born as a sentient being, there will be no happiness, by all means you will gravitate toward the sacred doctrine. The freedoms and advantages are hard to find. They are of great benefit, but such opportunities will not last for long. The basis on which these are attained is this very human body that is endowed with freedoms and advantages.

As for the freedoms and advantages: Among the latter there are five individual advantages and there are five circumstantial advantages.[379] Though they are hard to find, at times when these are obtained, you should take on board the essential points; for at such times as this the celestial realms of the next life, the nirvana of the lower vehicles, {206} and even omniscient buddhahood can all be attained. These freedoms and advantages that are hard to find are impermanent phenomena, so the opportunity will not last for a long time. This is because the life span of the beings of Jambudvīpa is uncertain. There are many disharmonious conditions, and the harmonious conditions are rare, so one does not know when one will die.

You should have confidence in causes and their results. Reflect on nonvirtuous actions, virtuous actions, and neutral actions. By engaging in the ten nonvirtuous actions to a greater, middling, or lesser extent, you will be reborn in the three aforementioned inferior realms. Since suffering arises from nonvirtuous actions, you should instantly desist from them. Through the maturation of having practiced the ten virtuous actions, the result is that you will be reborn in the blissful realms. You should consider that the three degrees of enlightenment[380] will be attained and that there are advantages in virtuous action. There are also neutral motivations that are not retained by any thought of virtue or nonvirtue, so whatever aspects of the actions of body, speech, and mind you might practice, these should be retained by enlightened mind.

Experiential Appearances

In terms of experiential appearances:[381] You should cultivate, in common, loving-kindness, compassion, and the altruism of enlightened mind. For ordinary friends and foes you should cultivate loving-kindness. With regard to compassion, you should rejoice in sentient beings who encounter happiness and the causes of happiness: "Pity those designated as sentient beings who suffer due to fundamental ignorance, even though sentient beings are established to be without self! Pity those who engage in the causes of suffering! Pity those sentient beings who suffer due to attachment to the notion of an individual person and to phenomena, even though these are established to be without genuine inherent existence!"

Then you should reflect, "Would that I, aspiring to enlightened mind, might attain buddhahood for the sake of all sentient beings! Like the thirsty who desire water, I should achieve whatever sentient beings may desire because they have been my mother!" Visualize sentient beings in front and abandon your self-cherishing. "May all the negative actions of sentient beings be ripened in myself! May my own happiness and virtuous actions be ripened in sentient beings!"

After making such reflections, {208} you should train in austerities—assuming the burdens of others and so forth. You should determine decisively that the happiness of yourself and the suffering of others, which are respectively the subject and object to be exchanged, are the perceptions of your own mind. They are nonexistent, that is to say, empty. You should hone this realization to the correct standard.

Then, once you have entered into the profound uncommon path, the experiential appearances that may arise are inconceivable. However, when these are subsumed, they number fifteen—the three paths, the three experiences, the three auspicious circumstances, the three aspects of warmth, and the three meditative stabilities.[382] You should meditate, thinking that since these attributes originate dependent on the auspicious circumstances of subtle energy, there is nothing harmonious that they should like, and there is nothing disharmonious that they should dislike.

Pure Appearances

As for pure appearances:[383] The inexhaustible buddha body denotes the inconceivable protuberance [and so forth] of the buddha body, which cannot be overtly examined; the inexhaustible buddha speech denotes the inconceivable speech that is heard without distinctions of proximity and remoteness; and the inexhaustible buddha mind denotes the inconceivable quantitative knowledge of buddha mind. You should meditate, thinking that innumerable enlightened attributes such as these are acquired through the experiential cultivation of the path.

Continuum of the Ground

At this point you should receive empowerment, which is the causal basis [or ground] among the three continua [of ground, path, and result]. After that, when you examine outer [appearances] and inner mind, outside there is nothing at all, and [internally] also, the mind is radiant in its essential nature and empty in its natural expression. When it is radiant, it is empty; and when it is empty, it is radiant. You should establish decisively and without wavering that the integration of these two [radiance and emptiness] indivisibly is the essential nature of mind. At that time, if thoughts are diffused, do not prolong them. Let any thoughts that arise be equipoised in that integrated disposition.[384]

Due to a misunderstanding of the three attributes [radiance, emptiness, and unity] that are present here and now, there are twenty-seven coemergent factors through which beings then roam in cyclic existence.[385] But mind is a magical display, without inherent existence, and there are four principal examples and four ancillary examples through which this nature of mind is established.[386] First, sleep and perception should be intermingled, and any distinction between dreams and the present waking state should be experienced. You should develop the certainty that fact is fiction. Then, afterward, the merit should be dedicated {209} with compassion for unrealized beings, and you should remember always the examples and their meanings.[387] That is to say, you should develop certainty according to the first example[—namely, sleep—]through the three phases of preparation, main practice, and conclusion. Even if this takes a long time, you should not transfer your focus to the second [visualization] onward. Next, you may also connect the [aforementioned] nine factors[388] with the remaining examples. To point out the essence of these [remaining] examples, they concern substances, illnesses, evil spirits, double vision, blurred vision, whirling fire, and rapid spinning. You should cut off conceptual elaboration, determining that, dependent on these examples, this world of appearances has not been created by chance, or by mighty Īśvara, or by indivisible particles and so forth, but is the emanation of your own mind.[389]

Next, to establish that mind is a magical display, there are the four principal examples—namely, magical display, mirage, the moon reflected in water, and lightning; and there are four ancillary examples—namely, Hari,[390] gandharva spirit towns, clouds, and rainbows. Through these examples you should cut off conceptual elaborations, determining that in mind itself there is no genuine inherent existence, and that transformations in relation to the nature of mind arise dependent on diverse causes and conditions.[391]

Next, there are four principal examples of dependent origination—namely, oral recitations, lamps, mirrors, and seals; and four ancillary examples—namely, magnifying fire crystal, seeds, sour tastes, and echoes. The point of these examples is that the causes and conditions of a magical display [and so forth] are without any genuine existence at all, that causes do not at all come into being as results, and that results do not at all arise dependent on causes, so that there is no coming or going, and no arising or ceasing.[392]

Next, there are four primary examples of the inexpressibility of mind—namely, the laughter of a child, the dreams of a mute, the tickling of a sensitive spot, and the bliss of the sexual organs; and there are four ancillary examples—namely, the pristine cognition of the third empowerment, union with a secret consort, waves of enjoyment,[393] and the circle of the maṇḍala. Although certainty arises that all things are dependently originated, you should remain equipoised in the absence of expression because [a specified] "this" cannot be expressed.[394] {210}

Once you have established the meaning of mind by means of thirty-two examples in that manner, these are then reduced to the four principal examples. The four points are individually established in accordance with their respective four examples, and [the nature of] mind should then be established. That is to say, these four examples concern magical display, the moon reflected in water, the seedling of dependent origination, and the tickling of a sensitive spot indicative of inexpressibility; and they respectively convey certainty with respect to the nature of mind, magical display, dependent origination, and inexpressibility. These should be intermingled with perception and experientially cultivated.

When these four are then reduced to a single example, certainty is developed as follows: The coemergent pristine cognition arises dependent on the "wave of enjoyment," and it should be established according to the [same] four attributes: the nature of mind, magical display, dependent origination, and inexpressibility. So this [practice of the "wave of enjoyment"] should be experientially cultivated in the aforementioned manner [of the four examples].[395]

You should meditate strongly and for a short session, without letting ordinary thoughts interrupt the generation stage of meditation. Finally, the middle eye [of a deity representing pristine cognition] becomes clear and the nature of mind is apprehended. Then slightly relax your effort. If there is no clarity, you should look at the middle eye of a painted icon and it should become clear. Then you should meditate, focusing on all its eyes. After that, you should meditate as before on the entire head and the entire body [of the deity], and so forth, together with the maṇḍala of seats, the celestial palace of the deity, and the protective circle.[396]

Continuum of the Path

[This has four aspects, corresponding to the four empowerments:]

1. Cultivating the Path according to the Vase Empowerment

Next, during the continuum of the path, having received [the vase] empowerment elaborately, you should apprehend with your mind Cittavajra[—that is, Akṣobhyavajra—]at the heart with an entourage of eight female deities, Amitābha at the throat with an entourage of sixteen female deities, Vairocana at the crown with an entourage of thirty-two female deities, Ratnasambhava at the navel with an entourage of sixty-four female deities, and Amoghasiddhi at the secret cakra with an entourage of thirty-two female deities. Then you should apprehend with your mind the six sense fields, the six sense objects, and the twelve major joints[397] as deities, and the parts of the body as the supporting celestial palace.

2. Cultivating the Path according to the Secret Empowerment

Next, after receiving instruction on consciousness transference at the time of death by means of globes of light,[398] you should enter into the path of the secret empowerment. {211} [Here, meditative concentration emphasizes the path of the fierce inner heat, and there are seven initial steps through which it can be activated—namely, (i) adamantine recitation on the path of breath control, (ii–iv) the three pith instructions concerning exhalation, (v–vi) the two pith instructions concerning inhalation or filling, and (vii) the union of the upper and lower winds that makes the pausing of breath into the path.][399]

(i) The Adamantine Recitation on the Path of Breath Control

At first you should begin with breath control, since this is analogous to the dispelling of defects. Focusing on the right side of the tip of the nose, you should be mindful that you are exhaling while exhaling, inhaling while inhaling, and pausing while the breathing is slightly paused. Having focused one-pointedly on this breathing, if extraneous thoughts do not move, that is the path that will dispel the [involuntary] inhalation.[400] In order to achieve success, you should [gradually] invigorate breath control.[401] To that end, the exhalation should be lengthened and the inhalation and pausing of breath shortened. You should then let meditative stability arise and begin with mindfully inhaling, pausing, and exhaling the vital breath. While inhaling you should visualize the syllable OṂ, while pausing visualize ĀḤ, and while exhaling visualize HŪṂ.[402]

As an ancillary practice contingent on that, the inhalation should then be lengthened and the exhalation shortened, and commensurately the mental faculty should also be mindful of lengthening the inhalation, pausing, and then shortening the exhalation.[403]

(ii–iv) The Three Ancillary Pith Instructions concerning Exhalation

Next you should cease that exertion and apply the pith instructions concerning exhalation. To that end, you should raise the head slightly and focus on the tip of the nose or else on the left nostril. Then you should block the [right] nostril with the raised [middle finger of the right hand] forming the gesture of menace, inhale a long breath, and then exhale forcefully through the left nostril. This is in order to dispel defects, [giving rise to the nonconceptual meditative stability].[404]

Next, exhale your breath vigorously through both nostrils, focusing consciousness on the hair ringlet between the eyebrows. Strengthen its passageway through the two nostrils, the vital places of wind, and forcefully exhale it from the body.[405] You should maintain this exhalation as long as possible and then focus the vital wind on the space in front, about the distance of one cubit, and after that focus it about the distance of one double arm span, then about the length of a spear, then about the distance of a wide valley, then about the distance of a journey, then the distance of the four continents, then the distance of the trichiliocosm, and finally the entire space occupied by the world systems.[406]

Last, when exhalation is accompanied with sound, {212} you should clench the teeth and focus the vital mind on the space forming the horizon, about one double arm span in extent. Then focus on the sound of *si* and exhale the vital wind between the teeth with the sound of *si*.[407]

As indications of success [in these three branches of exhalation], there will be a wind similar to the smoke of incense that will emerge from the rectum, and you should be aware that it circulates about one cubit below [the rectum]. Then you should compress the upper wind as much as possible and slightly draw in the lower wind. At that time also you should not allow the abdomen to swell.[408]

(v–vi) The Two Ancillary Pith Instructions concerning Inhalation

You should then cease that exertion and fill [the central channel] with vital breath. Visualize that the wind moves softly downward to the navel cakra within an eggshell-like globe that is white on the outside and yellow on the inside. Soundlessly swallow the spittle on which the wind rides and compress the wind as much as possible. It is said that the experiences of a mighty lord of yoga will indeed arise through this practice.[409]

Next, you should visualize that all the winds move softly downward to the navel cakra within a blue hexahedron. Open the mouth and soundlessly inhale a long and slow breath of wind through the mouth. On completing this, you should swallow the spittle soundlessly and shake the head.[410]

Last, you should focus on both of these visualizations in common, and immediately thereafter, in the navel cakra, which is the focal point of the meditation, you should visualize a fire, two or four finger widths in length. Within the navel cakra the hexahedron extends in size, commensurate with the earth. By compressing the wind, the hexahedron increases in size and finally it covers the entire earth. You should meditate that the wind enters within its empty interior and that it is indeed profound and deep in the manner of an ocean.[411]

(vii) The Union of the Upper and Lower Winds: The Fierce Inner Heat

There then ensues the union [of the upper and lower winds]: You should visualize that at the navel cakra, the fire of the channel of fierce inner heat in the shape of an ashé (the stroke of the letter *a*) is subtle, hot, sharp, and volatile.

First, draw in the lower wind slightly, and without a sound gradually draw in the upper wind with exertion, so that it almost reaches the head, and meditate that all this wind then dissolves into the fire at the navel cakra. {213} Once this [movement of] the upper wind is completed, you should swallow some spittle. Then strongly draw in the lower wind, unite the upper and lower winds in the navel cakra, and squeeze the stomach against the spine. The abdomen should be slightly pushed out, the Adam's apple slightly compressed, and the wind held as long as possible.[412]

The pith instructions of the fierce inner heat [that are not contingent on the cakras] are respectively named (i) sustaining the lamp flame, (ii) the lightning bolt of the fontanel, (iii) the yoga of the channels, (iv) the wheel of the kindling sticks, (v) the union of sun and moon vital essences at the heart cakra, (vi) the solitary hero at the navel cakra, (vii) the vital essence of bliss at the secret cakra, and (viii) the seed of white hair at the *ūrṇa*.[413] [In the case of those pith instructions that are contingent on the cakras] the practice will be sharp if it is contingent on one cakra, swift if contingent on two cakras, and stable if contingent on four cakras.[414]

There are seven phases [of this fierce inner heat practice] according to the key points of the pith instructions: (i) the pale-red fire, (ii) the blazing fire, (iii) the battle of the [white and red] vital essences, (iv) the visualization of the [fire at the navel] cakra, (v) the intensely blazing fire, [(vi) the greatly blazing fire,] and (vii) the totally blazing fire.[415]

3. Cultivating the Path according to the Empowerment of Pristine Cognition [based on] Wisdom

When engaging in the path according to [the empowerment of] discerning pristine cognition, there are three phases: the preparation in which blessing is conferred by means of three perceptions; the main practice, which concerns the recognition of the descent and retention [of the vital essence]; and the conclusion, which concerns the preservation [of the vital essence] without diminution, by means of its reversal and distribution.[416]

4. Cultivating the Path according to the Fourth Empowerment

When you engage in the path according to the fourth empowerment, this entails the practice named "waves of the physical body." Here you should adopt the [appropriate] physical posture. Cover the knees with the hands, straighten the waist, press the stomach against the spine, induct the upper wind by means of three exhalations and three inhalations, and compress [the lower wind] below the right and left buttocks, alternately contracting it gently and then drawing it in forcefully. If it were contracted forcefully, its strength would be dissipated. When you release these winds, the lower wind should be released first.[417]

Next comes the practice named "calm and intense waves of vocal inhalation." [In the case of calm vocal inhalation,] you should adopt the [adamantine] physical posture and cross the hands at the heart in the gesture of the adamantine fist. You should hunch the body forward without quite touching the ground. Then, with the intonation of the syllable I, inhale the wind through the teeth without making a sound. As the inner wind is drawn upward, you should slowly draw it in through the mouth as much as you can, {214} and in tandem with that you should gradually but strongly contract the base of the small intestine along with the lower wind. Finally, you should raise your head and cast the eyes upward. You should compress the winds as much as possible, and practice this three times in front, three times on the right side, and three times on the left side. Having experienced that, you should emit a sound like that of a flute.

In the case of the intense vocal inhalation, the vital points of body and speech should be positioned as before, but here you should inhale more and more intensely, in conjunction with the sound HŪṂ. At the conclusion, you should emit a sound like that of a brass horn heard from a distance.[418]

Last, there is the practice named "waves of the mind."[419] Here you should be instantly equipoised by means of three perceptions that are dependent on the seal of pristine cognition.[420] So it has three aspects, as follows:

[Firstly, there is the purification of the mental continuum of those endowed with skillful means:] Once the generative essences of both the male and the female appear at the extremity of the central channel, they are transformed into rays of light. Moving from the right channel they appear at the navel cakra—[the white vital essence] causing the navel cakra to vanish like darkness at the break of day, and [the red vital essence] causing it to radiate like the rising sun, while [the wind] causes it to swell like an inflated lung.

Again, moving from the right channel, the vital essences appear at the throat cakra, whereupon you are mindful of possessing the [same] three attributes [of whiteness, brightness, and inflation].

Again, moving from the right channel, the vital essences are diffused from the right ear in the form of rays of light, and from the entrance to those rays of light the maṇḍala of your preferred deity is emanated. Then the four empowerments are conferred in the mental continuum of sentient beings. The inhabited world is transformed into the celestial palace and its sentient inhabitants into your preferred deity. Then the entire inhabited world and its inhabitants are transformed into rays of light. Mingling with the rays of light that are [already] diffused afar, these are transformed into the elixir of nectar and enter through your fontanel. At the crown cakra you are mindful of possessing those three attributes [of whiteness, brightness, and inflation], at the throat cakra there is the splendor of one thousand suns, and, appearing at the heart cakra, these are transformed into five-colored lights as a sign that your own mental continuum has been transformed into the five buddha bodies.

You should then visualize that the pathway of the pure channels originates from the navel cakra {215} and that [the vital essences] abide as before in the secret cakra of the female consort. Thereby apprehended conceptual thoughts subside, the right channel is brought under control, and power is obtained over the [lower] wind of exertion. You should simply determine that signlessness, the gateway of liberation, has been actualized.

Then in the same manner you should repeat this practice from the left channel. Thereby the apprehending conceptual thoughts subside, the left channel is brought under control, and power is obtained over the [upper] wind of life breath. You should then visualize that aspirationlessness, the gateway of liberation, has been actualized.

Similarly, you should repeat this practice from the central channel. Thereby subtle conceptual thoughts of both aspects of the subject-object dichotomy subside, the central channel is refined, and power is obtained over the location of the winds. You should then visualize that emptiness, the gateway of liberation, has been actualized.[421]

Secondly, there is the purification of the mental continuum of those endowed with discriminative awareness: Here the visualization that refines the three channels of the female consort should be undertaken as before, but in this case, apart from [the vital essences] simply moving from the right and left channels to the orifices of both the left and right ears, there is no external diffusion. Whether or not these are diffused from and absorbed into the fontanel, this is said to be the case.[422]

Thirdly, there is the purification of disparate mental continua: Here the pure generative essence emerges from the central channel of the male consort in the form of light rays and vanishes into the supreme protuberance. The pure generative essence of the female consort similarly vanishes. Then you should simply be mindful that both of these become spontaneously present as the five buddha bodies.

It is said that there is no need for these experiences to occur in tandem with the rising and induction of the upper and lower winds, and that there is no need for the precision of the four [daily] sessions of meditation. At that time, you should spontaneously nurture whatever imprecise experiences arise. Consequently, the experience of the four delights ascending from below,[423] the view that is the utterly pure real nature of all things, will arise within your mental continuum. This is the instruction on the path of immaculate and innate pristine cognition, for those who are most lethargic.[424]

Here I have set forth in writing this oral teaching, this record of visualization,
The pinnacle of **delight**, derived from **all** modes of instruction,
Victory banner of **supreme** maturation and **liberation**,
Fluttering with the four sessions of experiential cultivation. {216}

This was compiled from the instruction manual of Chojé Pelden Lama Dampa Sonam Gyeltsen entitled *Elucidation of All the Concealed Meanings*.

44. Guidebook Entitled *The Inconceivables*[425]

This is the first of the *Eight Further Cycles of the Path*. After first taking refuge and setting the mind on enlightenment, you should hone the vital points of body, speech, and mind. After meditating on the teacher and cultivating divine pride, you should train outwardly, taking space as an exemplary model. Focus your own consciousness on the space that is up to four finger widths from the tip of your nose, and meditate, concentrating with both body and mind. After that, you should again train in the same manner, focusing on the space that is up to eight finger widths distant, and also in the same manner, focusing on the space that is anything from sixteen finger widths up to a double arm span distant. You should maintain [your concentration] in this manner, whatever experiences arise in the mind. For the most part, you will experience the emptiness of inherent existence.[426]

Then, in order to achieve success, you should focus your thoughts on the eastern direction, starting from a double arm span in distance and continuing as far as the limits of space. Whatever experiences of limitlessness, feebleness, or attachment to splendor might arise, you should maintain [your concentration] in this [uncontrived] manner. Then you should similarly train, focusing your thoughts on all the other directions of space, starting from the south.[427]

1–3. The Three Equipoises in the Nature of Reality

When you train in that manner [there then ensue the three equipoises in the nature of reality]: (i) you will be united in the inconceivable nonarising of names, which resembles the hatching of an egg; (ii) you will be united in the inconceivable nonarising of meanings, which resembles the release from a trap; and (iii) you will also be united in the inconceivable nonarising of meditative stability, which resembles the breaking open of a cocoon.

As to [the first of these], the thoughts that the yogin might grasp as names dissolve into the nature of mind, and the experience of unceasing luminosity arises. As for the inconceivable nonarising of meanings, you should meditate that intrinsic awareness, in the manner of space, does not arise, whether in terms of its initial causal basis,[428] its presently abiding nature, or its conclusive cessation. Then, as for the inconceivable nonarising of meditative stability, internally you should let [the mental faculty] rest without grasping, {217} and externally you should let [consciousness] relax. You should lighten your body and mind, and simply be mindful that consciousness is introverted. But if it does become diffused, you should let the sensory gates relax, and, free from attachment, the supreme coalescence of bliss and emptiness will arise.[429]

4. The Supportive Ancillary Practices

Then, with regard to the supportive ancillary practices,[430] you should place a flower at a suitable distance in front, and train in the four ancillaries that comprise the unchanging support, the unmoving body, the unclosing eyes, and the nongrasping mental faculty. You should recognize [pristine cognition] through sights, and, similarly, you should then also train with reference to [other sensory objects] such as sounds.[431]

At first when you meditate, objects will sometimes be harmful and sometimes beneficial, owing to their conditions. But when they arise as subtle appearances, they will be neither beneficial nor harmful; and [for those of highest capacity] as soon as an object and its conditions are encountered, supreme realization will internally arise.[432] These three phases are respectively known as the time when appearances arise as a spiritual mentor, the time when outer and inner phenomena are both intermingled [in a common savor], and the time when the five poisons are cognized as medications.[433]

Then you should eliminate dullness and mental agitation that are obstacles to meditative concentration. That is to say, you should eliminate the dullness and mental agitation that are purposeful, the dullness and mental agitation that arise through conditions, and the dullness and mental agitation that arise implicitly.[434] [Should these occur during the first session of meditative concentration,] they may be eliminated through regimen, through diet, or the power of mind.[435]

5. The Five Subsidiary Pith Instructions of Suppression

There are also five [subsidiary pith instructions] of suppression in which you should train:[436] (i) spinning a [visualized] wheel [in the navel cakra], (ii) rotating a threadlike [exhalation of wind from a visualized hole in the body], (iii) the practice of [exhaling wind forcefully through] multiple [visualized] holes [in the body], (iv) the dispelling of wind through the upper or lower cakras, and (v) the practice of [sinking into] the lowest pit.[437]

Here I have set forth in unprecedented writing
All instructions of the path of the five inconceivables,
Guiding your own mind to the glory of **delight**,
The perfection stage of **supreme** maturation and **liberation**.

This was compiled from the instruction manual of Jetsun Drakpa Gyeltsen.

45. Guidebook Entitled *The Nine Profound Methods*[438]

As for the instruction of Padmavajra, which is the second of the *Eight Further Cycles of the Path*: After refuge and setting the mind on enlightenment, there are nine pith instructions concerning the retention of the mind—namely, {218} (i) mental placement, (ii) perpetual placement, (iii) integrated placement, (iv) intensified placement, (v) control, (vi) calmness, (vii) quiescence, (viii) one-pointedness, and (ix) absolute placement [or meditative equipoise].[439]

(i) [As to the first, mental placement:] you should concentrate and meditate with utmost effort, starting from the yoga of reemergence until [the visualization of the deity] is secured in accordance with the lord of your enlightened heritage.[440]

(ii) Then [as for perpetual placement]: At the outset you should focus your mind on the central eye [of the deity]. If it is clear, even though it is clear, you should then discontinue the visualization. If it is unclear, even though it is unclear, you should discontinue the visualization. For [in both cases] the [distracting] defects of meditative concentration will arise. If, even following that discontinuation, the visualization should again become vibrant, [your meditative concentration] will be defective, so let the mind wander to another object such as a vase or a blanket, and then resume the meditation. Once again, if the visualization is clear, even though it is clear, you should discontinue it; and if it is unclear, even though it is unclear, you should discontinue it and let your mind wander. Through your meditating in this manner, the visualization should [gradually] be established.

If, however, such [distracting] defects of meditative concentration continue to arise, and even after repeated experience the visualization does not become clear, then you should cultivate the "visualization that follows speech." This has two aspects, among which the first is visualization by means of your own speech. Here you should say, "The central eye [of the deity] is the primary eye, red in color and wrathful," and then you should meditate while the defects of meditative concentration arise as before. If the visualization does not become clear even on that basis, you should have someone else say, "The central eye [of the deity] . . ." and meditate on that while the [distracting] defects of meditation arise. If the visualization does not become clear even on that basis, you should cultivate "visualization by means of observation." Draw an extremely beautiful central eye and look at it. Then meditate while the [distracting] defects of meditative concentration arise. These constitute the oral instructions of perpetual placement.[441]

(iii) As far as integrated placement is concerned, if your consciousness is diffused outwardly, {219} it can be swiftly drawn back if you think, "My consciousness has become agitated." In this way, the mind will quickly find its placement in the visualization.[442]

(iv) As for intensified placement, you should meditate with a single visualization that the defects of the mind in each session [of meditation] resemble the protuberance of the head, a crossed vajra, or the fangs in the face [of a wrathful deity]. This should be meditated on in conjunction with exhalation of breath.[443]

(v) As for control, you should know that meditative stability is endowed with innumerable enlightened attributes, and even at the time of engaging in conduct, although the visualization is not clear, you should control the mind by always recalling the form of the deity.[444]

(vi) As for calmness, if conceptual thoughts are diffused, at the time when the mind is displeased, the mind should be relaxed and calmed on the basis of that visualization.[445]

(vii) As for quiescence, when nonvirtuous thoughts arise, including malice, these should be made quiescent dependent on that visualization.[446]

(viii) As for one-pointedness, if the mind is present without [thoughts] being outwardly diffused, on that basis placement in one-pointedness is achieved.[447]

(ix) As for absolute placement, here meditative stability will arise without being purposefully achieved, on the basis of those visualizations.[448]

Through this oral instruction that holds the mind on a single facet of the body [of the deity] according to the generation stage of meditation, you should also transfer the visualization to other facets of the deity's body once the mind has been stabilized in the [initial] single facet of the deity's body. That is to say, during the first session [of the first day], you should meditate on the central eye [of the deity]. In the second, you should visualize the three eyes [of the deity]. In the third, [you should visualize] the wrathful frowns. And in the fourth, the nose [of the deity]. On the second and third days [of the retreat], you may also meditate in a clear manner on the three eyes [of the deity]. In brief, you should maintain steadfast visualization until the three eyes [of the deity] become clear if you want them to be clear, and invisible if you want them to be invisible.

In addition, during the first session of the second day, you should visualize the fangs [of the wrathful deity Hevajra]; {220} in the second session, the ears; in the third, the face; and in the fourth, the white right arm. During the first session of the third day, you should visualize the primary face and the right-sided white face. During the second session of that day, you should visualize the red left arm; in the third, the second face of the right side, which is black; and in the fourth, you should visualize the second face of the left side, which is black, and the upper face. During the first session of the fourth day, you should visualize the eight faces; during the second session, the protuberance of the head, the yellowish-red hair of the head, and the crossed vajra. During the third session of that day, you should visualize the ornaments of the head, including the wheel of bone and the earrings. During the fourth session, you should visualize most of the deity's body including the neck ornaments. During the first session of the fifth day, you should visualize the heads and most of the deity's body. During the second, you should visualize the eight right arms and their hand emblems. During the third, you should visualize the eight left arms and their hand emblems, along with the body ornaments, including human heads, and the [peripheral] mountain of fire. During the fourth, you should visualize the legs that suppress the four demonic forces. During the first session of the sixth day, you should visualize the principal deity [Hevajra] along with Gaurī; during the second, Caurī; during the third, Vetālī; and during the fourth, Ghasmarī. During the first session of the seventh day, you should visualize, in addition to the group of five comprising the principal deity and that entourage, Pukkāsī. In the second session of that day, you should visualize Śabarī; in the third, Caṇḍālī; and in the fourth, Ḍombī. In the first session of the eighth day, you should visualize all those nine deities, along with their celestial palace. In the second session of that day, you should visualize the charnel ground; in the third, the protective circle; and in the fourth, the three world systems—the inhabited environment and its inhabitants, along with the wheel of the maṇḍala. All these constitute the visualizations of the generation stage.[449]

Next you should focus also on the perfection stage, which resembles the tip of a flame.[450] [The aforementioned visualization,] from the three world systems to the wheel of the maṇḍala, is dissolved in succession; {221} and you should then meditate on the vital essence as a mass of light. If that is clear, you should focus your mind on the tip of a lamp flame; and if that is clear, on a line the thickness of a horse's tail hair; and one-hundredth of a horse's tail hair; and finally on emptiness, in the manner of warm breath evaporating on a mirror.[451]

Having undertaken clear visualizations in that manner, starting from then, when you want to place [the mind in meditation], you should commence the sessions of meditation on emptiness with the dissolving of the three world systems, and you should continue to dissolve them until they are empty. If you want to arise [from meditation], you should adopt [a postmeditative state] with pride that chiefly derives from the disposition of emptiness. You should recollect virtuous actions and recite adamantine songs and pure prayers of aspiration, and abide in accordance with the yoga of conduct.[452]

Here I have set forth in writing the clear instruction,
The sacred doctrine that exudes **delight**,
Having elucidated in the nine profound methods of the path
All enlightened intentions of Saroruhavajra,
The **supreme** path of **liberation**, resembling the tip of a lamp flame.

This was compiled from the instruction manual composed by Jetsun Drakpa Gyeltsen.

46. Guidebook Entitled *The Attainment of Coemergence*[453]

As for the instruction of Ḍombipā, which is the third of the *Eight Further Cycles of the Path*: After you have taken refuge and set the mind on enlightenment, there are two methods by which individuals may attain the path—through the [outer] way of austerities and the [inner] way of Buchung.[454] In both of these there are three things not to be squandered—that is to say, resources should not be squandered, the physical body should not be squandered, and the mind should not be squandered. The first of these requires that resources should not be squandered due to fire, water, foes, or demonic forces, and instead they should be dedicated to the three precious jewels and to the ḍākinīs. The second requires that the physical body should observe the three vows—namely, the vows of individual liberation, those of the bodhisattvas, and those of the awareness holders. The nonsquandering of the mind refers to the two aspects of enlightened mind—namely, the outer aspect, where thc relative enlightened mind comprises aspiration and application[455] and the ultimate enlightened mind denotes the absence of conceptual elaboration; and the inner aspect, where the relative enlightened mind comprises the generative essences and the ultimate enlightened mind denotes the [coalescence of] bliss and emptiness.[456]

Next there is the method of instruction on the path by means of the threefold coemergence: {222} (i) the coemergence of the causal basis naturally abides, (ii) the coemergence of skillful means denotes the methods that generate the three meditative experiences, and (iii) the coemergence of the result denotes the three gateways of liberation and the arising of the three buddha bodies.[457]

Confronting this coemergence are internal obstacles that are coemergent with the three humoral disorders and external obstacles that are coemergent with the three demonic forces. Among them, the former comprise disorders of wind, disorders of blood and bile combined, and disorders of phlegm. The three demonic forces comprise the class of male demons, the class of female demons, and the class of nāgas.[458]

The first aspect of the threefold coemergence, the coemergence of the causal basis, is the nonarising abiding nature—the actual nature of mind. The second, the coemergence of skillful means[—namely, the path—] denotes two methods of practice that accord with two sorts of individuals. That is to say, once individuals practicing austerity have first entered upon the path,[459] they should initially be mindful of the teacher on the crown of the head and cultivate the precious enlightened mind; and after that, they should be instantaneously mindful of deity yoga.

[Common to both the way of austerities and the way of Buchung,] there are twenty-seven pith instructions on the meditative experiences associated with physical exercises, dependent on which joy and bliss arise in the mind, harsh speech and so forth will arise, and you will suddenly cry out. Such is the meditative stability named "pervasion of body, speech, and mind with great desire."[460] When bliss arises, if consciousness is clear and light, and great compassion emerges, that is meditative stability.[461]

Next, since hatred is a culmination of radiance, hatred is also transformed into the path. It arises as the culmination of radiance due to the condition of unpleasant objects.[462]

Also, since there is no awareness and no conception of any object at all, this is [a state of] great fundamental ignorance. In this way, delusion, the afflicted mental state, arises on the path.[463]

Through the twenty-four ancillary pith instructions that accord with these [three primary pith instructions], the experiences of the coemergence of the path will develop.[464]

Here, I myself, of **supreme liberation,**
And with a totally **delightful** mind,
Set forth in writing this memorandum of precise aspects
Of **all** the nectar of Ḍombipā's speech. {223}

This was compiled from the instruction manual composed by Jetsun Drakpa Gyeltsen.

47. Guidebook Entitled *The Perfection of the Path of Fierce Inner Heat*[465]

As for the instruction of Kṛṣṇacārin, which is the fourth of the *Eight Further Cycles of the Path*: After first taking refuge and setting the mind on enlightenment, you should be seated on a comfortable mat [and conclusively practice the four phases: continuum, mantra, pristine cognition, and secrecy].[466]

(i) The Phase of the Continuum

You should let the visualizations of the generation stage dissolve [into the syllable HŪṂ within the heart cakra, and finally] Vajravārāhī also dissolves into the syllable AṂ [within the navel cakra].[467] When light has emerged from that AṂ, you should then visualize the two active cakras and the four higher cakras in descending order;[468] and then you should visualize the three channels—the right and left channels blocked by their [respective] seed syllables.[469]

(ii) The Phase of Mantra

The wind of the rectum causes the fire of the triple intersection to blaze, and this ignites the syllable AṂ at the navel cakra. You should then gulp in the upper wind, along with spittle, and meditate that it is compressed as much as possible. Visualize that the fire of AṂ burns uncontrollably, and then, without drawing in the lower wind, the fire continues to blaze uncontrollably.[470]

Moving in association with the right channel, [at the heart cakra] this fire will burn the five lords of enlightened heritage and their five female consorts,[471] and then, exiting from the right nostril, it will be diffused. You should do this initially only once, and then increase the practice from ten times and one hundred times to an inconceivable number of times. The fire should then gradually enter through the left nostril of the Tathāgata, [seated] in the space [above your head], and several times reverse upward or downward. In this way, it will cause the four cakras of the Tathāgata and the nectars of the elements to melt together, and these are then drawn along in the manner of blood drawn by a leech. The nectar flow enters through your own left nostril and strikes the syllable AṂ at your navel cakra, which is strongly aroused. Opening the central channel, it melts the syllables HŪṂ, AṂ, and HAṂ [which are located at your heart, throat, and crown respectively].[472]

(iii) The Phase of Pristine Cognition

The vital essence of generative fluid [thus formed] becomes stronger and stronger, and then from the crown of the head this generative fluid descends and falls to the tip of the vajra (penis), and the experiences of bliss, radiance, and nonconceptualization are perfected through the four aspects of delight that are subsumed within delight, the four aspects of delight that are subsumed within supreme delight, {224} the four aspects of delight that are subsumed within absence of delight, and the four aspects of delight that are subsumed within coemergent delight. Once these sixteen aspects of delight have been perfected, the practice should be discontinued.[473]

(iv) The Phase of Secrecy

You should then concentrate on the space between the nostrils, without any bridge between them, resembling an empty egg. You should meditate that within your body, the wind, like the smoke of incense, wafts toward the tip of the nose but does not escape. Having meditated in that manner, the ḍākinīs should grant their blessing.[474]

Here I have definitively set forth in writing
The experiential cultivation of the vital points
That bring forth the meaning of the continuum of bliss,
Bestowing the naturally **delightful supreme liberation**
Of **all** things in the unique path of the fierce inner heat.

This was compiled from the instruction manual composed by Jetsun Drakpa Gyeltsen.

48. Guidebook Entitled *The Straightening of Crooked Posture*[475]

As for the instruction of Acyutakāṇha, which is the fifth of the *Eight Further Cycles of the Path*: after first taking refuge and setting the mind on enlightenment, you should be seated on a comfortable mat and be mindful of your meditational deity.[476]

Then you should practice the yogic exercises: Place your hands on the knees, forming the gesture of the adamantine fist. Turn the eyes upward, let the tongue touch the palate, close the teeth, and open the mouth. Then you should unite the upper and lower winds, press the abdomen strongly toward the spine, and then gradually raise the hands above the knees so that the elbows almost reach the knees. If the calf muscles are taut, they may slightly tremble, but the wind will be secured. Whenever you do this practice, whether counting the sessions or not, as soon as you have performed that yogic exercise to some extent, you will progress toward the meditative stability of radiance and emptiness, and thereupon you will have completed [the first yogic exercise].[477]

In order to stabilize this practice [there are other yogic exercises]: Place your left fist upon the heart, raise the right fist, and then unite [the upper and lower] winds. Then, reversing that, you should raise the left fist.[478]

Also, you should position the right and left hands as if stretching a bowstring; or else raise both hands toward the sky, or meditate, securing the gesture of the closed fist, with the arms crossed at the heart.[479]

In whatever manner you secure these yogic exercises, the ineffable meditative stability will arise in your mental continuum {225} and you will reach the conclusion of this practice.[480]

Here I have set forth in writing the core instruction
On the vital points of the swift and blissful short path to buddhahood,
Which reveal **supreme liberation** from bondage in the central channel,
The abiding nature that brings the joy of the four **delights**
To **all** the channels, vital essences and winds.

This was compiled from the instruction manual composed by Jetsun Drakpa Gyeltsen.

49. Guidebook Entitled *The Path of the Female Mudra*[481]

As for the instruction of Indrabhūti, which is the sixth of the *Eight Further Cycles of the Path*: After first taking refuge and setting the mind on enlightenment, you should undertake the yogic exercises of the physical body: Cover your knees with both hands, cast the eyes downward toward the tip of the nose, and draw in the lower wind strongly. Then you should drag the syllable HŪṂ, slow and long, from the chest and compress it. At that time, if you have a pain in the perinephric area, you should shake the abdomen, sit up,[482] and tie soft material such as silk around your waist. If you have a headache, you should shake your head. If you have a pain in the upper part of the body, you should rock it. If you train in this manner for one week, a fortnight, or twenty-one days, you will acquire control over the downward purgative wind to some extent.[483]

Until then, you should initially maintain the view that is imbued with the following four defining characteristics: permeation of material entities in the abiding nature, imperishability due to formative conditioning, unchangeability through the three times, and understanding of the natural expression of all fields of knowledge.[484]

If you engage in this experiential cultivation, all phenomena will be radiant in the essential nature of your own mind, and empty when they are examined without impediment; this is termed the *inseparability of radiance and emptiness*. Alternatively, this radiant nature will be intrinsically aware and empty when examined experientially; this is termed the *inseparability of awareness and emptiness*. Alternatively, your physical body will arise in the form of supreme bliss, and all appearances will arise as supreme bliss, but these are indeed empty when examined; this is termed the *inseparability of bliss and emptiness*. These should be known, initially through study and reflection, {226} and then they should be nurtured spontaneously and the application of the winds should be refined.[485]

Having refined the winds in the above manner, you should then attain accomplishment dependent on the seal of pristine cognition. You and your female partner should, contingent on the pride of the meditational deity, consecrate the vajra (penis) and lotus (vagina) as a cross (*bsnol ma*). That is to say, the practitioner should visualize a hexahedron that derives from the syllable E within the lotus of the female consort and, within it a red lotus with eight petals and anthers that derives from the syllable A, each petal of which is marked with A. The visualization should then be stabilized by mantra syllables: [the female] should visualize the five-pronged vajra of the male marked with HŪṂ, and meditate that it has a gemstone derived from OṂ; a jewel crest derived from SVĀ; and at its orifice both a downward-facing dark blue HŪṂ and an upward-facing dark red PHAṬ, which meet at their extremities. The visualizations should be stabilized by those mantra syllables.[486]

Next the very nature of desire comprising ordinary attachment is made into the path, and gradually the very nature of ordinary desire is transformed into the generative essence, aroused and motivated by great compassion. You should reflect that thereby sentient beings may attain buddhahood.[487]

Here the pith instructions that are crucially retained are fivefold: (i) the vital essence of the generative fluids should descend, (ii) it should be retained, and (iii) there should be meditation on bliss; (iv) it should be reversed and made to permeate [the channels]; and (v) it should be conserved, without diminution.

You should gaze upward with the eyes open, let the tongue touch the palate, compress the upper wind, and focus on pushing it down from the lower gate, which resembles a vase with a leaking base. You should then imagine that it is drawn back by the upward-facing PHAṬ and the downward-facing HŪṂ, and then you should actually draw it upward by means of twenty-one slow and long HŪṂ syllables, and so forth.[488]

[In order to enhance bliss,] the lower wind should be slightly contracted, and then, with the eyes open, the breath should slowly and over a long time be drawn upward. {227} It should then be exhaled through both nostrils. Thereby the entire body will be permeated with the meditative stability of bliss and emptiness.[489]

You should then experientially cultivate the method of the sixteen aspects of delight, stabilized from below.[490] When the generative essence is reversed from the very tip of the vajra (penis), the reversal should be made in accordance with the six aspects of transformation. That is to say, you should undertake the visualization while contracting the two thumbs and the two big toes; you should press the abdomen against the spine, turn the tongue inward, intone the long syllable HŪṂ followed by HIK, let the HŪṂ of meditative stability draw in the syllable PHAṬ, and carry it to the crown of the head. Since there will be a residue of generative essence, it should be drawn upward in this manner for a second or third time.[491]

Then you should undertake the practice of permeation. If the generative essence does not spread through the body, you may fall ill and the like. Therefore, you should allow it to permeate in the following manner: shake the head, rock the upper body, turn the waist, wave the arms, dance, or cry out, and so forth. In these ways the generative essence will be carried to its natural place.[492]

You should not abandon your female partner in the manner of the pious attendants. If she were abandoned, your vital essence would not increase, just as when a cow is not milked, its teats will dry up. Therefore, if the vital essence is milked, in the manner of a cow, it will increase; and buddhahood will emerge on the basis of the vital essence.[493]

You should not ejaculate the generative essence in the manner of ordinary persons. If it is ejaculated, all the defects mentioned in the tantras will emerge. Therefore, by means of the descent and reversal of the vital essence, you should visualize that the coemergent pristine cognition is actualized, and so attachment is rejected. Filled with the vital essence, the meditative stability of bliss and emptiness will be uninterrupted.[494]

Here I have set forth in writing, among the two traditions that give rise
To **supreme** maturation and **liberation**,
The method that carries onto the path
Simply the seal of pristine cognition—
The support of **delight** comprising **all** classes of female mudra. {228}

This was compiled from the instruction manual composed by Jetsun Drakpa Gyeltsen.

50. Guidebook Entitled *The Great Seal Devoid of Letters*[495]

As for the instruction manual of Vagīśvarakīrti, which is the seventh of the *Eight Further Cycles of the Path*: After first taking refuge and setting the mind on enlightenment, you should meditate on your teacher at the crown of your head. Then visualize the meditational deity and hold the mind by the rope of recollection, wherever it goes. Do not let it escape elsewhere. Nurture this very visualization and retain it without searching for the past or future.[496]

If you cannot retain it, focus on the tip of a [previously consecrated] wooden stick or focus on the sun and moon. If even through that technique you cannot retain it, you should turn your gaze from the tip of the nose or the eyebrows to the navel and refocus the mind. Thereby the mind will be focused.[497]

If you cannot focus the mind with mindfulness, conceptual thoughts will revolve, and finally you will lapse. If that were to happen, you would become a pious attendant, so propel your mind toward a pillar, vase, or some other object, and after withdrawing from that, focus it elsewhere. In brief, when you have control over the mind's abiding nature and restrain its diffusion through mindfulness, it will be disciplined.[498]

When you see a mirage and mistakenly take it for a lake, while going toward it you should think, "There is no water; it is a mirage," and when you reach it you will not apprehend anything. You should similarly have certainty concerning the enemies, conflicts, allies, and friendships that may manifest in dreams.[499]

If strong hatred arises, you should realize that it is fictitious, and think that thoughts of hatred are without inherent existence. This is the Great Seal devoid of letters. Letters and conceptual thoughts are inexpressible. The inexpressible is the Great Seal.[500]

In the sky in front, you should offer to the teacher and meditational deity your enemies, friends, and even your own body, and train in the thought that these too are mind, that mind is a magical display, and that this magical display is without inherent existence.[501] As for the sufferings of being roasted and burned that denizens of hell in the underworld experience, these too are mind; that mind is a magical display, and that magical display is without inherent existence. Then again, {229} you should observe the buddha fields of the ten directions—including the east, south, west, and north—with Buddha Vairocana above, gazing upon the one hundred thousand buddhas below; these too are mind, that mind is a magical display, and that magical display is without inherent existence.[502]

You should intermingle this practice with afflicted mental states such as hatred. In one of those directions, for example, you should be attentive that hatred is a magical display or a dream, and realize spontaneously that all appearances and sounds, cyclic existence and nirvana, are at one and the same time the Great Seal devoid of letters and without inherent existence.[503]

When you practice without distinguishing between meditative equipoise and postmeditation, when appearances arise as the master, when afflicted mental states are carried on the path, when conceptual thoughts arise as pristine cognition, when the abyss of the six realms is cut off, and the citadel of the six classes of beings is subjugated, at that time you will realize that the Great Seal is the real nature, devoid of letters, transcending sounds and conceptual thoughts. This is reminiscent of effortlessly meeting a former acquaintance, without ideation or scrutiny.[504]

Here I have clearly and concisely set forth in writing
The method of instruction that reaches **supreme liberation,**
The mystery that is devoid of **all** letters,
The coemergent nucleus of **delight.**

This was compiled from the instruction manual composed by Jetsun Drakpa Gyeltsen.

51. Guidebook Entitled *The Attainment in Proximity to a Stupa*[505]

As for the instruction of Nāgārjuna, which is the eighth of the *Eight Further Cycles of the Path*: After first taking refuge and setting the mind on enlightenment, you should let the mind rest—relaxed, fresh, loose, naturally clear,[506] and uncontrived. Do not search for any virtuous or nonvirtuous actions and so forth that the mind may have acquired. Your mind should be focused thereby, but if it is not focused, post a sentinel and allow it to stray. In this way, your mind will [naturally] return. By practicing in that manner, it will be the norm that you focus on the innate state, in the manner of a hand that is placed wherever a gift is given.[507]

So, in this modality of uncontrived placement, you should inspect your own mind and be mindful that since it has neither beginning nor end, it resembles space; {230} since it has neither birth nor death, it resembles space; since it has neither going nor coming, it resembles space; and since it has neither middle nor extremes, it resembles space.[508]

If the mind does become diffused, you should not search for the past, you should not welcome the future, and you should be mindful of encountering the present. The essential instruction is that you should cultivate certainty in the absence of conceptual elaboration where the three times are without arising, ceasing, or abiding; and juxtapose the experiences of meditative equipoise with conduct during postmeditation.[509]

Here I have set forth in writing this quintessential crucial instruction
That is to be cultivated with confidence,
That generates **delight** in one's own mind, in **all** respects,
And that reveals **supreme liberation** from bondage.

This was compiled from the instruction manual composed by Jetsun Drakpa Gyeltsen.

52. Guidebook Entitled *The Mingling of Sutra and Tantra*[510]

After first taking refuge and setting the mind on enlightenment: You should refine the essential physical posture by means of meditative stability and clearly visualize your ordinary mental associations as your [meditational] deity.[511] The seed syllable within your heart is then diffused and absorbed, and its rays of light, through their upward diffusion, are offered to the sublime beings [at the crown of your head], entering into their hearts and then returning, so that the blessing of nondual pristine cognition enters into yourself. Through the outward diffusion of these rays of light, you should also visualize that the entire inhabited world is refined as the celestial palace, and its sentient inhabitants as male and female deities. You should then meditate on the teacher [on the crown of your head] and let [all the deities] dissolve therein.[512]

Then, confounded with great astonishment, you should inspect phenomenal existence and profoundly develop the certainty that all things of phenomenal existence are fictitious, like a magical display. You should not immediately contrive anything but determine absolutely that your doubts have been naturally pure from the beginning. You will then become resplendent in natural radiance, dissolved in natural liberation. This is termed the *liberation in the buddha body of reality, without duality of cyclic existence and nirvana*.[513]

Next, you should develop compassion for those who do not know and have not realized this. {231} The indivisible nature, so designated because it is the disposition of reality's expanse, is said to be "imbued with the essence of emptiness and compassion."[514]

Thereby you will effortlessly traverse the supreme path with natural momentum that is the essential meaning of the path. When definitively appraised from top to bottom and dynamically assessed from bottom to top, this comprises (i) the path of provisions, including the virtuous actions that are cultivated and retained; (ii) the path of connections that elucidates and determines general concepts dependent on the appropriate mental states of meditative concentration; (iii) the path of insight that is actualized thereby; (iv) the path of cultivation in which the propensities of afflicted mental states and the subtle impulses of the obscuration of knowledge subside due to that experience; and (v) the path of conclusion in which each subtle stain also becomes quiescent in reality's expanse, the enlightened attributes of renunciation and realization are perfected, and enlightened activities emerge spontaneously for the sake of sentient beings.[515]

This path should not be bestowed on those of feeble intelligence, who cannot connect with the meaning of the abiding nature. It should be retained by spiritual mentors and bestowed on those who understand the nature of cyclic existence, have abandoned the egotism of this life, and engage in practice in a concentrated manner.[516]

Here I have integrated in written form
The path that brings **delight** to the mind,
The method of guidance on **supreme liberation**,
Absorbing and mingling together the essence
Of **all** the sutras and tantras.

This was compiled from ancient writings.

53. Guidebook Entitled *The Dispelling of Obstacles due to External Demons*[517]

This instruction derives from the cycle of the *Dispelling of the Three Obstacles*. After first taking refuge and setting the mind on enlightenment: You should meditate on yourself as the deity, and from the syllable HŪṂ within your heart, light rays are transformed into a vajra, the center of which is marked with HŪṂ, and then diffused, densely filling all the pores of the body. With powerful resonance you should repeatedly intone HŪṂ, long and strong, and visualize that the light again is diffused, forming an adamantine wall in all the ten directions. {232} Then you should continue to intone HŪṂ. This is the best protection from the three sorts of external demonic force, for the mind does not waver from reality's expanse.[518]

Here I have also illustrated in writing
This guidance of **supreme liberation**
That generates **delight**, having dispelled
All obstacles due to external demons.

This was compiled from ancient writings.

54. Guidebook Entitled *The Dispelling of Obstacles due to the Agitation of the Physical Body by the Elements*[519]

This instruction derives from the cycle of the *Dispelling of the Three Obstacles*. After first taking refuge and setting the mind on enlightenment: You should visualize upon a moon cushion in the case of fevers of the upper body and on a sun cushion in the case of colds of the lower body, a five-pronged vajra within an enclosure formed by the central channel that is the axis of vitality, and within which there is a vital essence, the size of an average pea, at the center of which there is a sealed syllable HŪṂ, the size of a barley grain, or alternatively your root teacher, as appropriate.[520]

Next, you should exhale the stale air three times [and unite the upper and lower winds]. If you meditate for approximately a single session with clear and precise focus that [the wind] does not encircle the HŪṂ or your teacher but encircles the vajra and the vital essence, there is no doubt that this will protect against and alleviate all illnesses that agitate the physical elementals.[521]

Here I have also illustrated in writing
This guidance of **supreme liberation**
That generates **delight**, having dispelled
All obstacles that agitate the physical elements.

This was compiled from ancient writings.

55. Guidebook Entitled *The Dispelling of the Obstacles of Meditative Stability and Mind*[522]

This instruction derives from the cycle of the *Dispelling of the Three Obstacles*. After first taking refuge and setting the mind on enlightenment: The originally pure nature of your own mind constitutes the four seals. That is to say, it constitutes the commitment seal (*samayamudrā, dam tshig gi phyag rgya*), in which radiance and emptiness are indivisible. Here, "commitment" (*dam tshig*) implies the nontransgressing of radiance that is its defining characteristic, "hand" (*phyag*) suggests natural purity, and "seal" (*rgya*) suggests pervasion. "The nature of your own mind" also constitutes the phenomenal seal (*dharmamudrā, chos kyi phyag rgya*), in which appearances and emptiness are indivisible—appearances being the "attributes" (*chos*) of mind. It constitutes the action seal (*karmamudrā, las kyi phyag rgya*), in which bliss and emptiness are indivisible—"action" (*las*) implying contaminated bliss. {223} Lastly, it constitutes the Great Seal (*mahāmudrā, phyag rgya chen po*), in which all things are intrinsically empty—"great" (*chen po*) implying all things of radiant appearance and phenomenal existence. It is impossible for yogins who knows this to die [prematurely] because they are without obstacles.[523]

Here I have also illustrated in writing
This guidance of **supreme liberation**
That generates **delight**, having dispelled
All obstacles of meditative stability and mind.

This was compiled from ancient writings.

56. Guidebook Entitled *The Great Seal Dispelling the Three Sorts of Suffering*[524]

After you have taken refuge and set the mind on enlightenment, there are five profound essentials: (i) the profound essential for cultivating the innate truth is ascertainment of the meaning of the continuum [of the mind]; (ii) the profound essential for those who have not focused the mind is internal focus; (iii) the profound essential for success in maintaining [this stability] is skillful means; (iv) the profound essential for cutting off dangerous passageways of the mental faculty is decisive determination;[525] and (v) the dedication of merit, free from the poisons, is the profound essential for all.[526]

1. Ascertainment of the Continuum of the Mind

[The first of these five profound essentials] concerns the three sorts of suffering. With respect to the nature of cyclic existence, when the innate mind is perceived, if you understand the nature of the suffering of suffering, you will attain the buddha body of emanation. If you understand the nature of the suffering of change, you will attain the buddha body of perfect resource. If you understand the nature of the suffering of formative predispositions, you will attain the buddha body of reality. By understanding that all things are without inherent existence, you will be liberated from the three obscurations and attain the buddha body of essentiality.[527]

[As far as the experiential cultivation of this profound essential is concerned,] all that appears and exists, cyclic existence and nirvana, is mind. In terms of the skillful refinement of its radiance and emptiness, emptiness [is the nature of mind]. You should purify the poison of appearances, aware that appearances are the uncontrived innate mind, just as the sky and its clouds are indivisible. However all things without exception may appear internally and wherever all things without exception may appear externally, they are indeed of a single savor.[528]

2. Internal Focus

[As for the second of the five profound essentials:] You should focus the mind on the vital essence upon a moon cushion at the heart cakra and observe [the nature of the unelaborate mind]. During the day, bliss and emptiness or awareness and emptiness will arise; and during the night, you should focus on luminosity.[529]

Then you should focus the mind on the vital essence at the tip of the nose. During the day, radiance and emptiness or appearance and emptiness will arise; and during the night, you should focus on dreams.[530]

3. Skillful Means

[As for the third of the five profound essentials:] By intrinsically knowing the abiding nature of reality, you should leave it unchanged and also maintain it naturally in its own place. {234} Then you should engage in the skillful refinement that intensely maintains its stability.

4. Decisive Determination

[As for the fourth of those five profound essentials:] this includes the decisive determination that the parameters of your understanding will be resolved [through the introduction given by your teacher] and nothing beyond that will be found; and the decisive determination that, having engaged in experiential refinement by means of reflection and meditation, you will not be destitute.[531]

5. The Dedication of Merit

[As for the last of those five profound essentials:] without keeping [the fruit of this practice] to yourself, you should seal it by dedicating the merit for the sake of others.[532]

Here I have set forth in writing,
As a topic of aspiration for anyone whomsoever,
This guidance on the path that generates **supreme** natural **liberation**,
The disposition of **delight** and bliss
Regarding the source of **all** suffering.

This was compiled from ancient writings.

57. Guidebook Entitled *The Clear Recollection of the Innate State*[533]

After first taking refuge and setting the mind on enlightenment: You should be seated comfortably, with your body adopting the [sevenfold] posture of Vairocana completely. Then meditate on yourself as the deity, with the teacher on the crown of your head. After paying respectful homage, you should then dissolve [the visualization of the teacher into yourself].[534]

Next, after exhaling three stale breaths, [you should visualize yourself as] the supporting maṇḍala [of the celestial palace] and the supported maṇḍala [of the deities]: The soles of your feet are the adamantine ground and the crown of your head is the crest of the crossed vajra. Your rib cage is the adamantine tent, the pores of the skin are the network of ramparts, the nails are the burning volcanos, the open legs are the maṇḍala of wind, the channel of triple intersection is the maṇḍala of fire, the navel is the maṇḍala of water, the heart is the maṇḍala of earth, the spine is Mount Meru, the four joints of your double arm span are the symmetrical four corners of the walls, the eyes are the five bands [forming the walls], the teeth are the swags and half-length swags, the tongue and the lips are the platforms of the offering goddesses, the eight legs are the eight pillars, and the movements of the winds of the four elements from the four directions of the channel branches of the heart cakra are the four gates.[535]

At the secret cakra is green Amoghasiddhi, holding a sword and a bell—his female consort holds a curved knife and a skull, and they have an entourage of thirty-two female deities. At the navel cakra is yellow Ratnasambhava, holding a gemstone and a bell—his female consort holds a curved knife and a skull, and they have an entourage of sixty-four female deities. At the heart cakra is blue Akṣobhya, holding a vajra and a bell—his female consort holds a curved knife and a skull, and they have an entourage of eight female deities. At the throat cakra is red Amitābha, holding a lotus and a bell—his female consort holds a curved knife and a skull, and they have an entourage of sixteen female deities. At the forehead is white Vairocana, holding a wheel and a bell—his female consort holds a curved knife {235} and a skull, and they have an entourage of thirty-two female deities. At the protuberance is white Vajradhara, his legs in the adamantine posture, his hands in the gesture of teaching the sacred doctrine and holding a vajra and a bell—his female consort holds a curved knife and a skull, and they have an entourage of four female deities. The eyes are Kṣitigarbha, the ears are Vajrapāṇi, the nose is Ākāśagarbha, the tongue is Lokeśvara, the body is Nivāraṇaviṣkambhin, and the mental faculty is Samantabhadra. In sequence, these [male bodhisattvas] are embraced by the [corresponding female bodhisattvas], from Rūpavajrā to Dhātvīśvarī.[536]

All of these deities do not need to be generated from their [respective] seed syllables. They do not need empowerment, invitation, or a request to be present. You should recollect that they are naturally present, and from them there arises the pristine cognition of appearance and emptiness. That is to say, the vase empowerment will have been conferred.[537]

Next, the fire of the rectum blazes forth in the form of the short syllable A. The fire is radiant, the heat is empty, and it blazes with three attributes.[538] The deities are radiant like a lamp penetrating darkness. You should meditate on [the uniting of the upper and lower] winds, and then there will arise the pristine cognition of radiance and emptiness. That is to say, the secret empowerment will have been conferred.[539]

Next, the fire melts the syllable HAṂ. You should meditate that it flows [vertically] like the thread of a web, and there will arise the pristine cognition of bliss and emptiness. That is to say, the empowerment of discerning pristine cognition will have been conferred.[540]

Lastly, all phenomena of impure cyclic existence become the pure deities and the celestial palace. You should not meditate but simply remain with unwavering mindfulness, cognizing the innate state in the nature of the Great Seal where all things—appearance and emptiness, radiance and emptiness, and awareness and emptiness—are intrinsically empty. Then the pristine cognition of intrinsic emptiness will arise. That is to say, the fourth empowerment will have been conferred.

Such are the pith instructions concerning the meditation on the four empowerments conferred in a single sitting.[541]

Here I have set forth in writing
The essentials of the meditation on **supreme** radiance,
The method of nurturing natural unchanging **liberation**,
The disposition of the four **delights**
Present in **all** the innate deities.

This was compiled from ancient writings concerning the four empowerments.

58. Guidebook Entitled *The Three Purities*[542]

After first taking refuge and setting the mind on enlightenment, you should practice the three purities:

(i) The Purity of the Real Nature

When all external and internal entities are examined, there exists neither space nor time, {236} and no singularity is established in respect of the external and internal aspects of space and time. When there is no singularity, multiplicity will not arise. Their presence will not be established because there is neither singularity nor multiplicity, and when there is nothing that is present, neither will their absence be established in relation to that. Therefore, you should meditate, determining without doubt that all things are the natural expression of mind, free from conceptual elaboration.[543] You should also meditate thinking compassionately of sentient beings who have not realized that.[544] After meditating in that manner, you will not be inclined toward erroneous views, and the supramundane pristine cognition will arise.[545]

(ii) The Purity of an Individual Deity

Next, you should meditate on the generation stage, which concerns the purity of an individual deity, alone [and without consort], in the manner of a solitary hero. You should vibrantly visualize that the appearance of this deity is without inherent existence, in the manner of the reflection in a mirror. You should visualize with your focus on the central eye [of pristine cognition] in particular, and then meditate, as before, on all three eyes, the entire head, the entire body, and the seat. Having developed the clear and expanded visualization of the deity, you should meditate that this comes to permeate all worlds; and after that, you should gradually visualize that the deity contracts smaller and smaller, within a space the size of a mustard seed. By accomplishing that visualization, you will perfect the generation stage.[546]

(iii) The Purity of Intrinsic Awareness

Lastly, you should meditate on the purity of intrinsic awareness. To that end, you should refine the nine branches of meditative concentration.[547] [Specifically, when wind is refined in meditative concentration,] there are seven steps: [(i) You should meditate on the winds of exertion and life breath that regulate inhalation, pause, and exhalation.][548] [As for exhalation:] (ii) you should block the wind of exertion and exhale the wind of life breath,[549] (iii) you should exhale forcefully through both [nostrils],[550] and (iv) you should exhale noisily from the mouth.[551] [As for filling the channels with wind:] (v) you should block [the nostrils alternately] with the wind of exertion and fill [the central channel] with the wind of life breath,[552] and (vi) you should fill the central channel, breathing silently through the mouth.[553] Lastly, (vii) you should unite the [upper and lower] winds.[554]

For the practice of the fierce inner heat, your body should adopt the crouching posture, and you should secure the sealing gesture of the opposing stoves. Four finger widths below the navel, the fire of the channel of fierce inner heat is subtle, resembling one-hundredth part of a horse's tail hair. You should meditate that it has a fierce heat measuring half a finger width. Then you should compress the upper wind and bind the lower wind. If you cannot do this, breathe in slowly, and then by your practice of that meditation, a degree of warmth will arise. Once this has been perfected, {237} the warmth will arise without interruption and bliss will arise throughout the body.[555]

With regard to the yoga of the vital essence: Within the heart cakra, upon a moon disk the size of a round nail, you should focus on a white vital essence that is round, the size of a pea. Having experienced that, you should meditate as before on the vital essence in the space between the eyebrows. Having experienced that, you should meditate on a red vital essence within the secret cakra, and having experienced that, you should connect those three vital essences with a subtle thread of light. Next, when breathing out, you should meditate that the power of [the vital essence of] the secret cakra comes to rest in the heart cakra, and when you breathe in, the power of [the vital essence] of the space between the eyebrows comes to rest in the heart cakra. Thereupon you should meditate that the power of [the vital essence of] the heart cakra extends throughout all the elements within the ancillary channels of the physical body.[556]

[There then follows the method of meditating diversely on these three yogas of the winds, fierce inner heat, and vital essence:] Dependent on the cakras, within the physical body, there are three channels: the central channel, which is subtle; the right channel, which is red; and the left channel, which is white. Visualize that at the center of the sixty-four channel branches of the navel cakra there is a syllable A,[557] at the center of the eight channel branches in the heart there is a HŪṂ, at the center of the sixteen channel branches in the throat there is an OṂ, and at the center of the thirty-two channel branches in the crown there is a HAṂ.[558]

Next, you should arouse the wind, so that the blazing fire moves from the right channel and incinerates the cakra of the heart. It then also incinerates the cakra of the throat. Then the fire exits [your body] via the crown of the head and enters the feet of the Buddha [seated above your head] via the right ankle. Drawn by the power of the fire, the Buddha's generative essence then descends via the crown of your head, entering your left channel, and penetrating your crown and throat cakras and the syllable A of the navel cakra, from which subtle rays of light then enter within the central channel. From the syllable HAṂ at the crown cakra visualize that a subtle vital essence then flows downward. The crucial point is that it should permeate the channels and seed syllables within your body. Then the upper and lower winds should be united.[559]

The signs that this has been perfected are that the wind can remain to a certain extent within the channels, it can be exhaled at will to a certain extent, that ailments of the upper and lower body can be expelled respectively from within the upper and lower body, that the vital essences will increase, that the extrasensory powers will emerge, that the complexion is excellent, that miraculous abilities can be revealed, that wind and mind can be controlled, {238} that the supramundane pristine cognition will arise by refining the path of the third empowerment, and that the path may be traversed as far as the buddha level.[560]

Having absorbed **all** that is within the three purities,
Here I have definitively set forth in writing
The **supreme liberation** of the knots
Of the genuine continuum endowed with the four **delights**,
According to this aspect of the Path and Its Fruition
That have been excluded from the primary instructions.

This was compiled from the instruction manual of Chogyel Pakpa.

59. Guidebook Entitled *The Twenty-Nine Essential Visualizations of Self-Consecration*[561]

After taking refuge and setting the mind on enlightenment: The first essential visualization is of the fierce inner heat. You should visualize yourself as the deity according to the generation stage. With the vital points of your physical body, you should adopt the crouching posture, with both arms embracing the knees, and the head should be suitably positioned—neither too high nor too low. Next, at the middle of the navel cakra there arises a red AṂ, and in the middle of the heart cakra a blue HŪṂ. The channel branches are without any arrangement of letters, but these two cakras are connected via the subtle central channel. You should compress the wind and meditate that the fire of the AṂ burns, melting the HŪṂ.[562]

The second essential visualization is that at the middle of the cakra of emanation in the navel there is a syllable AṂ, with four stacked letters in the channel branches of the four cardinal directions and a single syllable in each of the four intermediate directions. Meditate that all these nine syllables assume the form of fire, and then compress the wind.[563]

The third essential visualization is that at the middle of the cakra of emanation in the navel there is a syllable AṂ, with two vowels in each of the [eight] channel branches. These assume the form of fire, and then you should compress the [upper] wind. Finally, [the peripheral vowels] should be dissolved into thc AṂ.[564]

The fourth essential visualization is that at the middle of the four cakras are respectively the syllables AṂ, HŪṂ, OṂ, and HAṂ, with the eight phonetic sets of syllables on the eight channel branches. [The four main syllables are respectively] white, blue, red, and white. When breathing out, you should visualize that they rise; when breathing in, you should visualize that they fall; and when pausing, you should meditate that the [peripheral sets of syllables] dissolve into their respective [central] seed syllables; and then you should compress the wind.[565]

The fifth essential visualization is that at the middle of the cakra of emanation in the navel there is the syllable AṂ, with the eight phonetic sets of syllables on the eight channel branches. You should compress the [lower] wind and meditate, visualizing that the seed syllables are moving [upward].[566]

The sixth essential visualization is that at the middle of the navel cakra of emanation there is the syllable AṂ, at the heart cakra of the phenomenal wheel there is VAṂ, at the throat cakra of perfect resource there is LAṂ, and at the crown cakra of supreme bliss there is YAṂ—their colors corresponding to the four respective elements. You should dissolve the wind into the AṂ and compress [the upper wind] as much as possible.[567]

The seventh essential visualization is that at the middle of the navel cakra of emanation there is the syllable AṂ with A, KA, CA, ṬA, TA, PA, YA, and ŚA at the eight channel branches; and at the middle of the heart cakra of the phenomenal wheel there is the syllable HŪṂ. [When breathing in,] you should dissolve the wind into the AṂ, {239} and [when breathing out,] you should clearly visualize and meditate on the HŪṂ.[568]

The eighth essential visualization is that at the middle of the heart cakra of the phenomenal wheel there is the syllable HŪṂ [or AṂ],[569] with A, Ā, AṂ, and AḤ in the four cardinal directions, adorned with vital essences, and Ṛ, Ṝ, Ḷ, and Ḹ in the four intermediate directions. You should meditate that when the wind is inhaled, it should be dissolved into the syllable HŪṂ or AṂ.[570]

The ninth essential visualization is that at the middle of the heart cakra of the phenomenal wheel, upon a moon disk the size of a split pea, there is the white syllable HŪṂ, the size of a mustard seed. You should compress the [upper] wind and meditate on that.[571]

The tenth essential visualization is that at the middle of the four cakras are respectively AṂ, HŪṂ, OṂ, and HAṂ, while the channel branches are without any arrangement of letters. You should meditate on [the contraction of the lower] wind and visualize that the fire [of pristine cognition] blazes forth, melting the syllable HŪṂ.[572]

The eleventh essential visualization is that at the middle of the navel cakra of emanation there is the syllable AṂ, its channel branches without any arrangement of letters. [When you breathe out,] the AṂ blazes as fire, which is inverted upward from the heart cakra, opening the space between the eyebrows and opening the vital points of the Tathāgata's body [above the crown of your head]. A stream of generative fluid then emerges and is absorbed into the AṂ at your navel. Then the upper and lower winds should be united.[573]

The twelfth essential visualization is that at the middle of the navel cakra of emanation there is the syllable OṂ, and its eight channel branches each have two of the sixteen seed syllables beginning with RA and HA, which then rise upward [to the heart cakra]. You should compress the [upper] wind and meditate on that.[574]

The thirteenth essential visualization is that at the middle of the heart cakra [of the phenomenal wheel], you should meditate that there is the syllable HŪṂ, with five channel branches, [marked] with the white syllables RA, HA, SA, YA, and E. Then you should compress the wind.[575]

The fourteenth essential visualization is that at the base of the uvula on the palate there is a four-petal lotus at the center of which is the syllable OṂ, with the red syllables RA, HA, SA, and YA on the four channel branches. During exhalation, the wind should be absorbed into these [five] seed syllables, so that it is not permitted to reenter.[576]

The fifteenth essential visualization is that A, KA, CA, ṬA, TA, PA, YA, and ŚA are arrayed at the branches of the heart cakra of the phenomenal wheel, and at its center there is a white vital essence. You should meditate that as the wind of life breath is inhaled, these move downward and that they are drawn upward by the wind of exertion.[577]

The sixteenth essential visualization is that at the middle of the navel cakra of emanation, at the middle of conjoined moon and sun disks the size of a split pea, there is a white vital essence the size of a mustard seed. When the breath is exhaled, you should meditate that the yellow wind of the earth element [is diffused, and during inhalation it] is absorbed into that vital essence. Similarly [during exhalation], the white wind of the water element, the red wind of the fire element, and the green wind of the wind element are diffused [and during inhalation they are absorbed into that vital essence].[578]

The seventeenth essential visualization is that at the middle of the heart cakra of the phenomenal wheel, you should visualize a white vital essence the size of a mustard seed. When breath is inhaled, it is absorbed into the left side [of that vital essence]. Then the [upper] wind should be compressed.[579]

The eighteenth essential visualization is that {240} at the middle of each of the four cakras you should meditate on a vital essence, and then you should compress the [upper] wind.[580]

The nineteenth essential visualization is that at the four cakras are the syllables AṂ, HŪṂ, OṂ, and HAṂ, which are [yellow,] blue, red, and white. When the breath is exhaled, rays of light are diffused through the two nostrils; and when it is inhaled, you should meditate repeatedly that [it is dependent on] those syllables.[581]

The twentieth essential visualization is that you should visualize the primordially abiding maṇḍalas of the four elements, draw in the [lower] wind, and meditate that the wind causes the fire element to burn, that that in turn causes the water element to boil, that the earth element melts, and that its vapor causes the syllable HAṂ at the crown cakra to melt.[582]

The twenty-first essential visualization is that at the navel cakra of emanation there is the syllable AṂ, with A, KA, CA, ṬA, TA, PA, YA, and ŚA at its channel branches, and with, at their periphery, two sets of [the sixteen] vowels [that rotate counterclockwise] and thirty-two consonants, minus HA and KṢA, [that rotate clockwise]. At the heart cakra of the phenomenal wheel there is the syllable HŪṂ, with Ā, Ī, U, and E in the four cardinal directions and YA, VA, RA, and LA in the four intermediate directions. At the throat cakra of perfect resource, there is the syllable OṂ on the inside with A, I, U, and E on the periphery, excluding the neuter vowels. At the crown cakra of supreme bliss there is the syllable HAṂ, with two sets of vowels on its channel branches. You should also visualize the two side channels. Then you should draw in the lower wind, and this causes fire to blaze. The syllable AṂ is set on fire, and the two cakras [above it] are incinerated. The fire is inverted three times, so that the syllable HAṂ [at the crown] is incinerated and a flow of generative fluid descends, causing the seed syllables to revive. [On contacting] the AṂ, it reignites, and in a most subtle form it burns through the central channel, causing the HAṂ to melt. Then you should unite the [upper and lower] winds.[583]

The twenty-second essential visualization is that you should visualize at the middle of the navel cakra of emanation the syllable AṂ. You should close the round anal orifice of the lower wind and focus consciousness on the AṂ.

Finally, the AṂ ignites, causing the generative fluid [of the upper cakras] to emerge at the navel.[584]

The twenty-third essential visualization is that at the heart cakra of the phenomenal wheel there is the syllable HŪṂ, with the syllables OṂ, TRAṂ, HRĪḤ, and KHAṂ in the four cardinal directions. You should dissolve the wind into those five seed syllables and compress [the upper wind].[585]

The twenty-fourth essential visualization is that at the heart cakra of the phenomenal wheel there is upon a moon disk the white syllable HŪṂ. Your inhaled breath should be absorbed into the HŪṂ, the upper wind should be compressed, and the HŪṂ then ignites. Finally, the naturally originated pristine cognition will arise.[586]

The twenty-fifth essential visualization concerns the yoga of the vital essence. At the fontanel there is a downward-facing white HŪṂ upon a split-open moon disk, and below it there is a downward-facing white SUṂ. When exhaling breath, you should visualize that from the SUṂ {241} nectar descends like a stream of milk. It should be reversed at the uvula and savored.[587]

The twenty-sixth essential visualization concerns the vital essences of the ten orifices.[588] You should visualize that at the heart cakra there is a white HŪṂ upon a moon disk, the light of which, when exhaling breath, penetrates all the nine orifices—ten including the space between the eyebrows—like a lamp penetrating darkness. You should then meditate that [when inhaling breath,] the rain of vital essence again flows down.[589]

The twenty-seventh essential visualization is that at the heart cakra of the phenomenal wheel there is a moon disk. When you exhale breath, [its light] illuminates the thirty-two [channels]; and when inhaling breath, you should meditate again and again that all the channels are filled with the vital essence of generative fluid.[590]

The twenty-eighth essential visualization concerns the vital essence of the fontanel. There is a white HŪṂ on a moon disk at the heart and a white HAṂ at the fontanel. When you exhale breath, [the light of the HŪṂ] touches the HAṂ, and you should meditate repeatedly that nectar flows from the HAṂ.[591]

The twenty-ninth essential visualization is that the AṂ at the navel cakra of emanation and the downward-facing HŪṂ at the heart cakra of the phenomenal wheel are connected through the extremely fine [central channel]. The AṂ causes the fire to blaze, and you should then focus on [the generative fluid] dripping from the HŪṂ. After that, you should meditate, [arousing the lower] wind [to some extent].[592]

Here I have expanded in written form
The list of visualizations for self-consecration,
Which is the exegetical basis of **all** the tantras,
The **supreme** path of great **delight** and coemergent **liberation**.

This was compiled from the ancient writings of Drokmi.

60. Guidebook Entitled *The Exegesis of the Concealed Path*[593]

After first taking refuge and setting the mind on enlightenment: You should prepare [an anal plug in the form of] a cone, made of clay, two thumbs in width and four digits in height, with a slightly tapering top, wrapped in silk, and so forth.[594] Then, resting on a pillow, your body should adopt the posture that resembles the ear of an elephant.[595] You should position the aforementioned plug directly below your anus, support it with your thighs alternately, and draw in the lower wind. [Then, after closing the anus, you should rest upon the plug.][596] If this is uncomfortable, you should reduce its size; and if it is comfortable, you should hold it in place.[597]

Next, you should visualize yourself as Hevajra, with your lungs assuming the form of a white lotus with eight downward-facing petals, your liver a dark red lotus with upward-facing petals, and from the place where these two lotuses virtually overlap at their tips, there appears the celestial palace. {242} At its center, the knot of the three channels [is marked with] HŪṂ, the essential nature of compassion, and from the HŪṂ you should simply visualize that there arises blue Vajraheruka, with bared fangs and three eyes—the right one like the sun, the left one like the moon, and the central one like Rāhu. With his right leg he oppresses the sun, not permitting the blood (*rakta*) of the right channel to spill; and with his left leg he oppresses the moon, not permitting the generative fluid of the left channel to spill. The transcendent lord is seated in the central channel, which is the pure nature of Rāhu, and in the midst of a blazing fire of pristine cognition, which is the pure nature of Ketu. His two hands hold the vajra and bell, crossed at the heart, inducting the winds of the sun and moon side channels into the central channel. The protuberance of his head holds together the three channels of the sun, moon, and planetary divinity [Rāhu], and he has six ornaments, symbolizing the six transcendent perfections.[598]

Next, you should cover your knees with your hands, shake the abdomen, rest the tongue against the palate, open your eyes slightly, draw in the upper wind with HIK, and compress it with the hissing sound of SIB.[599] Then you should draw in the lower wind and meditate, nurturing this practice by means of the appropriate diet and regimen. Externally appearances will then become completely white;[600] warmth and bliss will arise within the body, and your mind will directly reach the initial absorption of the sensory elements,[601] which is free from the subject-object dichotomy.

After one month, signs such as smoke will emerge. After three months, your body will become as light as a sheet of cotton and your mind will be free from the subject-object dichotomy. There will be no distinction between meditative equipoise and postmeditation, and you will directly reach the middling absorption of the sensory elements. Then appearances will arise as deities and the deities of the five palaces will become radiant. You should maintain nonconceptual meditative stability during meditative equipoise and during postmeditation; all sorts of extrasensory powers will emerge. In this way, you will reach the final absorption of the sensory elements. The path of insight will then arise through the power of that auspicious circumstance, in the manner in which the eyes are opened by a cataract scalpel.[602]

If one digit of the aforementioned plug is absorbed [into the anus], bliss will arise. If two digits are absorbed, the bliss will exceed that. If three digits are absorbed, there will be greater and greater bliss. And if four digits are absorbed, the path of insight will arise, but the plug should not be absorbed up to five digits because that would cause obstacles to the life span. {243} It is said that this plug will cause the penis to contract of its own volition.[603]

With regard to occasional activities: (i) After meals, you should refrain from meditating for a while, until the residue of the meal reaches the stomach. (ii) Then you should support the sides of your kidneys in accordance with the pith instructions. (iii) [In addition,] for the practice concerning the crown of the head, you should secure your head on the ground with your legs raised upward, and then repeatedly raise up and contract the legs. (iv) In order to enhance the physical constituents, you should cross your feet at the nape of the neck. Or else you should cross your ten toes at the nape of the neck. The eyes should remain wide open, and the upper and lower winds should then be united. It is important to turn the head to the right and left, with the eyes focused upward.[604]

Here I have definitively set forth in writing
The method of naturally obtaining **supreme liberation**,
This tract of exegesis, **delightful** to behold,
Concerning the concealed [path], hidden to **all**.

This was compiled from the instruction manual of Chojé Sakya Paṇḍita.

61. Guidebook Entitled *The Elucidation of the Symbolic Meaning*[605]

After first taking refuge and setting the mind on enlightenment: [The preliminaries entailing] the three refinements, three meditations, and the three points that hone the essentials should be revealed.[606]

(i) [As for the main practice, you should first determine in accordance with the view of discriminative awareness] that mind is a magical display, in accordance with a single example—the moon's reflection in water—[and establish that] it is an inexpressible, auspicious circumstance; and then you should meditate, associating the four [aspects of empowerment] with that single example.[607]

(ii) Then, in order to experientially cultivate that view through skillful means, you should meditate that the vase empowerment, the secret empowerment, the empowerment of discerning pristine cognition, and the fourth empowerment are conferred in the maṇḍala of the physical body, comprising either 157 deities, or five palaces, or the central male and female deities. The diffusion and absorption of the light rays within their hearts cause the inhabited world and its sentient inhabitants to appear respectively as the maṇḍala and the deities.[608] In accordance with the four verses that concern the receiving [of empowerment] in the middle-length empowerment [of Hevajra], you may perfectly receive [all four] empowerments in a single stream of generative essence.[609]

Specifically, in the case of the secret empowerment, you should meditate on (i) the seven applications of wind, or on (ii) the adamantine recitation and (iii) the eighteen yogic exercises focusing on the fierce inner heat; or, alternatively, you should meditate on (iv) the yoga of the channels according to the method of refining the pathways of the channels, (v) the four cakras according to the three complete methods of the fierce inner heat,[610] {244} (vi) the four applications of the vital essence according to the method that brings success, and (vii) the intense blazing of fire according to the method of eliminating obstacles—these seven steps. Alternatively, you may meditate exclusively on the burning and dripping [of the syllables] within the central channel.

In the case of the empowerment of discerning pristine cognition, according to the extensive path of the application of the wind of pristine cognition, in the main practice you should arouse the consort of pristine cognition [and apply] the four phases of the descent, retention, reversal, and pervasion [of the vital essence].

In the case of the fourth empowerment, the recitation should be undertaken, whether peaceful or wrathful, for seven moments of time, or for three moments of time, or for a single session of meditation.[611]

The Three Approaches to This Practice

(i) According to the extensive approach, the preliminaries comprise three focuses: one combining both accumulation and refinement; one combining the three refinements [of body, speech, and mind]; and one combining the remainder [of the preliminaries]. The determination [of doubts] by means of the view comprises thirty-seven aspects. The vase empowerment has seven aspects, including one for the generation of mindfulness, one each for the five palaces, and one for the ancillaries. [As for the secret empowerment,] the yogic application of wind has seven aspects, and the fierce inner heat has eighteen aspects. [As for the empowerment of discerning pristine cognition,] the melting bliss has eight aspects, including one for the refinement, five for the training, one for the union in equipoise, and one for the arousal. [As for the fourth empowerment,] the adamantine wave of blessing has nine aspects, including two for the peaceful and wrathful recitation and seven for the moments of time. So the extensive approach altogether has these eighty-nine aspects.

(ii) According to the middle-length approach, the preliminaries have three aspects, the view has four, the vase empowerment has three, the application of wind has seven, the fierce inner heat has seven, the melting bliss has four, and the wave of blessing has five, making altogether thirty-three aspects.

(iii) According to the abridged approach, the preliminaries have three aspects, the view has one, the vase empowerment has one, the application of wind has one, the fierce inner heat has one, the melting bliss has one, and the fourth empowerment has one, making altogether nine focuses.

As far as these three approaches—extensive, middle-length, and abridged—are concerned, without being rigidly [inclined toward] a single approach, you should understand that they are all magical transformations, like the eyes of a Chinese mask.[612]

Here I have just partially set forth in writing
This quintessence of the Path and Its Fruition
That generates the **delightful** mind surpassing **all**,
Combined with the essentials of the **supreme** path of **liberation**.

This was compiled from the instruction manual of Chojé Sakya Paṇḍita.

Regarding this guidebook, there is a sealed restriction to the effect that the glorious protector-lord Mahākāla and his sister will split open the head if it were written that one might ordinarily read this aloud. {245} Therefore it is inappropriate to write of this extensively, but there are annotations that elucidate misunderstandings and doubts to some extent.

62. Guidebook Entitled *The Five Stages of the Secret Assembly*[613]

After you have taken refuge and set the mind on enlightenment, in this instruction there are seven steps:

(i) The Yoga of a Singular Recollection

You should meditate relying on the foremost of mental focuses, until the inhabited world and its sentient inhabitants arise as the deities. This is called the "yoga of a singular recollection."[614]

(ii) The Yoga of Adamantine Buddha Body That Entails the Isolation of the Ordinary Body

The yoga of adamantine buddha body entails the isolation of the ordinary body:[615] In the context of this instruction, the main practice concerns either the single enlightened family that is most secret or the one hundred sacral aspects. For ease of understanding, the last mentioned comprise the five outer sense fields, the five inner sense fields, the five aggregates, the four elements—nineteen aspects, each of which is fivefold, making ninety-five aspects, and, with the inclusion of the five pristine cognitions that are universally pervasive, the number totals one hundred sacral aspects.[616]

You should meditate that, with regard to matter, shapes such as square, round, long, short, and so forth are Vairocana. The forms that appear as the dichotomy of self and others are Ratnasambhava—the precious origin of Vairocana. The material colors including blue and yellow are Amitābha—the boundless light of Vairocana. The luminous forms of sunlight, moonlight, and so forth are Amoghasiddhi—the successful accomplishment of Vairocana. The nonapperceived forms that manifest as objects of the mental faculty when the eyes are closed are Akṣobhya—the immovability of Vairocana.[617] Then you should examine this summarily, substituting "sound" and so forth for "matter."

When these one hundred aspects[618] are subsumed, they may be gathered in the following five groups: (i) [sights,] the sense faculty of the eyes, the aggregate of physical forms, and the earth element are associated with the enlightened family of Vairocana; (ii) sounds, the sense faculty of the ears, the aggregate of feelings, and the water element are associated with the enlightened family of Ratnasambhava; (iii) odors, the sense faculty of the nose, the aggregate of perceptions, and the fire element are associated with the enlightened family of Amitābha; (iv) tastes, the sense faculty of the tongue, the aggregate of formative predispositions, and the wind element are associated with the enlightened family of Amoghasiddhi; and (v) tangibles, the sense faculty of the body, the aggregate of consciousness, and the space element are associated with the enlightened family of Akṣobhya.

When these five are subsumed, they are gathered into the three adamantine realities of buddha body, speech, and mind; and when these three adamantine realities encompassing all appearances as body, speech, and mind are further subsumed, they are gathered in Vajradhara, the sixth enlightened family. Body and speech may also be gathered in mind, {246} so that there is a single enlightened family that is most secret.[619]

You should meditate that all things that appear as the dichotomy of self and others within the inhabited world and its sentient inhabitants are instantly and perfectly recollected as Vajradhara, with his three faces—blue, white, and red—and six arms—those on the right side, holding a vajra, wheel, and lotus; and those on the left, holding a bell, jewel, and sword. When you meditate on yourself as Vajradhara, if the visualization is unclear, you should generate the visualization and meditate while looking at an icon.

If it is still unclear, you should place an extremely clear mirror in front and display an icon of Vajradhara behind you, with its faces and the right and left arms inverted. Its reflection should then arise on the mirror, and you should make the visualization and meditate on it, looking at that reflection. Through your having meditated in that manner, the entire inhabited world and its sentient inhabitants will actually appear as Vajradhara. Thereby all ordinary conceptual thoughts will be reversed.[620] This meditation does not refer to any specific ritual of the generation stage, and it is not included in any specific aspect of the generation or perfection stages. As such, it resembles the borderline between mountains and plains.[621]

(iii) The Yoga of Adamantine Buddha Speech That Entails the Isolation of Ordinary Speech

The yoga of the adamantine buddha speech entails the isolation of ordinary speech.[622] To facilitate its understanding, briefly stated, wind generally has three phases: inhalation, pausing, and exhalation. The five primary winds comprise the life-sustaining wind, the ascending wind [associated with the vocal cords], the fire-accompanying wind [associated with digestion], the descending purgative wind, and the pervasive wind [associated with metabolism and muscular movement]. Their respective locations are the heart, the throat, the navel, the secret cakra, and the joints of the body. Their respective natures are the water, fire, wind, earth, and space elements. Their respective colors are white, red, green, yellow, and unclear azure blue. The names [of their respective enlightened families] are vajra, padma, ratna, karma, and [tathāgata, which is that of] the protector-lord Vairocana. Their respective dynamic functions are movement, precise movement, genuine movement, intense movement, and definitive movement. [Their respective orifices are] the eyes, the ears, the nose, the tongue, and the genitals. [Their respective sense objects] are sights, sounds, odors, tastes, and tangibles.[623]

In brief, in the course of a single twenty-four-hour day, wind has twenty-one thousand six hundred movements. These comprise twelve major cycles or twenty-four minor cycles {247}—each minor cycle with nine hundred movements.[624]

Since these are subsumed in inhalation, pausing, and exhalation, the experiential cultivation is as follows: You should be aware of the resonance of the syllable HŪṂ while exhaling, of OṂ while inhaling, and of ĀḤ while pausing.[625] You should count the number of breaths without error. Having understood that the winds and their nature are inseparable and without conceptual elaboration, you should then train according to the four-session yoga.

When you perceive the places from where the winds arise and their corresponding colors, the wind named Amoghasiddhi, arising from the navel, is exhaled through the left nostril and moves in a greenish-yellow color. The wind named Amitābha, lord of the padma family, arising from the throat, is exhaled through the right nostril and is red. The wind named Ratnasambhava, lord of the ratna family, arising from the secret cakra, is exhaled through both nostrils and is whitish yellow. The wind named Akṣobhya, lord of the vajra family, arising from the heart, is exhaled through both nostrils, without any escaping, and is white.[626]

So it is that there are four cycles of movement—one cycle from each of the left and right nostrils, one cycle from both nostrils, and one minor cycle of slow movement from both nostrils. In the course of a single day, this cycle will occur six times; and since each of these four winds moves six times per day, each of them has twelve major cycles, and when each of these is subdivided in two, it has twenty-four minor cycles.

Once you acquire familiarity with this, the winds of the four female deities are as follows: The two hundred and twenty-five downward movements of wind from the left nostril, pale green in color, denote Māmakī—the wind of the water element. The upward movements of wind from the left nostril, reddish-green in color, denote Pāṇḍaravāsinī—the wind of the fire element. The direct movements of wind from the left nostril, greenish-yellow in color, denote Buddhalocanā—the wind of the earth element. The shadowy[627] movements of wind from the left nostril, dark green in color, denote Tārā—the wind of the wind element. You should experientially cultivate the inhalation, pausing, and exhalation of these winds in this manner, without error. Similarly, there are four movements of wind from the right nostril—respectively, red, extreme red, yellowish-red, and dark red—respectively moving downward, upward, directly, and in the shadows; and they respectively represent the water, fire, earth, and wind elements. You should then experientially cultivate the [former] four that emphasize the earth element and the [latter] four that emphasize the water element, estimating the colors, as before.[628]

You should accomplish the four winds without impediment, {248} and the wind of the earth element will be impeded. With the proverbial strength of Nārāyaṇa, the wind of the water element will be impeded. Unburnable by fire, the wind of the fire element will be impeded. Impervious to water, the wind of the wind element will depart into space.[629]

(iv) The Yoga of Adamantine Buddha Mind That Entails the Isolation of Ordinary Mind

The yoga of the adamantine buddha mind entails the isolation of ordinary mind:[630] You should meditate in sequential order on luminosity, the spread of luminosity, and the approximate attainment of luminosity; and then you should meditate on these in reverse order.[631]

[With regard to luminosity:][632] You should visualize yourself as Vajradhara, with a solar disk in the heart. Upon it, there is an eight-petal red lotus, and at the navel there is a white AṂ.[633] Meditate on AṂ. Light is diffused from the AṂ; it penetrates the HAṂ at the crown and causes a stream of nectar to dissolve into the AṂ. Luminosity resembling sunlight will then appear and bliss will arise.[634]

With regard to the yoga of the spread of luminosity:[635] You should meditate on yourself as Vajradhara, with a solar disk in the heart. Upon it there is a red five-pronged vajra. At the navel you should visualize the syllable ĀḤ, with its visarga. Visualize that a hot red light from the ĀḤ penetrates the syllable HAṂ [at the crown], causing nectar to appear and dissolve into the AṂ. Luminosity resembling moonlight will then appear and bliss will arise.[636]

With regard to the yoga of the approximate attainment of luminosity:[637] You should visualize a red ĀḤ in the heart. From it there issues a faint ray of light that penetrates the syllable HAṂ [at the crown], causing it to dissolve into nectar. Intense great bliss will then arise, and once the luminosity has vanished, it will resemble darkness.[638]

Next, you should visualize the luminosity associated with the reverse sequence. The spread of luminosity will then arise from the preceding approximate attainment; and then from the spread of luminosity that resembles sunlight, the luminosity will arise. You should meditate that that is transformed into the red ĀḤ and the white OṂ.[639]

(v) The Illusory Body

Once the three isolations of ordinary body, speech, and mind have been perfected in that manner, you should experientially cultivate [the illusory body] as follows:[640] Meditative equipoise is a magical display, postmeditation is a magical display, and dreams are a magical display.[641] You should instantaneously and perfectly recall white Vajradhara, materialized simply from subtle energy. In terms of appearance, he is existent; and in terms of the subsequent [dissolution of the visualization], he is nonexistent. You should instantaneously visualize his body like the reflection in a mirror. {249} Each part of his body is fully perfected in a single facet of rainbow light. It is permeated by reflections, like the reflection of the moon that arises in water, like that of a full moon reflected in a lake, pool, river, or some other body of water. During postmeditation, whatever appears is that buddha body of magical display.

After that, you should apply the experiential cultivation of magical display with respect to dreams. That is to say, once you have familiarized yourself with the recollection of magical display in all circumstances of meditative equipoise and postmeditation, when lying down to sleep, you should fervently reflect that you will recognize the consciousness that is aware of dreams. When dreams indistinctly arise, you should recall the luminosity of the reverse sequence [that you previously practiced].

Others integrate with this practice the transformation of the path [of dreams] according to Nāropā, visualizing the letters A, NU, TA, RA in the throat cakra, but that does not accord with our own tradition of the Secret Assembly. By meditating in this manner, you will apprehend the movement of [dreamlike] appearances.

(vi) Luminosity

You should next meditate on the respective phases [of luminosity known as] "encompassing" and "dissolution":[642] To achieve the dissolution of the adamantine buddha body, there is encompassing of the syllable OṂ in the heart. Light rays are diffused from the OṂ, and the inhabited world and its sentient inhabitants melt into light. The adamantine buddha body then dissolves into the OṂ, in the manner of an eclipse.[643] With regard to both the adamantine buddha speech and the adamantine reality of buddha mind, you should undertake the corresponding encompassing and dissolution practices in the correct manner, from the syllables ĀḤ and HŪṂ respectively.[644]

Next, you should meditate on the encompassing [and dissolution] of the three adamantine realities and on the encompassing [and dissolution] of the five enlightened families. Visualize that upon a red lotus on a moon disk at the navel cakra, there is the short syllable A. When the wind is exhaled, it brings forth the sixteen vowels and thirty-four consonants to the tip of the nose. When it is inhaled, it brings them forth [in reverse] from KṢA[645] to ĀḤ visarga, and when it pauses [it brings them forth] from A to KṢA. The syllable KṢA at the end also vanishes, as it were, into rainbow light.[646]

In the case of the encompassing and dissolution of adamantine buddha speech, you should meditate on the vowels in the heart cakra where, upon a sun disk, there is a red eight-petal lotus with its perimeter; and in the navel cakra where there is a red ĀḤ with its perimeter. Light is diffused from the ĀḤ, and the inhabited world and its sentient inhabitants dissolve.[647]

In the case of the encompassing and dissolution of adamantine buddha mind, within the body in the central channel, {250} white in color, there is a coalescence of emptiness and radiance. Light is diffused from the central channel and dissolves into your own central channel, like a rainbow vanishing into the sky. In the dissolution phase, the inhabited world and its sentient inhabitants are dissolved by the light of the central channel.[648]

In the case of the encompassing and dissolution of the five enlightened families, there are five aspects: There are two encompassings and dissolutions associated with Vairocana, Amitābha, and Akṣobhya—these three—based as before on the syllables OṂ, ĀḤ, HŪṂ. There are two encompassings and dissolutions associated with Ratnasambhava, with another modulation based on the [aforementioned] syllables of the illusory body and so forth. There are two encompassings and dissolutions associated with Amoghasiddhi, with another modulation based on the syllable HAṂ.[649]

(vii) The Body of Coalescence

Having meditated in that manner for a long time, when luminosity and emptiness are realized, finally you will arise from luminosity in the body of coalescence; and the luminosity of the sequential and reverse phases arises as Vajradhara, materialized simply from subtle energy and adorned with the major and minor marks. This is the coalescence of the buddha body of perfect resource.[650]

Next, from your heart there emanates the consort embodying the awareness of pristine cognition. Consecrated by her secret cakra, you should enter into meditative absorption and then the maṇḍala perfectly arises from the vital essence within the secret cakra of the female consort. This is conducted into her heart cakra and diffused outward. Dissolving into yourself, it is then transformed into the adamantine reality of hatred.[651] The foregoing constitutes the coalescence [of the paths] of learning. When that continuum has been experienced and engaged, there ensues the coalescence [of the path] of no-more-learning.

So it is that in accordance with the practices of (i) singular recollection, (ii) isolation of the body, (iii) isolation of speech, (iv) isolation of mind, (v) illusory body, (vi) luminosity, and (vii) coalescence, you should know the number of procedures that the visualization entails and refine them energetically.

This sets forth in writing the pure list of visualization points
Of the unadulterated *Five Stages*,
The **supreme liberation** extrapolated with **delight**
From **all** the lecture scrolls of Go Lotsāwa.

This was compiled based on discussions ensuing from Vajradhara.[652]

63. Guidebook Entitled *The Vital Essence of Liberation*[653]

After first taking refuge and setting the mind on enlightenment: You should visualize yourself at the center of the protective circle {251} as Mañjuvajra. Within his body are the three channels and the four cakras.[654]

Focus your mind within the heart cakra on the being of pristine cognition, similar to your visualized self, and then within his heart cakra on the being of meditative stability, which is in the form of the syllable MAṂ, resting upon the handle of a sword.[655] Next, you should meditate that the MAṂ melts and becomes a red vital essence, the size of a small pea, emitting light rays of five colors, and that within it there are the vital essences of the supporting celestial palace and the supported deities. Smoke and other such signs will appear.[656] As a successful outcome, light will be diffused from the vital essences, and at its point the maṇḍala is emanated. It will fill the worlds of the ten directions, causing them to melt, and then it should dissolve.[657]

Your mind—the essential nature [of pristine cognition]—should then be equipoised in the vital essences:[658] There are sixteen white vital essences, and you should visualize that these are the sixteen vital essences present within the foundational physical body in the forms of the sixteen vowels. That is to say, you should visualize the syllable A on the base of the two big toes, Ā on the two calves, I on the two thighs, Ī on the genitals, U at the base of the abdomen, Ū on its upper part [i.e., the diaphragm], Ṛ on the breasts, Ṝ on the hands, Ḷ on the throat, Ḹ on the lips, E on the cheeks, AI on the eyes, O at the base of the ears, AU on the crown of the head, and AṂ and ĀḤ on all the joints. All these should be transported by the light of the heart cakra's vital essence, and they dissolve therein.[659] After that, [the light rays of the vital essence of the heart cakra] should summon the nectar of the buddhas, which also dissolves therein.[660]

[Next, there are the methods of the principal and conclusive meditations:] You should repeat the same visualization as before, from the sword handle up to the foundational physical body. The maṇḍala emanated from the point of the rays of light traverses infinite buddha fields and enters the mouths of the conquerors. Intermingling with nectar, it should then dissolve into the primary vital essence of the male from the right nostril and of the female from the left nostril. Finally, all phenomena should be absorbed within the mind.[661]

You should then be one-pointedly equipoised, exclusively on the vital essence of the mind, and home in on the imperishable vital essence. Light will blaze as before within the vital essence of the genitals and the vital essence of the heart, and then the three attributes of energy, dullness, and lightness[662] will flow down from the right, left, and central channels respectively. At the tip of the penis (*nor bu*) there is a vital essence, the thickness of a white mustard seed, [resting] upon the hand emblem—the handle of a blue sword, the size of a barley grain, endowed with light rays of five colors. {252} Within it, you should focus one-pointedly on the three-tiered principal beings [of commitment, pristine cognition, and meditative stability], in such a way that the vital essence is not enlarged and the maṇḍala is not diminished.[663]

To ensure a successful outcome, if the mind becomes sluggish or overactive, the vital essence will be ejaculated from your lower extremity. Therefore you should focus mindfully upon it as it descends toward the lower extremity of the female. Once sluggishness and overactivity have been purged,[664] you should focus on the primary vital essence, and consequently five signs of success will appear, including mirage, smoke, fireflies, burning lamps, and a cloudless sky.[665]

As far as [the phase of] recollection is concerned, you should generate the visualization of the deity without relying on a specific ritual and enter into meditative equipoise, having [instantly] recalled the buddhas of the five enlightened families, the four female buddhas, the wrathful deities, and so forth. You should then meditate on the melting vital essence [resulting from that visualization]. This is most profound. You should meditate on the lower extremity of the central channel and apply the particular methods of retaining the wind and of absorbing the subtle energy and mind.[666]

In the forehead, the throat, the heart, and between the breasts, there are [respectively] the buddha body, speech, and mind, along with the being of pristine cognition and the corresponding maṇḍalas of the wheel, lotus, vajra, and sword; as well as the maṇḍalas of wind, water, fire, and earth elements. At their centers, upon a moon disk, there are [respectively] white OṂ, red ĀḤ, blue HŪṂ, and MAṂ, in a form that neither goes, comes, or pauses.[667]

You should then undertake the yoga of the four elements and their recitations, and in this regard, persevere with the three phases of exhalation, inhalation, and pausing of breath in relation to the three seed syllables—inhalation with OṂ, pausing with ĀḤ, and exhalation with HŪṂ. Then, when [this visualization] has been internally absorbed, it should dissolve into the imperishable [vital essence].

The stabilizing wind[668] is located in the right channel, the life-sustaining wind in the left channel; the ascending wind is associated with the two water elements, and the descending purgative wind is associated with the two fire elements. You should make the adamantine recitations [of the seed syllables corresponding to these elements]. Specifically with regard to the wind located at the forehead [which is identified with the wind of the wind element], you should recite [OṂ, ĀḤ, HŪṂ respectively] in conjunction with the exhalation, inhalation, and pausing of breath.[669]

Then, from the seed syllable KṢUṂ, which represents the radiant aspect of the apperception of luminosity, and around which the letters KA, ṢA, RA, U, and MA are gathered,[670] light rays emerge, causing the three maṇḍalas [of water, fire, and earth] or the single maṇḍala [of wind] to melt in a coalescence of emptiness and radiance. Equipoised therein, you should focus principally on the aspect of radiance. Next, the vital essences should be gradually absorbed, and you should focus on the coalescence of appearance and emptiness, which resembles the maṇḍala of space; {253} and at this point you should focus principally on profound [emptiness]. Next, you should be equipoised in the disposition where the light rays of the coalescent vital essences, the three maṇḍalas, profound and radiant, are inseparable, like the moon reflected in water; and at this point you should focus principally on the nonduality of profundity and radiance.[671]

Consciousness Transference

There is a saying to the effect that those who have perseverance will attain buddhahood in this lifetime, those who are indolent will attain buddhahood in the intermediate state, and those who have obstacles will attain buddhahood through the course of their rebirths.[672] To that end, you should block the nine orifices—navel, eyebrows, crown of the head, eyes, ears, mouth, nose, anus, and urethra—with the syllable HŪṂ.[673] You should focus on a nine-pronged vajra fashioned of various precious gems and metals on the crown of your head; and at its center, there is another white five-pronged vajra representing your own mind. Both are upright. At the center of the five-pronged vajra, on a moon disk, there is a yellow vital essence, the size of a small pea. At this point the aspect of radiance is brought forth.[674]

Next, all appearances of the inhabited world and its sentient inhabitants should be absorbed into the vital essence of your own heart, radiant in the form of Mañjuvajra. Your mind then enters into the central channel and emerges unimpededly from the "golden orifice" (*gser sgo*) of the anterior fontanel on the crown of the head. The prongs at the lower end of the two vajras penetrate your central channel and should be absorbed in the vital essence at the center of the five-pronged vajra. Focusing in that manner, your own body is absorbed into the nine-pronged vajra, that in turn is absorbed into the five-pronged vajra, that in turn is absorbed into the vital essence, and that vital essence then is ejected to a distance of seven palm trees [through the anterior fontanel]. Then the vital essence becomes subtler and subtler, and finally it will be absorbed into luminosity. The buddha body of reality in which all conceptual elaboration is quiescent is actualized; and, simultaneously, you should be attentive to the buddha body of perfect resource in which the major and minor marks are radiant and perfect, and the buddha body of emanation that, in the perception of ordinary beings, demonstrates the way of the twelve deeds.[675]

This definitive framework of consciousness transference is not clearly revealed in the father tantras, except in *The Oral Transmission of Buddhajñānapāda*.[676]

Here I have set forth this rare consciousness transference
Including the sequence of visualization
Of the perfection stage, resembling an udumbara lotus.
It is the path of great **delight**, and **supreme liberation**,
That of **all**-seeing Mañjuvajra.

This was compiled from the memorandum of Jang Pukpa Kunlek.

64. Guidebook Entitled *The Unelaborate Practice of Red Yamāri*[677] {254}

After first taking refuge and setting the mind on enlightenment: You should visualize that from a syllable HŪṂ in the middle of an ordinary protective circle in the sky in front, upon a seat comprising a lion throne with lotus and sun cushions, and a red buffalo, your precious root teacher manifests in the form of red Mañjughoṣa Yamāntaka.[678] Encircling him on the periphery, on seats of precious gems with lotus and moon cushions, are the teachers of the lineage, the assemblage of meditational deities, buddhas, bodhisattvas, sublime pious attendants, hermit buddhas, heroes, ḍākinīs, and the hosts of doctrinal protectors. Through the light rays emanating from your teacher's heart, all sentient beings of the three world systems are transformed into meditational deities and established on that aforementioned periphery.[679]

OṂ VAJRA PUṢPE ĀḤ HŪṂ
OṂ VAJRA DHUPE ĀḤ HŪṂ
OṂ VAJRA ĀLOKE ĀḤ HŪṂ
OṂ VAJRA GANDHE ĀḤ HŪṂ
OṂ VAJRA NIVEDHYA ĀḤ HŪṂ
OṂ RŪPA VAJRĪ HŪṂ
OṂ ŚABDA VAJRĪ HŪṂ
OṂ GANDHE VAJRĪ HŪṂ
OṂ RASA VAJRĪ HŪṂ
OṂ SPARŚA VAJRĪ HŪṂ
OṂ DHARMADHĀTU VAJRĪ HŪṂ[680]

I will offer all my harmful enemies and obstructors to the sacred teacher, essential nature of all the buddhas of the three times!
Grant your blessing that I may be free from hatred!
I will offer all allies who are of benefit!
Grant your blessing that I may be free from attachment!
I will offer all neutral beings and all material possessions!
Grant your blessing that I may be free from grasping, attachment, and miserliness![681]

Glorious sacred teacher, please understand my thoughts!
Favor me with compassion!
Grant me your blessings!

The fragments of your body within your [severed] skull are then transformed into a great ocean of nectar, which is uncontaminated pristine cognition. OṂ ĀḤ HŪṂ![682]

I go for refuge to the monastic community!
I go for refuge to the sacred doctrine!
I go for refuge to the Buddha!
I go for refuge to the precious teacher—
Essential nature of all the buddhas of the three times![683] {255}

[After making those offerings, you should be equipoised in the unelaborate] state in which the body, speech, and mind of the teacher and your own body, speech, and mind are indivisible. Within this disposition, whatever suddenly arising consciousness manifests, at its very first initial appearance your mind should intimate to your own mind from where it has come, how it now abides, and where it will finally cease. Although from the start this consciousness has not come from anywhere at all, does not now abide anywhere at all, and in the end will not cease anywhere at all, it still appears to come, it appears to abide, and it appears to cease. At that very instant, you should be guided to conviction through certainty.[684]

The conceptual thoughts that you find by searching in that manner, whether subjective or objective, should be induced into your body through its nine orifices [in the manner of a storm]. Consequently, there will be a flash of light that resembles either the clear and radiant tip of a butter lamp flame or lightning, and finally, an opening will suddenly be breached from within the heart cakra. In the manner of an arrow fired by a [powerful] archer, [your bundle of thoughts] will reach the limitless shore of the great outer ocean. Your body, assuming the very form of Yamāntaka, will be light and mobile, like the leaves of a tree stirred by the wind, and you should then take your place alongside Amitābha in Sukhāvatī. OṂ ĀḤ HŪṂ! You should consolidate your mind, the essential nature of awareness, with the pristine cognitions of empty space, and let it be present, free from grasping.[685]

[Then, as far as postmeditation is concerned, there are two aspects, comprising the methods of setting the mind on enlightenment and the attributes that dispel obstacles. The former includes the six yogas,] which are as follows:[686]

1. Union with the Teacher Who Confers Blessings

After meditating that Mañjughoṣa Yamāntaka is actually present in the form of the teacher on the crown of your head, from the very depths of your heart, in words imbued with strong and fervent devotion, you should say, "I pray to the precious teacher, essential nature of all the buddhas of the three times!" After you pray with concentration, the teacher will dissolve into yourself, and you should remain equipoised in that disposition.[687]

2. Union of Peerless Compassion

Here, you should meditate, focusing on any sort of harmful enemy or obstructor. {256} That is to say, you should meditate, thinking, "How beautiful it is that over this and my many lives I have associated again and again with parents, siblings, and friends, and we have achieved mutual benefit! How pitiful are those harmful and injurious deeds that we inflict even now like a madman, aroused by past actions! May all those malign thoughts be calmed!"[688]

3. Union of the Primary Causal Basis

This may be uniquely exemplified by your own experience of toothache; for the loving-kindness that assumes the suffering of other sentient beings experiencing a similar sort of pain is not contrived. You should meditate thinking, "May this toothache of mine absolutely be of use for alleviating the toothache of all sentient beings!"[689]

4. Union of the Winds of Vital Breath and Exertion

Here, your own outer form manifests as Yamāntaka—empty inside, like an inflated red silk bag. With three HŪṂ syllables and three HA syllables, you should exhale any stale residue of the upper and lower winds respectively, and then unite the winds gently together. That is to say, these gentle winds should circulate through the stomach [and other parts of the body] sixteen times, clockwise and counterclockwise, and they should also be associated with the refinement of the five limbs.[690]

5. Union of the Sacraments of Auspicious Coincidence

This entails relying on the extraction of elixir that has been created through spiritual accomplishment and consecration.[691]

6. Union of Vajrabhairava

Next, your own body should be clearly visualized as Yamāntaka. Visualize that the teacher seated on the crown of your head melts into light and that the central channel, from the space between the eyebrows to the penis, is filled with the bluish-red wind of life breath and imbued with light rays of five colors.[692]

Seventh [in addition to those six unions or yogas], there are also the nails that dispel obstacles: You should take responsibility, as before, for familiarizing yourself with the transmitted teachings, scriptures, and pith instructions of the extremely unelaborate phase. Then, from that very disposition, you should resort to the crucial points of carefree and extensive conduct and bring forth the successful outcome of your former meditative stability. Should your mind waver toward objects due to thoughts of circumstantial appearance that may arise, and not hit the object of meditative concentration, you should accept these circumstantial appearances as a spiritual accomplishment and {257} pray one-pointedly by maintaining the union with the teacher who confers blessings, which is one of the aforementioned six methods of setting the mind on enlightenment, thereby transforming the appearance of the teacher into a deity. Finally, the teacher and your own mind will intermingle, and you should settle into that relaxed, open, and carefree mode.

Those of highest acumen should maintain their natural position, without wavering from their direct focus. Those of average acumen should cultivate settling into that basic position with respect to any conceptual objects that arise. Those of lowest acumen should carry whatever arises onto the path, prolonging it without foundation.

Furthermore, if the arising of masses of conceptual thoughts should occur without ceasing, then you should hold in your right hand the sharp sword of pristine cognition that appears from who knows where, and with that you should cut the arrogant conjectures that cherish the physical body into hundreds and thousands of pieces until not even the slightest remains. Offer these freely to harmful elemental spirits, so that they obtain satisfaction and unsurpassed joy. Imagine that all the venomous enmity of your mindstream, without exception, is pacified and that you possess the mind of enlightenment, endowed with spiritual and temporal well-being. Saying OṂ ĀḤ HŪṂ, you should then enter into meditative equipoise.[693]

If conceptual thoughts should suddenly resurface, then with regard to any actual painful thoughts that might occur, as in the aforementioned pith instruction on the luminosity of conceptual thought, you should distinguish between the supporting body and the supported mind and imagine that your own intrinsic awareness in the manner of the tip of a butter lamp flame dissolves into the heart of that deity of terrifying appearance [Vajrabhairava] and is turned toward the essence—the actual nature of mind. Then you should enter into meditative equipoise.[694]

If conceptual thoughts should suddenly arise yet again, you should focus from afar on the actual essential nature of the thoughts that arise, without wavering, and say, "If I myself am nondual pristine cognition, how should I regard you thoughts!"[695] In the manner of someone personally experiencing that it is a mistaken perception to see a multicolored rope as a snake and that it is actually a rope, your bewilderment will become groundless and baseless. You will triumph in battle with obstacles. {258}

Here I have set forth in writing in a few points,
This quintessential visualization of the **supreme** path,

Revealing the path of unelaborate **liberation**,
Bringing **delight** to minds endowed with **all** elaborations.

This was compiled from the lecture notes of Lowo Lotsāwa.

65. Guidebook Entitled *The Four-Stage Yoga*[696]

After you have taken refuge and set the mind on enlightenment, there ensue the four stages of yoga:

1. The Yoga of Form

The first of the four yogas is entitled "the yoga of form." This has three phases: (i) the self-consecration of the generation stage, (ii) the consecration of appearances, and (iii) the consecration of the coalescence.[697]

(i) With regard to the self-consecration of the generation stage: commencing from the central eye of the deity, you should focus on the whole body of the transcendent lord Yamāntaka, male-female in union.[698]

(ii) With regard to the consecration of appearances: You should clearly visualize the transcendent lord Yamāntaka, male-female in union, and imagine that there is a red syllable YA in his heart. Light is diffused from that, causing the entire inhabited world to melt into red light. Then visualize this very world as his celestial palace. Imagine that light is repeatedly diffused from it, penetrating its sentient inhabitants, so that all sentient beings become the body of the transcendent lord Yamāntaka, male-female in union.[699]

(iii) With regard to the consecration of the coalescence: You should meditate on the celestial palace and the body of the transcendent lord Yamāntaka, in whatever manner they are recalled, [arising] from the very perception of this inhabited world and its sentient inhabitants as they commonly appear. Since they are without inherent existence although they appear in that manner, they resemble the reflection of the moon in water. Such is the consecration of the coalescence.[700]

2. The Yoga of Mantra

The second of the four yogas is known as the "yoga of mantra." With regard to the sequence of the mantras, you should exhale wind from the mouth, intoning the three HA syllables one thousand times, and then you should exhale wind from the nose, intoning the three HŪṂ syllables. Next, you should hold the upper surfaces of your feet with your hands and visualize the three channels. Meditate that wind enters from the right channel into the central channel, where it is retained and secured. Similarly, wind enters from the left channel into the central channel, where it is retained and secured. Once these winds have entered into the central channel, you should aim to hold the wind as long as you can.[701]

With regard to consciousness transference [which is a subsidiary of the yoga of mantra]: You should visualize that the essential nature of your own mind is the red syllable HŪṂ. Below it is ĀḤ, {259} below that is HRĪḤ, and below that are two green YA syllables, back to back. Your nine orifices, including the eyes, are blocked in succession by two conjoined HŪṂ syllables. In front of you, on the crown of the head, like an open window, there is a palm tree that reaches as far as Tuṣita. Above it you should meditate that your own root teacher is seated, radiant in the form of the transcendent lord Yamāntaka, male-female in union. Then wind arises from the two YA syllables within the heart, drawing in the HRĪḤ, and that in turn draws in the ĀḤ, and that in turn draws in the HŪṂ, so that they all then merge from the crown of the head. Visualize that they penetrate the heart of the transcendent lord, your teacher, who is in front. Afterward, you should visualize that that same syllable HŪṂ is again present within your own heart cakra. Then recite HIK,[702] and visualize that the fontanel on the crown of the head is blocked by a [stabilizing] crossed vajra.[703]

3. The Yoga of Consecration

The third of the four yogas is known as the "yoga of consecration": Here the coalescence of bliss and emptiness is realized through the skillful means of the female mudra, commencing with those of the conch type.[704] Far from being a contaminated realization, this method actually effects the consecration in an uncontaminated manner.[705]

4. The Yoga of Pristine Cognition

The fourth of the four yogas is known as the "yoga of pristine cognition," according to which the stage of the real nature is introduced without conceptual elaboration.[706]

Here I have embellished in writing the essential visualization list
According to Drubchen Peldzin Zhepa,
Concerning the essentials of **all** the four stages of yoga—
The path of the four **delights** and **supreme liberation.**

This was compiled from the instruction manual of Lowo Lotsāwa.

66. Guidebook Entitled *The Mental Focus on the Horns of Bhairava*[707]

After first taking refuge and setting the mind on enlightenment, you should visualize yourself as Vajrabhairava, in the form of a "solitary spiritual warrior," without consort.[708] His horns are clear blue, wrinkled at the base, crooked in the middle, and sharp and tapering at the top.[709] They are translucent and radiant, like the interior of a beryl gemstone. Within the tip of each horn there is a shining, white vital essence, in the shape of a dewdrop. At his heart, upon a lotus and moon cushion, there is Mañjughoṣa, according to the Indian tradition (*rgya'i 'jam dbyangs*), reddish yellow, the color of saffron, shrouded in a mass of light. You should visualize that his right hand brandishes the sword level with his shoulder {260} and the left hand holds a book upon a lily. His feet are in the adamantine posture. He is adorned with silks and ornaments, the major and minor marks are clearly complete, and he has a smiling demeanor. His topknot of matted hair is adorned with ornaments and a garland of flowers. Having generated this visualization, you should settle into meditative equipoise.

Next, from the left and right vital essences in the tips of Vajrabhairava's horns, generative fluids, of the nature of bliss and the thickness of a spider's web, flow down and crisscross his cheeks, in the manner of threads fashioned of white or crystal rainbow light in a clear sky. From the throat they come together and enter into the heart through the central channel, where they dissolve into Mañjughoṣa, so that there then manifest the appearances of one hundred thousand solar rays. These outwardly diffuse from all your pores one million trillion points of light.

Consequently, you yourself become radiant as the deity Vajrabhairava, with a form perfectly radiant, like a torch raised aloft in a dungeon. From the broad nostrils of his buffalo face—fearsome, awesome, and wrathful—bluish-red life-sustaining breath swirls like a cloud of smoke. The frowns of his face are closely furrowed, like the waves of an ocean. His three eyes are bright, staring and open, and his eyelashes and eyebrows flash like lightning moving throughout the ten directions. The hair of his head is tawny yellow, blazing like fire, and at the tips of his hair intense flames are diffused—flickering and spreading forth. His incisors are white and his other teeth—sharp, tapering, and covered with blood—are snarling. His mouth is wide open, and its interior, with quivering tongue, incinerates malignant spirits and obstructors with a vortex of hot wind, resembling fire. His body is stout and short, with the folded muscles of a thick lingam. His abdomen is round, and his fingernails and toenails draw in enemies and obstructors with their hooklike forms. His two hands {261} hold a knife and a skull at the heart. His left leg is extended, standing upon a lotus and moon seat in a haughty manner. He is adorned with a whitish neckband with bone ornaments, a crown of dry skulls, and a necklace of human heads, dripping with blood. He wears a cross-band of poisonous snakes and stands in the midst of a burning fiery mass of pristine cognition.

Having visualized the body of Vajrabhairava in that manner, without wavering from supreme pride, naked and holding a knife and skull, around midnight you should, along with a female partner, refine the dance movements [of Vajrabhairava] in a place measuring up to seven steps. Consequently, you will attain the miraculous ability to move unimpeded through walls and barriers. At that time, you should frequent charnel grounds and so forth.

Furthermore, when your physical body is filled with luminosity from the body of Mañjughoṣa within the heart and with the vital essence from the horn tips, which are of the nature of generative fluids, and you have become like the sky permeated with white rainbow light, points of light will emerge gradually from the orifice of the thick lingam, in the manner of incense smoke, and your entire physical body, without exception, will be covered by that mist-like white semen. Consequently, pale-blue rays of light will be diffused, and the vital essence, resembling a globule of mercury, will become radiant as the deity. You should then meditate, focusing with one-pointed attention on bliss and emptiness.

It is said with regard to this instruction that it is to be investigated whether the seed syllables of the four cakras, the five enlightened families, the four female buddhas, and the eight female bodhisattvas commencing with Lāsyā are to be established in the channels and the cakras.

Here I have set forth in writing the **supreme** method
Of **liberation** of the knotted snake—
The dance in which you yourself move during the nighttime
With the natural descent of **delight** and bliss,
Focusing above **all** on the horns of Bhairava,
Which are your own mental faculty.

This was compiled from the writings of Kyoton.

67. Guidebook Entitled *The Central Channel Dependent on the Male Deity Cakrasaṃvara*[710]

After first taking refuge and setting the mind on enlightenment: You should adopt the adamantine posture and the gesture of meditative equipoise and then focus directly on the navel. In the navel cakra {262}, upon a moon disk the size of a split pea, you should visualize the vital essences comprising the winds of the five elements—blue in the center, yellow in the east, green in the south, red in the west, and white in the north.[711] Seven times you should induce the breath to movement, and then unite the upper and lower winds with a single rotation of the knees (*pus mo la bskor ba*) and a single finger snap.[712] When you are resting, you should undertake five short sessions during that period of rest, without rising from your seat, and after that you may engage in activities. Over a twenty-four-hour period, you should undertake altogether thirty short sessions, adding a single rotation [of the knees] and a single finger snap to each short session. The best will acquire the power of the fire element within three days, the average within seven days, and the feeblest within fifteen days.[713]

Next, you should be firmly established as the deity [Cakrasaṃvara]: Within your navel cakra, you should visualize that upon the syllable AṂ[714] there is a red vital essence. It is connected via the central channel with a white HAṂ in the crown cakra.[715] The wind of power at the back focuses on the vital essences at the lower extremities of the right and left channels, and at their upper extremities it penetrates the nostrils. The wind at the soles of the feet ignites the fire of the triple intersection channel and causes the lower gate to open and close. Consequently, the syllable AṂ ignites and, passing from the right and left channels, it strikes the wind [of power] at the back.[716] The flame is then conducted downward [through the central channel] from the white and red KṢUṂ located within the *anusvāra* above the syllable HAṂ, [which is known as] the "luminous fierce inner heat"; and the fire blazes upward from the dark red KṢUṂ located within the anusvāra of the syllable AṂ in the navel cakra, [which is known as] the "ordinary fierce inner heat." These two fires then collide together at the heart cakra, and in this way the upper and lower winds are intensely united.[717]

Next, you should visualize that the [four] primary elements and Mount Meru are present below you and your female mudra, who embodies pristine cognition. You manifest radiantly as Cakrasaṃvara, and at the tip of the vajra (penis) there is the syllable BYĀṂ. Your female mudra manifests radiantly as Vajravārāhī, and at the tip of her lotus anthers (vagina) there is the syllable DHYĀṂ. In the central channel of your own body there is a multicolored vajra with three upper and lower prongs. The generative essences derived from the meditative union of male and female then travel [upward] from their respective pathways of the central channel to their supreme location [at the crown of the head]. They are guided into that location with the resonance of the syllables HA, SIB, HRIṂ, RNIṂ, and HŪṂ, and the pathways of the upper and lower winds are refined.[718]

Consciousness Transference

As for consciousness transference: The syllable KṢUṂ is at the anus and urethra; the [stacked] syllables KṢAM RAṂ YAṂ are at the navel; the [stacked] syllables YAṂ RAṂ YAṂ are at the heart; the [stacked] syllables HAṂ MAṂ RAṂ YAṂ are at both shoulders; the [stacked] syllables SAṂ RAṂ YAṂ are at the throat; the syllable SUṂ is at the mouth; {263} the syllable YUṂ is at the two nostrils; the syllables YAB and YUṂ are at the two ears; the syllable HŪṂ is at the two eyes; the syllable SU is at the *ūrṇakeśa*; the syllable KṢUṂ is at the crown of the head; and the syllable HŪṂ is at the heart.[719] Then with the resonance of HIK KA KA KĀHI, these seed syllables of the deity, indicative of your own mind, are raised by the wind upon the moon disk and ejected through the supreme pathway [of the anterior fontanel].[720]

This briefly sets forth in writing
The elixir of essential visualization on the swift path,
The mystery of **supreme** natural **liberation**,
Delightful above **all**,
That causes the young lily to open.

This was compiled from the instruction manual of Jetsun Drakpa Gyeltsen.

68. Guidebook Entitled *The Central Channel Dependent on the Female Deity Vajravārāhī*[721]

After first taking refuge and setting the mind on enlightenment:[722] You should meditate on your teacher at the crown of your head, visualize an awesome protective circle of mantras, and practice the generation stage, along with the *Arraying of the Physical Body with the Four Empowerments of Khecarī*.[723]

Securely sealed with this armor, and mastering the vital points of the physical body, you should then meditate that in the navel cakra, the channel in the center, where the wind of the space element moves, resembles the cutting blade of a curved knife. The channel in the east, where the wind of the wind element moves, resembles a staff. The channel in the south, where the wind of the earth element moves, resembles a visarga. The channel in the west, where the wind of the water element moves, resembles a plow. The channel in the north, where the wind of the fire element moves, resembles a circular sphere. You should meditate that these all resemble minute drops. Then you should draw in the lower wind slightly and compress the upper wind slowly. Then draw in the lower wind strongly and hold it with the vase breathing. After that, you should focus on the channel in the center.

Over twenty-four hours you should undertake six sessions of this practice, including three during the daytime. Once five sessions have been completed, during the first session of the following morning you should snap a finger and desist from holding the [vase breathing] further.

In terms of the [division into] short sessions, each short session also ends with a finger snap, so that, incrementally, in the next morning session there will be five finger snaps; and in the next middle session of the day, there will be five finger snaps, making ten; and in the next evening session, there will be five finger snaps, making fifteen altogether. Until the following dawn there will be a further fifteen, making thirty. On the second day [of the retreat], this will become sixty; and on the third day, ninety. Adding these and refining the practice in that manner, those of superior acumen will develop the sensation of warmth within three or five days, those of middling acumen in seven or ten days, and those of lowest acumen {264} in fifteen days.

You should recognize the various adverse circumstances that may occur, such as pains in the channels, pains in the wind, an increase in afflicted mental states, and feelings of hunger and thirst, and you should take care.

The preliminary practice entails the refinement of the wind. Here you should visualize that the wind is in the soles of the feet, the fire is in the triple intersection channel, the short vowel AṂ (with anusvāra) is in the abdomen, and the downward-facing HAṂ is at the center of the crown of the head, directly in front of the space between the eyebrows. These two syllables are connected by the central channel, resembling a spider's thread, and to its rear is the wind of power. The right and left channels simply cannot be tolerated by the eyes, their roots converging at the syllable OṂ [between the eyes]. They then directly reach the base of the HAṂ, where they curl at their ends and enter the nostrils.

Next, the fire should be intensified by the movement of the wind; and from the AṂ in the navel, the wind that has the appearance of fire and the property of warmth enters from the pathways of the right and left channels, so that the pathways of the channels are refined. Compressed by the wind [of power] at the back, it is slowly inhaled from the nostrils, thereby reversing the fire of the right and left channels. Pressing down slowly on the syllable AṂ causes it to combust, so that an extremely minute flame from the syllable AṂ passes upward through the central channel and the upper and lower winds are united. Sparks are diffused from the physical body, and vital essences are diffused like stars and reabsorbed. Such are the sorts [of experiences] that may occur. That concerns your own superior state of abiding.

Next, you should visualize that in the navel cakra, within its sixty-four channel branches, the fifty primary vowels and consonants encircle in groups of eight with the six short vowels in the middle.[724] In view, within the anusvāra circle of the short syllable AṂ there is a rough and strong dark red KṢUṂ, and on the crown of the head there is a similar KṢUṂ within the anusvāra circle of the syllable HAṂ. You should visualize that the fire is aroused, as before, by the wind, so that an extremely subtle flame deriving from the KṢUṂ passes upward from the heart. The wind is exhaled slowly from the nostrils, so that the tailwind is increased, and the HAṂ rubs against the KṢUṂ. Then they descend within the central channel and intermingle.

Holding the wind, the main practice concerning the opening of [the central channel] is as follows: you should visualize that a burning lamp is released and the generative essence descends, flowing downward like a spider's thread, from the HAṂ, so that the AṂ is revitalized and the upper and lower winds are united.

With regard to the number of visualizations in this practice, there is one corresponding to the action of the wind, one corresponding to your own superior state, {265} one corresponding to the opening of the central channel, one corresponding to the main practice, or else two corresponding to the opening [of the central channel].

This sets forth in writing without omission or addition
This **supreme** quintessence of **liberation**—
The perfection stage of Khecarī,
Concerning the great **delight** of the fierce inner heat,
Which is superior to **all.**

This was written having distilled the essence according to the oral transmission.

69. Guidebook Entitled *The Five Stages according to Ghaṇṭāpāda*[725]

After you have taken refuge and set the mind on enlightenment, the five stages are as follows:

1. The Stage Conjoined with the Seed Syllables

You should instantly visualize yourself clearly as the deity [Cakrasaṃvara]. The female consort, in the form of light, dissolves into the syllable A in the navel cakra. You should pay homage and pray with devotion to your teacher; then focus on a pale-red vital essence, the size of a mustard seed, resting upon a moon disk, the size of a split pea, in the heart cakra. After that, you should focus your awareness on the white vital essences in the two eyes, the blue ones in the ears, the yellow one between the nostrils, the red one in the channel of the tongue, and the green one at the tip of the genitals. Above the aforementioned pale-red vital essence of the heart there is a pale-blue one. Each of these is, as before, resting upon a moon disk. The sense faculties associated with these vital essences should then be diffused toward their corresponding sense objects and engaged with them. If they do not become diffused toward the six sense objects, you should focus exclusively on the heart cakra. That is the first stage conjoined with the seed syllables.[726]

2. The Stage of the Crossed Vajra, in Which the Seed Syllables Are Absent

Next, you should meditate on the winds of the sun and moon in association with the right and left nostrils, with nothing in between the nostrils. You should visualize that when the wind is exhaled, it resembles the mist at the end of a mountain range; and when it is inhaled, it has the form of light that fills the physical body. If it is diffused toward the gates of the sense faculties, you should act as before; but if it is not diffused, it is said that there will be no error. Self-consecration is undertaken here without the seed syllables. The wind is exhaled and inhaled three times, after which you should visualize a crossed vajra on the crown of your head, its hub reflecting the colors of the [four] directions, with a hexahedron motif. Within that there is a pale-red vajra, at the center of which there is a moon disk with a blue HŪṂ, from which rays of light are diffused. These should dissolve into the buddhas and bodhisattvas. If it becomes diffuse, you should repeat this training in the heart and navel cakras, and [in the other orifices] from the eyes to the genitals. If the wind moves from the right nostril, you should visualize a sun disk on the ūrṇakeśa; and if it moves from the left nostril, you should visualize a moon disk. Above that you should visualize the vital essence {266}—blue in the center, white in the east, green in the north, red in the west, and yellow in the south. Meditating on this subtle energy constitutes the second stage—the crossed vajra, in which the seed syllables are absent.[727]

3. The Stage in Which the Gem Is Filled

Next, with regard to the commitment seal, you should meditate on yourself as the meditational deity in male-female union, and visually generate the lotus (vagina) and vajra (penis) associated with the secret cakra. At their tips, you should visualize the generative essences in the form of HŪṂ, and then enter into meditative absorption. If the action seal is physically present, the visualization is the same. With regard to the phenomenal seal, you should focus your awareness on the white HŪṂ at the orifice of the vajra, which is of the nature of a vital essence. When you have obtained bliss, it should be inducted upward through the secret channel, the navel, the heart, and the throat, to the crown of the head. With regard to the Great Seal, the bliss is established without contrivance, naturally descending and free from limitations. That constitutes the third stage in which the "gem" is filled.[728]

4. The Stage of Jālandharipā

Next, you should meditate as before that within the secret cakra there is a pale-red hexahedron within which there are five vital essences, resembling five clusters. You should focus the mind and finally visualize that a light of fire from these vital essences exits the body via the pathway of the right channel [and enters into the bodies of] the tathāgatas of the ten directions, where their generative essences are carried by the fire toward your nose, entering via the pathway of the left channel. You should meditate, gently uniting the upper and lower winds together. That constitutes the fourth stage, that of Jālandharipā.[729]

5. The Fifth Stage of the Inconceivable

Next, you should focus upon a moon disk in your own heart, resting on which there is a white HŪṂ. Finally, light is diffused from it and the entire inhabited world and its sentient inhabitants are absorbed into light, and then the lotus of the HŪṂ is absorbed into the HŪṂ, the body of the syllable into the head of the syllable HA, that into the crescent, and that into the biṇḍu. The vibration of that syllable also becomes like a vanishing cloud. You should then be equipoised in luminosity, where all things are empty. If the experience of emptiness is excessive, [the wind] will arise [again] as the vibration; and if the experience of bliss is excessive, you should do as before. That constitutes the fifth stage of the inconceivable.[730]

This definitively sets forth in writing
The method by which one attains **supreme liberation**—
The brief visualization list that confers **delight**,
Revealing **all** the experiential cultivations of the five stages.

This was compiled from the instruction manual of Tsokgom Kunga Pel. {267}

70. Guidebook Entitled *The Four Stages according to Kṛṣṇacārin*[731]

After first taking refuge and setting the mind on enlightenment: You should develop certainty, thinking that you yourself have been inducted into the maṇḍala by your teacher, and that the external appearance of your physical body is Cakrasaṃvara, with four faces and twelve arms; and the deities within this maṇḍala number sixty-two. You should meditate that the boot of your teacher rests on the crown of your head, develop devotion, and then dissolve that visualization. The inhabited world and its sentient inhabitants, assuming the form of the deity and the celestial palace, are then absorbed into you. Your faces are absorbed into the primary face, your arms are absorbed into the primary pair of arms, and the female consort Vajravārāhī, too, assuming the form of a red light, is absorbed into the syllable A in the navel cakra.

1. The Stage of the Continuum to Be Known

Next, you should mindfully and clearly visualize your external form as Innate Cakrasaṃvara, with the three channels and four cakras internally manifest, along with the two dynamic maṇḍalas of the wind and fire elements. You should meditate that the dark green maṇḍala of wind at the entrance to the anus resembles swirling smoke. Above it there is the triangular red maṇḍala of fire—the dark red blazing fire of the syllable KṢA. In the middle of the navel cakra, there is the syllable AṂ. Forming an inner circle around it are the eight syllables A, KA, CA, ṬA, TA, PA, YA, and ŚA. Outside these are the sixteen vowels, the thirty-four consonants, and the six long vowels. In the four cardinal directions of the heart cakra are the four short vowels A, I, U, and O; and in its four intermediate directions are YA, RA, LA, and VA. Within the throat cakra are the four encircling syllables Ā, Ī, Ū, and AI, with OṂ in the middle; and on an outer circle, on twelve petals, are the twelve vowels with the exception of Ṛ, Ṝ, Ḷ, and Ḹ. In the crown cakra, in the middle there is the syllable HAṂ, and on its petals two sets of the sixteen vowels. The syllable AṂ [in the navel] and HAṂ [in the crown] are connected via the central channel. In the right and left channels the vowels and consonants are multiplied. The fontanel of the head is blocked by the syllable OṂ, and the lower orifice by the syllables HŪṂ PHAṬ. That constitutes the first stage of the continuum to be known.[732]

2. The Stage of Mantra to Be Experientially Cultivated

Next, you should dissolve the upper wind into the syllable AṂ and induce this experience by means of the four signs of refinement, and the six signs of stability.[733] Meanwhile, the cakras of the navel, heart, and throat are melted by the fire. Flames burst forth from the point between the eyebrows and enter you via the legs of Cakrasaṃvara, the essential nature of your teacher, in whom all the tathāgatas of the ten directions are gathered. {268} Then the nectar of his body is invited [into your body], and the sixteen delights are individually enhanced in your crown, throat, heart, and navel cakras. After that the upper and lower winds should be united and reconnected. That constitutes the second stage of mantra to be experientially cultivated.[734]

3. The Stage of Pristine Cognition That Arises

Finally, the path that differentiates the sun and moon[—that is, the red and white generative fluids—]is gradually traversed in order to reverse upward the motion of the channels, winds, and vital essences. This constitutes the third stage of pristine cognition that arises.[735]

4. The Secret Stage

Next, your physical body becomes the rainbow body, and your mind, devoid of conceptual thoughts, is perfected in the coalescence of buddha body and pristine cognition. This constitutes the fourth or secret stage.[736]

Here I have set forth in writing the words of Kṛṣṇacārin,
Concerning experiential cultivation of **supreme liberation**,
Associated at **all** times with **delight** in the mind.

This was compiled from Venerable Sachen Kunga Nyingpo's *Commentary on Inciting the Path of the Four Stages.*

71. Guidebook Entitled *The Guidance of White Cakrasaṃvara*[737]

After first taking refuge and setting the mind on enlightenment, then with the words ŚRĪHERUKA AHAṂ ("I am Śrīheruka!"), you should adopt the skillful means whereby your awareness, clear and unimpeded, definitively assumes the form of the four buddha bodies. As such, you arise as Innate Cakrasaṃvara, the color of the moon, and the interior of your body resembles an inflated bag of white silk. In the middle [of that divine form] the three channels, including those to the right and left of the central channel, are filled with pure essences and with semen and blood in the form of the vowels and consonants. The maṇḍala of the wind element is at the anus and the maṇḍala of the fire element is at the triple intersection. In the middle of the navel cakra with its sixty-four branches there is the syllable AṂ. In its inner circle there are the eight letters representing the eight sets [of consonants and vowels], and outside these are all the vowels and consonants. At the heart cakra, in the middle there is the syllable HŪṂ, and in its four cardinal directions, the syllables BHRŪṂ, ĀṂ, JĪṂ, and KHĀṂ, and in the four intermediate directions, the syllables LAṂ, MAṂ, PAṂ, and TAṂ. At the throat cakra, in the middle is the syllable OṂ, and on its branches are the sixteen vowels. In the crown cakra there is the syllable HAṂ, with two sets of vowels. Here you should meditate that the letters are inside the channels.

Next, the fire is ignited by the wind, and the fire of the syllable AṂ incinerates the cakras. After training in the blazing and secretion [of the vital essence] that is warmed by the nectar of HAṂ, as a successful outcome you will be introduced to the eight sacred places of the maṇḍala of buddha mind with PU JĀ O A GO RĀ DE MĀ; {269} to the eight sacred places of the maṇḍala of buddha speech with KĀ O TRI KO KA LA KĀ HI; and to the eight sacred places of the maṇḍala of buddha body with PRE GṚ SAU SU NA SI MA KU—that is to say, you will be introduced to all the primary sacred places of the twenty-four lands.[738]

Finally, you should develop confidence in the level imbued with the seven aspects of union.[739]

Here I have embellished in writing the oral transmission
Of the perfection stage, praised as **supreme**,
Conferring **liberation** when **delight** is disclosed
With respect to **all** the instructions of Paṇchen Śākyaśrī of Kashmir.

This was compiled from the instruction manual of Chel Amogha.

72. GUIDEBOOK ENTITLED *THE FOUR ADAMANTINE SEATS*[740]

After first taking refuge and setting the mind on enlightenment: You should generate the visualization of yourself as Jñāneśvarī. You should visualize that in order to mature the seed syllables, at all the orifices of the body there are triangular hexahedrons fashioned of bone, and within [each of] them at the triangular channel knot there is a vital essence of generative fluid in the shape of a half-moon. You should meditate that these vital essences of generative fluid are virtually spinning around.[741]

Next, the four delights known as "delight," "supreme delight," "absence of delight," and "coemergent delight" are experientially cultivated [with reference to the four cakras], along with their four [corresponding subtle perceptions]: the subtle perception [of whiteness], the grand subtle perception [of redness], the approximate subtle perception [of blackness], and [the subtle perception of] coemergence.[742]

Pith Instruction of the Cow's Udder

As for the pith instruction entitled "cow's udder": In the navel cakra there is a channel resembling a coiled nāga (*nagendrakuṇḍalinī, klu dbang 'khyil ba*). Below it, at the triple intersection channel, there is a hexahedron, within which there is a yellow KṢUṂ with the property of fire. In the sole of each foot there is a syllable KṢUṂ. Within a red lotus in the heart cakra, resembling the "hoofprint of a bull," there is a vital essence of generative fluid, the size of a thumb. In its center there is a white HŪṂ, where the upper and lower winds clash. In the navel is the place where the wind of past actions gathers.

The fire then blazes from the yellow KṢUṂ, and it also blazes from the two soles of the feet. Everything within the channels burns with a reddish-yellow glow. Next, your mind should be concentrated on the crown of the head, where it dissolves into the syllable HAṂ. This is the coalescence—the nonduality of magical display and emptiness. Through your having meditated in that manner, the nine orifices of buddha body should be blocked, the four orifices of buddha speech should be blocked, and the two of buddha mind should be opened.[743] {270}

Pith Instruction of the Hoofprint of the Bull

Next, with regard to the pith instruction called the "hoofprint of the bull": You should meditate, as appropriate, dependent on either thirteen syllables or a single syllable. In the former case, there is a vital essence upon the open lotus of the heart cakra that resembles the hoofprint of a bull, and at its center there is a white syllable AṂ inserted within a vital essence, surrounded at its extremity by the twelve vowels, commencing with A. From the vital essence there arises on the right side a red hot wind, with the properties of fire and wind; and on the left side, there arises a white cold wind with the properties of earth and water. You should meditate that these two intermingle and collide, with the result that the vital essences alone spin, while the seed syllables do not spin.[744]

In the latter case, where the practice is dependent on a single syllable, you should meditate that upon the open lotus of the heart that resembles the hoofprint of a bull, there is a single white syllable AṂ. You should visualize that it starts to spin due to the conflict between the hot and cold winds, as above. The burnt offering of the flames should be dissolved in the white syllable A of the navel and the heart, and then the syllable A dissolved into the external body. It is said that this experience resembles the higher aspiration toward emptiness.[745]

Next, with regard to the central channel that resembles the awn of a plantain, in the heart cakra there is an eight-petal lotus. Opening on its right side there is an egg-shaped vital essence, with the properties of water, heavy and cool; and in its center there is a white HŪṂ. This egg-shaped vital essence opens in the manner, for example, of fruit that opens due to three conditions—warmth, seasonal moisture, and wind.[746]

In this context, you should visualize the coiled nāga at the navel, and below it a yellow KṢUṂ appears with the properties of fire and wind. It blazes within the central channel and melts the generative fluid. That fire then melts the syllable HAṂ, resembling the leaf of a tree. It flows down from its vital essence to the place between the eyebrows and is thereby rendered efficacious. Via the central channel, it then gradually dissolves into the white HŪṂ of the heart cakra and fills the body. You should then visualize that its whiteness extends from all the pores. You should visualize that, at this point, it does not diffuse outwardly, for at the heart cakra resembling the dome of a stupa, in the central channel resembling the awns of a plantain, the vital essence fills the inwardly opening eight-petal lotus [of the heart cakra]—the dome of the stupa, with the savor of bliss. On its four cardinal petals are the syllables A, A, AṂ, and A, {271} and on the four intermediate petals are the four neuter syllables. These are filled with the light of that vital essence, which outwardly permeates whiteness. You should meditate repeatedly in that manner.[747]

Pith Instruction on Consciousness Transference

As for the pith instruction on consciousness transference, when the outer and inner signs of death appear, you should endeavor to deceive impending death. But when you are definitely about to die, first you should cultivate the vase breathing twenty-one times, again and again. The orifices should be blocked in the following manner: the blue HŪṂ is at the two eyes; the white SUṂ is at the palate; the stacked syllables SAṂ MAṂ RAṂ YUṂ are at the throat; the stacked syllables HAṂ MAṂ RAṂ YUṂ are at both shoulders; the stacked syllables YAṂ MAṂ RAṂ YUṂ are at the heart; the stacked syllables KṢAṂ MAṂ RAṂ YUṂ are at the navel; HŪṂ is at the lower orifice of the urethra; and KṢUṂ is at the anus.[748]

Then you should fill [the abdomen with wind], as if filling a vase, and array six blue YUṂ syllables in the following six places: the two kidney cavities, the two armpits, and the two soles of the feet. You should meditate that the syllable HŪṂ in the middle of the heart cakra is surrounded at the periphery by four blue syllables, and that from the navel to the crown of the head twenty-one lotuses are vertically stacked, in the manner of a string of *dongtsé* coins.[749] You should meditate that in the middle of the navel cakra there is the syllable A, and on the crown of the head the syllable KṢUṂ at the orifice of the anterior fontanel. These last two are connected by a line of light that resembles a spider's thread. Saying HIK, you should meditate that the syllable A is drawn upward, as if being pulled by a rope, and it reaches the top of the [first] lotus. As you say HIK a further twenty-one times, that syllable A is drawn by the KṢUṂ all the way up to the lotus of the crown cakra. You should know that this resembles the drawing of water from a well. It is said that you should focus on the desirable place for rebirth by means of meditative stability, and then breathe HIK twenty-one times, before transferring consciousness from the crown of your head. By this means you will obtain the body that you desire—an awareness holder, the body of a god, and so on.[750]

Here I have combined **all** the pith instructions of the four adamantine seats
And presented them in writing, without addition or omission
According to the words of Ngok,
Integrated in the **supreme** path of **liberation** and great **delight**.

This was compiled from the ancient writings of Ngok Zhedang Dorjé.

73. Guidebook Entitled *The Great Magical Emanation*[751]

After first taking refuge and setting the mind on enlightenment, you should sit cross-legged upon a comfortable mat {272} with both hands in meditative equipoise. You should focus the mind and meditate that in the right channel are the consonants, ranging from top to bottom, and in the left channel are the vowels, ranging from bottom to top. Below the navel cakra, at the triple intersection of channels, upon a hexahedron, the fire is ignited by the wind. You should visualize that the syllable A is warm and hot to the touch. You should be mindful of this experience in each vertebra, and meditate without wavering.[752]

Having mastered this stability, through the movement of the vowels and consonants in the right and left channels, you should then meditate focusing on the letter A in the navel cakra, which has the properties of the fire and wind elements and is present within a white chamber of light formed by the hexahedron. A subtle flame burns noisily, incinerating the syllable HAṂ at the crown of the head, so that the generative fluid flows down, coats the extremity of the flame, and dissolves into the syllable A. You should meditate on that.[753]

The Yoga of Conclusive Attributes

[As far as the three phases of yoga are concerned:] From the perspective of the yoga of conclusive attributes, the complete path comprising all the three phases—lower forms, profound mantra, and conclusive attributes—is without error. But, even though you may have sequentially practiced first the lower forms, next the profound mantra, and finally the conclusive attributes, it is said that that sequence is not definitive.[754]

You should block the right and left channels with the garlands of vowels and consonants. A is in the navel cakra, HŪṂ is in the heart, AṂ is in the throat, HAṂ is in the crown of the head. The three higher syllables have the properties of the water element, while the syllable A in the navel has the properties of the fire and wind elements. From the syllable A the fire burns noisily. It penetrates and melts the syllables HŪṂ, AṂ, and HAṂ, which then directly flow down, forming a coating, and dissolve gradually into the syllable A.

The Yoga of Profound Mantra

With regard to the yoga of mantra, there are pith instructions of the upper gate and the lower gate, the former comprising three sorts [based on the cakras, the vital essences, and the subtle winds].[755] When buddhahood is attained, it is said to be secured through this very means.

The Meditation on the Middle of the Body

[More specifically, the pith instructions based on the vital essences are threefold, including the meditation on the upper extremity, the meditation on the lower extremity, and the meditation on the middle of the body.][756] [First] you should practice the yoga of lower forms [which accords with the generation stage]. Then [with regard to the meditation on the middle of the body]:[757] The crown of the head has the properties of the wind element, the heart has the properties of the earth element, the navel has the properties of the water element, and the genitals have the properties of the fire element. The three higher syllables have the properties of the water element.

As the wind moves toward the crown of the head, it causes the generative essence to appear at the syllable HAṂ, and subsequently that wind causes the white generative fluid to appear prominently in the heart, in the navel, and at the tip of the vajra (penis), after which it is reversed upward to the crown of the head, where it dissolves into the syllable HAṂ. [You should know that] as breath is exhaled, the vital essence appears prominently at the tip of the vajra (penis); and as breath is inhaled, it rises higher and dissolves into the syllable HAṂ.

Just as water from a single channel divides into two, at the upper extremity [of the central channel] {273} there are the right channel of the sun and the left channel of the moon. You should meditate in conjunction with the syllable OṂ when the breath is exhaled, in conjunction with the syllable

HŪṂ when breath is inhaled, and in conjunction with the syllable ĀḤ when the breath is diffused at the triple intersection of channels below the navel. Bliss will immediately arise.[758]

The Meditation on the Upper Extremity

Next, you should meditate on the form [of the deity] that accords with the generation stage, and as the eight attributes [of the eight elements] arise,[759] you will then connect with the perfection stage.

With regard to the visualization at the upper extremity of the upper gate,[760] you should meditate that at the heart cakra there is an open red lotus with four petals, and [at its center] there is a sun disk [with the properties of the fire and wind elements] and a moon disk with the properties of the earth and water elements, with a drop of generative essence between them. The sun and moon disks are conjoined around it [in the manner of an amulet]. There is a fine thread wound around them [back and front] in three strands, and on the side of the moon disk there are seed syllables wound around in three bands—with the thirty-two consonants on the upper thread and the sixteen vowels on the middle thread. On the side of the sun disk there are no seed syllables. You should focus your mind on the vital essence at the middle of this thread,[761] observing it there in a hollow in the center of the moon disk. With the sound of TOG, a syllable HŪṂ appears, piercing through the moon disk above. There is a fine thread attached to the HŪṂ, which winds around the moon disk in a circle, turning to the right, and then winds around the sun and moon disks from front [to back], thereby forming a cross. Once the HŪṂ has exited from the hollow, you should continue focusing on the vital essence. That is the form through which the deity is generated in the mantra syllables.[762]

You may then meditate on the [aforementioned] three phases of yoga[—that is, lower form, profound mantra, and conclusive attributes—]in their totality, and five signs will appear.[763]

When that vital essence is activated at the upper extremity of the upper gate, you should visualize that there is a vital essence at the center of the conjoined sun and moon disks, which resemble an amulet box, empty in the middle. At its periphery, strung by a fine thread, are the sixteen vowels, with A in the vanguard, and above that, also strung by a fine thread, are the thirty-six consonants, with KA in the vanguard. These strings of letters rotate one by one, without touching, just as gemstone beads are strung with a fine thread in such a way that they do not touch one another. You should then meditate that the wind slightly collides and breaches the top [of the amulet], so that it is loosened. KṢA, the final consonant in the string, brushes against the vital essence, and the syllable A [leading the vowels that follow it] is released, so that the KṢA is dislodged {274} and presses the syllable A inside. You should undertake this meditation repeatedly.

The Meditation on the Lower Extremity

When, on the other hand, the vital essence is activated dependent on the lower gate, you should look for a female consort with the appropriate signs. Having found her, you should undertake the "finger application" (*aṅguli'i sbyor ba*), and her channel will gently be opened. When that happens, you should not vigorously rub the vajra (penis) but engage in this experiential cultivation in an uncontaminated manner. Settle your mind on that, and later, even without discriminative awareness, realization will arise.[764]

Breathing

There are three ways of training the breath:[765] (i) relaxed breathing, (ii) counted breathing, and (iii) vase breathing [the last of which requires forceful training].

With regard to the first method: You should examine from where the wind has come, where it goes, and what is its action. Do not let it be purposeful. Even though you want to control it, you should not. Even though you want to inhale it, you should not. You should act freely and without effort.

As to the second method: After that, you should maintain awareness of the wind, counting the breaths. That is to say, you should visualize HŪṂ in the heart cakra. As you exhale breath, you should count or estimate three cycles of OṂ, revolving like a millstone; as you inhale breath, you should count or estimate three cycles of HŪṂ; and as you pause the breath, you should count or estimate the syllable ĀḤ. You should control your breathing by counting in that manner and prolong the pauses.

As to the third method: You should vigorously perform vase breathing, bumping on the ground and exhaling about ten times. Then you should inhale and restrict the breath within, filling the area below the navel. Do not exhale strongly or you will fill the abdomen in the wrong way. You should breathe out twenty-one times and fill the abdomen while maintaining the posture of the lion's play.[766]

You may also block the eyes, ears, mouth, and nostrils. Press the vajra (penis) between the thighs and block the anus with the heels. This constitutes the forceful method of breath control. With regard to the duration of this blocking, it should be equivalent to six finger snaps while placing the palms of the hands on the knees.[767]

Since the complete phases of mantra, form, and attributes appear in a nonarising manner, it is from the attributes that the [forms of the] deities and the mantras appear. Such are the pith instructions of the *Great Magical Emanation* that are unmistaken with regard to the entire path.

Here I have presented the heart elixir of Marpa,
The essentials that reveal **supreme** natural **liberation**,
Conferring the **delight** accrued from **all** the texts of Kukuripā on Māyā.

This was compiled from the ancient writings of Ngokpa.

74. Guidebook Entitled *The Kharamukha Cakrasaṃvara*[768]

After first taking refuge and setting the mind on enlightenment: {275} You should meditate that [you are present as Kharamukha Cakrasaṃvara and that] rays of light are diffused from the syllable HŪṂ in your heart cakra, absorbing the entirety of the inhabited world and its sentient inhabitants into your own body. Your female consort is also absorbed into your heart cakra from the left nostril. The visualization should then dissolve into a form in which you yourself appear as two-armed [Kharamukha Cakrasaṃvara], and your teacher is present on the crown of your head. With fervent devotion you should then pray, "May the genuine meditative stability grow in my mind!"[769]

Then you should visualize that within your heart cakra, there is a syllable A from which, upon a moon disk the size of a split pea, your own awareness is present as a white and red vital essence, the size of an average mustard seed. Hold this in mind! Then gradually you should gently unite the upper and lower winds. After familiarizing yourself with this practice, you should continue to hold it in mind, without letting your mental faculty be diffused elsewhere. As you abide one-pointedly, the meditative stability of bliss and radiance will arise.[770]

Dependent on that, your mind may become diffused toward other sense faculties, in which case you should undertake the preliminary practices as before. Then, with regard to the main practice, you should meditate on extremely minute white vital essences resting upon moon disks inside your two eyeballs. You should close the eyes and hold these in mind. After maintaining that practice for a while, you may then observe diverse sights, while focusing your mind on the vital essences, without permitting it to be diffused elsewhere. When you have familiarized yourself with this, the form of the vital essences will become radiant and meditative stability will arise on the basis of whatever sights you see. You should acquire some stability in this practice and meditate that those vital essences are absorbed into the heart cakra, whereupon the vital essence of the heart cakra becomes even more radiant and blazing than before. Through meditative equipoise the supreme meditative stability will then arise.[771]

Thereafter, your mind may become diffused toward the ears, in which case you should meditate on the preliminary practices, as before. Then, with regard to the main practice, you should meditate on two blue vital essences resting upon moon disks inside your two ears. You should hold in mind a direction where there is no sound. After maintaining that for a while, you may then hear diverse sounds, while focusing your mind on the vital essences, without permitting it to be diffused elsewhere. {276} When you have familiarized yourself with this, your visualization of the vital essences will become radiant and meditative stability will arise on the basis of whatever sounds you hear. You should acquire some stability in this practice and meditate that those vital essences are absorbed into the vital essence of the heart cakra, whereupon that vital essence becomes even more radiant and blazing than before. Through meditative equipoise the supreme meditative stability will then arise.[772]

Thereafter, your mind may become diffused toward the nose, in which case you should meditate on the preliminary practices, as before. Then, with regard to the main practice, you should meditate on yellow vital essences resting upon moon disks inside the cavity of each nostril. You should hold in mind a place where no odor is smelled. After maintaining that for a while, you may then smell diverse odors, while focusing your mind on the vital essences, without permitting it to be diffused elsewhere. When you have familiarized yourself with this, your visualization of the vital essences will become radiant and meditative stability will arise on the basis of whatever odors you smell. You should acquire some stability in this practice and meditate that those vital essences are absorbed into the vital essence of the heart cakra, whereupon that vital essence becomes even more radiant and blazing than before. Through meditative equipoise the supreme meditative stability will then arise.[773]

Thereafter, your mind may become diffused toward the tongue, in which case you should meditate on the preliminary practices, as before. Then, with regard to the main practice, you should meditate on a red vital essence resting upon a moon disk at the base of the tongue. You should hold this in mind, without tasting anything. After maintaining that for a while, you may then savor diverse tastes, while focusing your mind on the vital essence, without permitting it to be diffused elsewhere. When you have familiarized yourself with this, your visualization of the vital essence will become radiant and meditative stability will arise on the basis of whatever tastes you savor. You should acquire some stability in this practice and meditate that that vital essence is absorbed into the vital essence of the heart cakra, whereupon that vital essence of the heart cakra becomes even more radiant and blazing than before. Through meditative equipoise the supreme meditative stability will then arise.[774]

Thereafter, your mind may become diffused toward the body, in which case you should meditate on the preliminary practices, as before. Then, with regard to the main practice, you should meditate on a green vital essence resting upon a moon disk at your brow. You should hold this in mind, without touching anything. After maintaining that for a while, {277} you may then touch diverse tangibles while focusing your mind on the vital essence, without permitting it to be diffused elsewhere. When you have familiarized yourself with this, your visualization of the vital essence will become radiant and meditative stability will arise on the basis of whatever tangibles you touch. You should acquire some stability in this practice and meditate that that vital essence is absorbed into the vital essence of the heart cakra, whereupon that vital essence of the heart cakra becomes even more radiant and blazing than before. Through meditative equipoise the supreme meditative stability will then arise.[775]

Thereafter, you should visualize and meditate on the mental faculty that wanders everywhere, in which case you should meditate on the preliminary practices, as before. Then, with regard to the main practice, you should meditate on a pale-red vital essence that rests upon the red and white vital essence of the heart cakra but is even more subtle than that. You should hold this in mind, in a place that is extremely isolated. After maintaining that for a while, you may then meditate on topics imbued with social diversion. Those objects and thoughts to which your mental faculty becomes diffused should then themselves be absorbed into the pale-red vital essence. You should hold this in mind. When you have familiarized yourself with this, your visualization of the vital essence will become radiant and thoughts will not arise, or else they will arise only slightly and even vanish of their own accord. You should acquire some stability in this practice and meditate that that vital essence is absorbed into the red and white vital essence below it, whereupon that vital essence becomes even more radiant and blazing than before. Through meditative equipoise the supreme meditative stability of calm abiding will then arise.[776]

Thereafter, you should visualize and meditate on the afflicted mental faculty, in which case you should meditate on the preliminary practices, as before. Then, with regard to the main practice, you should meditate on a pale-red vital essence that rests upon the red and white vital essence of the heart cakra, and upon that there is a blue vital essence. You should hold this in mind, in a place that is extremely isolated. After maintaining that for a while, you may then meditate on topics imbued with objects where diverse afflicted mental states arise. This movement of afflicted mental states, including attachment, {278} should then be absorbed into the blue vital essence. You should hold this in mind. When you have familiarized yourself with this, your visualization of the vital essence will become radiant and afflicted mental states will not arise, or else they will arise only slightly and even vanish of their own accord. You should acquire some stability in this practice and meditate that that [blue] vital essence is absorbed into the pale-red vital essence below. That, in turn, is also absorbed into the red and white vital essence below. That, in turn, is absorbed into the moon disk. The moon disk, in turn, vanishes like clouds dissolving into space. Through meditative equipoise supreme calm abiding will then arise.[777]

At the end, when you arise from meditative equipoise, you should instantaneously see the appearances of the moon disk and the vital essence that are gradually formed. You should look upon yourself—the Heruka—and external phenomena to be without inherent existence, just as they appear. You should meditate in that manner until the respective signs [of realization] appear. When this is perfected, the meditative stability of calm abiding that is empty and of higher insight that is blissful and radiant will arise. Through that continuum of meditative stability, the pristine cognition of the path of insight will arise, so that buddhahood will be attained.

In brief, this method of training infinitely refines the meditative stability of composure with respect to the gates of the sense faculties, and then, in the main practice, you will settle upon the expressive energy of the imperishable vital essence. Finally, you should visualize that in the navel cakra resembling the coiled Kharamukha Cakrasaṃvara, the fire of the fierce inner heat darts like the tongue of a snake, so that it fills and permeates the interior of the central channel. You should meditate persistently on the union of the upper and lower winds.[778]

Here I have presented the **supreme** pith instruction,
The profound essentials that reveal **liberation**
From the fetters of attachments to the **delight** and bliss of existence,
Which are not found at **all** in other instructions.

This was written directly from the mouth [of Lowo Khenchen].

75. Guidebook Entitled *The Six Meditations of Vajravārāhī*[779]

After first taking refuge and setting the mind on enlightenment: (i) You should meditate on your own body as the body of Vajravārāhī. This is the first meditation—the training in visualizing her form. {279} (ii) Next, you should meditate upon a red four-petal lotus in the navel cakra, where there is a red syllable VAṂ. That is the second meditation—the training in the seed syllables. (iii) Next, you should compress the upper wind and meditate that it dissolves into the syllable VAṂ within the navel cakra. That is the third meditation—the training in subtle energy. (iv) Next, you should meditate that, owing to the movement of the maṇḍala of wind derived from the syllable YAṂ in your feet, the fire derived from the syllable RAṂ blazes as far as the genitals; then, through the warming of the syllable VAṂ in the navel cakra, light is on the verge of blazing from the syllable VAṂ, and as light blazes therefrom, the body is transformed into a mass of light. This is the fourth meditation—the training in the body of light. (v) Next, you should meditate that this light resembles hazy clouds vanishing in the sky or rainbow light vanishing in the atmosphere. This is the fifth meditation—the training in luminosity. (vi) Finally, within the disposition of this luminosity, you should visualize that there is a downward-facing white syllable HAṂ, directly positioned at the crown of the head, as before, and that there is an upward-facing red syllable VAṂ, directly positioned at the navel cakra. You should meditate that from that syllable HAṂ of the upper gate, generative essence drips as if on a spider's thread and penetrates the syllable VAṂ, so that the VAṂ is completely transformed, and consequently you become manifest as the coalescent female deity Vajravārāhī, in the manner of rainbow light. This manifestation arises in the nature of bliss, radiance, and nonconceptualization, but these attributes are not differentiated—they are coalesced owing to the inseparability of bliss and emptiness, and they are coalesced owing to the inseparability of radiance and emptiness. That is the sixth meditation—the training in coalescence.

Here I have elucidated in writing
A text praised for conferring **supreme** maturational **liberation**,
Composed by Chel **Kun**ga Dorjé,
Revealing the essentials of the six meditations of Vārāhī.

This was written according to the definitive ancient writings of Chel.

76. Guidebook Entitled *The Six Doctrines of Nāropā*[780]

After first taking refuge and setting the mind on enlightenment: You should settle your body into the exemplary sevenfold posture of Vairocana.[781] You should clearly regard and maintain the notion of your body as an empty frame and all its hairs, nails, and pores {280} hollow like a sieve. You should also regard and maintain the notion of the body of [your female consort, embodying] the transcendent lady Sahajā, with the nature of an empty frame.[782]

[Next, the practice of the six doctrines is as follows:]

1. The Fierce Inner Heat

When the core of your body is upright, you should imagine that the vertical central channel, extending from the genitals to the anterior fontanel, is straight as an arrow, hollow as straw, and radiant like a sesame oil lamp. The right and left channels both converge with the central channel at the upper and lower gates. At the upper gate they enter into the two nostrils. The cakra of the navel has sixty-four channel branches, the cakra of the heart has eight, the cakra of the throat has sixteen, and the cakra at the forehead has thirty-two. All these have the nature of an empty frame, and the network of the channels, extending as far as the horripilation of the pores, also constitutes an empty frame. This practice is called "holding the family-endowed basis."[783]

Next, you should expel the residual breath, and then slowly inhale breath that has the color of smoke and is directly in front, sixteen finger widths from the tip of the nose. It passes from the two pathways of the right and left channels into the lower end of the central channel. At this point you should also draw in the lower wind, and when you are ready to breathe out, you should visualize that it rises upward from the central channel through the anterior fontanel at the crown of the head. Without holding either the upper or lower wind, you should then push out your abdomen and fill it with the middle wind.[784]

Next, you should visualize that at the upper end of the central channel, which reaches the point between the eyebrows, there is a vital essence of generative fluid with four attributes—it is white, lustrous, round, and bright. As you inhale breath, at the same time you should visualize that vital essence descending within the central channel, pausing in the center of each respective cakra, and gradually appearing at the center of the secret cakra, after which it again rises upward, pale [in color], quickly reaching the upper extremity—the point between the eyebrows.[785]

Next, you should visualize that from the vital essence within the channel of fierce inner heat, an intensely burning flame spreads throughout all the cardinal and intermediate directions, along with the zenith and the nadir. This nature of fire, endowed with the four aforementioned attributes, then assumes the form of a celestial palace within an extensive and vast protective circle. {281} In this way, the channel of fierce inner heat should be transformed into your dwelling. When you are sitting and lying down, you should visualize that your seat and the ground also are of the nature of fire. In this way, the channel of fierce inner heat should be transformed into your seat. You should imagine that all the clothes that you wear are also of the nature of fire. In this way, the channel of fierce inner heat should be worn as clothing.[786]

2. The Illusory Body

With regard to the pith instructions concerning the illusory body, you should reflect and investigate that all the phenomena of cyclic existence, which are of the nature of suffering, and in particular the aggregates of your own body, and especially your mind, are impermanent and lacking independence, even for a single instant of time. That is to say, they are unreliable.[787]

On the other hand, since all that appears and exists has been present from the beginning in a pure cycle, you should regard your own physical body as the body of your preferred deity and develop certainty through the twelve similes of magical display. For, with regard to the completely perfect appearance of this buddha body, its lack of inherent existence resembles a reflection in a mirror. Its manifestation in any color whatsoever resembles a rainbow. Its manifestation of two from one resembles a mirage. Its formation from subtle energy and rays of light resembles an optical aberration. Its manifestation of a singular form as a multiplicity resembles the moon's reflection in water. Its indestructibility by any entity whatsoever resembles a human shadow. Its manifestation in diverse fields and arrays resembles a spirit town of gandharvas. These seven are the similes pertaining to buddha body. Its swift transformations resemble an echo. Its manifestation of a single savor as multiplicity resembles bubbles of water. These two are the similes pertaining to buddha speech. The lack of inherent existence in its experiences resembles a dream. Its manifestation as coemergence resembles a magical display. These two are the similes pertaining to buddha mind. Its swift engagement in enlightened activity resembles lightning. This is the simile pertaining to the essentiality of all three [buddha body, speech, and mind] combined. You should develop certainty and meditate through the approaches of these [twelve similes].[788]

3. Dream Yoga

With regard to the retention of dreams, you should visualize that at the center of the throat cakra is a lotus that has four petals, upon which is a red vital essence with the nature of the fire element. On its [center and] four petals there appear the syllables OṂ A NU TA RA. On falling asleep, you will definitely [know that you are dreaming].[789] {282}

As far as your activity [during dreams] is concerned, your dreams can then be transformed, increased, or refined.[790]

4. Luminosity

With regard to luminosity, during the daytime you should rely on the experience of luminosity in the disposition of nonconceptualization, and then through its power you will actualize the meditative stability of the luminosity associated with deep sleep, in which bliss, radiance, and nonconceptualization are combined.[791]

5. The Intermediate State

When the circumstances of the intermediate state arise after death, you should skillfully refine in accordance with your past experience the realization that whatever arises is pure appearance. In this way, you will actualize the buddha body of perfect resource during the intermediate state. You should abandon the sustenance of the present life and, until you grasp the next life, experientially cultivate your present circumstance as a corporeal being imbued simply with subtle energy and mind. You should also ascertain the notion that any appearances that arise at the present time contingent on past experiences in fact denote the intermediate state. In this way, the natural expression [of the intermediate state] will be actualized or else phenomena will be transformed into pure appearances.

By having naturally cultivated and experienced the appearances of the intermediate state in this disposition, you will arrive at [the true nature of] dreams. That is to say, whatever appearances of dreams might arise, they will be reminiscent of the intermediate state, and on that basis, you will refine them and take into your own hands the experiential cultivation of natural liberation.

If you have familiarized yourself with that, when the time of death arrives, the conceptual thoughts that partake of eighty natural expressions[792] will gradually dissolve, and through the phases of the three perceptions,[793] your presence in this life will yield. After you have died, when the appearances of the intermediate state arise in whatever forms, you will comprehend them according to the pith instructions that you previously experienced and, in this way, actualize the level of the buddha body of perfect resource during the intermediate state.[794]

6. Consciousness Transference

With regard to the pith instructions of consciousness transference, you should actually visualize in the sky, about one hand span above the crown of your head, your root teacher and the meditational deity in the form of Khecarī, in her celestial palace. You should then visualize within the central channel of your body, at the location of the throat, a white syllable OṂ, encircled by A NU TA RA. Breathe in and simultaneously imagine that from the syllable OṂ of the throat cakra a blue HŪṂ breaks off and appears at the heart cakra. From that, in turn, a red ĀḤ breaks off and comes to rest at the navel cakra. You should hold your breath as long as possible, and then breathe out. {283} After that, you should visualize simultaneously that the syllable ĀḤ of the navel cakra and the syllable HŪṂ merge, and that these in turn merge with the syllable OṂ of the throat cakra. Then the syllable OṂ, with its four surrounding letters, assumes the form of a vital essence that is the essential nature of your body, speech, and mind. Emerging from the anterior fontanel, it finally merges into the heart of your teacher.[795]

Here I have documented in the manner of a fragment of brocade
That has been extracted from molten gold
The **supreme liberation** of the knots of extensive **delight**,
Which derives from the **all**-pervasive *Six Doctrines of Nāropā*.

This was extrapolated from the *Molten Gold of the Six Doctrines* [of Karmapa Rangjung Dorjé] and then written down.

77. Guidebook Entitled *The Six Doctrines of Nigumā*[796]

After first taking refuge and setting the mind on enlightenment: You should meditate on the teacher upon a lotus and moon cushion on the crown of your head, and say, "I beseech you, Precious Teacher, to assuage my ailments and demons. I beseech you to purify my negativity and obscurations! I beseech you to let extraordinary meditative stability grow in my mindstream!" You should visualize that within your own head, there is a pristine white hexahedron, resting directly upon which there is a white syllable A, from which nectar arises, filling the body and expelling negativity, obscuration, and propensities in the form of smoky liquid.[797] Then your body is transformed, as if into a crystal ball. Cooling nectar will alleviate fevers; red nectar will alleviate colds; red and yellow nectar will alleviate wind disorders, purifying them by balancing heat and cold; and nectar that resembles boiling molten bronze will alleviate demonic possession.[798] Signs of this success will arise in actuality and in dreams.[799]

[The ensuing practice of the six doctrines is as follows:]

1. The Fierce Inner Heat

As for the fierce inner heat, in the preliminaries your physical body should be visualized as an empty frame that is of the nature of fire,[800] and then you should secure the posture of the "six opposing stoves" [of the hands, legs, and elbows].[801]

Next, you should become manifestly radiant as Vajrayoginī and visualize that the interior of her body is fine and translucent, like an inflated bag of red silk, and that to the left, right, back, and front of the kidney channels there are globes of fire.[802] You should then say, "Precious Teacher, I beseech you to let the meditative stability of bliss and warmth and the meditative stability of bliss and emptiness arise within me for the sake of all sentient beings!"[803] For the control of the gentle wind, you should perform the yogic exercise of stomach rotation, and thereby imagine that the [four globes of] fire fill the abdomen and clash together, causing pale-red sparks to scatter.[804]

Next, you should practice the "consumption of the channel of fierce inner heat" and visualize that the syllable RAṂ at the triple intersection of the channels is aroused by the fire and wind, and as the central channel widens, {284} it fills it with fire. Through the yogic exercises that stimulate the body and the yogic exercise of kindling fire with a rubbing stick, the winds below the navel, associated with speech, are united, and you should then focus one-pointedly on the blazing of the fire.[805]

Next, you should undertake the ancillary practices, known as the "wearing of clothing" that covers the body with fire down to the soles of the feet; the "spreading of the mat," through which you lie down like a sleeping dog at the gate; and the "riding of the horse," through which the goddess of wind lifts you up from under the armpits.[806]

You should [first] refine the [fourfold] "cycle of wind" twenty-one times.[807] The empowerment of conditioned existence will then be conferred and white nectar will flow from the body of the teacher at the crown of your head, filling [by stages] your crown, throat, heart, navel, and secret cakras. You should long for the four empowerments[808] and meditate on the places of the upper body where obstacles might arise as [precious] "three-eyed gems."[809] You should repeatedly visualize your body like a sieve and expel them. As you strongly intone the syllable HA and pound the back of your fist directly against your chest, diseases will then emerge in the form of steam.[810] As far as the lower part of your body is concerned, you should meditate that at the orifice of the vajra (penis), the generative essence wells up within the opening of the slender stem of a red lotus—the essential nature of blood (*rakta*)—and after adorning the soles of the feet, it is transferred to the crown of the head through the gesture of *vajroṣṇīṣa*. The visualization entails that the penis (*nor bu*) appears to be inverted upward into the small intestine, so that you focus your awareness on a red and translucent HŪṂ emerging via the pathway of the central channel as far as the anterior fontanel. Thereby ejaculations can be cut off six times. I have written this according to an oral teaching.[811]

2. The Illusory Body

With regard to the illusory body, you should engender a sense of disillusionment [with impermanent phenomena] and meditate on yourself as Innate Cakrasaṃvara. At the crown of your head is [your teacher in the form] Gathering of All Gurus. You should then say, "Precious Teacher, I beseech you that I might abandon self-grasping, that I might develop in my mind the sense that it is unnecessary, and that I might refine the illusory body and dreams!" The teacher should then dissolve into yourself, and thereafter, whatever appears arises as a magical display.

Those of superior acumen reinforce this during postmeditation, which is free from ideation. Those of average acumen resolutely assert that objective appearances exemplified by the manifestation of one's own body as Cakrasaṃvara are magical displays and dreams, equivalent to those that merely appear in mind and in speech. Those of lowest acumen abandon the four challenges that concern excessive movement, excessive migration, excessive thought, and excessive chattering; and then {285} they generate compassion for the six classes of living beings who are visualized as present within a hexahedron in the navel cakra.[812]

Next, you should draw in the lower wind and gradually compress the upper wind, so that six attributes arise—namely, blissful warmth, self-control of dreams, refinement of dreams, expansion [of dreams], the appearance of objective phenomena, and the natural arising [of magical display].

You should determine that illnesses are magical displays and lure demons into the hexahedron. Through the yogic exercise that agitates them, they then suddenly depart, and without attachment, you consider them as natural manifestations of magical display.[813]

3. Dream Yoga

With regard to dreams, you should say, "Precious Teacher, I beseech you that I might abandon self-grasping, that I might develop in my mind the sense that it is unnecessary, and that I might control [the recognition of] dreams!" You should imagine that there is a white vital essence derived from the syllable HAṂ in the crown cakra, and a red vital essence derived from the syllable HŪṂ in the secret cakra. When these [break away] and circle at the heart cakra, the vase empowerment is conferred; when they touch, the secret empowerment is conferred; when there is bliss arising from that touch, the empowerment of discriminating pristine cognition is conferred; and when they dissolve into one another, the fourth empowerment is conferred.[814]

[For the successful practice of dream yoga] there are nine unerring essentials: the three appropriate times—dawn, daybreak, and sunrise; the three physical postures—cross-legged, crouching, and the reclining of the lion; and the three visualizations—two with ideation and one without ideation. Thereby the white and red vital essences emerge from the right and left nostrils, and at the point between the eyebrows, these are clearly visualized as the male-female Cakrasaṃvara, who then vanishes into light. After that, you should visualize the syllable HŪṂ in the heart of the teacher, at your heart cakra. As you dissolve into the teacher and the teacher into the HŪṂ, and the HŪṂ vanishes into light, you should concentrate on and maintain your singular aspiration, saying, "This is itself a dream."[815]

With regard to the refinement of dreams, you should pray, "I beseech you that I might refine my dreams!" There are four phases of this refinement: (i) The refinement by the mind on the body is effected by visualizing Cakrasaṃvara when encountering a frightening precipice. (ii) The refinement of the mind by the body is effected by the absorption of the vital essences of the nine orifices and their subsequent vanishing. (iii) The refinement by means of Nairātmyā is effected by visualizing Nairātmyā in front, with a garland of A syllables in her lotus, and she is then invited into the adamantine gem [of the penis] in the form of blue light. (iv) The refinement by purposeful intent is effected by means of the one-pointed purposeful intent of Nairātmyā alone.[816]

With regard to the increasing of dreams, you should pray, "I beseech you that I might be able to increase them!" (i) You should increase the number of inanimate objects and sentient beings [in your dreams] from one to ten and so forth, and then reabsorb them into the originals. (ii) You should then increase the number of creatures who would train those beings, emanating cats for mice, {286} wolves for dogs, lions for tigers, cannibal ogres for human beings, and so forth, as well as garuḍas for nāgas, Vajrapāṇi for stroke-causing demons, Hayagrīva for king spirits and bewitchers, and Vajrabhairava for the lord of death; and then those beings will be tamed as you imagine they are struck with the appropriate hand emblems or incinerated by a mass of fire.[817]

With regard to the emanation of dreams, you should pray, "I beseech you for the power to emanate dreams!" and thereafter emanate whatever forms are appropriate, as before.[818]

With regard to the transformation of dreams, you should pray, "I beseech you for the power to transform dreams!" Then you may transform (i) sentient beings; (ii) subtle and gross phenomena; (iii) the diverse bodies of deities with different numbers of faces and arms; or (iv) empty appearances, free from attachment.[819]

[With regard to the perception of the objects that occur in dreams] you should pray, "I beseech you that I might determine the perception of objects!" Consequently, (i) [for those of superior acumen,] there will be clear understanding that there is no objective referent; (ii) [for those of average acumen,] there will be clear seeing of whatever is imagined; (iii) [for those of feeble acumen,] there will be the perception of the mental body flying through space; and apart from them, (iv) for those of lowest acumen, there will be perception of the objects they imagine.[820]

[As far as the last mentioned is concerned, the visualization is as follows:] Within a skull in a hexahedron at the navel cakra are the syllables OṂ, ĀḤ, HŪṂ, SVĀ, and HĀ. Therefrom Nairātmyā arises, resembling translucent crystal, emanating rays of light of five colors. At their tips the host of deities appears, resounding their respective mantras. Through your making outer, inner, and secret offerings to them, the impure inhabited world and its sentient inhabitants are refined. Then you should either (i) establish the desirable objects that you see within the heart of Nairātmyā, which is densely filled; or (ii) you should regard the objects that appear through the light visualized in the syllable A of Nairātmyā; or (iii) you should diffuse, as before, the objects appearing through the light rays visualized in the syllable A of Nairātmyā.[821]

4. Luminosity

With regard to luminosity, as before, you should engender intense disillusionment [with impermanent phenomena]. You should partake of sacramental substances and oily foods [in moderation], adopt a leisurely regimen, and abandon exertion that induces sweat. You should make a burnt offering of sacramental human flesh and human fat, and present an excellent array of communal offerings and torma offerings. Then you should pray, "I beseech you that I might apprehend the luminosity with a mind that actually sees the teachers, the buddhas!"[822]

Next, you should meditate on the translucent and radiant central channel within your own body. Settle the mind, without wavering, on the syllable A in the navel cakra. Above the cerebral membrane Nairātmyā appears, and the light of the syllable A in her heart purifies the brain, which is the natural expression of delusion.[823] Focus one-pointedly on the celestial palace, which is the cranium of the skull, and on the teacher within a radiant and translucent vital essence at the center of the heart cakra. {287} In his heart, too, there is a syllable HŪṂ imbued with the nature of a vital essence.[824]

Then you should practice the carrying of the three buddha bodies onto the path, and from within that disposition you should intermingle meditative equipoise and postmeditation through the perspective that radiance and emptiness are inseparable. You should above all develop and recognize the certainty that the coalescences of appearance and emptiness, bliss and emptiness, and radiance and emptiness are profound, calm, free from conceptual elaboration, and endowed with the two purities.[825]

You should persistently engage with the general and specific commitments, and then it will be important to discriminate the definitive dispelling of obstacles, the natural liberation of flaws, the resolution of doubts concerning the successful outcome of the practice, and the distinctions between daytime and nighttime experiences and realizations.[826]

5. Consciousness Transference

With regard to consciousness transference, you should pray with intensity, saying, "I beseech you that I may succeed in consciousness transference!"

Your own physical body then appears as a tent of blue silk. At the navel cakra within it there is a six-sided hexahedron, which cuts off the entrance to rebirth. Its three lower sides that face downward cut off the entrance to the path of the three lower realms, and the three upper sides face upward and to the right and left of the kidney channels. From within that hexahedron, the central channel rises upward to the dusty white aperture, resembling a skylight, at the crown of the head. In the navel cakra, light is diffused from a white syllable A, causing the abdomen to come into contact with the small of the back, so that the A shoots upward like an arrow through the main pathway of the central channel.

When it emerges from the skylight aperture at the crown of the head and vanishes into light, this denotes the consciousness transference into the reality of the buddha body of reality. When it dissolves into whichever meditational deity you revere—Cakrasaṃvara, Hevajra, and so forth—this denotes the consciousness transference into the coalescent meditational deity. When it enters into the secret womb of white or red Khecarī, whichever is appropriate, this denotes the consciousness transference into the unerring realm of the sky-farers. When it is transferred into the heart of the teacher, this denotes the consciousness transference of the guru's blessing.[827]

6. The Intermediate State

With regard to the intermediate state, you should pray to the teacher, saying, "I beseech you that I may attain the buddha body of perfect resource in the intermediate state!" Those of highest acumen should, during the luminosity of the first intermediate state, meditate on the child [luminosity that is encountered] within the disposition of the naturally arising mother luminosity. They will acquire the confidence of recognizing and recollecting the mother and child luminosities, as if meeting someone with whom they had been acquainted in the past. Those of average acumen, through the appearance of the body as a deity, of speech as mantra, and of mind as the natural expressive power of the nonarising Great Seal, will be free from the fear and trepidation that arise during the intermediate state of rebirth due to the forms of Yama and the sounds of the reversal of the four elements that manifest as shouts of "Strike, kill!" {288}

Those of lowest acumen will consider external appearances to be the celestial palace and the sentient inhabitants within it to be meditational deities, and then they should meditate on a blue hexahedron in front. You should reflect that those who do not realize this will enter into the womb of a mother, and those who do realize it will think that this is assuredly the palace of the expanse of reality, Akaniṣṭha. You should visualize that at its center, there is a blue HŪṂ diffusing light rays of five colors, so that it purifies your former womb entrances, refines your present womb entrance, and blocks your future womb entrances, all of which lead toward the four modes of birth. From that HŪṂ you become manifest as Cakrasaṃvara, and on the crown of your head is Jetsunma. On the crown of her head your teacher is seated, embodying light rays and bliss. He dissolves into Jetsunma, and therefrom rays of light, of the nature of bliss, penetrate you yourself. You should then meditate that on the right side of the hexahedron, objects giving rise to male hatred appear as the male consort Cakrasaṃvara alone, and that on the left side of the hexahedron, objects giving rise to female desire appear as the female consort Vajrayoginī alone. By presenting and refining mentally emanated offerings, you will attain buddhahood in the buddha body of perfect resource during the intermediate state.[828]

This clearly sets forth in writing
The natural, experiential cultivation of **supreme liberation**—
The instructions of the *Six Doctrines of Nigumā* that confer **delight**,
Perfect among **all** the profound instructions.

This was compiled from the instruction manual of Samdingpa Zhonu Drub.

78. Guidebook Entitled *The Amulet Tradition of the Great Seal*[829]

After you have taken refuge and set the mind on enlightenment, the preliminaries concern the three natural states [of body, speech, and mind, which are as follows]: (i) Undistracted by physical activities, your body should be seated in a relaxed manner, with your legs in the adamantine posture, your spine straight, and your hands resting upon your knees. (ii) As far as your speech is concerned, you should desist from speaking but keep your lips open, without closing them. (iii) As for your mind, throughout the three times you should sever the flow of conceptual thoughts and meditate while maintaining the innate natural state, without pondering, without reflecting, and without discursiveness. You should remain focused, uncorrupted by thoughts of desire, and {289} act spontaneously, without turning your gaze toward the front, the rear, the top, the bottom, the right, or the left, and without effort. You should chant the sutras, recite the mantras, and act out of that spontaneous disposition in all your conversations. If your awareness is sluggish, you should raise the gaze of your eyes, and if it is overactive, you should lower the gaze. Again and again you should meditate and maintain your perspective through the blessing of your teacher.[830]

As for the main practice, there are four defects to be naturally liberated: (i) though [the abiding nature of mind] is too familiar, its face is not seen; (ii) since [the Great Seal cannot be exemplified and] is too profound, it is not recognized; (iii) since [its establishment] is too easy, it is not convincing; and (iii) since [the three buddha bodies] are too noble, they do not enter into your mind. Recognition will come about once you have broken through these impasses.[831]

In conclusion, the four buddha bodies naturally arise—the buddha body of reality devoid of the conceptual thoughts of the mind, the buddha body of perfect resource imbued with intrinsic awareness, the buddha body of emanation that diversely appears, and the buddha body of essentiality in which these are inseparable. The outcome will be successful through compassion, through the generation stage, through the [control of] wind, and through devotion.[832]

Here and now I have set forth in written form
This **supreme liberation** from the knots of **delight**,
The instruction manual inscribed **entirely** on palm leaves—
A book that emerged from within an amulet.

This was compiled from the instruction manual of Samdingpa Zhonu Drub.

79. Guidebook Entitled *The Three Aspects Carried on the Path*[833]

After first taking refuge and setting the mind on enlightenment: You should meditate on the teacher, [seated] upon a lotus and moon cushion on the crown of your head. You should clearly recall the appearance of your teacher's body just as it is, the sound of your teacher's voice just as it is, and the understanding and enlightened intention of your teacher's mind just as it is. With fervent devotion you should have the power to dissolve outwardly [into that visualization], and inwardly your vacillating mind should hover around the tip of your nose. Consequently, you should determine that apparent physical forms are the body of the teacher, words are the speech of the teacher, and intrinsic awareness is the mind of the teacher.[834]

Thinking that it is through this genuine teacher endowed with the defining characteristics that you will be liberated from cyclic existence—hard to endure—and that consequently cyclic existence will be rendered nonexistent through your teacher's kindness, you should engage in the power of devotion that makes the hairs of the body stand on end and agitates the eyes with tears. {290} Then say, "I pay homage! I make offerings! I go for refuge! I pray that you turn the wheel of the sacred doctrine and do not pass into nirvana! May this virtuous merit become the causal basis for me being favored by my teacher!"[835]

In the same manner, you should meditate on the meditational deity, however that appears, and on the magical display [of appearances], however that appears; and these experiential cultivations should also be carried on the path, as above.[836]

Here I have illustrated in a few clear words
The guidance of **supreme liberation** in the **delightful** mind,
Which gathers **all** aspects carried on the path.
This augments the auspicious path of liberation.

This was compiled from the instruction manual of Samdingpa Zhonu Drub.

80. Guidebook Entitled *The Deathlessness of One's Own Mind*[837]

After first taking refuge and setting the mind on enlightenment: You should visualize yourself as Innate Cakrasaṃvara in male-female union. You should focus on a blue HŪṂ at the fontanel of the male deity, and the red syllable VAṂ at the fontanel of the female deity. The bodies of those deities will become lackluster owing to the blue and red radiance of those two seed syllables respectively. Then blue and red rays of light, of the nature of bliss, gradually emerge from these two syllables, exemplified by sunrise on a snow mountain peak, so that everything is filled and enveloped with the light.

Next, just as an aquamarine and a ruby covered with mud can be cleansed with water, that external radiance [of the syllables] transforms into the nature of internal radiance. You should visualize that at the top of the matted hair of the male deity there is a wish-granting gem, and on its left side a moon disk of the first lunar day. Just above the fontanel there is a crossed vajra supported on his matted hair, and on the black locks of his matted hair there is a circlet of bone and dangling bone ornaments. Between the crown ornaments comprising five dry skulls there are transverse vajras. He has the silken ribbons of a spiritual warrior and three red eyes—blue in the middle and pale at the periphery. The bridge of his nose is high, his brow large, his mouth closed, his earlobes long, his face smiling, and the tips of his upper and lower teeth and incisors are just about visible. His throat is bulbous, his upper body is broad, {291} and his two hands hold the vajra and the bell, embracing his female consort. All of his bone ornaments—the choker, earrings, necklace, shoulder bands, bracelets, waistband, and anklets—are completely white, and his tiger-hide garment is loose at the back. His right leg is drawn in and the left leg extended, pressing down upon lotus and sun cushions and [mats in the forms of] Bhairava and Kālarātrī. The female consort is smiling, wrathful, and energetic, the hair of her head disheveled; and she holds a curved knife and a skull, embracing the neck of the male. Her bone ornaments are shining white, her breasts prominent, her right leg extended, her left leg contracted, in union with the male; and they are sealed within an amulet of blue and red light.[838]

Consequent on that visualization, you should develop the conviction that your own mind is immortal, untainted by the stains of birth and death. You should equipoise your mind in the body of the deity that appears but lacks inherent existence.[839]

Here I have presented in writing
The natural face of **supreme liberation**,
The uncontrived natural state of mind,
The mental faculty that appears **totally delightful**
And that is free from transitions.

This was compiled from the instruction manual of Samdingpa Zhonu Drub.

81. Guidebook Entitled *The Six Doctrines of Sukhasiddhi*[840]

After you have taken refuge and set the mind on enlightenment, the Six Doctrines of Sukhasiddhi are as follows:

1. The Fierce Inner Heat

With regard to the practice of the fierce inner heat, you should secure the six stoves [of the hands, feet, and elbows] and visualize in your own navel cakra a four-petal lotus with five syllables. Next, you should focus on the wind of the rectum, which ignites the fire of the navel cakra, causing the syllable A in the center and the surrounding four syllables HA, RI, NI, and SA to blaze with fire—red and brilliant. Your body will be filled internally with the light of the fire. Then you should mentally repeat HA RI NI SA and maintain the union of the upper and lower winds.[841]

2. The Illusory Body

With regard to the practice of the illusory body, you should visualize that below the lotus of the navel cakra there is a hexahedron containing all sentient beings of the six classes. You should cultivate compassion, and the light of the seed syllables will purify the obscurations of sentient beings. The light itself will then emerge from your own fontanel, with a white radiance in the case of divine goddesses: {292} azure blue in the case of gandharvas, pale yellow in the case of brahmins, pink in the case of human beings, whitish yellow in the case of nāgas, and dark brown in the case of outcastes. These beings have an epicanthus on the eyes and an epicanthic fold on the lips. Below the navel, the lotus of their naked, secret cakra is extensive, with bristling anthers from which a stream of blissful generative fluid is released. It enters through the crown of your head and fills your body internally. You should imagine that bliss will then grow, and you should maintain this natural state of the illusory body.[842]

3. Dream Yoga

With reference to dream yoga, you should focus awareness on the natural experience of blissful warmth in the lotus of the navel cakra, and on the spinning of the letters. You should recognize that dreams are dreams and repeatedly practice their recognition, emanation, and transformation. Objective appearances will then reach the pathway of light that derives from the syllable A, in consequence of which you may see them, just as you wish.[843]

4. Luminosity

With reference to the practice of luminosity, you should focus your own mind radiantly on the syllable A, without contrivance, so that the experience of luminosity consequently arises.[844]

5. Consciousness Transference

With reference to the practice of consciousness transference, you should visualize the four syllables of the lotus petals as the four elements, and through the sequence of the dissolution of the elements, dissolve them into the syllable A. You should imagine that your consciousness will then emerge [from your body], some distance from the crown of your head, and vanish into the nonarising state.[845]

6. The Intermediate State

With regard to the practice of the intermediate state, from the present moment you should carry forward appearances as deities, sounds as mantra, and recollections and thoughts as reality.[846]

This tract without addition or omission
Concerns the six doctrines of **supreme liberation**
That energize the coemergence of the four **delights**,
Associated with the foremost of **all** the ḍākinīs of bliss.

This was compiled from the instruction manual of Khyenrab Chojé [Rinchen Chokdrub Pelzang of Zhalu].

82. Guidebook Entitled *The Inner Guidance of Nairātmyā*[847]

After first taking refuge and setting the mind on enlightenment: You should visualize yourself as the body of Nairātmyā. You should meditate that on each of the twenty-one articulations of her spine there is an inch-sized miniature representation of Nairātmyā and that in the middle of the body are the three channels, among which the right and left channels depend upon the central channel, just as creepers entwine around a tree. On the four-petal lotus in the navel cakra, the syllables HA, RI, NI, and SA surround the syllable A—pale blue on the front side, red on the right, yellow on the left, white on the rear, and green in the center. On the crown of the head, inseparable from Virūpa, is Hevajra, with one face and two arms, assuming a dancing demeanor. In the sky in front is Dampa Gyagar, {293} the lower part of his body covered in a woolen cloak. You should meditate that in his hands he holds a reed flute and he is facing toward you. Pray one-pointedly, and say, "Virūpa HŪṂ, Sukha ĀḤ, Dampa Gyagar OṂ!"[848]

Then you should visualize that from the syllable A resting within the navel cakra an arrow also in the form of the syllable A breaks off, and, dependent on the bow of the central channel, it is propelled by the whip of subtle energy and mind combined and moves upward. You should turn your body alternately toward the right and the left, with your legs in the adamantine posture, and your hands placed upon your pulse of vitality at the wrists. Your eyeballs, too, should move gradually upward. At that time, you should train the pathway of the central channel with the [tightening] noose of the right and left channels, and then the syllable A will emerge some distance above the crown of the head. There you will be blissfully transformed into Nairātmyā, inseparable from Sukhasiddhi, and embrace black Virūpa. You should imagine that the stream of generative fluid arising from this union then descends via the spine, filling the twenty-one aforementioned miniature representations of Nairātmyā, and finally from the navel—the fertile ground of the body—it permeates the entire body.[849] Your complexion will be invigorated, your optic nerves will be raised up, your consciousness captivated, and you will refine the empty nature of space, devoid of awareness as well as the fundamental nature of mind endowed with awareness. Having trained in this fundamental nature, you should be relaxed. By being relaxed you will achieve your goal. Such are the crucial points.[850]

Here I have turned into writing
Sukhasiddhi's method of adorning the cakra of great bliss—
Supreme liberation from the knots
Associated with the four **delights**,
Entirely inseparable from Hevajra.

This was compiled from the ancient instructions of Khyungpo Neljor.

83. Guidebook Entitled *The Coemergent Union of the Great Seal*[851]

After first taking refuge and setting the mind on enlightenment: You should meditate clearly on your teacher in the maṇḍala of your heart. In front you should position a slender stick and stare directly at it without closing the eyes and without moving. You should indeed focus your awareness lucidly on that object, but not settle on it with constraint. {294} Nor should you hold the object in esteem. Instead, without permitting awareness to wander, you should focus for that moment simply on a support where the mind is undistracted and let awareness rest completely in that state, relaxed in its natural modality.

It is important to distinguish quality in meditation. To enhance this state of abiding, you should take a break and rest for a while, before resuming your meditation. After undertaking many short sessions of this sort, you should engage in the four-session meditation. In all the intervals between sessions, you should not lose that disposition but act continuously and constantly with mindfulness. Your eyes may also gaze upon the tip of your nose, but not for long. All modes of activity—moving about, sitting, and so forth—should be undertaken [slowly], like the actions of an invalid.

Next, in the space between the eyebrows, you should visualize a white vital essence, the size of a pea, and focus your awareness upon that for a moment. In that disposition, let the mind relax into its natural modality. To enhance this state of abiding, take a break and rest for a while. After undertaking many short sessions of this sort, you should engage in four-session meditation. In all the intervals between sessions you should not lose that disposition but act as above [continuously and constantly with mindfulness].

Next, you should meditate briefly on a round black vital essence, resting upon a seat, and focus your awareness upon that for a moment. In that disposition, let your mind settle into its natural state of abiding.

In the course of these [visualizations], if you do not focus on [the tip of] the nose upon which [the mind] rests, you will incur the obstacle of having a mind that does not rest. All your thoughts will freely escape, and at that time you will be impeded by conceptual thoughts. So, from the start, you should recognize these thoughts without obstacle. You should grasp the crucial point of not being vexed by meditating, and thereby you will develop a focus on ever more subtle thoughts. By whatever means, you should then let all tarnished thoughts and all other thoughts that arise in the above manner relax directly, and permit all those thoughts that are present to move within a disposition in which the rope of mindfulness is not severed. You should regard them, however many they are; and without allowing even a single one to escape, you should recognize the first one that arises, you should recognize the second one that arises, {295} and you should recognize all those that subsequently arise. Thereby, through your focusing on those thoughts, the continuum of conceptual thoughts will be interrupted. Once conceptual thoughts have been interrupted, the state of abiding will be enhanced and the continuity of occasionally present [thoughts] will be rendered nonexistent.

If the strength of your constitution is impaired when your awareness is agitated due to many ephemeral thoughts, you should recuperate and rest just for a day, and then by resuming the meditation from the beginning you will recover. It is important to partake of nutritious food.

Now, you should meditate similarly, without any referential focus or support for meditation. Here your mind should relax at ease in its own modality, and you should meditate, looking gently wherever it arises, uncontrived, without ownership, and without supervision. Let your mind settle steadily into its natural state. You should for a moment maintain mindfulness of its state, simply without wavering. Otherwise, let it settle into its natural modality, without meditating at all. As far as the sessions are concerned, these should be shorter than before. You should remain calm, take a break, and rest for a while before resuming the meditation. You should meditate in this manner over four sessions, and in all the intervals between sessions you should act continuously and constantly with mindfulness. You may engage in activities in the aforementioned manner. When arising from meditation and taking a break, you should ask yourself how the mind is present, so that whenever you take a break it does not move anywhere; and whenever you stand up, your awareness is slow, relaxed, languid, hazy with regard to perceptions, and loose, without effort. If your awareness does not intentionally engage with objects, and it is said to be present without differentiating anything, the state of calm abiding will arise.

At this point, in order to stimulate your awareness somewhat, you should let it be lucid and vivid. Without wavering in this disposition, you should be mindful of it for a moment, clear and calm, and then take a break and rest, before resuming the meditation. You should meditate accordingly over four sessions, and in all the intervals between sessions you should act without losing that state. You may also engage in activities in the aforementioned manner.

After interrupting the abiding continuity of thoughts in that manner, {296} now, at this time when the quality of meditation is enhanced, you should regard the essential nature of mind with greater intensity. You should observe how the essential nature of mind is present, and you should observe any proper determination that it itself makes concerning itself. Then you should refrain completely, and rest for a while before resuming the meditation. When observing any [proper] determination, you should observe, with regard to yourself, whether recognition is present in your mind, whether emptiness is present without recognition, whether something is present entirely without emptiness, whether from the disposition of emptiness a naked radiance is present, or whatever. You should carry any such experiences [onto the path].

All the crucial points of instruction are contained in this practice: You should ask yourself in what manner the essential nature of mind is present; and consequently, if it is said that an emptiness is present, you are seeing simply one side of it and cannot be introduced to the essential nature of mind. If it is said that no emptiness at all is present, or that a lucidity and vividness is present, you should observe this properly. Until you recognize that state, you cannot be introduced to the essential nature of mind. If it is said that awareness is lucidly present without recognition, you have not seen its essential nature.

Therefore, with regard to this introduction: In general, meditation includes both calm abiding and higher insight. *Calm abiding* and *higher insight* are technical terms, the former denoting that a state of abiding is present and the latter denoting that a radiance or luminosity is present. But these alone are not beneficial. Instead, we great meditators must experientially cultivate the naked awareness directly. If that is introduced to you right now, when your mind settles in a relaxed manner into its natural modality, thoughts will subside and be calmed right where they are. If your mind is calmly present in its natural modality, this is said to be genuine calm abiding. Most persons who receive the oral instructions or great meditators should now meditate on that alone. If, on the other hand, you are proud and in addition have too many teachers, you will not be able to meditate, even a little. Yet without that practice there will be no way at all to progress. Within the disposition of genuine calm abiding {297} nothing remains that is deluded, indeterminate, nonsensical, or indifferent. When it is said that "the essential nature of mind is like this," there is indeed no recognition of anything that should be verbalized in speech, conceptualized by the mental faculty, scrutinized by the intellect, or expressed in words. While there is no such recognition, there should come to you a radiant and unimpeded awareness—exposed, trembling, stark, and distinct, seeing that which has not yet been seen and experiencing that which has not yet been experienced. And then if there is no lack of recognition with regard to this radiance that cannot be verbalized, this is said to be genuine higher insight.

As far as the terms *calm abiding* and *higher insight* are concerned, even though these two have a temporal sequence, you should actually meditate on them without differentiation. It is said that no fault will arise from meditating on them completely in that very instant of time. Since you are without all sorts of superimposition, you will not fall into the extreme of eternalism, and since you are intrinsically aware and accomplished through experience, you will not fall into the extreme of nihilism.

Now that you have calmed conceptual thoughts right where they are by relaxing the mind in its natural modality, the [formerly] unrecognized consciousness that is clear, sharp, intrinsic awareness, stark in its natural radiance, is said to be the enlightened intention of the mind of the buddhas. It is said to be the defining characteristic of the mind of sentient beings. It is said to be the abiding nature of all entities. That which is called your own mind is this [formerly] unrecognized, radiant, and sharp awareness, which is introduced by teachers and then cognized by disciples. So, that which was formerly unrecognized is said to be the mind that is now recognized. This is the case for those who attain buddhahood, for those who roam in cyclic existence, for those who have likes and dislikes—in short, for all those who engage with the phenomena of existence and quiescence. Having formerly been obscured by conceptual thoughts, they did not recognize the essential nature of mind, but now, cutting off the continuity of conceptual thought, they do recognize it. Even when the recognition of the essential nature of mind is entirely absent, it is still the intrinsic nature of mind. Even when radiance and vibrancy are absent, they are still the defining characteristics of mind. {298} In the essential nature of empty and radiant awareness, sharpness and clarity are the essential nature. You should achieve a stark recognition of this. Such is the introduction to the coemergent nature of mind.

Here there arises in the format of writing
The way that leads to **supreme liberation**,
The union in the equipoise of coemergent **delight**
That is the jewel crest of **all** instructions of the Great Seal.

This was compiled from the memorandum composed by Gyamawa [Lodro Gyeltsen], based on the teachings of Gyelsépa Tokmé Zangpo.

84. Guidebook Entitled *The Fivefold Great Seal*[852]

After you have taken refuge and set the mind on enlightenment, there ensues the fivefold experiential cultivation of (i) the enlightened mind, (ii) the meditational deity, (iii) the teacher, (iv) the Great Seal, and (v) the dedication of merit.

During this session, you should meditate sincerely, saying, "I will charge my body, speech, and mind to engage in virtuous action!" You should meditate that you instantaneously become Cakrasaṃvara in union with female consort, with a radiant form and steadfast pride. You should then pray, saying, "I pray to Vajradhara, precious teacher of all sentient beings and essential nature embodying all objects of refuge, seated upon a lotus, moon, and sun cushion on the crown of my head!"

Finally, Vajradhara dissolves into yourself and his buddha body, speech, and mind blend together with your own body, speech, and mind. In that state, from within a disposition devoid of sluggish and overactive thoughts of anything at all, you should settle the mind clearly and starkly, without becoming diffused toward anything at all; and you should then secure this by means of the dedication of merit.

Here I have embellished in writing
The essentials of experiential cultivation,

Combining skillful means and discriminative awareness,
The path of emancipation that reveals **supreme liberation**,
Giving rise to **delight** that gathers together
All the five essentials [of the Great Seal].

This was compiled from the instruction manual of Chen Ngawa.

85. Guidebook Entitled *The Four Syllables of the Great Seal*[853]

After you have taken refuge and set the mind on enlightenment, the four main points are explained. These comprise (i) the basis that eradicates obscuration, (ii) the presentation of the means of establishing the nature of mind, (iii) the severing of deviations, and (iv) the carrying of the nature of mind on the path.

1. The Basis That Eradicates Obscuration

The mind in the beginning is without point of origin, primordially empty and baseless. In the middle it is nonabiding, and its movement is empty of movement. In the end there is nowhere that it goes; {299} its movement is naturally liberated, and it is neither obstructed nor does it exist at all. Uncovered by the flaws of cyclic existence, it is primordial buddhahood.[854]

2. The Presentation of the Means of Establishing the Nature of Mind

There are six methods of establishing the nature of mind: Your body should assume the sevenfold posture of Vairocana and then: (i) You should be established without laborious effort in the uncontrived, innate disposition of mind, like a mighty garuḍa soaring in the sky. (ii) You should be established in the unwavering disposition of mind, like an ocean devoid of waves. (iii) You should be established in equipoise imbued with radiant space, like a cloudless sun. (iv) You should be established in unimpeded luminosity without grasping, like a small child looking at a temple. (v) You should be established in recognizing all the sensations that arise to be the nature of mind, like the waves of water. (vi) You should be established in awareness that leaves no tracks, like a bird flying in the sky.[855]

3. The Severing of Deviations

With regard to the severing of deviations, you should determine absolutely not to aspire for buddhahood above, not to harbor doubts toward cyclic existence below, not to be attached to appearances in between, and then your mental faculty should be unengaged.[856]

4. The Carrying of the Nature of Mind on the Path

With regard to the teaching concerning the carrying of the nature of mind on the path, this comprises six continuous yogas—namely, (i) the yoga that secures appearances during the daytime, (ii) the yoga that carries the attributes of desire on the path as an assist during mornings and evenings, (iii) the yoga that gathers the four powers at twilight, (iv) the yoga that induces knowable phenomena into the vase [of luminosity] at midnight, (v) the yoga that illuminates awareness at dawn, and (vii) the yoga that penetrates pristine cognition to its core at the time of death.[857]

This presents in writing the teaching concerning:
The eradicating of obscurations in the ground,
The means of establishing the nature of mind,
The severing of deviations,
And the carrying of the nature of mind on the path,
Which constitute the **supreme liberation** from bondage,
The **all**-encompassing **delight**
[Of the four syllables—A, MA, NA, SI.][858]

This was compiled from the instruction manual of Yagdé Paṇchen.

86. Guidebook Entitled *The Introduction to the Three Buddha Bodies*[859]

After first taking refuge and setting the mind on enlightenment: You should visualize yourself upon a lion throne with lotus and moon cushions, from the four corners of which Brahmā, Indra, Upendra [Viṣṇu], and Rudra appear, with heads bowed, as emanational supports, embellished with divine sacraments, clothing, and gems. Upon it you are seated in the form of Munīndra, {300} golden colored, adorned with the major and minor marks, wearing the three religious robes, the hands in the earth-touching gesture and the gesture of equipoise, and the legs in the adamantine posture. Commencing from the protuberance at the crown of the head, he has a hair ringlet at the forehead, a glorious *śrīvatsa* at the heart, and the entirety of his body radiates the [eighteen] distinct attributes of the buddhas.[860] Even to the extent of the hairs of his head, he is present throughout the three times. From his body, rays of light are diffused, transforming the inhabited world into a pure land and its sentient inhabitants into the body of the Conqueror. These then enter through the billion pores of your own body, so that you appear as the glorious lord-protector of living beings endowed with sight, hearing, memory, and awareness. This constitutes the introduction to the spontaneously present natural expression of the buddha body of emanation.[861]

Also, you should visualize yourself in the form of Avalokiteśvara, the buddha body of perfect resource, seated upon a lion throne with lotus and moon cushions, with one face and four arms—the first pair of hands in the union of meditative equipoise, the other right hand holding a crystal rosary, and the other left hand holding a lotus. His legs are in the adamantine posture, and in the front of his crown of matted hair there is Amitābha. He has a jacket of antelope hide, and the pores of his skin are filled with buddhas and bodhisattvas from whom light rays are diffused, resembling sunrise on a snow mountain. The inhabited world and its sentient inhabitants are then purified, and you are transformed into the buddha body of perfect resource, endowed with the five certainties.[862] This constitutes the introduction to the buddha body of perfect resource.[863]

Also, you should visualize yourself in the form of Vajradhara, the buddha body of reality, seated upon a throne endowed with excellence—azure blue, like the sky uncovered by clouds, with one face and two arms, holding a vajra and bell that are crossed at the heart. His legs are in the adamantine posture, and the major and minor marks are radiantly perfect. All the parts of his body, which is adorned with silks and gems, are filled with the maṇḍalas of the four classes of tantra, and therefrom rays of light are diffused and absorbed, purifying the inhabited world and its sentient inhabitants and then being reabsorbed into yourself. Your own manifestation also dissolves into this disposition of luminosity and bliss, phenomena are exhausted, and the conclusion is reached. This total withdrawal into the natural state, without verbalization, conception, or expression, which is profound, calm, unelaborate, and uncreated by the intellect, {301} constitutes the introduction to the buddha body of reality.

Here I have illustrated through writing
The **supreme** doctrine bestowed by Nāropā
Concerning natural **liberation**—
The teachings that generate **delight**,
The perfect conclusion to **all** the instructions of Pullahari.

This was compiled from the instruction manual of Venerable Rangjungwa [Karmapa III].

87. Guidebook Entitled *The Indivisibility of Subtle Energy and Mind*[864]

After you have taken refuge and set the mind on enlightenment: (i) There ensues the indivisibility of subtle energy and mind during the generation stage. Here, having abandoned differentiations between subtle energy and mind, you should nurture mindfulness, without distraction, of the innate personal experience of bliss associated with the body of the deity that manifests in and of itself.

(ii) Next, without [distinguishing between] meditative equipoise and postmeditation, and with certainty that the innate inner state is attained in the vitality of the subtle energy of fierce inner heat, clad in the fire that blazes from the ashé (the stroke of the letter *a*) of the navel cakra, you should control this wind in the manner of a man riding a horse, an analogy which some from our school of practice employ to describe subtle energy and mind.[865]

(iii) When control has been achieved, you should instantaneously nurture the naturally occurring radiant and abiding aspects of the original nature of mind and intermingle the perception of fire with the abiding aspect. Whatever arises then becomes the [coalescence of] appearance and emptiness devoid of attachment, the incontrovertible disposition of the illusory body in which subtle energy and mind are indivisible. You should be open and at ease, without discouragement even when under the sway of ill health and at the time of death, and you should develop the conviction that fervent devotion to the teacher alone constitutes the vitality of the path.[866]

(iv) Next, when you apply consciousness transference at the time of death, the subtle energy and mind will be indivisible. A blue and red vital essence, the size of a pea, in which subtle energy and mind are intermingled, will rise upward from the secret cakra and pass directly from the pathway of the central channel, upward through the anterior fontanel, and settle in the disposition of the abiding nature.[867]

This is the writing that discloses the **supreme**
Expanse of the Great Seal concerning natural **liberation**—
Through the mind of natural **delight**,
Which in **all** respects does not differentiate
The common savor of subtle energy and mind.

This was compiled from the instruction of Lhazik Repa.

88. Guidebook Entitled *The Six Doctrines according to the Sekharma Tradition*[868]

After first taking refuge and setting the mind on enlightenment: You should establish the scope of the view concerning the meditations of the *Fifteen Scrolls*,[869] [which conclude with the liturgy of] the protector of the transmitted teachings Kholpo Dartochen and so forth; and after that, you should focus on the three phases of essential visualization, {302} focusing on the conquerors of the five enlightened families, in whom the five poisons are the essential nature of the five pristine cognitions.

At the time when dark hatred arises, it is ascertained that the unchanging pristine cognition of reality's expanse and Akṣobhya are manifesting. Do not enter into the pathway of hatred. If you do enter, the prince will be without a father. Do not impose an antidote upon hatred. If you impose one, the prestige of the prince will be diminished. This is the intrinsic face that appears as hatred. You should establish its entirety, with corners unbroken and sides undamaged, to be the defining characteristic of the adamantine reality of hatred. Without your abandoning hatred, its inherent purity is the Great Seal. That is to say, you should meditate on the scroll that concerns the adamantine reality of hatred.

Then, modulating this according to the [other] enlightened families, pride is [inherently] pure as the pristine cognition of sameness and miserliness as Ratnasambhava, desire as the pristine cognition of discernment [Amitābha], jealousy as the pristine cognition of accomplishment [Amoghasiddhi], and delusion as the mirrorlike pristine cognition [Vairocana]. You should experientially cultivate these in the above manner. The implementation of the respective scrolls concerning these five poisons is sequentially established.

Then, at the conclusion of [the scrolls concerning] the six doctrines [of the perfection stage], there are the essential points concerning consciousness transference and resurrection:[870] You should smear the inside of a skull possessing the appropriate defining characteristics with black ink, and directly in the middle of that blackened skull you should inscribe a shining white HŪṂ, which is the seed syllable of the meditational deity. Entering retreat at an auspicious time when the ḍākinīs gather, you should hold a communal offering in general, and particularly on behalf of the ḍākinīs of Oḍḍiyāna and the ḍākinīs who undertake the devouring rites. Tormas adorned with human flesh, incense of human fat, and lamps of melted human fat are the three sacraments of commitment that it is improper to be without.

Once the ḍākinīs have gathered in the above manner, you should present these offerings and then meditate on yourself innately as Cakrasaṃvara or Hevajra, whichever you prefer. You should count [the corresponding mantra] HRĪḤ HA HA or DEVA PICU, as much as you can. Then, in an isolated grass hermitage, facing west in the morning and east in the evening, you should place the skull with its plinth nearby and in front, and train your gaze upon the syllable HŪṂ inside that skull, settling the mind without wavering. Consequently, {303} after a greater or lesser number of days commensurate with your resources and capacity, light will be diffused from the HŪṂ within the skull, and if smoke billows out, if it shakes or trembles and so forth, these are all signs of accomplishment. Thereupon you should wrap the skull in fine silk and venerate it. You should then cast a torma in the western direction and complete the concluding rite. As a test, you should place on the palm of your hand the corpse of a fly that has fallen into your meal, immediately after it has died. Then you should meditate on the deity and recite the [corresponding] mantra. Focus your own awareness, which was formerly focused on the syllable HŪṂ, directly upon the corpse [of the fly]. If it emits a buzzing sound and flies off, shaking and quivering, you should train repeatedly in that practice, not just once or twice, and then you will succeed [in resurrection]. Formerly the Venerable Marpa in the emanational form of an accomplished master performed this rite of resurrection on behalf of pigeons, lambs, and so forth. Apart from that, since it is difficult even for those who can perform consciousness transference on behalf of animals to reverse [the process], it will be important to exercise judgment.

Here I have extracted and set forth in writing the essentials
Derived from the **supreme liberation** acquired by Chowang,

The scrolls of instruction that bring **delight**
To **all** the disciples of Se
By means of certain secret doctrines.

This was extracted from among the treasure texts [of Chowang] and written down.

89. Guidebook Entitled *The Mingling and Transformation of the Three Poisons*[871]

After first taking refuge and setting the mind on enlightenment: You should experientially cultivate the essentials without abandoning the three poisons that are the basis of cyclic existence. This is achieved through the essentials that intermingle desire with the pristine cognition of empowerment, hatred with the generation and perfection stages, and delusion with luminosity.

As far as the original abiding nature is concerned, in the case of all sentient beings, natural luminosity denotes the buddha body of reality, the intermediate state denotes the buddha body of perfect resource, and birth denotes the buddha body of emanation.

As far as the modes of appearance [of all sentient beings] are concerned, their maturational body is present during the interval between birth and death, their body of propensities is present during the interval between sleeping and waking, and their mental body is present during the interval between the obstruction of the rebirth process and birth.[872]

As far as the modes of bewilderment [of all sentient beings] are concerned, these comprise {304} perceptions during the intermediate state from birth to death, propensities during the intermediate state of dreams, and the bewilderment of past actions during the intermediate state of the rebirth process.

As far as the modes of liberation [of all sentient beings] are concerned, those of superior acumen are liberated at the time of death when the two sorts of luminosity are mingled together.[873] Those of average acumen are liberated in the intermediate state after death when the three magical displays are present in the mental continuum.[874] Those of inferior acumen are liberated in the Great Seal during [the intermediate state] of this life, that is, in their modes of birth.

With regard to the modes of experience that arise on the path: bliss and radiance of the generation stage are refined on the path in the context of daytime appearances, luminosity is refined on the path during nighttime sleep, and aspiration is refined on the path during the intermediate state.

With regard to the modes of actualization in terms of the sense objects, desire is purified through the male-female union of the teacher, hatred for one's parents from whom one acquires rebirth is purified through the manifestation of that [union], and delusion embodying all fundamental ignorance is purified through the lamp of naturally radiant intrinsic awareness.

Commencing from the foregoing essentials concerning the intermingling [of the three poisons], when death occurs, those of highest acumen transfer consciousness into luminosity, those of average acumen transfer consciousness into the illusory body, and those of inferior acumen transfer consciousness into the grasping of birth. That is to say, if through the power of yogic experience you intrinsically recognize the luminosity of the ground, that will resemble an encounter with an old acquaintance. You may also, at will, transfer consciousness into a pure land where appearances resemble a magical display, or into the womb of a noble family, with parents who act in accordance with the sacred doctrine.

This indeed is the essential point of the aural lineage [of Ngok]—the cycle concerning intermingling and transformation—that is an instruction belonging to the four pronouncements.[875]

Here I have set forth in writing the quintessence
Of the nectar of the teachings through the lineage of Ngok,
The **supreme** path of **liberation**
Gathering the four **delights**—
The crucial instruction among **all** the four transmitted teachings.

This was compiled from the instruction manual of Ngok Zhedang Dorjé.

90. Guidebook Entitled *The Four Scrolls of the Aural Instructions*[876]

After first taking refuge and setting the mind on enlightenment: You should practice according to the first of these four scrolls, which concerns the conclusive meaning of the *Hevajra Tantra* and was the quintessential oral instruction of Nāropā. It teaches (i) the movement of the ashé by which one progresses from the level of sentient beings to buddhahood, (ii) the movement of the ashé from the navel cakra via the pathway of the central channel, and (iii) the movement dependent on the short path of skillful means that engages the winds of vital breath and exertion.[877] That is to say, you should visualize your own body as the deity and meditate on the ashé in the navel cakra, which resembles the moon reflected in a deep well and is the essential nature of awareness, the nature of mind. {305} Next, you should explore its passage through the subtle energy of life breath. Finally, the ashé passes directly upward from within the central channel, in the manner of a shooting star, and at the crown of the head settles into the Great Seal, the nonreferential abiding nature [of reality]. That is the first [of the four scrolls].

The second scroll concerns the conclusive meaning of the *Tantra of the Secret Assembly*, and it was the quintessential oral instruction of glorious Jñānagarbha. It teaches (i) the magical display of appearances, (ii) the luminosity of mindfulness and awareness, and (iii) the dissolution of the three phases of mind.[878] That is to say, the inhabited world and its sentient inhabitants resemble a dream or a magical display, mindfulness and awareness are the nonarising luminosity, and conviction is then found in the midst of bewilderment in your own experience of the three [phases of dissolution at the time of death]—namely, appearance, increase, and attainment.[879]

The third scroll concerns the conclusive meaning of the *Tantra of Great Magical Emanation*, and it was the quintessential oral instruction of Kukkurāja. It teaches the severing of conceptual elaboration. By severing the mass of intellectually generated conceptual elaborations in the unchanging essential nature, where ebbing and flowing are naturally liberated, you will be separated from the ebbing and flowing of the subject-object dichotomy, and then, entering into the genuine, innate middle way, your awareness will attain buddhahood in the buddha body of reality.[880]

The fourth scroll concerns the conclusive meaning of the *Tantra of the Four Adamantine Seats*, and it was the quintessential oral instruction of the yoginī Kadalīmañjarī. It teaches (i) the yogin's arrival at the time of death, (ii) the manifestation of convincing immediate signs [of death], and (iii) the absence of doubt concerning the attainment of buddhahood at the time of death. That is to say, when the general outer and inner signs of death have been ascertained, and in particular when the natural sound of the ḍākinīs of the three abodes who have gathered in the secret cave has faded, you should with certainty fix the time [of impending death] at no more than seven days. Then, from the citadel of the navel—the cakra of the coiled nāga, the offspring of awareness will fly, entering through the great pathway of the authentic central channel and come to linger just in front of the throat. On that support you should strongly inhale the outer breath through the two nostrils, and instead of compressing it downward, you should propel it upward. You should turn your eyeballs upward and, above all, bend back the occiput, pressing it with your fingers {306} as you draw the subtle energy upward. Focusing your awareness on that, you will consequently experience a sharp pain as a symptom at the anterior fontanel, and finally the fontanel will become swollen like the egg of a goose. You should then insert a blade of straw within it and achieve confidence [in this practice]. It is said that a yogin such as this will attain buddhahood at the time of death, penetrating pristine cognition to the core, and untainted by negativity and obscuration.[881]

Here I have set forth in writing the **supreme liberation**
That was conferred on Tsurton Wang-ngé,
Sung as a song of **delight**,
Including **all** the instructions of the four conclusive points,
Derived from Marpa's scrolls of aural [instruction].

This was compiled from the ancient writings of Tsurton Wang-gi Dorjé.

91. Guidebook Entitled *The Six Doctrines of Liberation through the Upper Gate according to the Aural Lineage*[882]

After you have taken refuge and set the mind on enlightenment, the six doctrines are as follows:

1. The Fierce Inner Heat

The method of igniting the fierce inner heat is as follows:[883] You should first focus on the ashé. At the triple intersection of the channels [below the navel], the needlelike ashé is extremely red and hot and propelled by the wind from the right and left pathways. Concentrate your body and mind within the central channel where the ashé is warmed by the crackling heat. Then you should adjust the visualization as follows: From wind blowing on the ashé, which has the essence of fire, {316} the fire slightly combusts, so that it becomes larger and larger, four digits in height, and then eight digits.

It has four defining characteristics, in that it is hot to the touch, sharp at the tip, gentle, and pliable.[884] You should refine this practice, generate the warmth, and at that time wear a cotton robe.

Next, at the crown of your head there is a white downward-facing syllable HAṂ. As the ashé blazes with fire, owing to its light, a cooling generative fluid then emerges from the white HAṂ, permeating everything with whiteness. You should not be distracted from that visualization.

Next, you should become familiar with the three seed syllables of adamantine recitation—HŪṂ during exhalation, OṂ during inhalation, and ĀḤ during the pausing of breath; and you should train in the five buddhas according to their respective colors.[885] The earth element is dependent on the bridge of the nose, the water element is dependent on the two lips, the fire element is dependent on retrograde motion (*phyi log*), and the wind element is dependent on upward motion (*steng*). Earth is yellow, water is white, fire is red, and wind is blue. Muscle tissue and complexion arise through the earth element. Oiliness of the body arises through the water element. Metabolism arises through the fire element. Lightness of body arises through the wind element. Absence of sensation in the entire body arises through the space element.

2. The Illusory Body

On the successful outcome [of this practice], there follows the magical display [of the illusory body], which resembles the alchemical transformation of gold: The nature of mind is a magical display, since it arises as the diverse causes and fruits of virtuous and negative actions, dependent on the diverse appearances of the propensities of past actions. Just as an illusionist can cause many phenomena such as a horse, an ox, a house, and so forth to appear dependent on material objects such as a pebble or a ceramic tile, but these are actually fictitious, in the same way you should refine the certainty that all things of cyclic existence appear but are without inherent existence, in the manner of a magical display, until this [refinement] arises resplendently from the depths [of your experience].[886]

Next, [you should refine the introduction to pristine cognition] through the light of the sun and moon. This includes [refinement] at times of transition, [introduction to the rays of sun and moon, and establishment of appearances as fictitious in accordance with the twelve similes of illusion].[887] Next, [you should untie the fictitious knots of] disparagement and praise.[888]

Next, all appearances will arise as evanescent experiences, and you should rely on a strong motivation to carry daytime perceptions into the dreams of the night.[889]

3. Dream Yoga

Here you should pray that you might retain your dreams.[890] Rest on your pillow, and lie down on your right side. {317} During deep sleep you should examine whether your dreams are retained or not retained. You should recognize your room and your bed. Retention ensues by refining your motivation. When dreams are retained, they are retained by your recognizing that they are dreams. While refining this practice, you should train your dreams by transforming larger appearances into smaller ones, and smaller ones into larger ones. There are four pervasions that are experienced in relation to dream yoga—namely, the pervasion of forgetfulness, the pervasion of wakefulness, the pervasion of bewilderment, and the pervasion of continuity.[891]

4. Luminosity

After completing the training in dream yoga, you should enter into luminosity during deep sleep.[892] While you are sleeping, you should have affection for and devotion to the teacher. Focus your mind on the heart cakra and rest in a disposition that is without distracted perception and without grasping. Thereby awareness will become radiant without any external reference and without being objectively recognized. Free from the covering of obscuration, the meditative stability of luminosity will emerge. You will awaken from sleep and all your present perceptions will become radiant, without being objectively recognized. You may then train without interruption in the disposition of the Great Seal and thereby traverse the path.

5. Consciousness Transference

If consciousness transference is to be applied [at death] in a timely manner,[893] you should adopt the essential physical posture and visualize the syllable HŪṂ directly at your heart cakra, with your teacher on the crown of your head. Next, visualize that the HŪṂ emerges from your anterior fontanel and is absorbed into the heart of the teacher. When resting in meditative equipoise, you should block the anterior fontanel with the syllable KṢA.

6. The Intermediate State

[With regard to the intermediate state after death:][894] Having practiced this in detail during dream yoga, at the time of death you will encounter luminosity, like a calf meeting its mother.[895] Once your awareness has awakened from obfuscation, it will become radiant, without being objectively recognized. The natural expression of the five lights will be perfected, without their intermingling.[896] Then, when the first weeks of reception and reconnection [with the propensities of your past life] have been completed,[897] at this time you should recall the following instruction that you formerly received [concerning the appearance of the mental body]:

> Having the bodily form of one's past and emergent existences,
> Complete with all sense faculties, and the power of unobstructed movement . . .
> Visible to those similar in kind and through pure clairvoyance . . .[898]

You should then meditate during this life[899] where the threefold intermingling of beings, similar in kind within cyclic existence, occurs,[900] {318} and starting from now, you should cut off doubts, such as wondering whether buddhahood may be attained. You should know that this is the way of the six doctrines through which you may experientially cultivate the path that escorts all things to their finality.

This commits to writing the abridged essentials
Of the **supreme** path, combining maturation and **liberation**—
The doctrines that bequeathed with **delight**
All the teachings of Mila into the heart of Rechungpa.

This was compiled from the guidance of Zhang Lotsāwa [Jangchub-o].

92. Guidebook Entitled *The Nine Doctrinal Cycles of Nirdehaḍākinī*[901]

After you have taken refuge and set the mind on enlightenment, there then ensues the [nine cycles of] instruction that the melodious voice of Nirdehaḍākinī [the disembodied ḍākinī of pristine cognition] imparted [to Tilopā].[902]

(i) The first instruction is as follows: "You should untie the knots of the mind through maturation and liberation."[903]

In this regard, in the path of provisions, the two provisions [of merit and pristine cognition] are carried on to the path. In the path of connection, the focus is devoid of attachment. In the path of insight, whatever arises is a facilitating instruction.[904] In the path of meditative cultivation, afflicted mental states are carried onto the path. In the conclusive [path of no-more-learning], there are the instructions that introduce the fruit.[905]

In order to sever attachment to the path of provisions, the path of connection has a focus devoid of attachment. In order to sever attachment to the path of connection, the path of insight carries as facilitators all desirable attributes of the senses that appear. Even simple attachment to those facilitators will be severed on the path of meditative cultivation by carrying afflicted mental states onto the path. This completes the first instruction: "You should untie the knots of the mind through maturation and liberation."

(ii) The second instruction is as follows: "The commitment is that you should look into the mirror of your own mind."[906]

In this regard, there are commitments concerning things to be prevented, commitments concerning things to be established, and commitments concerning things that are neither to be prevented nor established.

[Among the first of these categories,] you should not explain the empowerments and sacred doctrine to the immature. You should not reveal the higher paths to unworthy recipients. You should not reveal[907] sacred representations in inappropriate locations. You should not explain the sacred doctrine to those lacking devotion. You should not induce those without faith to engage in the path of provisions. You should not accept as a disciple one who is without commitment. You should not revere Hanuman as a teacher.[908] You should not befriend messengers. You should not cultivate instructions that rely on words.[909]

[Among the second category,] you should rely on teachers who are endowed with the lineage. You should cultivate the meditational deities that are the inheritance of your past actions. You should make offerings to the ḍākinīs who dispel obstacles. You should associate with friends who are of harmonious view and conduct. {319} You should cultivate the aural lineage that is the lineage of accomplished masters.[910]

[Among the third category,] you should not abandon afflicted mental states. You should not rely upon antidotes. You should not cultivate the attributes of the real nature. You should not search elsewhere for the fruit.[911] This completes the second instruction: "The commitment [to look into] the mirror of your own mind."

(iii) The third instruction is as follows: "The sacraments of the commitments bask in the sun of realization."[912]

In this regard, there are sacraments of commitment that give rise to cyclic existence, which is the basis of bewilderment, and those that are opposite, basking in the sun of nirvana. In general, the former include sacraments of commitment that generate the three poisons, sacraments of commitment that accumulate negative deeds, and sacraments of commitment that give rise to cyclic existence. Contrary to these are sacraments of commitment that abandon the ten nonvirtuous actions and do not give rise to the lower realms, and in addition to these, there are sacraments of commitment that engage in the ten virtuous actions and attain the higher realms [of gods and humans].[913]

As for sacraments of commitment that bask in the sun of nirvana, they include those that rely on the object of refuge, those concerning the actions and fruits associated with the vows of individual liberation, those concerning the altruistic mind of enlightenment, and those concerning the introduction to the way of Secret Mantra.[914] This completes the third instruction: "The sacraments of commitment bask in the sun of realization."

(iv) The fourth instruction is as follows: "In conduct you should strike water with a sword."[915]

In this regard, there is (i) conduct associated with the threefold vows of Samantabhadra,[916] (ii) conduct endowed with the commitments of secret practice, (iii) conduct that retains awareness with carefulness and mindfulness, and (iv) conduct associated with the central channel that is without referential object.

[As to the first of these categories,] you should engage in external conduct symbolizing circumstances that have arisen, you should engage in internal conduct through which the three media [of body, speech, and mind] block the entrances to the three lower realms, you should engage in secret conduct that carries the three poisons onto the path, and you should engage in authentic conduct that introduces bliss and radiance.

In addition, you should engage in physical conduct that pertains to the buddha body of emanation and the vows of individual liberation, verbal conduct that pertains to the buddha body of perfect resource and the bodhisattva vows, and mental conduct that pertains to the buddha body of reality and the vows of the awareness holders.

Furthermore, you should not turn the wheel of attachment and hatred associated with the three poisons. You should not profit from conduct that stockpiles merit. You should not run after this life[917] that is preoccupied with the eight worldly concerns. You should not disparage the sacred doctrine on account of your own opinions. You should not deprecate others on account of your own positive desires. You should not engage in study or reflection out of desire for cyclic existence. You should not serve as a household priest for friends or foes. You should not cling to isolation in the borders of your native land. You should not scatter the storm[918] of bias, including factionalism. You should not forsake [lowly] sentient beings out of pride. You should not draw the bowstring of enmity toward equals. You should not fire the arrows of jealousy upward.[919] {320}

[As for the second category,] secret conduct includes the physical conduct of nudity and loose hair; the conduct of wearing ornaments such as human ash and bone ornaments; and the conduct of holding hand emblems such as a khaṭvāṅga, bell, and ḍamaru drum.[920]

As for [the third category, which concerns] the conduct of awareness: you should act in the manner of a lion that is fearless and solitary, in the manner of a tiger that is unimpeded and without exhaustion, in the manner of an ox that is intrepid, in the manner of a dog or pig that is without impurity, and in the manner of a child who is without reflection or meditative cultivation.[921]

As for [the fourth category, which concerns][922] conduct associated with the central channel: you should engage in conduct that is without attachment to magical appearances; you should engage in conduct concerning the inexpressible luminosity of the nature of mind; you should engage in conduct that is nondual and free from activity, transcending the intellect; and you should engage in conduct of conclusive meditation that is free from temporal limitations.[923] This completes the fourth instruction: "In conduct you should strike water with a sword."

(v) The fifth instruction is as follows: "You should spin the wheel of the network of the channels and winds."[924]

This instruction comprises (i) the essential nature of the cakras of the channels and winds, and (ii) the activities pertaining to the network of the channels and winds.

[The former includes the channels, winds, and vital essences; and among these, the channels are explained in terms of their shapes, number, and location.] As for their shapes, they resemble a parasol, a rooftop, an amulet, or a lily. As for their number, the outer channels number seventy-two thousand; the inner channels number one hundred and twenty; the secret channels number thirty-two; and the authentic channels number three, which, when condensed, number one. As for their location, the outer channels are located in muscle tissue and skin, the inner channels are located in adipose tissue, the secret channels are located in bone tissue, and the authentic channels are located in secret places. [Among the outer channels,] the longer are a double arm span in length and the shorter are the size of a barley grain or needle, and they are all present within the network of physical channels. The inner channels pertain to conceptual thought, and the secret channels to bliss and emptiness.[925]

As far as the winds are concerned, these are of three types, resembling kings, ministers, and subjects. There are five primary winds that resemble kings, five ancillary winds that resemble ministers, and hundreds of thousands of winds that resemble subjects. The internal winds arouse the material elements. The secret winds regulate motion. And the wind of pristine cognition actualizes the three buddha bodies.[926]

As far as the vital essences are concerned [they are also of three types: outer, inner and secret]. Among them, the outer vital essences are the contaminated vital essences present within each of the channels, which number the same as the above [that is, seventy-two thousand]. When these are condensed, urine flows from the left channel, blood from the right channel, and generative fluid from the central channel. The inner vital essence is the naturally arising awareness, and the secret vital essence is the nondual pristine cognition.[927]

The arising [of the fruition] ensues when [their unelaborated nature] has been experientially cultivated.[928] {321}

[In terms of the natural unelaborate state:] the chyle of blood takes the form of light, the chyle of breath is present as the warmth in wind, and the chyle of the vital essences is clear and transparent.[929]

[In terms of the experiential cultivation of the path, there are four sorts of motion:][930] The first sort is the motion that derives from the winds of the five lights. The second is the motion that derives from the winds of breath. The third is the motion that derives from the winds of attachment. And the fourth is the motion that derives from the winds of the sense faculties.

As far as the [four] motions of consciousness indicative of past actions are concerned: the first is the motion that derives from the substratum consciousness, the second is the motion that derives from the mental consciousness, the third is the motion that derives from the afflicted mental consciousness, and the fourth is the motion that derives from the consciousnesses of the five sensory gates.[931]

As for the "lamp of the light of ideation and scrutiny,"[932] the thickness of its channel is one-tenth of a horse's tail hair, and its vital essence is the thickness of a white silk thread. The motion of its wind has five aspects: attachment is red, hatred is white, delusion is black, pride is yellow, and jealousy is green. In its center, giving rise to mindfulness, the light that is the support of the generative essence is present as nondual pristine cognition.[933] The pristine cognitions then arise [from the five poisons] in the following manner: The mirrorlike pristine cognition arises from hatred, the pristine cognition of discernment arises from attachment, the pristine cognition of reality's expanse arises from delusion, the pristine cognition of sameness arises from pride, and the pristine cognition of accomplishment arises from jealousy.[934]

In terms of their [fruitional] manifestation, the channels are the buddha body of emanation, the winds are the buddha body of perfect resource, [and the vital essence is the buddha body of reality].[935] This completes the fifth pith instruction: "[You should spin] the wheel of the network of the channels and winds."

(vi) The sixth instruction is as follows: "You should retain the precious [generative essence] according to the teachings of supreme bliss."[936]

This instruction includes (i) the disclosure of empowerment on the path of maturation, and (ii) the generation of the lamp of skillful means on the path of liberation. [As to the former,] empowerment is conferred on a female "action seal" endowed with the defining characteristics that enhance the mantras, and then [her body becomes the deity, her speech becomes mantra, and] her mind becomes innate [pristine cognition].[937]

[As to the latter,] this concerns the male-female union endowed with the three aspects of authentic perception.[938] The female is Vārāhī and the male is Cakrasaṃvara. The vajra and the lotus should be consecrated and slowly rubbed together. [The main practice then has five parts:] (i) the generative essence should descend; (ii) it should be diffused, absorbed, and retained by means of yogic exercises that constitute the elixir of the three buddha bodies; (iii) it should be reversed through essential practices of three sorts;

(iv) it should be intermingled, descending to the apertures of the channels; [and (v) the method of introducing pristine cognition should then ensue].[939]

That is to say, the descent [of the generative essence] should be controlled because it comes of your own power. For retention [of the generative essence], there are yogic exercises in which the body resembles a contracted tortoise, the vomiting of a grunting tigress, and a shooting star. For its reversal, there is the great nail of the syllable HŪṂ [as well as mantra recitation and meditative stability]. As the generative essence intermingles at the apertures of the channels, it has the [white] color of the moon or Vairocana; [and the channel through which it is reversed resembles] a tree or an opened parasol.[940] {322} This completes the sixth instruction: "The precious [generative essence] should be retained according to the teachings of supreme bliss."

(vii) The seventh instruction is as follows: "Awareness is the lamp of the pristine cognition."[941]

In this instruction [there are five aspects]: (i) the lamp that seeks conventional methods, (ii) the lamp that reveals the illustrative meaning, (iii) the lamp that unravels the symbolic meaning, (iv) the lamp that inspires experiential realization, and (v) the lamp of self-originating consecration.[942]

[The first of these lamps has two functions:] it illuminates the extremes of being and nonbeing, and it generates the lamp that transcends the intellect.

[In terms of the former it has four attributes:] (i) it is a material entity because it seeks to attain accomplishment through awareness, (ii) it is within perceptual range of the scriptures because it has contradictions, (iii) it is within the range of hearing because it illustrates the meaning of words, and (iv) it is conceptual because it is examined through discriminative awareness.

[In terms of the latter,] its generation of the lamp that transcends the intellect [has five attributes]: (i) it is not an object of awareness because it is devoid of refutation and proof; (ii) it is not within perceptual range of the scriptures because it is without contradiction; (iii) it is not within the range of hearing because it does not pursue words; (iv) it is not conceptual because, on examination, it is not found; and (v) it is revealed to be realized through the oral instructions of the teacher because it derives from essential [reality]. [This realization, in turn, has three aspects:] (i) realization that comes about when blessings are present, (ii) realization that comes about when there is conviction, and (iii) realization that comes about when there is experiential cultivation. Here, there is no realization[943] that comes about through scriptural authority because that to which one is attentive would be subsumed within the three world realms.[944]

As for the [second] lamp that reveals the illustrative meaning, [this also has five attributes:] (i) it may by exemplified by the knot of a snake that naturally uncoils, (ii) it may be exemplified by a natural bubble of water, (iii) it may be exemplified by clouds that naturally arise, (iv) it may be exemplified by crystal that is naturally clear, and (v) it may be exemplified by the horns of a hare that surpass intellectual understanding.[945]

As for the [third] lamp that unravels the symbolic meaning, this [has five aspects]: (i) symbols that realize the view, (ii) symbols that experience meditation, (iii) symbols that are blind and unseen, (iv) symbols that are dumb and soundless, and (v) symbols that are crazy and without attachment. [Among these, symbols that realize the view include] symbols that are pointed out but untouched, symbols of the sword that does not cut, symbols of the shoulder that does not stretch, and symbols of the fire that does not burn.[946]

As for the [fourth] lamp that inspires experiential realization, this [has two aspects]: experiential realization that is without attachment and unrecognized; and experiential realization that is naturally liberated, beyond the intellect.[947]

As for the [fifth lamp] of self-originating consecration, this [has three aspects]: (i) experience that is soundless in the manner of the bliss of a mute, (ii) experience that is without attachment in the manner of a small child, and (iii) experience that is naturally radiant in the manner of a butter lamp.[948] This completes the seventh instruction: "Awareness is the lamp of pristine cognition."

(viii) The eighth instruction is as follows: "The Great Seal is naturally liberating."[949]

In this instruction [there are three aspects: (i) the meditation that roams the mountain hermitage of the sky], (ii) the meditator who enacts the dance of the son of a barren woman, and (iii) the object of meditation that is [the ritual application of] the Great Seal. {323} The last of these [entails eleven procedures]: (i) you should prepare a formless fire pit; (ii) you should arrange [within it] a self-originating effigy; (iii) you should cut the firewood for the rite of Jarokpa; (iv) you should visualize the divine form of the original buddha; (v) you should induce the ritual summons with the blindfold; (vi) you should maintain an unsurpassed focus; (vii) you should scatter the ritual charms of turtle hair; (viii) you should thrust the ritual spike fashioned of the horn of a hare; (ix) you should combust the fire of the end of time; (x) you should offer the flowers of space; and (xi) with lion's milk as *rakta*, you should receive the spiritual accomplishment of the kingdom of the mental faculty.[950] This completes the eighth instruction: "The Great Seal is naturally liberating."

(ix) The ninth instruction is as follows: "Common savor is the mirror of external appearances."[951]

In this instruction [there are four parts: refinement of visualization, examination of ailments, the experience of common savor, and the expulsion of ailments. Among these, the refinement of visualization is as follows]: the wind of the upper gate and the wind of the lower gate are [separately] present, like heat and cold, or horses and yaks. Pristine cognition should then melt the two sorts of afflicted mental states frozen within the central channel, so that the wind of the upper gate and the wind of the lower gate are fused together.[952]

[As for the examination of ailments, if you are ill, you should undertake massage, unblock the winds, and sit up straight as an arrow.] You should circulate [the wind] in the manner of a wheel, attract it in the manner of a hook, and elevate it in the manner of the sky. If you are in pain, you should disrupt it by adopting the posture of the lion's play.[953] If you are lethargic, you should secure the lower gate. If you are overactive, you should inflate the base of the small intestine. If the wind is retained within, pristine cognition will arise. If it is dispersed externally, nothing at all will transpire.[954]

As for the experience of common savor, if the earth element indicative of the lower wind is excessive, you should dispense wind for the earth element and strongly practice the ascetic discipline of physical exercises. If the water element indicative of the upper wind is excessive, you should dispense fire for the water element, focus consciousness upward by means of yogic exercises, and ignite the fire from the syllable HAṂ that emerges from the mouth of the ogre (*srin po'i zhal nas*).[955] If the fire element indicative of the upper wind is excessive, you should focus on the female action seal and elevate the vital essence. If the wind element is excessive, you should dispense earth for the wind element, place the palms together at the crown of the head, stare into the distance, and partake of bone soup. If the fire and water elements are excessive, you should suppress the upper wind. And if the earth and water elements are excessive, you should ignite the lower winds. You should then dispense wind for the earth element, you should dispense earth for the wind element, you should dispense fire for the water element, you should dispense water for the fire element, you should dispense nonarising [space] for the wind element, you should dispense emptiness for bliss, and you should dispense bliss for emptiness.[956] This completes the ninth instruction: "Common savor is the mirror of external appearances."

Among these Nine Doctrinal Cycles of Nirdehaḍākinī, the first four cycles were arranged by Marpa {324} and the last five by Rechungpa, in accordance with the teachings of Tipuwa.

This excellently commits to writing the instructions of Nirdeha,
All the remainder of which Tipuwa bestowed upon Rechungpa.
Dancing with **delight**, he, in turn, offered their maturation and **liberation**
In the presence of the **supreme** Mila.

This was compiled from ancient writings.

93. Guidebook Entitled *The Elaborate Guidance according to Zhang Tselpa*[957]

After you have taken refuge and set the mind on enlightenment, there follows the consecration in the symbolic method that pertains to body, speech, and mind:

(i) You should instantly meditate on your meditational deity and ask yourself if the visualization is clear or not. If you say it is clear, you should ask yourself whether that vision was present a short while ago, or whether it was not. If you say it was not, you should then ask yourself whether it may be interrupted or not interrupted. If you say it may be interrupted, then it consists of adventitious thought. It is merely a fleetingly instantaneous support.

Then, again, you should meditate on a color in front. You should ask yourself if that patch of color clearly appears. If you say it does, you should ask yourself if it was present a short while ago, or whether it was not. If you say it was not, then that color is adventitious and fleetingly instantaneous. All phenomena are like that.

(ii) Furthermore, the buddha fields above, the fields of the hells below, and the intellect that apprehends those fields have been fabricated by the mind. These have arisen through conditions, but all thoughts present within the mental faculty are groundless and baseless.

(iii) With regard to the symbols that pertain to speech, you should ask yourself whether you can hear the bodhisattva Caryāmati residing in Cindhona, the citadel of Vajravārāhī.[958] If you say you can hear him, you should place your palms together toward him and ask whether you can hear his words. If you say you can hear them, you should ask whether you perceived Caryāmati a short while ago or did not. If you say, with your palms together, that you did not formerly perceive him, then that is an adventitious thought, without inherent existence.

Again, when it is said that the mighty lord of the gods Śakra is present in the divine assembly of Dharmabhadra in Trāyastriṃśa, you should understand that there is one example indicative of this that pertains to speech—namely, when the syllable PHAṬ is discerned in the sky. You should ask yourself whether your sense faculties will [later] not become oblivious to that. If you say that it will be repeated owing to a subsequent instance of that sound, then this is but an adventitious thought. {325} All sights and sounds are like that.

In brief, since there are many indefinite modes of physical conduct that are revealed, they arise through the condition of adventitious thoughts and so they are fleetingly instantaneous, essentially empty, indefinite, groundless, and baseless.

Illustrated by such diverse symbols, naked perception is directly introduced. All that appears is introduced to be adventitious, without inherent existence, like a dream, like a magical display, and like the sky.

If you ask how the five buddha bodies and pristine cognitions abide in relation to that, they are without any ground or basis: The buddha body of reality is nonarising, the buddha body of emanation arises through dependent origination, the buddha body of perfect resource is essentially empty and does not differentiate appearances and emptiness, and the buddha body of essentiality is their inseparability. Apart from their having simply and spontaneously experienced these four buddha bodies, there is no separate fruit that can be obtained by those who have refined a path and so forth. This constitutes the symbolic introduction to the direct path of the Great Seal.

This presents in writing **all** that arose from the mind of Zhang,
A pleasing and **delightful** tradition that establishes examples,
Abiding in the nature of mind, teacher of **supreme liberation**.

This was compiled from the elaborate guidance of Zhang Tselpa.

94. Guidebook Entitled *The Six-Branch Yoga according to Pelchen Ga Lotsāwa*[959]

After first taking refuge and setting the mind on enlightenment, then, on the path of pristine cognition, the supreme accomplishment, you should adopt the essential physical posture within a darkened room.

1. Composure

Just as ordinary visual consciousness engages with sights, the yogin should maintain composure with regard to any apparent signs and objects that arise. Just as two distinct thoughts are not assimilated simultaneously because, when [visual consciousness] is distracted by sights, the sound of a conch is not heard, the yogin should one-pointedly rest the mind on the very inception of anything that appears, so that the mind abides right where it is, uncaptivated by [extraneous] sensations due to past actions and perceptions, its disposition omnipresent, engaging with minimal sensations.

2. Meditative Concentration

Next, you should apply meditative concentration on smoke and other such [signs of meditative experience that arise], in association with the five sensory consciousnesses, and then direct your ideation and scrutiny imbued with joy and bliss, and your unmoving discriminative awareness, toward the inception of whatever arises. You should maintain composure and meditative concentration, integrating calm abiding and higher insight, in the manner of a mother and child meeting face to face. {326}

3. Breath Control and Adamantine Recitation

Next, you should go back and forth between breath control and adamantine recitation, uniting the sun and moon of the right and left channels and intermingling both subtle energy and mind. Without a sound, you should mentally recite the syllables HŪṂ, OṂ, and ĀḤ that arise from the power of their respective places [in the heart, forehead, and throat]. While maintaining that, you should forcefully induce the union [of the upper and lower winds] in the central channel by means of the vase breathing. In addition, with regard to the upper wind, you should repeatedly apply [the yogic exercise] named "wave of perfect rapture,"[960] blocking the movement of the winds of action from above and below and uniting them in the amulet of breath control.

4. Retention

Next, you should retain the intrinsic awareness that experiences bliss when the generative essence is melted by the fire of the fierce inner heat. At each moment of the natural descent of bliss, when the blissful sensations of the body that arise in and of themselves appear commensurate with the objects that appear, you should rest in the essential physical posture.

5. Recollection

While you are adopting the yogic gaze of skillful means, there will ensue recollection of that former bliss.

6. Meditative Stability

Finally, meditative stability that blocks the perception of suffering will naturally and abundantly arise. Since your body is permeated with chyle, you will actualize miraculous abilities and effortlessly overwhelm external appearances.

Glorious Kālacakrapāda has said, "Those of highest acumen initially acquire realization through the tantra."[961] This implies that there is a secret bond of firsthand guidance and innermost advice. By contrast, it is an essential point that those of inferior acumen will certainly develop the activated fierce inner heat[962] within seven days. The successful outcome of this practice was actually granted him by the ḍākinīs at Śītavana.

Accordingly, you should visualize yourself as the meditational deity. In the fireplace of the navel cakra, you should visualize your teacher in the form of the fire of pristine cognition, one inch in size, and the place where your teacher appears is vividly clear. You should fervently imagine that he or she embodies all the objects of refuge—buddha, sacred doctrine, and monastic community.

Then you should sit cross-legged, secure one hand with the other [in the gesture of meditation], bend your neck, straighten your spine and waist, stretch your shoulders,[963] and expel the residue of wind [three times]. After that (i) you should inhale gently, long, strongly, and completely, forcing the wind downward.[964] (ii) Next, you should hold and fill the upper and lower winds in equilibrium, circulating them back and forth, and filling [the abdomen] with wind. (iii) Next, you should expel this wind [from the abdomen to the apertures of the channels] and shake the body, visualizing that the body is permeated by wind. (iv) Next, you should exhale the wind actually through the nostrils {327} while visualizing that it exits from the tips of the pores.[965]

[There are seven phases of visualization that then ensue:][966] (i–ii) Firstly, you should concentrate your mind, as if inserting a thread into the eye of a needle, upon the fire at the navel cakra, the size of a pea, which diffuses sparks of flame and is imbued with warmth that can virtually burn the body.[967]

(iii) Consequently, the sunlike rakta derived from the pathway of the pea-sized vital essence that is of the material of fire blazes and darts in the form of a flame, four digits in height, resembling the tongue of a snake. You should one-pointedly focus on its movement that resembles the tip of a flame flickering in the wind. The tip of the flame then opens the aperture of the central channel. You should let your mind rest without wavering on this flame that is endowed with four attributes[968] and that resembles an upstretched yarn of red silk within the clear and transparent central channel, as if a thread were inserted within a crystal.

(iv) Next, you should visualize that from the top of the central channel a bluish-green smoke resembling the smoke of incense emerges from the crown of your head and billows like an open parasol upward into the sky, but you should continue focusing your visualization on the actual fire within the navel and meditate diligently.

(v) Even when that smoke covers your body in the manner of mist descending on a mountain, you should continue to meditate one-pointedly, honing your visualization on the fire burning within the body.[969]

(vi) Next, you should focus your mind on the twisting flames that emerge from both the crown of your head and your rectum, coiling like a noose and forming a ball of light. You should control this strongly with wind.

(vii) Lastly, you should mentally focus that from within the central channel, all the channel apertures of your body will be filled with fire; and the fire of the mighty disk of the sun outside your body in the four directions will virtually burn your body. Once the rays of the sun encounter the firelight diffused from your body, a conflict between the fiery rays will ensue, so that the outside and inside of your body will crackle with warmth.[970]

Then you should tense your calves and forearms and fill your body forcefully with wind. Do not pay attention to the freezing cold! Meditate that you are smitten by warmth, heat, and the light of one thousand suns![971]

This presents from within the profound essentials of Zhang
The foremost of **all** the secret advice of Ga Lotsāwa,
The elixir of **supreme** natural **liberation**, of **delightful** bliss,
The supreme medication, the actual experience of fierce inner heat. {328}

This was compiled from the guidance of Lama Zhang Tselpa.

95. Guidebook Entitled *The Cycle of Pagmodru Densatel*[972]

After first taking refuge and setting the mind on enlightenment: You should adopt the essential physical posture, straighten the joints, and adopt the gesture of meditative equipoise, with the eyes focusing on the tip of the nose. You should then ascertain the entrance [to this practice] through the symbolic empowerment of Vajravārāhī, which focuses on the three poisons; and relying on spiritual mentors who are free from two of the four conditions,[973] you should comprehend the defining characteristics of your own mind by means of discriminative awareness. That is to say, there is no possibility of arising or ceasing, and the four buddha bodies transcending the intellect are spontaneously present from the beginning. The defining characteristics of all things transcend their illustrative basis. The fish of meaning is caught from the river of words. Through your knowing the sameness of all things, the buddha bodies are fully perfected because all that arises is enjoyed as the shifting display of the buddha body of reality.[974]

The five distinctive paths, commencing with the path of provisions, should be refined, and in conclusion, you must comprehend through skillful means and discriminative awareness the thirty-seven factors conducive to enlightenment. These include the four applications of mindfulness, the four correct trainings, and the four supports of miraculous ability that derive from that path—their causal basis being based on faith, their path based on mindfulness, and their facilitator being the three modes of perseverance.[975]

They also include the five powers, the seven branches of enlightenment, and the noble eightfold path, which are the fruits of meditative stability.[976]

When in that manner conceptual thought is carried on the path by means of the armor of the view:[977]

> The defining characteristics of the mind are unknown,
> Just as [the extent of] the space element cannot be examined.
>
> One harboring positive and negative thoughts regarding illusory forms is mistaken,
> Like a small child grasping at a reflection as real.
>
> Both meditative equipoise and postmeditation wear each other out.[978]
>
> Cyclic existence and nirvana are indivisible,
> Alike in the nature of the buddha body of reality.
>
> All phenomena are the miracles of space.
> If one knows one's own shortcomings
> There will be no need for liberation from fetters.
>
> While nonexistent, appearances are a miraculous display of space.
> By knowing this, you will be liberated, as if awakening from a dream. {329}
> Diverse appearances are the flowers of space.[979]
> Are the joys and sorrows of children at all true for the aged?
> They are without advantages, natural manifestations of illusion.
> You should examine them, knowing them to resemble this spectacle of space.
>
> From physical forms to omniscience, all things are drawings of space.
>
> Whatever arises is without acceptance or rejection in the expanse of reality.
> Since all things are exaggerated and deprecated, they are exposed as fiction.
> All meditators determine exaggeration and deprecation to be mind.

You should realize the sole point
That nothing is to be renounced or adopted.

This is the supreme modality of undeviating liberation.

You should look at yourself and know your own shortcomings.

Do not grasp anything at all that arises!
There is nothing elsewhere higher than this supreme path.
These imperceptible, multifarious appearances conforming to habitual propensities
Are the seeds of mental concepts that can all be grasped by the intellect.

Look! Look! You should observe nothing at all!

Look at the one who cuts and severs the doubtful mind!

[And]:[980]

All hopes and doubts, cyclic existence and nirvana are quiescent in the expanse.
Thereby you will reach upward to the reality of entities.
Always examine this, as if awakening from a dream.
The genuine expanse is itself without speech, thought, and expression.
That which is free from the intellect is held to be the Great Seal.

The Fierce Inner Heat

Next, there is the path of skillful means, which concerns the fierce inner heat:[981] Your physical body should assume the empty frame of your meditational deity, and you should adopt, above all, the essential physical posture. The eyes should be concentrated in that manner, and you should meditate that, with the teacher present above your head, your three channels and four cakras are clear and transparent, and that the wind is moving from the left side. You should practice the fourfold application of wind, which entails inhalation, filling, crushing, and elevation, and thereby control the subtle energy and mind, commencing with the ashé (the stroke of the letter *a*) that is associated with the navel cakra.

You should develop certainty in the bliss and warmth as the fire, expanding from four digits to twenty in height, is progressively inducted through the navel, heart, throat, and crown cakras and throughout the entire body. The successful outcome of this practice is that [the vital essence] will blaze and drip down [through the central channel], like a bristling strand of hair.

To that end, you should rest for a longer time in meditative concentration, at the limits of nonconceptuality, and then chain all the winds together. During inhalation you should not rest. The RAṂ syllables are visualized in proximity to the two kidneys, with the red lotus of the fire element in the navel cakra, and at its center an ashé, which has the nature of fire. {330} You should expel the wind of the right and left channels [into the central channel], and as the fire increases to four, eight, and twelve digits in height, it fills the navel, heart, throat, and crown cakras with fire that is gross and subtle. The subtle and coarse[982] vital essence of the melting syllable HAṂ then descends, like a distended thread, so that it fills the cakras in succession. You should construct this visualization without attachment.

As for the method of refining this practice: You should focus on the blissful warmth that burns more intensely and engage in experiential cultivation that combines together the three phases of fierce inner heat—the activated fierce inner heat, the [experiential] fierce inner heat, and the supreme fierce inner heat.[983] The melting bliss of the five female buddhas, including Buddhalocanā, will then arise on the basis of subtle energy and mind.

The Illusory Body

With regard to the method of attaining buddhahood through the illusory body: The preliminaries are as in the practice of the fierce inner heat. (i) You should then meditate on yourself and all appearances as a magical display. (ii) Next, you should praise and criticize your reflection in a mirror. When it evokes neither pleasure nor displeasure, at that moment you should absorb the reflection into yourself and engage in praising and criticizing yourself. As in the case of your reflection, it is certain that no thoughts of pleasure or displeasure will arise. (iii) Next, you should go to a market or a similarly busy place and examine [the praise and criticism you receive] in the aforementioned manner. (iv) If these are rendered nonexistent, you should then have an image of your meditational deity and so forth reflected in a mirror, and once its reflection has appeared, you should absorb it repeatedly into yourself. When you have visualized your own body clearly as the deity, you will have refined the pure illusory body. (v) By refining that, you will attain the supreme accomplishment, if there is no distinction between meditative equipoise and postmeditation. If, however, that distinction persists, you will attain buddhahood during the intermediate state after death.

Dream Yoga

To practice apprehending dreams, your head should face toward the north. (i) You should actually perceive the Buddha as your teacher, above the crown of your head, and pray that you might apprehend your dreams. Set your mind on aspirational enlightenment, so that all sentient beings might attain the level of an adamantine holder by means of the illusory body. (ii) You should then visualize a red lotus with four petals in the throat cakra, and at its center, as the essential nature of your teacher, is the syllable OṂ. On its four petals the syllables A, NU, TA, RA—respectively, white, yellow, red, and green—are spinning, revolving in a forward motion. You should repeatedly intensify your aspiration to apprehend your dreams. (iii) Next, you should focus your awareness on the syllable A, and you will come to apprehend your dreams while you are asleep, late at night, at midnight, or at dawn. (iv) If you do not apprehend them, you should do so by focusing your awareness upon a glistening pea-sized red vital essence in the space between the eyebrows. {331} (v) If you apprehend and understand your dreams to be dreams, you should then prolong and nurture them. You may increase them from one to two, transform them, apprehend fearful and hazardous situations [as dreams], leap around, and so forth.

Luminosity

As for the practice of luminosity during sleep: You should transform all the entities of your dreams so that they resemble space, without extremes or center. Having nurtured that experience, you should then apprehend the luminosity of the time of death and attain supreme spiritual accomplishment. Consequently, facilitated by that, you should engage in experiential cultivation in the manner of Lawapa.[984]

Consciousness Transference

For the practice of consciousness transference: Lie down on your right side, with your head pointing north. If you transfer consciousness from within that former disposition of luminosity, those of highest acumen will attain supreme accomplishment, and at the very least, you will acquire a human body inclined toward the sacred doctrine.

You should visualize your own body as the deity, and the central channel the thickness of a bamboo cane. The inhabited world and its sentient inhabitants become radiant as appearances of light, and then melt and dissolve into yourself. You, in turn, are absorbed into the syllable HŪṂ, and then, in the manner of a shooting star, that dissolves into the heart of your teacher, in the form of Vajradhara, who is upon the crown of your head. You should then rest in meditative equipoise. This practice should be refined many times.

Those of highest acumen will master luminosity, those of average acumen will master the illusory body, and those of inferior acumen will transfer consciousness into the human body that they desire.

The Intermediate State

On the other hand, if you are attached to the past deeds you have accumulated, the reality is that you will wander into the intermediate state after death. So, after approximately three days have passed, the three signs of death will arise.[985] Your movement will not be impeded anywhere, with the exception of the Adamantine Seat and the womb of your next rebirth.[986]

To block your entrance into that womb, you should clearly visualize yourself as the meditational deity and block it by resting in luminosity. Alternatively, you may block that womb entrance by meditating on yourself and all appearances as your teacher in male-female union. You should refine this practice [of blocking the womb entrance] from now onward.

In addition, those in whom attachment arises when they encounter their [future] parents in sexual union should respectfully venerate those two as their teacher or meditational deity in male-female union. Through your making offerings and praying to them, the womb entrance will be blocked. Alternatively, those who are at fault due to harboring attachment or hatred [for their future mother or father] may block the womb entrance by reflecting that this is merely discrimination (*dbyed ri she snyams pa*).

If, even then, it is not blocked, you should visualize yourself and appearances as the deity, and the body of the deity as a rainbow-colored magical display. You should then intermingle that with luminosity. That is to say, you should rest your mind in the Great Seal, without apprehending clarity or radiance. Thereby it will be impossible for the womb entrance not to be blocked. It should be blocked thereby within the first week, and it should effortlessly be blocked also within the subsequent [six] weeks [of the intermediate state].[987] {332}

It is important to persevere in the roots of virtuous action for the sake of deceased persons, and you should emphasize the Great Seal itself, the all-pervasive luminosity that has previously been revealed. There is evidently nothing else apart from these essential points.

This presents in writing the elixir of the **entire** Great Seal of the Kagyu lineage,
The **delightful** enlightened intention of Dakpo [Lharjé],
The essential points of **liberation**,
And the lucid instructions of the Six Doctrines of Tel
According to the **supremely** secret practice of Pagmodrupa.

This was compiled and reproduced here from the *Collected Works* of Venerable Pagmodrupa.

96. Guidebook Entitled *The Unique Enlightened Intention according to the Drigung*[988]

After first taking refuge and setting the mind on enlightenment [you should understand the following forty-seven supplementary points]:

(i) [Some hold that] the teachings [of all the conquerors of the ten directions and three times] are distinct [and various], but [in this tradition it is stated that the sacred doctrines of all the buddhas and the descent of their teachings] are one.

(ii) [Some say that the sacred doctrines and philosophical systems of the buddhas are different, but in this tradition it is stated that the vehicles and] the philosophical systems are the auspicious circumstances [of the buddhas].

(iii) [Some hold that] the eighty-four thousand sections of the sacred doctrine [amount to a single ox load and so forth, but in this tradition it is stated that they] are antidotes for the eighty-four thousand afflicted mental states.

(iv) [Some hold that] the twelve branches of the scriptures are different, but [in this tradition it is stated that] all of them are complete in each one.

(v) [Some hold that] the five excellences are [not] completely present in teachings [that are noncanonical],[989] but [in this tradition it is stated that] the entirety of cyclic existence and nirvana is subsumed in the five excellences.[990]

(vi) [Some hold that] the three scriptural collections are [un]connected with each other, [but in this tradition it is stated that] all three are completely present in each one.

(vii) [Some say that, in general, the excellence of the sacred doctrine is not completely present in the introductory chapters of all the scriptures, but in this tradition it is stated that all five excellences are completely present to their fullest extent in all the teachings.][991]

(viii) [There are many opinions concerning] the Vinaya, [Sutras, and Abhidharma, but in this tradition it is stated that the teachings of] the common sutras[992] and the Cittamātrins are [included within the scriptural compilation of the] Abhidharma.

(ix) [Some hold that the truth will be seen] by entering into the ways of the extremists and the Bonpos, [but in this tradition it is stated that] there is no opportunity for them] to see the truth.

(x) [Some hold that] the extremists and the Bonpos [have nothing at all that is conducive to liberation, but in this tradition it is stated without contradiction that they] do have some elements that are conducive to liberation.

(xi) Some say that all the experiential cultivations of the extremists should be abandoned in that they are without vows or compassion, but [in this tradition it is stated that] the outsiders also keep vows and do have compassion.

(xii) [Some hold that buddhahood will be attained after three "countless" aeons[993] through the vehicle of causal characteristics, but in this tradition it is stated that] buddhahood may be attained within a single lifetime, even through the vehicle of causal characteristics.

(xiii) [Some hold that the buddhahood of] the vehicle of the mantras and the vehicle of causal characteristics are not the same, but in this tradition it is stated that] they attain a single buddhahood through their sacred doctrines and courses of experiential cultivation.

(xiv) [Some hold that the three sorts of vows become more open at the higher levels, but in this tradition it is stated that] the three sorts of vows become narrower at the higher levels.

(xv) [Some hold that] the thirty-seven factors conducive to enlightenment are [attributes of] the path and that the buddha level transcends them, but [in this tradition it is stated that] one progresses through the essence of the path [of provisions up to the conclusive buddha level].

(xvi) [Some hold that] pious attendants and hermit buddhas do not attain buddhahood because they are cut off from the family [of the Great Vehicle], but [in this tradition it is stated that] they will ultimately achieve great enlightenment [because they have the causal basis of buddhahood].

(xvii) [Some hold that the vehicles and philosophical systems are indefinable and various, but in this tradition it is stated that all vehicles and philosophical systems constitute the dependent origination of the buddhas].[994]

(xviii) [Some hold that cyclic existence has no end and some hold that it does have an end, but in this tradition it is stated that] cyclic existence is without end and without conceptual elaboration.

(xix) [Some hold that the eighty-four thousand sections of the sacred doctrine and so forth are specific antidotes for each afflicted mental state that is to be renounced, but in this tradition it is stated that] all aspects of the sacred doctrine are subsumed in each of the vows of individual liberation.[995]

(xx) [Some hold that the Vinaya of the sacred doctrine is dissimilar in each of the four orders, but in this tradition it is stated that the four scriptural transmissions of monastic discipline that are the roots of] the four orders are essentially identical.

(xxi) [Some hold that] there is no offense when semen is ejaculated during a dream, but in this tradition it is stated that even ejaculation in a dream is an offense.

(xxii) [Some hold that] after attaining the first bodhisattva level there is no fear of being reborn in lower existences, but in this tradition it is stated that even] after attaining the bodhisttva levels, one may be reborn in lower existences.

(xxiii) [Some hold that the provisions of merit constitute a lower accumulation of provisions, but in this tradition it is stated that] the accumulated provisions of merit constitute the [marvelous] experiential cultivations {333}—the provisions accumulated by *kuśāla* practitioners.[996]

(xxiv) [Some hold that] when illness and harm afflict practitioners, [outer and inner auspicious coincidences will be beneficial, but in this tradition it is stated that] generosity [and visualization] will be the supreme methods for dispelling these obstacles.

(xxv) [Some hold that the secret mantras are the fourth scriptural compilation, but in this tradition it is stated that] the secret mantras are the essence of all three scriptural collections [and of each of them].

(xxvi) Some hold that the empowerment [of the secret mantras] may not be obtained even though it has been conferred and that it may be obtained even though it has not been conferred, but [in this tradition it is stated that profound empowerment] rituals of [the lineage] are necessary for those of superior, average, and inferior acumen.

(xxvii) [Some hold that the deeds of the three buddha bodies are definitively three in number, but in this tradition it is stated that although this is so] all enlightened activities may be accomplished even through a single [meditational] deity.

(xxviii)[Some hold that] each [meditational] deity has its own [specific] name, but [in this tradition it is stated that] "preferred deity" may be accepted [as a name] for all [meditational] deities.

(xxix) [Some hold that the primary commitments are granted through the secret mantras in all their four phases,[997] but in this tradition it is stated that] there is no opportunity to grant the primary commitments through the [secret] mantras [in all their four phases].

(xxx) [Some say that one cannot engage with the meditational deity from the very beginning and that one has to engage gradually, but in this tradition it is stated that immediate engagement, or] nongradual engagement, with the [meditational] deity is the profound essential point.

(xxxi) [Some hold that] the number of recitations in ritual service is important for [stabilizing] the generation stage, but [in this tradition it is stated that] one should know accomplishment to emerge through a host of auspicious circumstances that concern the [meditational] deity.

(xxxii) [Some hold that] asceticism [and so forth] disparages the [meditational] deity, but [in this tradition] it is stated that [the meditational deity] is denigrated by [conceiving of] the ordinary body.

(xxxiii) [Some hold that] the first [three] of the four classes of tantra are [not profound because they are] of provisional meaning, and [they hold that] the unsurpassed tantras [are of definitive meaning because they] alone are profound; but [in this tradition it is stated that] all the teachings of provisional and definitive meaning require [extensive rituals].

(xxxiv) [Some hold that empowerments from the start require engagement in a single extensive ritual, but in this tradition it is stated that] this may be condensed in any [simple] rite in order to train beings.

(xxxv) Some hold that the protective circle formed of [the wrathful deities,] the adamantine fence, [and so forth] is profound, but [in this tradition it is stated that] the [marvelous] protective circle is the armor[998] of enlightenment.

(xxxvi) Some hold that the [marvelous, uncommon] experiential cultivation of the [secret] mantras is the [most] profound [oral instruction concerning] the channels and the winds, but [in this tradition it is stated that] training [of body, speech, and mind] is even more important than the channels and the winds.

(xxxvii) [Some say that it is necessary to purify the channels, winds, and vital essences that are impure due to the action of the three poisons, but in this tradition it is agreed that] the purification of the channels, winds, and vital essences that are corrupt and poisonous is especially profound.

(xxxviii) [Some hold that] the commitments [of the disciple] are [most] critical and [the commitments of the master are] not critical, but [in this tradition it is stated that] both master and disciple have commitments that are [reciprocally] equal.

(xxxix) [Some hold that even tenth-level bodhisattvas do not see the substratum consciousness apart from only a single part or aspect, but in this tradition it is stated that] the substratum consciousness may also be seen on other [occasions] by those endowed with blessings.

(xl) [Some hold that the excellent and positive [nonregressive] path commences from seeing the truth of reality, but in this tradition it is stated that] even one of the tenth level may fall into lower realms by having committed a nonvirtuous action.

(xli) Some hold that [the three trainings constitute the further graduated path of the secret mantras, the vehicle of adamantine reality, and that the paths of] the Vinaya, the transcendent perfections, and the secret mantras are not identical; but [in this tradition] it is stated that those [six transcendent perfections] constitute the path of all three vehicles.

(xlii) Some hold that the Great Seal is obscured by both virtuous action and nonvirtuous action, but [in this tradition it is stated that] the buddha body of reality cannot be obscured by the essence of virtuous actions.

(xliii) Some hold that the fruition separated [from obscurations] is without a cause, but [in this tradition it is stated that] there cannot be fruition without a cause.

(xliv) Some hold that the mingling of both the object of meditation and the meditator [in nonduality], as if they were two spaces, is conclusive, but [in this tradition it is stated that] freedom from all conceptual elaboration denotes [the clear realization of] the pious attendants.

(xlv) Some hold that the fourfold action of breath control [and so forth] is profound, but [in this tradition it is stated that] the profound essential is not to hold the breath but to leave it relaxed.

(xlvi) Some hold that consciousness transference denotes the transference into the heart of the teacher [or meditational deity] dependent on [recitation of] HŪṂ or seed syllables, {334} but [in this tradition it is stated that] the supreme consciousness transference should engage with the luminosity of the teacher.

(xlvii) Some hold that when a buddha has entered nirvana, this resembles a fire that has run out of firewood, as if the wood were exhausted and the fire exhausted; but in this tradition it is stated that nirvana is the natural form of enlightenment, the essential nature free from extremes.

The points explained here should be imparted as incremental steps in respect of the *Revered* [*Wheel of Vitality*] and *The Fivefold* [*Great Seal*]. That is to say, they are to be experientially cultivated.

This sets forth in writing the instructions of adamantine speech
That **supremely** reveal the natural **liberation,**
Delightfully and excellently discerning the single savor
Of **all** sacred doctrines in the expanse of enlightened intention.

This was compiled from *The Forty-Seven Adamantine Sayings.*[999]

97. Guidebook Entitled *The Six Doctrines according to Taklungpa*[1000]

After you have taken refuge and set the mind on enlightenment, the practice of the fierce inner heat is differentiated according to both lower and higher methods.[1001]

(i) [As to the former,] the wind of past actions should be compressed [by yogic exercises,] and there will be a gradual increase in the appearances [of heat, bliss, and nonconceptuality].[1002] The sessions of visualization are short but there are many essential points. You should diligently try to secure the physical posture known as the "six opposing stoves."[1003]

The inception of postmeditation is then taken as an example of the impure illusory body. From the time of its appearance its modality is empty of inherent existence.

Also, if you do not waver from the aspiration that arises when you lie down to practice dream yoga, the fierce inner heat associated with the wind of past actions will become the basis of your meditative equipoise and the impure illusory body will become your path of postmeditation. For the aspiration associated with dream yoga is an attribute that facilitates perception during the night.

(ii) The higher method, distinct from that, applies the four-session yoga and it emphasizes the fierce inner heat associated with [the wind] of pristine cognition. Here, the upper and lower winds should be united through breath control. The vital essence will then descend from the crown of the head to the [fire in the navel cakra] in the form of an ashé, and the experiences of bliss, radiance, and nonconceptual mind will then follow.

[In this higher method] the primordially pure expanse is the Great Seal, and the natural expressive power of its appearance is the innate fundamental state—the pure illusory body where [pristine] objects are atemporally present.

These pith instructions are the foundation of excellent remedies, resembling the alchemical transformation [of base metal] into gold. As for their practical implementation, once delusion, which resembles that base metal element, has been transformed, it is termed *luminosity*. Whatever the experiences of bliss and emptiness that arise may be, at that very moment they are spacious, without fabrication or contrivance. The luminosity [that is subsequently experienced] at the time of death is known as "the meeting of mother and child."

Those who would assume the dance of the mental body [in the intermediate state after death] should be attentive to consciousness transference {335} and recite HIK.[1004] The arrow and the bow of subtle energy and mind are the devices that direct this visualization. Consciousness transference through[1005] the syllable HŪṂ is the short path that subsumes the enlightened intention of the Six Doctrines.

This sets forth in writing the practical method of the Six Doctrines
Through the fierce inner heat, illusory body, dream yoga,
And, similarly, the luminosity that is the glow of **total delight**,
Its manifestations being the nature of **supreme liberation**.

This was compiled from the instruction manual of glorious Taklungpa the Great.

98. Guidebook Entitled *The Means for Attainment of the Guru, Auspicious Circumstances, and Common Savor*[1006]

After you have taken refuge and set the mind on enlightenment, [there follows the cycle of the Middle Drukpa, which has three aspects]:

1. Means for Attainment of the Guru

You should experientially cultivate the essential instructions that conceive of the teacher as the three buddha bodies of reality, perfect resource, and emanation. Rising when dawn covers one-eighth of the sky, you should array the visualization in the sky in front of yourself. That is to say, you should conceive of your teacher seated upon a particularly sublime ornate throne, as Prajñāpāramitā, the consort of the conquerors—the natural grace of the uncontaminated buddha body of reality. While verbally chanting the verses of the *Fourfold Cycle of the Mother of Space*,[1007] you should complete one thousand prostrations with your five limbs touching the ground, precisely and without mistaking the number, and then finally you should dissolve the great mother Prajñāpāramitā, who is the essential nature of the teacher, into yourself. Consequently, you should nurture the natural descent of naked intrinsic awareness, however it abides, as the buddha body of reality free from conceptual elaboration, uncovered by the stains of the trichotomy between subject, object, and interaction. You may then attend to [mundane] activities, such as eating at the end of the session.

Next, while conceiving of your teacher as Vajradhara, the buddha body of perfect resource in whom the major and minor marks are perfectly radiant, embodying all the lineage holders, you should do one thousand prostrations as before, and after dissolving that visualization into yourself, you should nurture the unimpeded natural glow of the buddha body of perfect resource that manifests in and of itself.

Next, with devotion you should conceive of your teacher as the buddha body of emanation, Śākyamuni, diffusing light rays in the ten directions, and do one thousand prostrations as before. After dissolving the visualization into yourself, you should hone your own awareness within the disposition where you yourself are the buddha body of emanation, effortlessly acting for the benefit of living beings. Then, finally, the three buddha bodies will have been perfected {336} and you should develop strong devotion and faith from the heart in your actual root teacher. Prostrate toward that teacher with your body, and with your speech recite the words, "All sentient beings who are equal to space go for refuge to the teacher who is the buddha body of reality, to the teacher who is the buddha body of perfect resource, to the teacher who is the compassionate buddha body of emanation, to the teacher who is the buddha body of essentiality, to the teacher who is the precious buddha, and to the venerable lord of the sacred doctrine who is the gracious buddha!"[1008]

With your mind you should completely abandon [all activities], out of regard for the expression "You know what is to be done!" You should concentrate your body, speech, and mind one-pointedly and be particularly strict while in retreat. In the night you should practice [dream] yoga while sleeping, and thereby you will perfect the provisions, purify obscurations, and forcefully draw the blessings of the body, speech, and mind of the teacher into your own mind, so that meditative experiences and realization gush forth and you become like a son who has followed in his father's footsteps.[1009]

2. Auspicious Circumstances

As for the guidance that determines auspicious circumstances,[1010] you should ascertain [the nature of] fundamental mind and not incite mental obfuscation through a multitude of unnecessary activities. That is to say, you should develop the [commonsense] understanding that vomiting or indigestion are gastric ailments that may occur if you overeat.

Just as [a farmer at the end of] the four agricultural seasons and a trader who has obtained a favorable price for tea may idly rest, after encountering the face of mind you should rely on the common savor without engaging in any activity.

Just as a herdsman on the high plateau is vigilant, wondering whether any enemy, thief, or wolf may approach or not approach his livestock, you should concentrate on the strength of awareness with unwavering vigilance.

Just as a wild ungulate sticks to its own habitat, you should meditate in the manner of a solitary juniper growing on a cliff in a snow range or forest.

You should move about and sit with your body, speak with your voice, and with your mind you should avoid all elaborations. You should not resort to agricultural activities.

Starting with a secluded house or remote dwelling, you should even erect a partition screen around your own bed.

You should cut off the continuity of speech, but when you do speak out, extol your teacher, the sacred doctrine, or spiritual siblings.

You should refine these four pith instructions concerning contentment, renunciation, dispassion, and withdrawal.[1011] {337}

If, in addition, you guard the three commitments of unwavering body, speech, and mind, auspicious circumstances will spontaneously emerge, like flies gathering on meat.

3. Common Savor

As far as the guidance on the common savor is concerned, you should pray fervently to your teacher. This direct liberation without grasping is profound. [Specifically, there are six pith instructions to be observed:][1012]

(i) The pith instruction of bringing negative views to the precipice that carries conceptual thoughts onto the path: Here you should discard [conceptual thoughts] with your mind, dispel hope and doubt, and precisely apprehend whatever arises. Even though thoughts might be abandoned, do not abandon them and do not pursue them. Do not rectify them. You should rest in a relaxed manner, wide-eyed and in equilibrium, and let go of egotistical grasping.

(ii) The pith instruction of transforming poison into nectar that carries afflicted mental states onto the path: In this regard, when hatred, delusion, pride, jealousy, or desire suddenly arise, you should precisely apprehend them, remain lucid, and purify them inherently, without abandoning them. You should realize them to be the pristine cognition of discernment, the mirrorlike pristine cognition, the pristine cognition of reality's expanse, the pristine cognition of sameness, and the pristine cognition of accomplishment, which are the natural expressions of the five families [of buddhas].

(iii) The pith instruction of accepting obstacles as spiritual accomplishments that carries gods and demons onto the path: Here you should precisely apprehend the face of demonic forces and the perception of fearful thoughts when they suddenly arise, and purify frightful perceptions inherently, without abandoning them. That should clearly transpire.

(iv) The pith instruction of enlightened mind that carries the sufferings of cyclic existence onto the path:[1013] here you should cultivate compassion for sentient beings and nurture the exchanging of yourself and others, without contrivance.

(v) The pith instruction of the common savor of the elements that carries ill health onto the path: Though you may fall ill, there will be nothing other than this practical technique [that will assist]. Recognize this and abandon [obstacles or ailments] with your mind! You should dispel hope and doubt, and starkly behold the discomfort of your pain. If you probe around your seat, you will not find anything [that will assist], so rest in that disposition! The apprehension of a self is the causal basis of hope and doubt and of ill health.

(vi) The pith instruction of introducing the mother and child that carries death onto the path: Here the "mother" is reality and the "child" is awareness, the true modality of appearances. At the time of death, you should meditate on your teacher. You should recognize conceptual thoughts and act with fervent devotion. You should remain relaxed. By your recognizing the awareness of the moment of death and resting in it, in an uncontrived manner, {338} it is said buddhahood will be attained.

This sets forth in writing buddhahood in the palm of the hand—
The **entirety** of the means for attainment of the teacher,
The auspicious circumstances, and the common savor,
Which delightfully with joy and responsiveness
Reveals the essentials of **supreme liberation.**

This was compiled from the instruction manuals of the glorious Drukpa [Tsangpa Gyaré].

99. Guidebook Entitled *The Fivefold Capacity of Lorepa*[1014]

After you have taken refuge and set the mind on enlightenment [there follows the cycle of the Lower Drukpa concerning the five capacities]:[1015]

1. The Capacity to Wear the Cotton Robe of the Fierce Inner Heat

Here the visualization is as follows: You should one-pointedly focus on yourself as Vajrayoginī, with a body of fire. Within an aureole of a blazing mass of fire, she appears, with the soles of her feet [resting on] a sun disk below, diffusing red and shining sparks of fire, as if being burned by fire. Above, also, her body blazes as the natural expression of fire, its six ornaments[1016] fiery red, blazing outwardly and inwardly on fire. With fervent devotion, until the [molten] fluid from her head almost flows down as far as her heels, you should say, "Grant your blessing that the pristine cognition of blissful warmth may arise!"[1017]

Finally, you should continuously practice the yogic exercise named "kindling fire with a rubbing stick"[1018] and develop strength in both the control of [the winds of] vital breath and exertion. When resting you should nurture your own true nature and do this without distraction.[1019]

2. The Capacity to Dwell in Mountains, Engaged in Secret Practice[1020]

Goaded on by diet and conduct,[1021] you should determine that whatever appearances arise, they are a magical display, and by crushing faintheartedness, you should determine that you have the capacity to master the signs that underlie the illusory body.

3. The Capacity to Agitate Diseases and Demonic Possession[1022]

At the inception of disease and demonic possession, whatever negative circumstances should arise, you should not grasp them but adroitly train in the capacity [to agitate diseases and demonic possession], based on the direct understanding that these are facilitators.[1023]

4. The Capacity to Apply Antidotes according to the Circumstances[1024]

Consequently, having taken onto the path whatever arises through the common savor of happiness and suffering, in an unconcerned manner, you should have the capacity to fathom the antidotes for diseases [and so forth].[1025]

5. The Capacity to Fathom the Great Seal[1026]

Those who are of happy disposition right now should examine without a trace of fear or apprehensiveness the voidness of inanimate and animate things, and sever their pride, with the capacity to die in the expanse of the Great Seal.[1027]

This propagates in writing **all** the instructions of the fivefold capacity,
The **supremely** compact path
That renounces this life and, with a mind of **delight** and felicity,
Severs pride concerning the **liberation** of bondage in the expanse.

This was compiled from the instruction manual of Dra Gandenpa. {339}

100. Guidebook Entitled *The Six Primary Essentials for the Mountain Retreat of Yangonpa*[1028]

After you have taken refuge and set the mind on enlightenment [there follows the cycle of the Upper Drukpa, which has six primary essentials—namely, (i) the primary essential of the five crucial procedures for vigorous breathing, (ii) the primary essential of the training in the red HŪṂ of consciousness transference, (iii) the primary essential of the six adamantine expressions of emptiness, (iv) the primary essential of the sacred doctrine of HŪṂ pertaining to evil spirits that bring diseases, (v) the primary essential of the dream yoga of secret conduct, and (vi) the primary essential of guarding against ejaculation along with the restricted injunction].[1029]

1. The Primary Essential of the Five Crucial Procedures for Vigorous Breathing

The five crucial procedures for vigorous breathing comprise inhalation, filling, crushing, ejection of breath in the manner of an arrow, and the union of the upper and lower winds through vase breathing. For the first crucial procedure, inhalation, you should distinguish between the defect [of not knowing] and the advantage [of knowing] the key points of inhalation. Similarly, when you practice the four subsequent crucial procedures[—filling, crushing, ejection, and union—]their practical application is revealed by the teacher in person because there is no tradition for recording these in writing.[1030]

2. The Primary Essential of the Training in the Red HŪṂ of Consciousness Transference

As for the red HŪṂ of consciousness transference, this is refined by training and application. [First the training is as follows:] Adopting the essential physical posture, you should meditate on the teacher at the crown of your head and imagine that the secret cakra of the teacher and your own anterior fontanel are directly level. Cultivate the utmost devotion! Then, at your navel cakra there is a red HŪṂ resembling coral. It falls freely to the secret cakra and diffuses rays of light like the sting of a bee, incinerating all impurities and filth within the physical body and transforming it, as if the cartilages were inflated with emptiness and radiance.

Next, there are interlinking HŪṂ syllables that break off individually from that red HŪṂ, and respectively block the rectum, the urethra, the navel, the mouth, the nose, the eyes, the ears, and the space between the eyebrows. You should imagine that the anterior fontanel at the crown of your head is suddenly opened and visualize that in the middle of your empty body the central channel has the thickness of a bamboo cane—at its lower extremity reaching the deepest entrails and at its upper extremity penetrating the anterior fontanel, empty and radiant. You should visualize that the HŪṂ of the secret cakra then reaches the navel cakra, shimmering red and causing it to shake and tremble.

[Secondly, the application is as follows:] From within that disposition, the HŪṂ is ejected afar in the manner of an arrow through the central channel, and it enters into the secret cakra of the teacher, so that it passes above the head of the teacher and comes to rest far off in the disposition of the Great Seal, upon the *amoliṅga* stone platform of Trāyastriṃśa.[1031]

3. The Primary Essential of the Six Adamantine Expressions of Emptiness

Reality is nothing at all. [In general,] there is the one-sided emptiness exemplified by nonexistence in relation to existence, {340} there is the ephemeral emptiness exemplified by a vase that is empty of water, there is the emptiness of synonyms that exaggerate and deprecate emptiness and its modalities, and there is the emptiness of the mental faculty that reflects on a single object that is not intellectually established. Here, on the other hand, there is [the modality of the emptiness of the ground], which denotes the emptiness of cyclic existence and nirvana, of everything that appears and exists, untainted by the stains of such [narrow perspectives]. There is also [the modality of the emptiness of the path], which denotes the great freedom from extremes that does not fall into bias. This comprises the emptiness of views, because inclusions such as the statement "my view is this" are not established; and it comprises the emptiness of nonviews, because preclusions such as the statement "it is not this" are not refuted.

Having been transformed in accordance with [the foregoing modality of the path, the modality of the emptiness of the fruition] is neither a profound aspect of the oral instructions of the teacher nor an understanding on the part of the wisdom of the disciples. The original, uncontrived abiding nature is present as such.

The six aspects established in the context of the six [adamantine] expressions comprise these three modalities of the emptiness of ground, path, and fruition, along with the compatibility of these modalities of emptiness, the establishing of emptiness, and, lastly, the defects and advantages that may arise in relation to emptiness.[1032]

4. The Primary Essential of the Sacred Doctrine of HŪṂ Pertaining to Evil Spirits That Bring Diseases

This has two aspects—namely, evil spirits that bring diseases on yourself, and evil spirits that bring diseases on others. [As to the former,] you should meditate on a thumbnail-sized blue HŪṂ in your own heart, and then, differentiated on the basis of heat and cold, you should visualize a white HŪṂ [in the case of fevers] and a red HŪṂ [in the case of colds], which are respectively cold and hot to the touch, within the upper and lower parts of your body. Just as a magnet attracts iron filings, your ailments will be gathered in one fell swoop and finally expelled afar from the crown of the head. [In the case of subsidiary diseases such as tumors,] you should visualize a blue HŪṂ in the place where there is a tumor and gather the disease, as before, expelling it from the fingertips.[1033]

With reference to evil spirits that bring diseases on others, this conforms with the [aforementioned practice] of expelling the HŪṂ in your own heart. In conjunction with vigorous breathing, you should visualize that a string of HŪṂ syllables, unbroken as a thread, enters though the nose of the invalid and fills their body. All diseases without exception should then be gathered and inhaled through your own nose, along with the string of mantra

HŪṂ syllables. Finally, on breathing out clearly, you should imagine that the manifestations of disease vanish like mist in the sky. This treatment for evil spirits that bring diseases appears to resemble the extraction of a painful thorn.[1034] {341}

5. The Primary Essential of the Dream Yoga of Secret Conduct

As for the dream yoga of secret conduct,[1035] if you carry this [understanding] of the aforementioned gods and spirits as an empty reflection onto the path, you should assume the essential physical posture and meditate as follows, saying, "Since these [gods and spirits] are my parents, I should cultivate loving-kindness. Since these are my teacher, I should pray to them. Since these are my meditational deity, I should request spiritual accomplishment. Since these are innate, I should rest in their disposition!"[1036]

6. The Primary Essential of Guarding against Ejaculation

You should visualize a reddish-yellow downward-facing syllable PHAṬ at the orifice of the vajra (penis). Next, imagine that from the tip of the vajra as far as the navel cakra, a string of white HŪṂ syllables is arrayed, and that from your pores the HŪṂ syllables half protrude and half remain submerged within. Then focus your awareness on the syllable HAṂ on the crown of your head and visualize that the string of HŪṂ syllables at the orifice of the vajra surges upward within the central channel to emerge from the crown of your head by a full span.[1037]

You should guard against ejaculation at six times: (i) If you are about to ejaculate in dreams, you should meditate at the time of falling sleep. (ii) [You should meditate if you are about to ejaculate when the experience of bliss arises, and so forth.] And (iii–vi) [you should meditate at the end of all the four sessions of practice].[1038]

As for [the restricted injunctions] on guarding against ejaculation by using a device: You should tie a span-sized stick from the waist by a cord and position it upright at the occiput, which is said to correlate with the sacred place of Arbuda. You should not make the mistake of tying the cord at the neck, which is said to correlate with the sacred place of Lampāka.[1039] Then close the left channel and there will be no ejaculation. This oral instruction [when it is effective] resembles the play of children.[1040]

Then there is the guarding against ejaculation by means of sacramental substances [which is a restricted injunction: If the aforementioned device does not help,] you should make a dough combining the following substances—frankincense, which represents the authentic dreadlocks of Yama; mustard, which is the sacramental charm for wrathful rites; menstrual blood; human ash; human brain; deer fat; and human fat. You should knead this with the urine of a [healthy] child under the age of eight, prepare mustard seed–sized pills, and let them dry in the shade. If these are inserted individually into the orifice of the vajra (penis), the pain will cease [and the remedy will be effective].[1041]

It is said:[1042]

> If you do not maintain all these six primary essentials
> From the crucial great corpus concerning mountain retreat,
> Even though you have many of the most crucial points,
> They will be incomplete, and for this reason
> It will be hard to understand the practical application, without error.

This presents in writing the terse and meaningful instructions
Of Yangonpa, endowed with the eye of the sacred doctrine,
Whose *Mountain Retreat* reveals **all delightful** key points,
The path of **supreme liberation** in six primary essentials. {342}

This was compiled from the *Mountain Retreat* itself.

101. Guidebook Entitled *The Four-Armed Mahākāla in the Form Kurakma*[1043]

After you have taken refuge and set the mind on enlightenment, whenever this body of yours engages in this practice, it is known as the "being of commitment," but when glorious Jñānanātha becomes vibrantly radiant, the being of pristine cognition is present.

[As to the former, the visualized being of commitment:] At the navel cakra within your body, which resembles a pure and transparent crystal offering lamp, at the triple intersection of the channels, you should visualize the three deities that are naturally present. That is to say, you should meditate vividly on Mahākāla in the form Jñānanātha in the center, raven-faced

Kākamukha to the right, and red Caṇḍikā to the left, standing on the channel branches that are the supporting basis of Mahākāla and his consort, and on the channels and vital essences. Next, the being of pristine cognition similar to your visualized form should arrive from the great Śītavana charnel ground and dissolve therein. After that, you should visualize your teacher in the form of the lord of enlightened heritage Innate Cakrasaṃvara, present directly at Mahākāla's head.

Within the heart cakra of Mahākāla you should visualize the syllable HŪṂ, within the heart cakra of raven-faced Kākamukha also the syllable HŪṂ, and within the heart cakra of Caṇḍikā the syllable BHYOḤ, surrounded by their own respective mantras. Then you should cultivate devotion for the teacher and recite approximately a rosary of the seven-syllable mantra [of Cakrasaṃvara]. From the body of your teacher, Innate Cakrasaṃvara, rays of light of the nature of bliss then appear, penetrating Mahākāla and his consort, so that they are pleased to the utmost. In consideration of the being of commitment, they then diffuse doctrinal protectors resembling themselves from your ten million pores, so that your body is covered, as it were, with armor. Imagining you are protected with the adamantine body, you should then count [the mantra recitations]: OṂ VAJRA KAWUVA VAPAŚAYA MAHĀKĀLA YA HŪṂ HŪṂ PHAṬ.[1044] Aroused by the light of these syllables, Caṇḍikā and raven-faced Kākamukha then diffuse forms resembling themselves and eradicate the enemies of the Buddhist teaching, absorbing the strength, capacity, and power of the three planes of existence.

Next, you should absorb these emanations inwardly through the pores of your own body, visualized as Mahākāla, and imagine that they dissolve into one another in the four channels of the navel cakra. {343} The vital essences of the channel branches are then absorbed in the manner of globules of mercury moving in fire and dissolve as offerings into Mahākāla and consort. Next, the ritual acolytes of Mahākāla and the female deities to the right and left also dissolve into the central Mahākāla, so that Mahākāla alone is visualized, and he, in turn, is transformed into the syllable HŪṂ. The parts of that syllable then dissolve in succession, from the subscript vowel U, to the nasalized vibration (*nāda*), and thence into the visage of your teacher in the form of Innate Cakrasaṃvara, seated in male-female meditative equipoise. Finally, your vitality of pure essence, in the disposition of bliss and emptiness, should settle into the Great Seal.

In that same manner, you should also meditate on the three [aforementioned] deities within the four other cakras—the secret cakra, the heart, the throat, and the crown of the head—and that in succession, these also dissolve into your teacher in the form of Innate Cakrasaṃvara, the disposition of bliss and emptiness.

Next, you should meditate that the three channels are respectively white, red, and pale blue, and that vital essences are present in the five cakras, in their five colors.

Finally, visualizing yourself as Mahākāla, at the secret cakra there is a hexahedron embodying bliss and emptiness, blue on the outside, red on the inside, and in the middle is the female consort Nandikeśvarī. You should meditate that within her womb there is a dark blue HŪṂ, the natural expression of Mahākāla, glistening and endowed with five-colored rays of light, with the brilliance of one thousand suns. This is the supremely crucial point concerning the secret support that is established within the body.

May insightful persons obtain pleasure
Through the higher teachings, trusted above **all**,
That are simply listed [here] with **delight** and enthusiasm,
Fulfilling aspirations for **supreme** natural **liberation**.

This was compiled and documented in accordance with ancient writings.

102. Guidebook Entitled *The Inner Guidance of Glorious Pañjaranātha*[1045]

After first taking refuge and setting the mind on enlightenment: You should visualize the three channels and five cakras of your own subtle body, radiantly manifest as Mahākāla. Within the navel cakra of emanation there is an ashé (the stroke of the letter *a*) indicative of nonarising, from which Ekajaṭī then arises. She melts into light that is transformed into four vital essences, among which the upper vital essence appears as your teacher in the form of the solitary hero Hevajra. In the middle of that, where the right, left, and central channels converge with the vital essence, is Mahākāla, with his copper knife–wielding emanation to the right and Śrīdevī to the left. The syllable YA is then diffused from the heart cakra of Mahākāla and the syllable MAṂ from Śrīdevī, giving rise respectively to the {344} male yakṣa and female yakṣinī. Two TRI syllables then diffuse from the male yakṣa and the syllable BHYOḤ from the female yakṣinī, and from these, in turn, Putra with his brother and sister appear.[1046]

The beings of pristine cognition should then dissolve into those visualizations, and the empowerments should be conferred. You should imagine that Akṣobhya [confers empowerment] on the teacher and Mahākāla, and that the crown ornament is conferred on the others by means of the five-pronged vajra, and that they are bound under an oath of allegiance by means of the teacher's handheld vajra, as he says:[1047]

> This vajra is the great vajra.
> It has the blessings of all the buddhas.
> If you transgress your oaths,
> There is no doubt that this will be terrifying!
> SAMAYASMARA SAMAYAMĀTI KRAMA
> SAMAYA RAKṢANTU

Thereafter the DEVA PICU mantra,[1048] the twelve-syllable mantra,[1049] and the RORU mantra[1050] should be recited, binding and suppressing them.

The [sequence of the] visualization is that your teacher arouses Mahākāla. Mahākāla then arouses the copper knife–wielding emanation and Śrīdevī. They, in turn, respectively arouse the male yakṣa and female yakṣinī,[1051] and they, in turn, respectively arouse Putra with his brother and sister.[1052] You should imagine that their messengers who fill the trichiliocosm eradicate enemies and obstructors. Then you should recite OṂ KĀLA YAKṢAYA KĀLĪ YAKṢISĪ YAKṢAPUTRAYE RUṬABHATRAYE RULU RAKṢASĪ HŪṂ BHYOḤ HŪṂ.[1053] Finally, the visualization is gradually dissolved; you should let your mind rest on a yellow vital essence, the size of a small seed, and maintain the gentle union of the upper and lower winds.

Next, in that same manner, you should focus on Ekajaṭī as she arises from the ashé (the stroke of the letter *a*) in each of the other cakras—the secret cakra, the heart, the throat, and the crown of the head—and then rest your mind respectively in the green, blue, red, and white vital essences. Finally, you should visualize the syllable HŪṂ within a hexahedron, which is the secret abode of the female deity in the navel cakra, and become established in that secret support, while meditating also according to the *Ritual Application of the Razor Cut*.[1054]

Here I have **supremely** established and clearly documented
The list of visualizations for the sacred doctrine
That **all** proclaim to be profound—
The guidance of the path to **liberation**
Where **delight** arises and there is a natural descent of bliss.

This was compiled and documented in accordance with the guidance of Yarlungpa Sengé Gyeltsen.

103. Guidebook Entitled *The Trilogy of Spiritual Songs*[1055] {345}

After first taking refuge and setting the mind on enlightenment: [You should understand that] the entirety of cyclic existence and nirvana is the arising modality of [the nature of] mind, and apart from that there is no entity that exists. Through this mind—the agent of causes and conditions—there is nothing to be done. It is empty, nothing whatsoever, and the expressive power of its awareness is unimpeded. Form and color are similarly nonexistent anywhere. The dichotomies of singularity and multiplicity, of eternalism and nihilism, and of extremes and freedom from extremes cannot be specifically pinpointed. Anything whatsoever may appear in your own meditative experience that transcends the intellect. That is to say, the nature of mind may manifest as anything whatsoever, it is unlimited, it does not fall into extremes, it is not attached to biased perspectives, it is without exhaustion or increase, and it is without discontinuity.

You should be introduced to this nature of mind through symbols. Concentrate the mind! Do not get lost in the past, and do not get lost in the future! Rest your mind instantly in its natural state, and intensely refine [the awareness] that is without support! You should maintain mindfulness without distraction and nurture the experience of awareness. When you have become familiar with the space [of reality], you will no longer have to exercise control through mindfulness. You will no longer have to depend on antidotes. There will be no discontinuity of your meditative experience that is naturally present, transcending the intellect.

Here I have lucidly set forth in writing
The path that generates delight,

Excellently combining **all** the essentials of *The Trilogy of Spiritual Songs*,
The **supreme** guidance that confers **liberation** from bondage.

This was compiled from the instruction manual of Parpuwa [Lodro Sengé].

104. Guidebook Entitled *The Six Doctrines of the Accomplished Masters*[1056]

After you have taken refuge and set the mind on enlightenment: your horizon should become luminosity, your body should become the illusory body, and the continuity of your past propensities after death should depend on dream yoga and the intermediate state.

The Fierce Inner Heat and Illusory Body

Once you have been reborn in whatever form, the period from your birth until your death constitutes the intermediate state. The path through which the maturational body is attained depends on the channels and winds. To that end, you should intermingle the practice of fierce inner heat with desire, train in magical display, and not transgress this reality.

Dream Yoga

For this practice, you should first develop a strong aspiration and repeatedly remind yourself that you should understand your dreams in the [nighttime] intervals between the daylight hours. With a high pillow and a comfortable mattress, you should lie down on your right side {346} and visualize in the throat cakra a red lotus with four petals, at the center of which is a white syllable A. When falling asleep, you should have fervent recollection. After sunset, you should focus your mind on a white vital essence between the eyebrows; at dawn, you should focus on the syllable ĀḤ at the throat; and when waking up, you should understand that all phenomenal existence resembles a dream. The signs of successful recognition are that even though you are confronted by water or fire, fall into an abyss, or are pursued or killed, and so forth, you will understand this to be a dream. You should maintain this practice.

The training is as follows: you should aspire in whichever way you can, pondering in your mind whether during dreams you will jump into water, be burned in a fire, behold the domain of Trāyastriṃśa or the twenty-four sacred places, be oppressed by the sun, behold the face of your meditational deity, or listen to the sacred doctrine, and so forth. That is the training.

When training in magical display and refining dreams, if you have thoughts of fear and anxiety because you have jumped into water and so forth, you should abandon your distress, thinking, "This is a dream. This is fictitious. What is terrifying?" You should not transgress this reality.

Luminosity

In refining your dreams, you should understand also that whatever transpires is bewilderment, and during sleep you should then enter into luminosity. You should meditate on the syllable HŪṂ at the center of the heart cakra—with A in front, NU to the right, TA to the rear, and RA to the left. In normal circumstances you should visualize the syllable A; when gross thoughts have subsided and deep sleep has arrived, you should visualize the syllable NU; when subtle thoughts have subsided, you should visualize the syllable TA; and when sleeping at dusk, you should visualize the syllable RA. When sleep is wearing out, these should be absorbed into the syllable HŪṂ. By sleeping accordingly, you will relish sleep as emptiness, experiencing the luminosity of bliss and emptiness.

The Intermediate State

When the maturational body of the intermediate state is investigated, the mental body consisting of past propensities endures through the intermediate state of the rebirth process, until another body is acquired. {347} At that time, without generating attachment toward a beautiful female form or hatred toward a beautiful male form, you should carry [this experience] as luminosity. [To that end, you should know that] after you have died, you will faint for three days, or for up to five or seven days, as if falling asleep. After waking up, you will be fearful simply of the extent of your dreams. After you have died, the thought will arise that you exist, whereupon the propensities accrued in your past life will finally be continued through reincarnation and you will experience the suffering of the three lower realms, including the hells. Therefore, instead of lapsing into ordinary afflicted mental states of the past, it is said that you should not mistake the thoughts [of the mental body in] the intermediate state for your own mental continuum but actualize them as the buddha body of reality, which is luminosity.

Here I have transformed into writing
The **supreme** natural **liberation** of **total delight**,
The elixir of the enlightened intention of all the accomplished masters,
The instructions that were conferred on the yakṣinī.

This was compiled from ancient writings.

105. Guidebook Entitled *The Gradual Path of Padmasambhava*[1057]

After first taking refuge and setting the mind on enlightenment, you should stay at an isolated hermitage. When there is sunlight, you should clearly focus on the rainbow light emerging from an egg-shaped crystal and rest [your mind] on the support of that perception. This is [known as] the "mirror of Vajrasattva" that manifests to disciples, in the manner in which Padmasambhava pointed it out to an old man with his staff and to an old woman with his finger.[1058]

Just as this light is not transformed into any existent entity but may arise as anything whatsoever on the basis of conditions, the entirety of cyclic existence and nirvana—all that appears and exists—is actually the unique vital essence that is not differentiated outwardly or inwardly; a spectacle, radiant and distinct in its rainbow lights. This unique vital essence of appearance and emptiness accommodates the fields of existence, exemplified even by this field of joyous Akaniṣṭha, the supremely secret abode. Indeed, all that may be designated as phenomena is permeated by the sameness of primordial purity and spontaneous presence, like a crystal and its light. You should visualize that though form and color together appear as the diversity of rainbow light, {348} they do not transgress these three characteristics: nonexistence, appearance, and pervasion.

In this timeless liberation, the unique vital essence is dazzling, vibrant, clear, pulsating, quivering, stark, and bright. It neither differentiates nor does it not differentiate between the expanse of reality and awareness. It is devoid of distinguished aspects and distinguishers. It emerges from the uncontrived expanse, as naturally present luminosity. Though it is present to all, there is no one at all who sees it. No one dares appraise it, just like the extent of space. It is radiant and brilliant, like the light of the sun. It is unchanging and steadfast, like Meru, king of mountains. It is profound and bottomless, like the depths of the ocean. It is untainted, like a lotus in the mud. It is intangible, like the moon reflected in water. It arises in all ways, like rainbow clouds in the sky. It is radiantly perfect, like the reflection in a mirror. It is unimpeded in all respects, like a meteorite from the sky. It is uninterrupted, like the flow of a great river. It is the substratum, like the mighty earth. Examples such as these indicate that the unique vital essence unites pristine cognition and the expanse.

Though this adamantine chain of awareness does not exist outwardly or inwardly, owing to the modalities of its appearance, it does appear outwardly and inwardly—outwardly as a precious enclosure of spontaneous presence,[1059] and inwardly as naturally radiant awareness and their offspring of pure essence. That is to say, it has three modalities: actual awareness, the natural light of awareness, and the natural conception of awareness, which correspond respectively to (i) the unchanging light of the male that resembles a vibrant painting, distinct and radiant; (ii) the channel enclosure of the female that is of luminous vital essence, radiant and empty; and (iii) the offspring that is the experience of bliss, radiance, and emptiness, born consequent on the entry of the former into the womb of the adamantine queen.

Wish-granting fruit ripens from the wish-granting tree. Waves of nectar emerge from the ocean of nectar. The rainfall of all that is desired cascades from the wish-fulfilling gem. You should not therefore pour nectar into a vase containing the vomit of suspicion that is the negative conceptualizing intellect. You should not grow poisonous fruits from medicinal seeds. {349} You should not cover the light of the sun with darkness. How wonderful! Exactly like this crystal before you, you should understand that internal awareness also has a radiant adamantine chain of light. Exemplified by the unimpeded colors of rainbow light that arise from this crystal, the luminosity of the inception [of awareness] occurs naturally, transforming the four material elements. All the self-manifesting appearances of the channels, winds, and vital essences may assume the form of smoke, mirage, fireflies, burning lamps, light resembling the moon, light resembling the sun, or Rāhu, the eclipser. All these indications that arise and these that do not arise are nonexistent. Indeed, the arising of the expanse and the liberating of the expanse are similar to the coiling and uncoiling of a snake, so you should not be agitated by the demonic forces that would grasp those signs. Exemplified by this crystal, which has no interior content but seems to manifest as appearances, you should not look anywhere apart from your own intrinsic awareness. Since all those apparent signs without exception exemplify the natural manifestation of natural radiance that is uncreated and without effort, they may be engaged without mistaking cause and result.

I have faith in this text that reveals
The **supreme** path to **liberation**
From the bondage of the mind,
Through **all** the essential teachings of Padma,
The symbolic method of the **delightful** crystal.

This was extracted from the essential instructions of *The Gradual Path of Padmasambhava*.

106. Guidebook Entitled *The Collected Injunctions of the King*[1060]

After you have taken refuge and set the mind on enlightenment [there then ensues the threefold guidance of buddha body, speech, and mind]:

(i) The guidance of buddha body concerns the uncommon preliminaries associated with the generation stage. You should confess acts of killing, stealing, and sexual misconduct committed by means of the body; and you should train in the acquisition of the three virtuous actions of the body. With certainty that your body has from the beginning been the body of the deity, through that disposition you should clearly visualize yourself as sublime Avalokita, the color of a stainless conch, with one face and four arms. It is said that when cultivating the generation stage, you should observe rainbows in the sky and develop certainty that appearances do exist as form but that tangible phenomena do not exist as form. {350}

Finally, there is the consciousness transference of buddha body in the manner of a mustard seed: you should visualize that the inch-sized being of pristine cognition in the heart cakra is transferred from the pathway of the central channel into the heart of the teacher, present in the sky in front, in the form of Amitābha surrounded by a host of divine princes and princesses, and is then invited onto a pathway of rainbow light, reaching Sukhāvatī.

(ii) The guidance of buddha speech concerns the recitation [of mantras]. You should confess the four [nonvirtuous actions of] lying, slander, verbal abuse, and nonsensical talk, and train so that your speech is never separated from the six-syllable mantra. With a mind that understands speech to be an empty echo from the beginning, you should chant the adamantine song of the six-syllable mantra. This recitation should resemble the sound of thirty-six beehives breaking open, and you should visualize plants, mountains, rocks, earth, stones, and all that appears and exists as the sound of the six-syllable mantra. You should recite OṂ MAṆI PADME HŪṂ without interruption, day and night.

[Finally,] there is the consciousness transference of buddha speech in the manner of a seed syllable: you should visualize that the syllable HRĪḤ, which is the support of awareness, the enlightened mind, in the navel cakra is instantly drawn from the pathway of the central channel through the anterior fontanel by the compassionate hook of the lord of enlightened heritage at the crown of your head, where it dissolves into the heart of the teacher, and that the teacher then ascends upward, reaching Sukhāvatī.

(iii) The guidance of buddha mind concerns luminosity. You should confess covetousness, vindictiveness, and wrong views, and develop certainty that mind is originally present as the buddha body of reality. You should adroitly determine the basis of the view that mind is spontaneous and leaves no trace. It is as if the sensations of dampness and warmth were to occur simultaneously in a tangible object, without one following the other. Consequently, you will not eat after satisfying your hunger. You will not drink after quenching your thirst. You will not put on clothes after feeling warm. And you will not search for something after finding it.

[Finally,] there is the consciousness transference of buddha mind into luminosity: this denotes the settling of the mind in the face-to-face encounter of the mother and child luminosities owing to the absence of both the object of consciousness transference and the agent of consciousness transference.

This is the brilliant gradual path of the ten virtuous actions—renouncing negativity,
Where the three transformations [of appearances, sounds, and thoughts] into buddha body, speech, and mind

Are to be cultivated with **total delight** {351}
And through which **liberation, supreme** buddhahood, is attained.

This was compiled from the instruction manual of Lharjé Gewabum.

107. Guidebook Entitled *The Liberation by Seeing according to Norbu Rinchen*[1061]

After you have taken refuge and set the mind on enlightenment, there then ensues the introduction to words [of symbolic expression] and their meaning.

First, the [words of] symbolic expression are as follows: (i) In the expanse of space, both the sun and moon arise as precious wish-fulfilling gems. (ii) The rainbow colors of the sky should be ensnared by the noose of wind. (iii) The gem of the ocean rides the supreme horse of crystal. (iv) Triumphing over sun and moon, the six classes of living beings incite the conflict[1062] of the five material elements and surpass Mount Meru. (v) The man of crystal imprisoned in the ravine of the three worlds instantly circumambulates the three worlds and goes to sleep in his own home.[1063]

The meaning of these expressions is respectively as follows:

(i) [Externally] in the expanse of space, when the gem of awareness arises as an [adamantine] chain [of light], it is perceived by both the sun and moon, which are the eyes. Internally, at the center of an aureole of light within the heart cakra, the light of the gem of awareness in the form of an adamantine chain then arises at both [optic] channels as the lamp of the empty vital essence, which is the pure essence of the eyes.[1064]

(ii) When the externally glowing chain [of light] arises in cloudless space and the internally glowing five lights of the expanse arise in the sky, you should focus awareness without distraction and interrupt the movement of wind, so that the vital essences neither quiver nor flicker.[1065]

(iii) The radiant awareness of the heart cakra then enters through a crystal tube.[1066]

(iv) It rises unimpededly above the two eyes, whereupon, owing to its nonrecognition, you would roam in cyclic existence. You should therefore not provoke the conflict of the six classes of living beings in the citadel of the five material elements.[1067]

(v) Then you will be instantly liberated through recognition of the mind, manifesting in the prison perceived as birth and death and you will go to sleep in that expanse, which is the disposition of the buddha body of reality. In brief, although your mind will roam through the three worlds, you will recognize the pure pristine cognition. {352} Fundamental ignorance will be eliminated, and you will maintain the originally secure fortress.[1068]

Although the essential nature of fundamental reality is not established in terms of cyclic existence and nirvana, the expressive power of awareness in its natural arising will arise as either cyclic existence or nirvana on the basis of whether awareness or fundamental ignorance is present. You should directly behold the awareness that is the natural expression of ultimate reality and that is unknown through words. Although there is neither increase nor decrease in the original seed of reality—the nucleus of the enlightened heritage that naturally abides—even so, because you have experientially cultivated it, the four visionary appearances will successively arise.[1069] Although there is nothing to be liberated in the fundamental nature of primordial purity, subtle energy and mind are purified in the expanse by means of these profound essentials. Although buddhahood is referenced through the vehicles in the course of time, liberation occurs instantaneously in the present. Although the aspects of meditative experience are immeasurable, their determination is made without wavering from the single essential nature.[1070]

This crucial text should be entrusted as a secret expression and concealed from those who are without good fortune.[1071]

Here I have presented in writing this quintessence
That gathers the most **delightful** of **all** [instructions]
Of the Great Seal and Great Perfection—
The enlightened intention of eight accomplished masters,
In Norbu [Rinchen's] **supreme liberation** by seeing.

This was compiled from the instruction manual of Drampa [Kunga Zangpo].

108. Guidebook Entitled *The Nature of Mind: The Wish-Fulfilling Gem*[1072]

After first taking refuge and setting the mind on enlightenment: You should develop fervent faith and devotion because this constitutes the aspiration for exclusive blessing. The esteemed expression "Great Seal" is said to denote the nature of your own mind. If it is not recognized, it becomes this [mundane] awareness harboring all sorts of fantasies. There is nothing at all to be cultivated. Let this awareness rest right where it is, naturally wide open. You should not hesitate, wondering whether this is or is not the Great Seal. From the start you should not indulge in hope for positive outcomes or doubt concerning negative outcomes. Do not pursue the myriad mists of thought. By training repeatedly in this manner, at one specific time you will recognize the nature of conceptual thoughts, and then you will clearly realize that these are without ground and devoid of basis. All attachments will be liberated right where they are. Instantly, the darkness of propensities will recede. {353} That is called buddhahood.

In this instantaneous natural dynamic of the mind, the key point is that appearances are themselves the mind. When you look directly at the essential nature of whatever arises, you are individually aware of all appearances externally, without exception, and of the mind, internally, without exception. Since their arising and liberation are simultaneous, you should focus one-pointedly on that which arises, and in that perspective, it will appear empty of the dualistic grasping and so forth, free from elaborate signs, without conceptual elaboration, empty without any experience at all, and empty without being precisely determined. And while things appear, they are empty, in a common savor in intrinsic awareness. As you abide therein without effort, abiding[1073] itself arises spontaneously. This is the yoga that is not to be cultivated.

Here I have set forth in writing the experience of unique liberation (*chig grol*),
The authentic secret that I received twice,
Which generates **supreme liberation** of the knots of the mind,
Through **delightful** enthusiasm for **all** classes of instruction.

This was compiled from an ancient text brought forth from Kala Dungtso.

Concluding Verses

So it is that I have here presented
Simply the gist of these one hundred and eight modes of guidance,
Complete in meaning and terse in expression,
In accordance with the writings that I myself obtained from wherever.

After the preliminaries of which all these partake,
Combining common and uncommon instructions,
The sequence of instruction in the main practices is individual and distinct,
Like the threads of a Chinese weaving.[1074]

Without entangling together the enlightened intentions
Of our predecessors, the supreme lineage holders,
My mind has emphasized the traditions from which they derive,
Without any stains of contrivance.
I have had the good fortune to hear such teachings,
Gathering all the profound essentials explained
By all the learned and accomplished masters of the past, none excepted—
The emanations of the buddhas, in India and here in Tibet.

It is wonderful and marvelous
That you may without hardship and at one time
Study the difficult points and doctrines that I acquired and searched
From each of these profound instructions.

Due to the prevalence of my former provisions [of merit],
I have passed this life in accordance with the lamp of the sacred doctrine,
Seeking, hearing, writing, and pondering;
And, finally, I have set these instructions forth in writing.

May this work nurture the propensities of the sacred doctrine
In my own future lives,
And if there are any interested in it at this time,
May it also be of benefit to them!

Colophon

These are the verses from the ocean of Drolchok consolidating the written memoranda of the *One Hundred and Eight Guidebooks*, which enable the essential points of the sacred doctrine to be realized easily and with little difficulty.

MAṄGALAṂ {355}

PART THREE
Supports

10. Marvelous Key to the Contents of the One Hundred and Eight Guidebooks

In this chapter, Kunga Drolchok explores the classifications of the one hundred and eight guidebooks, according to the primary distinction between sutras, tantras, and their integration. By his own calculation, there are altogether "twenty-five ordinary instructions, twenty-five instructions common to all traditions, twenty-five pertaining to the Sakya tradition, and thirty-three instructions pertaining to the Kagyu lineage."

Formal Title

Marvelous Key to the Contents of the One Hundred and Eight Guidebooks[1]
{356}

Introductory Verses

OṂ May this be auspicious!

The one hundred and eight rivers of these distinct guidebooks
That descend from the snow peaks of their respective lineages
Fill the vast Anavatapta Lake that is my own mind.
If one were to analyze their basis definitively, it is as follows:

Preamble

Here I will briefly comment on the listing of the one hundred and eight guidebooks, highlighting the definitive basis of their auspicious number.

This commences from the two great pathways of the Buddhist teaching, deriving from the two traditions of Sutra and Tantra, which are both the canonical teachings of the Conqueror. To explain, first there are the guidebooks that accord with the actual teaching of the precious sutras. Next there are guidebooks based on the integration of both the sutras and the tantras. Then there are the guidebooks derived from the short path of the Supreme Mantra.

The Sutra Section

The first of these, the sutra section, includes both the experiential cultivations of those guidebooks endowed with the greatness of the lineal descent of the transmitted teachings and the experiential cultivations of those that apply the words and meanings, mother and child, without error.

Among these, the former include *Parting from the Four Attachments* (1), which was actually spoken by Mañjughoṣa; *The Seven-Point Mind Training of the Great Vehicle* (2), which directly reveals the two modes of enlightened mind; *The Mind Training according to Sumpa Lotsāwa* (5), which was bestowed by both Vajravārāhī and Tārā; the guidance of *The Five Doctrines of Maitreya* (23), which were taught by Maitreya; {357} the guidance of the consequentialist *View of Intrinsic Emptiness* (24), which is the oral transmission of glorious Candrakīrti; and the guidance of *The View of Extraneous Emptiness* (25), which is the enlightened intent of Maitrīpā.

Next, with regard to the experiential cultivations of those that apply the words and meanings, mother and child, without error, this includes *The Three Sorts of Person* (9); *The Sequence of the Teaching* (10); *The Sameness of Existence and Quiescence* (11); *The Great Middle Way* (12); *The Hidden Guidance of Kadam* (13); the integrated *Parables of Potowa* (18); *The Six Descents of the Transcendent Perfection of Wisdom* (20); *The Five Paths of Pacification* (21), which is the elixir of the mind of Dampa; and *The Three Stages of Meditation—Beginning, Middle and Conclusive* (22).

The Integration of Both the Sutras and the Tantras

Secondly, there are the guidebooks based on the integration of both the sutras and the tantras. These include *The Heart of Dependent Origination* (3), *The Carrying of Happiness and Suffering on the Path* (4), *Severance* (6) of demonic forces, *The Three Essential Points* (7), *Resting in the Nature of Mind*

(8), the guidance of Kadam on Munīndra (14) that holds the mind in calm abiding, the guidance of Kadam on Avalokita (16) that is all-pervasive with compassion, the guidance of Kadam on Acala (15) that focuses on the fire [of pristine cognition], the guidance of Kadam on Tārā (17) that foreordains extrasensory powers, and *The Sixteen Spheres of the Heart* (19).

The Short Path of the Supreme Mantra

Thirdly, the guidebooks deriving from the short path of the Supreme Mantra comprise (i) those that are generic, revealing the tradition expounded by all the learned and accomplished masters of India and Tibet, and (ii) those that are specific, separately explaining the respective individual traditions of the Sakya and Kagyu lineages.

Generic Guidebooks

The former guidebooks are threefold: {358} (i) those arranged on the basis of the practical application of learned translators and paṇḍitas, (ii) those with lineages derived from the oral instructions of meditative experience vomited forth by accomplished masters, and (iii) those encompassing all the profound essential points of all the learned and accomplished masters.

The first of these has four aspects: (i) The father tantras include *The Five Stages of the Secret Assembly* (62) of Nāgārjuna, *The Vital Essence of Liberation* (63) of Buddhajñānapāda, *The Unelaborate Practice of Red Yamāri* (64), *The Four-Stage Yoga* (65), and *The Mental Focus on the Horns of Bhairava* (66). (ii) The mother tantras include *White Cakrasaṃvara* (71) according to the great paṇḍita Śākyaśrī of Kashmir, the subtle vital essence of *Kharamukha Cakrasaṃvara* (74) according to the Newar Mahābodhi, *The Six Meditations of Vajravārāhī* (75) according to Chelpa Kunga Dorjé, and *Vārāhī in the Form Kurmapādā* (38) according to Chak Lotsāwa. (iii) The yogatantras include the guidance of *Vajrapāṇi in the Form Mahācakra* (36) according to Marton Chokyi Gyeltsen and the guidance on *Vajrapāṇi in the Form Caṇḍa* (37). (iv) The nondual tantras include *The Aural Lineage of Kālacakra* (41) with *The Six-Branch Yoga* (40), *The Gradual Path of Secret Mantra according to Master Padmasambhava* (105), *The Collected Injunctions of the King* (106), and *Norbu Rinchen's Liberation by Seeing* (107).

Second, the guidebooks with lineages derived from the oral instructions of meditative experience vomited forth by accomplished masters include the guidance on *White Amitāyus* (29) according to Mitrayogin; *The Direct Guidance of Avalokiteśvara according to the Lakṣmī Tradition* (30); *The Direct Guidance of Avalokiteśvara according to the Candradhvaja Tradition* (31); *The Direct Guidance of Avalokiteśvara according to the Tsembupa Tradition* (32); *The Direct Guidance of Avalokiteśvara according to the Kyergangpa Tradition* (33); each of the two modes of direct guidance elaborated from the texts of Ānandavajra—namely, *The Direct Guidance of Cakrasaṃvara* (34) and *The Direct Guidance of Hevajra* (35); the guidance on *The Trilogy of Spiritual Songs* (103); and *The Six Doctrines of the Accomplished Masters* (104).

Third, the guidebooks encompassing all the instructions of the profound essential points of all the learned and accomplished masters include the clarification of all *The Concealed Meanings of Yogatantra* (26), which is divided into two hundred and thirty modes of guidance.

Lineage-Specific Guidebooks

The latter, those that separately explain the respective individual traditions, include guidebooks representing the Sakya and Kagyu lineages.

Sakya Guidebooks

Among them, first the cycle of the glorious Sakyapa comprises the cycle of the Path and Its Fruition, along with its ancillaries—namely, (i) those instructions associated with Hevajra, (ii) those extracted from the profound essentials of Cakrasaṃvara, and (iii) the concluding support of the protectors of the transmitted teachings. Therefore, this Sakya cycle includes the following guidebooks: the general text of *The Path and Its Fruition* (43), which comprises sixty works, along with its eight subsidiary cycles of the path (44–51); the spiritual connections [of Drokmi], with the six gatekeepers [of Nālandā] (52–57); *The Three Purities* (58); *The Twenty-Nine Essential Visualizations of Self-Consecration* (59); *The Exegesis of the Concealed Path* (60); *The Elucidation of the Symbolic Meaning* (61); the secret guidance of *Kurukullā* (39); {359} the gateways of the central channel dependent on the two deities Cakrasaṃvara and Vajravārāhī (67–68); *The Five Stages according to Ghaṇṭāpāda* (69); *The Four Stages according to Kṛṣṇacārin* (70); and *The Inner Guidance of Glorious Pañjaranātha* (102).

Kagyu Guidebooks

Next, the cycle of the precious Kagyu lineage has three aspects: (i) those derived from the great paṇḍita Nāropā, the elder brother; (ii) those derived from the sister Nigumā; and (iii) those derived from other accomplished masters.

The first, those derived from Nāropā, include *The Mingling and Transformation of the Three Poisons* (89), *The Four Adamantine Seats* (72), and *The Great Magical Emanation* (73), all of which descended from Ngokpa Choku Dorjé in accordance with the teaching of Venerable Marpa; *The Four Scrolls of the Aural Instructions* (90), which descended from Tsurton Wang-ngé of Dol; *The [Six Doctrines of Liberation through the Upper Gate, according to the] Aural Lineage of Cakrasaṃvara* (91), which descended from Milarepa; *The Six Doctrines according to the Sekharma Tradition* (88), which descended from Marpa's son Darma Dodé; the five supplementary instructions from *The Nine Doctrinal Cycles of Nirdehaḍākinī* (92), *The Guidance on Amitāyus* (27), and the guidance of the *Fierce Inner Heat* (47), all of which descended from Rechungpa; *The Introduction to the Three Buddha Bodies* (86), *The Indivisibility of Subtle Energy and Mind* (87), and *The Guidance on White Tārā* (28), all of which descended from the two streams of the Black Hat and Red Hat branches of the Karma Kamtsang school, originating from Karmapa Dusum Khyenpa Usé, who nurtured the enlightened intention and objectives of Venerable Dakpo Gampopa; *The Cycle of Pagmodrupa Densatel* (95); *The Unique Enlightened Intention* (96), and *The Fivefold Great Seal* (84), along with the *Revered Wheel of Vitality*, according to the Drigungpa; the cycle of *The Six Doctrines according to Taklungpa* (97); *The [Six Primary Essentials for] Mountain Retreat* (100) according to the Upper Drukpa; *The Ritual Service and Attainment of the Three Adamantine Realities according to Orgyanpa* (42); *The Means for Attainment of the Guru, Auspicious Circumstances, and Common Savor* (98) according to the Middle Drukpa; *The Fivefold Capacity of Lorepa* (99) according to the Lower Drukpa; and *The Elaborate Guidance of Lama Zhang Tselpa Yudrakpa* (93). In addition, all of the doctrinal cycles of Dakpo Gampopa each include the Six Doctrines and the Great Seal, so here I also recognize the *Molten Gold of the Six Doctrines of Nāropā* (76) and *The Coemergent Union of the Great Seal* (83), the last of which was written according to the teaching of Gyelsé Chodzongpa.

The second, those guidebooks derived from the lady Nigumā, include *The Six Doctrines of Nigumā* (77), *The Amulet Tradition of the Great Seal* (78),

The Three Aspects Carried on the Path (79), and *The Deathlessness of One's Own Mind* (80), all of which constitute four [of the Six] Golden Doctrines and their branches.

The third, those derived from other accomplished masters, include *The Six Doctrines of Sukhasiddhi* (81); *The Emanational Navel Cakra* [also known as *The Inner Guidance of Nairātmyā*] (82); the seven-day fierce inner heat [from *The Six-Branch Yoga according to Pelchen Ga Lotsāwa*] (94) and *Four-Armed Mahākāla in the Form Kurakma* (101)—the last two of which descended through the lineage from Ga Lotsāwa; {360} *The Four Syllables of the Great Seal* (85), which is extant through the lineage of Kyergompa; and *The Nature of Mind: The Wish-Fulfilling Gem* (108), which was retrieved as treasure by Dungtso Repa.

In brief, there are twenty-five ordinary instructions, twenty-five instructions common to all, twenty-five pertaining to the Sakya tradition, and thirty-three instructions pertaining to the Kagyu lineage. Altogether, this completes the enumeration of one hundred and eight.

Concluding Verses

Having in that manner devoutly touched with the crown of my head
The dust from the feet of holy beings, resembling a bank of lotus flowers,
I took from afar, as an anthill takes honey,
A fraction of their distinct doctrinal traditions.

Owing to my experience of the sacred doctrine accrued in the past,
I pondered the best of acquisitions in this life,
And so with resources, great effort, and perseverance,
I many times repeatedly sought all these profound instructions, without exception.

Unsatisfied even with all the peerless ones
Imbued with the glory of learning and accomplishment,
I was utterly exhausted searching for authentic lineage holders,
Possessing the eye of the sacred doctrine, from wherever they came.

I scorned the rest that my tired body and mind required,
And my mind indeed rejected the talk of fame elsewhere.
Without conceit, renouncing grandeur, and holding down my proud head,

For the sake of the sacred doctrine I have borne hardships.
Thus, in order to arrange each of these profound instructions,
I have again and again roamed throughout the land,
And on meeting travelers I have been bold, without trepidation,
To ask them correctly what sacred doctrine they possess.

Having stayed in colleges from the age of seven
Until the age of thirty-seven, my mind has been enriched
By these one hundred and eight guidebooks.
Rejoicing in this supreme era of ours,
My mind is happy and contented, in a disposition free from arrogance.

By virtue of the merit in this work,
Here and in other lives, may I act for the sake of others,
Abandoning disillusionment,
And may I certainly accomplish my aspiration, like the wish-fulfilling gem,
To guide beings on the path of liberation, endowed with the highest of realms. {361}

Colophon

This *Marvelous Key to the Contents of the One Hundred and Eight Guidebooks* was brought forth from the ocean of intelligence of Kunga Drolchok at the mountain hermitage of Cholung Jangtsé.[2] The role of the scribe was undertaken by one Kunga Lekgyal.

MAṄGALAṂ {363}

11. A List of the One Hundred and Eight Guidebooks with Their Protectors and Empowerments

In the penultimate chapter, Kunga Drolchok begins by enumerating the one hundred and eight guidebooks in verse, intimating how he personally assimilated their meaning in his practice. In the second part, he names the one hundred and eight protector deities for which he received empowerment, headed by the diverse aspects of Mahākāla, and at the end of that section he subsumes them all in twenty-seven classes. In the third and final part, he lists more than one hundred empowerments that he received often multiple times according to the diverse classes of tantra, individually naming the teachers who conferred them.

Formal Title

A Specific Listing of the One Hundred and Eight Guidebooks Along with the Listing of the Names of Their One Hundred and Eight Protectors and the Listing of the Names of Their One Hundred and Eight Empowerments[1] {364}

Listing of the One Hundred and Eight Guidebooks

As for the sacred doctrines that I heard from the words of my teachers
Through many efforts in this lifetime,
In the manner in which an anthill extracts honey [from hives],
The list of the titles of the one hundred and eight guidebooks is as follows.

On the basis of *Parting from the Four Attachments*,
I was pierced by the weapons of *The Seven-Point Mind Training* (1–2).

I trained my mind in equanimity through *The Heart of Dependent Origination* (3), *The Carrying of Happiness and Suffering on the Path* (4), and *The Mind Training of Sumpa Lotsāwa* (5),
And I cut off attachments with *The Severance of Machik* (6).

I relied on *The Three Essential Points* (7) and *Resting in the Nature of Mind* (8).
I was separately taught *The Three Sorts of Person* (9) and *The Sequence of the Buddhist Teaching* (10).
I applied *The Sameness of Existence and Quiescence* (11), the disposition of *The Great Middle Way* (12), *The Hidden Guidance of Kadam* (13), the nailing of the *Four Deities of Kadam* (14–17) and *The Parables of Potowa* (18).
Then were explained *The Sixteen Spheres of the Heart* (19).

I yoked the oxen of *The Six Descents of the Transcendent Perfection of Wisdom* and *The Five Paths of Pacification* (20–21).
I opened the doorbolt of *The Three Stages of Meditation* (22) with the key of *The Five Doctrines of Maitreya* (23).
I integrated the guidance of *The View of Intrinsic Emptiness* (24) and *The View of Extraneous Emptiness* (25).

The guidance of *The Concealed Meanings of Yogatantra* (26) illuminated all darkness.
The streams of *The Guidance of Amitāyus* (27), the long-life treasure of the mother *White Tārā* (28), the rite of attainment of *White Amitāyus* (29) that had been acquired by Maitrīpā, and the four sorts of *The Direct Guidance of Avalokiteśvara* (30–33) fell to me separately.
I obtained *The Direct Guidance of Cakrasaṃvara* and *Hevajra* (34–35)
According to the texts of Ānandavajra, {365}
Vajrapāṇi in the Form Mahācakra (36) who has an aureole of fiery light,
And *Vajrapāṇi in the Form Caṇḍa* (37) who bellows the sound of HŪṂ.
Through *Vārāhī in the Form Kurmapādā* (38) I perceived the magical display,
And *Kurukullā* (39) shook phenomenal existence.
Through *The Six-Branch Yoga of Kālacakra* (40) experiences of radiant perception and beauty naturally arose.

I leisurely pursued *The Aural Lineage of Kālacakra* (41),
And *The Ritual Service and Attainment of the Three Adamantine Realities according to Orgyanpa* (42) guided me on the path.

I examined the secret guidance of *The Path and Its Fruition* (43),
Along with its subsidiary instructions:
The Inconceivables (44), *The Nine Profound Methods* (45),
The Attainment of Coemergence (46), *The Perfection of the Path of Fierce Inner Heat* (47), *The Straightening of Crooked Posture* (48), *The Path of the Female Mudra* (49),
The Great Seal Devoid of Letters (50), *The Determination of the Mind* (51),[2]
And *The Mingling of Sutra and Tantra* (52),
As well as *The Dispelling of Three Kinds of Obstacles* (53–55),
Dispelling the Three Sorts of Suffering (56),
And *The Clear Recollection of the Innate State* (57).

On the basis of *The Three Purities* (58),
I applied *The Twenty-Nine Essential Visualizations of Self-Consecration* (59),
And through *The Exegesis of the Concealed Path* (60),
I practiced *The Elucidation of the Symbolic Meaning* (61).

I scaled the ladder of *The Five Stages of the Secret Assembly* (62),
Along with *The Vital Essence of Liberation* (63) and so forth.
From the expanse of *The Unelaborate Practice of Red Yamāri* (64),
The Four-Stage Yoga (65) then arose.

I applied *The Mental Focus on the Horns of Bhairava* (66)
And directed [the vital essence] upward in accordance with its nocturnal motion.
Based on the device of *The Central Channel Dependent on the Male Deity Cakrasaṃvara* (67),
I also brought forth *The Central Channel Dependent on the Female Deity Vajravārāhī* (68).
Through the path of *The Five Stages* [*according to Ghaṇṭāpāda*] (69) and *The Four Stages* [*according to Kṛṣṇacārin*](70) I aroused the sky-farers.

White Cakrasaṃvara (71) was the deity through whom I attained enlightenment.
I also mastered *The Four Adamantine Seats* (72)
Which concern the spleen, [kidney] cavities, [and so forth];
The Great Magical Emanation (73), which concerns [lower] forms and [conclusive] attributes; {366}
The Kharamukha Cakrasaṃvara (74), which concerns the subtle vital essence;
And *The Six Meditations of Vajravārāhī* (75), which are wondrous.

I sought refinement through the primer of *The Six Doctrines of Nāropā* (76).
The Six Doctrines of Nigumā (77) were the essential elixir of my experiential cultivation.
From within *The Amulet Tradition of the Great Seal* (78)
I extracted *The Three Aspects Carried on the Path* (79) and [*The*] *Deathlessness* [*of One's Own Mind*] (80).
I secured *The Six Doctrines of Sukhasiddhi* (81) with the nail of the *Emanational Navel Cakra* (82).[3]
I was revitalized by *The Coemergent Union of the Great Seal* (83),
The Fivefold Great Seal (84), *The Four Syllables of the Great Seal* (85),
The Introduction to the Three Buddha Bodies (86),
The Indivisibility of Subtle Energy and Mind (87),
The Six Doctrines according to the Sekharma Tradition of Marpa (88),
And *The Mingling and Transformation of the Three Poisons*, according to Ngok (89).

I secured the mighty pillar of *The Four Scrolls of the Aural Instructions* (90)
And wrote down the oral instructions of Milarepa
That Rechungpa received through an *Aural Lineage* (91–92),
Along with *The Elaborate Guidance of Zhang Tselpa* (93),
And *The Six-Branch Yoga* that was the secret counsel of Ga Lotsāwa (94).

I separately acquired the enlightened intention of *The Cycle of Pagmodrupa Densatel* (95),
Along with the instructions of Drigung and Taklung (96–97).
I gathered *The Means for Attainment of the Guru, Auspicious Circumstances, and Common Savor* (98), which is associated with the Middle Drukpa.

I grasped the distinctive doctrines of *The Fivefold Capacity of Lorepa* (99).
The Mountain Retreat of Yangonpa (100) resembled a three-eyed gem.

From within my waistbelt the vital heart essence of *Four-Armed Mahākāla* emerged in the form Kurakma (101).
I also acquired *Pañjaranātha* (102) according to the arrangement of Drachok Yarlungpa [Sengé Gyeltsen].

From the chest of *The Trilogy of Spiritual Songs* (103)
I extracted *The Six Doctrines of the Accomplished Masters* (104).
[My mind] was opened by the secret *Gradual Path of Padmasambhava* (105) and *The Collected Injunctions of the King* (106).
I entered upon *Norbu Rinchen's Liberation by Seeing* (107)
Through the [four] precious mothers and [seventeen] offspring (*ma nor bu smad*),[4]
And I reached the isle of guidance on *The Nature of Mind: The Wish-Fulfilling Gem* (108).

This complete listing of the One Hundred and Eight Guidebooks
Was brought forth from the lake that is the mind of Drolchok.

MAṄGALAṂ.

Listing of the One Hundred and Eight Protectors

As for the sacred doctrines that I heard from the words of my teachers
Through many efforts in this lifetime,
In the manner in which an anthill extracts honey [from hives],
The list of the names of the one hundred and eight protectors including Mahākāla is as follows:

Pañjaranātha according to the tradition of Bari Lotsāwa, and according to the tradition of Gayādhara. Pañjaranātha in the form Brother and Sister according to the tradition of Śākyaśrī.[5] Pañjaranātha with an assemblage of eight deities,[6] with an assemblage of five deities, with an assemblage of twelve deities,[7] and with an assemblage of seventeen deities. Pañjaranātha in union with a female consort;[8] in the outer, inner, and secret aspects of kīla; with a military banner; with faces focusing on the rites of service, attainment, practical application, and brahmanical [rituals concerning pollution]; in a form with [four] replicated faces,[9] in blue, yellow, red, green and white aspects;[10] {367} and with a retinue comprising the six black brahmin butcher spirits.

Four-armed Mahākāla in the form of a solitary hero.[11] Four-armed Mahākāla with two retainers,[12] with an assemblage of five deities,[13] with an assemblage of nine deities,[14] and with an assemblage of twelve deities. Four-armed Mahākāla in white and red aspects, in the form that has perfected the eleven aspects of the vase empowerment and the four empowerments, in the red silken form, in the lion-faced form,[15] and in the blazing lion-faced form.

Six-armed Mahākāla, dispeller of all obstacles.[16] Six-armed Mahākāla inseparable from the Teacher,[17] and in the form that [overpowers ḍākinīs and] evokes the essential point. Six-armed Mahākāla in the liver-colored form and in the pollution-dispelling form. Six-armed Mahākāla as [the Lord of Life in] blue, yellow, red, and green aspects.[18] Six-armed Mahākāla with ornaments, elaborate and unelaborate.

Mahākāla in the form with one thousand arms and one thousand eyes, and with Śrīdevī and her four retainers.[19]

Vaiśravaṇa in white, yellow, red, green, and black forms.[20] Vaiśravaṇa as the supreme dancer.[21] Vaiśravaṇa with a red spear.[22] Vaiśravaṇa in the form of secret attainment.[23] Vajramāradama in outer, inner, and secret forms,[24] and as the two yakṣas of the Maitrīpā tradition. Gaṇapati—white and red.[25] Jambhala—white and red,[26] along with the sixty protectors,[27] and the eighty white-robed guardians,[28] as well as the twelve liberators,[29] the twelve subterranean spirits,[30] the twelve protectresses of Vajrakīla,[31] and the white-clad demon.[32]

Mahākāla in the form of Lekden and his two brothers.[33] Knife-wielding Mahākāla with an assemblage of five deities.[34] Mahākāla with four conjoined aspects,[35] red-faced Mahākāla,[36] black-cloaked Mahākāla.[37] Mahākāla in the form Maning.[38] Mahākāla in the form Aghora.[39] Mahākāla in his tiger-riding form.[40] Trakṣad Mahākāla,[41] Trakṣad Mahākāla with the face of a dog,[42] and Trakṣad Mahākāla with the face of a wild yak.[43] Rock-faced Yakṣa, the Rāhu-faced five *gying* spirits,[44] the auspicious *tsen* spirits, the acolytes of Yama,[45] the Lord of the Charnel Ground,[46] and the Lord-Protector of the Aural Lineage.[47]

The Self-Arisen Queen,[48] Dhūmāṅgārīśrīdevī,[49] Rematī,[50] Caṇḍikā,[51] Śrīdevī,[52] the glorious mother [Ekajaṭī?] (*dPal ldan ma*), Tseringma,[53] [White] Gyeltang,[54] Varuṇa,[55] Yajña, the Lord of Mantra,[56] [Yakṣa] Aparājita,[57] Harisiddhi,[58] dark-yellow Jambhala,[59] Mahākāla holding a red club,[60] and the sky-clad Goddess.[61]

When these are all subsumed according to their classes, they comprise Pañjaranātha, Vaiśravaṇa, four-armed Mahākāla, six-armed Mahākāla, Lekden, Maning, Aghora, tiger-riding Mahākāla, Trakṣad Mahākāla, Vajramāradama, Gaṇapati, Red Jambhala, the sixty protectors, {368} the white-clad demon, the protectors of Vajrakīla, the Lord of the Charnel Ground, the black-cloaked Mahākāla, the red-faced Mahākāla, the acolytes of Yama, the rock-faced Yakṣa, the Rāhu-faced gying spirits, Dhūmāṅgārīśrīdevī, Rematī, Kṣetrapāla,[62] Śrīdevī, Tseringma, and White Gyeltang.

These are the protectors of Dolchok.

MAṄGALAṂ.

Listing of the One Hundred and Eight Empowerments

As for the sacred doctrines that I heard from the words of my teachers
Through many efforts in this lifetime,
In the manner in which an anthill extracts honey [from hives],
The definitive listing of the one hundred and eight empowerments is as follows.

Initially I requested twenty-one times the empowerment and mantra recitations of Hevajra, the highest of all the profound nondual tantras, according to the tradition of the pith instructions, based on the maṇḍalas of colored sand and cotton drawings (1). That is to say, I requested it seven times from Venerable Kunga Chogdrub, seven times from Lowo Khenchen Rinpoché, once from Venerable Sangyé Rinchen, three times from Lhachok Sengé, once from Doring Kunpangpa, and once from Pakchen Pelden Tashi. In addition, I requested Hevajra according to the tradition of Ḍombipā, and obtained it from Lowo Khenchen (2). I requested Hevajra according to the tradition of Saroruha from Lowo Khenchen (3). I requested Hevajra according to the tradition of Kṛṣṇacārin, including the four maṇḍalas that are distinguished in Hevajra—namely those of buddha body (4), buddha speech (5), buddha mind (6), and the nucleus (7). I received these from Lowo Khenchen Rinpoché.

I requested fourteen times[63] the empowerment and mantra recitations of the fifteen-deity assemblage of Vajranairātmyā, based on the maṇḍalas of colored sand and cotton drawings (8). That is to say, I received it once from Venerable Kunga Chogdrub, seven times from Lowo Khenchen Rinpoché, once from Venerable Sangyé Rinchen, three times from Lhachok Sengé, once from Doring Kunpangpa, and once from Phakchen Pelden Tashi.

I requested the empowerment of Hevajra with Rudra as his seat (9) from Lowo Khenchen Rinpoché, and from Kyagom Lekpa Gyeltsen. I requested the empowerment of the seventeen-deity assemblage [of Hevajra], and Nairātmyā with an assemblage of twenty-three female deities (10), from Rabsel Dawa Gonpo.

I requested the empowerment of Hevajra with an assemblage of thirteen weapon-wielding deities (11), and the empowerments of both the *Adamantine Tent* (12) {369} and the *Vital Essence of Union* (13) from Lowo Khenchen. I requested the empowerment of Hevajra according to the tradition of Ngok (14), and the empowerment of Nairātmyā with an assemblage of fifteen female deities according to the tradition of Ngok (15) from Lodro Pelzang, who is a familial descendant of Ngok. I requested the empowerment of the *Adamantine Tent* according to the tradition of Ngok (16), and the empowerment of Vajratārā (17) that is enunciated in the context of the *Adamantine Tent* from Rabsel Dawa Gonpo. I requested the empowerment of the five-deity assemblage of Kurukullā (18) and received it from Lowo Khenchen Rinpoché. So it was that I obtained eighteen empowerments pertaining to the cycle of Hevajra.

From the cycle of the Wheel of Time, the extensive nondual tantra, I requested the complete empowerment and mantra recitations of Kālacakra, including the seven neophyte empowerments [of water, crown, silk pendant hat, vajra with bell, ascetic discipline, name, and promissory initiation] in the maṇḍala of the glorious constellations, along with the four supreme empowerments and [empowerment of] the Great Identity; and I obtained them three times based on the maṇḍalas of colored sand and cotton drawings (19). That is to say, I received the tradition of Buton from Lochen, the tradition of the Jonangpa from Paṇchen Sherab Tashi, and the tradition of Pelden Lama from Mupa Konchok Drak, according to the actual individual maṇḍalas. The one that I received from Paṇchen Sherab Tashi was based on a cotton drawing, in contrast to the other two that were based on colored sand.

As for the six cakravartin tantras enunciated in the context of the Wheel of Time:[64] I requested the empowerments of the Secret Assembly with an assemblage of nine deities (20), with an assemblage of thirteen deities (21), with an assemblage of nineteen deities (22), with an assemblage of twenty-five deities (23), with an assemblage of thirty-two deities (24), and with an assemblage of thirty-four (25). Also, in terms of the mother tantras, I requested [the empowerment of] *Great Cakrasaṃvara* (26) on the basis of a visualization maṇḍala made by the Omniscient Dong (Lochen Rinchen Zangpo), and received it from Lowo Khenchen on the basis of the writings of paṇḍita Drakpa Gyeltsen; and I also requested it from Paṇchen Sherab Tashi based on the writings of Dakchen Namgyel Drakpa. I requested the empowerments of *Short Cakrasaṃvara* (27) and of *Vajravārāhī* with an assemblage of thirteen deities (28) according to the tradition of the Kulikā Viṣṇugupta and received these from Zelmo Drakpa Drakpa Yeshé. I requested the *Net of Magical Emanation* with an assemblage of forty-three deities (29), with an assemblage of forty-five deities (30), and with an assemblage of forty-nine deities (31). So it was that I obtained altogether thirteen empowerments pertaining to [the assimilated cycle of] the Wheel of Time.

As for the father tantras, within the cycle of the Secret Assembly, I requested two times the empowerment and mantra recitations of Akṣobhya with an assemblage of thirty-two deities according to tradition of Sublime Nāgārjuna (32), {370} and I received it from Rabsel Dawa Gonpo and from Khenchen Tashi Namgyel, the former on the basis of the visualization maṇḍala made by Dorjé Chang Kunga Zangpo, and the latter on the basis of the visualization maṇḍala made by Buton. I also requested two times the empowerment and mantra recitations of the *Secret Assembly* according to the tradition of Buddhajñānapāda (33). I obtained this from Rabsel Dawa Gonpo based upon the memorandum of Zarjang Pukpa, and from Khenchen Tashi Namgyel based on the writings of Buton.

I requested once the empowerment of Lokeśvara (34) and received it from Lochen, who had composed a liturgy based on the visualization maṇḍala made by Hor Kabzhipa Sengé Gyeltsen.

I requested the empowerment of the transcendent lord Vajrabhairava with an assemblage of forty-nine deities according to the tradition of Zhang Tselpa (35) and received it from Lowo Khenchen. I requested the empowerment of Vajrabhairava with an assemblage of seventeen deities according to the tradition of Kyo (36) and received it from Lowo Khenchen Rinchen. I requested the empowerment of Vajrabhairava with a retinue of eight zombies in the tradition of Sakya (37) and received it from Paṇchen Pelden Tsultrim. I requested the empowerment of Vajrabhairava with an assemblage of thirteen deities according to the tradition of Ra Lotsāwa (38) and received it from Lowo Khenchen Rinchen. I requested the empowerment of Vajrabhairava with a retinue of eight zombies according to the tradition of Ra Lotsāwa (39) and received it from Paṇchen Pelden Tsultrim. I requested the empowerment of Vajrabhairava with an assemblage of thirteen deities according to the tradition of Shangpa (40) and received it from Kyagom Lekpa Gyeltsen. I requested the empowerment of Vajrabhairava with an assemblage of nine deities according to the tradition of Nyo (41) and received it from Tenpei Gyeltsen, a familial descendent of Gori.[65]

I requested the empowerment of Black Yamāri with an assemblage of thirteen deities according to the tradition of Ra Lotsāwa (42) and received it from Lowo Khenchen Rinpoché. I requested the empowerment of Ṣaḍānana with an assemblage of twenty-one deities (43), also from Lowo Khenchen Rinpoché. I requested four times the empowerment of Red Yamāri with an assemblage of five deities (44) and received it based on a maṇḍala of colored sand from Venerable Kunga Chogdrub according to the lineage derived from Lowo Lotsāwa, and also according to the Chak tradition from Lowo Khenchen Rinpoché and Ngorchen Lhachok Sengé, and according to the Chel tradition from Khenchen Tashi Namgyel. I requested the empowerment of Red Yamāri with an assemblage of thirteen deities (45) and received it from Lowo Khenchen Rinpoché. So it was that I obtained fourteen empowerments pertaining to the father tantras.

As for the cycle of the mother tantra Cakrasaṃvara: {371} I requested three times the empowerment of Cakrasaṃvara according to Kṛṣṇacārin, based on the maṇḍala of colored sand and cotton drawing (46), and I received it based on the maṇḍala of colored sand from Lowo Khenchen Rinpoché, and based on the cotton drawing from Paṇchen Pelden Tsultrim and Khenchen Tashi Namgyel. I requested the empowerment of Cakrasaṃvara according to Luipā (47) and received it from Venerable Sangyé Rinchen. I requested three times [the empowerment of] the body maṇḍala [of Cakrasaṃvara] according to Ghaṇṭāpāda (48) and received it once each from Lowo Khenchen, Pelden Tsultrim, and Rabsel Dawa Gonpo. I requested the empowerment of Cakrasaṃvara with an assemblage of five deities according to Ghaṇṭāpāda (49) and received it from Lowo Rinpoché. I requested the empowerment of Cakrasaṃvara with an assemblage of thirteen deities according to Lawapa (50) and received it also from Lowo Khenchen Rinpoché. I requested the empowerment of Cakrasaṃvara with an assemblage of thirteen deities according to Maitrīpā (51), and the empowerment of his female consort Vajravārāhī with an assemblage of thirteen deities (52), both of which I received from Taklung Tulku Rinpoché.

I requested the empowerment of the *Adamantine Sky-Farers* (53) and received it from Lowo Khenchen Rinpoché. I requested the empowerment of the *Ocean of Sky-Farers* (54) and received it from Gyalton Wangchuk Wangyal. I requested the empowerment of *Buddhakapāla* with an assemblage of twenty-five deities (55) and received it from Lowo Khenchen Rinpoché. I requested the empowerment of *Buddhakapāla* with an assemblage of twenty-nine deities (56) and received it from Rabsel Dawa Gonpo. I requested two times the empowerment of the *Great Magical Emanation* (57) and received it from Lowo Rinpoché and Ngokpa. I requested the empowerments of *The Four Adamantine Seats*—the male Yogāmbara (58) and the female Jñānaḍākinī with an assemblage of thirteen deities (59)—and received them both from Lodro Pelzang, a familial descendent of Ngokpa. I requested the empowerments of the *Aural Lineage of Cakrasaṃvara*—the male with an assemblage of sixty-two deities (60) and the female with an assemblage of fifteen deities (61)—and received them both as an empowerment rite and a recited transmission from Lochen. I requested the empowerments of Cakrasaṃvara who abandons bewilderment—the male with an assemblage of sixty-two deities (62) and the female Vajravārāhī with an assemblage of thirty-seven deities (63)—and received them both from Rabsel Dawa Gonpo. I requested the empowerments of *Śrīherukābhyudaya*—the male form (64) and his female consort (65)—and I received them both from Zelmo Drakpa Drakpa Yeshé. I requested the empowerments of yellow Cakrasaṃvara—the male with an assemblage of sixty-two deities (66) and the female yellow Vajravārāhī with an assemblage of thirty-seven deities (67)—and received them both also from Rabsel Dawa Gonpo. I requested the empowerment of Cakrasaṃvara in the form Saṃvarodaya with an assemblage of thirteen deities (68) and received it from the great scholar Sangyé Ozer. I requested the empowerment of Kharamukha Cakrasaṃvara (69) and received it from Lowo Khen Rinchen. I requested the empowerment of Cakrasaṃvara according to the Six Cakravartins (70) and received it from Rabsel Dawa Gonpo. {372} I requested the empowerment of Cakrasaṃvara in the form Mañjuvajra with an assemblage of thirty-seven deities (71) and received it from Khepa Sangyé Ozer. I requested the empowerment of *Cakrasaṃvara Equal to Space* with an assemblage of five deities embodying the five enlightened families (72) and received it from Kyagom Lekpa

Gyeltsen. So it was that I obtained twenty-seven empowerments pertaining to the mother tantras.

I requested the empowerment of unsurpassed Acala with an assemblage of nine deities (73) and received it from Kyagom Lekpa Gyeltsen. I requested the empowerment of unsurpassed Tārā with an assemblage of seventeen deities (74) and received it from Ngorchen Lhachokpa. I requested the empowerment of the body maṇḍala of Tārā (75) and received it from Khepa Sang-o. I requested the empowerment of Vajrapāṇi in the form Mahācakra with an assemblage of eighteen deities (76) and received it from Lowo Khen Rinpoché. I requested the empowerment of Vajrapāṇi in the form Caṇḍa, with an assemblage of twenty-one deities (77) and received it from Rabsel Dawa Gonpo. I requested the empowerments of *Vajrakīla* (78) and *Nine-Lamp Śrīheruka* (79) and received them from Gyalton Jangchub Wangyal. I requested the empowerment of Avalokita Subduer of Beings (80) and received it from Yigdrukpa Sherab Peljor. I requested the empowerment of Amitāyus in the form Queen of Accomplishment with a divine multitude forming an assemblage of thirty-four deities (81) and received it from the venerable geshé Tashi Pelzangpo of Gyalkhar Chodzong. I requested the empowerment of Amitāyus in the form Queen of Accomplishment with an assemblage of thirteen deities (82) and received it from Rinchen Tashi, the monastic preceptor of Gendun Gangpa. I requested the empowerment of Amitāyus in the form Queen of Accomplishment with an assemblage of five deities (83) and received it from Dakchen Ngagi Wangchuk. I requested the empowerment of the Sixteen Spheres of the Heart according to Kadam (84) and received it from the omniscience great paṇḍita Gendun Gyatso. So it was that I also heard these twelve supplementary empowerments.

As far as the yogatantras are concerned, I requested the empowerment of Vajradhātu according to the tradition of Pelden Lama (85) and received it from Rabsel Dawa Gonpo. I requested the empowerment of *Sarvavidvairocana* according to the tradition of Sakya (86) and received it from Jetsun Kunga Chogdrub. I requested the empowerment of *Vajrapāṇi, Subjugator of the Lord of Death* (87) and received it from Yigdrukpa Sherab Peljor. I requested the empowerment of *Esoteric Mañjuśrī* (88) and received it from Ngok.

As far as the cycles of Kriyātantra and Caryātantra are concerned, I requested the empowerment of eleven-faced Avalokita with an assemblage of many deities according to the tradition of Lakṣmī (89), and I received it from Lowo Khen Rinpoché. I requested the empowerment of the *Adaman-*

tine Subjugator Maṇivajra with an assemblage of nineteen deities (90), and I received it also from Lowo Khen Rinchen. I requested the empowerment of the Five Protective Great Incantations (91), and I received it from Lowo Khenchen Rinchen. I requested the empowerment of the *Protuberance with the White Parasol* with an assemblage of many deities (92), and I received it from Lowo Khen Rinchen. I requested the empowerment of Amitāyus according to the tradition of Jetāri with an assemblage of nine deities (93), and I received it about one hundred times from seventeen lamas. {373} I requested two times the empowerment of Akṣobhya with an assemblage of nine deities (94), and I received it from Lowo Khenchen and from Yigdrukpa Sherab Peljor. I requested the empowerment of Mañjughoṣa in the form Arapacana with an assemblage of five deities (95) and received it from Lowo Khenchen Rinchen. I requested the empowerment of Marīcī with an assemblage of five deities (96) and received it from Lowo Khen. I requested the empowerment of Grahamātṛkā (97) and received it from Lowo Khen. I requested the empowerments of Munīndra in the form [*Kingly*] *Array of the Three Commitments* (98), and of the *Awakening of Vairocana* (99), and received them both from Jampa Konchok Pelzangpo. I requested the empowerment of all three classes [of Action Tantra deities] (100) and received it from Lowo Khenchen Rinchen. So it was that I received these sixteen empowerments of the lower tantras. Altogether I properly received the conferral of one hundred empowerments.

In order to receive the great empowerments of yogatantra, I went into the presence of Sonam Peljor, the official of Zhalu, and made a petition. With his permission I requested the scriptural transmission of the prayer entitled *He Whose Glory Is Gracious* by means of which Tuksé Lotsāwa Rinchen Namgyel had extolled Buton Rinpoché, along with the vitality empowerment of mule-faced Śrīdevī, but apart from that, after Chojé Gelongwa had passed away I did not find anyone else from whom to request these again.

As for the other sundry empowerments that I received,[66] I obtained from Gyalton Jangchub Wangyalwa the empowerments of the *Four Collections of the Guru* or their twenty aspects, according to the tradition of Chowang, which had been revealed as treasure. From Dakchen Atsewa I obtained the empowerment of the *Red Wrathful Guru* according to the tradition of Ngadak Nyang, and from Marlungpa Jampa Konchok Pelzangwa I obtained the empowerment of *Amitāyus and Hayagrīva Combined* and the empowerment of *Utterly Secret and Wrathful Hayagrīva* with an assemblage of nine deities. From Zhuben Chenchikpa I received the empowerment of *Hayagrīva with the Combined Assemblage of the Five Arrogant Spirits.* From Gyalton Jangwangpa I received the empowerment that manifestly reveals the signs and miracles associated with the *Seventeen-Deity Assemblage of Amitāyus,* which Padmākara of Oḍḍiyāna had actually conferred upon Rechen Peljor Zangpo at the Zilchen Cave in Tsāri. From Yarlungpa Norbu Rinchen I received the introduction to the instruction entitled *Buddha Field of Norbu's Liberation by Seeing,* along with the empowerments of the *Liberation by Hearing: The Wish-Fulfilling Gem.*

From some eighteen Sakya and Kagyu lamas I have also received about one hundred times the *One Deity One Vase* long-life empowerment according to the tradition of Drubgyalma. {374}

Furthermore, I completely received the four empowerments that are contingent on Mahākāla. Those that I specifically obtained contingent on Pañjaranātha, four-armed Mahākāla, six-armed Mahākāla, and Trakṣad accord with the listing presented in the foregoing section [of this chapter] concerning the protectors of the transmitted teachings.

Concluding Verse

May extensive benefits arise for the sake of the Buddhist teaching and
sentient beings.

MAṄGALAṂ.

Colophon

This is by Drolchok. {375}

12. Methods for the Conferral of the Empowerments

Losal Tenkyong

Although Kunga Drolchok had remarked that guidance should be given according to the individual guidebooks after the empowerments of Hevajra and so forth had been conferred, in later times only the chanting of the scriptural transmission survived. For this reason, Katok Tsewang Norbu during the eighteenth century introduced the so-called empowerment of the book, which transfers the blessings of the anthology—the actual volume containing the one hundred and eight guidebooks. The liturgical arrangement for this empowerment ceremony, which is the subject of this final chapter, was composed by Losal Tenkyong of Zhalu during the nineteenth century.

Formal Title

A Cornucopia of Blessings Documenting the Oral Instructions of My Teacher concerning the Method for the Conferral of Empowerments in Respect of the Volume Containing the One Hundred and Eight Guidebooks[1] {376}

Introductory Verse

Homage to the teacher (*NAMO GURAVE*)!

Regarding the procedure for conferring empowerments in respect of this anthology of the one hundred and eight guidebooks, you should present the maṇḍala offering and say three times the prayer that begins "Endowed with the aggregate of omniscient pristine cognition."[2] The disciples should then be visualized as deities and enter into meditation. The master, holding the volume of the One Hundred and Eight Guidebooks in his hand, should then say the following words:

> You should visualize the master as the glorious hero Kunga Drolchok Losel Gyatsodé, who has attained the accomplishment of Mañjunātha and who embodies all the rivers of the lineage. Contingent on your faith and devotion, the garland of vowels and consonants headed by a white OṂ emerges from the OṂ in the forehead of the master, in the manner of a string of white pearls, and it diffuses lights of five colors, along with a stream of white nectar. It enters through the crown of your head and completely fills all the channel branches of the cakra of supreme bliss. All negativity, downfalls, and degenerations and all the outer and inner negativities that obstruct your visualization, meditation, and experiential cultivation by means of the body are refined and purified right where they are. This arrangement of auspicious circumstances will be known by means of the one hundred and eight distinct guidebooks at the very time when you complete the path that refines the adamantine body, including the yogic gazes, the yogic exercises, and the visualization of the aggregates, sensory elements, and sense fields as deities. {377} Having understood all these words and meanings, without exception, you should believe that your mind will acquire the great nail that is unchanging!

Then the master places the volume of the One Hundred and Eight Guidebooks upon the head [of the disciple]. Incense should be lit and music played. Three times you should recite the vowels and consonants with the heart cakra as their support, and then you should scatter flowers [of offering].

> Then again, the garland of vowels and consonants headed by a red ĀḤ emerges from the ĀḤ in the throat of the master, in the manner of a string of coral, and it diffuses lights of five colors, along with a stream of red nectar. It enters through your throat and completely fills the channel branches of the cakra of perfect resources. All negativity, downfalls, and degenerations and all the outer and inner negativities that obstruct your recitation of

> mantra, cultivation of breath control, and so forth by means of speech are refined and purified right where they are. This arrangement of auspicious circumstances will be known by means of the one hundred and eight distinct guidebooks at the very time when you complete the path that refines the subtle and gross yoga of the winds, and that commences with the saying of prayers, mantra recitation, and the breathing that dispenses [compassion to others] and draws in [the suffering of others]. Having understood all these words and meanings, without exception, {378} you should believe that your mind will acquire the great nail that is unchanging!

Then [the master] places the volume [of the One Hundred and Eight Guidebooks] at the throat [of the disciple]. As before, incense should be lit and music played.

> Then again, the garland of vowels and consonants headed by a blue HŪṂ emerges from the HŪṂ in the heart of the master, in the manner of a string of aquamarine, and it diffuses lights of five colors, along with a stream of blue nectar. It enters through your heart and completely fills the central channel of the cakra of the phenomenal wheel. All negativity, downfalls, and degenerations and all the outer and inner negativities that obstruct your experiential cultivation of the path of subtle and gross meditative stability by means of mind are refined and purified right where they are. This arrangement of auspicious circumstances will be known by means of the one hundred and eight distinct guidebooks at the very time when you complete the path that cultivates devotion, detachment, loving-kindness, compassion, and enlightened mind and refines the real nature of ineffable coemergent pristine cognition. Having understood accordingly, you should believe that your mind will acquire the great nail that is unchanging!

Then [the master] places the volume [of the One Hundred and Eight Guidebooks] at the heart [of the disciple]. As before, incense should be lit and music played.

> Finally, you should visualize the master as the glorious hero Kunga Drolchok Losel Gyatsodé, who has attained the accomplishment of Mañjunātha. From the three places of his body[—forehead, throat, and heart—]three replicas [are diffused], each about three thumbs in size and each enclosed within a tent of five-colored light rays. These then dissolve into your own corresponding three places. Consequently, you will experientially cultivate, without error, all the words and meanings of the one hundred and eight profound guidebooks. This arrangement of auspicious circumstances will be known at the very time when you are filled like a vase to the brim with all the transmitted teachings of maturational empowerment and all the transmitted teachings of liberating guidance, and so forth, just as Venerable Kunga Drolchok Losel Gyatsodé, embodiment of all lineages, possesses them. {379} You should believe that you will acquire the transference of his authentic blessing, in the manner of a unique lineage!

Then [the master] places the volume [of the One Hundred and Eight Guidebooks] at the crown, throat, and heart [of the disciple]. JAḤ HŪṂ VAṂ HOḤ should then be recited three times, incense should be lit, and music played.

The precious garland of the one hundred and eight profound guidebooks,
The essence that churns the ocean of Sutra and Tantra traditions,
Has, as a beautiful ornament for the minds of fortunate disciples,
A stream of lineage blessings that does not vanish,
Just as the moist breath from the mouths of mātaraḥ and ḍākinīs does not fade.
Through the power of truth, may the blessing of the three supreme precious jewels,
Commencing with Jetsun Kunga Drolchok who embodies all teachers
And the trio—Cakrasaṃvara, Hevajra, and Guhyasamāja—
Embodying all meditational deities, enter into you, O fortunate disciples!

Then, while scattering flowers, you should recite the benedictions of good auspices—one quatrain of verse beginning with the words "Summit of the victory banner,"[3] one quatrain beginning with the words "Unchanging mountain,"[4] and one quatrain beginning with the words "[Without the need for] diligence and effort."[5]

Afterward, as in general, [you should recite the verses] that begin "Just as the lord [commands]."[6]

Conclusion

In this context of the One Hundred and Eight Guidebooks, the maturational empowerment in the maṇḍala of Hevajra—essential for the practical application of Jetsun Kunga Drolchok—should be conferred, and then after that the guidance should be given according to the individual guidebooks. In later times, however, apart from simply the chanting of its scriptural transmission, this guidance has for the most part been lost, not to mention its empowerments. Although there are one or two who proudly say they have this transmission of guidance, theirs does not appear to be authentic apart from the mere exegetical transmission. After the time of Venerable Katokpa [Tsewang Norbu], however, this [new] transmission of the empowerment of the book did emerge. To seek to acquire completely all the empowerments and guidance of the One Hundred and Eight Guidebooks through this alone would be extremely presumptuous. Even so, if one has listened to the scriptural transmission of these guidebooks completely, it may permissibly be conferred at the conclusion. Whether or not this was the intention of Venerable Drolchok himself, there is no contradiction. Having observed the correct procedure for their practical application, I have set forth this instruction in writing just as I obtained it from my own teacher.

Colophon

This was compiled by the vagabond renunciate Rinchen Mangto Losal Tenkyong [of Zhalu] on the third day (*rgyas pa gsum pa'i nyin*) of the waning half of the late-summer month of the earth pig year,[7] {380} to the east of the palace at the adamantine cave hermitage of glorious Sakya, the place of attainment where Mañjughoṣa had revealed his visage to the most merciful Jetsun Kunga Nyingpo.

SARVA MAṄGALAṂ

Concordance of Technical Terms

The following concordance gives precedence to the original Tibetan in the first column, with Sanskrit equivalents in the middle column and English translations or proper names in the third column.

Tibetan	Sanskrit	English
ka dag		primordial purity
kun tu'am rgyun du 'jog pa	saṃsthāpana	perpetual placement
kun btags	parikalpita	imaginary nature
kun da	kunda	generative essence (code word); lit., jasmine
kun 'dar	avadhūti	central channel
kun rdzob byang sems	saṃvṛtibodhicitta	relative enlightened mind
kun gzhi	ālaya	substratum
kun gzhi rnam par shes pa	ālayavijñāna	substratum consciousness
kun bzang sdom pa gsum ldan		threefold vows of Samantabhadra
kyi hud	hahava	hell of lamentations (fourth of eight cold hells)
kri ka		epicanthus
klags lung		recited transmission
klad kor	anusvāra	nasalization marker
klad rgya	mastakaluṅga	cerebral membrane
klu	nāga	serpentine water spirit
klu chen brgyad	aṣṭamahānāga	eight great nāgas

Tibetan	Sanskrit	English
klu dbang 'khyil ba	kuṇḍalinī	coiled nāga (latent energy at base of spine)
klong		space, aureole, vortex
dka' thub kyi lam	tapaścaryā	way of austerities
dka' thub gsum		three austerities
dkar po'i sa bon stobs	gaurībījabala	power of the seed of virtuous action (first of five powers)
dkon mchog gsum	triratna	three precious jewels
dkyil krungs	paryaṅka, āsana	cross-legged posture
dkyil 'khor	maṇḍala	maṇḍala
bka' rgya		sealed injunction, restricted teaching
bka' babs bzhi		four successions of the transmitted teachings
bka' ma		distant lineage of orally transmitted teachings
bka' bzhi	caturvacana	four transmitted teachings/ pronouncements
rkang mgyogs kyi dngos grub	jaṅeghākarasiddhi	accomplishment of swift-footedness
rkang mthil rlung	pādatalavāyu	wind at the soles of the feet
rkyang pa		single syllable
rkyang ma	lalanā	left channel
rkyen	pratyaya	condition, circumstance
rkyen snang		circumstantial appearance
skad cig ma'i rang 'gros		instantaneous natural dynamic
skal ldan rjes 'dzin		accepting of fortunate disciples
sku	kāya	buddha body
sku rdo rje	kāyavajra	adamantine reality of buddha body
sku rdo rje'i rjes gzhig		dissolution of the adamantine buddha body

Tibetan	Sanskrit	English
sku mi zad pa	akṣayakāya	inexhaustible buddha body
sku gsum	trikāya	three buddha bodies
sku gsum bla sgrub		attainment of the guru as the three buddha bodies
skyabs gnas	śaraṇa	refuge, object of refuge
skye sgo	utpattidvāra	entrance to rebirth, cervix
skye mched drug	ṣadāyatana	six sense fields
skye gnas bzhi	caturyoni	four modes of birth
skye ba ye shes kyi rim pa		stage of pristine cognition that arises (third of four stages)
skye med chig chod		unique determination of the unborn state
skye srid kyi dag byed		purification of rebirth (third of three purifications)
skyes bu chung ngu	kāpuruṣa	person of lesser capacity
skyes bu chen po	mahāpuruṣa	person of greater capacity
skyes bu 'bring	madhyamapuruṣa	person of middling capacity
bskyed rim	utpattikrama	generation stage (of meditation)
bskyed rim bdag byin gyis brlab pa		self-consecration of the generation stage
bskrad pa	uccāṭana	expulsion
kha ton	svādhyāya	oral recitation
kha nang du lta ba	antaramukha	introverted
kha sbyor yan lag bdun	saptasampuṭa	seven aspects of union
kha 'dzin		opinion
kha zas	bhojana	diet, food
khams	dhatu	sensory element, material element, seminal fluid, physical constitution
khams dangs ma		generative essence

Tibetan	Sanskrit	English
khams 'dus pa tha ma		final absorption of the sensory elements (i.e., stability)
khams 'dus pa dang po		initial absorption of the sensory elements (i.e., blazing of fierce inner heat)
khams 'dus pa bar ma		middling absorption of the sensory elements (i.e., dynamic movement)
khaṭvāṅga	khaṭvāṅga	khaṭvāṅga scepter
khu khrag		semen and blood
khu tshur	muṣṭi (mudra)	gesture of the fist
khyab byed	vyāna	pervasive wind (associated with metabolism and muscular movement)
khro rgyal	krodhajina, krodharāja	wrathful conqueror, wrathful king
mkha' 'gro ma	ḍākinī	ḍākinī, female muse, sky-farer
mkhal rken		perinephric area
mkhal rtsa		kidney channel
'khor ba		samsara, cyclic existence
'khor ba'i nyes dmigs	saṃsārādīnava	defect of cyclic existence
'khor lo	cakra	cakra, energy center, wheel-shaped anal plug
'khor lo sgyur pa	cakravartin	universal emperor
'khrul 'khor	yantra	yogic exercise, device
'khrul 'byams		pervasion of bewilderment (third of four pervasions)
gang zag	pudgala	individual person
gang zag gi bdag med	pudgalanairātmya	nonself of individual persons
gang zag gsum		three sorts of person
gu gul	guggula	frankincense

TIBETAN	SANSKRIT	ENGLISH
gud chung spun lnga		five sibling frailties
gus sbyor	satkṛtyaprayoga	devout application
gegs sel nges		definitive dispelling of obstacles
goms stobs	abhyāsabala	power of familiarity (third of five powers)
gol sa		deviation
gol sa bcad		severing of deviations (third of the four syllables of the Great Seal)
gos gyon		wearing of clothing (as an ancillary yogic practice)
gyen rgyu	udānavāyu	ascending wind (associated with the vocal cords)
grub mtha'	siddhānta	philosophical system, tenet
grogs chos spyod bcu		ten facilitating modes of doctrinal conduct
grong 'jug		resurrection
grol lam	muktimārga	path of liberation (guidance)
glang po che'i rna ba		posture that resembles the ear of an elephant
gleng gzhi	nidāna	introductory narrative
dgang	pūraka	filling (second of four applications of wind)
dga' 'khyil	nandyāvarta	swirl of delight (motif)
dga' spro		exaltation
dga' ba	ānanda	delight
dga' ba bcu drug	ṣodaśānanda	sixteen delights
dga' ba bzhi	caturānanda	four delights
dga' bral	viramānanda	absence of delight
dge ba	kuśala	virtuous action
dge ba chos sdud	kuśaladharmasaṃgrāhaka	discipline of gathering virtuous attributes
dgongs thun rjes ma		next evening session

Tibetan	Sanskrit	English
dgongs pa	abhisandhi	enlightened intention
dgra bgegs tshar gcod pa		eradication of hostile and obstructing forces
'gag pa'i bden pa	nirodhasatya	truth of cessation
'gyur ba rnam drug		six aspects of transformation (of generative essence)
'gyur ba'i sdug bsngal	viparināmaduḥkhatā	suffering of change
'gyur med yongs grub	avaivartasampanna	unchanging consummate nature
'gro 'dug mang po		excessive movement (first of four challenges)
rgya tshil		deer fat
rgya yan		carefree
rgyal		king spirits (of anger)
rgyal 'gong		king spirits and bewitchers
rgyal po rol pa	rājalalita	posture of royal ease
rgyal ba	jina	conqueror, buddha
rgyal ba rigs lnga	pañcajina	buddhas of the five enlightened families
rgyal rigs	kṣatriya	princely class
rgyal srid sna bdun	saptarājyaratna	seven insignia of royal dominion
rgyas gdab gsum	trimudraṇa	three sealings
rgyas pa'i las	pauṣṭikakarma	rite of enrichment
rgyu mthun spyod	niṣyandacaryā	causally concordant conduct
rgyu ba	gati	movement
rgyu lhan cig skyes pa		coemergence of the causal basis
rgyud	tantra	continuum, tantra text
rgyud sde bzhi		four classes of tantra
rgyud gsum		three continua (ground, path, and result)

Tibetan	Sanskrit	English
rgyun gyi rnal 'byor drug		six phases of continuous yoga
rgyun gcig tu byed pa	saṃsthāpanā	perpetual placement
rgyun du byed pa'am rtse gcig tu byed pa	ekotīkaraṇa	one-pointedness
rgyun 'byams		pervasion of continuity (fourth of four pervasions)
rgyu'i bdag med	hetunairātmya	nonself of the causal basis
sgo bcu	daśadvāra	ten orifices
sgom	bhāvanā	meditation, cultivation
sgom rim gsum	tribhāvanā	three stages of meditation
sgom lam	bhāvanāmārga	path of meditation/ cultivation
sgyu ma	māyā	magical display, illusion
sgyu ma'i dpe bcu gnyis		twelve similes of magical display
sgyu lus	māyākāya	illusory body
sgyur byed	vikāri	earth pig year
sgra	śabda	sound
sgrub chen	mahāsādhana	great attainment
sgrub pa	sādhana	attainment
sgrub pa po	sādhaka	practitioner
sgro btags	āropa	superimposition
nga bdag	ātma, svayam	self, myself
ngag 'dren pa		recitation, recite
ngag dben gsung rdo rje'i rnal 'byor		yoga of adamantine buddha speech that entails the isolation of ordinary speech
ngu 'bod	raurava	howling hell (fourth of eight hot hells)
ngu 'bod chen po	mahāraurava	great howling hell (fifth of eight hot hells)

Tibetan	Sanskrit	English
nges byed bzhi	caturniścaya	four grades of ascertainment (warmth, peak, acceptance, and supremacy)
nges gnas	niyatistha	real nature
nges pa lnga	pañcaniścaya	five certainties
nges pa gsum		three certainties
nges par rgyu ba	niścaraṇa	definitive movement
nges par 'jog pa'am bslan te 'jog pa	avasthāpanā	definitive or integrated placement
ngo bo nyid	svabhāva	essential nature, inherent existence
ngo bo nyid med gsum	trayaniḥsvabhāva	three essenceless natures
ngo bo nyid gsum	trisvabhāva	three essential natures
ngo bo sbyor ba bzhi		four essential applications
ngo bo'i bdag med	svabhāvanairātmya	nonself of the essential nature
dngos gzhi	maula	main practice
mngal sgo	yonidvāra	womb entrance
mngon dkyil		visualization maṇḍala
mngon rtogs brgyad	aṣṭābhisamaya	eight phases of clear realization
mngon shes lnga	pañcābhijñā	five extrasensory powers
rngub pa		inhalation (first of four applications of wind)
sngags	mantra	mantra, spell
sngags kyi rnal 'byor	mantrayoga	yoga of mantra
sngags pa	mantrin	practitioner of Mantra
sngo ba	pariṇāma	dedication of merit
sngon gyi gnas rjes su dran pa'i mngon par shes pa	pūrvanivāsānusmṛtyābhijñā	extrasensory power of the recollection of past lives
sngon 'gro	pūrvaka	preliminaries, preliminary practices

TIBETAN	SANSKRIT	ENGLISH
cang te'u	ḍamaru	skull drum
cer phog		direct focus
cong zhi	śaila	calcite
gcig bsgom mdud grol		knots unraveled in a singular meditation
gcig brjod kun khyab		permeating all things in a singular utterance
gcig shes kun grol		all things liberated through singular knowledge
bcas mtshams		prescribed boundary
bcud	sattva, rasa	(sentient) inhabitants, essence
bcud bsdus		condensed elixir
bcud len	rasāyana	extraction of elixir
lce'i dbang po	jihvendriya	sense faculty of the tongue
lce'u chung	lambikā	uvula
cha ga		epicanthic fold
cha shas kyi rten bcas		calm abiding with a partial support
chad lta	ucchedavāda	nihilism
chig brgyud		unique lineage (i.e., with a single lineage holder)
chig chod blo bde		ease of singular resolution
chu stod	āṣāḍha	late-summer month
chu bur can	arbuda	blistering hell (first of eight cold hells)
chu bur rdol ba can	nirarbuda	blister-bursting hell (second of eight cold hells)
chu bo rgyun gyi rnal 'byor		yoga of continuous flow
chu srung		water protection rite
chu'i dkyil 'khor	udakamaṇḍala	maṇḍala of water
chu'i khams	abdhātu	water element

Tibetan	Sanskrit	English
chud ma zos pa gsum		three things not to be squandered
chos kyi sku	dharmakāya	buddha body of reality
chos kyi khams	dharmadhātu	seed of reality, sensory element of phenomena
chos kyi 'khor lo gsum	trayadharmacakra	three promulgations of the doctrinal wheel
chos kyi bdag med	dharmanairātmya	selflessness of phenomena
chos kyi gnas tshul	dharmastithi	abiding nature of reality
chos kyi phyag rgya	dharmamudrā	phenomenal seal
chos kyi 'byung gnas	dharmodaya	hexahedron (motif); lit., "source of phenomena"
chos sku de bzhin nyid kyi 'pho ba		consciousness transference into the reality of the buddha body of reality
chos 'khor snying gi 'khor lo		heart cakra of the phenomenal wheel
chos gos rnam gsum	tricīvara	three religious robes
chos can	dharmin	apparent thing, subject, topic, attribute
chos nyid	dharmatā	reality, true nature of phenomena (i.e., emptiness)
chos dbyings ye shes	dharmadhātujñāna	pristine cognition of reality's expanse
chod tshad		evidence of determination (i.e., realization)
mchog	uttama, parama	supremacy
mchog dga'	paramānanda	supreme delight
mchog sbyin	varadānam	supreme generosity
mchog sbyin gyi phyag rgya	varadamudrā	gesture of supreme boon
mchod sdong	yaṣti	offering lamp
'chi khar ye shes zang thal du btang ba'i rnal 'byor		yoga that penetrates pristine cognition to its core at the time of death (sixth of six phases of continuous yoga)

Tibetan	Sanskrit	English
'chi bdag	Yama	lord of death
'chi ba slu		ritual on cheating death
'chi med	amartya	deathlessness
'chi srid kyi dag byed		purification of death (first of three purifications)
'chugs med mkha' spyod kyi 'pho ba		unerring consciousness transference into the realm of the sky-farers
'jam rlung	mṛduprāṇa	gentle breathing
'jam rlung dgang gtong		filling and release of gentle wind
'jam rlung bzung ba		control of gentle wind
'ja' lus	mahāsaṃkrāntikāya	rainbow body
'jigs pa brgyad	aṣṭabhaya	eight fears
'jug gnas sdang gsum		inhalation, pausing, and exhalation of breath
'jug pa'i rnal 'byor		yoga of engagement
'jug pa'i byang chub sems	prasthānabodhicitta	engaged enlightened mind
rjen rjen		stark
rjes thob	pṛṣṭalabdha	postmeditation
rjes dran	anusmṛti	recollection (fifth branch of six-branch yoga)
rjes dran lnga		five recollections (Kadampa)
rjes gnang	anujñā	initiation, permissory rite
rjes sbyor	upayoga	subsequent application
rjes gzhig		dissolution
brjed byang	ṭippaṇī	memorandum
brjed 'byams		pervasion of forgetfulness (first of four pervasions)
nyams		experience

Tibetan	Sanskrit	English
nyams rtogs bskul byed kyi sgron ma		lamp that inspires experiential realization (fourth of five lamps)
nyams len	upagamana	experiential cultivation
nyams len sngags rim		stage of mantra to be experientially cultivated
nyams rlung		degenerate wind
nyams gsum		three meditative experiences
nyal ba'i rnal 'byor	svapnayoga	sleeping yoga, dream yoga
nyi tshe dmyal ba	pratyekanaraka	ephemeral hells
nyin rtags drug		six signs indicative of daytime yoga
nyin mo snang ba rgyas gdab pa'i rnal 'byor		yoga that secures appearances during the daytime (first of six phases of continuous yoga)
nyin mo'i rnal 'byor	divāyoga	daytime yoga
nye 'khor dmyal ba	upāntanaraka	neighboring hells
nye bar 'jog pa	upasthāpanā	intensified placement
nye bar zhi bar byed pa	vyupaśamana	intensified calming, quiescence
nyes byas	duṣkṛta	minor (monastic) offenses
gnyan khrod		haunted mountain range
gnyan sa		rugged place
gnyis med	advaya	nonduality
gnyug ma'i don	ādyārtha	innate truth
gnyug ma'i lha	ādyādevatā	innate deity
gnyugs ma'i rang so		innate natural state
gnyen po rkyen thub		capacity to apply antidotes according to the circumstances (fourth of five capacities)
mnyam nyid kyi ye shes	samatājñāna	pristine cognition of sameness

TIBETAN	SANSKRIT	ENGLISH
mnyam gnas kyi rlung	samānavāyu	stabilizing wind
mnyam med snying rje'i rnal 'byor		union of peerless compassion
mnyam bzhag	samasaṃsthāpa	meditative equipoise, placement in meditative equipoise
snying gi thig le bcu drug		sixteen spheres of the heart (Kadampa)
snying rje	karuṇā	compassion
snying gtam		innermost advice
snying po ma		primary essential
snying po'i yang snying po		quintessential
snyems pa	parāmarśa	egotistical pride
snyems 'phrigs		arrogant conjecture
snyel byang		memorandum
bsnyen sgrub	sevāsādhana	ritual service and attainment
bsnyen pa	sevā	ritual service
bsnyen par rdzogs	upasampadā	full monastic ordination
ting nge 'dzin	samādhi	meditative stability (sixth branch of six-branch yoga)
ting 'dzin sems dpa'	samādhisattva	being of meditative stability
gtad so		focus
gti mug	moha	delusion
gtum mo	caṇḍālī	fierce inner heat, channel of fierce inner heat
gtum mo dmigs pa bco brgyad		eighteen visualizations of the fierce inner heat
gtum mo zad bza'		consumption of the channel of fierce inner heat (a yogic exercise)

Tibetan	Sanskrit	English
gtum mo ras thub		capacity to wear the cotton robe of the fierce inner heat (first of five capacities)
gter kha bco brgyad		eighteen treasure troves (of Guru Chowang)
gter ma	nidhi	treasure, revelation
gtor ma	bali	torma offering
rta zhon		riding of the horse (ancillary yogic practice)
rtag lta	śāśvatadṛṣṭi	eternalism
rtags lta	liṅga, cihna	sign
rten dkyil 'khor gyi thig le bzhi		four spheres of the supporting maṇḍala (Kadampa)
rten bcas kyi zhi gnas	sāśrayaśamatha	calm abiding with a support
rten 'brel	pratītyasamutpāda	dependent origination, auspicious circumstance
rten 'brel chig chod kyi khrid		guidance that determines auspicious circumstances
rten med kyi zhi gnas	anāsrayaśamatha	calm abiding without a support
rtog ge	tarka	sophistry
rtog pa	kalpa	ideation
rtog pa'i rnal 'byor	kalpayoga	conceptual yoga
rtog dpyod 'od kyi sgron ma		lamp of the light of ideation and scrutiny
rtogs pa	adhigama	realization
lta stangs	avalokita	yogic gaze
lta ba	dṛṣṭi	view
ltag par stobs kyi rlung		wind of power at the back
ltung ba	āpatti	downfall
lto ba ldebs pa		contracting the abdomen
ltos med bzhi	caturanapekṣa	four things to disregard
sta gon	adhivāsana	preparatory empowerment rite

Tibetan	Sanskrit	English
stan 'ding	āsanadāna	spreading of the mat (ancillary yogic practice)
stegs bu	vedikā	platform
steng gi skyil krung	ūrdhvaparyaṅka	upper posture
steng sgo	ūrdhvadvāra	upper gate
steng rlung	ūrdhvavāyu	upper wind
stong chen yig ge lnga		five syllables of great emptiness
stong pa nyid	śūnyatā	emptiness
stong pa'i byang chub	śūnyatābodhi	generative essence of emptiness
stong ra		empty frame
stod g.yogs	uttarīya	upper robe
stobs lnga	pañcabala	five powers
stobs bcu	daśabala	ten powers
brtan pa'i rtags drug		six signs of stability
brtan pa'i yan lag		supportive ancillary practices
brten pa lha'i thig le drug		six spheres of the supported deities (Kadampa)
bstan pa	śāsana	Buddhist teaching
tha snyad don 'tshol gyi sgron ma		lamp that seeks conventional methods (first of five lamps)
tha mal gyi gtum mo		ordinary fierce inner heat
thab 'gal gyi phyag rgya		sealing gesture of the opposing stoves
thabs	upāya	skillful means, method
thabs lta stangs		yogic gaze of skillful means
thabs lhan cig skyes pa		coemergence of skillful means
thal chen	mahābhasma	human ash
thig nag	kālasūtra	black line hell (second of eight hot hells)

Tibetan	Sanskrit	English
thig le	biṇḍu	vital essence, sphere, drop
thig le dkar dmar		red and white vital essences
thig le nyag gcig		unique vital essence
thig le stong pa'i sgron me		lamp of the empty vital essence
thig le yig ge drug		six syllables of vital essence
thig le longs spyod		resource of vital essences
thig le'i rnal 'byor		yoga of the vital essence
thugs	citta	buddha mind
thugs dam		steadfast meditation, meditational deity (hon.), postdeath meditation
thugs rdo rje	cittavajra	adamantine reality of buddha mind
thugs mi zad pa	akṣayacitta	inexhaustible buddha mind
thun	prahara, yāma, hāraka	session (of meditation), ritual charm
thun bzhi'i rnal 'byor	catuḥpraharayoga	four-session yoga
thub pa lnga		five capacities
thur sel	apānavāyu	descending purgative wind
theg pa chung	hīnayāna	Lesser Vehicle
theg pa chen po	mahāyāna	Great Vehicle
them yig		signpost
tho yig		memorandum, notes
tho rangs rig pa gsal char btab pa'i rnal 'byor		yoga that illuminates awareness at dawn (fifth of six phases of continuous yoga)
thod rgal	vyutkrānta	all-surpassing (realization)
mtha' brgyad	aṣṭānta	eight extremes
mtha' bzhi	caturānta	four limits
mthar thug lnga		five culminations of Khyungpo Neljor
mthar thug chos kyi rnal 'byor		yoga of conclusive attributes

Tibetan	Sanskrit	English
mthar phyin pa'i lam	niṣṭāmārga	path of conclusion
mthar lam	niṣṭāmārga	path of conclusion
mthun dpe		simile of compatibility
mthong lam	darśanamārga	path of insight
dag pa gsum		three purities
dag pa'i 'khor lo	śuddhacakra	pure cycle
dag pa'i sgyu lus	śuddhamāyākāya	pure illusory body
dag pa'i snang ba		pure appearance
dag byed gsum		three purifications
dang ba	prasāda	conviction (first of four modes of faith)
dangs ba'i rlung		lucid wind
dad pa	śraddhā	faith
dam pa rigs brgya		one hundred sacral aspects
dam tshig	samaya	commitment
dam tshig gi phyag rgya	samayamudrā	commitment seal
dam tshig sems dpa'	samayasattva	being of commitment
dam rdzas	samayadravya	sacrament of commitment
dal 'byor	kṣaṇasampat	freedoms and advantages
dug lnga	pañcaviṣa	five poisons
dug zhi ba		alleviation of poison
dug gsum	triviṣa	three poisons
dus sbyor kyi rlung		winds of temporal conjunction
de kho na nyid kyi rim pa		stage of the real nature
de bzhin nyid kyi dag pa		purity of the real nature (first of three purities)
don lnga		five solid viscera
don spyi	arthasāmānya	general concept
don lhan skyes dbu ma		genuine, innate middle way
drag gi las	krūrakarma	rite of wrath

Tibetan	Sanskrit	English
drag po'i thun rdzas		sacramental charm for wrathful rites
drag rlung		strong breathing
dran pa gcig pa'i rnal 'byor		yoga of single recollection
dri ma	mala, gandha	odor
dri za	gandharva	gandharva; lit., "odor eater"
dri za'i grong khyer	gandharvanagara	gandharva spirit town
dril bu	ghaṇṭā	bell
dregs pa		proud spirit
drod gsum		three aspects of warmth
dvangs cha		clarity aspect
dvangs ma		pure essence, chyle, semen
dvangs ma gsum		three pure essences (of channels, winds, and generative fluids)
dvangs ma'i khye'u chung		offspring of pure essence
dvangs ma'i srog		vitality of pure essence
gdangs	ojas	luster, glow, resonance, incandescence
gdong rtse		coinage with hole in the middle
gdon		malign spirit
gdol pa	caṇḍāla	outcaste
bdag	ātman	self, soul, I
bdag gi srung ba		protection of self
bdag nyid chen po	mahatma	great identity
bdag po'i 'bras bu	adhipatiphala	predominant result
bdag 'dzin	ātmagraha	self-grasping
bdag gzhan brje ba		exchanging of self and others
bdud rtsi lnga	pañcāmṛta	five nectars
bdud bzhi	caturmāra	four malevolent forces/devils

Tibetan	Sanskrit	English
bdun tshig		forty-nine-day ceremony
bde ba	sukha	bliss
bde ba'i rang nyams lhan cig skyes ma		innate personal experience of bliss
bde stong		bliss and emptiness
bde drod		blissful warmth, warmth of bliss
mdo	sūtra	discourse
'da' kha ma	ātyaya	time of death
'da' kha ma grong 'jug		resurrection at the time of death
'du byed kyi sdug bsngal	saṃskāraduḥkhatā	suffering of conditioned existence
'du byed kyi phung po	saṃskāraskandha	aggregate of formative predispositions
'du shes kyi phung po	aṃjñāskandha	aggregate of perceptions
'du shes gsum		three perceptions of male, female, and nondual union
'dul bar byed pa	damana	control
'dre		evil spirit
'dod chags	rāga	desire
'dod pa	icchā	longing (second of four modes of faith)
'dod ma'i gnas lugs		original abiding nature
'dod zad		dispassion
rdo rje	vajra	adamantine reality, vajra (emblem), penis
rdo rje skyil krung	vajraparyaṅka	cross-legged adamantine posture
rdo rje rgya gram	viśvavajra	crossed vajra
rdo rje 'jig byed kyi rnal 'byor		union of Vajrabhairava
rdo rje nor bu	vajramaṇi	adamantine gem (i.e., penis)
rdo rje gtsug gtor	vajroṣṇīṣa	adamantine protuberance

Tibetan	Sanskrit	English
rdo rje 'dzin pa'i sa		level of an adamantine holder (thirteenth buddha level)
rdo rje gsum gyi ril 'dzin		encompassing of the three adamantine realities
rdo rje'i gur	vajrapañjara	adamantine tent
rdo rje'i rba rlabs		adamantine waves of blessing (a yogic practice)
rdo rje'i bzlas pa		adamantine recitation
rdo rje'i lus	vajrakāya	adamantine body
rdo rje'i rva		vajra prong
ldang ba'i rnal 'byor		yoga of reemergence
ldog gi tshad		evidence of pitfalls
sdigs mdzub	tarjanīmudrā	gesture of menace
sdug bsngal gyi sdug bsngal	duḥkhaduḥkhatā	suffering of suffering
sdug bsngal gsum	triduḥkhatā	three sorts of suffering
sdud rim	saṃhārakrama	phase of absorption (of wind)
sde tshan brgyad	aṣṭavarga	eight phonetic sets of syllables (consonants and vowels)
sdod tshugs pa		withdrawal
sdom pa gsum	trisaṃvara	three vows
sdom pa'i khrims		discipline of observing vows
brda dbang		symbolic empowerment
brda' don 'grol ba'i sgron ma		lamp that unravels the symbolic meaning (third of five lamps)
bsdus 'joms	saṅghāta	crushing hell (third of eight hot hells)
nag khrid gsung bgros		black guidance that is discussed
nang gi skye mched lnga	pañcādhyātmikāyatana	five inner sense fields

Tibetan	Sanskrit	English
nang gi lhan cig skyes ma		innate inner state
nang bltas		internal inspection
nang nub 'dod yon grogs su 'khyer ba'i rnal 'byor		yoga that carries the attributes of desire on the path as an assist during mornings and evenings (second of six phases of continuous yoga)
nad gdon 'khrugs thub		capacity to agitate diseases and demonic possession (third of five capacities)
nā da	nāda	vibration
nam mkha'i khams	ākāśadhātu	space element
nam gung shes bya bum par gzhug pa'i rnal 'byor		yoga that induces knowable phenomena into the vase (of luminosity) at midnight (fourth of six phases of continuous yoga)
nor bu	maṇi	gem, penis
nor bu mig gsum		three-eyed gem
gnad	marma	crucial/essential point
gnad 'doms		essential point
gnad phyugs med dgu		nine unerring essentials (of dream yoga)
gnas kyi srung ba		protection of environment
gnas cha		abiding aspect
gnas brtan	sthavira	elder
gnas pa'i rnal 'byor		yoga of abiding
gnas tshad		correct standard
gnas lugs	sthiti	abiding nature of reality
gnas su dag pa		inherent purity
gnas sum mkha' 'gro		ḍākinīs of the three abodes
mnar med	avīci	hell of ultimate torment (eighth of eight hot hells)
rnam gcod	vyavaccheda	preclusion

Tibetan	Sanskrit	English
rnam rtog 'gyu tshad		plethora of fleeting conceptual thoughts
rnam thar sgo gsum	trivimokṣamukha	three gateways of liberation
rnam snang gi chos bdun	vairocanasaptadharma	sevenfold posture of Vairocana
rnam pa	ākāra	apparition, apparent form, sensum
rnam pa kun ldan gyi mchog dang ldan pa'i stong pa nyid	sarvākāraguṇopetaśūnyatā	emptiness in all its finest aspects
rnam par dpyad pa'i stong pa nyid	vicāraśūnyatā	analytical emptiness
rnam smin gyi 'bras bu	vipākaphala	ripening result of past actions
rnam smin gyi lus	vipākakāya	maturational body
rnam shes kyi phung po	vijñānaskandha	aggregate of consciousness
rnam shes sgo lnga		five sensory consciousnesses
rnam shes tshogs brgyad	aṣṭavijñānakāya	eight aspects of consciousness
rnal 'byor	yoga	yoga, union, engagement
rnal 'byor gyi srung ba		protection of engagement
rna'i dbang po	śrotrendriya	sense faculty of the ears
snang chen		grand subtle perception (of whiteness) (second of four subtle perceptions)
snang mched thob gsum		three phases of subtle perception, diffusion, and attainment (i.e., whiteness, redness, and blackness at the time of death)
snang ba	ābhāsa	appearance, perception, pure visionary appearance (Great Perfection), subtle perception (first of four subtle perceptions)
snang ba mched pa		diffusion of subtle perception (i.e., redness)

Tibetan	Sanskrit	English
snang [ba nyer] thob		attainment of subtle perception (i.e., blackness, third of four subtle perceptions)
snang ba byin gyis brlab pa		consecration of appearances
snang ba bzhi		four subtle perceptions, four pure visionary appearances (Great Perfection)
snang tshul		apparent modality
sna'i dbang po	ghrāṇendriya	sense faculty of the nose
snod	bhājana	inhabited world
snod drug		six hollow viscera
bsnol ma		cross
padma	padma	lotus, vagina
padma ltar gas pa	padmanaraka	hell of lotus-like cracks (seventh of eight cold hells)
padma ltar cher gas pa	mahāpadmanaraka	hell of large lotus-like cracks (eighth of eight cold hells)
po ti gdong ras can		labeled book
pod dbang		empowerment of the book
dpa' bo gcig po	ekavīra	solitary spiritual warrior (i.e., without consort)
dpa' bo chig chod		heroic determination
dpal be'u	śrīvatsa	heart-orb motif
dpe dang don gyi ye shes	upamārthajñāna	illustrative and genuine pristine cognitions
dpe don ston pa'i sgron ma		lamp that reveals the illustrative meaning (second of five lamps)
dpe'i ye shes	upamajñāna	exemplary pristine cognition
dpyod pa	vicāra	scrutiny
spang ba	parityāga, prahāṇa	renunciation

Tibetan	Sanskrit	English
spu gri'i thang	kṣuranaraka	plain of razors (third neighboring hell)
spu ris		subtle distinction, hairbreadth distinction
spyi sbyor		general application
spyi gtsug bde chen gyi 'khor lo		crown cakra of supreme bliss
spyil bu	kuṭi	grass hermitage
spyod lam	caryāmārga, īryāpatha	regimen
sprul pa lte ba'i 'khor lo		navel cakra of emanation
sprul pa'i sku	nirmāṇakāya	buddha body of emanation
spros pa	prapañca	conceptual elaboration
pha rgyud	pitṛtantra	father tantra
pha chos		inherited teaching, ancestral teaching
pha rol gyi sems kyi mngon par shes pa	paracittābhijñā	extrasensory power of knowledge of the minds of others
phag mo'i brda dbang		symbolic empowerment of Vajravārāhī
phung po	skandha	aggregate
phung po lnga	pañcaskandha	five aggregates
phur bus gtab pa	kīlitana	thrusting of the ritual spike
phur bus btab pa	kīlita	struck by the ritual spike
pho skor		yogic exercise of stomach rotation
pho zhe sdang skye ba'i yul		object giving rise to male hatred
phyag rgya chen po	mahāmudrā	Great Seal
phyag rgya chen po gding thub		capacity to fathom the Great Seal (fifth of five capacities)
phyag rgya chen po'i yi ge bzhi		four syllables of the Great Seal
phyag rgya bzhi	caturmudrā	four seals

Tibetan	Sanskrit	English
phyag rgyun		practical transmission
phyi bltas		external inspection
phyi'i skye mched lnga	pañcabāhyāyatana	five outer sense fields
phyin ci ma log pa'i yongs grub	aviparyāsaparinişpanna	incontrovertible consummate nature
phyir phul ba	pratyarpita	pushing out
phyir mi ldog pa	avinivartanīya	incontrovertibility (fourth of four modes of faith)
phyed skyil	ardhaparyaṅka	semi-cross-legged posture
phra rgyas	anuśaya	subtle impulse
phra thig gi rnal 'byor		yoga of subtle vital essence
phrag dog	īrṣyā	jealousy
phrin las	kārya, karma	enlightened activity
'phangs		elevation (fourth of four applications of wind)
'phen stobs	ākṣepabala	power of propelling intention (second of five powers)
'pho skyas		excessive migration (second of four challenges)
'pho chung	saṃkrānti	minor cycle (of wind)
'pho chen	mahāsaṃkrānti	major cycle (of wind)
'pho ba	saṃkrānti	transference of consciousness
'phrul sbyar ba'i dbang		transformative empowerment
ba nu'i man ngag		pith instruction named cow's udder
bag chags	vāsanā	propensity
bag chags kyi lus	vāsanākāya	body of propensities
bar thun rjes ma		next middle session of the day
bar do	antarābhava	intermediate state

Tibetan	Sanskrit	English
bar do'i dag byed		purification of the intermediate state (second of three purifications)
bar srid	antarābhava	intermediate state
bu chung gi lam		way of Buchung
bu 'od gsal		child luminosity
bum pa can	kumbhaka	vase breathing
bum dbang	kalaśābhiṣeka	vase empowerment
bur ston chen po		molasses feast
be'u bum		anthology of teachings
bon po		Bonpo
bya grub pa'i ye shes	kṛtyānusthānajñāna	pristine cognition of accomplishment
bya btang		renunciation
bya bral		freedom from activity
bya ma rta	cāra	messenger
bya ra	adṛsyapuruṣa	sentinel
byang chub	bodhi	enlightenment
byang chub kyi phyogs chos	bodhipakṣadharma	factors conducive to enlightenment
byang chub kyi sems	bodhicitta	enlightened mind, generative essence/fluid
byang chub lnga	pañcabodhicitta	five generative essences
byang chub sems kyi thig le		vital essence of generative fluid, sphere of enlightened mind
byang chub sems dpa'	bodhisattva	bodhisattva
byang chub sems dpa'i sdom pa	bodhisattvasaṃvara	vows of the bodhisattvas
byang sems gnyis		twofold enlightened mind
byams pa	maitrī	loving-kindness
bying ba	magna	mental dullness
bying rmugs		sluggish inertia
byin gyis rlabs pa'i rnal 'byor		yoga of consecration

TIBETAN	SANSKRIT	ENGLISH
byin rlabs	adhiṣṭhāna	blessing, consecration
byin rlabs bla ma'i rnal 'byor		union with the teacher (guru yoga) who confers blessings
byin rlabs bla ma'i 'pho ba		consciousness transference of the guru's blessing
byin rlabs bzhi	caturadhiṣṭhāna	four blessings
byin brlabs rang byung gi sgron ma		lamp of self-originating consecration (fifth of five lamps)
byis 'jug bdun		seven neophyte empowerments (in Kālacakra)
bye ba khrag khrig	koṭiniyuta	million trillion
byed pa rgyu mthun	kāraṇaniṣyandahetuphala	result corresponding to its cause on the basis of past activities
bram dze	brāhmaṇa	brahmin, priestly class
bris sku	citrapaṭa	icon
bla ma	guru	teacher
bla ma kun 'dus		Gathering of All Gurus (i.e., teacher)
bla rtsa		pulse of vitality
bla tshe		vitality
blo sna		excessive thought (third of four challenges)
dbang	abhiṣeka	empowerment
dbang gi yul	viṣaya	sense object
dbang gi las	vaṣitakriyā	rite of subjugation
dbang chog	abhiṣekakrama	empowerment rite
dbang bzhi	caturabhiṣeka	four empowerments
dbang bzhi pa	caturthābhiṣeka	fourth empowerment
dbang lag		orchid
dbu ma thal gyur ba	prāsaṅgika mādhyamika	consequentialist mādhyamika

Tibetan	Sanskrit	English
dbu ma rang rgyud pa	svāntantrika mādhyamika	syllogistic mādhyamika
dbu ma'i 'bar 'dzag		burning and dripping (of syllables/vital essence) within the central channel
dbu ma'i lam	madhyamapratipat	middle way
dbu mdzad		chant master
dbugs 'byung 'jug		cycle of respiration
dbyings	dhatu	expanse
dbyibs kyi rnal 'byor		yoga of form
dbye		ritual separation
dbye cha		distinguished aspect
dbye byed		distinguisher
'bogs lugs		conferral
'byams pa bzhi		four pervasions (in dream yoga)
'byung nye ba rnams	adhyāpatti	specific subsidiary downfalls
'byung ba bzhi	caturbhūta	four elements
'byongs pa'i rtags bzhi		four signs of refinement
'bras bu	phala	fruition
'bras bu bzhi	catuḥphala	four types of result
'bras bu lhan cig skyes pa		coemergence of the result
sbyang ba gsum	triviśodhana	three refinements
sbyin pa	dāna	generosity, gift
sbyin pa gsum		three aspects of generosity
sbyor lam	prayogamārga	path of connection
ma rgyud	mātṛtantra	mother tantra
ma dag pa'i sgyu lus	aśuddhamāyakāya	impure illusory body
ma dag pa'i snang ba		impure appearances
ma 'od gsal		mother luminosity
ma rig kun ldan gti mug		delusion embodying all fundamental ignorance

Tibetan	Sanskrit	English
mal		natural condition
mas brtan gyi dga' ba bcu drug		sixteen aspects of delight, stabilized from below
mas brtan gyi dga' ba bzhi		four delights ascending from below
mi bskyod pa		Akṣobhya, urine (coded term)
mi rtag pa	anitya	impermanence
mi rtog pa	avikalpanā	nonconceptualization
mi mthun pa'i dpe	pratidṛṣṭānta	simile of incompatibility
mi zad pa'i blo gros	akṣayamati	inexhaustible intelligence
mi slob pa'i zung 'jug		coalescence (of the path) of no-more-learning
mi'i klad pa	naragoda, mastaka	human brain
mi'i tshil		human fat
mig gi dbang po	cakṣurindriya	sense faculty of the eyes
mig thur ma		cataract scalpel
mig rtsa		optic nerve
mun khang	apavaraka	darkened room
me mnyam	samāna	fire-accompanying wind (associated with digestion)
me thab drug		six opposing stoves (posture of the hands, legs, and elbows)
me ma mur gyi 'obs	agnikhadā	pit of burning embers (first neighboring hell)
me long gi ye shes	ādarśajñāna	mirrorlike pristine cognition
me'i dkyil 'khor	agnimaṇḍala	maṇḍala of fire
me'i khams	tejodhātu	fire element
med snang khyab gsum		nonexistence, appearance, and pervasion
mo 'dod chags skye ba'i yul		object giving rise to female desire
mya ngan las 'das	nirvāṇa	nirvana

Tibetan	Sanskrit	English
myong ba rgyu mthun	anubhavaniṣyandahetuphala	result corresponding to its cause on the basis of past experience
dman pa dbyibs kyi rnal 'byor		yoga of lower forms
dmigs tho		list of visualizations
dmigs pa'i snying po dus gsum		three essential phases of visualization
dmigs pa'i gnas dril		quintessential points of visualization
rmi nyams		experience of dreams
rmi lam	svapna	dream yoga
rmi lam bsgyur ba		transformation of dreams
rmi lam spel ba		increase of dreams
rmi lam sbyang ba		refinement of dreams
rmi lam gzung ba		retention of dreams
rmongs	vyāmoha	obfuscation
smad dkris	ardhoruka	skirt
smar khrid mdzub btsugs		direct guidance that is pointed out
smin lam		path of maturation (empowerment)
smon pa'i byang chub sems	praṇidhibodhicitta	aspirational enlightenment
smon lam stobs	praṇidhānabala	power of aspirational prayer (fifth of five powers)
tsog bu	utkuṭaka	crouching posture
gtsug gtor	uṣṇīṣa	crown protuberance
gtsub shing me'i 'khrul 'khor		kindling fire with a rubbing stick (yogic exercise)
gtso bo sems dpa' sum brtsegs		three-tiered principal beings (of commitment, pristine cognition, and meditative stability)

TIBETAN	SANSKRIT	ENGLISH
gtso bo'i nga rgyal	pradhānāhaṃkāra	egocentricity of primal matter
btsan bkra		auspicious tsen spirit
btsan thabs	haṭha	forceful method
rtsa	nāḍi	channel
rtsa khyim		framework of channels
rtsa 'khor 'dab ma		channel branch
rtsa brgyud bla ma'i thig le drug		six spheres of the teachers of the root lineage (Kadampa)
rtsa dag sku rdo rje		channels as the adamantine reality of buddha body
rtsa mdud		channel knot
rtsa 'dab		channel branch
rtsa ba rgyu'i rnal 'byor		union of the primary causal basis
rtsa ba'i bla ma	mūlaguru	root teacher
rtsa ba'i rlung lnga	pañcavāta	five primary winds
rtsa ba'i sems	mūlacitta	fundamental mind
rtsa dbu ma	avadhūti	central channel
rtsa sbubs		channel enclosure
rtsa'i rnal 'byor	nāḍiyoga	yoga of the channels
rtsub rlung bstan thabs		forceful method of rough breathing
rtsub rlung bum pa can		rough vase breathing
rtsol ba	prayatna, samudyoga	articulation of sound, exertion
rtsol ba'i rlung		wind of exertion
brtse ba	prema	love
brtsegs kyi yi ge		stacked letter
brtson 'grus	vīrya	perseverance
tsha ba	tapana	heating hell (sixth of eight hot hells)
tshang bug	brahmārandha	fontanel

Tibetan	Sanskrit	English
tshad med bzhi	caturaprameya	four immeasurable aspirations
tshad rims kyis 'debs pa		affliction through fever
tshig brgyud chen po		great word transmission
tshig zin		memo
tshigs chen bcu gnyis		twelve major joints
tshul khrims	śīla	ethical discipline
tshe grub		long-life attainment
tshe dbang		long-life empowerment
tsheg drag	visarga	visarga (aspiration marker)
tshogs	sambhāra	accumulation, provision
tshogs	gaṇa	communal offering
tshogs lam	sambhāramārga	path of provisions
tshor ba'i phung po	vedanāskandha	aggregate of feelings
mtshan rtags bzhi		four signs indicative of nighttime yoga
mtshan dpe	lakṣaṇavyañjana	major and minor marks
mtshan ma lnga		five signs (of the dissolution of the elements)
mtshan mo'i rnal 'byor	rātriyoga	nighttime yoga
mtshams sbyor	anusandhi	reconnection (with propensities of past life), reincarnation
mtshogs ma		fontanel
mdzod spu	ūrṇakośa	hair ringlet
'dzin pa	grahaṇa	retention (fourth branch of six-branch yoga)
rdzu 'phrul gyi mngon par shes pa	ṛddhyābhijñā	extrasensory power of miraculous abilities
rdzogs pa chen po	mahāsandhi	Great Perfection
rdzogs rim	sampannakrama	perfection stage (of meditation)

TIBETAN	SANSKRIT	ENGLISH
wal wal		vibrant
zhi ba	śānta	calm
zhi ba'i las	śāntikriyā	rite of pacification
zhi bar byed pa	śamana	calming
zhi byed	śamana	pacification
zhun chen		melted human fat
zhe sdang rdo rje	dveṣavajra	adamantine reality of hatred
gzhan stong		extraneous emptiness
gzhan dbang	paratantra	dependent nature
gzhan 'byor lnga	pañcānyasampat	five circumstantial advantages
gzhal yas khang	vimāna	celestial palace
gzhi	ādhāra, āśraya, mūla	ground
gzhi gnas	śamatha	calm abiding
gzhi rtsa bcad		basis that eradicates obscuration (first of the four syllables of the Great Seal)
gzhi'i rgyud		continuum of the ground
gzhil ba	praśāntaka	crushing (third of four applications of wind)
bzhag thabs bstan		presentation of the means of establishing the nature of mind (second of the four syllables of the Great Seal)
za byed las		devouring rites
zab gnad lnga		five profound essentials
zab pa sngags kyi rnal 'byor		yoga of profound mantras
zung 'jug gi sku	yuganaddhakāya	body of coalescence

Tibetan	Sanskrit	English
zung 'jug yi dam kyi 'pho ba		consciousness transference into the coalescent meditational deity
zla ba chu shel	candramaṇi	pure crystal
gza'		stroke-causing demon
gza' gtad med		without referential object
gzugs	rūpa	sights, matter
gzugs kyi phung po	rūpaskandha	aggregate of physical forms
gzugs sku	rūpakāya	buddha body of form
bzung 'dzin	grāhyagrahaṇa	subject-object dichotomy, dualistic perception
bzod pa	kṣānti	tolerance
'og gi skyil krung		lower posture
'og sgo	pāyu	lower gate
'og rlung		lower wind
'od kyi gong bu		globe of light
'od kyi gtum mo		luminous fierce inner heat
'od gsal	prabhāsvara	luminosity
yang dag par rgyu ba		genuine movement
yang sos	sañjīva	reviving hell (first of eight hot hells)
yas thags		Bon ritual ingredients
yi ge 'god pa	akṣaranyāsa	arrangement of letters
yi ge drug ma	ṣaḍakṣara	six-syllable mantra
yi ge bdun ma	saptakṣara	seven-syllable mantra of Cakrasaṃvara
yi ge med pa'i brda thabs		unwritten symbolic method
yi dam	iṣṭadevatā	meditational deity
yi dam kun 'dus		Gathering of All Meditational Deities
yi dvags	preta	anguished spirit

Tibetan	Sanskrit	English
yid ches	adhimukti	confidence (third of four modes of faith)
yid lus	manomayakāya	mental body
yin nges rnam bzhi		four definitive presences
yin lugs		real nature
yungs kar	sarṣapa	mustard
yul mkhyen gsum		three aspects of objective understanding
yul can lnga	pañcaviṣayin	five sensory consciousnesses
yul drug	ṣaḍviṣaya	six sense objects
ye grol		timeless liberation
ye shes	jñāna	pristine cognition
ye shes kyi sku	jñānakāya	body of pristine cognition
ye shes kyi rnal 'byor	jñānayoga	yoga of pristine cognition
ye shes kyi phyag rgya	jñānamudrā	seal of pristine cognition
ye shes kyi rig ma		consort embodying the awareness of pristine cognition
ye shes lnga	pañcajñāna	five pristine cognitions
ye shes sems dpa'	jñānasattva	being of pristine cognition
yer yer		quivering
yo 'bog		elm tree
yon tan	guṇa	enlightened attribute
yon tan brgyad	aṣṭaguṇa	eight attributes (of the eight elements)
g.yas rol	ardhaparyaṅkalalita	posture of right-sided royal ease
g.yung drung	svāstika	svastika motif
g.yon rol	rājalalita	posture of left-sided royal ease
ra mo shag		Solomon's seal
rak ta	rakta	blood, menses
rang 'gros		natural momentum

Tibetan	Sanskrit	English
rang 'gyu		natural momentum
rang ngo		intrinsic nature/face
rang stong		intrinsic emptiness
rang dvangs		naturally clear
rang dran rig		intrinsic awareness
rang mdangs		natural glow
rang babs		natural state
rang babs rnam gsum		three natural states (of body, speech, and mind)
rang byin rlabs	svādhiṣṭhāna	self-consecration
rang 'byor lnga	pañcasvasampat	five individual advantages
rang bzhin	svabhāva	intrinsic nature, inherent existence
rang bzhin gyi rigs		buddha nature, enlightened heritage that naturally abides
rang bzhin brgyad cu'i rnam rtog		conceptual thoughts that partake of eighty natural expressions
rang rtsal		natural energy
rang rig	svasaṃvedana	intrinsic awareness
rang rig pa'i dag pa		purity of intrinsic awareness (third of three purities)
rang so	svadhārā	natural position
rab tu rgyu ba	pracāra	intense movement
rab tu byung ba	pravrajyā	mendicant ordination
rab tu tsha ba	pratāpana	intense heating hell (seventh of eight hot hells)
ral gri lo ma'i nags	asipatravana	forest of swordlike leaves (fourth neighboring hell)
rig gdangs		radiant awareness
rig pa	vidyā, saṃvedana	awareness
rig pa rten du gnas pa		resting of awareness on its support

Tibetan	Sanskrit	English
rig pa rdo rje'i lu gu rgyud		adamantine chain of awareness
rig pa'i ngo sprod		introduction to awareness
rig pa'i rang so		natural state of awareness
rig ma		female consort embodying awareness
rig 'dzin	vidyādhara	awareness holder
rig 'dzin gyi sdom pa	vidyādharasamvara	vows of the awareness holders
rigs	kula	enlightened family
rigs lnga	pañcakula	five enlightened families
rigs lnga yum lnga		five lords of enlightened heritage and their five female consorts
rigs lnga'i ril 'dzin		encompassing of the five enlightened families
rigs gcig	ekakula	single enlightened family
rigs ldan gyi gzhi gzung		holding the family-endowed basis
rigs ma		female partner
rim gyis pa		gradual
rim sbyor		sequential phases of application
ril 'dzin	piṇḍagrāha	encompassing
re khā nag po	kālarekhā	black outline
reg bya	spraṣṭavya	tangible
rengs pa	stambhana	paralysis
ro	rasa	taste
ro mnyam	samarasa	common savor
ro ma	rasanā	right channel
ro myags kyi 'dam		swamp of putrefied corpses (second neighboring hell)
rlung	vāyu	wind
rlung khug pa		cycle of wind
rlung gi dkyil 'khor	vāyumaṇḍala	maṇḍala of wind

Tibetan	Sanskrit	English
rlung gi khams	vāyudhātu	wind element
rlung gi bdag po		mastery of the winds
rlung rgyu ba'i byed las		dynamic functions of the movement of wind
rlung gnas		location of winds
rlung bum pa can	kumbhaka	vase breathing
rlung sbyor		union of upper and lower winds
rlung sbyor lnga		five applications of the winds (of the elements)
rlung sbyor bdun		seven applications of wind
rlung sbyor bzhi ldan		fourfold application of wind
rlung gzhil ba		exhalation of breath
rlung sems		subtle energy and mind
rlung sems dbyer med		indivisibility of subtle energy and mind
rlung srog rtsol	prāṇayāma	winds of vital breath and exertion
lag khrid		firsthand guidance
lam	mārga	path
lam khyer dgu		nine things carried on the path
lam 'khyer		carrying of the nature of mind on the path (fourth of the four syllables of the Great Seal)
lam gyi bden pa	mārgasatya	truth of the path
lam gyi rim gnyis		two stages of the path
lam lnga	pañcamārga	five paths
lam rim	paṭhakrama	graduated path
lam lam		dazzling
las	karma	ritual, action, impact of past deeds
las kyi phyag rgya	karmamudrā	action seal, female mudra

TIBETAN	SANSKRIT	ENGLISH
las kyi rlung	karmavāyu	wind of past actions
las mkhan		acolyte
las mgon		ritual acolyte of Mahākāla
las rgya	karmamudrā	action seal, female mudra
las rgyu 'bras		causes and results of past actions
las snang gyi dngos po		entities that appear on the basis of past actions
las byed pa'i 'khor lo gnyis		two active cakras
las tshogs	karmagaṇa	liturgical/ritual feast offering
las bzhi	catuḥkarma	four rites
las gshin		acolyte of Yama
lus kyi 'khrul 'khor		physical exercise
lus kyi dbang po		sense faculty of the body
lus dkyil	kāyamaṇḍala	body maṇḍala
lus dkrugs 'khor		yogic exercise that stimulates the body
lus nyams		experience of the body
lus gnad		essential physical posture
lus rnam gzhag		structure of the subtle body
lus dben sku rdo rje'i rnal 'byor		yoga of the adamantine buddha body that entails the isolation of the ordinary body
lus zungs		physical constituent
lus shin tu sbyangs pa	prasrabdhakāya	extreme physical refinement
le lan	aparādha	criticism, offense
log gnon rnam pa lnga		five (subsidiary pith instructions) of suppression
long gtam		excessive chatter (fourth of four challenges)
longs spyod kyi rlabs		wave of perfect rapture (a yogic exercise)

Tibetan	Sanskrit	English
longs spyod sgrin gyi 'khor lo		throat cakra of perfect resource
longs spyod rdzogs pa'i sku	sambhogakāya	buddha body of perfect resource
sha lnga	pañcamāṃsa	five meats
sha chen	mahāmāṃsa	sacramental human flesh
sha ba'i ril ma		deer droppings
sha ma li'i sdong po		hill of iron śālmali trees (fifth neighboring hell)
sha gzugs		monastic boots
shig ge		open
shel sbub can		crystal tube
shes sgrib	jñeyāvaraṇa	obscuration of knowledge
shes bya rgyud rim		stage of continuum to be known
shes rab	prajñā	wisdom
shes rab kyi pha rol tu phyin pa	prajñāpāramitā	transcendent perfection of wisdom
shes rab ye shes kyi dbang	prajñājñānābhiṣeka	empowerment of discerning pristine cognition
gshang rlung		anal wind
bshad tshom		public exegesis
sa	bhūmi	bodhisattva level
sa bdag	bhūmipati	spirit lords of the soil
sa gnon	bhūmisparśamudrā	earth-subduing gesture
sa bon	bīja	seed syllable, generative fluid
sa bon dang bcas pa'i rim pa		stage conjoined with the seed syllables (first of four stages)

TIBETAN	SANSKRIT	ENGLISH
sa bon med pa'i sna tshogs rdo rje		(stage of) the crossed vajra in which the seed syllables are absent (second of four stages)
sa rlung		wind of the earth element
sangs rgyas	buddha	buddha
sangs rgyas kyi ma 'dres pa'i chos bco brgyad	aṣṭādaśāveṇikabuddhadharma	eighteen distinct attributes of the buddhas
sad 'byams		pervasion of wakefulness (second of four pervasions)
sad bzhi		four challenges
sa'i kham		earth element
sal sal		clear
sing sing		pulsating
sun byin stobs		power of eradication (fourth of five powers)
sum mdo		channel of triple intersection (below the navel)
seng ge rnam rol phyag rgya	siṃhaśayyā	posture of the lion's play
seng ge'i nyal stabs		posture of a reclining lion
sems	citta	mind
sems skyil	sattvaparyaṅka	bodhisattva posture
sems bskyed	cittotpāda	setting the mind on enlightenment
sems can gyi don byed		discipline of acting for the benefit of sentient beings
sems 'jog	cittasthāpanā	mental placement
sems nyams	naṣṭacitta	experience of the mind
sems nyid	cittatva	nature of mind
sems gnas cha		abiding aspect of mind
sems dpa'i skyil krung	sattvaparyaṅka	bodhisattva posture

note: this was missing in 1st pass

Tibetan	Sanskrit	English
sems dben thugs rdo rje'i rnal 'byor		yoga of adamantine buddha mind that entails the isolation of ordinary mind
sems 'dzin	cittadhāraṇa	mental focus
sems gzung man ngag dgu		nine pith instructions concerning mental focus/ retention of mind
ser sna	mātsarya	miserliness
so tham pa	aṭaṭa	hell of chattering teeth (fifth of eight cold hells)
so thar gyi sdom pa	prātimokṣasaṃvara	vows of individual liberation
so ma	soma	fresh
so sor sdud pa	pratyahara	composure (first branch of six-branch yoga)
so sor rang rig	pratisamvedana	particularizing intrinsic awareness
sor 'jog nyid		unmodified basic state
sor rtog pa'i ye shes	pratyavekṣaṇajñāna	pristine cognition of discernment
sor sdud	pratyāhāra	composure (six-branch yoga)
sor sdud kyi ting nge 'dzin	pratyāhārasamādhi	meditative stability of composure
sor mo	aṅguli	digit, finger width
srid pa'i dbang		empowerment of conditioned existence
srid zhi'i mtha' gnyis		two extremes of existence and quiescence
srung 'khor	rakṣācakra	protective circle
srung ba bzhi		four protections
srog	prāṇa, āyuḥ	vitality, vital breath, aspiration (sound)
srog gi rlung	prāṇavāyu	wind of vital breath
srog gi srung ba	prāṇarakṣā	protection of life breath
srog sngags		life-extracting mantra

Tibetan	Sanskrit	English
srog snying		vital heart mantra
srog thig		vitality essence
srog thur bsre ba		mingling vital breath with downward purgative wind
srog dang rtsol ba	prāṇayāma	breath control (third branch of six-branch yoga)
srog rtsol gi rlung	prāṇāyāma	breath control (i.e., control of the winds of vitality and exertion)
srog rtsol rlung gi rnal 'byor		union of the winds of vitality and exertion, yoga of breath control
srog 'dzin	prāṇāyāma	breath control
srog rlung	prāṇa	life-sustaining wind, wind of vitality, wind of life breath
srog shing	yaṣṭi	axis of vitality (central channel), life-giving axis
srod la dbang po bzhi la bsdu ba'i rnal 'byor		yoga that gathers the four powers at twilight (third of six phases of continuous yoga)
slob pa'i zung 'jug		coalescence (of the paths) of learning
slob ma	śiṣya	disciple
gsang chen rigs gcig		unique and most secret enlightened family
gsang rten		secret support
gsang spyod ri thub		capacity to dwell in mountains, engaged in secret practice (second of five capacities)
gsang ba nor bu'i thig le		vital essence of the genitals
gsang ba'i snyoms 'jug	guhyasamāpatti	secret equipoise
gsang ba'i rim pa		secret stage (fourth of four stages)

Tibetan	Sanskrit	English
gsang dbang	guhyābhiṣeka	secret empowerment
gsang rlung		secret wind
gsal ba	prakāśa	radiance
gsal ba'i sems	prakāśacitta	luminous mind
gsal le gnas cha		radiant and abiding aspects
gsung	vāk	buddha speech
gsung rdo rje	vāgvajra	adamantine reality of buddha speech
gsung mi zad pa	akṣayavāk	inexhaustible buddha speech
gsung rabs kyi sde bcu gnyis	dvādaśāṅgapravacana	twelve branches of the scriptures
gsum pa'i ye shes		pristine cognition of the third empowerment
gser 'gyur gyi rtsi	rasāyana	alchemical transformation of gold
bsam gtan	dhyāna	meditative concentration (second branch of six-branch yoga)
bsam gtan gyi yan lag dgu	navadhyānāṅga	nine branches of meditative concentration
bsen		attachment spirit
bslab pa	śikṣā	precept
lha so so'i dag pa		purity of an individual deity (second of three purities)
lhag mthong	vipaśyanā	higher insight
lhag pa'i lha	adhideva	preferred deity
lhan skyes	sahaja	coemergence (fourth of four pure appearances)
lhan skyes dga' ba	sahajānanda	coemergent delight
lhan skyes gnas lugs		innate abiding nature
lhan skyes ye shes	sahajajñāna	coemergent pristine cognition
lhan cig skyes sbyor		coemergent union

Tibetan	Sanskrit	English
lhan cig skyes gsum		threefold coemergence
lhan lhan		bright
lha'i rna'i mngon par shes pa	divyaśrotrābhijñā	extrasensory power of clairaudience
lha'i mig gi mngon par shes pa	divyacakṣurābhijñā	extrasensory power of divine clairvoyance
lhun grub	anābhoga	spontaneous presence
lhun grub rin po che'i sbubs		precious enclosure of spontaneous presence
lhug pa		loose
a chu zer ba	huhuva	hell of groans (third of eight cold hells)
a ru ra gser mdog	harītakī	golden myrobalan
utpal ltar gas pa	utpala	hell of lily-like cracks (sixth of eight cold hells)

Concordance of Personal Names

The following concordance gives precedence to the romanized Sanskrit and Tibetan phonetic spellings in the first column. The Wylie transliterations are given in the second column.

Phonetic	Wylie Transliteration
Aba Drakpa	A ba grags pa
Abhayadattaśrī	Mi 'jigs sbyin pa'i dpal
Abhayākaragupta	'Jigs med 'byung gnas sbas pa
Acala	Mi g.yo ba
Aja, king (of Śambhala)	rGyal dka'
Ajātaśatru	Ma skyes dgra
Ajita Maitreya	Ma pham byams pa
Ākāśagarbha	Nam mkha'i snying po
Akṣayamati	bLo gros mi zad pa
Akṣobhya	Mi bskyod pa/Mi 'khrugs pa
Alalavajra	Ngo mtshar rdo rje
Amitābha	'Od dpag med
Amitāyus	Tshe dpag med
Amitāyus and Hayagrīva Combined	Tshe rta sbrag ma
Amitāyus in the form Queen of Accomplishment	Tshe dpag med grub pa'i rgyal mo
Amoghasiddhi	Don yod grub pa
Amoghavajra the Elder	Don yod rdo rje che ba
Amoghavajra the Younger	Don yod rdo rje chung ba
Analé	A na le
Ānanda	Kun dga' bo

Phonetic	Wylie Transliteration
Ānandagupta	Ā nanda
Ānandakīrti	Kun dga' grags pa
Ānandavajra	Kun dga' rdo rje
Anaṅgavajra	Yan lag med rdo rje
Ananta (king of Śambhala)	mTha' yas
Anantavijaya (king of Śambhala)	mTha' yas rnam rgyal
Andharapa	A ndha ra
Aniruddha, king of Śambhala	Ma 'gags pa
Anyen Dampa Kunga Drak	A mye dam pa kun dga' grags
Apo	A pho
Arkakīrti (king of Śambhala)	Nyi ma grags
Ārya Vimuktisena	'Phags pa rnam grol sde
Āryadeva	'Phags pa'i lha
Asaṅga	Thogs med
Aseng of Nenying	gNas rnying pa a seng
Asthikhaṇḍaḍākinī	Ḍā ki rus rgyan can
Asu, the Newar	Bal po a su
Aśvaghoṣa	rTa dbyangs
Aśvottama	rTa mchog
Atiśa	[Jo bo rje] A ti sha
Avadhūtipā (also known as Maitrīpā)	A ba dhu ti pa
Avadhūtipā Namgyel Drakpa	A ba dhu ti pa rnam rgyal grags pa
Avalokita	sPyan ras gzigs
Avalokita Subduer of Beings	sPyan ras gzigs 'gro 'dul
Avalokiteśvara	sPyan ras gzigs dbang phyug
Ayi Sengé	A'i seng ge
Bagton Tsultrim Gyeltsen	Bag ston tshul khrims rgyal mtshan
Bagton Zhonu Gyeltsen	Bag ston gzhon nu rgyal mtshan
Bagton Zhonu Tsultrim	Bag ston gzhon nu tshul khrims
Banrik Gyelkhampa	'Ban rigs rgyal khams pa
Barawa Gyeltsen Pelzang	'Ba' ra ba rgyal mtshan dpal bzang
Bardingpa Namka Gyeltsen	Bar sdings pa nam mkha' rgyal mtshan

Phonetic	Wylie Transliteration
Bareg Lotsāwa Sonam Gyeltsen	Ba reg lo tsā ba bsod nams rgyal mtshan
Bareg Tonkyab	Ba reg ston skyabs
Bari Lotsāwa Rinchen Drak	Ba ri lo tsā ba rin chen grags
Be Drum	dBas grum
Bengarwa Jampel Zangpo	Ban sgar ba 'jam dpal bzang po
Beton Zhikpo	sBas ston zhig po
Bhadra (king of Śambhala)	bZang po
Bhadrapāda	bZang po zhabs
Bhairava	'Jigs byed
Bhaṭṭāraka Vimuktisena	rJe btsun rnam grol sde
Bhaṭṭārikā Tārā	rJe btsun sgrol ma
Bhavyabodhi	sKal ldan byang chub
Bhṛṅgapadminī	[Lha mo] Bung ba'i pad ma
Bhuṣaṇa	Bhu ṣa ṇa
Bimbisāra, king	gZugs can snying po
Black Yamāri	gZhed nag
Black-cloaked Mahākāla	Ber nag can
Bodhiśrī Ngok Jangchub Peldrub	Bodhi shri rngog byang chub dpal grub
Bodong Paṇchen Jigdrel Sangwa Jin	Bo dong paṇ chen 'jigs bral gsang ba sbyin
Bodong Rinchen Tsemo	Bo dong rin chen rtse mo
Bodong Tsondru Dorjé	Bo dong brtson 'grus rdo rje
Brahmā	Tshangs pa
Brahmāṇī	Tshangs ma
Buddhadatta	Sangs rgyas byin
Buddhaguhya	Sangs rgyas gsang ba
Buddhajñānapāda	Sangs rgyas ye shes zhabs
Buddhalocanā	Sangs rgyas spyan ma
Buddhaśrī Sangyé Pel	Sangs rgyas dpal
Buton Rinchen Drub	Bu ston rin chen grub
Cakrasaṃvara	'Khor lo sdom pa
Cakrasaṃvara in Coemergent Union	bDe mchog lhan cig skyes sbyor

Phonetic	Wylie Transliteration
Cakrasaṃvara in the form Mañjuvajra	bDe mchog 'jam pa'i rdo rje
Cakrasaṃvara in the form Saṃvarodaya	bDe mchog sdom 'byung
Cakrasaṃvara Who Abandons Bewilderment	bDe mchog 'khrul spong
Cakrī, king of Śambhala	'Khor lo can
Caṇḍālī	Tsa ṇḍā lī
Caṇḍikā, protector	Tsantri ka
Candradhvaja/Jangsem Dawa Gyeltsen	Byang sems zla ba rgyal mtshan
Candrakīrti	Zla ba grags pa
Caryāmati, bodhisattva	sPyod pa'i blo gros
Caryāvajra (also known as Kṛṣṇacārin)	sPyod pa'i rdo rje
Caurayaśa (also known as Kālacakrapāda the Elder)	Tsau ra ya sha
Caurī	Tsau rī
Chagenpa	Cha gan pa
Chak Lotsāwa Chojé Pel	Chag lo tsā ba chos rje dpal
Chak Lotsāwa Drachompa	Chag lo tsā ba dgra bcom pa
Chak Lotsāwa Rinchen Chogyel	Chag lo tsā ba rin chen chos rgyal
Chakzampa Tulku Nyima Chopel	lCags zam pa sprul sku nyi ma chos 'phel
Chammo Yeshé Chok	lCam mo ye shes mchog
Changlungpa Zhonu Chodrub	sByang lung pa gzhon nu mchog grub
Changlungpa Zhonu Lodro	sByang lung pa gzhon nu blo gros
Chapa Chokyi Sengé	Phyva pa chos kyi seng ge
Chegom Dzogpaché Khakyong	lCe sgom rdzogs pa che kha skyong
Chegom Sherab Dorjé	lCe sgom shes rab rdo rje
Chekhawa Yeshé Dorjé	'Chad kha ba ye shes rdo rje
Chel Amogha	dPyal a mo gha
Chel Lotsāwa Chokyi Zangpo	dPyal lo tsā ba chos kyi bzang po
Chel Lotsāwa Kunga Dorjé	dPyal lo tsā ba kun dga' rdo rje
Chel Lotsāwa Kunga Drakpa	dPyal lo tsā ba kun dga' grags pa
Chen Nga Chokyi Gyelpo	sPyan snga chos kyi rgyal po
Chen Nga Drakpa Jungné	sPyan snga grags pa 'byung gnas

Phonetic	Wylie Transliteration
Chen Nga Nyernyipa Chokyi Gyelpo	sPyan snga nyer gnyis pa chos kyi rgyal po
Chen Nga Sonam Gyeltsenpa	sPyan snga bsod nams rgyal mtshan pa
Chen Ngawa Rinchen Den	sPyan snga ba rin chen ldan
Chen Ngawa Tsultrim Bar	sPyan snga ba tshul khrims 'bar
Chim Tsondru Gyeltsen	mChims brtson 'grus rgyal mtshan
Chim Tsondru Sengé	mChims brtson 'grus seng ge
Chimchen Namka Drak	mChims nam mkha' grags
Chimé Drub	'Chi med grub
Chimton Lobzang Drak	mChims ston blo bzang grags
Chiwo Lhepa	sPyi bo lhas pa
Cho Gyelwa	Chos rgyal ba
Chodrak of Dingri	Ding ri ba chos grags
Chodrak Zangpo	Chos grags bzang po
Chodrub Sengé	Chos grub seng ge
Chogowa Chopel Sherab	Chos sgo ba chos dpal shes rab
Chogyel Pakpa Lodro Gyeltsen	Chos rgyal 'phags pa blo gros rgyal mtshan
Chogyel Sherab Zangpo	Chos rgyal shes rab bzang po
Chojé Gewa Gyeltsen	Chos rje dge ba rgyal mtshan
Chojé Khewang Rinchen Chowang	Chos rje mkhas dbang rin chen chos dbang
Chojé Namka Tenpa	Chos rje nam mkha' bstan pa
Chojé Peldenpa of Jampeling	Byams gling chos rje dpal ldan pa
Chojé Rongchung	Chos rje rong chung
Chojé Rongpo	Chos rje rong po
Chojé Zung	Chos rje gzungs
Chokhor Gangpa	Chos 'khor sgang pa
Choklé Namgyel	Phyogs las rnam rgyal
Chokro Chokyi Gyeltsen	Cog ro chos kyi rgyal mtshan
Choku Lhawang Drakpa	Chos sku lha dbang grags pa
Choku Ozer	Chos sku 'od zer
Choku Śākya Rinchen	Chos sku shākya rin chen

Phonetic	Wylie Transliteration
Chokyi Gyeltsen	Chos kyi rgyal mtshan
Chokyi Wangchuk	Chos kyi dbang phyug
Chokyi Yungdrung	Chos kyi g.yung drung
Cholungpa Sonam Rinchen	Chos lung pa bsod nams rin chen
Chomden Rikpei Reldri	bCom ldan rig pa'i ral gri
Chopel Zangpo	Chos 'phel bzang po
Chorin	Chos rin
Choying Wangchuk	Chos dbyings dbang phyug
Chugompa	Chu sgom pa
Churak Lodro Gyeltsen	Chu rag blo gros rgyal mtshan
Cintāmaṇicakra Tārā	sGrol ma yid bzhin 'khor lo
Cintivilavavajra	Tsinti bi lāsya rdo rje
Cittavajra [Akṣobhyavajra]	Sems kyi rdo rje
Copper knife–wielding Mahākāla	Zangs gri can
Dakchen Dorjé Chang Lodro Gyeltsen	bDag chen rdo rje 'chang blo gros rgyal mtshan
Dakchen Drakpa Lodro	bDag chen grags pa blo gros
Dakchen Jamyang Namka Gyeltsen	bDag chen 'jam dbyangs nam mkha' rgyal mtshan
Dakchen Ngagi Wangchuk	bDag chen ngag gi dbang phyug
Dakpo Gomtsul Nyingpo	Dvags po sgom tshul snying po
Dakpo Lharjé Gampopa (also known as Sonam Rinchen)	Dvags po lha rje sgam po pa
Ḍamarupā	Ḍa ma ru pa
Dampa Sangyé	Dam pa sangs rgyas
Daṃṣṭrasena	mChe ba'i sde
Dānaśīla	sByin pa'i tshul khrims
Dark-yellow Jambhala	Dzam ser nag
Darma Sherab	Dar ma shes rab
Darpaṇa Acārya	Da rba na
Delek Gyeltsenpa	bDe legs rgyal mtshan pa
Densatel Khenchen Sherab Dorjé	gDan sa thel mkhan chen shes rab rdo rje

Phonetic	Wylie Transliteration
Devaḍākinī	De ba ḍā ki ni
Devākaracandra	De va ā ka ra tsandra
Devapūrṇamati	De ba pū rṇa
Dewa Pel	bDe ba dpal
Dhamapa	Dha ma pa
Dhārikpa	Dā rik pa
Dharmakīrti of Sumatra	gSer gling pa chos kyi grags pa
Dharmarakṣita	Dha rma ra kṣi ta
Dharmavaṃ (ḍākinī)	Dha rma vaṃ
Dharmaviṣā (ḍākinī)	Dha rma vi ṣa
Dhārmika	Chos kyi sde
Dhātvīśvarī	Chos dbyings ma
Dhītika	Dhi ti ka
Dhūmāṅgārīśrīdevī	Dud sol lha mo
Dīpaṃkarabhadra (also known as Atiśa)	Mar me mdzad bzang po
Dodé Bum	mDo sde 'bum
Dodé Rabjam	mDo sde rab 'byams
Dolpa Zangtalwa	Dol pa zang thal ba
Dolpopa Sherab Gyeltsen	Dol po pa shes rab rgyal mtshan
Ḍombipā	Ḍo mbi pa
Ḍombī (deity)	g.Yung mo
Dondarwa [Tingngedzin Dorjé]	lDong dar ba [ting nge 'dzin rdo rje]
Dondrub Pel	Don grub dpal
Dongtri Dulwadzin	gDong khri 'dul ba 'dzin
Donyo Drubpa	Don yod grub pa
Donyo Pel	Don yod dpal
Dorjé Chang Lhawang Drakpa	rDo rje 'chang lha dbang grags pa
Dorjé Rinchen	rDo rje rin chen
Dra Gandenpa	Grva dga' ldan pa
Drab Gompa Konchok Sungwa	Grab dkon mchog srung ba
Drak Burwa	Brag 'bur ba
Drak Marwa	Brag dmar ba
Drakar Sonam Rinchen	Brag dkar bsod nams rin chen

Phonetic	Wylie Transliteration
Drakarwa	Brag dkar ba
Drakchen [Donmoripa]	Grags chen [don mo ri pa]
Drakmar Kunga Tsepel	Brag dmar kun dga' tshe 'phel
Drakpa	Grags pa
Drakpa Gyeltsen, lotsāwa	Lo tsā ba grags pa rgyal mtshan
Drakpa Pelden Dondrub	Grags pa dpal ldan don grub
Drakpa Peljor	Grags pa dpal 'byor
Drakpa Sherab	Grags pa shes rab
Drakpa Tsultrim	Grags pa tshul khrims
Drakpa Zhonu	Grags pa gzhon nu
Drakpukpa Sonam Pelwa	Brag phug pa bsod nams dpal ba
Drakrom	Brag rom
Drakteng Yonten Tsultrim	Brag steng yon tan tshul khrims
Drakton Donchok	Grags ston don mchog
Drakton Pelden Dondrub	Grags ston dpal ldan don grub
Draktopa Choku Lhawang Drakpa	Brag stod pa chos sku lha dbang grags pa
Dramen Chikpa Sherab Zangpo	Gra sman gcig pa shes rab bzang po
Drampa Kunga Zangpo	Bram pa kun dga' bzang po
Drangti Darma Nyingpo	Brang ti dar ma snying po
Drapupa Chenpo	Gra phu pa chen po
Dremarwa Sangyé Yeshé	Bred mar ba sangs rgyas ye shes
Drenton Sherab Zangpo	Dran ston shes rab bzang po
Drenton Tadrel	Dran ston mtha' bral
Drigom Melton Yerpawa	'Bri sgom mal ston yer pa ba
Drigung IV Chen Nga Drakpa Jungné	'Bri gung gdan rabs bzhi pa spyan snga grags pa 'byung gnas
Drigungpa I Jigten Sumgon	'Bri gung pa 'jig rten gsum mgon
Drigungpa III On Sonam Drakpa	'Bri gung gdan rabs gsum pa dbon bsod nams grags pa
Drigungpa IX Chunyipa Dorjé Rinchen	'Bri gung gdan rabs dgu pa bcu gnyis pa rdo rje rin chen
Drigungpa V Telo Dorjé Drak	'Bri gung gdan rabs lnga pa te lo rdo rje grags

Phonetic	Wylie Transliteration
Drigungpa VI Tok Khawa Rinchen Sengé	'Bri gung gdan rabs drug pa thog kha ba rin chen seng ge
Drigungpa VII Tsamché Drakpa Sonam	'Bri gung gdan rabs bdun pa mtshams bcad grags pa bsod nams
Drigungpa X Nyergyepa Dorjé Gyelpo	'Bri gung gdan rabs bcu pa nyer brgyad pa rdo rje rgyal po
Drinchen Lobzang Tutob	Drin chen blo bzang mthu stobs
Drinchen Sengé Zangpo	Drin chen seng ge bzang po
Dro	'Bro
Drogon Chogyel Namka Pelzang	'Gro mgon chos rgyal nam mkha' dpal bzang
Drogon Dharaśrī	'Gro mgon dha ra shrī
Drogon Pagmodrupa Dorjé Gyelpo	'Gro mgon phag mo gru pa rdo rje rgyal po
Drogon Pelden Yeshé	'Gro mgon dpal ldan ye shes
Drogon Sangyé Tonpa	'Gro mgon sangs rgyas ston pa
Drogon Tonpa	'Gro mgon ston pa
Drokmi Lotsāwa Śākya Yeshé	'Brog mi lo tsā ba shākya ye shes
Drolmei Gonpo Tāranātha	Grol ma'i mgon po tā ra nā tha
Drolungpa Lodro Jungné	Gro lung pa blo gros 'byung gnas
Drom Namka Rinchen	'Brom nam mkha' rin chen
Drom Wangchuk Drakpa	'Brom dbang phyug grags pa
Drom Zhonu Lodro	'Brom gzhon nu blo gros
Dromoché Dutsi Drak	Gro mo che bdud rtsi grags
Dromton Gyelwei Jungné	'Brom ston rgyal ba'i 'byung gnas
Droton Kunga Gyeltsen	Gro ston kun dga' rgyal mtshan
Droton Namlatsek	sGro ston gnam la brtsegs
Drotonpa Dutsi Drak	Gro ston pa bdud rtsi grags
Dru Chok Yeshé	Gru mcog ye shes
Drubchen Kunlowa	Grub chen kun blo ba
[Drubchen] Tsembupa	Tshem bu pa
Drubpa Sengé	Grub pa seng ge
Drubpa Sherab (monastic preceptor of Nartang)	Grub pa shes rab

Phonetic	Wylie Transliteration
Drubtob Hūṃ Barwa	Grub thob hūṃ 'bar ba
Drubtob Lhabar	Grub thob lha 'bar
Drubtob Ngodrub	Grub thob dngos grub
Drukchen II Gyelwang Kunga Peljor	'Brug chen gnyis pa rgyal dbang kun dga' dpal 'byor
Drukchen Ngawang Chokyi Gyelpo	'Brug chen ngag dbang chos kyi rgyal po
Drung Peldenpa	Drung dpal ldan pa
Drungchen Norzang	Drung chen nor bzang
Drungtsun Pelden Gyelpo	Drung btsun dpal ldan rgyal po
Drungtsun Zangpo Tenpa	Drung btsun bzang po bstan pa
Drushulwa Chorab Drakpa	Gru shul ba chos rab grags pa
Duldzin Chewa Ratnapa	'Dul 'dzin che ba ratna pa
Dulkarwa	'Dul dkar ba
Dulwadzinpa Ngagi Wangpo	'Dul ba 'dzin pa ngag gi dbang po
Dulwadzinpa Ngawang Gyeltsen	'Dul ba 'dzin pa ngag dbang rgyal mtshan
Dung-gyu Rinchen Gyeltsen	gDung rgyud rin chen rgyal mtshan
Dungtsé Nyimalung	mDung rtse nyi ma lung
Dungtso Repa	Dung tsho ras pa
Durjayacandra	Mi thub zla ba
Dutsi Drak	bDud rtsi grags
Dzalongkar Lama Drubwang Kunzang Wangpo	rDza slong dkar bla ma grub dbang kun bzang dbang po
Dzilungpa Ozer Drakpa	rDzi lung pa 'od zer grags pa
Dzimchen Gyeltsen Pelzang	'Dzim chen rgyal mtshan dpal bzang
Dzinpa Rinchen Sherab	'Dzin pa rin chen shes rab
Dzongripa Konchok Zangpo	rDzong ri pa dkon mchog bzang po
Eighty white-robed guardians	dKar po brgyad cu
Eighty-four accomplished masters	Grub thob brgyad bcu rtsa bzhi
Ekajaṭī	E ka dzā ṭi, dpal ldan ma
Eleven-faced Avalokita	sPyan ras gzigs zhal bcu gcig
Four-armed Mahākāla	mGon po phyag bzhi pa

Phonetic	Wylie Transliteration
Four-armed Mahākāla in the blazing lion-faced form	Seng zhal 'bar ma
Four-armed Mahākāla in the form of a solitary hero	Phyag bzhi pa dpa' rkyang
Four-armed Mahākāla in the form that has perfected the eleven aspects of the vase empowerment and the four empowerments	Bum dbang bcu gcig dbang bzhi rdzogs
Four-armed Mahākāla in the lion-faced form	Seng gdong ma
Four-armed Mahākāla in the red silken form	Dar dmar ma
Gadenpa Kunga Sonam	dGa' ldan pa kun dga' bsod nams
Gadenpa Tashipel	dGa' ldan pa bkra shis dpal
Galung Jangchub Pel	sGa lung byang chub dpal
Gampopa Dakpo Lharjé	sGam po pa dvags po lha rje
Gaṇapati	Tshogs bdag
Gaṅgabhadra	Ghaṅga bha dra
Gangpa Rinchen Pelzangpo	Gangs pa rin chen dpal bzang po
Gangtropa Drakpa Gyeltsen	Gangs khrod pa grags pa rgyal mtshan
Gangtropa Gyelsé Konchok Bang (also known as Sempa Zhonu Gyelchok)	Gangs khrod pa rgyal sras dkon mchog 'bangs
Gar Lotsāwa Chokyi Zangpo	mGar lo tsā ba chos kyi bzang po
Gar Repa	mGar ras pa
Garbharipā	Garbha ri pa
Garjong Gonpo Gyeltsen	mGar ljongs mgon po rgyal mtshan
Gartsa Yonten Yungdrung	mGar tsa yon tan g.yung drung
Gaurī	Gau rī
Gayādhara	Ga ya dha ra
Gedingpa Choku Ozer	dGe sdings pa chos sku 'od zer
Gelong Adrakpa	dGe slong a grags pa
Gendun Gyatso	dGe 'dun rgya mtsho
Genmo Lhepa Jangchub Pel	rGan mo lhas pa byang chub dpal

Phonetic	Wylie Transliteration
Geshé Jayulwa Zhonu O	dGe bshes bya yul ba gzhon nu 'od
Geshé Langri Tangpa	dGe bshes lang ri thang pa
Geshé Neuzurpa Yeshé Bar	dGe bshes sne'u zur pa ye shes 'bar
Geshé Sharawa	dGe bshes sha ra ba
Geshé Shawo Gangpa	dGe bshes shva bo sgang pa
Geshé Zhangpa Chokyi Lama	dGe bshes zhang pa chos kyi bla ma
Ghaṇṭāpāda	Dril bu pa
Ghasmarī	Gha sma rī
Girpuwa Ngejung Dar	'Gir phu ba nges byung dar
Go Lotsāwa Khukpa Lhetsé	'Gos lo tsā ba khug pa lhas btsas
Gomiśra	Sa 'dres pa
Gonpawa of Kashmir	Kha che dgon pa ba
Gonpo Zhonu	mGon po gzhon nu
Gorampa Sonam Sengé	Go rams pa bsod nams seng ge
Gori	Go ri
Goton Cholo	mGo ston chos blo
Gotsangpa Gonpo Dorjé	rGod tshangs pa mgon po rdo rje
Gugé Paṇchen Drakpa Gyeltsen	Gu ge paṇ chen grags pa rgyal mtshan
Gugé Paṇchen Sonam Lhundrub	Gu ge paṇ chen bsod nams lhun grub
Guhyapati Vajrapāṇi	gSang bdag phyag na rdo rje
Guhyasamāja (Secret Assembly)	gSang ba 'dus pa
Guhyavijaya	Guhya rnam par rgyal ba
Guṇamitra	Gu ṇa mi tra
Gundharipā	Gundha ri pa
Guru Chokyi Wangchuk (also known as Guru Chowang)	Gu ru chos kyi dbang phyug
Gya Marwa	rGya dmar ba
Gyagom Lekpei Gyeltsen	rGya sgom legs pa'i rgyal mtshan
Gyagom Riwa Zhikpo	rGya sgom ri ba zhig po
Gyakar Tangbewa Pakpa Kyab	rGya dkar thang sbe ba 'phags pa skyabs
Gyalton Jangwangpa	rGyal ston byang dbang pa
Gyalton Wangchuk Wangyal	rGyal ston dbang phyug dbang rgyal
Gyamawa Lodro Gyeltsen	rGya ma ba blo gros rgyal mtshan

Phonetic	Wylie Transliteration
Gyamawa Yonten-o	rGya ma ba yon tan 'od
Gyanak Cherbu Sangyé Rabton	rGya nag gcer bu sangs rgyas rab ston
Gyangro Darma Gon	rGyang ro dar ma mgon
Gyangro Jangchub Bum	rGyang ro byang chub 'bum
Gyangro Serdingpa Zhonu O	rGyang ro gser sdings gzhon nu 'od
Gyaton Chagriwa	rGya ston lcags ri ba
Gyawo Khenchen Sonam Drak	rGya bo mkhan chen bsod nams grags
Gyelsé Kunga Zangpo	rGyal sras kun dga' bzang po
Gyelsé Lobzang Peljor	rGyal sras blo bzang dpal 'byor
Gyelsé Pomdrakpa Sonam Dorjé	rGyal sras spom brag pa bsod nams rdo rje
Gyelsé Sherab Bum	rGyal sras shes rab 'bum
Gyelsé[pa] Tokmé Zangpo	rGyal sras pa thogs med bzang po
Gyelshé, sthavira	gNas brtan rgyal she
Gyeltangpa Samten Ozer	rGyal thang pa bsod nams 'od zer
Gyeltsa Lungmang Chokyi Wangchuk	rGyal tsha lung mang chos kyi dbang phyug
Gyeltsa Ramo	rGyal tsha ra mo
Gyeltsab Kunga Wangchuk	rGyal tshab kun dga' dbang phyug
Gyelwa Bum	rGyal ba 'bum
Gyelwa Rinchen Gon	rGyal ba rin chen mgon
Gyelwa Tené	rGyal ba te ne
Gyelwa Yeshé	rGyal ba ye shes
Gyelwang Kunga Peljor	rGyal dbang kun dga' dpal 'byor
Gyergom Zhikpo	Gyer sgom zhig po
Gyijo Dawa Ozer	Gyi jo zla ba 'od zer
Hadu Karpo, the Newar	Ha du dkar po
Hanuman	rLung gi bu
Hari (king of Śambhala)	Seng ge
Haribhadra	Seng ge bzang po
Harisiddhi	Ha ri siddhi
Hayagrīva utterly secret and wrathful	rTa mgrin yang gsang khros pa

Phonetic	Wylie Transliteration
Hayagrīva with the combined assemblage of the five arrogant spirits	rTa mgrin dregs pa lnga dril
Heruka	He ru ka
Hevajra	dGes mdzad rdo rje he ru ka, kye rdo rje
Hevajra with an assemblage of thirteen weapon-wielding deities	Kye rdor mtshon cha can lha bcu gsum ma
Hor Kabzhipa Sengé Gyeltsen	Hor bka' bzhi pa seng ge rgyal mtshan
Hūṃ Gyel Lhundrub Rinchen	Hūṃ rgyal lhun grub rin chen
Hūṃchen Namka Neljor	Hūṃ chen nam mkha' rnal 'byor
Indra	[Lha] dBang
Indrabhūti	Indra bhū ti
Innate Cakrasaṃvara	bDe mchog lhan skyes
Intermediate Indrabhūti	Indra bhū ti bar pa
Īśvara	dBang phyug
Jadrel Ritro Rechenpa	Bya bral ri khrod ras chen pa
Jakchen Jampa Pel	'Jags chen byams pa dpal
Jālandharapāda (also known as Jālandharipā)	Dza landha ri pa, 'bar 'dzin
Jambhala	Dzam ba la
Jamgön Kongtrul Lodrö Tayé	'Jam mgon kong sprul blo gros mtha' yas
Jamkya Namka Pelden	'Jam skya nam mkha' dpal ldan
Jampa Konchok Pelzangpo	Byams pa dkon mchog dpal bzang po
Jamsarwa Sherab Ozer	'Jam gsar ba shes rab 'od zer
Jamyang Darma Ozer	'Jam dbyangs dar ma 'od zer
Jamyang Drakpa Gyeltsen	'Jam dbyangs grags pa rgyal mtshan
Jamyang Khyentsé Wangpo	'Jam dbyangs mkhyen brtse dbang po
Jamyang Konchok Zangpo	'Jam dbyangs dkon mchog bzang po
Jamyang Kunga Sengé	'Jam dbyangs kun dga' seng ge
Jamyang Lodro Sengé	'Jam dbyangs blo gros seng ge
Jamyang Sangyé Rinchen	'Jam dbyangs sangs rgyas rin chen
Jamyang Sherab Gyatso	'Jam dbyangs shes rab rgya mtsho

Phonetic	Wylie Transliteration
Jang Pukpa Kunlek	Byang phug pa kun legs
Jangchub Gyatso	Byang chub rgya mtsho
Jangchub Gyeltsen	Byang chub rgyal mtshan
Jangchub Tsemo	Byang chub rtse mo
Jangchub Yeshé	Byang chub ye shes
Jangchub Zangpo	Byang chub bzang po
Jangpa Sherab Bar	Byang pa shes rab 'bar
Jangsem Dawa Gyeltsen	Byang sems zla ba rgyal mtshan
Jangsem Gyelwa Yeshé	Byang sems rgyal ba ye shes
Jangsem Jadeng	Byang sems bya sdeng
Jangsem Jinpa Zangpo	Byang sems sbyin pa bzang po
Jangsem Konchok Gyeltsen	Byang sems dkon mchog rgyal mtshan
Jangsem Kunga	Byang sems kun dga'
Jangsem Radengpa	Byang sems rva greng pa
Jangsem Sonam Gyeltsen	Byang sems bsod nams rgyal mtshan
Jarokpa (protector deity)	Bya rog pa
Javaripā	Dza ba ri pa
Jayaśrījñāna	bSod snyoms [rgyal ba dpal gyi ye shes]
Jayulwa Zhonu O	Bya yul ba gzhon nu 'od
Je Dawa Gonpo	rJe zla ba mgon po
Jetsun Tsewa Chenpo (also known as Sachen Kunga Nyingpo)	rJe btsun brtse ba chen po
Jinadatta (also known as Sonyompa)	rGyal ba byin
Jinasāgara	rGyal ba rgya mtsho
Jīvabodhi	'Tsho ba'i byang chub
Jñānaḍākinī	Ye shes mkha' 'gro
Jñānagarbha	Ye shes snying po
Jñānanātha	Ye shes mgon po
Jñānaśrībhadra	Ye shes dpal bzang po
Jñānaśrībodhi	Ye shes dpal gyi byang chub
Jobum-ma, ḍākinī	Ḍā ki jo 'bum ma
Joden Ngaripa Zhang Joton	Jo gdan mnga' ris pa
Jonshing	lJon shing

Phonetic	Wylie Transliteration
José Khampa	Jo sras khams pa
José Namka-o	Jo sras nam mkha' 'od
José Zhangton Chokyi Lama	Jo sras zhang ston chos kyi bla ma
Joton Dzakhol Drubchen	Jo ston rdza khol grub chen
Jotsowa Pakpa Ozer	Jo gtso ba 'phags pa 'od zer
Jotsunpa	Jo btsun pa
Jowo Atiśa	Jo bo a ti sha
Jowo Rinpoche (image)	Jo bo rin po che
Kabzhipa Drakpa Zhonu	bKa' bzhi pa grags pa gzhon nu
Kachu Jangchub Pel	bKa' bcu byang chub dpal
Kachupa Zhonu Sengé	bKa' bcu pa gzhon nu seng ge
Kadalīmañjarī, yogini	Chu shing snye ma can
Kākamukha, raven-faced Mahākāla	Bya rog gdong can
Kālacakra	Dus kyi 'khor lo
Kālacakrapāda	Dus 'khor zhabs
Kālarātrī	Dus mtshan ma
Kam Yeshé Gyeltsen	Kam ye shes rgyal mtshan
Kamala, paṇḍita	Paṇ chen ka ma la
Kamalaśīla	Ka ma la shī la
Kambalapāda	Lva ba zhabs
Kandarayoginī	Ri sul gyi rnal 'byor ma
Kangyurwa Śākya Gyeltsen	bKa' 'gyur ba śākya rgyal mtshan
Karma Trinlepa	Karma phrin las pa
Karmapa I Dusum Khyenpa	Karma pa sku phreng dang po dus gsum mkhyen pa
Karmapa II Karma Pakshi	Karma pa sku phreng gnyis pa karma pak shi
Karmapa III Rangjung Dorjé	Karma pa sku phreng gsum pa rang byung rdo rje
Karmapa IV Rolpei Dorjé	Karma pa sku phreng bzhi pa rol pa'i rdo rje
Karmapa V Dezhin Shekpa	Karma pa sku phreng lnga pa de bzhin gshegs pa

Phonetic	Wylie Transliteration
Karmapa VI Tongwa Donden	Karma pa sku phreng drug pa mthong ba don ldan
Karmapa VII Chodrak Gyatso	Karma pa sku phreng bdun pa chos grags rgya mtsho
Karmavajra	Las kyi rdo rje
Karṇa	Karṇa
Karṇaripā	Karṇa ri pa
Kāśyapa	'Od srung
Katok Rigdzin Tsewang Norbu	Kaḥ thog rig 'dzin tshe dbang nor bu
Ketu (comet Enke)	Dus me
Khampa Aseng	Khams pa a seng
Khampa Dorjépel	Khams pa rdo rje dpal
Khampa Drakpa Gyeltsen	Khams pa grags pa rgyal mtshan
Khampa Jampel	Khams pa 'jam dpal
Khangsarwa Namka Ozer	Khang gsar ba nam mkha' 'od zer
Khanitra	Tog tse pa
Kharak Gompa	Kha rag sgom pa
Kharamukha Cakrasaṃvara	bDe mchog bong zhal can, (coiled) bong gdong 'khyil ba
Khasarpaṇi (Avalokiteśvara)	Kha sarpa ṇi
Khedrub Shangton	mKhas grub shangs ston
Khedrub Zhonu Drub	mKhas grub gzhon nu grub
Khenchen Jangchubsem	mKhan chen byang chub sems
Khenchen Ratna Jamyang Rinchen Gyeltsen	mKhan chen ratna 'jam dbyangs rin chen rgyal mtshan
Khenchen Rinchen Gyatso Neten Dorjedzin	mKhan chen rin chen rgya mtsho gnas brtan rdo rje 'dzin
Khenchen Sengé Pel	mKhan chen seng ge dpal
Khenchen Tashi Namgyel	mKhan chen bkra shis rnam rgyal
Khepa Sang-o	mKhas pa sangs 'od
Khepa Tsangnak Repa	mKhas pa gtsang nag ras pa
Khepa Yonten Tri	mKhas pa yon tan khri
Khetsun Ziji Gyeltsen	mKhas btsun gzi brjid rgyal mtshan
Khewang Lotsāwa Rinchen Zangpo	mKhas dbang lo tsā ba rin chen bzang po

Phonetic	Wylie Transliteration
Kholpo Dartochen (protector deity)	Khol po dar thod can
Khon Konchok Gyelpo	'Khon dkon mchog rgyal po
Khon Kyichuwa Dralha Bar	'Khon skyi chu ba dgra lha 'bar
Khonton Tukjé Rinchen	'Khon ston thugs rje rin chen
Khorewa Okyi Gyeltsen	Kho re ba 'od kyi rgyal mtshan
Khu Netso	Khu ne tso
Khugom Chokyi Sengé	Khu sgom chos kyi seng ge
Khuton Tsondru Yungdrung	Khu ston sangs rgyas g.yung drung
Khyenrab Chogdrub	mKhyen rab mchog grub
Khyentsé Tokden	mKhyen brtse rtogs ldan
Khyungpo Lhepa Zhonu Sonam	Khyung po lhas pa gzhon nu bsod nams
Khyungpo Neljor	Khyung po rnal 'byor
Khyungpo Tsultrim Gonpo	Khyung po tshul khrims mgon po
Khyungtsang Yeshé Lama	Khyung tshang ye shes bla ma
Knife-wielding Mahākāla with an assemblage of five deities	Gri gug lha lnga
Kodrakpa Sonam Gyeltsen	Ko brag pa bsod nams rgyal mtshan
Kokalī/Kokalilā, ḍākinī	mKha' 'gro kho ka li/kho ka li la
Konchok Dorjé	dKon mchog rdo rje
Konchok Gyeltsen	dKon mchog rgyal mtshan
Konchok Zangpo	dKon mchog bzang po
Kṛṣṇacārin	Nag po spyod pa, spyod 'chang dbang po, spyod nor
Kṛṣṇapā (also known as Kṛṣṇacārin), mahāsiddha	Grub chen nag po pa
Kṛṣṇocita	U tsi ṭa [nag po]
Kṣetrapāla, protector deity	Zhing skyong
Kṣitigarbha	Sa yi snying po
Kukkurāja	Kukku rā dza
Kulikā	Rigs ldan ma
Kundar Rema	Kun dar ras ma
Kunden Repa	Kun ldan ras pa
Kunga Chogdrub	Kun dga' mchog grub

Phonetic	Wylie Transliteration
Kunga Dondrub	Kun dga' don grub
Kunga Drolchok [Losel Gyatsodé]	Kun dga' grol mchog blo gsal rgya mtsho'i sde
Kunga Gyeltsen	Kun dga' rgyal mtshan
Kunga Lekgyal, scribe	Kun dga' legs rgyal
Kunga Nyingpo	Kun dga' snying po
Kunga Rinchen	Kun dga' rin chen
Kunga Tashi	Kun dga' bkra shis
Kunga Zangpo	Kun dga' bzang po
Kunglung Sangyé Pelzangpo	sKung lung sangs rgyas dpal bzang po
Kunīka, king	rGyal po ku nī ka
Kunkhyen Donyo Pelwa	Kun mkhyen don yod dpal ba
Kunpang Chokyi Nyima	Kun spangs chos kyi nyi ma
Kunpang Namka Pelyang	Kun spangs nam mkha' dpal dbyangs
Kunpang Tukjé Tsondru	Kun spangs thugs rje brtson 'grus
Kunzang Chojor	Kun bzang chos 'byor
Kunzang Choying Rangdrol	Kun bzang chos dbyings rang grol
Kunzang Wangpo	Kun bzang dbang po
Kūrmapādā	Rus sbal zhabs
Kurukullā	Ku ru kulle, rigs byed ma
Kusulu the Elder	Ku su lu che ba
Kusulu the Younger	Ku su lu chung ba
Kuyalwa Rinchen Gonpo	sKu yal ba rin chen mgon po
Kuzhang Khyenrab (also known as Rinchen Khyenrab Chogdrub)	sKu zhang mkhyen rab
Kyagom Lekpei Gyeltsen	rKya sgom legs pa'i rgyal mtshan
Kyapchewa	sKyabs che ba
Kyapjé Tokden Trewo Chokyi Gyatso	sKyabs rje rtogs ldan tre bo chos kyi rgya mtsho
Kyebu Sherab	sKyes bu shes rab
Kyebu Yeshé Dorjé	sKyes bu ye shes rdo rje
Kyebu Yonten Ga	sKyes bu yon tan dga'
Kyechok Monlampa	sKyes mchog smon lam pa

Phonetic	Wylie Transliteration
Kyemé Dopa Chokyi Sherab Jodenpa	sKye med jo gdan pa
Kyergangpa Chokyi Sengé	sKyer sgang pa chos kyi seng ge
Kyergom Zhikpo [Tsultrim Sengé]	sKyer sgom zhig po [tshul khrims seng ge]
Kyipukpa Tsultrim Dargyé	sKyid phug pa tshul khrims dar rgyas
Kyoton Monlam Tsultrim	sKyo ston smon lam tshul khrims
Kyoton Ojung	sKyo ston 'od 'byung
Kyoton Sonam Lama	sKyo ston bsod nams bla ma
Lachen Lodro Gyeltsen	bLa chen blo gros rgyal mtshan
Lachen Sonam Zangpo	bLa chen bsod nams bzang po
Lakṣmī	dPal mo
Lakṣmīkarā	Legs smin
Lalitavajra	sKegs rdor
Lama Dampa Sonam Gyeltsen	bLa ma dam pa bsod nams rgyal mtshan
Lama Shang Khyungpo Neljor	bLa ma shangs khyung po rnal 'byor
Lama Tokdenpa	bLa ma rtogs ldan pa
Lama Zhang Tselpa Tsondru Drak	bLa ma zhang tshal pa brtson 'grus grags
Langri Tangpa Dorjé Sengé	Lang ri thang pa rdo rje seng ge
Langtangpa Chen Nga Kunga Dorjé	Lang thang pa spyan snga kun dga' rdo rje
Lapchiwa Dokton Namka Gyeltsen	La phyi ba mdog ston nam mkha' rgyal mtshan
Lawapa (also known as Kambalapāda)	Lva ba pa, va ba pa
Lechungwa Sonam Pelzang	sLe chung ba bsod nams dpal bzang
Lekden Pelchen	Legs ldan dpal chen
Lentsangtsa Nyima Cham	gLan gtsang tsha nyi ma lcam
Lha Rinchen Wangyal	Lha rin chen dbang rgyal
Lhachok Sengé	Lha mchog seng ge
Lhading Jangchub Bum	Lha sdings byang chub 'bum
Lhading Kunga Gyatso	Lha sdings kun dga' rgya mtsho
Lhapa	Lha pa
Lharjé Gewa Bum	Lha rje dge ba 'bum

Phonetic	Wylie Transliteration
Lhaton Ozer Lama	Lha ston 'od zer bla ma
Lhatsun Gonserwa	Lha btsun dgon gser ba
Lhawang Drakpa	Lha dbang grags pa
Lhazik Repa	Lha gzigs ras pa
Lhodrak Jangchub Pelzangpo	Lho brag byang chub dpal bzang po
Lhopa Kunkhyen Rinchen Pel	Lho pa kun mkhyen rin chen dpal
Lhundrub Dechen Rabjampa	Lhun grub bde chen rab 'byams pa
Lhundrub Dorjé	Lhun grub rdo rje
Ling Repa Pema Dorjé	gLing ras pa padma rdo rje
Lobzang Tutob	bLo bzang mthu stobs
Lochen Rinchen Zangpo	Lo chen rin chen bzang po
Lodro Gyatso	bLo gros rgya mtsho
Lodro Gyeltsen	bLo gros rgyal mtshan
Lodro Pelzangpo	bLo gros dpal bzang po
Lodro Zangpo	bLo gros bzang po
Lokeśvara	'Jig rten dbang phyug
Lokya Lotsāwa Sherab Tsekpa	kLog skya lo tsā ba shes rab brtsegs pa
Longchen Rabjam	kLong chen rab 'byams
Lopon Chodrak	sLob dpon chos grags
Lopon Penyulwa Jangchub Nangwa	sLob dpon 'phan yul ba byang chub snang ba
Lopon Tontsulwa	sLob dpon ston tshul ba
Lord Khyenrab of Zhalu (also known as Rinchen Chogdrub Pelzang)	Zha lu mkhyen rab rje
Lord of Mantra (protector)	sNgags bdag
Lord of the Charnel Ground (protector)	Dur khrod bdag po
Lord-protector of the Aural Lineage	sNyan brgyud mgon po
Lords of the three enlightened families	Rigs gsum mgon po
Lorepa Darma Wangchuk Tsondru	Lo ras pa dar ma dbang phyug brtson 'grus
Losal Tenkyong of Zhalu	Zha lu blo gsal bstan skyong
Loton Chodrak	Lo ston chos grags
Lowo Khenchen Sonam Lhundrub	gLo bo mkhan chen bsod nams lhun grub

Phonetic	Wylie Transliteration
Lowo Lotsāwa Sangyé Sé	gLo bo lo tsā ba sangs rgyas sras
Lowo Lotsāwa Sherab Rinchen	gLo bo lo tsā ba shes rab rin chen
Luipā	Lu yi pa
Lungpuwa	Lung phu ba
Ma Chokyi Sherab	rMa chos kyi shes rab
Maben Chobar	rMa ban chos 'bar
Machik Angjo	Ma gcig ang co
Machik Labkyi Dronma	Ma gcig lab kyi sgron ma
Mahābala (king of Śambhala)	sTobs po che
Mahābodhi (the Newar)	Ma hā bo dhi
Mahācakra (also known as Vajrapāṇi)	'Khor chen
Mahākāla	Nag po chen po
Mahākāla holding a red club	Beng dmar
Mahākāla in the form Aghora	A gho ra
Mahākāla in the form Jñānanātha	Ye shes mgon po
Mahākāla in the form Maning	Ma ning
Mahākāla in the form of Lekden and his two brothers	Legs ldan gsum
Mahākāla with one thousand arms and one thousand eyes	Phyag stong spyan stong
Mahākāla in the tiger-riding form	sTag gzhon
Mahākāla Trakṣad	mGon po tra kṣad
Mahākāla Trakṣad with the face of a dog	Khyi zhal can
Mahākāla Trakṣad with the face of a wild yak	'Brong zhal ma
Mahākāla with four conjoined aspects	mGon po bzhi sbrag
Mahākāla with Śrīdevī and four retainers	Lha mo 'khor bzhi
Mahāmaitreya	'Byams pa chen po
Mahāvajradhara	rDo rje 'chang chen po
Maheśvara, king of Śambhala	dBang phyug chen po
Mahīpāla, king of Śambhala	Sa skyong
Maitreya[nātha]	'Byams pa [mgon po]

Phonetic	Wylie Transliteration
Maitrīpā	Mai tri pa
Mal Lotsāwa Lodro Drak	Mal lo tsā ba blo gros grags
Malton Yerpawa	Mal ston yer pa ba
Māmakī	Mā ma kī
Mangkhar Lotsāwa Chokden Lekpei Lodro	Mang mkhar lo tsā ba mchog ldan legs pa'i blo gros
Mangkharwa Dawa Gonpo	Mang mkhar ba zla ba mgon po
Mangkharwa Rabsel Dawa Gonpo	Mang mkhar ba rab gsal zla ba mgon po
Mangrawa Sengé Gyeltsen	Mang ra ba seng ge rgyal mtshan
Maṇidvīpa Sukhavajra	Nor bu gling pa bde ba'i do rje
Maṇiwa Drakpa Sonam	Ma ṇi ba grags pa bsod nams
Maṇiwa Lekpei Gyeltsen	Ma ṇi ba legs pa'i rgyal mtshan
Mañjughoṣa	'Jam pa'i dbyangs
Mañjughoṣa in the form Arapacana	'Jam dbyangs a ra pa tsa na
Mañjughoṣa Vādīsiṃha	'Jam dbyangs smra ba'i seng ge
Mañjuśrīmitra	'Jam dpal bshes gnyen
Mañjuvajra	'Jam pa'i rdo rje
Mar Chokyi Gyelpo	dMar chos kyi rgyal po
Mar Chokyi Gyeltsen	dMar chos kyi rgyal mtshan
Mar Sherab Dorjé	dMar shes rab rdo rje
Mar Tsondru Sengé	dMar brtson 'grus seng ge
Mar Tubpa Sherab	dMar thub pa shes rab
Mardo Chokyi Wangchuk	Mar do chos kyi dbang phyug
Mardo Lotsāwa	Mar do lo tsā ba
Marpa Dopa	Mar pa do pa
Marpa Lotsāwa Chokyi Lodro	Mar pa lo tsā ba chos kyi blo gros
Marton Chokyi Gyeltsen	dMar ston chos kyi rgyal mtshan
Marton Gyeltsen Ozer	dMar ston rgyal mtshan 'od zer
Marton Samgyelwa	dMar ston bsam rgyal ba
Mati Paṇchen Lodro Gyeltsen	Ma ti paṇ chen blo gros rgyal mtshan
Matiratna	Ma ti ratna
Menlung Guru Sonam Pel	sMan lung gu ru bsod nams dpal
Menlung Kunkhyen	sMan lung kun mkhyen

Phonetic	Wylie Transliteration
Menlungpa Mikyo Dorjé	sMan lung pa mi bskyod rdo rje
Menpa Gomchen Tsultrim Zangpo	sMan pa sgom chen tshul khrims bzang po
Milarepa	Mi la ras pa
Minyak Lotsāwa Mondrub Sherab	Mi nyag lo tsā ba smon grub shes rab
Mitrayogin, the younger Kusulu	Mi tra dzo gi
Mokchokpa Rinchen Tsondru	rMog lcog pa rin chen brtson 'grus
Mondzong Rechen Dawa Gyeltsen	Mon rdzong ras chen zla ba rgyal mtshan
Monlam Tsultrim	sMon lam tshul khrims
Mu Konchok Gyeltsen	Mus dkon mchog rgyal mtshan
Muchen Sangyé Rinchen	Mus chen sangs rgyas rin chen
Mule-faced Śrīdevī	dPal ldan lha mo zhal 'drel ma
Mumenpa Dutsi Charchen	Mus sman pa bdud rtsi char chen
Munīndra (also known as Śākyamuni)	Thub dbang
Nāgabodhi	Nā ga bo dhi
Nāgārjuna	kLu sgrub
Nāgayoginī	kLu yi rnal 'byor ma
Nagtso Lotsāwa Tsultrim Gyelwa	Nag 'tsho lo tsā ba tshul khrims rgyal ba
Nairātmyā	bDag med ma
Nālendrapā (also known as Kālacakrapāda the Younger)	Nā lendra pa
Nam Khawupa Chokyi Gyeltsen	gNam kha bu pa chos kyi rgyal mtshan
Namdrol Sengé Pelzangpo	rNam grol seng ge dpal bzang po
Namgyel Drakpa	rNam rgyal grags pa
Namka Chokyong	Nam mkha' chos skyong
Namka Gyeltsen	Nam mkha' rgyal mtshan
Namka Ozer	Nam mkha' 'od zer
Namka Pelzang	Nam mkha' dpal bzang
Namka Sengé	Nam mkha' seng ge
Namza Drakpuk Sonam Pelwa	Na bza' brag phug bsod nams dpal ba
Nanda	dGa' bo
Nandikeśvarī (consort of Mahākāla)	dGa' byed dbang phyug ma

Phonetic	Wylie Transliteration
Narasiṃha (king of Śambhala)	Mi'i seng ge
Nārāyaṇa	Sred med kyi bu
Nāropā [Jñānasiddhi]	Nā ro pa [Ye shes grub pa]
Nāyakapāda	'Dren mdzad zhabs
Neljor Choyung	rNal 'byor chos g.yung
Neljorpa Kyapsé	rNal 'byor skyabs sras
Nesar Zhonu Drub	gNas gsar gzhon nu grub
Net of Magical Emanation	sGyu 'phrul 'dra ba
Neten Sampenpa Jangsem Jinpa	gNas brtan bsam 'phan pa byang sems sbyin pa
Newu Repa	sNe'u ras pa
Nezur Yeshé Bar	sNe zur ye shes 'bar
Ngadak Nyangrel Nyima Ozer	mNga' bdag nyang ral nyi ma 'od zer
Ngapa Gyagar	Ngang pa rgya gar
Ngari Sherab Gyeltsen	mNga' ris shes rab rgyal mtshan
Ngari Ulekpa	mNga' ris u legs pa
Ngaripa Selnying	mNga' ris pa gsal snying
Ngawang Chogyel	Ngag dbang chos rgyal
Ngawang Drakpa Pelzangpo	Ngag dbang grags pa dpal bzang po
Ngawang Nampar Gyelwa	Ngag dbang rnam par rgyal ba
Ngawang Tulku [of Taklung]	Ngag dbang sprul sku
Ngenlampa Tsul Pak	Ngan lam pa tshul 'phags
Ngodrub, accomplished master	Grub thob dngos grub
Ngok Choku Dorjé	rNgog chos sku rdo rje
Ngok Dodé	rNgog mdo sde
Ngok Drakpa Peljor	rNgog grags pa dpal 'byor
Ngok Jangchub Peldrub	rNgog byang chub dpal grub
Ngok Konchok Pel	rNgog dkon mchog dpal
Ngok Kunga Dorjé	rNgog kun dga' rdo rje
Ngok Lekpei Sherab	rNgog legs pa'i shes rab
Ngok Loden Sherab	rNgog blo ldan shes rab
Ngok Lodro Pelzangpo	rNgog blo gros dpal bzang po
Ngok Lotsāwa Loden Sherab	rNgog lo tsā ba blo ldan shes rab

Phonetic	Wylie Transliteration
Ngok Nyima Sengé	rNgog nyi ma seng ge
Ngok Pakpa Lha	rNgog 'phags pa lha
Ngok Tashi Peldrub	rNgog bkra shis dpal grub
Ngok Tsa Choku Dorjé	rNgog tsha chos sku rdo rje
Ngok Yeshé Sengé	rNgog ye shes seng ge
Ngok Zhedang Dorjé	rNgog zhe sdang rdo rje
Ngokton Choku Dorjé	rNgog ston chos sku rdo rje
Ngokton Jangchub Pel	rNgog ston byang chub dpal
Ngokton the Great	rNgog ston chen po
Ngor Khenchen Sangyé Rinchen	Ngor mkhan chen sangs rgyas rin chen
Ngorchen Kunga Zangpo	Ngor chen kun dga' bzang po
Ngorchen Lhachok Sengé	Ngor chen lha mchog seng ge
Nigumā	Ni gu ma
Niḥsaṅgapāda	Gos bral zhabs
Nirdehaḍākinī	Lus med mkha' 'gro
Nīvaraṇaviṣkambhin	sGrib pa rnam sel
Norbu Rinchen	Nor bu rin chen
Nub Khulungpa Yonten Gyatso	gNubs khu lung pa yon tan rgya mtsho
Nubchen Sangyé Yeshé	gNubs chen sangs rgyas ye shes
Nubpa Rigdzin Drak	Nub pa rig 'dzin grags
Nubton Gyelyé	gNubs ston rgyal ye
Nur Chopak Gyeltsen	sNur chos 'phags rgyal mtshan
Nyag-gom Marpo	gNyags sgom dmar po
Nyagton Nyingpo Gyeltsen	gNyags ston snying po rgyal mtshan
Nyak Lotsāwa Yeshé Zhonu	gNyags lo tsā ba ye shes gzhon nu, gnyags dzñāna ku mā ra
Nyakpu Sengé Pelwa	gNyags phu seng ge dpal ba
Nyan Lotsāwa Darma Drak	gNyan lo tsā ba dar ma grags
Nyangton Konchok Dorjé	Nyang ston dkon mchog rdo rje
Nyangton Yeshé Jungné	Nyang ston ye shes 'byung gnas
Nya-on Kunga Pel	Nya dbon kun dga' dpal
Nyelwa Delekpa	gNyal ba bde legs pa
Nyemdo Kunga Dondrub	Nye mdo kun dga' don grub

Phonetic	Wylie Transliteration
Nyemdo Sonam Pel	Nye mdo bsod nams dpal
Nyemo Gyagom (also known as Nyipuwa Gyergom Zhikpo)	sNye mo rgya sgom
Nyen Repa Gendun Bum	gNyan ras pa sge 'dun 'bum
Nyenchenpa Sonam Tenpa	Nyan chen pa bsod nams bstan pa
Nyenton Chogyel	gNyan ston chos rgyal
Nyenton Chokyi Sherab	gNyan ston chos kyi shes rab
Nyenton Osung	gNyan ston 'od srungs
Nyenton Rigongpa Chokyi Sherab	gNyan ston ri gong pa chos kyi shes rab
Nyenton Rinchen Ngodrub	gNyan ston rin chen dngos grub
Nyenton Rinchen Tenpa	gNyan ston rin chen bstan pa
Nyima Chopelwa	Nyi ma chos 'phel ba
Nyima Gyeltsen	Nyi ma rgyal mtshan
Nyima Sengé	Nyi ma seng ge
Nyingpo Lodro Tayé	sNying po blo gros mtha' yas
Nyingpo Tayepa (also known as Nyingpo Lodro Tayé)	sNying po mtha' yas pa
Nyipuwa Gyergom Zhikpo	sNyi phu ba gyer sgom zhig po
Nyo/Nyopa	gNyos/gnyos pa
Nyonak Gyeltsen	gNyos nag rgyal mtshan
Nyukla Paṇchen Ngawang Drakpa	sMyug la paṇ chen
Olgom Janglingpa	'Ol sgom byang gling pa
Olkha Lama	'Ol kha bla ma
Omniscient Dong (also known as Lochen Rinchen Zangpo)	gDong thams cad mkhyen pa
On Dzalongkar Lama Kunzang Chojor	dBon rdza slong dkar bla ma kun bzang chos 'byor
On Repa Darma Sengé	dBon ras pa dar ma seng ge
On Sonam Gyelwa Choyang	dBon rgyal ba mchog dbyangs
One thousand buddhas of the Auspicious Aeon	bsKal pa bzang po'i sangs rgya stong rtsa
Onpo Chozang	dBon po chos bzang
Onpo Sonam Dar	dBon po bsod nams dar

Phonetic	Wylie Transliteration
Onsé Cholek	dBon sras chos legs
Orgyanpa Rinchen Pel	O rgyan pa rin chen dpal
Ozer Gyatso	'Od zer rgya mtsho
Padampa Sangyé	Pha dam pa sangs rgyas
Padmākara	Padma 'byung gnas
Padmapāṇi	Padma pā ṇi
Padmavajra	Padma rdo rje
Pagmodrupa Dorjé Gyelpo	Phag mo gru pa rdo rje rgyal po
Pago Jamyang Chojé	Pha rgod 'jam dbyang chos rje
Pak Chok Norzang	'Phags mchog nor bzang
Pak Chok Sonam Dar	'Phags mchog bsod nams dar
Pakpa Lodro Rinchen	'Phags pa blo gros rin chen
Pakton Samten Wang	Phag ston bsam gtan dbang
Paṇchen [Amogha] Donyo Drubpa	Paṇ chen don yod grub pa
Paṇchen Donyo Sengé	Paṇ chen don yod seng ge
Paṇchen Drakmar Kunga Tsepel	Paṇ chen brag dmar kun dga' tshe 'phel
Pāṇḍaravāsinī	Gos dkar mo
Pandeva	Pan de ba
Paṇḍita Sergyi Bumpa	Paṇḍita gser gyi bum pa
Pang Lotsāwa Lodro Tenpa	dPang lo tsā ba blo gros brtan pa
Pangton Drubpa Sherab	dPang ston grub pa shes rab
Pañjaranātha	mGon po gur
Pañjaranātha in a form with [four] replicated faces	Gur gdong gnyan can
Pañjaranātha in the form Brother and Sister	Gur lcam dral
Pañjaranātha in the outer, inner, and secret aspects of kīla	Gur phur bu phyi nang gsang ba
Pañjaranātha with faces focusing on the rites of service, attainment, practical application, and brahmanical	Zhal mgon bsnyen sgrub las sbyar [sbags chog] bram ze'i rig gtad
Pañjaranātha with a military banner	Gur ru mtshon

Phonetic	Wylie Transliteration
Pañjaranātha with a retinue comprising the six black brahmin butcher spirits	Bram nag shan pa drug skor
Parpuwa Lodro Sengé	Par phu ba blo gros seng ge
Patsab Gompa Tsultrim Bar	Pa tshab sgom pa tshul khrims 'bar
Patsab Nyima Drak	Pa tshab nyi ma grags
Pelchen Ga Lotsāwa Zhonu Pel	dPal chen rgva lo tsā ba gzhon nu dpal
Pelchen Kunlhunpa	dPal chen kun lhun pa
Pelden Dondrub	dPal ldan don grub
Pelden Dorjé	dPal ldan rdo rje
Pelden Gyelwa	dPal ldan rgyal ba
Pelden Lama Dampa Sonam Gyeltsen	dPal ldan bla ma dam pa bsod nams rgyal mtshan
Pelden Lekpa	dPal ldan legs pa
Pelden Tsultrim	dPal ldan tshul khrims
Pelden Zangpo	dPal ldan bzang po
Pendhapā	Pen dha pa
Penyawa Ratnabhadra, the Newar	Pe nya ba rin chen bzang po
Phamtingwa Abhayakīrti, the Newar	Pham mthing ba ['jigs med grags pa]
Phamtingwa Vāgīśvara, the Newar	Pham mthing ba [ngag gi dbang phyug]
Pokya Rinchen Sengéwa	sPos skya rin chen seng ge ba
Pomdrakpa Sonam Dorjé	sPom brag pa bsod nams rdo rje
Potowa Rinchen Sel	Po to ba rin chen gsal
Prajñāguhya	Shes rab sbas pa
Prajñākaramati	Shes rab 'byung gnas blo gros
Prajñāpāramitā	Shes rab kyi pha rol tu phyin ma
Prakāśaśīlā, nun	gSal ba'i tshul khrims
Pratibhākuṭa, deity	sPobs pa rtsegs pa
Puchung Rinchen Gyeltsen	Phu chung rin chen rgyal tshan
Pukkasī	Pukkasī
Puṇḍarīka (king of Śambhala)	Padma dkar po
Puṇyaśrī	Puṇya śrī
Purang Lochung of Kashmir	Pu hrang lo chung
Pūrṇavardhana	Gang spel

Phonetic	Wylie Transliteration
Putra with his brother and sister (protectors)	Putra ming sring gsum
Ra Lotsāwa	Rva lo tsā ba
Ra Yonten Pelzangpo	Rva yon tan dpal bzang po
Rabjor Sengé	Rab 'byor seng ge
Rabkar Jangzangwa	Rab dkar byang bzang ba
Rabsel Dawa Gon	Rab gsal zla ba mgon
Radengpa Śākya Sonam	Rva dengs pa śākya bsod nams
Rāhu	Rā hu, gza'
Rāhu-faced five gying spirits	Gying lnga gza' gdong
Rāhula (mahāsiddha)	Rā hu la
Raktapāṇi (king of Śambhala)	Phyag dmar
Ratnabhadra (elder Kusulu)	Rin chen bzang po
Ratnaguru	Rin chen bla ma
Ratnākara	Rin chen 'byung gnas
Ratnakīrti	Rin chen grags
Ratnasambhava	Ratna sambhava, rin chen 'byung gnas
Ratnavajra (also known as Younger Indrabhūti)	Rin chen rdo rje
Ratnavajriṇī, ḍākinī (also known as Jonang Jetsunma Kunga Trinlé Pelwangmo)	Rin chen rdo rje ma
Raton Yonten Pelzangpo	Rva ston yon tan dpal bzang po
Ratri Zangbarwa	Rva khri bzang 'bar ba
Rechen Lhundrubpa	Ras chen lhun grub pa
Rechen Namka Gyeltsen	Ras chen nam mkha' rgyal mtshan
Rechen Peljor Zangpo	Ras chen dpal 'byor bzang po
Rechen Ronyompa	Ras chen ro snyoms pa
Rechungpa Dorjé Drak	Ras chung pa rdo rje grags
Red Yamāri	bZhed dmar
Red-faced Mahākāla	mGon po zhal dmar can
Rematī	dMag zor ma
Remdawa Zhonu Lodro	Re mda' ba gzhon nu blo gros

Phonetic	Wylie Transliteration
Rigdzin Tsewang Norbu	Rig 'dzin tshe dbang nor bu
Rikgom Bepei Neljor	Rig sgom sbas pa'i rnal 'byor
Rinchen (son of Tsami)	Rin chen
Rinchen Chodar	Rin chen chos dar
Rinchen Chung	Rin chen chung
Rinchen Dorjé	Rin chen rdo rje
Rinchen Dorjéma Ratnavajriṇī	Rin chen rdo rje ma
Rinchen Gangpa Śākya Shenyen	Rin chen sgang pa śākya bshes gnyen
Rinchen Gyatso	Rin chen rgya mtsho
Rinchen Gyeltsen	Rin chen rgyal mtshan
Rinchen Khyenrab Chogdrub	Rin chen mkhyen rab mchog grub
Rinchen Mangto Losal Tenkyong	Rin chen mang thos blo gsal bstan skyong
Rinchen Ozer	Rin chen 'od zer
Rinchen Zangpo	Rin chen bzang po
Rinchen Zhonu	Rin chen gzhon nu
Ripa Zhonu Rinchen	Ri pa gzhon nu rin chen
Ritro Wangchuk	Ri khrod dbang phyug
Riwo Gangpa	Ri bo sgang pa
Rock-faced Yakṣa	gNod sbyin beg gdong
Rogton	Rog ston
Rok	Rog
Rok Tselha Gangpa	Rog rtse lha gang pa
Rongchung Sherab Pelden	Rong chung shes rab dpal ldan
Rongpa Ga Lotsāwa Namgyel Dorjé	Rong pa rgva lo tsā ba rnam rgyal rdo rje
Rongpa Sherab Gyeltsen	Rong pa shes rab rgyal mtshan
Rongpa Sherab Sengé	Rong pa shes rab seng ge
Rongtö Gungru	Rong stod gung ru
Rongton Sheja Kunrik	Rong ston shes bya kun rig
Rudra	Drag po
Rūpavajrā	gZugs rdo rje ma
Rutsam Gomchen	Ru mtshams sgom chen

Phonetic	Wylie Transliteration
Śabarī, deity	Śa va rī
Śabaripā Wangchuk, mahāsiddha	Ri khrod dbang phyug, śa va ri pa
Sabzang Mati Paṇchen Lodro Gyeltsen	Sa bzang ma ti paṇ chen blo gros rgyal mtshan
Sabzang Pakpa Zhonu Lodro	Sa bzang 'phags pa gzhon nu blo gros
Sachen Kunga Nyingpo	Sa chen kun dga' snying po
Ṣaḍānana	gDong drug
Sadāprarudita	rTag tu ngu
Sahajā, transcendent lady	bCom ldan 'das ma lhan cig skyes ma
Sajjana	Sadzdza na
Śakra	rGya byin
Śākya Bumpa	Śākya 'bum pa
Śākya Chokden	Śākya mchog ldan
Śākya Ozer	Śākya 'od zer
Sakya Paṇḍita Kunga Gyeltsen	Sa skya paṇḍita kun dga' rgyal mtshan
Śākya Pelzang	Śākya dpal bzang
Śākya Sengé	Śākya seng ge
Śākya Sonam	Śākya bsod nams
Śākya Yarpel	Śākya yar 'phel
Śākya Yeshé	Śākya ye shes
Śākya Zangpo	Śākya bzang po
Śākyamitra	Śākya bshes gnyen
Śākyamuni Buddha	Śākya thub pa
Śākyaśrī of Kashmir	Śākya śrī, kha che paṇ chen
Samādhibhadra	Ting nge 'dzin bzang po
Samādhivajra (also known as Dondarwa)	Ting 'dzin rdo rje
Samantabhadra, buddha body of reality	Kun tu bzang po
Samayavajra	Dam tshig rdo rje
Samdingpa Zhonu Drub	bSam dings pa gzhon nu grub
Samten Ozer	bSam gtan 'od zer
Samudravijaya, king of Śambhala	rGya mtsho rnam rgyal
Śāṇavāsika	Sha na'i gos can
Sangdak Drubchen	gSang bdag grub chen

Phonetic	Wylie Transliteration
Saṅgha, the brahmin	Bram ze saṅ gha
Sangyé Gelong	Sangs rgyas dge slong
Sangyé Gompa Sengé Kyab	Sangs rgyas sgom pa seng ge skyabs
Sangyé Nyingpo	Sangs rgyas snying po
Sangyé On[po] Drakpapel	Sangs rgyas dbon [po] grags pa dpal
Sangyé Pel Buddhaśrī	Sangs rgyas dpal, buddha śrī
Sangyé Pelzangpo	Sangs rgyas dpal bzang po
Sangyé Rechen Peldrak	Sangs rgyas ras chen dpal grags
Sangyé Repa	Sangs rgyas ras pa
Sangyé Rinchen	Sangs rgyas rin chen
Sangyé Tonpa Tsondru Sengé	Sangs rgyas ston pa brtson 'grus seng ge
Sangyé Yarjon	Sangs rgyas yar byon
Sangyé Zangpo	Sangs rgyas bzang po
Sangyé Zhonu	Sangs rgyas gzhon nu
Śāntarakṣita	Zhi ba'i 'tsho
Śāntipa	Śānti pa
Saraha	Sa ra ha
Saroruha	Sa ro ru ha, mtsho skyes
Saroruhavajra	mTsho skyes rdo rje
Śaśiprabha, king of Śambhala	Zla 'od
Sechilbupa Chokyi Gyeltsen	Se spyil bu pa chos kyi rgyal mtshan
Secret Assembly (Guhyasamāja)	gSang ba 'dus pa
Self-Arisen Queen	Rang byung rgyal mo
Semo Chewa Namka Gyeltsen	Se mo che ba nam mkha' rgyal mtshan
Semodru, of U	Se mo 'bru ba
Sempa Ché Sonam Sengé	Sems dpa' che bsod nams seng ge
Sempa Sogyel	Sems dpa' bsod rgyal
Sendhepa	Se ndhe pa
Sengé Gyelpo	Seng ge rgyal po
Sengé Gyeltsen	Seng ge rgyal mtshan
Sengé Sherab	Seng ge shes rab
Serdingpa Zhonu O	gSer dings pa gzhon nu 'od

Phonetic	Wylie Transliteration
Serkhang Tengpa Kunga Gyeltsen	gSer khang steng pa kun dga' rgyal mtshan
Seton Chenpo	Se ston chen po
Seton Kunrik	Se ston kun rig
Setsun Wangchuk Zhonu	Se btsun dbang phyug gzhon nu
Shangkarwa Rinchen Gyeltsen	Shangs dkar ba rin chen rgyal mtshan
Shangpa Rechen Sonam Chokgyur	Shangs pa ras chen bsod nams mchog 'gyur
Shangpa Rikpei Dorjé	Shangs pa rig pa'i rdo rje
Sharawa Yonten Drak	Sha ra ba yon tan grags
Sharwa (also known as Sharchen Yeshé Gyeltsen)	Shar ba/shar chen ye shes rgyal mtshan
Shawo Gangpa	Sha bo sgang pa
Shengom Rokpo	gShen sgom rog po
Sherab Bumpa	Shes rab 'bum pa
Sherab Dorjé	Shes rab rdo rje
Sherab Pel	Shes rab dpal
Sherab Rinchen	Shes rab rin chen
Sherab Yonten	Shes rab yon tan
Shik Chawa	Shig 'cha' ba
Shing Lopa	Shing lo pa
Shong Lotsāwa Dorjé Gyeltsen	Shong lo tsā ba rdo rje rgyal mtshan
Siddhirājñī	Grub pa'i rgyal mo
Siddhivajra	dNgos grub rdo rje
Śīlacandra	Tshul khrims zla ba
Siṃhabodhi	Seng ge byang chub
Siṃhavaktrā (ḍākinī)	Seng ge gdong ma
Śiṣyavajra	Slob pa'i rdo rje
Six-armed Mahākāla	Ṣaḍbhujamahākāla, mgon po phyag drug pa
Six-armed Mahākāla in the liver-colored form	[mGon po] mchin kha
Six-armed Mahākāla in the pollution-dispelling form	[mGon po] sgrib sel

PHONETIC	WYLIE TRANSLITERATION
Six-armed Mahākāla, dispeller of all obstacles	Phyag drug bar chad kun sel
Six-armed Mahākāla, inseparable from the Teacher	Bla ma mgon po dbyer med
Sky-clad Goddess (deity)	Lha mo nam mkha'i gos can ma
Sochung Gedunbar	So chung dge 'dun 'bar
Sok-on [Kabzhipa] Rigpei Reldri	Sog dbon [bka' bzhi pa] rig pa'i ral gri
Somadatta (king of Śambhala)	Zla bas byin
Somanātha (of Kashmir)	Zla ba'i mgon po
Sonam Drakpa	bSod nams grags pa
Sonam Drubpa	bSod nams grub pa
Sonam Gyelchok	bSod nams rgyal mchog
Sonam Gyeltsen	bSod nams rgyal mtshan
Sonam Gyelwa Choyang	bSod nams rgyal ba mchog dbyangs
Sonam Ozer	bSod nams 'od zer
Sonam Peljor (official of Zhalu)	Zha lu drung bsod nams dpal 'byor
Sonam Sengé	bSod nams seng ge
Sonam Tenpa	bSod nams bstan pa
Sonam Tsemo	bSod nams rtse mo
Sonam Wangchuk	bSod nams dbang phyug
Songtsen Gampo	Srong btsan sgam po
Śraddhākara[varman]	Dad pa'i 'byung gnas [go cha]
Śrībhadra	dPal bzang
Śrībrahmā	dPal tshangs pa
Śrīdevī	dPal ldan lha mo, dpal lha, lha mo
Śrīdhara	dPal 'dzin
Śrīpāla (king of Śambhala)	dPal skyong
Śrīsukha	dPal bde ba
Sthiramati	brTan pa'i blo gros
Subhadra	Nor bzang
Subhadra (king of Śambhala)	Shin tu bzang po
Sucandra (king of Śambhala)	Zla ba bzang po
Sukhadeva	bDe ba'i lha

Phonetic	Wylie Transliteration
Sukhamahāsiddha	Grub chen bde ba
Sukhanātha	bDe ba'i mgon po
Sukhasiddhi	Su kha si ddhi
Sumati	Blo gros bzang
Sumpa Lotsāwa Darma Yonten	Sum pa lo tsā ba dar ma yon tan
Sumpa Repa Rinchen Gyeltsen	Sum pa ras pa rin chen rgyal mtshan
Sunitra (king of Śambhala)	bShes gnyen bzang po
Śūnyatāsamādhivajra (also known as Śabaripā)	lDong ngar ba ting 'dzin rdo rje
Sureśāna (king of Śambhala)	Lha'i dbang ldan
Sureśvara (king of Śambhala)	Lha'i dbang phyug
Sureśvara (king of Śambhala)	Lha'i dbang po
Sūrya (king of Śambhala)	Nyi ma
Tagton Zhonu Dar	sTag ston gzhon nu dar
Taklung Ngawang Drakpa	sTag lung ngag dbang grags pa
Taklung Rinpoché [Ngawang Tulku]	sTag lung rin po che
Taklung Tulku Namgyel Tashi	sTag lung sprul sku rnam rgyal bkra shis
Taktsang Lotsāwa Drapa Sherab Rinchen	sTag tshang lo tsā ba sgra pa shes rab rin chen
Tanak Monlam Gom	rTa nag smon lam sgom
Tanak Rinchen Yeshépa	rTa nag rin chen ye shes pa
Tang Lotsāwa	Thang lo tsā ba
Tangpa Tashipel, of Taklung	Thang pa bkra shis dpal
Tangtong Gyelpo	Thang stong rgyal po
Tārā	sGrol ma
Tārā in the form Cintāmaṇicakra	sGrol ma yid bzhin 'khor lo
Tāranātha (also known as Drolwei Gonpo Kunga Nyingpo)	Tā ra nā tha, sgrol ba'i mgon po kun dga' snying po
Tashi Dorjé	bKra shis rdo rje
Tashi Gyeltsen	bKra shis rgyal mtshan
Tashi Lama	bKra shis bla ma
Tashi Namgyel	bKra shis rnam rgyal

Phonetic	Wylie Transliteration
Tashi Peltsek	bKra shis dpal brtsegs
Tashi Rinchen	bKra shis rin chen
Tashi Zangpo	bKra shis bzang po
Tazhi Jadrel	mTha' bzhi bya bral
Tejī, king of Śambhala	gZi brjid can
Tepuwa [Pārvātapāda]	Te phu ba
Tīlakakalāśa	dNgul gyi bum pa
Tilopā	Ti lo pa
Tokden Gangpa Rinchen Pelzangpo	rTogs ldan sgang pa rin chen dpal bzang po
Tokden Gonpo Gyeltsen	rTogs ldan mgon po rgyal mtshan
Tokden Khacho Wangpo	rTogs ldan mkha' spyod dbang po
Tokden Trewo Chokyi Gyatso	rTogs ldan tre bo chos kyi rgya mtsho
Trariwa Rinchen Gyelchok	Khra ri ba rin chen rgyal mchog
Tri Songdetsen	Khri srong lde'u btsan
Tropu Lotsāwa Jampapel	Khro phu lo tsā ba byams pa dpal
Trulzhik Darma Sengé	'Khrul zhig dar ma seng ge
Trulzhik Kundarma	'Khrul zhig kun 'dar ma
Trulzhik Kunga Chogyel	'Khrul zhig kun dga' chos rgyal
Trulzhik Namkei Neljorpa	'Khrul zhig nam mkha'i rnal 'byor pa
Trulzhik Tsultrim Gyeltsen	'Khrul zhig tshul khrims rgyal mtshan
Tsaktsa Śākya Dorjé	Tsak tsha śākya rdo rje
Tsami Lotsāwa Mondrub Sherab	Tsa mi lo tsā ba smon grub shes rab
Tsami Sangyé Drak	Tsa mi sangs rgyas grags
Tsangma Shangton	gTsang ma shangs ston
Tsangnak Tsondru Sengé	gTsang nag brtson 'grus seng ge
Tsangpa Dregurwa Dongtro Dulwadzin	gTsang pa 'bre sgur gdong khrod 'dul 'dzin
Tsangpa Gyaré Yeshé Dorjé (also known as Sangyé Rabdun)	gTsang pa rgya ras ye shes rdo rje
Tsawaripa	Tsha ba ri pa
Tsawarongpa Śākya Gyeltsen	Tsha ba rong pa śākya rgyal mtshan
Tse Gangpa	[Rog] rTse [lha] sgang pa

Phonetic	Wylie Transliteration
Tsen Khawoché	bTsan kha bo che
Tseringma, protector	Tshe ring ma
Tsetsa Repa Śāk Dor	rTsad tsha ras pa śāk rdor
Tsi Tonpa	rTsis ston pa
Tsok Khenchen Rinpoché	Tshogs mkhan chen rin po che
Tsokgom Kunga Pel	Tshogs sgom kun dga' dpal
Tsondru Zangpo	brTson 'grus bzang po
Tsulchen Sonam Sengé	Tshul chen bsod nams seng ge
Tsultrim Chogdrub	Tshul khrims mchog grub
Tsultrim Gonpo	Tshul khrims mgon po
Tsultrim Gyeltsen	Tshul khrims rgyal mtshan
Tsurpu Jamyang Dondrub Ozer	mTshur phu 'jam dbyangs don grub 'od zer
Tsurton Wang-gi Dorjé	mTshur ston dbang gi rdo rje
Tukjé Tsondru Chojé	Thugs rje brtson 'grus chos rje
Tukséwa Rinchen Namgyel	Thugs sras ba rin chen rnam rgyal
Tulku Jodenpa	sPrul sku jo gdan pa
Tumton Lodro Drak	gTum ston blo gros grags
Twelve liberators	sGrol ma bcu gnyis
Twelve protectors of Vajrakīla	Phur srung bcu gnyis
Twelve subterranean spirits	brTan ma bcu gnyis
Twenty-five Kulika kings of Śambhala	Rigs ldan nyer lnga
Umdzé Yonten Pel	dBu mdzad yon tan dpal
Upagupta	Nyer sbas
Upama	dBu pa ma
Upendra [Viṣṇu]	Nye dbang
Urawa	dBu ra ba
Uriwa	dBus ri ba
Uṣṇīṣasītātapatrā	gTsug gtor gdugs dkar can
Vagīśvara	Ngag gi dbang phyug
Vagīśvarakīrti	Ngag gi dbang phyug grags

Phonetic	Wylie Transliteration
Vairocana	rNam par snang mdzad
Vairocana in the form Himamahāsāgara	rNam par snang mdzad gangs can mtsho
Vairocanabhadra	rNam snang bzang po
Vairocanabhadra (also known as Ngulchu Bairo)	Bai ro tsa na bha dra
Vairotsana, the translator	Bai ro tsa na
Vaiśravaṇa	rNam sras, rnam mang thos sras
Vaiśravaṇa as the supreme dancer	Gar mkhan mchog
Vajrabhairava	rDo rje 'jigs byed
Vajrabhairava with a retinue of eight zombies	Ro langs brgyad bskor
Vajracaṇḍālī	rDo rje gtum mo
Vajradhara	rDo rje 'chang
Vajragarbha	rDo rje snying po
Vajraheruka	Badzra he ru ka
Vajrakīla	rDo rje phur ba
Vajramāradama (also known as Vaiśravaṇa)	rDo rje bdud 'dul
Vajranairātmyā	rDo rje bdag med ma
Vajrapāṇi	Badzra pā ṇi, Phyag na rdo rje
Vajrapāṇi in the form Caṇḍa	gTum po
Vajrapāṇi in the form Guhyapati	gSang ba bdag po
Vajrapāṇi in the form Mahācakra	Phyag na rdo rje 'khor lo chen po
Vajrapāṇi, of India	Phyag na pa
Vajrārali	Ra li
Vajrāsana the Elder	rDo rje gdan pa che ba
Vajrāsana the Younger (also known as Amoghavajra)	rDo rje gdan pa chung ba
Vajrāsanapāda	rDo rje gdan pa
Vajrasattva	rDo rje sems dpa'
Vajratārā	rDo rje sgrol ma
Vajravārāhī	rDo rje phag mo
Vajravārāhī in the form Chinnamuṇḍā	Phag mo dbu bcad ma
Vajravārāhī in the form Dvimukhā	Phag mo zhal gnyis ma

Phonetic	Wylie Transliteration
Vajrayoginī	rDo rje rnal 'byor ma
Valacaṇḍa	Va la tsaṇḍa
Vārāhī in the form Sarvārthasiddhā	Phag mo don grub ma
Vararuci	mChog sred
Varuṇa	Chu lha
Vasantatilaka	dPyid thig
Vasubandhu	dByig gnyen
Vasudhara	Ba su dha ra, nor rgyun
Vetālī	Ve tā lī, ro langs ma
Vibhūticandra	Bi bhū ti tsandra
Vidyākokila	Rig pa'i khu byug
Vijaya, king of Śambhala	rNam rgyal
Vikhyātadeva	rNam grags lha
Vikrama, king of Śambhala	rNam par gnon pa
Vilāsa	Bi lā sa
Vimalagupta	Dri med sbas pa
Vimalamitra	Dri med bshes gnyen
Vīṇapa	Bī ṇa pa
Vināyaka, deity	bGegs kyi rgyal po glang po che'i sna can
Vīraraśmi, paṇḍita	dPa' bo 'od gsal
Vīravajra	dPa' bo rdo rje ba
Virūpa	Bi rū pa
Viṣṇugupta, Kulika (king of Śambhala)	Rigs ldan khyab 'jug sbas pa
Visukalpa, king	Bi su ka va
Viśvamūrti (king of Śambhala)	sNa tshogs gzugs
Viśvarūpa (king of Śambhala)	sNa tshogs gzugs
Vṛddhaja	rGan po skyes
Wangchuk Gyeltsen	dBang phyug rgyal mtshan
White Gyeltang (deity)	rGyal thang dkar po
White-clad demon (deity)	dKar bdud

Phonetic	Wylie Transliteration
Yagdé Lotsāwa Sonam Sengé (also known as Yagdé Paṇchen)	g.Yag sde lo tsā ba bsod nams seng ge
Yagton Sangyé Pel	g.Yag ston sangs rgyas dpal
Yajña	mChog sbyin
Yakṣa Aparājita	A pa rā tsitta
Yakṣa, protector	gNod sbyin
Yakṣinī, protector	gNod sbyin ma
Yama, deity	gShin rje
Yamāntaka	gShin rje gshed
Yamkyilwa Lodro Chogyel	g.Yam skyil ba blo gros chos rgyal
Yangonpa Gyeltsen Pel	Yang dgon pa rgyal mtshan dpal
Yangtsewa Rinchen Sengé	Yang rtse ba rin chen seng ge
Yargom Sewo	Yar sgom se bo
Yargyab Kunpang Chokor Gangpa	Yar rgyab kun spangs chos 'khor sgang pa
Yarlungpa Lotsāwa Drakpa Gyeltsen	Yar lung pa lo tsā ba grags pa rgyal mtshan
Yarlungpa Norbu Rinchen	Yar lung pa nor bu rin chen
Yarlungpa Sengé Gyeltsen	Yar lung pa seng ge rgyal mtshan
Yaśas (king of Śambhala)	Grags pa
Yellow Cakrasaṃvara	bDe mchog ser po
Yellow Vajravārāhī	Phag mo ser mo
Yerpa Gomseng	Yer pa sgom seng
Yeshé Pelwa	Ye shes dpal ba
Yigdruk Sherab Peljor	Yig drug shes rab dpal 'byor
Yolton Chowang (known as Yolgom)	Yol ston chos dbang
Yongdzin Lama (also known as Kunga Chogdrub)	Yongs 'dzin bla ma
Yonten Gyatso	Yon tan rgya mtsho
Yorpa Yeshé Pelwa	Yor pa ye shes dpal ba
Yumo Mikyo Dorjé	Yu mo mi bskyod rdo rje
Yungtonpa Dorjé Pel	g.Yung ston pa rdo rje dpal
Zangpo Pel	bZang po dpal

Phonetic	Wylie Transliteration
Zangpo Tenpa	bZang po bstan pa
Zarjang Pukpa Kunga Lekpa Rinchen	Zar byang phug pa kun dga' legs pa rin chen
Zelmo Drakpa Drakpa Yeshé	Zal mo brag pa grags pa ye shes
Zewu Tsondru Drak	Ze'u brtson 'grus grags
Zhalu Khyenrab Chojé	Zha lu mkhyen rab chos rje
Zhalu Lotsāwa Losal Tenkyong	Zha lu lo tsā ba blo gsal bstan skyong
Zhamar II Khacho Wangpo	Zhva dmar mkha' spyod dbang po
Zhang Dodé Pel	Zhang mdo sde dpal
Zhang Jangchub Sherab	Zhang byang chub shes rab
Zhang Konchok Pel	Zhang dkon mchog dpal
Zhang Lotsāwa Drubpa Pel	Zhang lo tsā ba grub pa dpal
Zhang Lotsāwa Jangchub-o	Zhang lo tsā ba byang chub 'od
Zhang Lotsāwa Nyangenmé Pel	Zhang lo tsā ba mya ngan med dpal
Zhang Rinchen Ozer	Zhang rin chen 'od zer
Zhang Ring Kyitsa Ochen	Zhang ring spyi tsha 'od chen
Zhang Tangsagpa Yeshé Jungné	Zhang thang sag pa ye shes 'byung gnas
Zhang Tselpa Tsondru Drak	Zhang tshal pa brtson 'grus grags
Zhang Ukarwa	Zhang dbu dkar ba
Zhangton Chobar	Zhang ston chos 'bar
Zhangton Chokyi Lama	Zhang ston chos kyi bla ma
Zhangton Darma Gyeltsen	Zhang ston dar ma rgyal mtshan
Zhangton Drukdra Gyeltsen	Zhang ston 'brug sgra rgyal mtshan
Zhangton Gadenpa Kunga Sonam	Zhang ston dga' ldan pa kun dga' bsod nams
Zhangton Konchok Pel	Zhang ston dkon mchog dpal
Zhikpo Nyima Sengé	Zhig po nyi ma seng ge
Zhonu Chodrub	gZhon nu mchog grub
Zhonu Drakpa	gZhon nu grags pa
Zhonu Drubpa	gZhon nu grub pa
Zhonu Gyelchok	gZhon nu rgyal mchog
Zhonu Gyeltsen	gZhon nu rgyal mtshan
Zhonu Sengé	gZhon nu seng ge

Phonetic	Wylie Transliteration
Zhuton Tsultrim Gon	Zhu ston tshul khrims mgon
Ziji Drakpa	gZi brjid grags pa
Zilung Paṇchen Śākya Chokden	Zi lung paṇ chen śākya mchog ldan
Zur Dropukpa Śākya Sengé	Zur sgro phug pa śākya seng ge
Zur Śākya Pelwa	Zur śākya dpal ba
Zurchen Śākya Jungné	Zur chen śākya 'byung gnas
Zurchung Sherab Drak	Zur chung shes rab grags
Zurhaṃ Śākya Jungné	Zur haṃ śākya 'byung gnas
Zurhaṃ Shenyen	Zur haṃ bshes gnyen
Zurpukpa Rinchen Pelzang	Zur phug pa rin chen dpal bzang

Concordance of Place Names

The following concordance gives precedence to the romanized Sanskrit and Tibetan phonetic spellings in the first column. The Wylie transliterations are given in the second column.

Phonetic	Wylie Transliteration
Akaniṣṭha	'Og min
Anavatapta Lake	Ma pham mtsho
Andaman Sea	Phyi'i rgya mtsho'i klong
Aparagodānīya	Ba lang spyod
Arbuda	Ar bu ta
Baiḍūr Tsongdu	Bai ḍur tshong 'dus
Bartsik Lungtur, in Lower Matang	Bar tshigs lung thur
Bengal	Bhaūgala
Beta	Be ta'i yul
Central Tibet	dBus
Chimphu	mChims phu
Cholung Jangtsé (hermitage)	Chos lung byang rtse
Cholung Kunra	Chos lung kun ra
Cindhona, citadel of Vajravārāhī	Tsi ndho na
Densatel	gDan sa thel
Devagiri	Lha'i ri bo
Dharmabhadra, in Trāyastriṃśa	Chos bzang
Dingri	Ding ri
Dingri Langkor in Lato	La stod ding ri lang skor
Dragto, doctrinal palace	Brag stod chos kyi pho brang
Drakha in U	dBus kyi brag kha

Phonetic	Wylie Transliteration
Gelung in Olka	'Ol kha dge lung
Gyel	rGyal
India	rGya gar
Jambudvīpa	'Dzam bu gling
Jang Radeng	Byang rva sgreng
Jang Uri	Byang dbu ri
Kala Dungtso	Ka la dung mtsho
Kantamara in Saurāṣṭra	So raṣṭha'i yul gyi chas shas kanta ma ra
Kashmir	Kha che'i yul
Kathmandu	Ye rangs
Kham	Khams
Kharchu	mKhar chu
Lampāka	Lam pa ka
Langtang	Lang thang
Lhasa	Lha sa
Lhodrak	Lho brag
Lower Rongting	Rong gting smad
Lupuk Karchung, in Lhasa	kLu phug dkar chung
Magadha	Ma ga dha
Mahābodhi, at Vajrāsana	Byang chub chen po
Mangyul	Mang yul
Mount Meru	Ri rab
Mutso	Mus tsho
Nadong	Yul sna gdong
Nartang	sNar thang
Nepal	Bal yul
Netsedrum, in Lowo Matang	sNe tshe grum
Nezin in Pari	Phag ri'i sne zin
Ngari	mNga' ris
Ngor Evam Choden	Ngor evaṃ chos ldan
Nub Cholung	gNubs chos lung
Oḍḍiyāna	O rgyan yul
Olka	'Ol kha

Phonetic	Wylie Transliteration
Paro Drang-gyé	sPa dro 'brang rgyas
Penyul	'Phan yul
Prānta	Bas mtha'
Pullahari	Phul la ha ri
Pūrvavideha	Lus 'phags
Ratnagiri	Rin chen ri bo
Rinpung	Rin spungs
Rong	Rong
Sahalokadhātu	Mi mjed 'jig rten gyi khams
Sakya	Sa skya
Śambhala	Śa mbha la
Sekhar Gutok	Sras mkhar dgu thog
Sekhar Kyawo (in Drowolung)	Sras mkhar skya bo
Sewalung in Nyel	gNyal gyi se ba lung
Shong	Shong
Śītavana (charnel ground)	bSil bu tshal
Soldro Jetang (in Nub Cholung)	gSol gro bye thang
Sukhāvatī	bDe ba can
Tibet, Land of Snows	Bod kha ba can
Trichiliocosm	sTong gsum gyi stong chen po 'jig rten gyi khams
Tropu	Khro phu
Tsang	gTsang
Tsāri	Tsā ri
Tsetang	rTses thang
Tuṣita	dGa' ldan
Uru	dBu ru
Utsang	dBus gtsang
Uttarakuru	sGra mi snyan
Vajrāsana	rDo rje gdan
Vanaprastha	Nags khrod pa
Viśvakoṭacandana, isle of (source of wonder)	Bi śva ko ṭa tsandana gyi gling

Phonetic	Wylie Transliteration
Wangmopuk Monastery	dBang mo phug dgon
World of patient endurance	Mi mjed 'jig rten gyi khams
Yamdrok	Yar 'brog
Yang Gon in Rigongpel	Ri gong dpal gyi yang dgon
Yechung Pulung	Ye chung phu lung
Yumta Yulma, in Gyel	Yum lta yul ma
Zarjang Pukpa	Zar byang phug pa
Zhalu	Zha lu
Zilchen Cave, in Tsāri	Tsā ri zil chen phug
Zimkhang (in Sakya)	gZim khang

Abbreviations

BDRC Buddhist Digital Resource Center. Online catalog at www.tbrc.org.

Dg.K The Derge Kangyur (sDe dge bka' 'gyur) xylograph edition. 103 vols. Edited by Situ Chokyi Jungne. Freely accessible online at www.tbrc.org.

Dg. NGB The Derge xylograph edition of the Collected Tantras of the Nyingmapa (rNying ma'i rgyud 'bum). Edited by Katok Getse Gyurme Tsewang Chokdrub. 26 vols. Catalog by Thubten Chodar. Beijing: Mi rigs dpe skrun khang, 2000.

Dg.T The Derge Tengyur (sDe dge bstan 'gyur) xylograph edition. Edited by Zhuchen Tsultrim Rinchen. 213 vols. Freely accessible online at www.tbrc.org.

DNZ The Treasury of Precious Instructions (*gDams ngag rin po che mdzod*). Compiled by Jamgön Kongtrul. 18 vols. Delhi: Shechen Publications, 1999.

Drigungpa Anthology
The Great Treasury of the Drigung Kagyu (*'Bri gung bka' brgyud chos mdzod chen mo*). Edited by Agon Rinpoche. 151 vols. Lhasa 2004.

Drukpa Kagyu Anthology
Great Anthology of the Drukpa Kagyu Tradition (*'Brug lugs chos mdzod chen mo*). Compiled by Drukpa Kagyu Heritage Project. 101 vols. Kathmandu: Khams sgar gsung rab nyams gso rgyan spel khang, n.d.

GDKT Compendium of Tantra (*rGyud sde kun btus*). Compiled by Jamyang Loter Wangpo. 33 vols. Kathmandu: Sachen International, 2014.

Kadampa Anthology
Anthology of the Collected Works of the Kadampa (*bKa' gdams gsung 'bum phyogs sgrig*). The First Collection (I), 2006, contains vols. 1–30. The Second Collection (II), 2007, contains vols. 31–60. The Third Collection (III), 2009, contains vols. 61–90. The Fourth Collection (IV), 2015, contains vols. 91–121. Compiled by dPal brtsegs bod yig dpe rnying zhib 'jug khang. Chengdu: Sichuan mi rigs dpe skrun khang.

KPD Comparative edition of the Tibetan Kangyur (*bKa' 'gyur dpe bsdur ma*), largely based on the Derge Kangyur, input with annotations and references to alternative woodblock versions. 108 vols. Beijing: Krung go'i bod rig pa'i dpe skrun khang, 2006–9. The contents are now searchable online at www.tbrc.org.

Martin — Martin, Dan. 1997. *Tibetan Histories*. London: Serindia Publications.

NA — Not available; used of works that are probably not extant at the present time.

NK — The Collected Pronouncements of the Nyingmapa (*rNying ma'i bka' ma*). Currently 120 vols. in the most extended edition (*shin tu rgyas pa*), compiled and published by Khenpo Munsel and Khenpo Jamyang of Katok. Chengdu 1999.

NL — Not located; used of works that may be extant at the present time but have not yet been identified.

PZ — Pekar Zangpo, *mDo sde spyi'i rnam bzhag*. Beijing: Mi rigs dpe skrun khang, 2006. A sixteenth-century Tibetan-language summary of all the sutras preserved in the Kangyur

RTD — Treasury of Revealed Teachings (*Rin chen gter mdzod*), compiled by Jamgön Kongtrul. This is the new Shechen edition (2016), published in 72 vols.

SK — Collected Writings of the Five Founders of Sakya (*Sa skya' bka' 'bum*). This anthology contains the works of Sachen Kunga Nyingpo (1092–1158), vols. 1–2; Lobpon Sonam Tsemo (1142–1182), vols. 3–5; Jetsun Drakpa Gyaltsen (1147–1216), vols. 6–9; Sakya Paṇḍita Kunga Gyaltsen (1182–1251). vols. 10–12; and Chogyal Pakpa Lodro Gyaltsen (1235–1280), vols. 13–15, including the three supplementary volumes published by Khenpo Tsultrim Gyaltsen. Dehra Dun: Sakya Center, 1992–93.

SLC — Collection of the Sakya Path and Its Fruition (*Sa skya'i lam 'bras*). 43 vols. Originally compiled under the inspiration of Jamyang Loter Wangpo (1847–1914), and recompiled by Guru Lama. Kathmandu: Sachen International, 2008.

Skt. — Sanskrit.

T — H. Ui et al., *A Complete Catalogue of the Tibetan Buddhist Canons*. Tohoku University catalog of the Derge edition of the canon. Sendai 1934.

Tib. — Tibetan.

TPD — Comparative edition of the Tibetan Tengyur (*bsTan 'gyur dpe bsdur ma*), largely based on the Derge Tengyur, input with supplements, annotations, and references to alternative woodblock versions. 120 vols. Beijing: Krung go'i bod rig pa'i dpe skrun khang, 1994–2008. The contents are now searchable online at www.tbrc.org.

Notes

Translator's Introduction

1. In Tibetan, there are two extant autobiographical accounts of Jamgön Kongtrul's life, not to mention the writings of his student Karma Tashi Chopel, and the later abridged biographies contained in the Buddhist histories of Zhechen Gyaltsab (1910) and Dudjom Rinpoche (1964). Gene Smith was the first Western scholar to appraise the life and works of Kongtrul in his groundbreaking introduction to the Indian edition of *The Treasury of Knowledge*, published in 1970. The longest account in English is Richard Barron's (2003) translation, and there are also short hagiographies to be found in Dudjom Rinpoche 1991 and in Ringu Tulku 2006.
2. Jamgön Kongtrul's exhaustive studies are fully documented in the record of his received teachings (*gsan yig*), which was devotedly compiled by Karma Tashi Chopel.
3. This encyclopedic work has already been translated and published by Snow Lion in ten volumes, under the title *The Treasury of Knowledge*.
4. A searchable online catalog to the expanded seventy-two volume Shechen edition is accessible at http://rtz.tsadra.org/index.php/Main_Page.
5. This has a supplement, entitled *Treasury of Extensive Pronouncements*, which contains Jamgön Kongtrul's miscellaneous textual commentaries.
6. On the Tsadra Foundation's current project and aspiration to translate this entire anthology, see http://tsadra-wp.tsadra.org/translation/treasury-of-precious-instructions.
7. *gDams Ngag Mdzod* [A Treasury of Instructions and Techniques for Spiritual Realization], compiled by 'Jam-gon Kon-sprul Blo-gros-mtha'-yas. Reproduced from a xylographic print from the Dpal-spungs blocks (Delhi: Ngawang Lungtok and Ngawang Gyaltsen, 1971).
8. See also Jamgön Kongtrul's own detailed exposition of these eight lineages of spiritual attainment in Jamgön Kongtrul 2007, 63–339.
9. A brief account of the life of Sherab Ozer and his spiritual revelations is found in Yeshe Gyamtso 2011, 235–38. On Pelri Tekchokling Monastery in upper Chongyé, which he founded circa 1570, see Akester 2016, 438–39; see also Dorje 2009, 248. It was here that Rigdzin Jigmé Lingpa studied and practiced during his early formative years. The verses in question derive from Sherab Ozer's *Death-*

less Nectar of Meditation, which, together with his *Deathless Nectar of Study and Reflection*, is extant in Jamyang Khyentsé Wangpo, in his *Collected Works*, vol. 6, pp. 327–74. A translation and transliteration of this passage is found in Deroche 2009, 328–35. Jamgön Kongtrul reiterates the initial verses of this passage, as annotated by Jamyang Khyentsé Wangpo, in his introduction to *The Catalog of The Treasury of Precious Instructions*, *DNZ*, Book 18, p. 405 (Barron 2013, 35–36; also Kapstein 2007, 110–29). On this, see also Kapstein 1996, 277. Among the eightfold classification outlined here, much has been documented in recent decades regarding the origins, development, and revival of the Shangpa Kagyu tradition. See Kapstein 1980, 138–44; Namka Samdrub Gyeltsen, *Biographies of the Abbatial Succession of the Shangpa Kagyu*; Akester 2016, 549–50; and also Sheehy, forthcoming.

10. These include five scholars representing the early phase of Buddhist propagation in Tibet: Tonmi Sambhoṭa (early to mid-seventh century), Vairotsana (eighth to ninth century), Kawa Peltsek (eighth to ninth century), Chokro Lu'i Gyeltsen (eighth to ninth century), and Zhang Yeshedé (eighth to ninth century), along with five representing the later phase: Lochen Rinchen Zangpo (958–1055), Dromton Gyelwei Jungné (1005–1064), Ngok Lotsāwa Loden Sherab (1059–1109), Sakya Paṇḍita Kunga Gyeltsen (1182–1251), and Go Lotsāwa Khukpa Lhetsé (early eleventh century).
11. These miscellaneous writings for the most part concern the spiritual attainments of the foremost bodhisattvas: Avalokiteśvara, Mañjughoṣa, Vajrapāṇi, Amitāyus, Tārā, and Jambhala, as well as the instructions of Bodongpa, Rongton Sheja Kunrik, and Śāntigupta.
12. The catalog has already been translated in Barron 2013.
13. See Snellgrove 1989; also Peissel 1967, and Jackson 1976.
14. This biographical sketch of Kunga Drolchok derives from Cyrus Stearns, *Treasury of Lives*, https://treasuryoflives.org/biographies/view/Kunga-Drolchok/TBRC_P2387.
15. This undated manuscript from Dzamtang is digitally accessible at BDRC (W2MS2257).
16. Held at Tibet House, and digitally accessible at BDRC (W1CZ1130).
17. There is a two-volume manuscript accessible at BDRC (W4CZ15391); see also Kunga Drolchok, *The Outer, Inner, and Secret Biographies of Venerable Kunga Drolchok*.
18. This is the view that all the attributes of buddhahood are extraneously empty of mundane impurities and defilements, but not intrinsically empty in a nihilistic sense, their experience thereby transcending all notions of existence and nonexistence. On the life and work of Dolpopa, see the definitive study in Stearns 2010; also Ruegg 1963.
19. Contemporary descriptions of Takten Puntsoling and its environs are found in Peljam, *Abridged History of the Abbatial Succession of the Jonangwa*, pp. 27–31. See also Akester 2016, 615–28; and Dorje 2009, 348–50.

20. The philosophical and political controversies are clearly presented in Stearns 2010, 69–77.
21. On the Mongolian dimension, see Stearns 2010, 73–77.
22. His teaching career in these regions is narrated in Ngawang Namgyel, *A Brief Lucid Biography of Venerable Ngawang Trinlé.*
23. A detailed account of Dzamtang Monastery can be found in Peljam, *Abridged History of the Abbatial Succession of the Jonangwa*, pp. 39–59. For brief descriptions in English, see Gruschke 2001, 72–78; also Dorje 2009, 776–77.
24. The formal translations of these twelve chapter titles are as follows:

    1. Supplication to the Lineage of the One Hundred and Eight Guideboooks, Easy to Recite and Clearly Listing to Some Extent the Names of the Lineage Holders, pp. 1–37 by Kunga Drolchok, Rearranged by Jamgön Kongtrul
    2. Supplement to the Supplication of the Lineage of the One Hundred and Eight Guidebooks, p. 39 by Zhalu Choktrul Losal Tenkyong
    3. Life-Sustaining Verses Introducing the Source of the One Hundred and Eightfold Profound Guidebooks, pp. 41–46 by Kunga Drolchok
    4. Multiple Approaches of the Wondrous Doctrine, Enhancing the Summary of the One Hundred and Eight Guidebooks, pp. 47–66 by Kunga Drolchok
    5. Historical Anecdotes of the Lineage of the One Hundred and Eight Guidebooks, pp. 67–98 by Kunga Drolchok
    6. Supplement to the Historical Anecdotes of the Lineage of the One Hundred and Eight Guidebooks, pp. 99–116 by Tāranātha
    7. The Ordinary Preliminary Practices of the One Hundred and Eight Guidebooks, pp. 117–120 by Kunga Drolchok
    8. The Extraordinary Preliminary Practices of the One Hundred and Eight Guidebooks, pp. 121–126 by Kunga Drolchok
    9. The Actual Texts of the Profound One Hundred and Eight Guidebooks, pp. 127–353 by Kunga Drolchok
    10. The Marvelous Key Commenting on the Contents of the One Hundred and Eight Guidebooks, pp. 355–361 by Kunga Drolchok
    11. A Specific Listing of the One Hundred and Eight Guidebooks, Along with the Listing of the Names of Their One Hundred and Eight Protectors and the Listing of the Names of Their One Hundred and Eight Empowerments, pp. 363–374 by Kunga Drolchok
    12. A Cornucopia of Blessings Documenting the Oral Instructions of the Teacher concerning the Methods for the Conferral of Empowerment of the Book Containing the One Hundred and Eight Guidebooks, pp. 375–380 by Zhalu Choktrul Losal Tenkyong

Chapter 1: Lineage Prayers of the One Hundred and Eight Guidebooks

1. *Khrid brgya'i brgyud 'debs brjod bde brgyud pa'i mtshan sdom cung zad gsal bar bkod pa*, *DNZ*, vol. 18, pp. 1–37.
2. The four attachments (*zhen pa bzhi*) comprise (i) attachment to this life (*tshe 'di la zhen pa*), (ii) attachment to cyclic existence (*'khor bar zhen pa*), (iii) attachment to self-interest (*bdag don la zhen pa*), and (iv) attachment to prejudices (*phyogs 'dzin ltar zhen pa*).
3. These are the titles of the core chapters of Tokmé Zangpo's *Seven-Point Mind Training* as presented in his *Practical Implementation of the Bodhisattvas*.
4. These seven focuses (*dmigs yul bdun*) for the cultivation of loving-kindness and compassion include (i) one's own mother, (ii) all relatives headed by one's father, (iii) all human beings—extending from one's own compatriots to those of the four continents, (iv) denizens of the hells, (v) anguished spirits, (vi) animals, and (vii) gods. See Tokmé Zangpo, *The Heart of Dependent Origination*, in his *Collected Works*, p. 195.
5. The four malevolent forces or devils (*bdud bzhi*) to be severed comprise (i) the malevolent force of the afflicted mental states (*nyon mongs pa'i bdud*), (ii) the malevolent force of the psychophysical aggregates (*phung po'i bdud*), (iii) the malevolent force of the lord of death/impermanence (*'chi bdag gi bdud*), and (iv) the malevolent force of the divine prince (*lha bu'i bdud*). On this enumeration, see also Nordrang Orgyan, *Compendium of Buddhist Numeric Terms*, pp. 674–75.
6. Tib. *skye med chig chod.* This expression is also translated by Harding in Jamgön Kongtrul 2016 as the "unborn single cut."
7. These three essential points comprise (i) the yoga of continuous cultivation in this life (*tshe 'dir sgom pa rgyun gyi rnal 'byor*), (ii) the yoga of the transference of consciousness cultivated at the time of death (*'chi khar sgom pa 'pho ba'i rnal 'byor*), and (iii) the yoga of mingling and transference cultivated in the intermediate state (*bar dor sgom pa bsre 'pho'i rnal 'byor*).
8. Kusulu the Younger is generally identified with Mitrayogin, a teacher of Atiśa (982–1054) and contemporary of Dharmakīrti of Sumatra, but elsewhere he is mysteriously revered as a teacher of Tropu Lotsāwa (1173–1236).
9. The seven renunciations (*spong bdun*) are the forsaking of killing, stealing, sexual misconduct, falsehood, slander, verbal abuse, and futile chatter. See Nordrang Orgyan, *Compendium of Buddhist Numeric Terms*, p. 1677.
10. For illustrations and descriptive detail of these eight aspects of Tārā, who protects from the eight fears or dangers, see Mullin and Watt 2003, 79–96.
11. The four deities of the Kadam tradition are Munīndra, Acala, Avalokita, and Tārā. The three doctrines (*chos gsum*) comprise the sixteen heart spheres—namely, (i) the four spheres of the supporting maṇḍala (*rten dkyil 'khor gyi thig le bzhi*), (ii) the six spheres of the supported deities (*brten pa lha'i thig le drug*), and (iii) the six spheres of the guru of the root lineage (*rtsa brgyud bla ma'i thig le drug*).

12. The Six Descents (*bka' babs drug*) of the transcendent perfection of wisdom are sequentially associated with the following locations: the paradise of Tuṣita, source of happiness; the underworld of nāgas, source of resources; the learned paṇḍitas of Bengal, source of awareness; the southern land of Beta, source of enlightened attributes; the western land of Oḍḍiyāna, source of blessings; and the isle of Viśvakoṭacandana, source of wonder.
13. The five paths (*lam lnga*) are those of provisions, connection or preparation, insight, meditation, and conclusion or no-more-learning. The three austerities (*dka' thub gsum*) are the practices associated respectively with pious attendants, hermit buddhas, and bodhisattvas.
14. The three promulgations of the Buddhist discourses by Śākyamuni Buddha respectively concern (i) the path that leads to the cessation of suffering, (ii) the nature of emptiness, and (iii) the attributes of the buddhas. The three sorts of person are those of inferior, average, and superior acumen.
15. Otherwise known as Nyangro Kunga Dorjé.
16. Otherwise known as Pakton Samten Zangpo.
17. This refers to the commentary of Bodong Paṇchen entitled *Summation of the Real* (*dPal de kho na nyid 'dus pa'i snying po chos spyod rab tu gsal ba'i snye ma*), which is discussed below.
18. The four primary elements are earth, water, fire, and wind.
19. That is to say, in this context the preliminary practices extract elixir that reduces the weight of the physical constituents; the main practices control the movement of the vital essence within the body; and the subsequent practice engages with a female mudra, endowed with appropriate signs.
20. The six yogas of continuous flow (*chu bo rgyun gyi rnal 'byor rnam drug*) in this context may refer to the six doctrines (*chos drug*), culminating in the practices of consciousness transference and intermediate state, rather than the six-branch yoga (*sbyor drug*).
21. Also known as Mar Tsondru Dorjé.
22. The variant Khenchen Jangchubseng is also found.
23. These seven religious kings and the dates traditionally ascribed to them are (i) Sucandra (Zla ba bzang po, 977 B.C.E.), Sureśvara (Lha'i dbang po, 877 B.C.E.), (iii) Tejī (gZi brjid can, 777 B.C.E.), (iv) Somadatta (Zla bas byin, 677 B.C.E.), (v) Sureśvara (Lha'i dbang phyug, 577 B.C.E.), (vi) Viśvamūrti (sNa tshogs gzugs, 477 B.C.E.), and (vii) Sureśāna (Lha'i dbang ldan, 377 B.C.E.). See Henning 2007, 365.
24. The twenty-five Kulika kings of Śambhala and the dates traditionally ascribed to them are as follows: (i) Yaśas (Grags pa, 277 B.C.E.), (ii) Puṇḍarīka (Padma dkar po, 177 B.C.E.), (iii) Bhadra (bZang po, 77 B.C.E.), (iv) Vijaya (rNam rgyal, 24 C.E.), (v) Sunitra (bShes gnyen bzang po, 124), (vi) Raktapāṇi (Phyag dmar, 224), (vii) Viṣṇugupta (Khyab 'jug sbas pa, 324), (viii) Arkakīrti (Nyi ma grags, 424), (ix) Subhadra (Shin tu bzang po, 524), (x) Samudravijaya (rGya mtsho rnam rgyal, 624), (xi) Aja (rGyal dka', 806), (xii) Sūrya (Nyi ma, 1027), (xiii)

Viśvarūpa (sNa tshogs gzugs, 1127), (xiv) Śaśiprabha (Zla 'od, 1227), (xv) Ananta (mTha' yas, 1327), (xvi) Mahīpāla (Sa skyong, 1427), (xvii) Śrīpāla (dPal skyong, 1527), (xviii) Hari (Seng ge, 1627), (xix) Vikrama (rNam par gnon pa, 1727), (xx) Mahābala (sTobs po che, 1827), (xxi) Aniruddha (Ma 'gags pa, 1927), (xxii) Narasiṃha (Mi'i seng ge, 2027), (xxiii) Maheśvara (dBang phyug chen po, 2127), (xxiv) Anantavijaya (mTha' yas rnam rgyal, 2227), and (xxv) Cakrī ('Khor lo can, 2327). On discrepancies and for alternative listings, see Henning 2007, 365–66.

25. These components of the six-branch yoga according to the *Tantra of the Wheel of Time* are presented below.
26. These terms appear to reflect the inspiration that Menlung Guru may have derived from the revelations of Guru Chowang. See RTD, vol. 59, p. 5b. The five sibling frailties (*gud chung spun lnga*) comprise the three poisons with the addition of pride and jealousy.
27. The term *fierce inner heat* describes the function of the channel below the navel cakra, literally known as the "fierce one" (*caṇḍālī, gtum mo*). Whenever the term occurs throughout this text, it refers to practices associated with this specific channel, which assumes the form of an *ashé* (the stroke of the letter *a*, written as "|" and known as *a thung* or *a shad* according to its uncreated intrinsic nature and its shape, respectively). On the practice of the fierce inner heat, see also Jamgön Kongtrul's explanation in Jamgön Kongtrul 2007, 158–73.
28. These are the procedures outlined in Kṛṣṇacārin's *Perfection of the Path of Fierce Inner Heat*, which is contained in *DNZ*, vol. 6, pp. 43–53. Briefly stated, there are four phases of this practice, each of which has its distinct conclusion: (i) continuum (*rgyud*) refers to the "timeless presence of the three maṇḍalas based on the four cakras," (ii) mantra (*sngags*) refers to the blazing of the stroke of the letter *a* (*a thung*) at the navel cakra, (iii) pristine cognition (*ye shes*) refers to the diffusion of coemergent delight through the upward movement of vital essence through the central channel, and (iv) secrecy (*gsang ba*) refers to breath control.
29. In terms of these three channels of the subtle body, semen (*khu*) is here associated with the left channel, and blood (*khrag*) with the right channel.
30. At this point in the Tibetan text this lineage prayer is preceded by the number fifty, which has been moved for the sake of consistency to its rightful position below.
31. This appears as an alternative title for *The Attainment in Proximity to a Stupa*.
32. Here the text (p. 20, line 3) in error retranscribes dPal ldan tshul krims ba.
33. *Instruction Entitled Three Emerging from Two* (*gNyis las gsdum 'byung gdams pa*) refers to a text by Ngawang Chodrak, based on a pithy quatrain attributed to Ngorchen Kunga Zangpo. It suggests that the extensive, middling, and abridged visualizations originated from two lineage transmissions, long and short. The full text, entitled *The Way of Enacting the Blessings of the Elucidation of the Symbolic Meaning according to the Path and Its Fruition, Along with the Meaning of the Emergence of Three from Two*, SLC, vol. 19, pp. 121–27. Alternatively, it has been suggested that this terse expression could imply that the three extensive, middling, and abridged visualizations originated from the two aspects of the main

practice—the determining of the view of discriminative awareness and the experiential cultivation of the view through skillful means, which are outlined below.

34. The actual name of the brother of Kyoton (*skyo ston sku mched*) appears to be unknown.
35. The five vocalic syllables A, I, Ṛ, U and Ḷ, known as the "five syllables of great emptiness" (*stong chen yig lnga*), represent the transformation of the five psychophysical aggregates and are contained in the letter VAṂ. The six consonantal groups (velars, palatals, cerebrals, dentals, labials, and sibilants), known as the "six syllables of the vital essence" (*thig le'i yig drug*), are contained in the letter *E*. These are unified in the Great Seal union of bliss and emptiness. See Jamgön Kongtrul 2005, 187–97.
36. Specifically, the "application at the spleen and kidney cavities" (*mchan khung sbyor ba*) concerns the region below the navel, the "meditative concentration of the 'cow udder'" (*ba nu'i bsam gtan*) concerns the navel cakra, the "awns of the plantain" (*chu shing snye ma*) concerns the central channel within the heart cakra, and the "hoofprint of a bull" (*glang rmig rjes*) concerns the heart cakra.
37. These are the syllables HA, RI, NI, and SA, on which see below.
38. This guidebook is also substituted by *The Inner Guidance of Nairātmyā.*
39. Tib. *rang zhal lha yi sku.*
40. This insertion must only refer to Kunga Drolchok and his successors.
41. The entrustment seal (*gtad rgya*) denotes the transmission of an authoritative rediscovered or revealed scriptural treasure, in this case the *Sekharma* of Guru Chowang.
42. Elsewhere written as Ras chen ro skom pa.
43. Tib. *bCu chos gdams pa*. This refers to the title of a work by Jigten Gonpo, generally entitled *Drops of Nectar: Sacred Teachings of Drigungtel.*
44. The allusion here is to Tashipel, the founder of Taklung, whose work on the *Six Doctrines* is entitled *Wish-Fulfilling Gem* (*Yid bzhin nor bu*). The expression "auspicious mound of glory" (*bkra shis dpal rab rtsegs pa*) could refer either to his own name (Tashipel) or to the later lineage holder named Tashi Peltsek.
45. The positioning of Lorepa here, immediately following Rechungpa Dorjé Drak, would seem to be untenable.
46. That is to say, the four precious teachers of Yangonpa were Kodrakpa, Gotsangpa, Sakya Paṇḍita, and Drigung On.
47. The four rites are pacification, enrichment, subjugation, and wrath.
48. Drushulwa (Gru shul ba) is also written in our text as drag shul ba, and elsewhere as gro shul ba.
49. See their individual biographies by Abhayadatta, *Narrative of the Eighty-Four Great Accomplished Masters*, TPD, vol. 48, pp. 413–556.
50. Elsewhere written as Dza ma ri pa.
51. This figure is also known as Kangyurwa Śākya Zangpo.
52. The "four mothers and seventeen offspring" (*ma bzhi de bu bcu bdun*) appear to be mentioned only obliquely in the source text (see RTD, Delhi ed., vol. 92, p.

173). There is a sense that the four mothers are the four ḍākinīs of pristine cognition mentioned in the lineage prayer, in which case their seventeen offspring would include the treasure finder and subsequent lineage holders whose names are listed in RTD, Delhi ed., vol. 92, p. 173. Alternatively, the expression may possibly denote a series of primary and secondary instructions within this cycle of revelation.

53. On Namdrol [Sengé] Zangpo (ca. 1504–1573), see BDRC; see also *Treasury of Lives*. https://treasuryoflives.org/biographies/view/Namdrol-Zangpo/9923.

54. These comprise the eight freedoms (*dal ba brgyad*) and ten opportunities (*'byor ba bcu*), which are considered prerequisite for the successful practice of dharma. Birth as a human being with the freedom and opportunity to follow the Buddhist path is regarded as difficult to attain and a precious circumstance. In the preliminary practices of the tantra path, in order to establish an appreciation for the significance of human rebirth, the freedom one has from eight unfavorable rebirths is a focus of contemplation, together with contemplation of the ten favorable opportunities. The eight freedoms are the freedoms from the following eight states: birth in the hells, birth as an anguished spirit, birth as an animal, birth as an uncivilized or barbarous person, birth as a long-living god, birth into a society that holds mistaken beliefs, birth in an age devoid of Buddhism, and birth with limited faculties. Among the ten favorable opportunities, there are five that are personally acquired and five contingent on external factors. The former include the favorable opportunities of being born as a human being, in a civilized society, with perfect sense faculties, not being engaged in a conflicting lifestyle, and having confidence in Buddhism. The latter include the favorable opportunities of being born in an aeon when a buddha has appeared, when the sacred teachings have been taught, when they are still being practiced, and when one actively engages in their practice and finds a qualified spiritual mentor (*kalyānamitra*). See Patrul Rinpoche 1994, 19–37.

55. Kunga Lekgyel (Kun dga' legs rgyal) appears to be the name of a well-known scribe who was a contemporary of Tāranātha.

56. This is why, in the English translation, the names have been standardized and listed in the preambles that accompany the contracted variants of the Tibetan metrical verses.

57. This is the personal name of Jamgön Kongtrul, compiler of *The Treasury of Precious Instructions*.

Chapter 2: Supplementary Prayer to the Lineage

1. *Khrid brgya'i brgyud 'debs kha skong*, *DNZ*, vol. 18, p. 39.

2. In the verses that follow, the full name of each lineage holder has been given, integrating the author's verses and annotations. Draktopa Choku Lhawang Drakpa is an important lineage holder of the Kālacakra and Shangpa teachings. He was also the one who encouraged Tāranātha to write the *Supplement to the Historical*

Anecdotes, contained in chapter 6.

3. The author's annotation adds that her title is Jonang Jetsunma and her secret name is Ratnavajriṇī (Rin chen rdo rje ma).
4. The author here includes an annotation indicating that the lineage also descended from Kunzang Wangpo and Tsewang Norbu to Ngawang Namgyel, who was the nephew of Dzalongkar Lama.
5. This figure also appears to be known as Trulzhik Kunzang Choying Rangdrol.
6. The author's annotation here suggests that he was the vajra master of Jonang Puntsoling.
7. Another author's annotation suggests that he and his predecessor both transmitted the lineage to Zhalu Lotsāwa Losal Tenkyong.
8. There is a reference in Tsewang Norbu's *Inventory to the Meritorious Offerings Made to Jonang Takten Puntsoling* (in his *Collected Works*, vol. 2, p. 450) alluding to the instruction on the six-branch yoga that he himself received on six occasions from Lama Dampa Kunzang Wangpo, and to the offerings he presented to Jonang, in consideration of the future development of this tradition.

Chapter 3: The Life-Sustaining Prayer of the One Hundred and Eight Guidebooks

1. *Zab khrid brgya dang brgyad kyi khungs gleng ba'i zhabs rten tshigs su bcad pa*, *DNZ*, vol. 18, pp. 41–46.
2. Tib. *rgya mo'i thags kyi 'phrul 'dra'i mig yangs*. Ringu Tulku adds that Chinese silk weaving is exemplary because all delicate designs become clear when each thread is placed without mistake. This requires a very clear head and sharp eyes.

Chapter 4: An Autobiographical Record of the One Hundred and Eight Guidebooks Received

1. *Khrid brgya'i spyi chings rnam par spel ba ngo mtshar chos kyi sgo mang*, *DNZ*, vol. 18, pp. 47–66.
2. An epithet of the primordial buddha body of reality, here in the form Mahāvajradhara.
3. This quatrain includes the four-syllable signature of the author's name, Kunga Drolchok, as do the concluding verses of certain other chapters and each of the one hundred and eight individual guidebooks contained in chapter 9. The transliterated Tibetan is retained in parentheses in this first instance for the aid of the reader, but subsequently dropped. In Tibetan these signature syllables are conventionally marked by subscript circles, equivalent to underlining. In the translation they have been replicated by bolding.
4. See also Jamgön Kongtrul's succinct explanation of the four seals in the context of Śāntigupta's *Hevajra* transmission, translated by Guarisco and McLeod in Jamgön Kongtrul 2005, 165.

5. "She who is endowed with all the finest aspects" (*rnam kun mchog ldan ma*) is a metaphor for extrinsic emptiness (*gzhan stong*).
6. Tib. *myang ba stong pa'i dug ro*. Here, the analytical approach adopted by certain exponents of intrinsic emptiness (*rang stong*) is contrasted with the experiential approach of the exponents of extrinsic emptiness (*gzhan stong*).
7. The four great lakes (*rgya mtsho bzhi*) comprise Manasarovar, Namtso, Nubtso, and Kokonor. See Nordrang Orgyan, *Compendium of Buddhist Numeric Terms*, p. 555.
8. Inexhaustible intelligence (*akṣayamati, blo gros mi zad*) is the name of a bodhisattva to whom the *Akṣayamatinirdeśasūtra* (T 175) was revealed. In terms of its meaning, it is said to comprise eighty inexhaustible attributes that are retained. See Pekar Zangpo, *Structural Presentation of All the Discourses*, pp. 236–37.
9. Here the text has an annotation that reads "Such as [in disputation between] Sakya and Ngok, Sakya and Tropu, Sakya and Drigung, Sakya and Kagyu, Sakya and Geluk, or Jonang and Zhalu."
10. The eighteen schools of monastic discipline that were well documented in ancient India comprise the four basic monastic orders that were then subdivided into eighteen. Among them, the Mūlasarvāstivāda order had seven subdivisions—namely, the Kāśyapīya, Mahīśāsaka, Dharmagupta, Bahuśrutīya, Tāmrasatīya, Vibhājyavādin, and the basic subdivision known as Sarvāstivādin. These are the lineages derived from the students of Rāhulabhadra. Their language was Sanskrit, and their robes had between twenty-five and twenty-nine patches, with the motifs of the blue lotus (*utpala*), the lotus (*padma*), and the gemstone (*ratna*). The Mahāsaṃghika order had five subdivisions—namely, the Pūrvaśaila, Haimavata, Prajñāptivādin, Lokottaravādin, and the basic subdivision known as Uttaraśaila. These were the lineages derived from the students of Mahākāśyapa. Their language was Prakrit, and their robes had between twenty-three and twenty-nine patches, with the motifs of the svāstika and the glorious heart orb (*śrīvatsa*). The Sthavira order had three subdivisions—namely, the Jetavanīya, Abhayagirivādin, and Mahāvihāravādin. These are the lineages derived from the students of Mahākāṭyāyana. Their language was Apabhraṃśa, and their robes had between twenty-one and twenty-nine patches, with the motif of the conch shell. The Sammitīya order had three subdivisions—namely, the Kaurukullika, Āvantaka, and Vatsīputrīya. These were the lineages derived from the students of Upāli. Their language was Paiśācika, and their robes had the same number of patches as those of the Sthaviras, their motif being the *sorsika* flower.
11. The three kinds of faith (*dad pa gsum*) comprise confidence, conviction, and longing. See Nordrang Orgyan, *Compendium of Buddhist Numeric Terms*, p. 296.
12. The distribution of Kadampa instructions among the One Hundred and Eight Guidebooks accords with Kunga Drolchok's own analysis, on which see below, chapter 10.
13. Kunga Drolchok's analysis of the Sakya and Kagyu instructions contained in the One Hundred and Eight Guidebooks is found in chapter 10.

14. The two stages of the path (*lam rim pa gnyis*) comprise the generation and perfection stages of meditation, the former emphasizing the visualization of meditational deities and the latter emphasizing internal yogic practices. For Jamgön Kongtrul's explanation of the distinction between these stages and their respective attributes, see Jamgön Kongtrul 2008, 59–135.
15. The level of an adamantine holder (*rdo rje 'dzin pa'i sa*) denotes the thirteenth or buddha level.
16. The four reliances (*rton pa bzhi*) comprise (i) reliance on the sacred doctrine rather than individuals, (ii) reliance on meanings rather than words, (iii) reliance on pristine cognition rather than consciousness, and (iv) reliance on definitive meaning rather than provisional meaning. See Zhang Yisun et al., *Great Tibetan-Chinese Dictionary*, p. 1080.
17. Nubpa Rigdzin Drak is said to have been a disciple of Drakpa Gyeltsen.
18. There appears to be no extant writing contained in the *Collected Works of Chogyel Pakpa* that pertains to this cycle. There is, however, a short text entitled *Instruction on Parting from the Four Attachments* contained in the *Collected Works of Sakya Paṇḍita*, vol. 1, p. 470; and also *DNZ*, vol. 6, pp. 314–15, which is translated in Jinpa 2006, 525–26.
19. Zarjang Pukpa Kunga Lekpei Rinchen is said to have been a disciple of Ngorchen Kunga Zangpo.
20. This is Gorampa Sonam Sengé's *Mind Training: A Key to the Profound Essential Points of the Guidebook Entitled Parting from the Four Attachments*, translated in Jinpa 2006, 529–39.
21. This work by Kunga Tashi (1349–1425), who was given the title "doctrinal king of the Great Vehicle" (*theg chen chos kyi rgyal po*) by the Ming emperor, appears to be no longer extant. As indicated above, Changlungpa Zhonu Chodrub was active during the fifteenth and sixteenth centuries.
22. The root text of the *Mind Training of the Great Vehicle* is attributed to Atiśa and contained in *DNZ*, vol. 3, pp. 405–28; and translated with annotations in Jinpa 2006, 71–82. The original Tibetan formulation of mind training in seven points is recognized as the work of Chekhawa Yeshé Dorjé (1101–1175) and his disciple Sé Chilbupa Chokyi Gyeltsen (1121–1189), on which see the translations in Jinpa 2006, 83–132. Two traditions subsequently evolved based on the interpretation of the term *substratum* or *basis of all*—as emptiness in the view of Lhading Jangchub Bum (fl. twelfth century) and as the uncontrived natural mind, in the view of Gyelsé Tokmé Zangpo (1295–1369). It is the latter's instruction entitled *The Seven-Point Mind Training of the Great Vehicle* that Kunga Drolchok recognizes as the second of his One Hundred and Eight Guidebooks. See below, chapter 9, n. 4. On the background to this extensive literature, see Jinpa 2006, 1–15.
23. Jangsem Zhonu Gyelchok (fl. fourteenth century) compiled the core texts of mind training in a new anthology, entitled *Compendium of Eloquence on Mind Training*, which forms the basis of *The Great Collection*, translated in Jinpa 2006. He is said to have synthesized the approaches of both Lhading Jangchub Bum and

Gyelsé Tokmé Zangpo. A catalog of its contents is also included in *DNZ*, vol. 3, pp. 377–78. His disciple Mu Konchok Gyeltsen (1388–1469) assisted with that compilation and in addition authored a separate commentary entitled *Supplement to the Oral Tradition*, also translated in Jinpa 2006, 431–515, which is based on the *Great Public Exposition* of Sangyé Gompa (1179–1250) and represents a distinct tradition of mind training.

24. Ngulchu Chodzongpa is an alternative name of Gyelsé Tokmé Zangpo (1295–1369). Drogon Pelden Yeshé (fl. fourteenth century) was his disciple and biographer.
25. Hor Kabzhipa Sengé Gyeltsen (fl. late fourteenth–early fifteenth centuries) was the disciple of Drogon Pelden Yeshé. There is a brief biography contained in Kadampa Anthology III, pp. 3–10. His extensive five-notebook supplementary compilation does not appear to be extant, distinct from the *Great Aural Transmission of Mind Training*.
26. The preliminary practice entitled the *Supporting Doctrine* (*sNgon 'gro rten gyi chos*) constitutes the first of the seven points of mind training, and the setting of the mind on an altruistic attitude (*sems bskyed*) is the second. Kunga Drolchok's remark suggests that he received direct instruction on the remaining five points that constitute the main practice through a text entitled *Cycle That Adopts the Calmness of Visualization*, which has not yet been identified. It may possibly be a work associated with Kunga Drolchok's own teacher, Kunga Chogdrub.
27. This guidebook entitled *The Heart of Dependent Origination* is the redaction introduced by the Jonangpa master Muchen Gyeltsen Pelzangpo (fl. thirteenth–fourteenth centuries), on which see below, chapter 9, n. 18.
28. *The Carrying of Happiness and Suffering on the Path* is contained in the *Collected Works of Tokmé Zangpo*. On this transmission and its antecedents, see below, chapter 9, n. 25.
29. It is suggested there that Remdawa Zhonu Lodro (1349–1412), who received this instruction directly from Gyelsé Tokmé Zangpo, wrote the notes that formed the basis of the fourth guidebook. However, there does not appear to be any *Memorandum on the Teachings of Gyelsépa* in Remdawa's *Collected Works*, distinct from Tokmé Zangpo's text.
30. On *The Mind Training according to Sumpa Lotsāwa*, which is translated in Jinpa 2006, 215–16, see below, chapter 9, n. 33.
31. This *Direct Guidance of Avalokiteśvara according to the Tsembupa Tradition* is the thirty-second guidebook of the present anthology. See below, chapter 9, n. 273.
32. This is the eighty-third guidebook in the present anthology, on which see below, chapter 9, n. 851. The memorandum on the oral instruction was apparently committed to writing by Gyamawa Lodro Gyeltsen (1390–1448), although he is not named in the lineage prayer of chapter 1.
33. The six guidebooks associated with Tokmé Zangpo therefore comprise (i) *The Seven-Point Mind Training of the Great Vehicle*, (ii) *The Heart of Dependent Origination*, (iii) *The Carrying of Happiness and Suffering on the Path*, (iv) *The Mind*

Training according to Sumpa Lotsāwa, (v) *The Direct Guidance of Avalokiteśvara according to the Tsembupa Tradition*, and (vi) *The Coemergent Union of the Great Seal*.

34. Kunga Drolchok's sixth guidebook entitled *The Severance of Machik Labdron* is based on the revelation of Samten Ozer entitled *Wish-Fulfilling Gem: An Instruction on the Inner Meaning*, on which see below, chapter 9, n. 35. Our text misreads *spyod yul* for *gcod yul*.

35. These are possibly included among Kyemé Dopa Chokyi Sherab Jodenpa, *The Ten Approaches to the Oral Instruction*. These comprise (i) the approach to means for attainment and spiritual accomplishment (*sgrub thabs dngos grub sgo 'byed*), (ii) the approach to dream yoga and the sun and moon [channels] (*rmi lam nyi zla sgo 'byed*), (iii) the approach to liberating consciousness transference (*'pho ba thar pa'i sgo 'byed*), (iv) the approach to the intermediate state and inner radiance (*bar do 'od gsal sgo 'byed*), (v) the approach to dependent origination that dispels obstructions (*gegs sel rten 'brel sgo 'byed*), (vi) the approach to enlightened attributes that brings forth success (*bogs 'don yon tan sgo 'byed*), and (vii–x) the four rites of the approach to enlightened activity that benefits others (*gzhan don phrin las sgo 'byed*).

36. The "inner examples" denotes Śākya Chokden's *Guidebook on the Three Essential Points*, contained in his *Collected Works*, vol. 8, pp. 371–74.

37. The name "Great Guidance of Zhalupa" (*Zha lu pa'i khrid chen*) reflects the important contribution of Buton Rinchen Drub to this transmission, on which see below, chapter 9, n. 54.

38. Chimchen Namka Drak (1210–1285) was seventh in the abbatial succession of Nartang.

39. The *Commentary on the Transcendent Perfection of Wisdom in One Hundred Thousand Lines* (*'Bum ṭīk*) is contained in vols. 4–5 of the *Collected Works of Rongton Sheja Kunrik*.

40. On the lives of these three seminal figures in the early, intermediate, and later transmissions of Pacification, see Roerich 1949, 867–982. Their transmissions may be described as "later" in relation to that of Dampa Sangyé himself.

41. See below, chapter 9, n. 270.

42. On this instruction manual of Sherab Bumpa, which was compiled by his disciple Gyelsé Tokmé Zangpo, see above, chapter 4, n. 33, and below, chapter 9, n. 273. I have not yet located a distinct text entitled *Great Guidance* (*Khrid yig chen mo*) in the *Collected Works of Lama Dampa Sonam Gyeltsen*, which does, however, include several short texts of Avalokiteśvara mantra and *dhāraṇī* recitation (vol. 1, pp. 801–13).

43. That is to say, rather than this Barawa/Drukpa tradition, Kunga Drolchok counted the transmission outlined above, in the corresponding lineage prayer: Chiwo Lhepa, Drak Marwa, Lhatsun Gonserwa, Tukjé Tsondru Chojé, Sherab Bumpa, Gyelsé Tokmé Zangpo, Gyamawa Yonten-o, Lotsāwa Drakpa Gyeltsen, Jangsem Konchok Gyeltsen, and Kunga Chogdrub.

44. The term *solitary hero* (*ekavīra, dpa' bo gcig pa*) indicates a male meditational deity without a female consort.
45. Tib. *Phyag rdor gtum po'i gsang ba bsam gyis mi khyab pa*. See below, chapter 9, n. 282.
46. Tib. *Ku ru kulle'i gsang khrid*. See below, chapter 9, n. 289.
47. This "unwritten" *Aural Transmission of Kālacakra* (*Yi ge med pa'i dus 'khor snyan brgyud*) originated from Menlungpa Sonam Pel, who visited Śambhala in person and later appears to have been inspired by the revelations of Guru Chowang. See chapter 9, n. 330.
48. See below, chapter 9, n. 368. The origins of the system and this attribution are discussed in Davidson 2005, 183–89.
49. These eighteen traditions are outlined in Dhongthog Rinpoche 2016, 94–95.
50. Dhongthog Rinpoche 2016, 95–96.
51. On the eighteen traditions of common descent (*spyi babs srol bco brgyad*), the twenty-four or twelve extensive subdivisions, the four primary divisions (*rtsa ba'i gyes pa bzhi*), and the two traditions of Drokmi and Gyijo, see Dhongthog Rinpoche 2016, 94–96.
52. The tradition of the Great Vehicle (*theg chen lugs*) is associated with Sakya itself, and the tradition of Ngor (*ngor lugs*) with Ngorchen Kunga Zangpo and his abbatial succession.
53. This instruction manual, composed by Lama Dampa Sonam Gyeltsen, is contained in *DNZ*, vol. 5, pp. 329–423.
54. Tib. *ma pang du bu bcug pa*.
55. On these eight or nine subsidiary cycles of the path (*lam skor phyi ma brgyad/dgu*) that also descended through Drokmi, see Davidson 2005, 194–204; and Dhongthog Rinpoche 2016, 91–92. They were redacted in Tibetan by Drakpa Gyeltsen; their Indian origins are respectively attributed to Khanitra (*The Inconceivables*, guidebook 44, chapter 9, n. 425; *DNZ*, vol. 6, pp. 81–118), Saroruha/Padmavajra (*The Nine Profound Methods*, guidebook 45, chapter 9, n. 438; *DNZ*, vol. 6, pp. 19–41), Ḍombī Heruka (*The Attainment of Coemergence*, guidebook 46, chapter 9, n. 453; *DNZ*, vol. 6, pp. 7–17), Kṛṣṇacārin (*The Perfection of the Path of Fierce Inner Heat*, guidebook 47, chapter 9, n. 465; *DNZ*, vol. 6, pp. 43–53), Acyutakāṇha (*The Straightening of Crooked Posture*, guidebook 48, chapter 9, n. 475; *DNZ*, vol. 6, pp. 43–53), Indrabhūti (*The Path of the Female Mudra*, guidebook 49, chapter 9, n. 481; *DNZ*, vol. 6, pp. 119–36), Vāgīśvarakīrti (*The Great Seal Devoid of Letters*, guidebook 50, chapter 9, n. 495; *DNZ*, vol. 6, pp. 67–79), and Nāgārjuna (*The Determination of Mind*, or *The Attainment in Proximity to a Stupa*, guidebook 51, chapter 9, n. 505; *DNZ*, vol. 6, pp. 59–65). The order of the last three has been adjusted here to reflect their order in chapters 1 and 9.
56. All of the foregoing six guidebooks are contained in *DNZ*, vol. 6, pp. 289–303, under the collective title *Instruction Manuals with Spiritual Connections to the Six Gatekeepers* (*sGo drug la gsang ba'i sgo drug chos 'brel du grags pa'i khrid yig*). These six gatekeepers were the renowned custodians of Nālandā Monastery—

namely, Śāntipa, source of *The Mingling of Sutra and Tantra,* on which see chapter 9, n. 510); Prajñākaragupta, source of *The Dispelling of Obstacles due to External Demons*, on which see chapter 9, n. 517; Jñānaśrī, source of *The Dispelling of Obstacles due to the Agitation of the Physical Body by the Elements*, on which see chapter 9, n. 519; Ratnavajra, source of *The Dispelling of the Obstacles of Meditative Stability and Mind*, on which see chapter 9, n. 522; Nāropā, source of *The Great Seal Dispelling the Three Sorts of Suffering*, on which see chapter 9, n. 524; and Vāgiśvarakīrti, source of *The Clear Recollection of the Innate State*, on which see chapter 9, n. 533.

57. Here, the male is considered to be the "referential basis" (*ltos gzhi*) for this practice, and the female is the "referential object" (*ltos chos*). Our text misreads *ltos bzhi* for *ltos gzhi*.
58. Khyenrab Chojé of Zhalu is otherwise known as Rinchen Chogdrub Pelzang. Chapter 9 attributes the last of these four guidebooks to him and the previous three to Samdingpa Zhonu Drub.
59. Khyungpo Neljor's *Emanational Navel Cakra* is replaced in chapter 9 with *The Inner Guidance of Nairātmyā*.
60. On these sources, see below, chapter 9, n. 972.
61. This would appear to be Mu Sangyé Rinchen, the eighth preceptor of Ngor (1450–1524). In chapters 1 and 9, however, this guidebook is attributed to Yarlungpa Sengé Gyeltsen.
62. In the last three quatrains, the first two syllables of each line of the Tibetan verse exhibit the poetic ornament of repetition (*yamaka, sbyar ba*).

Chapter 5: Historical Anecdotes of the Lineage Holders

1. *Khrid brgya'i brgyud pa'i lo rgyus, DNZ*, vol. 18, pp. 67–98.
2. Presumably this refers to Kunga Chogdrub, the tutor and teacher (*yongs 'dzin bla ma*) of Kunga Drolchok.
3. In Tibetan, this quatrain exhibits the poetic ornament of repetition (*yamaka, sbyar ba*) with respect to the final syllable of one line and the first syllable of the next line.
4. Khon Konchok Gyelpo's dates are 1034–1102. This event would therefore have occurred circa 1113.
5. On the birth and life of Sachen Kunga Nyingpo, see Davidson 2005, 294–321; and Dhongthog Rinpoche 2016, 56–59.
6. *Eulogy to Sachen*, dated 1164, is contained in Sonam Tsemo, in his *Collected Works*, vol. 1, pp. 151–52.
7. The life and work of Jetsun Drakpa Gyeltsen, one of the sons of Sachen Kunga Nyingpo, are discussed in Davidson 2005, 341–70; also Dhongthog Rinpoche 2016, 60–62. The quotations here have not yet been identified.
8. See above, chapter 4, n. 25.
9. The source of this citation from the sutras has not yet been identified.

10. *The Wheel of Sharp Weapons* and *The Peacock's Neutralizing of Poison* are attributed to Atiśa's teacher Dharmarakṣita. See the translations in Jinpa 2006, 133–70.
11. *The Adamantine Song of Chanting Meditation* is attributed to Atiśa's teacher Mitrayogin, also known as Kusulu the Younger. See the translation in Jinpa 2006, 171–75.
12. For Atiśa's own account of his voyage across the Andaman Sea to Sumatra, see Jinpa 2006, 57–70.
13. *Stages of the Heroic Mind*, in one hundred and two quatrains, is attributed to Serlingpa Dharmakīrti. See the translation in Jinpa 2006, 177–94. The eighteen factors (*chos bco brgyad*) to be carried on the path are outlined in a separate work, also attributed to Serlingpa, entitled *The Leveling-Out of Conceptions*, on which see the translation in Jinpa 2006, 195–96.
14. *The Leveling-Out of Conceptions*, v. 3, translated in Jinpa 2006, 195.
15. On this compilation, see above, chapter 4, n. 23.
16. This citation is not found in Jinpa's (2006) translation of Zhonu Gyelchok's text. According to Ringu Tulku (oral communication, February 26, 2019), this passage may have been considered by some as an interpolation.
17. This citation has not been identified elsewhere.
18. This group of nine lesser paṇḍitas (*paṇ chung dgu*) included Sugataśrī, Jayadatta, Vibhūticandra, Dānaśīla, Saṅghaśrī, Jīvagupta, Mahābodhi, and Kālacandra.
19. See the translation of these verses in Jinpa 2006, 213–14.
20. These four monastic communities (*tshogs sde bzhi*) founded in Tibet by Śākyaśrī comprise Neudongtsé Tsokpa (sNe'u gdong rtse tshogs pa), Drachi Tsongdu Tsokpa (Grwa phyi tshong 'dus tshogs pa), Dranang Gyeling Tsokpa (Grwa nang rgyal gling tshogs pa, founded by Jangchub Pel), and Tsang Cholung Tsokpa (gTsang chos lung tshogs pa). See the recent study in Heimbal 2013.
21. This original *Severance* text by Āryadeva the Brahmin is variously entitled *Esoteric Instructions of the Transcendent Perfection of Wisdom*, *Fifty-Verse Poem*, or *Great Poem*. Its later inclusion in the Nartang edition of the Tengyur would not contradict the comment of Kunga Drolchok who notes its absence from the Tengyur manuscripts of the sixteenth century. See the translation by Harding in Jamgön Kongtrul 2016, 3–11.
22. These practices are contained in her *Great Bundle of Precepts: The Source Text of Esoteric Instructions on Severance: The Profound Transcendent Perfection of Wisdom*. See the translation by Harding in Jamgön Kongtrul 2016, 13–27.
23. The primary revelation of Samten Ozer, the so-called new pronouncement (*bka' gsar ma*), is formally entitled *Severance of Demonic Forces: Essence of Profound Meaning*. Its eight appendices (*le'u yan lag brgyad*) are enumerated in the bibliography. On Samten Ozer, see also Jamgön Kongtrul 2016, 233–44.
24. The full title of this text is *Esoteric Instructions on Resting in the Nature of One's Own Mind: Spoken by Sublime Avalokita to the Great Accomplished Master Mitrayogin*. It is contained in *DNZ*, vol. 16, pp. 497–523. The miraculous life of Mitrayogin is recounted in Roerich 1949, 1030–43.

25. *DNZ*, vol. 16, p. 500, line 1.
26. It is unclear whether Hor Kabzhipa's two doctrinal collections, large and small (*chos tshoms che chung gnyis*), are extant.
27. Following Dhītika, the succession is said to have passed through Micchaka (Bhi bhi ka la), Buddhānandin, Buddhamitra, Bhikṣu Pārśva, Punyayaśaḥ, Aśvaghoṣa, Nāgārjuna, Āryadeva, Rāhulata, Saṃghānandi, Bhikṣu Arhat, Saṃghayaśaḥ, Kumārata, Śayata, Vasubandhu, Manorhita, Haklenayaśaḥ, and Siṃhabodhi.
28. This incident is recounted by Tāranātha in Chattopadhayaya 1970, 141–42.
29. Cf. Tāranātha's account of the two brothers in Chattopadhayaya 1970, 154–75.
30. This is the final quatrain from Nāgārjuna's *Refutation of Disputed Topics* and is not found, as our text suggests, in *Sixty Quatrains on Reasoning*. Note also that in the first line, our text reads *gang gis rten cing* for *gang gis ston cing*.
31. These verses are found toward the end of Rongton's biography, entitled *Wondrous Ocean of Faith,* in *Collected Works of Rongton Sheja Kunrik*, vol. 1, p. 99.
32. Our text reads *gra'i sman gcig du sman gcig pa* for *gra sman gcig pa.*
33. See Roerich 1949, 347–50.
34. This denotes a particular type of Tibetan monastic footwear (*sha gzugs ma*), on which see Zhang Yisun et al., *The Great Tibetan-Chinese Dictionary*, p. 3362. It suggests that Candrakīrti was engaged in prostrations over some distance.
35. Tib. *g.yar*, literally "lent out." Stearns 2010 (p. 42) reads "rediscovered by."
36. See Stearns 2010, 42–43.
37. The expression "single-deity single-vase" transmission (*lha gcig bum gcig*) denotes a simple vase empowerment ceremony, generally associated with action tantra deities, especially the long-life empowerment of Amitāyus, but also in respect of other deities, such as Vajraviḍāraṇa.
38. The expression "my father, the great translator" (*pha lo chen*) suggests that sixteenth-century Lochen Rinchen Zangpo was the father of Kunga Drolchok.
39. Despite this assertion, there appears to be no evidence of special terminology derived from the extant versions of *Heruka Galpo* in Dg. NGB. The distinctive expressions that appear in the lineage prayer in chapter 1 do have a certain affinity with the terminology of Guru Chowang's revelations, as has already been noted.
40. The purification of the seven aspects of consciousness—the afflicted mental consciousness and so forth (*nyon yid bdun sbyong tshul*)—would denote the purification of the five sensory consciousnesses, along with mental consciousness and afflicted mental consciousness, but exclude the substratum consciousness.
41. On these transmissions stemming from Gayādhara, see Davidson 2005, 178–83; also Dhongthog Rinpoche 2016, 81–87.
42. These are all enumerated in Dhongthog Rinpoche 2016, 95–96.
43. Dhongthog Rinpoche 2016, 98–102.
44. Dhongthog Rinpoche 2016, 91–92; also Davidson 2005, 194–204.
45. Drakpa Gyeltsen mentions the empowerment of the profound path (*zab lam gyi dbang*) very briefly in his *Analysis of Empowerment*, SLC, vol. 11, p. 42, line 1.
46. On these seventy-two tantras, see Stearns 2001, 255n234. The four profound doc-

trines (*zab chos bzhi*) comprise (i) the secret path, (ii) the profound path, (iii) the protectors of Virūpa, and (iv) the Vajravidāraṇa. See Dhongthog Rinpoche 2016, 246n200.

47. Tib. *go 'byed rnam gsal dpe brjod skad gnyis zung sbyor*. Dhongthog Rinpoche 2016, 98–100.
48. See Tsongkhapa 2013, 140, 277, 281–83, 359, 438–39.
49. On Mu Konchok Gyeltsen (1388–1469), see Stearns 2006, 246–47, 304.
50. Chojé Zung (Chos rje gzungs), also known as Dzongpa Zung-gi Pelwa (1306–1389), is counted among the disciples of Lama Dampa Sonam Gyeltsen in the lineage of the Path and Its Fruition.
51. See Drakpa Gyeltsen, in his *Collected Works*, vol. 3, pp. 383–87 on Khecarī; and pp. 410–36 on the central channel.
52. Kunga Zangpo, *Useful Rites for All the Means for Attainments of Mahāyoga Entitled Ornament of All Secrets*, in his *Collected Works*, vol. 3, pp. 239–85.
53. This refers to Tsongkhapa's *Exegesis of the Five Stages according to Cakrasaṃvara Entitled Opening the Eyes of the View concerning the Concealed Meaning*, in his *Collected Works*, vol. 10, pp. 115–86.
54. This would be Taktsang Lotsāwa Sherab Rinchen's *Descriptive Basis of Cakrasaṃvara according to the Tradition of Ghaṇṭhāpāda*, in his *Collected Works*, vol. 4, pp. 260–79.
55. Drakpa Gyeltsen, *Elucidation of the Five Stages*, in his *Collected Works*, vol. 3, pp. 242–63.
56. Pakpa Lodro Gyeltsen, *Pith Instructions of the Five Stages*, *Collected Works*, vol. 2, pp. 278–91.
57. The text of Tsokgompa Kunga Pel (1210–1307) and the notes of Zhang Dodé Pel (fl. thirteenth century) do not appear to be extant.
58. There is an extant translation by Marpa Chokyi Wangchuk of Vāgīśvaragupta's *Pith Instruction of Nondual Meditative Concentration of Glorious Cakrasaṃvara Entitled Fierce Inner Heat of Yoga*, T 1508, TPD, vol. 11, pp. 1775–77.
59. Gungru Sherab Zangpo's *A General Description of the Four Stages* and *A Particular Exegesis of the Vital Essence of Spring* have not been located in his extant works.
60. This can be seen in the final chapter of the *Vital Essence of Spring*, TPD, vol. 11, pp. 833–37, which refers to all four cakras. I have not located the *Instruction Manual Entitled Oral Discussion* (*Khrid yig gsung bgros ma*), which should not be conflated with Mu Konchok Gyeltsen's *Mind Training: Supplement to the Oral Tradition*, translated in Jinpa 2006, 431–515.
61. Nub Cholung (gNubs chos lung). Sonam Rinchen appears to have flourished in the fourteenth century.
62. In 1435, Rinpung Norbu Zangpo (Rin pungs drung chen nor bzang) seized power from the Pagmodrupa dynasty following the death of King Drakpa Gyeltsen (r. 1409–1434). He became the governor (*drung chen*) of Tibet, and his son Donyo Dorjé inflicted a decisive defeat on the Pagmodrupa forces in 1478. Rinpung's

rule continued until they, in turn, were eclipsed by the Samdrubtsé fiefdom in 1565.

63. On the three appearances according to the Path and Its Fruition (*lam 'bras snang gsum*), see Stearns 2006, 25–27, and the commentary on pp. 319–94. Nordrang Orgyan (*Compendium of Buddhist Numeric Terms*, p. 330) enumerates them as (i) impure appearances, (ii) appearances of the sacred doctrine, and (iii) physical appearances.
64. This text may possibly be the *Instruction on Cheating Death* (T 2839), which is attributed to Ajitamitragupta, an epithet of Jetāri.
65. The eight freedoms and ten advantages (*dal 'byor bco brgyad*) form the initial contemplation of the common preliminary practices, which, in the context of the present work, are mentioned in chapter 7. They are enumerated above, chapter 1, n. 54.
66. Our text reads *bod gdong* for *bong gdong*.

Chapter 6: Supplementary Historical Anecdotes

1. *Khrid brgya'i brgyud pa'i lo rgyus kha skong*, *DNZ*, vol. 18, pp. 99–116.
2. The longer and shorter texts concerning Vajravārāhī in the form Dvimukhā (*Zhal gnyis ma'i gzhung che chung*) are Śūnyatāsamādhi's *Attainment of the Pristine Cognition of the Real*, T 1551, and his *Transference of Pristine Cognition*, T 1553.
3. The longer and shorter texts on Vajravārāhī in the self-decapitating form Chinnamuṇḍā (*dBu bcad ma'i gzhung che chung*) comprise Śrīmatī's *Means for Attainment of Decapitated Vajravārāhī*, T 1554, and Virūpa's *Means for Attainment of Decapitated Vajravārāhī*, T 1555. See English 2002, 94–103.
4. The longer and shorter texts concerning Vajravārāhī in the form Sarvārthasiddhā (*Don grub ma'i gzhung che chung*) comprise Avadhūtipā's *Means for Attainment of Sarvārthasiddhā*, T 1552, and Advayavajra's *Rite of the Means for Attainment of Vajravārāhī Entitled Sarvārthasiddhā*, T 1578.
5. *Rite of Burnt Offerings* (*sByin sreg gi gzhung*) is Buddhadatta's *Rite of the Burnt Offering of Vajrayoginī*, T 1556, on which see English 2002, 384n4.
6. On Vārāhī according to the pith instructions of Oḍḍiyāna (*oḍḍiyāna gsang ba'i man ngag gi phag mo*), see also English 2002, 75.
7. This is also attributed to Avadhūtipā. It is possible that this reference may denote another text attributed to Śabaripā entitled the *Means for Attainment of Vajrayoginī*, T 1550.
8. See English 2002, 50.
9. These denote the four successions of the transmitted teachings (*bka' babs bzhi*) that fell to Tilopā and Nāropā. Among them, the first line of succession was from Vajradhara through Indrabhūti the Great, Sahajayoginī, Bhisukalpa, Saraha, and Nāgārjuna. It concerned the *Tantra of the Secret Assembly*, the *Tantra of the Four Adamantine Seats*, and the oral instructions of illusory body and transfer-

ence of consciousness from the *Six Doctrines*. The second line of succession was from Vajradhara, through Jñānaḍākinī, Kukkurāja, and Caryāpā. It concerned the *Tantra of Mahāmāyā* and the oral instructions of dream yoga from the *Six Doctrines*. The third line of succession was from Vajradhara, through Vajrapāṇi, Ḍombī Heruka, Vīṇāpavajra, and Kambalapāda. It concerned the mother tantras headed by *Cakrasaṃvara*, and the oral instructions of luminosity from the *Six Doctrines*. The fourth line of succession was from Vajradhara, through Vajrapāṇi, Anaṅgavajra, Padmavajra, and Kusalibhadra. It concerned *Hevajra*, and the oral instructions of the fierce inner heat from the *Six Doctrines*.

10. On this guidebook attributed to Karmapa Rangjung Dorjé, which is contained in *DNZ*, vol. 9, pp. 17–37, see below, chapter 9, n. 780.
11. Elsewhere she is considered to have been Nāropā's sister.
12. The five culminations (*mthar thug lnga*) achieved by Khyungpo Neljor included Hevajra, the culmination of fierce inner heat; Cakrasaṃvara, the culmination of the action seal; Guhyasamāja, the culmination of the illusory body and luminosity; Mahāmāyā, the culmination of dream yoga; and Vajrabhairava, the culmination of enlightened activities. See Jamgön Kongtrul 2007, 233–36.
13. *Clarifying the Six Doctrines* (*Chos drug gi tshig gsal*) also known as *The Inventory* (*Thems yig*), by Khyungpo Neljor, copied down directly from Nigumā, is in *DNZ* vol. 11, pp. 9–10.
14. The general Nigumā and Shangpa cycles are contained in *DNZ*, vols. 11–12. The two tantras containing the quintessential Shangpa teachings—namely, the *Tantra of the Ocean of Vows* (*sDom pa rgya mtsho'i rgyud*) and the *Tantra of the Precious Ocean* (*Rin chen rgya mtsho'i rgyud*)—were not translated into Tibetan. Khyungpo Neljor received their teachings from Vajrāsanapāda. See Jamgön Kongtrul 2007, 248n47.
15. This quotation has not yet been identified.
16. The five signature Shangpa teachings are described in the mnemonic device of a tree as the roots, trunk, branches, flowers, and fruit. See Jamgon Kontrul 2007, 238–49.
17. *The Three Nails of the Pith Instructions of Secret Attainment* (*gSang sgrub man ngag gzer gsum*), committed to writing by Nyenton Chokyi Sherab based on the revelation of Sukhasiddhi, is contained in *DNZ*, vol. 12, pp. 315–28.
18. *The Six Doctrines of Sukhasiddhi* are contained in *DNZ*, vol. 12, pp. 299–313. Some chapters of the present anthology suggest that *The Emanational Cakra of the Navel* is a substitute or even an alternative title for *The Inner Guidance of Nairātmyā*, the guidebook that immediately follows.
19. These five aspects comprise enlightened mind (*byang sems*), divine body (*lha sku*), resolute devotion (*mos gus*), abiding nature (*gnas lugs*), and dedication (*bsngo ba*).
20. For an account of the legendary error of Buddhajñānapāda, who requested empowerment from an emanational maṇḍala rather than his teacher, see Dudjom Rinpoche 1991, 494–96.

21. *DNZ*, vol. 8, pp. 202–33.
22. Also known as Zhang Lotsāwa Jangchub-o (b. 1237).
23. There appears to be no extant teaching attributed to Tsami Sangye Drak and pertaining to Cakrasaṃvara, which is entitled *On a Single Seat* (*sTan thog gcig ma*).
24. Jigten Gonpo's *Tenfold Doctrinal Instruction* (*bCu chos*) is contained in Drigungpa Anthology, vol. 30, pp. 305–22. Note that our text reads *chos bcu* for *bCu chos*.
25. Jigten Gonpo's *The Threefold Doctrine* (*gSum chos*) is contained in Drigungpa Anthology, vol. 30, pp. 323–32.
26. These three stems (*sdong po gsum*) therefore comprise (i) the view that accords with the tradition of Gampopa (*lta ba sgam po lugs*), (ii) the oral instructions that accord with the tradition of Rechungpa (*gdams ngag ras chung lugs*), and (iii) the auspicious circumstances that accord with Tsangpa Gyaré's own tradition (*rten 'brel kho bo lugs*). Respectively they pertain to the *The Means for Attainment of the Guru*, *The Common Savor*, and *The Auspicious Circumstances.*
27. The eight great instructions (*khrid chen brgyad*) of Tsangpa Gyaré are enumerated in the *Ornament Adorning the Eight Great Instructions* (*DNZ*, vol. 10, pp. 173–87) and may be paraphrased as follows: (i) the instruction on devotion to the teacher; (ii) the instruction of *The Coemergent Union of the Great Seal* that introduces ordinary minds to the genuine pristine cognition; (iii) the instruction of the extraordinary path of skillful means that actually and uncontrollably confers the coemergent pristine cognition by refining the auspicious circumstances of subtle energy and mind in the adamantine body; (iv) the instruction of unerring secret conduct and reversal meditation that accomplishes all things, carrying all common and uncommon misfortunes as an aid, allowing all harmonious circumstances to arise on the path, and all obstacles to be rendered harmless; (v) the instruction of profound pure visions and purification; (vi) the instruction that is impartial with respect to the eight worldly concerns; (vii) the instruction of loving-kindness and compassion that enables fortunate individuals to traverse in a short time the key stages of all profound and excellent paths that lead to enlightenment; and (viii) the instruction of causes and fruition, dependent origination, through which all things are dependently originated.
28. In succession, these were On Repa Darma Sengé (1177–1238), Zhonu Sengé (1200–1266), Nyima Sengé (1251–1287), Sengé Sherab (1236–1280), Pokya Rinchen Sengéwa (1258–1313), Sengé Gyelpo (1289–1325), Jamyang Kunga Sengé (1314–1347), Dorjé Rinchen (fl. fourteenth century), and Jamyang Lodro Sengé (1345–1390).
29. See below, chapter 9, n. 1043. The instruction known as the "vitality essence" (*srog thig*) corresponds to Ga Lotsāwa's *Heart Essence of Mahākāla*, vol. 92, pp. 365–78.
30. This *Instruction on the Book with a Sash* (*Be bum sku rags la gdams pa*) would correspond to Ga Lotsāwa, *Means for Attainment of Glorious Four-Armed Jñānanātha Mahākāla with Two Cakras according to the Kurakma Indic Text*, *DNZ*, vol. 10, pp. 471–96. Pagmodrupa himself authored the *Essential Instruction on Kurakma*,

in his *Collected Works*, vol. 7, pp. 447–60; and *The Secret Attainment of Kurakma: A Pith Instruction of Profound Summation*, in his *Collected Works*, vol. 4, ff. 408b–426b.

31. Texts representing these aspects of raven-faced Mahākāla (*bya rog gdong can*) are found in Drigungpa Anthology, vols. 91–92. The aspects with four cakras are exemplified in the *Secret Attainment That Reveals the Oral Instruction of Glorious Mahākāla with Three Channels and Four Cakras*, vol. 92, pp. 315–30; and the aspects with five cakras are exemplified in *Uncommon Oral Instruction of Guidance on Mahākāla with Five Cakras*, vol. 92, pp. 331–48. The aspects with two cakras include *Secret Attainment of Kurakma with Two Cakras*, vol. 92, pp. 259–86; and those with a single cakra include *Kurakma: The Secret Attainment of Mahākāla with One Cakra*, vol. 92, pp. 177–88. On the iconography, see Willson and Brauen 2000, nos. 351–353, 356.
32. This refers to the distinction between the lower rites (*smad las*) of exorcism and so forth, and the higher rites (*stod las*) of spiritual accomplishment.
33. Possibly Ratnagiri (Rin chen ri bo) in Odiviśa and Devagiri (Lha'i ri bo) in Mahārāṣṭra, near Ajanta.
34. *The Seven Sections of Spiritual Attainment* (*Grub pa sde bdun*) comprise the seven treatises contained in the first part of volume *wi* of the Derge Tengyur (TPD, vol. 26, pp. 3–191; T 2217–2223), which are respectively by Saroruhavajra, Anaṅgavajra, Indrabhūti, Lakṣmīkarā, Dārikapa, Cito, and Ḍombī Heruka.

    The Six Essential Cycles (*sNying po bskor drug*) comprise (i) the *Treasury of Spiritual Songs* by Saraha (T 2224), (ii) the *Establishment of the Four Seals* by Nāgārjuna (T 2225), (iii) the *Pith Instructions of the Inconceivable Stage* by Togtsepa (T 2228), (iv) the *Purification of Mental Obscuration* by Āryadeva (T 1804), (v) the *Luminosity of Pristine Cognition* by Devākaracandra (T 2226), and (vi) the *Synthesis of Abiding* by Sahajavajra (T 2227).

    The Twenty-Four Doctrinal Cycles of Nonmentation (*Amansikāra*, *Yid la mi byed pa, a ma na si'i chos bskor nyi shu rtsa bzhi*) are the works of Maitrīpā (also known as Advayavajra) contained in the *Advayavajrasaṃgraha* and in vol. *wi* of the Derge Tengyur. They are variously said to number twenty-four, twenty-five, or twenty-six (T 2229–2254; TPD, vol. 26, pp. 288–523). In our text, the number is given as twenty-two, and these are supplemented by four further texts, collectively known as the *Four Doctrines Exhorted by Injunction* (*bKa' yis bskul ba'i chos bzhi*), making up the full cycle. On this corpus, see Higgins 2008, 255–303. Also on the variant listings of these texts, see Mathes 2009; and for a complete translation of the texts in this cycle, see Mathes 2015.
35. Translated in Guenther 1993, 106 (v. 75).
36. Generally, Luipā is given as the first and Vyāli as the last. See Robinson 1979. The order presented here—from the "holder of the sword, bull, and fish" (*ral gri khyu mchog ro tsa na*) to the "holder of the peacock and treasure vase" (*rma bya gter gyi bum pa*)—may perhaps suggest "from Khaḍgapa, Gorakṣa, and Luipā, to Śabaripā and Vyāli."

37. See Robinson (1979, 23), who gives the king's name as Kunji.
38. This is Abhayadattaśrī, *Narrative of the Eighty-Four Accomplished Masters*, pp. 413–556, translated in Robinson 1979; and Abhayadattaśrī with Vīraraśmi, *The Essence of the Realizations of the Eighty-Four Accomplished Masters and Their Significance*, pp. 562–667.
39. Dudjom Rinpoche 1991, 607–14.
40. Dudjom Rinpoche 1991, 617–35.
41. Dudjom Rinpoche 1991, 538–42; also 555–68.
42. This is the transmission of Aro Yeshé Jungné, on which see Dudjom Rinpoche 1991, 708n896.
43. Dudjom Rinpoche 1991, 510–13.
44. On the activities of Dungtso Repa, see Yeshé Gyamtso 2011, 201–2.
45. This would have been the year 1607.

Chapter 7: The Ordinary Preliminary Practices

1. *Khrid brgya'i sngon 'gro thun mong ba*, *DNZ*, vol. 18, pp. 117–20.
2. The verses of this quatrain in Tibetan are characterized by reduplication of the final syllable of each line, in the initial syllable of the following line.
3. See above, chapter 1, n. 54.
4. On this contemplation of impermanence and death, see Patrul Rinpoche 1994, 39–59.
5. Patrul Rinpoche 1994, 61–99.
6. Patrul Rinpoche 1994, 101–31.
7. Patrul Rinpoche 1994, 195–234.
8. Here, the emphasis is on the twofold practice of calm abiding (*śamatha*, *zhi gnas*) and higher insight (*vipaśyanā*, *lhag mthong*).
9. On the formulation of these "signature" quatrains of verse, see above, chapter 4, n. 3.

Chapter 8: The Extraordinary Preliminary Practices

1. *Khrid brgya'i sngon 'gro thun mong ma yin pa*, *DNZ*, vol. 18, pp. 121–26.
2. These verses concerning the consecration of the terrain, cited by many authors of diverse traditions, derive from the *Incantation Rite of the Extraordinarily Vast Aspiration of the Seven Sugatas Compiled from the Sutra*, TPD, vol. 38, p. 909.
3. Each aspect of this visualization has an apparitional or apparent form (*rnam pa*) and an underlying essential reality (*ngo bo*). The truth of cessation (*nirodhasatya*, *'gog pa'i bden pa*) denotes the fourth of the noble truths, the fruitional cessation of cyclic existence. The ten powers (*daśabala*, *stobs bcu*) mentioned here are those of the buddhas (*daśatathāgatabala*, *de bzhin gshegs pa'i stobs bcu*), comprising (1) qualitative knowledge that positive contingencies are indeed positive contingencies (*sthānasthānayathābhūtaprajñāna*, *gnas la yang gnas su yang dag pa ji lta ba*

bzhin du rab tu shes pa); (2) qualitative knowledge that negative contingencies are indeed negative contingencies (*asthānāsthānayathābhūtaprajñāna, gnas ma yin pa la yang gnas ma yin par yang dag pa ji lta ba bzhin du rab tu shes pa*); (3) qualitative knowledge through contingencies and causes of the maturation of the past, future, and present actions of sentient beings, and of those who undertake such actions (*atītānāgatapratyutpannasarvakarmasamādānahetuvipākayathābhūtaprajñāna, 'das pa dang ma 'ongs pa dang da ltar byung ba'i las rnams dang las yang dag par len pa rnams kyi rnam par smin pa gnas kyi sgo dang rgyu'i sgo nas yang dag pa ji lta ba bzhin du rab tu shes pa*); (4) qualitative knowledge of multiple world systems and diverse sensory bases (*nānalokadhātunānadhātuyathābhūtaprajñāna, 'jig rten kyi khams du ma pa khams sna tshogs pa yang dag pa ji lta ba bzhin du rab tu shes pa*); (5) qualitative knowledge of the diversity of volitions and the multiplicity of volitions with respect to other sentient beings and other individuals (*anyasattvpudgalanānādhimuktyanekādhimuktiyathābhūtaprajñāna, sems can gzhan dag dang gang zag gzhan rnams kyi mos pa sna tshogs nyid dang mos pa du ma nyid yang dag pa ji lta ba bzhin du rab tu shes pa*); (6) qualitative knowledge of other sentient beings and other individuals who are of supreme acumen and those who are not (*anyasattvpudgalendriyavarāvarayathābhūtaprajñāna, sems can gzhan dag dang gang zag gzhan rnams kyi dbang po mchog dang mchog ma yin pa nyid yang dag pa ji lta ba bzhin du rab tu shes pa*); (7) qualitative knowledge of the paths that lead everywhere (*sarvatragānīpratipadyathābhūtaprajñāna, thams cad du 'gro ba'i lam yang dag pa ji lta ba bzhin du rab tu shes pa*); (8) qualitative knowledge of all the dissonant and purified mental states associated with the faculties, powers, branches of enlightenment, aspects of liberation, meditative concentrations, meditative stabilities, and formless absorptions (*sarvendriyabalabodhyaṅgavim okṣadhyāna-samādhisamāpattisaṃkleśavyavadānavyuthānayathābhūtaprajñāna, dbang po dang stobs dang byang chub kyi yan lag dang rnam par thar pa dang bsam gtan dang ting nge 'dzin dang snyoms par 'jug pa'i kun nas nyon mongs pa dang rnam par byang ba dang ldang pa shes pa yang dag pa ji lta ba bzhin du rab tu shes pa*); (9) qualitative knowledge of the recollection of multiple past abodes, and of the transference of consciousness at death and birth in respect of all sentient beings (*anekapūrvanivāsānusmṛticyutyutpattiyathābhūtaprajñāna, sngon gyi gnas rnam pa du ma rjes su dran pa dang sems can rnams kyi 'chi 'pho dang skye ba yang dag pa ji lta ba bzhin du rab tu shes pa*); and (10) qualitative knowledge that through one's own supernormal cognitive powers one has actualized, achieved, and maintained in this very lifetime the liberation of mind and the liberation of discriminative awareness in the state that is free from corruption because all corrupt states have ceased (*āsrvavakṣayayathābhūtaprajñāna, zag pa zad pa yang dag pa ji lta ba bzhin du rab tu shes pa*).

4. On the significance of taking refuge, see Patrul Rinpoche 1994, 171–92.
5. These verses are found in the *Maṇḍala Rite of the Transcendent Lord Glorious Cakrasaṃvara*, TPD, vol. 11, p. 723, except for the last line, which reads *dpal ldan he ru ka rang bya*.

6. These verses are also found in Jamgön Kongtrul, *All Requisite Quintessential Oral Instructions of the New and Ancient Traditions Useful for the Yoga of Retreat Sessions*, GDKT, vol. 12, pp. 305–84.
7. Jamgön Kongtrul, *All Requisite Quintessential Oral Instructions*, GDKT, vol. 12, pp. 305–84.
8. This practice is analogous to the purification of Vajrasattva, on which see Patrul Rinpoche 1994, 263–80.
9. On the maṇḍala offering in general, see Patrul Rinpoche 1994, 283–95; and on the offering of the body maṇḍala in the context of Severance, see Patrul Rinpoche 1994, 297–307.
10. With regard to this conflation of macrocosm and microcosm, the substratum (*ālaya, kun gzhi*) denotes the ground-of-all, or its substratum consciousness. The four continents surrounding Mount Meru in traditional cosmology comprise Pūrvavideha, Jambudvīpa, Aparagodānīya, and Uttarakuru. The four immeasurable aspirations concern the cultivation of loving-kindness, compassion, empathetic joy, and equanimity. The solar and lunar channels are the right and left channels of the subtle body. The red and white vital essences in their coarsest forms are menses and semen; see Gyalwa Yangonpa 2015, 289–92. The seven insignia of royal dominion (*saptarājaratna, rgyal srid sna bdun*) are those enjoyed by universal emperors during an ideal perfect age—namely, the wheel, the gemstone, the queen, the minister, the elephant, the horse, and the general (or the householder). The five solid viscera (*don lnga*) comprise the heart, lungs, liver, spleen, and kidneys, while the six hollow viscera (*snod drug*) comprise the stomach, gallbladder, large intestine, small intestine, urinary bladder, and the "reservoir for reproductive fluid" (*sam se'u*). See the illustrations in Parfionovitch et al. 1992, 1:43–44, 2:199–200.
11. The seven aspects of sublime spiritual wealth (*'phags pa'i nor bdun*) comprise faith, ethical discipline, generosity, study, conscience, shame, and discriminative awareness. See Dudjom Rinpoche 1991, 2:153.
12. These verses of maṇḍala offering are found in several sources within the *Compendium of Sādhanas* (*sGrub thabs kun btus*) anthology.

Chapter 9: The One Hundred and Eight Guidebooks

1. *Zab khrid brgya dang brgyad kyi yi ge, DNZ*, vol. 18, pp. 127–353.
2. *Zhen pa bzhi bral gyi khrid yig.* The author's primary sources for the first guidebook are Nub Rigdzin Drak's *List of Instructions in the Form of a Memorandum, DNZ*, vol. 6, pp. 315–17, translated in Jinpa 2006, 527–28; and Sakya Paṇḍita's *Instruction on Parting from the Four Attachments*, in his *Collected Works*, vol. 1, p. 470; also *DNZ*, vol. 6, pp. 314–15, translated in Jinpa 2006, 525–26. On their antecedents, especially Drakpa Gyeltsen's *Root Verses of the Account of Sachen Kunga Nyingpo's Encounter with Mañjughoṣa*, and other related texts contained in the *Cycle of Mind Training: Parting from the Four Attachments, DNZ*, vol. 6, pp.

305–56, see the translations in Jinpa 2006, 517–66. As mentioned above, chapter 1, n. 2, the four attachments to be separated are (i) the attachment to this life, which is contrary to the sacred doctrine; (ii) the attachment to cyclic existence, which is contrary to emancipation; (iii) the attachment to self-interest, which is contrary to the enlightened mind; and (iv) the presence of grasping, which is contrary to the right view.

3. These are translated in Jinpa 2006, the former on pp. 527–28, and the latter on pp. 525–26.
4. *Theg chen blo sbyong don bdun ma'i khrid yig.* The primary source of the second guidebook is Tokmé Zangpo's *The Seven-Point Mind Training of the Great Vehicle, DNZ*, vol. 4, pp. 189–214, which is also contained in the *Collected Works of Tokmé Zangpo, Concise Interpretation of the Verses of the Aural Transmission of the Seven-Point Mind Training*, and more elaborately in *Great Aural Transmission of Mind Training.* The earlier texts of Chekhawa and Sechilbupa are translated in Jinpa 2006, 83–132. The seven points respectively concern (i) the preliminary supporting teachings (*sngon 'gro rten chos*); (ii) refinement in the twofold enlightened mind—relative and absolute—that constitutes the main practice (*dngos gzhi byang sems gnyis rab 'byongs*), (iii) transforming negative circumstances into the path (*rkyen ngan byang chub kyi lam du khyer ba*), (iv) integration of a lifetime's experiential cultivation (*tshe gcig gi nyams len chig sgril*); (v) the measure of mind training (*blo sbyong pa'i tshad bstan pa*), (vi) the precepts of mind training (*blo sbyong gi bslab bya bstan pa*), and (vii) the commitments of mind training (*blo sbyong gi dam tshigs bstan pa*).
5. Tokmé Zangpo, *DNZ*, vol. 4, p. 191. line 4–p. 192, line 2.
6. Tokmé Zangpo, vol. 4, p. 192, line 2–p. 195, line 6.
7. The substratum consciousness (*ālayavijñāna, kun gzhi rnam par shes pa*) is differentiated from the seven other aspects of consciousness (*rnam shes tshogs bdun*), including the five aspects of sensory consciousness, mental consciousness, and afflicted mental consciousness. See Jamgön Kongtrul's explanation in Jamgön Kongtrul 2012, 511–30.
8. Tokmé Zangpo, *DNZ*, vol. 4, p. 195, lines 3–4.
9. That is to say, in walking, strolling, sitting, and sleeping.
10. The practice of exchanging compassion for the suffering of others (*gtong len*) is explained in Patrul Rinpoche 1994, 223–28.
11. Tokmé Zangpo, *DNZ*, vol. 4, p. 195, line 6–p. 202, line 5.
12. Tokmé Zangpo, vol. 4, p. 200, line 7.
13. Tokmé Zangpo, vol. 4, p. 202, line 5–p. 204, line 5.
14. On these five powers (*stobs lnga*)—(i) the power of the seed of virtuous action (*dkar po'i sa bon stobs*), (ii) the power of propulsion (*'phen stobs*), (iii) the power of familiarity (*goms stobs*), the power of eradication (*sun byin stobs*), and the power of aspirational prayer (*smon lam stobs*)—see also Jinpa 2006, 112–15.
15. Tokmé Zangpo, *DNZ*, vol. 4, p. 204, line 5–p. 205, line 6.

16. Tokmé Zangpo, vol. 4, p. 205, line 6–p. 208, line 5.
17. Tokmé Zangpo, vol. 4, p. 208, line 5–p. 214, line 3.
18. *rTen 'brel snying po'i khrid yig.* The primary source is attributed to the Jonangpa master Muchen Gyeltsen Pelzangpo (fl. thirteenth–fourteenth centuries), although his name does not appear in the lineage outlined above in chapter 1. There is an extant work by him entitled *Profound Guidance on the Dependent Origination of Past Actions, Causes, and Fruition*, but any relationship between the two texts is yet to be determined. Another version attributed to Tokmé Zangpo is found in the *Collected Works of Tokmé Zangpo* (Zhigatse ed.), pp. 193–200, and also in Kadampa Anthology II, pp. 287–300. The lineage prayer in chapter 1, on the other hand, ascribes the origin of this instruction to Dromtonpa, from whom the related *Guide to the Heart of Dependent Origination*, translated in Jinpa 2006, 423–429, possibly derives—its authorship has been attributed to both Dromtonpa and Puchungwa Zhonu Gyeltsen (see Jinpa 2006, n. 811).
19. The annotation in the text reads *khyad par sngon 'gro.*
20. The annotation in the text reads *byams pa.*
21. The annotation in the text reads *snying rje.*
22. The annotation in the text reads *brje ba.*
23. The annotation in the text reads *gtong len.*
24. These three ancillary meditations are explained in Tokmé Zangpo, *Collected Works*, pp. 199–200; also Jinpa 2006, 427.
25. *sKyid sdug lam 'khyer gyi khrid yig.* The primary source is Remdawa Zhonu Lodro's *Memorandum on the Teaching of Gyelsépa*, which does not appear to be extant apart from the text contained in Tokmé Zangpo's *Collected Works* (Zhigatse ed.), pp. 201–5. See also above, chapter 4, nn. 28–29. A related instruction is also translated in Jinpa 2006, 213–14, who in his n. 335 discusses the antecedents of this instruction in the writings of Śākyaśrī (1127–1225) and Tropu Lotsāwa Jampapel (1173–1236).
26. The carrying of happiness on the path by means of relative enlightened mind, which is discussed in this paragraph, appears to be missing from the extant text of Tokmé Zangpo and may possibly reflect Remdawa's distinctive approach.
27. The introduction to happiness in the buddha body of reality (*skyid pa chos skur ngo sprad pa*) is discussed in Tokmé Zangpo, *Collected Works*, p. 202.
28. The introduction to happiness in the buddha body of perfect resource (*skyid pa longs skur ngo sprod pa*) is discussed in Tokmé Zangpo, *Collected Works*, pp. 202–3.
29. The introduction to happiness in the buddha body of emanation (*skyid pa sprul pa'i skur ngo sprod pa*) is discussed in Tokmé Zangpo, *Collected Works*, pp. 203–4.
30. Tokmé Zangpo, *Collected Works*, p. 203.
31. Tokmé Zangpo, pp. 204–5.
32. Tokmé Zangpo, p. 205.
33. *Sum pa'i blo sbyong gi khrid yig.* The primary source of this guidebook, attributed to Lama Dampa Sonam Gyeltsen (1312–1375), has not yet been identified in his

extant *Collected Works*. The significance here is that it was he who imparted the instruction to Gyelsé Tokmé Zangpo, in whose *Collected Works* there is an extant *Homage to the Teachers of the Aural Transmission of Sumpa Lotsāwa*. A related text entitled *Mind Training of Sumpa Lotsāwa* is translated in Jinpa 2006, 215–16.

34. The dangerous passageway of the mental body (*yid 'phrang*) refers to the pitfalls that the mental body may experience during the intermediate state of the rebirth process, after death. See Dorje 2005, 273–303.

35. *Ma gcig gi gcod kyi khrid yig.* The primary source is Nyakton Samten Ozer's *Wish-Fulfilling Gem: An Instruction on the Inner Meaning*, the third of the eight appendices to his *Severance of Demonic Forces: Essence of Profound Meaning*, pp. 71–96. Some phrases from that text have been inserted here in square brackets for the sake of clarity. Thanks to Sarah Harding for help in accessing these sources. Jamgön Kongtrul's anthology on Severance is contained in *DNZ*, vol. 14, and translated by Harding in Jamgön Kongtrul 2016.

36. An annotation in the text here accordingly reads *sngo 'gro lta ba | yum don sngo sprad pa*.

37. Nyakton Samten Ozer, *Wish-Fulfilling Gem*, p. 81, line 7–p. 82, line 2.

38. Nyakton Samten Ozer, p. 82, line 2–p. 83, line 2.

39. Nyakton Samten Ozer, p. 83, line 8–p. 84, line 2.

40. Nyakton Samten Ozer, p. 84, line 2.

41. Nyakton Samten Ozer, p. 84, line 7–p. 85, line 1.

42. Nyakton Samten Ozer, p. 85, lines 5–6.

43. The annotation in the text accordingly reads *bdud bzhi dbyings su gcod pa*. The four devils to be severed are enumerated here (Nyakton Samten Ozer, *Wish-Fulfilling Gem*, p. 86, lines 5–7) as (i) devil of impeded senses (*thogs bcas kyi bdud*), (ii) devil of unimpeded thoughts (*thogs med kyi bdud*), (iii) devil that induces exaltation (*dga' byed kyi bdud*), and (iv) demonic forces that induce egotistical pride (*snyems byed kyi bdud*).

44. Nyakton Samten Ozer, *Wish-Fulfilling Gem*, p. 87, lines 1–2.

45. Nyakton Samten Ozer, *Wish-Fulfilling Gem*, p. 87, line 3–p. 88, line 8. On this devil of impeded senses, see also Harding (2003) 2018, 117–18, 309–10; also Jamgön Kongtrul 2016, 303.

46. Nyakton Samten Ozer, *Wish-Fulfilling Gem*, p. 88, line 8–p. 90, line 7. On this devil of unimpeded thoughts, see also Harding (2003) 2018, 118–19, 310; also Jamgön Kongtrul 2016, 303.

47. Nyakton Samten Ozer, *Wish-Fulfilling Gem*, p. 90, line 7–p. 92, line 3. On this devil that induces exaltation, see also Harding (2003) 2018, 119, 310–13; also Jamgön Kongtrul 2016, 303.

48. Nyakton Samten Ozer, *Wish-Fulfilling Gem*, p. 92, line 3–p. 95, line 1. On this devil that induces egotistical pride or inflated pride, see also Harding (2003) 2018, 120–122, 313–316; also Jamgön Kongtrul 2016, 304.

49. An annotation in the text accordingly reads *rjes spyod pa*.

50. Nyakton Samten Ozer, *Wish-Fulfilling Gem*, p. 95, lines 1–8.

51. *sNying po don gsum gyi khrid yig.* The primary source, attributed to Mitrayogin and Tropu Lotsāwa, is contained in *DNZ*, vol. 16, pp. 605–7.
52. An annotation in the text indicates that these immediate perceptions refer to the intermediate state after death.
53. *DNZ*, vol. 16, pp. 605–7.
54. *Sems nyid ngal gso'i khrid yig.* The primary source is Yangtsewa Rinchen Sengé's text, which appears to be no longer extant. Its antecedents include the revelation that Avalokiteśvara imparted to Mitrayogin, entitled *Resting in the Nature of Mind*, which is contained in *DNZ*, vol. 16, pp. 497–523. Its immediate successors include the contributions of Yangtsewa's illustrious disciple Buton Rinchen Drub, whose compilation of relevant scriptural quotations from the sutras and tantras is found in *DNZ*, vol. 16, pp. 553–65.
55. The sevenfold posture of Vairocana that clarifies the meditative state of mind comprises (i) a straight spine, (ii) hands positioned in meditative equipoise, (iii) elbows slightly protruding, (iv) chin slightly lowered, (v) eyes unwavering, (vii) lips resting naturally with the tongue against the palate, and (vii) legs crossed in the adamantine posture. See Khenchen Thrangu 1993, 21–25, for a lucid and succinct explanation.
56. Tib. *glang skyong ba.*
57. On an earlier reference to the three metaphors of the swordsman, bull, and bird, see *DNZ*, vol. 16, p. 502, line 6–p. 503, line 3.
58. *sKyes bu gsum gyi khrid yig.* The primary source is Chimchen Namka Drak, *Excellent Path of the Three Sorts of Person*, contained in Kadampa Anthology II, vol. 47, pp. 227–66. Later works include Tāranātha's *Guidance on the Pith Instructions of the Three Sorts of Person on the Stages for Entering the Buddhist Teaching Entitled Nectar Essence*, *DNZ*, vol. 3, pp. 181–273.
59. Among these, (i) the ripening results of any contaminated virtue or nonvirtue may be exemplified by the contaminated psychophysical aggregates that one presently has; (ii) results corresponding to their causes on the basis of past experience may be exemplified by the enjoyment or prosperity experienced in future lives by one who has practiced generosity in this life; (iii) results corresponding to their causes on the basis of past activities may be exemplified by the desire to perform negative deeds in this life when one has already performed negative deeds in past lives; and (iv) predominant results may be exemplified by rebirth in a negative environment due to having practiced negativity in former lives, and rebirth in a positive environment due to having practiced virtue in former lives.
60. The five acquisitive aggregates (*pañcopadānaskandha*, *nyer len gyi phung po lnga*) comprise physical forms, feelings, perceptions, formative predispositions, and consciousness. See Jamgön Kongtrul's (2012, 477–531) presentation.
61. *bsTan rim gyi khrid yig.* The primary source of this guidebook, here attributed to Chim, is actually Drolungpa Lodro Jungné, *The Great Sequence of the Teaching*, Kadampa Anthology I, vol. 4, p. 35–vol. 5, p. 322. It takes the form of a commentary on Atiśa's *Lamp for the Path of Enlightenment*. There is also a summary by

the same writer, entitled *Synopsis of the Great Sequence of the Buddhist Teaching*, contained in Kadampa Anthology I, vol. 5, pp. 243–323. On this genre, see also Jackson 1996.

62. The text (p. 144, line 3) accordingly has the annotation *tshul gnas*.
63. On these distinctions from a Tibetan perspective, see Choying Tobden Dorje 2014, 242–54.
64. See Choying Tobden Dorje 2014, 255–91.
65. The text (p. 145, line 3) accordingly has an annotation that reads *thos bsam sgom*.
66. *Srid zhi mnyam nyid kyi khrid yig.* The primary source, the adaptation of Chimchen Namka Drak, has not yet been located elsewhere. There are other extant versions, including Rongton Sheja Kunrik, *Essence of the Key to the Guidance on the Sameness of Existence and Quiescence, according to the Tradition of Atiśa*, in his *Collected Works*, vol. 1, pp. 324–29; and Tsongkhapa Lobzang Drakpa, *Guidance on the View of the Sameness of Existence and Quiescence*, in his *Collected Works*, vol. 15, pp. 767–817.
67. This accords with the annotation *kun rdzob*, found in our text, p. 145, line 7.
68. This accords with the annotation *don dam*, found in our text, p. 146, line 5.
69. Literally "without negation or proof" (*dgag sgrub bral ba*).
70. *dBu ma chen po'i khrid yig.* The primary source, attributed to Jangsem Dawa Gyeltsen, has not yet been located elsewhere. There are other distinct but related texts, including the Sakya monk Yeshe Gyeltsen's *Pith Instruction of the Great Middle Way*, contained in Kadampa Anthology I, vol. 22, pp. 5–28; and also Chimchen Namka Drak's *Guidance on the Middle Way*, Kadampa Anthology II, vol. 17, pp. 171–208.
71. This accords with the annotation *sngon 'gro*, found in our text, p. 147, line 2.
72. The annotation here reads *shes rab*.
73. Here there is an annotation reading *thabs*.
74. Here there is an annotation reading *thabs byung*.
75. On the four sorts of physical activity (*spyod lam rnam bzhi*), see above, chapter 9, n. 9.
76. That is to say, the eight extremes (*mtha' brgyad*) of arising, cessation, nihilism, eternalism, coming, going, diversity, and identity.
77. See the alternative translation of this guidebook in Kapstein 1996, 282–83.
78. *bKa' gdams lkog khrid kyi khrid yig.* The primary source is said to be Shawo Gangpa's *Trilogy of Pulverizing*, which does not appear to be extant as a distinct work; nor does any adaptation by Chimchen Namka Drak appear to be extant.
79. *Thub pa'i khrid yig.* The primary source for guidebooks numbered fourteen to seventeen, collectively entitled *Four Deities of Kadam* (*bKa' gdams lha bzhi*), is Chimchen Namka Drak's *Instructions of the Four Deities of Kadam: Essential Fusion of the Path of Sutra and Mantra, DNZ*, vol. 4, pp. 367–433. These four guidebooks respectively concern Munīndra, Avalokiteśvara, Acala, and Tārā. On their antecedent in the transmission to Atiśa, see Jinpa 2008, 80–94; and for iconographic and liturgical details, see Willson and Brauen 2000, nos. 39, 103, 174.

80. The three religious robes (*tricīvara, chos gos gsum*) comprise (i) the outer robe (*saṃghāṭī, snam sbyar*), (ii) the upper robe worn by all mendicants (*uttarasaṅgha, bla gos*), and (iii) the inner robe (*antarāvāsa, mthang gos*).
81. Calm abiding may be practiced with an external support (*rten bcas kyi zhi gnas*)—that is, physically present; or without an external support (*rten med kyi zhi gnas*)—that is, with a visualized object. In the former case, calm abiding may have a partial support, such as a stone or any ordinary object (*cha shas kyi rten bcas*), or a perfect support (*rdzogs pa'i rten bcas*), such as a buddha image or seed syllable. On the practice of calm abiding, see Khenchen Thrangu 1993, 17–62.
82. The nine phases of calm abiding (*śamatha, gzhi gnas*) comprise (i) mental placement (*cittasthāpanā, sems 'jog*), (ii) total or perpetual placement (*saṃsthāpana, kun tu 'jog pa*), (iii) definitive or integrated placement (*nges par 'jog*), (iv) intensified placement (*upasthāpanā, nye bar 'jog*), (v) controlling (*damana, 'dul byed*), (vi) calming (*śamana, zhi bar byed*), (vii) intensified calming (*upaśamana, nye bar zhi bar byed*), (viii) perpetual or one-pointed placement (*rgyun gcig tu byed*), and (ix) placement in meditative equipoise (*samasaṃsthāpa, mnyam bzhag*). See Jamgön Kongtrul's presentation in Jamgön Kongtrul 2012, 428–29. Khenchen Thrangu (1993, 54) includes a chart depicting the relationship between these nine techniques of calm abiding and their associated mental powers and levels of engagement, which is based on Asaṅga's *Level of the Pious Attendants* (T 4036).
83. The practice of higher insight (*vipaśyanā, lhag mthong*) focuses on the nonself of individual persons (*pudgalanairātmya, gang zag gi bdag med*), (ii) the nonself of phenomena (*dharmanairātmya, chos kyi bdag med*), (iii) the nonself of the causal basis (*hetunairātmya, rgyu'i bdag med*), and (iv) the nonself of the essential nature (*svabhāvanairātmya, ngo bo'i bdag med*). On this practice in general, see Khenchen Thrangu 1993, 54, 65–107.
84. *Mi g.yo ba'i khrid yig.*
85. The eight great nāgas (*aṣṭamahānāga, klu chen brgyad*) comprise Ananta (mTha' yas), Takṣaka ('Jog po), Vāsuki (Nor rgyas), Śaṅkhapāla (Dung skyong), Padma (Pad ma), Mahāpadma (Pad ma chen po), Karkoṭa (sTobs rgyu), and Kulikā (Rigs ldan ma).
86. As below, the ten-syllable mantra (*yi ge bcu pa*) is OṂ CAṆḌA MAHĀROṢANA HŪṂ.
87. According to Vasubandhu (1988–90, chap. 3, vv. 85b–89c), one double arm span or bow span (*dhanus, mda' rgyang*) equals four cubits (*hasta, khru*), one earshot (*krośa, rgyangs grags*) equals five hundred bow or double arm spans, and one yoking distance (*yojana, dpag tshad*, approximately 7,315 meters) equals eight earshots.
88. On Nezur Yeshé Bar (1042–1118), see also *Treasury of Lives* and (TBRC P1316).
89. *sPyan ras gzigs kyi khrid yig.* The pervasion of space with compassion is the hallmark of this guidebook.
90. "Sunlight" (*sūryaprabha, nyi ma'i 'od*).
91. "Power of the conqueror" (*jinendra, rgyal ba'i dbang po*).

92. "Great medication" (*mahoṣadha, sman chen po*).
93. "King of diversity" (*chitrarāja, sna tshogs pa'i rgyal po*).
94. The twelve branches of scripture (*dvādaśāṅgapravacana, gsung rab yan lag bcu gnyis*) altogether comprise discourses (*sutra, mdo sde*), proverbs in prose and verse (*geya, dbyangs bsnyad*), prophetic declarations (*vyākaraṇa, lung bstan*), verses (*gāthā, tshig bcad*), aphorisms (*udāna, ched brjod*), legends or frame stories (*nidāna, gleng gzhi*), extensive teachings (*mahāvaipulya, shin tu rgyas pa*), tales of past lives (*jātaka, skyes rabs*), marvelous events (*adbhutadharma, rmad du byung*), narratives (*avadāna, rtogs brjod*), fables (*itivṛttaka, de lta bu byung ba*), and established instructions (*upadeśa, gtan phab*). See the analysis offered in Butön Rinchen Drup 2013, 17–18.
95. "King of victory banners" (*dhvajāgra, rgyal mtshan gyi rgyal po*).
96. *sGrol ma'i khrid yig.* The function of this guidebook is to offer protection from fears.
97. For illustrations and descriptive detail of these eight aspects of Tārā, who protects from the eight fears or dangers, see Mullin and Watt 2003, 79–96.
98. *Tā rā mkhyen.*
99. *Po to ba'i dpe chos kyi khrid.* The primary source of this guidebook, attributed to the writings of Hor Kabzhipa Sengé Gyeltsen, does not appear to be extant apart from this synopsis. Its antecedent is the seminal text of Potowa Rinchen Sel (1027–1105) entitled *The Parables of Potowa: A Heap of Gems*, which is not included in *DNZ* but is published in *Gangs can rig mdzod lde mig*. The text takes the form of parables pointing to the compatibility and incompatibility of persons of the three sorts of capacity to engage in the practice of the sacred doctrine.
100. Potowa Rinchen Sel, *Parables of Potowa*, chap. 2, pp. 17–19.
101. Mental inertia (*yid 'dus*) is here exemplified by meditative absorption, sleep, and torpor.
102. Potowa Rinchen Sel (*Parables of Potowa*, chap. 2, pp. 19–22), following Vasubandhu, adds faithlessness as a sixth stain to be abandoned.
103. Potowa Rinchen Sel, *Parables of Potowa*, chap. 2, pp. 22–23.
104. Potowa Rinchen Sel, chap. 2, pp. 23–25.
105. Potowa Rinchen Sel, chap. 4, p. 32. The citation is from *The Parables of Potowa: A Heap of Gems* (*dpe chos*), root verses, p. 1. Note that our text reads *sngon pa* for *ston pa*. There are two parables here indicating that this guidebook has been authentically transmitted and not fabricated. The methods by which genuine teachers grant instruction, illuminating the path, are (i) by imitating one's own teacher (that is, like a child in its father's voice), and (ii) offering a last will and testament to the wind, which may or may not be disregarded.
106. On these parables, including "the wedding invitation" (*gnyen sbron*), see Potowa Rinchen Sel, *Parables of Potowa*, chap. 5, pp. 32–44.
107. On these parables, including "the killing of a field mouse" (*bra ba bsad pa*), see Potowa Rinchen Sel, *Parables of Potowa*, chap. 5, pp. 44–50.
108. On the parables from "the grass on a castle roof" (*mkhar thog rtsva*) to "the watch-

tower" (*so kha'i mkhar*), see Potowa Rinchen Sel, *Parables of Potowa*, chap. 6, pp. 51–56.

109. On the parables from "the child losing its last morsel of food [in a time of famine]" (*byis pa'i sne zan*) to "cold sealing wax" (*la cha grang mo*), see Potowa Rinchen Sel, *Parables of Potowa*, chap. 6, pp. 56–60.

110. On the parables from "dislike for this transient state" (*'di na mi dga' ba*) to "the sthavira named Vṛddhaja" (rGan po skyes), see Potowa Rinchen Sel, *Parables of Potowa*, chap. 7, pp. 60–77.

111. On the parables from "clutching at death" (*shi sbar*) and continuing through to the parable of "grassland [unwarmed by the evening sun]" (*spang thang*), see Potowa Rinchen Sel, *Parables of Potowa*, chap. 7, pp. 77–81.

112. On the parables from "[positive actions] with positive returns" (*bzang lan*) to "[nonwithdrawal from the sacred doctrine] despite being enslaved by the trichiliocosm" (*stong gsum bran khol*) and "[not being swayed by hatred] even though one might be killed" (*bsad kyang rung*), see Potowa Rinchen Sel, *Parables of Potowa*, chap. 8, pp. 82–96.

113. On the parables from "the loss of good fortune" (*skal chad*) to "being stuffed with tea and cheesecake [but lacking faith]" (*ja thud 'grangs*), see Potowa Rinchen Sel, *Parables of Potowa*, chap. 8, pp. 96–104. Note that our text reads *ja thug drang* for *ja thud 'grangs*.

114. On the parables from "Nanda (dGa' bo)" to "seeing the [irreversible] goal" (*mtha' mthong*), see Potowa Rinchen Sel, *Parables of Potowa*, chap. 9, pp. 105–11. Nanda was the younger half brother of Śākyamuni Buddha who was shown the defects of cyclic existence by the Buddha and eventually renounced them to attain arhatship.

115. On the parables from "the monkey in a trap" (*rnyong la spre'u*) to "[the reversing of] a falling boulder of copper ore" (*zangs rbab [zlog]*), see Potowa Rinchen Sel, *Parables of Potowa*, chap. 9, pp. 112–20. Our text reads *zang sbab* for *zangs rbab zlog*.

116. On the parables from "bridling a horse" (*rta la srab*) to "the two divine princes" (*lha gnyis bzhin*), see Potowa Rinchen Sel, *Parables of Potowa*, chap. 10, pp. 120–27.

117. On the parable from "crossing a river without being able to ford a ditch" (*yur chu gtsang po*) to "the eagle and the monkeys" (*bya glag spre'u*), see Potowa Rinchen Sel, *Parables of Potowa*, chap. 10, pp. 127–34. Note that the latter parable is missing in our text, and that this section actually appears to have thirteen parables.

118. On the parables from "begging for alms" (*bsod snyoms*) to "two sibling monks of Gyel" (*rgyal btsun spun*), see Potowa Rinchen Sel, *Parables of Potowa*, chap. 11, pp. 135–37. The former parable is missing in our text. With regard to the latter, the story goes that one of the siblings drank ale and the other did not. Not surprisingly, however, when the one who did drink visited Radreng, he returned home as a nondrinker, but the one who did not drink visited Lhasa and returned home as a drinker.

119. On the parables from "feeding off an invalid when hungry, in the manner of Bon-

pos and wild horses" (*ltogs na nad pa bon po rta*) to "finding a small room [in a blizzard]" (*khang bu rnyed*), see Potowa Rinchen Sel, *Parables of Potowa*, chap. 11, pp. 137–42.

120. On the parables from "the well of gold bursting forth" (*gser gyi khron rdol*) to "the goat herder" (*ra 'ded*), see Potowa Rinchen Sel, *Parables of Potowa*, chap. 12, pp. 143–48. The former suggests that disciples should not be distracted whatever the teacher says. If the teacher preaches without practicing the sacred doctrine, there will be no practical application.

121. On the parable from "the [functionless] water mill made of wood" (*shing gi rang 'thags*) to "the [impotent] castrated bull" (*'og med glang 'dra*) and "an ordinary agate stone [instead of a wish-fulfilling gem]" (*mching bu*), see Potowa Rinchen Sel, *Parables of Potowa*, chap. 12, pp. 149–51. In the latter case, our text reads *'phying bu* for *mching bu*.

122. On the parables from "the two [breastfed] babies—one with a mouth and one without a mouth" (*bu chu kha can kha med*)—to "[Potowa's exemplary disciple] Sherab Yonten" (Shes rab yon tan), see Potowa Rinchen Sel, *Parables of Potowa*, chap. 13, pp. 151–55.

123. On the parables from "[Potowa's failed disciple] Ngapa Gyagar" (Ngang pa rgya gar) to "the child named Analé" (A na le), see Potowa Rinchen Sel, *Parables of Potowa*, chap. 13, pp. 155–61.

124. On the parables from "the baby and a chick who are both dependent on its mother" (*bu chung bye phrug ma la rag*) to "[Nāgabodhi] swallowing [Nāgārjuna's] spittle [and attaining the first bodhisttva level]" (*lud pa thob pa*), see Potowa Rinchen Sel, *Parables of Potowa*, chap. 14, pp. 161–66.

125. On the parables from "[Atiśa's disciple] Shik Chawa (Shig 'cha' ba) to "the monkey's [stolen] food" (*spre'u yi zas*), see Potowa Rinchen Sel, *Parables of Potowa*, chap. 14, pp. 166–69.

126. On the parables from "the sweet ball of molasses" (*bur sgor*) to "our past history, [which has brought about our present excellent condition]" (*nged kyi gna' gtam*), see Potowa Rinchen Sel, *Parables of Potowa*, chap. 15, pp. 169–71. Note that our text reads *rna gtam* for *gna' gtam*.

127. On the parables from "[the disconsolate bride] saying to her mother, 'I have been [harmed]!'" (*a ma nga ni*) to "[the accepting] of an [inferior] goat or bird [as compensation] rather than a [superior] horse or a yak" (*rta g.yag ra dang bya*), see Potowa Rinchen Sel, *Parables of Potowa*, chap. 15, pp. 171–72.

128. On the parables from "Atiśa (A ti sha) [who accumulated merits in former lives]" to "[meritoriously responding to Mangyul] while sitting on one's seat" (*stan la 'dug pa*), see Potowa Rinchen Sel, *Parables of Potowa*, chap. 16, pp. 173–81.

129. On the parables from "having acquired a body with unfavorable conditions" (*mi khom lus blangs*) to "having sold a [wish-fulfilling] gem [for a pittance]" (*nor bu btsongs pa*), see Potowa Rinchen Sel, *Parables of Potowa*, chap. 16, pp. 181–85.

130. That is to say, the four conducive factors (*'khor lo bzhi*) for monks are (i) living in a facilitating place, (ii) relying on a holy person, (iii) making aspirational prayers,

and (iv) accumulating merit. See Zhang Yisun et al., *Great Tibetan-Chinese Dictionary*, p. 413.

131. On the parables from "the pathway [to enlightenment]" (*'gro sa lam*) to "the resemblance of [remedial enlightened mind] to nectar" (*bdud rtsi 'dra ba*), see Potowa Rinchen Sel, *Parables of Potowa*, chap. 17, pp. 185–87.

132. On the parables from "[the essenceless] plantain" (*chu shing*) to "the [hibernating] marmot" (*'phyi ba*), see Potowa Rinchen Sel, *Parables of Potowa*, chap. 17, pp. 187–88. Note that our text reads *'chi ba* for *'phyi ba*.

133. On the parables from the "[mother's nurturing of an infant from the size of] a worm [to the size of a yak]" (*'bu srin [g.yag tsam]*) to "[the stabbing of] an enemy with a sword" (*ral gri dgra*), see Potowa Rinchen Sel, *Parables of Potowa*, chap. 18, pp. 188–91.

134. Tib. *ba gtor*. See Āryasūra 1895, 218–27. Note that our text reads *bu stor* for *ba gtor*.

135. Tib. *chus khyer*. See Āryasūra 1895, 234–44.

136. Tib. *ma skyes dgra*. See Potowa Rinchen Sel, *Parables of Potowa*, chap. 18, p. 191.

137. On the parables from "the mother's [love] for her child' (*ma ni bu la*) to "[the loving sthavira] Gyelshé (rGyal she), see Potowa Rinchen Sel, *Parables of Potowa*, chap. 19, pp. 192–95. On this figure, see also Roerich 1949, 1003. Our text reads *rgyal sho* for *rgyal she*.

138. On the parables from "the burning fire [of hatred]" (*sreg byed me ni*) to "[the limited loving-kindness of Jangpa Sherab Bar] in the face of his mother's suffering" (*ma la sdug*), see Potowa Rinchen Sel, *Parables of Potowa*, chap. 19, pp. 195–96. Our text reads *ma la sgrig* for *ma la sdug*.

139. On the parables from "[compassion] for the blind roaming in a wilderness" (*dmus long 'brog 'khyams*) to "[the incident] at Nadong [where Khampa Jampel's mother suffered a dog bite]" (*yul sna gdong*), see Potowa Rinchen Sel, *Parables of Potowa*, chap. 20, pp. 196–99.

140. On the parables from "the mantrin who slew a goat" (*sngags pa ra bsad*) to "the falcon and the wolf" (*khra spyang*), see Potowa Rinchen Sel, *Parables of Potowa*, chap. 20, pp. 199–200.

141. On the parables from "the desire [of a thirsty man] for water" (*chu 'dod*) to "training in the seven attributes [of a bodhisattva]" (*chos bdun bslab*), see Potowa Rinchen Sel, *Parables of Potowa*, chap. 21, pp. 202–13.

142. On the parables from "[inadequate aspiration] like a foe banished from the land" (*dgra bo yul 'byin*) to "the mantrin [deceitfully] selling butter" (*sngags pa mar 'tshong*), see Potowa Rinchen Sel, *Parables of Potowa*, chap. 21, pp. 214–24.

143. On these parables, from "the snake slithering from its hole" (*sbrul lkogs*) to "[Jowo Rinpoché saying,] 'I am skilled [in acts of liberality]'" (*kho mkhas*); as well as "the hermit monk" (*dgon pa'i dge slong*), "the reading aloud [of the sutras]" (*kha ton klog*), "the royal class [protecting the lowly]" (*rgyal rigs*), and "the mendicant dwelling in a fearsome place" (*'jigs sa'i rab byung*), see Potowa Rinchen Sel, *Parables of Potowa*, chap. 22, pp. 225–29.

144. On the parables, from "an [oblivious] skunk attracted to butter" (*mar la ti tos*) to "the [unclean] feast offered by northern [brigands]" (*byang pa'i ston mo*), as well as "the wild [brigand] burned by fire" (*mes tshig rgod*), "the lion [in mendicant's garb]" (*seng ge*) and "the [hypocrite] licking a butter lamp" (*kong bu ldag*), see Potowa Rinchen Sel, *Parables of Potowa*, chap. 22, pp. 229–31.

145. On the parables from "[the nonattachment to] grass or impurities" (*rtsva ba'am mi gtsang*) to "the gilded manuscripts of the Transcendent Perfection of Wisdom" (*gser 'bum*), as well as "the absorbing [of all things] with moisture" (*rlan gyis sdud*), "[the able-bodied] person with legs and eyes" (*rkang mig ldan*), and the parables from "parents acting without sadness" (*pha ma mi skyo*) to "[acting on behalf of others as you would in the case of] your own body" (*rang lus*), see Potowa Rinchen Sel, *Parables of Potowa*, chap. 23, pp. 234–49.

146. On the parables from "the [greedy] dog" (*khyi 'dra*) to "raising oneself up and then crashing down" (*btegs nas brdabs*), as well as "the incineration by the fire [of afflicted mental states]" (*mes bsregs*), "the wingless bird" (*'dab gshogs med pa'i bya*), and the parables from "selling a blanket at a loss" (*snam bu bor btsongs*) to "[the northern brigands] inflicting harm instead of benefit" (*phan gnod skyel*), see Potowa Rinchen Sel, *Parables of Potowa*, chap. 23, pp. 249–57.

147. On the parables from "the earth [that supports all things]" (*sa dang*) to "[the travails of] Sadāprarudita" (rTag tu ngu), see Potowa Rinchen Sel, *Parables of Potowa*, chap. 24, pp. 257–63.

148. On the parables from "the dog that cannot bear a load" (*khyi khal mi theg*) to "the glib [and false promise] of sweet [outcomes without prior effort]" (*kha bde mngar ba*), see Potowa Rinchen Sel, *Parables of Potowa*, chap. 24, pp. 263–67.

149. On the parables from "[Ma of Penyul] acquiring the fortress [of Dro]" (*phya mkhar thob 'dra*) to "drinking [completely] whatever little one has" (*nyung thug 'thung ba*), see Potowa Rinchen Sel, *Parables of Potowa*, chap. 25, pp. 267–74.

150. On the parables from "[old] tripe [shriveling in] fire" (*grod lkogs me*) to "[the misplaced efforts of] Semodru [of U]" (*se mo 'bru ba*), see Potowa Rinchen Sel, *Parables of Potowa*, chap. 25, pp. 274–77. Note that our text reads *drod lkog me* for *grod lkogs me*.

151. On the parables from "pure water in a clean container" (*dri med snod du chu gtsang*) to "seeing [one's past life] on the basis of an icon" (*sku mthong shig*), see Potowa Rinchen Sel, *Parables of Potowa*, chap. 26, pp. 278–84. Note the alternative reading: *sku mthong shi ba*.

152. On the parables from "the impure vessel" (*ma dag snod 'dra*) to "the lady of the North [inexperienced in farming but proud of her harvest]" (*byang pa mo bzhin*) and "[the meditator] without signs [of realization]" (*rtags med 'dra*), see Potowa Rinchen Sel, *Parables of Potowa*, chap. 26, pp. 284–89.

153. On the parables from "the sighted person [leading the blind]" (*skyes bu'i mig*) to "the excellent vase [that is never diminished]" (*bum bzang*), see Potowa Rinchen Sel, *Parables of Potowa*, chap. 27, pp. 289–314.

154. On the parables from "hundreds [of blind people without a guide]" (*brgya phrag*)

to "[a deer] chasing a mirage" (*smig rgyu snyegs pa*), see Potowa Rinchen Sel, *Parables of Potowa*, chap. 27, pp. 314–24.

155. On the parables from "handcrafted [buddhahood]" (*lag gi bzo byed*) to "[the disciple who became accomplished despite misinterpreting] the mantra MARAṆA JAḤ" (*ma ra [na] dza*), see Potowa Rinchen Sel, *Parables of Potowa*, chap. 28, pp. 324–26. On the parables from "[Atiśa finding] no [suitable teacher of mantras] in Tibet" (*bod na mi 'dug*) to "Apo [passing the buck and] saying he did not know" (*nga la cha med a pho zer*), see Potowa Rinchen Sel, *Parables of Potowa*, chap. 28, pp. 326–33.

156. On the parables from "[the irrigation pool] fed by a mountain spring" (*phu chu rdzing*) to "Atiśa [encountering Ḍombīpa who was] of an inferior social class" (*a ti sha dang rigs ngan bzhin*), see Potowa Rinchen Sel, *Parables of Potowa*, chap. 29, pp. 333–38.

157. On the parables from "the child who claimed not to be inferior to his] paternal ancestors" (*pha mes*) to "the brahmin who obtained the accomplishment of] swift-footedness" (*rkang mgyogs*), see Potowa Rinchen Sel, *Parables of Potowa*, chap. 29, pp. 338–40.

158. On the parables from "[the perfected workmanship] of a goldsmith or silversmith" (*gser dngul mgar ba*) to "[the boatman crossing a river] with a safety towrope" (*'brel thag can*), see Potowa Rinchen Sel, *Parables of Potowa*, chap. 30, pp. 340–46.

159. On the parables from "the [passing] comet [that self-destructs]" (*skar mda'*) to "offering someone a pull rope [after weighing him down with an anchor]" (*sdog pas phul*), see Potowa Rinchen Sel, *Parables of Potowa*, chap. 30, pp. 346–49. Note that the text reads *rtog pas phul* for *sdog pas phul.*

160. On the parables of "the conclusive investigation of enemies" (*dgra zin phye bar*), "[the balanced raising of a grain container from] its four corners," "[the accurate counting of Bon ritual ingredients required] for a single doughball" (*zan rdog gcig*), "the rubbing of sticks to make fire" (*gtsub shing me*), and "[the exemplary pursuits of] Sadāprarudita and Subhadra" (*rtag tu ngu dang nor bzang*), see Potowa Rinchen Sel, *Parables of Potowa*, chap. 31, pp. 350–53.

161. *Thig le bcu drug gi khrid yig.* The primary source is attributed to the memorandum of Nyukla Paṇchen Ngawang Drakpa (1458–1515) but seems not to be extant in his *Collected Works*. Kunga Drolchok also states that he himself rewrote it on the basis of the original. Related texts by Jamgön Kongrul and Konchok Tenpei Dronmé are contained in *DNZ*, including *Liturgy of the Means for Attainment and Empowerment Rite of the Sixteen Spheres Entitled Ornament of Compassionate Emanation*, *DNZ*, vol. 4, pp. 283–315; *Quintessential Practice of Meditation and Recitation for the Sixteen Spheres*, *DNZ*, vol. 4, pp. 317–26; and Jamyang Khyentsé Wangpo's *Quintessential Stages of Profound Guidance on the Sixteen Spheres according to Kadam Entitled the Boon of the Two Accomplishments*, *DNZ*, vol. 4, pp. 327–49. The commentary by Khenchen Nyima Gyeltsen (1223–1305) is translated in Jinpa 2008, 395–452.

162. On the cultivation of the four spheres of the supporting maṇḍala (*rten dkyil 'khor gyi thig le bzhi*), the six spheres of the supported deities (*brten pa lha'i thig le drug*), and the six spheres of the teachers of the root lineage (*rtsa brgyud bla ma'i thig le drug*), which find their coalescence in the sphere of enlightened mind (*byang chub sems kyi thig le*), see Jinpa 2008, 395–452.
163. Jinpa (2008, 427–28) refers to this sphere as the generation of one's own mind in the form of Mahākāruṇika.
164. Jinpa (2008, 428–30) refers to this sphere as the generation of oneself as Buddha Śākyamuni.
165. Jinpa (2008, 430–31) refers to this sphere as the generation of oneself as Avalokiteśvara with either four or forty arms.
166. Jinpa (2008, 432) suggests that this is associated with the third sphere, and that the visualization of Prajñāpāramitā has Atiśa Dīpaṃkara on the right and Śākyamuni on the left.
167. Jinpa 2008, 431–34.
168. Jinpa 2008, 434–38.
169. Jinpa 2008, 438–40.
170. In this context, the five recollections (*rjes dran lnga*) comprise (i) guruyoga, which is the recollection of the teacher (*bla ma rjes su dran pa'i bla ma'i rnal 'byor*); (ii) meditation on the nature of your body as the deity (*lus lha'i rang bzhin du sgom pa*); (iii) continuous recitation of mantra in your speech (*ngag la sngags kyi bzlas brjod dang ma bral ba*); (iv) meditations on emptiness, loving-kindness, and compassion, as the abiding nature of your mind (*sems kyi gnas lugs stong pa nyid du sgom pa dang / byams snying rje sgom pa*); and (v) the dedication of merit so that the roots of virtuous action might be perfected and refined (*dge rtsa rdzogs byang du bsngo ba*). See Dungkar Lobzang Trinle, *Great Dictionary of Dungkar*, p. 166.
171. *Shes phyin bka' babs drug gi khrid yig*. The primary source of this guidebook has not yet been identified in Rongton Sheja Kunrik's *Collected Works*. Mention is made, however, of these six descents (*bka' babs drug*) in his *Sequence of Practicing the Path of the Transcendent Perfection of Wisdom Entitled Lamp Clarifying Darkness*, in his *Collected Works*, vol. 4, p. 4. Accordingly, the Six Descents of the Transcendent Perfection of Wisdom are sequentially associated with the following locations: the paradise of Tuṣita, source of happiness; the underworld of nāgas, source of resources; the learned paṇḍitas of Bengal, source of awareness; the southern land of Beta (Vaidarbha), source of enlightened attributes; the western land of Oḍḍiyāna, source of blessings; and the isle of Viśvakoṭacandana, source of wonder. Another text in his *Collected Works* entitled *Safe Ford of the Path of Liberation Experientially Cultivating the Six Transcendent Wisdoms* (vol. 1, pp. 115–17) is dissimilar in content.
172. Among these eight phases of clear realization, the three understandings (*mkhyen pa gsum*) comprise understanding of all phenomena (*sarvākārajñāna*, *rnam mkhyen*), understanding of the aspects of the path (*mārgajñatā*, *lam gyi rnam pa shes pa nyid*), and understanding of omniscience (*sarvajñatā*, *thams cad shes pa*

nyid). The four applications (*sbyor bzhi*) comprise clear realization of all phenomena (*sarvākārābhisambodha, rnam kun mngon rdzogs rtogs pa*), culmination of clear realization (*mūrdhābhisamaya, rtse mor phyin pa'i mngon rtogs*), serial clear realization (*ānupūrvābhisamaya, mthar gyis pa'i mngon rtogs*), and instantaneous clear realization (*ekakṣaṇābhisamaya, skad cig ma gcig gis mngon par rtogs pa*). The fruition is the buddha body of reality (*dharmakāya, 'bras bu chos sku*). Interspersed through these eight phases of clear realization are seventy subtopics.

173. This most extensive version of the *The Transcendent Perfection of Wisdom* in sixteen volumes is not extant.

174. The sixfold summation (*don bsdus drug tu 'byed pa*) denotes the longer recensions, known as the "six mothers" (*yum drug*), which are respectively entitled (i) *The Transcendent Perfection of Wisdom in One Hundred Thousand Lines* (*Śatasāhasrikāprajñāpāramitā*, T 8, in twelve volumes, twenty-five fascicles, and seventy-two chapters); (ii) *The Transcendent Perfection of Wisdom in Twenty-Five Thousand Lines* (*Pañcaviṃśatisāhasrikāprajñāpāramitā*, T 9, in three volumes, seventy-eight fascicles, and seventy-six chapters); (iii) *The Transcendent Perfection of Wisdom in Eighteen Thousand Lines* (*Aṣṭādaśasāhasrikāprajñāpāramitā*, T 10, in two and a half volumes, sixty fascicles, and eighty-seven chapters); (iv) *The Transcendent Perfection of Wisdom in Ten Thousand Lines* (*Daśasāhasrikāprajñāpāramitā*, T 11, in one and a half volumes, thirty-four fascicles, and thirty-three chapters); (v) *The Transcendent Perfection of Wisdom in Eight Thousand Lines* (*Aṣṭasāhasrikāprajñāpāramitā*, T 12, in one volume, twenty-four fascicles, and thirty-two chapters); and (vi) *The Verse Summation of the Transcendent Perfection of Wisdom* (*Prajñāpāramitāratnaguṇasañcayagāthā*, T 13, in nineteen folios). The threefold summation (*gsum du 'byed pa*) denotes the reduction of these six to the long, medium, and short versions.

175. This refers to the analysis of the four sequential phases of application (*rim sbyor*; that is, phases iv–vii) and their many subtopics, including the four grades of ascertainment (*nges byed bzhi*) that denote the fourfold gradation of warmth, peak, acceptance, and supremacy experienced during the phase of culminating clear realization.

176. The pacification (*zhi byed*) of suffering is the theme of the next guidebook.

177. *Zhi byed lam lnga'i khrid yig*. This instruction originated in Tibet through Padampa Sangyé. The primary source of the present guidebook is attributed to Rongton Sheja Kunrik, although no text of this title is found in the ten volumes of his *Collected Works*, and his name does not figure in the corresponding lineage prayer in chapter 1. In content, however, the text corresponds to Nyemdo Sonam Pel's *Guidance of the Five Paths of the Pacification of Suffering, a Sacred Doctrine Derived from the Lineage of the Great Accomplished Master Dampa Sangyé, Entitled Oral Transmission of the Supreme Attainment of Taintless Light*, *DNZ*, vol. 13, pp. 409–38. It is possible that Rongton's notes were based on this work. The references that follow and the relevant comments in square brackets all derive therefrom. Coincidentally, the *Collected Works of Rongton Sheja Kunrik* (vol. 1,

pp. 64–69) contain an unrelated instruction entitled *Guidance on the Five Paths according to the Tradition of Atiśa*. Jamgön Kongtrul's complete anthology of the instructions on Pacification is translated by Harding in Jamgön Kongtrul 2019 (509–35), including Nyemdo Sonam Pel's text with appended biographical information concerning the author.

178. Nyemdo Sonam Pel (*DNZ*, vol. 13, p. 413, line 5) reads *bho lo ltar gzengs pa* (bristling or upturned like the leaves of an elm tree). According to this interpretation, *bho* would be equivalent to *ye 'bog* (elm tree).
179. This is a simplified version of the refuge tree. The added text derives from Nyemdo Sonam Pel, *DNZ*, vol. 13, pp. 413–14.
180. Tib. *gang du'ang ma 'ongs*. The sense of this incomplete phrase is suggested in Nyemdo Sonam Pel, *DNZ*, vol. 13, p. 416, line 4.
181. Nyemdo Sonam Pel, *DNZ*, vol. 13, pp. 417–18.
182. Nyemdo Sonam Pel, vol. 13, pp. 418–19.
183. Nyemdo Sonam Pel, vol. 13, p. 419.
184. Tib. *skam thag chu nang nas chod*. On this obscure expression, see Nyemdo Sonam Pel, *DNZ*, vol. 13, p. 420, line 5–p. 421, line 1. This is an example of an "essential point that is counterintuitive or paradoxical" (*gya log gi gnad*), stating the opposite of what is generally accepted, as, for example, treating fevers with heat and chills with cold. See Jamgön Kongtrul 2019, 519.
185. Nyemdo Sonam Pel, *DNZ*, vol. 13, pp. 421–22.
186. Nyemdo Sonam Pel, vol. 13, p. 424.
187. Nyemdo Sonam Pel, vol. 13, pp. 424–25.
188. Nyemdo Sonam Pel, vol. 13, pp. 425–26.
189. Nyemdo Sonam Pel, vol. 13, p. 426.
190. Nyemdo Sonam Pel, vol. 13, pp. 427–28.
191. Nyemdo Sonam Pel, vol. 13, pp. 428–29.
192. Nyemdo Sonam Pel, vol. 13, p. 430.
193. Nyemdo Sonam Pel, vol. 13, pp. 430–431. These words attributed to Kamalaśrīvajra are found in Nyemdo Sonam Pel, *DNZ*, vol. 13, p. 431, line 1.
194. Our text reads *ma bsnyes pa* for *bsnyes pa*.
195. Nyemdo Sonam Pel, *DNZ*, vol. 13, p. 431.
196. Nyemdo Sonam Pel, vol. 13, pp. 432–33.
197. Nyemdo Sonam Pel, vol. 13, pp. 433–34.
198. Nyemdo Sonam Pel, vol. 13, p. 434.
199. Nyemdo Sonam Pel, vol. 13, p. 435.
200. Nyemdo Sonam Pel, vol. 13, p. 435.
201. Nyemdo Sonam Pel, vol. 13, p. 436.
202. Cf. Nyemdo Sonam Pel, vol. 13, p. 436.
203. Nyemdo Sonam Pel, vol. 13, p. 437.
204. *sGom rim thog mtha' bar gsum gyi khrid yig*. The primary source is Rongtonpa's three-part commentary that comprises the *Commentary on the First Stage of Meditation Entitled Ornament Illuminating Calm Abiding and Higher Insight*,

the *Commentary on the Second Stage of Meditation Entitled Moonbeams of Abiding*, and the *Commentary on the Final Stage of Meditation Entitled Drumbeat of the Gods*. These are all found in his *Collected Works*, vols. 8–9. The antecedent is Kamalaśīla's original text *Three Stages of Meditation* (*Tribhāvanākrama*). Among the three stages of meditation, the first emphasizes calm abiding and textual exegesis; the second emphasizes the integration of calm abiding with higher insight, along with experiential cultivation of the path; and the last emphasizes higher insight and the refutation of alien perspectives.

205. *Byams pa'i chos lnga'i* [*sgom*] *khrid*. The primary sources of this guidebook are the commentarial writings of Chomden Rikpei Reldri, four of whose relevant treatises are still extant, namely, (i) *Flower Ornament Commentary on the Ornament of Clear Realization*, *Collected Works of Chomden Rikpei Reldri*, vol. 4; (ii) *Flower Ornament of Exegesis on the Ornament of the Sutras of the Great Vehicle*, Kadampa Anthology III, vol. 61, pp. 415–66, and *Collected Works of Chomden Rikpei Reldri*, vol. 2, pp. 33–188; (iii) *Flower Ornament Commentary on the Supreme Continuum of the Great Vehicle*, Kadampa Anthology III, vol. 62, pp. 745–74; and (iv) *Flower Ornament Commentary on the Distinction between Phenomena and Reality*, *Collected Works of Chomden Rikpei Reldri*, vol. 5, pp. 669–96. His *Flower Ornament Commentary on the Distinction between the Middle and Extremes* appears to be no longer extant.

206. See above, chapter 9, n. 175.

207. See next note.

208. *Ornament of Clear Realization* is translated by Conze in Maitreyanātha 1954 and Khenchen Thrangu Rinpoche 2004. See also the commentaries of Vimuktasena (T 3787) and Haribhadra (T 3791), translated in Sparham 2006–12. The practice of the six transcendent perfections—generosity, ethical discipline, tolerance, perseverance, meditative concentration, and wisdom or discriminative awareness—is the focus of the *Six Mothers*, on which see above, chapter 9, n. 174.

209. The three aspects of generosity (*sbyin pa gsum*) are material generosity (*zang zing gi sbyin pa*), fearless generosity (*mi 'jigs pa'i sbyin pa*), and doctrinal generosity (*chos kyi sbyin pa*).

210. The four additional transcendent perfections comprise method, power, aspiration, and pristine cognition. The refinement of the ten bodhisattva levels and the ten corresponding transcendent perfections is the focus of the *Sutra of the Ten Levels*.

211. *Ornament of the Sutras of the Great Vehicle* is translated in Maitreyanātha and Āryāsaṅga 2004, and with commentaries in Jamgön Mipham 2018. The points listed here suggest a progression from preparation through main practice to conclusion, and they appear to essentialize the content of the *Ornament of the Sutras of the Great Vehicle,* although the actual wording does not derive from that text, nor is it found in Chomden Rikpei Reldri's source text, *Flower Ornament of Exegesis on the Ornament of the Sutras of the Great Vehicle*, Kadam Anthology III, vol. 61, pp. 415–66. I am grateful to Stephen Gethin for his comments on this passage.

212. On the eight aspects of consciousness, see above, chapter 9, n. 7.

213. *Distinction between Phenomena and Actual Reality* is translated in Jamgön Mipham 2004.

214. *Distinction between the Middle and Extremes* is translated by the Dharmacakra Translation Committee in Maitreya and Jamgön Mipham 2006. The expression "causally concordant conduct" (*rgyu mthun spyod*) here denotes the practice of the transcendent perfections. See Maitreya and Jamgön Mipham 2006, 126.

215. Maitreya and Jamgön Mipham 2006, 125–26.

216. *Distinction between the Middle and Extremes*, chap. 5, vv. 4–6, on which see Maitreya and Jamgön Mipham 2006, 126–29.

217. The ten facilitating modes of doctrinal conduct (*grogs chos spyod bcu*) comprise transcribing the scriptures, making offerings, generosity, study, reading, memorizing, explaining, reciting, reflecting, and meditating. See *Distinction between the Middle and Extremes*, chap. 5, v. 9, and Maitreya and Jamgön Mipham 2006, 131–32.

218. *Distinction between the Middle and Extremes*, chap. 5, v. 11a–b, on which see Maitreya and Jamgön Mipham 2006, 133–42.

219. See *Five Treatises of Maitreya*, Tib. ed, p. 149.

220. *Supreme Continuum of the Great Vehicle* is translated in Takasaki 1966 and Arya Matreiya and Acarya Asanga 1985. The seven adamantine topics (*rdo rje'i gnas bdun*) comprise buddha, sacred doctrine, monastic community, buddha nature, enlightenment, enlightened attributes, and enlightened activities.

221. The nine examples (*dpe dgu*) indicative of the presence of naturally luminous buddha nature are the buddha in a decaying lotus, honey amid bees, grains inside their husks, gold in filth, a treasure underground, shoots piercing their fruits, a buddha icon inside tattered rags, a future monarch in a poor woman's womb, and an image of precious metal in a clay mold. See Arya Matreiya and Acarya Asanga 1985, 51–69.

222. *Rang stong gi lta khrid.* The primary source is said to be Patsab Nyima Drak's *Abridgement of the Essentials of the Root and Commentary of the Introduction to the Middle Way*, which does not appear to be extant. Patsab Nyima Drak is well known as the translator of Candrakīrti's *Autocommentary on the Introduction to the Middle Way*, which is an antecedent to this guidebook. Another important source is Remdawa Zhonu Lodro's *Great Commentary on the Introduction to the Middle Way*. *DNZ* (vol. 4, pp. 549–64) contains a later text by Ngamring Mangto Ludrub Gyatso (1523–1596) entitled *Essence of Nectar: An Instruction on the View of the Middle Way in Conformity with the Texts of the Two Great Promulgators*.

223. *gZhan stong gi lta khrid.* The primary source of this guidebook is stated to be Tsen Khawoché's *Hook of the Lotus*, which has not yet been located. *DNZ* (vol. 4, pp. 565–86) includes Jamgön Kongtrul's own instruction, entitled *Instruction on the View of Extrinsic Emptiness: Immaculate Moonlight of Adamantine Reality*.

224. The two buddha bodies of form (*gzugs sku gnyis*) comprise the buddha body of perfect resource (*longs spyod rdzogs pa'i sku*) and the buddha body of emanation

(*sprul pa'i sku*). On this distinction, see Dudjom Rinpoche 1991, 123–38; and on the three natures, see Jamgön Kongtrul's explanation in Jamgön Kongtrul 2012, 59–61.

225. *sBas don kun gsal gyi khrid yig.* The primary source is stated to be Kunga Drolchok's own writing, based on the advice of his teacher Zelmo Drakpa Drakpa Yeshé concerning the two hundred and thirty instructions of Bodongpa Choklé Namgyal's enormous compilation entitled *Summation of the Real*. The content of this guidebook relates to many others within the One Hundred and Eight Guidebooks of Jonang, and appropriate cross-references have been added. There is a text entitled *Elucidation of the Concealed Meanings* [*of Yogatantra*] contained in Bodongpa's *Collected Works* (vol. 71, pp. 417–503), but this focuses largely on Vajrabhairava and, with the exception of a single reference, it is not the source of Kunga Drolchok's presentation. There are also interesting parallels in the tantra sections of Bodongpa's *Cornucopia Clarifying the Essential Doctrinal Practices of the Glorious Summation of the Real*, pp. 313–412.

226. It is explained in Bodongpa Choklé Namgyal's *Elucidation of the Concealed Meanings* [*of Yogatantra*] (p. 2, lines 5–6) that the eradication of hostile and obstructing forces (*dgra bgegs tshar gcod pa*) is based on Vajrabhairava, and the acceptance of fortunate disciples (*skal ldan rjes 'dzin*) is based on Akṣobhyavajra.

227. *The Unelaborate Practice* (*sPros med*) and *The Four-Stage Yoga* (*rNal 'byor bzhi*) correspond respectively to Kunga Drolchok's guidebooks 64 and 65. See also Jamgön Kongtrul 2008, 148–52. In terms of Bodongpa's *Summation of the Real*, this section corresponds to vols. 70–73 of his *Collected Works*.

228. The first four of these are mentioned in Choying Tobden Dorje 2017, 276–77; and on the Lobo Lotsāwa tradition in particular, see Jamgön Kongtrul 2008, 151–52.

229. Jamgön Kongtrul 2008, 151–52; Choying Tobden Dorje 2017, 276–77.

230. According to Jamgön Kongtrul (2008, 152n80), this text of Devākaracandra was not included in the Tengyur.

231. The text reads *dag gdong* for *drug gdong*.

232. Of these texts, *The Mental Focus on the Horns of Bhairava* corresponds to guidebook 66 in the present anthology.

233. *Vajrapāṇi in the Form Mahācakra* corresponds to guidebook 36 in the present anthology, and *The Coemergent Union* [*of the Great Seal*] (*lhang cig skyes sbyor*) to guidebook 83.

234. See Tsongkhapa 2013, 46–47. In terms of Bodongpa's *Summation of the Real*, this section corresponds to vols. 59–70 of his *Collected Works*. Among these listed texts, the *Tantra Requested by Devendra* was not translated into Tibetan.

235. Tsongkhapa 2013, 60.

236. This corresponds to guidebook 62 in the present anthology.

237. Not extant in the *Collected Works of Marpa Lotsāwa Chokyi Lodro*. According to Tsongkhapa 2013, the *Five Stages Perfected on One Seat* (*Rim lnga'i gdan rdzogs*) is attributed to Serdingpa Zhonu O.

238. This corresponds to guidebook 63 in the present anthology.
239. The five syllables of great emptiness (*stong chen yig ge lnga*) are the five vowels, and the six syllables of the vital essence (*thig le yig ge drug*) are the six classes of consonants. See the detailed explanation in Jamgön Kongtrul 2005, 187–97. I have not yet located this in the *Root Tantra* (T 368), but there are references to EVAṂ in the *Tantra of the Origin of Glorious Samvara* (T 373).
240. The profound abodes are the twenty-four sacred places, divided into outer, inner, and extraneous categories of buddha body, speech, and mind. See below, chapter 9, n. 738. The ashé is visualized as the support of the fierce inner heat.
241. See guidebook 67 in the present anthology.
242. The one hundred sacral aspects (*dam pa rigs brgya*) are the psychophysical aggregates, elements, and consciousnesses in their purified state. See Dorje 2005, 388–94.
243. Cf. guidebook 73 in the present anthology.
244. Cf. guidebook 72 in the present anthology.
245. This pertains to guidebook 70 in the present anthology.
246. This corresponds to guidebook 69 in the present anthology.
247. See guidebooks 38, 68, and 75 of the present anthology.
248. This corresponds to guidebook 71 in the present anthology.
249. Cf. guidebook 34 in the present anthology.
250. These are exemplified in guidebooks 76–78, 81, and 90–92 of the present anthology. In terms of Bodongpa's *Summation of the Real*, this entire section on Cakrasaṃvara corresponds to vols. 74–93 of his *Collected Works*.
251. Cf. guidebook 58 in the present anthology.
252. Cf. guidebook 11 in the present anthology.
253. Cf. guidebook 1 in the present anthology.
254. The sixteen methods of guidance listed here accord with the Tibetan commentarial tradition on the perfection-stage practices. They comprise (i) the guidance of the three purities (*dag pa gsum khrid*); (ii) the guidance of the three coemergent states (*lhan skyes gsum khrid*); (iii) the continuous guidance of the profound and illuminating river (*zab gsal chu bo'i rgyin khrid*); (iv) the guidance on the view that equipoises existence and quiescence (*srid zhi mnyam sbyor lta khrid*); (v) the guidance that introduces the meaning of the four innate coemergent states (*gnyug ma lhan skyes bzhi don du ngo sprod khrid*); (vi) the guidance on secret conduct with respect to the central channel by means of coercion (*spyod pa thog rdzis kun 'dar gsang spyod khrid*); (vii) the guidance combining three concealed exegeses of the introductory narrative (*gleng gzhi sbas bshad gsum sbyor ba'i khrid*); (viii) the guidance on the six-branch yoga (*yan lag drug khrid*)—composure, concentration, breath control, apprehension [of the complete deity], subsequent recollection, and meditative stability; (ix) the guidance on the four aspects of mingling, transformation, and discriminative awareness (*bsre 'pho shes rab rnam bzhi*); (x) the guidance on the means of separation from attachment (*chags bral thabs*

khrid); (xi) the guidance of the alluring messenger (*chags can pho nya'i khrid*); (xii) the guidance on the balancing of the generation and perfection stages (*bskyed rdzogs cha mnyam khrid*); (xiii) the guidance on the perfection stage in which the body appears as a deity (*rdzogs rim lus lha khrid*); (xiv) the guidance on the final thoughts of clinging to the generation stage (*bskyed rim zhen rtog mthar khrid*); (xv) the attainment of the three roots combined (*rtsa gsum dril sgrub*); and (xvi) the guidance on devotion and the vitality of the teacher (*mos gus bla ma'i srog khrid*). In addition, there are sixteen extant commentaries on the *Tantra of Hevajra*, which are of Indian origin, and among these, two were not translated into Tibetan.

255. Cf. guidebook 43 in the present anthology.

256. Cf. guidebook 59 in the present anthology. In terms of Bodongpa's *Summation of the Real*, this entire section on Hevajra corresponds to vols. 94–102 of his *Collected Works*.

257. The eighteen yogic exercises focusing on the fire within the channel of fierce inner heat (*gtum mo'i me dmigs bco brgyad*) derive from the *Aural Lineage of Cakrasaṃvara* (*bDe mchog snyan brgyud*). They are described individually in Thupten Phuntsok, *Yogic Exercises of the Channels and Winds*, pp. 11–20.

258. Contained in SLC, vol. 10, pp. 293–97.

259. Cf. guidebook 40 in the present anthology.

260. See Jamgön Kongtrul 2007, 189–90. In terms of Bodongpa's *Summation of the Real*, this section on Kālacakra corresponds to vols. 113–18 of his *Collected Works*.

261. Cf. the seventeen transmissions outlined in Jamgön Kongtrul 2007, 290–91.

262. *Tshe khrid*. The primary source is stated here to be Kunga Drolchok's own instruction manual. Its antecedent is the *Guidance on Amitāyus according to the Tradition of Siddhirājñī*, which derives from the instruction of Barawa Gyeltsen Pelzang (1310–1391), founder of a subbranch of the Drukpa Kagyu school. A related work entitled *Profound Guidance on the Generation and Perfection Stages of Amitāyus according to the Tradition of Siddhirājñī: Ocean of Deathless Nectar* is found in Drukpa Kagyu Anthology, vol. 23, pp. 506–66.

263. The four lower elements (*'og 'byung ba bzhi*) comprise earth, water, fire, and wind.

264. These are the five pure essences (*dvangs ma lnga*) of the five gross material elements: earth, water, fire, wind, and space.

265. *sGrol dkar gyi khrid yig*. The primary source, attributed to the oral teachings of Atiśa and entitled *Instruction on Long Life through the Virtuous Lady Cintāmaṇicakra according to the Pure Tradition of Glorious Dīpaṃkara: A Basket of Nectar*, is contained in GDKT, vol. 4, pp. 569–98. For iconographic and liturgical details, see Willson and Brauen 2000, no. 4.

266. The mantra of Tārā in the form Cintāmaṇicakra is: OṂ TĀRE TUTTĀRE TURE MAMA ĀYUR PUṆYE JÑĀNA PUṢṬIM KURU SVĀHĀ. See Willson and Brauen 2000, 237–39.

267. These verses employ the poetic ornament of repetition, whereby the final word of each line is repeated in the first word of the immediately following line. This is a feeble attempt to recreate the pattern in translation.
268. Tib. *nang grub kyi skabs su 'khor 'das snod bcud kyi chos bcu bzhi*. This enumeration is found in Terdak Lingpa's *Outer Attainment and Long-Life Empowerment of Amitāyus, Lord of the Dance, Entitled Downpour of Nectar, from the Profound Path: Gathering of All the Sugatas*, RTD, vol. 24, no. 26, p. 390. This text states that these fourteen attributes are also found in other compatible modes of instruction, and adds that these all originate from the power and glory of the potent pure essences that are the attributes of the inhabited world and its sentient inhabitants.
269. *Tshe dpag med dkar po'i khrid yig*. The primary source, attributed to Chak Lotsāwa Chojé Pel, does not appear to be extant as a distinct text outside this anthology. The transmission stems from Mitrayogin. For iconographic and liturgical details, see Willson and Brauen 2000, no. 182.
270. *dMar khrid dpal mo lugs kyi khrid yig*. This guidebook is attributed to Atiśa's disciple Yolton/Yolgom Chowang and is contained in the *Cycles of Means for Attainment and Initiations for Eleven-Faced Sublime Avalokiteśvara according to the Tradition of the Nun Lakṣmī*, GDKT, vol. 3, pp. 51–82. There is another short text in *DNZ*, vol. 17, pp. 22–25, by Jamyang Khyentsé Wangpo, entitled *The Direct Guidance of Avalokiteśvara according to the Tradition of the Nun Lakṣmī: The Swift Path Integrating the Essentials of Experiential Cultivation*. For iconographic and liturgical details, see Willson and Brauen 2000, no. 104.
271. *dMar khrid zla rgyal lugs kyi khrid yig*. The primary source is attributed here to both Dzimchen Gyeltsen Pelzang and Rongton Sheja Kunrik, although the antecedent of these instructions is traced to the bodhisattva Candradhvaja. A related text entitled *Direct Guidance of Avalokiteśvara according to the Tradition of the Bodhisattva Candradhvaja* is found in *DNZ*, vol. 17, pp. 39–40. Rongton Sheja Kunrik's actual composition, *The Direct Guidance on Avalokiteśvara according to the Tradition of the Bodhisattva Candradhvaja Entitled White Lotus*, is contained in his *Collected Works*, vol. 1, pp. 398–402. I have not separately located either the brief notes of Zhang Ring Kyitsa Ochen or the extensive analysis by Dzimchen Gyeltsen Pelzang, although Kunga Drolchok states that these are all subsumed in the present guidebook.
272. The three deportments (*'khyer so gsum*) are those of buddha body, speech, and mind, on which see Nordrang Orgyan, *Compendium of Buddhist Numeric Terms*, p. 203.
273. *dMar khrid tshem bu lugs kyi khrid yig*. The primary source is attributed to Chojé Sherab Bumpa, a teacher of Tokmé Zangpo. It is not contained in *DNZ*, vol. 17, although it is listed in the catalog. See Jamgön Kongtrul 2013, 110n482. However, the text is found in Tokmé Zangpo, *Memorandum on Mind Training Along with the Memorandum on the Direct Guidance*, contained in Kadampa Anthology II, pp. 301–80; and in Sangyé Phuntsok, ed., *The Doctrinal Cycle of Mahākāruṇika according to the Tradition of Tsembupa*. On this transmission, see also Roerich

1949, 1043–44. Note that in the Tibetan text corresponding to this chapter 9, this guidebook precedes those of Lakṣmī and Candradhvaja, but the order has been rearranged here so as to conform to the earlier historical chapters.

274. In this context, the term *five awakenings* (*byang chub lnga*) would seem to refer to the five phases of manifest awakening (*mngon byang lnga*) experienced during the generation stage of meditation, commencing with the visualization (out of emptiness) of the moon disk, followed by the sun disk, the seed syllable, the symbolic attribute, and the complete form of the deity. There are also outer and inner explanations of these five awakenings (*mngon byang lnga*) that accord respectively with yogatantra and unsurpassed yogatantra, indicating how the physical body is formed. On this, see Gyalwa Yangonpa 2015, 224–30.

275. *dMar khrid skyer sgang pa'i lugs kyi khrid yig*. *DNZ*, vol. 17, pp. 8–19. The primary source attributed to Choku Śākya Rinchen appears not to be extant as a separate work outside this anthology.

276. *bDe mchog gi dmar khrid*. The primary source for this guidebook is Ghaṇṭāpāda's shorter means for attainment entitled *Coemergent Cakrasaṃvara* (*bDe mchog lhan skyes*, T 1436). There are also other extant means for attainment of Cakrasaṃvara in the solitary hero form by Ḍombipā (T 1464) and Nāropā (T 1472). Kunga Drolchok also associates this and the immediately following guidebook with a nonextant work of Tokmé Zangpo entitled *Direct Guidance on All the Meditational Deities in General*. The virtually identical wording in these two guidebooks suggests a common origin.

277. The five meats (*sha lnga*) comprise elephant, human, horse, dog, and ox or peacock. The five nectars (*bdud rtsi lnga*) comprise excrement, urine, human flesh, blood, and semen.

278. *Kye rdo rje'i dmar khrid*. The primary source of this guidebook is said to be Ānandavajra's means for attainment, possibly the one entitled *Glorious Hevajra* (T 1302). There is another extant text referring to the solitary hero form of Hevajra by Kṛṣṇacārin (T 1252). As stated above, Kunga Drolchok also associates this and the immediately preceding guidebook with an apparently nonextant work of Tokmé Zangpo entitled *Direct Guidance on All the Meditational Deities in General*.

279. *Phyag rdor 'khor chen gyi khrid*. The primary source of this guidebook is said to be Marton Chokyi Gyeltsen's *The Perfection Stage of Vajrapāṇi in the Form Mahācakra Endowed with Four Blessings*. The actual *Tantra of Vajrapāṇi in the Form Mahācakra* is contained in GDKT, vol. 8, no. 46. There is also a short but incomplete tract concerning this perfection-stage practice by Akhu Ching Sherab Gyatso (1803–1875) entitled *Continuing Explanation of the Perfection Stage of Vajrapāṇi in the Form Mahācakra*.

280. This alludes to the process through which, according to the ancient Indian philosophical system of Sāṃkhyā, all phenomena unfold from the dichotomy of "soul and egocentricity of primal matter" (*bdag gtso bo'i nga rgyal*). See, for example, the Tibetan account of Longchen Rabjam in Choying Tobden Dorje 2017, 25–32.

281. See the diagrams and description of these four cakras in Rangjung Dorjé 2014, 198–208. There is also a detailed description of the four cakras and their channel branches in Gyalwa Yangonpa 2015, 230–59.
282. *gTum po'i khrid.* The primary source of this guidebook, formally entitled *Inconceivably Secret Guidance of Vajrapāṇi in the Form Caṇḍa* (*Phyag rdor gtum po'i gsang ba bsam gyis mi khyab pa*), appears to be based on a Jonangpa text attributed to Sangdak Drubchen, the teacher of Tulku Jodenpa (ca. 1292–1361). For similar iconographic and liturgical details, see Willson and Brauen 2000, nos. 156–58.
283. This guidebook alludes to three main aspects of Vajrapāṇi corresponding to ground, fruition, and path. These commence with Vajrapāṇi who appears to the minds of living beings as a sentient being (*'gro rgyud sems can su snang ba'i phyag na rdo rje*).
284. Vajrapāṇi who appears to fruitional minds as a buddha (*'bras rgyud sangs rgyas su snang ba'i phyag na rdo rje*).
285. Vajrapāṇi who appears to the minds of those on the path as a sublime being (*lam rgyud 'phags par snang ba*).
286. Literally, "in his lap" (*pang na*).
287. *Phag mo kurma pā da'i khrid.* The primary source of this guidebook is attributed to Chak Lotsāwa Rinchen Chogyel, but there appears to be no extant version outside the present anthology. For iconographic and liturgical details, see Willson and Brauen 2000, no. 85.
288. The five symbolic regalia (*phyag rgya lnga*) with which female deities are endowed comprise the crown ornament, the earrings, the choker, the bracelets, and the girdle.
289. *Ku ru kulle'i khrid.* Formally entitled *The Secret Guidance of Kurukullā* (*Ku ru kulle'i gsang khrid*), this secret practice is associated with the Sakya lineage and found in a selection of instructions, exemplified in Drakpa Gyeltsen, *Collected Works*, vol. 3, pp. 488–92. There are several other means for attainment in the Tengyur (T 1314–1318). For iconographic and liturgical details, see Willson and Brauen 2000, nos. 201–5.
290. See the diagram in Rangjung Dorje 2014, 199.
291. See the diagram in Rangjung Dorje 2014, 205.
292. This verse is cited in several texts with variant readings, for example, Jālandharipā's *Brief Exegesis of the Means for Attainment of Hevajra Entitled Pure Adamantine Lamp*, TPD, vol. 5, p. 252.
293. *sByor drug gi khrid.* The primary source of this guidebook is Kālacakrapāda's *The Six-Branch Yoga* (T 1732), which is also contained in *DNZ*, vol. 15, pp. 6–13. The Sanskrit sources are summarized and elaborated by Tāranātha in his *Guidance on the Adamantine Yoga of the Profound Path Entitled Meaningful to Behold*, *Collected Works of Tāranātha*, vol. 7, pp. 1–107; *DNZ*, vol. 15, pp. 133–231; and in his *Tract on the Evidence of the Signs of Realization of the Six-Branch Yoga*, *Collected Works of Tāranātha*, *DNZ*, vol. 15, pp. 233–68. For Jamgön Kongtrul's presentation of the six-branch yoga, see Jamgön Kongtrul 2008, 154–61; and for

his own elaborate commentary, see Khedrup Norsang Gyatso 2004, 439–584.

According to the historical information presented in chapters 1, 4, and 5 of the present work, this instruction was originally recognized as the fortieth of the one hundred and eight guidebooks. It appears to have been moved later to become guidebook 90 in the sequence, as the numbering in the Tibetan text of chapter 9 suggests. For the sake of consistency, however, in this translation it has been moved to its more appropriate position, and the subsequent guidebooks from 41–90 have been renumbered throughout this present chapter.

294. See Thupten Phuntsok, *Treasure Ocean of Tibetan Lexicography*, p. 3451.

295. According to Tāranātha (*Collected Works of Tāranātha*, vol. 7, pp. 16–17; also *DNZ*, vol. 15, p. 150, lines 4–5), the four things to be disregarded (*ltos med bzhi*) are the resources of mundane body, speech, and mind, along with consciousness transference (*'pho ba*), but in this preliminary phase, only the first three are applicable.

296. The flow through the right nostril begins during each two-hour period with the wind of the earth element, and through the left nostril it concludes with the wind of the earth element. See Gyalwa Yangonpa 2015, 272. On the significance of the stabilizing wind of the earth element (*sa rlung*) for beginning the practice of the fierce inner heat, see also Gyalwa Yangonpa 2015, 276–77.

297. See Tāranātha, in his *Collected Works*, vol. 7, p. 32.

298. The monkey hour (*dgong cha*) refers to the late afternoon, before sunset. Our text reads *dgongs cha*.

299. Cf. the explanation of these ten signs in Tāranātha, in his *Collected Works*, vol. 7, pp. 33–35; also his *Tract on the Evidence of the Signs of Realization of the Six-Branch Yoga*, *DNZ*, vol. 15, pp. 240ff.

300. The expression "emptiness in all its finest aspects" (*sarvākāraguṇopetaśūnyatā*, *rnam pa mchog dang ldan pa'i stong pa nyid*) is elaborated in the context of extraneous emptiness (*gzhan stong*). It also denotes the continuum of the ground according to Great Madhyamaka. See Dudjom Rinpoche 1991, 169–77.

301. Jonang Kunpang Chenpo Mikyo Dorjé, *Quintessential Commentary on the Six Branches*, *DNZ*, vol. 15, p. 21, lines 2–4; also Tāranātha, in his *Collected Works*, vol. 7, pp. 41–42. The five ancillary aspects are (i) discriminative awareness, (ii) ideation, (iii) scrutiny, (iv) extraordinary joy, and (v) bliss of extreme physical refinement.

302. These are the certainties of place, time, and appearance endowed with the major and minor marks. See Tāranātha, *DNZ*, vol. 15, p. 249.

303. Cf. Tāranātha, in his *Collected Works*, vol. 7, p. 43–44; also Tāranātha, *DNZ*, vol. 15, pp. 249ff.

304. This posture is formed by the hands, legs, and elbows assuming the shapes of opposing triangles that resemble the stoves or hearths of a cooking tripod. These, in turn, have outer, inner, and secret aspects, so that they come to number eighteen. See Roberts 2011, 343. The posture is illustrated in Baker 2019, 157.

305. The gesture of the fist (*khu tshur*), also known as the "gesture of the adamantine

fist" (*vajramuṣṭi, rdo rje khu tshur*), is formed with the ring finger extended and the others drawn in.

306. This text is commented on by Tāranātha, in his *Collected Works*, vol. 7, p. 45. The six verses state (i) once the channels have been refined by the adamantine recitations of the preliminary practices, the vital breath is induced into the central channel by applying the filling and release of gentle wind (*'jam rlung dgang gtong*); (ii) the vital breath that has been induced into the central channel is secured by applying the rough vase breathing (*rtsub rlung bum pa can*); (iii) if the vital breath is not induced or is not secured by these methods, the right and left channels should be blocked by applying the forceful method of rough breathing (*rtsub rlung bstan thabs*); (iv) when the lower gate has been forcefully closed by that blockage, liberation will be attained through the application of the upper gate; (v) the elixir of internal nectar will be savored by the threefold movement of the uvula; and (vi) the intermingling of the vital breath with the downward purgative wind and the attainment of deathlessness will be achieved by applying the ignition of the fierce inner heat. The first four of these pertain to the branch of breath control and the last two to the branch of retention.
307. These practices known as "adamantine recitations" (*rdor zlas*) are discussed in Tāranātha, in his *Collected Works*, vol. 7, pp. 45–47.
308. Tāranātha, *Collected Works*, vol. 7, pp. 47–48.
309. Tāranātha, vol. 7, pp. 48–51.
310. Tāranātha, vol. 7, pp. 53–56.
311. Tāranātha, vol. 7, p. 47–48.
312. Tāranātha (*Collected Works*, vol. 7, p. 48) notes that it is at this time that the filling and release of wind and the vase breathing should be applied.
313. The text here misreads *song bsam dag* for *sor bsam dag*.
314. Tāranātha, *Collected Works*, vol. 7, pp. 51ff.; and also under the fourth branch, retention, *Collected Works*, vol. 7, p. 64.
315. Tāranātha, *Collected Works*, vol. 7, pp. 61–68, discusses the fourth branch in detail.
316. Tāranātha, *Collected Works*, vol. 7, p. 63.
317. Tāranātha, *Collected Works*, vol. 7, pp. 77–78; also Rangjung Dorje 2014, 198–202. Our text reads *rgya* for *brgyad*.
318. Tāranātha, *Collected Works*, vol. 7, pp. 64ff.
319. Our text here omits the heart cakra, which has four and eight channel branches. See Tāranātha, *Collected Works*, vol. 7, p. 78; also Rangjung Dorje 2014, 202–4.
320. See Tāranātha, *Collected Works*, vol. 7, p. 78; also Rangjung Dorje 2014, 202–4.
321. See Tāranātha, *Collected Works*, vol. 7, p. 78; also Rangjung Dorje 2014, 204–6.
322. See Tāranātha, *Collected Works*, vol. 7, p. 78; also Rangjung Dorje 2014, 206–8, on the forehead cakra.
323. See Tāranātha, *Collected Works*, vol. 7, p. 78; also Rangjung Dorje 2014, 211–12.
324. See Tāranātha, *Collected Works*, vol. 7, pp. 83–84, where it is explained that yogins of lowest capacity who have thin generative fluid should depend on the action seal in addition to the Great Seal and the seal of pristine cognition, those of slightly

thick generative fluid who are of average capacity should depend on the Great Seal and the seal of pristine cognition, while those of highest capacity who have extremely thick generative fluid should depend on the Great Seal alone.

325. That is to say, the seal of pristine cognition and the action seal. See Tāranātha, in his *Collected Works*, vol. 7, p. 84.

326. This fifth branch is discussed in detail in Tāranātha, in his *Collected Works*, vol. 7, pp. 69–86.

327. The text reads *dus sbor gyi rlung* for *dus sbyor kyi rlung*. These are the number of breaths taken by an average male in the course of a single day. On this term, see Thupten Phuntsok, *Treasure Ocean of Tibetan Lexicography*, p. 1513.

328. A single cycle of respiration (*dbugs 'byung 'jug*) comprises a single exhalation of breath followed by an inhalation of breath.

329. The sixth branch is discussed in Tāranātha, *Collected Works*, vol. 7, pp. 86–90; and on the attainment of the twelve levels in relation to the six cakras, see Tāranātha, in his *Collected Works*, pp. 100–101.

330. *Dus 'khor snyan brgyud kyi khrid*. The primary source of this guidebook is said to have been the writing of Khewang Rinchen Zangpo, who asserted his confidence in the unusual terminology of Menlungpa Sonam Pel. The latter had obtained this aural transmission of Kālacakra directly from Śambhala and integrated it with the terminology of the Great Perfection and *Heruka Galpo* cycles of the Nyingmapa, probably under the inspiration of Guru Chowang.

331. The following passage derives from Gampopa's *Synopsis of the Meditations of Sutra and Tantra*, which is contained in the latter's *Miscellaneous Works* (*gSung thor bu*). Words in square brackets reflect the original.

332. Our text reads *khong slod* for *khong glod*.

333. The exact source of this citation has not yet been identified. The title *Total Liberation through Singular Knowledge* (*gCig shes kun grol*) suggests some affinity with the revelations of Guru Chowang, as do the related Dzogchen terms mentioned above: "ease of singular resolution" (*chig chod blo bde*), "total liberation through singular knowledge" (*gcig shes kun grol*), "permeating all things in a singular utterance" (*gcig brjod kun khyab*), and the "unraveling of knots in a singular meditation" (*gcig bsgom mdud grol*). So far I have been unable to locate this passage in his extant writings, despite the occurrence of such terms in, for example, the *Opening of Pristine Cognition: A Tract concerning the Empowerment of the Expressive Power of Awareness of Buddhasamāyoga according to the Yangti Class of the Great Perfection, Along with the Extensive Empowerments of the Expressive Power of Awareness according to the Chiti Class and the Ordinary Class*, RTD, vol. 59, no. 1; the related *Naturally Arising Pristine Cognition, Gathering and Elucidating the Instruction Manual of the Buddhasamāyoga according to the Yangti Class of the Great Perfection: Essence of All the Tantras, Transmissions, and Pith Instructions*, RTD vol. 59, no. 2; and the *Introduction to the Path of Pristine Cognition, the Extracted Liturgy of the Preliminary Practices for Buddhasamāyoga according to the Yangti Class of the Great Perfection*, RTD, vol. 59, no. 3.

334. This long citation with verses of irregular length has not yet been identified.

335. The pure ten signs (*rtags bcu rnam dag*) are equivalent to the renowned monogram of the Kālacakra named *rnam bcu dbang ldan*, in which seven mantra syllables and three Sanskrit accents are vertically stacked. From top to bottom, the seven mantra syllables HA KṢA MA LA VA RA and YA, respectively, represent the blue realm of the gods of formlessness, the green realm of the gods of form, the multicolored realm of the gods of desire along with Mount Meru, the yellow earth element, the white water element, the red fire element, and the black wind element. The three accents comprise the visarga (*rnam bcad*), the biṇḍu (*rjes su nga ro thig le*), and the vibration (*nāda*).

336. These twenty-one thousand six hundred breaths are equivalent to sixty hours. See Khedrup Norsang Gyatso 2004, 602.

337. See above, chapter 1, n. 26.

338. *O rgyan bsnyen sgrub kyi khrid*. The primary source of this guidebook is attributed here to Dawa Sengé, *Connecting Exegesis of the Rites of Service and Attainment Entitled Wish-Fulfilling Gem*, *DNZ*, vol. 15, pp. 511–74. Its antecedents are to be found in the *Ritual Service and Attainment of the Three Adamantine Realities*, *DNZ*, vol. 15, pp. 499–509, and in the commentary of Sonam Ozer, which may no longer be extant.

339. The three postures of the upper, middle, and lower body, as explained below, respectively control the upper, middle, and lower winds. See Dawa Sengé, *Connecting Exegesis*, p. 514, lines 5–6.

340. Dawa Sengé, *Connecting Exegesis*, p. 517, lines 4–6–p. 518, line 1.

341. Dawa Sengé, *Connecting Exegesis*, p. 518, lines 4–5. On the primary and ancillary winds and their functionality, see also Gyalwa Yangonpa 2015, 264–70.

342. Here the text misreads *stong du 'tshang na*.

343. Dawa Sengé, *Connecting Exegesis*, p. 520, line 6–p. 521, line 2.

344. Dawa Sengé, p. 521, lines 3–4.

345. Dawa Sengé, p. 522, line 7–p. 523, line 2.

346. Dawa Sengé, p. 524, line 7–p. 525, line 4.

347. Dawa Sengé, p. 525, line 4–p. 526, line 1.

348. Dawa Sengé, p. 526, lines 1–5.

349. Dawa Sengé, p. 526, lines 5–7.

350. Dawa Sengé, p. 527, lines 4–6.

351. Dawa Sengé (*Connecting Exegesis*, p. 527, line 6) suggests that this should be done with mental focus on the movement of an individual's own breathing, and in a nonconceptual disposition.

352. Dawa Sengé, *Connecting Exegesis*, p. 527, line 4–p. 528, line 1.

353. Dawa Sengé (*Connecting Exegesis*, p. 528, line 2–p. 530, line 2), by contrast, suggests that the shapes of these four planetary divinities correspond to those of the four elements in the sequence wind, water, fire, and earth.

354. Alternatively, the wind element is repeated here.

355. Dawa Sengé, *Connecting Exegesis*, p. 531, line 1–p. 532, line 1.

356. Dawa Sengé, p. 532, line 3.
357. Dawa Sengé, p. 532, line 3–p. 533, line 6.
358. Dawa Sengé, p. 533, line 7–p. 534, line 5.
359. Dawa Sengé, p. 534, line 7–p. 535, line 3.
360. The fourfold union denotes (i) the lower wind through which the maṇḍala of the element and the seat are visualized, (ii) the upper wind through which the seed syllables are visualized, (iii) the middle wind through which the hand emblems are visualized, and (iv) their union through which the deity is generated.
361. Dawa Sengé, *Connecting Exegesis*, p. 536, line 7–p. 537, line 6.
362. Or alternatively, BHASUDHI.
363. Dawa Sengé, *Connecting Exegesis*, p. 537, line 6–p. 537, line 7.
364. Dawa Sengé, p. 537, line 7–p. 538, line 2.
365. Dawa Sengé, p. 538, line 2–p. 538, line 4.
366. The twelve great rites (*las chen bcu gnyis*) are enumerated in Nordrang Orgyan, *Compendium of Buddhist Numeric Terms*, p. 2774.
367. Dawa Sengé, *Connecting Exegesis*, p. 538, line 4–p. 539, line 2.
368. *Lam 'bras bu dang bcas pa'i khrid.* The primary source of this guidebook is Lama Dampa Sonam Gyeltsen's *Instruction Manual Elucidating the Concealed Meaning*, *DNZ*, vol. 5, pp. 329–423. Its antecedents include texts attributed to Virūpa and Sachen Kunga Nyingpo, such as the *Root Verses of the Path and Its Fruition*, which are contained in *DNZ*, vol. 5, pp. 1–11, translated in Davidson 2005, 189–94. The origins of the system and this attribution are discussed in Davidson 2005, 183–89; and the lives of the early lineage holders are presented in Stearns 2001.
369. This is the first of the three categories of appearances (*snang ba gsum*) according to the Path and Its Fruition, on which see Lama Dampa Sonam Gyeltsen, *DNZ*, vol. 5, p. 338, line 4–p. 351 line 7; also Stearns 2006, 338–76.
370. On these distinctions, see Stearns 2006, 338–376.
371. Stearns 2006, 338–60.
372. Stearns 2006, 346–50; also Patrul Rinpoche 1994, 63–66.
373. Stearns 2006, 339–46; also Patrul Rinpoche 1994, 68–69.
374. Stearns 2006, 350–53; also Patrul Rinpoche 1994, 66–71.
375. Stearns 2006, 356–59; also Patrul Rinpoche 1994, 72–76.
376. Stearns 2006, 359–60; also Patrul Rinpoche 1994, 76–78.
377. Stearns 2006, 360–63.
378. Stearns 2006, 363–76.
379. See above, chapter 1, n. 54; also Patrul Rinpoche 1994, 22–30.
380. These comprise the realizations of pious attendants (*śrāvaka*), hermit buddhas (*pratyekabuddha*), and buddhas.
381. This is the second of the three categories of appearances (*snang ba gsum*) according to the Path and Its Fruition, on which see Lama Dampa Sonam Gyeltsen, *DNZ*, vol. 5, p. 351, line 7–p. 358, line 2; also Stearns 2006, 377–90.
382. The three paths (*lam gsum*) comprise the path of eliminating entry, the path of

severing attachment, and the path of great enlightenment. The three experiences (*nyams gsum*) comprise physical experiences, mental experiences, and dream experiences. The three auspicious circumstances (*rten 'brel gsum*) comprise the reversal of the winds of past actions, the visionary appearance of signs such as smoke, and the sensations of flying and so forth experienced in dreams. The three aspects of warmth (*drod gsum*) comprise the warmth preceded by conceptual thought, the warmth associated with the gathering of the nine physical constituents (*khams dgu*), and the warmth of the blazing and gathering of vital essences. The three meditative stabilities (*ting nge 'dzin gsum*) comprise defining characteristics as variety, natural expression as emptiness, and essential nature as unity. See Stearns 2006, 25–26.

383. This is the third of the three categories of appearances (*snang ba gsum*) according to the Path and Its Fruition, on which see Lama Dampa Sonam Gyeltsen, *DNZ*, vol. 5, p. 358, lines 2–7; also Stearns 2006, 391–92.
384. On the continuum of the ground (*gzhi'i rgyud*), see Lama Dampa Sonam Gyeltsen, *DNZ*, vol. 5, p. 358, line 7–p. 368, line 6.
385. These twenty-seven coemergent aspects (*lhan skyes nyi shu rtsa bdun*) comprise confusion about radiance, emptiness, and unity; each of which gives rise to (i) the three primary afflicted mental states, (ii) subsidiary afflicted mental states, (iii) subtle winds, (iv) syllables, (v) channels, (vi) constituents, (vii) illnesses, (viii) evil spirits, and (ix) coarseness. See Stearns 2006, 418–21.
386. Stearns (2006, 430–34) enumerates these four primary examples (*gtso bo dpe bzhi*) as sleep, substances, illnesses, and evil spirits; and the four ancillary examples (*yan lag gi dpe bzhi*) as double vision, eye disease, whirling fire, and rapid spinning.
387. Stearns 2006, 430–31.
388. These are the same nine factors enumerated above, chapter 9, n. 385.
389. Stearns 2006, 431–35.
390. Stearns (2006, 438) indicates that Hari (*'phrog pa*) here may denote either the magical reflection of the southern city of Harikela in the sky or the phantom emanation of King Haricandra.
391. Stearns 2006, 435–39.
392. Stearns 2006, 439–42.
393. Stearns 2006, 446–47. The "wave of enjoyment" (*longs spyod kyi rlabs*) indicates a yogic exercise in which the carotid arteries are pressed at the left and right channels, adjacent to the throat cakra. See the illustration in Baker 2019, 185.
394. Stearns 2006, 443–46.
395. Stearns 2006, 447–48.
396. Lama Dampa Sonam Gyeltsen, *DNZ*, vol. 5, p. 374, line 7–p. 376, line 2; also Stearns 2006, 488ff.
397. The six sense fields (*skye mched drug*) are those of the eyes, ears, nose, tongue, body, and mental faculty. The six sense objects (*yul drug*) are sights, sounds, odors, tastes, tangibles, and mental phenomena. The twelve major joints (*tshigs chen bcu gnyis*) are those of the wrists, elbows, shoulders, ankles, knees, and hips.

398. See Stearns 2006, 521.
399. Lama Dampa Sonam Gyeltsen, *DNZ*, vol. 5, p. 377, lines 3–5.
400. Lama Dampa Sonam Gyeltsen (*DNZ*, vol. 5, p. 377, line 7–p. 378, line 1) notes that this path that will dispel [involuntary] inhalation (*'jug pa sel ba'i lam*) is contrasted with the two other paths of severing attachment and great enlightenment that are respectively indicated by one-pointed abiding in a nonreferential disposition and by the mental focus on signs such as smoke.
401. Our text mysteriously reads *rlung 2 phyir 1 rngan dags byin 3*, whereas Lama Dampa Sonam Gyeltsen, *DNZ*, vol. 5, p. 378, simply reads *rtsol ba la rngan dags rims kyis byin*.
402. Lama Dampa Sonam Gyeltsen, *DNZ*, vol. 5, p. 378; also Stearns 2006, 548.
403. Lama Dampa Sonam Gyeltsen, *DNZ*, vol. 5, p. 378, lines 3–4; also Stearns 2006, 548.
404. Lama Dampa Sonam Gyeltsen, *DNZ*, vol. 5, p. 379, lines 4–7; also Stearns 2006, 548.
405. Our text reads *drag shul du lus la gtad* for *drag tu shul la btang*, as found in Lama Dampa Sonam Gyeltsen, *DNZ*, vol. 5, p. 380, line 3.
406. Lama Dampa Sonam Gyeltsen, *DNZ*, vol. 5, p. 380, lines 2–6; also Stearns 2006, 548.
407. Lama Dampa Sonam Gyeltsen, *DNZ*, vol. 5, p. 380, line 7–p. 381, line 1; also Stearns 2006, 548.
408. Lama Dampa Sonam Gyeltsen, *DNZ*, vol. 5, p. 381, lines 3–5.
409. Lama Dampa Sonam Gyeltsen, *DNZ*, vol. 5, p. 381, line 5–p. 382, line 1; also Stearns 2006, 549.
410. Lama Dampa Sonam Gyeltsen, *DNZ*, vol. 5, p. 382, lines 2–5; also Stearns 2006, 549.
411. Lama Dampa Sonam Gyeltsen, *DNZ*, vol. 5, p. 382, line 5–p. 383, line 2.
412. Lama Dampa Sonam Gyeltsen, *DNZ*, vol. 5, p. 383, line 6–p. 384, line 2; also Stearns 2006, 549. This posture is illustrated in Baker 2019, 154.
413. Lama Dampa Sonam Gyeltsen, *DNZ*, vol. 5, pp. 385–92; also Stearns 2006, 550–53.
414. Lama Dampa Sonam Gyeltsen, *DNZ*, vol. 5, pp. 392–95; also Stearns 2006, 553–55.
415. Lama Dampa Sonam Gyeltsen, *DNZ*, vol. 5, pp. 395–98; also Stearns 2006, 555–56. Note that our text omits the sixth.
416. Lama Dampa Sonam Gyeltsen, *DNZ*, vol. 5, pp. 398–404; also Stearns 2006, 560–66.
417. Lama Dampa Sonam Gyeltsen, *DNZ*, vol. 5, p. 404, line 4–p. 405, line 1; also Stearns 2006, 566–67.
418. Lama Dampa Sonam Gyeltsen, *DNZ*, vol. 5, p. 405, lines 1–5; also Stearns 2006, 567.
419. Our text reads *sogs kyi rba rlabs*, but see Lama Dampa Sonam Gyeltsen, *DNZ*, vol. 5, p. 405, line 5.

420. These are the three perceptions (*'du shes gsum*) of the male, female, and their nondual union.
421. Lama Dampa Sonam Gyeltsen, *DNZ*, vol. 5, pp. 405–6; also Stearns 2006, 567–68. On the distinction between the lower wind of exertion (*rtsol rlung*) and the upper wind of life breath (*srog rlung*), see also Gyalwa Yangonpa 2015, 271.
422. Lama Dampa Sonam Gyeltsen, *DNZ*, vol. 5, p. 406.
423. On the experience of the four delights ascending from below (*mas brtan gyi dga' ba bzhi*) within the central channel, see, for example, the interpretation of Longchen Rabjam in Dorje 1987, 1015–17.
424. Lama Dampa Sonam Gyeltsen, *DNZ*, vol. 5, pp. 406–7.
425. *bSam mi khyab kyi khrid.* The primary source is Drakpa Gyeltsen's *Oral Instruction of the Inconceivables, Attributed to Glorious Khanitra*, *DNZ*, vol. 6, pp. 81–118, with commentary on pp. 231–54. On the original sources, see also Davidson 2005, 194–96; and Stearns 2006, 135.
426. Drakpa Gyeltsen, *DNZ*, vol. 6, p. 240, line 5–p. 241, line 3. The three cultivations of these ranges of external space correspond respectively to the meditative stability of method (*thabs kyi ting nge 'dzin*), the meditative stability of discriminative awareness (*shes rab kyi ting nge 'dzin*), and the meditative stability of their coalescence (*zung 'jug gi ting nge 'dzin*).
427. Drakpa Gyeltsen, *DNZ*, vol. 6, p. 241.
428. Our text reads *thog ma'i rgya* for *thog ma'i rgyu*.
429. Drakpa Gyeltsen, *DNZ*, vol. 6, p. 242, line 1–p. 244, line 2.
430. Drakpa Gyeltsen (*DNZ*, vol. 6, p. 244, lines 4–5) here points out that these supportive ancillary practices (*brtan pa'i yan lag*) are undertaken and experienced in all one's actions in order to liberate one from the bondage of attachment and hatred that might arise through incidental encounters, even though they no longer arise in meditative absorption.
431. Drakpa Gyeltsen, *DNZ*, vol. 6, p. 244, line 5–p. 245, line 2.
432. Drakpa Gyeltsen, vol. 6, p. 245, lines 2–5.
433. Drakpa Gyeltsen, vol. 6, p. 245, lines 5–7.
434. Drakpa Gyeltsen, vol. 6, p. 245, line 7–p. 246, line 6.
435. Drakpa Gyeltsen, vol. 6, p. 246, line 6–p. 249, line 7.
436. These five subsidiary pith instructions of suppression (*log gnon rnam pa lnga*) are undertaken in order to eliminate ill health.
437. Drakpa Gyeltsen, *DNZ*, vol. 6, p. 249, line 7–p. 251, line 5.
438. *Zab pa'i tshul dgu'i khrid yig.* The primary source is Drakpa Gyeltsen's *Generation Stage Adorned with Nine Profound Methods, Attributed to Padmavajra*, *DNZ*, vol. 6, pp. 19–41, and its commentary on pp. 151–80. On the original sources, see also Davidson 2005, 199–200; and Stearns 2006, 135.
439. Drakpa Gyeltsen, *DNZ*, vol. 6, p. 26, lines 5–7. Cf. the presentation in Jamgön Kongtrul 2012, 428–29; also Dakpo Rabjampa Tashi Namgyal's *Elucidation on the Sequence of Meditation according to the Great Seal of Definitive Meaning Enti-*

tled *Moonbeams of Eloquence*, pp. 367–80, and the translation in Dakpo Tashi Namgyal 2006; also Khenchen Thrangu (1993, 15–62), who includes a chart (p. 54) outlining the relationship between these nine techniques of calm abiding and their associated mental powers and levels of engagement, based on Asaṅga's *Level of the Pious Attendants*. See also Cha 2013, on the presentation of the nine techniques of calm abiding according to Asaṅga.

440. Drakpa Gyeltsen, *DNZ*, vol. 6, p. 26, line 7–p. 27, line 1. This text also explains that in the deity visualization of the generation stage of meditation, there are three phases: the yoga of engagement (*'jug pa'i rnal 'byor*), the yoga of abiding (*gnas pa'i rnal 'byor*), and the yoga of reemergence (*ldang ba'i rnal 'byor*). The nine pith instructions pertain to the yoga of abiding.

441. Drakpa Gyeltsen, *DNZ*, vol. 6, p. 27, line 7–p. 28, line 3.

442. Drakpa Gyeltsen, vol. 6, p. 28, lines 3–4.

443. Drakpa Gyeltsen, vol. 6, p. 28, lines 4–5.

444. Drakpa Gyeltsen, vol. 6, p. 28, lines 5–6.

445. Drakpa Gyeltsen, vol. 6, p. 28, line 6.

446. Drakpa Gyeltsen, vol. 6, p. 28, lines 6–7.

447. Drakpa Gyeltsen, vol. 6, p. 28, line 7.

448. Drakpa Gyeltsen, vol. 6, p. 28, line 7–p. 29, line 1.

449. Drakpa Gyeltsen, vol. 6, p. 29, line 3–p. 30, line 4.

450. Stearns (2006, 135) points out that Padmavajra, also known as Saroruhavajra, composed two treatises based on the *Two-Chapter Tantra of Hevajra*—namely, the *Method for Accomplishment* (*sGrub thabs*) and *Like the Tip of a Lamp Flame* (*Mar me'i rtse lta bu*), which respectively concern the generation and perfection stages.

451. Drakpa Gyeltsen, *DNZ*, vol. 6, p. 30, lines 4–5.

452. Drakpa Gyeltsen, vol. 6, p. 30, lines 5–7.

453. *Lhan cig skyes grub kyi khrid.* The primary source is Drakpa Gyeltsen's *The Attainment of Coemergence Attributed to Ḍombī Heruka*, *DNZ*, vol. 6, pp. 7–17, with its commentary on pp. 137–50. See also Davidson 2005, 196–97; and Stearns 2006, 134.

454. According to Drakpa Gyeltsen (*DNZ*, vol. 6, p. 139 line 4), the outer way of austerities (*dka' thub kyi lam*) is characterized as conceptual and the inner way of Buchung (*bu chung gi lam*) as nonconceptual.

455. Our text reads *sngon 'jug* for *smon 'jug.* See Drakpa Gyeltsen, *DNZ*, vol. 6, p. 9, line 6.

456. Drakpa Gyeltsen, *DNZ*, vol. 6, p. 8, line 3–p. 10, line 1.

457. Drakpa Gyeltsen, vol. 6, p. 10, lines 1–2.

458. Drakpa Gyeltsen, vol. 6, p. 10, lines 3–4.

459. The text here includes an annotation that reads "Though this is not in later versions, it seems that it does derive from *The Path and Its Fruition*."

460. Drakpa Gyeltsen, *DNZ*, vol. 6, p. 146, line 7–p. 147, line 2. The commentary

here mentions the twenty-four ancillary pith instructions rather than twenty-seven, which add the primary transformations of desire, hatred, and delusion, as indicated here.

461. Drakpa Gyeltsen, *DNZ*, vol. 6, p. 147, line 4.
462. Drakpa Gyeltsen, vol. 6, p. 147, lines 4–5.
463. Drakpa Gyeltsen, vol. 6, p. 147, line 7.
464. Drakpa Gyeltsen, vol. 6, p. 148, line 2.
465. *gTum mo lam rdzogs kyi khrid.* The primary source is Drakpa Gyeltsen's *Perfection of the Path of Fierce Inner Heat Attributed to the Master Kṛṣṇacārin*, *DNZ*, vol. 6, pp. 43–53, with its commentary on pp. 271–87. See also Davidson 2005, 200–201; and Stearns 2006, 135–36.
466. For Jamgön Kongtrul's somewhat different explanation of these four phases, see Jamgön Kongtrul 2008, 175–78.
467. Drakpa Gyeltsen, *DNZ*, vol. 6, p. 46, lines 4–5.
468. The two active cakras (*las byed pa'i 'khor lo gnyis*) are those of the rectum (*bshang sgo*) and the triple intersection (*sum mdo*) of the three main channels below the navel. The four higher cakras (*'khor lo gong ma bzhi*) are at the navel, heart, throat, and head.
469. Drakpa Gyeltsen, *DNZ*, vol. 6, p. 46, lines 5–6. The detailed visualization of the channels and syllables is found on p. 46, line 6–p. 47, line 4. This paragraph constitutes the phase of the continuum (*rgyud kyi rim pa*).
470. This paragraph constitutes the preliminary practice for the phase of mantra (*sngags kyi rim pa*).
471. The five lords of enlightened heritage and their five female consorts (*rigs lnga yum lnga*) are the male and female buddhas of the five enlightened families, representing the buddha body of perfect resource.
472. Drakpa Gyeltsen, *DNZ*, vol. 6, p. 48, line 6–p. 49, line 6. This paragraph constitutes the actual phase of mantra.
473. Drakpa Gyeltsen, *DNZ*, vol. 6, p. 49, line 6–p. 51, line 4. This paragraph constitutes the phase of pristine cognition (*ye shes kyi rim pa*). On the sixteen delights, see Longchen Rabjam's explanation in Dorje 1987, 900–914.
474. Drakpa Gyeltsen, *DNZ*, vol. 6, p. 51, line 4–p. 52, line 6. This section constitutes the phase of secrecy (*gsang ba'i rim pa*).
475. *Yol po bsrang ba'i khrid.* The primary source is Drakpa Gyeltsen's *Instruction on the Straightening of Crooked Posture, Attributed to Acyutakāṇha*, *DNZ*, vol. 6, pp. 55–57, with its commentary on pp. 181–88. See also Davidson 2005, 201; and Stearns 2006, 136.
476. Drakpa Gyeltsen, *DNZ*, vol. 6, p. 56, lines 2–3.
477. Drakpa Gyeltsen, vol. 6, p. 56, lines 3–6.
478. Drakpa Gyeltsen, vol. 6, p. 56, line 7.
479. Drakpa Gyeltsen, vol. 6, p. 57, line 1.
480. Drakpa Gyeltsen, vol. 6, p. 57, line 2.
481. *Phyag rgya'i lam khrid.* The primary source is Drakpa Gyeltsen's *The Cycle of the*

Path of the Female Mudra, DNZ, vol. 6, pp. 119–36, with its commentary on pp. 255–69. See also Davidson 2005, 202–204; and Stearns 2006, 134.

482. The commentary reads *gyen du drangs*. Our text reads *pang gyen du drangs*.
483. Drakpa Gyeltsen, *DNZ*, vol. 6, p. 123, lines 3–6.
484. Drakpa Gyeltsen, vol. 6, p. 124, lines 1–2.
485. Drakpa Gyeltsen, vol. 6, p. 124, lines 3–5.
486. Drakpa Gyeltsen, vol. 6, p. 124, line 7–p. 125, line 1.
487. Drakpa Gyeltsen, vol. 6, p. 125, lines 1–2. The commentary suggests that the practitioner "should attain perfect buddhahood for the sake of sentient beings." The three foregoing visualizations are said to make the three buddha bodies into the path—the sameness of body and speech (*lus ngag mnyam pa*) as the buddha body of emanation, the sameness of the consecration (*byin rlabs mnyam pa*) as the buddha body of perfect resource, and the sameness of desire (*'dod mnyam pa*) as the buddha body of reality.
488. Drakpa Gyeltsen, *DNZ*, vol. 6, p. 126, line 3–p. 127, line 3.
489. Drakpa Gyeltsen, vol. 6, p. 127, lines 3–4.
490. On these sixteen aspects of delight, stabilized from below (*mas brtan gyi dga' ba bcu drug*), see above, chapter 9, n. 473.
491. Drakpa Gyeltsen, *DNZ*, vol. 6, p. 127, line 6–p. 128, line 1.
492. Drakpa Gyeltsen, vol. 6, p. 128, lines 1–3.
493. Drakpa Gyeltsen, vol. 6, p. 128, lines 3–4.
494. Drakpa Gyeltsen, vol. 6, p. 128, lines 4–5.
495. *Phyag rgya chen po yi ge med pa'i khrid*. The primary source is Drakpa Gyeltsen's *Great Seal Devoid of Letters, Attributed to Master Vagīśvarakīrti, DNZ*, vol. 6, pp. 67–79, with its commentary on pp. 213–29. See also Davidson 2005, 198–99; and Stearns 2006, 136.
496. Drakpa Gyeltsen, *DNZ*, vol. 6, p. 73, lines 1–2.
497. Drakpa Gyeltsen, vol. 6, p. 73, lines 3–5.
498. Drakpa Gyeltsen, vol. 6, p. 73, line 1–p. 74, line 2.
499. Drakpa Gyeltsen, vol. 6, p. 74, lines 3–7.
500. Drakpa Gyeltsen, vol. 6, p. 74, line 7–p. 75, line 2.
501. Drakpa Gyeltsen, vol. 6, p. 75, lines 3–4.
502. Drakpa Gyeltsen, vol. 6, p. 75, line 5–p. 76, line 1.
503. Drakpa Gyeltsen, vol. 6, p. 76, lines 1–2.
504. Drakpa Gyeltsen, vol. 6, p. 77, lines 4–7. Our text reads *dgra* for *sgra*.
505. *mChod rten drung thob kyi khrid*. The primary source is Drakpa Gyeltsen's *Attainment in Proximity to a Stupa, Attributed to Master Nāgārjuna, DNZ*, vol. 6, pp. 59–65, with its commentary on pp. 189–212. See also Davidson 2005, 197–98; and Stearns 2006, 133–134. In the lineage prayers of chapter 1, this guidebook is known as *The Determination of Mind*. On this and other variant titles, see Davidson 2005, 197.
506. Our text reads "naturally compatible" (*rang 'thad*), but see Drakpa Gyeltsen, *DNZ*, vol. 6, p. 62, line 6, which reads *rang dvangs*.

507. Drakpa Gyeltsen, *DNZ*, vol. 6, p. 62, line 6–p. 63, line 2.
508. Drakpa Gyeltsen, *DNZ*, vol. 6, p. 63, lines 3–7.
509. Drakpa Gyeltsen, *DNZ*, vol. 6, p. 64, line 7–p. 64, line 3.
510. *mDo rgyud bse ba'i khrid.* The primary source is Drokmi Lotsāwa's *Experiential Cultivation of the Mingling of Sutra and Tantra: A Pith Instruction Attributed to Guru Śāntipa, DNZ*, vol. 6, pp. 290–93. This text is the first of Drokmi's *Spiritual Connections with the Six Gatekeepers.*
511. Drakpa Gyeltsen, *DNZ*, vol. 6, p. 291, lines 2–3.
512. Drakpa Gyeltsen, vol. 6, p. 291, lines 4–5.
513. Drakpa Gyeltsen, vol. 6, p. 292, lines 1–2.
514. Drakpa Gyeltsen, vol. 6, p. 292, lines 2–6.
515. Drakpa Gyeltsen, vol. 6, p. 292, line 7–p. 293, line 3.
516. Drakpa Gyeltsen, vol. 6, p. 293, lines 3–4.
517. *Phyi rol gdon gyi bar chad sel ba'i khrid yig.* The primary source is Drokmi Lotsāwa's *Dispelling of the Obstacles of External Demons: A Pith Instruction Attributed to Prajñākaragupta, DNZ*, vol. 6, pp. 293–94. This text is the second of Drokmi's *Spiritual Connections with the Six Gatekeepers*, and it more specifically belongs to the cycle of the *Dispelling of the Three Obstacles.*
518. Drokmi Lotsāwa, *DNZ*, vol. 6, p. 294, lines 2–4.
519. *'Byung ba lus 'khrugs kyi bar chad sel ba'i khrid yig.* The primary source is Drokmi Lotsāwa's *Dispelling of All Ailments That Agitate the Physical Elements: A Pith Instruction Attributed to Guru Jñānaśrī, DNZ*, vol. 6, p. 294. This text is the third of Drokmi's *Spiritual Connections with the Six Gatekeepers*, and it more specifically belongs to the cycle of the *Dispelling of the Three Obstacles.*
520. Drokmi Lotsāwa, *DNZ*, vol. 6, p. 294, lines 5–6.
521. Drokmi Lotsāwa, vol. 6, p. 294, lines 6–7.
522. *Ting nge 'dzin sems kyi bar chad sel ba'i khrid yig.* The primary source is Drokmi Lotsāwa's *Dispelling of the Obstacles of Meditative Stability and Mind: A Pith Instruction Attributed to Guru Ratnavajra, DNZ*, vol. 6, p. 295. This text is the fourth of Drokmi's *Spiritual Connections with the Six Gatekeepers*, and it more specifically belongs to the cycle of the *Dispelling of the Three Obstacles.*
523. Drokmi Lotsāwa, *DNZ*, vol. 6, p. 295, lines 1–5.
524. *Phyag chen sdug bsngal gsum sel gyi khrid yig.* The primary source is Drokmi Lotsāwa's *Great Seal Dispelling the Three Sorts of Suffering: A Pith Instruction Attributed to Glorious Nāropā, DNZ*, vol. 6, p. 300, line 5–p. 303, line 4. This text is the fifth of Drokmi's *Spiritual Connections with the Six Gatekeepers.*
525. Our text here reads *yid 'phreng* (threads of the mental faculty).
526. Drokmi Lotsāwa, *DNZ*, vol. 6, p. 300, line 7–p. 301, line 4. The source text enumerates nine profound essentials (*zab gnad dgu*) including the five mentioned here. The other four may be regarded as preliminary or subsidiary.
527. Drokmi Lotsāwa, *DNZ*, vol. 6, p. 301, lines 4–7.
528. Drokmi Lotsāwa, vol. 6, p. 301, line 7–p. 302, line 1.
529. Drokmi Lotsāwa, vol. 6, p. 302, lines 2–3.

530. Drokmi Lotsāwa, vol. 6, p. 302, lines 3–4.
531. Here the translation follows Drokmi Lotsāwa, *DNZ*, vol. 6, p. 302, lines 5–6. By contrast, our text reads *go bas mtha' rgya chod mtha' 'das sa ma rnye / bsam bsgom gyis nyams su sbyong / dbus sa ma rnyed*; that is, it reads *dbus sa* (center) for *dbul ba* (destitute).
532. Drokmi Lotsāwa, *DNZ*, vol. 6, p. 302, lines 6–7.
533. *gNyug ma dran gsal gyi khrid yig.* The primary source is Drokmi Lotsāwa's *Clear Recollection of the Innate State: A Pith Instruction Attributed to Vagīśvarakīrti*, *DNZ*, vol. 6, p. 295, line 7–p. 300, line 5. This text is the sixth and last of Drokmi's *Spiritual Connections with the Six Gatekeepers.*
534. Drokmi Lotsāwa, *DNZ*, vol. 6, p. 296, line 6–p. 297, line 1.
535. Drokmi Lotsāwa, vol. 6, p. 297, lines 1–4.
536. Drokmi Lotsāwa, vol. 6, p. 297, line 4–p. 298, line 6.
537. Drokmi Lotsāwa, vol. 6, p. 298, lines 6–7.
538. According to Drokmi Lotsāwa (*DNZ*, vol. 6, p. 299, line 2), the three attributes (*chos gsum ldan*) of the fierce inner heat are radiance, heat, and pliancy.
539. Drokmi Lotsāwa, *DNZ*, vol. 6, p. 299, lines 1–3.
540. Drokmi Lotsāwa, vol. 6, p. 299, lines 3–4.
541. Drokmi Lotsāwa, vol. 6, p. 299, line 7–p. 300, line 2.
542. *Dag pa gsum gyi khrid yig.* The primary source is Pakpa Lodro Gyeltsen's *The Three Purities: Enlightened Intention of the Sublime Tantra of the Adamantine Tent of the Ḍākinīs*, in his *Collected Works*, vol. 1, pp. 601–17; also in *DNZ*, vol. 5, pp. 491–505.
543. Pakpa Lodro Gyeltsen, *DNZ*, vol. 5, p. 494, lines 3–5.
544. Pakpa Lodro Gyeltsen, *DNZ*, vol. 5, p. 495, line 3.
545. Pakpa Lodro Gyeltsen, *DNZ*, vol. 5, p. 495, lines 6–7.
546. Pakpa Lodro Gyeltsen, vol. 5, p. 495, line 7–p. 497, line 4.
547. Pakpa Lodro Gyeltsen, vol. 5, p. 497, line 5–p. 498, line 5. These include the three refinements (*sbyang ba gsum*), the three practices that hit the essential point (*gnad la dbab pa gsum*), and the three preliminaries (*sngon 'gro gsum*)—all of which pertain respectively to ordinary body, speech, and mind.
548. This is missing in our text, but see Pakpa Lodro Gyeltsen, *DNZ*, vol. 5, p. 498, line 7–p. 499, line 5.
549. Pakpa Lodro Gyeltsen, *DNZ*, vol. 5, p. 499, line 6–p. 500, line 1.
550. Pakpa Lodro Gyeltsen, vol. 5, p. 500, lines 1–4.
551. Pakpa Lodro Gyeltsen, vol. 5, p. 500, lines 5–7.
552. Pakpa Lodro Gyeltsen, vol. 5, p. 500, line 7–p. 501, line 3.
553. Pakpa Lodro Gyeltsen, vol. 5, p. 501, lines 3–6.
554. Pakpa Lodro Gyeltsen, vol. 5, p. 501, line 6–p. 502, line 3. As indicated above, the lower wind is known as the "wind of exertion," and the upper wind as the "wind of life breath."
555. Pakpa Lodro Gyeltsen, *DNZ*, vol. 5, p. 502, line 3–p. 503, line 1.
556. Pakpa Lodro Gyeltsen, vol. 5, p. 503, lines 1–6.

557. Our text reads OṂ.
558. Pakpa Lodro Gyeltsen, *DNZ*, vol. 5, p. 503, line 6–p. 504, line 4. Our text reads HA for HAṂ.
559. Pakpa Lodro Gyeltsen, *DNZ*, vol. 5, p. 504, line 4–p. 505, line 2.
560. Pakpa Lodro Gyeltsen, vol. 5, p. 505, lines 2–7.
561. *Rang byin rlabs kyi dmigs pa nyer dgu'i khrid*. The primary source is Drokmi Lotsāwa, *Twenty-Nine Essential Visualizations of Self-Consecration*, SLC, vol. 11, pp. 70–83.
562. Drokmi Lotsāwa, SLC, vol. 11, p. 70, line 2–p. 71, line 2.
563. Drokmi Lotsāwa, vol. 11, p. 71, lines 2–5.
564. Drokmi Lotsāwa, vol. 11, p. 71, line 5–p. 72, line 1.
565. Drokmi Lotsāwa, vol. 11, p. 72, lines 1–3.
566. Drokmi Lotsāwa, vol. 11, p. 72, lines 3–5.
567. Drokmi Lotsāwa, vol. 11, p. 72, lines 5–6.
568. Drokmi Lotsāwa, vol. 11, p. 72, line 6–p. 73, line 3.
569. Drokmi Lotsāwa (SLC, vol. 11, p. 73, line 4) suggests the alternative visualization with AṂ at the center instead of HŪṂ.
570. Drokmi Lotsāwa, SLC, vol. 11, p. 73, lines 3–5.
571. Drokmi Lotsāwa, vol. 11, p. 73, line 5–p. 74, line 1.
572. Drokmi Lotsāwa, vol. 11, p. 74, lines 1–4.
573. Drokmi Lotsāwa, vol. 11, p. 74, line 4–p. 75, line 1.
574. Drokmi Lotsāwa, SLC, vol. 11, p. 75, lines 1–4.
575. Drokmi Lotsāwa, vol. 11, p. 75, lines 4–6.
576. Drokmi Lotsāwa, vol. 11, p. 75, line 6–p. 76, line 1.
577. Drokmi Lotsāwa, vol. 11, p. 76, lines 1–5.
578. Drokmi Lotsāwa, vol. 11, p. 76, line 5–p. 77, line 2.
579. Drokmi Lotsāwa, vol. 11, p. 77, lines 2–4.
580. Drokmi Lotsāwa, vol. 11, p. 77, lines 4–6.
581. Drokmi Lotsāwa, vol. 11, p. 77, line 6–p. 78, line 1.
582. Drokmi Lotsāwa, vol. 11, p. 78, lines 1–3.
583. Drokmi Lotsāwa, vol. 11, p. 78, line 3–p. 79, line 4.
584. Drokmi Lotsāwa, vol. 11, p. 79, lines 4–6.
585. Drokmi Lotsāwa, vol. 11, p. 79, line 6–p. 80, line 2.
586. Drokmi Lotsāwa, vol. 11, p. 80, lines 2–6.
587. Drokmi Lotsāwa, vol. 11, p. 80, line 6–p. 81, line 4.
588. The ten orifices (*sgo bcu*) of the body include the eyes, ears, nose, mouth, anus, genitals, and the space between the eyebrows.
589. Drokmi Lotsāwa, SLC, vol. 11, p. 81, lines 4–6.
590. Drokmi Lotsāwa, vol. 11, p. 81, line 6–p. 82, line 2.
591. Drokmi Lotsāwa, vol. 11, p. 82, lines 2–5.
592. Drokmi Lotsāwa, vol. 11, p. 82, line 5–p. 83, line 2.
593. *Lam sbas bshad kyi khrid yig*. The primary source by Sakya Paṇḍita is contained in SLC, vol. 11, pp. 342–53. A related text, Dakchen Dorjé Chang Lodro Gyeltsen's

Memorandum on the Pith Instruction Entitled the Exegesis of the Concealed Path, is also contained in *DNZ*, vol. 5, pp. 425–31. The antecedent of this instruction, as stated above, is the revelation that Virūpa imparted to Sachen Kunga Nyingpo.

594. Sakya Paṇḍita, SLC, vol. 11, p. 343, lines 3–4; also Lodro Gyeltsen, *DNZ*, vol. 5, p. 427, line 7–p. 428, line 1. This text claims, however, that the height of this anal plug should be six finger widths, and it may also be made of wood. An annotation adds that the silk covering may be softened with butter or fat.

595. Sakya Paṇḍita, SLC, vol. 11, p. 343, lines 5–6; also Lodro Gyeltsen, *DNZ*, vol. 5, p. 428, lines 1–2. The posture that resembles the ear of an elephant (*glang po che'i rna ba lta bu skyil krung*) entails that the heel of the right foot is positioned against the root of the penis, with the left foot in front of it and the knees on the ground.

596. Sakya Paṇḍita, SLC, vol. 11, p. 343, line 6–p. 344, line 1; also Lodro Gyeltsen, *DNZ*, vol. 5, p. 428, lines 2–3.

597. Sakya Paṇḍita, SLC, vol. 11, p. 344, line 1; also Lodro Gyeltsen, *DNZ*, vol. 5, p. 428, lines 2–4.

598. Sakya Paṇḍita, SLC, vol. 11, p. 344, line 1–p. 345, line 4; also Lodro Gyeltsen, *DNZ*, vol. 5, p. 428, line 6–p. 429, line 1.

599. Sakya Paṇḍita, SLC, vol. 11, p. 345, lines 4–5; also Lodro Gyeltsen, *DNZ*, vol. 5, p. 429, lines 2–3.

600. Sakya Paṇḍita, SLC, vol. 11, p. 345, lines 5–6; also Lodro Gyeltsen, *DNZ*, vol. 5, p. 429, line 5.

601. The initial absorption of the sensory elements (*khams 'dus pa dang po*) is an indication associated with the blazing of the fierce inner heat, in contrast to the middling absorption of the sensory elements (*khams 'dus pa bar ma*), which is associated with its dynamic motion, and the final absorption of the sensory elements (*khams 'dus pa tha ma*), which is associated with its stability.

602. Sakya Paṇḍita, SLC, vol. 11, p. 346, lines 1–5.

603. Sakya Paṇḍita, vol. 11, p. 346, line 6–p. 347, line 3.

604. Sakya Paṇḍita, vol. 11, p. 347, line 3–p. 348, line 6. Supporting the kidneys at the waist is said to help alleviate graying of the hair, wrinkles, eye diseases, and headaches.

605. *brDa don gsal ba'i khrid*. The primary source by Sakya Paṇḍita is contained in SLC, vol. 11, pp. 209–16, and immediately followed by the memorandum of his disciple Lhopa Kunkhyen Rinchen Pel, SLC, vol. 11, pp. 216–18. There is also a related text, Dakchen Dorjé Chang Lodro Gyeltsen's *Elucidation of the Symbolic Meaning*, contained in *DNZ*, vol. 5, pp. 433–57.

606. Sakya Paṇḍita, SLC, vol. 11, p. 211, lines 1–3; also Lodro Gyeltsen, *DNZ*, vol. 5, p. 433, lines 2–4. As indicated above, these bring about the transformation of ordinary body, speech, and mind.

607. Sakya Paṇḍita, SLC, vol. 11, p. 211, lines 3–5; also Lodro Gyeltsen, *DNZ*, vol. 5, p. 433, lines 4–6.

608. Sakya Paṇḍita, SLC, vol. 11, p. 211, line 5–p. 212, line 1; also Lodro Gyeltsen, *DNZ*, vol. 5, p. 433, line 6–p. 434, line 1.

609. Sakya Paṇḍita, SLC, vol. 11, p. 212, line 1; also Lodro Gyeltsen, *DNZ*, vol. 5, p. 412, lines 3–4.
610. The three complete modalities of the fierce inner heat (*gtum mo gsum tshang tshul*) are outer, inner, and secret, or ritual (*las*), experience (*nyams*) and supremacy (*mchog*). On the eighteen yogic exercises focusing on the fierce inner heat, see above, chapter 9, n. 257.
611. Sakya Paṇḍita, SLC, vol. 11, p. 211, line 2–p. 213, line 1.
612. On these three approaches—extensive, middle-length, and abridged—see Sakya Paṇḍita, SLC, vol. 11, p. 213, line 1–p. 214, line 2.
613. *gSang 'dus rim lnga'i khrid*. The primary source is said to be Mangkharwa Lodro Gyeltsen's *Memorandum of the Five Stages of the Secret Assembly*, which appears to be no longer extant as a distinct work. Its antecedents are found in Nāgārjuna's original commentary and the Tibetan writings of Go Khukpa Lhetsé and Serdingpa Zhonu O (fl. twelfth century). In the notes that follow, Tāranātha's *Instruction Manual of the Go Tradition on the Five Stages: Elucidating the Meaning of the Tantra* [*of the Secret Assembly*] (*Collected Works of Tāranātha*, vol. 9, pp. 156–93) has been referenced. Tsongkhapa's interpretation of the *Five Stages* is presented in Tsongkhapa 2013, and Jamgön Kongtrul's can be found in Jamgön Kongtrul 2008, 138–45. For iconographic and liturgical details, see Willson and Brauen 2000, no. 459.
614. The "yoga of a singular recollection" (*dran pa gcig pa'i rnal 'byor*) refers to coarse (*rags pa*) deity yoga in contrast to subtle (*phra ba*) deity yoga, which is known as "conceptual yoga" (*rtog pa'i rnal 'byor*). On this distinction, see Tāranātha, in his *Collected Works*, vol. 9, pp. 159–60; also Tsongkhapa 2013, 89–90.
615. Tsongkhapa 2013, 167–210.
616. Tāranātha, in his *Collected Works*, vol. 9, pp. 162–70; Tsongkhapa 2013, 181.
617. Tsongkhapa 2013, 181.
618. The text reads *brgyad po* for *brgya*.
619. Tsongkhapa 2013, 188–89.
620. Tāranātha, in his *Collected Works*, vol. 9, pp. 170–71; Tsongkhapa 2013, 208.
621. Tāranātha, *Collected Works*, vol. 9, p. 168.
622. Tāranātha, *Collected Works*, vol. 9, pp. 171–78; Tsongkhapa 2013, 213–329.
623. Tsongkhapa 2013, 219ff.; and Wayman 1977, 252–53.
624. Tsongkhapa 2013, 233; also Gyalwa Yangonpa 2015, 272–73.
625. Tāranātha, in his *Collected Works*, vol. 9, p. 173.
626. Tāranātha, vol. 9, p. 173.
627. Literally, *srib* (in the shade).
628. Tāranātha, in his *Collected Works*, vol. 9, pp. 173–74.
629. Tāranātha, vol. 9, p. 175.
630. Tāranātha, *Collected Works*, vol. 9, pp. 178–83; also Tsongkhapa 2013, 333ff.
631. Tāranātha, *Collected Works*, vol. 9, p. 179; and on their Tsongkhapa 2013, 341–46.
632. Defined in Tsongkhapa 2013, 346.
633. Our text reads OṂ for AṂ.

634. Tāranātha, in his *Collected Works*, vol. 9, p. 179.
635. Defined in Tsongkhapa 2013, 347.
636. Tāranātha, in his *Collected Works*, vol. 9, pp. 179–80.
637. Defined in Tsongkhapa 2013, 347.
638. Tāranātha, in his *Collected Works*, vol. 9, pp. 180–81.
639. Tāranātha, vol. 9, p. 181.
640. Tāranātha, *Collected Works*, vol. 9, pp. 182–85; also Tsongkhapa 2013, 379–417.
641. Tāranātha, *Collected Works*, vol. 9, pp. 182–83.
642. Tāranātha, in his *Collected Works*, vol. 9, pp. 185–90; also Tsongkhapa 2013, 453–61.
643. Tāranātha, *Collected Works*, vol. 9, p. 185.
644. Tāranātha, vol. 9, pp. 185–86.
645. Our text reads KA for KṢA, but see Tāranātha, *Collected Works*, vol. 9, p. 187.
646. Tāranātha, in his *Collected Works*, vol. 9, pp. 187–88.
647. Tāranātha, vol. 9, p. 188.
648. Tāranātha, vol. 9, p. 188.
649. Tāranātha, vol. 9, pp. 188–90.
650. Tāranātha, vol. 9, p. 191.
651. The adamantine reality of hatred (*dveṣavajra, zhe sdang rdo rje*) here denotes the buddha body of emanation.
652. An oblique reference perhaps to Mangkharwa Lodro Gyeltsen.
653. *Grol ba'i thig le'i khrid.* In this chapter, the primary source is attributed to the memorandum of Jang Pukpa Kunlek, whereas in chapter 5 it is attributed to the memorandum of Drakmar Kunga Tsepel. Neither of these has been separately identified. According to Tāranātha, the former was a disciple of Sabzang Pakpa Zhonu Lodro (1358–1412/24) and teacher of Sempa Sonam Rinchen Gyeltsen. The latter was a teacher of Rabsel Dawa Gon (fl. fifteenth century). The antecedent of both is Buddhajñānapāda's Indic commentary, *The Vital Essence of Liberation*, concerning the nineteen-deity assemblage of Mañjuvajra, according to the later interpretation of the *Tantra of the Secret Assembly*. Jamgön Kongtrul's explanation of this instruction is contained in Jamgön Kongtrul 2008, 145–48. For iconographic and liturgical details, see Willson and Brauen 2000, no. 457. Here, specific references are made to Sherab Rinchen's commentary entitled *Essential Vital Essence of the Perfection Stage according to Buddhajñānapāda*, contained in his *Collected Works*, vol. 3, pp. 119–34.
654. Sherab Rinchen, in his *Collected Works*, vol. 3, p. 121.
655. Sherab Rinchen, vol. 3, pp. 121–22.
656. Sherab Rinchen, vol. 3, p. 122.
657. Sherab Rinchen, vol. 3, p. 122.
658. Sherab Rinchen, vol. 3, p. 122.
659. Sherab Rinchen, vol. 3, p. 123.
660. Sherab Rinchen, vol. 3, p. 123.
661. Sherab Rinchen, vol. 3, pp. 123–24.

662. These are the three attributes of energy, dullness, and lightness (*rdul mun snying stobs kyi rang bzhin*) elucidated in the Sāṃkhyā philosophy of ancient India.
663. The three-tiered principal beings of commitment, pristine cognition, and meditative stability (*gtso bo sems dpa' sum brtsegs*) are contained, one within the other, in a manner reminiscent of Russian dolls. Cf. Sherab Rinchen, in his *Collected Works*, vol. 3, p. 124.
664. Tib. *sangs pa na*. Our text reads *sangs ma na*, but see Sherab Rinchen, in his *Collected Works*, vol. 3, p. 125, line 3.
665. Sherab Rinchen, in his *Collected Works*, vol. 3, pp. 124–25.
666. Sherab Rinchen, vol. 3, pp. 125–26.
667. Sherab Rinchen, vol. 3, pp. 126–27, which explains that these four respectively correlate with the four seals in the sequence: action seal, phenomenal seal, Great Seal, and commitment seal.
668. According to Thupten Phuntsok (*Treasure Ocean of Tibetan Lexicography*, p. 1236), the stabilizing wind (*mnyam gnas kyi rlung*) is equivalent to the fire-accompanying wind (*samāna, me mnyam*).
669. Sherab Rinchen, in his *Collected Works*, vol. 3, pp. 127–28. The two water and two fire elements are distinguished as internal and external.
670. Our text reads *kra śa u mra*.
671. Unidentified source, apart from the first sentence.
672. Tāranātha attributes this remark to earlier Tibetan teachers in his *Precious Cornucopia of Exegesis on the Summation of the Real, Collected Works of Tāranātha*, vol. 20, p. 62, perhaps referring to Śākya Chokden and Sonam Sengé.
673. Sherab Rinchen, in his *Collected Works*, vol. 3, p. 132.
674. Sherab Rinchen, vol. 3, p. 133.
675. Sherab Rinchen, vol. 3, pp. 133–34. The twelve deeds are those exemplified in the life of Śākyamuni Buddha. Various enumerations of the twelve deeds are found. The most popular enumeration comprises the residence in Tuṣita, the descent into the womb, birth, proficiency in the arts, enjoyment of consorts, renunciation of the world, the practice of asceticism, the reaching of the point of enlightenment, the vanquishing of demonic forces, the attainment of manifestly perfect enlightenment, the turning of the doctrinal wheel, and the passing into final nirvana.
676. TPD, vol. 21, pp. 961–74.
677. [*gZhed dmar*] *shin tu spros med kyi khrid yig*. The primary source, attributed to Lowo Lotsāwa Sherab Rinchen, appears to be no longer extant. Elsewhere, Kunga Drolchok mentions Ngorchen Kunga Zangpo's *Elucidation and Advice concerning the Extremely Unelaborate Instruction* [*of Red Yamāri*] *Entitled Beauteous Unelaborated Ornament* (Ngorchen Kunga Zangpo, *Collected Works*, vol. 3, pp.750–89). In the notes for this guidebook, however, Tāranātha's *Wondrous Instruction Manual of the Unelaborate Practice, Collected Works of Tāranātha*, vol. 11, pp. 369–92, which closely follows the present text, has been referenced. For Jamgön Kongtrul's brief explanation of the practices based on Red Yamāri, see Jamgön Kongtrul 2008, 148–51.

678. Tāranātha, *Collected Works*, vol. 11, p. 372.
679. Tāranātha, vol. 11, p. 373.
680. Tāranātha (*Collected Works*, vol. 11, p. 373) comments that the first five of these mantras consecrate emanational sacraments of offering, including flowers and so forth, while the last six consecrate the emanational attributes of the six sense objects, from sights to mental phenomena.
681. Tāranātha, in his *Collected Works*, vol. 11, pp. 373–74.
682. Tāranātha (*Collected Works*, vol. 11, p. 374) notes that while reciting these three syllables, the offerings of the skull are presented to the root teacher, the meditational deities and all the buddhas, and so forth.
683. Tāranātha, in his *Collected Works*, vol. 11, p. 374.
684. Tāranātha, vol. 11, pp. 374–76.
685. Tāranātha, vol. 11, p. 377.
686. Tāranātha, vol. 11, pp. 377–78.
687. Tāranātha, vol. 11, pp. 378–79.
688. Tāranātha, vol. 11, pp. 379–80.
689. Tāranātha, vol. 11, pp. 380–82.
690. Tāranātha, vol. 11, pp. 382–85.
691. Tāranātha, vol. 11, p. 385.
692. Tāranātha, vol. 11, pp. 386–87.
693. Tāranātha, vol. 11, pp. 388–89.
694. Tāranātha, vol. 11, pp. 389–90.
695. Tāranātha, vol. 11, p. 390.
696. *rNal 'byor bzhi rim gyi khrid yig*. The primary source, attributed to Lowo Lotsāwa Sherab Rinchen, appears to be no longer extant. Drubchen Peldzin Zhepa, who is mentioned in the concluding verses to this guidebook, appears to be an epithet of Yangonpa Gyeltsen Pel, whose *Memorandum on the Four-Stage Yoga*, in his *Collected Works*, vol. 1, pp. 285–302, is also highlighted as a secondary source by Kunga Drolchok. The notes that follow reference Tāranātha's *Guidance on the Four-Stage Yoga of Red Yamāri*, in his *Collected Works*, vol. 11, pp. 356–68. See also Jamgön Kongtrul's summary of the four-stage yoga in Jamgön Kongtrul 2008, 149.
697. Tāranātha, in his *Collected Works*, vol. 11, p. 356.
698. Tāranātha, vol. 11, p. 357.
699. Tāranātha, vol. 11, p. 358.
700. Tāranātha, vol. 11, p. 358.
701. For a much more elaborate explanation, see Tāranātha, *Collected Works*, vol. 11, pp. 358–61.
702. Our text reads KĀHI for HIK.
703. Tāranātha, in his *Collected Works*, vol. 11, pp. 362–64.
704. The various distinctions between the six types of female mudra, or muse (*mudra*), are examined by Longchen Rabjam in an extensive overview, on which see the translation in Dorje 1987, 900–10; also Longchenpa 2011, 469–75. Briefly stated,

the muse of the lotus type (*padma can ma*) is the consort of Samantabhadra, the primordial buddha. The muse of the conch type (*dung can ma*) is the consort of the tathāgata or buddha family. The muse of the marked type (*ri mo can ma*) is the consort of the ratna family. The muse of the doe type (*ri dvags can ma*) is the consort of the vajra family. The muse of the elephant type (*glang po can ma*) is the consort of the padma family; and the muse of the miscellaneous type (*sna tshogs can ma*) is the consort of the karma family.

705. Tāranātha, in his *Collected Works*, vol. 11, p. 365.
706. Tāranātha, vol. 11, pp. 365–66.
707. *'Jigs byed kyi rva rtse'i khrid yig*. The primary source is Kyoton Ojung Lotsāwa's *Mental Focus on the Horns of Bhairava*, which appears to be no longer extant as a distinct work. The sole reference that follows here derives from Tāranātha's *Method of Experiential Cultivation Combining All the Meanings of Tantra*, in his *Collected Works*, vol. 12, pp. 346–77.
708. See the illustrations of this "solitary spiritual warrior" (*ekavīra, dpa' bo gcig po*) form of Vajrabhairava without consort, in Jigmé Chokyi Dorjé, *Great Anthology of Buddhist Icons according to the Tibetan Lineages*, pp. 333–48.
709. Tāranātha, in his *Collected Works*, vol. 12, p. 353.
710. *Yab la brten nas rtsa dbu ma'i khrid yig*. The primary source is Drakpa Gyeltsen's *Elixir of the Buddha Mind of Nāropā*, also known as *Guidance on the Central Channel*, contained in SK, vol. 8, pp. 151–79. The integration of its two antecedents—Nāropā's *Vārāhī Khecarī of the Generation Stage* and his *Central Channel of the Perfection Stage* is attributed to Lama Dampa Sonam Gyeltsen. The present guidebook is also associated with Drakpa Gyeltsen's *Array of the Seats of the Syllables*, in his *Collected Works*, vol. 3 pp. 410–36.
711. Drakpa Gyeltsen, SK, vol. 8, p. 160.
712. Drakpa Gyeltsen, vol. 8, p. 161.
713. Drakpa Gyeltsen, vol. 8, pp. 161–62.
714. The text reads OṂ for AṂ.
715. Drakpa Gyeltsen, SK, vol. 8, pp. 163–64.
716. Drakpa Gyeltsen, vol. 8, p. 164.
717. Drakpa Gyeltsen, vol. 8, p. 167.
718. Drakpa Gyeltsen, vol. 8, p. 170.
719. Drakpa Gyeltsen, vol. 8, p. 173.
720. Drakpa Gyeltsen, vol. 8, p. 174.
721. *Yum la brten nas rtsa dbu ma'i khrid yig*. The primary source is Drakpa Gyeltsen's *Central Channel of Khecarī*, also entitled *Guidance on the Central Channel of the Perfection Stage*.
722. Here the text includes an annotation suggesting that this instruction also appears to be called *Phyags lhva ma*.
723. There is a short text of this title contained in the *Sakya Anthology of Khecarī*, vol. 2, pp. 265–66.
724. That is to say, the eight groups are those commencing with A, CA, ṬA, TA, PA,

YA, and ŚA, and the six short vowels are A, I, U, E, O, and AṂ. Cf. Drakpa Gyeltsen, SK, vol. 8, p. 166.

725. *Dril bu rim lnga'i khrid*. The primary source, attributed here to Tsokgom Kunga Pel, appears to be no longer extant as a distinct work. Elsewhere, Kunga Drolchok also mentions Drakpa Gyeltsen's *Elucidation of the Five Stages*, in his *Collected Works*, vol. 3, pp. 242–63; and Pakpa Lodro Gyeltsen's *Pith Instructions of the Five Stages*, in his *Collected Works*, vol. 2, pp. 278–91. Its original antecedent, Ghaṇṭhāpāda's Indic commentary (T 1433) is found in TPD, vol. 11, pp. 578–92. The sources referenced in the notes that follow include Tāranātha's *Guidance on the Five Stages of Glorious Cakrasaṃvara*, in his *Collected Works*, vol. 16, pp. 304–17; and Tsongkhapa's *Teaching on the Instruction Manual of the Five Stages by Ghaṇṭhāpāda, Documented by the Great Bodhisattva Cheton Kunga Zangpo*, in his *Collected Works*, vol. 10, pp. 173–94. For Jamgön Kongtrul's concise presentation, see Jamgön Kongtrul 2008, 172–74.

726. Tāranātha, in his *Collected Works*, vol. 16, pp. 305–7; also Tsongkhapa, in his *Collected Works*, vol. 10, p. 182.

727. Tāranātha, in his *Collected Works*, vol. 16, pp. 307–11; also Tsongkhapa, in his *Collected Works*, vol. 10, pp. 181–82.

728. Tāranātha, in his *Collected Works*, vol. 16, pp. 311–13; also Tsongkhapa, in his *Collected Works*, vol. 10, pp. 182–87.

729. Tāranātha, in his *Collected Works*, vol. 16, pp. 313–14; also Tsongkhapa, in his *Collected Works*, vol. 10, p. 187.

730. Tāranātha, in his *Collected Works*, vol. 16, pp. 314–15; also Tsongkhapa, in his *Collected Works*, vol. 10, pp. 187ff.

731. *Nag po rim bzhi'i khrid*. The primary source is Sachen Kunga Nyingpo's *Commentary on Inciting the Path of the Four Stages*, in his *Collected Works*, vol. 2, pp. 429–40. Elsewhere Kunga Drolchok mentions the memoranda on this text by Lowo Khenchen Sonam Lhundrub and Langtangpa Chen Nga Kunga Dorjé. The antecedent and original source is Kṛṣṇacārin's *Inciting the Path of the Four Stages* (T 1451), contained in TPD, vol. 11, pp. 961–69, a work related to his cycle of the *Vital Essence of Spring*, TPD, vol. 11, pp. 817–38. The notes that follow refer to Tāranātha's *Quintessence of Inciting the Path of the Four Stages: Its Enlightened Intention*, in his *Collected Works*, vol. 16, pp. 276–303; and to Ngawang Kunga Sonam's *Corrections to Chojé Rinpoché Sangyé Pel's Supplementing the Four Stages of Kṛṣṇacārin*, in his *Collected Works*, vol. 17, pp. 81–87; as well as to Sachen Kunga Nyingpo's *Commentary on the Vital Essence of Spring*, in his *Collected Works*, vol. 1, pp. 133–78. In the last of these, Sachen explains (pp. 133–34) that chapters 2–9 of the *Vital Essence of Spring* refer to the first of the four stages, and chapter 10 refers to the remaining three stages. For Jamgön Kongtrul's concise explanation of this instruction, see Jamgön Kongtrul 2008, 175–78.

732. Tāranātha, in his *Collected Works*, vol. 16, pp. 282–84; also Ngawang Kunga Sonam, in his *Collected Works*, vol. 17, pp. 82–83.

733. On the four signs of refinement (*'byongs pa'i rtags bzhi*), see Sachen Kunga

Nyingpo, in his *Collected Works*, vol. 1, pp. 162–65; and on the six signs of stability (*brtan pa'i rtags drug*), pp. 159–62.

734. Tāranātha, in his *Collected Works*, vol. 16, pp. 284–86; also Ngawang Kunga Sonam, in his *Collected Works*, vol. 17, pp. 83–85.

735. Tāranātha, in his *Collected Works*, vol. 16, pp. 286–87; also Sachen Kunga Nyingpo, in his *Collected Works*, vol. 1, pp. 166–69; and Ngawang Kunga Sonam, in his *Collected Works*, vol. 17, p. 85.

736. Tāranātha, in his *Collected Works*, vol. 16, p. 287; also Sachen Kunga Nyingpo, in his *Collected Works*, vol. 1, pp. 169–70; and Ngawang Kunga Sonam, in his *Collected Works*, vol. 17, pp. 85–87.

737. *bDe mchog dkar po'i khrid yig*. The primary source is Chel Amogha's *White Cakrasaṃvara*, which appears to be no longer extant as a distinct work, outside of this anthology. The antecedent is found in the transmission of *White Cakrasaṃvara* by Śākyaśrī of Kashmir.

738. On the twenty-four lands and their microcosmic correlations within the body, see Gray 2007, 54–62. More specifically, the eight seed syllables of the maṇḍala of buddha mind—PU, JĀ, O, A, GO, RĀ, DE, and MĀ—respectively represent Pullīramalaya, Jālandhara, Oḍḍiyāna, Arbuda, Godāvarī, Rāmeśvarī, Devīkoṭa, and Mālava; the eight seed syllables of the maṇḍala of buddha speech—KĀ, O, TRI, KO, KA, LA, KĀ, and HI—respectively represent Kāmarūpa, Oḍra, Triśakuni, Kośala, Kaliṅga, Lampāka, Kāñcī, and Himālaya; and the eight seed syllables of the maṇḍala of buddha body—PRE, GṚ, SAU, SU, NA, SI, MA, and KU—respectively represent Pretapuri, Gṛhadevata, Saurāṣṭra, Suvarṇadvīpa, Nagara, Sindhu, Maru, and Kulutā.

739. As stated in Nordrang Orgyan, *Compendium of Buddhist Numeric Terms* (p. 1618), the seven aspects of union (*kha sbyor yan lag bdun ldan*) comprise (i) the buddha body of perfect resource complete with major and minor marks; (ii) union with the self-manifesting consort, embodiment of awareness; (iii) the experience of physical and mental bliss dependent on the threefold dissolution of wind in the central channel; (iv) the realization of the lack of inherent existence, emptiness, as the mind abides in the essential nature of uncontaminated bliss; (v) the uninterrupted continuity of not passing into nirvana but remaining in the world as long as cyclic existence endures; (vi) the unwavering fullness of nonreferential compassion, acting for the sake of all sentient beings; and (vii) the never-ceasing engagement in enlightened activities.

740. *gDan bzhi'i khrid yig*. The primary source is stated to be Ngok Zhedang Dorjé's *Instruction Manual of the Four Adamantine Seats*, which appears to be no longer extant, outside the present anthology. The notes that follow refer to Tāranātha's *Instruction Manual of the Four Adamantine Seats Entitled Opening the Door of Pristine Cognition*, in his *Collected Works*, vol. 20, pp. 323–71. For Jamgön Kongtrul's presentation of this tantra's special terminology, see Jamgön Kongtrul 2008, 179–82, and 384–86.

741. Tāranātha, in his *Collected Works*, vol. 20, pp. 326–28.

742. On the relationship between the four delights (*dga' ba bzhi*) and the four subtle perceptions (*snang ba bzhi*) at the onset of death, see Tāranātha, *Commentary on the Spiritual Songs of Jālandharipā Entitled Secret Treasury*, in his *Collected Works*, vol. 19, p. 49.
743. Tāranātha, in his *Collected Works*, vol. 20, pp. 338–39.
744. There is an annotation in the text here, suggesting that these may be present or imagined.
745. Tāranātha, in his *Collected Works*, vol. 20, pp. 334–38; also 346–48.
746. Tāranātha, vol. 20, pp. 340–42.
747. Tāranātha, vol. 20, pp. 342–43.
748. Tāranātha, vol. 20, pp. 328–29.
749. This is a traditional type of coinage with a hole in the middle to facilitate stringing or stacking.
750. Tāranātha, in his *Collected Works*, vol. 20, pp. 350–53.
751. *Ma hā mā yā'i khrid.* The primary source, attributed to Ngok Zhedang Dorjé or Ngok Choku Dorjé, appears to be no longer extant as a distinct work. Antecedents include the Sanskrit commentaries of Kukkurāja. The following notes reference Tāranātha's *Instruction Manual of Glorious Mahāmāyā Entitled Noble Path of the Conquerors*, in his *Collected Works*, vol. 22, pp. 44–56; also Pema Karpo's *Gradual Path of Mahāmāyā Yielding the Desired Good Fortune*, contained in Drukpa Kagyu Anthology, vol. 27, pp. 339–74. For Jamgön Kongtrul's explanation of this practice, see Jamgön Kongtrul 2008, 183–86.
752. Tāranātha, in his *Collected Works*, vol. 22, pp. 45–46; also Pema Karpo, Drukpa Kagyu Anthology, vol. 27, pp. 347–48.
753. Tāranātha, in his *Collected Works*, vol. 22, p. 46; also Pema Karpo, Drukpa Kagyu Anthology, vol. 27, p. 348.
754. These three phases comprising the yoga of lower forms (*dman pa dbyibs kyi rnal 'byor*), the yoga of profound mantra (*zab pa sngags kyi rnal 'byor*), and the yoga of conclusive attributes (*mthar thug chos kyi rnal 'byor*) are arranged sequentially in Pema Karpo, Drukpa Kagyu Anthology, vol. 27, respectively on pp. 343–45, 345–66, and 366–69. In the present guidebook, the order appears to be reversed.
755. The three sorts of pith instructions pertaining to the upper gate are based respectively on the cakras, the vital essences, and subtle winds. See Tāranātha, in his *Collected Works*, vol. 22, pp. 45ff. Our text appears to be corrupted here, reading *sngags kyi rnal 'byor re / sgo / 'og sgo steng gsum gyi man ngag.*
756. Tāranātha, in his *Collected Works*, vol. 22, p. 47.
757. Tāranātha, vol. 22, pp. 50–51.
758. Tāranātha, *Collected Works*, vol. 22, p. 51; also Pema Karpo, Drukpa Kagyu Anthology, vol. 27, pp. 354–56.
759. These comprise the attributes of the five elements, along with those of the sun, moon, and pristine cognition. See Pema Karpo, Drukpa Kagyu Anthology, vol. 27, p. 365.
760. Tāranātha, in his *Collected Works*, vol. 22, pp. 47–50.

761. Tāranātha, vol. 22, p. 45.
762. Tib. *sngags la lha bskyed pa'i dbyibs*. Tāranātha, in his *Collected Works*, vol. 22, p. 49; also Pema Karpo, Drukpa Kagyu Anthology, vol. 27, pp. 354–57.
763. These five signs indicative of dissolution of the elements are discussed in Pema Karpo, Drukpa Kagyu Anthology, vol. 27, pp. 364–65. Among them, smoke indicates the dissolution of earth into water, mirages indicate the dissolution of water into fire, fireflies or celestial apparitions indicate the dissolution of fire into wind, a lamp flame indicates the dissolution of wind into mind, and a cloudless sky indicates the dissolution of mind into space.
764. Tāranātha, in his *Collected Works*, vol. 22, p. 50, refers briefly to this practice. For more detail, see Pema Karpo, Drukpa Kagyu Anthology, vol. 27, pp. 360–64.
765. Pema Karpo (Drukpa Kagyu Anthology, vol. 27, pp. 350–52) adds a fourth—namely, training in the color and form of the winds of the elements.
766. The posture of the lion's play (*seng ge rnam rol phyag rgya*) is the fourteenth of the eighteen yogic exercises focusing on the fierce inner heat that derive from the *Aural Lineage of Cakrasaṃvara* (see chapter 9, n. 257). Thupten Phuntsok (*Yogic Exercises of the Channels and Winds*, p. 18) offers the following description: "Blocking the mouth, nose, eyes, and nostrils with the fingers, you should rotate the upper body in the manner of a wheel, dispel the impediments of the channels, winds, and vital essences, and let the pure essence, or chyle, diffuse through the four cakras. When practicing consciousness transference, the most crucial point is that this yogic exercise guides the vital essence."
767. Tib. *pus mo la lag mthil yul pa gcig byas*. On this practice, see Tāranātha, in his *Collected Works*, vol. 22, pp. 52–53.
768. *bDe mchog bong zhal can gyi khrid yig*. The primary source is attributed to Samten Ozer and Khenchen Sonam Lhundrub, based on the guidance of the Newar Mahābodhi, but it is no longer extant apart from this text. In the notes, reference has been made to Jamyang Khyentsé Wangpo's *Quintessential Instruction Manual on the Generation and Perfection Stages of Glorious Kharamukha Cakrasaṃvara Entitled Vital Essence of Supreme Bliss*, contained in his *Collected Works*, vol. 7, pp. 263–80.
769. Jamyang Khyentsé Wangpo, in his *Collected Works*, vol. 7, pp. 273–74.
770. Jamyang Khyentsé Wangpo, vol. 7, p. 274.
771. Jamyang Khyentsé Wangpo, vol. 7, pp. 274–75.
772. Jamyang Khyentsé Wangpo, vol. 7, p. 275.
773. Jamyang Khyentsé Wangpo, vol. 7, pp. 275–76.
774. Jamyang Khyentsé Wangpo, vol. 7, p. 276.
775. Jamyang Khyentsé Wangpo, vol. 7, pp. 276–77.
776. Jamyang Khyentsé Wangpo, vol. 7, p. 277.
777. Jamyang Khyentsé Wangpo, vol. 7, pp. 277–78.
778. Jamyang Khyentsé Wangpo, vol. 7, pp. 278–79.
779. *Phag mo sgom drug gi khrid yig*. The primary source, attributed to Chel Kunga Dorjé, appears to be no longer extant outside this collection. The text is included

here, along with two other renowned sextets that follow: *The Six Doctrines of Nāropā* and *The Six Doctrines of Nigumā*. The antecedents of this guidebook are the six Sanskrit texts and supplement contained in TPD and attributed to Śūnyatāsamādhi (also known as Śabaripā) (T 1551 and T 1553), Avadhūtipā (T 1552), Śrīmatī (T 1554), Virūpa (T 1555), Advayavajra (T 1578), and Buddhadatta (T 1556).

780. *Nā ro'i chos drug gi khrid*. The primary source appears to be an independent composition, inspired by Karmapa Rangjung Dorjé's *Molten Gold of the Six Doctrines*, and its *Guidance on the Meditation of the Six Doctrines*, which are contained in *DNZ*, vol. 9, pp. 17–61. It broadly follows the content of Zhamar Chokyi Wangchuk's *Sessions of Experiential Cultivation of the Profound Six Doctrines of Nāropā Entitled Nectar Elixir*, contained in *DNZ*, vol. 9, pp. 193–229, translated in Roberts 2011, 333–72. However, the text is extremely terse and lacks much of the detail presented in those other writings. On the antecedent text of Nāropā, see also Guenther 1963.

781. See above, chapter 9, n. 55.

782. Karmapa Rangjung Dorjé, *DNZ*, vol. 9, p. 37; also Roberts 2011, 337–38.

783. On this practice called "holding the family-endowed basis" (*rigs ldan gyi gzhi gzung*), see Karmapa Rangjung Dorjé, *DNZ*, vol. 9, pp. 37–38; also Roberts 2011, 338–39.

784. Karmapa Rangjung Dorjé, *DNZ*, vol. 9, p. 38; also Roberts 2011, 339–40.

785. Roberts 2011, 340–41.

786. On the yoga of the fierce inner heat, see Karmapa Rangjung Dorjé, *DNZ*, vol. 9, pp. 39–42; also Roberts 2011, 341–47.

787. Roberts 2011, 348–49.

788. On the practice of the pure illusory body (*dag pa'i sgyu lus*), see Karmapa Rangjung Dorjé, *DNZ*, vol. 9, pp. 42–45; also Roberts 2011, 350–53.

789. Karmapa Rangjung Dorjé, *DNZ*, vol. 9, p. 45; also Roberts 2011, 353–54.

790. On the transformation (*bsgyur*), increase (*spel*), and refinement (*sbyang*) of dreams, see Karmapa Rangjung Dorjé, *DNZ*, vol. 9, pp. 45–49; also Roberts 2011, 354–58.

791. Karmapa Rangjung Dorjé, *DNZ*, vol. 9, pp. 49–51; also Roberts 2011, 358–62.

792. The conceptual thoughts that partake of eighty natural expressions (*rang bzhin brgyad cu'i rnam rtog*) coincide with the disintegration of the elements at the time of death. They include thirty-three natural expressions of conceptual thought that derive from hatred, forty that derive from desire, and seven that derive from delusion. These are all enumerated in Tselé Natsok Rangdrol 1987, 57–60.

793. This refers to the three perceptions (*snang ba gsum*) of redness, whiteness, and blackness, experienced as death approaches, on which see Tselé Natsok Rangdrol 1987, 49–74; also Dorje 2005, 173–77.

794. Karmapa Rangjung Dorjé, *DNZ*, vol. 9, pp. 51–59; also Roberts 2011, 362–66.

795. Karmapa Rangjung Dorjé, *DNZ*, vol. 9, pp. 59–60; also Roberts 2011, 366–69.

796. *Ni gu chos drug gi khrid*. This and the guidebooks that follow represent the

Shangpa Kagyu tradition. In the present case, the primary source is attributed to Samdingpa Zhonu Drub. Its antecedents, attributed to Khyungpo Neljor, include the *Adamantine Verses of the Six Doctrines of the Ḍākinī of Pristine Cognition: Foundation of the Golden Doctrines of the Shangpa*, *DNZ*, vol. 11, pp. 1–27. The notes that follow reference the commentary by Tāranātha, entitled *Extensive Instruction Manual of Profound Meaning on the Six Doctrines of Nigumā, the Profound Path*, in his *Collected Works*, vol. 24, pp. 213–314. On the life and teachings of Nigumā, see also Harding 2010.

797. Tāranātha, in his *Collected Works*, vol. 24, p. 221.
798. Tāranātha, vol. 24, pp. 222–24.
799. Tāranātha, vol. 24, pp. 224–25.
800. Tāranātha, vol. 24, p. 226.
801. Tāranātha, in his *Collected Works*, vol. 24, pp. 227–28. The stoves denote the feet, hands, and elbows. See above, chapter 9, n. 304; also Roberts 2011, 343.
802. Tib. *me gong*. Our text reads *me rgod*. Tāranātha, in his *Collected Works*, vol. 24, p. 228.
803. Tāranātha, in his *Collected Works*, vol. 24, p. 226.
804. Tāranātha, vol. 24, pp. 228–29.
805. Tāranātha, in his *Collected Works*, vol. 24, pp. 229–34; also Roberts 2011, 344–45.
806. The ancillary practices, known as the "wearing of clothing" (*gos gyon*), the "spreading of the mat" (*stan 'ding*), and the "riding of the horse" (*rta zhon*) are discussed in Tāranātha, in his *Collected Works*, vol. 24, pp. 234–36.
807. Tāranātha (in his *Collected Works*, vol. 24, p. 236) adds that this exercise is for those who have not yet mastered the vase breathing.
808. Tāranātha, in his *Collected Works*, vol. 24, pp. 237–39.
809. Tāranātha, vol. 24, p. 239.
810. Tāranātha, vol. 24, pp. 239–40.
811. Tāranātha (in his *Collected Works*, vol. 24, p. 240) declines to elaborate here on the grounds that this instruction is sealed with secrecy.
812. Tāranātha, in his *Collected Works*, vol. 24, pp. 248–49.
813. Tāranātha, vol. 24, pp. 241–54.
814. Tāranātha, vol. 24, pp. 255–56.
815. Tāranātha, vol. 24, pp. 257–62. According to the latter (p. 258), there are two sorts without ideation and one with ideation.
816. Tāranātha, in his *Collected Works*, vol. 24, pp. 262–66.
817. Tāranātha, vol. 24, pp. 266–69.
818. Tāranātha, vol. 24, pp. 269–71.
819. Tāranātha, vol. 24, pp. 271–74.
820. Tāranātha, vol. 24, pp. 274–75.
821. Tāranātha, vol. 24, pp. 275–79.
822. Tāranātha, vol. 24, pp. 279–82.
823. Tāranātha, vol. 24, pp. 282–84.
824. Tāranātha, vol. 24, pp. 284–86.

825. Tāranātha, vol. 24, pp. 286–91.
826. Tāranātha, vol. 24, pp. 291–99.
827. Tāranātha, vol. 24, pp. 299–305.
828. Tāranātha, vol. 24, pp. 305–9.
829. *Phyag rgya chen po ga'u ma'i khrid.* The primary source is Samdingpa Zhonu Drub's *The Amulet Tradition of the Great Seal*, *DNZ*, vol. 12, pp. 181–87. The notes that follow additionally reference Tāranātha's *The Amulet Tradition of the Great Seal, or the Instruction Manual Entitled Three Natural States*, which is contained in *DNZ*, vol. 12, pp. 237–49; and also in his *Collected Works*, vol. 39, pp. 179–91.
830. Samdingpa Zhonu Drub, *DNZ*, vol. 12, pp. 183–85; also Tāranātha, in his *Collected Works*, vol. 39, pp. 179–81.
831. Samdingpa Zhonu Drub, *DNZ*, vol. 12, pp. 183–85; also Tāranātha, in his *Collected Works*, vol. 39, pp. 185–86. The sequence presented in our text here seems to have been corrupted. This translation therefore followed Samdingpa Zhonu Drub, *DNZ*, vol. 12, p. 185, line 7–p. 186, line 3; and the commentary in Tāranātha, in his *Collected Works*, vol. 39, pp. 185–86.
832. Samdingpa Zhonu Drub, *DNZ*, vol. 12, p. 186; also Tāranātha, in his *Collected Works*, vol. 39, pp. 186–88.
833. *Lam khyer rnam gsum gyi khrid.* The primary source is Samdingpa Zhonu Drub's *The Three Aspects Carried on the Path*, which is contained in *DNZ*, vol. 12, pp. 187–92.
834. Samdingpa Zhonu Drub, *DNZ*, vol. 12, pp. 188–89.
835. Samdingpa Zhonu Drub, vol. 12, p. 189.
836. Samdingpa Zhonu Drub, vol. 12, pp. 189–92.
837. *Rang sems 'chi med kyi khrid.* The primary source is Samdingpa Zhonu Drub's *The Deathlessness of One's Own Mind*, contained in *DNZ*, vol. 12, pp. 192–98.
838. Samdingpa Zhonu Drub, *DNZ*, vol. 12, p. 193.
839. These practices are elaborated in Samdingpa Zhonu Drub, *DNZ*, vol. 12, pp. 193–98.
840. *Su kha chos drug gi khrid.* The primary source is Rinchen Chokdrub Pelzang's *Six Doctrines of Sukhasiddhi*, contained in *DNZ*, vol. 12, pp. 299–313.
841. Rinchen Chokdrub Pelzang, *DNZ*, vol. 12, p. 303, line 3–p. 304, line 3.
842. Rinchen Chokdrub Pelzang, vol. 12, p. 304, line 3–p. 305, line 5.
843. Rinchen Chokdrub Pelzang, vol. 12, p. 305, line 5–p. 306, line 6.
844. Rinchen Chokdrub Pelzang, vol. 12, p. 306, line 6–p. 307, line 5.
845. Rinchen Chokdrub Pelzang, vol. 12, p. 307, line 5–p. 308, line 5.
846. Rinchen Chokdrub Pelzang, vol. 12, p. 308, line 5–p. 309, line 6.
847. *bDag med ma'i nang khrid.* The primary source of this guidebook from the Shangpa Kagyu cycle is Khyungpo Neljor's *The Inner Guidance of Nairātmyā*, which seems to have had an antecedent in the writings of Āryadeva the Brahmin. This guidebook is later conflated with Rinchen Chokdrub Pelzang's *The Emanational Cakra of the Navel*, which is contained in *DNZ*, vol. 12, p. 286, line 7–p. 289, line 4, and also in the *Shangpa Texts*, vol. 7, pp. 568–70.

848. Rinchen Chokdrub Pelzang, *Shangpa Texts*, vol. 7, p. 568, line 3–p. 569, line 3; also *DNZ*, vol. 12, p. 286, line 7–p. 287, line 7. Here, Nairātmyā is replaced with Vajravārāhī, but otherwise the visualizations are similar.

849. Rinchen Chokdrub Pelzang, *Shangpa Texts*, vol. 7, p. 569, line 3–p. 570, line 2; also *DNZ*, vol. 12, pp. 288–89.

850. Rinchen Chokdrub Pelzang, *Shangpa Texts*, vol. 7, p. 570, lines 3–5.

851. *Lhan cig skyes sbyor gyi khrid*. The primary source is said to be Gyamapa's memorandum on Tokmé Zangpo's *Coemergent Union of the Great Seal*. The Gyamapa (rGya ma pa) in question is Gyamawa Lodro Gyeltsen (1390–1448), who does not figure in the lineage outlined above in chapter 1. The antecedent text by Tokmé Zangpo is contained in Kadampa Anthology II, pp. 259–78. *DNZ* includes several other works pertaining to this cycle, among which Karmapa Rangjung Dorjé's *Instruction Manual of the Coemergent Union of the Great Seal* (*DNZ*, vol. 9, pp. 1–16) is translated in Roberts 2011, 153–68. Commentarial works include Karma Wangchuk Dorjé's *Memorandum on the Coemergent Union of the Great Seal Entitled Essential Clear Lamp*, *DNZ*, vol. 9, pp. 71–105.

852. *Phyag rgya chen po lnga ldan gyi khrid*. The primary source is Chen Nga Nyernyipa Chokyi Gyelpo's *The Fivefold Great Seal*, *DNZ*, vol. 10, pp. 21–23. The latter's seminal writings include the *Jewel Garland Illuminating the Fivefold Great Seal*, contained in Drigungpa Anthology, vol. 49, pp. 1–36. Several related texts are found in *DNZ*, vol. 9, pp. 431–68, and, especially, *The Fivefold Great Seal according to the Tropu Kagyu Lineage*, in vol. 10, pp. 21–23. Outside *DNZ*, other related works include Kunga Rinchen's *Wish-Granting Gem Fulfilling the Hopes of Living Beings: An Instruction Manual concerning the Fivefold Great Seal*, which is contained in Drigungpa Anthology, vol. 54, pp. 56–62.

853. *Phyag rgya chen po yi ge bzhi pa'i khrid*. The primary source is Yagdé Paṇchen's *The Four Syllables of the Great Seal*, which has not yet been identified outside of the present anthology. It seems that there is no such instruction of that title among the extant texts of Yagdé Paṇchen Tsondru Dargyé cataloged in the *Precious Treasury of Knowledge* (*Shes bya'i gter mdzod*, vol. 3, pp. 305–7. Nor does his name figure in the lineage prayer above. Related texts according to the lineage of Rechungpa and Tropu Lotsāwa are contained respectively in *DNZ*, vol. 8, pp. 39–44; and vol. 10, pp. 25–29.

854. Rechungpa Dorjé Drak, *DNZ*, vol. 8, p. 41, line 3–p. 42, line 2.

855. Rechungpa Dorjé Drak, vol. 8, p. 42, line 2–p. 42, line 5.

856. Rechungpa Dorjé Drak, vol. 8, p. 42, line 5–p. 43, line 1.

857. Rechungpa Dorjé Drak, vol. 8, p. 43, line 1–p. 44, line 2.

858. See above, chapter 6, n. 34.

859. *sKu gsum ngo sprod kyi khrid*. The primary source is Karmapa Rangjung Dorjé's *The Introduction to the Three Buddha Bodies*, which is contained in *DNZ*, vol. 9, pp. 231–45.

860. The eighteen distinct attributes of the buddhas are as follows: (1) the tathāgatas are without clumsiness; (2) they are not noisy; (3) they are without false memo-

ries; (4) they are without differentiating perceptions; (5) they are without uncomposed minds; (6) they are without the indifference that lacks discernment; (7) they do not degenerate in their resolution; (8) they do not degenerate in their perseverance; (9) they do not degenerate in their recollection; (10) they do not degenerate in their meditative stability; (11) they do not degenerate in their wisdom; (12) they do not degenerate in their liberation, nor do they degenerate in their perception of liberating pristine cognition; (13) all the activities of their bodies are preceded by pristine cognition and followed by pristine cognition; (14) all the activities of their speech are preceded by pristine cognition and followed by pristine cognition; (15) all the activities of their minds are preceded by pristine cognition and followed by pristine cognition; (16) they engage in the perception of pristine cognition that is unobstructed and unimpeded with respect to the past; (17) they engage in the perception of pristine cognition that is unobstructed and unimpeded with respect to the future; and (18) they engage in the perception of pristine cognition that is unobstructed and unimpeded with respect to the present. See the analysis in Konow 1941, 41–44, which discusses the etymology of *āveṇika* ("unshared factors" of a buddha) and compares alternative listings; also Dayal (1932) 1970, 21–23, and Sparham 2006–12, 4:82.

861. Karmapa Rangjung Dorjé, *DNZ*, vol. 9, p. 241, line 1–p. 242, line 3.

862. The five certainties (*nges po lnga*) of the buddha body of perfect resource are those of teacher, teaching, retinue, time, and place. See Choying Tobden Dorje 2016, 48–53.

863. Karmapa Rangjung Dorjé, *DNZ*, vol. 9, p. 242, line 3–p. 243, line 3.

864. *rLung sems gnyis med kyi khrid.* The primary source is stated to be Lhazik Repa's *Memorandum on the Indivisibility of Subtle Energy and Mind.* Its antecedent is Karmapa III Rangjung Dorjé's *The Indivisibility of Subtle Energy and Mind*, *DNZ*, vol. 9, pp. 167–73. The specific terminology of this guidebook does not accord with the latter, which presents the indivisibility of subtle energy and mind in terms of (i) fierce inner heat (*gtum mo rlung sems gnyis med*), (ii) consciousness transference (*'pho ba rlung sems gnyis med*), (iii) illusory body (*sgyu lus rlung sems gnyis med*), and (iv) nonarising (*skye med rlung sems gnyis med*).

865. This second phase would correspond to the fierce inner heat (*gtum mo rlung sems gnyis med*).

866. This third phase would correspond to the illusory body (*sgyu lus rlung sems gnyis med*).

867. This fourth phase would correspond to consciousness transference (*'pho ba rlung sems gnyis med*).

868. *Chos drug sras mkhar ma'i khrid.* This quintessential doctrine of the New Translation is said to have been revealed as treasure from Sekhar Kyawo in Drowolung by Guru Chowang, and, as such, it belongs among his eighteen renowned treasure troves (*gter kha bco brgyad*). The text and a preamble concerning its inventory, reception from Nāropā by Marpa, and its subsequent revelation by Guru Chowang is contained in the *Collected Works of Lhodrak Marpa Lotsāwa*, vol. 6, pp.

103–208; and it is also found in RTD, vol. 55, pp. 1–134, and in Drigungpa Anthology, vol. 4, pp. 373–514. The present text, however, is not taken verbatim from these sources. On this instruction, see also Ducher 2016.

869. This cycle comprises fifteen scrolls, also known as the *Fifteen Cycles of Instruction concerning the Continuum of Buddha Mind*, which are enumerated in the *Collected Works of Lhodrak Marpa Lotsāwa*, vol. 6, pp. 109–10. These scrolls commence with the first on empowerment and conclude with the fifteenth on the protector deity Kholpo Dartochen. The original Tibetan translation of all fifteen is attributed to Marpa.

870. These practices of consciousness transference and resurrection are contained in the thirteenth scroll. The seven immediately preceding scrolls concern the six doctrines of the perfection stage. The detailed account of this practice is found in the *Collected Works of Lhodrak Marpa Lotsāwa*, vol. 6, pp. 189–92. On the expertise of Guru Chowang specifically in these rites of consciousness transference and resurrection, see Dudjom Rinpoche 1991, 766–70.

871. *rNgog pa'i bsre 'pho'i khrid.* The primary source, attributed to Ngok Zhedang Dorjé, does not appear to be extant, outside the present anthology. Its antecedent is Marpa Chokyi Lodro's *Profound Implementation of the Mingling and Transformation [of the Three Poisons], along with the History of the Pronouncements of the Four Oral Instructions*, in his *Collected Works*, vol. 5, pp. 150–72.

872. Marpa Chokyi Lodro, in his *Collected Works*, vol. 5, p. 151.

873. That is, the union of the mother and child luminosity at the time of death.

874. According to Pema Karpo, *Ornament of the Secret Assembly*, the three magical displays (*sgyu ma gsum*) comprise the magical displays of meditative equipoise, postmeditation, and the next life. According to Longchen Rabjam, *Trilogy on Resting*, they comprise the magical displays of ground, path, and fruition; and according to Tāranātha, *Instruction Manual of the Perfect Seat Free from the Stain of Bewilderment: Direct Guidance on the Five Stages of the Secret Assembly according to Nāgārjuna*, they comprise the magical displays of appearances, dreams, and the intermediate state.

875. The instructions belonging to the four pronouncements (*bka' bzhi gdams pa*) are those instructions imparted to Tilopā, which subsequently fell respectively to Nāgārjuna, Saraha, Kṛṣṇacārin, and Sumatibhadrī. See Marpa Chokyi Lodro, in his *Collected Works*, vol. 5, p. 150.

876. *sNyan gyi shog dril bzhi'i khrid.* The primary source, attributed to Tsurton Wang-gi Dorjé, appears to be no longer extant outside the present anthology. Its antecedent is Marpa Chokyi Lodro's *The Four Scrolls of Lama Marpa*, contained in the latter's *Collected Works*, vol. 2, pp. 41–46, and in his *History of the Four Scrolls of the Aural Instructions: An Extraordinary Teaching of Venerable Lhodrakpa, along with Its Appendix*, *Collected Works*, vol. 4, pp. 87–121; also *DNZ*, vol. 8, pp. 203–33. The presentation and wording of Tsurton Wang-gi Dorjé's synopsis is, for the most part, dissimilar.

877. Marpa Chokyi Lodro, in his *Collected Works*, vol. 4, pp. 93–101.

878. Marpa Chokyi Lodro, vol. 4, p. 101.
879. Appearance, increase, and attainment (*snang mched thob gsum*) are the three subtle phases associated with the dissolution of the elements as death approaches, giving rise respectively to the perceptions of whiteness, redness, and blackness.
880. Marpa Chokyi Lodro, *Collected Works*, vol. 4, pp. 102–4.
881. Marpa Chokyi Lodro, vol. 4, pp. 104–5, also pp. 109ff.
882. *sNyan brgyud steng sgo chos drug gi khrid*. The primary source is here attributed to Zhang Lotsāwa Jangchub-o, but its immediate antecedent is Rechungpa's *Guidance of the Six Doctrines That Confer Liberation through the Upper Gate, according to the Perfection Stage of the Aural Lineage of Cakrasaṃvara*. The latter derives from *The Aural Lineage of Rechungpa* and is contained in *DNZ*, vol. 7, pp. 501–33. A more extensive compilation from the aural lineage of Rechungpa can also be found in Drigungpa Anthology, vols. 58–62. Readers should note that, as stated above, chapter 9, n. 293, the guidebook entitled *The Six-Branch Yoga of Kālacakra* has been moved forward from its position here in chapter 9 to its position as the fortieth guidebook in the present anthology. This accords with Kunga Drolchok's clearly stated position in the earlier historical chapters of this text.
883. Rechungpa Dorjé Drak, *DNZ*, vol. 7, pp. 511–14.
884. Rechungpa Dorjé Drak, vol. 7, p. 511, lines 5–6.
885. Rechungpa Dorjé Drak, vol. 7, p. 512, lines 6–7.
886. As explained in Rechungpa Dorjé Drak, *DNZ*, vol. 7, p. 514, line 6–p. 515, line 5, the alchemical transformation of base metal into gold is a metaphor for the transformation of lower into superior, and, in the case of this practice of the illusory body, it may denote transformation through either the meditational deity, the teacher, or appearances.
887. Rechungpa Dorjé Drak, *DNZ*, vol. 7, p. 515, line 7–p. 517, line 3.
888. Rechungpa Dorjé Drak, vol. 7, p. 517, line 3–p. 518, line 4.
889. This section on the illusory body concludes on p. 519, line 4 in Rechungpa Dorjé Drak, vol. 7.
890. The detailed instruction of dream yoga is found on p. 519, line 4–p. 523, line 2 in Rechungpa Dorjé Drak, vol. 7.
891. The distinctions between these four are discussed in Rechungpa Dorjé Drak, *DNZ*, vol. 7, p. 522, lines 2–7.
892. The instruction on luminosity is discussed in Rechungpa Dorjé Drak, *DNZ*, vol. 7, p. 523, line 2–p. 526, line 5.
893. On consciousness transference, see Rechungpa Dorjé Drak, *DNZ*, vol. 7, p. 526, line 5–p. 530, line 4.
894. This present text appears to include intermediate state (*bar do*) as the sixth doctrine, rather than resurrection (*grong 'jug*), which is discussed in Rechungpa Dorjé Drak, *DNZ*, vol. 7, p. 530, line 4–p. 533, line 2.
895. This denotes the intermediate state of the time of death (*'chi ka'i bar do*).
896. This denotes the intermediate state of reality (*chos nyid bar do*).
897. This denotes the intermediate state of rebirth (*srid pa'i bar do*).

898. These well-known verses describing the experience of the mental body during the intermediate state of rebirth are cited from Vasubandhu, *Treasury of Phenomenology*, chap. 3, vv. 13–14. See the explanation in Dorje 2005, 274–77.
899. This denotes the intermediate state of our present natural existence (*rang bzhin bar do*).
900. An annotation in the text points out that this manifests within the womb following conception. The "threefold intermingling" would therefore denote ovum, sperm, and consciousness.
901. *Lus med mkha' 'gro'i chos skor dgu'i khrid.* The primary source of this guidebook appears to be Marpa Chokyi Lodro's *Teachings of the Nine Doctrinal Cycles of Nirdehaḍākinī*, in his *Collected Works*, vol. 4, pp. 225–51. *DNZ* also contains three texts pertaining to this cycle. The first of these is Rechungpa Dorjé Drak's *Root Text and Pith Instructions of the Nine Doctrinal Cycles of Nirdehaḍākinī*, *DNZ*, vol. 8, pp. 165–73, which is the root text of the cycle. The second, entitled *Teaching of Tilopā: The Nine Doctrinal Cycles of Nirdehaḍākinī*, *DNZ*, vol. 8, pp. 175–95, represents the oral lineage of Zurmang. And the third, entitled *Pith Instructions of the Aural Lineage concerning Nirdehaḍākinī*, or *Essence of the Nine Doctrinal Cycles of Nirdehaḍākinī*, *DNZ*, vol. 8, pp. 197–201, represents the oral tradition of Rechungpa. On this literature and the varying historical perceptions, see Roberts 2007, 154–82. The language of this guidebook is often enigmatic and hard to comprehend, even when structural content has been added in square brackets from the source text of Marpa Chokyi Lodro. It would be beyond the scope of the present work to elaborate further. Readers are therefore referred to those other texts within the cycle, which will be translated in volume 8 of the present series.
902. Among the Nine Doctrinal Cycles of Nirdehaḍākinī, the first four were introduced to Tibet by Marpa and the last five by Rechungpa. See Roberts 2007. The account of these transmissions is found in a number of sources, for example, Taklung Ngawang Namgyal's *Wondrous Ocean of Eloquence: Histories of the Taklung Kagyu Tradition*, pp. 153–154; and Roerich 1949, 437. On the life of Tilopā, see Marpa Chokyi Lodro 1995; also Sangye Nyenpa 2014.
903. Tib. *smin grol sems kyi rgya mdud bshig pa*. Marpa Chokyi Lodro, in his *Collected Works*, vol. 4, pp. 225–36.
904. Our text reads *grong gdams* for *grogs gdams*.
905. Marpa Chokyi Lodro, in his *Collected Works*, vol. 4, p. 225.
906. Tib. *dam tshig sems kyi rgya mdud ltos*. Marpa Chokyi Lodro, in his *Collected Works*, vol. 4, pp. 236–38.
907. Our text reads *brtan* for *bstan*.
908. Our text reads *rlung gi dbu mar mi bskur* for *rlung gi bu bla mar mi bkur*.
909. Marpa Chokyi Lodro, in his *Collected Works*, vol. 4, pp. 236–37.
910. Marpa Chokyi Lodro, vol. 4, p. 237.
911. Marpa Chokyi Lodro, vol. 4, pp. 237–38.
912. Tib. *dam rdzas rtogs pa'i nyi ma lde*. Marpa Chokyi Lodro, in his *Collected Works*, vol. 4, pp. 238–40.

913. Marpa Chokyi Lodro, in his *Collected Works*, vol. 4, pp. 238–39.
914. Marpa Chokyi Lodro, vol. 4, p. 239.
915. Tib. *spyod pa chu la ral gri thob*. Marpa Chokyi Lodro, in his *Collected Works*, vol. 4, pp. 240–42.
916. Our text misreads *som pa* for *sdom pa*.
917. Our text reads "horse of this life" (*tshe 'di'i rta*), whereas Marpa Chokyi Lodro, in his *Collected Works* (vol. 4, p. 241), omits *rta*.
918. Our text reads *bya ra mi dbram* for *char ba mi dgram*.
919. Marpa Chokyi Lodro, in his *Collected Works*, vol. 4, p. 241.
920. Marpa Chokyi Lodro, vol. 4, p. 241.
921. Marpa Chokyi Lodro, vol. 4, p. 242.
922. According to Marpa Chokyi Lodro (*Collected Works*, vol. 4, p. 242), this is the fifth category, and a fourth entitled the engagement in communal offerings (*tshogs spyod pa*) is added.
923. Our text reads "timely" (*dus tshod dang 'brel ba*) for *dus tshod dang bral ba*.
924. Tib. *rtsa rlung dra mig 'khor lo bskor ba*. Marpa Chokyi Lodro, in his *Collected Works*, vol. 4, pp. 243–45.
925. Marpa Chokyi Lodro, in his *Collected Works*, vol. 4, pp. 243. Cf. also Yangonpa's explanation of the energy channels, translated by Guarisco in Gyalwa Yangonpa 2015, 230ff.
926. Marpa Chokyi Lodro, in his *Collected Works*, vol. 4, pp. 243–44. On these primary and ancillary winds, see also Gyalwa Yangonpa 2015, 264ff.
927. Marpa Chokyi Lodro, in his *Collected Works*, vol. 4, p. 244. Cf. also Yangonpa's explanation of the vital essences, translated by Guarisco in Gyalwa Yangonpa 2015, 287ff.
928. This terse sentence follows Marpa Chokyi Lodro, in his *Collected Works*, vol. 4, p. 244.
929. Marpa Chokyi Lodro, in his *Collected Works*, vol. 4, p. 244.
930. Tib. *rgyu lugs bzhi*.
931. Marpa Chokyi Lodro, in his *Collected Works*, vol. 4, p. 244.
932. According to Marpa Chokyi Lodro (*Collected Works*, vol. 4, p. 244), this should read *rdo gcod kyi 'od kyi sgron ma*.
933. Marpa Chokyi Lodro, in his *Collected Works*, vol. 4, pp. 244–45.
934. Marpa Chokyi Lodro, vol. 4, p. 245.
935. Marpa Chokyi Lodro, vol. 4, p. 245. Our text reverses the buddha bodies associated with the channels and winds.
936. Tib. *bde chen gsung gi rin chen zungs*. Marpa Chokyi Lodro, in his *Collected Works*, vol. 4, pp. 245–47. Our text reads "diminish" (*bri/bris*) for "retain" (*zungs*).
937. Marpa Chokyi Lodro, in his *Collected Works*, vol. 4, p. 246.
938. The three aspects of authentic perception (*'du shes gsum ldan*) are those of the male, the female, and their nonduality.
939. Marpa Chokyi Lodro, in his *Collected Works*, vol. 4, p. 246.
940. Marpa Chokyi Lodro, vol. 4, pp. 246–47.

941. Tib. *rig pa ye shes sgron me*. Marpa Chokyi Lodro, in his *Collected Works*, vol. 4, pp. 247–48.
942. Marpa Chokyi Lodro, in his *Collected Works*, vol. 4, p. 247.
943. Our text reads *lung gis rtogs* for *lung gi mi rtogs*.
944. Marpa Chokyi Lodro, in his *Collected Works*, vol. 4, pp. 247–48.
945. Marpa Chokyi Lodro, vol. 4, p. 248.
946. Marpa Chokyi Lodro, vol. 4, p. 248.
947. Marpa Chokyi Lodro, vol. 4, p. 248.
948. Marpa Chokyi Lodro, vol. 4, p. 248.
949. Tib. *rang grol phyag rgya chen po*. Marpa Chokyi Lodro, in his *Collected Works*, vol. 4, pp. 248–49.
950. Marpa Chokyi Lodro, in his *Collected Works*, vol. 4, pp. 248–49.
951. Tib. *ro snyoms spyi'i me long*. Marpa Chokyi Lodro, in his *Collected Works*, vol. 4, pp. 249–51. Our text reads *phyi* for *spyi*.
952. Marpa Chokyi Lodro, in his *Collected Works*, vol. 4, p. 249.
953. On the posture of the lion's play (*seng ge'i rnam rol*), see also above, chapter 9, n. 766.
954. Marpa Chokyi Lodro, in his *Collected Works*, vol. 4, pp. 249–50.
955. This denotes Agni, the god of the fire element.
956. Marpa Chokyi Lodro, in his *Collected Works*, vol. 4, p. 251.
957. *Zhang gi zab rgyas khrid yig*. The primary source of this guidebook has not yet been identified in the *Collected Works of Zhang Tselpa Yudrakpa*. It is neither the *Conclusive Supreme Path of the Great Seal, DNZ*, vol. 8, pp. 429–62, nor the *Unrivaled Pith Instruction of Zhang Tselpa: Preliminary and Main Practices in the Great Meditation of the Great Seal, DNZ*, vol. 8, pp. 463–84.
958. This bodhisattva is said to intimate the empowerment of word (*tshig gi dbang*).
959. *dPal chen rgva lo'i sbyor drug gi khrid*. The primary source, attributed to Zhang Tselpa, is not contained in his *Collected Works*, but there is an antecedent text, Pelchen Ga Lotsāwa Namgyel Dorjé's *Pith Instructions of the Six-Branch Yoga*, vol. 35. The last part of the present guidebook follows the seven-point visualization presented in Yangonpa's *Seven Days of Fierce Inner Heat according to Ga Lotsāwa*, which is extant in various compilations, for example, Drigungpa Anthology, vol. 48, pp. 148–63. The first part, summarizing the six branches, is dissimilar.
960. The yogic exercise named "wave of perfect rapture" (*longs spyod kyi rlabs*) entails pressing the carotid arteries adjacent to the throat cakra with the two thumbs. See above, chapter 9, n. 393.
961. Tib. *rab kyis dang por rgyud las rtogs*. The actual expression found in *The Aural Transmission of Kālacakrapāda: Pith Instructions of the Six-Branch Yoga* (*DNZ*, vol. 15, p. 7) is *rab kyis dang po rtogs pa'o* (the best attain realization from the beginning) in contrast to the "average who practice breath control and so forth, and the inferior who gradually cultivate all the six branches."
962. This "activated fierce inner heat" (*las kyi gtum mo*) induced by the refinement of mind, subtle energy, and physical posture contrasts with the "blazing fierce inner

heat" (*'bar ba'i gtum mo*) and the "fierce inner heat of the Great Seal" (*phyag chen gyi gtum mo*), or else with the "experiential fierce inner heat" (*nyams pa'i gtum mo*) and the "supreme fierce inner heat" (*mchog gi gtum mo*).

963. According to Yangonpa's *Seven Days of Fierce Inner Heat according to Ga Lotsāwa* (Drigungpa Anthology, vol. 48, p. 154), you should sit with the legs crossed like interwoven netting, secure your hands [in the gesture of meditation] in the manner of a noose, bend your neck like a hook, straighten your spine and waist like as an arrow, and stretch your shoulders like the wings of a vulture.
964. Our text reads *snad du gcun* for *smad du sgyur*. See Yangonpa, Drigungpa Anthology, vol. 48, p. 155.
965. Inhalation, filling, crushing, and elevation or ejection are enumerated as the four applications of wind (*rlung sbyor bzhi*). See above and also Yangonpa, Drigungpa Anthology, vol. 48, pp. 155–56.
966. Yangonpa (Drigungpa Anthology, vol. 48, p. 159) states that the following seven visualizations should be undertaken on successive days, or else over two or three days each.
967. Yangonpa, Drigungpa Anthology, vol. 48, p. 156.
968. The four attributes (*chos bzhi*) are redness, heat, sharpness, and intensity. See Yangonpa, Drigungpa Anthology, vol. 48, pp. 156–57.
969. Yangonpa, Drigungpa Anthology, vol. 48, pp. 157–58.
970. Yangonpa, Drigungpa Anthology, vol. 48, p. 158.
971. Yangonpa, Drigungpa Anthology, vol. 48, p. 159.
972. *Phags gru thel skor gyi khrid.* The precise sources of the first and third parts of this guidebook have not yet been identified among the *Collected Works* of Gampopa and Pagmodrupa. The second part derives from Gampopa's *Defining Characteristics of Mind: Revelation of the Hidden*. The comment at the end may suggest that the content was compiled from various other sources within the collected works of Pagmodrupa, not simply one or two specific texts. The historical account given above in chapter 4 mentions the *Verses on the Great Seal* (possibly *DNZ*, vol. 9, pp. 349–67) and the *Verses on the Path of Skillful Means*, which are contained in Pagmodrupa, in his *Collected Works*, vol. 16, pp. 91–94.
973. This perhaps may refer to the objective and immediate conditions.
974. The exact source of this passage has not yet been identified.
975. The three modes of perseverance (*grogs brtson 'grus gsum*) are donning the armor, engagement in virtuous actions, and engaging in the benefit of sentient beings. See Nordrang Orgyan, *Compendium of Buddhist Numeric Terms*, p. 386.
976. The thirty-seven factors conducive to enlightenment that are pursued by bodhisattvas comprise the four applications of mindfulness, the four correct exertions, the four supports for miraculous ability, the five faculties, the five powers, the seven branches of enlightenment, and the noble eightfold path. Among these, the four applications of mindfulness (*catuḥsmṛtyupasthāna, dran pa nye bar gzhag pa bzhi*) concern the physical body, feelings, the mind, and phenomena. The four correct exertions (*catuḥprahāṇa, yang dag par spong ba bzhi*) concern the

noncultivation of future nonvirtuous actions, the renouncing of past nonvirtuous actions, the cultivating of future virtuous actions, and the maintaining of former virtuous actions. The four supports for miraculous abilities (*catvāra ṛddhipādāḥ, rdzu 'phrul gyi rkang pa bzhi*) concern the meditative stabilities of resolution, perseverance, mind, and scrutiny. The five faculties (*pañcendriya, dbang po lnga*) and the five powers both comprise faith, perseverance, recollection, meditative stability, and discriminative awareness. The seven branches of enlightenment (*saptabodhyaṅga, byang chub kyi yan lag bdun*) comprise recollection, doctrinal analysis, perseverance, delight, mental and physical refinement, meditative stability, and equanimity. The noble eightfold path (*aṣṭaṅgāryamārga, 'phags pa'i lam yan lag brgyad*) comprises correct view, correct ideation, correct speech, correct action, correct livelihood, correct effort, correct recollection, and correct meditative stability. See Dayal (1932) 1970, 80–164.

977. The verses that follow are a rearrangement of Gampopa's *Defining Characteristics of Mind: Revelation of the Hidden*, which belongs to his miscellaneous writings (*gsung thor bu*) and is found in various collections. I have translated the words as they appear in the present text, although readers should understand that original lines of verse have frequently been omitted, and even the wording of the included verses has often been changed.

978. Literally, "iron exhausted, whetstone exhausted" (*lcags zad brdar zad*).

979. Gampopa's *Defining Characteristics of Mind: Revelation of the Hidden* (p. 414, line 2) reads "empty drawings" (*stong pa'i ri mo*) for "flowers of space" (*nam mkha'i me tog*).

980. The source of the following verses has not yet been identified.

981. The source of this passage among the extant texts of Pagmodrupa on fierce inner heat has not yet been identified.

982. Here our text reads *rigs pa* for *rags pa*.

983. See above, chapter 9, n. 962.

984. This would corroborate the identification of Lawapa with Kambalapāda. See Dudjom Rinpoche 1991, 485–87; also Robinson 1979, 117–20.

985. The three signs of death (*'chi ba'i rtags gsum*) comprise appearance, increase, and attainment, each of which has outer and inner signs. See Roberts 2011, 363–65.

986. The mental body assumed during the intermediate state of the rebirth process is said to have the capacity to roam anywhere except in Vajrāsana (Bodh Gaya), the seat of the Buddha's enlightenment, and in the womb where the consciousness of the deceased will next take birth, owing to the impact of past actions.

987. This period of forty-nine days is said not to be absolute, but nonetheless is attested in Tibetan works such as Karma Lingpa's revelations (Dorje 2005) and in traditional Indic Abhidharma sources.

988. *dGongs pa gcig gi khrid*. The primary source is Drigung Jigten Gonpo's *Forty-Seven Supplements to the One Hundred and Fifty Adamantine Teachings*, contained in his *Root Text, Supplement, Summary, and Framework of Unique Enlightened Intention, the Sacred Doctrine of Glorious Drigungpa*, *DNZ*, vol. 9, pp. 395–401 (of pp.

369–408). The words in square brackets in the present translation correspond to that text, which is also translated in Roberts 2011, 390–95. The related text, mentioned here, is Jigten Gonpo's *Revered Wheel of Vitality*, contained in Drigungpa Anthology, vol. 96, pp. 193–206.

989. Our text reads *bka' thams cad . . . tshang* for *bka' min la ma khyab.*
990. In our text the order of this and the following point is reversed.
991. Omitted in our text.
992. The "common sutras" (*thun mong gi mdo*) denote those sutras of the first turning of the wheel that include Vinaya and Abhidharma content. See Roberts 2011, 391n680.
993. One to the power of fifty-nine.
994. Omitted in our text. Similar to the second point listed above.
995. This is positioned out of order in our text, between numbers thirty-nine and forty.
996. The *kuśāla* are virtuous practitioners who undertake visualizations such as the body offering of the Severance practice.
997. The four phases of Secret Mantra (*gsang sngags nas / kyi dus bzhi*) could refer either to the four classes of tantra or to the four empowerments. Roberts (2011, 393n687) suggests the latter.
998. Our text reads "mind" (*sems*) but see Drigung Jigten Gonpo, *DNZ*, vol. 9, p. 400, line 4, which reads "armor" (*go cha*); also Roberts 2011, 393.
999. Our text here reads "forty-eight adamantine sayings" (*rdo rje'i gsung zhi brgyad pa*).
1000. *sTag lung pa'i chos drug gi khrid.* The primary source would seem to be Taklungpa Tashipel's *Wish-Fulfilling Gem: The Six Doctrines of Glorious Nāropā*, which is part of the *Wish-Fulfilling Gem: Adamantine Stanzas on the Short Text of the Guidebook Entitled Coemergent Union of the Great Seal*, *DNZ*, vol. 10, pp. 1–19, specifically pp. 5–19. However, the actual wording of this present guidebook is distinct.
1001. The former pertains to the controlling of the wind of past actions (*las kyi rlung*) and the latter to the wind of pristine cognition (*ye shes kyi rlung*).
1002. See Roberts 2011, 341–47.
1003. Tib. *lus me 'gal drug.* See above, chapter 9, n. 304.
1004. In our text this is reversed and written as KA HI.
1005. Our text reads *gi* for *gis.*
1006. *bLa sgrub rten 'brel ro snyoms kyi khrid.* This is an amalgam of three distinct instructions attributed to Tsangpa Gyaré, which are presented here in the context of a single guidebook. All three are also represented in *DNZ* in the later writings of Pema Karpo, specifically (i) *The Means for Attainment of the Teacher as the Three Buddha Bodies*, which is also entitled *The Outer, Inner, and Secret Attainments of the Teacher*, *DNZ*, vol. 10, pp. 131–41; (ii) *The Basket of Sacred Doctrines: Meditation Sequence of Auspicious Circumstance*, *DNZ*, vol. 10, pp. 123–30; and (iii) *Surmounting the Experiential Cultivation of the Six Cycles of Common Savor*, *DNZ*, vol. 10, pp. 115–22. The notes that follow also reference other related texts

by Tsangpa Gyaré, including his *Oral Teaching of the Single Sufficient Synopsis of Auspicious Circumstances*, Drukpa Kagyu Anthology, vol. 55, pp. 417–22; and his *Extracting the Essence of All Instructions of My Own Tradition on Auspicious Circumstances*, Drukpa Kagyu Anthology, vol. 55, pp. 618–20; as well as Gotsangpa's *Guidance of Profound Auspicious Circumstances*, Drukpa Kagyu Anthology, vol. 55, p. 530; and three other works of Pema Karpo, which are respectively entitled *Extracting the Essence of All Instructions of Tsangpa Gyaré's Own Tradition on Auspicious Circumstances*, in his *Collected Works*, vol. 24, p. 315; *Oral Transmission of Drogon: Embracing the Definitive Common Savor*, in his *Collected Works*, vol. 24, pp. 39–51; and *Contents of the Guidance on Common Savor*, in his *Collected Works*, vol. 24, pp. 289–94.

1007. *Fourfold Cycle of the Mother of Space* is a work of Barawa Gyeltsen Pelzang (1310–1391).

1008. The actual source of these words has not yet been identified.

1009. The actual source of these words has not yet been identified.

1010. Cf. Tsangpa Gyaré, Drukpa Kagyu Anthology, vol. 55, pp. 417–22, which contains four pith instructions concerning withdrawal (*sdod tshugs pa*), renunciation (*bya btang*), contentment (*chos shes*), and dispassion (*'dod zad*). The wording of our text partly reflects this source. Other related texts by Tsangpa Gyaré (Drukpa Kagyu Anthology, vol. 55, pp. 618–20) and Gotsangpa (Drukpa Kagyu Anthology, vol. 55, p. 530) allude to some of the terminology found in our text, although they are dissimilar.

1011. See also Pema Karpo, in his *Collected Works*, vol. 24, p. 315.

1012. These six pith instructions are discussed in Pema Karpo, in his *Collected Works*, vol. 24, pp. 39–51, 289–94.

1013. Our text reads "demons that immediately arise" (*gdon thul*) for "sufferings of cyclic existence."

1014. *Thub pa lnga ldan gyi khrid.* The primary source is attributed to Dra Gadenpa, a disciple of Lorepa. Its antecedent is Lorepa's *Natural Arising of the Buddha Body of Reality: Instructions of the Fivefold Capacity—a Distinctive Doctrine of the Glorious Lower Drukpa Kagyu Tradition*, which is contained in *DNZ*, vol. 10, pp. 223–41.

1015. Among the five capacities (*thub pa lnga*), the first four are regarded as ancillaries to the last, which is the basic capacity. See Lorepa, *DNZ*, vol. 10, p. 224, lines 4–5.

1016. The six ornaments (*rgyan drug*) comprise crown (*dbu rgyan*), earrings (*snyan rgyan*), necklace (*mgul rgyan*), bracelets or anklets (*gdu bu*), sash (*se ral kha*), and waistband (*'og pag*).

1017. Lorepa, *DNZ*, vol. 10, p. 230, line 1.

1018. Lorepa, vol. 10, p. 230, lines 3–6.

1019. Lorepa, vol. 10, pp. 228–31.

1020. Lorepa, vol. 10, pp. 231–35

1021. Diet (*zas*) here refers to the five meats and five nectars, and conduct (*spyod pa*) to sacred song and dance. See Lorepa, *DNZ*, vol. 10, p. 234, line 7–p. 235, line 1.

1022. This title has been omitted in our text.

1023. Lorepa, *DNZ*, vol. 10, pp. 235–39.
1024. This title has been omitted in our text.
1025. Lorepa, *DNZ*, vol. 10, pp. 239–42.
1026. This title has been omitted in our text.
1027. Lorepa, *DNZ*, vol. 10, pp. 224–28.
1028. *Ri chos snying po ma drug gi khrid.* The primary source is Yangonpa's *Trilogy on Mountain Retreat*, especially the first part, which is entitled *Profound Instruction of the Six Primary Essentials for Mountain Retreat: Origin of All Enlightened Attributes*, and also contained in *DNZ*, vol. 10, pp. 243–96. The other two parts are entitled *Liberation from the Dangerous Passageway of the Intermediate State* and *Concealed Exegesis of the Adamantine Body*. On the life of Yangonpa, see Gyalwa Yangonpa 2015, 113–217.
1029. The six primary essentials are listed in Yangonpa, *DNZ*, vol. 10, p. 243, as (i) the primary essential of the five crucial procedures for vigorous breathing (*drag rlung gnad lnga ma*), (ii) the primary essential of the training in the red HŪṂ of consciousness transference (*'pho ba HŪṂ dmar ma*), (iii) primary essential of the six adamantine expressions of emptiness (*stong nyid rdo rje'i tshig drug ma*), (iv) the primary essential of the dream yoga of secret conduct (*gsang spyod rmang lam ma*), (v) the primary essential of the sacred doctrine of HŪṂ pertaining to evil spirits that bring diseases (*nad gdon HŪṂ chos ma*), and (vi) the primary essential of guarding against ejaculation along with the restricted injunction (*'dzag srung bka' rgya ma*).
1030. Yangonpa, *DNZ*, vol. 10, pp. 243–56.
1031. Yangonpa, vol. 10, pp. 256–62. The *amoliṅga* stone platform (*gnas rdo*) is the name of the teaching platform of Indra in Trāyastriṃśa.
1032. The source text for this paragraph is incomplete in Yangonpa, *DNZ*, vol. 10, p. 262. For further detail on all six adamantine expressions, each of which has two subsidiary aspects, see *Six Adamantine Verses on Emptiness*, Drigungpa Anthology, vol. 47, pp. 528–45.
1033. Yangonpa, *DNZ*, vol. 10, pp. 291–92.
1034. Yangonpa, vol. 10, pp. 292–93.
1035. Our text reads *gsang gcod rnal lam ma*.
1036. This section appears to be incomplete in the extant source texts for the Mountain Retreat (*Ri chos*), as, for example, in Yangonpa, *DNZ*, vol. 10, pp. 263–75, lines 11a–17a.
1037. Yangonpa, *DNZ*, vol. 10, p. 294. The term *span* (*mtho*) denotes the distance from the extended thumb to the tip of the middle finger.
1038. Yangonpa, *DNZ*, vol. 10, p. 294.
1039. Arbuda (Ar bu ta) and Lampāka (Lam pa ka) are two of the twenty-four sacred places, correlated with the subtle body, according to the Cakrasaṃvara cycle. See above, chapter 9, n. 738; also Gray 2007, 54–62.
1040. Yangonpa, *DNZ*, vol. 10, pp. 294–95.
1041. Yangonpa, vol. 10, p. 295.

1042. Yangonpa, vol. 10, p. 295, lines 6–7.

1043. *mGon po sku rags ma'i khrid.* The primary source of this guidebook on the four-armed protector Jñānanātha, known here as Mahākāla in the form Kurakma/Mekhalā (*sKu rags ma/sKu regs ma*), has not yet been identified. Several texts are contained in Drigungpa Anthology, vols. 91–92. Among them, the background narrative is found in the *Tantra of the Emergence of Kurak* (*sKu rags mngon byung gi rgyud*), vol. 91, pp. 103–8. The instruction known as the "vitality essence" (*srog thig*) corresponds to Ga Lotsāwa's *Heart Essence of Mahākāla*, vol. 92, pp. 365–78. Other related texts include Pagmodrupa Dorjé Gyelpo's *Secret Attainment of Kurakma: A Pith Instruction of Profound Summation*, in his *Collected Works*, vol. 4, ff. 408b–426b; as well as the *Secret Attainment That Reveals the Oral Instruction of Glorious Mahākāla with Three Channels and Four Cakras*, Drigungpa Anthology, vol. 92, pp. 315–30; the *Uncommon Oral Instruction of Guidance on Mahākāla with Five Cakras*, Drigungpa Anthology, vol. 92, pp. 331–48; the *Secret Attainment of Kurakma with Two Cakras*, Drigungpa Anthology, vol. 92, pp. 259–86; and *Kurakma: The Secret Attainment of Mahākāla with One Cakra*, Drigungpa Anthology, vol. 92, pp. 177–88. Apart from that anthology, other related texts include Ga Lotsāwa's *Means for Attainment of Glorious Four-Armed Jñānanātha Mahākāla with Two Cakras according to the Kurakma Indic Text* (also entitled *Instruction on the Book with a Sash*), *DNZ*, vol. 10, pp. 471–96; and Pagmodrupa's *The Kurakma Instruction of Four-Armed Mahākāla* (also entitled *The Essential Instruction on Kurakma*), in his *Collected Works*, vol. 7, pp. 447–60. On the iconography of this transmission from Ga Lotsāwa through Pagmodrupa, see Willson and Brauen 2000, 342–43.

1044. This is the special heart mantra of four-armed Mahākāla. See Willson and Brauen 2000, 343.

1045. *dPal gur gyi mgon po'i nang khrid.* The primary source, attributed to Yarlungpa Sengé Gyeltsen (or else Mu Sangyé Rinchen of Ngor) has not been located outside the present anthology. Related texts include *Means for Attainment and Initiation for the Eight-Deity Assemblage of Glorious Adamantine Mahākāla in the Form Pañjaranātha Entitled Strong Blaze of Splendor*, contained in *DNZ*, vol. 6, pp. 403–24. On the iconography of Pañjaranātha, see Willson and Brauen 2000, nos. 357–61.

1046. Cf. *DNZ*, vol. 6, p. 407.

1047. These verses of consecration employing the vajra are found in many diverse scriptures representing different traditions.

1048. OṂ DEVA PICU VAJRA HŪṂ HŪṂ PHAṬ SVĀHĀ.

1049. The twelve-syllable mantra (*yi ge bcu gnyis pa*) is OṂ ŚRĪ MAHĀKĀLAYA HŪṂ HŪṂ PHAṬ SVĀHĀ. See Willson and Brauen 2000, 346.

1050. The RORU mantra (*ro ru*) is the heart mantra of Śrīdevī, on which see Willson and Brauen 2000, 346.

1051. Black Yakṣa (Nag po gnod sbyin) and Black Yakṣī (Nag mo gnod sbyin), on which see Willson and Brauen 2000, 346.

1052. Putra (Pu tra) and his brother Black Putra (Pu tra nag po) along with their sister Ekajaṭā Rākṣasī (*srin mo ral gcig ma*). See Willson and Brauen 2000, 346.

1053. This is the combined mantra of the male and female yakṣas, along with Putra and his brother and sister.

1054. *Ritual Application of the Razor Cut* (*sPu gri so 'debs kyi las sbyor*), also entitled *Caturmukha'i zhal gdams snying gi dum bu*, is mentioned in the Sakya writings of Ngawang Kunga Sonam and Zhuchen Tsultrim Rinchen.

1055. *Do hā skor gsum gyi khrid*. The primary source is Parpuwa Lodro Sengé's *Synopsis of the Spiritual Songs of Glorious Saraha*, *DNZ*, vol. 7, pp. 22–28. The actual *Trilogy of Spiritual Songs* that is its antecedent comprises *The Spiritual Songs of the Populace* (T 2224; also *DNZ*, vol. 7, pp. 7–22), *The Spiritual Songs of the Queen* (T 2264), and the *The Spiritual Songs of the King* (T 2263), which are all translated in Guenther 1993, 89–211. *DNZ* also contains Śabaripā's *Pith Instruction of the Great Seal Entitled Treasury of Spiritual Songs*, *DNZ*, vol. 7, pp. 28–33.

1056. *Grub thob chos drug gi khrid*. The primary source of these perfection-stage practices is attributed to Tsami Lotsāwa Mondrub Sherab. Its antecedents include Abhayadattaśrī's *Pith Instruction Entitled Precious Garland* (Skt. *Ratnamālā*), TPD, vol. 48, pp. 671–74; and Vīraraśmi and Abhayadattaśrī's *The Essence of the Realizations of the Eighty-Four Accomplished Masters and Their Significance*, TPD, vol. 48, pp. 562–667. The inspirational legends of the eighty-four accomplished masters of India and their disciples were compiled in Abhayadattaśrī's *Narrative of the Eighty-Four Accomplished Masters*, TPD, vol. 48, pp. 413–556, translated in Robinson 1979.

1057. *Padma lam rim gyi khrid*. This instruction integrates the Great Perfection practices of "cutting through resistance to primordial purity" (*ka dag 'khregs chod*) and all-surpassing realization of spontaneous presence (*lhun grub thod rgal*). The primary source is Padmasambhava's *The Uncommon Gradual Path of Sutra and Mantra regarding External Phenomena: A Heap of Gems*, NK, vol. 82, pp. 137–72; also *DNZ*, vol. 2, pp. 257–82. Other relevant sources include Longchen Rabjam's revelation, *Entering the Enclosure of Luminosity*, in his *Collected Works*, vol. 8, pp. 71–77; and Dalai Lama V, *The Extensive Pronouncements and Profound Revelations of the Ancient Way of Secret Mantra*, in his *Collected Works*, vol. 2, pp. 224–92.

1058. These instructions were given by Padmasambhava respectively to an old man named Ngok Sherab Gyelpo and an old woman named Gedenma, along with her servant Rinchentso. Both instructions were redacted by Khandro Yeshé Tsogyel and are contained in Padmasambhava, *Uncommon Gradual Path of Sutra*, NK, vol. 82, pp. 137–72; and *DNZ*, vol. 2, pp. 276–82. See also the reference in Dalai Lama V, in his *Collected Works*, vol. 2, p. 282.

1059. On the precious enclosure of spontaneous presence (*lhun grub rin po che'i sbubs*), see Dudjom Rinpoche 1991, 448.

1060. *rGyal po bka' 'bum gyi khrid*. The primary source, attributed here to Lharjé Gewabum, purports to summarize the essence of *The Collected Injunctions of the King concerning Oṃ Maṇi Padme Hūṃ* (*Maṇi bka' 'bum*), which was elaborated and redacted by Drubtob Ngodrub and Nyanrel Nyima Ozer from an earlier core text that the Tibetan tradition attributes to King Songtsen Gampo. On its compilation and anachronisms, see Martin 1997, no. 16, p. 30; Mills 2007; Aris 1979, 8–24; and Kapstein 1992. The related text concerning Mahākāruṇika entitled *The Delightful Way of the Sublime Essential Experiential Cultivation: The Direct Guidance of Mahākāruṇika according to the Tradition of the King*, is extant in a later compilation by Jamyang Loter Wangpo, also in *DNZ*, vol. 17, pp. 43–51.

1061. *Nor bu mthong grol gyi khrid*. The primary source of this guidebook concerning all-surpassing realization of the Great Perfection is attributed to Norbu Rinchen, a teacher of Kunga Drolchok, but based on Drampa Kunga Zangpo's revelation entitled *Precious Liberation by Seeing: Coalescence of the Great Seal and Great Perfection*, RTD, vol. 60, pp. 149–64; also RTD (Delhi ed.), vol. 92, pp. 173–77.

1062. Our text reads "train" (*gcun*), whereas RTD (Delhi ed., p. 175, line 4) reads "incite conflict" (*dmag gi gcug nas*).

1063. RTD (Delhi ed.), vol. 92, p. 175, lines 3–5.

1064. RTD (Delhi ed.), vol. 92, p. 175, lines 5–6.

1065. RTD (Delhi ed.), vol. 92, p. 175, line 6–p. 176, line 1.

1066. RTD (Delhi ed.), vol. 92, p. 176, line 1.

1067. RTD (Delhi ed.), vol. 92, p. 176, line 2.

1068. RTD (Delhi ed.), vol. 92, p. 176, lines 2–4.

1069. With regard to these four visionary appearances (*snang ba bzhi*): (i) The visionary appearance of actual reality (*chos nyid mngon sum gyi snang ba*) occurs at the time when an awareness holder with power over the life span first perceives the pristine cognition of luminosity as smoke and so forth. (ii) The visionary appearance of ever-increasing experience (*nyams gong du 'phel ba'i snang ba*) occurs when that diffusion intensifies so that outer and inner signs are perceived. (iii) The visionary appearance that reaches the limit of awareness (*rig pa tshad phebs kyi snang ba*) occurs when the field of the buddha body of perfect resource is perceived. And (iv) the visionary appearance of the cessation [of cyclic existence] in actual reality (*chos nyid zad pa'i snang ba*) occurs when that, too, becomes inward quiescence, so that there is no subjective apprehension. Then, when the effulgence of the field of the buddha body of perfect resource dissolves in the original disposition, the ground is directly reached, and it is present without being seen, within a precious enclosure of spontaneous presence (*lhun grub rin po che'i sbubs*). See the description of Longchen Rabjam in Dorje 1987, 1011–44.

1070. RTD, vol. 92, p. 176, line 4–p. 177, line 1.

1071. RTD, vol. 92, p. 177, line 1.

1072. *Sems khrid yid bzhin nor bu'i khrid*. The primary source, attributed to Tokden Chonyi Rangdrol and transmitted through the aural lineage of Zurmang, is based on Drogon Dungtso Repa's revelation of *The Nature of Mind: The Wish-Fulfilling Gem*, contained in *The Cycles of Thirteen Great Instructions of the Aural Lineage*, vol. 1, pp. 663–98. However, the texts are somewhat dissimilar in content.

1073. Our text reads *ba nas pa* for *gnas pa.*

1074. On the expression *rgya mo'i thag so'i dpe,* which should perhaps read *rgya mo'i thags so'i dpe,* see above, chapter 3, n. 2.

Chapter 10: Marvelous Key to the Contents of the One Hundred and Eight Guidebooks

1. *Khrid brgya'i sa 'grel ya mtshan 'phrul gyi lde mig, DNZ,* vol. 18, pp. 355–61.
2. Cholung Jangtsé (Chos lung byang rtse) is the name of Jonang Monastery, the residence of Kunga Drolchok and his reincarnation, Tāranātha. See Akester 2016, 621.

Chapter 11: A List of the One Hundred and Eight Guidebooks with Their Protectors and Empowerments

1. *Khrid brgya'i mtshan tho dmigs bsal mgon brgya'i mtshan tho dbang brgya mtshan thos nges gnas dang bcas pa, DNZ,* vol. 18, pp. 363–74.
2. This is alternatively titled *The Attainment in Proximity to a Stupa.*
3. This is alternatively named *The Inner Guidance of Nairātmyā.*
4. On the expression "[four] precious mothers and [seventeen] offspring" (*ma nor bu smad*), see above, chapter 1, n. 52.
5. Willson and Brauen 2000, 345–46; Nebesky-Wojkowitz 1975, 49.
6. Jigmé Chokyi Dorjé, *Great Anthology of Buddhist Icons according to the Tibetan Lineages,* pp. 975–76; Willson and Brauen 2000, 346–47; Nebesky-Wojkowitz 1975, 49–51.
7. Nebesky-Wojkowitz 1975, 51.
8. Jigmé Chokyi Dorjé, *Great Anthology of Buddhist Icons,* p. 977; Willson and Brauen 2000, 347–48; Nebesky-Wojkowitz 1975, 51.
9. Jigmé Chokyi Dorjé, *Great Anthology of Buddhist Icons,* p. 1014; also Nebesky-Wojkowitz 1975, 64–65. Willson and Brauen 2000 (365) reads *gnyan gdong can.*
10. Jigmé Chokyi Dorjé, *Great Anthology of Buddhist Icons,* pp. 1011–14.
11. Jigmé Chokyi Dorjé, *Great Anthology of Buddhist Icons,* pp. 967–70; Willson and Brauen 2000, 340–44; Nebesky-Wojkowitz 1975, 44–45.
12. Jigmé Chokyi Dorjé, *Great Anthology of Buddhist Icons,* pp. 966–67.
13. Nebesky-Wojkowitz 1975, 45.
14. Jigmé Chokyi Dorjé, *Great Anthology of Buddhist Icons,* pp. 969–70; Nebesky-Wojkowitz 1975, 56.
15. Nebesky-Wojkowitz 1975, 65.
16. Jigmé Chokyi Dorjé, *Great Anthology of Buddhist Icons,* pp. 958–59; Willson and Brauen 2000, 336–37; Nebesky-Wojkowitz 1975, 38–39.
17. Willson and Brauen 2000, 344.

18. Jigmé Chokyi Dorjé, *Great Anthology of Buddhist Icons*, pp. 960–66; Willson and Brauen 2000, 338–40.
19. Willson and Brauen 2000, 366–67.
20. Jigmé Chokyi Dorjé, *Great Anthology of Buddhist Icons*, pp. 1027–34; Willson and Brauen 2000, 320–25.
21. Jigmé Chokyi Dorjé, *Great Anthology of Buddhist Icons*, pp. 1034–35; Willson and Brauen 2000, 322–23; Nebesky-Wojkowitz 1975, 70–71.
22. Jigmé Chokyi Dorjé, *Great Anthology of Buddhist Icons*, p. 1039; Willson and Brauen 2000, 321–22, Nebesky-Wojkowitz 1975, 69–70.
23. Similar perhaps to the form of Vaiśravaṇa known as the "supreme dancer."
24. Willson and Brauen 2000, 332–33; Nebesky-Wojkowitz 1975, 77–80.
25. Jigmé Chokyi Dorjé, *Great Anthology of Buddhist Icons*, p. 1064–71; Willson and Brauen 2000, 334–35; Nebesky-Wojkowitz 1975, 80.
26. Jigmé Chokyi Dorjé, *Great Anthology of Buddhist Icons*, pp. 942, 946–48; Willson and Brauen 2000, 327–29.
27. Associated with the *Tantra of the Wheel of Time*.
28. A group of guardian deities holding the lay (*upāsaka*) vows, associated with the Kadampa tradition of Atiśa. See also Nebesky-Wojkowitz 1975, 73–76.
29. Another group of Kadampa protectors.
30. Jigmé Chokyi Dorjé, *Great Anthology of Buddhist Icons*, pp. 1058–63; Nebesky-Wojkowitz 1975, 181–98.
31. The twelve protectresses in the retinue of the meditational deity Vajrakīla are said to have offered their services to Padmasambhava as he meditated on Vajrakīla in Nepal. They include the four of the rosewood family—namely, Śvanamukhā, Srira, Sṛgāla, and Kukkura; the four of the iron family—namely, Rematī, Remajā, Remajū, and Remajī; and the four of the conch family—namely, Yajin (Ya byin), Dejin (De byin), Sejin (bSe byin), and Pakjin (Phag byin). For iconographic details and further background, see Rigdzin Dorje 2013, 277–80.
32. The white-clad demon (*dkar bdud*) is a Sakya protector, said to "undertake outer, inner, and secret rites" (*phyi nang gsang las mkhan dkar bdud*).
33. Jigmé Chokyi Dorjé, *Great Anthology of Buddhist Icons*, p. 987; Willson and Brauen 2000, 351; Nebesky-Wojkowitz 1975, 52–53.
34. A group of Mahākāla figures corresponding to body, speech, mind, attributes, and activities, each of them without a female consort. See Jigmé Chokyi Dorjé (*Great Anthology of Buddhist Icons*, pp. 992–95), who emphasizes the seventeen-deity and nine-deity assemblages; also Willson and Brauen 2000, 352–53.
35. Jigmé Chokyi Dorjé, *Great Anthology of Buddhist Icons*, p. 991; Willson and Brauen 2000, 353–54; Nebesky-Wojkowitz 1975, 54–55.
36. Nebesky-Wojkowitz 1975, 54.
37. Jigmé Chokyi Dorjé, *Great Anthology of Buddhist Icons*, p. 995; Willson and Brauen 2000, 356; Nebesky-Wojkowitz 1975, 56.
38. Jigmé Chokyi Dorjé, *Great Anthology of Buddhist Icons*, p. 1002; Willson and Brauen 2000, 361.

39. Jigmé Chokyi Dorjé, *Great Anthology of Buddhist Icons*, p. 998; Willson and Brauen 2000, 351; Nebesky-Wojkowitz 1975, 53.
40. Jigmé Chokyi Dorjé, *Great Anthology of Buddhist Icons*, p. 985; Willson and Brauen 2000, 349; Nebesky-Wojkowitz 1975, 34, 52.
41. Jigmé Chokyi Dorjé, *Great Anthology of Buddhist Icons*, pp. 997–1001; Willson and Brauen 2000, 357–64; Nebesky-Wojkowitz 1975, 39, 57–60.
42. Jigmé Chokyi Dorjé, *Great Anthology of Buddhist Icons*, p. 1004; Willson and Brauen 2000, 361–62.
43. Jigmé Chokyi Dorjé, *Great Anthology of Buddhist Icons*, p. 1003; Willson and Brauen 2000, 361; Nebesky-Wojkowitz 1975, 229.
44. There are torma rites dedicated to this group of protectors entitled *gying lnga gza' gdong gi gtor chog*.
45. Jigmé Chokyi Dorjé, *Great Anthology of Buddhist Icons*, pp. 1020–24; Willson and Brauen 2000, 371–72; Nebesky-Wojkowitz 1975, 83–84.
46. Willson and Brauen 2000, 372; Nebesky-Wojkowitz 1975, 85–86.
47. A form of Mahākāla associated with Lhodrak.
48. Jigmé Chokyi Dorjé, *Great Anthology of Buddhist Icons*, pp. 1044–45; Willson and Brauen 2000, 367–68.
49. Jigmé Chokyi Dorjé, *Great Anthology of Buddhist Icons*, pp. 1040–42; Nebesky-Wojkowitz 1975, 24.
50. Jigmé Chokyi Dorjé, *Great Anthology of Buddhist Icons*, pp. 1042–43, 1046–49; Willson and Brauen 2000, 366–69; Nebesky-Wojkowitz 1975, 24–31.
51. Jigmé Chokyi Dorjé, *Great Anthology of Buddhist Icons*, p. 971; Willson and Brauen 2000, 344; Nebesky-Wojkowitz 1975, 48.
52. Nebesky-Wojkowitz 1975, 22ff.
53. Jigmé Chokyi Dorjé, *Great Anthology of Buddhist Icons*, pp. 1052–57; Willson and Brauen 2000, 376–77; Nebesky-Wojkowitz 1975, 177–81.
54. A group of three siblings (*rgyal thang dkar po mched gsum*) who are protectors of the instructions of Severance.
55. The Vedic deity representing the water element. See Jigmé Chokyi Dorjé, *Great Anthology of Buddhist Icons*, p. 1206; Nebesky-Wojkowitz 1975, 477.
56. Nebesky-Wojkowitz 1975, 273.
57. Willson and Brauen 2000, 333–34.
58. A Kagyu protectress, described as a "holder of mantras" (*sngags 'chang ma*).
59. Willson and Brauen 2000, 326.
60. Jigmé Chokyi Dorjé, *Great Anthology of Buddhist Icons*, p. 1005; Nebesky-Wojkowitz 1975, 67.
61. Jigmé Chokyi Dorjé, *Great Anthology of Buddhist Icons*, pp. 1049–50; Willson and Brauen 2000, 370; Nebesky-Wojkowitz 1975, 35.
62. Nebesky-Wojkowitz 1975, 39–42.
63. The text reads "seven times" (*lan bdun*), although Kunga Drolchok clearly states that he received this empowerment fourteen times.
64. The expression "six cakravartin tantras" (*rgyud 'khor los sgyur ba drug*) denotes

the assimilation of the following tantras with the cycle of the Wheel of Time: *Guhyasamāja*, *Mahāsaṃvarodaya*, *Laghusaṃvara*, *Vajravārāhī*, and *Māyājāla*.

65. Our text reads *go rig dung brgyud pa* for *go ri gdung brgyud pa*.
66. That is to say, the empowerments that he received from within the Nyingma tradition.

Chapter 12: Methods for the Conferral of the Empowerments

1. *Khrid brgya'i bod dbang byed tshul bla ma'i zhal shes yi ger bkod pa byin rlabs kyi za ma tog*, *DNZ*, vol. 18, pp. 375–79.
2. Tib. *kun mkhyen ye shes phung po can*. This prayer, found in many liturgical texts, is said when requesting empowerment. The verses are as follows: "Omniscient One, endowed with the aggregate of pristine cognition, purifying the cycle of existence! Through the precious words that you explain today, please bestow, O Lord, your kindness upon me! O Lord, I will not go for refuge to another, abandoning your lotus feet! Empower me definitively in accordance with the Great Sage, hero among living beings!" (*kun mkhyen ye shes phung po can / srid pa'i 'khor lo rnam sbyong ba/ de ring bshad pa'i rin chen gyis / gtso bo bdag la bka' drin stsol / khyod zhabs padma spangs nas ni / gtso bo gzhan la skyabs ma mchis / 'gro ba'i dpa' bo thub chen gyis/ bdag la nges par dbang bskur cig*). See, for example, *Tantra of the Great King Chapter Entitled Victory of Nondual Sameness* (T 452, KPD vol. 82, chap. 71, p. 717).
3. The full quatrain reads: "May the glorious teachers have good auspices—they who with the kingly power of the victory banner's summit adorn the crowns of their preferred deities and confer supreme accomplishment on practitioners!" (*rgyal mtshan rtse mo dbang gis rgyal po ltar / lhag pa lha yi gtsug gi rgyan gyur pa / sgrub pa po la dngos grub mchog stsol ba'i / dpal ldan bla ma rnams la bkra shis shog*). See, for example, Longchen Rabjam, *Precious Treasury of the Attainment Maṇḍala of the Peaceful and Wrathful Conquerors*, in his *Collected Works*, vol. 25, p. 385.
4. The full quatrain reads: "May there be good auspices of buddha body—the unchanging mountain! May there be good auspices of buddha speech with its sixty aspects! May there be good auspices of buddha mind—limitless and unbewildered! May there be good auspices of the body, speech, and mind of the conquerors!" (*mi 'gyur lhun po sku yi bkra shis shog / yan lag drug cu gsung gi bkra shis shog / mtha' bral 'khrul med thugs kyi bkra shis shog / rgyal ba'i sku gsung thugs kyi bkra shis shog*). See its occurrence, for example, in Pema Karpo, *Ritual Array Commenting on the Connections with the Empowerments of the Nine-Deity and Five-Deity Assemblages of Amitāyus according to the Drubgyel Tradition Entitled Noble Vase of Nectar*, Drukpa Kagyu Anthology, vol. 23, pp. 461–84.
5. The full quatrain reads: "Without the need for diligence and effort, fulfilling the hopes of sentient beings like the wish-fulfilling gem and wish-granting tree, may there be good auspices of aspirations attained!" (*'bad dang rtsol ba mi dgos*

pa'i / yid bzhin nor bu dpag bsam shing / sems can re ba bskong mdzad pa / bsam pa 'grub pa'i bkra shis shog). See Tāranātha, *Description and Long-Life Attainment of White Tārā according to the Tradition of Jowo Atiśa*, in his *Collected Works*, vol. 27, pp. 243–47.

6. The full verses read: "May I do just as the lord commands!" (*gtso bo'i ji ltar bka' stsal pa / de bzhin bdag gis bgyid par 'tshal*). See, for example, Tāranātha, *Maṇḍala Rite of Glorious Cakrasaṃvara Entitled Ford of Supreme Bliss*, in his *Collected Works*, vol. 13, pp. 232–88.
7. The year would have been either 1839 or 1899—the last being after the death of Jamyang Khyentsé Wangpo in 1892.

Bibliography

Bibliographical references for this volume are presented in five alphabetically arranged sections: (1) Vinaya Scriptures; (2) Sutra and Tantra; (3) Treatises of Indic Origin; (4) Tibetan Treatises and Spiritual Revelations; and (5) Works in Other Languages.

1. Vinaya Scriptures

Analysis [of Monastic Discipline for Monks]
Vinayavibhaṅga
['Dul ba] rnam 'byed
Dg.K. 'Dul ba vols. *ca*, f. 21a–*nya*, f. 269a; KPD, vol. 5, p. 62–vol. 8, p. 634; T 3.

Analysis [of Monastic Discipline for Nuns]
Bhikṣuṇīvinayavibhaṅga
['Dul ba] rnam 'byed
Dg.K. 'Dul ba vol. *ta*, ff. 25b–328a; KPD, vol. 9, pp. 72–784; T 5.

Four Scriptural Transmissions of Monastic Discipline
'Dul ba lung sde gzhi
Dg.K. 'Dul ba vols. *ka–pa* (1–13); KPD, vols. 1–13; T 1–7.

Ground Rules of Monastic Discipline
Vinayavastu
'Dul ba gzhi
Dg.K. 'Dul ba vols. *ka–nga*; KPD, vols. 1–4; T 1.

2. Sutra and Tantra

Ārali Trilogy
A ra li skor gsum
A collective name for the texts contained in T 426–27 and possibly T 385.

Collection of Aphorisms [of the Arhat Dharmatrāta]
Udānavarga

Ched du brjod pa'i tshoms
Dg.K. mDo sde vol. *sa*, ff. 209a–253a; KPD, vol. 72, pp. 602–704; T 326.
Summarized in PZ, pp. 491–92. See Brough 2001.

Five Protective Great Incantations
Pañcarakṣā
gZungs chen grva lnga
A collective title for T 558–59 and T 561–63; KPD, vol. 90, pp. 176–351 and pp. 355–476. See also Dudjom Rinpoche 1991, vol. 2, p. 228.

Root Tantra of the Secret Assembly
[Sarvatathāgatakāyavākcittarahasya] Guhyasamāja-nāma-mahākalparāja
De bzhin gshegs pa thams cad kyi sku gsung thugs kyi gsang chen gsang ba 'dus pa zhes bya ba brtag pa'i rgyal po chen po [short title: gSang ba 'dus pa rtsa rgyud]
Dg.K. rGyud vol. *ca*, ff. 90a–148a; Dg.NGB vol. *na* (12), no. 3, ff. 89a–147a; KPD, vol. 81, pp. 442–578; T 442.
Translated in Fremantle 1971.

Subsequent Tantra of the Secret Assembly
Guhyasamājottaratantra
gSang 'dus rgyud phyi ma
Dg.K. rGyud vol. *ca*, ff. 148a–157b, KPD, vol. 81, pp. 584–606; T 443.

Supreme Tantra of Clear Expression
Abhidhānottaratantra
mNgon par brjod pa'i rgyud bla ma
Dg.K. rGyud vol. *ka*, ff. 247a–370a, KPD, vol. 77, pp. 708–1005; T 369.

Sutra of the Cornucopia of Avalokiteśvara's Attributes
Āryakaraṇḍavyūha-nāma-mahāyānasūtra
'Phags pa za ma tog bkod pa zhes bya ba theg pa chen po'i mdo
Dg.K. mDo sde vol. *ja*, ff. 200a–247b; KPD, vol. 51, pp. 529–640; T 116.
Translated in Roberts and Tulku Yeshi 2013.

Sutra of the Ten Levels
Daśabhūmikasūtra
Sa bcu pa'i mdo
Dg.K. Phal chen vol. *kha*; KPD, vol. 36, pp. 355–603; T 44.
Summarized in PZ, pp. 12–14. Translated in Cleary 1993.

Sutra of the Transcendent Perfection of Wisdom in Eight Thousand Lines
Aṣṭasāhasrikāprajñāpāramitā
Shes rab kyi pha rol tu phyin pa brgyad stong pa
Dg.K. Shes phyin vol. *ka*, ff. 1b–286a; KPD, vol. 33; T 12.
Summarized in PZ, pp. 410–12. Translated in Conze 1973.

Sutra of the Transcendent Perfection of Wisdom in Eighteen Thousand Lines
Aṣṭādaśasāhasrikāprajñāpāramitā
Shes rab kyi pha rol tu phyin pa khri brgyad stong pa
Dg.K. Shes phyin vols. *ka*, f. 1b–*ga*, f. 206a; KPD, vol. 29, p. 3–vol. 31, p. 495; T 10.
Summarized in PZ, pp. 402–6. Translated and edited in Conze 1975.

Sutra of the Transcendent Perfection of Wisdom in One Hundred Thousand Lines (also known as *Extensive Mother*, Yum rgyas pa)
Śatasāhasrikāprajñāpāramitā
Shes rab kyi pha rol tu phyin pa stong phrag brgya pa
Dg.K. Shes phyin vols. *ka*, f. 1b–*a*, f. 395a; KPD, vols. 14–25; T 8.
Summarized in PZ, pp. 395–99.

Sutra of the Transcendent Perfection of Wisdom in Ten Thousand Lines
Daśasāhasrikāprajñāpāramitā
Shes rab kyi pha rol tu phyin pa khri pa
Dg.K. Shes phyin vols. *ga*, ff. 1b–91a, and *nga*, ff. 92b–397; KPD, vol. 31, pp. 530–763, and vol. 32, pp. 3–763; T 11.
Summarized in PZ, pp. 406–10. Translated in Padmakara Translation Group 2018.

Sutra of the Transcendent Perfection of Wisdom in Twenty-Five Thousand Lines
Pañcaviṃśatisāhasrikāprajñāpāramitā
Shes rab kyi pha rol tu phyin pa stong phrag nyi shu lnga pa
Dg.K. Shes phyin vols. *ka*, f. 1b–*ga*, f. 381a; KPD, vols. 26–28; T 9.
Annotated Sanskrit edition of the recast manuscript in Dutt 1934 and Kimura 1986–2007.
Partially translated in Conze 1975. Summarized in PZ, pp. 399–402.

Sutra Revealed by Akṣayamati
Āryākṣayamatinirdeśasūtra
'Phags pa blo gros mi zad pas bstan pa
Dg.K. mDo vol. *ma*, ff. 79a–174b; KPD, vol. 44, pp. 494–511; T 175.
Summarized in PZ, pp. 235–39.

Tantra Entitled Compendium of the Adamantine Reality of Pristine Cognition
Vajrajñānasamuccaya-nāma-tantra
Ye shes rdo rje kun las btus pa zhes bya ba'i rgyud
Dg.K. rGyud vol. *ca*, ff. 282a–286a; KPD, vol. 81, pp. 962–74; T 447.

Tantra of Acala
Āryācalakalpatantrarāja
Mi g.yo ba'i rgyud
Dg.K. rGyud vol. *ca*, ff. 1b–12a; KPD, vol. 81, pp. 3–39; T 432.

Tantra of Buddhakapāla
Śrībuddhakapāla-nāma-yoginītantrarāja
[dPal] sangs rgyas thod pa [zhes bya ba'i rnal 'byor ma'i rgyud kyi rgyal po]
Dg.K. rGyud vol. *nga*, ff.143a–167a; KPD, vol. 80, pp. 434–505; T 424.

Tantra of Cakrasaṃvara
Tantrarājaśrīlaghusaṃvara-nāma (also known as *Short Cakrasaṃvara*, sDom chung)
rGyud kyi rgyal po dpal bde mchog nyung ngu zhes bya ba
Dg.K. rGyud vol. *ka*, ff. 213b–246b; KPD, vol. 77, pp. 604–89; T 368.
Translated in Gray 2007.

Tantra of Great Magical Emanation
Śrīmahāmāyātantrarāja
[dPal] sgyu 'phrul chen mo [zhes bya ba'i rgyud kyi rgyal po]
Dg.K. rGyud vol. *nga*, ff. 167a–171a; KPD, vol. 80, pp. 505–17; T 425.

Tantra of Heruka Galpo
Yang dag thugs rgyud he ru ka gal po
Dg. NGB vol. 18, nos. 15–16, and vol. 19, no. 1.

Tantra of Hevajra
Hevajratantrarāja
Kye'i rdo rje zhes bya ba rgyud kyi rgyal po [short title: *Two-Chapter Tantra of Hevajra*, brTag gnyis pa]
Dg.K. rGyud vol. *nga*, ff. 1b–30a; KPD, vol. 80, pp. 3–92; T 417–18.
Edited and translated in Snellgrove 1959.

Tantra of Inconceivable Rali Cakrasaṃvara
Śrīcakrasaṃvaraguhyācintyatantrarāja
Ra li bsam gyis mi khyab pa'i rgyud
Dg.K. rGyud vol. *ga*, ff. 196a–199a; KPD, vol. 79, pp. 561–71; T 385.

Tantra of Nine-Lamp Śrīheruka
dPal yang dag me dgu
Here used as a generic title for the texts contained in Dg. NGB vol. 13, no. 2; vol. 18, nos. 15–16; and vol. 17, nos. 1–4.

Tantra of the Adamantine Garland
Vajramālābhidhānamahāyogatantrasarvatantrahṛdayarahasyavibhaṅganāma
rNal 'byor chen po'i rgyud dpal rdo rje phreng ba mngon par brjod pa rgyud thams cad kyi snying po gsang ba rnam par phye ba
Dg.K. rGyud vol. *ca*, ff. 208a–277b; KPD, vol. 81, pp. 752–917; T 445.

Tantra of the Adamantine Sky-Farers
Vajraḍākanāmamahātantrarāja
rGyud kyi rgyal po chen po pal rdo rje mkha' 'gro

Dg.K. rGyud vol. *kha*, ff. 1b–125a; T 370.
An explanatory tantra pertaining to the cycle of Cakrasaṃvara.

[*Tantra of the*] *Adamantine Subjugator Maṇivajra*
Vajravidāraṇanāmadhāraṇī
rDo rje rnam par 'joms pa [zhes bya ba'i rtsa ba'i rgyud] (also known as *Sutra of Ablution through the Indestructible Subjugator*, rDo rje rnam par 'joms pa khrus pa'i mdo)
Dg.K. rGyud vol. *dza*, ff. 265b–266b; KPD, vol. 95, pp. 785–91; T 750.

Tantra of the Adamantine Tent
Ḍākinīvajrapañjaramahātantra
[mKha' 'gro ma rdo rje] gur gyi rgyud
Dg.K. rGyud vol. *nga*, ff. 30a–65b; KPD, vol. 80, pp. 93–207; T 419.

Tantra of the Awakening of Vairocana
Mahāvairocanābhisambodhivikurvitādhiṣṭhānavaipulyasūtrendrarāja
rTsa rgyud rnam snang mngon par byang chub pa (also known as *Sarvavidvairocana*, Kun rig)
Dg.K. rGyud vol. *tha*, ff. 151b–260a; KPD, vol. 86, pp. 436–756; T 494.
Translated in Hodge 2003.

Tantra of the Black Slayer of Death
Śrīkṛṣṇayamāritantrarājatrikalpa
dPal gshin rje'i gshed nag po'i rgyud kyi rgyal po rtog pa gsum pa
Dg.K. rGyud vol. *ja*, ff. 164a–167b; KPD, vol. 83, pp. 522–31; T 469.
Also: Sarvatathāgatakāyavākcittakṛṣṇayamāri-nāma-tantra
De bzhin gshegs pa thams cad kyi sku gsung thugs gshin rje gshed nag po shes bya ba'i rgyud
Dg.K. rGyud vol. *ja*, ff. 134b–151b; KPD, vol. 83, pp. 429–84; T 467.

Tantra of the Coalescent Union of the Four Yoginīs
Caturyoginīsampuṭatantra
rNal 'byor ma bzhi'i kha sbyor gyi rgyud
Dg.K. rGyud 'bum vol. *ga*, ff. 44b–52b; KPD, vol. 79, pp. 129–48; T 376.

Tantra of the Emancipation of Śrīheruka
Śrīherukābhyudayatantra
dPal khrag 'thung mngon par 'byung ba
Dg.K. rGyud vol. *ga*, ff. 1b–33b; T 374.

Tantra of the Emergence of Cakrasaṃvara (also known as *Great Cakrasaṃvara*, sDom chen)
Śrīmahāsaṃvarodayatantrarāja
dPal bde mchog 'byung ba zhes bya ba'i rgyud kyi rgyal po chen po
Dg.K. rGyud vol. *kha*, ff. 265a–311a; KPD, vol. 78, pp. 774–883; T 373.

Tantra of the Emergence of Kurak
sKu rags mngon byung gi rgyud
Drigungpa Anthology vol. 91, pp. 103–8.

Tantra of the Four Adamantine Seats
Śrīcatuḥpīthamahāyoginītantrarāja
rNal 'byor ma rgyud kyi rgyal po chen pod pal gdan bzhi pa
Dg.K. rGyud vol. *nga*, ff. 181a–231b; KPD, vol. 80, pp. 549–685; T 428.

Tantra of the Great King Chapter Entitled Victory of Nondual Sameness
Advayasamatāvijayākhyānakalpamahārāja
gNyis su med pa mnyam pa nyid rnam par rgyal ba zhes bya ba'i rtog pa'i rgyal po chen po
Dg.K. rGyud vol. *cha*, ff. 58b–103a ; KPD, vol. 82, pp. 150–265; T 452.

Tantra of the Habitual Practice of the Yoginīs
Yoginīsañcāryatantra
rNal 'byor ma kun spyod kyi rgyud
Dg.K. rGyud vol. *ga*, ff. 34a–44b; T 375.
An explanatory tantra pertaining to Cakrasaṃvara.

Tantra of the [Kingly] Array of the Three Commitments
Trisamayavyūharāja-nāmatantra
Dam tshig gsum bkod pa'i rgyal po zhes bya ba'i rgyud
Dg.K. rGyud vol. *da*, ff. 181a–247a; KPD, vol. 87, pp. 543–742; T 502.

Tantra of the Litany of the Names of Mañjuśrī
Mañjuśrījñānasattvasyaparamārtha-nāma-saṅgīti
'Jam dpal [gyi] mtshan [yang dag par] brjod [pa] (also known as *Net of the Magical Emanation of Mañjuśrī*, 'Jam dpal sgyu 'phrul drva ba)
Dg. NGB vol. *tha* (10), ff. 123a–135b; Tingkye NGB vol. 15, pp. 97–118; Dg.K. rGyud vol. *ka*, ff. 1b–13b; KPD, vol. 77, pp. 3–31; T 360.
Translated in Choying Tobden Dorje 2016, Wayman 1983, and Davidson 1981.

Tantra of the Ocean of Sky-Farers [of Cakrasaṃvara]
Ḍākārṇavamahāyoginītantrarāja
[bDe mchog] mkha 'gro rgya mtsho [rnal 'byor ma'i] rgyud
Dg.K. rGyud vol. *kha*, ff. 137a–264b; KPD, vol. 78, pp. 404–773; T 372.

Tantra of the Ocean of Vows
sDom pa rgya mtsho'i rgyud
Not translated in Tibetan.

Tantra of the Ornament of the Nucleus of Adamantine Reality
Vajrahṛdayālaṃkāratantra
rDo rje snying po rgyan gyi rgyud
Dg.K. rGyud vol. *cha*, ff. 36a–58b; KPD, vol. 82, pp. 89–149; T 451.

Tantra of the Precious Ocean
Rin chen rgya mtsho'i rgyud
Not translated in Tibetan.

Tantra of the Vital Essence of Union
Śrīsampuṭatilaka-nāma-yoginītantrarāja
dPal kha sbyor thig le zhes bya ba rnal 'byor ma'i rgyud kyi rgyal po [short title: Kha sbyor thig le'i rgyud]
Dg.K. rGyud vol. *ga*, ff. 158b–184a; KPD, vol. 79, pp. 410–69; T 382.

Tantra of the Wheel of Time
[Paramādibuddhoddhṛtaśrī]kālacakratantrarāja
[mChog gi dang po'i sangs rgyas las phyung ba] rgyud kyi rgyal po dpal dus kyi 'khor lo
Dg.K. rGyud vol. *ka*, ff. 22b–128b; KPD, vol. 77, pp. 57–311; T 362.
Partially translated in Newman 1987 (chap. 1); and Wallace 2001 (chap. 2) and 2010 (chap. 4).

Tantra of Vajrakīla
rDo rje phur pa
A generic title for the texts contained in Dg. NGB vol. 13, no. 4; vol. 20, nos. 10–13; vol. 21, nos. 1–28; vol. 22, nos. 1–7; and the fragment contained in Dg.K. rGyud vol. *ca*, ff. 43b–45b; T 439.

Tantra of Vajrapāṇi in the Form Caṇḍa
Caṇḍamahāroṣanatantrarāja
dPal gtum po khro bo chen po'i rgyud kyi rgyal po [dpa' bo gcig pa]
Dg.K. rGyud 'bum vol. *nga*, ff. 304b–343a; KPD, vol. 80, pp. 889–1009; T 431.

Tantra of Vajrapāṇi in the Form Mahācakra
Phyag na rdo rje 'khor chen rgyud
GDKT vol. 8, no. 46.

Tantra Requested by Devendra
Lha'i dbang pos zhus pa
NL.

Tantra Requested by Four Goddesses
Caturdevīparipṛcchātantra
Lha mo bzhis yongs su zhus pa'i rgyud
Dg.K. rGyud 'bum vol. *ca*, ff. 277b–281b; KPD, vol. 81, pp. 946–61; T 446.

Verse Summation of the Transcendent Perfection of Wisdom
Prajñāpāramitāsañcayagāthā
Shes rab kyi pha rol tu phyin pa sdud pa tshigs su bcad pa
Dg.K. Shes phyin vol. *ka*, ff. 1b–19b; KPD, vol. 34, pp. 3–44; T 13.
Summarized in PZ, p. 412. Translated in Conze 1973.

3. Treatises of Indic Origin

Abhayadattaśrī

Narrative of the Eighty-Four Great Accomplished Masters
Caturaśītisiddhapravṛtti
Grub thob brgyad cu rtsa bzhi'i lo rgyus
TPD vol. 48, pp. 413–556.
Translated in Robinson 1979.

Pith Instruction Entitled Precious Garland
Ratnamālā
Man ngag rin chen 'phreng ba
TPD vol. 48, pp. 671–74.

Abhayadattaśrī with Vīraraśmi

The Essence of the Realizations of the Eighty-Four Accomplished Masters and Their Significance
Grub thob brgyad cu rtsa bzhi'i rtogs pa'i snying po dang de'i don 'grel
TPD vol. 48, pp. 562–667.

Advayavajra (also known as Maitrīpā)

Rite of the Means for Attainment of Vajravārāhī
Vajravārāhīkalpasarvārthasādhana
rDo rje phag mo'i sgrub thabs kyi cho ga don thams cad grub pa
Dg.T. rGyud vol. *'a*, ff. 9b–10a; TPD, vol. 24, pp. 788–90; T 1578.
One of the *Six Texts concerning Vajravārāhī* (*Phag mo'i gzhung drug*); an antecedent of Guidebook 75.

The Twenty-Four Doctrinal Cycles of Nonmentation
Amansikāra (also known as Advayavajrasaṃgraha)
Yid la mi byed pa/A ma na si'i chos bskor nyi shu rtsa bzhi/drug
Dg.T. rGyud vol. *wi*, ff. 104b–177a; TPD, vol. 26, pp. 288–523; T 2229–54.
They are variously said to number twenty-four, twenty-five, or twenty-six, the last enumeration including the supplementary *Four Doctrines Exhorted by Injunction* (*bKa' yis bskul ba'i chos bzhi*). The complete cycle is translated in Mathes 2015.

Ajitamitraguptya (also known as Jetāri)

Instruction on Cheating Death
Si tao bi jiao xun (Chinese)
'Chi ba slu ba'i gdams pa
Dg.T. rGyud vol. *na*, ff. 180b–181a; TPD, vol. 37, pp. 650–52; T 2839.

Amoghavajra, Lalitavajra, and Mañjuśrīmitra

The Nocturnal Motion
mTshan mo rgyu ba
NL.

Ānandavajra

The Direct Guidance of Hevajra
Kye rdo rje'i dmar khrid
Guidebook 35

Glorious Hevajra
Śrīhevajra-nāma-sādhanopadeśa
dPal kye'i rdo rje'i sgrub thabs zhes bya ba'i man ngag
Dg.T. rGyud vol. *ta*, ff. 205b–209a; TPD, vol. 5, pp. 1512–22; T 1302.
Antecedent to Guidebook 35.

Anon

[Instruction Entitled] Oral Discussion
[Khrid yig] gsung sgros ma
NL.

Āryadeva

Esoteric Instructions of the Transcendent Perfection of Wisdom
Shes rab kyi pha rol du phyin pa'i man ngag (also known as *Fifty-Verse Poem*, Tshigs su bcad pa lnga bcu pa; or *Great Poem*, Tshigs bcad chen mo)
Translated in Jamgön Kongtrul 2016, 3–11.

Guidance on the Four Yogas
rNal 'byor bzhi khrid
NL.

Asaṅga

Level of the Pious Attendants
Śrāvakabhūmi
Nyan thos kyi sa
Dg.T. Sems tsam vol. *dzi*, ff. 1b–195a; TPD, vol. 73, pp. 3–522; T 4036.

Level of the Bodhisattvas
Bodhisattvabhūmi
Byang chub sems dpa'i sa
Dg.T. Sems tsam vol. *wi*, ff. 1b–213a; TPD, vol. 73, pp. 525–1094; T 4037.
Translated in Ārya Asaṅga 2016.

Atiśa

Guidebook Entitled White Tārā
sGrol dkar gyi khrid yig
Guidebook 28

Instruction on Long Life through the Virtuous Lady Cintāmaṇicakra according to the Pure Tradition of Glorious Dīpaṃkara: A Basket of Nectar
dGe ba can ma yid bzhin 'khor lo'i tshe khrid dpal ldan mar me mdzod kyis lugs gtsang lam 'dres pa bdud rtsi'i za ma tog

GDKT vol. 4, pp. 569–98.
Antecedent to Guidebook 28.

Lamp for the Path of Enlightenment
Bodhipathapradīpa
Byang chub lam gyi sgron ma
Dg.T. Jo bo'i chos 'byung, ff. 1b–4b; TPD, vol. 64, pp. 1641–49; T 4465.
Translated in Sherbourne 2000, 328–45.

Mind Training of the Great Vehicle
Theg chen blo sbyong
DNZ vol. 3, pp. 405–28.
Translated with annotations in Jinpa 2006, 71–82; an antecedent of Guidebook 2.

Avadhūtipā
Means for Attainment of Sarvārthasiddhā
Sarvārthasiddhisādhana
Don thams cad grub pa zhes bya ba'i sgrub thabs
Dg.T. rGyud vol. *za*, ff. 202a–202b; TPD, vol. 12, pp. 597–600; T 1552.
One of the *Six Texts concerning Vajravārāhī* (*Phag mo'i gzhung drug*); an antecedent of Guidebook 75.

Buddhadatta
Rite of Burnt Offerings of Vajrayoginī
Vajrayoginīhomavidhi
rDo rje rnal 'byor ma'i sbyin sreg gi cho ga (also known as *Text on Burnt Offerings*, sByin sreg gi gzhung)
Dg.T. rGyud vol. *za*, ff. 208a–208b; TPD, vol. 12, pp. 621–23; T 1556.
Supplement to the *Six Texts concerning Vajravārāhī* (*Phag mo'i gzhung drug*); an antecedent of Guidebook 75.

Buddhajñānapāda
The Vital Essence of Liberation
Mukhāgama
Zhal lung grol ba'i thig le (also known as *The Oral Transmission of Buddhajñānapāda*)
Dg.T. rGyud vol. *di*, ff. 47a–52a; TPD, vol. 21, pp. 961–74; T 1859.

Candrakīrti
Autocommentary on the Introduction to Madhyamaka
Madhyamakāvatārabhāṣya
dBu ma la 'jug pa'i bshad pa
Dg.T. dBu ma vol. *'a*, ff. 220b–348a; TPD, vol. 60, pp. 600–928; T 3862.

Clarifying Lamp: [An Extensive Exegesis of the Tantra of the Secret Assembly]
Pradīpodyotana-nāma-ṭīkā

sGron ma gsal bar byed pa zhes bya ba'i rgya cher bshad pa
Dg.T. rGyud vol. *ha*, ff. 1b–201b; TPD, vol. 15, pp. 3–676; T 1785.

Dharmakīrti of Sumatra
The Leveling-Out of Conceptions
rTog pa 'bur 'joms
Translated in Jinpa 2006, 195–96.

Stages of the Heroic Mind
Sems dpa'i rim pa
Translated in Jinpa 2006, 177–94.

Dharmarakṣita
The Peacock's Neutralizing of Poison
rMa bya dug 'joms
Translated in Jinpa 2006, 155–70.

The Wheel of Sharp Weapons
mTshon cha 'khor lo
Translated in Jinpa 2006, 133–53.

Ghaṇṭāpāda
Coemergent Cakrasaṃvara
Sahajasamvarasādhana
bDe mchog lhan skyes sgrub thabs
Dg.T. rGyud vol. *wa*, ff. 233a–233b; TPD, vol. 11, pp. 594–96; T 1436.
An antecedent of Guidebook 34.

The Direct Guidance of Cakrasaṃvara
bDe mchog gi dmar khrid
Guidebook 34

Five Stages
Śrīcakrasamvarapañcakrama
[dPal 'khor lo sdom pa'i] rim pa lnga pa
Dg.T. rGyud vol. *wa*, ff. 224b–227a; TPD, vol. 11, pp. 578–92; T 1433.

Jālandharipā
Brief Exegesis of the Means for Attainment of Hevajra Entitled Pure Adamantine Lamp
Hevajrasādhanavajrapradīpa-nāma-ṭippaṇīśuddha
Kye rdo rje'i sgrub thabs kyi mdor bshad pa dag pa rdo rje sgron ma
Dg.T. rGyud vol. *nya*, ff. 73a–96a; TPD, vol. 5, pp. 209–358; T 1237.

Kamalaśīla
Three Stages of Meditation
Tribhāvanākrama
De kho na nyid bsdus pa'i dka' 'grel

Dg.T. dBu ma vol. *ki*, ff. 22a–68b; T 3915–17.
Antecedent of Guidebook 22.

Kālacakrapāda

The Aural Transmission of Kālacakrapāda: Pith Instructions of the Six-Branch Yoga
Ṣaḍaṅgayogopadeśa
[Dus zhabs snyan brgyud] sbyor ba yan lag drug gi man ngag
Dg.T. rGyud vol. *pa*, ff. 224a–226b; TPD, vol. 7, pp. 1413–21; T 1372; also contained in *DNZ* vol. 15, pp. 6–13; the primary source of Guidebook 40.

Guidebook Entitled the Six-Branch Yoga
sByor drug gi khrid
Guidebook 40

Kṛṣṇacārin

Inciting the Path of the Four Stages
Olapatituṣṭaya
Nag po rim bzhi'i khrid/lam slong
Dg.T. rGyud vol. *wa*, ff. 355b–358b; TPD, vol. 11, pp. 961–69; T 1451.
An antecedent of Guidebook 70.

Vital Essence of Spring
Vasantatilaka
Dg.T. rGyud vol. *wa*, ff. 298b–306b; TPD, vol. 11, pp. 817–38; T 1448.
An antecedent of Guidebook 70.

Kukuripā

Extremely Unelaborate [*Perfection Stage*]
Shin tu spros med
Probably a reference to his *Six Arrays of Esoteric Meaning* (Ṣaḍguhyārthadharavyūha, T 1664–69, and especially T 1665.

Luipā

Perfection Stage of Great Yoga
rNal 'byor chen po'i rdzogs rim
NL.

Maitreya

Distinction between Phenomena and Actual Reality
Dharmadharmatāvibhāga
Chos dang chos nyid rnam par 'byed pa
Dg.T. Sems tsam vol. *phi*, ff. 46b–49a; TPD, vol. 70, pp. 916–34; T 4022.
Translated in Jamgön Mipham 2004.

Distinction between the Middle and Extremes
Madhyāntavibhāga
dBus mtha' rnam par 'byed pa'i tshig le'u byas pa

Dg.T. Sems tsam vol. *phi*, ff. 40b–45a; TPD, vol. 70, pp. 902–13; T 4021.
Translated in Dharmachakra Translation Committee 2006.

Five Treatises of Maitreya
Byams chos sde lnga
Comprising the five individual works of Maitreya (T 3786, T 4020–22, T 4024)
Beijing: Mi rigs dpe skrun khang 1991; also Sichuan: Mi rigs dpe skrun khang 1992.

Ornament of Clear Realization
Abhisamayālaṃkāra-[nāma-prajñāpāramitopadeśaśāstrakārikā]
[Shes rab kyi pha rol tu phyin pa'i man ngag gi bstan bcos] mngon par rtogs pa'i rgyan
Dg.T. Shes phyin vol. *ka*, ff. 1b–13a; TPD, vol. 49, pp. 3–30; T 3786.
Translated in Conze 1954 and Khenchen Thrangu 2004.

Ornament of the Sutras of the Great Vehicle
[Mahāyāna]sūtrālaṃkārakārikā
[Theg pa chen po] mdo sde'i rgyan zhes bya ba'i tshig le'ur byas pa
Dg.T. Sems tsam vol. *phi*, ff. 1b–39a; TPD, vol. 70, pp. 805–90; T 4020.
Translated in Maitreyanātha and Āryāsaṅga 2004; Maitreya and Jamgön Mipham 2014; and (with the commentary of Mipham Rinpoche) in Jamgön Mipham 2018.

Supreme Continuum of the Great Vehicle
Mahāyānottaratantraśāstra
Theg pa chen po rgyud bla ma'i bstan bcos
Dg.T. Sems tsam vol. *phi*, ff. 54b–73a; TPD, vol. 70, pp. 935–79; T 4024.
Translated in Takasaki 1966; Arya Matreiya and Acarya Asanga 1985; Brunnhölzl 2014; and Charrier 2019.

Mitrayogin

The Adamantine Song of Chanting Meditation
Gyer sgom rdo rje'i glu
Translated in Jinpa 2006, 171–75.

Esoteric Instructions on Resting in the Nature of One's Own Mind: Spoken by Sublime Avalokita to the Great Accomplished Master Mitrayogin
Svacittaviśrāmopadeśapañcaviṃśatikāgāthā
'Phags pa spyan ras gzigs kyi grub chen mi tra dzo gi la gsungs pa'i rang gi sems nyid ngal gso'i man ngag (also known as *The Fourteen Quatrains on Resting in the Nature of Mind*, Ngal bso'i sha lo ka bcu bzhi pa)
Dg.T. rGyud vol. *tshi*, ff. 175b–176b; TPD, vol. 25, pp. 523–26; T 2129; also contained in *DNZ* vol. 16, pp. 497–523.
An antecedent of Guidebook 7.

Miscellaneous Authorship

The Seven Sections of Spiritual Attainment
Grub pa sde bdun
Dg.T. rGyud vol. *wi*, ff. 1b–70b; TPD, 26, pp. 3–191; T 2217–23.
These seven treatises are respectively by Saroruhavajra, Anaṅgavajra, Indrabhūti, Lakṣmīkara, Dārikapā, Cito, and Ḍombī Heruka.

The Six Essential Cycles
sNying po bskor drug
These comprise (i) the *Treasury of Spiritual Songs* (Do hā mdzod, T 2224) by Saraha, (ii) the *Establishment of the Four Seals* (Phyag rgya bzhi gtan la dbab pa, T 2225) by Nāgārjuna, the *Pith Instructions of the Inconceivable Stage* (bSam gyis mi khyab pa'i rim pa'i man ngag, T 2228) by Togtsepa, (iv) the *Purification of Mental Obscuration* (Sems kyi sgrib sbyong, T 1804) by Āryadeva; (v) the *Luminosity of Pristine Cognition* (Ye shes gsal ba, T 2226) by Devākaracandra, and (vi) the *Synthesis of Abiding* (gNas pa bsdus pa, T 2227) by Sahajavajra.

Nāgārjuna

Five Stages
Pañcakrama
Rim pa lnga pa
Dg.T. rGyud vol. *ngi*, ff. 45a–57b; TPD, vol. 18, pp. 129–60; T 1802.
See Tsongkhapa 2013.

Refutation of Disputed Topics
Vigrahavyāvartanī
rTsod pa zlog pa'i tshig le'ur byas pa
Dg.T. dBu ma vol. *tsa*, ff. 27a–29a; TPD, vol. 57, pp. 74–82; T 3828.

Sixty Verses on Reason
Yuktiṣaṣṭikā
Rigs pa drug cu pa
Dg.T. dBu ma vol. *tsa*, ff. 20b–22b; TPD, vol. 57, pp. 74–82; T 3825.

Nāropā

The Central Channel of the Perfection Stage
rDzogs rim rtsa dbu ma
An antecedent of Guidebook 67.

The Erect Penis of Bhairava
[Nā ro pa'i man ngag] mtshan ma gyen bsgrengs
NL; an antecedent of Guidebook 66.

The Six Doctrines of Nāropā
Ṣaḍdharmopadeśa
Nā ro chos drug gi man ngag (imparted by Tilopā)

Dg.T. rGyud vol. *zhi*, ff. 270a–271a; TPD, vol. 26, pp. 1725–29; T 2330.
Translated in Guenther 1963; an antecedent of Guidebook 76.

Vārāhī Khecarī of the Generation Stage
bsKyed pa'i rim pa phag mo mkha' spyod
Possibly related to T 1579; an antecedent of Guidebook 67.

Padmasambhava
The Gradual Path of Padmasambhava
Padma lam rim gyi khrid
Guidebook 105

The Uncommon Gradual Path of Sutra and Mantra regarding External Phenomena: A Heap of Gems
Phyi chos mdo sngags thun min gi lam rim rin chen spungs pa
NK vol. 82, pp. 137–72; also *DNZ* vol. 2, pp. 257–82.
An antecedent of Guidebook 105.

Padmavajra (also known as Saroruha)
Like the Tip of a Lamp Flame: [An Instruction concerning Glorious Hevajra]
[dPal kyes rdo rje'i] mar me'i rtse mo lta bu'i gdams pa
Dg.T. rGyud vol. *nya*, ff. 19a–20b; TPD, vol. 5, pp. 52–56.

Method for Accomplishment [of Glorious Hevajra]
Śrīhevajrasādhana
[dPal dgyes pa rdo rje'i] sgrub thabs
Dg.T. rGyud vol. *nya*, ff. 1b–7a; TPD, vol. 5, pp. 3–17.

Puṇḍarīka
Commentary on the Tantra of the Wheel of Time [Entitled Taintless Light]
Vimalaprabhānāmamūlatantrānusāriṇīdvādaśasāhasrikālaghukālacakratantra-rājaṭīkā
bsDus pa'i rgyud kyi rgyal po dus kyi 'khor lo'i 'grel bshad rtsa ba'i rgyud kyi rjes su 'jug pa stong phrag bcu gnyis pa dri ma med pa'i 'od, also known as Dus 'khor 'grel chen; also 'grel chen
Dg.K. Dus 'khor 'grel bshad vol. *śrī*, ff. 1b–469a; KPD, vol. 99, pp. 3–815; T 845.
Skt. ed. in Jagannatha Upadhyaya, Bibliotheca Indo-Tibetica, vols. 11–13. Sarnath, Varanasi: Central Institute of Higher Tibetan Studies, 1986. See Khedrup Norsang Gyatso 2004.

Ratnarakṣita
Practical Guidance on the Five Stages
Rim lnga lag khrid
Possibly related to his magnum opus, Śrīsaṃvarodayamahātantrarāja-nāma-pañjikā.

Śabaripā Wangchuk

Means for Attainment of Vajrayoginī
rDo rje rnal 'byor ma'i sgrub thabs
Dg.T. rGyud vol. *za*, ff. 197a–199a; TPD, vol. 12, pp. 580–86; T 1550.
An antecedent of Guidebook 75.

Pith Instruction of the Great Seal Entitled Treasury of Spiritual Songs
Do hā mdzod ces bya ba phyag rgya chen po'i man ngag
Dg.T. rGyud vol. *zhi*, ff. 122a–124a; TPD, vol. 26, 1266–72 (attributed to Saraha); also in *DNZ* vol. 7, pp. 28–33.

[*Pith Instructions of the Short Lineage of the Wheel of Time Entitled*] *Six-Branch Yoga*
Yogaṣaḍaṅga
[Dus 'khor nye brgyud kyi man ngag] yan lag drug pa
Dg.T. rGyud vol. *pa*, ff. 251a–251b; TPD, vol. 7, pp. 1488–90; T 1375; also in *DNZ* vol. 15, pp. 13–14; related to Guidebook 40.

Śākyaśrī

Six Adamantine Verses
rDo rje'i tshig drug

Śāntarakṣita

Incantation Rite of the Extraordinarily Vast Aspiration of the Seven Sugatas Compiled from the Sutra
De bzhin gshegs pa bdun gyi sngon gyi smon lam gyi khyad par rgyas pa'i mdo sde bklag cing de bzhin gshegs pa bdun mchod de smon lam gdab pa'i cho ga mdo sde las btus te rim par bklag pa
Dg.T. rGyud vol. *pu*, ff. 295b–301b; TPD, vol. 38, pp, 863–934; T 3134.

Śāntideva

Compendium of Lessons
Śikṣāsamuccaya
bsLab pa kun las btus pa
Dg.T. dBu ma vol. *khi*, ff. 3a–194b; TPD, vol. 64, pp. 1009–1519; T 3940.
Translated in Santideva 1971.

Introduction to the Conduct of a Bodhisattva
Bodhisattvacaryāvatāra
Byang chub sems dpa'i spyod pa la 'jug pa
Dg.T. dBu ma vol. *la*, ff. 1b–40a; TPD, vol. 61, pp. 951–1048; T 3871.
Translated in Shantideva 1997; commentary in Kunzang Pelden 2007.

Stanzas of the Compendium of Lessons
Śikṣāsamuccayakārikā
bsLab pa kun las btus pa'i tshig le'u byas pa
Dg.T. dBu ma, vol. *khi*, ff. 1b–3a; TPD, vol. 64, pp. 1005–8; T 3939.

Saharа

Introduction to the Innate
gNyug ma ngo sprod
NL.

The Spiritual Songs of the King
Dohākośa-nāma-caryāgīti
Do ha mdzod ces bya ba spyod pa'i glu (also known as rGyal po'i do hā)
Dg.T. rGyud vol. *zhi*, ff. 26b–28b; TPD, vol. 26, pp. 1013–19; T 2263.
Translated in Guenther 1993.

The Spiritual Songs of the Populace
Dohākośagīti
Do ha mdzod kyi glu (also known as dMangs kyi do hā)
Dg.T. rGyud vol. *wi*, ff. 70b–77a; TPD, vol. 26, pp. 193–208; T 2224; also in *DNZ* vol. 7, pp. 7–22.
Translated in Guenther 1993.

The Spiritual Songs of the Queen
Dohākośopadeśagīti
Mi zad pa'i gter mdzod man ngag gi glu (also known as rGyal mo'i do hā)
Dg.T. rGyud vol. *zhi*, ff. 28b–33b; TPD, vol. 26, pp. 1020–34; T 2264.
Translated in Guenther 1993.

Trilogy of Spiritual Songs
Do ha skor gsum
Comprising *The Spiritual Songs of the King* (T 2263), *The Spiritual Songs of the Queen* (T 2264), and *The Spiritual Songs of the Populace* (T 2224).

Smṛtijñānakīrti

Esoteric Mañjuśrī
Mañjuśrīguhyaka
'Jam dpal gsang ldan
This includes both the *Means for Attainment* (T 2585) and its *Commentary* (T 2584).
Dg.T. rGyud vol. *ngu*, ff. 107b–151a; TPD, vol. 33, pp. 360–479.

Śrīdhara

Four-Stage Yoga of Red Yamāri
Svādiṣṭhānacaturyogatattvopadeśa
rNal 'byor bzhi'i de kho na nyid ces bya ba rang byin gyis brlabs pa'i man ngag (also known as gShed dmar rnal 'byor bzhi)
Dg.T. rGyud vol. *tsi*, ff. 110b–113b; TPD, vol. 24, pp. 1114–22; T 2025.

Śrīmatī

Means for Attainment of Decapitated Vajravārāhī
Chinnamuṇḍāvajravārāhīsādhana

rDo rje phag mo dbu bcad ma'i sgrub thabs
Dg.T. rGyud vol. *za*, ff. 205a–206a; TPD, vol. 12, pp. 609–12; T 1554.
One of the *Six Texts concerning Vajravārāhī* (*Phag mo'i gzhung drug*); an antecedent of Guidebook 75.

Śūnyatāsamādhi[vajra] (also known as Śabaripā)
Attainment of the Pristine Cognition of the Real
Tattvajñānasiddhi
De kho na nyid ye shes yang dag par grub pa
Dg.T. rGyud vol. *za*, ff. 199a–202a; TPD, vol. 12, pp. 587–96; T 1551.
Sanskrit text in Pandey 2000. This is one of the *Six Texts concerning Vajravārāhī* (*Phag mo'i gzhung drug*); an antecedent of Guidebook 75

Means for Attainment of Jowo Bhugama
Jo bo bhugama'i sgrub thabs
NL.

Transference of Pristine Cognition
Jñānāveśa
Ye shes 'pho ba
Dg.T. rGyud vol. *za*, ff. 202b–204b; TPD, vol. 12, pp. 601–8; T 1553.
One of the *Six Texts concerning Vajravārāhī* (*Phag mo'i gzhung drug*); an antecedent of Guidebook 75.

Śūra
Garland of Birth Stories
Jātakamālā
sKyes pa'i rabs kyi rgyud
Dg.T. sKyes rabs, vol. *hu*, ff. 1b–135a; TPD, vol. 94, pp. 3–385; T 4150.
Translated in Āryasūra 1895.

Vāgīśvaragupta
Pith Instruction of Nondual Meditative Concentration of Glorious Cakrasaṃvara Entitled Fierce Inner Heat of Yoga
dPal 'khor lo sdom pa'i gnyis su med pa'i bsam gtan gyi man ngag rnal 'byor gyi gtum mo
Dg.T. rGyud vol. *zha*, ff. 274b–275b; TPD, vol. 11, pp. 1775–77; T 1508.

Vajrahāsya
Array of the Staircase Differentiating the Stages
Rim par phye ba'i them bkod
NL.

Vasubandhu
Treasury of Phenomenology
Abhidharmakośakārikā

Chos mngon pa'i mdzod kyi tshig le'ur byas pa
Dg.T. mNgon pa vol. *ku*, ff. 1b–25a; TPD, vol. 79, pp. 3–59; T 4089.
Translated from the French in Vasubandhu 1988–90.

Virūpa
Means for Attainment of Decapitated Vajravārāhī
Chinnamuṇḍāsādhana
dBu bcad ma'i sgrub thabs
Dg.T. rGyud vol. *za*, ff. 206a–208a; TPD, vol. 12, pp. 613–20; T 1555.
One of the *Six Texts concerning Vajravārāhī* (*Phag mo'i gzhung drug*); an antecedent of Guidebook 75.

Root Verses of the Path and Its Fruition
gSung ngag rin po che lam 'bras bu dang bcas pa'i gzhung rdo rje'i tshig rkang
DNZ vol. 5, pp. 1–11.
An antecedent of Guidebook 43.

4. Tibetan Treatises and Spiritual Revelations

Akhu Ching Sherab Gyatso
Continuing Explanation of the Perfection Stage of Vajrapāṇi in the Form Mahācakra
Phyag rdor 'khor chen gyi rdzogs rim rtsom 'phro
Collected Works of Akhu Ching Sherab Gyatso, vol. 2, pp. 837–46.
Lhasa: Zhol par khang, 1998.

Anon.
Cycle That Adopts the Calmness of Visualization
dMigs pa'i zhi ba len lo bskor ma
NL.

Kurakma: The Secret Attainment of Mahākāla with One Cakra
'Khor lo gcig ma gsang sgrub sku rags ma
Drigungpa Anthology vol. 92, pp. 177–88.

Ritual Application of the Razor Cut
sPu gri so 'debs kyi las sbyor (also known as Caturmukha'i zhal gdams snying gi dum bu)
NL.

Secret Attainment of Kurakma with Two Cakras
sKu rags ma 'khor lo gnyis ma'i gsang bsgrub
Drigungpa Anthology vol. 92, pp. 259–86.

Secret Attainment That Reveals the Oral Instruction of Glorious Mahākāla with Three Channels and Four Cakras

dPal nag po chen po'i zhal gyi gdams pa rtsa gsum 'khor lo bzhi la bstan pa'i gsang sgrub
Drigungpa Anthology vol. 92, pp. 315–30.

Uncommon Oral Instruction of Guidance on Mahākāla with Five Cakras
'Khor lo lnga ma'i khrid yig zhal gdams thun mong ma yin pa
Drigungpa Anthology vol. 92, pp. 331–48.

Barawa Gyeltsen Pelzang
Fourfold Cycle of the Mother of Space
Ma nam mkha' ma bzhi skor
This work has not yet been identified in the *Collected Works of Barawa Gyeltsen Pelzang*. 14 vols. Dehradun: Ngawang Lungtok and Ngawang Gyaltsen, 1970.

Guidance on Amitāyus according to the Tradition of Siddhirājñī
Grub pa'i rgyal mo'i lugs kyi tshe khrid
NL. An antecedent to Guidebook 27.

Profound Guidance on the Generation and Perfection Stages of Amitāyus according to the Tradition of Siddhirājñī: Ocean of Deathless Nectar
Tshe dpag med grub pa'i rgyal mo lugs kyi bskyed rdzogs zab khrid kyi yi ge 'chi med bdud rtsi'i chu gter
Drukpa Kagyu Anthology vol. 23, pp. 506–66. Related to Guidebook 27.

Bodongpa Chole Namgyal
Collected Works of Bodongpa Chole Namgyal
Bo dong phyogs las rnam rgyal gyi gsung 'bum
137 vols. New Delhi: Tibet House, 1969–81.

Cornucopia Clarifying the Essential Doctrinal Practices of the Glorious Summation of the Real
dPal de kho nyid 'dus pa'i snying po chos spyod rab tu gsal ba'i snye ma
Collected Works, vol. 119, pp. 1–715; also Beijing: dPal brtsegs bod yig dpe rnying zhib 'jug khang, 2012.

Elucidation of All the Concealed Meanings of Yogatantra
sBas don kun gsal
Collected Works, vol. 71, pp. 417–503. An antecedent of Guidebook 26.

Summation of the Real
De kho nyid 'dus pa
This corpus comprising the main tantra sections of Bodongpa's massive *Collected Works* forms the antecedent of Guidebook 26.

Buton Rinchen Drub
History of Buddhism
Bu ston chos 'byung gsung rab rin po che'i mdzod

Xining: mTsho sngon mi rigs dpe skrun khang, 1988.
Translated in Butön Rinchen Drup 2013 by Lisa Stein and Ngawang Zangpo; partial translation by Eugene Obermiller in Bu-ston Rin-chen-grub 1932.

Scriptural Quotations from the Sutras and Tantras concerning the Root Text of the Great Seal: Resting in the Nature of Mind
Phyag rgya chen po sems nyid ngal gso'i rtsa ba mdo yi lung dang sbyar ba
DNZ vol. 16, pp. 553–65. These pertain to Guidebook 8.

Chak Lotsāwa Chojé Pel
Guidebook Entitled White Amitāyus
Tshe dpag med dkar po'i khrid yig
Guidebook 29

Chak Lotsāwa Rinchen Chogyel
Guidebook Entitled Vārāhī in the Form Kurmapādā
Phag mo kurma pā da'i khrid (also known as Chag lugs kyi phag mo ser mo kurma pā da'i khrid)
Guidebook 38

Chekhawa Yeshé Dorjé
Seven-Point Mind Training
bLo sbyong don bdun ma
Translated in Jinpa 2006, 83–85; an antecedent of Guidebook 2.

Chel Amogha
Guidebook Entitled White Cakrasaṃvara
bDe mchog dkar po'i khrid
Guidebook 71

Chel Kunga Dorjé
Guidebook Entitled the Six Meditations of Vajravārāhī
Phag mo sgom drug gi khrid yig
Guidebook 75

Chen Nga Nyernyipa Chokyi Gyelpo
Guidebook Entitled the Fivefold Great Seal
Phyag rgya chen po lnga ldan gyi khrid
DNZ vol. 10, pp. 21–23.
Guidebook 84

Jewel Garland Illuminating the Fivefold Great Seal
Phyag rgya chen po lnga ldan gsal byed nor bu'i phreng ba
Drigungpa Anthology vol. 49, pp. 1–36. Primary source of Guidebook 84.

Chim[chen] Namka Drak
Excellent Path of the Three Sorts of Person

sKyes bu gsum gyi lam legs pa
Kadampa Anthology II vol. 47, pp. 227–66. Primary source of Guidebook 9.

Four Deities of Kadam: Munīndra, Avalokiteśvara, Acala, and Tārā
bKa' gdams lha bzhi'i khrid yig
Contained in *Instructions of the Four Deities of Kadam: Essential Fusion of the Path of Sutra and Mantra*
bKa' gdams lha bzhi'i khrid kyi yi ge mdo sngags lam gyi bcud 'dus
DNZ vol. 4, pp. 367–433.
Guidebooks 14–17

Guidance on the Middle Way
dBu ma'i khrid
Kadampa Anthology II vol. 17, pp. 171–208.

Guidebook Entitled Sameness of Existence and Quiescence
Srid zhi mnyam nyid kyi khrid yig
Guidebook 11

Guidebook Entitled the Sequence of the Buddhist Teaching
bsTan rim gyi khrid yig
Guidebook 10

Guidebook Entitled the Three Sorts of Person
sKyes bu gsum gyi khrid yig
Guidebook 9

Choku Śākya Rinchen
Guidebook Entitled the Direct Guidance of Avalokiteśvara according to the Tradition of Kyergangpa
dMar khrid skyer sgang pa'i lugs kyi khrid yig
DNZ vol. 17, pp. 8–19.
Guidebook 33

Chomden Rikpei Reldri
Flower Ornament Commentary on the Distinction between Phenomena and Reality
Chos dang chos nyid rnam par 'byed pa'i rgyan gyi me tog
Collected Works of Chomden Rikpei Reldri, vol. 5, pp. 669–96.
Lhasa: Khams sprul bsod nams don grub, 2006. A primary source of Guidebook 23.

Flower Ornament Commentary on the Distinction between the Middle and Extremes
dBus mtha' rnam 'byed rgyan gyi me tog
NL. A primary source of Guidebook 23.

Flower Ornament Commentary on the Ornament of Clear Realization
mNgon rtogs rgyan gyi 'grel pa'i rgyan gyi me tog
Kadampa Anthology III vol. 63, pp. 21–648. A primary source of Guidebook 23.

Flower Ornament Commentary on the Supreme Continuum
rGyud bla ma'i rgyan gyi me tog
Kadampa Anthology III vol. 62, pp. 751–80. A primary source of Guidebook 23.

Flower Ornament of Exegesis on the Ornament of the Sutras of the Great Vehicle
mDo sde rgyan gyi rnam par bshad pa rgyan gyi me tog
Kadampa Anthology III vol. 61, pp. 415–66. A primary source of Guidebook 23.

Flower Ornament of the Tales of Past Lives
sKyes rabs rgyan gyi me tog
Kadampa Anthology II vol. 51, pp. 349–592.

Guidebook Entitled [Cultivation of] the Five Doctrines of Maitreya
Byams pa'i chos lnga'i [sgom] khrid
Guidebook 23

Dakchen Dorjé Chang Lodro Gyeltsen
Elucidation of the Symbolic Meaning
brDa' don gsal ba'i khrid yig bdag chen rdo rje 'chang gis mdzad pa
DNZ vol. 5, pp. 433–57. Related to Guidebook 61.

Memorandum on the Pith Instruction Entitled the Exegesis of the Concealed Path
Lam sbras te bshad pa man ngag gi zin bris
DNZ vol. 5, pp. 425–31. Related to Guidebook 60.

Dakpo Rabjampa Tashi Namgyal
Elucidation on the Sequence of Meditation according to the Great Seal of Definitive Meaning Entitled Moonbeams of Eloquence
Nges don phyag rgya chen po'i sgom rim gsal bar byed pa'i legs bshad zla ba' 'od zer
Translated in Dakpo Tashi Namgyal 2006 by Lobsang P. Lhalungpa; also Callahan 2019.

Dalai Lama V Ngawang Lobzang Gyatso
The Extensive Pronouncements and Profound Revelations of the Ancient Way of Secret Mantra
gSang sngags snga' 'gyur gyi rgya che ba bka' ma dang zab pa gter ma gnyis kyi skor
Collected Works, vol. 2, pp. 224–92.
Beijing: Krung go'i bod rig pa dpe skrun khang, 2009.

Dawa Sengé

Connecting Exegesis of the Rites of Service and Attainment Entitled Wish-Fulfilling Gem
bsNyen sgrub kyi 'brel bshad yid bzhin nor bu
DNZ vol. 15, pp. 511–74. Primary source of Guidebook 42.

Guidebook Entitled the Ritual Service and Attainment of the Three Adamantine Realities according to Orgyanpa
O rgyan bsnyen sgrub kyi khrid
Guidebook 42

Dra Gadenpa

The Fivefold Capacity of Lorepa
Thub pa lnga ldan gyi khrid
Guidebook 99

Drakmar Kunga Tsepel

Guidebook Entitled the Vital Essence of Liberation
Grol ba'i thig le'i khrid
Guidebook 63

Memorandum on the Vital Essence of Liberation
Grol thig gi zin bris
NL. One of two primary sources for Guidebook 63.

Drakpa Gyeltsen

Analysis of Empowerment
dBang gi rab dbye
SLC vol. 11, pp. 41–43.

Array of the Seats of the Syllables
Yi ge gdan bkod
Collected Works, vol. 3, pp. 410–36. A primary source of Guidebook 67.

The Attainment in Proximity to a Stupa Attributed to Master Nāgārjuna
sLob dpon klu sgrub kyis mdzad pa'i mchod rten drung thob
DNZ vol. 6, pp. 59–65, with its commentary on pp. 189–212. Primary source of Guidebook 51.

The Attainment of Coemergence Attributed to Ḍombī Heruka
Dombi he ru kas mdzad pa'i lhan cig skyes grub
DNZ vol. 6, pp. 7–17, with its commentary on pp. 137–50. Primary source of Guidebook 46.

Collected Works of Drakpa Gyeltsen
rJe btsun grags pa rgyal mtshan gyi gsung rab
5 vols.
Beijing: Krung go'i bod rig pa dpe skrun khang, 2007.

The Cycle of the Path of the Female Mudra Attributed to Master Indrabhūti
sLob dpon indra bhū ti'i mdzad pa'i phyag rgya'i lam skor
DNZ vol. 6, pp. 119–36, with its commentary on pp. 255–69. Primary source of Guidebook 49.

Eight Further Cycles of the Path
Lam skor phyi ma brgyad
Collective name for Guidebooks 44–51 (which are listed separately in this section).

Elixir of the Buddha Mind of Nāropā
Nā ro pa'i thugs kyi nying khu (also known as *Guidance on the Central Channel*, rTsa dbu ma'i khrid)
SK vol. 8, pp. 151–79. A primary source for Guidebook 67.

Elucidation of the Five Stages [according to Ghaṇṭāpāda]
Rim pa lnga'i gsal byed
Collected Works, vol. 3, pp. 242–63. A primary source of Guidebook 69.

Generation Stage Adorned with Nine Profound Methods Attributed to Master Padmavajra
sLob dpon padma badzra gyis mdzad pa'i bskyed rim zab pa'i tshul dgus brgyan pa
DNZ vol. 6, pp. 19–41, and its commentary on pp. 151–80. Primary source of Guidebook 45.

The Great Seal Devoid of Letters, Attributed to Master Vāgīśvarakīrti
sLob dpon ngag dbang grags pas mdzad pa'i phyag rgya chen po yi ge med pa
DNZ vol. 6, pp. 67–79, with its commentary on pp. 213–29. This is the primary source of Guidebook 50.

Guidebook Entitled Kurukullā
Ku ru kulle'i khrid
Guidebook 39

Guidebook Entitled the Attainment in Proximity to a Stupa
mChod rten drung thob kyi khrid (also known as *The Determination of Mind*, Sems mtha' gcod pa)
Guidebook 51

Guidebook Entitled the Attainment of Coemergence
Lhan cig skyes grub kyi khrid
Guidebook 46

Guidebook Entitled the Central Channel Dependent on the Female Deity Vajravārāhī
Yum la brten nas rtsa dbu ma'i khrid yig (also known as *The Central Channel*

of Khecarī, mKha' spyod dbu ma, or *The Central Channel according to the Perfection Stage*, rDzogs pa'i rim pa rtsa dbu ma)
Guidebook 68

Guidebook Entitled the Central Channel Dependent on the Male Deity Cakrasaṃvara
Yab la brten nas rtsa dbu ma'i khrid yig
Guidebook 67

Guidebook Entitled the Great Seal Devoid of Letters
Phyag rgya chen po yi ge med pa'i khrid
Guidebook 50

Guidebook Entitled the Inconceivables
bSam mi khyab kyi khrid
Guidebook 44

Guidebook Entitled the Nine Profound Methods
Zab pa'i tshul dgu'i khrid yig
Guidebook 45

Guidebook Entitled the Path of the Female Mudra
Phyag rgya'i lam khrid
Guidebook 49

Guidebook Entitled the Perfection of the Path of Fierce Inner Heat
gTum mo lam rdzogs kyi khrid
Guidebook 47

Guidebook Entitled the Straightening of Crooked Posture
Yol po bsrang ba'i khrid
Guidebook 48

Instruction on the Straightening of Crooked Posture, Attributed to Acyutakāṇha
Nag po u tsi ta 'chi ba med pas mdzad pa yon po srong ba'i gdams pa
DNZ vol. 6, pp. 55–57, with its commentary on pp. 181–88. Primary source of Guidebook 48.

Oral Instruction of the Inconceivables, Attributed to Glorious Khanitra
dPal tog tse ba'i bsam gyis mi khyab gyi gdams ngag
DNZ vol. 6, pp. 81–118, with commentary on pp. 231–54. Primary source of Guidebook 44.

Perfection of the Path of Fierce Inner Heat, Attributed to Master Kṛṣṇacārin
sLob dpon nag po spyod pas mdzad pa'i gtum mo lam rdzogs
DNZ vol. 6, pp. 43–53, with its commentary on pp. 271–87. Primary source of Guidebook 47.

Root Verses of the Account of Sachen Kunga Nyingpo's Encounter with Mañjughoṣa
'Jam dbyangs dang sa chen 'jal ba'i lo rgyus rtsa tshig
DNZ vol. 6, p. 310; also in *Collected Works*, vol. 5, p. 331.
Translated in Jinpa 2006, 517; an antecedent of Guidebook 1.

Secret Guidance of Kurukullā
Ku ru kulle'i gsang khrid
Collected Works, vol. 3, pp. 488–92.
Primary source of Guidebook 39.

Songs of Meditative Experience
rJe btsun gyi nyams mgur rnams
Seven sacred songs in the genre of *rnyams dbyangs* or *mgur*.
Collected Works, vol. 5, pp. 335–50.
An antecedent of Guidebook 1.

Versified Instruction on Parting from the Four Attachments
rJe btsun rin po che grags pa rgyal mtshan gyi khrid yig tshigs bcad ma
DNZ vol. 6, pp. 310–14; also in *Collected Works*, vol. 5, pp. 331–35.
Translated in Jinpa 2006, 519–23; an antecedent of Guidebook 1.

Yogic Exercises of the Thirty-Two Activities
Phrin las sum cu rtsa gnyis ky̥i 'khrul 'khor
SLC vol. 10, pp. 293–97.

Drampa Kunga Zangpo
Precious Liberation by Seeing: Coalescence of the Great Seal and Great Perfection
Phyag rdzogs zung 'jug nor bu mthong grol
RTD (Delhi ed.), vol. 60, pp. 149–54.
Antecedent of Guidebook 107.

Drogon Dungtso Repa
The Nature of Mind: The Wish-Fulfilling Gem
Sems khrid yid bzhin nor bu
Contained in *The Cycles of Thirteen Great Instructions of the Aural Lineage* (sNyan brgyud khrid chen bcu gsum skor), vol. 1, pp. 663–98. Katok 2004.
Antecedent of Guidebook 108.

Drogon Pelden Yeshé
Memorandum on the Mind Training of the Great Vehicle
Theg chen blo sbyong gi zin bris
Redaction of Guidebook 2.

Drokmi Lotsāwa Śākya Yeshé
Clear Recollection of the Innate State: A Pith Instruction Attributed to Vāgīśvarakīrti

sLob dpon ngag gi dbang phyug grags pa'i gnyug ma dran gsal
The sixth and last of Drokmi's *Spiritual Connections with the Six Gatekeepers* (sGos drug chos 'brel).
DNZ vol. 6, p. 296, line 7–p. 300, line 5. Primary source of Guidebook 57.

Dispelling of All Ailments That Agitate the Physical Elements: A Pith Instruction Attributed to Jñānaśrī
'Byung ba 'khrugs pa'i nad thams cad sel ba
The third of Drokmi's *Spiritual Connections with the Six Gatekeepers*, more specifically belonging to the cycle of the *Dispelling of the Three Obstacles* (Bar chad gsum sel).
DNZ vol. 6, p. 294–95. Primary source of Guidebook 54.

Dispelling of the Obstacles of Meditative Stability and Mind: A Pith Instruction Attributed to Guru Ratnavajra
bLa ma rin chen rdo rje'i ting nge 'dzin sems kyi bar chad sel ba'i man ngag
The fourth of Drokmi's *Spiritual Connections with the Six Gatekeepers*, more specifically belonging to the cycle of the *Dispelling of the Three Obstacles.*
DNZ vol. 6, p. 295. Primary source of Guidebook 55.

Dispelling of the Obstacles of External Demons: A Pith Instruction Attributed to Prajñākaragupta
Shes rab 'byung gnas sbas pa'i man ngag phyi rol gdon gyi bar chad sel ba
The second of Drokmi's *Spiritual Connections with the Six Gatekeepers*, more specifically belonging to the cycle of the *Dispelling of the Three Obstacles.*
DNZ vol. 6, pp. 293–94. Primary source of Guidebook 53.

Experiential Cultivation of the Mingling of Sutra and Tantra: A Pith Instruction Attributed to Guru Śāntipa
bLa ma śānti pa'i man ngag mdo rgyud bsre ba'i nyams len
The first of Drokmi's *Spiritual Connections with the Six Gatekeepers.*
DNZ vol. 6, pp. 290–93. Primary source of Guidebook 52.

Great Seal Dispelling the Three Sorts of Suffering: A Pith Instruction Attributed to Glorious Nāropā
dPal nā ro pa'i phyag rgya chen po sdug bsngal gsum sel
The fifth of Drokmi's *Spiritual Connections with the Six Gatekeepers.*
DNZ vol. 6, p. 300, line 5–p. 303, line 4. Primary source of Guidebook 56.

Guidebook Entitled the Clear Recollection of the Innate State
gNyug ma dran gsal gyi khrid yig
Guidebook 57

Guidebook Entitled the Dispelling of the Obstacles of External Demons
Phyi rol gdon gyi bar chad sel ba'i khrid yig
Guidebook 53

Guidebook Entitled the Dispelling of the Obstacles of Meditative Stability and Mind
Ting 'dzin sems kyi bar chad sel ba'i khrid yig
Guidebook 55

Guidebook Entitled the Dispelling of the Obstacles Due to Agitation by the Physical Elements
'Byung ba lus 'khrugs kyi bar chad sel ba'i khrid
Guidebook 54

Guidebook Entitled the Great Seal Dispelling the Three Sorts of Suffering
Phyag chen sdug bsngal gsum sel gyi khrid
Guidebook 56

Guidebook Entitled the Mingling of Sutra and Tantra
mDo rgyud bse ba'i khrid
Guidebook 52

Guidebook Entitled the Twenty-Nine Essential Visualizations of Self-Consecration
Rang byin rlabs kyi dmigs pa nyer dgu'i khrid
Guidebook 59

The Twenty-Nine Essential Visualizations of Self-Consecration
Rang byin rlabs kyi dmigs pa nyer dgu
SLC vol. 11, pp. 70–83. Primary source of Guidebook 59.

Drolungpa Lodro Jungné
The Great Sequence of the Buddhist Teaching
bsTan rim chen mo
A commentary on Atiśa's *Lamp for the Path of Enlightenment.*
Kadampa Anthology I vol. 4, p. 35–vol. 5, p. 322. A primary source of Guidebook 10.

Synopsis of the Gradual Path according to the Great Sequence of the Buddhist Teaching
bsTan rim chen mo'i don bsdu'am lam rim
Kadampa Anthology I vol. 5, pp. 243–323. A primary source of Guidebook 10.

Drubtob Ngodrub and Nyangrel Nyima Ozer
The Collected Injunctions of the King concerning Oṃ Maṇi Padme Hūṃ
Ma ṇi bka' 'bum
Translated in Trizin Tsering 2007. This work may not have reached its final form until the fifteenth century.

Dungkar Lobzang Trinle
Great Dictionary of Dungkar

Dung dkar tshig mdzod chen mo
Beijing: Krung go'i bod rig pa dpe skrun khang, 2002.

Dzimchen Gyeltsen Pelzang
Extensive Analysis of the Direct Guidance of Avalokiteśvara according to the Tradition of the Bodhisattva Candradhvaja
[Zla rgyal lugs gyi dmar khrid] rgyas par phye ba
NL.

Ga Lotsāwa
Heart Essence of Mahākāla
mGon po'i snying thig
Drigungpa Anthology vol. 92, pp. 365–78.

Means for Attainment of Glorious Four-Armed Jñānanātha Mahākāla with Two Cakras according to the Kurakma Indic Text
dPal ye shes mgon po phyag bzhi pa sku regs ma'i rgya gzhung dang 'khor lo gnyis ma'i sgrub thabs kyi khrid yig (also known as *Instruction on the Book with a Sash*, Be bum sku rags la gdams pa)
DNZ vol. 10, pp. 471–96.

Gampopa Sonam Rinchen
Collected Works of Gampopa Sonam Rinchen
Khams gsum chos kyi rgyal po mnyam med sgam po pa 'gro mgon bsod nams rin chen mchog gi gsung 'bum yid bzhin nor bu
4 vols. Kathmandu: Khenpo S. Tenzin and Lama T. Namgyal, 2000.

Defining Characteristics of Mind: Revelation of the Hidden
Sems kyi mtshan nyid gab pa mngon phyung ba
Collected Works, vol. 2, pp. 405–22. Kathmandu: Khenpo S. Tenzin and Lama T. Namgyal, 2000.

Synopsis of the Meditations of Sutra and Tantra
mDo sngags kyi sgom don bsdus pa
Collected Works, vol. 3, pp. 269–308. Kathmandu: Khenpo S. Tenzin and Lama T. Namgyal, 2000.

Gewa Gyeltsen
Memorandum on the Mental Focus on the Horns of Bhairava
Rwa rtse'i khrid yig gu zin bris
NL.

Gorampa Sonam Sengé
A Key to the Profound Essential Points: A Meditation Guide to Parting from the Four Attachments
bLo sbyong zhen pa bzhi bral gyi khrid yig zab don gnad kyi lde'u mig

Collected Works, vol. 8, pp. 316–25. Beijing: Krung go'i bod rig pa dpe skrun khang, 2013.
Translated in Jinpa 2006, 529–39.

Gotsangpa Gonpo Dorjé
Guidance of Profound Auspicious Circumstances
Zab mo rten 'brel gyi khrid
Drukpa Kagyu Anthology vol. 55, p. 530.

Gungru Sherab Zangpo
A General Description of the Four Stages
Rim bzhi spyir bstan
NL.

A Particular Exegesis of the Vital Essence of Spring
dPyid thig bye brag tu 'chad pa
NL.

Guru Chowang
Four Collections of the Guru
Gu ru zlum po bzhi
Collective name for the four-volume revelations of Guru Chowang, which have twenty aspects.

Guidebook Entitled the Six Doctrines according to the Sekharma Tradition
Chos drug sras mkhar ma
RTD vol. 55, pp. 1–134; and Drigungpa Anthology vol. 4, pp. 373–514. Primary source of Guidebook 88.

Introduction to the Path of Pristine Cognition, the Extracted Liturgy of the Preliminary Practices for Buddhasamāyoga according to the Yangti Class of the Great Perfection
rDzogs pa chen po yang ti sangs rgyas mnyam sbyor gyi sngon 'gro'i 'don cha zur du bkol ba ye shes lam 'jug
RTD vol. 59, no. 3, pp. 137–51.

Natural Arising Pristine Cognition Gathering and Elucidating the Instruction Manual of the Buddhasamāyoga according to the Yangti Class of the Great Perfection: Essence of All the Tantras, Transmissions, and Pith Instructions
rGyud lung man ngag thams cad kyi nying khu rdzogs pa chen po yang ti sangs rgyas mnyam sbyor gyi khrid yig 'dus shing gsal ba ye shes rang shar
RTD vol. 59, no. 2, pp. 51–136.

Opening of Pristine Cognition: A Tract concerning the Empowerment of the Expressive Power of Awareness of Buddhasamāyoga according to the Yangti Class of the Great Perfection, along with the Extensive Empowerments of the

Expressive Power of Awareness according to the Chiti Class and the Ordinary Class

rDzogs pa chen po yang ti sangs rgyas mnyam sbyor gyi rig pa'i rtsal dbang dang spyi ti dang thun mong ba'i rig pa'i rtsal dbang rgyas par bskur ba'i yi ge ye shes sgo 'byed

RTD vol. 59, no. 1, pp. 1–49.

[*Tantra of Union with All the Buddhas:*] *Total Liberation through Singular Knowledge*

[Sangs rgyas mnyam sbyor gyi rgyud] gcig shes kun grol (also known as sLob dpon padma'i sangs rgyas mnyam sbyor)

2 vols. Paro: Ugyen Tempai Gyaltsen, 1980; also Potala Archive, ms. ed., vol. 5, nos. 19–20 (dkar chags, p. 149); and RTD vol. 59, nos. 1–3.

Gyamapa Lodro Gyeltsen

Guidebook Entitled the Coemergent Union of the Great Seal

Lhan cig skyes sbyor gyi khrid (also known as *Memorandum on the Coemergent Union of the Great Seal*, Lhan cig skyes sbyor gyi zin bris)

Guidebook 83

Gyelwa Ten-né

Inconceivable Blessing

bSam mi khyab kyi byin rlabs

NL.

Gyelwa Yeshé

Instruction [*on the Direct Guidance of Avalokiteśvara according to the Tradition of Drubchen Tsembupa*]

[Grub chen tshem bu pa lugs kyi dmar khrid kyi] gdams pa

NL.

Hor Kabzhipa

Guidebook Entitled the Parables of Potowa

Po to ba'i dpe chos ngo sprod kyi khrid

Guidebook 18

Jamgön Kongtrul

All Requisite Quintessential Oral Instructions of the New and Ancient Traditions Useful for the Yoga of Retreat Sessions

Thun mtshams rnal 'byor la nye bar mkho ba gsar rnying gi gdams ngag snying po bsdus pa dgos pa kun tshangs

Treasury of Extensive Pronouncements, vol. 12, pp. 305–84.

Instruction on the View of Extrinsic Emptiness: Immaculate Moonlight of Adamantine Reality

gZhan stong dbu ma chen po'i lta khrid rdo rje'i zla ba dri ma med pa'i 'od zer

DNZ vol. 4, pp. 565–86.

Liturgy of the Means for Attainment and Empowerment Rite of the Sixteen Spheres Entitled Ornament of Compassionate Emanation
bKa' gdams thig le bcu drug gi sgrub thabs dbang bskur ba'i cho ga bklag la chog tu bsdebs pa thugs rje rnam par rol pa'i rgyan
DNZ vol. 4, pp. 283–315.

Treasury of Extensive Pronouncements
rGya chen bka' mdzod
20 vols. Paro: Lama Ngodrup at the order of Dilgo Khyentse Rinpoche, 1975–76.

Treasury of Instructions
gDams ngag mdzod
DNZ.

Treasury of Jamgön Kongtrul's Own Uncommon Revelations
Thun mong ma yin pa'i mdzod
These are all contained in RTD.

Treasury of Kagyu Mantras
bKa' brgyud ngag mdzod
8 vols. Paro: Lama Ngodrub and Sherab Drimey, 1982; 3 vols. Baijnath: Palpung Sungrab Patrun Khang, 2010.

Treasury of Knowledge
Shes bya kun khyab mdzod
3 vols. Beijing: Mi rigs dpe skrun khang. 1982.
Translated in 10 vols. Ithaca/Boston: Snow Lion Publications/Snow Lion, 1995–2012.

Treasury of Spiritual Revelations
Rin chen gter mdzod
RTD.

Jamyang Khyentsé Wangpo

The Direct Guidance of Avalokiteśvara according to the Tradition of the Nun Lakṣmī: The Swift Path Integrating the Essentials of Experiential Cultivation
Thugs rje chen po'i dmar khrid dpal mo lugs kyi nyams len snying por dril ba zung 'jug myur lam
DNZ vol. 17, pp. 22–25.

Quintessential Instruction Manual on the Generation and Perfection Stages of Glorious Kharamukha Cakrasaṃvara Entitled Vital Essence of Supreme Bliss
dPal 'khor lo bde mchog bong bu'i zhal can gyi bskyed rdzogs kyi khrid yig snying po dril ba bde chen thig le
Collected Works, vol. 7, pp. 263–80. Gangtok: Gonpo Tseten, 1977–80.

Quintessential Stages of Profound Guidance on the Sixteen Spheres according to Kadam Entitled the Boon of the Two Accomplishments
bKa' gdams thig le bcu drug gi zab khrid kyi rim pa snying por dril ba grub gnyis mchog sbyin
DNZ vol. 4, pp. 327–49.

Jamyang Khyentse Wangpo and Jamyang Loter Wangpo, eds.
Compendium of Sādhanas
sGrub thabs kun btus
Kangara, H.P. India: Indo-Tibetan Buddhist Literature Publisher and Dzongsar Institute for Advanced Studies, 1902. BDRC W23681.

Jamyang Loter Wangpo
The Delightful Way of the Sublime Essential Experiential Cultivation: The Direct Guidance of Mahākāruṇika according to the Tradition of the King
Thugs rje chen po'i dmar khrid rgyal po lugs kyi nyams len snying por dril ba 'phags pa dgyes pa'i lam srol
DNZ vol. 17, pp. 43–51.

Jamyang Sangyé Rinchen
The Treasure That Brings Forth Accomplishment
dNgos grub 'byung gter
NL.

Jang Pukpa Kunlek
Memorandum on the Vital Essence of Liberation
Grol thig gi zin bris
One of the two primary sources of Guidebook 63.

Jangchub Tsemo
Biography [of Lama Dampa Sonam Gyeltsen] Arraying the Physical Body with the Four Empowerments of Khecarī
mKha' spyod ma dbang bzhi lus sgrigs
A short text of this title is contained in the *Sakya Anthology of Khecarī*, vol. 2, pp. 265–66. Related to Guidebook 68.

Jangsem Dawa Gyeltsen
Guidebook Entitled the Great Middle Way
dBu ma chen po'i khrid yig
Guidebook 12

Jangsem Zhonu Gyelchok (also known as Konchok Bang of Bulé), and Mu Konchok Gyeltsen
Compendium of Eloquence on Mind Training
bLo sbyong legs bshad kun btus/'dus (also known as *The Great Collection*)
Translated in Jinpa 2006; an antecedent of Guidebook 2.

Jigmé Chokyi Dorjé
Great Anthology of Buddhist Icons according to the Tibetan Lineages
Bod brgyud nang bstan lha tshogs chen mo
Xining: Qinghai mi rigs dpe skrun khang, 2001.

Jigten Gonpo
Drops of Nectar: Sacred Teachings of Drigungtel
'Bri gung thel chos bdud rtsi'i thigs pa (also known as *Tenfold Doctrinal Instruction*, bCu chos gdams pa)
Drigungpa Anthology vol. 30, pp. 391–416.

Guidebook Entitled the Unique Enlightened Intention
dGongs pa gcig gi khrid (also known as *Forty-Seven Supplements to the One Hundred and Fifty Adamantine Teachings*, rDo rje gsung brgya lnga cu pa'i lhan thabs bzhi cu rtsa bdun)
Contained in *Root Text, Supplement, Summary, and Framework of Unique Enlightened Intention, the Sacred Doctrine of Glorious Drigungpa*, dPal 'bri gung pa'i dam chos dgongs pa gcig pa'i rtsa ba lhan thabs dag bcas pa'i gzhung chings khog dbub dang bcas pa.
DNZ vol. 9, pp. 395–401 (of pp. 369–408).
Translated in Roberts 2011, 390–95.
Guidebook 96

Revered Wheel of Vitality
Mos gus srog 'khor
Drigungpa Anthology vol. 96, pp. 193–206.

Six Adamantine Verses on Emptiness
sTong nyid rdo rje tshigs drug ma
Drigungpa Anthology vol. 47, pp. 528–45.

The Threefold Doctrine
gSum chos
Drigungpa Anthology vol. 30, pp. 323–32.

Jonang Kunpang Chenpo Mikyo Dorjé
Quintessential Commentary on the Six Branches
Yan lag drug gi 'grel pa snying po bsdus pa
DNZ vol. 15, pp. 1–14.

Karmapa Rangjung Dorjé
Guidance on the Ritual Service and Attainment of Orgyanpa
O rgyan snyan sgrub kyi khrid yig
NL.

Guidance on the Six Doctrines
Chos drug gi khrid
DNZ vol. 9, pp. 37–61.

Guidebook Entitled the Introduction to the Three Buddha Bodies
sKu gsum ngo sprod kyi khrid
Guidebook 86

The Indivisibility of Subtle Energy and Mind
rLung sems dbyer med
DNZ vol. 9, pp. 167–73.
An antecedent of Guidebook 87.

Instruction Manual of the Coemergent Union of the Great Seal
Phyag rgya chen po lhan cig skyes sbyor gyi khrid yig
DNZ vol. 9, pp. 1–16.
Translated in Roberts 2011, 153–68.

The Introduction to the Three Buddha Bodies
sKu gsum ngo sprod kyi khrid
DNZ vol. 9, pp. 231–45.
Primary source of Guidebook 86.

Molten Gold of the Six Doctrines
Chos drug gser zhun ma
DNZ vol. 9, pp. 17–37.
An antecedent of Guidebook 76.

Karmapa Wangchuk Dorjé
Memorandum on the Coemergent Union of the Great Seal Entitled Essential Clear Lamp
Phyag rgya chen po lhan cig skyes sbyor gyi khrid zin bris snying po gsal ba'i sgron me
DNZ vol. 9, pp. 71–105.

Khewang Rinchen Zangpo
Guidebook Entitled the Aural Lineage of Kālacakra
Dus 'khor snyan brgyud kyi khrid (also known as Yi ge med pa'i dus 'khor snyan brgyud)
Inspired by Menlung Guru.
Guidebook 41

Khyenrab Chojé Rinchen Chokdrub Pelzang
Guidebook Entitled the Six Doctrines of Sukhasiddhi
Su kha chos drug gi khrid
Inspired by Khyungpo Neljor.
Guidebook 81

Secret Attainment: The Emanational Cakra of the Navel
gSang sgrub lte ba sprul 'khor
DNZ vol. 12, p. 286, line 7–p. 289, line 4. A primary source of Guidebook 82.

The Six Doctrines of Sukhasiddhi
Su kha chos drug
DNZ vol. 12, pp. 299–313. Primary source of Guidebook 81.

Khyungpo Neljor
Adamantine Verses of the Six Doctrines of the Ḍākinī of Pristine Cognition: Foundation of the Golden Doctrines of the Shangpa
Ye shes kyi mkha' 'gro ma'i chos drug rdo rje'i tshig rkang| shangs pa'i gser chos skor gyi rtsa ba
DNZ vol. 11, pp. 1–27.

Guidebook Entitled the Inner Guidance of Nairātmyā: The Emanational Navel Cakra
bDag med ma'i nang khrid
Conflated with Khyenrab Chojé Rinchen Chokdrub Pelzang's [*Secret Attainment:*] *The Emanational Cakra of the Navel*; antecedent attributed to Āryadeva the Brahmin.
Guidebook 82

Kodrakpa
Dispelling of Obstacles Entitled Ocean-Like Visualizations of Ha
Gegs sel ha dmigs rgya mtsho
NL.

Instruction Manual on the Path and Its Fruition
Lam 'bras khrid yig
NL.

Konchok Tenpei Dronmé
Quintessential Practice of Meditation and Recitation for the Sixteen Spheres
Thig le bcu drug gi sgom bzlas nyams su len tshul snying por dril ba
DNZ vol. 4, pp. 317–26.

Kunga Drolchok
Guidebook Entitled Guidance on Amitāyus
Tshe khrid
Guidebook 27

Guidebook Entitled the Elucidation of the Concealed Meanings [*of Yogatantra*]
sBas don kun gsal gyi khrid yig
Guidebook 26

The Outer, Inner, and Secret Biographies of Venerable Kunga Drolchok
rJe btsun kun dga' grol mchog gi phyi nang gsang gsum gyi rnam thar
Beijing: Mi rigs dpe skrun khang, 2005.

Kunga Rinchen

Wish-Granting Gem Fulfilling the Hopes of Living Beings: An Instruction Manual concerning the Fivefold Great Seal
Phyag chen lnga ldan gyi khrid yig yid bzhin gyi nor bu skye dgu'i re skong
Drigungpa Anthology vol. 54, pp. 56–62.

Kunga Tashi

Guidance on Parting from the Four Attachments
Zhen pa bzhi bral gyi khrid yig
NL.

Kyeme Dopa Chokyi Sherab Jodenpa

The Six Approaches of the Profound Meaning [*according to the Tradition of Kyeme Dopa*]
Zab don sgo drug skye med do pa'i lugs
These are possibly included among his *Ten Approaches to the Oral Instruction.*

The Ten Approaches to the Oral Instruction from the Heart Essence of Profound Meaning
Zab don thugs kyi snying po las zhal gdams sgo 'byed bcu
Limi Collection of Texts on Severance, BDRC W23390, pp. 216–46.

Kyoton Ojung Lotsāwa

Guidebook Entitled the Mental Focus on the Horns of Bhairava
'Jigs byed kyi rwa rtse'i khrid yig rva rtse sems 'dzin
Guidebook 66

Lama Dampa Sonam Gyeltsen

Great Guidebook [*on the Direct Guidance of Avalokiteśvara according to the Tradition of Drubchen Tsembupa*]
Khrid yig chen mo
NL.

Guidebook Entitled the Mind Training of Sumpa Lotsāwa
Sum pa'i blo sbyong gi khrid yig
Guidebook 5

Guidebook Entitled the Path and Its Fruition
Lam 'bras bu dang bcas pa'i khrid
Guidebook 43

Instruction Manual Elucidating the Concealed Meaning
Khrid yig sbas pa'i don kun gsal
DNZ vol. 5, pp. 329–423. Primary source of Guidebook 43.

Langtangpa Chen Nga Kunga Dorjé
Memorandum on the Four Stages
Rim bzhi'i zin bris
NL. This pertains to Guidebook 70.

Lharjé Gewabum
Guidebook Entitled the Collected Injunctions of the King
rGyal po bka' 'bum gyi khrid
Guidebook 106

Lhazik Repa
Guidebook Entitled the Indivisibility of Subtle Energy and Mind
rLung sems gnyis med kyi khrid
Guidebook 87

Memorandum on the Indivisibility of Subtle Energy and Mind
rLung sems gnyis med kyi khrid kyi zin bris
Primary source of Guidebook 87.

Lhopa Kunkhyen Rinchen Pel
Memorandum on the Elucidation of Symbolic Meaning
Lam 'bras lho pa'i zin bris.
SLC vol. 11, pp. 216–18.

Longchen Rabjam
Collected Works of Longchen Rabjam
Kun mkhyen klong chen rab 'byams kyi gsung 'bum
26 vols. Beijing: Krung go'i bod rig pa dpe skrun khang, 2009.

Entering the Enclosure of Luminosity
'Od gsal sbubs 'jug
mKha' 'gro yang tig
Collected Works, vol. 8, pp. 71–77.

Precious Treasury of the Attainment Maṇḍala of the Peaceful and Wrathful Conquerors
rGyal ba zhi khro'i sgrub dkyil rin po che'i gter mdzod
Collected Works, vol. 25, pp. 360–87.

Trilogy on Resting
Ngal gso skor gsum
Comprising (i) *Resting in the Nature of Mind* (Sems nyid ngal gso), (ii) *Resting in Illusion* (sGyu ma'i ngal gso), and (iii) *Resting in Meditative Concentration* (bSam gtan ngal gso).
Collected Works, 3 vols., dPal brtsegs bod yig dpe rnying 125–127, pp. 1–364. Beijing: Krung go bod ri pa dpe skrun khang, 2009.
Translated in Longchenpa 2018–19 by Padmakara Translation Group; also Guenther 1975–76.

Lorepa Darma Wangchuk Tsondru

Natural Arising of the Buddha Body of Reality: Instructions of the Fivefold Capacity—a Distinctive Doctrine of the Glorious Lower Drukpa Kagyu Tradition
dPal ldan smad 'brug bka' brgyud kyi khyad chos thub pa lnga'i gdams khrid chos sku rang shar
DNZ vol. 10, pp. 223–41. Primary source of Guidebook 99.

Lowo Khenchen Sonam Lhundrub

Memorandum on the Four Stages
Rim bzhi'i zin bris
NL. Related to Guidebook 70.

Lowo Lotsāwa Sherab Rinchen

Essential Vital Essence of the Perfection Stage according to Buddhajñānapāda
Zhabs lugs rdzogs rim snying gi thig le
Collected Works, vol. 3, pp. 119–34. Beijing: Krung go'i bod rig pa dpe skrun khang, 2007. Related to Guidebook 63.

Guidebook Entitled the Four-Stage Yoga
rNal 'byor bzhi rim gyi khrid yig
Guidebook 65

Guidebook Entitled the Unelaborate Practice of Red Yamāri
gZhed dmar shin tu spros med kyi khrid
Guidebook 64

Machik Labkyi Dronma

Great Bundle of Precepts: The Source Text of Esoteric Instructions on Severance, The Profound Transcendent Perfection of Wisdom
Shes rab kyi pha rol du phyin pa zab mo gcod kyi man ngag gi gzhung bka' tshoms chen mo
Translated by Sarah Harding in Jamgön Kongtrul 2016, 13–27.

Mangkharwa Lodro Gyeltsen

Guidebook Entitled the Five Stages of the Secret Assembly
gSang 'dus rim lnga'i khrid
Guidebook 62

Memorandum on the Five Stages of the Secret Assembly
gSang 'dus rim lnga'i zin bris
NL. Primary source of Guidebook 62.

Marpa Lotsāwa Chokyi Lodro

Collected Works of Lhodrak Marpa Lotsāwa
Lho brag mar pa lo tsa'i gsung 'bum
7 vols. Beijing: Krung go'i bod rig pa dpe skrun khang, 2011.

Fifteen Scrolls
Shog dril bco lnga (also known as *Fifteen Cycles of Instruction concerning the Continuum of Buddha Mind*, Thugs rgyud gdams skor bco lnga)
Collected Works, vol. 6, pp. 103–208

The Four Scrolls of Lama Marpa
bLa ma mar pa'i shog dril bzhi pa
Collected Works, vol. 2, pp. 41–46.
Antecedent of Guidebook 90.

History of the Four Scrolls of the Aural Instructions: An Extraordinary Teaching of Venerable Lhodrakpa, along with Its Appendix
rJe btsun lho brag pa'i khyad par gyi gdams pa snyan gyi shog dril bzhi'i lo rgyus gzhung lhan thabs dang bcas pa
Collected Works, vol. 4, pp. 87–121; also in *DNZ* vol. 8, pp. 203–33.

Profound Implementation of the Mingling and Transformation [of the Three Poisons], along with the History of the Pronouncements of the Four Oral Instructions
Zhal gdams bka' bzhi lo rgyus dang bcas pa bsre 'pho lag len du dril ba zab mo
Collected Works, vol. 5, pp. 150–72.

The Six Doctrines according to the Sekharma Tradition
Chos drug sras mkhar ma
Collected Works, vol. 6, pp. 103–208.

Marpa Lotsāwa Chokyi Lodro with Rechungpa Dorjé Drak
Guidebook Entitled the Nine Doctrinal Cycles of Nirdehaḍākinī
Lus med mkha' 'gro'i chos skor dgu'i khrid
Guidebook 92

Teachings of the Nine Doctrinal Cycles of Nirdehaḍākinī
Lus med mkha' 'gro'i chos skor dgu
Collected Works, vol. 4, pp. 225–51. Primary source of Guidebook 92.

Marton Chokyi Gyeltsen
Guidebook Entitled Vajrapāṇi in the Form Mahācakra
Phyag rdor 'khor chen gyi khrid
Guidebook 36

The Perfection Stage of Vajrapāṇi in the Form Mahācakra Endowed with Four Blessings
Phyag rdor 'khor chen gyi rdzogs rim byin rlabs bzhi ldan
NL. Primary source of Guidebook 36.

Mu Konchok Gyeltsen
Mind Training: Supplement to the Oral Tradition

bLo sbyong gsung bgros ma' kha skong
Translated in Jinpa 2006, 431–515; an antecedent of Guidebook 2.

Muchen Gyeltsen Pelzangpo
Guidebook Entitled the Heart of Dependent Origination
rTen 'brel snying po'i khrid yig
Guidebook 3

Profound Guidance on the Dependent Origination of Past Actions, Causes, and Fruition
Las rgyu 'bras rten 'brel gyi khrid yig zab mo
N.d., BDRC W8LS37365.

Namka Samdrub Gyeltsen
Biographies of the Abbatial Succession of the Shangpa Kagyu
Shangs pa bka' brgyud bla rabs kyi rnam thar
Lhasa: Bod ljongs mi dmangs dpe skrun khang, 1996.

Ngamring Mangto Ludrub Gyatso
Essence of Nectar: An Instruction on the View of the Middle Way in Conformity with the Texts of the Two Great Promulgators
Shing rta chen po gnyis kyi gzhung dang rjes su mthun pa'i dbu ma'i lta khrid bdud rtsi'i snying po
DNZ vol. 4, pp. 549–64.

Ngawang Chodrak
The Way of Enacting the Blessings of the Elucidation of the Symbolic Meaning according to the Path and Its Fruition, along with the Meaning of the Emergence of Three from Two
Lam 'bras kyi brda don gsal ba'i byin rlabs kyi bya tshul gnyis las gsum byung gi go don dang bcas pa
SLC vol. 19, pp. 121–27.

Ngawang Kunga Sonam
Collected Works of Ngawang Kunga Sonam
dPal sa skya pa chen po sngags 'chang thams cad mkhyen pa ngag dbang kun dga' bsod nams kyi gsung 'bum
29 vols. Kathmandu: Sa skya rgyal yongs gsung rab slob gnyer khang, 2000.

Corrections to a Memorandum of Venerable Ludrub Gyatso, Differentiating the Precious Teachings in Terms of Public Exegeses and the Exegeses Given to Disciples
gSung ngag rin po che slob bshad dang tshogs bshad kyi dbye ba rje klu grub rgya mtsho'i gsung gi zin bris la slar yang rje nyid kyis zhus dag mdzad pa
Collected Works, vol. 22, pp. 211–38.

Corrections to Chojé Rinpoché Sangye Pel, Supplementing the Four Stages of Kṛṣṇacārin
Nag po rim bzhi'i zur 'debs chos rje rin po che sangs rgyas dpal bas mdzad pa'i dpe ma dag pa'i zhu dag
Collected Works, vol. 17, pp. 81–87.

Ngawang Namgyel
A Brief Lucid Biography of Venerable Ngawang Trinlé
rJe ngag dbang 'phrin las kyi rnam thar nyung ngu rnam gsal
Unpublished manuscript, courtesy of the Jonang Foundation.

Ngok Zhedang Dorjé
Guidebook Entitled the Great Magical Emanation
Ma hā mā yā'i khrid
Guidebook 73

Guidebook Entitled the Four Adamantine Seats
gDan bzhi'i khrid yig
Guidebook 72

Guidebook Entitled the Mingling and Transformation of the Three Poisons
rNgog pa'i bsre 'pho'i khrid
Guidebook 89

Ngorchen Kunga Zangpo
Collected Works of Ngorchen Kunga Zangpo
Ngor chen kun dga' bzang po'i bka' 'bum
4 vols. Dehradun: Sakya Centre, 1993.

Elucidation and Advice concerning the Extremely Unelaborate Instruction [of Red Yamāri] Entitled Beauteous Unelaborated Ornament
Shin tu spros med kyi khrid yig gi zhal shes dang gsung sgros spros med mdzes rgyan
Collected Works, vol. 3, pp. 750–89. Related to Guidebook 64.

Memorandum on the Four Stages according to Kṛṣṇacārin
Nag po rim bzi'i zin bris
NL.

Religious History of the Path and Its Fruition
Lam 'bras chos 'byung (also known as *Extensive Sunlight Revealing the Origins of the Pith Instructions of the Path and Its Fruition*, Lam 'bras kyi man ngag gi byung tshul bstan pa rgyas pa'i nyi 'od)
Collected Works, vol. 1, pp. 435–508.

Useful Rites for All the Means for Attainments of Mahāyoga Entitled Ornament of All Secrets

rNal 'byor chen po'i sgrub thabs thams cad la nye bar mkho ba'i cho ga gsang ba kun rgyan
Collected Works, vol. 3, pp. 239–85.

Norbu Rinchen
Buddha Field of Norbu's Liberation by Seeing
Nor bu mthong grol gi zhing khams
NL.

Guidebook Entitled Norbu Rinchen's Liberation by Seeing
Nor bu mthong grol gyi khrid
Guidebook 107

Nordrang Orgyan
Compendium of Buddhist Numeric Terms
Chos rnam kun btus
3 vols. Beijing: Krung go'i bod rig pa dpe skrun khang, 2008.

Nubpa Rigdzin Drak
Guidebook Entitled Parting from the Four Attachments
Zhen pa bzhi bral gyi khrid yig
Guidebook 1

List of Instructions in the Form of a Memorandum
Zin bris su byas pa'i khrid tho
DNZ vol. 6, pp. 315–17. A primary source of Guidebook 1.
Translated in Jinpa 2006, 527–28.

Nyakton Samten Ozer
Guidebook Entitled the Severance [of Machik Lapdron]
gCod yul gyi khrid
Guidebook 6

Wish-Fulfilling Gem: An Instruction on the Inner Meaning
Don khrid yid bzhin nor bu
The third of the eight appendices to his *Severance of Demonic Forces: Essence of Profound Meaning*, bDud gcod zab mo don gyi nying khu.
BDRC W27506, pp. 71–96; also in Limi Collection of Texts on Severance, pp. 296–309. Primary source of Guidebook 6.

Nyakton Samten Ozer et al.
The New Pronouncement and Eight Appendices
bDud gcod zab mo don gyi nying khu (*Severance of Demonic Forces: Essence of Profound Meaning*)
BDRC W27506, pp. 1–351; also in Limi Collection W23390, pp. 246–412.
The *Eight Appendices* are as follows: (i) *Pearl Rosary of Legendary Tales* (gTam rgyud mu tig phreng ba), (ii) *Ocean of Empowerments and Blessings* (dBang bskur byin brlabs rgya mtsho), (iii) *Wish-Fulfilling Gem: An Instruction*

on the Inner Meaning (Don khrid yid bzhin nor bu yin), (iv) *Taking Accomplishments in Hand through Experiential Cultivation* (Nyams len dngos grub lag bcangs), (v) *Essential Key to the Dispelling of Obstructions* (Gags sel gnad kyi sde mig), (vi) *Treasure Store of Enlightened Attributes That Bring Forth Success* (Bogs don yon tan gter mdzod), (vii) *Brocade Cloth of Pith Instructions* (Man ngag za 'og ras ma), and (viii) *Supplement That Brings Forth All Needs* (Lhan thabs dgos 'dod kun 'byung).

Nyangrel Nyima Ozer
Red Wrathful Guru
Gu ru drag dmar
RTD vol. 11, no. 67, pp. 1013–14.

Nyenchen Sonam Tenpa
Anthology [on the Heart of Dependent Origination]
[rTen 'brel snying poi'i] be'u bum
NL.

Nyenton Chokyi Sherab
The Three Nails of the Pith Instructions of Secret Attainment
gSang sgrub man ngag gzer gsum
DNZ vol. 12, pp. 315–28.

Nyima Gyeltsen
Elucidation of the Spheres of the Heart
sNying gi thig le'i gsal byed
Translated in Jinpa 2008, 395–452.

Nyukla Paṇchen Ngawang Drakpa and Kunga Drolchok
Guidebook Entitled the Sixteen Spheres of the Heart
sNying gi thig le'i khrid
Guidebook 19

Orgyan Rinchen Pel
Ritual Service and Attainment of the Three Adamantine Realities
gDams ngag rdo rje gsum gyi bsnyen sgrub kyi gzhung
DNZ vol. 15, pp. 499–509.
Antecedent to Guidebook 42.

Pagmodrupa Dorjé Gyelpo
The Coemergent Union of the Great Seal
Phyag chen lhan cig skyes sbyor
Collected Works, vol. 4, pp. 272–98.

Guidebook Entitled the Cycle of Pagmodru Densatel
Phags gru thel skor gyi khrid
Guidebook 95

Verses on the Great Seal
Phyag chen tshigs bcad ma
NL.

Verses on the Path of Skillful Means
Thabs lam tshigs bcad ma
Drigungpa Anthology vol. 16, pp. 91–94; also in *Collected Works*, vol. 4, pp. 91–94.

Pakpa Lodro Gyeltsen
Collected Works by Pakpa Lodro Gyeltsen
'Gro mgon chos rgyal 'phags pa'i gsung 'bum
4 vols. Beijing: Krung go'i bod rig pa dpe skrun khang, 2007.

Guidebook Entitled the Three Purities
Dag pa gsum gyi khrid
Guidebook 58

Pith Instructions of the Five Stages
Rim pa lnga pa'i man ngag
Collected Works, vol. 2, pp. 278–91.

The Three Purities: Enlightened Intention of the Sublime Tantra of the Adamantine Tent of the Ḍākinīs
'Phags pa mkha' 'gro ma rdo rje gur gyi rgyud kyi dgongs pa dag pa gsum gyi khrid yig
Collected Works, vol. 1, pp. 601–17; also in *DNZ* vol. 5, pp. 491–505. Primary source of Guidebook 58.

Parpuwa Lodro Sengé
Guidebook Entitled the Trilogy of Spiritual Songs
Do hā skor gsum gyi khrid
Guidebook 103

Synopsis of the Spiritual Songs of Glorious Saraha
dPal sa ra ha'i gdams pa do hā'i bsdus don
DNZ vol. 7, pp. 22–28. Primary source of Guidebook 103.

Patsab Lotsāwa Nyima Drak
Abridgement of the Essentials of the Root and Commentary of the Introduction to the Middle Way
dBu ma 'jug pa rtsa 'grel gyi gnad rnams lta sgom spyod pa gsum du bsdus pa'i lan 'debs
NL. Primary source of Guidebook 24.

Analytic Meditation
dPyod sgom (the text reads *spod sgom*, "spicy/fragrant meditation")
NL.

Eight Sacral Aspects
Dam pa rigs brgyad
NL.

Guidebook Entitled the View of Intrinsic Emptiness
Rang stong gi lta khrid
Guidebook 24

Pekar Zangpo
Structural Presentation of All the Discourses
mDo sde spyi'i rnam gzhag
Beijing: Mi rigs dpe skrun khang, 2006.

Pelchen Ga Lotsāwa Namgyel Dorjé
Pith Instructions of the Six-Branch Yoga
sByor drug gi man ngag
Jo nang dpe tshogs, vol. 35. Beijing, 2014.
An antecedent of Guidebook 94.

Peljam
Abridged History of the Abbatial Succession of the Jonangwa
Jo nang ba'i gdan rabs mdor bsdus drang srong rgan po'i zhal lung
Beijing: Mi rigs dpe skrun khang, 2005.

Pema Karpo
Collected Works of Pema Karpo
Kun mkhyen padma dkar po'i gsung 'bum
24 vols. Darjeeling: Kargyud sungrab nyamso khang, 1973–74.

Contents of the Guidance on Common Savor
Ro snyoms khrid kyi sa bcad
Collected Works, vol. 24, pp. 289–94.

Extracting the Essence of All Instructions of Tsangpa Gyaré's Own Tradition on Auspicious Circumstances
rTen 'brel kho bo lugs gyi khrid chos thams cad kyi snying po len pa
Drukpa Kagyu Anthology vol. 55, pp. 618–20; also in *Collected Works*, vol. 24, p. 315.

Gradual Path of Mahāmāyā Yielding the Desired Good Fortune
sGyu ma chen mo ma hā māyā'i lam rim skal bzang 'dod 'jo
Drukpa Kagyu Anthology vol. 27, pp. 339–74.

Oral Transmission of Drogon: Embracing the Definitive Common Savor
Ro snyoms nges pa can 'chang thabs 'gro mgon zhal gyi lung
Collected Works, vol. 24, pp. 39–51.

Ornament of the Secret Assembly
gSang ba 'dus pa'i rgyan
Collected Works, vol. 16, pp. 63–146.

Ritual Array Commenting on the Connections with the Empowerments of the Nine-Deity and Five-Deity Assemblages of Amitāyus according to the Drubgyel Tradition Entitled Noble Vase of Nectar
Grub rgyal lugs kyi tshe dpag med gong khug lha dgu dang lha lnga'i dbang gis mtshams sbyor 'grel chog tu bkod pa bdud rtsi'i bum bzang
Drukpa Anthology vol. 23, pp. 461–84.

Potowa Rinchen Sel
The Parables of Potowa: A Heap of Gems
dPe chos rin chen spungs pa
Gangs can rig mdzod lde mig, vol. 17.
Beijing: Nationalities Press, 1987.
Primary source of Guidebook 18.

Precious Treasury of Knowledge
Shes bya'i gter mdzod
Chengdu: Si khron mi rigs dpe skrun khang, 1997. BDRC W19837.

Ra Lotsāwa
The Profound and Extensive Training
Zab pa rgya che la slob tshul
NL.

Rechungpa Dorje Drak
The Aural Lineage of Rechungpa
Ras chung snyan brgyud
Drigungpa Anthology vols. 58–62

Guidance of the Six Doctrines That Confer Liberation through the Upper Gate, according to the Perfection Stage of the Aural Lineage of Cakrasaṃvara
bDe mchog snyan brgyud kyi rdzogs rim steng sgo rnam par grol ba'i chos drug gi khrid
Part of *The Aural Lineage of Rechungpa.*
DNZ vol. 7, pp. 501–33.

Guidebook Entitled the Nine Doctrinal Cycles of Nirdehaḍākinī
Lus med mkha' 'gro'i chos skor dgu'i khrid
Guidebook 92

Pith Instructions of the Aural Lineage concerning Nirdehaḍākinī
Lus med mkha' 'gro'i snyan rgyud kyi man ngag gi khrid yig (also known as *Essence of the Nine Doctrinal Cycles of Nirdehaḍākinī*, Lus med mkha' 'gro'i chos skor dgu yi snying po)
DNZ vol. 8, pp. 197–201.

Root Text and Pith Instructions of the Nine Doctrinal Cycles of Nirdehaḍākinī
rJe btsun ras chung pa'i khyad chos lus med mkha' 'gro'i chos skor dgu'i gzhung man ngag dang bcas pa
DNZ vol. 8, pp. 165–73. Primary source of Guidebook 92.

Remdawa Zhonu Lodro
Great Commentary on the Introduction to the Middle Way/Guidance on the View of the Middle Way
dBu ma 'jug pa'i 'grel chen
Delhi: Ngawang Topgyay, 1974; Sarnath, 1983. Related to Guidebook 24.

Guidebook Entitled the Carrying of Happiness and Suffering on the Path
sKyid sdug lam 'khyer gyi khrid yig (also known as *Memorandum on the Teaching of Gyelsépa*, rGyal sras pa'i gsung la zin tho)
Guidebook 4

Rinchen Namgyel
He Whose Glory Is Gracious
dPal gang drin ma
Prayer in praise of Buton Rinchen Drub.

Rongton Sheja Kunrik
Biography of Śākya Gyeltsen Pelzangpo Entitled Wondrous Ocean of Faith
rJe btsun thams cad mkhyen pa bshes gnyen shākya rgyal mtshan dpal bzang po'i zhal snga nas kyi rnam thar ngo mtshar dad pa'i rol mtsho
Collected Works, vol. 1, pp. 1–108.

Collected Works of Rongton Sheja Kunrik
Rong ston bka' 'bum
10 vols. Chengdu: Sichuan Nationalities Publishing House, 2008.

Commentaries on the Three Stages of Meditation
sGom rim gsum gyi 'grel pa
Comprising (i) *Commentary on the First Stage of Meditation Entitled Ornament Illuminating Calm Abiding and Higher Insight* (sGom rim dang po'i 'grel pa zhi lhag gsal bar byed pa'i rgyan), (ii) *Commentary on the Second Stage of Meditation Entitled Moonbeams of Abiding* (sGom rim bar pa'i 'grel pa gnas kyi zla zer), and (iii) *Commentary on the Final Stage of Meditation Entitled Drumbeat of the Gods* (sGom rim tha ma'i 'grel pa lha'i rnga sgra).
Collected Works, vol. 8, p. 499–vol. 9, p. 124. These pertain to Guidebook 22.

Commentary on the Transcendent Perfection of Wisdom in One Hundred Thousand Lines
'Bum ṭīk
Collected Works, vols. 4–5. Chengdu: Sichuan Nationalities Publishing House, 2008.

Direct Guidance of Avalokiteśvara according to the Tradition of the Bodhisattva Candradhvaja
Byang sems zla rgyal lugs
DNZ vol. 17, pp. 39–40. This pertains to Guidebook 31.

Direct Guidance on Avalokiteśvara according to the Tradition of the Bodhisattva Candradhvaja Entitled White Lotus
Thugs rje chen po'i dmar khrid padma dkar po
Collected Works, vol. 1, pp. 398–402. Related to Guidebook 31.

Essence of the Key to the Guidance on the Sameness of Existence and Quiescence, according to the Tradition of Atiśa
Srid zhi mnyam nyid kyi khrid yig gnad kyi snying po jo bo chen po'i lugs
Collected Works, vol. 1, pp. 324–29.

Guidance of the Five Paths of the Pacification of Suffering, a Sacred Doctrine Derived from the Lineage of the Great Accomplished Master Dampa Sangyé, Entitled Oral Transmission of the Supreme Attainment of Taintless Light
Grub chen dam pa sangs rgyas nas brgyud pa'i dam chos sdug bsngal zhi byed kyi lam lnga'i khrid yig dri med snang ba grub pa mchog gi zhal lung
Redacted by Sherab Zangpo.
DNZ vol. 13, pp. 409–38. Related to Guidebook 21.
Translated by Sarah Harding in Jamgön Kongtrul 2019, pp. 509–35.

Guidance on the Five Paths according to the Tradition of Atiśa
Lam lnga'i khrid yig jo bo'i lugs
Collected Works, vol. 1, pp. 64–69.

Guidebook Entitled the Five Paths of Pacification
Zhi byed lam lnga'i khrid yig
Guidebook 21

Guidebook Entitled the Six Descents of the Transcendent Perfection of Wisdom
Sher phyin bka' bab drug gi khrid yig
Guidebook 20

Guidebook Entitled the Three Stages of Meditation—Beginning, Middle, and Conclusive
sGom rim thog mtha' bar gsum gyi khrid yig
Guidebook 22

Safe Ford of the Path of Liberation Experientially Cultivating the Six Transcendent Wisdoms
Phar phyin drug gi nyams su len tshul thar lam bde ba'i 'jug ngogs
Collected Works, vol. 1, pp. 115–17. A source of Guidebook 20.

Sequence of Practicing the Path of the Transcendent Perfection of Wisdom Entitled Lamp Clarifying Darkness

Shes rab kyi pha rol tu phyin pa'i lam nyams su len pa'i rim pa mun sel sgron me
Collected Works, vol. 4, pp. 341–492. Related to Guidebook 20.

Rongton Sheja Kunrik with Dzimchen Gyeltsen Pelzang
Guidebook Entitled Direct Guidance of Avalokiteśvara according to the Candradhvaja Tradition
dMar khrid zla rgyal lugs kyi khrid yig
Guidebook 31

Sachen Kunga Nyingpo
Commentary on Inciting the Path of the Four Stages
Rim bzhi lam slong gi 'grel pa
Collected Works, vol. 2, pp. 429–40.
An antecedent of Guidebook 70.

Commentary on the Vital Essence of Spring
dPyid thig gi ṭīkā
Collected Works, vol. 1, pp. 133–78.

Concordance of Bilingual Examples
Go byed rnam gsal dpe brjod skad gnyis zung sbyor
NL.

Cycle of Mind Training: Parting from the Four Attachments
bLo sbyong zhen pa bzhi bral gyi skor
DNZ vol. 6, pp. 305–56.
An antecedent of Guidebook 1.

Oral Transmission of Venerable Mañjughoṣa: Parting from the Four Attachments
rJe btsun 'jam pa'i dbyangs kyi zhal lung zhen pa bzhi dang bral ba'i gdams pa
An antecedent of Guidebook 1.

Śākya Chokden
Guidebook on the Three Essential Points
sNying po don gsum gyi khrid yig
Collected Works, vol. 8, pp. 371–74.
Kathmandu: Sachen International, Guru Lama, 2006; rDzong sar khams bye: rDzong sar khams bye'i slob gling thub bstan dar rgyas gling, 2006–7.

Sakya Paṇḍita
Guidebook Entitled the Elucidation of the Symbolic Meaning
brDa don gsal ba'i khrid
The original is contained in SLC vol. 11, pp. 209–16.
Guidebook 61

Guidebook Entitled the Exegesis of the Concealed Path
Lam sbas bshad pa
The original is contained in SLC vol. 11, pp. 342–53.
Guidebook 60

Instruction on Parting from the Four Attachments
Zhen pa bzhi bral gyi gdams pa
Collected Works, vol. 1, p. 470; also in *DNZ* vol. 6, pp. 314–15. An embellishment of Guidebook 1.
Translated in Jinpa 2006, 525–26.

Samdingpa Zhonu Drub

The Amulet Tradition of the Great Seal
Phyag chen ga'u ma
DNZ vol. 12, pp. 181–87. Primary source of Guidebook 78.

The Cycle of the Six Doctrines of Nigumā
Ni gu chos drug gi skor
The basic text is *Adamantine Verses of the Six Doctrines of Jñānaḍākinī* (Ye shes kyi mKha' 'gro ma'i chos drug rdo rje'i tshig rkang)
DNZ vol. 11, pp. 1–27. The full cycle is contained in *The Golden Doctrines of the Shangpa* (Shangs pa'i gser chos). Primary source of Guidebook 77.

The Deathlessness of One's Own Mind
Rang sems 'chi med
DNZ vol. 12, pp. 192–98. Primary source of Guidebook 80.

Guidebook Entitled the Amulet Tradition of the Great Seal
Phyag rgya chen po ga'u ma'i khrid
Guidebook 78

Guidebook Entitled the Deathlessness of One's Own Mind
Rang sems 'chi med kyi khrid
Guidebook 80

Guidebook Entitled the Six Doctrines of Nigumā
Ni gu chos drug gi khrid
Guidebook 77

Guidebook Entitled the Three Aspects Carried on the Path
Lam khyer rnam gsum gyi khrid
Guidebook 79

The Three Aspects Carried on the Path
Lam khyer rnam gsum gyi khrid
DNZ vol. 12, pp. 187–92. Primary source of Guidebook 79.

Samten Ozer and Sonam Lhundrub
Guidebook Entitled the Kharamukha Cakrasaṃvara
bDe mchog bong zhal can gyi khrid yig
Guidebook 74

Sangdak Drubchen
Guidebook Entitled Vajrapāṇi in the Form Caṇḍa
gTum po'i khrid
Guidebook 37

Inconceivably Secret Guidance of Vajrapāṇi in the Form Caṇḍa
Phyag rdor gtum po'i gsang ba bsam gyis mi khyab pa
Primary source of Guidebook 37.

Sangye Gompa
Great Public Exposition
Tshogs bshad chen mo
Translated in Jinpa 2006, 313–417; an antecedent of Guidebook 2.

Sé Chilbupa Chokyi Gyeltsen
A Commentary on the Seven-Point Mind Training
bLo sbyong don bdun ma'i 'grel pa
Translated in Jinpa 2006, 87–132; an antecedent of Guidebook 2.

Serdingpa Zhonu O
Five Stages Perfected on One Seat
Rim lnga'i gdan rdzogs
NL.

Shangpa Texts
Shangs chos (Indian Source Texts of the Dharma Cycle of Five Golden Dharmas of the Glorious Shangpa)
dPal ldan shangs pa'i chos 'khor gser chos rnam lnga'i rgya gzhung
Edited by Karma Rangjung Kunkhyab (Kalu Rinpoche). 11 vols. Sonada, India: Samdrup Darje Ling Monastery. n.d.

Shawo Gangpa
The Hidden Guidance of Kadam
bKa' gdams lkog khrid (also known as *Trilogy of Pulverizing*, rDung 'thag bskor gsum)
Primary source of Guidebook 37.

Sherab Bumpa
Guidebook Entitled the Direct Guidance of Avalokiteśvara according to the Tsembupa Tradition
dMar khrid tshem bu lugs kyi khrid yig
Guidebook 32

Sherab Ozer

Deathless Nectar of Meditation (bsGom pa 'chi med bdud rtsi) and *Deathless Nectar of Study and Reflection* (Thos bsam 'chi med bdud rtsi)

Contained in Jamyang Khyentsé Wangpo, *Collected Works*, vol. 6, pp. 327–74. Gangtok: Gonpo Tseten, 1977–80.

Sonam Ozer

Instruction Manual on the Ritual Service and Attainment [of the Three Adamantine Realities] according to Orgyanpa

O rgyan snyan sgrub kyi khrid yig

NL. An antecedent of Guidebook 42.

Sonam Tsemo

Eulogy to Sachen

Sa chen la bstod pa

Collected Works, vol. 1, pp. 150–52. Beijing: Krung go'i bod rig pa dpe skrun khang, 2007.

Taklung Ngawang Namgyal

Wondrous Ocean of Eloquence: Histories of the Taklung Kagyu Tradition

sTag lung chos 'byung ngo mtshar rgya mtsho

Lhasa: Bod ljongs bod yig dpe rnying dpe skrun khang, 1992.

Translated in Dorje, *Wondrous Ocean of Eloquence: Histories of the Taklung Kagyu Tradition*, forthcoming.

Taklungpa Tashipel

Guidebook Entitled the Six Doctrines according to Taklungpa

sTag lung pa'i chos drug gi khrid

Guidebook 97

Wish-Fulfilling Gem: The Six Doctrines of Glorious Nāropā

dPal nā ro'i chos drug yid bzhin nor bu (also known as *Wish-Fulfilling Gem: Adamantine Stanzas on the Short Text of the Guidebook Entitled Coemergent Union of the Great Seal*, Phyag rgya chen po lhan cig skyes sbyor gyi khrid yig gzhung chung rdo rje'i tshig rkang yid bzhin nor bu)

DNZ vol. 10, pp. 1–19.

Taktsang Lotsāwa Sherab Rinchen

Descriptive Basis of Cakrasaṃvara according to the Tradition of Ghaṇṭāpāda

bDe mchog dril bu lugs kyi mngon rtogs

Collected Works, vol. 4, pp. 260–79. Beijing: Krung go'i bod rig pa dpe skrun khang, 2007.

Tāranātha

The Amulet Tradition of the Great Seal, or the Instruction Manual Entitled Three Natural States

Phyag chen ga'u ma'am rang babs rnam gsum zhes bya ba'i khrid yig
DNZ vol. 12, pp. 237–49; also in *Collected Works*, vol. 39, pp. 179–91.

Commentary on the Spiritual Songs of Jālandharipa Entitled Secret Treasury
Grub chen dzālandha ra'i do ha'i 'grel pa gsang ba'i mdzod
Collected Works, vol. 19, pp. 1–105.

Description and Long-Life Attainment of White Tārā according to the Tradition of Jowo Atiśa
sGrol dkar jo bo lugs kyi mngon rtogs tshe sgrub dang bcas pa
Collected Works, vol. 27, pp. 243–47.

Extensive Instruction Manual of Profound Meaning on the Six Doctrines of Nigumā, the Profound Path
Zab lam ni gu chos drug gi khrid yig zab don thang mar brdal ba
Collected Works, vol. 24, pp. 213–314.

Guidance on the Adamantine Yoga of the Profound Path Entitled Meaningful to Behold
Zab lam rdo rje'i rnal 'byor gyi 'khrid yig mthong ba don ldan
Collected Works, vol. 7, pp. 111–388, also in *DNZ* vol. 15, pp. 133–231.

Guidance on the Five Stages of Glorious Cakrasaṃvara
dPal bde mchog rim lnga'i khrid yig
Collected Works, vol. 16, pp. 304–17.

Guidance on the Four-Stage Yoga of Red Yamāri
gShed dmar rnal 'byor bzhi rim gyi khrid
Collected Works, vol. 11, pp. 356–68.

Guidance on the Three Sorts of Person on the Stages for Entering the Buddhist Teaching Entitled Nectar Essence
rGyal ba'i bstan pa la 'jug pa'i rim pa skyes bu gsum gyi khrid yig bdud rtsi'i nying khu
DNZ vol. 3, pp. 181–273.

Instruction Manual of Glorious Mahāmāyā Entitled Noble Path of the Conquerors
dPal sgyu 'phrul chen mo'i khrid yig rgyal ba'i lam bzang
Collected Works, vol. 22, pp. 44–56.

Instruction Manual of the Four Adamantine Seats Entitled Opening the Door of Pristine Cognition
rDo rje gdan bzhi'i khrid yig ye shes sgo 'byed
Collected Works, vol. 20, pp. 323–71.

Instruction Manual of the Go Tradition on the Five Stages: Elucidating the Meaning of the Tantra [*of the Secret Assembly*]

Rim lnga 'gos lugs kyi khrid yig rgyud don gsal ba
Collected Works, vol. 9, pp. 156–93.

Instruction Manual of the Perfect Seat Free from the Stain of Bewilderment: Direct Guidance on the Five Stages of the Secret Assembly according to Nāgārjuna
gSang 'dus 'phags lugs rim lnga smar khrid gdan rdzogs kyi khrid yig 'khrul ba'i dri bral
Collected Works, vol. 9, pp. 194–222.

Instruction Manual of the Six Doctrines of Nigumā Entitled Unraveling the Meaning
Zab lam ni gu chos drug gi khrid yig zab don thang mar brdal ba
Collected Works, vol. 24, pp. 213–314.

Lamp of the Real Nature
De kho na nyid sgron ma
Collected Works, vol. 22, pp. 57–207.

Maṇḍala Rite of Glorious Cakrasaṃvara Entitled Ford of Supreme Bliss
dPal 'khor lo sdom pa'i dkyil 'khor gyi cho ga bde chen 'jug ngogs
Collected Works, vol. 13, pp. 232–88.

Method of Experiential Cultivation Combining All the Meanings of Tantra
rGyud don thams cad dril nas nyams len tshul
Collected Works, vol. 12, pp. 346–77. Related to Guidebook 66.

Precious Cornucopia of Exegesis on the Summation of the Real
De nyid 'dus pa'i rnam par bshad pa rin chen snye ma
Collected Works, vol. 20, pp. 1–67.

Quintessence of the Inciting of the Path of the Four Stages: Its Enlightened Intention
dGongs don rim bzhi lam slong snying por dril ba
Collected Works, vol. 16, pp. 276–303.

Tract on the Evidence of the Signs of Realization of the Six-Branch Yoga
rNal 'byor yan lag drug pa'i rtags tshad kyi yi ge
Collected Works, vol. 8, pp. 324–55; also in *DNZ* vol. 15, pp. 233–68.

Wondrous Instruction Manual of the Unelaborate Practice
sPros med kyi khrid yig ngo mtshar can
Collected Works, vol. 11, pp. 369–92.

Terdak Lingpa

Outer Attainment and Long-Life Empowerment of Amitāyus, Lord of the Dance, Entitled Downpour of Nectar, from the Profound Path: Gathering of All the Sugatas

Zab lam bde gshegs kun 'dus las padma gar dbang tshe dpag tu med pa phyi ltar sgrub pa tshe dbang dang bcas pa bdud rtsi'i char 'bebs
RTD vol. 24, no. 26, p. 390.

Thupten Phuntsok
Treasure Ocean of Tibetan Lexicography
Bod kyi tshig gter rgya mtsho
Chengdu: Sichuan mi rigs dpe skrun khang, 2012–13.

Yogic Exercises of the Channels and Winds
rTsa rlung 'phrul 'khor
Chengdu: Sichuan mi rigs dpe skrun khang, 1995.

Tokden Chonyi Rangdrol
Guidebook Entitled the Nature of Mind: The Wish-Fulfilling Gem
Sems khrid yid bzhin nor bu
Guidebook 108

Tokden Gangpa Rinchen Pelzangpo
The Striking
rTogs ldan dpal bzang pos bsdebs pa
NL.

Tokden Khacho Wangpo
Instruction [*on the Direct Guidance of Avalokiteśvara according to the Tradition of Drubchen Tsembupa*]
Grub chen tshem bu pa'i lugs kyi dmar khrid kyi gdams pa
NL.

Tokmé Zangpo
The Carrying of Happiness and Suffering on the Path
sKyid sdug lam khyer
Collected Works, pp. 201–5.
Translated in Jinpa 2006, 213–14; an antecedent to Guidebook 4.

The Coemergent Union of the Great Seal
Phyag chen lhan cig skyes sbyor gyi khrid yig
Kadampa Anthology II, pp. 259–78.
An antecedent of Guidebook 83.

Collected Works of Tokmé Zangpo
rGyal ba'i sras po thogs med bzang po'i bka' 'bum
1 vol. Lanzhou: Gansu Nationalities Publishing House, 2011.

Concise Interpretation of the Verses of the Aural Transmission of the Seven-Point Mind Training

bLo sbyong don bdun ma'i snyan brgyud kyi tshig rnams yi ge nyung ngu'i sgo nas bkrol ba
Collected Works, vol. 1, ff. 74b–108b. Lanzhou: Gansu Nationalities Publishing House, 2011. An elaboration of Guidebook 2.

Direct Guidance on All the Meditational Deities in General
sPyir yi dam thams cad kyi smar khrid
NL. An additional source of Guidebooks 34 and 35.

Great Aural Transmission of Mind Training
bLo sbyong snyan brgyud chen mo
Collected Works, vol. 1, ff. 226b–297b. Lanzhou: Gansu Nationalities Publishing House, 2011. An elaboration of Guidebook 2.

Guidance on the Coemergent Union of the Great Seal
Lhan cig skyes sbyor gyi khrid
Kadampa Anthology II, pp. 259–78; also in *DNZ* vol. 9, pp. 1–16.
An antecedent of Guidebook 83.

The Heart of Dependent Origination
rTen 'brel snying po
Collected Works, vol. 1, ff. 137b–142a; also Kadampa Anthology II, pp. 287–300.
An antecedent of Guidebook 3.

Homage to the Teachers of the Aural Transmission of Sumpa Lotsāwa
Sum pa lo tsā ba'i snyan brgyud kyi brgyud pa'i bla ma rnams la phyag 'tshal ba
Collected Works, vol. 1, p. 35.

Instruction on the Coemergent Union of the Great Seal
Phyag chen lhan cig skyes sbyor gyi khrid yig
Kadampa Anthology II, pp. 259–78.

Memorandum on Mind Training along with the Memorandum on the Direct Guidance
bLo sbyong zin bris dang dmar khrid zin bris bcas
Kadampa Anthology II, pp. 301–80. An elaboration of Guidebooks 2 and 32.

Mind Training of Sumpa Lotsāwa
Sum pa lo tsā ba'i blo sbyong
Translated in Jinpa 2006, 215–16. Related to Guidebook 5.

Practical Implementation of the Bodhisattvas
rGyal sras lag len [so bdun ma]
Collected Works, vol. 1, pp. 43–46.
Translated in Kunzang Pelden 2007 by Padmakara Translation Group.

The Seven-Point Mind Training of the Great Vehicle
Theg chen blo sbyong don bdun ma
DNZ vol. 4, pp. 189–214. Primary source of Guidebook 2.

The Three Essential Points
sNying po don gsum
DNZ vol. 16, pp. 605–16. Related to Guidebook 7.

Tsami Lotsāwa Mondrub Sherab
Guidebook Entitled the Six Doctrines of the Accomplished Masters
Grub thob chos drug gi khrid
Guidebook 104

Tsangpa Gyaré
Extracting the Essence of All Instructions of My Own Tradition on Auspicious Circumstances
rTen 'brel kho bo lugs kyi khrid chos thams cad kyi snying po len pa
Drukpa Kagyu Anthology vol. 55, pp. 618–20.

Guidebook Entitled the Means for Attainment of the Guru, Auspicious Circumstances, and Common Savor
bLa sgrub rten 'brel ro snyoms
This is an amalgam of three distinct instructions, which are all represented in *DNZ*, respectively, (i) *The Outer, Inner, and Secret Attainments of the Guru* (bLa ma phyi nang gsang sgrub pa'i gzhung), vol. 10, pp. 131–41; (ii) *The Basket of Sacred Doctrines: Meditation Sequence of Auspicious Circumstances* (rTen 'brel gyi sgom rim dam pa'i chos kyi za ma tog), vol. 10, pp. 123–30; and (iii) *Surmounting the Experiential Cultivation of the Six Cycles of Common Savor* (Ro snyoms skor drug gi nyams len sgang du dril ba), vol. 10, pp. 115–22.
Guidebook 98

Oral Teaching of the Single Sufficient Synopsis of Auspicious Circumstances
rTen 'brel gyi gnad bsdu chig chog ma'i zhal gdams
Drukpa Anthology vol. 55, pp. 417–22.

Ornament Adorning the Eight Great Instructions
Khrid chen brgyad mdzes par byed pa'i rgyan
DNZ vol. 10, pp. 173–87.

Tsawarongpa Śākya Gyeltsen
Memorandum on the Mental Focus on the Horns of Bhairava
Rwa rtse'i khrid yig gi zin bris
NL.

Tsen Khawoché

Guidebook Entitled the View of Extraneous Emptiness
gZhan stong gi lta khrid
Guidebook 25

Hook of the Lotus
Padma'i lcags kyu
NL. Primary source of Guidebook 25.

Tsewang Norbu

Inventory of the Meritorious Offerings Made to Jonang Takten Puntsoling
Jo nang rtag rten dga' ldan phun tshogs gling du dge rgyun sbyar ba'i dkar chag
Collected Works, vol. 2, pp. 449–51. Beijing: Krung go'i bod rig pa dpe skrun khang, 2006.

Tsokgompa Kunga Pel

Guidebook Entitled the Five Stages according to Ghaṇṭāpāda
Dril bu rim lnga'i khrid
Guidebook 69

Tsongkhapa Lobzang Drakpa

Collected Works of Tsongkhapa Lobzang Drakpa
rJe tsong kha pa'i gsung 'bum
18 vols. Labrang: Labrang Monastery, 199?.

Exegesis of the Five Stages according to Cakrasaṃvara Entitled Opening the Eyes of the View concerning the Concealed Meaning
bDe mchog rim lnga'i bshad pa sbas don lta ba'i mig rnam par 'byed pa
Collected Works, vol. 10, pp. 115–86.

Guidance on the View of the Middle Way
dBu ma'i lam gyi lta khrid
Collected Works, vol. 18, pp. 811–26.

Guidance on the View of the Sameness of Existence and Quiescence
Srid zhi mnyam nyid kyi lta ba'i khrid
Collected Works, vol. 15, pp. 767–817.

Teaching on the Instruction Manual of the Five Stages by Ghaṇṭāpāda, Documented by the Great Bodhisattva Cheton Kunga Zangpo
Dril bu rim lnga'i khrid yig rje'i gsung bzhin sems dpa' chen po lce ston kun dga' bzang pos mdzad pa
Collected Works, vol. 10, pp. 173–94.

Tsurton Wang-gi Dorjé

Guidebook Entitled the Four Scrolls of the Aural Instructions
sNyan gyi shog dril bzhi'i khrid
Guidebook 90

Yagdé Paṇchen Tsondru Dargyé
Guidebook Entitled the Four Syllables of the Great Seal
Phyag rgya chen po yi ge bzhi pa'i khrid
Guidebook 85

Yangonpa Gyeltsen Pel
Guidebook Entitled the Six Primary Essentials for Mountain Retreat of Yangonpa
Ri chos snying po ma drug gi khrid
Guidebook 100

Memorandum on the Four-Stage Yoga
rNal 'byor bzhi'i rim gyi zin bris
As documented by his disciple Gyen Chen Nga Rinchen Den
Collected Works, vol. 1, pp. 285–302. Thimphu, Bhutan: Tango Monastic Community, 1984.

Seven Days of Fierce Inner Heat according to Ga Lotsāwa
rGwa lo'i gtum mo zhag bdun ma
Drigungpa Anthology vol. 48, pp. 148–63. A primary source of Guidebook 94.

Three Crucial Points of the All-Pervasive Coemergent Union That Brings Forth the Miraculous Ability of the Esoteric Instructions
Man ngag 'phrul gyi thon pa'i kun 'gro lhan cig skyes sbyor gnad gsum
NL.

Trilogy on Mountain Retreat
Ri chos skor gsum
Comprising (i) *Source of All Attributes* (Yon tan kun 'byung); that is, *Profound Instruction of the Six Primary Essentials for Mountain Retreat: Origin of All Enlightened Attributes* (Ri chos yon tan kun 'byung gi snying po ma drug gi gdams zab), *DNZ* vol. 10, pp. 243–96; (ii) *Liberation from the Dangerous Passageway of the Intermediate State* (Bar do 'phrang sgrol); and (iii) *Concealed Exegesis of the Adamantine Body* (rDo rje lus kyi sbas bshad).
Primary source of Guidebook 100

Yangtsewa Rinchen Sengé
Guideboook Entitled Resting in the Nature of Mind
Sems nyid ngal gso'i khrid yig
Guidebook 8

Yarlungpa Sengé Gyeltsen (or else Mu Sangyé Rinchen of Ngor)
Guidebook Entitled the Inner Guidance of Glorious Pañjaranātha
dPal gur gyi mgon po'i nang khrid
Guidebook 102

Yeshe Gyeltsen (Sakya monk)
Pith Instruction of the Great Middle Way
dBu ma chen po'i man ngag
Kadampa Anthology I vol. 22, pp. 5–28.

Yolton/Yolgom Chowang
Cycles of Means for Attainment and Initiations for Eleven-Faced Sublime Avalokiteśvara according to the Tradition of the Nun Lakṣmī
'Phags pa spyan ras gzigs bcu gcig zhal dpal mo lugs kyi sgrub thabs rjes gnang dang bcas pa'i skor rnams
GDKT vol. 3, pp. 51–82. Primary source of Guidebook 30.

Guidebook Entitled Direct Guidance of Avalokiteśvara according to the Lakṣmī Tradition
dMar khrid dpal mo lugs kyi khrid yig
Guidebook 30

Zarjang Pugpa Kunga Lekpa Rinchen
Essence of the Focus on Guidance
Khrid dmigs kyi ngo bo
DNZ vol. 6, pp. 317–43.
Translated in Jinpa 2006, 541–66.

Zhamar Chokyi Wangchuk
Sessions of Experiential Cultivation of the Profound Six Doctrines of Nāropā Entitled Nectar Elixir
Zab mo na ro'i chos drug gi nyams len thun chos bdud rtsi'i nying khu
DNZ vol. 9, pp. 193–229.
Translated in Roberts 2011, 333–72.

Zhang Lotsāwa Jangchub-o
Guidebook Entitled the Six Doctrines of Liberation through the Upper Gate, according to the Aural Lineage
sNyan brgyud steng sgo chos drug gi khrid
Guidebook 91

Zhang Ring Kyitsa Ochen
Brief Notes [on the Direct Guidance of Avalokiteśvara according to the Tradition of the Bodhisattva Candradhvaja]
Tho chung
NL.

Zhang Śāntipa
The Inner Yoga of the Communal Offering: A Vase of Nectar
Tshogs 'khor nang gi rnal 'byor bdud rtsi bum pa
NL.

Zhang Tselpa Yudrakpa

Conclusive Supreme Path of the Great Seal
Phyag rgya chen po'i lam mchog mthar thug
DNZ vol. 8, pp. 429–62; also in *Collected Works*, vol. 4, pp. 78–149.

Guidebook Entitled the Elaborate Guidance according to Zhang Tselpa
Zhang gi zab rgyas khrid yig
Guidebook 93

Guidebook Entitled the Six-Branch Yoga according to Pelchen Ga Lotsāwa
dPal chen rgva lo'i sbyor drug gi khrid
Guidebook 94

Unrivaled Pith Instruction of Zhang Tselpa: The Preliminary and Main Practices in the Great Meditation of the Great Seal
Phyag rgya chen po sgom ma mo chen mo'i sngon 'gro dngos gzhi zhang rin po che zhes 'gran gyi do med de'i man ngag
DNZ vol. 8, pp. 463–84; also in *Collected Works*, vol. 9, pp. 29–72.

Zhang Yisun et al.

The Great Tibetan-Chinese Dictionary
Bod rgya tshig mdzod chen mo
3 vols. Beijing: Mi rigs dpe skrun khang, 1984.
Volume 1 translated in Nyima and Dorje 2001.

5. Works in Other Languages

Akester, Matthew. 2016. *Jamyang Khyentse Wangpo's Guide to Central Tibet*. Chicago: Serindia Publications.

Aris, Michael. 1979. *Bhutan: The Early History of a Himalayan Kingdom*. Warminster, UK: Aris and Phillips.

Ārya Asaṅga. 2016. *The Bodhisattva Path to Unsurpassed Enlightenment*. Translated by Artemus B. Engle. Boulder, CO: Snow Lion.

Arya Matreiya, and Acarya Asanga. 1985. *The Changeless Nature*. Translated by Kenneth Holmes and Katia Holmes. Eskdalemuir: Karma Drubgyud Darjay Ling.

Āryasūra. 1895. *The Jātakamālā of Āryasūra*. Translated by J. S. Speyer. London: Pali Text Society.

Baker, Ian A. 2019. *Tibetan Yoga: Principles and Practices*. London: Thames and Hudson.

Brough, John. 2001. *The Gandhari Dharmapada*. Delhi: Motilal Banarsidass

Brunnhölzl, Karl, trans. 2014. *When the Clouds Part: The Uttaratantra and Its Meditative Tradition as a Bridge between Sūtra and Tantra*. Boston: Snow Lion.

Bu-ston Rin-chen-grub. 1932. *History of Buddhism*. Translated by Eugene Obermiller. Heidelberg: Harrassowitz.

———. *See also* Butön Rinchen Drup.

Butön Rinchen Drup. 2013. *Butön's History of Buddhism in India and Its Spread to Tibet: A Treasury of Priceless Scripture.* Translated by Lisa Stein and Ngawang Zangpo. Boston: Snow Lion.

———. *See also* Bu-ston Rin-chen-grub.

Cha, Sangyeob. 2013. "The Yogācārabhūmi Meditation Doctrine of the 'Nine Stages of Mental Abiding' in East and Central Asian Buddhism." In *The Foundation for Yoga Practitioners: The Buddhist Yogācārabhūmi Treatise and Its Adaptation in India, East Asia, and Tibet,* edited by Ulrich Timme Kragh, 1166–91. Harvard Oriental Series 75. Cambridge, MA: Harvard University Press.

Chattopadhyaya, Alaka, and Lama Chimpa, trans. 1970/1990. *Tāranātha's History of Buddhism in India.* Delhi: Motilal Banarsidass.

Choying Tobden Dorje. 2014. *The Complete Nyingma Tradition from Sutra to Tantra, Books 1 to 10: Foundations of the Buddhist Path.* Translated by Ngawang Zangpo. Boston: Snow Lion.

———. 2016. *The Complete Nyingma Tradition from Sutra to Tantra, Books 15 to 17: The Essential Tantras of Mahayoga.* Translated by Gyurme Dorje. Boulder, CO: Snow Lion.

———. 2017. *The Complete Nyingma Tradition from Sutra to Tantra, Book 13: Philosophical Systems and Lines of Transmission.* Translated by Gyurme Dorje. Boulder, CO: Snow Lion.

Cleary, Thomas, trans. 1993. *The Flower Ornament Scripture.* Boston: Shambhala Publications.

Conze, Edward, trans. 1973. *The Perfection of Wisdom in Eight Thousand Lines and Its Verse Summary.* Bolinas, CA: Four Seasons Foundation.

———, trans. 1975. *The Large Sutra on Perfect Wisdom.* Berkeley: University of California Press.

Dakpo Tashi Namgyal. 2006. *Mahāmudrā: The Moonlight—Quintessence of Mind and Meditation.* Translated by Lobsang P. Lhalungpa. Boston: Wisdom Publications.

———. 2019. *Moonbeams of Mahāmudrā.* Translated by Elizabeth M. Callahan. Boulder, CO: Snow Lion.

Davidson, Ronald M., trans. 1981. "The Litany of Names of Manjushri: Text and Translation of the Manjushri-nama-samgiti." In *Tantric and Taoist Studies, in Honour of R. A. Stein,* edited by Michel Strickmann, 1–69. Vol. 20 of Mélanges Chinoises et Bouddhiques. Brussels: Institut Belge des Hautes Études Chinoises.

———. 2005. *Tibetan Tantric Buddhism in the Renaissance: Rebirth of Tibetan Culture.* New York: Columbia University Press.

Dayal, Har. (1932) 1970. *The Bodhisattva Doctrine in Buddhist Sanskrit Literature.* London: Routledge & Kegan Paul. Reprint, Delhi: Motilal Banarsidass. Citations refer to Banarsidass edition.

Deroche, Marc-Henri. 2009. "'Phreng po gter ston shes rab 'od zer (1518–1584) on the Eight Lineages of Attainment: Research on a Ris med Paradigm." In *Contemporary Visions in Tibetan Studies. Proceedings of the First International Seminar of*

Young Tibetologists, edited by Brandon Dodson, Kalsang Norbu Gurung, Georgios Halkias, and Tim Myatt, 328–35. Chicago: Serindia Publications.

Dhongthog Rinpoche. 2016. *The Sakya School of Tibetan Buddhism: A History.* Translated by Sam Van Schaik. Somerville, MA: Wisdom Publications.

Dorje, Gyurme. 1987. "The Guhyagarbhatantra and its XIVth Century Tibetan Commentary *Phyogs bcu mun sel.*" 3 vols. PhD diss., University of London, School of Oriental and African Studies.

———, trans. 2005. *The Tibetan Book of the Dead.* London and New York: Penguin.

———. 2009. *Tibet.* Bath, UK: Footprint Handbooks.

———, trans. Forthcoming. *Histories of the Taklung Kagyu Tradition.* Boulder, CO: Shambhala Publications.

Ducher, Cecile. 2016. "bKa' brgyud Treasure and rNyingma Revealer: The Sras mkhar ma of Mar pa Lo tsā ba." *Revue d'Etudes Tibétaines* 37 (December): 98–126.

Dudjom Rinpoche. 1991. *The Nyingma School of Tibetan Buddhism: Its Fundamentals and History.* 2 vols. Translated by Gyurme Dorje with Matthew Kapstein. Boston: Wisdom Publications.

Dutt, Nalinaksha. 1934. *Pañcaviṃśatisāhasrikā Prajñāpāramitā*, edition of the recast Sanskrit manuscript (Part One). Calcutta Oriental Series 28. London: Luzac.

English, Elizabeth. 2002. *Vajrayoginī: Her Visualizations, Rituals, and Forms.* Boston: Wisdom Publications.

Fremantle, Francesca. 1971. "A Critical Study of the Guhyasamāja Tantra." PhD diss., University of London, School of Oriental and African Studies.

Gray, David B., trans. 2007. *The Cakrasaṃvara Tantra.* New York: American Institute of Buddhist Studies.

Gray, David, Shaman Hatley, Olga Serbaeva, and Péter-Dániel Szántó., trans. Forthcoming. *Appendix to the Discourse Tantra.* (*Abhidhānottaratantra*). 84000: Translating the Words of the Buddha. https://84000.co/.

———. Forthcoming. *Ocean of Ḍākas: A Yoginītantra.* (*Ḍākarṇavamahāyoginītantrarāja*). 84000: Translating the Words of the Buddha. https://84000.co/.

Gruschke, Andreas. 2001. *Amdo.* Vol. 2, *The Gansu and Sichuan Parts of Amdo.* The Cultural Monuments of Tibet's Outer Provinces. Bangkok: White Lotus Press.

Guenther, Herbert V. 1963. *The Life and Teaching of Naropa.* Oxford: Clarendon Press.

———. 1993. *Ecstatic Spontaneity: Saraha's Three Cycles of Dohā.* Berkeley: Asian Humanities Press.

Gyalwa Yangonpa. 2015. *Secret Map of the Body: Visions of the Human Energy Structure.* Translated by Elio Guarisco. Merigar: Shang Shung Publications.

Harding, Sarah, trans. (2003) 2018. *Machik's Complete Explanation: Clarifying the Meaning of Chöd.* Ithaca, NY: Snow Lion Publications. Revised, Boston: Snow Lion.

———. 2010. *Niguma: Lady of Illusion.* Ithaca, NY: Snow Lion Publications.

Heimbal, Joerg. 2013. "The Jo gdan tshogs sde bzhi: An Investigation into the History of the Four Monastic Communities in Śākyaśrībhadra's Vinaya Tradition." In *Nepalica-Tibetica Festgabe For Christophe Cüppers*, vol. 1, edited by Franz-Karl Ehrhard and Petra Maurer, 187–241. Andiast, Switzerland: International Institute for Tibetan and Buddhist Studies.

Henning, Edward. 2007. *Kālacakra and the Tibetan Calendar*. New York: American Institute of Buddhist Studies.

Higgins, David. 2008. "On the Development of the Non-mentation (*Amansikāra*) Doctrine in Indo-Tibetan Buddhism." *Journal of the International Association of Buddhist Studies* 29 (2): 255–303.

Hodge, Stephen, trans. 2003. *The Mahā-Vairocana-Abhisaṃbodhi Tantra with Buddhaguhya's Commentary*. London: RoutledgeCurzon.

Jackson, David. 1976. "The Early History of Lo (Mustang) and Ngari." *Contributions to Nepalese Studies* 4 (1).

———. 1996. "The *bsTan rim* ('Stages of the Doctrine') and Similar Graded Expositions of the Bodhisattva's Path." In *Tibetan Literature: Studies in Genre, Essays in Honor of Geshe Lhundrup Sopa*, edited by José I. Cabezón and Roger Jackson, 220–43. Ithaca, NY: Snow Lion Publications.

Jamgön Kongtrul Lodrö Taye. 2003. *The Autobiography of Jamgön Kongtrul: A Gem of Many Colors*. Translated by Richard Barron. Ithaca, NY: Snow Lion Publications.

———. 2005. *The Treasury of Knowledge, Book 6, Part 4: Systems of Buddhist Tantra*. Translated by Elio Guarisco and Ingrid McLeod. Ithaca, NY: Snow Lion Publications.

———. 2007. *The Treasury of Knowledge, Book 8, Part 4: Esoteric Instructions*. Translated by Sarah Harding. Ithaca, NY: Snow Lion Publications.

———. 2008. *The Treasury of Knowledge, Book 8, Part 3: The Elements of Tantric Practice*. Translated by Elio Guarisco and Ingrid McLeod. Ithaca, NY: Snow Lion Publications.

———. 2012. *The Treasury of Knowledge, Book 6, Parts 1 and 2: Indo-Tibetan Classical Learning and Buddhist Phenomenology*. Translated by Gyurme Dorje. Boston: Snow Lion.

———. 2013. *The Catalog of The Treasury of Precious Instructions*. Translated by Richard Barron. New York: Tsadra Foundation.

———. 2016. *The Treasury of Precious Instructions: Essential Teachings of the Eight Practice Lineages of Tibet*. Vol. 14, *Chöd: The Sacred Teachings on Severance*. Translated by Sarah Harding. Boulder, CO: Snow Lion.

———. 2019. *The Treasury of Precious Instructions: Essential Teachings of the Eight Practice Lineages of Tibet*. Vol. 13, *Zhijé: The Pacification of Suffering*. Translated by Sarah Harding. Boulder, CO: Snow Lion.

Jamgön Mipham. 2004. *Maitreya's Distinguishing Phenomena and Pure Being*. Translated by Jim Scott. Ithaca, NY: Snow Lion Publications.

———. 2018. *A Feast of the Nectar of the Supreme Vehicle.* Translated by Padmakara Translation Group. Boulder, CO: Shambhala Publications.

Jinpa, Thupten, trans. 2006. *Mind Training: The Great Collection.* Boston: Wisdom Publications.

———, trans. 2008. *The Book of Kadam: The Core Texts.* Boston: Wisdom Publications.

Kapstein, Matthew T. 1980. "The Shangs-pa bKa'-brgyud: An Unknown School of Tibetan Buddhism." In *Tibetan Studies in Honour of Hugh Richardson: Proceedings of the International Seminar on Tibetan Studies,* edited by Michael Aris and Aung San Suu Kyi, 138–44. Warminster, UK: Aris and Phillips.

———. 1992. "Remarks on the Maṇi bKa'-'bum and the Cult of Avalokiteśvara in Tibet." In *Tibetan Buddhism: Reason and Revelation,* edited by Steven D. Goodman and Ronald M. Davidson, 79–93. Albany: SUNY Press.

———. 1996. "gDams ngag: Tibetan Technologies of the Self." In *Tibetan Literature: Studies in Genre,* edited by Jose Ignacio Cabezón and Roger R. Jackson, 275–89. Ithaca, NY: Snow Lion Publications.

———. 2007. "Tibetan Technologies of the Self, Part II: The Teachings of the Eight Great Conveyances." In *The Pandita and the Siddha. Tibetan Studies in Honour of E. Gene Smith,* edited by Ramon N. Prats, 110–11. Dharamsala: Amnye Machen Institute.

Khedrup Norsang Gyatso. 2004. *Ornament of Stainless Light.* Translated by Gavin Kilty. Boston: Wisdom Publications.

Khenchen Thrangu. 1993. *The Practice of Tranquillity and Insight.* Ithaca, NY: Snow Lion Publications.

———. 2004. *The Ornament of Clear Realization: A Commentary on the Prajnaparamita of the Maitreya Buddha.* Translated by Ken Holmes, Katia Holmes, and Cornelia Weishaar-Gunter. Auckland: Zhyisil Chokyi Ghatsal Charitable Trust Publications.

Kimura, Takayasu. 1986–2007. *Pañcaviṃśatisāhasrikā Prajñāpāramitā.* 8 parts. Tokyo: Sankibo Busshorin.

Konow, Sten. 1941. *The First Two Chapters of the Daśasāhasrikā Prajñāpāramitā: Restoration of the Sanskrit Text, Analysis and Index.* Oslo: I Kommisjon Hos Jacob Dybwad.

Kunzang Pelden. 2007. *The Nectar of Manjushri's Speech: A Detailed Commentary on Shantideva's Way of the Bodhisattva.* Translated by Padmakara Translation Group. Boston: Shambhala Publications.

Longchenpa. 1975–76. *Kindly Bent to Ease Us.* 3 parts. Translated by Herbert V. Guenther. Emeryville, CA: Dharma Publishing.

———. 2011. *The Guhyagarbha Tantra: Secret Essence Definitive Just as It Is.* Translated by Lama Chönam and Sangye Khandro. Ithaca, NY: Snow Lion Publications.

———. 2018–2019. *The Trilogy of Rest.* Translated by Padmakara Translation Group. 3 vols. Boulder, CO: Shambhala Publications.

Maitreya, and Jamgön Kongtrul Lodreu Thayé. 2019. *Traité de la Continuité suprême du Grande Véhicule: Mahāyāna-uttaratantra-śāstra, avec le commentaire de Jamgön Kongtrul Lodreu Thayé: L'Incontestable Rugissement du lion*. Translated and annotated by Christian Charrier and Patrick Carré. Plazac, France: Éditions Padmakara.

Maitreya, and Jamgon Mipham. 2006. *Middle Beyond Extremes: Maitreya's Madhyāntavibhāga with Commentaries by Khenpo Shenga and Ju Mipham*. Ithaca, NY: Snow Lion Publications.

———. 2014. *Ornament of the Great Vehicle Sūtras: Maitreya's Mahāyānasūtrālaṃkāra with Commentaries by Khenpo Shenga and Ju Mipham*. Translated by Dharmachakra Translation Committee. Boston: Snow Lion.

Maitreyanātha. 1954. *Abhisamayālaṅkāra*. Translated by Edward Conze. Serie Orientale Roma 6. Rome: Istituto Italiano per il Medio ed Estremo Oriente.

Maitreyanātha and Āryāsaṅga. 2004. *The Universal Vehicle Discourse Literature*. Translated by American Institute of Buddhist Studies team. New York: American Institute of Buddhist Studies.

Marpa Chokyi Lodro. 1995. *The Life of the Mahāsiddha Tilopa*. Translated by Fabrizio Torricelli and Achārya Sangye T. Naga. Dharamsala: Library of Tibetan Works and Archives.

Martin, Dan. 1997. *Tibetan Histories*. London: Serindia Publications.

Mathes, Klaus-Dieter. 2009. "Maitrīpa's Amanasikārādhāra ('A Justification of Becoming Mentally Disengaged')." *Journal of the Nepal Research Centre* 13, pp. 5–32.

———. 2015. *A Fine Blend of Mahāmudrā and Madhyamaka: Maitrīpa's Collection of Texts on Non-conceptual Realization (Amanasikara)*. Vienna: Verlag der Österreichischen Akademie der Wissenschaften.

Mills, Martin A. 2007. "Reassessing the Supine Demoness: Royal Buddhist Geomancy in the Srong btsan sgam po Mythology," *Journal of the International Association of Tibetan Studies* 3 (December): 15–21.

Mullin, Glenn H., and Jeff J. Watt. 2003. *Female Buddhas*. Santa Fe, NM: Clear Light Publishers.

Nebesky-Wojkowitz, René de. 1975. *Oracles and Demons of Tibet: The Cult and Iconography of the Tibetan Deities*. Graz, Austria: Akademische Druck-u.

Newman, John. 1987. "The Outer Wheel of Time: Vajrayāna Buddhist Cosmology in the Kālacakra Tantra." PhD diss., University of Wisconsin.

Nyima, Tudeng, ed., and Gyurme Dorje, trans. 2001. *An Encyclopaedic Tibetan-English Dictionary*. Beijing: Nationalities Publishing House/School of Oriental and African Studies.

Padmakara Translation Group, trans. 2018. *The Transcendent Perfection of Wisdom in Ten Thousand Lines*. 84000: Translating the Words of the Buddha. http://read.84000.co/translation/toh11.html.

Pandey, Janardan Shastri, ed. 2000. *Tattvajñānasaṃsiddhiḥ of Śūnyasamādhipada with Marmakalikāpañjikā of Vīryaśrīmitra*. Sarnath, Varanasi: Central Institute of Higher Tibetan Studies.

Parfionovitch, Yuri, Gyurme Dorje, and Fernand Meyer. 1992. *Tibetan Medical Paintings: Illustrations to the Blue Beryl Treatise of Sangye Gyamtso (1653–1795)*. London: Serindia Publications.

Patrul Rinpoche. 1994. *The Words of My Perfect Teacher*. Translated by Padmakara Translation Group. San Francisco: HarperCollins.

Peissel, Michel. 1967. *Mustang: A Lost Tibetan Kingdom*. New Delhi: Faith Books.

Rangjung Dorje. 2014. *The Profound Inner Principles*. Translated by Elizabeth M. Callahan. Boston: Snow Lion.

Rigdzin Dorje. 2013. *Gathering the Elements*. Translated by Matthew Boord. Berlin: Wandel Verlag.

Ringu Tulku. 2006. *The Ri-me Philosophy of Jamgön Kongtrul the Great*. Boston: Shambhala Publications.

Roberts, Peter Alan. 2007. *The Biographies of Rechungpa: The Evolution of a Tibetan Hagiography*. London: Routledge.

———, trans. 2011. *Mahāmudrā and Related Instructions: Core Teachings of the Kagyu Schools*. Boston: Wisdom Publications.

Roberts, Peter Alan, and Tulku Yeshi, trans. 2013. *The Basket's Display*. 84000 Online: Translating the Words of the Buddha. https://read.84000.co/translation/toh116.html.

Robinson, James B. 1979. *Buddha's Lions: The Lives of the Eighty-Four Siddhas*. Berkeley: Dharma Publishing.

Roerich, George, trans. 1949. *The Blue Annals*. 1st ed. Delhi: Motilal Banarsidass.

Ruegg, D. S. 1963. "The Jo Nang Pa, a School of Buddhist Ontologists according to the Grub mTha' Sel Me Long." *Journal of the American Oriental Society* 82 (1): 73–91.

Sangyes Nyenpa. 2014. *Tilopa's Mahamudra Upadesha: The Gangama Instructions with Commentary*. Translated by David Molk. Boston: Snow Lion.

Santideva. 1971. *Śikṣā Samuccaya*. Translated by Cecil Bendall and W. H. D. Rouse. Delhi: Motilal Banarsidass.

———. *See also* Shantideva.

Shantideva. 1997. *An Introduction to the Way of the Bodhisattva: A Translation of the Bodhicharyāvatāra*. Translated by Padmakara Translation Group. Boston: Shambhala Publications.

———. *See also* Santideva.

Sheehy, Michael R. 2019. "The Case of the Missing Shangpa in Tibet." In *Reasons and Lives in Buddhist Traditions: Studies in Honor of Matthew Kapstein*, edited by Daniel Arnold, Cecile Ducher, and Pierre-Julien Harter. Boston: Wisdom Publications.

Sherbourne, Richard, trans. 2000. *The Complete Works of Atiśa*. Delhi: Aditya Prakashan.

Snellgrove, David L., trans. 1959. *The Hevajra Tantra.* 2 parts. London: Oxford University Press.

———. 1989. *Himalayan Pilgrimage: A Study of Tibetan Religion by a Traveller through Western Nepal.* 2nd ed. Boston: Shambhala Puplications.

Sparham, Gareth, trans. 2006–12. *Abhisamayālaṃkāra with Vṛtti and Ālokā.* 4 vols. Fremont, CA: Jain Publishing.

Stearns, Cyrus. 2001. *Luminous Lives: The Story of the Early Masters of the Lam 'bras Tradition in Tibet.* Boston: Wisdom Publications.

———. 2006. *The Buddha from Dolpo: A Study of the Life and Thought of the Tibetan Master Dolpopa Sherab Gyaltsen.* Ithaca, NY: Snow Lion Publications.

———, trans. 2010. *Taking the Result as the Path: Core Teachings of the Sakya Lamdré Tradition.* Boston: Wisdom Publications.

Takasaki, Jikido. 1966. *A Study on the Ratnagotravibhāga (Uttaratantra).* Serie Orientale Roma 33. Rome: Istituto Italiano per il Medio ed Estremo Oriente.

Trizin Tsering Rinpoche, trans. 2007. *The Mani Kabum.* Singapore: Evergreen Buddhist Culture Service.

Tselé Natsok Rangdrol. 1987. *The Mirror of Mindfulness.* Translated by Erik Pema Kunsang. Kathmandu: Rangjung Yeshe Publications.

Tsongkhapa. 2013. *A Lamp to Illuminate the Five Stages.* Translated by Gavin Kilty. Boston: Wisdom Publications.

Vasubandhu. 1988–90. *Abhidharmakośabhāṣyaṃ.* 4 vols. Translated by Leo M. Pruden. Berkeley: Asian Humanities Press.

Wallace, Vesna A. 2001. *The Inner Kālacakratantra: A Buddhist Tantric View of the Individual.* New York: Oxford University Press.

———, trans. 2004. *The Kālacakratantra: The Chapter on the Individual Together with the Vimalaprabhā.* New York: American Institute of Buddhist Studies.

———, trans. 2010. *The Kālacakratantra: The Chapter on Sādhanā Together with the Vimalaprabhā Commentary.* New York: American Institute of Buddhist Studies.

Wayman, Alex, trans. 1977. *Yoga of the Guhyasamāja: The Arcane Lore of Forty Verses: A Buddhist Tantra Commentary.* Delhi: Motilal Banarsidass.

———, trans. 1983. *Chanting the Names of Mañjuśrī: The Mañjuśrī -Nāma-Saṃgīti Sanskrit and Tibetan Texts.* Delhi: Motilal Banarsidass.

Willson, Martin, and Martin Brauen. 2000. *Deities of Tibetan Buddhism: The Zurich Paintings of the Icons Worthwhile to See.* Boston: Wisdom Publications.

Yeshe Gyamtso, trans. 2011. *Biographies of the Hundred Tertöns.* Woodstock, NY: KTD Publications.

Index

Aba Drakpa, 177
Abhayadattaśrī, 115, 203, 645n38, 711n1056
Abhayākaragupta, 102–3, 182
Abhidharma, 466, 706n987, 707n992
abodes, profound, 277, 666n240
Abridged History of the Abbatial Succession of the Jonangwa (Peljam), xxiv–xxv
Abridgement of the Essentials of the Root and Commentary of the Introduction to the Middle Way (Patsab), 170
Acala, 22, 23, 157, 166–67, 245–47, 258, 259, 501, 518, 626n11, 652n79
action seal, 310, 450, 453, 642n12, 672n324
activities, occasional, 365, 685n604
Acyutakāṇha, 343, 636n55
adamantine body (vajrakāya), 56, 288, 307, 482, 522, 643n27
adamantine chain of light, 489–90, 492
Adamantine Garland, 278
adamantine holder, 136, 463, 633n15
adamantine recitation, 328, 377, 443, 456–57, 677n400
Adamantine Sky-Farers empowerment, 517
Adamantine Song of Chanting Meditation (Mitrayogin), 158, 638n11
Adamantine Subjugator Maṇivajra empowerment, 518–19
Adamantine Tent empowerment, 514
Advayavajra, 694–95n779
afflicted mental consciousness, 175, 639n40, 648n7
afflicted mental states
  abandoning, 226, 271
  antidotes for, 465
  arising of, 340
  buddha nature and, 270
  calming, 269
  carrying onto path, 474
  dependent phenomena and, 271
  increase in, 391
  as magical display, 347
  melting of, 453
  movement of, 408
aggregates, five, 237, 369, 412, 629n35, 651n60, 666n242
Agni ("mouth of ogre"), 453, 704n955
Ajātaśatru, 253
Akaniṣṭha, 421, 488
Ākāśagarbha, 355
Akṣayamati, 157
Akṣayamatinirdeśasūtra, 632n8
Akṣobya, 665n226
  deity assemblage of, 275
  empowerments of, 515, 519
  encompassing and dissolution of, 374
  enlightened family of, 369
  hatred and, 437
  at heart, 327, 355
  palace of, 177
  visualizations, 263, 265, 484
  wind, 371
  See also Mañjuvajra
Alalavajra, 53, 63, 64
alchemical transformation, 443, 471, 701n886
altruistic mind, 138, 216, 289, 323, 447, 634n26. *See also* enlightened mind
Amdo, xxv
Amitābha, 381
  desire and, 437
  encompassing and dissolution, 374
  enlightened family of, 369
  lineages, 34, 117–18

Amitābha (*continued*)
red, 263, 355
at throat cakra, 327, 355
in transference, 490–91
visualizations, 265, 286, 289, 290, 291, 292, 293, 327, 435
wind, 371
Amitāyus, 624n11
empowerments, 518, 519, 520, 639n37
lineages, 35, 36
visualization, 283–85
white, 287–88
Amoghasiddhi
encompassing and dissolution of, 374
enlightened family of, 369
jealousy and, 437
at secret cakra, 327, 355
wind, 371
Amoghasiṃha, 103
Amoghavajra. *See* Vajrāsana the Younger (a.k.a. Amoghavajra)
Amoghavajra the Elder, 72–73
Amulet Tradition of the Great Seal, 510
classification, 503
historical account, 193
lineage prayer, 85–86
practices, 421–22
source, 697n829
transmission, xxi, 149
anal plug, 364, 365, 685n594
analysis and logic, 225, 313, 314
Analysis of Empowerment (Drakpa Gyeltsen), 178
Ānanda, 168
Ānandagupta, 32
Ānandakīrti, 32
Ānandavajra, 41, 42, 142–43, 173, 502, 508, 669n278
Anaṅgavajra, 52–53, 55–56, 641–42n9, 644n34
Andhara, 73–74
animals, 227, 237, 322, 438, 626n4, 630n54
Anuyoga tantra, 204
Anyen Dampa Kunga Drak, 69–70
Apabhraṃśa, 632n10
Apo, 256
appearances, 298, 316
awareness as, 475
consecration of, 384
as deities, 365
and emptiness, indivisibility of, 352, 419, 436, 494
examining, 242–43
four visionary, 493, 712n1069
habitual propensities and, 461
impure, 321–23, 641n63
as magical displays, 416, 423, 460, 462, 476
as mind, 494
purifying, 353
relative, 240, 272
as spiritual mentors, arising, 335, 347–48
See also pure appearances
Ārali Trilogy, 279
Aro Yeshé Jugné, 645n42
Array of the Seats of the Syllables (Drakpa Gyeltsen), 147, 690n710
Array of the Staircase Differentiating the Stages (Vajrahāsya), 273
Arraying of the Physical Body with the Four Empowerments of Khecarī, 390
Āryadeva, 11, 19, 57, 67–68, 111, 166, 276, 278, 639n27
Āryadeva the Brahmin, 162, 194, 638n21
Asaṅga, 6, 14–15, 16, 29, 168
ascertainment, four grades, 260, 661n175
asceticism. *See* austerities
Aseng of Nenying, 148
ashé, 277, 284, 329–30, 436, 440–41, 442–43, 462, 471, 483, 484, 628n27, 666n240
aspirationlessness, 332
aspirations, 253, 268, 440, 493
in dream yoga, 417, 463, 471, 486, 487
higher, 269, 399
prayers of, 223, 289, 339
transcendent perfection of, 663n210
See also four immeasurable aspirations
Asthikhandaḍākinī, 98
Asu, the Newar, 202
Aśvaghoṣa, 111, 639n27
Aśvottama, 51–52
Atiśa (a.k.a. Dīpaṃkarabhadra), xv, 135, 253, 256, 626n8
historical accounts, 158–59, 171
lineages, 6, 8, 14–15, 16, 17, 20, 21, 22–23, 24, 29, 35, 37, 40, 69–70, 141, 164, 173
oral instructions of, 192, 287, 667n265
tradition of, 172, 182, 276, 278

visualizations, 258, 259, 660n166
works, 142, 202, 633n22
attachment, 232, 448, 462
to entities, 221
to five paths, 446
four types, 5, 220–21, 626n2, 647–48n2
in intermediate state, 464, 487
liberating, 494
winds of, 449
Attainment in Proximity to a Stupa/ Determination of Mind, 509, 628n31, 713n2
historical account, 176
lineage prayer, 57
practices, 348–49
source, 681n505
transmission, xx, 145, 636n55
Attainment of Coemergence, 509
historical account, 176
lineage prayer, 53–54
practices, 339–41
source, 679n453
transmission, xx, 145, 636n55
Attainment of the Pristine Cognition of the Real (Śabaripā), 190
Aural Lineage of Cakrasaṃvara, 517, 667n257, 694n766
Aural Lineage of Kālacakra, 509
classification, 501
historical account, 174–75
lineage prayer, 48–49
practices, 312–16
source, 673n330
transmission, xxi, 144, 636n47
auspicious circumstances, 182, 199, 467, 468
instructions on, 473–74, 643n27, 708n1010
Middle Way and, 168
power of, 365
sacraments of, 382
three, 324, 675–76n382
austerities, 27, 324, 339, 340, 468, 627n13, 679n454
Avadhūtipā. *See* Maitrīpā (a.k.a. Avadhūtipā)
Avadhūtipā Namgyel Drakpa, xxii, 24–25, 106–7, 515
Avalokiteśvara, 624n11, 626n11, 652n79
attainment of, 204
deity assemblage of, 275
empowerments of, 515, 518
Jinasāgara, 258
Khasarpaṇi, 13, 163, 164, 179, 234
lineages, 12, 22–23, 37, 38–39, 40, 61, 117–18
Mahākāruṇika, 289, 290, 293, 660n163
path manifesting as, 229
visualizations, 227, 247–48, 435, 490, 660n165
aversion, 222, 232
awakenings, five, 291, 294, 295, 669n274
awareness
clarity/luminosity of, 231, 441
conduct of, 447, 448
direct introduction to, 430–31
and emptiness, inseparability of, 344
and expanse, mingling of, 316
expressive power of, 493
as lamp of pristine cognition, 451–52
natural, 235, 314
nature of, 381
nonarising, 221
nurturing, 485
settling, 242, 304
vigilance in, 473
See also intrinsic awareness
axis of vitality. *See* central channel
Ayi Sengyé, 192

Bagton Tsultrim Gyeltsen, 29–30, 32–33, 71, 82
Bagton Zhonu Gyeltsen, 31
Bagton Zhonu Tsultrim, 29–30, 31, 71, 82, 115
Baiḍūr Tsongdu, 160
Bangarwa Jampel Zangpo, 83–84, 93–94
Banrik Gyelkhampa, 116–17
Barawa Gyeltsen Pelzang, 49–50, 103, 110, 141, 142, 172, 283, 667n262, 708n1007
Bardingpa Namka Gyeltsen, 175
Bareg Lotsāwa Sonam Gyeltsen, 29–30
Bareg Tonkyab, 29–30
Bari Lotsāwa Rinchen Drak, 41, 156–57, 511
Barron, Richard, 623n1
Barwa Gyeltsen Pelzang, 34, 49–50, 103, 110, 141, 142, 172, 283, 667n262, 708n1007
Be Drum, 28

Beauteous Unelablorate Ornament, 146
Bengal, 260, 660n171
Bengarwa Jampel Zangpo, 83–84, 93–94
Beta (Vaidarbha), 260, 660n171
Beton Zhikpo, 37–38
bewilderment, 220–21, 237, 271, 281, 447, 487
Bhadrapāda, 29–30, 51–52
Bhaṭṭāraka Vimuktisena, 6, 14–15, 16
Bhaṭṭārikā Tārā, 9, 10, 11
Bhavyabodhi, 81
Bhisukalpa, 641n9
Bhṛṅgapadminī, 55–56
Bhuṣaṇa, 51–52
Bimbisāra, 253
Biography of Lama Dampa Sonam Gyeltsen (Jangchub Tsemo), 180
birth, 421, 439, 440, 492–93
blessings, 260, 262, 469, 493
  of book empowerment, 521
  of buddhas, 284, 484
  of ḍākinīs, 342
  forcefully drawing, 473
  four types, 143, 297–98
  guru's, consciousness transference of, 420
  on intrinsic nature, 285–86
  lineage of, 167, 196, 200
  of long-life empowerment, 172
  of nondual pristine cognition, 349
  of teachers, 223, 262, 422
bliss, 298, 318
  arising of, 340, 357, 372, 403
  descent of, 457
  and emptiness, coalescence of, 334, 339, 344, 352, 385, 410, 419, 454
  enhancing, 345
  excessive, 394
  experiencing, 242, 342, 471
  great/supreme, 271, 303, 311, 312, 315, 372, 450–51
  increasing, 470
blood (*khrag*, *rakta*), 216, 243, 265, 295, 364, 387, 397, 416, 449, 481, 628n29, 669n277
bodhisattvas, 239, 247, 269, 355, 467. *See also* ten bodhisattva levels
Bodhiśrī Ngok Jangchub Peldrub. *See* Ngok Jangchub Peldrub
Bodong lineage, xxii, 76–77, 624n11
Bodong Paṇchen Jigdrel Sangwa Jin, 33
Bodong Rinchen Tsemo, 159–60
Bodong Tsondru Dorjé, 76
Bodongpa Choklé Namgyal, 34, 172, 283, 627n17, 665nn225–27, 666n250, 667n256, 667n260
body, maturational, 439, 486, 487
body, mental, 230, 418, 439, 445, 471, 487–88, 650n34, 702n898, 706n986
body, physical, 478
  bliss and emptiness permeating, 345
  as blue silk tent, 420
  cherishing, 383
  as deity, 395, 412
  as empty frame, 410, 415, 461
  maṇḍala of, 366
  not squandering, 339, 679n454
  sparks diffused from, 391
  as support, 236
Bokar Gon, xv
Bonpo tradition, xiv, 466
Book of Kadam, 140, 259
Brahmā, 281, 434
Brahmāṇī, 55–56
breathing, 449, 470
  adamantine recitation and, 328, 456–57, 677n400
  exhalation, pith instructions on, 328–29
  in fierce inner heat, 628n28
  inhalation, pith instructions on, 329
  in mind training, 221, 224
  in perfection stage, 282
  respiration cycle, 312, 673n328
  in six-branch yoga, 307–9
  training, methods of, 404–5, 694n765
  vigorous, 477, 479
  See also vase breathing
Buchang, inner way of, 339, 340, 679n454
buddha bodies
  five, 332, 333, 443, 455
  four, 222–23, 397, 422, 459
  two form, 272, 664n224
buddha bodies, three, 299, 422, 468, 681n487
  arising of, 340
  carrying onto path, 419
  happiness and suffering as, 160
  prayer to, 233–34
  spontaneous presence of, 315
  and sufferings, three, 353

as teacher, 472–73
in transference, 378
buddha body of emanation, 47, 229, 439
channels as, 450
coalescence of, 375, 687n651
conduct and, 447–48
introduction to, 435
visualization, 264–65
buddha body of essentiality, 422, 455
buddha body of perfect resource, 47, 229
coalescence of, 374
five enlightened families as, 680n471
as intermediate state, 439
in intermediate state, 413, 420, 421
introduction to, 435
in signs, 318
verbal conduct and, 448
visualization of, 262–63
winds as, 450
buddha body of reality, 47, 228–29, 314, 460, 469
attaining, 441
direct perception of, 277
disposition of, 493
as fruition, 260
in intermediate state, 488
introduction to, 435
liberation in, 349
mental conduct and, 448
as natural luminosity, 439
shifting display of, 459
transference into, 420
vital essence as, 450
buddha fields, 347, 454
buddha nature, 270
Buddha Śākyamuni, 21, 251, 655n114
definitive presence of, 198
lineages, 4, 6, 8, 14, 16, 17, 18, 20, 23, 24, 25, 27, 28, 29, 31, 32, 101–2
mantra of, 259
monastic succession of, 168, 639n27
three promulgations of, 627n14
twelve deeds of, 378, 688n675
visualizations, 258, 463, 472, 660n164, 660n166
Buddhadatta, 82, 641n5, 694–95n779
Buddhaguhya, 204, 261
buddhahood, 135, 312, 402, 493, 494
aspiration for, 129, 214
aspiration for others', 238
attaining, 221, 244
capacity for, 378
at death, 475
for others' sake, 345, 681n487
primordial, 433
three vehicles and, 467
time needed to attain, 466
Buddhajñānapāda, 69–70, 176, 197, 275, 276, 501, 515, 642n20, 687n653
Buddhakapāla, 278, 517
Buddhalocanā, 371, 462
buddhas
eighteen distinct attributes of, 435, 698n860
five female, 462
nectar of, 376
three certainties of, 307, 671n302
twelve deeds of, 378, 688n675
Buddhaśrī Sangyé Pel, 36, 50–51, 58, 59, 62, 64–65, 66, 67, 82
Burushaski, 204
Buton Rinchen Drub, 164, 171, 514, 515, 519
historical accounts, 181, 182, 183
lineages, 12–13, 68–69
transmissions of, 173, 283, 635n37

cakras
active and higher, 341, 680n468
correspondences of, 370, 371
five, 288, 312, 394, 415
in Kurakma Mahākāla, 201, 481–83, 644n31
six, 310, 311, 321
vital essences and, 282
cakras, four, 174, 180
consecrations of, 262
of deities, 375–76
elements of, 402
in fierce inner heat, 461–62
four empowerments and, 263, 264, 265
in Innate Cakrasaṃvara, 395–96
in self-visualization, 360–63
Cakrasaṃvara, 142–43, 181, 183
attainment of, 642n12
definitive presence of, 198
empowerments of, 515, 516–17
generation stage, 198
Innate, 173, 395–96, 397, 416, 423, 438, 482, 483

Cakrasaṃvara (*continued*)
in intermediate state, 421
Kāṇha tradition, 176
Kharamukha, 185–86, 405, 409, 517
lineages of, 78, 81, 101–2, 150
perfection stage, 176, 278–79
sacred places and, 709n1039
traditions of, 277–78
in union, 319, 417, 423, 432, 450
visualizations, 294, 388–89, 392
white, 182
calm abiding, 167, 242, 270, 430–31, 645n8
arising of, 408
and higher insight, integrating, 240, 292, 456
nine phases of, 244, 335–38, 653n82, 678–79n439
posture for, 213, 217
supports for, 244, 267, 653n81
Candalī, 338
Candikā, 482, 512
Candradhvaja. *See* Jangsem Dawa Gyeltsen (Candradhvaja)
Candrakīrti, 19, 31, 57, 67–68, 141, 166, 170, 276, 500, 639n34, 664n222
capacity/acumen, 135, 193, 464
for buddhahood, 378
at death, 440
in dream yoga, 418
empowerment and, 468
fire element and, 388
in illusory body, 416
in intermediate state, 420–21
for liberation, 439
in meditative stability, 457, 704n961
in ordinary preliminaries, 209, 210–11
in postmeditation, 383
in six-branch yoga, 310, 311, 672n324
for warmth, 390
in yogatantra, 272–73
Carrying of Happiness and Suffering on the Path, 508, 634n33
classification of, 500
historical account, 160–61
lineage prayer, 9–10
practices, 228–29
sources, 649n25
transmission of, xx, 138, 634n28
Caryāmati, 454–55, 704n958
Caryāpā, 641–42n9
Caryātantra, 518–19
Caryāvajra. *See* Kṛṣṇacārin (a.k.a. Kṛṣṇapā)
Caurayaśa. *See* Kālacakrapāda the Elder (a.k.a. Caurayaśa)
Caurī, 338
central channel, 180
ashé in, 440–41
cakras and, 309–10, 311, 321
conduct associated with, 447, 448
in deity visualizations, 284–85, 288
encompassing and dissolution in, 374
in fierce inner heat, 409, 410–12, 415, 628n28
fire in, 458–59
generative fluid in, 399
within heart cakra, 80, 629n36
in luminosity yoga, 419
opening, 342, 391–92
retention of wind in, 385
in self-visualization, 388–89
subtle energy and mind in, 305, 307
syllables within, 367
training pathway of, 427
in transference, 292, 378, 414, 464, 478, 490, 491
vital essence in, 351
winds in, 318
Central Channel Dependent on the Female Deity Vajravārāhī, 509, 637n57
historical account, 179–80
lineage prayer, 75–76
practices, 390–92
source, 690n721
transmission of, xx, 147
Central Channel Dependent on the Male Deity Cakrasaṃvara, 509
historical account, 179
lineage prayer, 73–75
practices, 388–91
source, 690n710
transmission of, xx, 147
Central Channel of the Perfection Stage, 179
Chagenpa, 42–43, 72–73
Chak Lotsāwa Chojé Pel, 36–37, 45, 143, 288, 668n269
Chak Lotsāwa Drachompa, 36–37
Chak Lotsāwa Rinchen Chogyel, 36–37, 45, 174, 302, 502, 670n287

Chak tradition, 146, 516
Chakzam tradition, 148
Chakzampa Tulku Nyima Chopel, 123, 124, 631n7
Chammo Yeshé Chok, 118
Changlungpa Zhonu Chodrup, 633n21
  lineages, 27, 35–36, 41–42, 49–50, 87–88, 91, 92–93, 104, 120
  transmissions from, xx–xxi, 137, 139, 140, 141, 142, 143, 144, 149, 150, 151–52
Changlungpa Zhonu Lodro, 35–36
channels, 277
  blocking, 341
  of deities, 375–76
  in fierce inner heat, 410–12, 461–62, 486
  of fierce inner heat, 415
  importance of, 469
  knot of, 364
  purifying, 307
  refining, 332–33
  right and left, 216, 308, 401–3, 456, 647n10
  self-manifesting appearance of, 489–90
  shapes, number, location, 449
  three, 55, 358, 483, 628n29
  winds, vital essences, combined, 302
  See also central channel
Chapa Chokyi Sengé, 32
charnel grounds, 228, 236, 294, 296, 338, 387. *See also* Śītavana
Chegom Dzogpaché Khakyong, 23–24
Chegom Sherab Dorjé, 40
Chegompa Sherab Dorpa, 173
Chekhawa Yeshé Dorjé, 6–7, 35, 159, 633n22, 648n4
Chel Amogha, 147, 397, 692n737
Chel Lotsāwa Chokyi Zangpo, 82
Chel Lotsāwa Kunga Dorjé, 82, 148, 191, 410, 502, 694n779
Chel Lotsāwa Kunga Drakpa, 82
Chel Lotsāwa Sonam Gyeltsen, 191
Chel tradition, 516
Chen Nga Nyernyipa Chokyi Gyelpo, 105, 149, 433, 698n852
Chen Nga Sonam Gyetsenpa, 198
Chen Ngawa Richen Den, 34, 89–90, 103, 110, 158
Chen Ngawa Tsultrim Bar, 17–18, 35
Chim Tsondru Gyeltsen, 28
Chim Tsondru Sengyé, 28
Chimchen Namka Drak, 139, 165, 635n38
  lineages, 14–15, 17–18, 19, 20, 21, 35–36
  works, 240, 241, 244, 249, 651n58, 652n66, 652nn78–79
Chimé Drub, 48–49
Chimphu, 202
Chimton Lobzang Drak, 14–15, 16–17, 19, 20, 21, 35–36, 165
Chinese Hoshang, 204, 645n42
Chinese silk weaving, 127, 495, 631n2
Chiwo Lhepa, 39–40, 635n43
Cho Gyelwa, 80
Chodrak Zangpo, 24–25
Chodrub Sengé, 99–100, 101
Chogowa Chopel Sherab, 114
Chogyel Pakpa. *See* Pakpa Lodro Gyeltsen
Chogyel Sherab Zangpo, 27
Chogyur Dechen Lingpa, xiii
Chojé Dratsang, xxv
Chojé Gewa Gyeltsen, 147
Chojé Lama Dampa Sonam Gyeltsen. *See* Lama Dampa Sonam Gyeltsen
Chojé Namka Tempa, 186
Chojé Pelden Lama, 138, 186
Chojé Rongpo, 183, 184
Chojé Zung, 179, 640n50
Chokhor Gangpa, 151
Choklé Namgyel, 47–48
Chokro Chokyi Gyeltsen, 181–82
Chokro Lu'i Gyeltsen, 624n10
Choku Śākya Rinchen, 142, 293, 669n276
Chokyi Gyeltsen, 97
Chokyi Wangchuck, 47
Chokyi Yungdrung, 8, 160
Cholung Jangtsé. *See* Jonang Monastery
Cholung Kunra, 165
Cholungpa Sonam Rinchen, 24–25
Chomden Rikpei Reldri, 17–18, 140, 165, 270, 663n205, 663n211
Chopel Zangpo, 87–88
Chorin, 11–12
Choying Wangchuk, 120
Chugompa, 118
Churak Lodro Gyeltsen, 118
Cindhona, 454–55
Cintivilavavajra, 52–53
Cito, 644n34
Cittamātrins, 466

clear realization, eight phases of, 660nn171–72
Clear Recollection of the Innate State, 145, 509
 lineage prayer, 62–63
 practices, 354–56
 source, 683n522
 transmission of, xx, 636–37n56
coalescence, body of, 374–75
Coalescent Union of the Four Yoginīs, 278
coemergence, threefold, 340
Coemergent Union of the Great Seal, 510, 634–35n33, 643n27
 classification of, 503
 historical accounts, 194–95, 199–200
 on introduction to coemergent nature of mind, 430–32
 lineage prayer, 89–90
 on meditation with support, 428–29
 on meditation without support, 429–30
 source, 698n851
 transmission of, xxii, 138, 149, 698n851
Collected Injunctions of the King, 511
 classification, 501
 historical account, 204
 lineage prayer, 117–19
 practices, 490–92
 source, 711n1060
 transmission of, xxii, 151
Collected Works (Tāranātha), xxiv
Commentary Entitled Taintless Light, 174
Commentary on Inciting the Path of the Four Stages (Kunga Nyingpo), 181, 396
Commentary on the Tantra of the Kālacakra, 143
Commentary on the Transcendent Perfection of Wisdom in One Hundred Thousand Lines, 140
commitment beings, 287, 376, 481, 482
commitments, 419, 468
 of master and disciple, equality of, 469
 of mind training, 224, 225
 sacraments of, 438, 447
 three, 474
 types of, 446–47
 violations, confession of, 215
common savor, 200, 233, 453–54, 473, 474–75, 476, 494
compassion, 135, 316, 345, 349, 422, 643n27
 for all sentient beings, 214
 cultivating, 9, 160, 240, 254, 323–24, 475, 626n4
 emerging, 340
 meditations on, 227, 238, 381
 misplaced, 226
 natural state of, 290
 of outsiders, 466
 placing in front, 163
 for sentient beings, 214, 323–24, 356
Compendium of Eloquence on Mind Training (Zhonu Gyelchok), 137, 159, 633n23
composure, 242, 277, 279, 304–6, 307, 309, 409, 456
conceptual elaboration, 221, 227, 242, 271, 289, 339, 348, 356, 441, 467, 470
conceptual thoughts, 332, 370, 494
 afflictions and, 270
 appearances as, 269
 carrying on path, 460, 474
 dispelling, three methods, 383
 eighty natural expressions of, 413, 695n792
 five eyes and, 263
 induced into one's body, 380–81
 interrupting, 429, 431–32
 as pristine cognition, 347–48
 revolving, 347
 severing, 232, 267, 421
 suppressing, 244, 306
conduct, 708n1021
 categories of, 447–48, 703n922
 causally concordant, 270, 664n214
 physical, 455
 pure, 252
 secret, 279, 447, 448, 477, 480, 643n27
 ten modes of doctrinal, 270, 664n217
confession, 215, 239, 490, 491
consciousness
 eight aspects of, 269, 302, 648n7, 666n242
 five sensory, 450, 456
 four motions of, 449–50
 relaxing, 334
 seven aspects of, 175, 222, 639n40, 648n7
consciousness transference, 223, 234, 378–79, 438, 470, 471, 641n9
 in Acala practices, 246
 acumen in, 440

in aural lineage of Rechungpa, 444
in Avalokiteśvara practices, 289, 290, 292
of buddha body, speech, mind, 490–91
in Cakrasaṃvara practices, 294–95, 389
at death, 327, 400, 436–37
in Hevajra practices, 296
lion's play posture in, 694n766
in mantra yoga, 385
Nāropā tradition, 414
Nigumā tradition, 419–20
in Padmodrupa cycle, 464
Sukhasiddhi tradition, 426
in Yangonpa instruction, 478
consecration, 316
symbolic method of, 454–55
of terrain, 213–14, 645n2
yoga of, 385
See also self-consecration
Cornucopia of Avalokiteśvara's Attributes, 166
crossed vajra, stage of, 393
crown cakra of supreme bliss, 428
branches of, 310, 358
deities at, 355
in empowerments, 332
generative fluid of, 311, 320
in self-visualization, 388
Vairocana at, 327
white Amitāyus in, 284–85
crystal, symbolic method of, 488–90
cutting through resistance to primordial purity, 711n1057
Cycle of Pagmodru Densatel, 510
classification, 503
on dream yoga and luminosity, 463
entrance to, 459–61
on fierce inner heat, 461–62
historical account, 198
on illusory body, 462–63
on intermediate state, 464–65
lineage prayer, 103–4
source, 705n972
on transference, 464
transmission of, xxi, 150
Cycle That Adopts the Calmness of Visualization, 138
cyclic existence, 447
arising of, 493
attachment to, 220
defects of, 237, 251
as deities and palace, 356
emptiness of, 479
as endless, 467
impermanence of, 322
as lacking inherent existence, 221
as magical display, 443
modalities of, 240
as nature of mind, 485
and nirvana, indivisibility of, 460
resolve for emancipation from, 210
as vital essence, 488

Dakchen Atsewa, 519
Dakchen Dorjé Chang Lodro Gyeltsen, xvii, 112–13, 684n593, 685n605
Dakchen Drakpa Lodro, 111–12, 113
Dakchen Jamyang Namka Gyeltsen, 112–13
Dakchen Ngagi Wangchuck, 518
ḍākinīs, 342, 457
aural lineage of, 278
dedicating resources to, 339
of four families, 265
of Oḍḍiyāna, 438
of pristine cognition, 119, 192, 203, 204, 629–30n52
texts from, 198
of three abodes, 441
Dakpo Gomtsul Nyingpo, 101–2, 198
Ḍamarupā, 50–51
Dampa Gyagar, 261, 276, 427
Dampa Sangyé, 11, 140, 168–69, 194, 500, 635n40
Daṃṣṭrasena, 29–30
Dānaśīla, 45, 46, 273, 638n18
dance, 387, 708n1021
Darchar Rinchen Zangpo, xxiii
Dārikapa, 644n34
Darma Sherab, 31
Darpaṇa Ācārya, 71
Dawa Sengé, 144, 321, 674n338
death, 220, 434, 440, 441, 445, 475, 487, 492–93
contemplating, 210, 236
four subtle perceptions at, 398
in Great Seal, 477
luminosity at, 463, 471
mind training and, 224, 230
premature, dispelling, 352

death (*continued*)
three perceptions at, 413, 695n793, 701n879
three signs of, 464, 706n985
transference at, 400, 413, 444
Deathlessness of One's Own Mind, 510
classification, 504
historical account, 194
lineage prayer, 86–87
practices, 423–24
source, 697n837
transmission, xxi, 149
decisive determination, 353–54
defects, four, 422
Delek Gyeltsenpa, 11–12
delight
coemergent, 628n28
four types, 311, 333, 398
meditative concentration and, 318
sixteen aspects of, 342, 345
delusion, 340, 419, 439, 440
demonic forces, 340, 350, 417, 474, 476, 490
Densatel Khenchen Sherab Dorjé, 115
dependent origination, 326, 455, 467, 643n27
Dergé, xiii
desire, 324, 437, 439, 448, 486
abandoning, 224
in intermediate state, 421
path of, 316
pristine cognition and, 437
purifying, 440
as thoughts, 232, 317, 422
transforming, 345, 474
desire realm, 237
Determination of Mind. See *Attainment in Proximity to a Stupa/Determination of Mind*
Devaḍākinī, 36, 141, 172–73
Devagiri temple, 202, 644n33
Devākaracandra, 56, 273, 276, 644n34, 665n230
Devapurṇamati, 42–43
devils, four (Severance), 12, 231–33, 626n5, 650n43
devotion, 283, 395, 422, 472, 478, 493
at death, 475
to doctrinal traditions, 133
to lineages, 137
nondegeneration of, 225
to teachers, 423, 436, 444, 473, 482
Dewa Pel, 6–7, 9
Dhamapa, 51–52
Dhārikapa, 73–74
Dharmakīrti of Sumatra, 6, 8, 14–15, 16, 17–18, 20, 35, 626n8
Dharmarakṣita, 158, 638n10
Dharmavaṃ (ḍākinī), 115
Dharmaviṣā (ḍākinī), 203
Dhārmika, 51–52
Dhātvīśvarī, 355
Dhītika, 168
Dhūmāṅgārīśrīdevī, 512, 513
Dilgo Khyentse Rinpoche, xiv–xv
Dingri Langkor (Lato), 169
Dīpaṃkarabhadra. *See* Atiśa (a.k.a. Dīpaṃkarabhadra)
Direct Guidance of Avalokiteśvara according to the Candradhvaja Tradition, 166, 508, 668n271
classification, 502
lineage prayer, 38–39
practices, 290–91
source, 142, 668n271
transmission, xx, 142
Direct Guidance of Avalokiteśvara according to the Kyergangpa Tradition, 508
classification, 502
lineage prayer, 40–41
practices, 293
source, 669n275
transmission, xxi, 142
Direct Guidance of Avalokiteśvara according to the Lakṣmī Tradition, 508
classification, 502
historical account, 173
lineage prayer, 37–38
practices, 289–90
source, 688n270
transmission, xx, 142
Direct Guidance of Avalokiteśvara according to the Tsembupa Tradition, 508, 634–35n33
classification, 502
lineage prayer, 39–40
practices, 291–93
source, 668n273
transmission, xx, 138, 142

Direct Guidance of Cakrasaṃvara
classification, 502
historical account, 173
lineage prayer, 41–42
practices, 294–95
source, 669n276
transmission, xx–xxi, 142–43
Direct Guidance of Hevajra
classification, 502
historical account, 173
lineage prayer, 42
practices, 295–96
source, 669n278
transmission, xx–xxi, 142–43
Direct Guidance on All the Meditational Deities in General (Tokmé Zangpo), 143, 173
disciples, characteristics of, 252
discriminative awareness, 136, 156, 242–43, 332, 366, 459
determining view, 628–29n33
emptiness as, 238
meditative concentration and, 318
severing thoughts with, 267
unmoving, 456
writings of, 314
Dispelling of Obstacles due to External Demons, 509
lineage prayer, 59–60
practices, 350–51
source, 682n517
transmission, xx, 145, 636–37n56
Dispelling of Obstacles due to the Agitation of the Physical Body by the Elements, 509
lineage prayer, 60
practices, 351
source, 682n519
transmission, xx, 145, 636–37n56
Dispelling of Obstacles Entitled Ocean-Like Visualizations of Ha (Kodrakpa), 175
Dispelling of the Obstacles of Meditative Stability and Mind, 509
lineage prayer, 60–61
practices, 351–52
source, 682n522
transmission, xx, 145, 636–37n56
Dispelling of the Three Obstacles (Drokmi Lotsāwa Śākya Yeshé), 350, 351, 682n517, 682n519, 682n522
Distinction between Phenomena and Actual Reality (Maitreya), 165, 169, 269
Distinction between the Middle and Extremes (Maitreya), 169, 269–70
divine pride, 290, 297, 302, 333, 344
Doctrinal Palace of Dragto, 206
Dodé Bum, 95–96, 196, 503
Dodé Rabjam, 199
Dolpa Zangtalwa, 11
Dolpopa Sherab Gyeltsen, xxiii, xxiv, xxv, 47–48, 171
Ḍombī (deity), 176, 177, 338, 636n55
Ḍombīpā, 53, 55–56, 63, 64, 71, 176, 256, 339, 513, 641–42n9, 644n43
Dondrub Pel, 80, 97
Dongtri Dulwadzin, 29–30
Donyo Dorjé, 640n62
Donyo Drubpa, Paṇchen Amogha, xvii–xviii, xxi–xxii, 31–32, 33, 114, 151
Donyo Pel, 29–30, 140
Dorjé Rinchen, 107–8, 111–12, 643n28
doubts, 121, 285, 367, 434, 441, 494
cutting, 196, 223, 445, 461
dispelling, 474, 475
as naturally pure, 349
resolving, 419
in sacred doctrine, 136, 241
Dra Gandenpa, 109, 477, 708n1014
Drab Gompa Konchok Sungwa, 47
Drachok Yarlungpa. *See* Yarlungpa Sengé Gyeltsen
Drak Burwa, 114
Drak Marwa, 39–40, 635n43
Drakar Sonam Rinchen, 43, 143
Drakarwa, 23–24
Drakchen Donmoripa, 69–70, 72–73
Drakhar (U), 175
Drakmar Kunga Tsepel, Paṇchen, 69–70, 146, 687n653
Drakpa, 101–2
Drakpa Gyeltsen, 157, 515, 633n17
historical account, 178
lineages, 4–5, 41, 50–51, 58, 62, 63–64, 65, 66–67, 69–70, 74, 75, 76, 104
works, 137, 147, 177–78, 180, 335, 343, 344, 346, 348, 349, 390, 670n289, 678n425, 678n438, 679n453, 680n465, 680n475, 680n481, 681n495, 681n505, 690n710, 690n721, 791n725

Drakpa Gyeltsen, Lotsāwa, 9, 37–38, 39–40, 635n43
Drakpa Pelden Dondrub, 139
Drakpa Peljor, 119
Drakpa Sherab, 14–15, 17, 19, 20, 21
Drakpa Tsultrim, 78
Drakpukpa Sonam Pelwa, 4–5, 10, 41–42, 46, 50–51, 63–64, 65–66, 74, 77, 175, 180
Drakrom, 8
Drakteng Yonten Tsultrim, 112–13
Drakton Donchok, 101–2
Drakton Pelden Dondrub, 16, 18, 19, 20, 21
Draktopa Choku Lhawang Drakpa, 4–5, 123, 630n2
Dramen Chikpa Sherab Zangpo, 169
Drampa Kunga Zangpo, 119, 204, 493, 712n1061
Drangti Darma Nyingpo, 28
Drapupa Chenpo, 24–25
dream yoga, 471, 473, 486–87, 641–42n9
  in aural lineage of Rechungpa, 444
  culmination of, 642n12
  Nāropā tradition, 412
  Nigumā tradition, 417–19
  Padmodrupa cycle, 463
  Sukhasiddhi tradition, 425–26
  Yangonpa's instruction, 480
dreams, 318
  certainty concerning, 347
  ejaculation in, 467, 480
  intermediate state and, 413
  internal focus on, 353
  as magical display, 373
  and waking state, intermingling, 325
Dremarwa Sangyé Yeshé, 78
Drenton Sherab Zangpo, 79
Drenton Tadrel, 79
Drepung Monastery, xxiv
Drida Zelmogang, xiii
Drigom Melton Yerpawa, 198
Drigung Kagyu, 34, 91–92, 105–6, 195, 199, 503, 510
Drigungpas
  Chen Nga Drakpa Jungné (fourth), 34, 104, 198
  Chunyipa Dorjé Rinchen (ninth), 91, 105
  Jigten Sumgon (first), 34, 91, 104, 105, 150, 195, 199, 643nn24–25, 706n988
  Nyergyenpa Dorjé Gyelpo (tenth), 91, 105
  On Sonam Drakpa (third), 91, 105, 110, 629n46
  Telo Dorjé Drak (fifth), 91, 105, 110
  Tok Khawa Rinchen Sangyé (sixth), 91, 105, 110
  Tsamché Drakpa Sonam (seventh), 91, 105, 110
Drinchen Lobzang Tutob, 123, 124, 631n6
Drinchen Sangyé Zangpo, 112–13
Drogon Chogyel Namka Pelzang, 48–49
Drogon Dharaśrī, 99–100, 101
Drogon Dungtso Repa, 120, 494, 712n1072
Drogon Pagmodrupa. *See* Pagmodrupa Dorjé Gyelpo
Drogon Pakpa, 157
Drogon Pelden Yeshé, 6–7, 8, 23–24, 137–38, 158, 159, 634nn24–25
Drogon Sangyé Tonpa, 192
Drokmi Lotsāwa Śākya Yeshé, xv, 144, 682n510
  historical account, 175
  lineages, 50–51, 52, 53–54, 55–56, 57, 59, 60, 61, 62, 63
  works, 682n510, 682n517, 682n519, 682n522, 682n524, 683n533, 684n561
Drolungpa Lodro Jungné, 14–15, 32, 164, 651n61
Drom Namka Rinchen, 24–25
Drom Wangchuk Drakpa, 31
Drom Zhonu Lodro, 24–25
Dromton Gyelwei Jungné, xv, 202, 258, 259, 624n10, 649n18
  historical account, 202
  lineages, 6–7, 8, 16–17, 18, 20, 24–25, 35, 159
  visualization, 259
Drongpa Tradun, xvii
Droton Kunga Gyeltsen, 16–17, 18, 19, 20, 35–36
Droton Namlatsek, 47
Drotonpa Dutsi Drak, 14–15, 16, 17–18, 19, 20, 21, 165, 166
Dru Chok Yeshé, 28
Drubchen Kunlowa, 47–48
Drubchen Namka Gyeltsen, 84–85, 86, 87, 88–89
Drubchen Peldzin Zhepa. *See* Yangonpa Gyeltsen Pel
Drubchen Tsembupa, 39, 138, 173

Drubpa Sengé, 32–33
Drubpa Sherab, 146
Drubtob Hūṃ Barwa, 115
Drubtob Lhabar, 59
Drubtob Ngodrub, 204
Drukchen II Gyelwang Kunga Peljor, 90, 107–8
Drukchen Ngawang Chokyi Gyelpo, xxii, 90
Drukpa Kagyu, 667n262
  lineages, 44, 89–90
  Lower, 109, 150, 200, 475, 503
  Middle, 150, 199, 200, 472, 503, 510
  Upper, 110–11, 151, 200, 477, 503
Drung Peldenpa, 186
Drungtsun Pelden Gyelpo, 78
Drungtsun Zangpo Tenpa, 157–58
Drushulwa Chorab Drakpa, 113–14
Dudjon Rinpoche, 623n1
Duldzin Chewa Ratnapa, 37–38
Dulkarwa, 32
Dulwadzinpa Ngagi Wangpo, 91, 105
Dulwadzinpa Ngawang Gyeltsen, 92–93
Dung-gyu Rinchen Gyeltsen, 72–73
Dungtsé Nyimalung, 98
Dungtso Repa, 205, 504
Durjayacandra, 53–54, 63, 65
Dzalongkar Lama Drubwang Kunzang Wangpo, 123, 124, 631n4
Dzamtang, xxv
Dzilungpa Ozer Drakpa, 19, 166
Dzimchen Gyeltsen Pelzang, 142, 290, 668n271
Dzinpa Rinchen Sherab, 42–43, 72–73
Dzongripa Konchok Zangpo, 44
Dzongsho, xv

eight extremes, 242, 271, 652n76
eight freedoms and ten opportunities, 121, 186, 210, 250–51, 323, 630n54, 641n65
Eight Further Cycles of the Path, 176–77, 335, 339, 341, 343, 344, 346, 348
eight lineages of spiritual attainment, xiv, xv–xvi, xvii, xxiii
eight worldly concerns, 210, 448, 643n27
eighteen schools of monastic discipline, 133, 632n10
eighty-four mahāsiddhas, 115, 116, 203, 644n36, 711n1056
ejaculation, guarding against, 480–81
Ekajaṭi, 113, 483, 484, 512
Elaborate Guidance according to Zhang Tselpa, 510
  classification, 503
  historical account, 198
  lineage prayer, 101–2
  practices, 454–55
  source, 704n957
  transmission, xxi, 150
elements
  correspondences of, 370, 371
  at death, 695n792, 701n879
  dissolving, 309, 426
  eight, 403, 693n759
  enlightened families and, 369
  five, 318–20, 492, 674n351
  four, 35, 283–84, 287, 361, 362, 377, 420, 443, 627n18, 667n263, 688nn668–69
  nectars of, 342
elixir
  extraction of, 382
  of four elements, 283–84
  nutritious, 285
  of three buddha bodies, 332
  visualization, 332
Elucidation of Symbolic Meaning, 509
  classification, 502
  historical account, 178
  lineage prayer, 66–67
  practices, 366–68
  source, 685n605
  transmission, xx, 146
Elucidation of the Concealed Meanings of Yogatantra, 508
  on Cakrasaṃvara, 277–79
  capacity for, 272–73
  on eradicating hostile forces, 273–75
  on four-stage adamantine reality, 282–83
  on Guhyasamāja, 275–77
  on Hevajra, 279–82
  historical account, 171–72
  lineage prayer, 33–34
  source, 665n225
  transmission, xxii, 141
Emanational Cakra of the Navel. See *Inner Guidance of Nairātmyā/Emanational Navel Cakra*
empathetic joy, 222, 226, 267
empowerments, 484
  of book, 521

empowerments (*continued*)
as causal basis, 325
of conditioned existence, 415
Kunga Drolchok receipt of, 513–20
long-life, 172, 184
maturational, 147, 176–77, 183, 192, 524, 525
of profundity, 194
of secret mantra, 468
vase, 172, 639n37
empowerments, four, 313, 327–33, 332, 520
in dream yoga, 417
four cakras and, 263, 264, 265
longing for, 415
in single sitting, 355–56
in single stream of generative essence, 366–67
three approaches to, 367–68
wisdom, 326, 330, 359
emptiness, 247, 271, 293, 333
actualizing, 332
analytical, 132, 632n6
and awareness, inseparability of, 344
disposition of, 290
examining, 242–43
excessive, 394
extraneous/extrinsic (*gzhan stong*), xxiii, 132, 171, 624n18, 632nn5–6, 671n300
higher aspiration toward, 399
intrinsic (*rang stong*), 632n6
in its finest aspects, 305, 306–7, 310, 316, 671n300
and magical display, nonduality of, 398
meditation on, 238
and radiance, coalescence of, 307, 344, 352, 419
six adamantine expressions of, 478–79
views of, 633n22
vital essence of, 315
See also under appearances; bliss
encompassing and dissolution, 373–74
enlightened activities, 350, 468, 642n12
enlightened attributes, 259, 260, 269, 302, 324, 337, 350, 627n12, 664n220
enlightened families, 290, 374, 474
correspondences of, 370, 371
encompassing and dissolution of, 374
in fierce inner heat, 341–42, 680n471
five poisons and, 437
maṇḍalas of, 377–78
single most secret, 686n614
enlightened mind
aspirational, 463
cultivating, 160, 238, 323–24
nonsquandering of, 339
relative, 210, 228, 229
self-manifesting sphere of, 259
two aspects of, 135, 221–22, 226
ultimate, 177, 228–29, 285
enlightenment
aspirational, 254
impediments to, 220
for the sake of others, 269
six methods of setting mind on, 381–82, 383
three degrees of, 323, 675n380
entrustment seal, 96, 629n41
Erect Penis of Bhairava (Nāropā), 179, 274
Essence of the Focus on Guidance (Kunga Lekpa), 137
eternalism, 18, 267, 270, 431, 485
ethical discipline, 210, 237, 238–39, 251–52, 254–55, 268
Eulogy to Sachen, 157, 637n6
exchanging of compassion for others' suffering (*gtong len*), 222, 223, 227, 238
Exegesis of the Concealed Path, 509
classification, 502
historical account, 177–78
lineage prayer, 65–66
practices, 364–66
source, 684n593
transmission, xx, 146
expanse of reality, 18, 231, 316, 349, 350, 421, 460, 461, 488–90
experiential cultivation, 313
for beginners, 242
of composure, 277
of confidence, 293
of ethical discipline, 239
fruits of, 324
of ground, 270–71
lineage of, 128, 167
of mantra stage, 396
metaphors for, 164, 235
of mind, 353
in mind training, 225
of natural liberation, 413
in ordinary preliminaries, 210, 211
of path, 449

of Perfection of Wisdom teachings, 168
of Sangaka Drubchen, 174
of winds, 370–71
Extensive Mother, 260, 661n173
extrasensory powers, 307, 318, 359, 365
Extremely Unelaborate Perfection Stage (Kukuripā), 278
extremists, 466
eyes, five, 263

faith, 127, 129, 135, 250, 493, 632n11
fame, 134, 135, 163, 504–5
father tantra class, 261, 277, 379, 501, 515–16
fear, 128
in dreams, 487
in intermediate state, 420, 487
protection from eight, 167, 249, 654n96
female mudras/consorts, 389
absorption of, 405
in Amitāyus practice, 288
body as empty frame, 410
finger application and, 404
types of, 689n704
in yoga of consecration, 385
fierce inner heat (*caṇḍālī, gtum mo*), 54, 174, 180, 195, 357, 358, 436, 628nn27–28
ancillary practices, 415
in aural lineage of Rechungpa, 442–43
culmination of, 642n12
and desire, intermingling, 486
Hevajra tradition, 282, 667n257
in Kharamukha Cakrasaṃvara, 409
Lorepa tradition, 475–76
lower and higher methods, 470, 471, 707n1001
luminous and ordinary, 389
Nāropā tradition, 410–12
Nigumā tradition, 415–16
in Padmodrupa cycle, 461–62
phases of, 327–30, 457, 462, 704n962
recollection and, 311
in self-visualization, 359
Sukhasiddhi tradition, 425
syllables of, 88, 629n37
three attributes of, 355, 683n538
three modalities of, 366, 686n610
works on, 187, 641–42n9
yogic exercises on, 282, 366, 415, 667n257, 694n766
Fifteen Scrolls, 437, 700nn869–70
five certainties, 435, 699n862
five culminations, 192, 642n12
Five Doctrines of Maitreya, 508
classification, 500
historical account, 169–70
lineage prayer, 29–30
practices, 268–70
source, 663n205
transmission, xx, 140
five excellences, 466
five meats and five nectars, 294, 296, 669n277, 708n1021
five paths, 27, 350, 446, 627n13
coalescence of, 375
path of conclusion, 264–65
path of connection/preparation, 262–63, 269
path of insight, 263–64, 365, 409
path of meditation, 264
path of provisions, 261–62, 268–69, 280
refining, 459
Five Paths of Pacification, 508
classification, 500
historical account, 169
lineage prayer, 27
path of conclusion, 264–65
path of connection, 262–63
path of insight, 263–64
path of meditation, 264
path of provisions, 261–62
source, 661n177
three austerities, 266
transmission, xx, 140
five powers, 223–24, 648n14
Five Protective Great Incantations, 519
five sibling frailties, 49, 316, 628n26
Five Stages (Nāgārjuna), 178
Five Stages according to Ghaṇṭāpāda, 278, 509
classification, 502
historical account, 180
lineage prayer, 76–77
practices, 392–94
source, 791n725
transmission, xx, 147
Five Stages of the Secret Assembly, 509
buddha mind, 372
buddha speech, 370–72
classification, 501

Five Stages of the Secret Assembly (*continued*)
coalescence body, 374–75
illusory body, 372–73
lineage prayer, 67–69
luminosity, 373–74
singular recollection and buddha body, 368–70
source, 686n613
transmission, xxi, 146, 276
Five Stages Perfected on One Seat, 276
Fivefold Capacity of Lorepa, 511
classification, 503
historical account, 200
lineage prayer, 109
practices, 475–77, 708n1015
source, 708n1014
transmission, xxi, 150
Fivefold Great Seal, 470, 510
classification, 503
historical account, 195
lineage prayer, 90–92
practices, 432–33
source, 698n852
transmission of, xxi, 149
Flower Ornament of the Tales of Past Lives (Rikpei Reldri), 165
focuses, seven, 9, 626n4
forehead cakra, 297, 310, 311, 355
Forty-Seven Adamantine Sayings, 470
four adamantine realities, 273
Four Adamantine Seats, 187, 278, 510
classification, 503
historical account, 182
lineage prayer, 79–80
practices, 398–401
source, 692n740
transmission, xxi, 148
Four Collections of the Guru empowerment, 519
Four Deities of Kadam, 508
Acala, 245–47
Avalokita, 247–48, 653n89
classification, 501
historical account, 166–67
lineage prayers, 21–23
Munīndra, 244–45
source, 652n79
Tārā, 248–50, 654n96
transmission, xx, 139
Four Doctrines Exhorted by Injunction, 202, 644n34
four immeasurable aspirations, 216, 647n10
"four mothers and seventeen offspring," 119, 511, 629n52
four profound doctrines, 178, 639n46
four reliances, 136, 633n16
Four Scrolls of the Aural Instruction, 510
classification, 503
historical account, 197
lineage prayer, 98–99
practices, 440–42
source, 700n876
transmission, xxi, 150
four seals, 132, 273, 274, 352, 393–94. *See also* action seal; Great Seal
Four Stages according to Kṛṣṇacārin, 509
classification, 502
historical account, 180–82
lineage prayer, 77–78
practices, 395–96
source, 691n731
transmission, xx, 147
Four Syllables of the Great Seal, 510
classification, 504
historical account, 195
lineage prayer, 92–93
practices, 433–34
source, 698n853
transmission, xxi, 149
four transmitted teachings, 191, 641n9
four visionary appearances, 493, 712n1069
Four-Armed Mahākāla in the Form Kurakma, 511
classification, 504
historical account, 201
lineage prayer, 111–12
practices, 481–83
source, 710n1043
transmission, xxi, 151
Fourfold Cycle of the Mother of Space (Barawa), 472
Four-Stage Yoga, 273–75
Four-Stage Yoga, 509
classification, 501
historical account, 179
lineage prayer, 72
practices, 384–86
source, 689n696
transmission, xx

Four-Stage Yoga of Red Yamāri (Śrīdhara), 179
Fourteen Quatrains on Resting in the Nature of Mind (Mitrayogin), 163, 638n24

Ga Lotsāwa, 643nn29–30, 710n1043
Gadenpa Tashi Pel, 69–70
Galung Jangchub Pel, 24–25
Gampopa Dakpo Lharjé, 705n972
historical accounts, 193, 195
lineages of, 34, 83, 89–90, 91, 92, 94–95, 104, 105, 106, 107–8, 109, 110, 120
tradition of, 199, 205, 465, 503, 643n26
Gaṇapati, 258, 512, 513
Ganden Palace, xxiv
Gaṅgabhadra, 29–30
Gangtropa Drakpa Gyeltsen, 44, 69–70, 72–73
Gar Lotsāwa Chokyi Zangpo, 42–43
Gar Rep, 98
Garbharipā, 53, 63, 65
Garjong Gonpo Gyeltsen, 120
Gartsa Yonten Yungdrung, 28
Gathering of All Gurus, 291, 292, 294, 295, 416
Gathering of All Meditational Deities, 291, 292, 294, 295
Gaurī, 338
Gayādhara, 50–51, 52–53, 54, 55, 175, 279, 511
gazes, 428
awareness and, 422
five types, 263
to refocus mind, 347
in Severance, 231
in six-branch yoga, 304, 305, 307, 308
of Vairocana, 317
yogic, 457
Geden Puntsoling (formerly Takten Puntsoling), xxiv
Gedingpa Choku Ozer, 47–48, 68, 92
Geluk system, 172
Gelung (Olka), 195
Gendun Gangpa, 518
Gendun Gyatso, 518
General Description of the Four Stages (Gungru Sherab Zangpo), 181, 640n59
generation stage, 326–27, 335–38, 402, 422, 436, 468
bliss and radiance of, 439–40
dissolving, 341
five awakenings in, 669n274
preliminaries for, 490
purity of deity in, 357
self-visualization of, 384
three phases of, 679n440
generative essences/fluid, 275, 288, 311
in central channel, 331
downward flow, 401
in fierce inner heat, 342, 443
melting, 399, 457
permeation of, 346
pure, 332–33
of relative enlightened mind, 339
retaining, 450–51
reversal of, 345
syllables and, 320, 321
types, 310, 672n324
generosity, 239, 254, 268, 633n209
Genghis Khan clan, xxiv
Genmo Lhepa Jangchub Pel, 115
gestures
earth-touching, 303, 435
fist, 308, 343, 671n305
of meditative equipoise, 217, 267, 303, 388, 401, 435, 459
of opposing stoves, 357
teaching, 355
vajroṣṇīṣa, 416
Ghaṇṭāpāda, 54, 76, 77, 173, 278, 516, 669n276, 691n725
Ghasmarī, 338
Girpuwa Ngejung Dar, 109
Go Lotsāwa Khukpa Lhetsé, 67–68, 146, 178, 375, 624n10
Golok, xxv
Gomiśra, 67–68
Gonpawa of Kashmir, 29–30
Gonpo Zhonu, 111–12
Gorampa Sonam Sengé, 137, 633n19
Goton Cholo, 198
Gotsangpa Gonpo Dorjé, 89–90, 110, 200, 629n46, 707–8n1006, 708n1010
Gradual Path of Padmasambhava, 511
classification, 501
historical account, 204
lineage prayer, 116–17
practices, 488–90
source, 711n1057
transmission, xx, 151

Great Commentary on the Transcendent Perfection of Wisdom in Eight Thousand Lines (Haribhadra), 169
"Great Guidance of Zhalupa," 139, 635n37
Great Magical Emanation, 510
  on breathing, 404–5, 694n765
  classification, 503
  historical accounts, 183–85
  lineage prayer, 80–81
  on lower-extremity meditation, 404
  on mid-body meditation, 402–3
  source, 693n751
  transmission, xxi, 148
  on upper-extremity meditation, 403–4
  on yoga of conclusive attributes, 401–2, 693n754
Great Middle Way, 166, 508
  classification, 500
  on discriminative awareness, 241–42
  historical account, 165–66
  lineage prayer, 18–20
  on skillful means, 242–43
  source, 652n70
  transmission, xx, 139
Great Mother Prajñāpāramitā, 11, 258, 259, 472, 660n166
Great Perfection, 174, 204, 219, 493, 673n330, 711n1057
Great Seal, 204, 219, 273, 312–13, 352, 394, 422, 437, 441, 469
  accomplishing, 301
  bliss and emptiness in, 629n35
  capacity and, 311, 672n324
  capacity to fathom, 476–77
  disposition of, 444, 478
  eleven teachers of, 261
  five essentials of, 432–33
  free from intellect, 461
  guidance on, 278
  as nature of mind, 493–94
  nonarising, expressive power of, 420
  pure expanse of, 471
  ritual application of, 452–53
  settling into, 465, 482
  symbolic introduction to, 454–55
Great Seal Devoid of Letters, 509
  historical account, 176
  lineage prayer, 56–57
  practices, 346–48
  source, 681n495
  transmission, xx, 145, 636n55
Great Seal Dispelling the Three Sorts of Suffering, 509
  lineage prayer, 61
  practices, 352–54, 682n526
  source, 682n524
  transmission, xx, 145, 636–37n56
Great Vehicle, 137, 144, 145, 168, 253, 271
Ground Rules of Monastic Discipline, 239
Gugé Paṇchen Drakpa Gyeltsen, 63–64, 72–73, 74, 76–77, 81, 82, 185, 186
Gugé Paṇchen Sonam Lhundrub, xxii, 46, 143
Guhyajñānā (ḍākinī), 172
Guhyasamāja, 176, 275–77, 642n12
Guhyavijaya, 76
Guidance of Amitāyus, 508
  classification, 502, 503
  historical account, 172
  lineage prayer, 34–35
  practices, 283–85
  source, 667n262
  transmission, xxi, 141
Guidance of White Amitāyus, 508, 627n19
  historical account, 172–73
  lineage prayer, 36–37
  practices, 287–88
  source, 688n269
  transmission, xxii, 141
Guidance of White Cakrasaṃvara, 510
  classification, 501
  historical account, 182
  lineage prayer, 78–79
  practices, 396–97
  source, 692n737
  transmission, xxii, 147
Guidance of White Tārā, 508
  classification, 503
  historical account, 172
  lineage prayer, 35–36
  practices, 285–87
  source, 667n265
  transmission, xx, 141
Guidance on Amitāyus according to the Tradition of Siddhirājñī (Barawa), 667n262
Guidance on the Four Stages (Āryadeva), 278

Guidance on the View of the Middle Way (Tsongkhapa), 159, 166
Guṇamitra, 6
Gundharipā, 51–52
Gungru Sherab Zangpo, 181
Guru Chowang (a.k.a. Guru Chokyi Wangchuk), 96, 150, 174–75, 628n26, 629n41, 636n47, 639n39, 673n330, 673n333
  treasures of, 196, 439, 519, 699n868
gurus. *See* teachers
Gya Marwa, 32
Gyagom Lekpei Gyeltsen
  empowerments from, 514, 516, 517–18
  lineages, 40–41, 84–85, 86, 87, 88–89
  transmissions from, xviii, xxi, 141, 142, 148
Gyagom Riwa Zhipo, 8
Gyakar Tangbewa Pakpa Kyab, 68
Gyalton Jangwangpa, 518, 519, 520
Gyalton Wangchuk Wangyal, 517
Gyamawa Lodro Gyeltsen, 138, 432, 634n32, 698n851
Gyamawa Yonten-o, 37–38, 39–40, 635n43
Gyanak Cherbu Sangyé Rabton, 11
Gyangro Darma Gon, 28
Gyangro Jangchub Bum, 35–36
Gyarong, xxv
Gyaton Chagriwa, 8
Gyawo Khenchen Sonam Drak, 78
Gyelsé Kunga Zangpo, 26, 27
Gyelsé Lobzang Peljor, 36–37, 45
Gyelsé Sherab Bumpa. *See* Sherab Bumpa
Gyelsé Tokmé Zangpo. *See* Tokmé Zangpo
Gyeltsa Lungmang Chokyi Wangchuk, 112–13
Gyeltsa Ramo, 79
Gyeltsab Kunga Wangchuk, 4–5, 69–70
Gyelwa Bum, 64–65, 177
Gyelwa Rinchen Gon, 111–12
Gyelwa Tené, 25–26, 27
Gyelwa Yeshé, 142
Gyergom Zhikpo, 114
Gyijo Dawa Ozer, xvi, 144, 175
Gyurmé Tsewang Chokdrub, xiv
Gyurmé Tutob Namgyal, xiii

Hadu Karpo (Newar), 82, 191
Haribhadra, 6, 14–15, 16, 169
Harisiddhi, 513, 715n58
hatred, 340, 347, 375, 437, 440, 448, 464, 487, 687n651
Hayagrīva, 418, 519–20
heart cakra of phenomenal wheel, 80, 167, 285, 341, 358, 487, 629n36
  Akṣobhya at, 327
  ashé in, 284, 405
  branches of, 297, 310, 355, 672n319
  deities at, 355
  in empowerments, 332
  encompassing and dissolution in, 374
  luminosity and, 444
  of Mahākāla, 482
  opening, 381
  in self-visualization, 388, 392, 393
  in transference, 444, 490
  in upper-extremity visualization, 403
  vital essence in, 278, 398, 399–400, 406, 407
Heart of Dependent Origination, 508, 634n33
  classification, 500
  historical account, 159–60
  lineage prayer, 8–9
  main practices, 227–28
  preliminary practices, 226–27
  sources, 649n18
  transmission, xx, 138, 634n27
hells, 322, 347, 454, 488
hermit buddhas, 240, 247–48, 263, 266, 268, 467, 627n13, 675n380
Heruka, 278, 408
Hevajra, 142–43, 150, 174, 483
  attainment of, 196, 642n12
  empowerments of, 279–80, 282–83, 513, 514, 525
  innate, 173, 438
  perfection stage, 176, 279–82
  six-branch yoga of, 178
  visualizations, 295–96, 337–39, 364, 427
Hidden Guidance of Kadam, 166, 508
  classification, 500
  historical account, 166
  lineage prayer, 20–21
  practices, 243–44
  source, 652n78
  transmission, xx, 139

higher insight, 242, 270, 430–31, 645n8
arising of, 408–9
and calm abiding, integrating, 240, 292, 456
nonself in, 245, 653n83
Hook of the Lotus (Tsen Khawoché), 141, 171
Hor Kabzhipa Sengé Gyeltsen, 165, 515, 634n25
lineages, 6–7, 8, 10, 14–15, 23–24, 118
works, 138, 140, 159, 257, 654n99
Hūṃ Gyel Lhundrub Rinchen, 48–49, 175
Hūṃchen Namka Neljor, 48–49, 175

icons, 301, 369–70
ignorance, fundamental, 323, 340, 440, 493
illnesses, 453
carrying onto path, 475
as magical displays, 417
protection and treatment, 351, 365, 414–15, 467, 476, 479–80, 685n604
illusory body, 372–73, 436, 641n9
in aural lineage of Rechungpa, 443–44
culmination of, 642n12
empowerment of, 192
Lorepa tradition, 476
Nāropā tradition, 412
Nigumā tradition, 416–17
in Padmodrupa cycle, 462–63
pure and impure, 471
Sukhasiddhi tradition, 425
transference into, 440
impermanence, 210, 236, 251, 266, 322, 323
Inciting the Path of the Four Stages (Kṛṣṇacārin), 181, 691n731
Inconceivables, The, 509
historical accounts, 176, 177
lineage prayer, 51–52
practices, 333–35
source, 678n425
transmission, xx, 145, 636n55
India, 3, 135, 150, 161, 170, 174, 191
destruction of Buddhist temples, 168
eighteen monastic schools of, 632n10
lineages from, 11, 12–13, 25–26, 27, 34–35, 36–37, 41–42, 43–44, 76, 81–82, 162
Mahākāla in, 201
Tibetans traveling to, 170, 197
See also Sāṃkhya system
Indivisibility of Subtle Energy and Mind, 510
classification, 503
historical account, 196
lineage prayer, 94–95
practices, 436–37
source, 699n864
transmission, xxi, 149
Indra, 281, 434, 709n1031
Indrabhūti, 51–52, 53, 55, 67–68, 176, 344, 636n55, 641n9, 644n34
Middle, 55–56
Younger (a.k.a. Ratnavajra), 55–56, 60, 69–70, 190, 636–37n56
"inexhaustible intelligence," 133, 632n8
inhabited world and sentient inhabitants, 338
absorption of, 405
coalescence of, 384
as deities and maṇḍalas, 366, 368, 395
encompassing and dissolution of, 373, 374
fourteen attributes of, 287, 668n268
as magical display, 441
purification of, 435
recollected as Vajradhara, 369–70
refining, 349, 418
in transference, 378, 464
Innate Cakrasaṃvara (Ghaṇṭāpāda), 173
Inner Guidance of Glorious Pañjaranātha, 511
classification, 502
historical account, 201
lineage prayer, 112–13
practices, 483–85
source, 710n1045
transmission, xxii, 151
Inner Guidance of Nairātmyā/ Emanational Navel Cakra, xxi, 194, 510, 629n38, 642n18
classification, 504
lineage prayer, 88–89
practices, 427–28
source, 697n847
transmission, xxi, 149
Inner Yoga of the Communal Offering (Śāntipa), 179, 274
Instruction Entitled Three Emerging from Two (Ngawang Chodrak), 628n33

Instruction Manual (Kodrakpa), 175
Instruction Manual Elucidating the Concealed Meaning (Sonam Gyeltsen), 144, 636n53
Instruction Manual Entitled Oral Discussion, 181
Instruction on the Book with a Sash, 201, 643n30
intermediate state, 234, 486, 650n34, 651n52
  buddhahood in, 463
  length of, 465, 706n987
  levels of, 701nn895–97, 702n899
intermediate state yoga, 487–88
  in aural lineage of Rechungpa, 445
  Avalokiteśvara in, 289, 292, 293
  in Cakrasaṃvara practices, 295
  in Hevajra practices, 296
  Nāropā tradition, 413
  Nigumā tradition, 420–21
  in Padmodrupa cycle, 464–65
  Sukhasiddhi tradition, 426
  three deportments in, 290
intrinsic awareness, 270, 272, 383, 490
  appearance of, 285, 289
  common savor in, 494
  descent of, 472
  individual, 287–88
  nonarising of, 334
  purity of, 357
  radiance of, 315
  retaining, 457
Introduction to the Innate (Saraha), 278
Introduction to the Three Buddha Bodies, 510
  classification, 503
  historical account, 195–96
  lineage prayer, 93–94
  practices, 434–36
  source, 698n859
  transmission, xxii, 149
introductions, 262, 354
  mother and child, 475
  to naked perception, 455
  to nature of mind, 430–32, 485
  to nature of reality, 136
  to pristine cognition, 443, 451
  to three buddha bodies, 434–35
  to words of symbolic expression, 492–93
Inventory Clarifying the Six Doctrines (Khungpo Neljor), 192
Īśvara, 55, 325
Jadrel Ritro Rechenpa, 40–41, 84–85, 86, 87, 88–89
Jakchen Jampa Pel, 148, 149
Jālandharapāda (a.k.a. Jālandharipā), 54, 76, 394, 670n292
Jambhala, 512, 513, 624n11
Jambudvīpa, 248, 323, 647n10
Jamgön Kongtrul Lodrö Taye, xi, xiii, xiv, xvii, 3, 122, 123, 623n1, 625n24, 630n57, 659n161
Jamkya Namka Pelden, 183
Jampa Konchok Pelzangpo, 519
Jampa Lingpa, xviii
Jampel Lodro, Khentrul, xxv
Jamsarwa Sherab Ozer, 47
Jamyang Darma Ozer, 29–30, 32–33
Jamyang Drakpa Gyeltsen, 12–13
Jamyang Khyentsé Wangpo, xiii, xiv, xxii, xxvi, 3, 4–5, 123, 124, 219, 659n161, 717n7
Jamyang Konchok Zangpo, 47–48
Jamyang Kunga Sengé, 107–8, 643n28
Jamyang Lodro Sengé, 107–8, 643n28
Jamyang Sangyé Rinchen, 145
Jamyang Sherab Gyatso, 26, 28–29, 71
Jang Pukpa Kunlek, 379, 687n653
Jang Radeng, 173
Jang Uri, 200
Jangchub Gyatso, 106–7
Jangchub Gyeltsen, 36–37
Jangchub Tsemo, 10, 14–15, 28–29, 180
Jangchub Yeshé, 58, 59
Jangchub Zangpo, 99–100, 101, 142
Jangpa Sherab Bar, 254
Jangsem Dawa Gyeltsen (Candradhvaja), 19, 38–39, 165–66, 173, 243, 290, 652n70, 668n271
Jangsem Gyelwa Yeshé, xxiii, 28, 47–48, 92, 142
Jangsem Jadeng, 78
Jangsem Jinpa Zangpo, 148
Jangsem Konchok Gyeltsen. *See* Mu Konchok Gyeltsen
Jangsem Kunga, 25–26, 27
Jangsem Radengpa, 41–42
Jangsem Sonam Drakpa, 159
Jangsem Sonam Gyeltsen, 99–100, 101
Jangsem Zhonu Gyelchok, 137, 159, 633n23
Javaripā, 42–43
Jayaśrījñāna, 53, 63, 65

Jayulwa Zhono O, 17–18, 35, 165
Jetāri, 184, 519, 641n64
Jigmé Lingpa, 623n9
Jigten Gonpo, 629n43
Jinadatta, 82
Jīvabodhi, 81
Jñānaḍākinī, 51–52, 72, 80, 517, 641–42n9
Jñānagarbha, 441
Jñānanātha, 481, 710n1043
Jñānaśrībhadra, 29–30, 636–37n56
Jñānaśrībodhi, 55–56, 60–61
Jñāneśvarī, 398
Jobum-ma (ḍākinī), 47
Joden Lama Ngaripa Zhang Joton, 113–14, 202
joints, twelve major, 327, 676n397
Jomo Nagyel Mountain, xxiii
Jomo Ngak Gyelmo, xxiii
Jonang Monastery, xviii, xix, 505, 713n2
Jonang Puntsoling, 631n6
Jonang tradition, xvi, xxii, xxiii–xxv
  appellation, meaning of, xvii
  Geluk suppression of, xxiv
  Kongtrul's affinity with, xiv
  Kunga Drolchok's connection with, xviii, xxi, 514
  lineages, 47, 113–14, 123–24
  Six-Branch Yoga in, xvi, 143
Jonshing, 177
José Khampa, 72–73
José Namka-o, 181, 182
José Zhangton Chokyi Lama. *See* Zhangton Chokyi Lama
Joton Dzakhol Drubchen, 114
Jotsowa Pakpa Ozer, 68
Jotsunpa, 31

Kabzhipa Drakpa Zhonu, 6–7, 9, 96, 104
Kachu Jangchub Pel, 118
Kachupa Zhonu Sengé, 48
Kadalīmañjarī, 79, 441
Kadam tradition, xv, xvi, xvii
  empowerments of, 518
  four deities and three doctrines of, 626n11
  guardians of, 512, 714nn28–29
  in Jonang guidebooks, xx, xxiii, 135, 139–40, 164–67, 172, 219
  lineages of, 6, 8, 9, 10, 14, 16, 17, 20, 21–23, 24, 35, 37–38
  six renowned texts of, 165
  three lineages of, 259
Kadampa Namka Bum, 183
Kagyu tradition, xvii, 172, 196, 715n58
  empowerments in, 520
  Great Seal of, 465
  in Jonang guidebooks, xxiii, 136, 219, 503–4
  Jonang political alliance with, xxiv
  Kunga Drolchok's connection with, xviii
Kālacakra, xxiv
  empowerments of, 514–15, 715n64
  Great Perfection and, 174, 673n330
  lineages, 48, 102–3
  monogram of, 674n335
  in union, 319
Kālacakrapāda the Elder (a.k.a. Caurayaśa), 47, 457, 627n24
Kālacakrapāda the Younger (a.k.a. Nālendrapā), 47
Kālarātrī, 424
Kam Yeshé Gyeltsen, 140
Kamala, Paṇchen, 115
Kamalaśīla, 28, 140, 169, 662–63n204
Kamalaśrīvajra, 264
Kambalapāda, 641–42n9, 706n984
Kanaśrī, 273
Kandarayoginī, 69–70
Kangyurwa Śākya Gyeltsen (a.k.a. Kangyurwa Śākya Zangpo), 115–16, 629n51
Karma Kagyu lineages, 83–84, 94–95
Karma Kamtsang tradition, 196, 503
Karma Lingpa, 706n987
Karma Tashi Chopen, 623nn1–2
Karma Trinlepa, xxii, 93–94, 149
Karmapas
  Chodrak Gyatso (seventh), 83–84, 93–94
  Dezhin Shekpa (fifth), 83–84, 93–94
  Dusum Khyenpa (first), 83, 94–95, 503
  Karma Pakshi (second), 83, 93–94, 95, 195–96
  Rangjung Dorje (third), 83, 93–94, 95, 144, 149, 436, 642n10, 698n851, 698n859, 699n864 (see also *Molten Gold of the Six Doctrines*)
  Rolpei Dorjé (fourth), 83–84, 93–94, 95, 141
  Tongwa Donden (sixth), 83–84, 93–94
Karmavajra, 43–44

Karṇa, 51–52
Karṇaripā, 44, 179
Katok, xiv
Katok Rigdzin Tsewang Norbu, 123, 124, 521, 631n4
Kawa Peltsek, 624n10
Ketu, 319, 364
Kham, xiii, 181
Khampa Aseng, 111–12, 201
Khampa Dorjé Pel, 69–70
Khampa Drakpa Gyeltsen, 116–17
Khangsarwa Namka Ozer, 47
Khanitra, 51–52, 636n55
Kharak Gompa, 59
Kharamukha Cakrasaṃvara, 510
  classification, 501
  historical account, 185–87
  lineage prayer, 81
  main practices, 406–9
  preliminaries, 405–6
  source, 694n768
  transmission, xx, 148
Kharchu, 200
Khasarpaṇi. *See under* Avalokiteśvara
Khawu Drakdzong, xvii
Khecarī, 414, 420
Khenchen Jangchubsen, 44, 627n22
Khenchen Ratna Jamyang Rinchen Gyeltsen, 24–25
Khenchen Sangyé Pel, 96
Khepa Sang-o, 518
Khepa Tsangnak Repa, 14–15
Khepa Yongten Tri, 112–13
Khetsun Ziji Gyeltsen, 99–100, 101
Khewang Lotsāwa Rinchen Zangpo, 317, 624n10, 639n38
  lineages, 47–48, 49, 99–100, 101
  transmissions from, xviii, xxi, 143–44
  works, 317, 673n330
Kholpo Dartochen, 437, 700n869
Khon Konchok Gyelpo, 62, 156, 637n4
Khon Kyichuwa Dralha Bar, 57–58, 61
Khonton Tukjé Rinchen, 72–73
Khorewa Okyi Gyeltsen, 175
Khu Netso, 191
Khugom Chokyi Sengé, 11
Khuton Tsondru Yungdrung, 28
Khyenrab Chojé Rinchen Chokdrub Pelzang (a.k.a. Kuzhang Khyenrab), 149, 194
  lineages, 12–13, 14, 27, 49–50, 87–88, 120
  works, 426, 637n58, 697n840, 697n847
Khyentsé Tokden, 107–8
Khyung Lhepa Zhonu Sonam, 68–69, 76–77, 183
Khyungpo Neljor Tsultrim Gonpo, xv
  historical accounts, 192, 193, 194, 642n12, 642n14
  lineages, 62, 84, 85, 86–87, 88–89
  works, 149, 428, 637n59, 642n13, 695–96n796, 697n847
Khyungpo Tsultrim Gonpo, 40–41, 79, 84–85, 86, 87, 88–89, 98
Khyungtsang Yeshé Lama, 99–100, 101
Kodrakpa Sonam Gyeltsen, 110, 175, 629n46
Kokalī (ḍākinī), 115
Kokolilā (ḍākinī), 203
Konchok Dorjé, 114
Konchok Gyeltsen, 184
Konchok Tempei Dronmé, 659n161
Konchok Zangpo, 116–17
Kriyātantra, 518–19
Kṛṣṇacārin (a.k.a. Kṛṣṇapā), xix, 513, 516, 700n875
  lineages, 46, 50–51, 52–53, 54, 55, 57, 67–68, 76
  works, 181, 278, 341, 628n28, 636n55, 640n60, 691n731
Kṛṣṇocita, 55
Kṣetrapāla, 513
Kṣitigarbha, 355
Kukkurāja, 80, 441, 641–42n9, 693n751
Kukuripā, 278, 405
Kulikā, 277
Kundar Rema, 103
Kunden Repa, 99–100, 101
Kunga Chogdrub, xvii, xviii, xix–xx, 634n26
  empowerments from, 513, 514, 516, 518
  epithets of, 131, 156, 637n2
  lineages, 4–5, 6–7, 8, 9, 10, 12–13, 15, 16–17, 18, 19, 20, 21, 23–24, 29–30, 37–38, 39–40, 50–51, 58, 59, 62, 64–65, 66, 67, 71, 116–17, 635n43
  teachings received from, 136–37, 139, 140, 142, 144, 146, 147, 151
Kunga Drolchok, xvi, 5
  biographical information, xvii–xviii, 4, 504–5

Kunga Drolchok (*continued*)
empowerments received, 513–20
personal practices, 507–11
previous lives of, xvii, xix
"signature" quatrains, 131, 132, 211, 631n3
supplication to, 123
transmissions received, xviii, xix–xxii
works, xviii–xix, xxii, xxv, 3, 129, 155, 625n24, 665n225, 667n262
Kunga Lekgyel, 121, 154, 505, 630n55
Kunga Pelzang, xviii
Kunga Rinchen, 116–17
Kunga Tashi, 137, 633n21
Kunglung Sangyé Pelzangpo, 40–41, 84–85, 86, 87, 88–89
Kunīka, King, 203, 645n37
Kunkhyen Donyo Pelwa, 140
Kunpang Chokyi Nyima, xxi, 13–14, 45, 139, 140, 141, 143, 149, 151
Kunpang Doringpa, xvii, xviii, 513, 514
Kunpang Namka Pelyang, 106–7
Kunpang Tukjé Tsondru, xxiii, 39–40, 47–48, 92, 635n43
Kunzang Chojor, 4–5, 123–24
Kunzang Choying Rangdrol, 4–5, 631n5
Kunzang Dechen Oseling, xiii
Kunzang Wangpo, 4–5, 123–24, 631n4, 631n8
Kurukullā, 302–3, 514
kuśāla practitioners, 467, 707n996
Kusalibhadra, 276, 641–42n9
Kuyalwa Rinchen Gonpo, 106
Kyapchewa, 34
Kyapjé Tokden Trewo Chokyi Gyatso, 83–84, 94–95
Kyebu Sherab, 205
Kyebu Yeshé Dorjé, 120
Kyebu Yonten Ga, 29–30
Kyechok Monlampa, 109, 110, 114
Kyemé Dopa Chokyi Sherab Jodenpa, 11–12, 138, 635n35
Kyergangpa Chokyi Sengé, 40, 84, 85, 86, 87–88, 89, 173, 293
Kyergom Zhikpo Tsultrim Sengyé, 92, 195
Kyipukpa Tsultrim Dargyé, 96
Kyo tradition, 179, 515
Kyoton Ojung Lotsāwa, 72–73, 273, 274, 388, 690n707
Kyoton Sonam Lama, 11
Lachen Lodro Gyeltsen, 162
Lachen Sonam Zangpo, 98
lakes, four great, 133, 632n7
Lakṣmī, 37, 173, 289, 518
Lakṣmīkarā, 51–52, 53, 55–56, 81–82, 644n34
Lalitavajra, 12–13, 51–52, 72, 179
Lama Dampa Sonam Gyeltsen, 157, 283
historical accounts, 173, 179–80
lineages, 4–5, 10, 41, 46, 50–51, 58, 59, 62, 64, 65–66, 74
works, 142, 144, 161–62, 230, 333, 636n54, 649n33, 675n368
Lama Shang Khyungpo Neljor. *See* Khyungpo Neljor Tsultrim Gonpo
Lama Tokdenpa, 101–2
Lama Zhang. *See* Zhang Tselpa Tsondru Drak
lamps
of empty vital essence, 492
of light of ideation and scrutiny, 450
of pristine cognition, 451–52
of skillful means, 450
Langri Tangpa Dorjé Sengé, 21, 166
Langtang, 166
Langtangpa Chen Nga Kunga Dorjé, 147, 691n731
Lapchiwa Dokton Namka Gyeltsen, 91, 92–93, 105
Lavapa the Younger, 191, 192
Lawapa, 463, 516, 706n984
Lechungwa Sonam Pelzang, 110–11
Lekden Pelchen, 45
Lentsangtsa Nyima Cham, 68
Lesser Vehicle, 158–59, 168, 224, 240
Lha Rinchen Wangyal, 96, 196
Lhading Jangchub Bum, 6–7, 633nn22–23
Lhading Kunga Gyatso, 6–7
Lharjé Gewa Bum, 118, 492, 711n1060
Lhasa, xviii, 162, 173, 655n118
Lhaton Ozer Lama, 6–7
Lhatsun Gonserwa, 39–40, 635n43
Lhawang Drakpa, 189
Lhazik Repa, 149, 437, 699n864
Lhodrak area, 96
Lhodrak Jangchub Pelzangpo, 9
Lhopa Kunkhyen Rinchen Pel, 24–25, 685n605
Lhundrub Dechen Rabjampa, 101–2
Lhundrub Dorjé, 44

liberation, 198, 230, 239, 268, 474, 493
Liberation by Seeing according to Norbu Rinchen, 511
  classification, 501
  historical account, 204–5
  lineage prayer, 119
  practices, 492–93
  source, 712n1061
  transmission, xxii, 151
life span, 285, 288, 323, 365
Ling Repa Pema Dorjé, 44, 89–90, 107–8, 109, 110, 145, 200
Litany of the Names of Mañjuśrī, 186
Lobzang Tutob, 4–5, 123–24
Lochen Rinchen Zangpo, 112–13, 144, 150, 152, 174, 276, 515, 624n10, 639n38
Lodro Gyatso, 26, 169
Lodro Namgyel, xxiv, xxv
Lodro Zangpo, 92–93
Lokeśvara, 355
Lokya Lotsāwa Sherab Tsekpa, 75
Lopon Chodrak, 99–100, 101
Lopon Penyulwa Jangchub Nangwa, 23–24
Lopon Tontsulwa, 31
Lord of the Charnel Ground, 512, 513
lords of the three enlightened families, 48–49
Lorepa Darma Wangchuk Tsondru, 107–8, 109, 200, 629n45, 708n1014
Losal Tenkyong, Zhalu Lotsāwa, xxii, xxv, 3, 4–5, 123–24, 521, 525, 625n24, 631n24
Loton Chodrak, 28
Lotsāwa Rinchen Zangpo. *See* Khewang Lotsāwa Rinchen Zangpo
lotus (vagina), 344–45, 389, 393, 450
love, cultivating, 210, 214, 239
loving-kindness, 135, 241
  cultivating, 9, 160, 240, 253–54, 323, 480, 626n4
  instruction on, 643n27
  meditation on, 227, 381–82
Lowo Khenchen Sonam Lhundrup, 691n731
  empowerments from, 513, 514, 516, 517
  historical account, 185–86
  lineages, 26, 28–29, 63–64, 72–73, 74, 76–77, 81, 82
  transmissions from, xx, 140, 144, 145, 146, 148, 409, 694n768
Lowo Lotsāwa Sangyé Sé, 71
Lowo Lotsāwa Sherab Rinchen, 71, 146, 147, 384, 386, 688n677, 689n696
Lowo Matang, xvii, xviii
Luipā, 73–74, 278, 516, 644n36
luminosity, 394, 440, 487, 641–42n9, 642n12
  in aural lineage of Rechungpa, 444
  of conceptual thoughts, 383
  delusion and, 439
  encompassing and dissolution of, 373–74
  innate, 285
  in intermediate state, 488
  internal focus on, 353
  meditation on, 372
  mother and child, 420, 439, 471, 491, 700n873
  Nāropā tradition, 413
  natural, 270, 489
  Nigumā tradition, 419
  nonarising, 441
  in Padmodrupa cycle, 463
  signs of, 305–6
  Sukhasiddhi tradition, 426
  of two stages, integrating, 276
Lungpuwa, 58, 59, 62, 66–67
Lupuk Karchug (Lhasa), 173

Ma Chokyi Sherab, 140
Maben Chobar, 191
Machik Angjo, 99–100, 101
Machik Labkyi Dronma, xv, 11, 138, 162, 231
Mādhyamikas, 166. *See also* Prāsaṅgika Mādhyamikas; Svātantrika Mādhyamikas
Magadha, 191
magical display
  appearances as, 416, 423, 460, 462, 476
  deity body as, 297
  mind as, 325–26, 347, 366
  in ordinary preliminaries, 210–11
  in postmeditation, 242, 269, 271, 373
  relative truth as, 242
  three types, 439, 700n874
  training in, 487
  twelve similes of, 412
Mahābodhi (Newar), 81, 148, 185, 186–87, 501, 638n18, 694n768

Mahābodhi temple (Vajrāsana), 161
Mahākāla, 113, 368, 483–84
aspects of, 644n31
forms of, 512, 513, 520, 714n34, 715n47
Kākamukha, 201, 481–83
Mahākāruṇika. *See under* Avalokiteśvara
Mahākāśyapa, 632n10
Mahākāṭyāyana, 632n10
Mahāmāyā, 642n12
Mahāsaṃghika, five subdivisions, 632n10
Mahāvajradhara, 631n2
epithets of, 132, 631n2
lineages, 39, 41, 42–43, 44, 49, 50, 51–52, 53, 54, 55, 57, 63, 64, 65, 66–67, 68, 73–74, 75, 76, 77, 79, 80, 83, 84, 85, 86–87, 88, 89–90, 91, 93, 94–95, 96, 97, 98, 99, 100, 101–2, 103–4, 105, 106, 107–8, 109, 110, 111, 112–13, 114, 115, 120, 641n9
Maitreya/Mahāmaitreya/Maitreyanātha, xxiii, 168, 170, 171, 260, 500
lineages, 6, 8, 14–15, 16, 17–18, 20, 25–26, 29–30, 32
visualizations, 234, 259
Maitrīpā (a.k.a. Avadhūtipā), xv, xix, 512, 516, 641n4, 641n7
historical accounts, 169, 197
lineages, 32, 45, 50–51, 82, 93, 113–14, 193, 195
oral instructions of, 192
works, 500, 508, 644n34, 694–95n779
Mal Lotsāwa Lodro Drak, 73–74, 75, 76, 112–13, 180
Malton Yerpawa, 101–2
Māmakī, 371
maṇḍalas, 176, 177
body, 275
emanational, 192, 197, 375, 376, 642n20
of enlightened families, 377–78
four elemental, 319, 362
induction into, 395
of physical body, 366
sand and cotton, 184, 513, 514, 516
self-visualization as, 354–55
two dynamic (wind and fire), 395, 397
Mangkhar Lotsāwa Chokden Lekpei Lodro, 28, 71
Mangkharwa Lodro Gyeltsen, 146, 686n613, 687n652
Mangkharwa Rabsel Dawa Gonpo, 687n653
empowerments from, 514, 515, 516, 517, 518
lineages, 44, 68–69, 70
transmissions from, xxi, 143, 146, 147
Mangrawa Sengé Gyeltsen, 67–68
Mangyul, 253
Maṇidvīpa Sukhavajra, 112–13
Mañjughoṣa/Mañjuśri, 122, 128, 259, 274, 500, 624n11
Arapacana, 157, 519
emanations and embodiments of, 157
empowerments of, 518, 519
in heart, 275, 386, 387
homage to, 155–56, 209, 213
lineages, 4, 18–19, 23–24, 27, 28, 31, 57–58, 69–70, 71
Vādisiṃha, 11, 27
vision of, 157, 525
See also Yamāntaka
Mañjuśrimitra, 72–73, 179
Mañjuvajra, 70, 146, 176, 275, 276–77, 375, 378, 379, 517, 687n653
mantras, 256, 384–85
of Amitāyus, 283–84
as buddha speech, 491
of Cintāmaṇicakra Tārā, 286, 667n266
eight-syllable (Padmasambhava), 262, 264, 265
fruitional recitation form, 300
Hevajra, 296
Kurukullā, 302–3
of Mahākāla, 482, 710n1044
protectors, 484, 710nn1048–50
of Red Yamāri, 379, 689n680
of Śākyamuni, 259
seven-syllable (Cakrasaṃvara), 482
six-syllable (Avalokita), 247, 248, 259, 289, 290, 291–92, 293, 491
ten-syllable (Acala), 245–46, 259, 653n86
ten-syllable (Tārā), 249, 250, 259
of Vajrapāṇi, 297
of yakṣas, 711n1053
Mar Chokyi Gyelpo, 42–43
Mar Sherab Dorjé, 42–43
Mar Tsondru Sengé (a.k.a. Mar Tsondru Dorjé), 42–43, 175, 627n21
Mar Tubpa Sherab, 42–43
Mardo Chokyi Wangchuk, 180, 181–82, 640n58

Marīcī empowerment, 519
Marlungpa Jampa Konchok Pelzangwa, 519
Marpa Dopa, 181–82
Marpa Kagyu tradition, xv, xvi, xxi, 150
Marpa Lotsāwa Chokyi Lodro, 146, 148, 276
  historical accounts, 181–82, 196–97, 438
  lineages, 79, 80, 83, 89–90, 91, 92, 94–95, 195
  transmissions, xv, 196, 405, 442, 454, 503
  works, 699n868, 700n869, 700n871, 700n876, 702n901
Marton Chokyi Gyeltsen, 42–43, 173, 501, 669n279
Marton Gyeltsen Ozer, 115–16
Marton Samgyelwa, 31
Mataṅgi, 276
Mati Paṇchen Lodro Gyeltsen, 42–43, 69–70, 72–73, 78
Matiratna, 12, 13, 93
Means for Attainment of Jowo Bhugama (Śabaripā), 190
Means for Attainment of the Guru, Auspicious Circumstances, and Common Savor, 510, 643n26
  classification of, 503
  historical account, 199–200
  lineage prayer, 107–8
  practices, 472–75
  source, 707n1006
  transmission, xxii, 150
Means for Attainment of the Guru as the Three Buddha Bodies, 200
measurements, 246, 653n87
meditation
  breaks, advice for, 428, 429–30
  distinguishing quality in, 428, 430
  on mothers, 222, 227
  reversal, 643n27
  sessions, 333, 388
  times for, 304–5, 318
meditative concentration, 135
  five ancillary aspects of, 306, 318, 671n301
  nine branches, 357, 683n547
  perfection of, 255–56, 268
  posture for, 217
  refining, 292
  resting in, 462
  in six-branch yogas, 306–7, 456
meditative equipoise, 336
  free from extremes, 271
  as magical display, 373
  in mind training, 226
  in nature of reality, 334
  on path of meditation, 264
  remaining in, 288
  sky-like, 210
  wind of past actions as basis, 471
  See also under postmeditation
meditative experiences, 493
  arising of, 298
  in fierce inner heat, 342
  nondifferentiated, 410, 413
  physical exercises and, 340
  signs of, 456
meditative stability, 292, 340, 343, 457, 678n426
  ancillary practices, 334–35, 678n430
  of bliss and emptiness, 345, 346
  of continuous flow, 157, 180
  defects of, meditation on, 237
  of luminosity, 444
  nonarising of, 334
  seven phases of visualization in, 458–59, 705n966
  in six-branch yoga, 312
  supreme, 406, 407
  three types, 324, 675–76n382
meditative stability beings, 376
Melungpa Mikyo Dorjé, 118
Memorandum on the Teaching of Gyelśépa (Zhonu Lodro), 138, 634n28
Meñja Lingpa, 190
Menlung Guru Sonam Pel, 48–49, 79, 174, 175, 283, 317, 628n26, 636n47, 673n330
Menlung Kunkhyen, 79
Menpa Gomchen Tsultrim Zangpo, 91, 92–93, 105
mental faculty, 304, 310, 334, 355, 407–8, 454
Mental Focus on the Horns of Bhairava, 274, 509
  classification, 501
  historical account, 179
  lineage prayer, 72–73
  practices, 386–88
  source, 699n707
  transmission, xx, 147

merit
accumulating, 253, 467
dedicating, 129, 160, 229, 256, 289, 292, 354
power of, 127, 228
Meru, Mount, 216, 354, 389, 489, 492, 647n10, 674n335
"Methods for the Conferral of the Empowerments," xxii
Milarepa
lineages of, 34, 83, 89–90, 91, 92, 94–95, 99, 104, 105, 106, 107, 109, 110, 120, 172, 195
transmissions of, 150, 445, 454, 503, 510
mind, 242
ascertainment of, 352–53
buddha and ordinary, mingling, 316
in central channel, 305
as deathless, 230
as groundless, 293
knots of, untying, 446
as lacking inherent existence, 238
observing, 430
purifying, 239, 267, 493
recognizing, 492–93
resting/relaxing, 234, 264
spontaneous, 491
and subtle energy, indivisibility of, 436–37, 456
of teacher and disciple, intermingling, 313, 383
twenty-seven coemergent factors, 325, 676n385
uncontrived, 348, 633n22
mind training, 135, 257, 261–62, 633n22, 634n26
Mind Training (Gorampa Sonam Sengé), 137, 633n19
Mind Training according to Sumpa Lotsāwa, 508, 634n33
classification, 500
historical account, 161–62
lineage prayer, 10–11
practices, 230
sources, 649n33
transmission, xx, 138
mindfulness, 235, 240, 347, 429, 450
of bliss, 436
of deity yoga, instantaneous, 340
empowerment for, 367
establishing, 247
maintaining, 485
as nonarising luminosity, 441
of syllables, 309
of thoughts, 230
unwavering, 304, 356
Mingling and Transformation of the Three Poisons, 510
classification, 503
historical account, 196–97
lineage prayer, 97–98
practices, 439–40
source, 700n871, 700n875
transmission, xxi, 150
Mingling of Sutra and Tantra, 509
lineage prayer, 57–58
practices, 349–50
source, 682n510
transmission, xx, 145, 636–37n56
Minyak Lotsāwa Mondrub Sherab, 203
miraculous abilities, 307, 359, 387, 457, 705–6n976
mirror of Vajrasattva, 488
Mitrayogin (younger Kusulu)
historical accounts, 163, 164
lineages, 6, 12–13, 14–15, 16, 36, 119, 141, 172–73, 626n8, 638n11
transmissions of, 288, 502, 668n269
works, 234, 638n11
Mokchok Tulku, xxiv
Mokchokpa Rinchen Tsondru, 84, 85, 86–87, 88–89, 193
Molten Gold of the Six Doctrines (Rangjung Dorjé), 148, 191, 414, 695n780
monastic community, 238–39, 253, 632n10, 656n130
Mondzong Rechen Dawa Gyeltsen, 49–50
Mongolia, xxiv, xxv
Monlam Tsultrim, 14–15, 17–18, 19, 20, 21
mother tantra class, 178, 261, 277, 278, 501, 516–17, 641–42n9
Mu Konchok Gyeltsen, 9, 37–38, 39–40, 179–80, 184, 633–34n23, 635n43, 640n60
Mu tradition, 148
Muchen Gyeltsen Pelzangpo, 138, 228, 634n27, 649n18
Muchen Sangyé Rinchen, xxii, 78, 147, 151, 637n61, 710n1045

Muktinath, xviii
Mūlasarvāstivāda, seven subdivisions of, 632n10
Mumenpa Dutsi Charchen, 17–18, 20, 165, 166
Munīndra, 121, 167, 168, 626n11, 652n79
empowerments of, 519
lineages, 15, 18, 20–21, 24, 25, 26, 27, 28, 29, 31, 32
visualizations, 244–45, 434–35
Mutso, 177

Nāgabodhi, 67–68, 252, 276, 656n124
Nāgārjuna, 170, 252, 348, 639n27
lineages, 18–19, 31, 57, 67–68, 73–74, 97, 111, 113–14, 166, 641n9
tradition of, 276, 515, 700n875
visualization of, 261
works, 168, 178, 502, 636n55, 639n30
nāgas, 243–44, 260, 660n171
as demonic forces, 340
eight great, 245, 653n85
kings, patronage of, 164
Nāgayoginī, 67–68
Nagtso Lotsāwa Tsultrim Gyelwa, 40, 202
Nairātmyā
empowerment of, 184, 514
lineages, 39, 42, 46, 50, 53, 63, 64, 65–66, 87–88, 89, 173
visualizations, 281, 417–18, 419, 427
Nālandā monastery, six gatekeepers of, 636n56
Nālendrapā. *See* Kālacakrapāda the Younger (a.k.a. Nālendrapā)
Nam Khawupa Chokyi Gyeltsen, 69–70
Namdrol Sengé Pelzangpo, 121, 153
Namka Chokyong, 47–48
Namka Gyeltsen, 40–41, 84–85, 86, 87, 88–89
Namka Ozer, 11–12
Namka Pelzang, 47–48
Namka Sengé, 49–50, 142
Namza Drakpuk Sonam Pelwa. *See* Drakpukpa Sonam Pelwa
Nanda, 251, 655n114
Nandikeśvara, 483
Nāropā Jñānasiddhi, xv, 197, 278
historical account, 196
lineages, 61, 73–74, 75, 83, 89–90, 91, 92, 94–95, 96, 97, 99, 100, 103–4, 105, 106, 107–8, 109, 110, 120, 641n9
Nigumā and, 191, 642n11
oral instructions of, 192, 440
transmissions of, 179, 181, 194–95, 276, 373, 436, 503, 699n868
works, 274, 636–37n56
Nartang Monastery, 14, 16, 139, 146, 164–65
nature of mind, 221–22, 313, 315–16, 383
abiding aspect of, 231
carrying on path, 434
emptiness and radiance of, 325, 344, 353, 485
instructions on, 195
as magical display, 443
recognizing, 494
six methods of establishing, 433
thirty-two examples, 325–26, 676n386
visualizing, 246
Nature of Mind, 511
classification, 504
historical account, 205
lineage prayer, 120
practices, 493–94
source, 712n1072
transmission, xxi, 135, 152
navel cakra of emanation, 335, 341
ashé in, 440–41, 462
branches of, 297, 302, 309–10, 358, 390
coiled nāga channel in, 398, 399, 441–42
deities at, 284–85, 327, 355
encompassing and dissolution in, 374
in fierce inner heat, 329, 342, 409, 628nn27–28
meditative concentrations of, 80, 629n36
in self-visualization, 359, 388, 392, 393
six classes of beings in, 416, 425
syllables in, 391, 401, 690n724
in transference, 420, 478, 491
vital essence at, 331
Nāyakapāda, 45
Nelingma, 176
Neljor Choyung, 195
Neljorpa Kyapsé, 37–38
Nepal, xvii, xviii, 190, 191, 201, 202, 714n31
Nesar Zhonu Drub, 44
Net of Magical Emanation empowerment, 515

Neten Sampenpa Jangsem Jinpa, 6–7, 8, 10, 15, 23–24
Netsedrum, 185
Neuzurpa Yeshé Bar, 167
New Pronouncement and Eight Appendices (Samten Ozer), 138
Newu Repa, 120
Nezin (Pari), 160
Nezur Yeshé Bar, 21, 246
Ngadak Nyangrel Nyima Ozer, 117–18, 204, 519, 711–12n1060
Ngamring Mangto Ludrub Gyatso, 664n222
Ngamring Monastery, xviii
Ngapa Gyagar, 252
Ngari Sherab Gyeltsen, 24–25, 166
Ngari Ulekpa, 177
Ngaripa Selnying, 57–58, 61
Ngawa, xxv
Ngawang Chodrak, 628n33
Ngawang Chogyel, xxii, 105, 107–8
Ngawang Drakpa Pelzangpo, 24–25, 91, 92–93, 106–7, 111–12, 114
Ngawang Lobsang Gyatso, Fifth Dalai Lama, xxiv
Ngawang Nampar Gyelwa, 123, 124, 631n5
Ngawang Tenzin Namgyel, xxv
Ngawang Trinlé, xxiv–xxv
Ngawang Tulku. *See* Taklung Rinpoché (Ngawang Tulku)
Ngenlampa Tsul Pak, 26
Ngodrub, 117–18
Ngok Choku Dorjé, 97, 183, 503, 693n751
Ngok Dodé, 80
Ngok Drakpa Peljor, 103, 119
Ngok familial lineage, 79–80, 97–98, 517
Ngok Jangchub Drakpa, 79–80, 96, 97, 98–99
Ngok Jangchub Peldrub, 79–80, 96, 97, 98
Ngok Konchok Pel, 79
Ngok Kunga Dorjé, 80, 97
Ngok Lekpei Sherab, 14–15, 24–25, 164–65
Ngok Lodro Pelzangpo, xxi, 79–80, 96, 97, 98–99, 148, 514, 517
Ngok Lotsāwa Loden Sherab, 29–30, 32, 624n10
Ngok Nyima Sengé, 68
Ngok Pakpa Lha, 68
Ngok Tashi Peldrub, 79, 80, 96, 97, 98–99
Ngok tradition, 79, 97, 148, 149–50, 514
Ngok Tsa Choku Dorjé, 79
Ngok Yeshé Sengé, 68
Ngok Zhedang Dorjé, 79, 97, 401, 405, 440, 692n740, 693n751, 700n871
Ngokton Chokyu Dorjé, 79, 80
Ngokton Jangchub Pel, 79, 80, 96, 97, 98–99
Ngokton the Great, 119
Ngor Evaṃ Choden, 184
Ngor Khenchen Sangyé Rinchen, 112–13, 513, 514, 516
Ngor Monastery, xviii, 183
Ngor region, 182, 184–85
Ngorchen Kunga Zangpo, 206
  historical accounts, 183, 184–86
  lineages, 4–5, 43, 46, 50–51, 58, 59, 62, 63–64, 65, 66, 67, 68–69, 70, 72–73, 74, 76–77, 78, 82
  tradition of, 144, 636n52
  works, 144, 145, 628n33, 688n677
Ngorchen Lhachok Sengé, xviii, 518
  empowerments from, 513, 514, 516
  lineage, 112–13
  transmissions from, xxii, 137, 144–45, 146, 147, 151
Ngorpa transmission, 174
Ngulchu Bairo. *See* Vairocanabhadra (a.k.a. Ngulchu Bairo)
Ngulchu Chodzongpa. *See* Tokmé Zangpo
Nigumā, xv, 148, 191–92, 193, 276, 642n11
  lineages, 84, 85, 86, 87
  transmissions of, 276, 278, 503–4
  vision of, xviii
nihilism, 18, 267, 270, 431, 485
Niḥsaṅgapāda, 55–56
Nine Cycles of the Path, 177
Nine Doctrinal Cycles of Nirdehaḍākinī
  classification, 503
  historical accounts, 197, 200
  lineage prayer, 100–101
  practices, 445–54
  source, 702nn901–2
  transmission, xxi, 150
Nine Profound Methods, 509
  generation stage, 335–38
  historical account, 176
  lineage prayer, 52–53

perfection stage, 338–39
source, 678n438
transmission, xx, 145, 636n55
Nine-Lamp Śrīheruka empowerment, 518
Nirdehaḍākinī, 100, 101, 445
nirvana, 240, 267, 447, 460, 470, 479, 485, 488, 493
Nivāraṇaviṣkambhin, 355
Nocturnal Motion, 179
nonconceptuality, 242, 298, 342, 470, 471
nondegenerations, three, 225
nondistraction, three metaphors for, 164
nondual tantra class, 501, 513, 514
nonsectarian tradition, xi, xiii–xiv, xxiv
nonself, 245, 653n83
nonseparations, three, 225
nonvirtuous actions, 186, 323, 348, 447
Norbu Rinchen, xxii, 119, 493, 520, 712n1061
Norchen Kunga Zangpo, 182, 633n19
lineages, 4–5, 43, 46, 50–51, 58, 59, 62, 63, 64–65, 66, 67, 68–69, 70, 72–73, 74, 76–77, 78, 82
works, 180
Nub Cholung, 183, 184
Nub Khulungpa Yonten Gyatso, 116
Nub Namkei Nyingpo, xxiii
Nubchen Sangyé Yeshé, 116, 204
Nubpa Rigdzin Drak, 137, 221, 633n17, 647n7
Nubton Gyelyé, 191
Nur Chopak Gyeltsen, 38–39
Nyag-gom Marpo, 98
Nyagton Nyingpo Gyeltsen, 64–65
Nyak Lotsāwa Yeshé Zhonu, 116
Nyakpu Sengé Pelwa, 98–99
Nyakton Samten Ozer. *See* Samten Ozer
Nyan Lotsāwa Darma Drak, 69–70
Nyangrel Nyima Ozer, 204
Nyangton Konchok Dorjé (a.k.a. Nyangro Kunga Dorjé), 29–30, 627n15
Nyangton Yeshé Jungné, 116
Nya-on Kunga Pel, 28–29, 47–48
Nyelwa Delekpa, 115, 116–17
Nyemdo Kunga Dondrub, 26, 48–49, 98
Nyemdo Sonam Pel, 26, 27, 661n177
Nyemo Gyagom. *See* Nyipuwa Gyergom Zhikpo
Nyen Repa Gendun Bum, 34, 83, 90, 94–95
Nyenchen Sonam Tenpa, 8, 160
Nyenton Chogyel, 72–73
Nyenton Chokyi Sherab, 84–85, 87–88, 89, 194, 642n17
Nyenton Osung, 72–73
Nyenton Rigonpa Chokyi Sherab, 40–41
Nyeton Rinchen Ngodrub, 42–43
Nyeton Rinchen Tenpa, 72–73
Nyima Chopelwa, 4–5
Nyima Gyeltsen, 36–37, 659n161
Nyima Sengé, 107–8, 643n28
Nyingma tradition, xv, xvi, xvii, 116–17, 204, 219, 317, 673n330, 716n66. *See also* Great Perfection
Nyingpo Tayepa (a.k.a. Nyingpo Lodro Tayé), 4–5, 123, 124
Nyipuwa Gyergom Zhikpo, 8, 35–36, 114, 160
Nyo tradition, 516
Nyonak Gyeltsen, 116–17
Nyo/Nyopa, 59, 196, 516
Nyukla Paṇchen Ngawang Drakpa, 115–16, 140, 259, 659n161

obstacles, 340, 350–54, 382–83, 391, 431, 474
Ocean of Sky-Farers, 278, 517
Oḍḍiyāna, xvi, 48, 190, 197, 260, 438, 520, 660n171
offerings
burnt, 419
communal/feast, 201, 438
maṇḍala, 216, 647n10
mentally emanated, 421
outer, inner, secret, 418
torma, 419, 438
Olgom Janglingpa, 96
Olkha Lama, 111–12
On a Single Seat, 198, 643n24
On Dzalongkar Lama Kunzang Chojor, 123, 124
On Repa Darma Sengé, 107–8, 643n28
On Sonam Gyelwa Choyang, 111–12, 113
One Deity One Vase empowerment, 520
One Hundred and Eight Guidebooks of Jonang, xvi–xvii
analysis of, xxiii, xxv
compilation of, xix–xxii, xxiii–xxiv, 131
content of, xxv–xxvi, 625n24
as distinct undertakings, 219, 494–95

One Hundred and Eight Guidebooks of Jonang (*continued*)
 empowerment ceremony for, 521–25, 716nn2–5, 717n6
 generic Supreme Mantra class, 501–2
 life-sustaining prayer, 125–30
 lineage prayer composition and recitation, 3, 121, 122, 137
 lineage-specific, 502–4
 memorandum style of, 219
 from oral instructions, 501–2
 order of, 219–20, 701n882
 restrictions in, 368, 493, 696n811
 sutra and tantra integration, 500–501
 sutra section, 500
one hundred sacral aspects, 277, 368–69, 666n242
Onpo Chozang, 101–2
Onpo Sonam Dar, 109
Onsé Cholek, 11–12
Oral Discussion (Marpa Dopa), 181
Oral Transmission of Buddhajñānapāda, 379
Orgyanpa Rinchen Pel, xvi, 49, 93, 196, 283
orifices
 of buddha body, speech, mind, 398
 at death, 400
 nine, 378, 380, 385
 ten, 363, 684n588
Ornament of Clear Realization (Maitreya), 169, 268
Ornament of the Sutras of the Great Vehicle (Maitreya), 165, 169, 269, 663n21
Ozer Gyatso, 109

Pacification and Severance tradition, xv, xvi, 169, 192, 219, 635n40, 715n54
Padampa Sangyé, xv, 25–26, 27, 661n177
Padmapāṇi, 258
Padmasambhava/Padmākara, xv, 117, 204, 205, 520, 711nn1057–58
 lineages, 116, 117–18, 119
 protectors of, 714n31
 revelations of, xiii–xiv
 sacred sites of, xxiii
Padmavajra (a.k.a. Saroruha/Saroruhavajra), 339, 513
 lineages, 51–52, 53, 55–56, 641–42n9
 visualization, 261
 works, 176, 335–36, 339, 636n55, 644n34, 679n450
Pagdru Kagyu lineage, 92–93
Pagmodrupa Dorjé Gyelpo, 150, 195, 199
 lineages of, 34, 89–90, 91, 92, 94–95, 104, 105, 106, 107–8, 109, 110, 111–12
 transmissions of, 198, 201, 465
 works, 643n30, 705n972
Pagmodrupa dynasty, 640n62
Pago Jamyang Chojé, 103
Paiśācika, 632n10
Pak Chok Norzang, 118
Pak Chok Sonam Dar, 115
Pakchen Pelden Tashi, 513, 514
Pakpa Lodro Gyeltsen, 180
 lineages, 4–5, 10, 41–42, 46, 50–51, 65, 69, 77
 works, 137, 183, 359, 633n18, 640n56, 683n542, 791n725
Pakpa Lodro Rinchen, 118, 145, 147
Pakton Samten Wang (a.k.a. Pakton Samten Zangpo), 31, 627n16
Palpung Monastery, xiii, xiv
Paṇchen Donyo Sengé, xxii, 103
Pāndaravāsinī, 284, 371
Pandeva, 69–70
paṇḍitas, nine lesser, 160, 638n18
Pang Lotsāwa Lodro Tenpa, 28, 63–64, 77
Pangton Drubpa Sherab, 16–17, 18–19, 20, 21, 29–30, 32–33, 35–36, 71
Pañjaranātha, forms of, 511–12, 513, 520
Parables of Potowa, 256–57, 508, 654n105
 on aspirations, merit, gratitude, 253
 classification, 500
 on compassion, enlightenment, 254
 on ethical discipline, 251–52
 historical account, 167
 on impermanence, past actions, cyclic existence, 251
 lineage prayer, 23–24
 on loving-kindness, 253–54
 on refuge, 250–51
 source, 654n99
 on teachers, disciples, veneration, 252, 256
 on transcendent perfections, 254–56
 transmission of, xx, 140
paradoxical essential point, 262, 662n184
Paro Drang-gyé, 172
Parpuwa Lodro Sengé, 113–14, 486, 711n1055

Particular Exegesis of the Vital Essence of Spring, 181
Parting from the Four Attachments, 507
  classification, 500
  historical accounts, 156–57, 177
  lineage prayer, 3, 4–5
  practices, 220–21
  sources, 647n2
  transmission, xix, 134, 136–37
past actions, 449–50
  acceptance and rejection of, 135, 240
  appearances and, 230, 443
  attachment to, 464
  dependent phenomena and, 271
  in exchanging compassion for others' suffering, 222
  meditating on, 236
  parables on, 251
  rebirth and, 439
  residual inheritance of, 133
  ripening of, 210
  sensations due to, 456
  signs arising from, 307
Path and Its Fruition, 509
  classification, 502
  on experiential appearances, 323–24
  on fourth empowerment, 330–33
  on ground, 325–27
  historical account, 175
  on impure appearances, 321–23
  lineage prayer, 50–51
  on pure appearances, 324
  on secret empowerment, 327–30
  source, 675n368
  transmission, xx, 144
  on vase empowerment, 327
  on wisdom empowerment, 330
Path and Its Fruition tradition, xv, xvii, xviii, 177, 178, 184, 641n63
Path of the Female Mudra, 509
  historical account, 176
  lineage prayer, 55–56
  practices, 344–46
  source, 680n481
  transmission, xx, 145, 636n55
Patient Endurance, 257, 258
Patrul Rinpoche, 209
Patsab Gompa Tsultrim Bar, 25–26, 27
Patsab Lotsāwa, 141, 276
Patsab Nyima Drak, 31, 170, 271, 664n222
Peacock's Neutralizing of Poison (Dharmarakṣita), 158, 638n10
Pelchen Ga Lotsāwa Namgyel Dorjé, 102–3, 178, 198, 504, 510, 704n959
Pelchen Ga Lotsāwa Zhonu Pel, 101–2, 111
Pelchen Kunlhunpa, 27, 169
Pelden Dondrup, 164
Pelden Dorjé, 50–51, 58, 59, 62, 64–65, 66, 67
Pelden Gyelwa, 112–13
Pelden Lekpa, 118
Pelden Tsultrim
  lineages, 4–5, 32–33, 46, 50–51, 58, 59, 62, 63–65, 66–67, 74, 77, 82
  transmissions from, xxii, 141, 146, 147
Pelden Zangpo, 6–7, 8, 10, 14–15, 23–24
Peljam, xxiv–xxv
Pelri Monastery, xvi
Pendhapā, 98
Penyawa Ratnabhadra, 19, 165–66
Penyul, 168
Perfection of the Path of Fierce Inner Heat, 180, 509
  classification, 503
  historical account, 176
  lineage prayer, 54
  practices, 341–43, 628n28
  source, 680n465
  transmission, xx, 145, 636n55
perfection stage, 273, 275, 278, 279, 338–39, 666n254
Perfection Stage of Great Yoga (Luipā), 278
perseverance, 268, 459, 705n975
person, three sorts, 29, 627n14
Phamtingwa Abhayakīrti, 73–74, 75, 76
Phamtingwa Vāgīśvara, 75
pious attendants, 240, 263, 266, 268, 346, 347, 467, 470, 627n13, 675n380
Pith Instruction Entitled Precious Garland, 203
Pith Instructions of the Five Stages, 147
planetary divinities, 319, 364–65, 674n353
pointing-out instructions, 159. *See also* introductions
poisons
  five, 335, 437, 450, 474
  three, 439–40, 447, 448, 459, 469, 628n26
Pokya Rinchen Sengéwa, 107–8, 643n28
Pomdrakpa Sonam Dorjé, 83, 94–95

positive actions. *See* virtuous actions
postmeditation, 348
  in Avalokiteśvara practices, 289, 290, 292
  dispelling obstacles in, 383
  illusory body in, 416, 470–71
  as magical display, 242, 269, 271, 373
  and meditative equipoise, indistinguishable, 347–48, 365, 436, 463
  and meditative equipoise, mingling, 233, 268, 282, 307, 419
  and meditative equipoise, wearing each other out, 460
  in mind training, 226
  ordinary preliminaries and, 210
  in Pacification, 262
  on path of meditation, 264
  pride in, 339
  setting enlightenment mind in, 381–83
  in Severance, 233
postures, 213, 221, 457, 705n963
  adamantine, 215, 217, 247, 262, 267, 303, 308, 388, 421, 427
  bodhisattva, 248, 303, 308
  crouching, 357
  for darkened room, 456
  of deities, 263
  in dream yoga, 417
  elephant ear, 364, 685n595
  essential, 307, 308, 309, 321, 349, 444, 456, 457, 459, 461, 478, 480
  kurmapāda ("turtle feet"), 301
  lion's play, 405, 694n766
  lotus, 215
  of Maitreya, 292
  reclining, 264
  refining, 349
  sevenfold Vairocana, 235, 354, 410, 433, 651n55
  sitting, 264
  six opposing stoves, 308, 415, 425, 470, 671n304, 696n801
  standing, 264
  of upper, middle, lower body, 321–22, 674n339
  for "waves of physical body," 330–31
Potālaka, 290
Potowa Rinchen Sel, 6–7, 8, 16–17, 20, 23–24, 654n99
Practical Guidance on the Five Stages (Ratnarakṣita), 278
Prahevajra, 278
Prajñāguhya, 55–56
Prajñākaragupta, 636–37n56
Prajñākaramati, 59
Prajñāpāramitā. *See* Great Mother Prajñāpāramitā
Prakāśīlā, 168
Prakrit, 178, 632n10
Prāsaṅgika Mādhyamikas, 141
Pratibhākuṭa, 157
precepts, 224–25, 238–39. *See also* vows
preliminary practices
  extraordinary, 213–17, 490
  four things to disregard, 304, 671n295
  ordinary, 210–11, 641n65
  Supporting Doctrine, 138, 634n26
  in Vajravārāhī, 391
pride, 233, 431, 437
pristine cognition, 221, 280, 315
  of appearance and emptiness, 355
  arising stage, 396
  of bliss and emptiness, 355
  body of, 312
  and buddha body, coalescence of, 396
  coemergent, 643n27
  conceptual thoughts as, 347–48
  of empowerment, 439
  of empty space, 381
  and expanse, uniting, 489
  in fierce inner heat, 628n28
  fire of, 457
  five types, 437, 450, 455, 474
  four types, 263, 278
  immeasurable, 288
  innate, 270, 281, 333
  of intrinsic emptiness, 356
  nonconceptual, 262, 269, 270, 306
  nondual, 349, 383, 449, 450
  of radiance and emptiness, 355
  recognizing, 493
  seal of, 331, 344–45, 346, 678n420
  supramundane, 356, 359
  yoga of, 385–86
pristine cognition beings, 289, 292, 375, 377, 481, 484, 490
Profound and Extensive Training (Ra Lotsāwa), 274
prostrations, 472, 473

protections, four, 296–97
protective circles, 338, 375, 379, 390, 469
Protuberance with the White Parasol empowerment, 519
pronouncements, four, 440, 700n875
Puchung Rinchen Gyeltsen, 24–25
Puchungwa Zhonu Gyeltsen, 159, 649n18
Pukkāsī, 338
Pullahari, 94, 180, 436
pulse of vitality, 427
Puntsok Namgyel, xxiv
Puṇyaśrī, 29–30
Pupak Monastery, xvii, xviii
Purang Lochung, 180, 181
pure appearances, 324, 413
pure lands, 213–14, 292, 440
pure vision, 153, 643n27
purification
  of consciousness, 175, 639n40
  in extraordinary preliminaries, 213, 215–16, 647n8
  of mental continuum, 331, 332–33
  of negativity, xxv
  of subtle body, 469
  three types, 297
purity
  primordial, 488, 493, 711n1057
  two types, 419
Pūrṇavardhana, 6
Putowa, 158
Putra, 484, 711nn1052–53

Ra Lotsāwa, 273, 274, 515, 516
Ra Yonten Pelzangpo, 164
Rabjor Sengé, 99–100, 101
Rabkar Jangzangwa, 24–25
radiance
  and emptiness, inseparability of, 307, 344, 352, 419
  experiencing, 342, 471
  in generation stage, 439–40
  of intrinsic awareness, 315
  of nature of mind, 325, 344, 353, 485
  of pristine cognition, 355
  signs of, 489, 490
Radreng, 655n118
Rāhu, 314, 319, 364–65, 489
Rāhula, 40, 192
Rāhulabhadra, 632n10
Rāhulata, 639n27
rainbow body, 190, 396
rainbow light, 488–90, 491
Rati Zangbarwa, 28
Ratnabhadra (elder Kusulu), 6, 14–15, 16
Ratnagiri temple, 202, 644n33
Ratnaguru, 106, 115
Ratnākara, 106–7
Ratnakīrti, 69–70
Ratnarakṣita, 278
Ratnasambhava, 263, 265, 327, 355, 369, 371, 374, 437
Ratnavajra. *See* Indrabhūti: Younger (a.k.a. Ratnavajra)
Ratnavajriṇī (ḍākinī, a.k.a. Jonang Jetsunma Kunga Trinle Pelwangmo), 123, 124, 631n3
Raton Yonten Pelzang
  lineages, 6–7, 8, 10, 15, 16–17, 18, 19, 20, 21, 23–24, 26, 28–29, 30, 71
  transmissions received, 139, 140
rebirth, 420, 439, 650n34
  aspiration for, 128–29
  in intermediate state, 445, 701n897
  in lower existences, 467
  past propensities and, 487–88
  ripening at, 237
  suffering and, 322
  transference and, 400
Rechen Lhundrubpa, 103
Rechen Namka Gyeltsen, 116–17
Rechen Peljor Zangpo, 148, 520
Rechen Ronyompa, 103
Rechungpa Dorjé Drak, 34, 44, 99–100, 101, 107–8, 150, 172, 197
  aural lineage of, 445, 503
  tradition of, 199, 454, 643n26
  treasures of, 200
  works, 701n882, 702n901
recollections, five, 259, 660n170
reduplication, 209, 645n2
refuge, 210, 214, 217, 237, 457, 645n3
Refutation of Disputed Topics (Nāgārjuna), 168, 639n30
Religious History of the Path and Its Fruition (Norchen Kunga Zangpo), 144–45
Rematī, 512, 513, 714n31
Remdawa Zhonu Lodro, 9, 138, 141, 166, 229, 634n29, 649nn25–26, 664n222
renunciation, 17, 350, 626n9

repetition (*yamaka, sbyar ba*), 153, 156, 286, 637n3, 637n62, 668n267
Resting in the Nature of Mind, 508
classification of, 500
historical account, 164
lineage prayer, 13–14
practices, 235–36
sources, 651n54
transmission, xxi, 139
results, four types, 237, 651n59
resurrection, 438, 701n894
retention, 157, 457
Revered Wheel of Vitality (Jigten Gonpo), 150, 470, 503
Rigdzin Tsewang Norbu, xiv
Rikgom Bepei Neljor, 48–49
Rinchen Chodar, 103
Rinchen Chung, 96
Rinchen Dorjé, 104
Rinchen Dorjéma Ratnavajriṇī, xxii, 3, 4–5
Rinchen Gangpa Śākya Shenyen, 162
Rinchen Gyatso Neten Dorjedzin, xxiv, 4–5, 99–100, 101, 123–24
Rinchen Gyeltsen, 96, 104, 111–12, 116–17
Rinchen Khyenrab Chogdrub. *See* Khyenrab Chojé Rinchen Chokdrub Pelzang (a.k.a. Kuzhang Khyenrab)
Rinchen Ozer, 11–12
Rinchen Zangpo, 80, 97
Rinchen Zhonu, 11–12
Ringu Tulku, 623n1, 631n2
Rinpung Norbu Zangpo, 183–84, 640n62
Ripa Zhonu Rinchen, 114
Rite of Burnt Offerings (Buddhadatta), 190, 641n5
rites
devouring, 438
distinctions between, 644n32
enrichment, 307
four, 112, 629n47
Jarokpa, 452
pacification, 307
torma, 715n44
twelve great, 320
water protection, 157
wrathful, 481
Ritro Wangchuk, 26
Ritual Application of the Razor Cut, 484
Ritual Service and Attainment of the Three Adamantine Realities according to Orgyanpa, xvi, 175, 219, 509
on buddha body, 317–18
on buddha mind, 321
on buddha speech, 318–20
classification, 503
lineage prayer, 49–50
source, 674n338
transmission, xxi, 144
Riwo Gangpa, 44
Riwo Genden tradition, 167, 179
robes, monastic, 244, 632n10, 653n80
Rok Tselha Gangpa, 98
Rongchung Sherab Pelden, 183, 185
Rongpa Ga Lotsāwa Namgyel Dorjé, 82
Rongpa Sherab Gyeltsen, 40
Rongpa Sherab Sengé, 82
Rongtö Gungru, 27
Rongton Sheja Kunrik, 163, 624n11
historical accounts, 167–69, 182
lineages, 26, 28–29, 30, 31, 32–33, 37–38
works, 140, 142, 261, 266, 268, 652n66, 660n171, 661n177, 662n204, 668n271
Rongton the Great, 168
Rongyab Pema Lhatsé, xiii
Root Tantra of Cakrasaṃvara, 277, 278
Root Tantra of Hevajra, 196, 279
Root Tantra of the Secret Assembly, 275
Root Verses of the Account of Sachen Kunga Nyingpo's Encounter with Mañjughoṣa, 136–37
Rudra, 281, 434
Rūpavajrā, 355
Rutsam Gomchen, 96

Śabaripā (a.k.a. Śūnyatāsamādhi), 204–5, 644n36, 694–95n779
historical accounts, 190–91, 202, 283
lineages, 42–43, 45, 73–74, 93, 113–14, 119
transmissions of, 283
visualization, 338
works, 190, 278, 641n7, 694–95n779
Sabzang Mati Paṇchen Lodro Gyeltsen. *See* Mati Paṇchen Lodro Gyeltsen
Sabzang Pakpa Zhonu Lodro, 43, 69–70, 72–73, 78, 687n653
Sachen Kunga Nyingpo, 525, 684–85n593
historical accounts, 156–57, 175, 178

lineages, 4, 41, 50–51, 57–58, 61, 62, 63, 65–66, 69–70, 74, 75, 76, 112–13
works, 181, 396, 675n368, 691n731
sacred doctrine, 132, 152–53
of all buddhas as one, 465
attachment to, 232
counterfeit forms, 125, 127, 128
eighty-four thousand sections of, 291–92
five excellences in, 466
melody of, 247
purity of, 135
Ṣaḍānana, 273–74, 516
Sadāprarudita, 257
Sahajā, 278, 410
Sahajayoginī, 641n9
Sajjana, 32, 171
Śakra, 322, 455
Śākya Bumpa, 101–2
Śākya Chokden, xvii, 31–32, 35–36, 41–42, 68–69, 91, 92–93, 120, 139, 635n36, 688n672
Sakya Monastery, xvii, 4, 525
Śākya Ozer, 11–12
Sakya Paṇḍita Kunga Gyeltsen, 137, 157, 624n10, 629n46
historical account, 180
lineages, 4–5, 10, 41–42, 46, 50–51, 58, 62, 63–64, 65–66, 67, 69–70, 74, 75, 76, 77, 78, 110
works, xviii, 221, 366, 368, 647n7, 684n593, 685n605
Śākya Pelzang, 116–17
Śākya Sengé, 116–17
Śākya Sonam, 101–2, 143
Sakya tradition, xv, xvi, xvii, 128, 146, 172, 174
Black Yamāri in, 273
empowerments of, 515, 518, 520
four stages of path in, 181
Great Vehicle tradition of, 144, 636n52
and Jonang, affiliation between, xxiii
in Jonang guidebooks, xix–xx, 136, 144–45, 219, 502, 636n52, 670n289
lineages of, 10, 41–43, 46, 50–51, 52, 53, 54, 55–56, 57, 59, 60, 61, 62, 69, 74, 76, 112, 162
protectors of, 714n32
Vajrabhairava in, 274
Śākya Yarpel, 107–8
Śākya Yeshé, 101–2
Śākya Zangpo, 116–17, 118
Śākyamitra, 67–68
Śākyaśrī, 397, 511, 649n25
lineages, 9, 45, 78, 511
monastic communities of, 160–61, 182, 638n20
realization of, 182
transmissions, 248, 276, 278, 308, 397, 501, 692n737
Samādhibhadra, 37–38
Samādhivajra (a.k.a. Dondarwa), 82
Samantabhadra, 116, 119, 259, 314, 355, 447, 689–90n704
Samayatārā, 215
Samayavajra, 215, 276
Śambhala, 48, 636n47, 673n330
seven religious kings, 47, 48, 627n23
twenty-five Kulika kings, 47, 627n24
Samdingpa Zhonu Drub, 148, 149, 421, 422, 423, 424, 637n58, 695–96n796, 697n829, 697n833, 697n837
Samdrubtsé fiefdom, 640–41n62
Sameness of Existence and Quiescence, 166, 508
classification, 500
historical account, 165
lineage prayer, 17–18
practices, 240–41
source, 652n66
transmission, xx, 139
Samitīya order, three subdivisions of, 632n10
Sāṃkhya system, 688n662, 699n280
Samten Ozer, 11–12, 81, 138, 162, 185–87, 635n34, 638n23, 650n35, 694n768
Śāṇavāsika, 168
Sangdak Drubchen, 44, 143, 174, 301, 670n282
Saṅgha the Brahmin, 29–30
Sangyé Gelong, 11
Sangyé Gompa Sengé Kyab, 14–15, 17–18, 19, 20, 21, 35–36, 166, 633–34n23
Sangyé Gyatso, xxiv
Sangyé Nyingpo, 101–2
Sangyé Onpo Drakpapel, 26, 37–38, 96, 114
Sangyé Pel, xix, 131, 134
Sangyé Pelzangpo, 106
Sangyé Rechen Peldrak, 83, 94–95
Sangyé Repa, 109

Sangyé Rinchen, 101–2
Sangyé Tonpa Tsondru Sengé, 40–41, 84–85, 86, 87–88, 89
Sangyé Yarjon, 106
Sangyé Zhangpo, 44
Sangyé Zhonu, 101–2
Sanskrit, 178, 632n10
Śāntarakṣita, 28
Śāntigupta, 624n11
Śāntipa, 57–58, 179, 275, 276, 636–37n56
Saraha, 67–68, 73–74, 113–14, 119, 204–5, 261, 278, 641n9, 644n34, 700n875
Saroruhavajra. *See* Padmavajra (a.k.a. Saroruha/Saroruhavajra)
scriptural transmission, 521, 525
scripture
  authority of, 225
  common sutras, 466, 707n992
  provisional and definitive, 468
  three collections, 466, 468
  twelve branches of, 248, 466, 654n94
Śe Chilbupa Chokyi Gyeltsen, 6–7, 633n22
Secret Assembly empowerments, 514–15
secret cakra
  Amoghasiddhi at, 327
  branches of, 310
  deities at, 355
  of female consort, 332, 374–75
  four seals and, 393–94
  generative fluid from, 288
  in transference, 478
  vital essence in, 358
Secret Guidance of Kurukullā, 508
  classification, 502
  historical account, 174
  lineage prayer, 46
  practices, 302–3
  source, 670n289
  transmission, xxii, 143
seed syllables, 263
  of buddha body, speech, mind, 692n738
  channels, blocked by, 341
  diffusion and absorption, 349
  dissolution of winds in, 363
  of elemental winds, 319, 320, 675n360
  in illusory body, 425
  maturation of, 398
  stage of, 392–93
  stage without, 393
  in transference, 491
Sekhar Gutok, 95–96, 196
Sekhar Kyawo, 699n868
Sekharma (Guru Chowang), 629n41
Self-Arisen Queen, 512
self-consecration, 280, 359–64, 384, 393
self-grasping, 224, 239, 267
self-interest, 220–21, 265
semen (*khu*), 387, 397, 467, 628n29, 647n10, 669n277
Semo Chewa Namka Gyeltsen, 47
Sempa Ché Sonam Sengé, 12–13
Sempa Sogyel, 43
Sempa Sonam Rinchen Gyeltsen, 687n653
Sendhepa, 196
Sengyé Gyelpo, 107–8, 643n28
Sengyé Sherab, 107–8, 643n28
sense faculties, 392–93, 406–7, 409, 445, 449, 455
sense fields, six, 327, 676n397
sense objects, 232, 263, 327, 370, 392–93, 440, 676n397
sensory elements, three absorptions of, 365, 685n601
sensory gates/organs, 232, 263, 317, 334, 355, 369
sentient beings
  compassion for, 214, 323–24, 356
  meditation on, 222
  modes of, three, 439
  as one's parent/mother, 240–41, 253
  See also inhabited world and sentient inhabitants
Sequence of the Buddhist Teaching, 508
  classification, 500
  historical account, 165
  lineage prayer, 16–17
  practices, 238–40
  sources, 651n61
  transmission, xx, 139
Serdingpa Zhonu O, 68, 92, 178, 195, 665n237, 686n613
Serdokchen Monastery, xvii, xviii
Sergyi Bumpa, 161
Serkhang Tenpa Kunga Gyeltsen, 101–2
Serlingpa Dharmakīrti, 158–59
Seton Chenpo, 116–17
Seton Kunrik, 50–51, 59, 60–61, 63, 175
Setsun Wangchuk Zhonu, 28

Seven Days of Fierce Inner Heat according to Pelchen Ga Lotsāwa (Yangonpa), 150, 198, 704n959, 705n963
seven insignia of royal dominion, 216, 647n10
Seven Sections of Spiritual Attainment, 202, 644n34
Seven-Point Mind Training of the Great Vehicle (Tokmé Zangpo), 507, 633n22, 634n33
  classification, 500
  enlightened mind in, 221–22, 226
  experiential cultivation, integrating, 223–24
  historical account, 157–59
  lineage prayer, 6–7
  mind training: measure, commitments, precepts, 224–25
  misplaced understandings, 225–26
  sources, 648n4
  transforming negative circumstances into path, 222–23
  transmission, xx, 137–38
Severance of Demonic Forces (Samten Ozer), 162, 638n23
Severance of Machik Labdron, 508, 635n34
  classification of, 500
  historical account, 162
  lineage prayer, 11–12
  preliminary practices, 230–31
  severance of four devils, 231–33
  sources, 650n35
  transmission, xxii, 138
Sewalung (Nyel), 195
Shang, xv
Shangkarwa Rinchen Gyeltsen, 40–41, 84–85, 86, 87, 88–89
Shangpa Kagyu tradition, xv, xvi, xvii, 192, 697n847
  empowerments of, 516
  in Geluk tradition, xxiv
  Golden Dharmas of, 193, 504, 642n16
  guidebooks in, xxii
  in Jonang guidebooks, xxi, xxiii, 149, 219, 695–96n796
  Kongtrul's affinity with, xiv
  Kunga Drolchok's connection with, xviii
  lineages, 84–85, 87–89
Shangpa Rechen Sonam Chokgyur, 33
Shangpa Rikpei Dorjé, 87–88
Shangton, 192
Sharawa Yonten Drak, 6–7, 16–17, 20, 159, 164, 165, 170
Sharwa (Sharchen Yeshé Gyeltsen), 4–5, 46, 63–64, 68–69, 74, 76–77
Shawo Gangpa, 20, 139, 166, 652n78
Shengom Rokpo, 59, 60–61
Sherab Bumpa, 8, 39–40, 90, 142, 293, 635nn42–43, 668n273
Sherab Dorjé, 31
Sherab Ozer, xvi, 623n9
Sherab Pel, 31, 45
Sherab Rinchen, 31
Sherab Tashi, 514, 515
Sherab Yonten, 252
Shik Chawa, 252
Shong area, 184
Shong Lotsāwa Dorjé Gyeltsen, 28
sibling monks of Gyel, 252, 655n118
Siddhirājñi, 34, 141, 172
Siddhivajra, 55–56
signlessness, 247, 332
signs, 396
  of accomplishment, 365, 376, 415, 438
  of dissolution of elements, 403, 694n763
  in dream yoga, 486
  of luminosity, 305–6
  of meditative experience, 456
  of natural radiance, 489, 490
  of realization, 408
Śīlacandra, 46
Siṃhabodhi, 168, 639n27
Siṃhavaktrā (ḍākinī), 42–43
single savor, 287–88, 310, 353, 412
"single-deity single-vase" transmission, 172, 639n37
Śiṣyavajra, 67–68
Śītavana, 198, 201, 203, 457, 482
Situ Chokyi Jungné, xiii, xiv
Situ Pema Nyinjé, xiii
Six Adamantine Verses, 308, 672n307
Six Approaches of the Profound Meaning, 138
six classes of living beings, 248, 249, 315, 348, 492
  as Avalokita, 292
  compassion for, 227, 241, 289, 416
  meditating on, 237
  navel cakra of emanation, 416, 425
  as one's parents, 239

Six Cycles of Common Savor, 200
Six Descents of the Transcendent Perfection of Wisdom, 508
classification, 500
historical account, 167–68
lineage prayer, 25–26
practices, 260–61
source, 660n171
transmission, xx, 140
Six Doctrines according to Taklungpa
classification, 503
historical account, 199, 200
lineage prayer, 106–7
practices, 470–72
source, 707n1000
transmission, xxi, 150
Six Doctrines according to the Sekharma Tradition, 510
classification, 503
historical account, 196
lineage prayer, 95–97
practices, 437–39
source, 699n868
transmission, xxi, 149–50
Six Doctrines of Liberation through the Upper Gate, according to the Aural Lineage, 510
classification, 503
historical account, 197
lineage prayer, 99–100
practices, 442–45
source, 701n882
transmission, xxi, 150
Six Doctrines of Nāropā, 199, 510
classification of, 503
historical account, 191
lineage prayer, 83–84
practices, 410–14
source, 695n780
transmissions, xxi, 148, 641n9
Six Doctrines of Nigumā, xviii, 510
classification of, 503
consciousness transference, 419–20
dream yoga, 417–19
fierce inner heat, 415–16
historical account, 191–92
illusory body, 416–17
intermediate state, 420–21
lineage prayer, 84–85
luminosity, 419
preliminaries, 414–15
source, 695n796
transmission, xxi, 148
Six Doctrines of Sukhasiddhi, 510
classification, 504
historical account, 194
lineage prayer, 87–88
practices, 425–26
source, 697n840
transmission, xxi, 149
Six Doctrines of the Accomplished Masters, 511
classification, 502
historical account, 203
lineage prayer, 115–16
practices, 486–88
source, 711n1056
transmission, xxi, 151
Six Essential Cycles, 202, 644n34
Six Meditations of Vajravārāhī, 510
classification, 501
lineage prayer, 81–83
practices, 409–10
source, 694n779
transmission, xx, 148
six ornaments, 476, 708n1016
Six Primary Essentials for the Mountain Retreat of Yangonpa, 511, 709n1020
classification, 503
on consciousness transference, 478
on dream yoga, 480
on ejaculation, guarding against, 480–81
on emptiness, 478–79
on evil spirits and disease, 479–80
historical account, 200
lineage prayer, 110–11
source, 709n1028
transmission, xxii, 151
on vigorous breathing, 477
six yogas of continuous flow, 42, 627n20
Six-Branch Yoga (Kālacakrapāda), 670n293
Six-Branch Yoga according to Pelchen Ga Lotsāwa, 510
classification, 504
historical account, 198
lineage prayer, 102–3
practices, 456–59
source, 704n959
transmission, xxii, 150

Six-Branch Yoga of Kālacakra, xvi, xviii, xxiv, 508, 628n25
on breath control, 307–9
classification, 501
on composure, 304–6
historical account, 174
lineage prayer, 47–48
on meditative concentration, 306–7
on meditative stability, 312
preliminaries, 303–4
on recollection, 311–12
on retention, 309–10
source, 670n293
transmission, xxi, xxiii, 143
Sixteen Spheres of the Heart, 508
classification of, 501
historical account, 167
lineage prayer, 24–25
source, 659n161
on supporting maṇḍala, 257–58, 660nn163–66
on teachers of root lineage, 259
transmission, xxii, 140
skillful means, 242, 353, 366, 459, 628–29n33
coemergence of, 340
compassion as, 238
of generation stage, 280
path of, 198, 441, 461, 643n27
perfection of, 270
writings of, 314
sleep, 292, 296, 307, 325, 413, 444, 487
Smith, Gene, 623n1
So Chung Gedunbar, 140
Sok-on Kabzhipa Rikpei Reldri, 83–84, 93–94
Soldro Jetang (Nub Cholung), 184
solitary hero, 143, 357, 386–87, 483, 636n44
Somanātha, xvi, xxiii, 47, 48, 143, 174
Sonam Drakpa, 6–7, 9, 37–38, 159
Sonam Drubpa, 101–2
Sonam Gyelchok, xxii, 110–11
Sonam Gyeltsen, 98, 104
Sonam Ozer, 24–25, 49–50, 144, 674n338
Sonam Peljor, 519
Sonam Sengé, 31
Sonam Tsemo
lineages, 4, 41, 50–51, 58, 62, 63, 65–66, 69–70, 74, 75, 76, 157
works, 637n6
Sonam Wangchuk, 12–13, 14, 78
Songtsen Gampo, 117–18, 204
soul and matter, dichotomy of, 297, 699n280
space, 460, 489
blessing of real nature and, 298
element, 318, 319, 320, 369, 370, 390, 443, 460
meditative stability on, 333–34, 678n426
mind resembling, 348
nonarising, 454
as not established, 356
spirits
anguished, 322
assault by, 243
elemental, 383
evil, 479–80
tsen and *gying*, 512, 513
Spiritual Connection with the Six Gatekeepers, 145, 177, 636n56
spiritual mentors, 267, 335, 347–48, 350, 459
spiritual songs, 203
spontaneous presence, 488, 489, 711n1057
Śraddhākaravarman, 35, 112–13
Śrībhadra, 37–38
Śrībrahmā, 55–56
Śrīdevī, 113, 483–84, 512, 513, 519, 710n1050
Śrīdhara, 52–53, 54, 55, 57, 71, 179
Śrīherukābhyudaya empowerment, 517
Śrīmatī, 694–95n779
Śrīsukha, 69–70
Stages of the Heroic Mind (Serlingpa), 158
stains, 250, 654nn101–2
Sthavira order, three subdivisions of, 632n10
Sthiramati, 29–30
Straightening of Crooked Posture, 509
historical account, 176
lineage prayer, 55
practices, 343
source, 680n475
transmission, xx, 145, 636n55
Striking, The (Tokden Pelzangpo), 138
study, reflection, meditation, 239, 267
stupas, xxiii, 185, 233
Subhadra, 257
subject and object, threefold interaction of, 268

Subsequent Tantra of the Secret Assembly, 275, 276
substratum (*kun gzhi*), 221–22, 489, 633n22, 647n10
substratum consciousness (*kun gzhi rnam par shes pa*), 450, 469, 639n40, 647n10, 648n7
subtle energy, 298, 305, 324, 436–37, 456, 493. *See also* winds
suffering
 blocking perception of, 457
 carrying onto path, 229, 474–75
 of contaminated phenomena, 266
 of cyclic existence, 210, 240
 of hell beings, 347
 in intermediate state, 487
 meditating on, 237
 of others, 381–82
 three types, 322–23, 352–53
 transforming, 223
Sukhadeva, 31
Sukhanātha, 113–14
Sukhasiddhi, 11, 87–88, 89, 192, 193, 194, 261, 278, 427, 428, 642n17
Sukhāvatī, 381
Sumati, 71
Sumatibhadrī, 700n875
Summation of the Real (Bodongpa), 34, 172, 283, 627n17, 665n225, 665n227, 665n234, 666n250, 667n256, 667n260
Sumpa Lotsāwa Darma Yonten, 10, 161
Sumpa Repa Rinchen Gyeltsen, 44, 107–8, 200
Śūnyatāsamādhi. *See* Śabaripā (a.k.a. Śūnyatāsamādhi)
suppression, five subsidiary instructions on, 335, 678n436
Supreme Continuum of the Great Vehicle (Maitreya), 169, 171, 270, 664nn220–21
Supreme Tantra of Clear Expression, 278
Sutra of the Ten Levels, 633n210
Sutra of the Transcendent Perfection of Wisdom in Eight Thousand Lines, 164
Sutra of the Transcendent Perfection of Wisdom tradition, 26, 627n12
Svātantrika Mādhyamikas, 140, 169
syllables, 399
 burning and dripping of, 367
 five of great emptiness, 76, 277, 278, 629n35, 666n239
 in Innate Cakrasaṃvara, 395, 397
 one hundred, 277
 recitation of, 262, 263, 264
 in right and left channels, 401–2
 six of vital essence, 76, 277, 278, 629n35, 666n239
 ten pure signs, 314, 674n335
 three, 292, 328, 377, 383, 404, 443
 in transference, 400
 variant times and, 487
 See also seed syllables

Tagton Zhonu Dar, 115
Taklung Kagyu, 106–8, 109, 110–11, 510, 629n44
Taklung Ngawang Drakpa. *See* Ngawang Drakpa Pelzangpo
Taklung Rinpoché (Ngawang Tulku), xxi, 101–2, 109, 150, 151
Taklung Tulku Namgyel Tashi, xxi, 105, 106–7, 111–12, 517
Taklungpa Tashipel, 106, 472, 629n44, 707n1000
Takten Puntsoling Monastery, xxiv
Taktsang Lotsāwa Drapa Sherab Rinchen, 180, 640n53
Tanak Monlam Gom, 23–24
Tanak Rinchen Yeshépa, 23–24, 171
Tang Lotsāwa Shing Lopa, 43–44
Tangtong Gyelpo, 148
tantra, four classes of, 468
Tantra of Cakrasaṃvara, 641–42n9. See also *Root Tantra of Cakrasaṃvara*
Tantra of Clear Expression, 187
Tantra of Great Magical Emanation, 197, 278, 441, 517
Tantra of Guhyasamāja, 191, 197, 641n9
Tantra of Heruka Galpo, 175, 317, 639n39, 673n330
Tantra of Hevajra, 191, 197, 279, 280, 440–41, 641–42n9. See also *Root Tantra of Hevajra*; *Two-Chapter Tantra of Hevajra*
Tantra of Mahāmāyā, 641–42n9
Tantra of the Adamantine Sky-Farers, 278
Tantra of the Adamantine Tent, 279, 280
Tantra of the Black Slayer of Death, 273
Tantra of the Emancipation of Śrīheruka, 278

Tantra of the Emergence of Cakrasaṃvara, 278
Tantra of the Four Adamantine Seats, 191, 197, 441, 517, 641n9
Tantra of the Habitual Practice of the Yoginīs, 278
Tantra of the Ocean of Vows, 192, 642n14
Tantra of the Precious Ocean, 192, 642n14
Tantra of the Secret Assembly, 178, 179, 276, 441, 687n653. See also *Root Tantra of the Secret Assembly*
Tantra of the Victory of Nondual Sameness, 275
Tantra of the Vital Essence of Union, 176, 279, 280
Tantra of the Wheel of Time, xvi, 628n25, 714n27
Tārā, 167, 500, 624n11, 626n11, 652n79
  Cintāmaṇicakra, 35, 286, 667n266
  definitive presence, 198
  empowerments, 518
  lineages, 23, 24–25, 56–57, 62, 101–2
  visions, 161
  visualizations, 248–50, 258
  wind, 371
  See also Samayatārā
Tāranātha, xxiv, xxvi, 219, 630n55
  contributions of, 155, 189, 206
  in Jonang guidebooks, xxii, xxv, 625n24
  Kunga Drolchok as, xvii
  lineages, xiv, 3, 4–5
  supplication to, 123, 124
  works, 630n2, 651n58
Tarpa Lotsāwa, 273, 283
Tashi Dorjé, 29–30
Tashi Gyeltsen, 118
Tashi Lama, 106
Tashi Namgyel, xxii, 43, 143, 515, 516
Tashi Peltsek, 106–7, 629n44
Tashi Zangpo, 76–77
tathāgatagarbha sutras, xxiii
Tazhi Jadrel, 118
teachers
  attachment to, 232
  genuine, 654n105
  meditation on, 422–23
  root, 210, 216–17, 256, 473
  as three buddha bodies, 472–73
  union with, 381, 382–83, 440
  venerating, 252, 656n120
  See also spiritual mentors
Ten Approaches to the Oral Instruction (Kyemé Dopa), 635n35
ten bodhisattva levels, 269–70, 467, 633n210
"ten great pillars," xvi, 624n10
Tenfold Doctrinal Instruction (Jigten Gonpo), 106, 199, 629n43, 643n24
Tengyur, 162, 638n21
Tenpei Gyeltsen, 516
Tepuwa Pārvātapāda, 34, 93, 107–8
thirty-seven factors conducive to enlightenment, 459–60, 467, 705n976
Three Aspects Carried on the Path, 510
  classification, 504
  historical account, 193
  lineage prayer, 86
  practices, 422–23
  source, 697n833
  transmission, xxi, 149
Three Crucial Points of the All-Pervasive Coemergent Union That Brings Forth the Miraculous Ability of the Esoteric Instructions (Yangonpa), 275–76, 277
three essenceless natures, 271–72, 280–81
Three Essential Points, 508
  classification of, 500
  historical account, 163
  lineage prayer, 12–13
  practices, 233–34
  sources, 651n51
  transmission, xx, 139
Three Nails of the Pith Instructions of Secret Attainment (Nyeton Chokyi Sherab), 194, 642n17
three promulgations (vehicles), 29, 627n14
Three Purities, 509
  classification, 502
  historical account, 177
  lineage prayer, 63–64
  source, 683n542
  on three purities, 356–57
  transmission, xx, 145
  on vital essence yoga, 358–59
three sealings, 193
Three Sorts of Person, 166, 508
  classification, 500

Three Sorts of Person (*continued*)
greater capacity, 238
historical account, 164–65
lesser capacity, 236–37
lineage prayer, 14–16
middling capacity, 237
sources, 651n58
transmission, xx, 139
Three Stages of Meditation, 508
classification, 500
historical account, 169
lineage prayer, 28–29
practices, 266–68
source, 662n204
transmission, xx, 140
three trainings, 469
Threefold Doctrine (Jigten Gonpo), 199, 643n25
three-tiered principle beings, 376, 688n663
throat cakra of perfect resource, 285
Amitābha at, 327
branches of, 297, 310, 358
deities at, 355
in dream yoga, 412, 463, 486
in empowerments, 332
vital essences at, 331
Tibet, xxiv, 135, 257, 258
Tīlakalalāśa, 170
Tilopā, 94, 276, 278, 445, 465, 700n875
historical account, 197
lineages, xv, 12–13, 73–74, 76, 83, 89–90, 91, 92, 95–96, 97, 99, 100, 103–4, 105, 106, 107–8, 109, 110, 120, 641n9
time, 356
Tokden Chonyi Rangdrol, 152, 712n1072
Tokden Gangpa Rinchen Pelzangpo, 11–12, 138
Tokden Gonpo Gyeltsen, 83, 94–95
Tokden Khacho Wangpo, 142
Tokmé Zangpo, 158, 159, 626n3
lineages, 6–7, 8, 9, 10, 37–38, 39–40, 41–42, 90, 635n43
works, 138, 143, 149, 162, 173, 226, 229, 432, 503, 633–34nn22–24, 634n29, 634n33, 635n42, 648n4, 649–50n33, 698n851
tolerance, 239, 255, 268
Tongdrol Chenmo stupa, xxiii, xxiv
Tonmi Sambhoṭa, 624n10
Tonpa Yolgom Chowang, 173
Total Liberation through Singular Knowledge, 313
Transcendent Perfection of Wisdom in One Hundred Thousand Lines, 168, 169
Transcendent Perfection of Wisdom teachings, 168, 231, 232, 260, 661n173
transcendent perfections, six, 248, 664n214
parables on, 254–56
practicing, 268–69, 663n208
symbols of, 365
in three vehicles, 469
transcendent perfections, ten, 269, 633n210
Trariwa Rinchen Gyelchok, xxii, 36–37, 141, 143
Trāyastriṃśa, 455, 478, 487, 709n1031
Treasure That Brings Forth Accomplishment (Sangyé Rinchen), 145
treasure tradition, 95–96, 119, 150, 196, 200, 204, 205, 439, 504, 519, 699n868
Treasury of Extensive Pronouncements (Kongtrul), 623n5
Treasury of Knowledge (Kongtrul), xi, xiv, 219, 623n1
Treasury of Precious Instructions (Kongtrul), xi, xiii, xiv–xvi, 123
Treasury of Spiritual Songs (Saraha), 644n34
Treasury of Valid Cognition (Sakya Paṇḍita), xviii
Trewo Chokyi Gyatso, Kyapjé Tokden
lineages, 34, 83–84, 94–95, 115–16
transmissions from, xxi, 141, 142, 144, 148, 149, 151
Tri Songdetsen, xv, 117–18
Trilogy of Pulverizing. See *Hidden Guidance of Kadam*
Trilogy of Spiritual Songs, 511
classification, 502
historical account, 202
lineage prayer, 113–14
practices, 485–86
source, 711n1055
transmission, xxii, 151
Trilogy on Mountain Retreat (Yangonpa), 200, 481, 709n1028
Tropu, 163
Tropu Lotsāwa Jampapel, 9, 12, 13, 139, 160, 163, 234, 626n8, 649n25, 651n51
Trulzhik Darma Sengyé, 27

Trulzhik Kundarma, 119
Trulzhik Kunga Chogyel, 49–50
Trulzhik Namkei Neljorpa, 107–8
Trulzhik Tsultrim Gyeltsen, 12–13, 120
Tsadra Rinchen Drak, xiii
Tsaktsa Śākya Dorjé, 116–17
Tsami Lotsāwa Mondrub Sherab, 203, 711n1056
Tsami Sangyé Drak, 102–3, 111, 198, 201, 643n23
Tsang, xxiv, 184
Tsangma Shangton, 40–41, 84–85, 86, 87–88, 89
Tsangnak Tsondru Sengé, 164
Tsangpa Dregurwa Dongtro Dulwadzin, 32
Tsangpa Gyaré Yeshé Dorjé (a.k.a. Sangyé Rabdun), 145
  instructions of, 199–200, 475, 643nn26–27, 707n1006
  lineages, 89–90, 107–8, 109, 110
  vision of, 200
Tsangwa Dratsang, xxv
Tsāri, 205, 520
Tsawaripa, 115
Tsawarongpa Śākya Gyeltsen, 147
Tsechu Dratsang, xxv
Tselpa lineage, 101–2
Tsen Khawoché, 32, 140, 141, 170, 171, 272, 664n223
Tserang, 174–75
Tseringma, 512, 513
Tsetsa Repa Śāk Dor, 11–12
Tsewang Norbu, xiv, xxii, 3, 4–5, 123, 124, 521, 525, 631n4, 631n8
Tsi Tonpa, 37–38
Tsok Khenchen Rinpoché, 146
Tsokgom Kunga Pel, 64–65, 147, 180, 394, 640n57, 691n725
Tsokha Gon, xv
Tsondru Zangpo, 67–68
Tsongkhapa, 159, 167, 180, 181, 640n53, 652n66
Tsulchen Sonam Sengé, 118
Tsultrim Chogdrub, 111–12
Tsultrim Gonpo, 79, 98
Tsultrim Gyeltsen, 87–88
Tsurpu Jamyang Dondrub Ozer, 94–95
Tsurpu Monastery, xviii
Tsurton Wang-gi Dorjé, 98, 197, 442, 503, 700n876
Tukjé Tsondru Chojé. *See* Kunpang Tukjé Tsondru
Tuksévwa Rinchen Namgyel, 12–13, 519
Tulku Jodenpa, 44, 670n282
Tumton Lodro Drak, 14–15, 16, 164, 165
Tushiyetu Khan, xxiv
Tuṣita, 168, 234, 252, 260, 660n171
Twenty-Four Doctrinal Cycles of Nonmentation, 202, 644n34
twenty-four sacred places, 397, 480, 487, 692n738, 709n1039
Twenty-Nine Essential Visualizations of Self-Consecration, 509
  classification, 502
  historical account, 177
  lineage prayer, 64–65
  practices, 359–64
  source, 684n561
  transmission, xx, 146
two stages, 136, 219, 633n14
  borderline between, 370
  conflating, 180
  hatred and, 439
  indivisibility of, 281
  integrating, 276, 296–98
  in yogatantra, 272
  See also generation stage; perfection stage
two truths, coalescence of, 238
Two-Chapter Tantra of Hevajra, 279, 679n450

Umdzé Yonten Pel, 6–7
uncommon path, 324, 675n382
Unelaborate Practice of Red Yamāri, 509
  classification, 501
  historical account, 179
  lineage prayer, 71–72
  offerings, 379–80
  on postmeditation, 381–83
  source, 688n677
  transmission, xx, 146
union, 163
  coemergent, 274, 275, 277
  in extraordinary preliminaries, 215
  referential basis and referential object, 146, 179, 637n57
  with secret consort, 326
  seven aspects of, 397, 692n739
  three aspects of authentic perception in, 450, 703n938

Unique Enlightened Intention according to the Cycle of Drigung
  classification, 503
  forty-seven supplementary points in, 465–70
  historical account, 199
  lineage prayer, 104–6
  source, 706n988
  transmission, xxi, 150
universal emperors, 322
Upagupta, 168
Upāli, 632n10
Upama, 55–56
Upendra, 281, 434
Urawa, 31
Uriwa, 44
Uru, 257, 258
Utsang, xvii, xix, 134, 138, 159, 162, 166, 181, 638n21

Vagīśvaragupta, 640n58
Vagīśvarakīrti, 35, 56, 62, 121, 346, 636–37nn55–56
Vairocana, xiii, 347
  blessing body of, 297–98
  at crown, 327
  delusion and, 437
  encompassing and dissolution of, 374
  enlightened family of, 369
  at forehead cakra, 355
  Himamahāsāgara, 258
  Sarvavid, 184
  visualizations, 263, 265, 451
Vairocanabhadra (a.k.a. Ngulchu Bairo), 14–15, 16, 101–2, 198
Vairotsana, 204, 624n10
Vaiśravaṇa, 512, 513, 714n23
vajra (penis), 344–45, 389, 393, 404, 405
  consecration of, 450
  ejaculation and, 480, 481
  in six-branch yoga, 305, 308, 311, 312
  upward inversion of, 416
Vajrārali, 274
Vajrabhairava, 383, 424, 665n226
  attainment of, 642n12
  in dream yoga, 418
  empowerments of, 515–16
  generation stage, 273, 274
  lineages of, 72
  self-visualization, 386–87
  union of, 382
Vajracaṇḍālī, 300
Vajradhara, 180, 374, 432, 464
  at crown, 355
  enlightened family of, 369
  in extraordinary preliminaries, 216–17
  as one's teacher, 472
  recollection of, instant, 373
  self-visualization, 369–70, 372, 435
  See also Mahāvajradhara
Vajradhātu empowerment, 518
Vajragarbha, 92
Vajragarbha Ḍākinī, 183
Vajrahāsya, 273
Vajraheruka, 364
Vajrakīla, 512, 513, 518, 714n31
Vajramāradama, 512, 513
Vajranairātmyā, 513–14
Vajrapāṇi, 355, 624n11
  aspects of, 299–300, 670n283
  Caṇḍa, 299–300
  in dream yoga, 418
  empowerments of, 518
  Guhyapati, 59, 60–61, 174
  lineages, 43–44, 67–68, 73–74, 641–42n9
  Mahācakra, 274, 297–98
Vajrapāṇi in the Form Caṇḍa, 508
  classification, 501
  historical account, 174
  lineage prayer, 43–44
  practices, 299–300
  source, 670n282
  transmission, xxi, 143
Vajrapāṇi in the Form Mahācakra, 508
  classification, 501
  generation stage, 296–97
  historical account, 173
  lineage prayer, 42–43
  perfection stage, 297–98
  source, 669n279
  transmission, xxii, 143
Vajrapāṇi of India, 113–14
Vajrāsana, 111, 192, 276, 642n14
Vajrāsana (Bodh Gaya), 161, 168, 706n986
Vajrāsana the Elder, 41
Vajrāsana the Younger (a.k.a. Amoghavajra), 41, 56, 72–73, 179

Vajrasattva, 33, 116, 172, 314, 316, 488, 647n8
Vajravārāhī, 172, 277, 455
absorption of, 395
blessings of, 187
Chinnamundā, 190, 641n3
definitive presence of, 198
deity assemblage of, 278
dissolving, 341
Dvimukha, 190, 641n2
empowerments of, 459, 515, 517
Kurmapādā, 54, 76, 301
lineages, 10, 41, 45, 49, 54, 75, 76, 81, 94–95, 101–2
Sarvārthasiddhā, 190, 197, 641n4
self-visualization, 409–10
transmissions from, 182, 500
in union, 278, 279, 294, 389, 450
visions of, 161
works on, 190, 641nn2–6
Vajravidāraṇa, 639n37, 639–40n46
Vajrayoginī, xvi, 33, 78, 81–82, 99, 415, 421, 475–76
Valcaṇḍa, 44
Vanaprastha, 53, 63, 65
Vanaratna, Paṇchen, 143, 283
Vārāhi. *See* Vajravārāhī
Vārāhī in the Form Kurmapādā, 508
classification, 501
historical account, 174
lineage prayer, 45
practices, 301–2
source, 670n287
transmission, xxi, 143
Vārāhī Khecarī of the Generation Stage, 179
Vararuci, 112–13
Varuṇa, 512, 715n55
Vasantatilaka, 278
vase breathing, 288, 309, 310, 390, 404, 456, 696n807
at death, 400
gentle, 311
rough, 308, 477, 672n312
Vasubandhu, 6, 14–15, 16, 29, 168, 639n27, 653n87, 654n102
Vasudhara, 281
veneration, 252, 656n120
Verses on the Great Seal, 150, 705n972
Verses on the Path of Skillful Means, 150, 198, 705n972
Versified Instruction on Parting from the Four Attachments (Drakpa Gyeltsen), 137
Vetālī, 338
Vibhūticandra, 182, 200, 283
Vidyākokila, 19, 29–30
View of Extraneous Emptiness, 508
classification, 500
historical account, 171
lineage prayer, 32–33
practices, 271–72
source, 664n223
transmission, xxii, 141
View of Intrinsic Emptiness, 508
classification, 500
historical account, 170–71
lineage prayer, 31–32
practices, 270–71
source, 664n222
transmission, xxi–xxii, 141
view(s)
armor of, 460
and conduct, integration of, 268
emptiness of, 479
erroneous, 356
four defining characteristics of, 344
free from extremes, 282
of genuine reality, 293, 333
of natural liberation, 271
of spontaneous mind, 491
uncontrived, 192, 292
Vikhyātadeva, 45
Vilāsa, 46
Vimalagupta, 69–70
Vimalamitra, xv, 100–101, 204
Vimuktisena, 6, 14–15, 16
Vīṇapa, 51–52
Vīṇāpavajra, 641–42n9
Vinaya, 466, 467, 469, 707n992
Vināyaka, 245
Vīraraśmi, 115, 203, 645n38, 711n1056
Vīravajra, 51–52, 53–54, 57, 63, 65
virtuous actions
adopting, 236, 267
emphasizing, 271
mature roots of, 240
not searching for, 348
as path, 237
persevering in, 228
ten, 323, 447, 490–91

Virūpa, xv, 273, 427, 694–95n779
lineages, 46, 50–51, 65–66, 67, 71, 82, 87–88
protectors of, 639–40n46
transmissions from, 175, 178, 179, 684–85n593
works, 675n368, 694–95n779
viscera, 216, 647n10
Visukalpa, 67–68
Viśvakoṭacandana, 260
Vital Essence of Liberation, 276, 509
classification, 501
on consciousness transference, 378–79
historical account, 179
lineage prayer, 69–70
on recollection, 377–78
on self-consecration, 375–76
source, 687n653
transmission, xxi, 146
Vital Essence of Spring (Kṛṣṇacārin), 181, 278, 640n60
Vital Essence of Union empowerment, 514
vital essence(s), 243, 277
of appearance and emptiness, 488
black, 428–29
blazing and secretion, 397
descent and reversal of, 346
elevating, 453
in fierce inner heat, 411, 471
five properties of, 307
five types, 392, 394, 406–8, 483
four phases of, 367
of great emptiness, 315
imperishable, 376, 409
internal focus on, 353
as mass of light, 338
melting, 377
mind blessing and, 298
pith instructions on, 402–4
red and white, 216, 284–85, 321, 331–32, 405, 407–8, 647n10
retention of, 320
self-manifesting appearance of, 489–90
spinning, 398, 399
subtle and coarse, 462
three types, 449
in transference, 436–37
visualizing, 292
white, 361, 362
white, sixteen types, 375–76
in wisdom empowerment, 330
yoga of, 280, 282, 358–59, 363
"vitality essence," 201, 643n29
vows, 251–52, 339, 447–48, 466, 467

Wangchuk Gyeltsen, 21
Wangmopuk Monastery, 199
warmth, 198, 324, 365, 675–76n382
waves of enjoyment (*longs spyod kyi rlabs*), 326, 676n393
wealth
material, 130
spiritual, seven aspects of, 216, 647n10
wheel of sacred doctrine
first turning of, 266–67
second turning, 267
three turnings of, 171
Unique Enlightened Intention as, 199
Wheel of Sharp Weapons (Dharmarakṣita), 158, 638n10
White Gyeltang, 512, 513
winds, 277, 298, 358, 393, 422, 448–50
applications of, 310, 458, 461–62, 705n965
correspondences of, 370–71
deities of, male and female, 371
elemental, 304, 318–20, 377, 388–89, 453–54, 671n296, 674n351, 688nn668–69
of exertion, 332, 357, 361, 683n554
fourfold cycle of, 415, 696n807
fourfold union of, 320, 675n360
gentle, controlling, 415
importance of, 469
life breath, 184, 284, 287, 296, 297, 320, 321, 332, 357, 361, 382, 441, 683n554
of past actions, 398, 470, 471, 707n1001
primary and ancillary, 317
of pristine cognition, 367, 471, 707n1001
refining applications of, 344, 357, 391
riding on consciousness, 306
secret, 288
self-manifesting appearance of, 489–90
of temporal conjunction, 312, 673n327
three types, 321, 449
uniting upper and lower, 284–85, 329–30, 351, 355, 357, 382, 388, 389, 394, 405, 409, 425, 471, 477, 484
visualization, 307

Wish-Fulfilling Gem (Samten Ozer), 138, 162, 635n34
womb, 706n985
  of adamantine queen, 489
  entrance to, 421, 440, 464–65
  meditation on, 483
  threefold intermingling in, 445, 702n900
Words of My Perfect Teacher (Patrul), 209
world. *See* inhabited world and sentient inhabitants
world systems, three, 220, 275, 289, 294, 315, 338, 339, 379

Yagdé Lotsāwa Sonam Sengé (a.k.a. Yagdé Paṇchen), 78, 149, 163, 434, 698n853
Yajña, Lord of Mantra, 512
Yakṣa Aparājita, 512–13
yakṣas (male), 483–84, 512, 710n1051
yakṣinīs (female), 203, 483–84, 710n1051
Yama, 281, 420, 481, 512, 513
Yamāntaka, 71, 72, 274, 379–81, 382, 384–85. *See also* Vajrabhairava; Yamāri
Yamāri
  Black, 273–74, 516
  Red, 273, 516
Yamdrok, 181
Yamkyilwa Lodro Chogyel, 109
Yangonpa Gyeltsen Pel
  lineages, 34, 89–90, 103, 110
  works, 150, 151, 200, 275–76, 277, 386, 481, 689n696, 709n1028
Yangton Sangyé Pel, 28–29, 30, 32–33
Yangtsewa Rinchen Sengé, 12–13, 76–77, 139, 236, 651n54
Yargom Sewo, 112–13
Yargyab Kunpang Chokor Gangpa, 110–11
Yarlungpa Lotsāwa Drakpa Gyeltsen, 48–49
Yarlungpa Norbu Rinchen, 520
Yarlungpa Sengé Gyeltsen, 111–12, 113, 201, 485, 511, 637n61, 710n1045
Yechung Pulung, 199
Yerpa Gomseng, 59
Yeshé Pelwa, 36–37, 45
Yigdruk Sherab Peljor, xxii, 11–12, 118, 138, 151, 518, 519
yoga, three essential points, 13, 233–34, 626n7
Yogābara, 517
yogatantra class, 501, 518, 519–20
yogic exercises, 178, 343, 344, 450–51, 453, 470, 522
  in fierce inner heat, 282, 366, 415, 667n257, 694n766
  kindling fire with rubbing stick, 476
  wave of perfect rapture, 457, 704n960
Yogic Exercises of the Thirty-Two Activities, 282
Yolton/Yolgom Chowang, 37–38, 142, 173, 290, 668n270
Yong Gon (Rigongpel), 194
Yonten Gyatso, xxiii, 47, 48
Yorpa Yeshé Pelwa, 94–95
Yumo Mikyo Dorjé, xxiii, 47
Yumto Yulma, 168
Yungtonpa Dorjé Pel, 93–94, 98

Zanabazar, xxiv
Zangpo Pel, 36–37
Zangpo Tenpa, 140
Zarjang Pukpa Kunga Lekpa Rinchen, 137, 515, 633n19
Zelmo Drakpa Drakpa Yeshé, xxii, 33, 141, 515, 517, 665n225
Zewu Drakpa Dherab, 19, 20
Zewu Tsondru Drak, 14–15, 19, 20, 21
Zhalu Khyenrab Chojé, 152
Zhalu Lotsāwa Losal Tenkyong, 123, 124, 631n7
Zhalu tradition, xvi, 143
Zhama tradition, 144, 175
Zhamar Chokyi Wangchuk, 695n780
Zhamar II Khacho Wangpo, 83–84, 93–94, 149
Zhang Dodé Pel, 180, 640n57
Zhang Jangchub Sherab, 62, 66–67
Zhang Konchok Pel, 4–5, 10, 41–42, 46, 50–51, 77
Zhang Lotsāwa Jangchub-o, 99–100, 101, 445, 643n22, 701n882
Zhang Lotsāwa Nyangenmé Pel, 38–39
Zhang Rinchen Ozer, 38–39
Zhang Ring Kyitsa Ochen, 38–39, 142, 173, 668n271
Zhang Tangsagpa Yeshé Jugné, 31
Zhang Tselpa Tsondru Drak, 101–2, 103, 455, 459, 515, 704n959
Zhang Ukarwa, 38–39
Zhang Yeshedé, 624n10

Zhangpa Chokyi Lama, 166
Zhangton Chobar, 50–51, 63, 175
Zhangton Chokyi Lama, 14–15, 17–18, 19, 20, 21, 37–38
Zhangton Darma Gyeltsen, 24–25
Zhangton Drukdra Gyeltsen, 38–39
Zhangton Gadenpa Kunga Sonam, 63–64, 65–66, 69–70, 74
Zhangzhong Dorjeden, xv
Zhechen Gyaltsab, 623n1
Zhechen Monastery, xiii
Zhigatse, xxiv
Zhikpo Nyima Sengé, 25–26, 27
Zhonu Drakpa, 35–36
Zhonu Drubpa, 58, 59, 62, 66–67, 192
Zhonu Gyeltsen, 36–37, 45
Zhonu Sengé, 107–8, 643n28
Zhuben Chenchikpa, 519–20
Zhuton Tsultrim Gon, 87–88
Ziji Drakpa, 80, 97
Zilchen Cave, 520
Zilung Paṇchen Śākya Chokden, 92–93
Zur Dropukpa Śākya Sengé, 116–17
Zur Śākya Pelwa, 116–17
Zurchen Śākya Jungné, 116–17, 204
Zurchung Sherab Drak, 116–17
Zurhaṃ Śākya Jugné, 116–17
Zurhaṃ Shenyen, 116–17
Zurmang lineages, 702n901, 712n1072
Zurpukpa Rinchen Pelzang, 34, 89–90, 103, 110